THE
HORNER PAPERS

FRONTISPIECE: Francis Horner, an engraving by S. W. Reynolds from an oil painting by Sir Henry Raeburn, 1812.

THE
HORNER PAPERS

Selections from the
Letters and Miscellaneous Writings of
Francis Horner, M.P.
1795–1817

edited by
KENNETH BOURNE
and
WILLIAM BANKS TAYLOR

EDINBURGH UNIVERSITY PRESS

The order of authors is alphabetical.
Both authors contributed equally to this work.

© Kenneth Bourne and William Banks Taylor, 1994

Edinburgh University Press Ltd
22 George Square, Edinburgh

Typset in Linotron Goudy
by Koinonia Ltd, Bury, and
printed and bound in Great Britain
by The University Press, Cambridge

A CIP record for this book is available
from the British Library

ISBN 0 7486 0398 0

Contents

Section II: The Edinburgh Reviewer, 1802–1809

Section III: The Front-Bench Politician, 1810–1817

Preface

The seed of this edition of Francis Horner's papers was William Banks Taylor's Ph.D thesis, 'The Foxite Party and Foreign Politics, 1806–1815' (University of London, 1974), which was directed by Dr Kenneth Bourne, Professor of History in the London School of Economics and Political Science. This volume is therefore the product of a collaborative effort by a former student and his mentor.

Yet in December 1992, when the work was in page proof, Professor Bourne died unexpectedly at his home in London. He is mourned by his grateful former students, among them a saddened co-editor who completed this, Kenneth Bourne's final contribution to historical scholarship.

The documents herein have been selected from two principal manuscript collections. The larger is the Francis Horner papers in the British Library of Political and Economic Science in London. It consists of nearly a thousand letters and amounts to more than 2,200 folios in addition to a supplementary volume of miscellaneous writings, to which has been added a lengthy family memoir by Horner's sister Frances, 'Memoirs of her Parents Mr and Mrs Horner, by F.C. Byrne'. The second collection remains in the family possession at Kinnordy House, near Kirriemuir in Scotland. It consists principally of some two hundred letters, Horner's journals, and a large number of miscellaneous notes, including his most notable comment on economic matters.

Other manuscript collections, some of which have become accessible to scholars only in recent years, have also provided valuable material. Among them the most important are the Holland House Papers in the British Library, which include the papers of John Allen. The editors have also examined the James Reddie papers, those of the Earls of Minto, and a number of miscellaneous Horner materials at the National Library of Scotland, the papers of the 2nd Earl Grey at Durham University, the Samuel Whitbread papers at the Bedfordshire County Record Office, the papers of Brougham, Bentham, and Creevey at University College, London, the papers of the 11th Duke of Somerset at the Buckinghamshire County Record Office and of his brother Lord Webb Seymour at the Devon County Record Office (the bulk of which, however, have been rendered illegible by damp), the Lacaita-Shelburne papers and those of the 2nd Earl of Shelburne in the University of Michigan, and the papers of the 1st and 2nd Lords Auckland, Bentham, Mackintosh, Macvey Napier, and Peel at the British Library.

A debt of gratitude is therefore owed above all to the Right Honourable Lord Lyell, and to Lady Lyell, who graciously allowed the publication of selections from the Horner papers at Kinnordy, to the British Library of Political and Economic Science for permission to use its collection of Horner papers, and to the late Sir John Langman for generously depositing there Frances Byrne's 'Family Memoirs'. Thanks also go to the Trustees of the British Museum and of the National Library of Scotland, the Bedfordshire County Record Office and Mr S. C. Whitbread, the Buckinghamshire County Record Office, Durham University Archives and Special Collections, the Library, University College, London, and the Trustees of the Whitfield Estate Office, and the William L. Clements Library in the University of Michigan. And the surviving editor must acknowledge with gratitude the kindness of the Director of the Board of Trustees of Kanto Gakuen University and to Dr Trevor Hughes Parry for generously permitting the inclusion of a hitherto unknown letter of Malthus (Doc. 377), and the sight of some associated documents.

Others who have been instrumental in bringing this project to fruition include Mr Patrick Davis, formerly Publications Officer at the London School of Economics and Political Science, and a number of accommodating archivists and librarians in both Great Britain and the United States of America, most notably Miss Angela Raspin at the British Library of Political and Economic Science, Miss A. Whitelegge at the University of London Library, and those at the National Library of Scotland and the Institute for Advanced Study, Princeton. Kenneth Bourne owed to the Nuffield Foundation a Social Sciences Fellowship that enabled him nearly to complete his share of the project; and William Taylor is similarly indebted to the Institute of Anglo-American Studies and to its Director, Dr Tim W. Hudson. To Dr Morris Perlman, Mr Ernest Thorp, Dr Peter Urbach, and Professor Basil Yamey of LSE is owed a considerable debt of help and encouragement; and to Professor Donald Winch of the University of Sussex also the avoidance of many errors of fact or judgement. Finally, profound thanks go to the University of Southern Mississippi, to the British Academy, to the LSE Publications Committee, and to the Suntory-Toyota International Centre for Economics and Related Disciplines at LSE for furthering the publication of this volume.

WBT

Editorial Note

Substantial passages or whole documents previously published are placed within angled brackets thus, ‹. . .›, and the source of the published version is similarly shown in brackets in the document heading. Omissions from the manuscript or previously published version are indicated by ellipses, and, in the latter cases, ellipses not enclosed in angled brackets indicate that at least part of the passage or passages omitted is also lacking in the previously published version.

The original text of the manuscripts has been retained throughout save that headings have been standardized and minor slips, such as inadvertent repetitions of a word or two, have been omitted and occasional small changes have been made in the spelling and punctuation. 'Ye', for example, has been rendered 'the', and the spelling of such words as 'expences', 'chuse', 'controul', 'publick', 'honor', 'shew', and 'œconomists' (which Horner often resorted to at random and quite inconsistently) modernized throughout. Horner's occasional errors with names have been retained where – as in the case of James Mill – they may have some significance, though his various renderings of Cobbett, Fremantle, Perceval, and Pigott have been made consistent and his habitual misspelling of 'accomodation' corrected. Most abbreviations – such as 'wh.' for 'which' and 'Ld' for 'Lord' – have been spelled out in full, and '&c' replaced by 'etc.'

Almost all the notes are those of the present editors; others marked * are, as indicated, those of Francis Horner himself or from his brother's published Life. Wherever possible persons mentioned in the documents have been identified in the notes, but to avoid unnecessary elaboration attention is drawn in appropriate cases to the *Dictionary of National Biography* (*DNB*), though the dates it gives have occasionally been corrected.

Reference is occasionally made in the notes to the 'Kinnordy set' of the *Edinburgh Review*. This is not, unfortunately, Horner's own collection which would apparently have yielded important new information, for among the papers noted by the editors at Kinnordy is Horner's undated holograph 'key' to the authors of the early articles in the *Review*. It is probably of an early date and incomplete even for the period it covers, though the last four names it contains appear to have been added subsequently to the initial list. Without the set to which it refers, it apparently confirms only one hitherto uncertain speculation, that Dr W.G. Maton contributed to at least one article – presumably to article 26 in the first issue. But it is reproduced here in the hope that one day some vigilant scholar or librarian will realize that he has before him Horner's own surviving set of the *Review*:

WRITERS IN THE *EDINBURGH REVIEW*

a. – Francis Jeffrey, advocate
b. – Rev. Sydney Smith
c. – Alexander Hamilton
d. – Francis Horner
e. – John Archibald Murray, advocate
f. – Thomas Brown, now MD
g. – Henry Peter Brougham
h. – John Thomson, surgeon, Edinr
i. – Thomas Thomson, advocate
k. – Rev. Peter Elmsley
l. – John Eyre
m. – Gregory Watt
n. – Walter Scott, advocate
o. – Humphry Davy, of the Royal Institution
p. – Andrew Duncan, jun. MD
q. – James Loch, advocate, and of Linc. I.
r. – Joseph Phillimore, LLD
s. – Honble William Herbert
t. – John Allen
u. – Thomas Campbell, author of the Pleas. of Hope

P. – Professor John Playfair
W. – Mr Wilberforce, MP
M. – Dr Mayton
K. – Richard Payne Knight, author of the work on Taste

The 'set' of the Review referred to in the notes to the documents printed here consists, rather, of a later edition of issues i–lxxi (vols i–xxxv, 1802–1821), given by John Horner to his daughter Anne Williams Power in 1822. The early numbers of this set in particular contain some manuscript identifications of contributors. The source of this information is not apparent. It does not seem to have been Cockburn since, while he was a close friend of the family, at least one entry (on art. 5) is at odds with information derived more directly from him, nor even for the early years Horner, whose record clearly contained much more information. The details are too many and the results too meagre to be worth recording here in full. For almost all merely correspond with those already well-established. But there are some possibly significant variations. Thus the Kinnordy set attributes article no. 5 to Brougham rather than Hamilton; 6 to Brougham and Jeffrey, not Hamilton; 26 to Brougham, not Jeffrey; 40 to Jeffrey as well as Stoddart; 49 to Reeve, not Thomson; 51 first to Murray and then, in a later pencil amendment, to Jeffrey rather than Smith; 53 to Brougham as well as Jeffrey; 97 to Jeffrey, not Eyre; 129 to John Thomson; and 340 to Murray, not Jeffrey.

Abbreviations

Sources frequently cited in the notes have been abbreviated as follows; unless otherwise stated the place of publication is London:

Addington: *The Life and Correspondence of the Right Honble Henry Addington, First Viscount Sidmouth*, by George Pellew (3 vols, 1847)

AR: *Annual Register*

Aspinall: Arthur Aspinall, *Lord Brougham and the Whig Party* (Manchester, 1927)

Bacon: *The Works of Francis Bacon*, ed. James Spedding, Robert Leslie Ellis, and Douglas Denon Heath (14 vols, 1857–74)

Bentham: *The Correspondence of Jeremy Bentham*, ed. Timothy L.S. Spragge, Ian R. Christie, Alexander Taylor Milne, John Dinwiddy, and Stephen Conway (in progress, London and Oxford, 1968–)

BLG: *Burke's Landed Gentry*

BLPES: The British Library of Political and Economic Science at the London School of Economics

BPP: *British Parliamentary Papers*

Brougham: *The Life and Times of Henry Lord Brougham written by himself* (3 vols, Edinburgh & London, 1871)

Brougham, *Historical Sketches*:
Henry, Lord Brougham, *Historical Sketches of Statesmen who Flourished in the Time of George III* (3 vols, 1839–43)

Brougham and Friends:
Brougham and His Early Friends: Letters to James Loch 1798–1809, ed. R.H.M. Buddle Atkinson and G.A. Jackson (3 vols, 1908)

Brown: David Welsh, *Account of the Life and Writings of Thomas Brown, MD* (Edinburgh, 1825)

Buckingham: *Memoirs of the Court of England during the Regency, 1811–1820*, ed. The Duke of Buckingham and Chandos (2 vols, 1856)

Burke: *The Correspondence of Edmund Burke*, ed. Thomas W. Copeland (10 vols, 1958–78)

Byrne Memoirs: 'Memoirs of her Parents Mr and Mrs Horner by F.C. Byrne', in the BLPES

Cantor: Geoffrey N. Cantor, 'The Academy of Physics at Edinburgh 1797–

1800', *Social Studies of Science*, v (no. ii, May 1975), 109–34

Chitnis: Anand C. Chitnis, *The Scottish Enlightenment and Early Victorian English Society* (1986)

Clive: John Clive, *Scotch Reviewers: The Edinburgh Review, 1802–1815* (Cambridge, Mass., 1957)

Cobbett: G.D.H. Cole, *The Life of William Cobbett* (1924)

Cockburn: Henry, Lord Cockburn, *Memorials of His Time* (1909)

Colchester: *The Diary and Correspondence of Charles Abbot, Lord Colchester*, ed. by his son (3 vols, 1861)

Constable: *Archibald Constable and his Literary Correspondents*, ed. Thomas Constable (3 vols, Edinburgh, 1873)

Creevey: *The Creevey Papers*, ed. Sir Herbert Maxwell (2 vols, 1904)

DNB: *Dictionary of National Biography*

Dropmore MSS: Historical Manuscripts Commission, *The Manuscripts of J.B. Fortescue, Esq., preserved at Dropmore* (10 vols, 1892–1927)

ER: *Edinburgh Review*

EW: *The Economic Writings of Francis Horner in the Edinburgh Review, 1802–6* (1957), ed. Frank Whitson Fetter and published as Number 13 of the London School of Economics and Political Science Series of Reprints of Scarce Works on Political Economy

Farington Diary: *The Farington Diary*, by Joseph Farington, ed. James Greig (8 vols, 1922–8)

Fetter, 'The Bullion Report Re-examined':
                    Frank Whitson Fetter, 'The Bullion Report Re-examined', *Quarterly Journal of Economics*, lvi (1941–2), 655–66

Fontana: Biancamaria Fontana, *Rethinking the Politics of Commercial Society: the Edinburgh Review 1802–1832* (Cambridge, 1985)

Fox: The Earl of Ilchester, ed., *The Journal of the Hon. Henry Edward Fox (afterwards fourth and last Lord Holland) 1818–1830* (1923)

George III: *The Later Correspondence of George III*, ed. A. Aspinall (5 vols, Cambridge, 1962–70)

Gore, Creevey: *Creevey's Life and Times: A Further Selection from the Correspondence of Thomas Creevey Born 1768 – Died 1838*, ed. John Gore (1934)

Gray, Perceval: Denis Gray, *Spencer Perceval: The Evangelical Prime Minister 1762–1812* (Manchester, [1963])

Grenville: Peter Jupp, *Lord Grenville 1759–1834* (Oxford, 1985)

Grey: George Macaulay Trevelyan, *Lord Grey of the Reform Bill* (1920)

Hawes: Frances Hawes, *Henry Brougham* (1957)

Heckscher: Eli Philip Heckscher, *The Continental System; An Economic Interpretation*, ed. Harald Westergaard (Oxford, 1922)

HHDB: Holland House Dinner Books, BL Add. MSS 51950–2

Hilton: Boyd Hilton, *Corn, Cash, Commerce: The Economic Policies of the Tory Governments 1815–1830* (Oxford, 1977)

HL: *Catalogue of a portion of the library of the late Francis Horner, containing many scarce articles on political economy, . . . which will be* sold by auction ... by Mr Francis Edwards ... on Wednesday, March 30, 1831 (1831)

Holland's Further Memoirs:
>   Further Memoirs of the Whig Party, 1807–1821. With Some Miscellaneous Reminiscences, by Henry Richard Vassall, Third Lord Holland, ed. by Lord Stavordale (1905)

Holland House: Leslie Mitchell, Holland House (1980)

Holland House Chronicles:
>   The Earl of Ilchester, Chronicles of Holland House, 1820–1900 (1937)

Holland House Circle:
>   Lloyd Sanders, The Holland House Circle (1908)

Holland Memoirs: Memoirs of the Whig Party During My Time by Henry Richard Lord Holland, ed. by his son (2 vols, 1852)

Home of the Hollands:
>   The Earl of Ilchester, The Home of the Hollands 1605–1820 (1937)

Horner: Memoirs and Correspondence of Francis Horner, M.P., edited by his brother, Leonard Horner (2nd ed., 2 vols, Boston and London, 1853)

Hume: David Hume, Essays Moral, Political, and Literary, ed. Thomas Hill Green and Thomas Hodge Grose (2 vols, 1882)

Inglis: Brian Inglis, Men of Conscience (New York, 1971)

Jeffrey: Life of Lord Jeffrey with a Selection from his Correspondence, ed. Lord Cockburn (2nd ed., 2 vols, Edinburgh, 1852)

King: A Selection from the Speeches and Writings of the Late Lord King, ed. Earl Fortescue (1844)

Lady Holland's Journal:
>   The Journal of Elizabeth Lady Holland, ed. the Earl of Ilchester (2 vols, 1908)

Lady Holland's Spanish Journal: The Spanish Journal of Elizabeth Lady Holland, ed. the Earl of Ilchester (1910)

Lean: E. Tangye Lean, The Napoleonists: A Study in Political Disaffection 1760–1960 (New York and Toronto, 1970)

Leonard Horner: Memoir of Leonard Horner, ed. Katharine M. Lyell (2 vols, 1890)

Letters to 'Ivy':   Letters to 'Ivy' from the First Earl of Dudley, ed. S.H. Romilly (1905)

Longford: Elizabeth Longford, Wellington: Pillar of State (1972)

Malthus: Patricia James, Population Malthus: His Life and Times (1979)

MC: Morning Chronicle

Medd: Patrick Medd, Romilly (1968)

Mitchell: Austin Mitchell, The Whigs in Opposition, 1815–1830 (Oxford, 1967)

Moore: Memoirs, Journal, and Correspondence of Thomas Moore, ed. Lord John Russell (8 vols, 1853–6)

Murray: Samuel Smiles, A Publisher and his Friends: Memoir and Correspondence of the late John Murray (2 vols, 1891)

Napier: Selections from the Correspondence of the late Macvey Napier, ed. by his son Macvey Napier (1879)

New: Chester New, *The Life of Henry Brougham to 1830* (Oxford, 1961)
NLS: The National Library of Scotland, Edinburgh
Palmerston Letters:
                              The Letters of the Third Viscount Palmerston to Laurence and Eliza-
                              beth Sulivan, 1804–1863, ed. Kenneth Bourne, Royal Historical
                              Society, Camden Fourth Series, xxxiii (1979)
Parl. Hist.:   *Cobbett's Parliamentary History of England*, published by Cobbett
                              in 1804–1812 and thereafter by T.C. Hansard
Parr: *The Works of Samuel Parr . . . with Memoirs of his Life and Writings*,
                              ed. John Johnstone (8 vols, 1828)
PH: *The History of Parliament: The House of Commons 1790–1820*, ed.
                              R.G. Thorne (5 vols, 1986)
Pitt: *Life of the Right Honourable William Pitt*, by Earl Stanhope (2nd ed.,
                              4 vols, 1862)
Plumer Ward: *Memoirs of the Political and Literary Life of Robert Plumer Ward*, ed.
                              Edmund Phipps (2 vols, 1850)
POW: *The Correspondence of George, Prince of Wales 1770–1812*, ed. A.
                              Aspinall (8 vols, 1963–72)
PR: *Cobbett's Weekly Political Register*
QR: *Quarterly Review*
Reid, *Sydney Smith*:
                              Stuart J. Reid, *A Sketch of the Life and Times of the Rev. Sydney*
                              Smith . . . (2nd ed., 1884)
Ricardo: *The Works and Correspondence of David Ricardo*, ed. Piero Sraffa
                              and M.H. Dobb (10 vols, Cambridge, 1951–5)
Roberts: Michael Roberts, *The Whig Party, 1807–1812* (1939)
Rogers: P.W. Clayden, *Rogers and his Contemporaries* (2 vols, 1889)
Romilly: *Memoirs of the Life of Sir Samuel Romilly, written by himself*, ed. by
                              his sons (2nd ed., 3 vols, 1840)
Romilly–Edgeworth Letters:
                              Romilly–Edgeworth Letters, 1813–1818, ed. Samuel Henry Romilly
                              (1936)
Ross: B.W. Ross, 'The Educational Works and Ideas of Lord Brougham',
                              M.A. thesis, University of London, 1951
Sack: James J. Sack, *The Grenvillites 1801–29: Party Politics and*
                              Factionalism in the Age of Pitt and Liverpool (University of Illinois
                              Press, 1979)
Sharp: [R. Sharp], *Letters and Essays in Prose and Verse* (1834)
Shine: Hill Shine and Helen Chadwick Shine, *The Quarterly Review*
                              under Gifford: Identification of Contributors 1809–1824 (Chapel
                              Hill, 1949)
Smith Letters: *The Letters of Sydney Smith*, ed. Nowell C. Smith (2 vols, Oxford,
                              1953)
Speculative Society:
                              History of the Speculative Society of Edinburgh from its Institution in
                              MDCCLXIV (Edinburgh, 1845)

Stewart's *Works*: Dugald Stewart, *The Collected Works*, ed. Sir William Hamilton (11 vols, Edinburgh, 1854–60)

Talleyrand: *Memoirs of the Duc de Talleyrand*, ed. Duc de Broglie(5 vols, 1891–2)

Taylor: William Banks Taylor, 'The Foxite Party and Foreign Politics, 1806–1815' (Ph.D. thesis, University of London, 1974)

Thomson: *Memoir of Thomas Thomson, Advocate*, ed. James T. Gibson Craig and C. Innis (Edinburgh, 1854)

Tierney: H.K. Olphin, *George Tierney* (1934)

Two Brothers: *Correspondence of Two Brothers: Edward Adolphus, Eleventh Duke of Somerset, and His Brother, Lord Webb Seymour, 1800 to 1819 and After*, by Lady Guendolen Ramsden (1906)

Webster: Sir Charles Webster, *The Foreign Policy of Castlereagh, 1815–1822: Britain and the European Alliance* (2nd ed., 1934)

Whishaw: *The 'Pope' of Holland House: Selections from the Correspondence of John Whishaw and His Friends 1813–1840*, ed. Lady Seymour (1906)

Whitbread: Roger Fulford, *Samuel Whitbread 1764–1815: A Study in Opposition* (1987)

WI: *The Wellesley Index to Victorian Periodicals, 1824–1900*, ed. Walter E. Houghton *et al.* (5 vols, Toronto, 1966–89)

Wilberforce: *The Life of William Wilberforce*, ed. Robert Isaac Wilberforce and Samuel Wilberforce (5 vols, 1838)

Winch: Donald Winch, 'The System of the North: Dugald Stewart and His Pupils', and 'Higher Maxims: Happiness versus Wealth in Malthus and Ricardo', in Stefan Collini, Donald Winch, and John Burrow, *That Noble Science of Politics: A Study in Nineteenth-Century Intellectual History* (Cambridge, 1983), pp. 23–61 and 63–89

WN: Adam Smith, *An Inquiry into the Nature and Causes of the Wealth of Nations*, ed. R.H. Campbell, A.S. Skinner, and W.B. Todd (2 vols, Oxford, 1976). (Individual references follow the system given in that edition; hence I. x. b. 1 is Book I, chapter x, section (i.e., 'Part' or 'Article') b, paragraph 1.)

WSD: *Supplementary Despatches, Correspondence, and Memoranda of Field Marshal Arthur Duke of Wellington*, ed. the Duke of Wellington (15 vols, 1858–72)

Ziegler: Philip Ziegler, *Addington* (1965)

General Introduction

Francis Horner (1778–1817) was one of those remarkable young men who studied under Professor Dugald Stewart at Edinburgh University during the final decade of the eighteenth century, founded the *Edinburgh Review* in 1802, and through that and other activities established themselves as a leading group of thinkers in a new era of British politics. The most famous of the group were Henry Brougham (1778–1868), the future Lord Chancellor of England, and Francis Jeffrey (1773–1850), the long-time editor of the *Review*. But it included also Sydney Smith (1771–1820), whose sagacious commentary figures so prominently in the history of the age, John Allen (1771–1843), later the sage of Holland House, and a number of others who were to earn considerable reputations. Horner, however, was the first to win both literary and political honours.

Among literary historians Horner is remembered as a founder of and early contributor to the *Edinburgh Review* and as its principal agent in London during the first decade of the nineteenth century. Political historians remember him as an important member of the Holland House circle and as a parliamentarian who, after a respected but rather inactive career from November 1806 until the end of the session of 1809, gradually emerged as a notable figure on the Whig bench between 1810, when he chaired the famous Bullion Committee, and 1816, when his active opposition to the Vienna Settlement and to British fiscal policy made a deep impression on the public at large. Historians of economic thought recall his scholarly essays on questions of political economy in the *Review*, his role in the bullion controversy, and his several parliamentary speeches criticizing British grain policy during the last years of the Napoleonic Wars.

Horner's reputation is based largely on the published memoirs, lives, and letters of his contemporaries. There is frequent mention of him and also a considerable amount of his correspondence in those of Brougham, Jeffrey, Smith, and his brother Leonard (1785–1864), but the published works of his early friends Lord Cockburn (1779–1854) and Thomas Thomson (1773–1852) and those of many other contemporary figures include materials on him as well. By far the most important single published source for him, however, is the two-volume *Memoirs and Correspondence of Francis Horner, MP*, edited by his brother and published in its most extended form in 1853.[1] That work draws heavily on Horner's

---

1. Leonard Horner began to collect materials shortly after his brother's death but produced

and correspondence and constitutes a substantial body of source material.

These were the principal sources used by late Georgian and early Victorian writers, though some of them had also known Horner personally, and until about the middle of the nineteenth century he enjoyed some reputation as an influential political economist of the classical school. In July 1852 the Scottish journalist William Weir maintained that Horner's early essays in the *Edinburgh Review* and his later advocacy of bullionist doctrine in Parliament were crucial to the success of the 'work to which Peel applied a finishing hand in 1819'. Lord Campbell, however, probably paid Horner the greatest tribute in recalling him as 'the first man in England to make the doctrines of political economy intelligible to the House of Commons'.[2]

Subsequently Horner's reputation rather languished in others' shadows until formerly inaccessible manuscript collections became available and regenerated interest in him. In 1941 an article by Frank Whitson Fetter reaffirmed his importance in the bullion controversy, and a second article in 1953 focused attention on his significance as both a reviewer of economic literature and a solicitor of reviews from Malthus and other economic thinkers. Four years later Fetter selected eight of his more important essays in the *Review*, and reprinted them together with an introductory summary of his life and works, and of his place in the history of economic thought. John Clive, the principal historian of the *Review*'s first fourteen years, provided further insight in 1957 with an analysis of the economic doctrine propounded by the early reviewers, and most subsequent works dealing with the years of the Bank restriction and with the wartime debate on corn policy include comment on Horner.[3]

Horner's name also appears with some regularity in the modern biographies of his political colleagues, in the various histories of the Holland House circle, and in the works of James Sack, Michael Roberts, and Austin Mitchell, the historians of the Grenvillites and the Whig party of the early nineteenth century. And of course Horner has a prominent place in the several publications produced by the relatively recent revival of scholarly interest in the *Review* and its dissemination of the 'Scottish Enlightenment'.[4]

Yet Horner remains a somewhat obscure figure. Perhaps his early reputation for brilliance and his failure to fulfil the high expectations he inspired have detracted

nothing until 1843, when the first edition of the *Memoirs and Correspondence* was published in Edinburgh. Two subsequent editions appeared, one at Edinburgh in a condensed form in 1849, and the other in a slightly enlarged form in London and in Boston, Massachusetts in 1853. For the purposes of this work the editors have used the 1853 edition, hereafter cited as *Horner*.

2. *Westminster and Foreign Quarterly Review*, lviii (July 1852), 105; Campbell quoted by Reid, *Sydney Smith*, p. 64.

3. Frank Whitson Fetter, 'The Bullion Report Re-examined', *Quarterly Journal of Economics*, lvi (1941–2), 655–66, and 'The Authorship of Economic Articles in the *Edinburgh Review*, 1802–47', *The Journal of Political Economy*, lxi (1953), 232–59. See also *Ricardo*, iii. 9–12, and, for an example of a subsequent work that, without yielding its subject's pride of place, gives considerable attention to Horner, Samuel Hollander, *The Economics of David Ricardo* (1979).

4. The most comprehensive account is Clive's *Scotch Reviewers*, but see also James A. Greig, *Francis Jeffrey of the Edinburgh Review* (1948). Among more recent works on their wider influence, especially in the economic sphere, are those by Chitnis, Fontana, and Winch.

from his fame. For he was regarded as a prodigy. He towered over his early school-mates, succeeding Brougham as *dux* of the rector's class at the High School of Edinburgh, and before his twentieth birthday contributing a memoir to the English translation of Euler's *Elements of Algebra*.[5] Later he enjoyed a lofty reputation in the debating societies of the university, emerged as Dugald Stewart's favourite, earned considerable reputation with his essays on economic questions in the early numbers of the *Review*, appeared before the bar of the House of Lords in his twenty-fifth year, and entered Parliament some two years later. But afterwards his accomplishments disappointed virtually everyone.

Horner's career at the English Chancery Bar was undistinguished; notwith-standing the patronage of well-placed friends, he never got his share of briefs and on several occasions was forced to turn for financial assistance to his family and friends.[6] As an Edinburgh reviewer he began with a flourish but effectively with-drew from Jeffrey's stable before the end of 1805. Of the fourteen completed articles generally assigned to him, twelve appeared in the first thirteen numbers of the *Review*, and only five of those essays contributed significantly to his reputation as a political economist.[7]

Horner's summary and analysis of Henry Thornton's *Inquiry into the Nature and Effects of the Paper Credit of Great Britain* (1802), which appeared in the first number, was his most important contribution. That learned essay on the theory of money was followed in January 1803 by his review of N.F. Canard's *Principes d'Economie Politique* (Paris, 1801), which displayed an uncommon grasp of economic philosophy but fell far short of the treatise on Physiocratic thought Horner had actually planned. In July of the same year he expanded in a review of Lord King's *Thoughts on the Restriction of Payments in Specie at the Banks of England and Ireland* (1803) the bullionist doctrine he had advanced in his earlier critique of Thornton. In October 1804 he contributed a perceptive analysis of the policy of export and import bounties on corn. And in October 1805 his review of the Earl of Selkirk's *Observations on the Present State of the Highlands of Scotland* (1805) reasoned expertly within the established principles of population.[8]

The quality of these essays was excellent, but there was nothing extraordinary about Horner's other reviews, and he somehow never got around to reviewing the leading economic treatises of his time. He delayed a review of Malthus's *Essay on Population* (1798) for years before finally abandoning it. He happily allowed

5. 'A Memoir of the Life and Character of Euler', in *Elements of Algebra, By Leonard Euler, Translated From the French With the Notes of M. Bernoulli, etc. and the Additions of M. De La Grange*, by the Rev. John Hewlett (3rd ed., 1822).

6. *Brougham*, i. 261–2, and Horner to his father, [?26 Apr. 1804], to Seymour, 30 Nov. 1805, to Leonard Horner, 24 and 30 Mar. 1808, to Murray, 7 July 1809, and to his father, 20 Aug. 1809, BLPES ii. 96–7 and 235–6, iii. 230–33, iv. 92–3, and *Horner*, i. 496–7.

7. *Brougham*, i. 259, claimed that in the first twenty numbers of the *Review* there were eighty articles by himself, seventy-five by Jeffrey, twenty-three by Smith, and fourteen by Horner, and this account has generally been accepted. For a bibliographical essay on the authorship of the *Review's* early articles, see Clive, p. 15; but see also the additions and corrections in *WI* and below p. 14 n. 48.

8. *ER* i (no. i, Oct. 1802), 172–201, (no. ii, Jan. 1803), 431–50, ii (no. iv, July 1803), 402–421, v (no. ix, Oct. 1804), 190–208, and vii (no. xiii, Oct. 1805), 185–202 (*EW*, pp. 28–56, 57–76, 77–95, 96–114, and 115–32).

Brougham to review Lauderdale's *Inquiry into the Nature and Origin of Public Wealth*, which put forward the first connected theory of the nature of profit. Despite his keen interest in the wartime carrying trade of neutral nations, he successfully encouraged others to review Stephen's celebrated *War in Disguise*. Furthermore, he neglected to comment in the *Review* on the numerous publications produced by the bullion controversy in 1810 and 1811, and by the debate on corn policy in 1814 and 1815.

As early as 1804 at least one of Horner's literary associates had decided that he was unreliable,[9] and by 1806 his reputation as a procrastinator was firmly established and Jeffrey no longer depended on him for reviews of even economic literature. Walter Scott, hardly an admirer of the Edinburgh reviewers, compared him to Obadiah's bull, 'who, though he certainly never did produce a calf, nevertheless went about his business with so much gravity, that he commanded the respect of the whole parish'.[10] Brougham, who was more charitable than Scott, nevertheless commented in his *Life and Times* on Horner's disappointing literary performance, and even Sydney Smith, who adored Horner, once described him as 'a sort of literary tiger, whose den is strewed with ten times more victims than he can devour'.[11]

Nor did Horner fulfil the high expectations of him in politics. After moving to London in the spring of 1803 he rose rapidly within the ranks of the Whig party. By the end of 1805 he was a fixture at Holland House, a colleague of Sir Samuel Romilly, Sir James Mackintosh, and the set of lawyers who were later to distinguish themselves on the Opposition bench in the Commons, and in November 1806, some months after Charles James Fox, the Grenvilles, and their 'Ministry of All the Talents' had come to power, he was returned to Parliament in the Whig interest. During the decade that followed, however, he displayed little inclination to step forward. Horner seemed more comfortable in the privacy of his study, at Brooks's, and at the dinner table of Holland House than in the public spotlight. In the House of Commons he displayed flashes of brilliance but tended to follow the lead of others, and much of his time was devoted to the work of committees charged to investigate social and legal issues well outside the mainstream of politics. His tendency to hold back, to avoid giving offence at all cost, cast him as a harmless back-bencher and frustrated the high expectations of his peers no less than his apparent procrastination as an Edinburgh reviewer. Jeffrey scolded him unmercifully for failing to assert himself in the Commons, but except for his involvement in the bullion controversy of 1810–11, Horner made no great mark in Parliament until the last years of his life.[12]

Ironically, the altogether unanticipated success of his belated parliamentary offensive, and the fact that he died shortly after it, also detracted from his reputation. In 1815 and 1816, when he at last asserted himself among the leaderless Whig bench in the Commons, his powerful speeches on grain policy, on monetary policy, and on the terms of the treaties of peace impressed the House and inspired high expectations among friends and rivals alike. But they led shortly afterwards only to regrets for what might have been had he lived.[13]

9. Smith to Jeffrey, April or May 1804, *Smith Letters*, i. 96.
10. Quoted by Clive, p. 82.
11. *Brougham*, i. 261; Smith to Jeffrey, 30 Nov. 1803, *Smith Letters*, i. 91.
12. For a systematic survey of Horner's discernible activities as an MP, see Frank Whitson Fetter, *The Economist in Parliament: 1780–1868* (Durham, NC, 1980).
13. Horner's most famous speeches of the 1815 and 1816 sessions were published as an

After some of the most influential members of the Commons had participated in a memorial tribute on 3 March 1817, Romilly protested in his diary that George Canning 'spoke of Horner only as a person who was rising into great eminence as a politician'. But every speaker then and those who eulogized him privately said much the same thing as Canning, and even Romilly told the Commons that if he had lived, 'he would have discovered powers not yet discovered to the House, and of which perhaps he was unconscious himself'.[14]

This was the view of Horner, emphasizing unfulfilled expectations to the virtual exclusion of real accomplishments, that adorned the inscription on Chantrey's monument to him in Westminster Abbey, and it was strengthened by the sentimental tributes of poets and by the martyrdom customarily assigned to fallen heroes by the Whig faithful. Poetry represented the dead Horner as 'the Friend of the Oppressed' and as a patriot whose 'arm was stretched' to save the realm, and all of it stressed that he had died on the eve of bigger things. At a dinner for Lord Erskine held in Edinburgh in 1820, Cockburn toasted Horner and remarked in the best of Whig tradition that 'if it had been known that he was to be at his post . . . some of the recent inroads which have been made upon our liberties would never have been even dared to be proposed'.[15]

Similar interpretations of Horner's unfulfilled potential were expressed in the years that followed. As an elder statesman, Lansdowne told a group of friends that death alone had prevented the young Scot from rising to the highest posts in the state. That view of Horner stuck; in 1906, for example, Lord Durham's biographer noted that Horner died 'just after he had risen from obscurity'.[16]

appendix in the second volume of *Horner*. They include those on the transfer of Genoa to Sardinia (Feb. 1815: *Horner*, ii. 519–22), the corn laws (Feb. 1815: Doc. 553), the treaties of peace (Feb. 1816: Doc. 599), the Alien Act (April and May 1816: *Horner*, ii. 555–62), and the resumption of cash payments by the Bank of England (May 1816: Doc. 609). *Home of the Hollands*, p. 317, relates Tierney's 1815 opinion that Horner was destined for a great career in the Commons. See also *Creevey*, i. 251, for the begrudgingly favourable opinion of Charles Callis Western, afterwards Baron Western (1767–1844: *DNB*), Horner's Whig rival on corn policy, and i. 249, for the restless Brougham's comment of 14 Jan. 1816 that the affairs of the party were likely to be carried on by 'a *coterie* at Lady Holland's elbow' led by Horner and Tierney in the Commons. For an analysis of the corn debates of 1814 and 1815 with comment on Horner's delicate position within the Whig party, see Hilton, pp. 13–29. See also Brougham's assessment of Horner's speeches on the treaties of peace in his *Historical Sketches*, ii. 180–81.

14. *Romilly*, iii. 281. The tributes given in the Commons on the occasion of a new writ being moved for Horner's vacated borough of St Mawes appear in *Horner*, ii. 443–54. They were also printed for private circulation by Lord Holland and translated into Italian by Ugo Foscolo. See also the eulogy and partial account of the parliamentary tributes in *The Edinburgh Annual Register for 1817*, x. 209–213. A number of private tributes appear in *Horner*, ii. 439–43 and 455–69.

15. The inscription in the Abbey mentions 'expectations which premature death could alone have frustrated'. A list of those who subscribed to the monument appears in *Horner*, ii. 489. Other partial lists of subscribers are in BL Add. MSS 34459, ff. 254–5, and in NLS MSS 2218, f. 1. The latter also includes the other quotations from anonymous poems entitled 'Imagination' (f. 3) and 'To the Memory of Francis Horner' (f. 4), and that from Cockburn (f. 2).

16. Moore, vii. 142; Stuart J. Reid, *Life and Letters of the First Earl of Durham, 1792–1840* (2 vols, 1906), i. 109.

The notion that Horner was an obscure figure for most of his life was strengthened by the perceived break in history occasioned by the conclusion of the Napoleonic Wars. Horner was not a Whig leader in Parliament during the 'Age of Napoleon', and was not so regarded by his contemporaries. His spirited parliamentary exertions during 1815 and 1816, moreover, encompassed only a short and relatively inconsequential period within the so-called 'Age of Reform'. Hence even his contemporaries tended to lose him in the process of historical transition, and their omissions inevitably affected the interpretations of later generations of historians.

Professor Roberts's *Whig Party, 1807–1812*, relegates Horner to a minor role in party affairs. There is a lamentable gap in the historiography of the Whig party for the years 1813 and 1814. But Austin Mitchell's *Whigs in Opposition, 1815–1830*, which offers but fleeting comment on the years immediately following the war, also mentions Horner only briefly as one who had been important at an earlier time.

The specialization that has come to characterize historical writing has also contributed to Horner's obscurity. Professor Clive's otherwise excellent account of the early history of the *Review* fails to give adequate consideration to the political circumstances that framed Horner's later relationship with Jeffrey. The work of economic historians is even more narrowly focused, tending to dwell, not on Horner as a man or as a rising Whig politician, but instead on his role in a narrow sphere of public policy. More recently he has fared better at the hands of intellectual historians. But while giving full acknowledgement to the 'courage and merit' of some of his writings, Dr Fontana tends still to emphasize that he 'was to a certain extent the prisoner of his own diligent and unimaginative scholarship', and Dr Chitnis merely concludes, rather lamely, that 'Horner is a well-documented example of the conscious transmission, through connection, of "Scotch knowledge".' However, Professor Winch, in a sympathetic and perceptive review of Horner's lifelong application to study, concludes despite his failings that 'it was certainly not fanciful to believe that he would have been a natural candidate for the Chancellorship of the Exchequer in any future Whig ministry'.[17] Yet political historians, too, are guilty of glaring omissions; Professor Roberts inexplicably excluded questions of fiscal policy from his evaluation of party politics, thereby ignoring the principal reason for Horner's standing among his contemporaries.

Horner's reputation suffered still further from the worship of originality so characteristic of the years immediately following the conclusion of the Napoleonic Wars and from the narrow view of history to which later generations subscribed. Horner spent most of his political career in futile opposition to Tory governments, he was directly responsible for no major legislation, and most of his labours in Parliament bore fruit only after his death. Those facts apparently led later editors and authors to ignore or underrate him; they generally focused on those who carried their causes to fruition and awarded Horner little more than footnotes.

The young Peel, for instance, was apparently influenced very profoundly by Horner, and two major pieces of legislation with which Peel is credited – the restoration of cash payments by the Bank of England and the repeal of the corn laws – were causes for which Horner laboured and with which the wartime generation of

17. Fontana, p. 59; Chitnis, p. 98; Winch, pp. 51–2.

Britons associated his name. Yet none of Peel's Victorian biographers made more than passing reference to Horner, and Kitson Clark does not even mention him.[18]

Horner's place in the history of economic thought has been moulded by similar factors. Cobbett was particularly unkind to his memory. In 1819, as Peel moved for cash payments, Cobbett wrote:

> Pray keep your eye on the praises (from all parts of the dens) bestowed on the memory of lawyer Horner; that stupid oaf, who always looked as if he had just had a bout at sucking his thumbs. The doctrines, which are now coming in vogue, are ascribed *to him*, when it is notorious, that the foolish fellow proposed, in 1811 (in *war*) to *compel the Bank to pay in specie at the end of two years!* Though now, at the end of *four years of peace*, it is found, that it cannot pay in specie at the end of *four years* yet to come! It is all a lie; it cannot pay *then*; but, at any rate, here is, upon the showing of the fellows themselves, quite enough to justify all that I have ever said about the foolish notions of this dead lawyer.

Two years later Cobbett was still referring sneeringly to 'Oracle Horner' in the fifth of his 'Letters to Landlords'.[19]

Although less unkind, the editor of Huskisson's *Speeches* in 1831 considered Huskisson's role in the bullion controversy and concluded that he, rather, was 'the first financier of the age'. Misleadingly, but with enough validity to detract from Horner's reputation, Brougham assigned full credit to Lord King for 'the detection and the proof of the effects actually produced by [the] fatal' bank restriction. Other Victorian writers, perhaps following the interpretation offered by David Ricardo's brother and surely influenced by Ricardo's later reputation, portrayed Ricardo as the driving force behind the Bullion Report, and as late as 1924 one scholar represented Horner as nothing more than Ricardo's spokesman in the Commons.[20]

The interpretations of modern biographers have added to the fog. G.D.H. Cole

---

18. François Guizot, *Memoir of Sir Robert Peel* (1857); Sir Lawrence Peel, *A Sketch of the Life and Character of Sir Robert Peel* (1860); J. R. Thursfield, *Peel* (1891); the 8th Earl of Rosebery, *Sir Robert Peel* (1891); Charles Stuart Parker, ed., *Sir Robert Peel from his Private Papers* (3 vols, 1891–9), where Horner is confused in the index with his brother; George Kitson Clark, *Peel and the Conservative Party* (1929). Cf., however, Norman Gash, *Mr Secretary Peel. The Life of Sir Robert Peel to 1830* (1961), pp. 241–3, and Benjamin Disraeli, *Lord George Bentinck. A Political Biography* (1852), p. 306, noting that Horner and Romilly had great influence on Peel during his 'sallet-days'.

19. PR xxxv. 222 (2 Oct. 1819) and xxxvi. 925–6 (20 Oct. 1821).

20. *The Speeches of the Right Honourable William Huskisson* (3 vols, 1831), i. 54; Brougham, *Historical Sketches*, ii. 182.

   Lord King's contributions to the bullion controversy included his 1803 pamphlet on the *Restriction of Payments in Specie*, a number of speeches in the Lords, and, perhaps most notably, his refusal in 1810 to accept rents in Bank paper, a political tactic that later forced Government to introduce legislation declaring Bank notes legal tender. See *King*.

   In 1824, when Horner was receiving a great deal of posthumous but well-deserved credit for the recent triumph of his bullionist doctrine, one of Ricardo's brothers depreciated Horner's role in the controversy and assigned his kinsman total credit for developing the 'perfect' theory of money then in vogue. (See 'A Memoir of David Ricardo', *The Annual Biography and Obituary*, viii (1824), 368–77. See also *Ricardo*, x. 8 and 14–15, and N.J. Silberling, 'Ricardo and the Bullion Report', being the second of two articles on the 'Financial and Monetary Policy of Great Britain during the Napoleonic Wars', *Quarterly Journal of Economics*, xxxviii (1923–4), 429–30.)

mentioned Horner's name only once in his account of Cobbett's crusade for the restoration of cash payments. H.K. Olphin somehow concluded that George Tierney, Horner's colleague on the Opposition bench, was 'the leading Whig financier' during the bullion debates. And Standish Meacham, the biographer of Henry Thornton, portrayed his man as the leading figure in the bullion inquiry to the virtual exclusion of Horner.[21]

One must suspect that the nature of Horner's economic doctrine, as much as others' claims to fame, also tended to diminish his reputation among later generations. For Horner was not an 'economist', even as the early Victorians defined the word. Throughout his life he remained the devoted student of Dugald Stewart and the jealous guardian of his old professor's reputation,[22] and his intellectual focus was that of an eighteenth-century moral philosopher. He therefore subscribed to a broad, metaphysical view of economic phenomena and believed that great national interests often transcended demands arising from the ups and downs of the market.

While that interpretation contrasted strikingly with the more narrowly focused views of Ricardo, J.R. McCulloch, and later generations of economists, Horner's prejudices and normative methodology also placed him at odds with post-classical economic thought. He distrusted the motives of commercial men so profoundly that he favoured their exclusion from parliamentary committees charged with investigating economic matters; he viewed the works of 'political arithmeticians' very suspiciously; and he abhorred the exaggerated use of algebraic symbols in economic analysis.[23]

Horner clung to David Hume's emphasis on historical example, and to a method of analysis much akin to the old *histoire raisonnée* of the French. He accordingly interpreted contemporary problems and the statistics and calculations of contemporary writers as little more than pieces of a broad historical puzzle, and he repeatedly referred to an unchanging human nature that adapted to changing historical circumstances. He therefore advanced no economic 'law' and thus no original 'concept' that could be represented by Victorians as a distinct step along the way to an 'enlightened' present.[24]

There are those who have suggested that Horner has been badly misrepresented by historians. Fetter attempted with some success to correct the pervasive notion that Ricardo's influence fashioned the report of the Bullion Committee, which even now is regarded as one of the most important documents in the history of British

---

21. *Cobbett*, p. 170; *Tierney*, p. 148; Standish Meacham, *Henry Thornton of Clapham* (Cambridge, Mass., 1964), pp. 72–80.

22. *Home of the Hollands*, p. 220, notes that Samuel Rogers once provoked a terrible reaction from Horner and Allen by attacking Stewart's published works and describing his metaphysics as 'sometimes trite and shallow and sometimes obscure'. See also Doc. 149.

23. For one of many examples see Horner's review of Canard (*EW*, p. 65). For comment see *ibid.*, p. 8, and Fontana, pp. 51–3. Horner, however, was by no means consistent in this respect. Fontana points out, p. 121, that in his review of Thornton he had gone out of his way to praise the contributions of business men. Since he also argued there against the prejudices generated by the 'spirit of system', this may have been due to his well-developed sense of caution and discretion. But in May 1814 he also criticized the Commons Report on the Corn Laws for failing to take evidence from 'practical' men (*Hansard*, xxvii. 1023–4).

24. For a summary of Horner's general economic doctrine see *EW*, pp. 12–17.

monetary policy. After all, stressed Fetter, Horner chaired the committee, wrote large sections of its report, and propounded bullionist doctrine that differed appreciably from that of Ricardo.[25] As a senior statesman Brougham also questioned the meagre historical reputation of his childhood friend and observed that even some of Horner's most zealous supporters, notably Cockburn, had 'greatly underrated his talents, and really suppressed some of the most extraordinary instances of their successful display'.[26] The *Edinburgh Review* quite agreed, but laid the blame at the feet of Horner's brother Leonard.

The review of the first edition of the *Memoirs and Correspondence of Francis Horner* tactfully observed that the editor had 'confined his functions within very moderate limits.' Indeed, it was clear 'that portions of the correspondence important to the history and to the biography' of Horner's times 'must have been kept back' in deference to the feelings of living personages. The result was that the two volumes contained 'many fragments of observation . . . which we would have wished to see completed; many outlines which it would have been most desirable to have seen filled up'.[27]

The evaluation was astute. Leonard Horner was a geologist and educational reformer who knew little about politics and nothing about political economy. He had undertaken an edition of his brother's papers only after more qualified individuals had abandoned it and had selected documents with an eye to paying 'a debt that was felt to be due to the memory' of his brother.[28] The result was an incomplete and rather mundane biographical memoir stressing personal virtues and so reinforcing an already distorted view of Horner's life and works. The review was quite right, moreover, in stating that important correspondence had been suppressed so as to avoid giving umbrage to Horner's surviving contemporaries. For Leonard Horner excluded a large number of very revealing letters and a considerable amount of other important materials; he bowdlerized some of those he included; and despite the *Review*'s critical remarks he made but modest improvements in the later editions of the work.

Perhaps the most incomprehensible of Leonard Horner's omissions were those relating to his brother's formative years in Edinburgh. At Kinnordy House are drafts of Horner's two most celebrated speeches to the Speculative Society and his meticulous notes on the *Wealth of Nations*, the system of the French 'Economists', and the philosophical writings of Bacon. None of those documents, or any extracts from them, appeared in the *Memoirs and Correspondence*, and Leonard Horner also excluded a number of significant entries in his brother's journal.

25. See Fetter's general arguments in 'The Bullion Report Re-examined'. See also *EW*, p. 18, for his short observations on the extent to which Ricardo's name has overshadowed Horner's in the history of economic thought. See also *Ricardo*, x. 8 and 91–2, for the questionable conclusion that the doctrine Ricardo advanced in early 1810 included all the ideas put forward in the Bullion Report, and for the editors' critical assessment of Professor Silberling's theory of the relationship between Horner and Ricardo that influenced the Bullion Report.

26. *Brougham*, i. 262.

27. *ER* lxxviii (no. clviii, Oct. 1843), 262–3. The review was by Thomas Spring-Rice, afterwards 1st Baron Monteagle (1790–1866: *DNB*), who had had some contact with Horner in 1816 (Doc. 613 n. 1).

28. *Horner*, i. vii–viii.

The unpublished journal entries, complemented by Frances Horner's family memoir and by several miscellaneous notes and unpublished letters found elsewhere, shed much light on the origins of Horner's economic, social, and political views, on the nature, sequence, and impact of his political and economical readings, and on Dugald Stewart and the celebrated circle of young men with whom Horner associated at university. Providing much insight into Horner's earliest views on political economy are the drafts of his two speeches to the 'Spec', especially his 1800 foray into the troubled world of Malthus and the theory of population, which he entitled 'Overgrowth of the Metropolis' (Doc. 44).

Of all Horner's early papers, however, the most significant are his notes on Smithian and Physiocratic doctrine, and to a lesser extent those on Bacon's philosophical writings, which often reflect a fascination with economic and political phenomena. McCulloch, who reviewed those manuscripts in 1824, observed that the notes on the French 'Economists' were 'very valuable', containing 'several éclaircissements, modifications, and corrections' of interest, and being written with 'equal acuteness, discrimination, and candour'. He discovered 'little or no original disquisition' in Horner's other writings on political economy but observed that they 'would be a treasure to anyone who was investigating the history of the science, and the progress of civilization in the British Empire'.[29]

McCulloch neglected to comment on the most interesting feature of Horner's notes on political economy. For there, in Horner's good hand, are the results of his histoire raisonnée of both the corn trade and the theory of money; and there, too, is clear evidence that before 1802 he had developed much of the doctrine, and in some cases even the wording, of his earliest essays in the Review, of the sections he contributed to the Bullion Report, and of his later speeches in Parliament. After 1802 he added a number of passages to his notes but never departed from the general point of view he developed as a student at Edinburgh, and it appears that throughout his life he made frequent reference to his early researches.

Horner's notes on political economy are complemented by a number of other unpublished documents that reflect the considerable extent of his economic inquiries, displaying his early command of economic literature, and explaining several hitherto curious facts and observations in the published writings of his contemporaries. Certainly the depth of research and analysis that characterize those documents goes far to account for Dugald Stewart's high esteem for Horner's intellectual endowments and promise, for his stature among his peers at university, and for Macvey Napier's later comment that he had been as well suited for an academic chair as for a political career.[30] The economic notes also help explain why his collaborators in the founding of the Review selected him as the principal reviewer of economic literature,[31] and why the leaders of the Whig party later came to regard him as a valued adviser in economic matters.

29. McCulloch to Leonard Horner, 28 Mar. 1824, with Horner's 'Notes on my Progress in Studying the System of the Economists' in the Kinnordy MSS.
30. Home of the Hollands, p. 318, noting a comment made in 1843 by Macvey Napier (1776–1847: DNB), Jeffrey's successor as editor of the ER, when he asked Allen to review the first edition of the Memoirs and Correspondence.
31. Brougham, i. 252.

Horner's unpublished papers also provide conclusive evidence of his high standing as a political economist during his lifetime. Even Fetter tended to underestimate the impact of the first numbers of the *Review* on London society, the fame that Horner enjoyed when he arrived in the English capital in March 1803, and the considerable reputation that was afterwards attached to his name. That reputation was born of his contributions to the early numbers of the *Review*; it was based on the subject matter of those essays – monetary and grain policy in particular; and it was later carried to even greater heights.[32]

As early as February 1805, when Horner's several essays in the *Review* constituted his only claim to fame, Sydney Smith told Jeffrey that Horner's 'worth and talents are acknowledged by the world at a more early period than those of any independent and upright man I ever remember'. Some eight months later Smith informed Mackintosh that Horner's reputation as a political economist was so high that he was being feted everywhere.[33] And in late 1806, when Horner first entered Parliament, a London journalist assessed the leading men on the Government bench in the Commons and added:

> we must not omit to mention a new candidate for popular attention, who bids fair to make a good figure in the House. . . . This Gentleman is a MR HORNER. . . . He brings to the business of Parliament, a mind much better stored with liberal information than the majority of our Representatives. He appears to have studied the policy of Foreign States, and the interests of the British Empire, in a more serious school than many of our Legislators, whose information on these topics has been acquired from mere conversation, and whose principles seem to have been fixed by the animated conviviality of public dinners.[34]

This reputation mounted in subsequent years because of Horner's continuing affiliation with the *Review*, because questions of political economy became progressively more important in public affairs, because of a profound ignorance of economic phenomena among even the most enlightened politicians, and because there was no other public man who could draw on a greater reservoir of historical fact in propounding economic philosophy. By all indications, beginning with the bullion controversy of 1810, and continuing until the spring of 1816, no economic thinker in Great Britain stood higher in public estimation.

Such stature ensured that Horner exerted influence on other political economists, and the extent of that influence is at least partly revealed by a number of hitherto unpublished letters. His correspondence with Lauderdale either has not survived or remains inaccessible.[35] But a number of his letters to Jeffrey and others provide enlightenment on the turbulent relationship between the Foxites' Scottish chieftain and the Edinburgh reviewers that arose from disagreement on economic

---

32. The considerable impact of the first numbers of the *Review* and the reasons for it are discussed in some detail by Clive, pp. 29–41, Fontana, and Chitnis.
33. Smith to Jeffrey, 16 Feb. 1805, *Smith Letters*, i. 102; *Chronicles of Holland House*, p. 83, quoting from a letter of 1 Oct. 1805.
34. Clipping from an unidentified London newspaper, NLS MSS 2218.
35. See *Economists' Papers, 1750–1950: A Guide to Archive and Other Manuscript Sources for the History of British and Irish Economic Thought*, comp. R.P. Sturges (London and Basingstoke, 1975), pp. 66–7.

doctrine, and also on the small circle of economic thinkers who met Lauderdale and Horner at Holland House and influenced the public views expounded by the Whigs.

Others who engaged in those discussions on a regular basis were John Allen, whose early economic researches had influenced Horner at university, and Lord King, with whom he formulated tactics that in 1811 led the Whig hierarchy publicly to embrace bullionist doctrine. Horner's correspondence with both men, and with others, casts new light on the wartime commercial policy of the Whig party, the bullion controversy, the factors behind Whig disagreement on corn policy in 1815, and the thought underlying his influential criticism of British fiscal policy in 1816.

Fetter examined Horner's correspondence with Malthus at the British Library of Political and Economic Science and commented at some length on the nature and importance of their relationship.[36] But Fetter saw neither the Kinnordy manuscripts nor a number of Horner's letters in other collections which together reveal a closer and more important link between the two economists. Of special interest is Horner's influence on Malthus's view of the Bank restriction in 1810 and 1811 and the debate between them on corn policy in 1814 and 1815.

There exists no known unpublished correspondence between Horner and Ricardo. Based on available evidence, however, Fetter concluded in 1941 that 'assertions regarding the doctrinal or political influence of Ricardo on the Bullion Report' were supported by nothing more than 'a general tradition that feeds on itself.'[37] Such a conclusion, of course, should have shifted the spotlight from Ricardo to Horner, who after all chaired the Bullion Committee, but Fetter did not have access to all the pertinent manuscripts and so was unable fully to develop his line of reasoning.

The unpublished Horner papers not only strengthen Fetter's argument but also magnify the importance of several published sources suggesting that Horner may well have exerted substantial influence on Ricardo's economic doctrine. Ricardo read and commented extensively on Horner's early essay on corn bounties in the *Review*, engaged in discussions with friends after reading his other economic treatises, and while still an obscure financier associated with an already famous Horner at the meetings of the Geological Society of London.[38] Furthermore, there is little reason to believe the claim that Ricardo's published views were responsible for Horner's famous motion for parliamentary inquiry into the high price of bullion.[39]

On the contrary, Horner's correspondence suggests that political considerations otherwise unrelated to the high price of bullion inspired Horner to step forward in Parliament. Moreover, his comments in the House on the occasion of his famous motion were consistent with the doctrine laid out in his university notes and in his

36. *EW*, pp. 9–11.
37. 'The Bullion Report Re-examined', p. 655.
38. For evidence of the influence on Ricardo of Horner's economic essays in the *Review*, see *Ricardo*, i. 302–303, 307–308, 315, and vii. 246. *EW*, p. 12, notes that Horner and Ricardo were elected to the seven-member board of trustees for the Geological Society of London in April 1810.
39. See *Ricardo*, x. 14–15. For an opposing interpretation arguing that the *ER*, and thus Horner, was 'the parent, nurse, and champion of the Bullion Committee', see the anonymously published pamphlet by J.C. Herries, *A Review of the Controversy Respecting the High Price of Bullion and the State of Our Currency* (1811), pp. 5–6.

earlier articles in the *Review*, and that doctrine differed so strikingly from Ricardo's that it inspired the financier to write several contentious letters to him.[40] After the Bullion Committee released its report it was Horner's 'bullion glory' that figured in contemporary letters,[41] and it was surely to him that the nation looked as the bipartisan leader of the bullionist forces, and during Horner's lifetime to Ricardo merely as one of his supporters.

Ricardo himself acknowledged Horner's stature as one of the leading economic thinkers of his time. Horner was, he wrote, 'a powerful supporter of all the good principles of Political Economy' and one who was 'much superior to the general race of young politicians'.[42] Perhaps Ricardo's greatest tribute to Horner, however, was his utilization of the Edinburgh reviewer's 1804 essay on corn bounties as a point of departure in his analysis of how changes in the prices of food, rather than changes in the prices of other commodities as Horner had reasoned, affected profits.[43]

Horner's unpublished papers, therefore, establish an important link between his early economic notes, his essays in the *Review*, and his later role as the leading political economist in Parliament. In turn that linkage sheds new light on a long-standing void in the history of economic thought extending from 1776, when the *Wealth of Nations* appeared, until 1819, when Ricardo produced his unsettling revisions of Smith's doctrine.

In but few cases do the manuscripts suggest that Horner merits the acclaim that posterity assigns to creativity; clearly there was little originality in the historical synthesis that constituted his doctrine. But he enjoyed relative superiority over the other economic thinkers of his time; his contemporaries, if not later generations, placed him in the first rank of economists; and there is no doubt that he exerted considerably more influence on economic thought than that with which he is usually credited. Indeed, his literary and parliamentary contributions to political economy lead one to reflect on Professor Burtt's remark that 'it is the attempt to build a theoretical system that marks the beginning of a discipline, not its content, or the policies it supports, or even the internal consistency of its doctrines'.[44]

Horner's hitherto unpublished correspondence also forces one to reassess his role in the early development of the *Edinburgh Review*. His contributions to the first number, especially his lengthy review of Thornton's treatise on the Bank restriction, impressed the public, adding much credibility to the journal and enhancing his already considerable standing among the inner circle of reviewers.[45] Smith, who edited the first number, afterwards promoted him to the exclusion of Brougham, and

40. See the account of Horner's speech in the *AR* lii (1810), 126–7, and Ricardo's letters to Horner dated 1 and 6 Feb. 1810, *Ricardo*, vi. 1–10.

41. See, for example, Smith to Lady Holland, 3 Nov. 1810, *Smith Letters*, i. 191.

42. Ricardo to McCulloch, 28 Feb. [1820], *Letters of David Ricardo to John Ramsay McCulloch, 1816–1823*, ed. J.H. Hollander (New York: Publications of the American Economic Association, No. x, n.d.), pp. 5–6; Ricardo to James Mill, 3 Nov. 1822, *Ricardo*, ix. 227–8.

43. See the chapter on 'Bounties on Exportation, and Prohibitions of Importation' in Ricardo's *Principles of Political Economy and Taxation* (1817). For comment see *EW*, p. 2.

44. Everett J. Burtt, jun., *Social Perspectives in the History of Economic Theory* (New York, 1972), p. 13.

45. Clive, p. 39, observes that Horner's review of Thornton's *Inquiry* probably produced more of 'an impression of competence and learning' than any other article in the first number. See also below, pp. 199–202.

Jeffrey came to revere his designated reviewer of economic literature. Constable, the publisher, also developed a 'reverent' attachment to him, and when Horner moved to London in early 1803 his strategic position in the English capital and the high esteem of Constable and Jeffrey assured him great influence over the *Review*'s content and editorial slant.[46]

No doubt Horner disappointed Jeffrey on numerous occasions, and no doubt the writings of Jeffrey, Brougham, and to a lesser extent Smith dominated the early numbers of the *Review*. But Horner's failure to meet Jeffrey's expectations had no apparent effect on the degree of influence he exerted on editorial policy. A large amount of unpublished correspondence for the years 1803–1810 mirrors Horner's role in the mounting Whig bias of the *Review*, in the utilitarian philosophy that began to creep in about 1806, in the selection of various reviewers, and in the exclusion, inclusion, or amendment of a number of reviews.

Moreover, the correspondence now printed perhaps gives new meaning to Brougham's later comment that 'Horner often said that his dissertation[s] would in all probability have been in his portfolio had the *Review* not existed'. Noting that no unpublished tracts were found among Horner's papers, Brougham dismissed the possibility that his old friend might have written more than was generally acknowledged with the observation that he 'now and then deceived himself'.[47]

Brougham's assessment is questionable. Horner's unpublished correspondence confirms that he began and laboured extensively on a number of reviews that later appeared bearing traces of his structured prose and general point of view. The authorship of several of those reviews remains unknown or in dispute. It therefore seems reasonable to suggest that Horner wrote and sent Jeffrey partial reviews on several occasions, that Jeffrey put them in final form, and that the result was confusion about authorship among contemporaries and historians alike.[48]

Horner would not have objected to such confusion; unquestionably, a timidity attributable to political considerations figured very prominently in his disappointing career as a reviewer. His correspondence indeed reveals mounting concern about the controversial nature of the *Review*, especially after 1804 when he publicly committed himself to the Whigs. Thereafter he sought with some success to maintain his advantageous relationship with Jeffrey, influencing editorial policy and setting the tone of several reviews by sending the editor extensive comment on a number of published works.

---

46. New, pp. 17–18; *Jeffrey*, i. 107; *Constable*, ii. 226.
47. *Brougham*, i. 261.
48. In both the introduction to the *EW*, and his 'Authorship of Economic Articles in the *Edinburgh Review*', Fetter suggested that Horner might have written several of the economic articles for which authorship remains in doubt. Fetter, however, did not develop that thesis or consider Horner's possible influence on a number of other reviews. There are numerous suggestions in the Documents of otherwise unknown reviews contemplated or even, apparently, begun; but few positive, let alone conclusive, indications of accomplishment. There is reasonably conclusive new evidence, however, that he was the author of a two-page notice in the Jan. 1806 issue of a speech on India, and it seems likely that he was at least joint author of the October 1806 notice of Foster's *Essay on Commercial Exchanges*, and possibly also of the October 1807 article on the Poor Law. (See pp. 217, 219 and 222–3.)

Whether Horner provided Jeffrey with partial reviews remains speculative, a thesis grounded on circumstantial evidence. After relocating in London, however, he played a double game – attempting on the one hand to influence the content and tone of the *Review* and seeking on the other to distance himself from the controversy bred by the prolific Brougham's reckless articles.[49]

Horner's papers also reveal substantial omissions and misinterpretations in the works of political historians. Here the blame can be assigned almost entirely to Leonard Horner, for the picture of his brother's political life painted by the *Memoirs and Correspondence* is greatly distorted. There he emerges as an altruist, which he was not; as a Whig hero who never compromised his fixed principles, which is not true; and as a charitable man who seldom uttered a harsh word about anyone, which is believable only if one accepts the veracity of published letters that were selected on dubious grounds and sometimes bowdlerized.

Yet posterity has generally accepted Leonard Horner's portrayal of his brother. All in all, Horner emerges as a doctrinaire saint or a sort of boy scout in the politics of his time. No wonder, then, that one recent writer should refer to him as 'the brilliant and lovable Francis Horner', and that another, who examined the politics of the Holland House circle, should find him too inconsequential for even a footnote.[50]

In considering Horner's political career, John Clive came closer to the truth when he observed that he 'epitomized a new kind of Whig – one who preferred financial and commercial statistics to the social whirl of the great country houses, and whose hagiology was headed not by Algernon Sydney but by Adam Smith'.[51] Even that description, however, is misleading. As the son of a merchant, Horner was of course 'a new kind of Whig', and no doubt his knowledge of the history of economic thought, including Smithian doctrine, set him apart from most of his political colleagues. But as his papers indicate, his hagiology was not headed by Adam Smith. He perceived that there were numerous omissions and errors in Smith's 'system', and the monetary doctrine for which he is best remembered borrowed virtually nothing from the *Wealth of Nations*. Horner's economic views, rather, were formed by Dugald Stewart's interpretations, by his own analysis of historical evidence, and, among the authors he read, perhaps more by Hume, Malthus, Turgot, the elder Mirabeau, and the others of Quesnay's set, than by Smith.

No economic thinker, however, headed Horner's hagiology; from first to last he was, as Sydney Smith remembered, 'an English whig, and no more than an English whig'.[52] Steven Watson rightly observed that Horner was among those who gave 'a new colour to politics' and brought philosophical freshness and depth to the whiggery of Fox, Grey, and the 'long-enduring, rather tired, band of brothers' they led.[53] But neither Steven Watson nor any other historian has identified Horner's most outstanding trait: his lifelong quest for political honours. Horner's papers

---

49. Note the assessment by Professor New, p. 17.
50. *Malthus*, p. 112, and Lean; Horner receives barely more attention in *Holland House*, pp. 175–6.
51. Clive, p. 83.
52. Smith to L. Horner, 26 Aug. 1842, *Horner*, ii. 467.
53. J. Steven Watson, *The Reign of George III, 1760–1815* (Oxford, 1960), pp. 436–7.

confirm that he ever bowed before the tired litany of English whiggery, that after 1802 virtually all of his behaviour was with a view to political advancement, and that once in the Whig camp he pondered financial and commercial statistics far less than he involved himself in the 'social whirl of the great country houses'.

Horner was no less ambitious than Brougham, just more adept in circumventing the barriers imposed by the aristocratic cast of early-nineteenth-century British politics. He always jockeyed to position himself in the Whig centre, and that tactic influenced his economic and political opinions. His style, however, was extra-ordinarily deceptive, and it is misunderstood even today. Perhaps Leonard Horner's worst fault as an editor was his failure to publish materials revealing his brother's burning ambition for political fame, his clever efforts to attain it, and the historical significance of his success.

The real Horner, then, provides a case study in early-nineteenth-century political manoeuvre. His is the story of a Scot of relatively humble origins who devoted countless hours to an analysis of the characters and styles of great men and to the structures and processes of English social and political life, exploiting his accurate conclusions for personal advancement and becoming, as an elderly Lansdowne remembered, the first 'mere man of the people' to be accepted by the great Whig party.[54]

Horner was a calculator, continually drafting outlines of personal strategy and tactics, and his political career can be divided into three stages, each of which was carefully plotted. The first stage, beginning in early 1802 and ending in November 1806 when he first entered Parliament, is most notable for his studied courtship of the Foxite Whigs. The second, extending from late 1806 to the end of the parliamentary session of 1814, encompasses the years in which he sought quietly to broaden his political influence, more especially with the Grenvillite faction of the Whig coalition to which he owed his seat in Parliament after May 1807.[55] The last stage, beginning in 1815 and concluding during the following session when terminal illness forced him to abandon public life at the age of thirty-seven, was the period of his great parliamentary offensive, the culmination of a long, measured rise to political eminence that was ironically thwarted by premature death.

The fount of Horner's whiggery was necessity. There was nothing peculiarly whiggish about his upbringing; as a young man he had little more in common with Lauderdale and the Scottish Whigs than with Henry Dundas and the dominant Pittite faction, and his political opinions remained undeveloped as late as December 1800.[56] But he contemplated a political career quite early in life, and over the years the course of his education and the context of politics in Edinburgh led him away from the Pittites, if not into the camp of Fox. At university, however, his reputation for godless Humeian sympathies and for radical political views made the Whigs his only

54. Moore, vii. 141.
55. Horner was not returned for St Ives in the general election of May 1807, but in a by-election of July 1807 he was chosen for Wendover through the influence of Lord Carrington, a political associate of the Grenville family. Carrington's desire to provide for a nephew cost Horner his seat in 1812, but in March 1813 he was offered St Mawes by Grenville's nephew, the Marquess of Buckingham. He accepted the offer, re-entered Parliament the following month, and sat for St Mawes until his death.
56. Cockburn, p. 167; Clive, p. 84; and Horner's journal entry of 11 Dec. 1800 in Horner, i. 130.

political option, and in 1802 he made the two most important decisions of his life.

The first, his decision to move to London and the English Bar, reflected his mounting ambition for a political career and his logical conclusion that advancement within the Whig ranks was unobtainable in Edinburgh. The second, his decision to collaborate in the founding of the *Edinburgh Review*, was influenced by the first; he saw the *Review* as a vehicle for the advancement of his political career.

Denied access to pertinent manuscript sources, and badly misled by published materials, historians have not fully comprehended the relationship between Horner the Edinburgh reviewer, Horner the political economist, and Horner the rising Whig politician.[57] For in striking contrast to Brougham, Horner never sent Jeffrey a completed review of a truly contentious nature; his contributions to the *Review* all expressed carefully measured political views; and his correspondence reveals his reluctance to review a number of leading economic works lest he offend important men. Furthermore, the great majority of his known contributions either embraced discernible Whig causes very cleverly or flattered prominent Whig politicians at timely moments.

Horner's papers confirm that, contemplating a political career under the banner of Fox, he was actively courting both the Scottish and the English Whigs when he wrote his first articles for the *Review*. When it is analysed in that light, one can perhaps discern calculations of political advantage in the economic doctrine propounded in his celebrated review of Thornton's treatise on paper credit. For that article embraced the long-standing Foxite view that the ill effects of the restriction of cash payments by the Bank of England were compounded by Pitt's subsidies to the continental powers.[58]

Calculations of political advantage are also apparent in two of the reviews Horner wrote shortly after establishing residence in London in March 1803. His early days in London were most notable for an active courtship of influential Whigs, among them Mackintosh, the respected but rather tedious philosopher of whiggery, and the lawyer Whishaw, who represented an important bridge to Holland House. All the while Horner expressed attachment to Fox and Whig principles in several letters to well-placed friends, most notably in those to John Allen, who had accepted an appointment as personal physician to Lord and Lady Holland and had accompanied them and Fox to Paris shortly before the appearance of the first number of the *Review*.

It would be an amazing coincidence if Horner's two contributions to the July 1803 number of the *Review* were not written with an eye to his political ambitions. His review of the trial of John Peltier – a curious subject for a literary journal to be sure – was nothing less than a paean of praise for the constitutional principles advanced in the speech of Peltier's attorney, Mackintosh.[59] And surely, too, Horner

---

57. Winch (especially pp. 58–9) perhaps comes nearest to such an appreciation, though from a rather different point of departure. See also below, p. 32.

58. See *EW*, p. 53, where Horner wrote:
      it must be remarked, though Mr Thornton seems studiously to have kept this out of view, that, by their indirect and unavoidable operation, these loans of the Bank to Government [for continental subsidies] contributed to aggravate that distress of the circulation, which was mainly produced by other causes.

59. *ER* ii (no. iv, July 1803), 476–84.

was aware of the political ramifications of his very favourable review of Lord King's treatise on the unhappy effects of the Bank restriction. For while enhancing his reputation in the domain of public finance, that article also flattered the work of a young Foxite peer who was closely connected with Holland House.

Equally significant were the publications Horner failed to review at pivotal moments. One must suspect that his almost comical procrastination in reviewing Malthus was owing in part at least to a fear of offending a man whose friendship he actively pursued. But it probably also had something to do with the intellectual problems it presented.[60] He certainly backed away from other works because they were too controversial. The outstanding example is his behaviour in regard to Lauderdale's *Inquiry*. That work, which attacked Adam Smith's shaky doctrine of value and produced outrage in Edinburgh, was published in 1804 when Horner was actively engaged in courting Whig leaders and when the unexpected support of Lauderdale was opening doors for him. The subject of the pamphlet was well within his purview, and its appearance placed him in a very delicate situation. Hence he voiced little protest when an unwitting Brougham insisted on reviewing the offending pamphlet and so saved his friend from the wrath of a Whig peer whose active support he probably had to have.[61]

There is reason to suggest that most of Horner's later contributions to the *Review* were also politically motivated. In October 1805, as Fox and Grenville were nearing coalition, the Earl of Selkirk, who was then affiliated very closely with the Opposition, had every reason to be pleased with Horner's favourable review of his recent book assessing the causes and probable consequences of emigration from the Scottish highlands. Three months later, at a time when Fox and Grenville were preparing to form a ministry, the slant of Horner's short, critical review of a new edition of the *Wealth of Nations* accorded with Grenville's pronounced Smithian predilections and reminded the nation of the reviewer's superior command of economic literature.[62]

Horner's last known contribution to the *Review*, which appeared in October 1809, only months before his famous motion for parliamentary inquiry into the high price of bullion, was clearly the work of a politician. It was a review of a French translation of Fox's *History of the Early Part of the Reign of James the Second* (1808). The awkward compilation of Fox's disjointed, partial narrative had been edited by

60. Fontana goes so far as to suggest (p. 56) that 'it was essentially because he felt he had not achieved sufficient clarity about the important theoretical implications of Malthus's anti-populationist argument'.

61. Lauderdale's treatise advanced the important idea that value was determined by the interaction of demand and scarcity and followed the traditional Foxite criticism of Pitt's sinking fund by arguing that money was useless unless it was spread. The work was apparently the first to put forward a connected theory on the nature of profit, but Lauderdale was needlessly critical of Adam Smith's omissions, his analysis sketchy, his style prolix and repetitious, and his reasoning in places weak. Brougham's subsequent critical review (*ER* iv (no. viii, July 1804), 343–77) earned him Lauderdale's enmity. (See Docs 165–6, 169, 171, 173, and 178. See also Herbert Fergus Thomson, jun., 'Lauderdale's Early Pamphlets on Public Finance', *History of Political Economy*, ii (1970), 344–80, and, for brief comments on Brougham's review, Fontana, pp. 63–8.)

62. Horner's review of William Playfair's *The Wealth of Nations, with Notes, Supplementary Chapters, and a Life of Dr Smith* (3 vols, 1805) appeared in *ER* vii (no. xiv, Jan. 1806), 470–71 (*EW*, pp. 133–4).

Lord Holland, and Horner's uncritical tribute did nothing to damage his cause at Holland House.[63]

While the effect of Horner's reviews was to advance his political career, several uncommon personal attributes, some natural, some contrived, enabled him also to impress the Whig society into which literary fame carried him. By every account Horner's physical appearance alone served him well. According to his younger sister Fanny, he had a 'monumental honesty' about him.[64] Sydney Smith agreed. 'There was', Smith recalled, 'something very remarkable in his countenance – the commandments were written on his face, and I have often told him there was not a crime he might not commit with impunity'.[65]

Horner was also 'wonderfully elegant in his looks and manners', well-schooled in English composition, grammar, and pronunciation,[66] and possessed of a solemnity that accentuated his considerable intellect and splendid education. His grave demeanour, one must suspect, was owing partly to chronically poor health, partly to an uneasiness attributable to humble origins; but it was also a trait he cultivated with great care. Well before his twentieth birthday he concluded that men devoted to study were devoid of 'those strong, complicated passions, which are contracted amidst the vicissitudes and tumult of public life'.[67] Later he laboured to emulate the formal, structured prose of Gibbon, and still later, when he began to reflect on the advantages of a political career, Locke's opinion that rhetoric equated with wrong ideas made a deep and lasting impression on him.[68]

Horner's upbringing and study of great men equipped him with several other personal characteristics that proved advantageous in later life. Among them were modesty and deference to social rank, a prudence that almost always kept him from stepping on the toes of others, a patience that allowed him to avoid the appearance of being personally ambitious, and an appreciation of the hold of Edmund Burke on the class of men who ruled Britain.[69] Throughout his political life an appreciation of tradition and established institutions and a measured view of change complemented his grave, scholarly demeanour and his carefully phrased remarks both in and out of Parliament. These were the traits that led Sydney Smith to refer to him as 'the aged Horner', the 'sage', and 'the frumentarious philosopher'; on one occasion Smith raised eyebrows by introducing him as 'Solon'.[70]

63. *ER* xv (no. xxix, Oct. 1809), 190–97.
64. Byrne Memoirs, p. 21.
65. Smith to L. Horner, 26 Aug. 1842, *Horner*, ii. 464.
66. Byrne Memoirs, p. 21; Hewlett to John Horner, 16 Oct. 1797, *Horner*, i. 40.
67. Horner's 'Memoir of Euler', p. xx.
68. Ricardo to James Mill, 9 Nov. 1817, *Ricardo*, vii. 89–90. Horner examined Locke's manuscripts during his visit to London in the spring of 1802. See Horner to Malcolm Laing, 15 May 1802, *Horner*, i. 200–201.
69. During his visit to London in the spring of 1802 Horner was surprised and troubled by the failure of Mackintosh and other Whig lawyers to qualify their praise of Burke. However, on 25 Jan. 1808, when William Dundas accurately observed in the Commons that Burke's view of sinecure places had changed appreciably during the course of his career, Horner rose 'for the purpose of repelling the aspersions which had been thrown upon the memory of one of the proudest ornaments of this or any other country'. (*Ibid.*, i. 185 and 445).
70. Smith to Jeffrey, [1 Aug.] 1801 and 13 Nov. 1804, *Smith Letters*, i. 65 and 100, and *A Memoir of the Reverend Sydney Smith . . . with a Selection from His Letters*, by Lady Holland, ed. Mrs Austin (2 vols, 4th ed., 1855), i. 136.

Nowhere were Horner's tactics more successful than at Holland House. After the Hollands returned from the continent in the summer of 1805, his cause was promoted by Allen, Whishaw, Mackintosh, Lauderdale, King, and Lord Henry Petty (afterwards Marquess of Lansdowne), the *beau enfant* of the Foxites who earlier had studied with him at Edinburgh University, and, according to Sydney Smith, Lady Holland came to admire Horner's 'young and muscular' body no less than his knowledge.[71] Smith's assertion may or may not have been true, but at all events both Lord and Lady Holland came to regard Horner 'almost as a son',[72] and in November 1806, some months after the ill-fated Fox–Grenville Ministry had taken office, he was returned to Parliament for the closed borough of St Ives through the influence of Petty and Lord Kinnaird.[73]

Horner's subsequent social conduct and his inactivity in the Commons brought him criticism from several of his contemporaries and from later generations of historians. Professor New found him 'as lacking in humour as a man could be and yet live', an admiring Lloyd Sanders conceded that he was 'a trifle dull', and John Clive concluded that he 'did not have it in him to strike hard at any time'.[74] Such views of Horner mistake calculated behaviour for character. For his papers suggest that, beginning in late 1806 and continuing for almost a decade, he was engaged in the second phase of a well-developed scheme for political advancement. They suggest, moreover, that his plan centred on a studied attempt to avoid controversy, and that his failure to 'strike hard' was largely responsible for his rising political stock.

Horner's tactics were evidently developed quite early in life. Winch stresses the importance of his early intellectual training and the price he subsequently paid by his unending pursuit of universal truth:

> Looking back . . . on his Scottish education, Mackintosh said that when so much activity was devoted to uncertain, speculative, and metaphysical subjects: 'Strength was exhausted in vain leaps to catch what is too high for our reach.' The grandiose projects left uncompleted by Mackintosh and Horner testify to this exhaustion.[75]

But there were other, rather more mundane, factors also at work. While assessing Brougham's political prospects in November 1802, Horner expressed concern that his friend 'might attempt to fix himself . . . too soon, before he had gone through . . . a necessary routine of subordination'. This was an astute observation, but one that revealed the first principle of his concept of political manoeuvre. He was willing to proceed slowly, to pose as a disinterested follower of others, to cultivate the support of diverse groups, and to seize opportunities whenever they appeared. Never did he betray impetuosity or force an issue, and Ricardo probably discerned the key to Horner's success when he observed that unlike Brougham, Horner never went 'beyond the mark', never endeavoured 'to prove too much'.[76]

71. *Holland House Chronicles* , p. 83, quoting from Smith's letter to Mackintosh of 1 Oct. 1805.
72. *Holland House Circle*, p. 71.
73. Charles, 8th Baron Kinnaird (1780–1826: *DNB*), who had also been at Edinburgh, was a staunch Whig. Later, Horner said of him: 'he had prematurely attained [?at Edinburgh] all that he was destined to acquire, and accordingly has been at a stand for some time.' (Chitnis, p. 92; see also Doc. 128.)
74. New, p. 11; *Holland House Circle*, p. 264; Clive, pp. 82–3.
75. Winch, p. 57.
76. Doc. 103; Ricardo to Mill, 9 and 17 Nov. 1817, *Ricardo*, vii. 89–90 and 206.

Horner certainly did not go 'beyond the mark' in Parliament between 1806 and 1814; instead he displayed great modesty, contenting himself with a subservient, advisory role and employing his pen to please the Whig leadership. During the short tenure of the 'Ministry of All the Talents' he advised party leaders on commercial policy and shamelessly attempted to bring Jeffrey round to the Government's point of view. When the Ministry fell in 1807 he co-operated in the production of a pamphlet that constituted its official defence[77] and continued his attempts to influence Jeffrey. In 1809 he edited a draft Lord Holland had sent him from Spain, and in the resulting pamphlet laid before the nation his patron's views on Spain and the Peninsular War.[78] All the while he courted the Whig rank and file at the Fox Club, at the Whig Club, and at Brooks's, to which he was admitted as a member in May 1808 on the motion of Fox's old cohort Lord Robert Spencer.[79]

Horner also developed connections with prominent figures outside the ill-defined Whig party. By all appearances he abhorred the African slave trade and earnestly believed in a national system of education for the poor, in a thorough reform of poor relief, and in sweeping changes in the harsh penal laws of Britain. But his support of those causes also broadened his influence in the House of Commons. On virtually all occasions he collaborated with William Wilberforce and the 'Saints', perhaps the most important 'swing group' in Parliament, and with the revered Romilly, 'the atrocious soul of Cato' whose principles were said to be 'eternal, and totally independent of events'.[80]

Horner also established and maintained a close relationship with Jeremy Bentham. He first met Bentham in 1805 and afterwards corresponded with him on the subject of Scots judicature. Horner, renouncing his earlier opinions, shortly afterwards sought to bring Jeffrey round to Benthamite views, and it was surely no coincidence that the *Review* almost immediately reversed its traditional criticism of the doctrine of utility.[81]

Horner apparently called on Bentham frequently. A previously unpublished document among his papers records his impressions of a conversation with the American Aaron Burr at Bentham's home in 1808 (Doc. 311). That same year Horner and Bentham discussed the political prospects of Spain so often that Sydney Smith facetiously reported that they had sent a 'list of pains and pleasures' to Spain accompanied by 'a smaller ditto of emotions and palpitations', and they planned to sail in September 'with laws, constitutions, etc.'.[82]

Although Horner usually attended Parliament when he was not on circuit, he spoke infrequently; and when he spoke his orations were short and didactic except on those rare occasions when there was general agreement among the leaders of the

77. The anonymous pamphlet, A Short Account of a Late Short Administration (1807), which was written jointly by Horner and H.G. Bennet, is reprinted as an appendix in Horner, i. 550–54.
78. See Doc. 339.
79. Memorials of Brooks's (1907), p. 65. Lord Robert Spencer (d. 1831) was the youngest son of the 3rd Duke of Marlborough.
80. Smith to Lady Holland, 27 Jan. 1810, Smith Letters, i. 181.
81. See Doc. 264 n. 3 and Clive, p. 93.
82. Smith to Lady Holland, 22 Aug. [1808], Smith Letters, i. 142.

Whig coalition. Indeed, between 1806 and 1814 a picture emerges of a young man who had the good sense to dissociate himself from the factious bickering that undid the Whigs.

Horner studiously avoided the turf of others. He followed the lead of Romilly in the reform of the criminal law, that of Whitbread in the reform of poor law, that of Lauderdale in the reform of Scots judicature, that of Brougham in educational reform, and that of Wilberforce in the attack on the African slave trade.[83] He refused to align himself with any faction in the Commons, instead moving in the company of Lord Holland, whom he knew to be a catalyst for party unity, and never voicing political opinions that were contrary to the principal tenets of what he rightly interpreted as the Foxite creed.

On all occasions Horner condemned either the principle or the practice of the Tory Government's policy. In league with the Foxite centre in Parliament, he supported Whitbread's motion for peace negotiations with France in 1808 and Thomas Brand's motions for parliamentary reform in 1809 and 1810.[84] In 1810 he aligned himself with long-standing Foxite precedent, if not with a majority of his closest friends, in championing the privilege of the Commons during the trial of Sir Francis Burdett, and later in the year he opposed the Government's restrictions on the Regency in a well-researched oration that leaned heavily on Fox's earlier example.[85]

Whenever possible Horner embraced causes that promised to appeal to both the Foxite and Grenvillite wings of Opposition. The greatest single source of party harmony after 1807 was Catholic Emancipation. Perhaps no member of the Whig coalition more adamantly supported the Catholic claims than Horner, albeit in his private correspondence. There he represented the issue on which the Whigs had fallen in 1807 in much the same way that an earlier generation of Whigs had represented Fox's old India Bill, as a rallying point and as a political *sine qua non*.

At other times, especially after 1807 when he was returned to Parliament by Grenville's friend Lord Carrington, Horner displayed remarkable flexibility in his political opinions. The greatest single source of disagreement within the party was the issue of war and peace. After initially lending silent support to the pacific views of Whitbread, Horner embraced warlike views in the name of Whig unity upon the outbreak of the Spanish revolution in 1808 and then returned to pacific language in 1814 when the very war he had supported in the Iberian peninsula at last bore fruit for Britain.[86]

Horner's view of economic and parliamentary reform also changed appreciably over the years. Initially he took a strong stand against reversionary appointments, but his later correspondence discloses a view of sinecure places largely consistent with that of the Grenvilles. The same trend is discernible in his notions about parliamentary reform. Early in his political career he felt that the support of the middle classes was the only hope for the Whigs; later he modified his opinion and

83. In 1815 Horner prepared a *Special Report of the Directors of the African Institution* that defended the Institution against charges that had recently been brought against it.
84. Roberts, pp. 112, 252, and 256.
85. See pp. 583–4.
86. Roberts, pp. 118, 149; Taylor, pp. 225–35, 362, 373, and 377–8.

came to agree with Grenville's more sceptical view of the reformers.[87]

Horner's papers suggest that calculations of political advantage also figured prominently in his famous motion for parliamentary inquiry into the high price of bullion and in the lead he took in the subsequent controversy. His motion was made early in the 1810 session, shortly after a desperate void in leadership on the Opposition bench had developed owing to the elevation of Lord Henry Petty to the House of Lords and, perhaps still more significantly, immediately after Horner had learned that his rival Brougham was at last to be brought into Parliament in the Whig interest. His timing may seem inopportune, with Horner getting more support in Parliament from disaffected Tories than Whig grandees and being 'left alone to stand for the principles of political economy and the defence of the constitution'. But, the immediate issue apart, this is not necessarily true, and it certainly seems a gross exaggeration to conclude that 'the issue itself was not regarded as particularly popular or politically rewarding'.[88] For 'hard money' was popular among all factions of the Whig coalition, with Grenville in particular, and in no other sphere of public policy had Horner's earlier contributions, even to the *Review*, brought him greater reputation. It was, however, utterly true to form, for Horner largely to dissociate himself from the heated bullion controversy after the debates of 1811, thereby following his tactic of never going 'beyond the mark', and he did not resume the attack until 1816.

Nor can one ignore the broader political context of Horner's parliamentary campaign for free trade in corn during 1814 and 1815. The collapse of Napoleonic France heightened tensions between the Foxite and Grenvillite wings of Opposition; Bonaparte's escape from Elba forced an open breach on the question of war or peace; and as always Horner aligned himself with the Foxite centre at Holland House. During the Hundred Days his difference of opinion with the Grenvilles over foreign policy was so pronounced that he offered to resign his seat in Parliament, and after Waterloo he agreed with Lord and Lady Holland that the British Government was 'wanting in generosity' in its treatment of the deposed French Emperor.[89] Meanwhile, however, he said little about foreign politics in the Commons and instead came forward as a leading opponent of the Government's revision of the corn laws. There is no reason to suggest that he was insincere in what he said, any more than in what he left unsaid; but, interestingly, what he did have to say about corn conflicted with Smithian doctrine and also with Malthus's concept of demand, and it placed him at odds with his bullionist colleagues, with Lauderdale, and with a united Foxite squirearchy. But while he remained relatively quiet where he differed with Grenville, his stand on the secondary issue of corn was entirely consistent with the views of Grenville at a crucial moment in his, Horner's, political career.[90]

Perhaps the greatest tribute to Horner's tactical skill is that Brougham alone among his contemporaries seemed to discern and resent his calculated conduct, and that the resulting troubled relationship between them did Brougham no good.

87. Roberts, pp. 191, 235, and 252; Horner to Jeffrey, 15 Sept. 1806 and 12 June 1809, *Horner*, i. 398 and 494–5; New, p. 148; and below, p. 581, and Docs 391–2.
88. Fontana, p. 121.
89. See Taylor, pp. 366–416, especially pp. 377–8, 392, 397, 400, 402, 406, 409–10, and 413–15; *Holland House Circle*, p. 40.
90. Hilton, pp. 13–16 and 28–9.

Virtually everyone attributed Brougham's attitude to dishonourable motives, and one of his biographers, accepting the contemporary view of Horner's virtues, concluded that his strained relationship with Brougham arose entirely from jealousy on the latter's part.[91]

Professor New hinted that Horner himself might have shared responsibility, but neither he nor any other historian has fully exploited the materials that suggest Horner was at the heart of Brougham's early problems with the Whigs. Brougham, indeed, remained on the periphery of Whig politics until well after Horner's death despite Lord Grey's high regard, and it is significant that Brougham himself once complained of 'the long-continued and bitter spite with which I was favoured by Lady Holland', the 'wronged' Horner's greatest advocate.[92]

Horner somehow evaded criticism even on those occasions when his native intolerance should have offended those around him. He once stormed from the room, refusing to come back and pouting for a fortnight, after Sydney Smith and J. W. Ward, later 1st Earl of Dudley, had jested about a political issue. But Smith attributed Horner's behaviour to a profound love of truth. On another occasion Ward reported that Horner had a foul temper, that he was 'impatient of contradiction', and that his friends found it necessary 'utterly to banish from conversation any subject on which they differ from him materially'. Ward, however, at the same time gave him the benefit of the doubt, attributing everything to poor health.[93]

People of all political persuasions were inclined to give Horner the benefit of the doubt. One of Constable's Scottish friends felt that he was 'as extraordinary a genius as any that ever came from our side of the Tweed'. Another acute observer reported that he had 'enough sense in his eyes only, for half a generation' and that others thought him 'the most delightful and eloquent person that ever lived'. Ward 'never met with any person . . . whose feelings were so correct, so delicate'. The left-leaning Creevey considered him to be one of only two lawyers liked by the House of Commons. Canning, whose political views were almost diametrically opposed to Creevey's, also held a high opinion of him, and Wilberforce, who generally had little in common with the Whigs, regarded him as one of the brightest stars in the Commons. Horner, wrote Sydney Smith with his usual perspicacity, 'pleases the best judges, and does not offend the worst'.[94]

Horner's measured conduct and resulting popularity made him an important

91. Note, for example, Lord Holland's opinion in *Home of the Hollands*, p. 308. Horner's sister recalled (Byrne Memoirs, p. 157) the 'envy which Henry bore to Frank' and 'his bad conduct towards him on more than one occasion'. See also Hawes, p. 54.

92. New, pp. 17–18; *Creevey*, i. 108; Clive, pp. 80–82; Brougham to Grey, 5 Jan. 1814, *Brougham*, ii. 99–102. See also *Holland House*, pp. 177–9.

93. Smith to L. Horner, 26 Aug. 1842, *Horner*, ii. 465; *Letters to 'Ivy'*, Aug. or Sept. 1810, p. 118.

94. Hunter to Constable, 7 Mar. 1807, *Constable*, i. 100; Lady Harriet Cavendish to Lady Georgiana Morpeth, early 1806, *Hary-O: The Letters of Lady Harriet Cavendish, 1796–1809*, ed. Sir George Leveson Gower and Iris Palmer (1940), p. 148; *Letters to 'Ivy'*, p. 50, quoting from Ward's letter of April 1807; *Creevey*, i. 278 (Sydney Smith made the same observation in a letter to Leonard Horner, 26 Aug. 1842, *Horner*, ii. 465). Canning's tribute in the Commons represented Horner, who had sat for a closed borough, as an example of the efficacy of the unreformed electoral system (*Horner*, ii. 446–8). For Whishaw's account of Wilberforce's tribute to Horner at the African Institution, see *Home of the Hollands*, p. 318. Smith to Jeffrey, 16 Feb. 1805, *Smith Letters*, i. 101.

bridge between the several factions within the Whig coalition.[95] He was intimate with Lansdowne, whose guest he frequently was at Bowood, and he also stopped regularly at the country estates of other influential Whigs while on the Western Circuit. He apparently enjoyed greater favour at Holland House than any other politician. He was said to be not only Lady Holland's favourite but also her political 'reporter-in-chief', and Allen, who exerted considerable behind-the-scenes influence as Lord Holland's political adviser, acknowledged that he consulted him 'on every event and project'.[96] To Lady Holland's dinner table Horner brought Brougham, Jeffrey, and a number of other young Scots; his influence can be seen in the appointment of Dugald Stewart to the diplomatic mission to Paris in 1806; and his correspondence reveals that he was an important link between the English and Scottish Whigs.

Despite his low opinion of Grey and Lauderdale, Horner wooed Fox's old lieutenants so successfully that they looked to him for leadership in the Commons. Despite his steady support of the coalition's leaders, he somehow maintained a close relationship also with Whitbread, Creevey, and the more 'radical' Foxites who refused to follow the temporizing politics of the party hierarchy.[97] And although he was extremely critical of Grenville in his private correspondence, he was the only politician identified with the Foxites who sat for a Grenvillite borough, visited Dropmore and Camelford House on a regular basis, and enjoyed Grenville's confidence. Grenville indeed had a very high opinion of him and recommended him for the position of Secretary of the Treasury in 1811 when a Whig Ministry was thought to be imminent.[98]

In all probability Horner held the esteem and enjoyed the confidence of a greater number of diverse personalities than any other figure within the Whig party. That, surely, to a large extent explains his historical importance. His early contributions to the Edinburgh Review, his later influence on Jeffrey, and his exertions in Parliament were all significant enough, and certainly he occupies an important place in the history of economic thought; but it was his grasp of political currents, his understanding of men and events, his immense popularity, and his resulting emergence as a 'repository of Whig secrets'[99] that made him unique among his contemporaries.

Leonard Horner's biographical account generally excluded materials reflecting the real political side of his brother, thereby relegating him to the status of a procrastinating Edinburgh reviewer, a political economist who functioned in the shadows of others, and a fringe politician. The Edinburgh Review, which knew better, could only express the hope in its 1843 notice of the Memoirs and Correspondence 'that at some future day, when restraints of delicacy no longer exist, a more full publication may take place'. 'The history of our times', it concluded, 'cannot but

95. Sack, pp. 156–7, goes so far, indeed, as to speculate that had he lived Horner might have served as the vital link between Grenvillites and Foxites and so averted the schism of 1817.
96. Holland House Circle, pp. 71–2 and 264; Allen to John Horner, 3 Mar. 1817, Horner, ii. 441.
97. See, for example, Creevey's note of 8 Nov. 1809 in Creevey, i. 111.
98. Grenville to Horner, 22 Jan., and Horner to Murray, 30 Jan. 1811, Horner, ii. 54–6.
99. Holland House Circle, p. 264.

profit by the unreserved disclosure of all judgements, whether negative or affirmative, passed by Francis Horner upon men and things.'[100]

Agreeing as they do with this view of the unfortunate *Memoirs and
Correspondence*, and feeling no 'restraints of delicacy', the editors of these volumes
have undertaken the task of examining the considerable quantity of Horner's
surviving papers and related manuscripts, comparing them with the documents
published by his brother, and selecting from them previously unpublished or
bowdlerized materials that shed new light on the great political and economic
debates to which he so significantly contributed. For clarity's sake some previously
published material has necessarily been included, but the editors have eschewed
Leonard Horner's first principle – selecting materials with an eye to biography – and
included, rather, substantial extracts from Horner's notes on political economy, as
well as from his correspondence.

The documents printed here have been arranged chronologically in three
sections, each of which is preceded by an introduction that seeks to give context to
the documents and notes that follow.

Section I, entitled 'The Education of a Political Economist, 1795–1802',
comprises those materials relating to the young Horner's residence in Middlesex
between 1795 and 1797 and to his later studies under the guidance of Dugald
Stewart at Edinburgh University. Section II, entitled 'The Edinburgh Reviewer,
1802–1809', includes most of Horner's known correspondence with Jeffrey as well as
the notes and letters of a rising politician. Section III, entitled 'The Front-Bench
Politician, 1810–1817', consists mainly of notes and correspondence commenting
on important individuals, political alignments and speculations, and the leading
controversies and events of the time.

100. *ER* lxxviii (no. clviii, Oct. 1843), 263.

Section I

The Education of a Political Economist
1795–1802

Introduction

THE EARLIEST of Francis Horner's surviving papers is a letter of 23 November 1795 addressed to his father from Shacklewell in Middlesex, where only recently he had taken up residence under the care of an English tutor.[1] That letter, which outlines the academic regimen of a lonely seventeen-year-old boy, prefaced the final six years of his formal education. Thereafter, until February 1802, when he and his friends conceived the *Edinburgh Review*, his correspondence, journal entries, and miscellaneous papers mirror his intellectual growth and shed much light on the last years of the Scottish Enlightenment.

The course of Horner's life between late 1795 and early 1802 was influenced very profoundly by the events and associations of his youth. He was born in Edinburgh on 12 August 1778, the second of seven children and the eldest son of John Horner, a linen merchant of that city, and Joanna Baillie Horner.[2] He was a sickly infant and a delicate child, and even in late adolescence his physical weakness and narrow chest were causes of concern.[3] His mother, who blamed his slow development on the indiscretions of a suckling nurse, initially thought him dull. In his fourth year, however, he suddenly began to display unusual powers of memory and a surprising degree of theatrical talent. For about a year he seemed a precocious actor who wore makeshift costumes and entertained his family and their friends with impressive recitations.[4]

---

1. *Horner*, i. 6–7.
2. The eldest child, Anne, died in infancy. Of the other five two were boys, John (1782–1802), who also predeceased Francis, and Leonard (1785–1864: *DNB*), who achieved some distinction as a geologist and educationist. Of his three surviving sisters, only the eldest, Elizabeth, was married during Francis's lifetime, in August 1802 to a London businessman, G. Leckie (d. 1812). The two youngest girls, Anne ('Nancy') and her twin sister Frances ('Fanny') were both married later, Anne to a Major William or Williams Power, Frances to the United Irishman Miles Byrne (1780–1842: *DNB*), whose memoirs she edited for publication. Francis was evidently very close to them all, corresponding regularly with them (except perhaps Mrs Leckie, who was after all close by in London most of the time) as well as with Leonard's wife Susan Lloyd, whom he married in October 1806.
3. Byrne Memoirs, p. 21, and *Horner*, i. 43, quoting from a letter written by Horner's tutor shortly after his death in 1817.
4. Joanna Horner to Leonard Horner, 23 Mar. 1820, Kinnordy MSS.

Such behaviour was probably inspired by Horner's earliest friend, Henry Brougham, with whom he played on the pavement before the Horner household in St David Street. Brougham was a striking personality, possessed of a quick mind, relentless energy, and an extraordinary ability to display his talents.[5] For many years Horner was awed by his friend, and as a four-year-old boy he apparently attempted to emulate the theatricality that characterized the clever Brougham, relying on rote to hold his own in the presence of one whom he perceived to be his intellectual superior. It was an unequal contest, however, and Horner soon abandoned the game. In 1783, when Brougham went off to school and left his younger friend behind, Horner began to return to his quieter ways.

In 1784 Horner himself began to attend school and forged there an enduring friendship with another clever youngster, John Archibald Murray, later Lord Advocate of Scotland. In marked contrast to Brougham, Murray was a modest boy most notable for hard study and quiet reflection, and he became Horner's constant companion.[6] While Brougham dazzled his tutors and schoolmates, Horner and Murray studied quietly together, plodding along in his wake, but achieving a degree of academic distinction of their own.

Horner was a successful student from the first. After standing his initial examination, during which he recited a poem, his mother overheard an examiner ask the name of that 'fine boy', and later his private tutor, who saw him in the evenings, 'gave him the highest praise'. Soon his studies consumed him to such an extent that his mother thought 'his anxiety to learn his lessons made him indifferent about his meals', and the 'gravity and earnestness of character' that would distinguish him for the remainder of his short life began to emerge.[7]

In all probability Horner's accomplished father was the principal source of the anxiety he felt about his studies. According to his daughter Frances, John Horner was 'no ordinary man'. As a youngster he was put as an apprentice in the shop of a retail silkmaker in Edinburgh, where his hard work later earned him a partnership. At one point he rescued the business by buying linens from the manufacturers of Dunfermline, which he bleached and sold to wholesale linen-drapers in London. In the end he enjoyed 'a very handsome income', displayed 'a sense of honour of the highest stamp', and stood as a man of some reputation among the rising Scots commercial class of which Adam Smith wrote in 1776.[8]

John Horner rightly perceived that upward social mobility was possible for the bourgeoisie and had high hopes for his eldest son. From young Horner's earliest years his father 'treated him as a rational being', 'cultivated his fine talents with care', and impressed upon him the pragmatic value of formal education.[9]

While the careful guidance of his father influenced Horner's early devotion to study, the teachings of his mother and maternal grandparents helped inculcate the love of literature and the arts that played such an important role in his later life. Joanna Horner sought every educational opportunity for her children, developing in

5. New, pp. 3 and 5.
6. Byrne Memoirs, pp. 52 and 160.
7. Joanna Horner to Leonard Horner, 23 Mar. 1820, Kinnordy MSS; *Horner*, i. 2–4.
8. Byrne Memoirs, pp. 5 and 8–10. John Horner, sen., died in 1829.
9. *Ibid.*, p. 39; and John Horner to Horner, 10 Sept. 1796, *Horner*, i. 19, wishing him 'not only to be as well educated as others that are to follow the law' but also 'better educated'.

them a fondness for music and dance and reading to them history, biography, travel literature, and the best of English poetry. Her father, John Baillie, owned considerable lands in Gladsmuir and East Lothian, but he did not like the lifestyle of a gentleman farmer, refusing to associate with his country neighbours and spending most of his time in Edinburgh. Rather, he possessed tastes and inclinations more like those Francis Horner later showed. He was a member of the Society of Writers to the Signet, and was fond of music and literary pursuits; he owned a choice library and was often to be seen on the streets of Edinburgh with violin in hand.[10]

Horner's maternal grandmother, Anne Broughton Baillie, apparently also influenced his early development. Before coming to Edinburgh with her father, an excise officer from Hampshire, she had learned French and Latin at a boarding school in Basingstoke, and she often spoke those languages with her grandchildren. She had, moreover, 'a very superior understanding', and her liberal social and political opinions were reinforced by her brother, the Reverend Thomas Broughton, who visited Edinburgh from time to time and impressed the Horner children with his uncommonly charitable view of religion.[11]

In 1786 Horner was sent to the High School of Edinburgh. There, for some four years, he was the pupil of William Nichol, who taught him the elements of Latin, until early 1790 when he came under the tutelage of the rector, Dr Alexander Adam.[12] Adam, who was described by Cockburn as a man 'born to teach Latin, some Greek, and all virtue', left an indelible mark on Horner. From the rector he imbibed an intellectual diversity that both delighted and frustrated him in later years. Upon Adam's death in 1809 Horner expressed a debt of gratitude 'for the love he gave me in early life, for the pursuits which are still my best source of happiness, as well as for the most valuable impressions in all subjects of political opinion'.[13]

On 10 August 1792, when Horner succeeded Brougham as *dux* of Adam's class, he delivered a 'well composed and well spoken' Latin oration that made one young listener conclude he was a god.[14] Some months later he began attending classes at the University of Edinburgh, where he would remain until the summer of 1795. At university he continued his study of Latin and Greek, became fairly familiar with French, acquired the elements of mathematics and natural philosophy, and attended lectures in rhetoric, logic, and moral philosophy.[15]

Horner's favourite subjects at university were chemistry, mathematics, and moral philosophy, and among the faculty he liked John Playfair, professor of mathematics, better than the rest.[16] No man, however, affected his intellectual development more than the moral philosopher Dugald Stewart, student and biographer of Adam Smith.[17]

10. Byrne Memoirs, pp. 16–17, 28, and 38.
11. *Ibid.*, pp. 11–13. Thomas Broughton (1712–1777: *DNB*) was secretary of the SPCK.
12. *Horner*, i. 3; Alexander Adam (1741–1809: *DNB*).
13. *Cockburn*, p. 5; Horner to Murray, 23 Dec. 1809, *Horner*, i. 514.
14. Byrne Memoirs, p. 96; *Cockburn*, p. 9.
15. *Horner*, i. 5.
16. John Playfair (1748–1819: *DNB*) was Professor of Mathematics and, from 1805, Professor of Natural Philosophy at Edinburgh. He achieved fame in 1802 with the publication of *Illustrations of Huttonian Theory*, a work through which Hutton's conception of great changes produced by slow processes passed into other sciences.
17. For an interesting essay on the influence on his pupils of Dugald Stewart (1753–1828: *DNB*), Professor of Moral Philosophy at Edinburgh, see Winch, pp. 25–61.

Devoted though he was to the professor and pervasive though Stewart's teachings were in both his thought and action, Horner was by no means blindly uncritical. Indeed, he sometimes thought him 'academic' and timid. In the spring of 1811 Stewart sent a stream of comment on bullion in Horner's direction, and disappointed that it seemed not to have effected any influence, afterwards gently complained: 'I have sometimes wished that I had seen the *Report* before it was printed, as nothing would have given me greater pleasure than to have contributed anything, however trifling, towards its improvement.' Dr Fontana rather unkindly observes: 'it is sufficient to glance briefly at the labyrinth of erudite quotations and elaborate references to the classical literature in Stewart's comments, to realize that his notes could have been of little use to Horner in his task as chairman of the Committee.' In earlier years, when he had his pupil more at his mercy and inculcated in him his integrated view of philosophy and history, Stewart might, she could perhaps also have suggested, have been responsible for Horner becoming what she calls 'the prisoner of his own diligent and unimaginative scholarship'. Professor Winch takes a much more sympathetic view of Stewart's influence. At a practical level, he comments:

> Horner was aware that his academic projects, and more especially his mastery of law and political economy, had particular relevance to his prospects in life. To a man of talents who lacked political connections, Stewart's teaching offered a way of serving the noble cause of human advancement by means that were largely independent of forms of government.

Moreover while that same teaching, by introducing to him a grand vision of thought and action and a commitment even to something resembling what is nowadays called *éducation permanente*, may have made it more difficult for Horner ever to complete anything in either field, it contributed something much more important. Whether Horner would have achieved more had he lived, Winch suggests, 'is less important than the nature of the ideal', and the distinction between amateur and professional scholar in his case essentially misleading. For

> Horner's Scottish education furnished him with criteria of liberal accom-plishment which overrode this distinction. His studies were partly undertaken to mitigate 'the illiberality of professional character', but the effort went so far beyond mere diversion that it deserves to be treated as evidence of an ideal character formation or *Bildung*.

Hence in the field of politics he quotes with approval Bagehot's citing of Horner as proof that 'Whiggism is not a creed, it is a character'.[18]

Be all this as it may, between late 1792 and the summer of 1795 Stewart introduced Horner to the French *philosophes* and the British empiricists, to his own celebrated concept of the philosophy of mind, and to a Humeian view of the laws and manner of philosophical inquiry.[19] Afterwards Horner always subscribed to the historicism of Hume and believed that the linear progression of mankind was guided by laws discernible in nature. Rousseau, his favourite philosopher in adolescence, probably influenced his darker view of society's 'artificial' checks on the scheme of nature, but whatever the case, by the end of his seventeenth year his lifelong faith in natural law and inductive metaphysics was already well-established.

18. Chitnis, pp. 121–4; Fontana, pp. 59 and 126; Winch, pp. 59 (citing Doc. 60) and 49.
19. Horner to Murray, 26 Nov. 1796, *Horner*, i. 27.

Horner's early education also enhanced his skills in public speaking and debate. Rector Adam schooled his boys in the techniques of the great orators of antiquity and encouraged *disputationes academicæ* among them.[20] Later at university Horner and his friends engaged in 'intellectual gladiatorship' at the meetings of the Juvenile Literary Society. There Brougham dominated the proceedings, but Horner took an active part, acquitting himself honourably and soon commanding his peers' respect.[21]

In the summer of 1795 Horner committed himself, *faute de mieux*, to a career in law,[22] and in November he was sent to Shacklewell, where for some two years he studied English grammar, composition, and pronunciation under the tutelage of the Reverend John Hewlett.[23] During that period his correspondence with family and friends in Edinburgh was not extensive, but a total of nineteen previously unpublished or only partially published letters (Docs 1–19) – six written to Murray and thirteen received from Brougham – contain a substantial amount of information regarding the formative years of Horner and his closest friends.

Horner's earliest letters to Murray (Docs 1 and 3) describe his studies at Shacklewell and reveal the longings of a young Scot who was troubled by the prejudice of Englishmen against the metaphysics of the schoolmen, was very critical in turn of the quality of oratory in the House of Commons, and pleaded for *disputationes academicæ* by post. His later letters to Murray (Docs 11, 15, 16, and 18) contain metaphysical essays drawing on the works of Locke, Priestley, and the principal Scottish empiricists. In these, which reflect the influence of Stewart and display Horner's concern for the vocabulary of philosophical inquiry and his early powers of enumeration and analysis, can be observed the nature and the depth of his earliest speculations on the philosophy of the mind, a branch of metaphysics to which he would later assign Adam Smith's chapter on the division of labour (Doc. 74, para. 6).

The absence of Horner's letters to Brougham is much to be regretted, but those Brougham wrote to Horner are of considerable importance. Five letters Brougham wrote between January and August 1796 (Docs 2, 4, 5, 6, and 7) provide much insight into the nature of both his own and Horner's studies as well as interesting comment on politics, on the demise of the Juvenile Literary Society, on the graduation of Horner's circle of friends to the Literary Society, and on leading personages in Edinburgh.

Among Brougham's later letters, none perhaps is more significant than that of 21 September 1796 (Doc. 8). For here is a rare glimpse of the young Brougham's hopes, fears, and aspirations. He is unusually frank in describing the several professional avenues open to him and the role of his father in his calculations; and the letter confirms that already he and Horner were speculating on the advantages of practice at the English Bar, considering the possibility of seats in the Commons, and weighing Horner's perception that a law career might compromise his political prospects.

The same letter contains what is surely the first reference to the formation of Edinburgh's Academy of Physics, and a subsequent one (Doc. 9) suggests that

20. New, p. 4.
21. *Ibid.*, pp. 4–5; *Brougham*, i. 84–6.
22. *Horner*, i. 6.
23. John Hewlett (1762–1844: *DNB*) was also a distinguished biblical scholar.

Horner responded in October with a letter developing the plan for the Academy that Brougham afterwards launched in his friend's absence. Brougham's later correspondence includes important comment about the men involved in the Academy's early proceedings (Docs 9, 10, 12, 13, 14, 17, and 19).

Also in Brougham's correspondence with Horner is evidence of a certain tension between the two future Edinburgh reviewers. Brougham is clearly the dominant figure; he is vain and intimidating, quick to associate himself with eminent figures, but cruelly critical of others. His replies to the solicitous Horner's mathematical queries are condescending. He scolds Horner for a failure to study mathematics and the 'exact' sciences properly. He dismisses as nonsense an essay Horner had sent to him, and on one occasion he criticizes Professor Stewart and warns pompously of the dangers inherent in inductive metaphysics, the only branch of learning in which Horner then felt competent to write a paper for the Academy (Docs 6, 13, and 14). Understandably Horner never submitted a paper while he was at Shacklewell, and the two young men, each appearing to jockey for an advantageous position, failed to agree even on the selection of a subject they could dispute by post.

After his return to Edinburgh in the autumn of 1797, Horner made law the first priority of his studies, but his philosophical turn of mind made him abhor the memorization needed (Docs 22 and 26). He bemoaned his legal researches on numerous occasions, falling behind in his notes, attending his law lectures less and less frequently, and giving them up altogether after a terrible altercation with his civil law professor.[24] With Brougham's assistance he somehow passed his law trials and was called to the Scottish Bar in the summer of 1800.[25] But afterwards his legal

24. Professor David Hume (1757–1838: DNB), the nephew of the famous philosopher, taught Horner civil law at Edinburgh. In 1799 Hume brought charges of atheism and democratic leanings against Horner, Brougham, Jeffrey, and James Loch, evidently with an eye to their expulsion from the university. Horner's sister recalled:

> Mr Hume did not make an open charge in the Senatus Academicus against these young men, with a view to have them reprimanded or punished for their errors, but in a mean intriguing manner summoned some of the professors to meet him at a tavern where he laid the matter before them. Of course such men as Mr Dugald Stewart or Professor Playfair were not called to the meeting. . . . He called Dr Hunter, the Professor of Divinity, Dr Gregory, etc., flattering himself they would join in the cabal, but he mistook his men; they indignantly reproached him for his meanness and said he wanted to expel the flower of the college. Poor Frank was very ill at the time . . . and was greatly worse for a long conversation he had with Lord Webb Seymour on the matter, and my Mother could not comprehend as she was sitting by his bed–side his repeating so often in the delirium of fever 'Why don't they investigate?'

> After Hume's attack was broken off, and after Horner had recovered, the young men resolved to challenge their professor to a duel and cast lots to determine who would issue the challenge. Jeffrey was duly chosen, he selected Horner as his second, and the two then called on Hume and demanded satisfaction. Hume declined and turned the matter over to the sheriff, who summoned the young rebels, forced them to post bail, and made them swear to keep the peace. Principal Robertson summoned them as well, but with the exception of Brougham, all of them either defiantly refused to appear or, by other, more plausible, accounts, pleaded illness or absence out of town. The Senate's investigations found the Speculative's debates not to be seditious; but discussion of the political affairs of the day was subsequently prohibited and the ban not removed until 1826. (Byrne Memoirs, pp. 48–52. See also Letters to 'Ivy', pp. 31–2; Brougham, i. 52; Cockburn, p. 74; Chitnis, p. 61.)

25. New, p. 9; Hawes, p. 30. See also Horner's journal entries of April, May, and June 1800 in Horner, i. 110–13.

practice was desultory; he received few briefs and found practice in the Court of Session boring (Doc. 49). His life in Edinburgh therefore centred mainly on a search for intellectual diversions (Docs 21, 25, 27, 43, 44, 45, 47, 65, and 66).

Such diversions were plentiful in the 'Athens of the North' during the last years of the eighteenth century. Among them was the Speculative Society, and no man was more active in it than Horner. He was admitted a member along with Brougham on 21 November 1797. Thereafter he seldom missed a meeting, and he served as one of three presidents during 1799 and 1800. He was also a zealous participant in the proceedings of the Academy of Physics, for which he was secretary during 1798–9 (Doc. 27), and he was quite active too in the Literary Society and in the Chemical Society, which he, Brougham, and John Thomson founded in 1800.[26]

Horner was also admitted to membership in Walter Scott's select Friday Club, where he associated with the city's intellectual élite, and he attended the periodic meetings of the Brown Toast Club, a society sponsored by Lady Carnegie and Lady Minto where, reluctantly following the example of Hume, he tolerated 'philosophers in petticoats'.[27]

Through these diverse activities Horner cultivated friendships that would bear strongly on the course of his later career. Almost everyone liked him, and his parents' new house in York Place became a regular meeting-place for his growing circle of friends. They included not only his oldest acquaintances – Brougham, Murray, Cockburn, Thomas Thomson, James Moncreiff, James Loch, Tom Millar, and George Bell[28] – but also several new ones. Among them were the surly Francis Jeffrey, then an unsuccessful Scottish lawyer and sometime literary critic, the caustic Sydney Smith, an English preacher without a flock who jolted Horner's serious turn of mind with his biting wit, and the condescending John Allen, a physician without a practice who astonished everyone with his command of esoteric information.

Jeffrey, Smith, and Allen were unlikely friends for the serious-minded Horner, but throughout his life he always gravitated towards genius. While cultivating relationships with the young men with whom he would later collaborate to launch the *Edinburgh Review*, he delighted in his quiet, secluded moments with the studious Murray, in whose company he felt more comfortable, and developed a close friendship with the dour Lord Webb Seymour, a young English aristocrat and fellow student with whom he regularly read (Doc. 28).[29] His oldest friends, as well as Jeffrey

26. *Ibid.*, i. 56; Ross, p. 53. Dr John Thomson (1765–1846: *DNB*) was afterwards professor at the university; see also Doc. 45 n. 1.
27. Ross, p. 53, and New, p. 19; *Life and Letters of Sir Gilbert Elliot First Earl of Minto From 1751 to 1806*, ed. the Countess of Minto (3 vols, 1874), i. 404 and iii. 230. See also *Horner*, i. 139–40.
28. James Wellwood Moncreiff (1776–1851: *DNB*) afterwards, as Lord Moncreiff, became a distinguished Scottish judge. James Loch (1780–1855: *DNB*; see also Eric Richards, *The Leviathan of Wealth. The Sutherland Fortune in the Industrial Revolution* (1973)), another advocate, afterwards abandoned the law for estate management and Parliament. The Byrne Memoirs, p. 52, do not identify Tom Millar; but possibly he was the youngest surviving son, who afterwards became a Writer to the Signet, of John Millar (1735–1801: *DNB*), Professor of Law at Glasgow and an acquaintance of Jeffrey. George Joseph Bell (1770–1843: *DNB*) afterwards became Professor of Scots Law at Edinburgh.
29. Lord Webb John Seymour (1777–1819), the younger brother of the 11th Duke of Somerset, was a dedicated if undistinguished scholar who, after passing some years at Oxford, left at the end of 1797 to pursue his studies in Edinburgh. His manuscript diaries,

and Seymour, were 'constantly about the house, at dinner and evening parties and in the forenoons'. Smith and Allen also called frequently, and occasionally Professor Stewart, whose early attachment to Horner was extraordinary, thrilled his students by coming to tea or dinner.[30]

Between late 1797 and 1800 Horner pursued a very diverse course of study. He read *belles lettres*, natural science, political philosophy, and history, all the while dabbling with astronomy and geology, conducting chemical experiments, and fagging at law. He recorded his thoughts in a journal, attempted with some success to develop a Gibbonesque style, and celebrated his intellectual acquisitions by writing a number of essays and reading them before the several debating societies of the university.

Horner presented his first essay to the Speculative Society on 18 December 1797, less than a month after he became a member (Doc. 20). Entitled 'On the Political Effects of the General Diffusion of Knowledge', it recommended an expanded system of education as a check on the baseness of Britain's emerging commercial society. This was a thesis to which Horner would subscribe throughout life, and it inspired a great deal of interest among the members of the Speculative. John Hay Forbes, afterwards Lord Medwyn, apparently contested it on 13 March 1798, and another member ventured an opinion on 12 March 1799.[31]

Meanwhile Horner presented a second essay that bore no less strongly on the course of his future life, this one entitled 'Remarks on the Opposition Party in the British Parliament'. He regarded that paper as a failure, however, and in his embarrassment unfortunately burned it. At other times he opened debates at the Speculative on emigration policy, the influence of physical causes on national character, the impressment of British seamen, the expediency of standing armies, and the immortality of the soul.[32]

Horner also presented to the Academy of Physics papers on 'the peculiarities of the Chinese language', 'a reform of the laws', and 'Disposing Affinity'. In addition, he began but never finished a treatise on 'the formation of the Delta or lower Egypt', and wrote, but apparently never presented, essays on 'imagination', 'the dramatic unities', 'the marvellous', and 'imitation'.[33]

Horner's active participation in the proceedings of the various debating societies earned him considerable stature among his peers,[34] but his journal reveals that he was unhappy between late 1797 and the early months of 1800. Quite simply, he lacked direction. He constantly protested about the drudgery of legal study, looked

one of the few items still legible among his papers at the Devon County Record Office, like Horner's own, closely document their studies together and attendance at Edinburgh societies. (See also *Two Brothers*.)

30. Byrne Memoirs, pp. 52–3. See also *Horner*, i. 154, for Horner's interesting assessment of the role of his friends in his intellectual improvement.
31. *Speculative Society*, pp. 215 and 386–8. John Hay Forbes, afterwards Lord Medwyn (1776–1854: *DNB*), later became a distinguished Scottish judge.
32. *Speculative Society*, pp. 216 and 387–90, which, however, do not confirm that Horner spoke on the last topic. But see Cockburn's account in *Jeffrey*, i. 56, and Doc. 26 n. 2.
33. Clive, p. 21; Ross, p. 52; but see also Docs 21 and 26 n. 2.
34. Cockburn (*Jeffrey*, i. 56), for example, ranked Horner's address on 'the immortality of the soul' among the three best orations he ever heard. The other two were by Brougham and Jeffrey, also at the Speculative.

with horror to a career at the Scottish Bar, and consoled himself with thoughts of professional and political honours in England instead. At the same time he dreamed of literary reputation, but shifting from one subject to another, bemoaned the fact that natural indolence and versatility rendered him intellectually superficial, and in a fit of frustration he destroyed most of his early essays (Docs 22, 23, 24, and 26 n. 2).

During 1798 Horner's diverse intellectual interests began very slowly to narrow, at first focusing on political history generally and then on historical inquiries into questions of political economy. Initially his interest in historical research was sparked by an attempt to study law as a science; he sought to view law within the broader context of what he called 'philosophical history', thereby rendering legal study an exercise in arrangement and reasoning rather than one of mere memory. Such an attempt was doomed from the beginning, for law is not a science; but in November 1798 Horner announced that he would suspend his study of the natural sciences, drew up a plan of study emphasizing readings in history, politics, moral philosophy, and law, and thereby committed himself to the researches that would frame his later career (Docs 26 and 36 n. 1).

From the beginning economic phenomena figured prominently in Horner's historical analysis of English law, government, and manners owing to the influence of Dugald Stewart. Stewart's lectures in moral philosophy had always included commentary on economic philosophy, but in the summer of 1798 the professor announced that he would offer a regular course of lectures in political economy during the 1799–1800 academic session. Thereafter Horner and his friends became ever more interested in economic speculations.

The new emphasis on economic philosophy was reflected in the proceedings of the Speculative Society. Prior to 1798 questions of political economy had not figured prominently in its deliberations. In November 1798, however, the members heard a paper assessing the policy of Pitt's funding system, and others followed on banking practice and paper money (5 Mar. 1799), the political regulation of exports and imports of corn (9 Apr. 1799 and 14 Jan. 1800), the relative advantages of agricultural and commercial economies (7 May 1799), and a number of similar subjects.[35]

As early as July 1798 Horner observed that 'political science' was a largely ignored sphere of scholarly endeavour in which one might acquire literary honours and asked Murray, who was about to depart for London, to procure four economical treatises. These included Malthus's anonymously-published *Essay on Population*, English editions of Isaac Pinto's *Circulation and Credit* and Turgot's *Reflections on the Formation and Distribution of Wealth*, and Campomanes's *Amortizacion* (Doc. 24).

By all appearances the nineteen-year-old Horner enjoyed relative superiority over his peers in economic speculations. His education in economics had evidently begun with his father's teachings; he once noted the value of John Horner's command of the details of commerce (Doc. 46), and scattered among his early papers are a number of passages that display a general comprehension of commercial exchange and an awareness of facts arising from the transactions of Scottish and English merchants. Then, too, no Scottish schoolboy of the late eighteenth century escaped the long shadow of Adam Smith, who after all lived until 1790 as a legend

35. *Speculative Society*, pp. 388–9.

in his own time. Horner was introduced to Smith's works quite early in life, reading parts of the *Wealth of Nations* while still at school (Doc. 75), and between 1792 and 1795 having his interest in Smith's moral and economic reasonings whetted by Professor Stewart's lectures.

Indeed, Horner's first letter to Murray from Shacklewell (Doc. 1) included an appeal to the philosophical authority of Smith, and preceded a second perusal of the *Wealth of Nations*. He undertook an analysis of the work and attempted to write an abstract of its contents, but abandoned the project because of confusion over Smith's troubled doctrine of value and perplexing distinction between nominal and real price (Doc. 75).

The letters Horner wrote and received during his residence in Middlesex also reveal his early fascination with the theory of money. His reading list included a number of treatises on law recommended by the Scottish advocate James Reddie, an older friend in Edinburgh to whom Horner's father looked for guidance in plotting his son's legal career (Doc. 8).[36] Among them were the works of Bentham. Initially Horner was perplexed by Bentham's philosophy and declined Brougham's invitation to dispute the doctrine of utility by post (Doc. 4), but he apparently read and pondered Bentham's *Defence of Usury* (1787), a work that he later listed among the premier publications on the theory of money (Doc. 84).

Horner's correspondence with Murray confirms that he also read David Hume's *History* and various philosophical writings while at Shacklewell, and probably Hume's essay 'Of Interest' was among them. At all events, Horner evidently wrote a short essay on monetary interest, posted it to Brougham in July 1796, and unsuccessfully proposed the subject as one worthy of academic disputation (Doc. 6).

Horner probably read Hume's essay 'Of Money' as well. Certainly Hume's quantity theory of specie flow had a profound effect on his later monetary doctrine, including the view he took initially of the restriction of payments in specie by the Bank of England. In March 1797, less than three weeks after the Bank had announced its shocking departure from long-standing monetary policy, Horner told his father that 'Paper money still circulates without depreciation, and must be found, in the mean time, a great relief to the market; for many reasons, especially the enlargement of the Bank discounts'. Even as an eighteen-year-old boy, however, he questioned the wisdom of the Bank restriction. 'All political reasonings', he observed, 'point out the increase of paper currency as a most pernicious evil; but it is to be hoped, that matters may yet go on well, provided it be used only as a temporary expedient.'[37]

Horner's economic researches at Shacklewell were accompanied by a number of mathematical speculations that evidently also influenced his later view of analysis and enumeration. He committed countless hours to his partial translation of Euler, and Hewlett, who was astonished by the breadth and depth of his knowledge, his 'natural good sense', and his 'practice to make memoranda of every thing new or

36. See also Horner to his father, 10 Oct. 1796, *Horner*, i. 21–2. James Reddie (1773–1852: *DNB*), a member of the Scots Bar, was afterwards town clerk and legal assessor of Glasgow and author of a number of legal works. But see Doc. 14 n. 1 for possible confusion with his son and brother.

37. Horner to his father, 17 Mar. 1797, *Horner*, i. 34–5.

important that was communicated to him', thought that project fostered the 'talent for analysis, close investigation, and logical inference, which he . . . afterwards displayed in so eminent a degree'.[38]

On the eve of his departure from Shacklewell, Horner had written a lengthy document which he entitled 'Plan of My Future Studies'.[39] In it he committed himself to future metaphysical speculations and noted that 'it is only on a complete and scientific knowledge of the principles of human nature and the theory of morals, that the path is laid towards the elements of legislative science'. He also pledged himself to write essays and disquisitions only 'on subjects of general law and politics' for the several literary societies of Edinburgh. Among the three topics he promised to investigate, two were within the realm of economic philosophy – the legislative control of gaming and the inequalities of rank in society. And the first paper he read before the Speculative Society dealt broadly with the moral ramifications of commercial wealth (Doc. 20).

Horner was therefore no novice in economic speculations when the prospect of Professor Stewart's first lectures in political economy inspired interest among the students of the university. By all indications Horner and his friends each sought to carve out a sphere of economic philosophy in which they could specialize. Later developments confirm that Allen undertook an examination of Physiocratic doctrine (Doc. 69) and that Brougham set out to stake his claim to the subject of colonial policy.[40] A paper Jeffrey read to the Academy of Physics in April 1800 suggests that his initial researches broached the theory of productive and unproductive labour (Doc. 45). Horner selected the theory of population.

Among Horner's first readings were Turgot's *Reflections* and the theories of population advanced by Condorcet and William Godwin. During the spring of 1799, when he considered writing a paper on population for the Academy, he read from the economic works of Lord Kames, Gaetano Filangieri, and Richard Price, perused Condorcet's *Vie de M. Turgot*, studied Spanish so that he could read Campomanes, and closely examined Malthus's *Essay on Population* (Docs 29, 30, 31, 32, 33, 34, and 35).

Horner's journal entries (Docs 31 and 32) reveal that he was surprised by the scope of Malthus's treatise; that work, he observed, went far beyond the traditional confines of population theory and to some extent offered a model connecting the various branches of economic philosophy. He was especially impressed by the author's remarks on the various definitions of national wealth, which apparently kindled his interest in the works of the French 'Economists', and by Malthus's strictures on Adam Smith's optimistic theories about the relationship between national prosperity and the wages of labour.

The effect of the *Essay on Population* on Horner was considerable; later he would write of the 'new world' discovered by Malthus (Doc. 226) and classify all economic

---

38. Hewlett to John Horner, 16 Oct. 1797, and to Leonard Horner, [?March-May 1817], *ibid.*, i. 40–47.
39. *Ibid.*, i. 48–53, omitting several passages to be found in the manuscript at Kinnordy.
40. In early 1800 Brougham spoke at the Speculative on colonial policy, and in 1803 he published his two-volume *Inquiry into the Colonial Policy of the European Powers*. (*Speculative Society*, p. 390; New, pp. 14, 18, and 23; see also Docs 103, 124, 128, 135, and 144.)

philosophy under two heads – population and money (Doc. 84). The immediate effect of Malthus's treatise on him, however, was inspirational; after completing the work he abandoned his planned paper on population and instead committed himself to a thorough examination of Montesquieu's *Esprit des Lois*, Smith's *Wealth of Nations*, and Physiocratic doctrine (Doc. 34 n. 2).

In late August, after he had squandered the summer on superficial geological inquiries, Horner read Bolingbroke, solicited the opinion of his friend Allen, and sketched out yet another ambitious plan for the study of history and politics. He placed the *Wealth of Nations* at the top of his reading list and began an analysis of Smithian doctrine that would continue intermittently for well over two years (Doc. 36).

Horner's brief initial notes on the *Wealth of Nations*, which are dated August and September 1799 and incorporated with those of a later date, reflect confusion over the division of labour and Smith's definition of exchangeable value (Doc. 74, paras 12 and 13). Like countless future students, he could not understand Smith's reasonings on the wages of labour or on nominal price and real price, but was left initially with the vague impression, later recorded in his journal (Doc. 45), that a distinction could be drawn between productive and unproductive labour. In September he perused Smith's chapter on money, and noting its omissions, identified the subject as one which he would have to investigate at a later date (Doc. 37).

Horner's interest in metaphysics generally and in economic philosophy in particular mounted after November 1799, when Stewart began his much-anticipated first course of lectures on political economy. Significantly, Horner attended the lectures while simultaneously collecting Turgot's writings and examining Hume's metaphysical essays with Seymour (Doc. 38). Turgot's economic essays impressed him very deeply, and during January 1800 he planned an English edition of Turgot's political and philosophical works, securing promises of collaboration from Jeffrey and several other future Edinburgh reviewers, but abandoned the project upon receiving an unfavourable opinion from a London bookseller (Docs 39 and 84). He found the metaphysics of Hume no less inspiring. On 21 January he opened debate at the Speculative Society by challenging a basic assumption in Hume with the question, 'Is commerce prejudicial to morality?'[41] In February he outlined another abortive scheme for a grand treatise on the principles of philosophical inquiry (Doc. 40) and began to correspond on philosophical subjects with Seymour's brother, the Duke of Somerset (Doc. 41).

In March 1800, shortly after Brougham had sparked debate at the Speculative with his remarks on colonial policy, Horner decided to present a paper on the circulation of money, the subject that had most intrigued him during his recent perusal of the *Wealth of Nations*. He laboured on that project for some two weeks and noted his progress in his journal (Doc. 42). Thus not only during his residence at Shacklewell but also on at least two occasions in his twenty-first year Horner examined and pondered the theory of money. Early on, it appears, he perceived that the controversy arising from the restriction of cash payments by the Bank of England offered a rich field for literary reputation.

41. *Speculative Society*, p. 389.

In the end Horner abandoned his plan to address the Speculative on the circulation of money. The subject was simply too obscure; Smith and other economic writers offered but little instruction in monetary theory, he noted, and there was not enough time to write a conscientious paper (Doc. 43). He therefore re-examined his earlier notes on population and hurriedly composed an essay on the economic, social, and political ramifications of London's emerging commercial wealth. But he carefully filed his notes on the circulation of money with an eye to later development; in 1801 he would incorporate them with the notes produced by a further foray into monetary theory (Doc. 74, paras 10–14).

The paper Horner therefore read before the Speculative Society on 8 April 1800 was that he entitled 'On the Overgrowth of the Metropolis' (Doc. 44). It incorporated the established principles of population and borrowed heavily from the general doctrines of Hume, Smith, and Malthus – Seymour, to whom Horner read it again a few days later, described it as 'an elegant declaration rather than an investigation of the subject' – but it reflected mature thought and an ability to synthesize diverse information, and constituted a renunciation of his earlier, negative view of commercial society. In essence it advanced an optimistic view of the effects of commerce on Britain, questioning the works of 'political arithmeticians' who drew contrary conclusions and disputing three popular notions: that all great cities were destructive of population; that they generated a profligacy of manners; and that the immense wealth of London monopolized trade and detracted from the prosperity of the rest of the nation.[42]

Hitherto Horner had studied only the general theory of political economy and had formulated far more questions than answers. His queries mounted as a result of Professor Stewart's first lectures, which offered little more than an introduction to essential principles, and after April 1800 he began to search for inductions capable of confirming or refuting existing theory. His correspondence and journal entries of the spring and summer of 1800 reveal close study of the details of commerce, which was enhanced by discussions with his father, and of the processes of iron manufacturing, which included visits to factories, troublesome interviews with labourers, and chemical experiments that depleted Joanna Horner's supply of towels (Docs 46–9).[43]

Horner's search for inductive facts was interrupted in early August when he learned of the furore sparked by Chief Justice Kenyon's recent decisions on forestalling and engrossing. These had resulted in the conviction of intermediaries trafficking in grain for pecuniary profit and focused public attention on Adam Smith's general view of the constructive function of middlemen. Horner immediately sensed the political import of the litigation, procured a number of the pamphlets inspired by the controversy, and studied Smith's chapter on corn, Turgot's *Lettres sur les Grains*, and the related works of several continental authors (Docs 50–52 and 70). In September 1800, in the midst of his first analysis of the theory of grain, he again expressed deep reservations about the ignorance that seemed to accompany Britain's mounting commercial opulence (Doc. 53).

42. Lord Webb Seymour's Diary, 13 Apr. 1800, Devon Record Office. See also Fontana, pp. 48–9.
43. Byrne Memoirs, p. 66.

Smith's chapter on corn largely moulded Horner's lifelong view of grain policy; he considered it accurate and profound, as well as an ingenious model of argumentative composition (Doc. 50), and he noted that its principal reasonings were confirmed by Turgot's *Lettres*, which he studied simultaneously (Doc. 52).

Horner's main series of notes on the *Wealth of Nations*, which he began in October 1800 (Doc. 54), were written in the form of paragraphs responding to points made by the author and posing queries for future investigation. They advanced speculations regarding the determinants and the relativity of the 'natural' and market prices of grain, noted the connection between Smith's grain theory of wages and Malthus's fundamental principle of population, and displayed a mature comprehension of Smith's several omissions, among them his curious failure to acknowledge the importance of the French 'Economists'. Horner realized, however, that Smith's work merely pointed the way to further inquiry. A full comprehension of the theory of grain, he observed, would require a more complete understanding of the historical relationship between trends in the price of grain and the price of silver, and the progress of the various branches of domestic industry.

Shortly after completing his initial researches on grain policy Horner undertook with Seymour a careful analysis of Bacon's philosophical writings. That project, he noted revealingly, might bring system to his study of human affairs, prepare him to reform political institutions, and allow him to extend the boundaries of legislative science.[44] His resulting notes (Docs 55, 63, and 67), which responded to passages in Bacon's writings with a sequence of numbered paragraphs and continued until 10 May 1801, say a great deal about his emerging view of political phenomena.

Horner contemplated Bacon with reference to the works of Gibbon, Hume, Smith, and Stewart, ever searching for the proper confines of the different sciences, for the just rules of scholarly inquiry, and for the framework within which one might write 'philosophical history'. Again the influence of Hume is evident. Horner noted that philosopher's emphasis on 'particular facts' arising from history, his admonitions against reasoning too finely from a lengthy chain of observable circumstances, and his disdain for hurried generalization (Doc. 67, para. 42). Those facets of Hume's method assumed new importance in the light of Bacon's comments on the unhappy effects of premature system on the progress of scientific endeavour (Doc. 63, paras 14 and 15), and indeed Horner noted in his journal that perhaps even Adam Smith's 'system' had been developed precipitously (Doc. 56). Like Smith, however, he depreciated the importance of mathematics in political speculations; the methods of the mathematician, he observed, were employed with greater advantage in the more precise realm of the natural sciences (Doc. 63, para. 14).

Intermittently Horner's notes on Bacon depart from methodology and turn to a number of generalizations about philosophical history. They contain a short critique of the political and commercial factors that had determined the history of economic speculations and conclude that the annals of a free nation animated by commerce best enable the historian to penetrate the core and to blend political and economic phenomena in the historical narrative (Doc. 55, para. 6; Doc. 63, para. 19). The notes observe, moreover, a dearth of facts pertaining to political economy and

44. See Winch, pp. 52–3.

criticize earlier political writers, especially Bacon and Montesquieu, for ignoring the 'particular facts' underlying political change (Doc. 55, para. 5; Doc. 67 n. 14).

Interestingly, Horner concluded that 'particular facts' were most notably discernible in the parliamentary history of Britain. Parliamentary discussions, he noted, chronicle the factors underlying the progress of commerce and its regulation ('police'), and indeed a general history of eighteenth-century Britain might well focus on the aberrations of the corn and provision trade (Doc. 55, para. 4). Here, then, was the blueprint for his *histoire raisonnée*.

Horner's notes on Bacon also include comment that appeared years later in his doctrine as a parliamentary economist. One passage observes the debilitating effects of poor relief and the ingratitude of its beneficiaries (Doc. 67, para. 44). Another, which anticipated Ricardo's views to some extent and would underlie Horner's controversial speeches on corn policy some fourteen years later, equates the manufacturers' spirit of money-making with progress and the agriculturalists' reverence for established customs with decadence (Doc. 55, para. 1).

These notes on Bacon's philosophical writings were clearly influenced by Horner's concurrent researches into economics. In December 1800 he began a course of reading on the details of political economy with a view to Stewart's second series of lectures, which were to commence later in the month. He opened with a further investigation of the corn trade, not only because of its general importance but also because of its contemporary political relevance. First he read Herbert's *Police des Grains*, from which he gleaned many hints for further inquiry, and studied the law of Scotland with respect to agricultural leases. Later in the month he examined several recent pamphlets and some extensive notes of evidence being collected by the House of Lords on the corn trade which Seymour had received from his brother. As he proceeded, he also read from Gibbon, planned a general commercial history of Britain, and dreamed again of historical eminence and professional reputation (Docs 57, 58, and 59).

Horner's journal entries of 17 December 1800 (Doc. 60) and of 16 January 1801 (Doc. 62) record his impressions of the remarks that introduced Stewart's second course of lectures on political economy. They include his assessment of the professor's definitions, delineations, and omissions as well as an interesting passage criticizing Stewart's political timidity and cautious view of change. But above all else they display the growing confidence of an economist, and of one who admired Stewart's didactic oratory but found his economic speculations somewhat narrow and largely devoid of 'particulars'.

Notwithstanding these criticisms, Horner's interest in questions of political economy mounted with the progress of Stewart's lectures. Late in February 1801 he was intrigued by a discussion at the Speculative Society on the consequences of a free commercial intercourse between China and the rest of the civilized world (Doc. 65).[45] A week later, apparently anticipating another debate at the Speculative,[46] he investigated the commercial rights of neutral nations in wartime (Doc. 66), a

---

45. *Speculative Society*, p. 391.
46. On 24 Mar. 1801 Horner's boyhood friend James Moncreiff opened debate at the Speculative on the question, 'Ought the right of belligerent powers of searching neutral vessels for contraband goods, to be recognized in the international law of Europe?' (*idem*).

subject with which he would later concern himself as a Whig politician, and about the same time Stewart's lectures led him to contemplate the writers of the Physiocratic school.

Horner's interest in the works of the French Economists had been sparked some time earlier by his study of Turgot, Malthus's comments on national wealth, and Smith's confusing doctrine of exchangeable value. Now, in late February 1801, Professor Stewart led his students into the complex world of Physiocratic doctrine. Horner and Seymour, who discussed Stewart's lectures on a regular basis, promptly ran aground on the subject of productive labour, and at the beginning of March, prior to a meeting of the Chemical Society, they sought clarification from the encyclopedic Allen (Doc. 66).

Allen, who earlier had read the works of Quesnay and the elder Mirabeau, not only provided a number of helpful hints but also allowed Horner to copy an abstract he had written on the principal tenets of Physiocratic doctrine (Doc. 69). This apparently inspired Horner's first notes of April 1801 on 'the system of the Economists' (Doc. 68). These brief notes, which were written with reference to Stewart's continuing discussion of the corn trade (Doc. 70), reflect the shaky reasoning of a young man who was confused about the meaning of exchangeable value and inclined to believe that perhaps Smith's grain theory of price formed a close alliance between the two great branches of 'economical science', wealth and population.

The month of April 1801 was pivotal in Horner's intellectual development. His journal entry of the 12th (Doc. 71) noted that Bacon's philosophical writings, and to a lesser extent Sir Joshua Reynolds's *Discourses*, had at last brought system to his studies, and that his destiny was largely fixed. Already he had resolved sooner or later to pursue a career at the English Bar.[47] But his long-standing desire for literary and political reputation now consumed him, and economic speculations were foremost in his mind. On the 24th he accompanied Allen and Seymour to Stewart's home, where they heard anecdotes about Adam Smith's character and curious habits (Doc. 72), and three days later Horner committed himself to a systematic course of reading in political economy (Doc. 73).

The researches Horner conducted between April 1801 and the early months of 1802 were of considerable importance in the evolution of his economic doctrine. Formerly his speculations had bogged down amidst confusion about Adam Smith's view of the real measure of value, his distinction between nominal and real price, and his comments on the price of labour. That confusion, in turn, had thwarted all of Horner's reasonings on reciprocal value, including that of the various denominations of coined and paper money. Hitherto the difficulty of the subject had led him to evade it; but now a pamphlet by Lauderdale and a lecture by Stewart inspired confidence and determined the course of his readings (Doc. 75).

Evidently Horner's primary object during 1801 was to clarify his view of exchangeable value and then to apply his conclusions to the theory of money. He pursued that object with reference to the principles of scholarly inquiry propounded by Hume and Bacon, at once seeking materials from which he could deduce and induce conclusions of his own. He proceeded with his researches both independently and with his friend Seymour. Horner and Seymour met in Horner's room

47. See Horner's journal entries of 22 Nov. 1801 and 3 May 1802, *Horner*, i. 174 and 198.

twice each week, where they read silently, took notes, and then engaged in discussions in which they sought to confirm or refute general principles (Doc. 74 n. 1). Between late April and the end of the year they read and analysed the first six chapters of the *Wealth of Nations* and Rice Vaughan's *Coin and Coinage*, which had attracted Horner's attention during his earlier researches on the circulation of money (Docs 75, 77, 79, and 83).

Simultaneously Horner conducted much more detailed researches on his own. Initially he attempted to compare the doctrine of the *Wealth of Nations* with that advanced by Turgot's *Reflections* and the elder Mirabeau's *Philosophie rurale*. When he and Seymour completed Smith's third chapter early in May 1801, however, he expressed disillusionment with Turgot's doctrines and bewilderment with Mirabeau's terminology, and noted that he was hampered by a failure to procure Quesnay's published works (Doc. 74 n. 7).

Thereafter Horner and Seymour proceeded, without reference to the French writers, to Smith's fourth chapter, 'Of the Origins and the Use of Money', and fifth chapter, 'Of the Real and Nominal Price of Commodities, or of their Price in Labour and their Price in Money'. Again the reasonings of the fifth chapter confounded them; so they suspended their perusal of the *Wealth of Nations* and turned to Vaughan's treatise on money (Doc. 75).

While he and Seymour together conducted a meticulous examination of Vaughan late into September, Horner searched independently for 'particular facts'. He gathered information on the political economy of the Swiss cantons and on the Republic of Geneva through the medium of a Swiss friend at university (Doc. 76). He conducted considerable researches on the theory of money that focused on the circumstances surrounding key events in monetary history. And his later correspondence (Doc. 84) suggests that he examined also the reports of parliamentary committees, a number of pamphlets dating back to the reign of Elizabeth, and two histories distinguished by their heavy reliance on illustration – Adam Anderson's *Origin of Commerce* and John Smith's *Memoirs of Wool*.

In October 1801 Horner at last procured Quesnay's writings and conducted an independent analysis of Physiocratic thought. That project, which was restricted to an examination of the subjects of wealth and exchangeable value, anticipated a further perusal of the *Wealth of Nations*. Then, in November 1801, he began with Seymour an analysis of Smith's sixth chapter, 'Of the Component Parts of the Price of Commodities', which continued until the early months of 1802.

These researches produced two sets of notes. The first, which is dated April 1801 but evidently includes later notations as well, constitutes a continuation of Horner's notes on the *Wealth of Nations* (Doc. 74). The second, dated October 1801, is a continuation of his notes on 'the system of the Economists' (Doc. 82).

Collectively these documents reveal conclusions of later significance. Horner states emphatically that Smith misunderstood the nature of exchangeable value and that the relative price of commodities was determined solely by the interplay of demand and supply, not by the quantity or quality of labour expended in producing them. That clarification of Smith's comments on natural and market price is accompanied by a denial of the existence of a standard measure of value, by repeated emphasis on the effect of competition on price, and by a passage noting the utility of

Smith's tactic of comparing prices at different times and places (Doc. 74, paras 16, 17, and 20). Horner notes, moreover, the simplicity of an analysis of price. Ever considering value with reference to the actual state of competition, he observes that such an analysis is nothing more than an examination of the proportions in which the price paid for any article is distributed among three parties: the landlord, in the form of rent, the labourer, in the form of wages, and the capitalist, in the form of profit (Doc. 74, paras 21–4).

Horner's notes on 'the system of the Economists' extend the conclusions at which he had arrived in his earlier study of Smith. He distrusts Quesnay's entire context of thought; that famous physician, he observes, was apparently misled by feudal habits and by the peculiarities of the means of production in his native France, and Quesnay's language, even that employed in expressing his fundamental idea that wealth was born of the earth, was insufficiently precise (Doc. 82, paras 3, 5, and 9).

Horner also dismisses Quesnay's notion that wealth equates with exchangeable value. That idea, he observes, is nothing but a relic of the old and mistaken premise that wealth consists in precious metals. It is, moreover, illogical, even within the context of Physiocratic doctrine. If, as Quesnay reasons, wealth equates with exchangeable value, and if, as all the French writers concede, manufacturing labour enhances the exchangeable value of a raw material born of the earth, then how can manufacturing labour be deemed barren? Since the second proposition is indisputable, Horner concludes, Quesnay's definition of wealth is erroneous. Wealth may well be born of the earth, and certainly the produce of the manufacturer uses up some measure of the produce of the land. That measure, however, is variable – contingent on the efficiency of the manufacturing process – and greater efficiency minimizes the consumption of agricultural riches, reduces manufacturing expenses, lowers the price of manufactured commodities, and thus increases the productive powers of agriculture (Doc. 82, paras 10–14).

National wealth, Horner notes, is nothing more than goods and services, the supply of commodities satisfying human needs and wants; and exchangeable value, he emphasizes yet again, is nothing more than a combination of scarcity and utility (Doc. 82, para. 10).

Horner's conclusions on exchangeable value influenced the course of his early researches on the theory of money. In the spring of 1800, when he had attempted unsuccessfully to write a treatise on circulation for the Speculative Society, his analysis had evidently revolved around Hume's economic writings, most notably his essays 'Of Money' and 'Of Interest'. Hume had reasoned that, owing to the effects of specie flows on prices in trading nations, the amount of specie in each nation naturally tended towards an equilibrium between imports and exports. The amount of specie a nation was capable of attracting and retaining was determined exclusively by the peculiarities of the domestic economy, not by political contrivance, and thus attempts to increase the amount of specie beyond its 'natural' level were doomed to failure. Any 'unnatural' influx of specie would raise the nation's prices relative to other trading nations, reduce exports and increase imports, and thereby generate a return outflow of specie.

These earlier researches reveal that Horner's first systematic examination of the theory of money focused on historical precedents, in particular on the effects of former attempts to raise the value of coin, the unsuccessful monetary policy of the reign of James I, and the effects of an influx of silver from the New World. Now, during the course of 1801, his new researches (Docs 74 and 79) further developed his monetary doctrine. In every instance, he observes, the reciprocal value of coined metals was determined by competition, by the proportion of demand and supply (Doc. 74, para. 17). Proportion is affected by numerous circumstances. The relative exchangeable value of precious metals on the bullion market constitutes the 'natural' bullion ratio; that ratio varies from day to day and is affected by an influx of specie of one denomination or another, as in the case of silver from the mines of South America. However, each country arbitrarily establishes proportions of value between minted coins, thereby creating a gulf between the bullion ratio, which floats, and the mint ratio, which remains fixed. That gulf is widened by the inevitable wear on metallic coins, which alters the value of currency relative to both the bullion price and the mint price, and also by political and commercial forces within each nation which add to or subtract from the relative value of precious metals and thus widen the gulf.

These several factors, Horner notes, combine to cause embarrassment at the mint. Contraband dealers melt down the coin which is under-valued by the mint and counterfeit the coinage which is over-valued, and merchants are encouraged to traffic in the exportation and importation of the precious metals (Doc. 74, paras 18 and 19).

As late as September 1801 Horner noted in his journal that, while his historical inquiries continued, he had neither arranged the subject of money nor reduced his facts to analytic order (Doc. 80). Clearly, however, by year's end he had developed much of the doctrine he later propounded in the *Edinburgh Review* and in the Bullion Report. For in his notes are the seeds of his fundamental disagreement with Ricardo – his insistence that it was not only the inflationary tendencies of the restriction of cash payments by the Bank of England but also a wide range of wartime commercial and political factors that bore on the British monetary dilemma.

Horner's interest in British politics mounted during the course of 1801. James Loch, the first of his Edinburgh friends to move to London, sent him political intelligence, and as early as February Horner wrote a letter which displayed an uncommon understanding of parliamentary alignments and concluded that the nation would at last turn to Fox (Doc. 64). Afterwards his economic speculations were interrupted from time to time by studies which examined the personal characteristics of great men (Doc. 71) and the essence of fine writing (Doc. 77).

In June 1801 Horner began to correspond with the Duke of Somerset on the issue of inclosures (Doc. 78). Somerset sent him accounts of the parliamentary discussions that had accompanied the defeat of the Inclosure Bill of 1801, and in September Horner responded with a critical treatise which reasoned confidently on the political economy of inclosures and the tithe to the Established Church (Doc. 81). A week later, following several conversations with the visiting Mackintosh, Horner was expressing fascination with the '*beaux-esprits* of London', and by mid-October, while he was still engaged in his examination of Physiocratic doctrine, he was asking Loch to send him information on the English Bar (Doc. 83 n. 1). In November, while he and Seymour were perusing the sixth chapter of the *Wealth of Nations*,

Horner noted in his journal that he would visit London to seek the opinions of English lawyers and then make a final determination during the coming spring vacation (Doc. 83).

By the last months of 1801, therefore, Horner's plans for the future were well-advanced. For years he had expressed interest in literary honours and political reputation. The one, he understood, could enhance the other; and the realization of both objectives was dependent on his presence in London, Britain's literary and political hub. Now, as he looked towards the English Bar and the party of Fox, his command of economic literature, and thus his vehicle for literary honours, was impressive indeed.

In mid-January 1802 Horner wrote a lengthy essay on the bibliography of political economy at the request of the Duke of Somerset (Doc. 84). Interestingly, he placed the essays of Turgot at the head of all works in economic philosophy. Otherwise he assigned considerable importance to Steuart's *Principles of Political Economy*, made but passing reference to Adam Smith, and recommended Mirabeau's *Philosophie rurale* as the most systematic and elaborate statement of Physiocratic principles, which he described as an admixture of error and truth.

Horner's bibliographical essay divided economic philosophy into two branches – money and population. In the doctrine of money he assigned special importance to Pinto's *Circulation and Credit* and to Vaughan's *Coinage*, listed Harris on coins, Bentham's *Defence of Usury*, and Locke's tracts, and mentioned the existence of numerous other publications. To 'population' he assigned all else, including, most prominently, the works he had consulted in his researches on the theory of grain.

The essay concluded with an acknowledgement of Horner's dissatisfaction with existing theory and of his continuing focus on 'particular facts' arising from history. The inductive facts contained in the reports of parliamentary committees and in the large number of obscure pamphlets written for ephemeral purposes, he observed, record the authentic materials of contemporary speculation, thereby illustrating principles already known or suggesting further generalization. That comment assumed importance about a month later when with Allen, Jeffrey, and Smith he conceived the *Edinburgh Review*.

1. To J.A. Murray

BLPES i. 3–4 ⟨Horner, i. 8–9⟩   Shacklewell, 24 Nov. 1795

⟨I leave the Port Royal Grammar and Lexicon of Hedericus[1] to refresh myself in your company, to inform you where I have taken up my winter quarters, and to interrogate you rigidly with regard to your plans at college, and the proceedings of that most polite, learned, and scientific body, the *Juvenile Literary Society*.[2]

⟨On Friday, 6th Nov., I fixed my abode at Shacklewell⟩ . . . ⟨The rev. gentleman, under whose superintendence I am, keeps a boarding-school for boys, on which account I have my bed and study at a room in a different part of the village; by this means I am at a distance from the boys, the music of whose motions is not always exactly the same with that which Pythagoras ascribed to the celestial spheres, so harmonious as not to be heard. At Mr Hewlett's house, however, I take all my meals; and he generally sits with me about an hour every day in my own room. He is a most agreeable man; an elegant and general scholar, in the most extensive sense of the words. I consider myself peculiarly happy in having fallen into his hands, and believe I shall pass the ensuing twelvemonth with much more pleasure and much more profit than I expected when I saw you last.

⟨This detail⟩ (equalling the longwinded metaphors of Ephraim, yea the longwinded arguments of Donaldson)[3] ⟨I have given you because I believe you would be as glad to hear of my having found an agreeable situation, as I am anxious about every thing that interests you. Write me, my dear friend, as soon as possible. You may believe with what pleasure I must seize every letter from Edinburgh.

⟨Tell me⟩ how your respectable mother keeps her health – ⟨how you are managing your studies, what classes you attend, and what books you are devouring.⟩ I hope we shall have many touches yet on the progressive and unlimited improvement of the species, luxury, etc. – and by the bye ⟨I see nothing to prevent us carrying on our *Disputationes Academicæ*, though we are four hundred miles asunder. Metaphysics can roar loud enough, and I can get franks every week. Come, I order you in the name of Hume, and Smith, and Dugald Stewart, to select a question immediately, and to begin upon it in your very first letter. The controversy would be much the better for our friend Brougham's assistance, and I shall give him a hint. In the meantime remember me to him.⟩ By way of appendix to your reasonings, give me your opinion of the bill 'now pending in Parliament'.[4] Here it is very unpopular; even a few of Mr Pitt's advocates, who enjoy not a sleep so profound and unbroken as the others, deem it an unnecessary stretch of power; the violent on the other side reprobate it in that canting phraseology which Rousseau I think invented and the French Revolution made common, while the staunch friends of the Constitution bless it as the happiest measure that could have been devised to hasten the fall of a minister who has brought many calamities on his country, and seems to have formed the design of overthrowing its liberties. . . .

1. The Greek and Latin grammars commonly in use were those emanating from the Abbey of Port Royal, together with the Greek Lexicon of Benjamin Hederich.
2. The Juvenile Literary Society had been established in Dec. 1792 with Brougham as first

president and with Horner among its charter members. See Cantor, pp. 110–11, *Brougham*, i. 84–6, and the Brougham MSS, UCL ff. 2445, 13976–80, 22910, 34170, 36691, 38429, 39485, and 39502, for lists of its members, rules, minutes, etc. The lists include twenty-one names over the life of the Society, with a limit on membership at any one time of sixteen (not twenty, as Cantor says). They met every week in term-time, at 8 a.m. in the class-room of the professor of agriculture, Andrew Coventry (not Playfair, as in Cantor), and there was an extensive system of fines for non-attendance or lateness and for showing 'disrespect' or making interruptions. At each meeting the programme for the following week would be arranged, with one member (who also acted for the occasion as chairman or 'President') designated to read an essay and others to debate a motion. Contemporary 'party politics' were banned by the rules, but this prohibition seems to have been very liberally interpreted and it did not prevent, for example, discussion of such a topic as the liberty of the press. Horner was an assiduous attender, never failing to be present until 15 Nov. 1794, when the surviving record ends, and only rarely incurring a fine for lateness or an interruption. During that period he read two essays, 'On the different virtues of Man' and 'On Fear', and among the debates for which he was named speaker most were on subjects of classical history, but it was he who won the argument, mentioned in *Brougham*, that theatrical representations were friendly to virtue, and lost that in favour of the unrestrained liberty of the press, by stressing overmuch the word 'unrestrained'.

3. See Doc. 2.
4. For the prevention of seditious meetings.

2. From Henry Brougham

BLPES i. 5 6   Edinburgh, 9 Jan. 1796

I wish you a good new year.

When I look at the date of your letter, and compare it with that of my answer, and of your arrival in London, I am struck with your goodness in writing so soon, and my own laziness in not answering till now. Murray (who has been a *better boy* than me) told you I suppose, that the [Juvenile Literary] Society died of what he calls an *abscess* in the side. I foresaw this on the first meeting, and moved, in order to prevent it, that an adjournment of 2 months should take place, but this was not agreed to. *Donald* resigned his office. I thought he wanted some *flattery* and gave him a damned large dose of it. *Forbes*, however, came closer to the point, for he moved a Book to him. This *infamous* measure had the desired effect. The funds were dilapidated, and Erskine's *Institutes* in folio were bought for £2. 2s., but I gave him to understand how much against my will it was, by refusing to let him have any inscription prefixed to it. As soon as *Ephraim* heard of this, he sent in his resignation, for fear of his purse, and has not yet been prevailed upon to contribute his shilling. Donaldson, Copland, and Watson are become members of the Literary [Society], of which I am *secretary*![1] Donaldson is [as] much despised here as in the other, a clear proof that fools are fools everywhere. I have become a member of the Natural History Society. You would see by the papers that Webb, is one of the *presidents*, as also of the Royal Medical [Society] together with Reid.[2] Such is all the Society news. As to the *parcel*, I believe it *has* gone to Jacobi.[3] Whether he has sent it or not I can't say, but am rather of the latter opinion. However if you could devise any way of ascertaining this, it might be of use, as the academy does not decide till *next June*. Do you ever go to the Royal

Society? Tell me if you hear any thing from that quarter. You was not mistaken about Spankie, he *is* reporter to the *Morning Chronicle*, at the salary of 2 guineas per week.[4] I'll take the liberty of troubling you with a commission. Be kind enough to look in any of the shops, for a book called, the *Mathematical Repository* published, I think, half yearly, and write me an account of the contents.[5] For I have not been able to find the book here.

. . .

1. There was no one named Donald among the members of the Juvenile Literary Society (or its successor, the Literary Society); but the recipient of the *Institutes of the Law of Scotland* (1773) by John Erskine (1695–1768: *DNB*), was evidently Hay Donaldson (d. 1822), afterwards a Writer to the Signet and Provost of Haddington. Ephraim Lockhart of Barmagatchan (d. 1850) also later became a Writer. Alexander Copland, a nephew of Andrew Hunter (1743–1809: *DNB*), the Professor of Divinity at Edinburgh, became an active member of the Speculative and a debater of some reputation. On 25 Nov. 1799 Horner made the following notation in his journal (*Horner*, i. 94):

   > I mean to practise myself in replying; and I think it will be a good plan to confine myself at first to one antagonist, Copland, for instance, and to study most accurately his peculiar style of speaking, his habits of association both in point of illustration and argument, and the most successful plan of encountering him.

   Copland became an advocate but died of consumption at an early age in 1809 (*Speculative Society*, p. 222). David Watson has not otherwise been identified.
2. William Webb, a student from Hampshire, was quite possibly William Webb (1780–1831), a cadet of the Webbs of Odstock, several members of whose immediate family were or became distinguished scholars. John Reid (1776–1822: *DNB*) was then a medical student in Edinburgh.
3. Perhaps Baron Jacobi-Klöst (1745–1817), the Prussian minister in London till 1817, rather than the German philosopher, Friedrich Heinrich Jacobi (1743–1819).
4. Robert Spankie (c.1774–1842), a London lawyer of Scots birth, was afterwards 'first assistant to James Perry, editor of the *Morning Chronicle*, and subsequently Attorney-General of Bengal'. (See H.R. Fox Bourne, *English Newspapers. Chapters in the History of Journalism* (2 vols., 1887), i. 268, and the AR lxxxiv (1842), 299–300.) He too was elected a corresponding member of the Academy of Physics.
5. *The Gentleman's Diary; or the Mathematical Repository* had been published annually in London since 1742.

3. To J.A. Murray

BLPES i. 7–8 ⟨*Horner*, i. 9–11⟩   London, 15 Feb. 1796

. . .

⟨It gives me very great satisfaction to find that you have such a relish for the new branch of science on which you have lately entered. All my former labours in that way are of little use to me, I find, in England; ignorance of the improvement of late years extends the influence of that well-founded opinion, which the English literati and all unlearned men have formed against the absurd and trifling metaphysics of the schoolmen, and the dangerous refinements of modern materialists. This prejudice, however, will of course wear gradually away, and there can be but little rashness or unfounded expectation, in believing that in the revolution of a century the science of the human mind will hold the same rank, be as generally cultivated, and applied to practical uses equally important as the science of experimental philosophy is at present. The free communication of sentiments, which subsists between us, my dear Murray, will, I am sure, suffer me to give you, from my own experience, an advice with regard to the first prosecutions of this study, viz., to write on all the subjects which the professor prescribes. The advantages, in every respect, which attend this, I believe to be immensely great. With regard to Reid, the arguments against the fidelity of the senses must be refuted (in the logical treatise which you mention), I should apprehend, in a manner different from his, as it rests entirely on what is thought his greatest improvement in the science, the accurate distinction which he has established betwixt sensation and perception.

⟨I should be much obliged to you, if you will give me an abstract of what *The Art of Thinking* says on this subject.[1] I am not at all surprised at your disliking, on first perusal, *The Inquiry into the Human Mind*. The style in which it is written, as well as many other *Aberdonian* productions that were published about the same time, would be indecent, even in a common political pamphlet. If you have not yet read Mr Stewart's book, I can assure you that you have high pleasure in store.[2]

⟨You ask, my dear Murray, for an account of my studies; at present, I confine them to the impressing on my mind more strongly those very few branches of knowledge which I had cultivated before leaving Edinburgh; mathematics, languages, and your science of *nousology* occupying each a portion of my daily employment. This I am obliged to do, on account of the time which I must spend in considering the principles of English pronunciation, and English composition. In prosecution of the last of these, I sometimes attempt myself, sometimes translate from my favourite Rousseau – carrying on at the same time, under the direction of my friend Mr Hewlett, a very rigid examination of the style of Mr Hume in his *History*, which I am astonished to find abound so much both in inaccuracies and inelegancies.⟩

Since I have come to London, I have been at one or two most luxurious banquets – but neither aldermen, orators, nor turtle. The chief dishes were philosophy and literature. I was most entertained by one at which I was about a fortnight ago, where I enjoyed the company of Nicholson,[3] the celebrated experimental philosopher and of several other eminent literary characters. I was to have dined on Friday last in a party with Mr Walcott,[4] but the Cousin of old Pindar failed to make out his engagement.

⟨I have not been at the House of Commons so frequently as you would suppose. Added to the distance, and the inconvenience of getting home after midnight, when it is above five miles off, and part of that, too, in the country, I must confess that I was greatly disappointed in my expectations with regard to the eloquence of the British Senate. The best of them – and the good are very few – speak with such an unaccountable tone, they have so little grace in their action and delivery, and such a set of cant appropriated phrases have crept into use, that he who has previously formed ideas of eloquence from what he has read of that of Greece and Rome, must find the speeches even of Fox and Pitt miserably inferior. The one, indeed, speaks with great animation, and, I am convinced, from the warmest sincerity of heart; and the other has a most wonderful fluency and correctness, approaching almost to mechanical movement. But neither of them has proceeded so far as the observance of Shakespeare's rule; for the one *saws the air* with his hands, and the other with his whole body.⟩

I am happy that you and Brougham have fallen in with the idea which I proposed in my first letter.[5] As it was in my power, I have that side of your question which coincides with my real opinion, which has now become almost familiar to my mind, and by which I endeavour to regulate as much as possible not only conduct – but even my feelings. I am convinced that the principles of conduct ought to be founded only on the duties which the reason of every man points out to him as belonging to the rank which he holds in the scale of intellectual beings – all the views of our former state of existence, and of what shall hereafter become of us appear to be subjects of mere speculative curiosity. You will see that I have just drawn up, in as great haste as possible an abstract of arguments; on which I shall enlarge according to the objections which you propose.

. . .

I. I think, in this dispute, we ought to leave out all considerations with respect to the nature of the Soul. It is a subject on which it seems impossible to come to any conclusion. Knowing nothing either of mind or body in their essence, we have no facts on which we can ground any reasonings. Immateriality will not prove Immortality. Materialism would indeed necessarily lead to the doctrine of the Soul's mortality. But for my part, I do not go so far as to assert the mortality of the Soul; but only that the arguments which have been adduced to prove its immortality are insufficient, and that all our inquiries on the subject must end in ignorance and obscurity.

II. The great argument is drawn from our supposed instinctive longings after immortality, and dread of annihilation. But these feelings are neither instinctive nor natural. And even if they were, it is evident that they have been always connected with the idea of future happiness or misery. Now there is no species of intellectual happiness which will suit two different minds, as it [is] merely relative; so that if we admit the conclusiveness of the argument drawn from the desire of immortality, we must also suppose that each person shall enjoy a different system of happiness.

III. Before we can prove the question from the unlimited perfectibility of the species, that fact, which has led philosophers to many visionary notions, must be proved.

IV. Neither can we argue in the least from the wisdom, the power, and the goodness of the Deity. All His plans are hid from our view: We can form [?no] notion of His ideas or His feelings. Besides, our knowledge of the First Cause, and all our notions of His attributes are derived from a consideration of the universe; so that it is not merely unphilosophical, but absurd, to argue from that Cause again to the effect. If the Soul were shown to be immortal, that fact would be additional proof of the wisdom, the power, and the goodness of God; but it is impossible for us to argue, at present, from our ideas of those attributes, with regard to that fact.

. . .

1. The Abbé Antoine Arnauld's *Art de Penser*, familiarly known as the Port-Royal Logic, was still very popular in England.

2. The first volume of Dugald Stewart's *Elements of the Philosophy of the Human Mind* (1792) and its companion textbook, *Outlines of Moral Philosophy* (1793), brought the author great reputation and sparked lively debate among his students. The two poles in the debate were David Hume's *Treatise of Human Nature* (2 vols, 1739), which contended that man knew only mental states, never a 'mind' additional to them, and Thomas Reid's *Inquiry into the Human Mind on the Principles of Common Sense* (1764), which attacked Hume's contention that man knew only sensations and ideas, ridiculed the reasonings of metaphysicians as solitary flights from the objective realities of the real world that undermined the distinctions framing human values, and argued than man knew things directly and immediately. In Horner's fifteenth year, he and the other members of the Juvenile Literary Society had debated the question, 'Are there any innate ideas in the human mind?' In 1843 Allen recalled that Horner was more inclined to Hume's metaphysics than to Reid's. (See New, pp. 4–5, and Allen to Macvey Napier, 25 Mar. 1843, *Napier*, p. 425.)
3. William Nicholson (1753–1815: *DNB*), inventor.
4. John Wolcot (1738–1819: *DNB*), physician and, under the name 'Peter Pindar', satirist and poet.
5. For academic disputation by post, solicited by Horner in Doc. 1.

4. From Henry Brougham

BLPES i. 11–12   [Edinburgh], Wednesday [?9] Mar. 1796[1]

I received yours with very great pleasure and take this opportunity of a frank from Park Place,[2] to write you a few lines; you see I have paid you in kind, by *beginning* on large paper – but I do not promise to *finish* better than you did – namely: by tantalizing me with filling the sheet only one half and then speaking of my patience being tried. *Your* opinion of Mr Nicholson differs widely from that of *others*; however you have *induction of facts* on your side. His works I have read – and my opinion of them is, that you may read from beginning to end, without ever *thinking* of the author. At best he is a *second Hand*; understands his subject, and has read much on every branch of Natural science; but never *spouts* an original idea. His chief publications are, as you well know, a compendium of Chemistry; ditto of Natural Philosophy and the Chemical Dictionary (allowed to be a *bookmaking job*) and translations without number.[3] I have however no doubt that your account is quite reconcilable with this for who was a more agreeable companion than Goldsmith? As N. is a man of learning, taste and general views, I am sorry we must rank him among the *too* many instances of neglected merit – for if the accounts which I have heard are true, he is, I am afraid, in the hands, not of creditors, but of those *worse harpies*, booksellers; and his Dictionary to say the truth, gives some countenance to such a surmise. But enough of Mr N.

Literary news is very *scarce* here. The Literary Society goes on vastly well. We have 30 attending members and shall have *more* before it gives up – besides a number of *Visitors* each night – our laws are printed; and we are about to begin a fund for a Library: having demolished 5 or 6 pounds of former fund, by word of mouth; i.e. having *eat* and *drank* it.

Poor *Donald* is a very useful animal – he copies over, reports, extracts, etc., etc., for me – in his menial office of undersecretary or clerk – but he took it into his head to speak every meeting on the Question. So we interrupted him at the end of every sentence, and then stopped him altogether – since that his speeches have been much fewer and shorter.

We have 2 or 3 dominies – them also we have *silenced*, by dint of interruption etc. – thus, observing one beginning a long reply to *Donald*, and every sentence consulting a long *roll* of *Notes* or *heads*, I slyly *subtracted* his paper and burnt it, substituting an *equal* and *similar* blank paper – when the poor animal looked round for further fuel to his eloquence, he was struck at this seeming *miracle* (for indeed he was speaking on *Divine interposition*) and immediately sunk down *speechless*, to the joy of the company. Since that he has never opened his mouth. . . .⁴

You are now tired of the L. Society. Perhaps you may have heard of my *Paper* on *light* having been read before the *Royal Society* of London. An abstract containing an account of the experiments, and discoveries in it, is to be published in the *Philosophical Transactions* for May next.⁵ If you have not heard of it – you need not mention the thing. (When do you think of returning?) A report has reached me, that Dugald Stuart means to publish my paper on Dreaming as a refutation of his (or Melvil's) theory.⁶ Did he ever mention it to you? For my own part I think it more than Stuart could bring himself to – as the theory was among the few original things in his book. I hope you will answer me *very soon* and begin a controversy on any subject you please – in which John Murray will join. What think you of the *Utility* question? I will support the side of *utility* – but as you please.

1. The date has been amended by Brougham to 'Mar. 8', and the cover is twice endorsed 'March 15'. But both dates were Tuesdays and the frank is indecipherable.
2. The Horners' house in Edinburgh until the autumn of 1799 (Byrne Memoirs, p. 34).
3. In addition to translating J. A. Chaptal's *Elements of Chemistry* (3 vols, 1795), Nicholson was author of *Introduction to Natural Philosophy* (2 vols, 1782) and *A Dictionary of Chemistry* (2 vols, 1795).
4. The following seven lines have been obliterated in the MS.
5. 'Experiments and Observations on the Inflection, Reflection, and Colours of Light', read on 28 Jan. and published in the *Philosophical Transactions of the Royal Society*, lxxxvi (1796), Pt I, 227–77.
6. Thomas Melvill (1726–53: *DNB*), experimental philosopher. A paper on dreaming, read by Dugald Stewart to a literary society in Glasgow in 1771 or 1772, was incorporated in his *Elements of the Philosophy of the Human Mind*. There is no evidence that Stewart published Brougham's paper.

5. From Henry Brougham

BLPES i. 17–20   Edinburgh, 14 June 1796

This letter may *suffice* to show that I am not a ceremonious correspondent: and but little hackney'd in the theory of D[ebit] and C[redit]. Your metaphysical acumen will also infer from the receipt of it, that I subscribe to the old proverb, 'that *no* news is *good* news'.

I hope you continue to like your quarters at Mr Hewlett's, of whom I hear good accounts; your father tells me, he is a good mathematician, and pretty preacher –

two qualities very different; but with *one* of which at least, neither you nor I will be inclined to quarrel. As I devoutly and faithfully expect an answer to this (at your leisure) I wish you would give me a more particular touch of his character, and of your own studies; for instance – whether you pursue your old topics; whether you have added to the number of them. ...[1]

Now, to change the subject, just as a polite man puts his hand into his pocket and courteously says, 'Sir will you eat an apple?' – just so do I say, 'Sir will you have a *simile?*' As the atmosphere serene and freed from corrupt effluvia, with elastic spring and increased pressure raises the *penetrating* fluid in the barometer; so does the breeze of liberty (perhaps only in reality a semblance of that blessing diffused through the stagnate medium, choaked by the foul vapors of a 6 years Parliament and Treasury), raise my spirits to unusual height; when I hear of *Combe's* glorious election, Tooke's vigorous opposition – and still more the overthrow of the *Lowther* and *Pitt* interest in Westmoreland.[2] Are we not brave fellows in Cumberland and Westmoreland? – Returning 6 Opposition members without contest. I dare say you join with me in devoting your prayers ... to Fox and Horne Tooke. The latter I take to be without any exception, the greatest demagogue and acutest metaphysician of Modern Europe. If he loses Westminster he'll get a Borough. On the whole it is rumoured that Opposition will be almost *doubled.*

So much for Politics. You seem anxious next for *Literary* news. The two societies, those centres of light, broke up in *glory.* The good which the Literary Society, or at least the zeal of some of its members, has wrought this session is extraordinary. How much it has diffused freedom of opinion I before told you ...

I have been of late busy with the prosecution of those inquiries part of which have been published (I believe by this time) in the *Philosophical Transactions.* A letter about the beginning of May informed me that the Royal Society had honoured it with the earliest place. Namely, the first part for 1796 published in May. May I solicit your attention to its remarks *s'il vous plait.* I am arranging materials (collected since September the date of my last) for a second paper to appear in November next.[3] At intervals I apply to my favourite subject the higher geometry to which I hope you continue to give attention. ...[4]

1. There follows a carefully deleted passage. It is now impossible to make out but appears to have contained some cynical comments on Brougham's, or even Horner's, religious convictions. There are similarly indecipherable deletions in the next two paragraphs.
2. In the general election of May 1796, Harvey Christian Combe (1752–1818) was placed third in the poll for the City of London, John Horne Tooke (1736–1812: *DNB*) was last in that for Westminster. But Brougham's assertions about Cumberland and Westmorland are at best confusing. The two counties between them of course returned only four members, though counting also the few boroughs within them there were ten seats in all, of which only two (those at Carlisle) were contested, being won by Opposition men. In Appleby also, where there had previously been an agreed division of interest, two members were returned this time against the Lowthers. But elsewhere, including both seats in the county of Westmorland as well as two at Cockermouth and one in Cumberland, the Lowther interest prevailed without an official challenge. (*PH.*)
3. Brougham's 'Farther Experiments and Observations on the Affections and Properties of Light' was read on 15 June 1797 and published in the *Philosophical Transactions of the Royal Society,* lxxxvii (1797), Pt II, 352–85.
4. There follow two geometrical propositions.

6. From Henry Brougham

BLPES i. 27–8   Edinburgh, 22 July 1796

You see by this that I have (*pro tempore*) waved my liking to one species of *Franks*; though at the same time my predilection for another I trust remains unimpaired (There's a genteel *complimentary* pun). I therefore shall sacrifice this sheet to answer your very agreeable letter; giving you full liberty to sacrifice it over again when you have read it, or half read it at another *shrine*, which shall be nameless. And as Aristotle with his usual acuteness and sagacity observes, '*First* of the *first*' – I saw *Robertson* yesterday for the first time; having missed him 3 weeks ago, when he called with your letter (for which by the bye, this must also be the return).[1] His language is certainly good, though far from perfect: He always spoke well, but had a damned trick of sounding *â* like *awe* which he has not left off: you I doubt not will excel him. He tells me you think of repeating the *Newtonian Experiments* with Mr Hewlett. You ought to pray to Appollo [*sic*] (whom I take to be the god of optics) for better opportunities than he has given me this summer. Altogether I have not had 10 good days since the 1st of June. And most part of these were employed in showing my Experiments to such as asked it. Among whom *Forbes* and Reddie (who had seen them *last* summer) both were perfectly satisfied. If the weather permits may I hope to come in for a share of your attention: if so write me the result, though I shall not be surprised if they do not all succeed, as I believe there never was an instance of a person repeating another's experiments with perfect success in his absence: however if you state your trials, I shall endeavour to assist you by *letter*. Robertson also informed me that you have been applying wholly to Maths which rejoices me exceedingly. It was always my idea that no science can be thoroughly studied unless it is for some time the sole object of attention.

The mathematical part of your letter both *pleased* and *disappointed* me. I was pleased to see you had made fluxions and the higher geometry an object of your attention; but expected a solution of the questions by Archimedes' exhaustion. There would have been considerable difficulty in this: none in the other. I state this, that you may not think I meant them as a task for a modern analyst, who would justly think it an insult. There is an *error* in your second demonstration. . . . [*sic*] I shall fill up the remainder of my letter with some [questions] of greater *importance* and *difficulty*, and deferring an answer to the *damned nonsense* which composed the remainder of your letter (about *interest*, etc.) shall expect an answer to this as soon as you please.

. . .[2]

---

1. This is perhaps the 'Bob' Robertson mentioned in Doc. 8, but more probably the 'Bob' was intended to distinguish him from this Robertson who therefore may have been James Robertson, formerly a member of the Juvenile Literary Society and listed as a member of the Speculative Society in 1798.
2. Brougham goes on to pose several 'Questions on Fluxions – Pure'.

7. From Henry Brougham

BLPES i. 29–30   Edinburgh, 25 Aug. [1796]

I take this opportunity of *boring* you with a letter; as my hairdresser, is going to London, and offers to take care of it.

I am extremely sorry to think there is a great chance of my not seeing you when you come North. My present plan is to enter at the Temple in November, and I trouble you with this chiefly to request information. I have conversed with your father about accommodation, and he informs me that he inquired *in vain* for a proper situation for you in London. My own wishes lead me to think of *trying* to succeed you in *Mr Hewlett's*: and your f[ather] referred me to you for information on this head: (not, however, that I wish you to speak to Mr Hewlett on the subject).

A number of walking parties are gone off to different parts of the Highlands – Forbes and Company to the Hebrides. In his corps is Stuart, alias writer; alias *Porcupine*; alias *Quill driver*; alias *Broadbottom*.[1] He has however returned before the rest of his party, either per *Stage* or *Carrier* I don't know which. *Reddie* and a friend are at *Blair in Athol* – William Erskine, *solus*, at Lochlomond.[2] I have been (with my father) at Loch Leven, etc. and am thinking of another jaunt *on foot*, with James[3] and some others, to the North western Lochs.

The Town is miserably dull. My only amusements are *music* and *shooting*; and stuffing the birds (if rare) which I kill. I shall mention an anecdote that I met with yesterday because it surprised me vastly. Inquiring at the *Library*, for *Citoyenne Roland's Appeal*, Gordon told me he *had sold it*: and that none of *these* books are ever kept. A gentleman standing by, informed me that, all the novels etc. go the same way![4]

How d'ye like the public affairs? Will Pitt's gang keep in do you think? It is said here, that the Portlands are to leave their places.[5] How cursedly has Pitt duped them?

I shall now conclude this letter (long I fear for the goodness) and, '*May God bless what has been said*', for never had a *sermon* more need of blessing.[6]

1. Although the editors of *Brougham and Friends* seem elsewhere (i. 63) to confuse him with Charles Stuart, afterwards Baron Stuart de Rothesay (1779–1845: *DNB*), whom *Brougham*, i. 88, describes as his 'most intimate friend', a letter in that work (i. 68) to Loch dated 13 Sept. 1799, appears to identify him as James Stuart (1775–1849: *DNB*), who afterwards achieved notoriety by killing Sir Alexander Boswell in a duel and is clearly identified by his address in the membership lists as a leading member of the Juvenile Literary Society.
2. William Erskine (1773–1852: *DNB*), John Erskine's grandson, was afterwards a distinguished orientalist.
3. His brother, James Brougham (1780–1833).
4. Duke Gordon (1739–1800: *DNB*) was assistant librarian at Edinburgh University.
5. The Duke of Portland remained in the Government.
6. There follow a postscript telling of Sir Joseph Banks's failure to honour a financially-secured pledge of marriage after he returned with Cook from the South Seas and a lengthy poem written by Brougham (ff. 31–5) entitled 'The Bankiad. A mock Epic Poem. Fragment or No. 1 (by me; the next by *you*).'

8. From Henry Brougham

BLPES i. 41–4 Edinburgh, 21 Sept. 1796

I received a few days ago your letter, which I confess pleased me not a little; so that I shall have to thank you for 'repaying evil with good'. To me *flattery* is as much an object of contempt, as it appears to be with you. But you would have just reason to accuse me of *pride*, were I not made *vain* by the *approbation* of a sincere and discerning friend. In science, fools alone court popularity; the commendations, of a few competent judges, ought to satisfy the expectations, the hopes, nay the wishes of a wise man – and however low my claims may stand to that denomination, I trust I have acquired as much of the essentials to it, as concerns the present purpose. Allow me to return you my sincere and hearty thanks for the whole of your advice. Where *you blame*, I myself am inclined to go *much* farther; as to the rest, I own myself rather undermined. Science is unquestionably a far finer field for mental exertion than *Law* or even Politics: but worldly things have their weight and their sweats: an independent spirit revolts from the idea of subsisting wholly on any man's bounty, even on a father's, and although I have no manner of doubt that my father would be well enough pleased that I should follow the plan you hint at; yet during his life I must be dependent and must either live in a style which is beneath the middle rank of life, or oblige him to part with more money than would be consistent with the schemes of a man who has a family to provide for, and who would think it beneath him to part with an *acre* of that land which has been handed down to him from ancestors whom he is proud to represent. I have thus, My Dear Horner, entrusted you with what is perhaps no secret; viz., that my father has a very common *foible*, the desire of providing for his family, joined to a fear of encroaching on his paternal estate. If I never mentioned this to you before, I have only to plead *prudence* in my defence. But even allowing, that I should be content to live the life of a country squire, or recluse philosopher if you will, during the most valuable of my years, is there no chance of a *tedium*, etc., coming on through want of some active profession, when it is too late to think of pursuing such? I own this has far more weight than the other reason, and both together induce me to think of the *law*. I only fear that even another *limitation* must be thought of, viz., the *Scotch Bar*. I believe I told you that my father was against the English law for a *beginning*; and pleads his own experience, the advice of his brother-in-law and that of William Adam.[1] Since I have thought a second time on the plan, I am *not cooled*: for I still think the Scottish Bar a miserable object, as an *ultimate* object:[2] but am induced to consider whether your plan of *beginning* with it may not be consistent with propriety; however as I am still in doubt, I expect much *light* from your answer, especially as to the English law and its incapacitating for the *House of Commons*, which I have great reason (from the experience of others) to fear.

Can you pardon my selfishness in devoting so much of your time and patience to my own concerns? or will an additional demand to speak of your own affairs make up for the transgression?

Your father will probably inform you by this packet, of the plan he has been laying for keeping you at Shacklewell another year. On this he did Murray and me the honour of asking our opinion: he also desired me to introduce *Reddie* to him; and received such information from him with respect to the study of Civil Law, as rather tended to strengthen his *opinion*. I shall now give you the substance of what Murray and I stated at different times to your father. First we doubted (or rather denied) the possibility of your preserving *pure* the English accent, even if you were to stay with Mr Hewlett another year: secondly, allowing the possibility of this, we questioned whether it was an advantage equal to those which you would by remaining there forego, and which are, the society of friends; the acquisition of worldly knowledge; the custom of public speaking; the formation of connections with those who may be of use in your profession; the display of your uncommon abilities; the pleasures of Literary intercourse and friendly society, for a year, the 50th part of what remains of your life; and, last though not of trivial import (at least in my mind) the opportunity of hearing *Robinson* deliver his first course, and of consequence his best; and of hearing *Black* lecture, in all probability more than he has done for 6 *years*, from the improved state of his health.³ Your father is not so much convinced as I am of the utility of societies nor is Murray.⁴ For my own part I look upon them as the *schools of politics* in a small scale, and no less funds of pleasure than instruction. The Literary Society is in its *Zenith* (to speak pompously) [and of its influence two anecdotes are sufficient. 1st it is the *terror* of all the orthodox divines. 2nd among others, a very sensible genteel young man, a cousin of Bob Robertson, entered the Divinity hall last year – but lately wrote in from the country, that the Literary Society had done him infinite good, thanked me and some others for opening his mind, and expressed *great* doubts about continuing in the *church*].⁵

Before I thought of London, I had promised myself great pleasure from meeting you there, and from endeavouring with your assistance to form another for speculation rather than speaking, and I confess that next to the reasons I before stated, those and the like would be great inducements to my continuing here, till I became a member of some profession. And they will certainly if I leave Edinburgh be the enjoyments the loss of which will give me the greatest regret. I believe you heard of the Death of the Juvenile Literary Society. Its members are many of them in the Literary Society. *Forbes* is not, but has given up the Banking house and turned his *talents* to bless and adorn the Bar – in conjunction with Tytler, Davison, Swinton, Kenneth (who passed his Civil Law trials at the same time with Reddie) and H. McKenzie, who indeed deserves not to be placed in the above group.⁶

Before concluding this tiresome harlequin Epistle, I must trouble you with 3 requests, first an immediate and long answer, secondly to let me know what in the Literary way is going on in Town, particularly if Mrs Radcliffe is writing a new novel,⁷ and lastly to beg of *Elmsley* the first time you are in his shop; that he will cause the following *erratum* to be inserted in Part II. *Philosophical Transactions* for 1796 (which surprises me exceedingly) – Page 276, line 6 from the bottom for *least* read *greatest* (according to the tenor of the paper). If Elmsley refuses to do this without leave of the Society, you need not (unless he seems to take the thing easily) insist upon it. I beg you will excuse this trouble and that of reading [the] greatest part of my letter.⁸

1. William Adam (1751–1839: *DNB*), the Foxite politician, was a nephew of the architects, Robert and James, and therefore a distant relative of Brougham's. See *Brougham*, i. 38.
2. See New, p. 6.
3. Apparently Brougham meant John Robison (1739–1805: *DNB*), Professor of Natural Philosophy at Edinburgh. The copy at Kinnordy reads 'Robison', and has been so corrected in the original MS. Joseph Black (1728–99: *DNB*) was Professor of Medicine and Chemistry at Edinburgh.
4. For correspondence relating to the decision for Horner to remain at Shacklewell a second year see John Horner to Horner, 27 Sept., Horner to John Horner, 10 Oct., and to Mrs John Horner, 13 Oct., and Mrs John Horner to Horner, 19 Oct. (*Horner*, i. 20–24).
5. The passage between square brackets, which is deleted in the BLPES original, has been supplied from the copy at Kinnordy. 'Bob Robertson' was Robert Robertson, afterwards Robertson-Glasgow of Montgreenan (1775–1845).
6. Forbes's father, Sir William (1739–1806: *DNB*), was a banker. William Fraser Tytler (1777–1853) was the eldest son of Alexander Fraser Tytler (1747–1813: *DNB*), Professor of Universal History at Edinburgh and afterwards Lord Woodhouselee. John Swinton, afterwards Campbell-Swinton of Broadmeadows and then Kimmerghame (1777–1867), was elected a member of the Speculative shortly before Brougham himself, but eventually entered the army. One of the Mackenzies is positively identified in *Brougham*, i. 84, as Joshua Henry Mackenzie (1777–1851), afterwards Lord Mackenzie, the eldest son of Henry Mackenzie (1745–1831: *DNB*), the novelist. Kenneth Mackenzie became an advocate, but died in November 1805. There is no Davison among the lists of the Juvenile Literary Society; but this was evidently Robert Davidson of Ravelrigg (1776–1856), a close relation of Joshua Mackenzie and another advocate, who was afterwards a land-agent and antiquary.
7. Ann Radcliffe's last novel, *The Italian*, appeared the following year.
8. Peter Elmsley (1736–1802: *DNB*) was a bookseller in the Strand. His nephew, the classical scholar of the same name (1773–1825: *DNB*), later became a close acquaintance of Horner's in London. Whether or not Elmsley inserted the erratum slip requested – and he may well have not since Brougham, with characteristic carelessness, meant his contribution in Pt I, not Pt II, of 1796 – no such correction appeared in the printed errata in subsequent parts, though there was at the end of Pt II for 1796 another supplied by Brougham in July correcting major errors in his mathematical calculations. Hence No. VI in the summary of his 'propositions' at the end of his first contribution to the Royal Society's *Transactions* continued to read: 'The rays which are most refrangible are least reflexible, or make the least angle of reflexion.'

9. From Henry Brougham

BLPES i. 51–4   Edinburgh, 6 Nov. 1796

On Saturday last I received yours, and cannot claim much praise for answering it so soon, as I only take the opportunity of Robertson. I agree perfectly with you on the propriety of being choice in our members, and indeed on every other point you touch upon.[1]

I *augur* very favourably even already. The following is a sketch of the plan which (if it meets with your approbation), I intend to follow.

I shall speak first of all to *Reddie*; who from what passed last winter, previous to his leaving town, will, I am sure be warm in the scheme. We shall then talk to *William Erskine*, whom also I have before sounded, and next to *Robert Robertson*. These three have *all* the requisites for making good members. *Gillespie* too, has an accurate knowledge of Chemistry and Natural History, and a very tolerable acquaintance with *Physics*.[2] But his *forte* is that sort of *Physiology*, and mixture of anatomy with metaphysics, in which *Darwin* shines.[3] Like him too, Gillespie excels in *fancy*, has strong inventive powers and is a good poet. But he follows the Philosopher of Derby into his faults, wants steadiness, and is rather too fanciful in his theories. This account may satisfy you that he will make an excellent member, though not just a good *founder*.

Robert Robertson is very much Gillespie's reverse. His knowledge is accurate and well digested and various. He can simplify and examine the opinions of others, with greater success than strike out new lights. Yet he can often think for himself and defend his opinions. *Erskine* has applied more to Metaphysics, and the *Belles Lettres*, than to physical subjects. Yet in these his knowledge is far from contemptible and is daily increasing, by following a plan of study in forming which he condescended to consult Reddie and your Humble Servant. Part of this is mathematical reading, and attending *Robison*. His *fortes* are, in metaphysics, speculative Politics and theoretical history, in Physics, animal, vegetable, and atmospherical *Electricity*. On the character of Reddie I shall not enlarge. He joins the good qualities of *every one*. Languages, Politics, Law, Metaphysics, Physics, and History are almost equally his and in all he is *original* and *true* when he pleases.

Another member is *Lang*.[4]

He is possessed of a mind whose *soundness* is truly great. His imagination is that of a mere Metaphysician, or if you will Mathematician. On *all* subjects in which he attends he thinks for *himself*, and to almost all his knowledge extends. He began to *think* about 6 years ago, for till then he lived with a *seceder*. His thoughts took a total change, for till then they were those of a *Calvinist*. His opinions are now free, yet (I hope and think) true; for he has *studied Berkeley, Rousseau, and Hume*. I need only add that his *candour* is equal to his judgement – and his heart to his head if you'll excuse a quaint phrase.

Thomas Browne is my next subject.[5] First as to, *who he is*. You may remember him reading an *abominable* essay on *Pneumonatology* at Finlayson's [logic class], and then at *Stewart's* [moral philosophy class] giving in a paper on *dreaming*. He was educated at Kensington and has been almost all his life in England. Now he resides here with his mother's family. Now as to *what he is*. He is a poet, without a poet's failings, and a classical scholar without the faults of a linguist. His mind is well stored with Physical and Metaphysical knowledge, as will be soon seen, when his Pamphlet in answer to Darwin's *Zoonomia* is published. Stuart[6] and Reddie have read and admired it. It will not add to its praise to join my suffrage.

Let me add, *John Leydon* whom (in spite of his quizzity and several other qualities that are philosophically speaking no faults) the more I know, the more I admire. He excels in Historical research. His mind is a store house of facts. His *fancy* is *Phantasy*, and his knowledge is very extensive. He is studying physics more minutely. He has long been an acute disputant and always a sublime poet. Many excellent judges (particularly Dr Anderson who writes the critiques on the Poets and their lives in the new edition published here), agree 'that he comes wonderfully near to *Gray* and *Milton*!'[7]

I have little doubt that we shall have all these for members, and afterwards others will occur – for instance, Peter Erskine, John Reid (Scottish), and more whom I omitt [sic].[8] In the mean time, I think those that I have mentioned are sufficiently select and numerous to begin with. I shall, therefore, set about it as soon as possible, *after your answer*, in which I expect:

1. Your consent to have your name enrolled, *exactly as if you were here*, and that, of course, if we begin this winter, you should transmitt [*sic*] papers in your turn, and receive accounts of our proceedings, so that you will join us in person, just as if you had been away for a few meetings and find yourself quite at home.

2. Your opinion on the members I have mentioned.

and 3. Some hints concerning *regulations*.

Permit me, Dear Horner, to thank you for giving me a proof as good as *Demonstration* of your attention to my commissions, viz., an *induction of facts*. I am busy with another *paper* which will be ready in a month or so, and which I hope you will find curious.

. . .

1. Brougham refers to the formation of the society 'for speculation rather than speaking' which he had mentioned briefly in Doc. 8. Horner evidently responded enthusiastically to the proposal and laid out a plan in a subsequent letter. The result was the Academy of Physics, which began in January 1797 and flourished for at least three years. See Cantor, pp. 109–134, and *Brown*, pp. 77–8, who also prints, pp. 498–506, the Academy's 'laws' and extracts from minutes of the first year. The NLS has a manuscript volume (Acc. 10073/1, formerly in the Royal Society of Edinburgh) of selections from the minutes from 7 Jan. 1797 until 10 Feb. 1798 when it breaks off in mid-sentence; on the inside cover there is a list of members made in April 1850 by one of its surviving members, William Erskine. The NLS also has two volumes (MSS 755 and 756) from what appears by the numerals on the covers to have been a much larger number of so-called 'Correspondence Books'. These latter cover the period 6 Feb. 1798 – 6 Dec. 1799, and are mostly written by Brougham as 'corresponding secretary' with Horner substituting during his absence.
2. William Gillespie (1776–1825: *DNB*), poet and cleric, was afterwards a corresponding member of the Academy of Physics.
3. Erasmus Darwin (1731–1802: *DNB*), grandfather of Charles Darwin, was founder of the Philosophical Society of Derby and author of *Zoonomia, or the Laws of Organic Life* (2 vols, 1794–6).
4. Two Langs appear as members of the Academy. One was Alexander Lang of Overton (d. 1835), who was afterwards an advocate; the other was James Lang, whom Erskine lists merely as 'a law student'. From a mention in Brougham's initial letter to Reddie (see Doc. 10), it seems to be the latter who is meant here and, though absent from the first meeting of the Academy, was chosen treasurer.
5. Thomas Brown (1778–1820: *DNB*) succeeded Dugald Stewart as Professor of Moral Philosophy at Edinburgh in 1810. He had attended the lectures on logic given in 1792 by Professor James Finlayson (1758–1808: *DNB*). He joined the Literary Society in 1796 and the Academy of Physics in 1797. His *Observations on the Zoonomia of Erasmus Darwin* was published in 1798.
6. See Doc. 7 n. 1.
7. John Leyden (1775–1811: *DNB*), the poet and physician, attended the first meeting of the Academy and was elected its joint secretary. Robert Anderson (1750–1830: *DNB*), editor of *A Complete edition of the Poets of Great Britain* (13 vols, 1792–5) and editor of the *Edinburgh Magazine*, became the Academy's first honorary member.
8. 'Peter' was perhaps one of William Erskine's brothers, but is probably a slip or nickname for William Erskine himself, who presided at the first meeting of the Academy. John Reid (1775–1811), the son of an Edinburgh merchant and afterwards an advocate, is probably the individual distinguished here from the physician previously mentioned (Doc. 2), who was English; but he seems never to have had anything to do with the Academy.

10. From Henry Brougham

BLPES i. 59–60   Edinburgh, 29 Dec. 1796

I received with great pleasure your letter dated November 27. And begin from this time a *regular* correspondence with you. I expect at least two letters per month, and shall give you (if you desire it) the same number. I certainly ought sooner to have answered yours, but you'll excuse the omission when I tell you its cause. This is the first day I can call my own. My 2nd paper to the Royal Society took up so very much of my time. Wilde's[1] class and reading to keep up with him, added to a circumstance which I am presently to state, occupied fully the rest, except what was spent in Societies. Lastly, I wished to wait till I could tell you something *final* about the *Academy*. The reasons I just now mentioned prevented my application to Reddie, and the other fellows whom I spoke of to you. Last week I wrote a long letter to Reddie stating very fully the absolute necessity of a society of investigation, considering the degraded state of Mathematical and Mechanical Philosophy, the inefficacy of *debating clubs* to prevent its fall, and chiefly the abominable politics, trifling pursuits and vile aristocracy which sway the Royal Societies of London and Edinburgh.[2] I also gave a long account of the plan concerted between you and me, and *demanded* his *immediate* and *peremptory* and *warm* concurrence, as a friend of science. My demands were instantly complied with. He entered as warmly into it as if he had been the prime mover; and we directly attacked *Erskine*. He became as zealous as any of us; and on Christmas day I met them by appointment. We there settled our ideas on the subject from a paper which I took the liberty of presenting to them containing a general view of the sciences in which certainty can be expected (in different kinds of *evidence*) and concluding with the plan. This paper was in substance delivered to Browne, Lang and Copland, and lastly to Leydon. All these became *zealous*, and approved exceedingly of the division of knowledge suggested by it.

Leydon immediately laid the scheme before a Mr Logan, an excellent arguer and good Natural Philosopher and chemist, but whose principal good quality (for us) is having daily, nay free hourly access to the *first apparatus in Scotland*, Sir James Hall's (who will be an honorary member). Logan entered most eagerly into it, as did also *Dr Robert Anderson*, a man of great abilities, author of the Lives and critiques affixed to the new edition of the poets, and of Johnson's life published separately and so much admired. He will be an honorary and contributing member. Several others for ordinary (and we shall begin with 14 ordinary and 20 correspondents including Rogerson and the *famous Wallis*) are also engaged, and I doubt not I shall get *Professor Robinson* [sic] to be honorary president as soon as we begin, which will be the second or 3rd day of the new year. I have become acquainted with that illustrious philosopher and *habile* Mathematician. Having read my optical paper (on the recommendation of Professor Wilson at Glasgow) he wrote a most flattering and modest letter, requesting an interview. You may easily guess the delight with which this was accorded. I was quite charmed with him, perhaps not less because I found him a convert to my deductions. We spent several hours in *condolence* over the state of Physical science and in Mathematical reveries. He was so condescending as to communicate some observations and conjectures which he wished to see investigated by induction and we began an experimental inquiry, interrupted by his journey to London. On his return I am very sure of his concurrence to the plan. I have only room to desire an answer and in it a specification of your *subjects*. You are an ordinary member. No bad *precedent* can arise, for if there were 50 like you, we would again break our rules 50 times. I fear we shall not do it *once* again.[3]

1. John Wilde was joint Professor of Civil Law at Edinburgh.
2. Brougham's interesting letter to Reddie, dated 17 Dec. and quoted by Cantor, pp. 116 and 117, is NLS MSS 3704, ff. 1–3. It says of Horner, who was expected to join them later, that his 'great ability will be a lasting asset to us. He has taken up the plan (as proposed by me to him) with enthusiasm, and will contribute papers during his residence in London.'
3. Thomas Logan, MD, minister of Dunglass, attended the first meeting of the Academy and was elected joint secretary with Leyden; his patron was Sir James Hall, 4th Bart (1761–1832: *DNB*), geologist and chemist. Playfair became an honorary member, as well as Anderson and Robison. Nothing seems to be known about James Rogerson except that according to Erskine's list he was 'a mathematician of great promise who died young'. But William Wallace (1768–1843: *DNB*), who became a corresponding member, was afterwards Professor of Mathematics at Edinburgh. Patrick Wilson (1748–1811) was Professor of Astronomy at Glasgow.

11. To J.A. Murray

BLPES i. 63–4   Shacklewell, 16 Jan. 1797

Though, after what has passed, I have no right to be positive, I think I now see clearly our misunderstanding with regard to Junius. While you alluded to *grammatical* correctness, I imagined you meant those matters of style which are to be judged of by *Taste*: you did not object to the praise that was bestowed on the letter to the Duke of Bedford, because you thought it *less* faultless than was represented; but because you did not see any reason to *distinguish* it from the rest, and were surprised that only one letter, of a writer so classical as Junius, should be found grammatically correct. I never had any idea of examining the book on this point, as I never doubted its accuracy.[1]

. . .

I perfectly agree with you in thinking that it would be premature in us to enter now into a discussion of the questions relating to volition, conception, etc. I will proceed therefore in this letter to the *prima libamina*, and consider, nearly in the same order which you have followed, the rules of investigation, the classification of the powers of the mind, and then the subject of perception and sensation. I believe it will greatly facilitate the prosecution of our inquiries, to proceed with strict regularity, as by that means the conclusions to which we are led in our investigation, may with justice be adopted as principles in conducting that which succeeds.

1. The first thing to be done is evidently to form a precise statement of the subject which we propose to inquire into. I cannot think we are yet competent to lay down a scheme of the science of mind, and arrange the different objects which it does or which it ought to comprehend. Fortunately, this is not requisite for our immediate

purpose; all that we need care for at present is to know the limits of that particular branch of the science which now attracts our curiosity. To me it appears, then, that our business is only to ascertain the *facts* concerning the human mind: we know ourselves to be thinking beings; we sometimes observe a degree of regularity in our thoughts, and we observe much variety; we know ourselves susceptible of various kinds of pleasure and pain, and of various degrees under each kind. The first division, therefore, of the science of human nature, ought to ascertain all the facts of this description that our consciousness informs us of; to discover the principles of the regularity, and enumerate and classify the varieties; to trace the dependence of one fact on another; and thence to lay down the General Facts, upon which the particular phenomena of thinking, etc. are to be explained. . . . [*sic*] This sketch, you observe, does not exactly coincide with the views of any of the metaphysical writers; it excludes some speculations which are too frequently blended with the subjects which I have enumerated, and takes in others which have for the most part been treated as a different branch of science. For it takes in the subject of the emotions, and all that relates to the capacity of *feeling*: but it does not comprehend the discussion of materialism, liberty, and necessity, etc., questions, which I by no means consider as unimportant, but as belonging to a separate *chapter* in the science, requiring a different *method* of inquiry, and especially as being posterior in the *order* of inquiry to the general laws of thought, emotion, etc. A true system of those laws will not only afford us the proper criterion of the utility of those questions, but the means also of a satisfactory solution. The same theory will likewise give us through the great moral phenomena of the universe, such as relate to the history of the species, the principles of Character both individual and national, and various branches in the most important of all sciences, those of Government and Education. . . . [*sic*] Such are the ideas which have struck me with respect to the Object of our inquiries. I beg of you to subject the plan to the most rigorous scrutiny; spare not a single one of its mistakes; let us make it as exact as we can; and when we have done so, let us fix it strongly in our mind. The consistency of our future deductions will depend on the steadiness, with which we keep our object in view; and the truth of them on the accuracy with which it is originally formed.

2. We are already agreed on the source from which we are to draw the facts, as that is the subject you begin with in your last letter. Since you have started the idea of deriving information from Language, let me request you to illustrate your opinion on that head fully: for I am rather disposed to consider this medium of information greatly inferior to Consciousness. The language of other men cannot communicate to us any simple operation of feeling, of which we ourselves have never been conscious. Your next letter will probably enable me to form a decided opinion.

3. But whatever use we make of popular language in order to arrive at facts, let us pay it no respect in expressing those facts for ourselves. It may give us information with respect to the mind of the speaker, provided we take his words, not on their strict import, but as they would obviously strike every person who uses the same dialect: but when we state that information to ourselves, with the view of philosophizing, we need not be confined to the expressions in which we received it, but should make use of the closest terms, such as cannot possibly suggest any meaning different from their strict import. To me it is past a doubt, that

philosophers should have a peculiar language, for expressing the facts and conclusions which they arrive at in the course of their inquiries. At the same time your observations, on the liberties they have taken with popular language, appear to me extremely just; and you will perceive, when you read this § a second time, that your excellent remarks led me to the distinction which I have attempted to mark. Metaphysicians, by not understanding common language in the common way, involved themselves in absurdity; and became more ridiculous by finding fault with what they had abused. But it must likewise be allowed, that much of their inconsistency and confusion arose from their having been restricted to common language in the explanation of their reasonings. By prudence and care we may avoid both these errors, these by-paths that join the high road to the temple of science; into either of which if we enter, we may be assured beforehand that we continually go farther from the object of our journey, and, after much perplexity and wandering, shall have the mortification to find ourselves at the identical spot from which we had set out. ... [sic] When we have discerned an operation of mind, which deserves to be distinguished by a particular name, let us represent it by a word that exactly comes up to our idea, suggesting no extraneous association or analogy; but if that word belong to popular language, which I think we ought to decline, let us carefully remember, when it is used in popular discourse, to understand it just as the speaker intended, and not according to the meaning which we have annexed to it in our philosophy.

4. Having considered the objects of our inquiry, and the language proper to be used in speaking of them, the next point is the *rules* of investigation. On this account only, I have numbered it in order. For as it will be of advantage to you, and of much greater to me, to have this matter discussed by your abilities, I shall proceed now to the fifth article, that I may examine some parts of your last letter.

5. We may expect to find difficulties in forming a proper division of the mental operations. Those hitherto given are quite unsatisfactory. Hume's, as you observe, is particularly so. I have not yet considered with full attention the principles on which the Classification should be conducted, but this we must settle, before advancing far in our research. Some cautions, indeed, are obvious; no classification can be just, which cannot be reconciled with facts already known; the facts must not be made subordinate to the division, but the division to the facts. Perhaps it would be better, therefore, to reserve the classification till the facts have been collected and examined: When we have accurately analysed the different operations of mind, we shall be able to discern in what circumstances two or more agree together, which must be the principle of classification. ... [sic] This is not an improper place to take notice of the distinction which is often made between *simple* and *pure*, and *compound* or *complex* operations. I had implicitly admitted the authority of Finlayson, Stewart and Reid, on this point; till I heard an observation made by Brougham, at one of the Literary Societies, where we were debating on the difference between animals and the human species. From circumstances which I have forgotten, I have an idea that it did not come originally from Brougham; but I sufficiently remember, he made it so clear and placed it in so strong a light, that in one and the same moment I heard it and was convinced of its truth. With like hopes of success, let me try whether I can produce a similar effect. As we know nothing of mind but by its operations, nothing

of the substance to which those operations belong, we can form no other notion of it than that it is a simple being, an *unum quid*; and it would be absurd to suppose it divided into parts. Speaking of its different faculties, we mean its different modes of operation; no two of which can exist together, but only successively. When we are told that Imagination, for instance (using that word in Stewart's sense of it), is a compound faculty or operation, let us demand its component parts; if we receive only a list of some simple operations already known to us, it is evident that Imagination is only a particular succession of acts of the mind, and deserves not an appropriate name; if in the enumeration we find also another simple act, not yet denominated, we conclude that this – and this alone – constitutes imagination, a simple and not a compound faculty. The mixture of two chemical simples may make a new substance; but two operations, sublimation and distillation, for example, can never make a new operation.

I shall be impatient for your answer, as I am become quite ardent in the plan in which you have engaged me, and the adequate execution of which will so much depend upon yourself.

1. Hewlett impressed upon Horner that Junius was 'a model of English writing', and in late 1796 Horner and Murray began to exchange letters in which they debated his literary virtues. On 18 Dec. Horner wrote (*Horner*, i. 28–9) 'that were I to write political invective and satire, I should aspire to the style of Junius'. Edmund Burke, the acknowledged author of *A Letter . . . to a Noble Lord, on the attacks made upon him . . . by the Duke of Bedford* (1796), was widely believed to have been the author of the Junius letters.

12. From Henry Brougham

BLPES i. 65–6   Carlisle, 17[1] Jan. 1797

Yours came here from Edinburgh and I now take a few moments leisure to return [an] answer to your very natural, and, to a friend of the Academy, very pleasing inquiries, about its success and proceedings. After adding several to the stock of members, we had our first meeting on *Saturday*, January 7 – at 8 o'clock in the morning, when we settled a few regulations from the copy which I had drawn up, but of the materials of *our* correspondence. I shall send you by the first opportunity an abstract of these and a list of members. *Rogerson* is the man you speak of: how I should have prefixed a *professorship* to his name, I really cannot tell, but rather suspect that you have read wrong.[2] So far from wondering at this *erratum*, I rather marvel that you ever read a word right, considering the *character* in which I usually (for reasons known to us both) choose to write.

He is an ordinary and active member. *Wallis* you must of course have heard of. . . . [*sic*] There was little else done at our first meeting. Some *news* was given in; and several *committees* of *examination* appointed, to report on new publications.

Unfortunately, I was obliged to leave town that very night, on half an hour's warning. My Grandmother, who has lived *here* since her husband's death, was declared to be at the very point of death. My father's ill health, kept him from coming, so that I had to travel post all night and arrived in 18 hours, or rather less, so that you see no time was lost. Since coming, the old lady, now in her 84th year, has recovered, or rather, was never very ill.[3] I should have returned immediately (as I wished much to be at the Literary Society and the Academy) but have been *tortured* by *visits*; and been forced to run up and down the country, to be introduced to neighbours that have come to estates and titles since we were last here. This has kept me here and will detain me till the beginning of next week. At that time I must go into *Westmoreland*, and may be kept at *Brougham* some days, and after that, shall go into *Lancashire* and *Yorkshire* in order to have interviews with the two celebrated Mathematicians, *Gough*; and *Dawson* of Sedberg: the famous man who refuted *Matthew Stewart* (and whom *Playfair* calls *Dawson* of *Sudbury* in his life of Stewart).[4] Both of these I propose, if you please, making *Honorary* members of the Academy and am not without hopes of a memoir from *Dawson*. What passes, I shall tell you in another letter after my journey. I must be in Edinburgh by the 7th of February, for on that day the whole Literary Society (*Number above* 70) is to dine together, celebrating *the anniversary*, and I would not for a great deal be absent, as I am to be in the Chair.

Be kind enough to give me a few lines, in return and direct to me, *Castle Street, Carlisle*. Let it come as soon as possible, in case I don't return by this way.

You ask what memoirs have been given in? Except reports of Committees, I know of none as yet, but one which I sent the other day, from hence, containing about a dozen of Geometrical propositions, chiefly *porisms*, in the ancient style.[5] I gave only such as I could think of at the time [for I] brought as you may easily believe no notes with me. But I thought it better to send them such as they were, as I had undertaken to give a paper. My next will be on the higher geometry, and the doctrine of central forces, as applied thereto. *Rogerson* is writing on infinite series, and some chemical memoirs are to be given in by myself and others. Lastly, committees of experiment are to be appointed.

Any paper you may write, be it even in *your* very worst style (which to us will be a *perfect novelty*) will be highly esteemed by the Academy. It is incumbent on you to give a memoir immediately as your name is almost at the top of the list of ordinaries. Except a paper, nothing is more acceptable than *news* of science, particularly what is done in the *Royal Society*, and how *Cavendish*,[6] etc. are employed – what new works and how received. Do you think Hewlett would give us a paper? At any rate write me immediately, for unless, by my Grand[mother]'s death, I should have to attend a funeral expedition of above 30 miles (and God forbid both cause and effect, especially the latter) I shall set off from hence on Monday next.

Your friends are all well, as James tells me, and I am My Dear H. one of the most sincere of them.

1. 19 Jan., according to the copy at Kinnordy, but the original MS appears rather to bear the date given here.
2. See Doc. 10. Brougham had not prefixed a professorship to Rogerson's name. His introduction of that name without elaboration, however, certainly added to the muddle he created by confusing the names of Robertson, Robinson, and Robison.
3. Mrs (Mary) Brougham died in 1807, aged 93.

4. John Gough (1757–1825: *DNB*), the blind scientific writer, and John Dawson (1734–1820: *DNB*) of Sedbergh, the surgeon and mathematician, both became honorary members. Dawson had pointed out the error in calculations about the distance of the earth from the sun made by Dugald Stewart's father Matthew (1717–1785: *DNB*), Professor of Mathematics at Edinburgh. See John Playfair's 'Account of Matthew Stewart' in the *Transactions of the Royal Society of Edinburgh*, i (1788), 68.
5. This probably became the basis for Brougham's third paper, on 'General Theorems, Chiefly Porisms, in the Higher Geometry', published in the *Philosophical Transactions of the Royal Society*, lxxxviii (1798), Pt II, 378–96.
6. Henry Cavendish (1731–1810: *DNB*).

13. From Henry Brougham

BLPES i. 67–8   Carlisle, Friday [?27 Jan. 1797][1]

I was made happy by finding yours, on my return from Yorkshire. My visit to *Dawson* fully answered expectation, and my absence from home was protracted, by a stay in Westmoreland. I shall go north in a week, and your next may be addressed to Edinburgh.

Your question I can answer, but not without a *degree* of hesitation. You may spare yourself the trouble of saying, 'you cannot spout new ideas on such and such subjects.' Begging your pardon (for the bluntness, not the falsity of the assertion) this is *not true. You have not tried sufficiently.* When I saw you last, you had not studied *physics* above *3 months* under a poor enough teacher, and in a bad season for patient or deep thought. Nor had you applied for any length of time to the higher branches of Mathematics. How then was it to be expected, that you *possibly could* spout new ideas on subjects difficult even when known; and, at any rate, almost unknown to you? Newton, McLaurin, Euler; names so deservedly revered for their great attainments, and for their *early* attainments too, were distinguished for the ease, the almost supernatural facility, which attended their studies of the works of others, but, though in early life, their discoveries were brilliant, yet they were preceded by a thorough knowledge of the sciences as they stood. Our great countryman, we are told, read *Des Cartes* and *Kepler*, as you or I would study *Euclid's elements*; yet, still, he had known these, unless he saw their substance by inspiration, before he either attempted the others, or wrote the *Principia*. I beseech you, therefore, to lay aside such *quaint* and unjust misapprehensions, not only of your own talents, but also of the subject to which you foolishly dread applying them. If, indeed, other avocations prevent your applying sufficiently to the principles, or acquiring that readiness (which I termed in another letter *habileté*), or giving your attention for the length of time, and with the constancy, required in order to explore a new field, in that case, you ought to turn your labours to what requires less time. But where shall we find this pursuit whose importance of purpose and certainty of means, can satisfy us after contemplating the science of *demonstration*, or even that of physical induction? You mention *inductive Metaphysics*. This indeed is one of our divisions, under the title of '*Physics of Mind*', and any paper from you on this subject will be highly acceptable. But beware falling into *Darwin's error*. See what a mass of theories he has raised upon a sort of induction. I have my doubts whether there be not more of *form* than of *substance* in what we have usually seen under the title of *moral experiments*, etc. I need not instance Stewart and *Beattie*.[2] However, I am *sure* you will not fall into *their* errors. I own I think, that (after the sciences of certainty) the next in rank, both as to *evidence* and *importance* is *politics*. I mean general politics, what in our division is called, the second branch of the Physics of mind, that is the true operations of *General or Universal Mind*, as opposed to *individual* [?politics]. I have no further information to give you. Pray think well before you choose a subject, I mean before you decide against the mathematical and mixed mathematical sciences. Whatever you choose will be esteemed a great favour, and the sooner it is conferred the greater (*bis dat, qui,* etc.) Write me soon and give me some news from the Royal Society, etc. I wrote the news you gave me before to the Academy.

1. The letter is endorsed in pencil, and may possibly also be franked, 30 Jan. 1797. Probably it was not posted until after the weekend.
2. James Beattie (1735–1803: *DNB*) was Professor of Natural Philosophy at Aberdeen and author of *Elements of Moral Science* (2 vols, 1790–93).

14. From Henry Brougham

BLPES i. 69–70   Edinburgh, 27 Feb. 1797

I shall not begin the *following* letter by *many* apologies for having delayed so very long to write it: my excuse is, a very pressing series of employment in matters which concerned others and which, consequently, could not with propriety be postponed for such as *chiefly* regarded myself. Of this last description I always must consider the pleasure of a little conversation with a friend. What I mean by the business of others, you will readily perceive from the few lines I have at present leisure to write you, concerning the *Academy of Physics*. That institution is flourishing exceedingly. Our meetings have been regular and well attended, the business highly interesting. Of this I shall give you a specimen, in a short detail of proceedings at the public sitting of Saturday last (Feb. 25). After proposing and discussing *freely*, the merits of several candidates for seats, and referring farther consideration of their requests, to the general election, next week, several corresponding members were voted on the list, among others, *Spankie* (in London) and the celebrated Geometrician *Wallace* at Perth. Philosophical news then became the topics of conversation, and several new publications were noticed. Reports were attended to from several academicians appointed to look out for a convenient set [of] apartments to lodge our collections, accommodate our meetings, and furnish our *Elaboratory*. The farther decision of this point was postponed till more proposals could be collected, and we shall most likely be *fixed* in our lodgings next week. After a few forms, etc., reports of committees of *analysis were received.* These produced interesting accounts of papers in the 2nd part of *Philosophical Transactions*, chiefly chemical and one mathematical. No other analysis was given this meeting except this (by myself). My associates are to give in theirs next meeting. Reddie, then, gave in a most excellent communication from his brother in *Jamaica* containing a beautiful and important account of the manners, customs, etc. of the unknown *Eboe* nation in the interior of Africa, collected from *slaves* brought thence.[1] Your humble servant then read a report of a committee of experimental inquiry. We (viz. myself and another) had been desired to repeat with every precaution possible, a *very important* chemical experiment, submitted to the Academy by Dr Harrington in Carlisle.[2] The result of this was such as had led me to a great number of others, in prosecuting which new and curious facts and substances were brought to light. I had, therefore, presented the Academy (at the same time that I drew up the report of the committee's labours) with a farther detail of these experiments, and also a large collection of preparatives, etc., the result of each step of the inquiry, thus being almost enabled to exhibit all my experiments over again before them. The course is far from finished and will be continued with great ardour as soon as we remove to our rooms, and as soon as a new associate shall be named to me. You may form some idea from this, how busy I have been since I received your last, for, except *one hour*, I never had the assistance or even presence of my associate, and the experiments continued, almost day and night from about the time I received yours, to last Wednesday, and on Wednesday, Thursday, Friday and Saturday, I had a public society to attend each evening. I may, however, promise not to allow the business again to interfere; for, when we get into our laboratory, any experiments I may be engaged in, will be overlooked by assistants and thus consume less time.

From this detail you may form some idea of the way in which business is carried on. As to the funds, they w[ere] very flourishing. Entry money 5s., and each academician to pay 6d. every meeting. This clears us (supposing no more admissions) £22 the first year, and, indeed, we have a shower of petitions for seats not yet determined. Accurate chemical knowledge and acquaintance with Physics (strictly called) are *sine-qua-nons*. We have as yet taken in no papers (except mathematical) that do not contain facts. And (except Reddie's communication) these *facts* have been always Physical, chiefly chemical. And from the present aspect of our affairs, strong hopes *are* forming that at no far distant period we may have a *volume for the press* of *Physical and Mathematical* papers, being the *Memoirs of the Academy of Physics*.[3] Hasten, therefore, *your paper*. I fear I have left no room to answer your Mathematical question *if I do find it out*, for I have been prevented as yet from considering it. . . .[4]

1. James Reddie's elder brother John was probably a merchant in West Africa, their father, also called John, being a shipowner. Whether or not the business prospered, his information certainly served his family well in other ways; for James's son John, afterwards Justice of St Lucia, subsequently also presented to the Speculative Society, to which he was admitted in 1825, an essay entitled 'Manners and Customs of the Eboe Nation' (*Speculative Society*, p. 307; *Brougham*, i. 243, in common with some other sources, confuses the son (who died in 1851) with the father).
2. There is in the Academy's 'Correspondence Books' a prolonged and somewhat ill-tempered series of communications with Robert Harrington (fl. 1815: DNB), a believer in Phlogiston.
3. No such publication appeared (Cantor, p. 131), although notes by Brougham and Horner in the Academy's second 'Correspondence Book' record that the proposal had been approved on 13 July 1799, a committee appointed to select the contents, and at least one

prospective author (Lockhart Muirhead) approached immediately afterwards. The Academy's papers were, however, bound up annually, though no such volume has come to light.

4. There follows a short answer to a geometrical problem posed by Horner.

15. To J.A. Murray

BLPES i. 71–2   Shacklewell, 27 Feb. 1797

. . .

In the course of my disappointment as to [not] hearing from yourself, I have frequently had recourse to some of your former Epistles; from the contents of which I form very sanguine prospects of success in our philosophical researches. Perhaps we may have it in our power to add some small improvement to science; at all events, we shall not fail to promote our own improvement, and that in the most agreeable manner. In a judicious examination of general mind, we shall find the best access to the knowledge of individual character, and such other information of the kind as may be useful, not merely in our profession, but through the whole business of active life, which I hope you and I are destined to pass together. And indeed this method of correspondence gives us an excellent opportunity for the discovery as well as the attainment of knowledge: we have no peculiar theory in view, for the service of which we may insensibly be tempted to pervert facts; on the contrary, we give up our opinions and conjectures to each other for free scrutiny, and by these means avoid the circumstances by which laudable curiosity is naturally discouraged, or rendered nugatory.

. . .

16. To J.A. Murray

BLPES i. 75–8   Shacklewell, 13 and 21 Mar. 1797

Monday, 13 Mar.

Your letter of the 3rd of March was quite a banquet to me; excellent however as it is, it has not given me amends for its long delay, but made me more sensible of my loss. My answer returns so speedily, that you may have an opportunity of reparation, or rather that I may have a right to that claim. But before I enter on the subject, which now monopolizes our correspondence, I must give myself the pleasure of telling you, that a few days ago, I met with an old school-fellow of ours, Robert Boyd.[1] He has lately returned from the continent, in the different capitals of which he has resided, since he left Edinburgh, for the purpose of acquiring the languages – this however with a mercantile view. He is now in his brother's banking house, which you must have heard of as being concerned in the late government loans. Bob urged very much to be remembered to Mr Murray; and I assure you, that the pleasure of meeting with him was not greater than I took in our talking together of you.

Let me begin with reporting progress: we are agreed that the present object of our curiosity and investigation is to ascertain the general *Facts* of mind: we are agreed on the means we possess for arriving at those facts, *Consciousness* – the original source of all information on this subject, and *Language* – which is a secondary medium of inquiry, admitting us to the consciousness of other men; here, permit me to acknowledge the favour of your excellent remarks: we are agreed, therefore, on the points that are marked *first* and *second* in my former letter [Doc. 11]. I proceed, as you desire, to explain myself more fully on the 3rd.

A philosophical language, distinct from that which serves the purposes of ordinary intercourse, seems open to objection only for one reason. It may give science an air of mystery, and appears to detach its conclusions from the maxims of common understanding; a separation, which, if actually effected, must lead it into degeneracy, and deprive mankind of the advantages which true Philosophy is calculated to bestow. This evidently refers to the jargon of the Peripatetics, with the mischievous effects of which inquirers even of the present day still find themselves embarrassed. But it appears to me to furnish no solid argument against a philosophical language, however useful it may be as a caution with regard to the principles on which such a language should be formed, and the manner in which employed. I am led to think so, from the modern improvements in logic, and our superior acquaintance with the objects of science, and with the laws and limits of inquiry. The error of the schoolmen was this: they did not employ their terms as arbitrary marks for real existencies [sic] and the discoveries of observation, but made experience, if ever they stumbled upon experiments, subordinate to their system of words: their terms, often uncouth – always obscure, were the representatives, not of facts, but of hypotheses, not of the things of nature, but of fictitious causes. I have this distinction fully in view, when I recommend adopting new terms of denomination in the course of our inquiries: for it not only shows that such a measure might be attended with advantages real and important, but by showing at the same time that it may be abused, describes the limits within which that advantage is to be looked for. At first sight, indeed, the answer to the objection which I have been combating might be this: that our speculations being confined to ourselves, it is a matter of indifference what terms (intelligible to ourselves) we employ, however they might seem mysterious to others, and veil our doctrines from all eyes but our own. But I am very far from allowing this consideration to weigh with me, on the subject of what I am proposing to you. On the contrary, I believe that were we to dress up our opinions in such a manner as to be understood by none else without our initiation, the same means of mystery would lead us also astray; you have remarked, with great truth, in your last letter, that men are liable to misinterpret the information of their own consciousness; and I am convinced, that without vigilant circumspection they are liable to practise all the arts of sophistry upon their own understanding, not only where self-interest or passion has been roused, but likewise in exploring metaphysical subjects where neither passion nor interest can be concerned. We run a great risk of entangling ourselves in the absurdities with which the schoolmen tortured their brain[s], if we imagine that by inventing names we philosophize, and explain causes: but if we consider language as subservient to inquiry, and as nothing but artifice for retaining and exhibiting our conclusions as we advance, I firmly believe, it would be found to facilitate our progress. I shall now state my reasons for this belief, as well as for thinking that the same effect would not follow from the use of more popular language. . . . [sic] It must be of great consequence, as we go on, to have our preceding acquisitions always at hand; and we may easily conceive, that this advantage would be proportioned to the conciseness and perspicuity of their form of expression. That this precision may be attained, the language ought to suggest nothing more nor less than the exact ideas which we intend to describe. If a simple idea, suppose a simple feeling or operation of mind, let us fix upon some sign which is never employed to represent any thing else: now I expect to find this impracticable, if we decline giving up popular language. Again, if the idea be compound, let the sign, by which we express it, be made up of the respective signs by which we had previously expressed the several components of the idea: unless we make it lawful to form peculiar terms, we shall find ourselves still more at a loss in this than in the former case. It is in very few instances, indeed, that the popular expressions of compound ideas have any reference to the simple component ideas; and this is more to be reproached to the English, than to either of the ancient languages, or several others of the modern. The representative of a compound idea should accurately suggest that idea to everyone acquainted with the simple components and their signs. This is hardly ever the case in popular languages; otherwise, the study of them would be found much easier than it is, and a much better exercise to the understanding. On the other hand, the popular expressions of simple ideas seldom suggest them individually to the mind; in proof of which, we find that different minds receive them with different shades of meaning. Some indistinct analogy, some tacit association, continually floats, as it were, loosely about the idea: a circumstance, which I will allow productive of many beauties in fine writing, but which occasions perpetual inaccuracy in philosophical disquisitions. . . . [sic] A new nomenclature, regularly constructed, might afford considerable advantage in another point of view: it would remove the necessity of formal *definitions*, a most tedious and clumsy instrument of scientific communication. Real logical definitions are incompatible with reasonings drawn from experience and induction. The case is different as to abstract reasonings. The definitions of geometry are the principles of the science, they are indeed hypotheses, every geometrical demonstration involves an hypothesis of the figure to which it is applied, they must all be subsequent and dependent on the definitions. In the subjects of inductive philosophy, we have the reverse of this; here the properties are not hypothetical, but exist in nature, and it is only when we have exhausted the consideration of them, that we can pretend to draw up a definition, which even then cannot be logical, but will no more than amount to a description in synonymous expressions. *Simple* ideas, we know, admit not of definition. And might not the awkward and prolix sentences, which are called definitions of *compound* ideas, be happily got rid of, by the concise expedient of bringing into the word which stands for the compound idea, the several words which originally represent the component simple ideas? . . . [sic] Give me leave to notice a farther assistance which we might

derive from a nomenclature, distinct from those which metaphysicians have hitherto employed. It would furnish the best key to a well-founded *classification*, after the
'general facts' of mind shall have been ascertained. But this consideration is so
closely connected with what I have already said on the subject of definition, that a
particular illustration is unnecessary. Indeed this article has already been spun out to
a length which I little expected, but it was your desire, that I should justify my
fondness for a philosophical language. At the same time, confidently as I seem to
have given my opinion in the former letter, I will confess to you, that I have been
farther confirmed in it while writing this. I have been led to consider it in several
points of view which I was not in possession of when I sat down first – and in none
of these have I met with any grounds of objection. Some weeks hence, perhaps, were
I to review my arguments, I should be sharper-sighted: but fortunately the present
instance affords me a better resource than even the cooling corrective of time, in the
ingenuity and candour of my dear friend.

You have very justly detected an inconsistency in my *5th* article,[2] after the
removal of which, I still am of the same opinion with respect to the impropriety of
dividing the operations of mind into simple and compound. However, whether this
division be well-founded or not, is a question which, according to our plan of
investigation, ought not to be considered till we have ascertained the 'general facts'
of mind. We are to lay wholly aside, the question of the materiality or immateriality
of the thinking principle; and in examining the modification of thought, we are
even to keep out of mind all reference to supposed powers: for the operations alone
are what we know really to exist.

As I am anxious to enter upon the subject of Perception, before another letter
passes between us, I must break the promise with which I began; and postpone the
continuation of this long-winded epistle, till my next day of leisure.

21 March
6. We cannot enter upon this subject without acknowledging the important
services of Dr Reid. You and I have both, I believe, imbibed a partiality, for his
doctrines concerning the powers of external Perception, which is by no means
universal even at Edinburgh. Of this partiality it becomes us to beware; and I think
it incumbent on us as we proceed, not only to examine his authority with strictness,
but also to study the arguments that have been advanced against his system,
particularly by Dr Priestley.[3] This I have not done yet, but I intend it shortly. Since
Monday, I have read one or two chapters in the *Intellectual Powers*, and shall state to
you some notions which the perusal suggested to me, and which I am inclined to
think an improvement of Reid's account of Perception.

The leading principle of that account is the distinction betwixt *Perception* and
Sensation. This distinction appears to me well-founded, and necessary to render the
function of the senses intelligible; but it has not yet been stated in the full extent
and accuracy which it admits of. We may effect this, however, by combining it with
another distinction which I think equally well-founded, viz. that of the qualities of
matter into *Primary* and *Secondary*. If you are acquainted with any objections to the
solidity of the foregoing distinctions, I beg you will mention them. Taking them for
granted, their union gives us a very simple analysis of the operations of the External

Senses. . . . [sic] Reid's descriptions of Perception and Sensation are very excellent;
but the doctrine which I see reason to combat, is this, which runs through the whole
of his writings upon the subject and is concisely expressed in p. 92 of Stewart's
Elements, that all our perceptions are preceded by corresponding sensations.[4] In p.
226 of the *Intellectual Powers*, indeed, Reid asserts this of *almost* all our perceptions.[5]
Consciousness informed him, as it probably does every one, that there are
perceptions which are unaccompanied with sensations. What particular perceptions
are they? I say, our *perceptions of the Primary qualities of matter*. So far as I may
generalize what I find true of myself, the Primary qualities never excite sensation;
the perceptions of them are often, no doubt accompanied with sensations, but then
we know that those sensations proceed from Secondary qualities, which happen to
be presented, to the organs of perception, in combination with the Primary. When
there are no Secondary qualities combined, no sensation is blended with the
Perception of the Primary. When Secondary qualities are combined, but their
corresponding sensations happen from frequent repetition etc. to have become
indifferent, we are not conscious of any other sensations as if proceeding from the
Primary. Reid and Stewart have, in various passages, assumed as a fact, that the
perception of a primary quality is always preceded by a peculiar sensation; for the
most explicit mention of it, that I can at present recollect, look at Stewart's *Outlines*,
p. 22.[6] In this passage, you will observe the improper and pernicious use of final
causes; the *intention of nature* is a thing we can know nothing about. There is one
observation there, however, which deserves attention, as an argument for the
existence of sensations impressed by the primary qualities – inasmuch as it shows
that sensations of that kind might exist and be overlooked. But they would still be
discoverable, by reflection; whereas no effort of reflection can point them out to me.
I have sometimes imagined that I had perceived one, but on examination it has
always proved to proceed from a secondary quality.

So much then for what my own Consciousness determines on this point;
according to §2,[7] I must apply to Language, to know how far it agrees with the
Consciousness of others; and this, I believe, gives me the same decision – for the
secondary qualities are spoken of by all men as an immediate source of agreeable
sensations, but no pleasures of taste are ever traced to primary qualities, except
where there has been a strong association, that may easily be analysed. Have I not
reason then to conclude, that *the primary qualities of matter excite no sensations in the
mind?* . . . [sic] I proceed to another proposition: *we have no perception of the Secondary
qualities of Matter*. Reid speaks of our perceiving the secondary, as well as the primary
qualities.[8] But let us attend to the fact. In the perception of a primary quality, the
mind is not conscious of any sensation; it only thinks of the particular quality
existing in a piece of matter. When the presence of a secondary quality is recognized,
the mind is chiefly occupied with a sensation: we know, indeed, that there must be
some quality in the matter, causal of our sensation; and from habit, we make this
reference very readily. But we have no perception of the quality; on the contrary, the
great business of natural philosophy is to ascertain from what circumstances in
matter our sensations proceed. Take a person unacquainted with the explanations,
which physical inquirers have given of the sensations of colour and sound; [passage
torn away] by which the former is referred to the action of light on the surfaces of

bodies, and the latter to vibrations transmitted through the pneumatic medium: ask this person to analyse the operation of his mind, when the colour – red, or a note from a musical instrument, is present to it. It would be impossible for him to find any thing really distinct from the sensations. He might talk, indeed, of *perceiving* the colour, red – but he does not perceive it – and we know that association has led him to the mistake. He has only a sensation of the colour red, in the same manner as he has only a sensation of the sound. That you may not misunderstand my meaning, observe, that when a colour is presented, there is indeed both a perception and a sensation; but then the sensation proceeds from the colour, which is a secondary quality; the perception is of the figure and extension, which are primary qualities. But take an instance of a sense, to which the primary qualities are not addressed; smelling, for example. 'When I smell a rose, (says Reid, p. 226) there is [in this operation] both sensation and perception.'9 There is evidently a sensation, but I think there is no perception: for in fact, had I never possessed any other sense than the olfactory, I should have had no idea even of the existence of matter.

In your next letter I hope you will review with freedom the various subjects of this, and enter upon some other branch of Perception. We must pay peculiar attention to the subject of the original and acquired Perceptions of Light.

1. Robert Boyd (d. 1815), a Writer to the Signet, was evidently the younger brother of the banker Walter Boyd (1753–1837: *DNB*).
2. Evidently a reference to the last of the numbered sections in Doc. 11, which are continued with the following paragraph 6 in this document.
3. In *Disquisitions relating to Matter and Spirit* (1777), Joseph Priestley (1733–1804: *DNB*) reduced everything, even the soul, into matter. In *The Doctrine of Philosophical Necessity Illustrated*, published in the same year, Priestley followed Hartley and Hume in denying the freedom of will.
4. Stewart had written in the first, 1792 edition of his *Elements* that Reid was the first to have had the courage to make the

    plain statement of fact ... that the mind is so formed, that certain impressions produced on our organs of sense by external objects, are followed by correspondent sensations; and that these sensations, (which have no more resemblance to the qualities of matter, than the words of a language have to the things they denote,) are followed by a perception of the existence and qualities of the bodies by which the impressions are made; and that all the steps of this process are equally incomprehensible; and that, for any thing we can prove to the contrary, the connection between the sensation and the perception, as well that between the impression and the sensation, may be both arbitrary: that it is therefore by no means impossible, that our sensations may be merely the occasions on which the correspondent perceptions are exerted; and that, at any rate, the consideration of these sensations, which are attributes of mind, can throw no light on the manner in which we acquire our knowledge of the existence and qualities of body.

5. Horner used the first edition of Thomas Reid's *Essays on the Intellectual Powers of Man* (Edinburgh, 1785); the page referred to is the first in Essay II, chapter xvi, 'Of Sensation'.
6. In his passages on 'the laws of Perception in the case of our different senses' in the first (1793) edition of his *Outlines of Moral Philosophy*, Stewart had written:

    16. It is necessary also to attend to the distinction between *Primary* and *Secondary* qualities. The former, although perceived in consequence of certain sensations excited in our minds, are always apprehended as external and independent existences; and the notions of them we form have in general no reference to the sensations by which they are suggested. The truth seems to be, that these sensations were intended by nature to perform merely the office of signs, without attracting any notice to themselves; and, as they are seldom accompanied either with pleasure

or pain, we acquire an habitual inattention to them in early infancy, which is not easily to be surmounted in our maturer years. . . .

17. Our notions of secondary qualities are merely relative; the sensations which correspond to them informing us of nothing but of the existence of certain unknown causes by which they are produced. What we know of the nature of these causes is the result of subsequent philosophical investigation. . . .

7. I.e., of the first page of Reid's Essay II, chapter xvi.
8. In Essay II, chapter xvii, 'Of the Objects of Perception; and, first, of Primary and Secondary Qualities'.
9. Para 4 of Essay II, chapter xvi.

17. From Henry Brougham

BLPES i. 79–82   Edinburgh, 27 Mar. 1797

I received your letter (*the day before yesterday*) with great pleasure, although I am concerned at your silence about returning. You must surely have been in a happy humour for writing, since both your father, Murray and I received each of us a letter from you in the course of a week. To show you that I am inclined to enter on a dispute, and, at the same time, to set you a good example, by obeying the injunction you lay upon me, in the emphatical *soon*, I sat down with 2 sheets before me, on the second day after receipt of yours, though you will probably be a week or two longer of receiving it, as I shall give it next Sunday for a frank to your Father, with whom I am that day to have the pleasure of dining.

The very night on which yours arrived, Robertson was made, according to request, a corresponding member; a letter was received, also, from Wallace, the great geometrician, expressive of the most grateful thanks for the same honour being conferred on *him*, with a promise of a paper immediately. I wish Robertson could, or even would follow his example, and send us *a paper* on any scientific subject. The promise to communicate *papers*, I think too vague; at least, it comes from all the correspondents, and generally comes alone.

Your picture of the Royal Society, is exactly in conformity to several others which I have received from eye-witnesses. The *experiments on impregnation* must, however, have been wretchedly contrived, if they do not prove interesting. The subject is important in the highest degree, as Naturalists have, with their usual discrimination, totally neglected it. The field was opened by Spallanzani, whose researches, though scanty, I was much pleased with: he thought of prosecuting the subject, instigated, I believe, by the late King of Prussia; but his farther endeavours were not crowned with success.[1] Be kind enough, therefore, to give me a short sketch of the paper you heard, for it has raised my curiosity, and a few lines will satisfy it. Did the author succeed in his attempts to impregnate these animals? And how often was injection necessary? Did he succeed in producing *muline*[2] *animals*? And in these trials, was a syringe used? With or without motion and consequent emission on the part of the female?

. . .

You do not tell me in what you are engaged. I expect an account of your studies by your next letter: what books you have been pleased with, for you surely don't *waste* time in reading disagreeable ones, what speculations you have been engaged in, what exercises you have used to keep alive facility of composition. A propos of composition – Have you ever found the bad effects of intense thinking, upon fluency of speech? I lately have had personal proofs of them. After being engaged for a week in close mathematical labours, I found myself extremely dull, stiff and unanimated in the Society on a most interesting question. Is not this dreadful encouragement? My time is occupied at present, with speculations on Curve lines, the Societies, and *Artillery*, to which I now belong.

For this year and half past I have been constantly engaged with Historical and Political reading, as I doubt not you have been also. If you don't like the subject on which my remarks are now to be made, let me have a new combat with you on some *point* in that *line*.

STRICTURES ON THE ARGUMENT FROM FINAL CAUSES

The reasoners in favour of a Deity's existence, have in general, and especially of late, had recourse to the arguments *a posteriori*, in support of their delightful but delusive theory. After soaring in vain, into the regions of lofty and abstruse metaphysics, in search of necessary and independent proofs, they found that even the genius of a Newton or a Clarke was unable to do more, than lull the reason asleep, by the confused noise of unintelligible sounds. The argument *a priori*, the fruit of these reveries, vanished with the smoke of language which had been supposed to conceal it. Simpler appeals, far more dangerous to truth, were now made to the natural world, its regularity and its beauty; the happiness arising from it to productions which animate the scene. The result was twofold; that these things must have a cause: and that this cause must be a benevolent being. Consequences the most favourable to human wishes, the most pleasing to the fancy and seducing to the reason of a weak being, were drawn with the pomp and presumptions of demonstration. Mankind placed in their certainty an implicit trust, because they wished their truth, and thinking their happiness connected with their belief, they received faith among their virtues and denounced atheism as a crime. David Hume pulled down the fabric [illegible word] – he showed the difference between causation and coexistence, reasoned from hence, that from seeing only the effect we cannot infer the cause, and that even though we could, that cause, being in every respect limited by the effect, cannot be what we call *deity*. In this state of the question, I shall suppose two arguers to be placed. My theist has adduced his proofs, first as supporting the positive side of the question; these have been proved by my Atheist to be *nugatory*, or at best quite *insufficient*. And he now proceeds with the *reserved fire*.

A.[3] I have heard those arguments by which you pretended to prove the existence of supernatural beings – arguments whose strength ought to have been proportioned to the extraordinary nature of the position. Having, I trust, repelled them, I now attack in my turn, and prove the impossibility of your assertions by positive facts. Look to the very quarter whence your proofs were drawn. Is the benevolent design so often insisted upon, as indubitable as you have supposed?

1. In the polar regions, the colour of animals is white. This prevents the scanty light of their shortened sun, from producing that genial heat which the more

favoured climates enjoy. The colour of the ground, too, is in general the same; hence its barrenness, hence its disagreeable effects in producing ophthalmic complaints. In the equatorial regions, on the other hand, the prevailing colour is black; hence the rays of a vertical sun are rendered the more intense. Here then we see either malevolence or folly. The greatest expense is where the materials are the scarcest; where they are superfluous the greatest saving. All redounds to the misery of the creature.

2. The researches of naturalists have furnished us with singular proofs of the almost infinite quantity of animal death by which animal life is supported.

3. In the deserts [sic] of Egypt, far from the fertilizing influence of the Nile, lies a spot bereft of every living production but Man. There no break in the dreary waste of sand relieves the weary eye. There no green thing exists. No cooling breeze refreshes the miserable native; no stream slakes his burning thirst. The morning dew exhales in noxious vapour. The evening's breeze is the deadly whirlwind of the desert. The same blast which carries in its bosom the destruction of man brings, also, the only sustenance of the surviving few. On its wings are born annual swarms of locusts, which have but lately laid waste happier lands. *The famished Arab satiates his hunger.* But even this miserable sustenance is not long continued. The life it maintains is short as well as wretched. At an early age, the body is corrupted. A total reviviscence takes place. Those animals that were once the preservers, become now the destroyers of life. Thus does nature plant these wretches in a situation destitute of all sustenance – to support the existence of her offspring she sends the annual swarms. The native eats and dies. To the famished lips of a rational being, she presents the cup. She starves him if he refuses to drink – if he obeys her orders, he has swallowed poison.

I shall not multiply proofs (or facts) of the malevolence of nature. The earth teems with them, for its fecundity in animation is unbounded.

Theist – These are partial evils resulting from design hid from our eyes – all is for the best.

Atheist – Truly the design is hidden, but that the evil is partial and all is for the best I deny. Show me your proof. The omnipotence of a deity being proved I [?allow] the conclusions of an optimist: but till we assume these *very conclusions*, how do we show the deity's existence and attributes? The argument is evidently, reasoning in a circle. Granting the evil to be partial, what then? Is it consistent with infinite wisdom to produce good by evil? A being who is infinite, has power over contingencies. He can turn the laws of nature and they are changed, or he can make, unmake and alter and annull [sic]. He can produce fertility without overflows, bestow a happy climate untainted by the breath of the poisonous reptiles and cleanse the air without the tempest to destroy. The matter crowds in upon me.[4]

1. The English translation of the work by Lazzaro Spallanzani (1729–99) had been published in two volumes in London in 1784 under the title of *Dissertations relative to the natural history of animals and vegetables.*
2. Hybrid (as a mule).
3. There appears to be no 'B'.
4. Horner did not answer this letter (see Doc. 19) and indeed seems to have ended his correspondence with Brougham from Shacklewell altogether with that acknowledged at the beginning of this document.

18. To J.A. Murray

BLPES i. 83–4   [Shacklewell], 14 May 1797

I have felt it a great restraint indeed to be kept so long from writing to you. Various engagements, almost all of them inferior to that in point of pleasure, have day after day run away with the time which I had intended for the study of your late letters. At length, however, having a forenoon at my disposal, I have placed Locke on my right hand, Condillac and Reid on my left, and Murray before me; resolved not to move, till I have finished the sheet. NB. Not having a larger [?sheet] at hand, I write as small as my eyes will suffer.

I am pleased with the way in which you define, that is, describe *Matter*. The old definition 'extended substance' should be suspended at least, till the issue of the discussion, brought forward by Boscovich,[1] whether extension be really a property of body, or inherent in space only: some ingenious reasons, and some plausible facts, have been adduced for the negative. But it is perhaps of very slight importance, by what formula we express our signification annexed to the word *Matter*; since a just definition is not to be had. The operations of mind on this subject are well investigated by Locke, in that excellent chapter, 23rd of the Second Book;[2] from the contents of which some of our Scottish metaphysicians have borrowed much, without thinking it necessary to acknowledge the debt. He shows, with great acuteness of metaphysical analysis, and a rich variety of illustration, that the mind can fix no other notion on the term *Matter*, than that of a supposed, but wholly unknown, substratum to a collection of various qualities; and that the mention of one, or other, or all, of those general qualities, describes matter as compleatly [sic] as it can be described. Your own definition, you seem to think, is ultimately resolvable into this, but I prefer it on the grounds you point out, as, without an enumeration of the qualities of body, it refers immediately to that which informs us of their existence. For notwithstanding the fact, that matter and its qualities exist independently of our perception; and notwithstanding the obvious evidence of the conjecture, that matter might have existed with the same qualities as at present, though minds, capable of perceiving them, had never had being: still, in distinguishing a particular class of our ideas from the rest, the understanding finds it satisfactory to form the distinction with a reference to the source from which those ideas, and no others, are desired.

With regard to the question in your last letter, 'Whether there are any facts which explain the different perceptions we form, according to the senses from which we have sensations': this question takes for granted Reid's theory, viz. that all our perceptions are preceded by corresponding sensations, from a comparison or combination of which they are formed. This I have not received sufficient proofs to admit, and in my last I offered a mere sketch of what seemed a theory more agreeable to fact, in order that you might correct the outline, and that we might work together in filling it up and finishing the colours. That theory however being intimately connected with the distinction between primary and secondary qualities, our previous business is to examine this distinction. ... [sic] All this, I confess, wears rather an odd appearance for an answer to a question about *facts*; which of course must exist, or not exist, whatever hypothesis we adopt, and whether we take up any hypothesis at all. But observe, though you desire me to look about for facts – yet those facts required are to be explanatory of a particular proposition which I doubt being true, and the falsity of which must evidently involve the non-existence of the facts for which you inquire.

I shall now attempt to settle what meaning we are to annex, in the prosecution of our inquiry, to the word *Sensation*. We should of course keep near to the common idiom; without carrying our compliance, however, farther than adopting one of the many senses in which we shall find it employed. If we do not confine our metaphysical use of it to *one* distinct signification, there must be an end of all precision. We have two or three English nouns, such as *feeling, emotion, sensation* – that express mental phenomena of a common genus, but differing specifically. The existence of a specific difference is indicated by this circumstance, that though no person whatever perhaps could on demand sketch the boundaries of distinction, yet all, who have any taste in speech or composition, find that those words are far from being altogether synonymous, and that there are several occasions where one cannot be substituted for another, without vitiating the expression – and those, not mere cases of idiomatic variety, the decision resting with the particular habits of the auditory organs, but distinctions which we perceive to be founded in the real nature of things. All such peculiarities of language are to be considered as guides to corresponding peculiarities of mental phenomena. These ravelled complications of popular phraseology it is the business of the metaphysician to untwine, and, by analysing with vigilance what passes before his consciousness, to obtain a full and a steady view of that original structure, which because carefully looked at by common minds and seen in part only, cannot but be indistinctly and partially described in common discourse. I don't recollect that the English language possesses any word peculiarly appropriated to the genus, under which the three species above-mentioned are comprehended. *Feeling* is the most general word, and therefore may be made use of in describing what we are to understand by Sensation – Wherefore,

> Sensations are those *feelings* which are impressed on the mind thro' the organs of the body.

I flatter myself this coincides with the notion you have explained in your letter of the 28th of March; but the phrase, 'result of our senses', appeared to me by much too general. I trust you will dissect the preceding description of mine, with as much freedom as I did yours. The best instrument that I can furnish you with for that purpose, is to state the grounds on which I have given it the preference. In the first place, I think that, with sufficient distinctness, this definition appropriates the word to mental phenomena which are known to exist, and which ought to be classified together by a common name. Secondly, so far as I have observed either in books or in conversation, this appears to be the import of the word in pure classical English. I have frequently found it, I allow, used without this exact limitation; never by those, however, who in other respects manifested a defective expression, whether they were led away from the standard by false taste, or from inattention and awkwardness had never come into it. I cannot avoid giving a particular instance of the former, as it struck me very much when I had little idea of the subject now before me; I allude to the singular way in which the word *sensation* is used in the late pamphlet by

Erskine,[3] and that repeatedly, thrice, I believe, within the first five pages. But I ask pardon: on any occasion, but a verbal discussion, I should have been ashamed to take notice of such a trifle: I might with great justice be required to sacrifice all cavils of criticism for the pleasure of reading a few of the pages of that publication, which are wrought in such a noble strain, as amply to counterbalance the general inferiority of the reasoning and carelessness of the composition. But to return to my definition; you will observe that I don't restrict the word *Sensation* to the impressions made at the five organs of external perception, but give it to all the feelings experienced by the mind in consequence of impressions made on the bodily organization. So that the corporeal frame may be considered as the occasional cause of sensations; and we are in the frequent habit of seating our sensations in that particular part of the bodily frame where the impression commences. By sensations, therefore, I understand not only the feelings excited by the smells, colours, etc. of matter, but likewise those irritations etc. which take place within our body itself, such as the pleasure of tickling, etc., the pain of hunger, cramp, fainting, etc., in short, the feelings arising from some peculiar state of the vital functions, or irregularity in the motions of the animal machinery.

I have purposely expressed the above definition so as to include nothing more than the known fact; without reference to a supposed faculty or power. This, you remember, we agreed on as a rule of inquiry. And indeed to talk of a *power* would be particularly improper in the present example, where the mind is passive, unless we adopt Locke's odd phrase of *passive power*. Independent of this, suppose we should use the word *capacity* instead of *power* – to speak of the mind, having a capacity of sensation, is only a roundabout expression of the bare fact, that the mind has sensations; and may be classed with the identical proposition, that because we have sensations, we are sentient beings.

With regard to the arrangement of sensations into pleasant, disagreeable, and indifferent – it is a question of fact, and of course our opinion must be determined by an appeal to experience.

You have been too severe, I think, on Reid's description of sensation. It appears to be by no means proper for a description or definition of that, on more than one account; but if you take it as the enunciation of a particular circumstance in which sensation, (we might say more comprehensively, in which Feeling) differs from other modes of mind – in fact, the basis of the distinction between the sensitive and the cogitative parts of human nature, the observation does not strike me as superficial or unimportant.

My Father, I expect, leaves Edinburgh tomorrow, and brings among other things a code of metaphysics from you. I will not dispute, that in this I expect more than I deserve; but this I have got the habit of, in consequence of your long friendship. Should I be disappointed, you shall hear from me very soon.[4]

1. Ruggiere G. Boscovich (1711–87), Italian mathematician and natural philosopher.
2. 'Of the complex ideas of Substances', in the *Essay on Human Understanding*, Book II.
3. Perhaps *Doctrinal and Occasional Sermons* (Edinburgh, [1795]), by the Reverend John Erskine (1719–1803: *DNB*), William Erskine's uncle.
4. Murray responded to this letter with another metaphysical discourse, but apparently Horner did not write to him again until 24 Oct., shortly before he ended his residence at

Shacklewell. That letter (BLPES i. 93–4) apologizes for a long break in correspondence; but the published version (*Horner*, i. 38–40) omits a key passage in which Horner expresses a very grim view of human nature.

19. From Henry Brougham

BLPES i. 89–90   Edinburgh, 5 Sept. 1797

It is unusual to begin a letter to a good correspondent by saying, 'I received yours of the — date, for which I return, etc., etc.' I may begin this, by saying that I have *not* received yours, and though, of course, I can return no thanks, yet I conjecture many sufficient excuses, have regularly heard of your welfare from your Father, and am by no means such a fool as to stand upon the ceremony so common to that tribe of letter writers, which you and I have often joined in despising. I must, however, add in case of mistakes, that I wrote you the first week of April last, and sent the letter (a double one I believe) to your Father for a frank. It contained some remarks on the problem, and others on a question in Natural Religion – and was written the day after I had received yours.[1]

The *Academy* has gone on with great success. It lately had a recess of about 6 weeks which opportunity I took to make a pretty extensive (and most agreeable) tour through the North of Scotland, walking in a little more than a fortnight, above 400 miles. My jaunt was productive of several curious mineralogical remarks, which I propose shortly to submit to the Academy. The whole of Scotland (particularly Perthshire, East Lothian and Berwickshire) is in a state of the greatest discontent. More spirit is manifested than one could ever have expected. But it may be dangerous to speak on these subjects in a letter which will run a risk of being opened at the Post Office, a hint which you may use if you have not already thought of it.

I know you care not about (what is commonly [?called]) news, and indeed, need not, as long as you have access to newspapers, for nothing can be more ridiculous than to stuff a sheet of paper with tattle which the same post brings much more fully and in far greater abundance. Our artillery corps is under *strict orders*, to be ready at a moment's notice. We have got 3 or 400 rounds of Cannister [*sic*] and round shot, new swords, etc., and Friday first is the *day of mob*, if such is to take place. I have little more time at present, from a similar cause, viz, a preparatory *field day*, in about an hour, before which I have to dress and dine. To this add the horrors of a *pen* bad beyond description, the sad remembrance of a half a dozen other letters just written, the hungry yearnings of the inward man, a sore finger and a headache – And I am sure your good nature will excuse the being who is burdened with so many ills, if indeed, your selfishness does not rather call on him to cease.

1. This seems to be a reference, not to a letter of April, but to Doc. 17.

20. 'On the Political Effects of the General Diffusion of Knowledge'[1]

Kinnordy MSS   18 Dec. 1797

In estimating the effects of civilization on the human race, it is often proposed as a topic of inquiry, whether in a state of refinement we find more or less virtue, than under the barbarism of primæval manners. Some writers, warm with their conviction of the various benefits that are derived from the sciences and arts, launch into the extravagancies [sic] of enthusiasm, feeling, in the past records of history, that vice is less hideous as it becomes less gross, and yielding to that fascinating delusion of interpreting wishes into reasonable expectations, they dare to anticipate the events of unknown futurity, delineate in glowing colours the gradual emancipa-tion of mankind from prejudice and from crimes, till they close the beauteous landscape with the fair but shadowy forms of perfect knowledge and perfect virtue. Another set of declaimers, less addicted to this visionary but amiable philanthropy than to an insatiable appetite for paradox, have reversed the scene; and pointing to the savage condition as the reign of innocence, would enforce the dreary and mortifying prospect that as we remove from the original state, we sink from the dignity of our nature, and that the farther we advance in science and refinement, we only plunge the deeper in corruption. Now, there is no objection to either of these as themes of academical disputation, or rhetorical exercise; but to calm serious inquiry, they have not the slightest reference. The one is false, because it contradicts fact; the other cannot be considered as true, because, unsupported by experimental probability, it contradicts the fundamental law of philosophizing, that the course of events is uniform and will be in future what has been in time past. Whatever arguments can be adduced, either from history or from an abstract examination of the human mind, point all to this conclusion, that taking one with another, we find but little variation in the sum total of virtue and vice. If there be any difference at all, it is in favour of the state of society which is most refined. No doubt, it is only in the period of cultivation, that we find those examples of flagrant villainy, which are suggested by the rapacity of avarice, and the high claims of uncontrollable ambition; but let it likewise be recollected that it is at this same period, when the arts have polished and science has enlightened, that we view the sublime exertions of courage, of justice, and of patriotism; that courage, which maintains truth in the face of persecution; that justice, which rouses to arms in defence of injured virtue, and in assertion of violated rights; that patriotism, which, scorning a sphere of action so confined as the politics of the native city, of the petty cabals of a senate, dictates even to the monarch, on the throne of power, that the prosperity of his people is most effectually secured by promoting general happiness, and by establishing a liberality and toleration that have no other limits than the world.

As every effect must bear a proportion to the intensity of its cause, the influence of science on national character must follow the same progress in which the diffusion of scientific acquirements proceeds. The improvement of manners, which it naturally tends to produce, cannot take place, unless the cultivation of knowledge has previously circulated through the various ranks of the people; and once they are enlightened, the corresponding improvement will as necessarily follow, as any physical phenomenon from its cause, subject only to the law, which restricts all causes, whether they operate in the moral or the material system, of being retarded in their course, and modified in their power, by the counteraction of causes of a different description.

Farther, it is of the utmost importance to remark, that this mutual counteraction and intermixed operation of different causes introducing one particular appearance or effect, is of much less frequent occurrence in the material world, than among what are called intellectual phenomena, whether moral or political. In our specula-tions upon the former, we can often perceive the individual action of a single cause, the force of gravity, for instance, without opposition or modification from any other; and the great movements of the planetary system are explained by the composition of but two causes, the force of gravity with that of projection: {When we carry our curiosity, indeed, into the corpuscular constitution of matter, we find, or think that we find gravity, electricity, magnetism, cohesion, elective attraction, acting and reacting one upon another in all varieties of combinations, though even here we have great reason to suspect.}[2] But in political philosophy, it rarely happens, that we have not a combination of many various causes, the operation of each of which we have to analyse, and the several effects to develop, before we can be sure of having an accurate explanation of the result ultimately produced. Numberless examples of this will occur to everyone who has had the most moderate experience in investigations of this kind; but it cannot be better illustrated than by the instance at present before us. For while science is operating by its general diffusion, the national character is at the same time exposed to a variety of other causes; of consequence the total change induced presents an appearance extremely complicated and admits of no satisfactory explication, until we have carefully analysed it into its component parts, and assigned to each of them its appropriate origin. Beside the circumstances of physical situation, historical vicissitudes, diplomatic connections, and religious establishment, which differ of course in every {individual}[3] instance, but which have all a very powerful influence; beside these, the direct operation of science upon manners must be modified and restricted by causes of a more general nature, according to the progress which has been made in commerce, in agriculture, in the fine arts and in those arts that are called mechanical.

To give the subject due consideration, therefore, it would be necessary to investigate it on this extensive plan; to view it under all the aspects that I have pointed out. But this is much more than I can pretend to, on the present occasion. All that I shall attempt, is a general sketch of the natural and direct consequences of knowledge on national character. The more curious and more difficult investigation, of the manner in which this immediate influence is modified by the counteraction of other causes, I flatter myself with the prospect of laying before the Society at some future period.

When we speak of a national character we mean to say, that we have distinguished a peculiar turn in the manners of almost all the inhabitants of that particular nation. And when we speak of a change of national character, from the influence of some cause, we mean, that such a change had been observed to take place in the manners of almost all of those inhabitants. We are not, however, to estimate this general change of national manners by what the effect would be in the case of a single mind influenced by the changing cause: we are not to measure the improvement, which the national character receives from a general diffusion of science, by the improvement which the same degree of knowledge would produce on the mind of an insulated individual. Were we to proceed on this supposition, our estimate would fall far short of what is actually found to be the fact. For we must farther take into account that by the very progress of diffusion, science is continually increasing its beneficial influence. By being reflected from one to another they acquire a habit of vigorous thought and liberal opinion, that can only be roused by this communication of sentiments. While it flows and spreads with successive gradations, new objects are continually supplied to the imitative principle; which, being the main spring of improvement, actuates all the passions and energies that depend on it, and preserves the whole mechanism in motion. And as that command, which the poet is ambitious to exercise over our feeling, displays itself most successfully in the crowded theatre, where the sympathy is caught from a thousand breasts; in the same manner does science invigorate the activities of intellect and genius, with accumulated power, when by circulating through the social system it is enforced by the action of those attributes of our nature which constitute the principles of improvement, and direct the individual to look for the development of his own powers in the perfectibility of the species.

National character, it has already been observed, is nothing but an average of individual characters. When we assert, therefore, that national character receives much higher improvement from knowledge, than the same degree of knowledge would produce on an individual mind; nothing else can be meant than this, that the inhabitants of a nation are more improved by the portion which they possess of the general knowledge, than they would have been, if we suppose it possible for them to have acquired the same share of knowledge individually, and independent of each other. This last supposition is indeed a cause that never has been, and never can be, verified by the fact; but it is a just standard for measuring the progress of national refinement, and its non-existence does not make it less so. It is somewhat analogous to an artifice much employed in the application of geometry to physics, when, having a curve to investigate, we suppose the deflective force to be suspended, that the motion may proceed in a tangent from the point of suspension; in this hypothesis, we evidently destroy the essential circumstances of the subject which we are to investigate; but we obtain what is absolutely necessary to the investigation, a resolution of the moving forces, and a medium of comparison without which we could deduce no demonstration. In the same manner, though we can have no instance of a single person having either by his own individual exertions, or from peculiar inspiration, attained to philosophy and science, yet so long as we argue, not upon the origin of attainments so extraordinary, but from what their effects would be, the supposition is not inadmissible, since, from our knowledge of the human mind, those effects might be ascertained; and when these are ascertained, we have analysed the composition of that motion in which national improvement is carried forward, and which consists, first, of the effect immediately and separately induced on the mind of each citizen, and, secondly, of the enhancement which this immediate effect receives from the co-operation of the social principles. And here, I think, a fine scene is opened for those who delight in finalizing, where they might exercise their ingenuity, and what would be more to their taste, where they might display their eloquence, in tracing the thoughts of the Supreme First Cause, and in painting that connection which He, in His wisdom, designed, and by His power established, between the existence of political society and this law of the human mind with respect to the progress of knowledge. But a more humble province is as much as I feel myself adequate to, that of stating and submitting to your examination this valuable fact; that not only has the great body of science, of which the world is in possession, been raised by the successive and united labours of ages, but that {those benefits which accompany the diffusion of philosophy in a nation, and which we observe accruing to individuals from a liberal education, are not so much the immediate and direct consequence of science itself, and of the mind being stored with facts and classifications, as of the intellectual habits which are thereby formed, and the free, constant, universal communication of opinion. It is this freedom of intellectual intercourse, the birth-right and beyond all comparison the noblest privilege of Man, which alone can inspire us with that liberality for the sentiments of one another, true independence in framing our own creed, and which can alone lead us into the path towards a national and just philosophy. For the mind is naturally so partial to its own performances, so secure of acquisitions once made, so confident in what has hitherto occupied its conviction, that all the influence of a mutual comparison and opposition of sentiments is required to preserve us from absolute bigotry and dogmatism on every topic of opinion or belief. As long as this intercourse is left perfectly free, truth will always appear to those who seek for her, and even where this previous disposition does not exist, will sooner or later force herself upon the view. But as soon as it is confined or obstructed, that moment discovery is at an end; and even what had already been made out is gradually darkened in consequence of its own imperfections, and at length lost sight of amid accumulating inconsistencies and errors. When a philosopher of antiquity says of himself, in the genuine spirit of liberality, *Si cum hac exceptione detur*, etc. – when Seneca delivers this manly sentiment, it is not merely the suggestion of an enlightened benevolence, which, disdaining a selfish monopoly of science, would diffuse its blessings over the universe; but it is also the declaration of what he had himself experienced in the study of knowledge – that it can neither be acquired nor preserved pure, unless our opinions be constantly overlooked, freely communicated to our neighbours for their examination, and brought into rigorous comparison with the notions which views and inquiries, different from ours, have induced them to adopt.}[4] Were an individual, according to the hypothesis formerly explained, to acquire science without this communication with society, his knowledge, however extensive and however accurate, would not be accompanied with that beneficial influence over his mind, which philosophy is found to operate over national character. It would not beget liberality of sentiment, for no opinion had ever been proposed to him different from his own; it would not beget *independence* of sentiment, for he had never experienced what it is to unshackle the understanding from the doctrines of education; and with all his store of knowledge, he could not ever possess the facility of distinguishing, among contradictory opinions, the true from the false, because, from the manner in which that knowledge had been impressed on his mind, he had not learned how to elicit truth from the heterogeneous systems and conflicting prejudices of the world.

Such, as it appears to me, is the natural and direct tendency of science to influence the national character. For the very rapid and imperfect view I have taken of it, I shall not presume to offer any apology; because I am convinced that no apology would be sufficient. I have already proposed my intention of prosecuting the inquiry farther, particularly of endeavouring to ascertain how far this immediate effect is counteracted by the operation of other circumstances. Before I conclude, however, the present branch of the subject suggests a few hints on the counteraction which this immediate influence of science opposes to certain causes that are usually found to act on national character at the same time.

The first of these is Commerce; the obvious and the experienced tendency of which is, undoubtedly, while it multiplies the wealth, to degrade the manners of a state. The corrective is found in the cultivation of science, which, by constantly keeping up a circulation of objects on which the higher faculties of the mind may be employed, preserve the tone and temper of the national character. As avarice, the vilest and also the most encroaching of all passions, is the original spring of commerce, it naturally tends to turn the whole attention and industry of a people to the accumulation of wealth, as the ultimate and universal pursuit; but when a passion for science is once thoroughly established, it coalesces with the commercial spirit, and the projects of the latter come in most cases to have a reference, in many cases to be subservient, to the speculations of the former. {This, etc.}[5]

The influence of Philosophy on National Character may likewise be considered as of the most important utility, in regulating the influence of the fine arts, which, otherwise, while they soften and humanize, are found to enfeeble and corrupt the mind. But the benefits of a general diffusion of science are most conspicuous, when we observe how wonderfully they counteract the pernicious consequences of that almost infinite subdivision of labour, which takes place in an opulent commercial nation. There, however, a wide field opens to us of investigation equally curious, important, and intricate; but on which I cannot, on the present occasion, pretend at all to enter.

1. On a page preceding the essay and dated June 1820, Leonard Horner writes:
    Extract from the Minute Book of the Speculative Society Edinr. 18 December 1797. Mr Horner read an Essay 'On the Political Effects of the General Diffusion of Knowledge.' He had been admitted a member of the Society on the 21 Nov. preceding, being then 19 years of age. I found the scattered sheets of this Essay, which are here bound together.
    On the facing page is another note written by Leonard Horner: 'I have an extract from this in the Memoir, beginning at page 13 – 7th line from bottom to following page 15 – 5th line from bottom.' The extract, however, does not appear in *Horner*.
2. This sentence is crossed out in the MS.
3. The word 'individual' appears to be crossed out.
4. The brackets that frame this lengthy passage are Horner's; perhaps they indicate his intention to omit the passage from his speech.
5. The brackets are Horner's; perhaps he had some additional notions or materials in mind for verbal elaboration.

21. To John Hewlett

BLPES i. 101–102   Edinburgh, 14 Mar. 1798

In addition to your kind letter, I have to thank you for the present it announced, and which has since arrived. I have been looking over the Spelling Book, and find it a complete work of its kind, were it not for having your name on its title-page: It will surely appear a paradox to the critics of posterity, that the mind which had produced Hewlett's Sermons, could descend to the composition of a Spelling-Book.[1] The physiognomy of Euler fully answers the description you gave me of your medallion, as well as the indistinct image which had formed itself in my own mind, while I was composing the Memoir.[2] I had made no provision indeed for the mouth, which, I fear, if the engraver has not done it injustice, expresses something worse than the imbecility of goodness: it is true, one finds in the lower part of the face, an indication of his grandmother-like love of children; but is there not likewise somewhat approaching to avarice, or some such passion of a selfish nature? I presented one of the heads to Mr Playfair, our very learned and ingenious professor of mathematics; he considered it as a great compliment, as in his opinion it greatly excels the only other likeness of Euler he had ever seen, which was among a collection of portraits of eminent mathematicians in Flamsteed house. I have also given Mr Playfair a copy of the *Algebra*.

You are so kind as [to] inquire about our Literary Society, and it is with much satisfaction I can assure you that, considering its infancy, it goes on well. I cannot answer your second question, with respect to my contributions, so confidently or with so much credit to myself. I am one of the least active among the members. I have as yet given only one communication, on a subject of some importance, the peculiarities of the Chinese language.[3] But I have another at present on the anvil, or the stocks, or in the womb, or in whatever situation it best becomes an author to speak of his embryo works. The subject of this is, the formation of the Delta or lower Egypt. You must remember the curious conjecture of Herodotus, that that land had been all formed out of travelled soil, brought from the interior of Abissynia [sic], and deposited during the inundations of the Nile. My object is to examine the proofs of this conjecture on geological principles, and from a comparison of ancient historians with modern travellers to ascertain whether any farther accumulation has taken place since the age of Herodotus. In your next letter, will you favour me with some remarks on this subject, and on what you would recommend as the best style of composition for such an investigation.[4]

The Academy of Physics, for so our Society is called, has of late acquired several valuable corresponding members, in England as well as Scotland; and we are in hopes of extending our correspondence, for that is the mainspring of every scientific institution, to the continent. We meet regularly once a week; the paper or communication intended for each meeting is in the mean time circulated among such of the members as are to be present at the public reading, in order that they may be masters of the subject, and give it a full and free discussion; we are collecting, slowly indeed, apparatus and specimens in natural history, so that we can perform such experiments as are not very complicated or expensive. We esteem it also a valuable part of our business, that we allot a certain portion of each meeting to conversation on literary news, and to the hearing of analyses or reviews of such new publications on subjects of philosophy, as individual members have had leisure to peruse. For instance, I have lately been reviewing several astronomical memoirs of Herschell. But you have had enough of the Academy of Physics.

I have scarcely left myself room to answer some particulars of your letter. I have not got either vol. of Euler's letters, nor can I recollect any circumstance by which I can conjecture how it could have been mislaid at Shacklewell. As for Monk's bill of 18/-, I cannot be certain, but think, though not made a separate article of in the account, it was included along with Bagster's in one article.[5] This you can ascertain immediately, and settle it with my father, who is lately gone to London . . .

1. John Hewlett's *Sermons on different subjects* had first been published in 1786. His *Introduction to reading and spelling* had been published in 1797.
2. Hewlett's 1822 edition of Leonhard Euler's *Elements of Algebra* revealed that Horner was both the anonymous translator and the author of the memoir in the 1797 edition.
3. The minutes of the Academy of Physics show that Horner had made his first appearance there on 18 Nov. 1797 and that it was to that body that he delivered his 'Report of facts with respect to the Peculiarities of the Chinese Language' in two parts, on 13 and 27 Jan. 1798. On 13 Jan. he also took over as treasurer, subsequently on 10 Feb. taking Leyden's place as joint secretary, and from May acting also as correspondence secretary whenever Brougham was absent. However, by the time the Academy came to an end, apparently two years later, Brown had become secretary.
4. The MS minutes of the Academy break off in mid-sentence in February 1798; but, while those reproduced in *Brown* (pp. 502–506) cease even earlier, it mentions (p. 77) that the subject of discussion at the last recorded meeting, on 1 May 1800, was Egypt.
5. Samuel Bagster the elder (1772–1851: *DNB*) was a bookseller in the Strand; Monk was probably a shoemaker or tailor.

22. Journal

Kinnordy MSS   23 Apr. 1798

Being about to begin a more regular course of studies, it is proper that before setting out I should furnish myself with a map of my route and make myself acquainted with the several stages I have to pass through in order to get to the end of my journey.[1] During this summer, I have much to do, much knowledge to acquire, and much already imperfectly acquired, to complete and to confirm. My great and indispensable business is, the elements of civil law, the elements of philosophical politics, and the elements of modern history. Next to those, my attention is required to English composition, and improvement in the three languages Greek, Latin and French; in the first, I aspire to read Demosthenes as a model for eloquence and style; in the second I must absolutely before the end of summer have read through Cicero, Virgil, Livy, Horace, and Tacitus, entirely and minutely; the last, I must gratify myself to speak and write like my own mother tongue. I have farther to acquire an elementary knowledge of chemistry; and a complete knowledge of any two branches of mechanical philosophy. This, with a few dissertations for the Academy, and a few

Literary Essays, make up my prospect for the Summer. It is multifarious and complicated, perhaps more than I shall be able to accomplish; certainly much more, if I go
on as I have of late – indolence, procrastination and versatility gain upon me – and
I may be seriously alarmed at the prospect of such habits. A great exertion will do
much; persevering regularity will do everything.[2]

1. Horner was fully aware that the diversity of his intellectual interests posed a considerable
   threat to systematic study, and so between late 1797 and 1800 he wrote out several similar
   plans of study and repeatedly admonished himself for failing to adhere to them. The most
   detailed statement of his intellectual goals, entitled 'Plan of my Future Studies', was written
   in late October 1797, shortly before he left Shacklewell for Edinburgh. It reveals that his
   main object was 'to become a consummate lawyer both in practice and in science'. In
   pursuit of that object he planned to master Latin and Greek, to acquire 'an eloquence and
   facility of English style both in writing and in speaking', to become proficient in the general
   principles of philosophy, and to emerge as 'a compleat master, if possible, of law as a
   science'. He identified Cicero as his model and committed himself to a thorough
   examination of the leading works of antiquity. He committed himself further to
   mathematical philosophy and to moral philosophy, through which, he noted, 'the path is
   laid towards the elements of legislative science'. So as to give system to his studies, he also
   pledged to keep a journal into which he would register daily his intellectual progress as well
   as his general observations. The bulk of the 'Plan' was published in *Horner*, i. 48–53. The
   manuscript, which contains several interesting passages omitted from the published
   version, is at Kinnordy.
2. During the last week of April, the entire month of May, and the first two weeks of June
   Horner pursued a course of study in French, reading at least one French novel and
   translating from the works of Cardinal de Retz, Condillac, and Rochefoucault.
   Simultaneously he examined Chesterfield's letters with an eye to English idioms and
   analysed the 44th chapter of Gibbon so as to enhance his skills in English composition and
   gain a fundamental knowledge of Roman jurisprudence. Later he turned to Arthur Duck's
   De Usu et Auctoritate Romanorum (1653) and to Justinian's *Institutes*. In mid-June he joined
   the first regiment of Edinburgh Volunteer Infantry. (See Horner's journal entries of 1, 3, 4,
   5, and 7 May, and his letter to Murray of 25 June in *Horner*, i. 57–60. The published journal
   entry of 1 May omits a passage about his study of French.)

23. To J.A. Murray

BLPES i. 103–104   Edinburgh, 16 June 1798

I learned with much satisfaction, from your letter to myself as well as those to the
good people in George St that you have passed your time in London as you ought –
'not in a manner (you affect to say) likely to produce any solid advantage' – in which
I must differ from you entirely. I thought we had agreed as to the *solid advantage* of a
knowledge of life and the acquisition of manners, and the value of good company
and fashionable well-regulated dissipation as leading to that acquisition. At least for
my part, if it were practicable, I would willingly dispose of a pretty large portion of
any commodity I may be possessed of, for an equivalent in that said article. You
know I have long and grievously felt my deficiencies in that particular; and you will
therefore please to observe, my dear friend, that your visit to London, and profit
thereby, is doubly interesting to me, on my own account as well as yours. You

remember our frequent conversations on the importance of the *tournure du monde*, and the value of experience in characters; so that I expect with pleasure the renewal of the topic, when you come home furnished with new observations on character and on manners – of which we shall try, no doubt, to make an application. It is one of the happy circumstances of our long acquaintance, that being habitually freed from reserve in matters so interesting to us, we can with confidence join our property as to experience in a stock-purse; like other traders, indeed, we often push our speculations beyond the amount of our real capital – but I think we always have the satisfaction, on balancing accounts, to find a small accumulation of profit going on.

You frequently see our friend Lord H. Petty; pray remember me to his Lordship. He is one of those I respect and admire much, for his great and original good sense, and for an affability of manners far superior to what one usually finds in those of his rank at his age.[1]

As to the English Bar, I am somewhat surprised at the little information you seem to have obtained. Can you determine this question; Whether a man might insure a moderate chance of success at the English Bar, if, in addition to the common routine of legal erudition, he should undertake the toil of making himself a good pleader? It is on this, that I think the whole seems to depend. But after all, my preference of the English Bar often flags, and is upon the whole much cooled.[2] By good or by ill luck we are natives of Edinburgh; and I do not know but we may vegetate as well here as elsewhere. Besides, the times are not in the same situation [as] when we chose our profession. In this country, things are irrecoverably altered. We may proceed farther, inclining either to the right hand or to the left – but to return back seems impossible. To me, the aspect of politics becomes every day more troubled and dismal; and by the time we arrive at the active years of our life, we may perhaps find it impossible to look upon the game or those engaged in it, without disgust and contempt, perhaps without apprehension and horror. . . .

1. Lord Henry Petty, afterwards 3rd Marquess of Lansdowne (1780–1863: *DNB*), had studied at Edinburgh University with Horner and Murray.
2. At this time Horner was admittedly ignorant of civil law. In early July he was attending pleadings before the Court of Session 'with a view to learn what style of oratory it ought to be my ambition to acquire'. A journal entry of 6 July reveals that the prospect of memorizing and systematizing substantive law intimidated him, and that the rhetorical method of law remained 'a desideratum in my education'. (*Horner*, i. 61–4.)

24. To J.A. Murray

BLPES i. 107–108   Edinburgh, 14 July 1798

You perceive I make no delay in answering your letter, which indeed I only received about an hour ago. You *insist* upon a speedy reply, which I take as a great compliment, since I believe you would at any time trust to me for the gratification of whatever request you might make, provided it lay within my power.

When I look over the remarks which fill the first two pages of your letter, I do not feel inclined to trouble you at present with any farther queries on that interesting subject which occupied my last.[1] Not that I am at all convinced of what your modesty would persuade me, that you have no information in this way to communicate. But I can gather from the manner in which you express that ignorance, and indeed I might have inferred from the nature of the subject itself, that I must wait with patience till we renew the pleasures of daily conversation. Your remarks must of course have been suggested to you on a variety of particular occasions, and it is therefore in the occasional topics of future conversation that they will be best communicated. Indeed I should suppose that they, who are desirous of acquiring a knowledge of character, cannot fall into a greater mistake, than that of generalizing too much by a habit of considering their observations apart from the incidents which gave them birth.

I heard a good deal of Mainauduc's system before I left London[2] – enough indeed to amuse me extremely, and to convince me that the days of credulity are not yet gone. The Lectures were not published at that time, so that all my information was derived from some of the pupils whom I met with. They did not betray the secret to me an uninitiated profane, but by all the arguments which could be used for such a purpose they made many a stout attempt to convert me. I recollect particularly an old Quaker lady, well known in the literary circles of London, of the name of Knowles, a woman of masculine manners – but of more than masculine understanding, who, though not much given to faith in other respects, was an absolute bigot in this sect.[3] But then she had paid 50 guineas for the secret, and I suspect thought it more creditable to continue an appearance of belief in the delusion than to acknowledge she had been gulled out of so much money. She used much rhetoric to persuade others also – and related facts, as consistent with her own personal knowledge, which if true went to a complete proof of the doctrine. But is there a single miracle related of any of the legendary saints, for which you could not at the time have procured the personal averment of intelligent and worthy people? Imagination has at times such power over the senses, or rather over the inferences which we draw from sensations, that if you admit this sort of testimony for miracles, it will be impossible for [you] to reject a single one of the popular superstitions that have successively tyrannized over the human understanding.

I am sorry you have not got Pinto nor Campomanes; as they are books of great reputation abroad, and very little known here.[4] You have procured, I hope, Turgot's *Reflections on Wealth*.[5] You know I am anxious to form a library of books on political science. They are not very numerous; it is at present the great field for the acquisition of literary honours. A pamphlet has been lately advertised in the Reviews, 'On Population, in opposition to the doctrines of Godwin and Condorcet.'[6] I wish you would look into it, and bring it down, if it contains any thing new.

The paper won't allow me to proceed much farther. I must therefore apologize to you if what I have written shall appear to you more than usually heavy. The truth is, that I was in bed the whole of yesterday with an excruciating head-ache, for which I was indebted to one of those riotous banquets which still prove the barbarity of Scotland. The consequence is that I feel myself still so nervous, that my hand shakes in writing, and the train of ideas is still more lame than usual.

1. Horner's letter to Murray of 25 June (*Horner*, i. 59–60), like his earlier letter of 16 June (Doc. 23), sought information on prospects at the English Bar. Apparently Murray and Brougham had gone up to London to investigate the pros and cons of practice there. During their visit they visited Hewlett, to whom Horner wrote a letter on 17 July that revealed a lofty opinion of Brougham (*ibid.*, i. 65–7): 'He is an uncommon genius, of a *composite order*, if you allow me to use the expression; he unites the greatest ardour for general information in every branch of knowledge, and, what is more remarkable, activity in the business, and interest in the pleasures of the world, with all the powers of a mathematical intellect.' On 17 Aug., after Brougham and Murray had returned to Edinburgh, Horner noted in his journal (*ibid.*, i. 67–8) that he had 'enjoyed a good deal of profitable conversation with my friend Brougham, whose studies are at present political, and whose conversation always affords me improvement'. Clearly Brougham inspired Horner to focus his studies on works of political economy (which is what Horner meant by the term 'political science'), and to contemplate a career at the English Bar and politics.

2. Dr J.B. Mainauduc's lectures on animal magnetism were published in London in 1798.

3. Mrs Mary Knowles (1733–1808: *DNB*).

4. Isaac Pinto (1715–1817), a Portuguese Jew, published in Amsterdam in 1771 his *Traité de la circulation et du crédit* in which he described stock exchange transactions and advanced the theory that public debt enhanced national prosperity. A note by Horner in the manuscripts at Kinnordy states that Dugald Stewart lent him Adam Smith's copy of the English edition; such an edition, *An essay on circulation and credit, in four parts; and a letter on the jealousy of commerce. From the French of Monsieur de Pinto, Tr., with annotations, by the Rev. S. Baggs, M.A.* (J. Ridley, 1774), was in Horner's library when it was sold at auction (*HL* no. 179). Pedro Rodriguez, Conde de Campomanes (1723–1802), published several works treating of the general theory of political economy. His *Tratado de la Regalia de Amortizacíon* (Madrid, 1765) was also included in the sale of Horner's books (*HL* no. 231).

5. An English edition of Turgot's *Reflections on the formation and distribution of Wealth* was published in London in 1793, but it does not appear to have been in Horner's library when it was sold.

6. The first edition of Malthus's famous *Essay on the Principle of Population*, published anonymously in 1798.

25. Journal

Kinnordy MSS   13 Aug. 1798

In the evening, I attended the Academy. Our business was an analysis, by Brougham, of Millar's treatise on the English Government.[1] This author divides the history of English Government into three great periods – the Anglo-Saxon, or, feudal aristocracy – the feudal monarchy, from the Conquest to the accession of the Stuarts – and the commercial government, from James I to the present times. The two first periods only are discussed in what he had already published; but Reddie said this evening that, from what Mr Millar had told him, he could gather that another volume was written out containing the last period which was delayed and only by the present political temper. In the conversation of the analysis, the following queries were started for farther information: What was the state of tenantry under the Roman Republic and Empire? Did any changes take place in the system of Roman provincial government in Britain, during the interval between the conquest and the departure of the Romans from the island? When were the terms *duke* and *count*, as names of Roman provincial governors, first introduced? Pinkerton[2] says that in the middle ages there were no titular nobility in Sweden and Denmark, an exception to the general state of Europe at that time; causes?

1. John Millar, An Historical View of the English Government (2nd ed., 1790); HL no. 150.
2. The source referred to is perhaps John Pinkerton, Dissertation on the Origin and Progress of the Scythians or Goths, being an Introduction to the Ancient and Modern History of Europe (1787).

26. To John Hewlett

BLPES i. 111–14   Edinburgh, 6 Nov. 1798

. . . I have turned over many volumes both ancient and modern, collected a great mass of notes, and having completely made up my mind, and arranged the proofs in my own head, have been so indolent as never to commit that arrangement to writing.[1] It is so much more agreeable to be on the chase for new game, than to fag at the mechanical drudgery of writing a journal of former sport.

I have some time since come to the resolution of interrupting, almost entirely for some time, the pursuit of scientific studies, in which I still feel myself extremely deficient; but it is absolutely necessary to concentrate my attention to law, and the subjects connected with it. For I by no means think that the proper study of that profession consists in the mere detail of municipal forms and positive institutions. I am labouring to study it as a science, and by uniting it with philosophical history to render it an exercise of the reasoning and arranging faculties, not of mere memory. I can find very few authors indeed who teach me any thing in this way; I should wish not only *general results*, but to be taught the *habit* of generalizing, and the *logic* (as it were) of legislative science. Would you be so good as [to] communicate to me your ideas on the most advantageous and philosophical plan of studying history? I am confident you could aid me in this respect.[2]

. . .

1. Horner refers to the paper on Egypt mentioned in Doc. 21.
2. Initially Horner followed a plan of studying the general history of English law, government, and manners, reading from the works of both Hume and Millar. On 13 Nov., however, the university's winter session commenced, and his plan of study fell prey to yet another intellectual tangent. On 5 Feb. 1799 he noted in his journal that he had finished a week-long project – a paper 'On the Opposition Party in Parliament' – and that he had studied 'nothing of civil law'. On 11 and 12 April 1799 Webb Seymour mentioned that they spent three hours and three and a half hours respectively reading two essays by Horner on Imitation.

> They were written by him in 1795 [Seymour wrote], when first attending Stewart's lectures, & are an extraordinary production for a person of his age, which was only sixteen. He attacks the doctrine of *instructive* imitation, arguing that the whole of what appears to be so may be resolved into *deliberate* imitation in children, who are induced in it from experiencing the utility of the actions they imitate, & that having thus acquired the habit, men are led at a more advanced age by appreciation to imitate actions which their judgement would regard as indifferent, or even disapprove. He contends further that sympathy which is observed in crowds, & the

infection (if it may be so called of nervous diseases) is to be attributed, not, as is commonly done to mechanical imitation, but to the effects of imagination in the nervous system. His arguments are ill arranged, but he displays great closeness of reasoning, & has taken a very comprehensive view of the subject.

In November that same year, Seymour also read 'some philosophical remarks' of Horner's on languages.

They were written [he commented] in the year '94, when he was only fifteen or sixteen, and they display uncommon acuteness for a person of that age. The remote sources from which the observations are collected shew a mind capable of concentrating its whole attention on whatever subject it proposed to investigate . . .

Several years later Horner himself noted that 'This morning a bundle of my own works fell into my hands, essays on imagination, the dramatic unities, the marvellous, imitation, the national character, the Opposition party in Parliament, etc., the offspring of former labours, the nurselings of former self-applause: but I was so mortified with them, that I committed them without mercy to the flames'. Contrary to the conclusion Fontana draws from this, however, he did not burn all his Speculative Society essays: see Doc. 20. (Lord Webb Seymour's Diary, 11 and 12 Apr. and 7 and 9 Nov. 1799, Devon Record Office; *Horner*, i. 68–9.)

27. To Francis Jeffrey

BLPES i. 115–16   Academy, Tuesday morning [?6 Nov. 1798]

In capacity of Secretary to the Academy have I been penning circular cards, till my quill is worn to a stump, and my head so confused and giddy with that labour, only equalled in dignity by that of a horse in a mill, that I can go on with it no longer. I felt great refreshment, when I arrived at your name in the list, because I thought I might take the freedom of rising above my official duty. I am afraid you were detained from us last night by indisposition; if not, you have reason to congratulate yourself, as nothing occurred but private business. Next night, however, we are to have a paper from Brown, which; from what I hear of it, as well as from what we know of his ingenuity, will certainly afford much entertaining discussion. The subject is the metaphysical philosophy of heat.[1]

You promised me a visit, which I hope you will not forget. I should like a walk any fine forenoon that you are disposed for it. In your present state of health, you should persevere in regular exercise.

That I may not omit the substance at least of [a] circular letter, if I have [?taken] the liberty of neglecting the [?form], I must inform you, that our meetings are to be on Saturday during the winter – and that your attendance is accordingly requested on Saturday next – the 10th inst.

1. According to *Brown*, pp. 464–5, this was an unoriginal fragment which Brown always planned to expand but had still not completed at the time of his death.

28. Journal

Kinnordy MSS ⟨Horner, i. 71–2⟩   21 Feb. 1799

⟨I am going on in the plan of conversation with Lord Webb, and am willing to believe that I have already acquired a little more *habileté* in argument.[1] It is not an argumentative *mania* that I wish to form, but to avoid that unfortunate habit, at the same time that I acquire some practical skill in the exercise of the reasoning faculty. I find that undivided attention, and a skill in stating propositions to myself in clear and precise language, form the great constituents of that faculty.

⟨I have also dabbled a little in the Pandects, and finished this morning the subject of 'Pledge'.

⟨Lord Webb Seymour entered into his twenty-sixth year yesterday. I am not sure that his genius is of a high order, but he possesses several of the most essential constituents to the character of a true philosopher: an ardent passion for knowledge and improvement, with apparently as few preconceived prejudices as most people can have. A habit of study intense almost to plodding – a mild, timid, reserved disposition with respect to the communication of such sentiments as he feels to be contrary to public prejudices. On this last head, in giving me a hint that he requested and expected confidential secrecy, he made an observation, the truth of which struck me forcibly, from what I am conscious of with regard to my own character, viz., that those who are most forward and bold in proclaiming their own paradoxes, are least to be trusted in the deposit of such of our opinions as we are inclined to make known only to private friends.⟩ I fear I may have made some enemies by the unnecessary and untimely declaration of sentiments, that, are interesting indeed to myself, but by which I have more than once scandalized persons of an opposite creed. I trust I shall never violate the confidence with which Seymour honours me.

⟨There is a style of behaviour with which I am not at all acquainted, but which I should aim at, as an invaluable possession, by which it is possible to keep certain sentiments within one's own breast, or at least within the circle of a few friends, and at the same time fall into no corrupt hypocrisy or unmanly acquiescence in the opinions of whatever company we happen to meet.⟩

1. An assiduous rather than distinguished scholar, Lord Webb Seymour formed a close friendship with Horner soon after arriving in Edinburgh. On 19 Feb. Horner noted in his journal (*Horner*, i. 70–71) that he had entered on a plan of discussing Professor Stewart's lectures with Lord Webb, that already the plan had been pursued 'for three or four days', and that Seymour's regular habits 'will perhaps insure mine'.

29. Journal

Kinnordy MSS ⟨Horner, i. 72–3⟩   10 Apr. 1799

⟨Read a little Spanish, the novel of 'Impertinent Curiosity', in the second volume of *Don Quixote*. In learning this language, I follow a plan recommended (I think) by Gibbon, endeavouring to acquire a readiness of translation before taking up the grammar. I was tempted a few days ago to undertake this language, from the simple motive of wishing to read Campomanes.

⟨Read half the first canto of Delille's *Jardins*.[1] This, as an exercise of taste in composition; the precepts of Delille to the gardener, admit of an easy application to the subject of style; and his own manner furnishes a continual commentary of examples and illustration.

⟨On the subject of population, which I am considering at present with a view to a paper for the Academy, I read Filangieri, and one of Kames's sketches.[2] Hitherto I have learnt nothing, but to doubt of the general principles which are laid down as certain. I doubt that number is in itself a direct object of legislative solicitude; I suspect the proposition, that a people will always people up to its resources, to be contrary to fact; and even the fundamental idea, the connection between population and subsistence, though I can hardly entertain a question of its truth, is in neither of these authors explained in that clear, simple, or direct manner which ensures conviction. I have not for a long time met with a more eloquent passage than the description in Filangieri, pp. 69 and 70, of the exaction of taxes. The conclusion shows true genius in the selection of circumstances: – 'il letto sul quale essa aveva pochi giorni indietro dato un cittadino allo Stato; quella ruvida veste colla quale essa cercava di nascondere la sua miseria nel giorno destinato ad assistere alla mensa del Signore', etc.

⟨. . .⟩

1. Jacques Delille, *Les Jardins, ou l'Art d'embellir les paysages: poëme* (Paris, 1782).
2. A copy of the five-volume edition of *La Scienza della Legislazione* (Filadelfia, 1799) by Gaetano Filangieri (1752–88) was among the sale of Horner's books (*HL* no. 101). But at this point he was evidently using volume ii of the four-volume Milan edition of 1784–6, part of which still survives in the Edinburgh University Library. The passages cited, and in part quoted, are from the opening paragraphs of Book II, chapter vi, 'Tributa eccessiva, dazi insupportabili, maniera violenta d'esigerli: quart'ostacolo alla popolazione'. Filangieri's economic doctrine was eclectic, a connecting link between mercantilist and Physiocratic thought. While never mentioning Adam Smith, he advocated free trade and a single tax but steadfastly maintained that a favourable balance of trade was an essential factor in national wealth. [Henry Home, Lord Kames], *Elements of Criticism, and Sketches of the History of Man* (6 vols, 1788), was also in *HL* no. 255.

30. Journal

Kinnordy MSS ·   22 Apr. 1799

. . .

   Read about an 100 pages of an anonymous *Essay on the Principle of Population.*[1] The subject is not directly population, but to show the chimerical nature of the late doctrines concerning the perfectibility of society, from a view of the misery which must for ever arise from the checks which are by necessity imposed on the progress of population. It is the work of an ingenious man, but not of one who thinks profoundly or comprehensively; the style is abominably inflated and affected. I . . . do not yet see my way in the subject of population; I have arranged in my head a number of facts, and a variety of detached views; but have not forced them into any arrangement.

   1. The first part of this journal entry, which further assesses the character of Lord Webb Seymour, is represented as the complete entry in *Horner*, i. 74–5, the whole of Horner's initial notes on the first edition of Malthus's *Essay* being omitted.

31. Journal

Kinnordy MSS   24 Apr. 1799

. . . Read the *Essay on Population,* pp. 113–303. A single argument on Population runs through the whole, and is tolerably well enforced; but Population is the least subject of the book. The author treats Godwin and Condorcet with great candour and mildness; his language, indeed, and his turn of thought seem to have been formed very much in their school.[1] He refutes their notions on the subject of perfectibility with great ability; as a serious answer, his arguments are complete; but I doubt whether such doctrines as the organic improvement of man, the indefinite prolongation of human life, and the extinction of the sexual passion, are entitled to a serious confutation. I need none for myself. . . .

   1. The works of Marie Jean Antoine Nicolas Caritat, Marquis de Condorcet (1743–94) and William Godwin (1756–1836: *DNB*), were evidently among the first of Horner's readings on political economy. Condorcet's *Esquisse d'un tableau historique du progrès de l'esprit humain* (Paris, [1794]) was an attempted summary of the Enlightenment and a blueprint for what the author regarded as a coming utopia. In 1798 an English edition of Condorcet *On Population* was published in London, and it is apparently to that version that Horner refers (*HL* no. 97). Godwin's utopian doctrine was expressed most notably in *Enquiry Concerning Political Justice and its Influence on Morals and Happiness* (1793), and in *The Enquirer: Reflections on Education, Manners and Literature* (1797).

32. Journal

Kinnordy MSS ⟨Horner, i. 75–6⟩   25 Apr. 1799

⟨Began *Vie de M. Turgot*, by Condorcet, and read to p. 60.[1] Interesting in the highest degree, though somewhat too much of a panegyric; a little of the cant of philanthropy, and the style, though extremely elegant, rather laboured and heavy. But it is a book from which I may depend on deriving much advantage if read well; the development of the views of such a man as Turgot not only tend to enlarge our own views, but cherish that emulation and that admiration of genius, which are the great springs of intellectual improvement. I was much struck with the following observation:

> Se comparer aux autres hommes pour s'enorgueillir de sa supériorité, lui paroissoit une foiblesse: comparer ses connoissances à l'étendue immense de la nature, lui sembloit une philosophie fausse et propre à produire une inaction dangereuse. C'étoit entre ses connoissances personelles et celles qu'on peut avoir dans le siècle où l'on se trouve, qu'il croyoit qu'un homme raisonnable devoit établir cette comparaison, pour bien juger de l'étendue de ses propres lumières: et il n'est personne que cette comparaison ne doive encore rendre très modeste.⟩[2]

Finished the *Essay on Population*. What I read of it this evening contained discussions very different in their nature. The first consisted of some strictures on Adam Smith's idea, that every increase of national revenue is an increase of the funds for the maintenance of labour, and consequently meliorates the condition of the mass of society. Together with some remarks on the different definitions that are given by that author and by the Economists, of national wealth, these observations do not appear to be very profound, but they are plausible and ingenious. The two last Chapters of the essay are the worst it contains; together with some trial causes for the misery produced in society by the principle of population, we are presented with a mystical metaphysical theory of the evolution or existence of mind out of matter by the impressions and stimulants which are received during our situation on earth. I am not much versed in these sort of speculations, but I suspect this theory is by no means so original with respect to our author as he would hold out. It seems a mixture of Helvettius[3] and Godwin.

1. Murray apparently brought the English edition of Turgot's *Reflections on Wealth* and the first edition of Malthus's *Essay on Population* to Horner from London in July 1798. On 17 Aug. 1798 Horner noted in his journal (*Horner*, i. 68) that he had read parts of Turgot's *Reflections* and thought the work 'truly denominated, by Condorcet, the germ of Adam Smith's Inquiry'. Although there is no further reference to Turgot's economic writings in Horner's surviving notes and correspondence between August 1798 and April 1799, it is very probable that he perused the *Reflections* at some point during that period, that he came to regard Turgot as a key figure in the history of economic thought, and that he accordingly turned to Condorcet's *Vie de M. Turgot* for further insight. As *Horner* states (i. 75), he used the Berne 8vo edition of 1787.
2. Quoting from p. 51.
3. Claude Adrien Helvetius (1715–71), an Encyclopedist and disciple of Locke, published *De l'Esprit* in Paris in 1759. The work represented self-interest as the axis around which human affairs turned, reasoned within the pain–pleasure thesis of human behaviour, assessed the

social ramifications of an inequality of wealth, and argued that the state must redistribute wealth by gradually decreasing the size of landed estates and increasing the number of landlords. The Italian legal philosopher Cesare Beccaria was greatly influenced by the general arguments of Helvetius, as were the British Utilitarians.

33. Journal

Kinnordy MSS ⟨Horner, i. 76–7⟩ 27 Apr. 1799

⟨Proceeded with Condorcet, p. 135 to 193. I have now got to his sketch of Turgot's Philosophical Opinions. Here the author seems more at his ease, at least I have felt more at mine. The former part I read very curiously, though with considerable interest, because I did not find that the author entered sufficiently into detail, either of facts or reasonings, to excite me to investigation. But I have now found materials for reflection; and a single page in this part of the work occupies me as much as ten in the preceding. At the same time, I must remark an instance of the effect of habit, and the bad effect of giving way to the practice of reading without *l'attention suivie*: the discussion into which the author enters (before coming to the sketch I have spoken of), with respect to the conversion of indirect taxes into one direct territorial tax, gave me some difficulties, and I passed it over as a reserve for the second perusal. So much for pretending to read well!⟩

34. Journal

Kinnordy MSS 29 Apr. 1799

... Did a little on the subject of Population; that is to say, ran over one of Price's essays in his first volume of *Observations*,[1] but without really reading it – formed one or two conjectures – and wrote out some queries with respect to matters of fact.[2]

1. Horner refers to the fifth edition of *Observations on reversionary payments; on schemes for providing annuities for Widows* (2 vols, 1792), by Richard Price (1723–1791: DNB), author of the sinking fund (HL no. 111).
2. The published journal entry of this date relates that Horner was simultaneously reading the second volume of Gibbon's posthumous works, dwelling on the historian's journal of studies, and identifying with him. Next day, Horner admonished himself for not following a systematic plan of study and noted that he had reflected 'more than I ever did on the necessity of arranging my knowledge, on the limits within which I should confine myself in the pursuit of science, and on the advantage of having certain definite objects in view'. On 1 May he read Heineccius's sections on consensual and innominate contracts, Henry Addington's recent speech on the Irish Union, and pages 205 to 231 of Condorcet's *Vie de Turgot*. Then, following Gibbon's example, he wrote yet another plan of study that arranged his objects under four heads: law, physical science, political philosophy, and English composition. Second only to law in his stated priorities, but in fact clearly a first priority, was the further study of political philosophy, history, and natural jurisprudence.

'With respect to these studies,' he wrote in his journal, 'I am engaged in the first place by an essay on *Population* for the Academy.' After completing that essay, he planned to read Montesquieu's *Esprit des Lois*, to analyse the *Wealth of Nations*, to examine 'the system of the French Economists', and then, 'in order to correct the habit of mind that may thereby be formed, to give a little time to the perusal of books of fact, such as a few of the most classical histories, and one or two of the most judicious travellers' (*Horner*, i. 77–83).

35. Journal

Kinnordy MSS ⟨*Horner*, i. 83–4⟩   2 May 1799

⟨. . . Read Condorcet, *Vie de Turgot*, from p. 231 to 258, the end: upon the whole I have derived much pleasure from this book, and I think some instruction – that, however, not so much on the subject of political philosophy (for I met with little else than the assertion of opinions) as with respect to some more enlarged notions that it has given me on the subject of intellectual improvement and discipline, especially as to systematizing one's knowledge in the memory. The latter part of the volume I have read with great care, but I ran over the first half in so hasty a manner, that I am not entitled to think I have read the book, till after another perusal: I found it in that part too long and too short; too short in each article of the detail, and too long from the number that are brought together. The second perusal I must defer till I come to study the system of the Economists.⟩

36. Journal

Kinnordy MSS ⟨*Horner*, i. 88–91⟩   28 Aug. 1799

. . .

⟨In the afternoon, I employed my thoughts on the best plan of studying history – ran over Bolingbroke on this subject.[1] As I am about to enter on a course of historical and political reading, and am ambitious of studying those important subjects, not in an irregular miscellaneous manner, but with an attention to general principles, and a serious attempt to systematize the knowledge which I may be able to amass, it is of some importance, as conducive to that end, to form a distinct view of the objects I mean to pursue. At present, I am sensible it would be no easy matter for me to state to my own mind a distinct conception of those objects; but by endeavouring to arrange such floating ideas as are already in my head, it will be more easy for me to correct and to expand those ideas, as I make some progress in my investigations. Before I enter therefore upon these inquiries, I shall endeavour to form as accurate a notion as I am fit to form of the proper objects of history, of the best mode of studying it, and of the manner in which it should be combined with the elements of political philosophy, in order that each may throw light and strength on the other.

⟨I imagine the events of history might, with convenience, be divided into two classes; viz. *general* and *particular* – not that I mean, by the word general, any allusion to a classification into genus and species, but as such events as are not single, but made up of a number of particular occurrences, which altogether have such a relation and connection that they appear one great transaction. The American, or English, or French revolutions are what may be called *general* events; the reformation also, the revival of Letters, the irruption of the northern barbarians.

⟨Mr Hume has observed, and I believe with great truth, that it is of such general events alone of which we can attempt, philosophically, to investigate the causes; particular events depending on such complicated combinations of minute causes as we are quite unable to develop, and which we therefore denominate chance or accident.[2]

⟨The effect of particular events, however, it may frequently be interesting and useful to trace in the course of historical inquiries. But upon the whole, the consequences of any general event present a wider and more noble field of investigation.

⟨But I do not mean to affirm that the causes even of particular events are entirely to be overlooked; all speculations with respect to them may probably be resolved into the study of individual characters – and a most attractive study that will ever be found. Some authors, Tacitus and Davila especially, and perhaps De Retz, excel in this line of writing; they have been accused of refining too much sometimes; an error indeed which it must be extremely difficult to avoid. I must leave it among my desiderata upon [?the] subject, to settle the rules that ought to be attended to here, in order to reach the proper medium.

⟨With respect to the investigation of general events, Allen made an excellent observation to me this forenoon, when I was mentioning to him my plans of historical reading; he proposed to divide history into its general events, and, before studying, *tout de suite*, the annals of the world in chronological order, to take those great events, one after the other, and investigate their several causes and various consequences. I rather think this would be the best species of historical reading that I could possibly carry on, along with my political inquiries. I shall attempt to enumerate some of them:

1. The Feudal System; its rise, fall, consequences, and what the permanence of those consequences.
2. The Revival of Letters – prosecuting the history of European literature.
3. The Reformation – consequences upon science, letters, taste, politics, etc.
4. The French Revolution.
5. The Discovery of America.
6. The Influence of the commercial spirit on politics, letters, and manners of Europe.
7. The Rise and Establishment of Christianity, and of Mahometanism.
8. The Age of Lewis XIV.

⟨In order to assist me in the prosecution of these reflections, and to form proper notions on the true spirit of historical reading, I shall consult Bolingbroke and

Chesterfield; and extract from them what I find most worthy of notice. 'History is Philosophy teaching by examples.'[3]

⟨The plan I propose for the occupation of the ensuing two months is, all the morning to study history and politics; and, in the afternoon, rhetoric and composition: I shall begin with Smith's *Wealth of Nations*, next Voltaire's *Histoire Générale*, and then *L'Esprit des Lois*. My studies in rhetoric should consist chiefly of actual composition, and an attentive study of a few of only the best models.⟩

1. As always, Horner wrote out a new plan of study whenever it dawned on him that he had wandered from his last. His journal entry of 13 Nov. 1798 had set out rules for future intellectual development focusing on moral philosophy, law, history, politics, and a regular attendance at the Speculative, but those rules were not followed during the winter or spring and Horner squandered the summer of 1799 on superficial geological readings and activities. (Journal, 25 and 26 June, and 1, 2, and 8 July 1799, *Horner*, i. 85–6.) On 11 July 1799 he made the following marginal note on his journal entry of 13 Nov. 1798 (Kinnordy MSS):

> It is truly melancholy to find, that not one of these rules has ever been observed. I have studied no civil law, attended college very irregularly, fallen immensely behind in my Scots law notes, read hardly a paper of general science, and scarcely thought of the Speculative Society out of it, at least of its literary business. I have been always in the way of taking up books but I have *read* nothing.

2. See Doc. 67.
3. Letter 2 of Bolingbroke's *On the Study and Use of History*.

37. Journal

Kinnordy MSS   17 Sept. 1799

Studied the remainder of what Smith delivers on the subject of money; so far as he goes, he seems accurate, but he goes very little way. I should wish to investigate this subject completely; but for the present I must satisfy myself with knowing where the desiderata lie, without attempting to fill them up.[1]

1. Horner read parts of the *Wealth of Nations* during August and September 1799 and took several notes that he later incorporated with those resulting from his more systematic analysis in April and May 1801 (Doc. 74).

38. Journal

Kinnordy MSS ⟨*Horner*, i. 92⟩   3 Nov. 1799

⟨. . .

⟨I this day resumed, with Seymour,[1] the investigation we attempted last spring into the nature of probable evidence; taking Hume's Metaphysical Essays, by no means as our text-book or creed, but as furnishing topics for our own reflections.[2] Meta-physics I find a most improving exercise; fixing the powers of attention, and sharpening those of apprehension. Metaphysics and history, says Lord Bolingbroke in a very fine passage of his *Letters*, are the vantage grounds which a lawyer must seize, if he means to make a science of his profession.⟩3

1. On 29 Oct. Horner had written in his journal (*Horner*, i. 91):
> My two English friends, the Rev. Sydney Smith and Lord Webb Seymour, are again come to Edinburgh for the winter; and I promise myself much pleasure and much instruction from their conversation. I shall perhaps improve my powers of argumentative dexterity, which are still very low; and, at any rate, I cannot but learn candour, liberality, and a thirst for accurate opinions and general information, from men who possess in so remarkable degree these valuable dispositions.

Seymour became a member of the Academy of Physics, and Smith is thought also to have attended (Cantor, pp. 113–14).

2. Horner read from the two-volume edition published in 1793 (*HL* no. 82).

3. In letter 6 *Of the Study and Use of History* Bolingbroke wrote of the law:
> in its nature the noblest and most beneficial to mankind, in its abuse and debasement the most sordid and the most pernicious. . . . there have been lawyers who were orators, philosophers, historians . . . There will be none such any more, till in some better age, true ambition or the love of fame prevails over avarice; . . . Till this happens, the profession of the law will scarcely deserve to be ranked among the learned professions: and whenever it happens, one of the vantage-grounds to which men must climb is metaphysical, and the other historical, knowledge. They must pry into the secret recesses of the human heart, and become well acquainted with the whole moral world, that they may discover the abstract reason of all law; and they must trace the laws of particular states, especially their own, from the first rough sketches to the most perfect draughts; from the first causes or occasions that produced them, through all the effects, good and bad, that they produced.

For the remainder of the year Horner pursued an uncommonly regular course of legal study, dabbled with chemistry, and attempted to hone his skills in argument at the Speculative Society. On 13 Dec. he read a paper on 'Disposing Affinity' before the Academy of Physics. Apparently that paper has not survived, though according to Seymour he read another version to the Academy on 20 Feb. 1800. (Journal entries of 5 and 25 Nov., and of 3, 8, 13, and 31 Dec. in *Horner*, i. 92–9; Lord Webb Seymour's Diary, 20 Feb. 1800, Devon Record Office.)

39. To William Erskine

⟨*Horner*, i. 99–102⟩   Edinburgh, 23 Jan. 1800

⟨. . .

⟨Reddie, Brown, and I have lately projected a translation of the political and philosophical writings of Turgot, and we are anxious to engage you in the undertaking. There is no collection of those valuable dissertations even in the original language, and one only has hitherto appeared in English, so that the plan is a very promising one. Reddie, as you might guess, insists that his share in the execution should be kept a secret; Brown and Jeffrey make no objection of any kind; and Murray and Lord W. Seymour are both desirous to have a portion of the task allotted them. By means of this subdivision, I think it may be accomplished without toil to any one. I have written to a London bookseller (Johnson), to have his commercial opinion of the project. The works of Turgot which we have collected are, his letters on the corn laws, on provincial administrations, on the interest of money, on toleration, on the policy of the administration of mines, on the iron manufactory, his outlines of the theory of national wealth, five articles in the Encyclopédie, and a short letter on the poetry of savage nations: some others may perhaps be found by a more diligent search, but these alone would make a valuable present to the public; their contents are at once so important and so unknown.[1] We think it would be proper, too, to include a new translation of Condorcet's biographical account, with extracts from the more detailed memoirs of Dupuy.[2] That the translation might do us credit, and not be a mere job, it is proposed that each of us should not only subject his own translation to the criticism of the rest, but also undertake to revise that of his associates.[3]

⟨Professor Stewart has lately begun a course of lectures on Political Economy; and though his plan is not so comprehensive as he proposes to render it next winter, yet I promise myself great instruction; and I hope he will at least have the influence to make this captivating science more popular than it has been for some time past, and that he will render us familiar with those liberal enlarged views which he forms upon sciences. Hitherto he has been occupied with preliminary disquisitions on the history of the science, and the best mode of prosecuting its inquiries. We had an admirable lecture on Godwin's system; in the discussion of which Stewart displayed, with his usual eloquence, more than usual acuteness; at least it was quite a new view of that system to me, to consider it as a *reductio ad absurdum* of Hutcheson's principle of universal benevolence.[4] If you are willing to enter into a correspondence, I shall be very happy to give you an account of Stewart's speculations, as well as such other literary news as may occur from time to time.⟩

1. *Lettres sur les grains*; *Les principes de l'Administration provinciale*; *Mémoires sur le prêt à intérêt, et sur le commerce des fers*; *Le Conciliateur*; *Mémoire qui contient les principes de l'administration politique des carrières et des mines*; *Réflexions sur la formation et la distribution des richesses*; 'Etymologie', 'Existence', 'Expansibilité', 'Foires', and 'Fondations'; and 'Lettres sur les poésies erse' (Gustave Schelle, ed., *Œuvres de Turgot* (5 vols, Paris, 1913–23, i. 624–7).
2. Louis Dupuy, *Eloge historique de M. Turgot* [Paris, 1782].
3. Evidently the opinion of Joseph Johnson, the bookseller and publisher in St Paul's Churchyard, was against the project and it therefore never saw the light. (See Doc. 84.)
4. Francis Hutcheson (1694–1746: *DNB*), Professor of Moral Philosophy at Glasgow from 1729 until his death, was one of Adam Smith's teachers. His principal works were *Inquiry Concerning Moral Good and Evil* (1725) and *Ideas on Beauty and Virtue* (1725).

40. Journal

Kinnordy MSS ⟨Horner, i. 102–105⟩   2 Feb. 1800

⟨Plan. – I have long been feeding my ambition with the prospect of accomplishing, at some future period of my life, a work similar to that which Sir Francis Bacon executed almost two hundred years ago. It will depend upon the success and the turn of my speculations, whether they shall be thrown into the form of a discursive commentary on the *Instauratio Magna* of that illustrious author, or shall be entitled to an original form, under the title of a 'View of the Limits of Human Knowledge, and a System of the Principles of Philosophical Inquiry'.

‹I shall say nothing at present of the audacity of such ambition. No presumption is culpable, while it only stimulates to great undertakings; it becomes excessive when it appears ridiculous by the inadequacy of what is performed, when contrasted with what is attempted. If I have vanity enough to think myself – I do not say *equal* to such a scheme, but *capable* of rendering myself equal to it, I trust I shall retain pride and discretion enough to be conscious all along how far my acquisitions are adequate to my aims.

‹The chief difficulties I shall have to encounter, arise from the vast extent of the plan itself, from the necessity of making it but a secondary object during the greater part of my life, and from my natural indolence and versatility. To the proper remedy of these evils, and the proper counterpoise of these obstacles, I must pay a solicitous and persevering attention; above all, to the most effectual means of economizing intellectual labour, and of methodizing the distribution of time. But I do not mean to enter upon these details at present. My object in committing myself to paper on this occasion is very different. In order to reduce my views within the span of probable longevity, I must look forward with courage, but at the same time with discretion and prudence, to the *quantum* of science which it is practicable for me to attain, in compatibility with my professional pursuits, within the next twenty years. It is proper for me to know how much I should aspire to, and then to arrange the order of my journey. At present, I am of all men that pretend to be informed the most superficial: I have dabbled in languages, mathematics, chemistry, metaphysics, the fine arts, even physiology and physiognomy: on all of them I can talk very fluently before the ignorant, but on none of them am I profoundly, or even accurately, informed, or capable of thinking for myself, either with originality or with precision. I see therefore what remains to be done, viz. to take up one science after another, and work doggedly through its details; to content myself, as far as vanity is concerned, with the reputation, which every superficial man acquires, of being a profound *savant* on those subjects on which I still remain superficial; and, as far as ambition is concerned, to content myself with the consciousness that my claim to real information and science will be progressively augmenting.

‹Before I enter upon this course, I am not sure but it may be advisable to extend my surface a little farther; that is, previous to the particular investigation of any one science through its details, to make myself master of the elements merely of all the different sciences. This idea I adopt, not merely from a conviction, that it is in early life that elements are most easily acquired; but likewise from its appearing to suit more happily, than any other plan, the project I have in view as the end of all my labours. For by thus embracing an elementary view of all the sciences, I shall obtain probably, in the same proportion, an elementary and imperfect conception of that *Prima Philosophia* which I mean to extract from my studies.

‹So much am I convinced of the propriety of keeping my final object always in sight, and of making references to it in every state of my advancement, that I intend to attempt even at present, in the crude state of my elementary knowledge, a sketch of my ultimate plan. It will be the scrawl of a child, who has for the first time laid his hands on a pencil; without proportion, without transition, without mind, without shading, without perspective, almost without form.

⟨Sketch, etc. – 1. It will probably be long ere I can decide, whether the best plan is to throw the 'view of the object of science', and the 'system of logic', into two separate treatises, as Bacon has done, or to combine them into one great regular structure. At present I am disposed to prefer the latter idea; but I am still ignorant whether Bacon explains his reasons for adopting the other.

⟨2. Philosophy is the knowledge of those numerous existents or beings that compose the universe, and of those various events which compose the phenomena of the universe. The rules and method of philosophical investigation are directed to the means of acquiring and of preserving this knowledge with the greatest accuracy, security, and facility. A knowledge of the beings that compose the universe seems to consist in a proper classification of them; and constitutes Natural History. Such classifications appear at first sight to be nothing more than artificial assistances to memory: if they are nothing else, it remains to inquire, upon what general principles such classifications should be constructed, so as most effectually to answer the purpose which they are intended to serve. This discussion, however, belongs to another part of the arrangement; here we have only to determine how far the knowledge of existents lies in classification, and how far the utility of classification consists in aiding the memory.

⟨A knowledge of the *events* which compose the phenomena of the universe consists also in a classification of those events; in other words, in the reduction of them to general facts or events, which are commonly but improperly called *general laws*. There appears to be some essential and fundamental distinctions between this classification and the former, though I cannot yet point out on what it depends.⟩[1]

> 1. Leonard Horner observes that this 'plan' was written on a separate paper, that it was stitched into his brother's journal, and that the following note dated 12 July [?1800] was on the margin of the page (Horner, i. 105):
>> The annexed plan fell into my hands among other scrawls, and I looked at it as if it had fallen from heaven. I have an indistinct recollection, however, of having written this dream one rainy afternoon, when I dreamt of a resolution to be a great man. – 'Parce, PUER, stimulis, etc. -'

41. To the Duke of Somerset

BLPES i. 119–20 ⟨Horner, i. 106–109⟩   Edinburgh, 14 Feb. 1800

⟨I have⟩ long ⟨been prevented by indisposition from acknowledging the letter with which you lately honoured me, and in which you communicate to me some idea of your views with respect to the improvement of language. . . .[1]

⟨. . . Your condescension in writing to me upon the subject, encourages me to believe that mutual and free discussion was what you intended. I shall therefore make no apology for the metaphysical aspect of the present letter; into which I have been betrayed, by your compliment to Scotland for her attachment to a science as unalluring, it is usually conceived, as her own soil and climate. That compliment, my Lord, I swallowed with the more exquisite relish, under recollection of the mortification which I have often experienced in England, on account of the same national peculiarity. The unpopularity of metaphysics in England has retarded very much the general progress of the science. For we can scarcely preserve ourselves in Scotland from falling into a sort of sect, and yielding of course to the unphilosophical spirit of sectaries, sometimes perhaps to the still more unphilosophical temper of persecuted sectaries. In our moments of candour, however, we cannot fail to recollect, that whatever the case may be at present, the light of rational metaphysics first broke upon us from England, the venerable source of all our learning, and all our improvement. You can put no author in competition with Hume, for importance of metaphysical research and admirable perspicuity of metaphysical language; but his is the single name we can oppose to those of Locke and Berkeley. At the same time, it must be confessed, that the name of the latter illustrious man is almost forgotten in England; and a sound national [sic] Scotsman, priding himself sincerely on his admiration of Locke, might insinuate, perhaps with plausibility, that even that philosopher owes the reputation he enjoys among his countrymen more to his Whig pamphlets than to his *Essay on Human Understanding*.⟩

1. On 3 Dec. 1799 Horner had noted in his journal (*Horner*, i. 95) that, at Somerset's suggestion, he and Seymour were entertaining the idea of a philological society 'with a view to the invention of a real character' (as in *pasigraphy*, a system of writing for universal use, in which the characters were to represent ideas rather than words: see Doc. 78). Here he summarizes the difficulties of such an undertaking and lays out his views in much the same manner as he had done in Docs 11, 16, and 18.

42. Journal

Kinnordy MSS ⟨*Horner*, i. 109⟩   26 Mar. 1800

⟨In a fortnight it will be my turn to read a paper at the Speculative Society, for the subject of which I have chosen 'the Circulation of Money'. This forenoon I endeavoured to meditate, and made out a few queries; all I can hope to do for some days to come. . . .⟩[1]

1. Horner had apparently begun in mid-September 1799 to read up on the circulation of money (Doc. 37), perhaps with an eye to his paper for the Speculative. He continued to read the subject intermittently for some six months, but did not attack it systematically until mid-March 1800. On 21 Mar. he wrote in his journal, 'I find the circulation of money a very dark subject though a few gleams of light have struck me.' (Kinnordy MSS; erroneously combined with the journal entry of 26 Mar. in *Horner*, i. 109.) At that time Horner was attending Professor Stewart's lectures on political economy and again reading Adam Smith's chapter on money. From the first, it seems, Stewart's general comments on the circulation of money, Smith's omissions on the subject, and the mercantilist facets of Hume's 'Quality Theory Specie Flow Doctrine' convinced Horner that monetary theory was a fertile field in which to make his name.

43. Journal

Kinnordy MSS ⟨Horner, i. 109⟩   8 Apr. 1800

⟨The circulation of money I found a subject of too great difficulty; and what Smith and others have written on it too controvertible to allow me to draw up a paper on it within so short a time. After running myself within four days of this date, I have been forced to change the subject of my paper for the Speculative; and I read this evening some remarks on the influence of the great commercial metropolis on the prosperity of the state. I had often made this a topic of reflection; so that I had little to do but putting together. I rather congratulate myself that I wrote above one half of the disquisition at one sitting this forenoon, and that I read the whole of it from the first draught, without being reduced, as formerly, to the sad task of copying. I must now apply with unremitting diligence to Scots law, as I mean to pass my trials in the course of two months.⟩

44. 'On the Overgrowth of the Metropolis'

Kinnordy MSS   8 Apr. 1800

The great height which the Commerce and Wealth of Great Britain have attained, while it calls forth much congratulation from all good Citizens, is already become a topic of speculation with those whose profession or taste it is to doubt and to inquire about every thing. They profess some fears that our progress especially of late years, may have been too rapidly accelerated; and as a matter not of curiosity merely, but of anxious concern, they strive to conjecture from this influx and accumulation of commercial opulence, what revolutions may ensue in the government and manners of our own Country, or destinies of the great commonwealth of Europe.

An idea – somewhat akin to these alarms has gained a degree of currency of the overgrowth of the City of London, considered in its relation to the rest of the Country. Though more plausible perhaps to vulgar apprehension, this notion is evidently of a less enlightened complection than the former. It must be very liberal views of its own true interest, that will lead a state to call in question the soundness of that prosperity, which gives it a domineering empire over its neighbours. It requires but a very ordinary sense of self interest to suggest to a state or a town that the prosperity of a neighbour may be injurious to theirs. The speculation first mentioned would require a great compass of historical reasoning, and upon some future occasion I may have the honour of leading the Society into the investigation. But the other idea, which I have chosen as a subject of discussion for the evening, appears to me a prejudice which it will not be very difficult to overthrow.

Though in the following remarks I shall endeavour to turn the discussion upon general principles; yet I beg it may be understood, that it is chiefly the Capital of this empire which I have all along in view. In the present state of political science I am convinced much advantage is gained by moulding our abstract reasonings on the particular circumstances of a given instance; provided we are careful not to generalize our conclusions beyond the limits of the induction from which they are derived. It is evident that the degree of benefit or prejudice, with which a large Capital may be supposed to affect the country in which it is situated, must be various according to the circumstances of the Country and according to the circumstances of that City itself.

When the territories of a nation present a dull waste unanimated by trade, it is impossible they can be pervaded by the fashions, manners and literature of the great central town as when that centre shoots out ramifications of commercial intercourse intersecting the country through its whole extent. Those capitals which are composed almost entirely of the profuse, the vicious and the idle, such as are exhibited in the last days of a declining government and diseased legislation, must impart to the general system that corruption which they foster; and may with justice be described as overgrown, how contracted soever the circumference of their walls may be, and however small their population. But situated in an industrious, improving and enlightened country, over which it distributes the means of improvement while it exerts within itself the most sufficient resources of human industry, how such a Metropolis of such a country can by any growth become overgrown I am at a loss to imagine, nor can I devise within what terms we are to proscribe that magnitude and stature, by exceeding which the health and prosperity of the state are endangered.[1]

In order to bring the discussion into some shape, it is necessary to observe, that, in the first place, all great cities are understood to be destructive to population; in the second place, they are supposed to engender a dissolute profligacy of manners; and lastly it is sometimes represented that London, by its immense wealth monopolizes the trade of the island and maintains a disadvantageous balance against the rest of the Country.

1. Political Arithmeticians[2] assure us, that great towns are constantly draining the country of its inhabitants, for as the number of annual deaths within a city constantly exceeds in a large proportion the number of annual births, the difference can only be explained by a constant recruit from without; upon this show of arithmetical evidence, it is not difficult to frame a presumption that in furnishing such a supply the country delivers over a portion of the virtuous husbandman of her soil to the devouring abyss of debilitating and unproductive luxury, and in this manner, the characters and ratios of algebra are made to pander for topics of declamation, on the decay of agriculture, the corruption of morals, and the dissolution of empire. The calculations of Political Arithmeticians have not yet established their claim to implicit credit, whether we consider the immense number of facts from which every single calculation must be deduced, the extreme difficulty of ascertaining the accuracy of these fundamental *data* or the irreconcilable discrepancy of the results that are presented to us by different inquirers: the fact at present in question seems better ascertained indeed than almost any other in the statistical tables; but with respect to the real influence of great cities upon population, it is so far from being equivocal, that it leads to some inconsistent conclusions. The excess of deaths above the number of births, shows nothing further

than this, that the town affords maintenance and occupation to a greater number of human beings than are born within its walls. This may be explained by supposing that in consequence of luxurious manners and unhealthy situations, the number of yearly births being depressed below the natural rate of propagation, is not adequate to the consumption of the yearly subsistence and employment; or it may be explained by supposing that from the multiplication of productive power which is the consequence of the progressive subdivision of labour, the yearly supply of maintenance and employment exceeds the rate at which population naturally advances. These two suppositions are equally probable if the total number of Citizens has always remained the same, but if this number is increasing, which is unquestionably the case with London, the latter supposition is much more probable than the former.

But to confirm us the more in our distrust of all these calculations from the bills of Mortality, suppose the above-proportion exactly reversed; would the excess of births above deaths be a symptom of a less dubious appearance? Such an excess would certainly accompany a constant decrease; But neither excess affords of itself a sure indication of the real increment or decrement of numbers; because both excesses may be produced by other combinations of circumstances. An emigration of inhabitants from a town would make the births exceed the deaths, and an influx of inhabitants would make the deaths appear more numerous than the births. The Bills of Mortality in China must make the deaths all over the empire, exactly equal to the births; but when the deserts of Muscovy and Lapland were pouring their starved barbarians upon the Roman Empire, the births – if numbered – would have always exceeded the deaths. In London the deaths are said to be more numerous. In Paris on the contrary, the births more numerous. Shall we therefore affirm that London is destructive to Population and Paris favourable? or shall we not more reasonably conclude that such estimates furnish no decision upon the subject.

But if it were accurately true, that in great cities the increase of population is repressed by the prevalence of luxiourious [sic] habits, and even by the physical obstacles of an impure atmosphere and want of exercise, the whole population of the Kingdom would not therefore be exposed to diminution. – It is the excess of resources alone that draws a supply from the country; suppose that supply to be granted, and there remains an excess of resources in the Country itself, where no obstacles exist to the action of that great participle of nature, which repairs the devastation of pestilence or of war, and will effectually counteract that influence by which commercial prosperity may be alledged [sic] to waste the numbers of the human species. If there is a demand from the Capital for inhabitants, the country will produce and rear such an additional number of men, as may answer that demand, besides maintaining its own stock. The whole numbers of the Kingdom will at least suffer no real diminution and instead of the villages being drained of inhabitants, population will there assume a more thriving appearance. Many whose infant constitution would have withered under the chilling air of penury are preserved to augment the mass of active industry, and many are restored to the propensities of nature whom the prospect of scanty subsistence had condemned to barrenness.

2. It is however a very partial view of the influence of commercial cities upon the

general population of a state to represent them merely as deriving from its fruitfulness a compensation for their own deficiency. By distributing a portion of the riches that are poured in by trade, as still more by diffusing the spirit and habits of industry, a powerful excitement is maintained to call forth the resources of the country itself, and to open those stores of opulence which nature confers with multiplied increases on the exertions of agricultural labour. It is sufficient to percieve [sic] an augmentation in the wealth and produce of a nation, without demanding a further proof of the increase of its population; for in every point of view, we trace the great physical law of animal reproduction, by which numbers are kept on a level with the means of subsistence.

However abundant the wealth which a great city may derive from foreign Commerce, it is dependent on the Country which surrounds it for the original supply of rude produce, not only for its own consumption but for what it manufactures with a view to foreign exchange. No increase it is evident can take place either in its consumption or in its foreign trade, without a proportional increase of demand upon the Country for rude materials; the raising of which is by far the most productive employment, to which the labour of the country can be turned. Every enlargement therefore of commercial and manufacturing enterprise gives a new impulse to agricultural industry.

But in return for the rude produce which the Country furnishes the Capital, it can only receive some portion of the same produce manufactured in different shapes, or some portion of the foreign commodities which have been purchased with such manufactures. No increase it is evident can take place with the quantity of rude produce which the Country sends into the Capital without a proportional increase in the quantity of foreign or manufactured commodities which the Country receives in pay. Every improvement therefore of agricultural industry multiplies the accommodations of agricultural life.

It is in this manner that commercial opulence invigorates the general industry of the Country; not only by holding out a constant demand for the produce of that industry, but by creating among the furnishers of rude produce a reciprocal demand upon the industry of the Merchant and Manufacturer, a taste is diffused for foreign luxuries and the productions of Manufacturing ingenuity; enjoyment heightens the relish; conveniences successively take their place among the necessities of life, and the ornamental devices of a moment are often adopted as conveniences not to be dispensed with.

While it communicates these habits of industry and this taste for the accommodations of polished society the great Metropolis of the Kingdom affords in a great measure, the funds and stocks by which the industry of the Country is rendered effective.

When commerce is conducted on a large scale, the profits of trade become proportionably [sic] smaller; and for the same reason it can afford a much slower return of Capital. Those who bestow any reflection on the present unparalleled prosperity of Great Britain, must have learned that, while ready Money is in almost every instance paid to the Merchants of the Continent for the commodities which they furnish, a long credit, generally of a twelve months duration, is granted to them for the purchases which they make of our Manufactures or Merchandise. It is evident that this must not only secure to Britain a predominating influence in the foreign market; but must powerfully contribute to the encouragement of industry abroad, by the augmentation which the Capital of those foreign traders necessarily receives in consequence of so long a credit. Now the same relation that Britain holds in this respect to the other commercial nations of the world, London the centre of British commerce, holds to the rest of the island. When a merchant at Manchester or at Glasgow ships goods for London the same post carries the invoice and a bill drawn payable at sight; when this Merchant orders goods from London he is allowed sometimes three months, but more frequently six months credit. The capital of the Country Merchant returns to him immediately; that of the London Merchant does not return till after it has remained some time in the hands of the Country Merchant; who, by means of this credit, can bring into his trade, not only his own capital which returns to him so fast, but a certain portion of the Capital belonging of [sic] the different London Merchants with whom he has transactions, and which they consent that he should return to them slowly.

London, therefore, is the great organ of commercial circulation,[3] in which [?as] the common centre all the channels of trade terminate, and from which the vital stream of industry is impelled through the whole system.

3. But while we thus acknowledge the benefit which an extensive territory derives from a great commercial Metropolis, there may be some reason to doubt whether its prosperity is equally favourable to the character of its own inhabitants. This point of view indeed gives a sort of vantage ground to those who indulge themselves in deploring the corruption of public spirit and of public Morals. It furnishes for their dismal pictures, some groupes [sic] which we recognize as brought from real life. There is not at this moment a Capital in Europe which does not openly exhibit the most profligate violation of every principle of Morality; and in which a vast number of human beings are not immersed in the gratification of every licentious passion, or engaged in the systematic pursuit of every species of crime. 'Divitiæ invexere avaritiam, et abundantes voluptates desiderium per luxum atque libidinem pereundi perdendique omnia.'[4]

That such disorders actually exist and to a degree of enormity which no sophistry can palliate, it would be vain to dispute; they strike too obviously not to command the earliest notice of every spectator, and too strongly not to leave the deepest impression. I shall not however hesitate to affirm that such evils do not necessarily flow from the wealth which a City derives from commerce; but on the contrary that, the only hope of alleviating such irregularities in the political system lies in the assistance which the commercial spirit naturally contributes in seconding the establishment of wise laws.

That the Wealth with which commerce overflows modern nations, must be as essentially different in its consequence to their welfare, as in the mode of its acquisition from that which ruined the republics of Antiquity, is a general remark of common place notoriety, but its application is too much neglected in the detail of political reasonings. The treasures which occasional conquests transferred to Rome accumulated all at once in the hands of some individuals the means of venality, dissipation and faction. The riches which commerce pours into London, flow with a steady and equable stream, and distribute through the various classes of the industrious the just rewards of their labour, their diligence and their skill. When money by the influence of some Malignant star is suddenly showered into the coffers of the idle, all those passions that idleness begets are let loose to prey upon the community. But the regular replacement of mercantile capital, breathes health and activity through the political fabric, realizing in the course of its circulation the credit that has already been advanced and fixing in its natural representative the labour which has already been expended. In proportion as the Capital employed is more extensive, the accumulation of profits will form a larger heap, and opulence will flow back – with more abundance; but the capital employed can only become more extensive by bringing more industry into action, and the progress of commercial wealth cannot be accelerated, except by quickening the rate at which it is distributed through all the productive labourers of the Nation. It ought, on no account, therefore, to be placed on the same footing with that Wealth, which was amassed in ancient times by violence and rapine, and was dispersed in feeding the idle and bribing the corrupt; nor ought the mercantile circulation of property which enriches equally the hand that receives, and that which gives away, to be confounded with the exchanges that subsist between the prodigal and those who seduce him to profusion. The former constitutes the life of the political union; the latter seems a hereditary disease with which its constitution is tainted.

The degree in which prodigality and its consequences to public character must be limited, I apprehend by the degree in which industry and Economy predominate. In other words, the influence of that luxury which is baneful to the manners of a people must bear an inverse proportion to the enlargement of Commerce.

But while nature seems thus to have herself provided a counteraction for her own irregularities, much is yet left to the wisdom of man, for the first principle of legislation is to beware of offering violence to her provisions by expedients of artificial institution. The second enjoins us to devise such laws as shall most effectually second her various provisions, and direct their operation to the happiness and tranquillity of the human race. But immense as the progress is which we have made in this matter of experience, no self congratulation should blind us to the disorders by which the political system is still deformed. The enormities that range our Metropolis in defiance of public decency, and in a systematic war upon private rights, might recall to our imagination these scenes of licence and depredation which are described by the philosophical poets to have preceded the establishment of property and the institution of Marriage. That law is adequate to the restraint of these disorders, no one will presume to doubt who knows the situation which he holds with all its rights and all its comparative security, amidst the complicated Mechanism of Society, nor can any one reflect on what law has already accomplished and prescribe a limit to its future achievements. No field opens so promising a harvest to the exertions of legislative genius, as the reformation of the criminal code and of those arrangements which affect the purity of manners. I am not a very sanguine advocate for the metaphysical hypothesis of perfectibility; but I am sanguine as to the influence of public opinion if properly directed in restraining the excesses of immorality: and I am sanguine as to the power of laws if framed with wisdom in detecting and punishing crimes. While the planet on which we live shall revolve in the present system, a portion of her inhabitants seems doomed by a fixed law of nature to poverty and to guilt; but the laws which men make for themselves should give all an equal chance, and counterbalancing the caprices of fortune by industry, and destroying by means of knowledge one prolific source of vice, should confine that sad destiny as much as possible to the victims of innate depravity and irreclaimable passion.

After having allowed the full extent of the immoralities that prevail in our commercial Metropolis as well as in other great cities, it is necessary to recollect that they occupy a very small proportion in the immense scale of transaction which it comprehends. The least quantity of evil is unquestionably the test by which political prosperity is to be tried; but that *minimum* of evil must be measured not by its own magnitude, but by its proportion to the quantity of good. The disorders by which our police is disgraced would scarcely perhaps depress the balance against those splendid exhibitions of public benificence [sic] which justly distinguish from all other countries the Metropolis of the English Nation. But these disorders to use Milton's expression would quick fly up, etc., were we to place in the opposite scale the accumulated stock of private virtues and private talents. For the incidents of Municipal notoriety, like the events of historical record consist in the irregularities with which human intercourse is disfigured; while the domestic and unobtrusive portions of industry, liberality, honour, intelligence are lost in the undistinguishable frequency of their occurrence. The Metropolis may be viewed as an unbound theatre, on which all the varieties of human character are performed, and all the catastrophes of human life mingled in one representation; all the virtues and all the vices of our mind are indulged to an extreme; every passion finds its object, and every talent its field of display. It is the intricacy of the drama that makes us exclaim against the size of the stage; and I am persuaded that the Magnitude of London and its transactions, has more frequently given birth to the opinion of its being overgrown, than any distinct deduction of the consequences with which that Magnitude may be accompanied. The Shepherd's boy, in Virgil, had framed to himself a conception of Rome, upon the model of the hamlet in which he was born; the rivulet, the downs, and the well known beech trees marked out an object which his fancy could embrace without effort. But the endless diversity of occupations, the infinite subdivisions of pursuits, in which the thousands of a great Capital are constantly engaged, the undefinable shades of character and varieties of genius, and combinations of passion, that are perpetually shifting before our sight, exhibit no arrangement on which our thoughts can distinctly dwell and abandon our imagination to all the restlessness of distracted curiosity and unrelieved amazement. To reduce it to a subject of practicable discussion, we must analyse it into a few particulars: and our conclusion with respect to the overgrowth of London, will probably be determined by those results which we obtain in tracing its influence on manners, on trade, and on population.

1. Throughout life, Horner's economic doctrine was greatly influenced by the published works of David Hume, most notably by Hume's essays 'Of Money', 'Of Interest', 'Of Taxes', and 'Of Public Credit' which were first published in 1752 in his *Political Discourses* (Hume, i. 309–21, 321–30, 356–60, and 360–74). In this paper Horner almost certainly leaned heavily on Hume's celebrated distinction between wealth generated by conquest and wealth generated by commerce as well as on Hume's general argument that the lively flow

of capital generated by manufacturing within a system co-ordinated by commerce promoted general happiness, led to the growth of knowledge, nurtured humane feelings,
enhanced social harmony, and stimulated political liberty.

2. Here, Fontana, p. 50, suggests, Horner had in mind George Chalmers, *An Estimate of the
Comparative Strength of Great Britain* (1782). Horner certainly had a low opinion of
Chalmers (see also Docs 109 and 412); but Professor Winch has suggested to the editors
that the more likely target here is Richard Price, whose gloomy predictions about cities and
depopulation Adam Smith helped Chalmers refute.

3. *I find it asserted by Talleyrand, that almost all the bills drawn by America upon the
continent are made payable in London.

4. Livy, I, pref. 112.

45. Journal

Kinnordy MSS   17 Apr. 1800

Three hours in the forenoon on the subject of *Redeemable Rights*. – In the evening at
the Academy, where Jeffrey read a paper on productive and unproductive labour; he
denies the distinction; but I think the circumstance of immediate consumption in
the one case, and of permanent exchangeable value in the other, is sufficient to
afford foundation for a distinction when we regard the effects of the two kinds of
labour upon the increase of national wealth.[1] – After the Academy, Brown, Jeffrey
and I supped with Hamilton in Hill Street; where we met L.D. Campbell, the editor
of Hugh Boyd's works, and of the new *Asiatic Register*, nothing remarkable in the
man, one way or other.[2]

1. This appears to be the last mention Horner made of the Academy, which after three years
of regular meetings, seems to have held its last meeting on 1 May. Apparently at Horner's
own suggestion and in concert particularly with Brougham and Dr John Thomson, it was
then merged with the Natural History Society to form a new Chemical Society. (Thomson
to Allen, n.d., John Thomson, William Thomson, and David Craigie, *An Account of the
Life, Lectures, and Writings of William Cullen* (2 vols, 1859), i. 15–16; Cantor, pp. 111–12;
and *Horner*, i. 112.)

2. Alexander Hamilton (1762–1824: *DNB*), a distinguished orientalist, was one of the first
contributors to the *Edinburgh Review*. After the breakdown of the Peace of Amiens he was
imprisoned by the French but released in 1806, becoming Professor of Sanskrit and Hindu
Literature at Haileybury. Lawrence Dundas Campbell, editor of *The Miscellaneous Works of
Hugh Boyd, the author of the Letters of Junius with an account of his Life and Writings* (2 vols,
1800), commenced *The Asiatic Annual Register* in 1800 and continued it until 1811.

46. Journal

Kinnordy MSS ⟨*Horner*, i. 111⟩   11 May 1800

⟨Did not read a syllable of Scots law, but lounged all the morning over some
commercial details,[1] till Brougham called on me, in company with Miller,[2] who is
come to town with a view of passing his trials in civil law. Walked out with my

father to dine with Sir Patrick Inglis.[3] As we went along, I got some valuable commercial information. Indeed, if I were awake to the opportunities that I daily possess, I might receive from my father a great deal of information in that line; to an extensive experience, he has added the habit of viewing that experience upon enlightened general principles.⟩

1. Although Horner studied law with especial diligence during the spring of 1800, his interest in political economy continued to mount, no doubt owing to Professor Stewart's lectures. On 18 Apr. he noted in his journal that Stewart had given an account of the poor laws of England and Scotland. On 8 May he read parts of Isaac Pinto's *Circulation and credit*, and at this point his mind began to turn to the details of commerce, from which he hoped to glean 'particular facts' either supporting or challenging established principles. (See the journal entries of 18 Apr. and 8 May in *Horner*, i. 110–11.)
2. *[Thomas Hamilton Miller (d. 1843) was the] ⟨Son of Mr [Patrick] Miller of Dalswinton, in Ayrshire.⟩
3. *⟨His father's partner in business. – Ed.⟩ [Sir Patrick Inglis, the 5th and last Bart of Cramond, died unmarried in Nov. 1817. According to the notes made by Mrs Byrne in her copy at Kinnordy of *Horner*, he was a weak individual and an incompetent businessman whom her father had to carry.]

47. Journal

Kinnordy MSS ⟨*Horner*, i. 112–13⟩   26 May 1800

⟨Another day of chemical dissipation. In the afternoon, I met Kennedy and Thomson, and enjoyed a miscellany of chemical conversation. I went with Kennedy to see the manufacture of tobacco-pipes, which is a very neat operation.[1] A knowledge of the arts, as they are practised in different parts of the country, is what I am desirous to possess on many accounts; but especially the subserviency of such knowledge to the study of political economy. To collect information from workmen is a matter of some address, for they are in general mere machines, and not unfrequently more ignorant, literally speaking, than the tools which they employ. I may gain sufficient practice of this address in the few manufactories that are in the neighbourhood of this place, to prepare me for more ample opportunities. But I must reflect on the best mode of acquiring this *habileté* of interrogating the lower orders; Locke and Franklin are said to have possessed this power in an eminent degree; the latter acquired it of course spontaneously by his early habits, the former must have made it a matter of study.⟩

1. Readings and experiments in chemistry detracted from Horner's legal studies no less than from readings in political economy during the spring of 1800. On 19 May he noted in his journal 'that my objects must be simplified, my views systematized, my ambition concentrated'. Next evening, however, he confessed that despite the near approach of his Scots law trials, 'the day was given up to a chemical debauch'. On 24 May Horner, Seymour, and Kennedy attended the Chemical Society and 'arranged the business that is to occupy us during the summer'. Their plan, which allied chemistry and political economy – now Horner's two favourite branches of learning – called for an examination of the chemical processes employed in manufacturing via on-site visits to a number of local

factories. (*Horner*, i. 111–12.) According to a note on the copy of this letter at Kinnordy, 'Kennedy' was Dr Robert Kennedy, FRSE (d. 1803), a physician, rather than the individual of the same name mentioned in Doc. 151.

48. Journal

Kinnordy MSS ⟨*Horner*, i. 114⟩   7 July 1800

⟨I had quite forgot my journal; my life for some weeks past has been pretty uniform.[1] I have to walk the Outer House[2] every forenoon; which gives me a constant headache, and debilitates me for the remainder of the day. I have had three or four causes to study, which have been my sole occupation in that way: even my favourite chemistry has been neglected till this day.

⟨I have been with Seymour and Kennedy to visit the manufactory of steel at Cramond; we got a tolerable notion of the process, and are to take another view of it next Friday. I hope I shall regularly persevere in my plan of acquiring a knowledge of the various arts and manufactures, on which so much of the prosperity, independence, and happiness of this country depends. The manufacture of iron, in its various stages, presents itself as the most prominent object in such a survey; iron is not only the soul of every other manufacture, but the main-spring perhaps of civilized society. The study of this, in its various relations, is a most complicated subject, and will require a comprehensive survey. I shall keep a journal of my progress in this speculation.⟩[3]

1. Horner had stood and passed his Scots law trials on 6 June (*Horner*, i. 113).
2. ⟨*The old Parliament House, the Westminster Hall of Edinburgh.⟩
3. Apparently this journal has not survived.

49. Journal

Kinnordy MSS   23 July 1800

. . .

This afternoon and evening, I studied with some degree of attention, and a moderate degree of ease, the iron manufacture considered in a general political view.[1] Without opening a book, I endeavoured to draw from my own source, and made some advances in a collection of queries and notes for investigation. Taking up this insulated manufacture I am endeavouring to draw out in the first place such a sketch or map of the subject, as will both guide my inquiries into the matter of fact, and serve as an artificial memory for the recollection of such information as I may think up. In the second place, by analysing theoretically and a priori the economy of the iron manufacture, and by reason on the establishment both in this commercial and opulent country, and in the general system of European markets, I hope either to strike out some general views with regard to the principles of manufacturing industry or to obtain illustration and corrections of such as I have already made familiar to my mind. The only speculation of the kind that I pursued this evening, related to the proper distinctive use of the expression – raw material, a few remarks on which I wrote out. Some other views suggested themselves to me, which I hope to examine tomorrow.

I may reckon fully *eight* hours this day of decent study; besides two hours I enjoyed in conversation with my friend *Allen*.

1. On 12 July, when the law session closed, Horner noted in his journal that he was 'delivered from few fees and many headaches'. That afternoon he again visited the steel factory at Cramond and 'gathered some additional information'. On 17 July he read 'part of a memoir, inserted among those of the Academy for 1786 [sic], drawn up by Vandermonde, Berthollet, and Monge, on the manufacture of iron' ([Alexandre Théophile Vandermonde, Gaspard Monge et Ch.-L. Bertholet], 'Avis aux ouvriers en fer', *Mémoires de l'Institut national des sciences et arts: sciences morales et politiques*, i (Paris, 1796). On 20 July he lighted his furnace for the first time, noted the folly of a 'Scots lawyer spending the live long day in distilling sulphuric acid!', but rationalized that chemical experiments enhanced his understanding of 'the principles of philosophical inquiry' and were therefore compatible with the study of law. (*Horner*, i. 114–15.)

50. Journal

Kinnordy MSS ⟨Horner, i. 117⟩   5 Aug. 1800

⟨Still I am loitering.[1] The late trials in England for forestalling and engrossing,[2] are talked of as such a complete refutation of the speculations of theorists on the subject of the corn trade, that I was driven to re-peruse Smith's noble chapter on it; and I have risen from it once more with the most thorough satisfaction in the profoundness and accuracy of his reasonings. In spite of Lord Kenyon, and the juries who have agreed with him in opinion, regrating is a public benefit; and whenever it is practised with a different intention, or with a different tendency, it provides for itself the most ample and efficacious punishment.

⟨Besides these reflections, the perusal of this beautiful chapter of Smith, on the Corn Trade, has suggested to me the propriety of studying his work as a model of argumentative composition. I should imagine, that his style of reasoning, so artificial and yet so perspicuous, so ingeniously minute and yet so broad and comprehensive, would be admirably adapted to the subjects of law. A treatise of law written in such a manner would be a masterpiece; nor would it be less suited, I apprehend, even to pleadings at the Bar. Spent the evening with Allen.⟩

1. Horner noted on 4 Aug. (*Horner*, i. 116–17) that he had been 'indulging for some days past in the indolence of miscellaneous reading', that a perusal of Hume's historical writings had aroused in him dreams of eighteenth-century British history, and that he was 'alternately intoxicated with visions of historic laurels and of forensic eminence'.
2. The terms 'forestalling', 'engrossing', and (below) 'regrating' refer to the operations of middlemen between producers and consumers. Until 1800 such practices were held to be a

violation of the Corn Laws and middlemen were prosecuted despite the critical observations advanced in Smith's *Wealth of Nations*. In 1800 a British subject bought wheat at 41/- and sold it at 43/-. He was tried before Lord Kenyon, who referred critically to Smith's observations in his remarks to the jury, and the conviction opened the door to some four hundred prosecutions. A great deal of protest erupted, a division of judicial opinion ensued, and prosecutions were discontinued. (*R. v. Rusby*, in T. Peake, *Additional Cases in Nisi Prius*, p. 189; see also Doc. 70.)

51. Journal

Kinnordy MSS ⟨Horner, i. 117–18⟩   7 Aug. 1800

⟨In the evening of yesterday, and this forenoon, I have read a Memoir by Talleyrand on the commercial relations of England and the United States of America.[1] That intriguing politician visited the American republic within these few years; and though we cannot, under the recollection of the infamous negotiations at Paris, trust him as an impartial judge of American manners and character, yet this memoir challenges in every page the acknowledgement, that he had observed them with a penetrating eye, and has delineated them with a nervous pencil. It is easy to detach the parade of unnecessary abstractions, with which, like the present French writers of every class, he has thought it necessary to introduce and to close his dissertation; and it requires no extraordinary vigilance to be aware of the false refinement, by which he endeavours to resolve all the peculiarities of the American character into a single passion: but with this caution, and after this separation, I have found in this memoir several most important views of the commercial relations, the domestic manners, and the national character of the United States. The style is mixed like the substance, but the good predominates greatly; for, independent of some affected conceits, and a few idiomatic inelegancies (if I may presume to judge of such a matter), his composition abounds in excellent characteristic painting. This Memoir is in Vol. II, *Sciences Morales et Politiques* of the Memoirs of the National Institute.

⟨In the evening, studied some pages of Turgot's *Lettres sur les Grains*, with a view to make myself master of this important subject. This has been in some degree a day of study; yet, as in my late days of idleness, both chemistry and law have been neglected.⟩

1. Charles Maurice de Talleyrand-Périgord, Prince of Benevento (1754–1838), 'Mémoire sur les relations commerciales des Etats-Unis avec l'Angleterre', *Mémoires de l'Institut national des sciences et arts: sciences morales et politiques*, ii (Paris, 1797).

52. Journal

Kinnordy MSS ⟨Horner, i. 118–19⟩   10 Aug. 1800

⟨After reading a little Scots law, I went to sit with Murray, who is confined; we went over together those fine chapters of Tacitus in which he delineates the death of Britannicus, and the first development of Nero's savage disposition.

⟨Till the heat of the day was over, I indulged my listless imagination with some pages of Price *On the Picturesque*;[1] I then took up Turgot's *Lettres sur les Grains*, which I studied with deep attention for above three hours. The admirable views that are opened up in every page of this little book, not only on the subject of the corn trade, but with respect to the various relations of political society, must afford me incalculable instruction, if studied throughout with as eager and profound attention as I have been able to exert this evening.⟩

> 1. Sir Uvedale Price, *An Essay on the Picturesque* (2 vols, London and Hereford, 1794–8), developed the author's views on garden landscape and natural beauty.

53. To William Erskine

⟨Horner, i. 121⟩   23 Sept. 1800

⟨... It may reasonably be questioned whether, upon the common chances of probability, we can expect the progress of national instruction to go on so rapidly, as to keep down the baleful effects of overgrown commerce, and to repress the growth of that odious character which a nation receives from the combination of opulence and ignorance. Am I too sanguine, or am I even correct, in fancying that some good effects may result from a fashion which carries the Edinburgh citizen to the lakes of Westmoreland, and brings the London citizen to the falls of the Clyde? ...⟩

54. Notes on Smith's *Wealth of Nations*[1]

Kinnordy MSS   October 1800

1. (II. 74.)[2] This paragraph suggests several doubts and inquiries. What is the system of the inland corn trade in England and Scotland? Is the great bulk of the grain annually consumed raised in particular districts, or are the consumers over the country in a great measure supplied from the lands in their vicinity? Large towns, it is evident, must draw their supply in a great proportion from a distance; the County of Midlothian does not raise ⅓ of its own consumption, and London must require a supply equal to the produce of several counties. It is obvious, therefore, that some

counties both in England and Scotland must raise a produce much greater than their own consumption. What, then, is the general system of markets throughout the country in this great branch of inland trade?

First, what are the districts of the island in which a produce is annually raised that exceeds the annual consumption of the neighbourhood? to what markets, respectively, do such [districts] send their surplus? and to what circumstances either of physical situation and soil, or of accidental improvement, is the superior production of each to be ascribed?

Secondly, from which particular districts of the country are the chief towns supplied?

Thirdly, is it a regular practice in any districts both to export and import grain; or does every district, that can afford to export a surplus, reserve its own supply out of its own crops?

Fourthly, in the general system of the trade, how many traders intervene between the cultivator and the consumer?

If it is true, that 'the corn which grows within a mile of the market fetches the same price as that brought from a distance',[3] the fact seems to suggest a modification of certain principles, which, in other respects, are well established. – Wherever the seller meets with rivals in the market, he will be disposed to content himself with what is called the natural price of his commodity, or with a price which replaces the stock and wages he has advanced together with a fair ordinary profit. If by residing nearer the market than his rivals, he saves the expense of carriage, it is evident that the whole sum he advances is less by this saving than what it is necessary for his competitors to advance; and his commodity may be sold in the market for a less price than that of his competitor, and yet secure to himself exactly the same profit. It is clearly for his interest to undersell his rivals, because a small increase of profit, upon a given quantity of goods, can never in the end prove so lucrative as an increase in the quantity of goods sold at the fair ordinary profit. – How then does it happen, that the farmer in the vicinity of the market does not undersell the farmer at a distance? it can only be from this reason, that it is not in the power of the farmer, as it is in the power of the manufacturer, to increase his commodity at pleasure. The fields in the vicinity of the town are unable to furnish a sufficient supply; the market is under the necessity of receiving additional supplies from a distance; but it is equally necessary that the farmers, who send grain from a distance, should have the natural profit upon their stock. Their grain must fetch a price, which shall afford them that profit, besides replacing the advances. It would be to no purpose, therefore, that the farmers in the neighbourhood should undersell those at a distance; for the town must buy the corn of the latter, and they must have the natural price.

I cannot make *the comparison* which Smith desires, in any instance that affords a confirmation of his remark. At London, Edinburgh, and many other cities that might be named, the fact is notoriously the reverse. In spite of the advantages of manure, the cultivators around Edinburgh acknowledge their vast inferiority to those of Berwickshire, Moray, and the Carse of Gowrie. There is not a field of wheat to be seen within many miles of London; and scarcely a road branches from that vast metropolis, which does not lead, within an hour's ride, to extensive tracts of uncultivated land. – B[ook] IV. *Wealth of Nations*; chap. 8. p. 259.[4] I think it has been asserted that much of the French Revolution, both in its good and bad circumstances, has been owing to the doctrines of the Economists. If this conjecture be well-founded, how short-sighted was Smith, when he thought so contemptuously of the possible consequences of that system! He regarded it indeed as merely speculative, but it would [appear?] that this very circumstance has rendered it pernicious.

WEALTH OF NATIONS. I.

p. 110.[5] In visiting any country or great town, this should always be one of my questions, as leading to an estimate of its state in the progression of prosperity: viz., what is the legal interest and what is the market rate of interest? The height of the rate of interest will show, by the rule of direct ratio, the profits of stock; and that, by the rule of inverse ratio, the capital of stock. – and according as the market interest stands with respect to the rate which is established by law, so we have the means of determining whether the fluctuation of profits have been in the prosperous or retrograde direction.

p. 111.[6] This is an instance of the bad effects of chopping the materials of a sentence into different periods. By this dissolution of thought, real obscurity is produced. For the several circumstances, which are only accessory, being here thrown into distinct sentences, are thereby rendered principals; and the distinction of light and shade, if we may [say] so, is totally lost.

p. 19.[7] The student of human nature should give particular attention to the rank which man holds in the creation, ascertaining by observation and inquiry his rank in the visible creation, and ascertaining by just reasoning and scientific deduction what rank he holds in that part of the creation which is not laid open to our senses. The observations which Smith has here thrown out, on the propensity to contract and traffic, may suggest some hints on the mode of prosecuting this important and interesting subject. The reciprocal and reactive connection which he points out between this propensity and the inequality of human talents, give a glimpse of that unity of design which appears to pervade every portion of Nature; and seems to show, that whereas animals have so far an affinity with the human race as to preserve the scale of being, and constitute them both parts of one common world, yet the differences which distinguish man from the lower species are so intimately blended with the animal principles of his constitution and at the same time so wonderfully consistent and congenial among themselves, as to present in man, to the attentive and meditating eye, an image as it were of a world within himself.

p. 73.[8] The secret may be concealed with greatest ease and certainty, when the change of price consists in a sinking of the natural price, not in an increase of the market price. For the same market price, the same quantity of labour – or commodities – or of money that is actually given to the seller, may, in different circumstances, bear a very different proportion to the natural price. For instance, if a manufacturer discovers a cheaper method of manufacturing his commodity, though the market price continues exactly the same as before, yet it is more above the natural price than before, and he is paid more for his commodity. It should be the business, therefore, of Legislature, to establish the means, either by reward or otherwise, of preventing the concealment of such discoveries.

p. 73.[9] The different causes, by which the market price may be kept above the natural price, might have been arranged in the following manner. I. Those causes which raise the market price, while the natural price remains the same; or in general those causes, by which the market supply is kept under par. II. Those causes which sink the natural price, while the market price remains the same: and these causes may be subdivided, according as the natural price is sunk by one or other of its component parts – by diminishing the quantity of labour, while the wages given in the market remain the same – by diminishing the quantity of stock, while the profits received continue the same – by diminishing the quantity of money advanced for land, while the same compensation is made by the market for rent.

p. 93.[10] Where is the proof to be had, that grain was dearer, in *France*, during the last century than during this?

p. 100.[11] I should like to know whether this is the fact. It is not a proof of it that the health and strength of the workman is greatly impaired, if not destroyed, in the course of a few years; for that may be as much the consequence of their excessive dissipation during one part of the week, as of their hard industry during the other; and though this laborious application may, and does, require to be refreshed by a period of moderate indulgence and ease, yet the sudden and violent transitions between extreme labour and extreme indulgence are probably more detrimental to the constitution of the human body, than an almost unvaried course either of the one or of the other.

p. 104.[12] I must endeavour to inform myself accurately of the seats of the different manufactures in the United Kingdoms; and likewise of the particular state and history of the manufactures, with regard to their being in a progressive, stationary, or declining state; the connection of their history with the history of grain and silver, and with the history of taxes and legislative regulations.

Having read over once the chapter on the wages of labour, I state now as I can what are the objects of it, or rather what instruction I have derived from it.

The wages, or recompense of labour, are in proportion to the progress of the society. They are highest, when the society is striving and advancing, and when the society is retreating in point of wealth they are not more than the lowest subsistence of the labourer. When the society is stationary, wages are little above this. The rate of wages is an effect, and therefore may be considered as a natural symptom of the wealth and prosperity of a nation. They are an operative cause on population: liberal wages enable the labouring part of the community, and they are the great mass, to rear more children than they ever can in a state of poverty and limited subsistence.

He also considers the connection between the price of labour and the price of provisions.

1. Evidently Horner's decision to enter into a systematic analysis of the *Wealth of Nations* at this time was owing to his interest in the controversy surrounding the recent English legal

holdings on forestalling and engrossing, and to the prospect of Professor Stewart's first comprehensive course of lectures in political economy, which were slated to begin in December 1800. The notes below seem to indicate that he read, in sequence, Book III, chapter I ('Of the natural Progress of Opulence'), Book IV, chapters V ('Of Bounties'), IX ('Of the agricultural Systems'), and VIII ('Conclusion of the Mercantile System'), and Book I, chapters X ('Of Wages and Profit in the different Employments of Labour and Stock'), I ('Of the Division of Labour'), VI ('Of the component Parts of the Price of Commodities'), VII ('Of the natural and market Price of Commodities'), and VIII ('Of the Wages of Labour').

With the exception of some of the entries in this Document, Horner used a three-volume edition, evidently (from the statement in Doc. 154 and the slightly erroneous entry in *HL* no. 69), that of 1796. However, with the curious exception of that in the first paragraph, the references in this Document are to the 1st or 2nd ed. Specific references have been located and explained wherever it would seem helpful; but it should be noted that Horner's apparent quotations from the original are not always precise, but often paraphrases or rough approximations. In each a corresponding reference has been made to the 'Glasgow Edition', as under *WN* in the list of abbreviations..

2. There is no distinct paragraph on this page of vol. ii of the 1796 edition; but Horner evidently means the first paragraph (pp. 73–5) of *WN* III. i., in which Smith opens his examination 'of the natural Progress of Opulence' with the following sentence: 'The great commerce of every civilized society, is that carried on between the inhabitants of the town and those of the country.'

3. Smith actually wrote (*WN* III. i. 1): 'The corn which grows within a mile of the town, sells there for the same price with that which comes from twenty miles distance.'

4. This reference is to vol. i of the two-volume edition of 1776 or 1778, as are all the others in the rest of this Document. In that edition 'chap. 8' is Book IV. ix in the 1796 edition, 'Of the agricultural Systems', the second paragraph of which begins (*WN* IV. ix. 2):

> That system which represents the produce of land as the sole source of the revenue and wealth of every country, has, so far as I know, never been adopted by any nation, and it at present exists only in the speculations of a few men of great learning and ingenuity in France. It would not, surely, be worth while to examine at great length the errors of a system which never has done, and probably never will do, any harm in any part of the world.

5. Smith wrote (*WN* I. ix. 7): 'It generally requires a greater stock to carry on any sort of trade in a great town than in a country village.'

6. *WN* I. ix. 8.

7. Smith writes in *WN* I. ii. 4: 'The difference of natural talents in different men is, in reality, much less than we are aware of.'

8. *WN* I. vii. 22: 'Secrets in manufactures are capable of being longer kept than secrets in trade.'

9. The reference is evidently to *WN* I. vii. 21.

10. *WN* I. viii. 34.

11. *WN* I. viii. 44: 'Workmen . . ., when they are liberally paid by the piece, are very apt to over-work themselves, and to ruin their health and constitution in a few years.'

12. In *WN* I. viii. 50, Smith makes some general comparisons about the state in the mid-eighteenth century of linen manufacture in Scotland and coarse woollens in the East Riding.

55. Notes on Bacon's *Philosophical Writings* 1800–1802[1]

Kinnordy MSS   23 Nov. 1800

1. (suggested by Bacon, *De Augmentis*, p. 48.)[2] It is the commercial spirit of money-making, that principally drives forward the improvements of the mechanical arts; it is the reverence for long-established customs and practice that chiefly retards their progress. The authority of a great name can scarcely affect their improvement; for there are but rare instances of sudden and [word missing?] revolutions in the history of any mechanical art. If we could suppose any such art communicated all at once in a very improved state to a people, unaccustomed to the spirit of commercial or manufacturing enterprise, this might perhaps be attended with consequences similar to those to which science is exposed by the achievements of a great discoverer and reformer. Such perhaps might be the effect of presenting the steam-engine, or the cotton-machinery, in their present very perfect form, to the infant manufacturers of Ava; such perhaps will be the effect of attempts which the Emperor of that active and generous people is said to have made, to introduce among his people the manufacture of glass by a translation of some English treatises upon the subject. It is in agriculture, almost solely, that England suffers from the prejudices in favour of established customs, while manufacturers have all the enthusiasm and rage of innovation; in China, on the other hand, manufactures are altogether stationary, and in some instances even declining; while their agriculture enjoys the benefits of active improvement. Whence all this?

2. (Suggested by a word in p. 47 of Bacon)[3] All the abstract words that form so great a part of common language, were originally the names of some sensible object, or the descriptive expressions of some sensible image: we daily and hourly use them, however, without any remembrance of this primitive meaning, and indeed it frequently costs the etymologist some trouble to trace their real origin. This fact may be added to many others, in illustration of the real function which general terms perform in the economy of the human understanding. It might be curious to illustrate this important truth, by a sort of detailed *Histoire Raisonnée* of general terms; comprehending a judicious and agreeable selection of examples. By a comparison of the abstract terms of different languages, and of the different metaphors from which they were invented in order to express the same idea, we might throw some light on the curious varieties of national character and manners; and perhaps ascertain some general facts or laws with regard to this operation of the human mind. And in order to render the investigation still more complete, we ought to search for analogies among the metaphorical derivations of different abstract words in the same language. — I may here observe, as the remark has presented itself in the course of this train of reflections, that one of the tricks of that style of writing, in which quaintness and point are affected, consists in suggesting to the imagination of the reader the sensible origin of abstract words. This speculation occurs frequently in the composition of Johnson, especially where he crowds together a number of synonymous expressions, under the appearance of discriminating their shades of

meaning with ostentatious precision. The reader often delights himself with the ideal possession of a nice distinction in the thought presented to him, while he is in truth amused away from the real object of reflection by verbal witticism and levity. I have not leisure to search at present for instances; but I cannot be mistaken in my general recollection of the fact.

3. (Suggested by Bacon, p. 25.)[4] General speculations on the policy of the ancient republics, with respect to the equalized distribution of property. It was no more than an appearance of equalization, the reality of which is best preserved by leaving the chances of acquisition and the circulation of wealth equally open to all, and consists, not in an equal distribution, but in a distribution proportioned to skill, industry and talents.

4. (Suggested by studying Corn trade.) The composition of history, upon the philosophical plan of incorporating the variations of legislative and economical prosperity with the narrative of civil events, would require infinite attention to arrangement, and would give great scope to the display of skill in design. The periodic and chronological statements, introduced by some writers such as Pliny, with regard to the minute particulars of every art and science and every form of human industry or political arrangement, are the mere annals from which a philosophical historian would select the most remarkable fact and deduce his general results. But it obviously requires much nicety, both of judgement and of taste, to determine at which points of the civil narrative those results should be introduced. There are certain implications in the political structure of a nation, which break out only at times into serious disorder; and as these inconveniences fall in with the succession of civil occurrences, an opportunity is thus successively presented of stating the origin, the extent, and (if it ever takes place) the course of the disorder, and at the same time of enlarging upon such in the manners and character of the people as either retard the application of a proper remedy, or they are at length silenced by the combined efforts of enlightened discussion and of severe experience: such, perhaps, may be the plan upon which a future historian of the 18th century will endeavour to elucidate the history of the corn and provision trade in Great Britain. There are other irregularities in domestic economy and law, of which the influence does not become apparent by any public or general distress, but which are gradually removed in proportion as experience becomes more enlightened and the relations of society placed on a more liberal footing: The most successful mode of describing these is perhaps, from a variety of similar instances of improvement, to form a general fact with regard to the progress of policy, and illustrate it by the most striking and general examples. It is also evident, that the narrative of occurrences must be filled up with views of the state of society and manners, as may convey in a general degree the proper impression, and mould the details of political revolutions into harmonious uniformity with the pictures of national economy. – These are important hints upon a subject which will require much reflection. – *vide infra* no. 51.[5]

5. (Bacon, p. 76.)[6] In all this laboured panegyric upon the character of Alexander, Lord Bacon appears altogether unaware of that great man's views with regard to the commercial intercourse of nations; though that is the chief light in which we are at present inclined to view his greatness. In Lord Bacon's

time national industry and wealth made no great figure in political philosophy.

6. (Suggested by Bacon, p. 109.)[7] In writing history upon a philosophical plan, the author should beware of sacrificing, in the prosecution of that view, what is no less valuable, the lessons of practical morality as adapted to public life. This is one of the great charms of historical compositions; by a skilful combination with the general development of the political machine, it may be made still more interesting and dignified.

7. (by Bacon, p. 160)[8] I once formed the idea of a dissertation on the history of that universal and very natural prejudice, which in all ages of the world has more or less prevailed, which assumes the subjection of the human mind to supernatural influence. This influence in some periods has been supposed permanent, at all times, has been believed to be occasional. The history of demoniacal possession illustrates the latter; that of the doctrine of fate and predestination and grace illustrates the former. The ideas are naturally suggested by the constitution of the human imagination; and when they are once embodied among the articles of popular belief, they soon exercise the casuistical ingenuity of divines and moralists.

8. (Bacon, p. 161.)[9] How singular are the revolutions in metaphysical philosophy! that the doctrine of Necessity should have been rejected by Epicurus! – that Lord Bacon should reprobate Epicurus for having rejected it!

9. (Bacon, Lib. III. cap. 1.)[10] In the composition of this very singular chapter, of which the general idea and design is so magnificent, but of which the execution is so inadequate, Lord Bacon seems to have been misled by two causes of error. In the first place, he appears to have been altogether unaware of the imperfections of the language in which the philosophers of his time were accustomed to express their several principles; and of which the abstract terms, being partly borrowed from the popular dialect, and partly invented upon gratuitous and hypothetical assumptions, suggested by a very rude or fallacious description the abstract ideas which they were used to convey. Secondly, he appears in this passage of his work to have formed an imperfect idea of that intellectual proof by which the principles of science are generalized and classified; and which [word illegible] to have forgotten that the labour of analysis by strict rule differs from the analogical sports of fancy, and that the province of the philosopher is separated by a distinct and strong boundary from those wider and more varied regions in which the poet and the wit have a licence to range.

10. (Bacon, De Augm. Lib. III. c. 4.)[11] In one and the same chapter we find Lord Bacon rejecting the Copernican system, and excluding the application of Geometry to Astronomy, and asserting the powers of man to predict the return of the comets. Is not this characteristic of his genius, rather comprehensive than accurate?

11. (Bacon, p. 206)[12] Was Bacon a Realist?

12. (Bacon, p. 210)[13] What is contained in this chapter on the subject of Astronomy is a great and singular deviation from the enlightened views which Bacon embraced with regard to the other sciences. He appears, so far from pointing out the path of astronomical investigation, to have even missed that which was already trod by some of his predecessors and contemporaries; he appears to censure that mode of Inquiry, which has in fact led to our very perfect [?] theory. It is worth inquiring by what circumstances in his education Bacon was left so instructed in

Mathematics, and by what circumstances in the nature of the subject, his accustomed perspicacity failed here to enlighten him.

13. (Bacon, p. 212)[14] Collect the history of this great institution by which the days of the year are grouped into weeks of seven days. Was it suggested by any astronomical phenomenon? by the *four* quarters of the *moon*? Is it from the Jews, that Europe has derived the institution? When was it adopted by a general law of the Roman Empire?

1. On 22 Nov. Horner and Seymour began to meet regularly, to read silently from the works of Bacon, and then to exchange difficulties and illustrations arising from their readings. Horner thought the exercise would improve his literary habits and transport him 'from the dust, and the jostling, and the loungers of the Outer House' (*Horner*, i. 124). The editors have been unable to determine which editions of Bacon Horner used. However, wherever possible, they have located the relevant passages in the Ellis and Spedding edition (cited as *Bacon*), but cite the English translation except where Horner directly quotes the Latin, when both are given.

2. Horner appears here to be reflecting on Bacon's assertion that among the greatest obstacles to the advancement of learning is the substitution for 'the last or furthest end of knowledge' of the pursuit of 'lucre and profession'. (*Bacon*, iii. 294; see also Doc. 56.)

3. The 'word' has not been identified but Horner evidently refers to *Bacon*, iii. c. 294.

4. Perhaps a reference to the supposed lack of regard for wealth in ancient Rome (*Bacon*, iii. 275).

5. Evidently a later cross-reference to the last paragraph of the notes on Bacon: see Doc. 67 n. 14.

6. *Bacon*, iii. 307ff.

7. This appears to be a general reference to *De Augmentis*, Book II, chapter vi, 'The First Division of Civil History', and chapter vii, 'The Division of Perfect History' (*Bacon*, iv. 303–308).

8. This appears to be a reference to the passage on the 'Fates or Destinies of things' in *Bacon*, iv. 320–21.

9. 'Indeed Epicurus seems not only to be profane, but also foolish, when he says, "That it is better to believe in the fable of the gods, than to assert the power of fate"' (*Bacon*, iv. 321).

10. 'Division of Science into Theology and Philosophy' (*Bacon*, iv. 336–40).

11. Cf. *Bacon*, iv. 348 and 353.

12. Presumably a reference to the beginning of *De Augmentis*, Book III, chapter iv, 'The division of Speculative doctrine concerning nature into Physic (special) and Metaphysic' (*Bacon*, iv. 344).

13. Evidently a reference to *De Augmentis*, Book III, chapter iv (*Bacon*, iv. 347ff.), where Bacon had 'missed' the work of Kepler and Tycho. The criticism that Bacon had taken a wrong-headed view of the role of mathematics in science had been common even in the mid-sixteenth century.

14. *Bacon*, iv. 349–50.

56. Journal

Kinnordy MSS ⟨*Horner*, i. 125–8⟩   1 Dec. 1800

⟨This forenoon was spent with Bacon and Seymour. We went over that portion of the first book *De Augm. Scient.* which enumerates the various obstacles that arise to the progress of science, from the defects of literary character; after running over the paragraphs separately, we examined them minutely together, with a view to illustrate them by such practical instances as had fallen under our own observations. The whole passage abounds in ideas so profound, and so beautifully expressed, that I cannot resist the temptation of culling some of the sweets, and serving up another banquet to my delighted imagination. In describing the opposite prejudices of a blind reverence for ancient opinions, and a raging appetite for paradox and innova-tion, Lord Bacon quotes a quaint maxim, which suggested to me an idea entirely new; '*Antiquitas seculi, juventus mundi:*' whence is it that our ordinary associations on this subject are so fallaciously founded on an analogy, directly the reverse? '*Nostra profecto sunt antiqua tempora, cum mundus jam senuerit.*'[1] Bacon speaks of the evil effects of premature system upon the progress of science, and he insists upon the superior advantage of arranging our knowledge into detached aphorisms, which leave the passage always open to farther additions and improvements.[2] If this observation refers to the propriety of confining our theoretical arrangements within the precise limits of actual and legitimate induction, it appears to be so well founded, that no real progress can be made in any science without implicit obedience to the precept.

⟨In all my future studies and investigations with regard to the complicated relations of political economy, and the principles of general jurisprudence, I wish I could keep this rule steadily and habitually in view. Did not Adam Smith judge amiss, in his premature attempt to form a sort of system upon the wealth of nations, instead of presenting his valuable speculations to the world under the form of separate dissertations? As a system, his work is evidently imperfect; and yet it has so much the air of a system, and a reader becomes so fond of every analogy and arrangement, by which a specious appearance of system is made out, that we are apt to adopt erroneous opinions, because they figure in the same fabric with approved and important truths. That illustrious philosopher might therefore have contributed more powerfully to the progress of political science, had he developed his opinions in detached essays; nor would he have less consulted the real interests of his reputation, which indeed may have been more brilliant at first, by his appearance as the author of a comprehensive theory, but will ultimately be measured by what he shall be found to have actually contributed to the treasures of valuable knowledge. I cannot refrain from copying at length the following sentence: – 'Omnium autem gravissimus error in deviatione ab ultimo doctrinarum fine consistit. Appetunt enim homines scientiam, alii ex insita curiositate, et irrequieta; alii anima causa et delectationis; alii existimationis gratia; alii contentionis ergo, atque ut in disserendo superiores sint; plerique *propter lucrum et victum*; paucissimi ut donum rationis divinitus datum in usus humani generis impendant.'[3] Must I confess it to myself with shame, that, except under the temporary elapses of philosophical enthusiasm, I cannot be numbered 'inter hos paucissimos?' Of the former motives to the prosecution of science, I must own, that except one (of which I am not in the smallest degree conscious), I feel them all in some degree. Yet the passions which I should encourage in my mind are an inviolable attachment to truth *for its own sake* in every speculative research, and an habitual reference of every philosophical acquisition to the improvement of my practical and active character: 'Hoc enim illud est quod revera doctrinam atque artes condecoraret, et attolleret, si contemplatio et actio arctiore quam adhuc vinculo copularentur.'[4]

⟨In the evening, I read over with attention that sketch of the general principles of jurisprudence, which Bacon has given in the eighth book of this treatise.[5] It suggested materials for much reflection and future investigation. In particular, it presented the idea of a work which might, perhaps, be entitled 'Elements of *Judicial*

Logic'; and which would contain not only those general principles of equity, by which the decisions of a judge ought to be guided when cases occur to which no principle already established is applicable; but likewise a set of rules, with respect to the interpretation of statutes, the proper limits of the authority which is due to precedents, and the gradual development of consuetudinary law; and besides these, the general rules and principles of evidence.

⟨This day has therefore been usefully employed, though not distinguished by laborious diligence: I shall endeavour to devote one day of the week, as regularly as I can, to the study of Lord Bacon's writings, or of works on a similar plan. In this way I may flatter myself with the reflection of making an effort at least, to preserve my mind untainted by the illiberalities of professional character; if not to mould my habitual reflections upon those extensive and enlightened views of human affairs, by which I may be qualified to reform the irregularities of municipal institutions, and to extend the boundaries of legislative science.⟩

1. *Bacon*, i. 458–9 (transl. iii. 291).
2. *Bacon*, iii. 292.
3. *Bacon*, i. 462; transl. iii. 294 (the emphasis is Horner's):
   But the greatest error of all the rest is the mistaking or misplacing of the last or furthest end of knowledge. For men have entered into a desire of learning and knowledge, sometimes upon a natural curiosity and inquisitive appetite; sometimes to entertain their minds with variety and delight; sometimes for ornament and reputation; and sometimes to enable them to victory of wit and contradiction; and most times for *lucre and profession*; and seldom sincerely to give a true account of their gift of reason, to the benefit and use of men.
4. *Bacon*, i. 462–3; transl., iii. 294: 'But this that which will indeed dignify and exalt knowledge, if contemplation and action may be more nearly and straitly conjoined and united together than they have been.'
5. I.e., in the 97 aphorisms at the conclusion of Book VIII of *De Augmentis* (*Bacon*, v. 88–110).

57. Journal

Kinnordy MSS ⟨*Horner*, i. 128–9⟩   2 Dec. 1800

⟨This forenoon I began a course of reading on the details of political economy, with a view to Stewart's lectures, which I propose to attend. I have commenced with the investigation of the *Corn Trade*; partly determined by its general importance, and partly induced by the interest which it excites at present in this country; when all enlightened reasoners are awaiting that accomplishment of the first genuine triumph of political philosophy, which the candid and liberal coalition of the two parliamentary parties has so fondly predicted. I read about fifty pages of the *Essai sur la Police Générale des Grains*.[1] In the evening went over, in a cursory manner, the general doctrine of the law of Scotland with respect to agricultural leases.⟩

1. By Claude Jacques Herbert (1700–1758), published in Berlin in 1755.

58. Journal

Kinnordy MSS ⟨Horner, i. 129⟩   3 Dec. 1800

⟨This forenoon, after returning home from the Parliament House, I ran through the remainder of the *Essay on the Police of Grain*. I have perused it in so hasty a manner, merely with a view to prepare myself, by a general idea of its contents, for a minute and *reflective* examination of its principles. I scarcely imagine, however, that it will detain me long; the views contained in it are delivered with so much perspicuity and eloquence, and accord so entirely with all that I have ever believed upon the subject, that I hope it will cost me very little trouble to select and appropriate to myself either what is new in argument and fact, or what is happy in point of expression. I was not entirely occupied, however, even this day, with the inactive impressions of cursory readings; many passages set my own thoughts to work, and I shall prosecute in the remainder of the week the hints that suggested themselves with respect to the general analysis of the corn trade. Not a day passes over me, whatever be my immediate object of inquiry, without a visionary and brilliant prospect of the position which the results of all my researches will hold in my general history of Britain.⟩[1]

> 1. In early December 1800 Horner received three copies of Pinto's *Circulation and Credit* from an anonymous party in London (Horner to Loch, 9 Dec., BLPES i. 122). The gift was certainly unsolicited, since Pinto's essay was already among the growing number of works on political economy in Horner's library.

59. Journal

Kinnordy MSS ⟨Horner, i. 129–30⟩   11 Dec. 1800

⟨For some days past my hours have been pretty regularly distributed between idleness and occupation. To the former side of the account, I must place the whole evening spent in the Parliament House; and which I can only occasionally relieve by attending a pleading, or by reading a law paper. On the other side, I may note a couple of hours devoted, after my return home, to the economical details of the corn trade; an hour immediately after dinner, while the rapid progress of digestion clouds the powers of apprehension, employed in the lighter labour of culling flowers from the style of Gibbon; and the remainder of the evening filled up with the study of my friend Bell's new publication on the bankrupt law.[1]

⟨The corn trade, the elegances of Gibbon, and the bankrupt law, are all coupled, in my dreaming imagination, with two glorious visions, historical reputation and professional eminence. I have of late been haunted, likewise, with numberless reflections on the propriety of investigating my political opinions with impartial perseverance, and of forming some short rules of conduct in this particular:

solvendum est problema difficillimum, to ascertain the maximum of absolute and enlightened independence, and the happy medium between the prostitution of faction and the selfish coldness of indifference.⟩

1. George Joseph Bell, A *Treatise on the Law of Bankruptcy in Scotland* (2 vols, Edinburgh, 1800–1804).

60. Journal

Kinnordy MSS ⟨Horner, i. 130–32⟩   17 Dec. 1800

⟨In addition to the employments and speculations described in the preceding article, I now attend Stewart's Lectures on Political Economy, which he delivers three times a week. I do not expect to find that he has enlarged his materials much beyond what he communicated to his hearers last winter; but it is not so much from the detail of particulars that I derive improvement from this amiable philosopher's lectures, as from the general manner and spirit with which he unfolds his speculations, and delivers, in chaste and impressive language, the most liberal and benevolent sentiments, the most comprehensive and enlightened views. Something of this taste may perhaps be caught, by the frequent opportunities of so pleasing an example. His plan embraces the various branches of what he properly terms Political Economy: the general principles of population, the theory of national wealth including an illustration of the doctrine of free trade as well as of the circulation of money, regulations with respect to the poor, plans for the education of the lower classes, for a system of preventive police, etc. He omits altogether the theory of jurisprudence, civil and criminal; a noble field for the future achievements of philosophical genius, and from which even the genius of Smith seems to have shrunk: he relinquishes also the theory of government, because he conceives (in my apprehension most justly) that compared with the investigations of political economy, it is at all events of secondary consideration, and perhaps of subordinate importance. He proposes, in all these subjects which he is successively to discuss, to remark the striking contrast of ancient and of modern policy.

⟨Stewart insisted this morning, with great elegance and force, on his favourite remark, that the general principles of internal economy and regulation, are far more worthy of the interest and attention of the political philosopher, because more immediately connected with the public happiness, than discussions with regard to the comparative advantages of different constitutions.[1] This view of political speculation falls in with the train of reflections on which my mind has lately dwelt a good deal, as to the share which the contagious spirit of party disputation almost insensibly leads most people to take in the parties of the day; a subject on which I ought soon to bring myself to a decision. The plan of sentiment and conduct can scarcely be difficult to form in my situation, and with my views; at too great a distance from the scene of public action for a man of liberal ambition to entertain any desire of political eminence, it can be no arduous task for me to fix myself in uncontrollable independence, and, by the entrenchments of liberal opinion and candid judgement of character, to insulate myself altogether from all forms of faction. My great difficulty is to ascertain the exact degree and tenor to which an interest in public transactions and in the general welfare of the state, ought to be kept up; for a scepticism or cold indifference about these seems to me both criminal and contemptible. Perhaps the remark of Dugald Stewart, to which I have already alluded, may help me to a solution of this problem; and I may enlighten as well as fortify my resolutions, by recourse to some of the ancient moralists, particularly the elegant writers of the Stoical school. Such resolutions, and such a plan of life, it imports me to form deliberately and boldly; whether I flatter myself with eminence professional, historical, or philosophical.⟩

1. A student of Adam Ferguson and Thomas Reid and a close acquaintance of Adam Smith, Stewart was apparently the first academician to detach political economy – speculations bearing on the improvement of political society – from the theory of government and to treat each as a distinct branch of 'political science'. While criticizing Adam Smith's doctrine of exchangeable value and strictures against the Physiocrats in his lectures, Stewart went along with Smith in advocating liberty of individual enterprise and unrestricted exchange. He was especially critical of the Navigation Laws and the Corn Laws and keenly interested in public policy relating to the relief and maintenance of the poor, including the education of the lower orders. His surviving lecture notes were included in Stewart's *Works*.

61. Journal

Kinnordy MSS ⟨Horner, i. 132–3⟩   18 Dec. 1800

⟨I still carry on my inquiries into the details of the corn trade; I have been much gratified with some late pamphlets on the subject, both on account of the information which they convey, and of the spirit in which they are written: *Magna quidem, magna est veritas, et prævalebit.*[1] In this investigation, I have enjoyed the advantage of perusing some very full notes of the evidence which the House of Lords is at present employed in collecting and arranging; these notes are written by the Duke of Somerset, who sends them down by parcels to his brother.

⟨My afternoon and evening are religiously given to legal studies; except the regular relaxation at the Chemical Society, and in the works of Bacon, and the occasional relaxation at the Speculative Society. Four evenings in the week I strictly command; and I extend the sitting for more than five, or sometimes six hours. I have made some progress in Bell's publication; and the arrangements of the bankrupt law interest me extremely; but the loss is, I cannot always keep in remembrance that I ought to prepare myself for business by the accumulation of authoritative details, but frequently awake out of a dream about the illustrations, which I *ought to find* in these details, of the general theory of jurisprudence, and about the prospects which break upon me at a distance of general commercial history. ...⟩

1. The celebrated English legal decisions on forestalling and engrossing combined with an extraordinary increase in the price of grain to inspire a number of pamphlets during the second half of 1800. The pamphlets to which Horner refers cannot be identified with certainty, but six focusing generally on the corn trade and the wages of labour and all published in 1800, were grouped together in HL nos 31–7, when it was sold at auction in 1831. These included Sir Thomas Turton's anonymous *Address to the good sense and candour of the people in behalf of the dealers in corn*; FitzJohn Brand's *Determination of the Average Depression of the Price of Wheat in War*; Edmund Burke's *Thoughts and Details on Scarcity*, written in 1795 and published posthumously; Arthur Young's *The Question of Scarcity plainly stated*; T. R. Malthus's *Investigation of the Cause of the present High Price of Provisions*, which assigned the high price of grain to increased allowances by poor-law authorities; and J. S. Girdler's *Observations on the pernicious consequences of forestalling, regrating and ingrossing*.

62. Journal

Kinnordy MSS ⟨*Horner*, i. 136⟩   16 Jan. 1801

⟨. . .

⟨I . . . attend Stewart's lectures, and strive to imbibe some portion of that elegant taste and comprehensive spirit which are diffused over his speculations. At the same time, I confess that I begin to suspect him of excessive timidity on the subject of political innovation, and the practicability of improvement by individual exertion. And I am not sure, if the great elegance and sensibility of his compositions have not in some degree an unfavourable effect in the investigation of truth and the communication of knowledge: in so pleasing a dress, error and involuntary sophistry might insinuate themselves undetected, because without suspicion; and even truth itself finds admission too easy, when the severities of attention have been lulled into reverie by the charms of the most select diction and the most attractive imagery.⟩

63. Notes on Bacon's *Philosophical Writings*
1800–1802[1]

Kinnordy MSS   18 Jan. 1801

14. (Bacon, *De Augm.*, p. 255.)[2] The distinction here laid down, as the test by which the truth of the system of astronomy ought to be tried, appears to be just. Bacon seems to remark that an hypothesis, with which the appearances of the heavens are consistent, is not a complete system of astronomy, if it does not show that the motions, on which these appearances depend, are produced according to the same laws which we observe in the motions on the surface of the earth, and the improvement, introduced by the Newtonian doctrine of gravitation, consisted in

fact in making this addition to the hypothesis of Copernicus. It would seem, therefore, that Bacon's objection to the Copernican hypothesis was founded upon the idea that the rotation of the earth was irreconcilable with the physical laws of motion. Lord Bacon's conception of those laws must be collected from the other parts of his writings, in which he perhaps explains at greater length his argument against that innovation in astronomical philosophy, which (he confesses) was already become the prevailing opinion.

A criticism, similar to that which Bacon has here passed on the astronomical reasoners of his time, may perhaps be applied to the experimentalists of the present day. Our chemists and physiologists have devoted their useful labours to the accumulation of particular facts and to the arrangement of phenomena: but they have perhaps shown an excessive timidity, in their reluctance to subject those phenomena to the precision of mathematical analysis, and to include them in an analogy with the general laws of dynamics. Not that these philosophers fall under the censure of irregular speculations; but that it may be regretted that they have not done enough. So far as they have proceeded, they are unquestionably upon the right paths; but their progress might have been more rapid and their journey more productive, had they associated mathematical science as the companion of their way, to conduct their steps and to simplify their labour.

This defect, however, in the conduct of philosophical inquiry, is infinitely more pardonable than that of which their predecessors may deservedly be accused; who ignorant both of the proper confines of the different sciences and of the just rules of inductive investigation, disdaining the patient perseverance of observation, and indulging the most licentious reveries of analogy, hurried forward at once to seize a complete system; and with blind precipitation applying general principles, of the real use and just relations of which they were unconscious, to phenomena with which they were still more imperfectly acquainted, flattered themselves with the confidence of having unfolded the accounts of nature in comprehensive theories, and retarded the progress of true philosophy by throwing in its way so many more obstacles to remove. The error of those writers on natural Jurisprudence, who attempted to extend the views and methods of their peculiar department to the whole theory of morals, may be classed with the prejudices of the philosophers last mentioned; while those of the former description may, in some degree, be compared to such speculators on the philosophy of law, as have dignified the municipal regulations of ancient Rome or the arbitrary institutions of modern states with the title of general principles of natural law.

15. (Suggested by the foregoing train of thought.) How far is the disposition of the mind to trace analogies between all insulated objects of perception and some part or other of that systematic train which has taken habitual possession of its reflections; how far is this propensity the same, or a different, phenomenon of mind, from its love of classification and its anxiety to assist the imagination and the memory, by the adoption of general principles? It may also be proper to inquire how far this natural disposition to classify and generalize, differs from the acquired and artificial habit which regulates the train of ideas and their association in the mind of a philosopher?

16. (Bacon, p. 257.)[3] This well known story of Ascham is now rendered more

intelligible and more credible by coupling it with the similar anecdote related of Phillidor, the celebrated chess player.

17. (Bacon, IV, c. 1.)[4] Some objection may be made to the arrangement which Bacon has here adopted, and even to the manner in which the subjects of his own arrangements are unfolded. The investigation of those general facts, which are observed with regard to the connection between the mind and the body, would be more correctly placed, I apprehend, subsequently to the separate investigations of the corporeal and of the mental phenomena.

The views of man's general condition in the universe, if not more properly a practical than a philosophical subject, is more correctly considered by Bacon as forming a distinct discussion from the inquiries with regard to mind and to body. The speculation, however, would be introduced perhaps with great accuracy of method, and certainly with a greater rhetorical effect, at the conclusion than at the commencement of those inquiries; to which, if conceived with enlightened comprehension and executed with eloquence, it would form a very noble and sublime peroration. The proper mode of treating it might perhaps be attained, by adopting the views of that speculation which professes to trace the scale of being. The place which man holds in the general system of the universe, embraces his relation to the mystical and the animated world on the one hand, and on the other his dependance [sic] upon that mind which is supposed to pervade the infinite expanse. The speculation would include the varieties of human misery which flow from the multiplied sources of physical as well as moral evil; and it would aspire to describe the infinite perfectibilities of human power, and the latent seeds of improvement in his organization, in his sensibility, and in his understanding. While those capacities yearn to promise a more elevated rank to the human race in the scale of the universe, the unconquerable fate, which has doomed our present condition to imperfection, recalls our hopes within those bounds which are never to be passed: and leaves us no other consolation than that of admiring that adjustment, by which the destiny of our nature is fulfilled, and which, while it renders our imperfections subservient to exertion, converts our capacities and our ambition of improvement into sources of disappointment and infelicity.

18. (Bacon, p. 261.)[5] How far may the effects of animal magnetism be explained upon some of the same principles, with the phenomena of dreaming?

19. The annals of a free nation seem most susceptible of being delineated upon the plan of a philosophical history. For where the people have themselves a voice and influence in public affairs, and when the rulers feel it necessary to pay some regard to public opinion, the progress and the changes of national manners form an essential link in the connected chain of historical narration. Whereas the resolutions of a despotism form a scene, as much detached from the general situation of the subjects who are unhappily enslaved, as the adventures and romance of any private family. When the free nation, whose history we describe, owes its liberty and opulence to trade, we have a still more favourable opportunity of blending with the narrative of political events, the progress of national industry, domestic economy, and foreign intercourse.

20. (suggested by I Gibbon, 261.) What, according to Buffon and other naturalists, are the circumstances in the organization or in the habits of the Rein-

deer, which prevents him from subsisting in any country to the south of the Baltic? The question may be extended and generalized, so as to comprehend other animals or plants, which are found to be peculiar to any one climate or latitude. I propose the query with reference to the subject of final causes. The naturalist perhaps says that Lapland was created for the rein-deer; the political philosopher maintains that the rein-deer was created for Lapland. Is this false logic amended, by the more comprehensive proposition – that they were created for each other?[6]

21. (suggested by I Gibbon, 269.) In the rude, as well as in the most cultivated states of the political union, we may observe the tendency and capacity of the human mind to embrace very remote views of general utility. What but such a view, whether generated by sympathy or by some other mechanism of the mind, could have imprinted (at least originally) on the mind of an ancient German the strong sense of a debt of honour at play?[7]

22. (by I Gibbon, 271.)[8] To that enumeration of beautiful topics, which Dugald Stewart has suggested for the investigation of the effects of landed appropriation on the manners and history of the human race, we may perhaps [?add] its influence in overcoming the national habits of emigration and the national passion for foreign conquest and plunder. – Copied II aph. 1.[9]

23. . . .

31. (Bacon, 292.)[10] This speculation, about the prolongation of life, was quite suited to the habits of Lord Bacon's imagination; yet he does not appear to have viewed it in that light which he usually throws over such subjects. His distinction between those precautions which secure health and such as may contribute to the prolongation of life, seem altogether unfounded. And in the variety of precepts which he gives for this vast object, he has forgotten that maxim, which pervades his reflections upon most other occasions, with regard to the provisions and arrangements which nature has made to effect her own purposes, and with regard to the subservient and ministerial rank to which the efforts of human art must necessarily be confined.

32. (Bacon, 297.)[11] When Bacon's views with regard to the imperfections of human society were so wide, and his confidence so enlightened in the practicability of curing them; why was he still unable to break that vulgar association, and to dispel from his own mind that vulgar prejudice which leads every age to deplore its own degeneracy from the virtues of its predecessors, and which authorizes even barbarians to ascribe their vices and corruptions to an excess of refinement and cultivation?

33. (Bacon, 304.)[12] It would be interesting to collect a list of the deviations into which Bacon has fallen from the general train of his philosophical views; and to ascertain how far they are to be ascribed to the defects of his own education, to the deficiency of his information upon certain subjects, to the state of science in his day, or to his attachment to certain prejudices.

34. (suggested by Bacon, p. 326.)[13] Much light may be thrown on the subserviency of language to the progress of accurate science, by a correct view of the syllogistic art; attending to its actual efficiency as an instrument of reasoning. If we examine the structure of a syllogism it is clear that no syllogism could ever lead the understanding to the discovery of a new truth; and yet it would be absurd to deny the

fact, that the syllogism is one form of argument by which the conviction or assent of the understanding to a proposition may be obtained. What then is that process or train of thought by which a syllogism leads in any instance to conviction? The truth of the conclusion is implied in that of the major, and was (if not actually, at least virtually) admitted by the mind, when the major proposition was first formed. It seems therefore to be by a process of *recollection* that the mind is conducted to acquiesce in the syllogistic conclusion; the memory is called to witness, that that conclusion was formerly admitted to be true. *At any rate*, the conviction, which a syllogism effects, consists in the perception that the particular proposition, expressed by the conclusion, is involved in the terms of that more general truth which was stated in the major. So that in running over a series of syllogisms, the mind is solely employed in settling the meaning and extent of general terms; and in considering whether certain individual instances belong, or do not belong, to certain general classes. If the terms were philosophically accurate, the syllogistic exercise of mind would be of trifling facility, and of constant occurrence; in those sciences of which the abstract language still labours under the defects of loose analogy, false generalization, and popular usage, the prosecution of syllogistic reasonings is equally endless and unprofitable. The trite reproach against the schoolmen, that their speculations are disputes about words, is only a reproach because the differences were never reflected; so the most necessary and the most profitable investigation, to which a scientific mind can apply itself, is that of words.

In the preceding note, I have merely wished to mark a gleam of light which came across me upon this curious subject; the prosecution of the same idea would lead me into a variety of topics, which appear to me at present in a very indefinite form. The speculation ought to be pursued chiefly with a view to the improvement of philosophical nomenclature, and to the illustration of that particular theory of nominalism, which Markoff and Stewart have professed themselves unable to comprehend.[14]

35. (Bacon, p. 326.)[15] Does Bacon mean to assert, that the syllogism is properly applied (*locum habere*) in the moral sciences? It can no more lead to the discovery of truth in these, than in physics; in these, as well as in physics, it can only be employed in tracing the classifications and the definitions of our abstract terms. If he fell into this mistake, it is an unfortunate limitation of the grandeur of his philosophical views; and must have originated in his ignorance of the proper subserviency and real use of language in the art of logic, a circumstance already remarked in one of the preceding notes.[16]

36. (suggested by Seymour,[17] in conversing on the subject of the two preceding notes.) '1st we have one verb which may be employed in all propositions expressing the connections of *co-existence*; might it not be an improvement in language to have one verb to express all the connections of *succession?*' – 2. 'May not the rare introduction of subjects of physical science into common conversation, have favoured the progress of that kind of science, by preserving the language of it definite?' On the other hand, the terms of moral and political science have always been liable to corruption, by the familiar and vague use of them in the common reasonings of men of every degree of talent; and of various habits of thinking.

1. Horner noted in his journal on 18 Jan. (*Horner*, i. 137–8), that the morning 'was spent with Lord Webb Seymour in reading Bacon, *De Dign. et Augm. Sc.*', that he 'wrote several pages in consequence of a conversation which we had started', and that Seymour sometimes reproached him for 'affecting fine composition even in my notes and memorandums'. The opening paragraph here continues the numerical sequence established in Doc. 55.

2. ?*Bacon*, iv. 353–4.

3. Not traced.

4. Chapter i of Book IV (*Bacon*, iv. 372–8) is entitled: 'Division of the doctrine concerning the *Philosophy of Humanity* and *Philosophy Civil*. Division of the *Philosophy of Humanity* into doctrine concerning the *Body of Man* and the *Soul of Man*.'

5. ?*Bacon*, iv. 361–2.

6. In chapter vi on 'The State of Germany', Edward Gibbon, *The History of the Decline and Fall of the Roman Empire* (6 vols, 1776–88), p. 261, citing Buffon, *Hist. Nat.*, xii. 79 and 116, wrote:

   > The rein deer, that useful animal, from whom the savage of the North derives the best comforts of his dreary life, is of a constitution that supports, and even requires, the most intense cold . . . at present he cannot subsist, much less multiply, in any country south of the Baltic.

7. This entire paragraph is crossed out in the MS. However, Gibbon, i. 269, reads: 'They [the Germans] gloried in passing whole days and nights at table; and the blood of friends and relations often stained their numerous and drunken assemblies. [Yet] Their debts of honour . . . they discharged with the most romantic fidelity.'

8. *Ibid.*, i. 271:

   > the national distress [occasioned to the Germans by famine] was sometimes alleviated by the emigration of a third, perhaps, or a fourth part of their youth. The possession and the enjoyment of property are the pledges which bind a civilized people to an improved country. But the Germans, who carried with them what they most valued . . ., cheerfully abandoned the vast silence of their woods for the unbounded hopes of plunder and conquest.

9. This entire paragraph has been crossed out in the MS. The concluding reference to the aphorism (*Bacon*, iv. 119) seems to have been added later, after Horner had begun to read Book II of the *Novum Organum*. There follows, numbered 23–30, a series of short and seemingly unimportant observations and queries with regard to the sections on human physiology and medical science in *De Augmentis* (*Bacon*, iv. 379–96).

10. *Bacon*, iv. 391: 'men should rightly observe and distinguish between those things which conduce to a healthy life, and those which conduce to a long life.'

11. *Bacon*, iv. 395: 'I fear that this our age of the world, as being somewhat upon the descent of the wheel, inclines to arts voluptuary'.

12. ?*Bacon*, iv. 399–401.

13. *Bacon*, iv. 411.

14. Markoff has not been identified.

15. *Idem*.

16. Here Horner has himself interpolated a later note: 'I then misunderstood Bacon's language about syllogisms.'

17. Presumably Lord Webb Seymour.

64. To James Loch

BLPES i. 125–6   Edinburgh, 18 Feb. 1801

I return you many thanks for the budget of political information which I received from you yesterday. It gives some small consolation to us who live at such a distance from the spot, where so many interesting things are passing, to find that you who are nearer at hand scarcely see more clearly than we do. We all observe the motions of the scene, but the machinery that moves it is hid from both; we see what puppet stalks up to the Treasury bench, and what puppet slinks off from it, but we are quite ignorant who pulls the wires. We do not even know *whether the master juggler*,[1] who sits behind the curtain *at present, is a being of sufficient reflection and discernment* to be amused with all the profound and ridiculous conjectures in which we spectators indulge ourselves upon this business.

The newspaper of this morning has brought us, it pretends, the final list; in which I do not find the name of Loughborough[2] – what is the reason of this? We understood here all along that he had a principal share in the new arrangement. Pelham[3] also is placed upon the Board of Control; where has he learned any thing of Indian politics, or has that presidency ceased to be a situation of real business?

I observe you take it for granted that the new Chancellor of the Exchequer has played false to his predecessor and friend, and that the exchange has taken place without a mutual understanding between them.[4] I am disposed to give every human being a large portion of political dishonesty, and I have implicit faith in the impotency of ambition to resist temptation; but I have not yet brought myself to believe that Addington could have the folly to throw away at once a reputation which he has earned literally by the sweat of his brow, and which rests solely upon the public opinion of his integrity. As a man of erudition in the forms of parliamentary procedure, of prompt and steady command of that sort of knowledge in the place where it is wanted, of tolerable (and but tolerable) impartiality among the noisy wranglers of St Stephen's, – as a man also of a tall person, a strong voice, and a large nose – we all know Addington very well: but he is utterly obscure to us, a mere upstart, if we think of him in the situation of a statesman, Minister of Britain, and Leader of the House of Commons; and we have much reason to suspect that twelve years drudgery at Hatsell's *Precedents*[5] and the details of private road and inclosure bills, is not the most eligible education for the conduct of that great system and the discussion of those great interests, which the administration of this empire involves.

I am waiting in great patience for the end of all things – that is, the reign of the Saints[6] – when we shall see a new heavens and a new earth under the reign of the hermit of St Ann's Hill.[7] It requires neither the spirit of prophecy, nor the sanguine confidence of a true believer, to foresee that we must come to him at last, or at least to his measures. Do let me know what you hear of him at present; does the history go on?[8] Is he still talked of as a thing to be feared, in the ex-Ministerial circles – or will the quondam alarmists soon be forgotten? Is it expected that he will soon appear in the Imperial Parliament? If Pitt would but strenuously coalesce with him for one debate upon the Emancipation, I could almost forgive the former a large portion of his disastrous measures. . . .

1. Horner surely refers to William Pitt, whose recent resignation had led to the formation of Henry Addington's Government. Brougham's kinsman, William Adam, probably summed up consensus opinion among Scottish Whigs with the observation that Addington's Government was merely '*locum tenens* for Pitt'. (W. Adam to C. Adam, 18 Feb., Blair-Adam Papers, Blair Adam, Fife, Scotland.)
2. Alexander Wedderburn, 1st Baron Loughborough and afterwards 1st Earl of Rosslyn (1733–

1805: *DNB*). As Lord Chancellor he had vigorously prosecuted the sedition trials of the 1790s. Loughborough resigned the Great Seal on 14 Apr. 1801 after Addington ousted him in favour of John Scott, 1st Earl of Eldon (1751–1838: *DNB*).

3. Thomas Pelham, afterwards 2nd Earl of Chichester (1756–1826: *DNB*). He had moved the appointment of Addington as Speaker of the House of Commons on 22 Jan. 1801. On 4 Apr. he was appointed chairman of the secret committee on the affairs of Ireland, and on the 14th he moved for leave to bring in a bill to suspend the Habeas Corpus Act in Ireland. Pelham became Home Secretary in Addington's Ministry.

4. As was then customary when the Prime Minister sat in the Commons, Addington succeeded Pitt as Chancellor of the Exchequer as well as First Lord of the Treasury.

5. John Hatsell, *Precedents of Proceedings in the House of Commons* (4 vols, 1785–96).

6. The name generally assigned to the small but influential parliamentary group led by William Wilberforce (1759–1833: *DNB*), James Stephen (1758–1832: *DNB*), and Henry Thornton (1760–1815: *DNB*) who together advocated the philanthropic causes of the 'Clapham Sect'.

7. Having led his followers out of Parliament in 1797, Fox afterwards cloistered himself in his country house at St Anne's Hill.

8. For some years Fox had worked on a definitive political history of England since the Glorious Revolution, through which he hoped to justify his own political behaviour. It was never finished, but some two years after Fox's death his nephew Henry Fox, Lord Holland, published a fragment entitled *A History of the Early Part of the Reign of James the Second by the Right Hon. Charles James Fox* (1808).

65. Journal

Kinnordy MSS ⟨*Horner*, i. 142–3⟩   24 Feb. 1801

⟨. . .

⟨I went to the Speculative Society this evening, where I heard a very indifferent discussion of one of the most interesting subjects which can engage the attention of a political philosopher; the consequences of a free commerce and intercourse between China and the rest of the civilized world. There cannot be a more splendid prospect, than that of this new world being unfolded to the curiosity and the observations of European science. . . .⟩

66. Journal

Kinnordy MSS ⟨*Horner*, i. 144–5⟩   1 Mar. 1801

⟨. . . I read over after dinner Lord Mansfield's celebrated State Paper of 1753, with regard to the condemnation of prize vessels, and the refusal of the King of Prussia to discharge the debts which were secured upon the duchy of Silesia.[1] The demonstration of this memorial is so condensed and so perspicuous, that while it keeps up a lively interest, it requires a very keen and constant effort of attention. I finished the perusal about seven o'clock, and went to the Chemical Society; where exertions of a different kind were called forth: previous to the proper business of the meeting, Allen, Lord Webb, and I joined in very active conversation upon the theory of the Economists with regard to productive labour. Allen confessed the same difficulties of apprehension upon the subject which we had experienced, and threw out a variety of ingenious hints which had occurred to his astute mind in labouring to dispel the unpleasant obscurity: the chemical paper before the Society was an analysis of Scheele's famous theory of phlogiston and fire,[2] which it cost me much pains to follow throughout, from my ignorance of his terms, as well as from my familiarity with a different nomenclature. From these diversified exercises, I transported myself to a scene of a different kind; where I was seated for two hours at the *whist* table; a game, the ingenious combinations of which interest me enough to rouse my attention, but puzzle me enough to make that attention an effort. After all this, I went late to bed; . . . After breakfast I worked with Lord Webb upon the beginning of the fifth book of Bacon *De Augmentis*, which suggested various topics of interesting conversation: we were occupied at home till two o'clock, but the thread of discussion was farther prolonged throughout a walk of several miles. . . .⟩

1. William Murray, afterwards 1st Earl of Mansfield (1705–1793: *DNB*), drafted a report justifying in international law England's seizure of Prussian merchant ships suspected of carrying contraband to France after the Prussian King had withheld payment of interest on the Silesian loan. Horner apparently read of the case in Martens, *Cours Diplomatique et Droit de l'Europe* (4 vols, Gothenburg, 1801); *HL* no. 73.
2. Karl Wilhelm Scheele (1742–1786), the Swedish chemist whose experiments in 1772 anticipated Priestley's discovery (1774) of what Lavoisier (1779) was the first to call oxygen. Horner refers here to Scheele's *Chemical Treatise on Air and Fire* (1777), which described the author's early experiments with 'fire-air' (oxygen) and 'vitiated air' (nitrogen).

67. Notes on Bacon's *Philosophical Writings* 1800–1802

Kinnordy MSS   March 1801[1]

37. (Bacon, pp. 339 and 340.)[2] Bacon evidently falls into an inconsistency of apprehension, when he thus considers *cold* and *shadow* as positive existences as well as *heat* and *light*. He must have been led into this mistake in consequence of different and distinct words being assigned to what are only degrees of the same thing. I have a notion that this very common blunder in reasoning illustrates the same general principles which Stewart has illustrated at p. 176 by a mathematical instance.[3] We use the words *heat* and *cold*, as distinct in our reasonings, not keeping in mind the necessary and fundamental hypothesis that they are relative terms, and denote degrees only of one and the same effect. If in reasoning upon heat and cold we preserve a distinct conception or picture in the mind, of a thermometrical scale, we shall thus obtain that sort of diagram which gives assistance in geometrical demonstration, by making distinctly a relation which abstract words alone are insufficient to express.

Some illustrations of the same error may probably be actuated in the disquisition *de gravi et levi* which Lord Bacon subjoins as an example of Topical Investigation.[4]

38. (Bacon, p. 382.)[5] What probability is there that in the course of a few centuries all the different nations of Europe, perhaps of the world, may be brought to speak and to write one language in common? The familiar use of the French language among the civilized nations of Europe, and the extension of the English language over the continent of North America and the Dominions of Hindustan, almost foretell that the competition for the universal adoption will be carried on between these two, and perhaps that the universal language will ultimately be a mixed dialect of both. We have often occasion to remark that analogy which assimilates the progressive improvement of individual mind to that of a nation and even of the human race; there is an analogy of the same kind, between that progressive enlargement of intercourse among the different provinces of a single kingdom which brings their manners and their language to a common standard, and that which is gradually opening up a communication of opinions and arts among the several kingdoms which compose the common-wealth of the civilized world. The dialects of France and Britain are scarcely more different at present, than those of Scotland and of England were some hundred years ago.

39. (Bacon, p. 386.)[6] Does not the fluctuating state of popular pronunciation arise in a great measure from the want of that accurate correspondence between it and orthography, which Bacon apprehends could not be established on account of that fluctuation?

40. (Bacon, p. 383.)[7] Adam Smith has endeavoured to explain the origin of this difference between the ancient and modern languages.[8] His theory has the air of great simplicity, but I am not sure that it is quite satisfactory. On referring to his dissertation, we find that he smooths over, by means of the convenient word '*naturally*', what is the chief difficulty he had to account for. If the new settlers originally spoke a language in which prepositions were used for the declension of nouns, and auxiliaries performed the functions of conjunctions, his account of the matter is quite intelligible so far as the languages of modern Europe are concerned. But in the general theory of language, this only removes the difficulty one step, without explaining it at all. If the two languages that are brought into contact are themselves original and uncompounded, and therefore furnished each with artificial inflections, I do not perceive that a native of the one, when attempting to express himself in the other, should *naturally* substitute prepositions for declension, and the substantive and possessive verbs for conjugation. Such a process implies a very singular effort of abstraction.

41. (Bacon, 469.)[9] There are several passages in this work *De Augm.* in which Bacon speaks of the Jesuits in the highest degree of admiration; see pp. 28, 66, 467, and 472.[10] In Bacon's time, what degree of prosperity had the Society of Jesus attained, and what general estimation throughout Europe? Had they already made themselves known by their learning and policy? – A candid and accurate history of the Jesuits is, I fancy, altogether a desideratum in European literature. Are the materials abundant?

42. The very profound and just observation of Hume, quoted by Stewart at p. 237, with regard to the error of reasoning too finely, and by too long a chain of consequences, with regard to *particular* affairs, is somewhat loosely expressed, and

might perhaps be stated with more precision. It is of great consequence, both to the political philosopher and to the practical statesman, that it should be understood accurately, in its proper light, and to its full extent. It is to the one a fundamental rule of logic; and to the other a fundamental maxim of conduct.[11]

43. (Chapt. 2 Book VIII.)[12] The latter part of this chapter, in which the underling tricks by which courtiers may rise into royal favour and political intriguers to public eminence are described with such familiar complacency, forms a most unpleasing contrast to that elevated tone of rectitude, dignity and simplicity which pervades the philosophical sentiments of Lord Bacon. Had *he himself* submitted to this servitude? – This part of the chapter might, along with Chesterfield's letter, be a good manual in studying the diplomatic intrigues of modern history. It suggests likewise a more general speculation, with regard to the general laws of that deception and false sympathy by which so many false estimates of character are daily formed, and with regard to those diversified weaknesses and follies of character which originate in the vanity of effecting excellencies not possessed and of dissembling real imperfections.

44. (Bacon, p. 595.)[13] It is remarked in the country of Scotland, that the lame poor, who are carried on barrows from door to door by the neighbours, are generally of a choleric irritable temper; which they express without reserve to the very people from whom they are receiving this charitable office. This can hardly be stated as an illustration or analogy of the fact which Bacon mentions in this case; but the one suggested the recollection of the other. It may perhaps be said more properly to illustrate one effect of the poor laws of England, the uniform certainty of which teaches the poor to demand with insolence as a right, what they ought to consider as a gift of beneficence.[14]

1. While 'March 1801' has been written in the margin opposite paragraph 37 (continuing the sequence from Doc. 63), these notes probably include entries of April and May as well. Horner and Seymour finished their analysis of Bacon on 10 May (*Horner*, i. 160–62).
2. *Bacon*, iv. 418.
3. *Elements of the Philosophy of the Human Mind* (1792), chapter iv, section ii:
    In algebraical investigations, it is well known, that the practical application of a general expression, is frequently limited by the conditions which the hypothesis involves; and that, in consequence of a want of attention to this circumstance, some mathematicians of the first eminence have been led to adopt the most paradoxical and absurd conclusions. Without this cautious exercise of the judgement, in the interpretation of the algebraical language, no dexterity in the use of calculus will be sufficient to preserve us from error. Even in algebra, therefore, there is an application of the intellectual powers perfectly distinct from any process of reasoning; and which is absolutely necessary for conducting us to the truth.
4. *Bacon*, iv. 424ff.
5. *Bacon*, iv. 441.
6. *Bacon*, iv. 444.
7. *Bacon*, iv. 442.
8. In Adam Smith's 'Dissertation on the Origin of Languages', added to the 1761 edition of his *Theory of Moral Sentiments*.
9. ?*Bacon*, iv. 494–6.
10. ?*Bacon*, iii. 277, 300, and 416n.
11. In chapter iv, section viii, of his *Elements*, Stewart had quoted at length from the second paragraph of Essay I, 'Of Commerce' (Hume, i. 287–8), beginning:
    When a man deliberates concerning his conduct in any *particular* affair, and forms schemes in politics, trade, economy, or any business in life, he never ought to draw

his arguments too fine, or connect too long a chain of consequences together. Something is sure to happen, that will disconcert his reasoning, and produce an event different from that which he expected. But when we reason upon *general* subjects, one may justly affirm, that our speculations can scarcely ever be too fine, provided they be just.

12. *Bacon*, v. 75–7.
13. ?*Bacon*, v. 50.
14. There follow, numbered 45–50, paragraphs containing short quotations from Bacon's scientific principles in *Cogitata et Visa*, together with brief notations by Horner which end with a personal observation numbered 51: 'The history of Britain during the 18th [century] must consist in a very great degree in the narrative of its parliamentary discussions. This affords the best opportunity of introducing different views of the progress of commerce and police.' The notes on Bacon then continue with diverse but generally uninteresting comment on the *Novum Organum*. However, below paragraph 57, which observes that Bacon apparently 'had a distinct conception of the philosophy of mind, as forming one branch of the science of Nature', Horner has made a later interpolation noting the great value of Bacon's method of 'generalizing by induction in the subject of mind'; and paragraph 59, referring to aphorism 98 – 'men of learning, but easy withal and idle, have taken for the construction or for the confirmation of their philosophy certain rumours and vague fames or airs of experience, and allow to these the weight of lawful evidence', etc. (*Bacon*, iv. 94–5) – notes the inadequate 'present state of facts in political economy' and the metaphysical shortcomings of Montesquieu in that branch of political science.

68. Notes of my progress in studying the system of the Economists[1]

Kinnordy MSS   8 Apr. 1801

1. It is evident that, in a year of scarcity, the produce of a farm rises in exchangeable value; not only is the money-price of corn greater, but its real price also; for it is to the average, and not to the temporary money-price of corn, that the money-price of other commodities adjusts itself. In a year of scarcity, the farmer gets more money for the same quantity of grain than in the preceding year of ordinary plenty; and yet for the same quantity of money he gets the same, or nearly the same quantity, of manufactured commodities: It is evident, therefore, that with the surplus portion of money he may purchase an additional quantity of those commodities.

It never can be supposed, however, that in the case of a deficient crop, the labour of the husbandman has added more to the sum of national wealth than in a year of ordinary plenty, nor indeed that he has added so much; yet the exchangeable value of the whole crop of the country is as great as if it had been an average crop, and indeed is generally greater than if [it] had been [an] average crop, since the price of corn is found in most countries to rise in a greater proportion than the crop falls short. Here, therefore, we appear to have obtained one illustration, that an increase in exchangeable value is not always an increase of the national wealth.

And this may perhaps show, that the profits of the merchant or artisan, however they may add to the wealth of an individual, do not therefore augment the wealth of the nation.

2. {Perhaps the fundamental principle of the theory of Population, viz. that every

country will people itself in proportion to the quantity of subsistence which it produces, may afford a more direct and satisfactory demonstration, than Smith has given, of the great principle, that the price of the necessaries of life never varies, that the wages of common labour accordingly remain equally stationary, and that labour therefore is the best measure of exchangeable value. I have not here expressed any of those principles properly; neither have I taken notice of the necessary limitations, with which each ought to be stated; but if my idea is correct, it suggests a very simple and beautiful view of the close alliance which connects the two great branches of Economical Science, Wealth and Population.}[2]

1. On 6 Apr. Horner noted in his journal (*Horner*, i. 148), that his 'only drudgery has been writing out very full notes of a few of Stewart's lectures on the corn trade'. Stewart's lectures on corn policy offered a favourable view of Physiocratic doctrine, thereby leading Horner to undertake an analysis of the 'system of the Economists'.
2. The brackets framing this paragraph are Horner's and perhaps denote a train of thought which he deemed worthy of further development. Here, however, Horner's initial notes on Physiocratic doctrine end. They do not resume until October 1801 (Doc. 82).

69. Abstract of Physiocratic Doctrine

Kinnordy MSS[1]   8 Apr. 1801

This short abstract of the fundamental arguments of the Economists was copied, by permission, from the notes which John Allen lately drew up, after perusing the work entitled *Physiocratie*.[2]

'The question [at] issue with the Economists appears to be, what are the classes of society who contribute directly, by their labour, to the production of national wealth, meaning by wealth that which is vendible, or has exchangeable value.

'Such is the physical constitution of man, that, in order to prolong his existence, he must consume daily a variety of articles, which from their usefulness and scarcity derive exchangeable value. Every man is, therefore, necessarily a consumer of national wealth; but many, even of the industrious and useful classes of mankind, take no part in its production.

'It is almost superfluous to remark that however honourable, the professions of the magistrate, of the judge or of the soldier, they add not in the most inconsiderable degree to the sum of national wealth. It is their business to protect from violence and secure from fraud the other members of society; and in return for these useful and important services, they receive from producers of wealth, an adequate portion for their own consumption.

'It is equally clear, that the professions of physics and divinity, that the teachers of youth, that domestic servants, and those who administer to the amusements of the public, however useful or agreeable their services, are mere consumers and in no respect producers of wealth.

'There is a very numerous class in every society, who are employed in transporting wealth from one place to another, purchasing it where it abounds, and selling it again where it is wanted. To this class belong the merchant, the sailor, the carrier, etc. The usefulness of these occupations is not to be questioned; but, that they are not productive of wealth, is almost self-evident. In this department of society, we meet with the carriers, but not with the makers of wealth; we perceive the circulation, but not the production of riches. It is in vain to object, that the merchant sells again *with profit*; for the profit as well as the expense of the merchant must be defrayed, in part by the raiser of the article in which he deals, and in part by its consumer who exchanges with it a portion of his surplus produce. Society is benefited by every internal improvement which facilitates the transportation of goods, and considers itself enriched by that competition in trade which lessens the profits of its merchants. How then can the profit of the merchant be placed to the account of national wealth? In what other point of view can the merchant appear a productive labourer, since he merely accomplishes the exchange of articles that abound in remote parts of the globe and neither adds to the quantity, nor improves the quality of the merchandise that passes through his hands?[3]

'There are but two divisions of society, who can be supposed to increase, by their labour, the wealth of the community, to which they belong. These are the husbandman, and the manufacturer.

'That the Husbandman, with whom one classed the Shepherd and the Fisher, is the chief source of national wealth, appears from this consideration, that his labour affords not only the funds for his own subsistence, but supplies with the necessaries of life the other members of Society, and furnishes the raw material of almost every manufacture.

'It is admitted by the Economists that the manufacturer, by changing the form and improving the qualities of rude produce, adds to its exchangeable value; but, it is contended, that the value which he communicates to any portion of rude produce by his manufacture, is precisely equal to the value of his own subsistence while employed in that manufacture. As he takes nothing from, so he adds nothing to the wealth of society. He produces not, but merely continues the existence of riches. Like every other class he depends on the labour of the husbandman for the necessaries of life; but he differs from the other classes in this respect, that his labour replaces, though under a different form, the wealth he consumes. He lessens not, but neither does he increase national riches. His labour, therefore, is not productive of wealth.

'This argument, it is obvious, rests entirely on the assertion that the additional value, which manufacturing labour confers upon rude produce, is precisely equal to the value of the subsistence of the manufacturer. But how these two values are to be rigidly compared, is not at first sight very evident. Of the general assertion, the following argument is the first proof adduced by the Economists.

' "Avouez-le franchement, etc. . . . la *réalité* d'une véritable production de richesses. . . . Il faut distinguer une *addition*, etc. – ne paroît plus d'aucune considération."[4]

'It is not to be dissembled, that there is a fatal error in the preceding argument which takes away entirely from its conclusiveness. The whole value that has ever been supposed to belong to manufactured goods, may be resolved into three distinct parts; first, the value of the raw materials which may be expressed by a, second, the value of the subsistence of the manufacturer, which may be expressed by b; third, the supposed additional value, which the skill and labour of the manufacturer confer on the manufactured goods, and in consequence of which his labour is supposed to augment the stock of national opulence. Let this supposed quantity be x, and the expression of the whole value will be = a + b ± x. In this notation x is an unknown quantity, the import of which it was the object of the preceding reasoning to investigate. Were x = o, the theory of the Economists were well-founded; were x a minus quantity, the manufacturer not deriving subsistence from his trade, must betake himself to some other occupation; were x a positive quantity, it would follow, that the labour of the manufacturer is productive of wealth. In every case, the value of manufactured goods = a + b ± x, and the expression to be investigated is the import of x; but the whole of the preceding argument relates to b, and turns upon the effect of raising or of lowering b, in regulating the price of the manufactured produce. The amount of the argument is, that a ± x ‹ a + b ± x; an evident truth, but from which it does not follow that x = o.

'In order to show that x = o; or in other words that the subsistence of the manufacturer is equal in value to the produce of his labour, it is necessary to advert to the difference in the principles, which determine the value of subsistence and the value of manufactured goods.

'Whatever be the physical limits to the production of subsistence, there are the same and no other limits to the increase of population. The number of mankind will be always in proportion to their means of subsistence. The average demand for subsistence, therefore, will always have the same ratio to the average production of subsistence. But the value of the article is directly as the demand, and inversely as the quantity, or it may be expressed by a fraction having for its numerator the demand, and for its denominator the quantity. Let m be the average quantity; and n the average demand for subsistence; the value of subsistence will be n/m: but, though m and n be variable quantities, they are always in the same ratio to one another, and consequently the quotient n/m is an invariable quantity. The average value of subsistence is, therefore, invariable, however much the price of subsistence may occasionally fluctuate.

'The case is different with manufactured goods. From causes which it is unnecessary to specify; from the accumulation of capital; from improvements of machinery; and from the increase in the productive powers of labour, the quantity of goods annually manufactured increases with the progress of society; but this increase in the quantity has no direct effect to the increase in the demand. The man who should permanently double the subsistence of society, would soon find its population doubled; but the man who should double the number of shoes annually provided for society, would not thereby double the number of feet to wear them, and must content himself with one half of his shoes remaining unsold, or must reduce the price in order to encourage people to wear out their shoes the faster. Every increase in the productive powers of the manufacturer has therefore no other effect but to reduce the value of the manufactured goods; while every increase in the productive powers of the husbandman extends the market for his produce. The manufacturer is forced, by competition, to reduce the price of his manufactured goods, in order to procure subsistence for himself and his family; and he is recomposed by a similar necessity on every other manufacturer. It is obvious that he *must* quit his trade, unless he derive from it a livelihood, and the means of support-ing his family; and it [is] obvious, that he *will* quit his trade, unless his rate of subsistence, unless the accommodations and enjoyment of life which he is able to command, equal the common rate of subsistence in the rank of society to which he belongs. When therefore, it is said, that the subsistence of the manufacturer is equal in value to the produce of his labour, it is this average subsistence which is meant; and from this, in a flourishing society, it is commonly in the power of the manufacturer to secure a portion, for his subsistence in old age, or from the accumulation of a capital.

'To show that the value of manufactured goods must be lessened by every increase in their quantity, while the demand for them continues unchanged, let p = quantity, q = demand, and v = value; then $v = q/p$, and $vp = q$. Consequently, q remaining the same, as p increases, v must diminish.

'It follows,

'1. That the average value of the rude produce of land is at all times invariably the same, though as society advances, it is exchanged for a larger and larger portion of manufactured produce; but, then, it is not the value of the rude produce which rises, but the value of the manufactured produce which sinks. There is always an exchange of value for value, the value being fixed by the ratio of the demand and quantity.

'2. That the rate of subsistence, in every trade and in every profession, will be reduced by competition to a level; but this average will be more or less strictly limited in different professions, according to the certainty or uncertainty of success etc.

'3. That the recompense of the manufacturer for his labour being reduced, by competition, to his subsistence, estimated by the average rate of subsistence in the rank of society which he holds, the value which his labour annexes to the raw material of his manufacture, must be equal to, since it is exchanged for, the value of his subsistence; and consequently his labour, though it perpetuates, is not productive of wealth.

'There is still a specious, though far from solid objection to be considered.

'During the progressive improvement of manufactures, it continually happens, that one manufacturer, more ingenious or more pain-taking than his neighbours, executes, in the same time and with the same expense of subsistence, a greater quantity of work than they can accomplish; and by this superiority in the effective powers of his labour, accumulates riches. How can it be said, that this man, whose greater skill and industry produce wealth to himself, produces none to the community in which he lives?

'Every increase in the quantity lowers the value and extends the circulation of the manufactured goods. The diminution of value is not confined to the additional produce, but is diffused over the whole of the manufacture. The manufacturer who had increased the quantity of his goods, is more than compensated for the diminution of price by the increase of his sales; while the loss is sustained by his less skilful or less industrious neighbour, and perhaps even extends beyond his own to collateral branches of manufacture. Every one who partakes in the loss, is stimulated to greater exertion, and in his turn raises the quantity and lowers still farther the value of his work.

'By this mutual competition and rivalship among manufacturers, society is benefited. Its wants are more fully supplied, if its riches be not augmented. This seeming paradox will disappear, when it is considered, that if every man could supply himself with every accommodation and every enjoyment of life, national opulence would vanish, the idea and the very name of riches would be forgotten.'

1. This copy of Allen's abstract is appended to Doc. 68, which suggests that Horner turned to his learned friend for clarification shortly after beginning his analysis of Physiocratic doctrine in April 1801.

2. Horner refers here to [François Quesnay], *Physiocratie, ou constitution naturelle du gouvernement le plus avantageux au genre humain*, edited by [Pierre Samuel] Dupont [de Nemours]. At this point he used the six-volume edition published in Yverdon in 1768–9. Later, however (in 1802: Docs 85 and 86), he used the earlier, one-volume edition published in two parts by the same editor in Leyden and Paris in 1767 or 1768 (*HL* no. 118). Dupont's *Exportation et importation des grains* (Soissons and Paris, 1764) gave the Physiocrats their name. A colleague of Turgot, Dupont also edited *Mémoires sur la vie et les ouvrages de M. Turgot* (Paris, 1788).

3. *Vide Tab. Econ.* [Vol. i], p. 63 and p. 106 – in *Physiocr.* [Horner refers to the *Tableau Economique* first printed by François Quesnay in 1758 but not published until 1759. Victor Riquetti, Marquis de Mirabeau (1715–1789), edited the first English edition, which was published in London in 1760 as *The Economical Table by the Friend of Mankind*. Dupont reprinted it, along with the 'Maximes Générales du Gouvernement Economique d'un royaume agricole', in both his editions of *Physiocratie*. The versions cited here are those in i. 35–78 and 79–139 of the six-volume edition. Other references at this period are, as indicated, to vol. ii, 'Discussions et Développemens'.]

4. *Physiocratie*, ii. 163–7.

70. To J.A. Murray

BLPES i. 130–31 ⟨*Horner*, i. 151⟩   York Place, [Edinburgh,] 10 Apr. 1801

⟨. . . In consequence of your request, I have taken notes from Dugald [Stewart]'s late lectures with my accustomed copiousness; he has given the subject of the corn trade a very ample and interesting discussion; Lord Lloyd Kenyon did not escape some very pointed allusions, sharpened in Stewart's best manner. . . .⟩[1]

1. When considering the corn trade in his Lectures on Political Economy and in particular the advantages to the grower of his crop being bought in advance by the merchant, Stewart had contrasted the attitudes of the judiciary in Scotland and England, averring that 'the progress of truth and liberalism does not appear, in this instance at least, to have been equally rapid' in the latter case, and citing the opinions of Chief Justice Kenyon against the practice of 'forestalling articles of food'. (Stewart's *Works*, ix. 89–91; see Doc. 50.)

71. Journal

Kinnordy MSS ⟨Horner, i. 151–2⟩   12 Apr. 1801

⟨. . . It is more than two years, I believe, since the idea first struck me of composing a practical treatise, which should bear the quaint title of 'The Economy of Intellectual Labour'; and which, professing to teach this most important art, should be ornamented and rendered interesting by a selection of such anecdotes with respect to the literary habits and intellectual resources of great philosophers and artists, as may be found either in the accounts left by themselves, or in the biographical repositories of Bayle, Fontenelle, Vasari, D'Alembert, Johnson, Condorcet, etc. The idea is not at present much more matured in my mind, than it was upon the original suggestion; but I still think it a promising scheme, provided the materials be wrought out of my own experience. Indeed it is now high time that my plans of study should be much more systematized, the distribution of my time more rigidly regular, and my literary habits more formal than they have hitherto been; for the destiny of my future life seems now to be pretty well fixed in most particulars. . . .

⟨I may here notice that, next to the writings of Bacon, there is no book which has more powerfully impelled me to revolve these sentiments than the *Discourses* of Sir Joshua Reynolds. He is one of the first men of genius who have condescended to inform the world of the steps by which greatness is attained: the unaffected good sense and clearness with which he describes the terrestrial and human attributes of that which is usually called inspiration, and the confidence with which he asserts the omnipotence of human labour, have the effect of familiarizing his reader with the idea that genius is an acquisition rather than a gift; while with all this there is blended so naturally and so eloquently the most elevated and passionate admiration of excellence, and of all the productions of true genius, that upon the whole there is no book of a more *inflammatory* effect.⟩[1]

1. During the spring of 1801 Horner paid special attention to the methodology of scholarly inquiry and arrived at conclusions that seemingly influenced his future career. After concluding his study of Bacon's works, he wrote (Journal, 10 May, *Horner*, i. 162) that Bacon 'anxiously reminds the philosopher that, it is not his sport to soar among the clouds, but his business to labour on the surface of the earth; and at the very time that he inflames our emulation by clothing philosophy in attributes that belong to immortality, he domesticates her charms to our cooler judgement, by the admirable intermixture of those plain and concise maxims, which an enlightened experience in study and an acute observation of the world has suggested to himself'. A day earlier Horner had read Burke's two speeches on American affairs 'in order to study this celebrated writer's style of composition', and also parts of the *Discourses* of Sir Joshua Reynolds, 'endeavouring to apply to my art the admirable criticisms which he delivers upon painting'. Horner noted that Reynolds 'constantly referred to the liberal precepts which he urges with regard to the study and imitation of great masters' and confidently accepted the thesis 'that the general rules of excellence in all the arts are the same'. (*Horner*, i. 160.)

72. Journal

Kinnordy MSS ⟨Horner, i. 155–6⟩   24 Apr. 1801

⟨. . . The afternoon I spent at Dugald Stewart's, where I met Alison; the rest of the company were Allen, Lord W. Seymour, and Lord Sempil.[1] The general conversation after dinner was of that rambling, light, literary kind, which Stewart seems studiously to prefer: he never will condescend in company to be original or profound, or to display those powers of observation which he possesses in an eminent degree, but shuns the least approach towards discussion. He told us some very interesting particulars of Adam Smith's character and habits, to which he has alluded but slightly in his biographical account. . . .⟩

>   1. Archibald Alison (1757–1839: *DNB*), student of natural history and author of *Essay on the Nature and Principles of Taste* (1790), had in early life become intimate with Dugald Stewart at Glasgow, and in 1800 had been elected minister of the episcopal chapel, Cowgate, Edinburgh. Hugh, 14th Lord Sempill (1758–1830: *DNB*), had apparently been deprived of his army commission in November 1792 for corresponding with the 'Friends of Freedom' in France.

73. Journal

Kinnordy MSS ⟨Horner, i. 157⟩   27 Apr. 1801

⟨I employed the whole forenoon in writing to the Duke of Somerset, upon the subject of philosophical language.[1] I had delayed this from time to time for nine months past.

⟨In the afternoon, I read with Lord Webb. He lately came to the resolution of passing another year in Edinburgh, as the political situation of the Continent is still unfavourable to travellers, and as in that time he may prosecute pretty far his mathematical studies under Mr Playfair. He has challenged me to continue during the ensuing year our studies of philosophical logic in the works of Lord Bacon; and likewise proposed that we should read together Smith's *Wealth of Nations*. I have agreed to both proposals. His more intimate acquaintance with many facts in the interior situation of the country, in consequence of having travelled a great deal both in England and in Scotland, will contribute a large portion of illustrations which will be valuable to me in the progress of the investigation. I hope to date from this day the commencement of a regular course of political economy.⟩

>   1. Horner to Somerset, 28 Apr., BLPES i. 132–5.

74. Notes on Smith's *Wealth of Nations*[1]

Kinnordy MSS   27 Apr. 1801

1. (p. 3)[2] Might not these two subjects, which he proposes to consider together in the first book, have been treated of more advantage separately?

2. (p. 6)[3] Beside the division of labour, is there any other cause to which the improvement in the effective powers of labour may in part be ascribed?[4]

3. (p. 10)[5] It can hardly be imagined, that the same quantity of agricultural labour is not much more effective or productive in an opulent and improved than in a poor country.[6] No doubt, the division of labour cannot be carried so far in agriculture, as in most manufactures;[7] but there are causes of the improvement of the effective power of labour beside that subdivision. There is an immense difference between the agricultural *skill* of an improved and of a poor country: is this additional *skill* accompanied by little or no increase in the effective powers of agricultural labour?

4. (p. 11)[8] This is an embarrassing illustration. Not only because, by the introduction of the idea of comparative cheapness, he anticipates certain doctrines, and those not altogether of a very simple nature, which are not brought forward till a subsequent part of the book. But also, because it is not found to be a very satisfactory illustration, even after we are apprised of those doctrines. The curious fact, 'that the corn of a poor country comes often as cheap to market as the corn of a rich country', affords no inductive proof of the general proposition 'that the agricultural labour of the rich country is not always much [more?] productive, or effective, than that of the poor': neither does this general proposition furnish, synthetically, sufficient explanation of that fact. For the price of corn is not, like the price of manufactures, necessarily reduced by the improvement in effective power of that labour which produces it: the fundamental law of population tends to maintain the value of corn at the same level from age to age, by constantly keeping up the number of consumers, that is the demand, in proportion to the increase of produce. This not only holds true with respect to each nation considered in itself, but with respect to all nations considered as forming one great community.

The illustration in question, however, describes a very curious fact, which probably depends upon a very complicated combination of circumstances, and of which the investigation would embrace a variety of discussions.[9]

5. (p. 5)[10] This introduction was evidently written without any regard to the situation of his readers, who had not yet read his system, and consequently are unable to understand justly that variety of general terms which are here employed.

6. (p. 19) This is a very superficial and unnecessary chapter; all that is valuable in the doctrine of it might be stated in a single sentence. The disquisition belongs rather to the philosophy of mind than to political economy: and as a metaphysical investigation, it is treated in a very slight and unsatisfactory manner. The first paragraph, however, of the chapter expresses an important truth in political philosophy.[11]

7. (p. 27)[12] If a pane of glass is broke in the Isle of Sky, they must [go] to Inverness for another. There are instances in the western parts of Inverness-shire, of the smith

having a forge and anvil, but not having capital enough to keep a stock either of iron or coals; the gentlemen in the neighbourhood keep a few bars of iron by them, and when a horse wants shoeing, they send iron and coals along with him to the smith. WS[13]

8. (p. 27) He has illustrated the important proposition of this chapter only [in] the effect of communication by water in extending the market, of which the effect is no doubt the most remarkable; but this part of his work might have afforded a proper opportunity for showing the beneficial consequences of the introduction and multiplication of *roads*. *Vide* p. 229 of the same volume.[14]

9. (p. 32) This is stated too strongly.[15] The rivers of Siberia, it is true, do not branch out into any great number of canals, but they are not at a great distance from one another; on the contrary, if we except that narrow neck of land which lies between the stream of the Ket and that of the Jenesai, and through [which] it was proposed at the beginning of the late century to cut a canal, there is one immense line of inland navigation from the mouth of the Wolga to the Baikal Sea and perhaps still further eastward. It is obstructed indeed during a great portion of the year by frost: but on the other hand it is not obstructed by running through the territories of different and hostile nations.

10. (p. 58) This seems a curious fact: how are the exchanges of the poor carried on at all, without proper money?[16] And how did it happen, that after having gone on so long without it, it became at length necessary,[17] more especially as the abundance and consequent cheapness of the more precious metals were every day increasing?[18]

Whence the word *Farthing*? Did these copper coins contain their intrinsic value of that metal, or were they merely tokens?

Perhaps the commerce and exchanges of the poor were previously facilitated by some species of base money.

11. (p. 58) [WN, I. v. 25–6] At what period were gold coins introduced into Germany, France, etc.?[19] Before either of the precious metals is coined in a country, it must have been long in use not only as a commodity, but as a commodity which frequently passed in exchange. In this view, it is natural to inquire, whether any records are preserved of the demand that prevailed for gold, and of the uses for which it was required, in England or in any other kingdom, previous to the employment of it as coin. It is not improbable, that it was actually considered as a representative pledge and as a medium of exchange among traders for some time before it [was] stamped for their use by public authorities; and perhaps that they had already adopted a stamp, or devised some other means of security against fraud either in its fineness or its weight. The researches of antiquaries are of more importance to the political philosopher, than I have hitherto been led to consider them.

12. (pp. 12 and 14) See annexed[20] a note written in August 1799.

13. (p. 4)[21]

3. (p. 7)[22] August 1799. This might be illustrated by a comparison between the state of Edinburgh and London as to the division of labour, both in manufacture, trade, the profession of a lawyer, and a thousand others.

14. (p. 60)[23] One of these cases seems to have been realized in England in the ninth year of James I's reign, in consequence of the proclamation that the gold coin should be raised in value 2 shillings in pound sterling. The consequences of which

regulation are described by Rice Vaughan to have been that 'all the weighty silver coin was melted or exported, it was extremely difficult to get a gold piece changed into silver, and almost all payments were made in gold'. Chapt. 8.[24] It is however not easily to be reconciled to this, that Leake, p. 273 and 275,[25] states that the very reason, why the gold coin was thus raised in value was that it had come (in consequence of the influx of silver from America into Europe) to bear a less proportion in our mints to the silver, than it bore in the bullion market of the Continent:[26] by reason of which, 'Gold became so scarce in *England*, that for near two years there was not any usual payment made in gold.'[27] He quotes the authority of a proclamation preserved by Stowe, p. 912. It is very possible, indeed, that when the exportation of gold coin became inconvenient, the remedy adopted by James, by an alteration of the mint proportion of the two metals, may have proved more than sufficient to restore the equilibrium, and may have led to the opposite evil of an exportation of the silver. It appears from p. 280 of Leake's work, that in the subsequent part of James's reign, proclamations were repeatedly issued to prohibit the exportation of gold and bullion; but it does not appear, from his vague abridgement whether these proceeded merely from his Majesty's general anxiety to prevent the decrease of national wealth, or from the inconvenience actually experienced from an exportation of *one* or *other* of the metals. See the proclamation in Rymer's *Fœdera*, tom. 17. p. 133, 376, 605. Indeed that this was the real state of the fact, is not only rendered extremely probable, by the distinct manner in which Rice Vaughan expresses himself, as well as by the appearance of intelligence and correct information which distinguishes his treatise; but is in some measure rendered certain by the confirmation which I have found in Martin Folkes's *Table of English Silver Coins*, where [p. 69] he mentions that 'silver was excessively scarce during some part of the reign of [James I], and the coinages of it [were] very small'; he further adds [p. 70], 'This scarcity of silver was the subject of much consideration and inquiry at the time: several proclamations were issued against the exportation of it, and several schemes were proposed for the drawing it into the mint. It was particularly advised that the weight of the money should be lessened: and this proceeded so far that directions were actually given to the attorney-general, the 21st February 1619, to prepare new indentures of the mint, whereby the pound weight Troy of standard silver should be coined into 66 shillings. But these directions were soon after recalled, and the designed alteration of the silver coin was ordered to be suspended for twelve months; upon a report made to the council, ... by several eminent merchants, whose advice had been desired in a consultation with the Ministers on that occasion. This intended alteration does not appear after this to have been thought of any more; and indeed silver about the same time began[28] to come again to the mint, in greater plenty than it had done for some years before,' though it does not appear what was the occasion of this change. p. 70. He does not quote his authority for all this; but the facts are very probably to be found in the volume of Rymer's above quoted. There appears to be very little reason to doubt, therefore, that at the beginning of James's reign, gold was exported and became scarce, and that afterwards silver was rendered scarce in the same manner; whether the explanation I have suggested be the right one, will appear from the result of further research.

15. (p. 58)[29] Was it not formerly, if not still, the custom in Sweden, to keep accounts in denominations of *copper* money?[30]

16. (p. 44)[31] *Non sequitur*. The exchangeable value, of every commodity depends, at any one time, on the proportion of demand and supply. This is subject to continual fluctuation. If of two commodities, the demand of the one is increased at a particular time while the supply remains unaugmented, and the demand of the other is diminishing while the supply remains undiminished; it is manifest, that, at that particular time, the respective quantities of the two commodities exchanged for each other may have cost very unequal quantities of labour in their production.[32]

If a greater quantity of labour does sometimes purchase or exchange for a less quantity of labour, {and it is improbable that quantities of labour accurately equal are ever exchanged for each other},[33] it is absurd to consider labour as a measure of exchangeable value. – If it were metaphysically correct to say, that in every bargain the buyer really purchases so much labour, I do not perceive that the proposition would lead to any important inference, either in theory or practice; because there is no strict proportion between the quantity of labour exchanged in any one bargain, and those exchanged in any other. But at any rate, it is not true, that in every bargain, the thing purchased is merely so much labour; for the value of the raw material on which that labour has been employed, can neither be rejected as nothing, nor estimated as a constant quantity; the value of raw materials, like that of manufactured articles, and of labour itself, varies with the proportion of supply and demand.[34]

17. (p. 43) In this, and the two subsequent chapters,[35] Smith appears to have missed the distinct view of the nature of exchangeable value, and of the real principle by which it is at all times regulated. He has even confounded very frequently those two meanings of the word *value*, which at the end of the fourth chapter he has been at pains to distinguish. In the following notes, I shall use the word *value* only in the sense of 'exchangeable value' for the phrase of 'value in use' is more concisely and properly expressed by the single word *utility*.

The value of any commodity, therefore, is the assignable quantity of any other commodity for which an assigned quantity of the former may be exchanged: in this respect, every one commodity may be considered as exchangeable for every other; and, therefore, what we call the value of any one, may be expressed by assigning a quantity of any other. In this general respect too we comprehend, under the name of commodities, not only rude produce and manufactured articles of every sort, but money likewise or the coined metals of every denomination, and labour of every description.[36]

The reciprocal value of any two commodities, i.e. the respective portions of each which are exchanged for one another, is determined in every instance of exchange by the competition; or by the proportion between the supply and demand of each of the two commodities. The reciprocal value, therefore, of any two commodities, is liable to vary with the variation of four circumstances and will depend upon the result of the variations of all combined together: these four circumstances are the demand and the supply of the one commodity, and the demand and the supply of the other. Whoever attempts to ascertain the variation of prices from one age to another, must, with respect to every couple of commodities compared together, take into consideration all of these four circumstances.

There can be no doubt, that the exchange value of labour, i.e. the quantity of corn or cloth for example which is given in exchange for a certain quantity of labour, is regulated at all times by the result of the four circumstances above-mentioned: the supply of that particular species of labour which is in question, demand for that particular labour, the supply of corn or of the particular kind of cloth in question, and lastly the demand for corn or for that cloth. All and each of these several circumstances affect the reciprocal value of any one kind of labour as exchanged for any one kind of grain or for any one kind of cloth. Let us take, for an instance, the labour of a common ploughman and let us estimate the exchangeable value of that quantity which is understood to be included in a day's work, in terms of one particular species of grain, such as oats. It is evident that the quantity of oats, given in exchange for a day's labour at the plough, will become greater, if there is either a diminished supply of ploughmen, or an increased demand for them, or an increased supply of oats, or a diminished demand for them. On the other hand, the quantity of oats, given in exchange for a day's labour at the plough, will become less, if there is either an increased supply of ploughmen or a diminished demand for them, or a diminished supply of oats, or an increased demand for them. In each of these single exchanges, while the three other circumstances remain permanent, the change of relative price will take place as already described; but it is evident that two or more or all of the four circumstances, on which exchangeable value depends, may be fluctuating at one time; and the final result of value depends upon the degree in which the several variations co-operate, or counteract the effect of each. – The same comparison may be instituted between the above species of labour and any commodity whatever, in short, between any two commodities.

Though the preceding view of the principles by which exchangeable value is regulated appears the true result of an accurate analysis; it is by no means steadily maintained by Smith. In various passages of these three chapters, he presents a very different notion, that the exchangeable value of any commodity depends on the quantity of labour that has been employed in producing it, that it really consists in the quantity of labour purchased; and that in the natural state of the market, we always exchange for each other certain quantities of commodity, which in their acquisition or production have cost equal quantities of labour. It has been shown, both in the present and preceding note, that this is an erroneous view of the subject; leading to conclusions inconsistent with facts; and not being itself justified by strict analysis. That the wages of labour employed in production form a component part of price,[37] is an undeniable principle; in other words the quantity of the commodity bought must be adequate to replace, by a circuit of other exchanges, the whole commodities advanced or consumed in the production of the commodity sold. But the proper introduction of this principle into the theory of exchangeable value, is to view it as regulating or limiting the eventual supply of each commodity. If the whole quantity of commodities advanced or consumed in the production of an article, be not replaced by its exchangeable value in the market, the supply of that particular commodity will certainly be lessened so far until by the influence of this diminution upon its value that replacement is complete. But in the actual exchange of any one commodity for any other, no regard is paid to the quantity of labour employed in producing either;[38] the quantities reciprocally exchanged are proportioned by the competition between the supply and demand for both.

The erroneous notion, that every commodity has a real value independent of its actual exchangeable value,[39] and that we may conceive the quantity of labour employed in its production to constitute that real value, appears to have been one of the circumstances which led Smith to call labour a measure of exchangeable value. In his conception and statement of this idea, there seems to prevail a still greater confusion than in his explanation of the former. The proposition that labour is the only real measure of the exchangeable value of all other commodities, can only be understood in this sense, that the exchangeable value of labour is a measure of the exchangeable value of other commodities: though even in this form, it is scarcely a very distinct, and certainly not at all a true proposition. It is not distinct, because it is by no means obvious, that the exchangeable value of any two commodities, even if altogether permanent, can be compared with the exchangeable value of two different commodities, whether permanent or variable. It is not true, because the exchangeable value of labour is itself extremely different according to the particular commodity by which it is at any one time expressed, and because the value of labour in any one commodity varies from time to time according to the many circumstances by which the exchangeable value of all commodities is affected. But by the above proposition Smith does not mean to say that the prices of other commodities are to be measured by the price of labour; his idea is altogether different from this. For it is evident that in the following passages, he changes upon his reader the meaning of the word *value*:[40] 'a commodity which is itself continually varying in its own *value*, can never be an accurate measure of the *value* of other commodities. Equal quantities of labour, at all times and places, may be said to be of equal value to the labourer. ... The price which he pays must ... always be the same, whatever [may be the] quantity of goods [which] he receives in return for it', etc. It is clearly absurd to talk of the *value* of any one thing independent of all reference to anything else; because the definition of value includes two things, and expresses a certain relation between them. The value of labour cannot be said to remain the same, unless it is shown that the assignable quantity of some one or more commodities, for which an assigned quantity of labour is exchanged, remains the same from age to age. When Smith talks of an equal quantity of labour being at all times of equal value to the labourer he really means nothing more, than that an equal quantity of labour always costs the labourer an equal effort or exertion of muscular force and intellectual skill; which hardly amounts to more than that an equal quantity of labour is always equal. But the same may be said of all other commodities and with much more truth than of labour. The sum of force expended by a labourer in the course of a day's work, is merely an abstract and very vague average; because it varies not only with the endless diversities of skill and dexterity in different individuals but with the daily and even hourly fluctuations of health, strength and spirits in the same individual: nay the most correct assay [?] we can form, must be different for the different climates of the globe. But the quantities of all other commodities, except labour, may be mathematically ascertained either by weight or by measures of length or capacity; equal quantities of all such commodities may strictly be said to be at all times equal, because at all times consisting of the same momentum of gravitating particles, or of the same volume or of the same extension.

The object, which Smith appears to have propounded by the use of a measure of value is to compare the value of commodities at different times and places. This is certainly of much importance in the details of political economy, as well as in historical investigations; more particularly, as it enables us to estimate the distribution of national wealth at different periods, and the degree in which the several orders of the community have enjoyed the accommodations of life.[41] The only way, however, in which this seems practicable, depends upon the number of minute facts with respect to prices that have been preserved in ancient records; by the comparison of which with each other, we may form very probable conjectures as to the opulence and enjoyment of the various ranks of that community. After a little explanation in such calculations, several artifices of abridgement easily suggest themselves, and even a few general rules of utility and importance. But as for a standard measure of value to guide us, no such has yet been discovered; nor is it by any means obvious, what is really meant by that expression.

18. (p. 61)[42] '– the value of the most precious metal regulates the value of the whole coin.' This appears to me very indistinct, and at best a nugatory proposition: If he means *exchangeable* value in both cases, the proposition only amounts to this, that the exchangeable value in other coins of the most precious metal regulates the exchangeable value in gold of the other coins: If in the first use of the word value he means the quantity of gold contained in coin of that metal, the proposition then amounts to this, that the quantity of gold contained in coins of that metal regulates the gold value of the other coins. But these propositions seem to be almost identical; and it would be equally correct and important to say, that the value of the silver coin regulates the value of the gold coin, as to say that the value of the gold coin regulates the value of the silver coin.

It is not altogether nugatory however to say, that the value of the most precious coin, if at its just standard, raises the value of the less precious coins especially if they are worn or debased below their standard; because the quantity of metal contained in these last coins, when exchanged for the precious coins, exchanges for a greater quantity of the precious metal, than according to the proportion of the bullion market and perhaps, a general proportion may be more correctly expressed thus; that, supposing the mint proportions to correspond with those of the bullion markets, the coin of whatever metal which is nearest its standard, will raise the value of any other coin that falls shorter. This is a consequence from the very nature of exchangeable value.

19. (p. 61)[43] Gold and silver, like any other two commodities, have, in the bullion market, a relative exchangeable value; which, like the exchangeable value of any other two commodities, is subject to constant variation according to the numerous circumstances which alter the demand or the supply of either.

The governments of almost all countries have deemed it expedient to coin gold and silver into pieces of money, and, by a farther regulation of law, they have ordained that so many pieces of the one metal should be a legal tender for so many pieces of the other; or that the pieces of each should have a certain value in the money; in other words, that, in the exchange of coins, the one metal should have a fixed proportion of value to the other.

The former may be called the bullion ratio of the two metals; the latter may be called their mint ratio. The former may vary from day to day; the latter remains fixed, so long as the law, by which it was enacted, remains unrepealed or not in desuetude. It is evident, that these two ratios cannot be expected, for any length of time, to continue the same; and the reciprocal value of the two metals in the bullion market must generally be different from the reciprocal value which is assigned by the regulations of the mint.

But the currency of every state is, generally, more or less degraded by wear; and it can scarcely be supposed, that the wear of the one metal in coin should go on at the same rate as the wear of the other. A consequence of this is that the exchangeable rate of the two coins, in the actual currency, deviates more or less from the rate assigned by the regulations of the mint.

Two causes, then, may be considered as constantly operating to prevent the rate of the metals in the actual currency from coinciding precisely with their rate in the bullion market.

This want of coincidence will occasion considerable embarrassment and trouble to the mint, or to that department of the offices of state, to which the superintendence of the current coin is committed. It will tempt the contraband dealers to melt down the metal which is under-valued and to counterfeit the coinage of that metal which is over-valued.

This want of coincidence will likewise present an opportunity of profit which will tempt the merchants to traffic in the exportation or importation of the precious metals. Beside these two consequences, one of a commercial nature and the other relating to a matter of police, I do not at present perceive any consequences that result from this want of coincidence between the bullion and the mint proportions of the two metals.

20. (p. 70)[44] It seems to me clear, that the only rule by which the exchange of all things must at all times be determined, is the competition of the contracting parties; the comparative value of a deer and a beaver in the savage state will be determined by the comparative proportion of supply and demand, as much as the comparative value of venison and mutton in a civilized society. It is mentioned, I believe, by Robertson in his *History of America*, that a savage will in the morning sell for a trinket the hut which on the preceding evening no consideration would have tempted him to part with. It is evident that the elapse of the night would not diminish the labour which he had employed in building the hut, though the circumstance of his having already slept would diminish his immediate demand for a covering.

21. (p. 77)[45] This is indistinctly expressed, and suggests at first a meaning which is certainly fallacious. The rate of profit being the same, the sum of profits must always bear an exact proportion to the capital employed; if the rate of profit is variable, the sum of profits cannot be said to bear a proportion to the capital.

As to what is said of 'every subsequent profit being greater than the foregoing', he can only be supposed to mean that, if the rate of successive profits is the same, the whole sum of profits upon each successive capital will constantly increase. There seems to be no reason, however, that the rate should continue the same, or that it should either increase or diminish. Of the three suppositions, it is more likely that the rate should go on diminishing; according to the general fact in merchandise, that trade may be carried on upon smaller profits when the capital is greater: as the rate goes on diminishing it may very easily happen that the subsequent profits shall be less than the foregoing, if the rate of profit diminishes in a greater proportion than whole capital increases.

22. (p. 71)[46] How imprecise to introduce such phrases, as 'some allowance [will] naturally [be] made for [the] superior hardship', and 'the esteem which men have for dexterity and ingenuity'! That these feelings may operate in certain combinations of circumstances, in consequence especially of previous habits in the mind of purchasers with regard to the value of the particular subject, may be very true; but in an analysis of the theory of exchangeable value, the proper place for introducing the notice of such a fact is in the subordinate enumeration of the various circumstances by which the effective demand may be influenced: it is the competition of demand and supply, we are forced eternally to remark, that alone determines price; and the direct manner, in which either the hardship of particular kinds of labour, or the scarcity of that ingenuity which it presupposes, influences exchangeable value, is by contributing to limit the supply.

When a family, accustomed to the high prices of the metropolis take up their residence during summer in any of those provinces, such as Yorkshire or the counties of Wales, where, from the imperfect communication with other parts of the country, the prices are still very low, they are placed in the situation above eluded [sic] to, and everyone has observed in others or in himself a disposition to give higher prices than what are actually demanded: such is the effect of former habits, that it even costs some reflection to overcome the suspicion, that there is a kind of unfairness and injustice in not giving the sellers more than they ask.

23. (p. 72) 'As soon as stock has accumulated in the hands of particular persons, some of them will *naturally* be employed [*recte* employ it] in setting to work industrious people,[47] whom, etc.'[48] This observation implies a view, which appears to me erroneous, of the historical progress of society towards the establishment of that order of men, who, by employing the industry of others, make a profit upon their own capital. Instead of their being led to this, however obvious and *natural*, by any plan or foresight, I believe the actual history of past time shows it to have been the gradual result of a different arrangement. In the rude ages of society, the head of every family considers himself as the proprietor of everything that belongs to the family; and the produce of the labour which his children, his women, or his slaves employ, forms a part of the family property of which he has the disposal and the power to exchange. The progress of the lower orders in modern Europe has consisted in the gradual emancipation of the husbandmen and artificers from the masters, who viewed them and the produce of their labour as property. – The same view of history will apply, with scarcely any other change than that of the names, to the cultivation of land; the progress from slaves to independent tenantry is analogous to the progress from slaves to independent artificers. Land is a species of capital stock; and the improvement of land exemplifies the accumulation of fixed capital.

24. (p. 70) This is, upon the whole, a valuable and well-arranged chapter: though

the object and result of the investigation which it contains is nowhere distinctly stated, and the title prefixed does not appear to have been very happily chosen.[49] An analysis of the component parts of price, appears to mean nothing more than an examination of the proportions in which the price paid in exchange for any article is distributed among the several individuals, who contributed their industry in the progress of its manufacture; whether those parts of the price actually go to them as the reward of their contributions or go to replace the credit which paid them that reward in advance. This analysis establishes a very curious and beautiful fact, in the general description of commercial circulation; that the price of every article, though determined by competition replaces the price of every portion of industry or stock that has been employed in its production, and may therefore be conceived to be composed of all those several prices accumulated successively. The value of this principle, however, does not so properly consist in adding any new attribute to our idea of price, as in showing, from a tolerably distinct point of view, the circulation of produce and price which takes place in a commercial community. – In a country where the division of labour is established every article of commerce may be considered as the production of a multitude of individuals, who contribute either their industry or their capital stock to its formation. If among these some contribute to its formation in one way, and some in another, or if the whole multitude admits of being separated into distinct orders, by certain marks of obvious and permanent difference: it is evident, that such a classification must prove very convenient in many of our political reasonings, and must especially facilitate the description of that circulation of wealth which is constantly going on in a commercial nation, and of that progress according to which the produce of national industry is distributed amongst the mass of the population. Now, it is evident, that one very large portion of the community contribute nothing but their manual labour; while another class furnishes the means of employing these, by contributing their property of accumulated produce; and a third, whose property consists in land, furnish the whole of the rude produce upon which labour can be employed, or at least the source or fund from which all that rude [produce] is derived. In every country, where the division of labour is established, the labourers, capitalists and landholders form three great orders, of which the distinctions are both permanent and obvious. The classification might be presented in many points of view, because it occurs very frequently in our investigations of political economy; one point of view, for instance, from which it may be considered, is the analysis of what Smith calls the component parts of price. As every individual who contributes to the production of an exchangeable article, is induced by a consideration which to him is equivalent, each of the three classes, taken together, may be viewed as contributing its share in the system of national industry by the consideration, to which, as it is paid to a distinct class, a distinct name may be given. In the same manner, as the three classes have received appropriate appellations in popular language, on account of the palpable distinction between them; so, different names have been likewise appropriated to the respective equivalents or considerations by which they are induced. But the whole equivalent, paid in exchange for an article, must be apportioned among the individuals who contributed to its production, and therefore may be considered as portioned out among the several classes into which those individuals are properly arranged: the price of an article, accordingly, is considered as portioned out among the labourers, the capitalists, and the landholders; and in this sense it may be said to consist of wages, profit, and rent.

Though this classification of the several orders of the community, viewed as contributing to produce, is consecrated by popular usage, it is necessary for the political economist to reflect, how far it is warranted by an accurate analysis of the subject, or will be found useful in the prosecution of economical inquiries. A correct opinion on this subject, can only be the result of a very comprehensive view; the following misc[ellaneous?] hints occur to me at present. – ^^50

1. Apparently Horner's notes on the *Wealth of Nations* dated 27 Apr. include those he took between that date and 24 May. On 30 Apr. he made the following entry in his journal (*Horner*, i. 157–8):

> In the afternoon, Lord Webb and I made our second attack upon Smith's *Wealth of Nations*; and finished, for the present, the subject of the Division of Labour. Our mode of reading is, first to go through each chapter with a minute attention to the accuracy of the argument, endeavouring at the same time to recollect all the illustrations by which we can either confirm, contradict, or modify his general principles: when we have read as many chapters as make a complete subject of itself, we review the whole in a more general manner, and take a note of such subjects of future investigation as seem necessary to complete the theory. It may be proper here to mention, that I have for some days past been in the practice of turning over, for an hour, not more, after dinner, any of those books in my room which are likely to present authentic facts, which may be turned to account in the philosophy of commerce and political economy. I wish to impose it upon myself as a rule not to listen to any fact, without an attempt at least to refer it to some general principle; thus reversing the order to which I subject the train of my thoughts when I read any general or theoretical treatise, and allow myself to admit no general principle, without summoning all the details of particular illustration which my memory can furnish.

Horner and Seymour continued to read and discuss the *Wealth of Nations* on Tuesday and Friday afternoons (Journal, 16 May, *Horner*, i. 163) until 24 May (Doc. 75).

2. In his 'Introduction and Plan' (*WN* i. 5) Smith had indicated his intention to examine the causes of the improvement in the productive powers of labour and its distribution among the different ranks of society.

3. The opening sentence of *WN* I. i. 2.

4. *The *accumulation of stock* is a cause of improvement in the effective powers of labour.

5. Horner accurately paraphrases *WN* I. i. 4.

6. *Smith afterwards mentions, I, p. 292 [*WN* I. xi. e. 28], a circumstance which in his opinion nearly counterbalances the increase of the effective power of agricultural labour; viz., 'the [continually] increasing price of cattle, the principal instruments of agriculture.'

7. *This necessary imperfection in agriculture should always be kept in view, as it may considerably limit our conclusions with respect to the general causes of improvement, and affect materially the reasonings of the Economical School.

> [On 3 May Horner made the following note in his journal (*Horner*, i. 160):
>
> This afternoon I gave a second or third sitting to the doctrine of the French Economists, which I perceive will cost me many an hour before I comprehend their meaning in the first place, and in the next place form my opinion on the justness of their principles. I have not yet been able to procure Quesnai's original work. I can *understand* Turgot's treatise on the formation and distribution of riches, but I see no reason to admit his doctrines; but as to Mirabeau's *Philosophie Rurale*, of which I have read a few chapters, I can scarcely attach a meaning to his terms.
>
> Here Horner refers to Quesnay's *Tableau Economique*, Turgot's *Richesses*, and the elder Mirabeau's *Philosophie rurale ou économie générale et politique de l'agriculture* (3 vols, Amsterdam, 1763).]

8. *WN* I. i. 4 actually reads:

In agriculture, the labour of the rich country is not always much more productive than that of the poor; or, at least, it is never so much more productive, as it commonly is in manufactures. The corn of the rich country, therefore, will not always, in the same degree of goodness, come cheaper to market than that of the poor.

9. *From what circumstances does it arise, that it is from poor countries often that corn is exported? And what are those circumstances in the economical situation of a country, upon which the power of exporting a surplus quantity of grain, or the necessity of importing in order to supply its own deficiency, depends?

I shall only note further that Smith does not distinctly express in what market he considers the prices of the two kinds of corn; whether he supposes them to be brought together into competition, in the market of a third country; or he compares the price which each bears separately in the market of the same country where it is raised.

10. The last paragraph of Smith's 'Introduction and Plan' (WN i. 9).

11. Horner refers to the opening sentence in 'Of the Principle which gives occasion to the Division of Labour' (WN I. ii. 1): 'This division of labour, from which so many advantages are derived, is not originally the effect of any human wisdom, which foresees and intends that general opulence to which it gives occasion.'

12. In 'That the Division of Labour is limited by the Extent of the Market' Smith assesses the influence of natural waterways in the development of commerce in various parts of the world (WN I. iii).

13. 'WS' presumably denotes an illustration offered by Lord Webb Seymour.

14. In 'Inequalities arising from the Nature of the Employments themselves' Smith went on to emphasize the importance of roads as well as other means of communication (WN I. x. b).

15. WN I. iii. 8:

The sea of Tartary is the frozen ocean which admits of no navigation, and though some of the greatest rivers in the world run through that country, they are at too great a distance from one another to carry commerce and communication through the greater part of it.

16. The 'curious fact' to which Horner refers cannot be identified with certainty, but it would seem to be the following (WN I. v. 25):

The northern nations who established themselves upon the ruins of the Roman empire, seem to have had silver money from the first beginning of their settlements, and not to have known either gold or copper coins for several ages thereafter.

This note seems to have been written after Horner had read this chapter and the preceding one on 'the Origins and Use of Money' (WN I. iv), which he had annotated with an eye to presenting a paper to the Speculative on the subject of the circulation of money. That project, however, he had abandoned because of the confusion he felt about Smith's definitions of 'value in use', 'value in exchange', 'real price', and 'nominal price' (Docs 37, 42, and 43). It would appear that at this point he began to incorporate in his notes on the Wealth of Nations the results of his earlier researches on the subjects of exchangeable value and the circulation of money.

17. *See Coll. I. [not identified] for the historical account. One circumstance should be particularly attended to, that during the greater part of the reign of James I, silver coin was extremely scarce; vide infra, note 14. During the reign of Elizabeth, there were coined in silver above £100,000 per annum; but in four years of the reign of James I, from 1 April 1617 to 4 Feb 1620, there was only coined the sum of £1,070. 15s. 4d. Folkes's Engl. Silv., p. 70. [Martin Folkes (1690–1754: DNB) published A Table of English Gold Coins from the Eighteenth year of King Edward the Third in 1736 and followed that with A Table of English Silver Coins . . . with their Weights, intrinsic Values and some Remarks upon the several Pieces in 1745.] On this account alone, a great inconvenience must have been experienced from the want of a medium of exchange for small purchases.

18. *The following circumstances may have contributed to occasion this remarkable fact, though I think they are scarcely sufficient to explain it entirely.

Previous to the Reformation the number of the poor, who were obliged to purchase their subsistence, was much more limited than it became afterwards; because a multitude was constantly fed by the hospitality of the convents and abbeys. The number was still smaller at that more early period of our history, when the lower orders formed a class of slaves or villeins entirely supported by their proprietors.

For a long time after the fall of the feudal system, and even after the completion of the Protestant establishment in England, the daily accommodations of the lower ranks were so few, that they scarcely needed any variety of coins smaller than the amount of their wages: the expense of new cloathing or household furniture occurred but rarely and at distant periods, even to those who did not supply these articles by their own occasional industry: and their food, almost the only want, admitted no variety of viands. Another circumstance must likewise be attended to. Even when the people required more articles than one, they must have generally purchased all of them from the same dealer, as in those early times there was little subdivision in the retail trade.

All these circumstances put together are, however, inadequate to explain this; why the want of small coins was early felt in Scotland, though not in England. Is it to be supposed, that, whereas copper coin was introduced into England and France merely to accommodate the poor in their necessary exchanges, it was from the first used in Scotland (as in ancient Italy) for a medium of exchange and a measure of value. Yet copper was very early an article of English commerce, I believe from the time of Richard II; and I do not remember that any copper mines were anciently worked in Scotland. The problem will be most easily solved, by a generalization of the fact with others of the same kind, if such are to be found.

19. *It is not very easy to understand how the Roman coins of silver and gold, which were circulating in great abundance throughout Europe at the time of the Barbarian irruption, were entirely thrown out of exchange. Gold was first coined at Venice; and had probably been brought from the East.

Did not some of the Barbarous nations adopt at their first settlement the use of coins, or is it merely a fond fable of Boulainvilliers when he asserts [Henri de Boulainvilliers (1658–1722), *Mémoires présentés à Monseigneur le duc D'Orléans, contenant les moyens de rendre ce royaume très-puissant, et d'augmenter considérablement les revenus du roy et du peuple* (2 vols, The Hague and Amsterdam, 1727)], I. 21, that the Franks found the silver money of the Romans grievously debased, and immediately struck coins of a pure and ample standard? If the use of coined money was utterly lost in the west of Europe, it is perhaps a more complete proof, than any that has yet been detected, of the change and desolation which the Barbarians occasioned.

20. *4. (pp. 9 and 11) This arrangement is not quite accurate. For though it is true a certain length, that the division of labour gives occasion to improvements and new inventions in manufacturing machinery, yet the immediate effect of machinery upon the labour of manufacturers is the very reverse of subdivision; and that principle by which the work of one man is distributed among many, cannot with propriety be said to effectuate its acknowledged improvement of industry by rendering it possible to have the work of many performed by one man. The division of labour, therefore, and the invention of machinery, ought to be stated as *separate and distinct causes* of improvements in the produce of industry. Those two causes have indeed some connection with one another inasmuch as Smith is correct in stating that to the division of Labour we owe many, though not all, of the greatest inventions in machinery. Still, however, the causes are distinct; by the one, the division of Labour, the produce of labour is increased by the improvements of dexterity and the saving of time: by the other, there is a positive saving of labour, and that work, which till then consumed a certain quantity of human exertion, is now performed by the combination of mechanical forces. If what required the labour of *four* men before is now performed by means of a machine which a *single* man can attend to sufficiently, a saving of labour is to be estimated by deducting from the value of four men's labour the labour of one man plus the value (estimated in labour) of the machinery and expense attending it. It is evident, that the operation of machinery, in improving the produce of labour is very different from that of the division of labour.

[The relevant passages on pp. 9 and 11–12 of Smith (*WN* I. i. 4–5) read respectively:
The division of labour . . . occasions, in every art, a proportionable increase of the productive powers of labour. The separation of different trades and employments from one another, seems to have taken place, in consequence of this advantage.

This great increase of the quantity of work, which, in consequence of the division of labour, the same number of people are capable of performing, is owing to three different circumstances; first, to the increase of dexterity in every particular workman; secondly, to the saving of the time which is commonly lost in passing from one species of work to another; and lastly, to the invention of a great number of machines which facilitate and abridge labour, and enable one man to do the work of many.

Page 14 (*WN* I. i. 8) elaborates the third of these 'circumstances'.]

21. 'The policy of some nations has given extraordinary encouragement to the industry of the country; that of others to the industry of towns.' (Smith's 'Introduction and Plan', *WN* i. 7.)

22. This note, which was evidently no. 3 of his earlier set, seems to be a comment on Smith's contention, stated in *WN* I. i. 2 and elaborated, that: 'The effects of the division of labour, in the general business of society, will be more easily understood, by considering in what manner it operates in some particular manufactures.'

23. *WN* I. v. 28:

> If the regulated value of a guinea . . . was either reduced to twenty, or raised to two-and-twenty shillings, all accounts being kept and almost all obligations for debt being expressed in silver money, the greater part of payments could in either case be made with the same quantity of silver money as before; but would require very different quantities of gold money; a greater in the one case, and a smaller in the other.

24. The apparent quotation is really a paraphrase of a sentence on pp. 70–71 of chapter viii, 'Of the low Price of our Silver', in Rice Vaughan, *A Discourse of Coin and Coinage*, ed. Henry Vaughan (1675).

25. Stephen Martin Leake, *Nummi Britannici Historia; or, an Historical Account of English Money, from the Conquest to the Uniting of the Two Kingdoms by King James I., and of Great Britain to the Present Time* (1726). Leake's chronological descriptive handbook of English coins was the first of its kind. A second edition appeared in 1745, and a third, from which Horner read, was published in 1793. The 'quotation' that follows (from p. 276) is again slightly adapted.

26. *Some phrases in these proclamations may be copied from Stowe [*Annales, or, A generall chronicle of England. Begun by John Stow: continued and augmented . . . by Edmund Howes* (1631)]; there were two, one on 18 May 1611, prohibiting the melting and exporting of money – the second on 23 November following raising the denomination of the gold coin 2/- in the £ sterling. The first of these does not state the practice of culling [?], melting and exporting, as confined to the gold coin but practised upon all sorts of money. But the second proclamation, which was published after more minute inquiry, refers to the gold only, and states that 'very great quantities of English gold were exported by merchants, as well as English, French, as Dutch, but *chiefly by the Dutch*.' 'So as English gold was verie plentiful in foraine nations, and very great payments were thus ordinarily made thereof etc.' – 'the piece called Unitie, which is here worth but 20 shillings, *was valued in foreign parts at 22 shillings*' – 'seeing that neither penalties nor diligent searches could keep gold within this kingdom' – 'by advice of his Privy Council, and conference with divers gentlemen of qualitie and discretion and with *merchants of every trade*, officers of the Mint, and *goldsmiths of best experience*, having judiciously looked into this matter.' Stowe subjoins a note, which is probably inaccurate, because inconsistent with the proclamation† above quoted from Rymer [Thomas Rymer, *Fœdera* (20 vols, 1704–1732)]; 'from the second year of his Majesty's reign, and for six years after, there was more plenty of gold than ever was before: and so would have continued, if it had not been so much exported.' 31 July 1619, a Proclamation for reformation of divers coins of gold; as follows; *vide* Howes' *Stowe*, p. 1032.

†Not altogether inconsistent for we may suppose that proclamation to have produced its intended effect though that is extremely improbable on Vaughan's authority, p. 85.

27. *In the second year of James, his 'Procl. de monet. ref. et de nunism. super unione Regnor. credendo', which is dated 16 Novr 1604, states 'that the English coins of gold are not, in regard of the silver coins, of the true proportion between gold and silver accustomed in all nations – which hath been a great cause of the transportation of gold out of this realm into foreign countries in such quantities as of late years have been used, because the gold monies are more worth in their true value than they are here allowed.' Rymer. The end of the Proclamation declares that the several new coins shall be exchanged 'at the several rates and values contained in the table hereunder, written expressing their true values and weights'.

But this table, Rymer has not published.

28. *This is rather inconsistent with what Rice Vaughan states, that 'the scarcity of silver is so great, etc.' p. 71. Now it is clear from pp. 22, 70 and 86, that he wrote his treatise after the year 1622.

[Here Horner refers to the first two pages of Vaughan's eighth chapter, entitled 'Of the low Price of our Silver'. Vaughan observes (pp. 70–71) that government's arbitrary decision to raise the price of gold two shillings in the pound, and a subsequent failure to raise the price of silver, resulted in the coining of more gold than silver, the melting or exportation of the weightiest silver, and thus a scarcity of silver coin and an imbalance between the two mediums of exchange. This passage prefaces a conclusion by Vaughan (pp. 71–2) that later appeared in Horner's bullionist doctrine:

> and the scarcity thereof is so great, that a man might go into a great many shops in *London*, of great Trade and Commerce before he shall get a 20s piece in *Gold* to be chang'd into *Silver*: and for the greatest part of all paiments is made now in Gold, contrary to the former times; whereas the true Rule for the good of the Commonwealth is, That there should be such a Proportion kept between *Gold* and *Silver*, as that they might equally abound, and of the two, Silver most abound: the Reason whereof is, That the greatest part of the Commerce of the Kingdom, and almost all the Inland Commerce, is made in *Silver*, the want whereof doth greatly prejudice the same. The remedy of this *Inconvenience* is plain and easy in the general, and *Theory*, which is to reduce the *Gold* and *Silver* to an equal Proportion . . .]

29. In *WN* I. v. 25 Smith had stated his belief that all modern European nations computed the value of goods in silver.

30. There is facing the first line of the next section, '*** anecdote of old Mr Waugh', presumably referring to the query relating to the use of copper coins in Sweden. Mr Waugh is not identified.

31. In *WN* I. v. 2 Smith had asserted that the exchangeable value of any commodity 'to those who possess it and who want to exchange it for some new productions, is precisely equal to the quantity of labour which it can enable them to purchase or command'.

32. *Quantities of labour, very nearly equal, are probably expended, in order to send to the London market the finest black and the finest blue woollens. But a sudden death in the Royal Family will raise the price of black cloth to the height of twice or thrice that of blue; one yard of the former, therefore may be considered as exchanging for two or three yards of the latter; that is, a certain quantity of labour, according to Smith's language, is given on the one side for twice or thrice that quantity of labour on the other. {In precisely the same manner we know that a yard of Bengal muslin will exchange, perhaps, for two yards of British muslin of the same fineness: yet the labour employed to manufacture a yard of the former, cannot be double of the labour employed to manufacture a yard of the latter; on the contrary, the actual time and toil expended by the weavers are probably the same in both cases; and the reward received by the Bengal weaver for the same expense of both, is less than that received by the British artisan.} [This final sentence is crossed out in the MS, presumably by Horner.]

33. The brackets are Horner's.

34. *In some manufactures, indeed, the value of the raw material bears a proportion almost infinitely small to that of the labour employed: for example, the value of the flax in 5 pair of lace ruffles, that of the kelp and sand in a vessel of cut glass, that of the iron and carbon in a steel-watch spring. But in all these instances, the supply of the raw material is abundant. There are other manufactures, in the producing of which the value of the raw material does not bear by any means so small a proportion to that of the labour: in a shawl of cashmere, for example, the value of the wool, which is of a very rare kind, greatly exceeds the value of all the labour employed to weave and embroider it; for those shawls greatly exceed in price the shawls made of other wool, upon which the quantity of labour employed cannot be very different.

35. *WN* I. v, 'Of the real and nominal Price of Commodities', I. vi, 'Of the Component Parts of the Price of Commodities', and I. vii, 'Of the Natural and Market Price of Commodities'.

36. In the margin opposite this section there is a pencil note, 'Used in the Review of Canard', referring to Horner's review of N.F. Canard's *Principes d'Economie Politique* (Paris, 1801), which was published in *ER* i (no. ii, Jan. 1803), 431–50.

37. *Vide infra*, notes 24 and 74. [Horner added this note later. It refers to the numbered

paragraphs in his notes on the *Wealth of Nations*: paragraph 24 below in this document and paragraph 74 in his August 1804 notes on corn policy (Doc. 168).]

38. *Vide infra*, note 20. [Again referring to his own paragraph 20 below.]

39. *Vide infra*, note 74. [Again referring to his own paragraph 74 (Doc. 168).]

40. *So in a passage, vol. III, p. 357. [*WN* V. ii. k. 39: 'The value of money is in proportion to the quantity of the necessaries of life which it will purchase. That of the necessaries of life is altogether independent of the quantity of money which can be had for them.' Corrections to Horner's quotation (from *WN* I. v. 7) have been indicated by insertions in the text; but the underlinings are his.]

41. *Hint – However the money price of corn and of wages may vary from time to time, we may compare the real wages of the labourer at different times, by estimating the proportion at each time between that part of his wages which must be employed in merely feeding himself and family, and the surplus which is over and above that part. The labourer will be more or less liberally rewarded, more or less comfortable, as that surplus is greater or smaller. In one period of society, the whole of his annual wages may not amount to more than twice or three times the price of food which he must purchase, and in another period may amount to four or five times that sum. The surplus is of course employed in purchasing the produce of the labour of other labourers. – Besides this difference of proportion, we must likewise take into account the changes that have taken place in the effective powers of labour – *vide infra*. note 74 *ad. fin*. [This note, which is dated in the margin 6 Sept. 1804, again refers to paragraph 74 (Doc. 168).]

42. *WN* I. v. 29.

43. *WN* I. v. 32.

44. *WN* I. vi. 1:

> In that early and rude state of society which precedes both the accumulation of stock and the appropriation of land, the proportion between the quantities of labour necessary for acquiring different objects seems to be the only circumstance which can afford any rule for exchanging them for one another.

45. *Recte* p. 76 (*WN* I. vi. 14):

> As any particular commodity comes to be more manufactured, that part of the price which resolves itself into wages and profit, comes to be greater in proportion to that which resolves itself into rent. In the progress of the manufacture, not only the number of profits increase, but every subsequent profit is greater than the foregoing; because the capital from which it is derived must always be greater.

46. In *WN* I. vi. 2–3, Smith talks about the implications of different 'species of labour'. The first of Horner's 'quotations' has been corrected in the text; the second is really a paraphrase.

47. *See Lord Lauderdale's *Inquiry*. [Added at a later time, this note refers to Lauderdale's *Inquiry into the nature and origin of Public Wealth and into the means and causes of its Increase* (Edinburgh, 1804).]

48. The underlining is Horner's. The quotation, from *WN* I. v. 5, continues: 'whom they will supply with materials and subsistence, in order to make a profit by the sale of their work, or by what their labour adds to the value of the materials'.

49. *WN* VI. i.

50. Despite Horner's reference to 'hints' that are to follow, and despite the insertion marks, there appear to be no more passages to be inserted. Indeed, although there is no date on the manuscript, this passage evidently concluded Horner's notes of 1801 on the *Wealth of Nations*. His journal entry of 24 May (Doc. 75) states that he and Seymour had suspended their analysis because of difficulties with Smith's fifth chapter, and the next paragraph in Horner's notes on the *Wealth of Nations*, which is numbered 25 and thus continues the numerical sequence, has no date but mentions Henry Thornton's *An inquiry into the nature and effects of the paper credit of Great Britain*, which was published in London in early 1802 (Doc. 95).

75. Journal

Kinnordy MSS ⟨Horner, i. 164–5⟩   24 May 1801

⟨. . .

⟨We have been under the necessity of suspending our progress in the perusal of the *Wealth of Nations*, on account of the insurmountable difficulties, obscurity, and embarrassment in which the reasonings of the fifth chapter are involved. It is amusing to recollect the history of one's feelings on a matter of this kind: many years ago, when I first read the *Wealth of Nations*, the whole of the first book appeared to me as perspicuous as it was interesting and new. Some time afterwards, while I lived in England, I attémpted to make an abstract of Smith's principal reasonings; but I was impeded by the doctrine of the real measure of value, and the distinction between nominal and real price: the discovery that I did not understand Smith, speedily led me to doubt whether Smith understood himself, and I thought I saw that the price of labour was the same sort of thing as the price of any other commodity; but the discussion was too hard for me, and I fled to something more agreeable because more easy. The next incident that I can recollect of this narrative, is the pleasure I received from finding in a pamphlet by Lord Lauderdale, of which Professor Dalzel gave me a copy, that what had puzzled me appeared decidedly erroneous to him, and was rejected without ceremony.[1] Mr Stewart also devoted an elaborate lecture to this curious subject; his refutation of Smith's argument appeared to me at the time demonstrative, but the principles he proposed to substitute were not quite so satisfactory. The subject has again come before me, and I hope, with Lord Webb's aid, not to quit it without making something of it. In utter despair, however, of conducting the investigation successfully without more materials than Smith furnishes, we have betaken ourselves to some treatises in which the doctrine of money is examined in a more elementary manner. We are at present engaged with Rice Vaughan's little book. . . .⟩

1. Lauderdale, *Plan for altering the manner of collecting a large part of the public revenue, with a short statement of the advantages to be derived from it* [1799], pp. 38ff. Andrew Dalzel (1742–1806: *DNB*), was Professor of Greek at Edinburgh.

76. Miscellaneous notes on Political Economy

Kinnordy MSS   [?May 1801][1]

SWITZERLAND

In spring 1801, I applied to M. Roches to inform me in what books I might obtain the most correct information of the political economy of Switzerland.[2] As he had not paid any particular attention to that subject himself, he proposed to write to some of his literary countrymen, who were acquainted with the authentic repositories of such information. For this purpose, I gave him a note of the following articles: viz.

'The number of inhabitants, and the proportion in which the population is distributed between the country and the towns. Have any comparative estimates been attempted between the actual population and that of former periods?

'The subsistence of the people, particularly of those orders who reside in the country – the species of food most generally consumed – and the annual consumption of individuals on an average.

'The average prices of the different sorts of grain for a course of years past, particularly of that sort which forms the principal fund of subsistence.

'The present and former rate of labouring wages, manufacturing and agricultural industry being distinguished.

'Details with regard to the present system of practical husbandry and rural economy, compared with the practice of former periods.

'Details with regard to the property of land; the tenures upon which it is possessed; the proportion in which it is distributed among large or small proprietors. Is the land chiefly cultivated by the proprietors themselves, or by tenants? If there are leases, what are the usual terms of such contracts and upon what footing of security and independence are the tenants placed?

'What is the usual routine of markets, by which the farmer disposes of his crops? Does he bring it directly to the consumer, or are any middle-traders interposed?

'The domestic manufactures and occupations of the peasantry.

'In what degree is the peasantry educated in the elements of reading, writing, and accounts?

'Are there any books in which details may be found with regard to the municipal and criminal codes, and the administration of courts of Justice?

'I wish to procure a list of those books, either of ancient or recent date, from which information may be collected with regard to the political economy and statistics of the Swiss Cantons and the Republic of Geneva.'

M. De Roches applied for me to Professor Pictet of Geneva, who wrote to a friend of his that was particularly conversant in the history of Switzerland, having been the author of some books upon that subject. He wrote to M. Pictet, enclosing a note of books, which, along with the letter, was transmitted here to M. De Roches. The letter contains such a distinct picture of some circumstances in the present political situation of that charming country, that I shall take a copy of it.[3]

1. This note was evidently not written in 1801 but it would seem appropriate to place it at the approximate date of the inquiries to which it relates.

2. Jean Jacques De Roches, the son of a Professor of Theology at Geneva, was then studying medicine at Edinburgh. In Dec. 1804 Horner was recommending him as 'a very particular friend', for a job in London, where he did practise for a time, but in 1811 he returned to Geneva to become an associate professor of medicine. Later, in 1830–41, he was also a Councillor of State. (*Horner*, i. 169; Horner to Hewlett, 23 Dec. 1803 or 1804, BLPES ii. 66, and *Dictionnaire Historique et Biographique de la Suisse*, ed. Marcel Goudet *et al.* (8 vols, Neuchâtel, 1921–34).)

3. Horner's copy of the letter to Charles Pictet (1755–1824), and the list of books it contained, follow in the manuscript notebook, but the correspondent is not identified.

77. Journal

Kinnordy MSS ⟨Horner, i. 165–6⟩   11 June 1801

⟨Since I entered my last record, my application has been chiefly to law, and that in a desultory manner, which is alone practicable during the time of session. . . .

⟨I have gone on reading Bacon with Lord Webb,[1] but our economical speculations have been much interrupted by the incomplete command which I at present possess over the disposition of my hours.

⟨I have again been visited by the passion for composition and fine writing, and I feed the resolution, and mature the plan, of acquiring an habitual fluency of correct, forcible, and ornamental expression. With this view, I have made out a list of the authors, in different languages, whose works comprehend the various models of taste and genius; and I have rioted an hour or two to-day in the enjoyment of one or other. I have made it a subject of particular and painful attention to form in my mind a conception of the proper mode of pursuing this study; and it puzzles me much, where to point the medium which shall be equally distant from vicious imitation of any one author, and from a motley patchwork of inconsistent excellencies, where to mark the line of true elegance, between affected simplicity and affected ornament. I will take care to describe the result as soon as I prove more successful.⟩

1. Apparently Horner took sporadic notes on Bacon's *Novum Organum* and consolidated them in early October 1801. At all events, paragraphs 62–72 of his 'Notes on Bacon's Philosophical Writings 1800–2', which dwell on the mechanics of inductive methodology in the natural sciences and in metaphysics, are dated 4 Oct. 1801.

78. To the Duke of Somerset

BLPES i. 136–7   Edinburgh, 17 June 1801

I thank your Grace for the two letters which you have sent me for perusal . . .[1]

. . .

From the imperfect accounts which reach this distant quarter of what is going on in the literary world, it appears that considerable attention is given to the philosophy of Language by some men of learning at Paris. Various schemes of Pasigraphy and Real Character have been published. Has your Grace seen any of these? One is mentioned in the last Number of the *Monthly Magazine*, but I forget the author's name.[2] These Books never arrive in Edinburgh, till they are out of date, and supplanted by successors who have made greater advances or at least larger promises.

Can we indeed flatter ourselves with much hope of success in these splendid projects of philosophical innovation, when we observe the fate of some plans of improvement which have every appearance of practicable simplicity, and of which the necessity is undeniably most imperious? I allude to the loss of the inclosure bill, the draught of which your Grace sent to Lord Webb several months ago. In this part of the island, we have been accustomed to the benefits of a similar plan for more than a century; and we are utterly at a loss to conceive where the difficulty lies of applying the same provisions, or how this opposition to the measure can wear the countenance of plausibility. The repositories of old prejudice must be ransacked for such objections. We suspect that the same professional contraction infects the Law Lords of Parliament, which dictated to Chief Justice Kenyon his extraordinary charges on the subject of forestalling.

1. Copies of letters to the Duke from Peter Elmsley, 5 June 1800, and Francis Leighton, 13 May 1801, both dealing with philosophy of language, are in BLPES i. 138–42.
2. *The Monthly Magazine; or, British Register* for June 1801 (xi. 430) mentions a forthcoming work by Jacques Cambry (1749–1807) on 'a *general language*, different from the *Pasigraphy*'; but it was not until 1805 that Cambry's *Manuel interprète de correspondance, ou Vocabulaires polyglottes* was published in Paris.

79. Journal

Kinnordy MSS ⟨Horner, i. 169–70⟩   30 July 1801

⟨I have been reading a good deal since I entered the last notice, but not with the regularity which I have so often enjoined to myself, and always to no purpose. . . .¹

⟨My studies in political economy (which I compare twice a week with Lord Webb, though the compass I take in is much wider than he has at present time for, and more in detail than it would be consistent with the plans of his life to prosecute), have gone on with more regularity.² The theory of metallic or coined money is my present subject; and while Seymour reads with me Rice Vaughan's admirable little treatise, to which we were driven in consequence of stumbling at Smith's fifth chapter, I am going through Harris,³ Bodin,⁴ Lowndes,⁵ Locke,⁶ etc.

⟨But I must confess that all my active enthusiasm has been employed on books of taste. The projects of historical composition are uppermost in my mind; the ambition for eloquence in pleading being remembered only in the second place. . . .⟩

1. For accounts of Horner's diverse readings during June and July 1801, which apparently did not include works in political economy, see his journal entries of 21 and 28 June and of 15 July in *Horner*, i. 166–9.
2. On 15 July Horner noted in his journal (*Horner*, i. 168–9), that Professor Pictet had recently visited Edinburgh, that he had spent two afternoons with him, and that he had also walked with De Roches and obtained 'some curious information with regard to the canton of Berne'.
3. Joseph Harris (1702–1764: *DNB*), assay master of the mint, published *Essay on Money and Coins* in two parts in 1757–8. Harris did not subscribe to the mercantile theory of wealth. The first part of his *Essay* treated the whole subject of money and foreign exchanges with uncommon clarity and dwelt on the relationship between the minimum standard of subsistence and the cost of production. The second part demonstrated the evil effects that accompany a debasement of coinage and provided an historical account of the variations in the standard.

4. Jean Bodin (1530–1596), precursor of Montesquieu, published two pamphlets attacking the mercantile theory of wealth advanced by Seigneur De Malestroit, a member of the royal council of France and comptroller of the mint. Following the appearance of Malestroit's *Les Paradoxes sur le fait des Monnaies* (Paris, 1566), Bodin published *Réponse aux paradoxes de M. de Malestroit touchant l'enrichessement de toutes les choses et des monnaies* (Paris, 1568) and *Discours sur le rehaussement et diminution des monnaies, pour réponse aux paradoxes du sieur de Malestroit* (Paris, 1578). The debate between Bodin and Malestroit raised issues in monetary theory to which Horner would refer years later during the British bullion controversy (Doc. 403).

5. William Lowndes (1652–1724), Secretary to the Treasury, *A Report containing an Essay for the Amendment of the Silver Coins* (1695).

6. Horner almost surely refers to Locke's *Further Considerations Concerning the raising the value of money, wherein Mr Lowndes' arguments for it in His late report concerning 'An Essay', etc., are particularly examined* (1695), which argued that a devaluation of coin would confuse trade and cause inflation, and perhaps to *Some Considerations of the Consequences of the Lowering of Interest, and Raising the Value of Money* (1691), in which Locke reasoned that the interest rate was determined by nature and thus could not be prudently regulated by law. These and other writings on political economy were reprinted in London in 1796 under the title of *Several papers relating to money, interest and trade etc.*

80. Journal

Kinnordy MSS ⟨Horner, i. 171–2⟩   6 Sept. 1801

⟨During this interval, I have been reading much more constantly than for a long time, though not much more systematically; I have been entirely immersed in law, political economy, and history; and have scarcely felt a moment's inclination to read either eloquence or poetry. As to political economy, I have not yet arranged the subject of money, nor reduced to analytic order either the facts or the queries which I have accumulated. I have taken a cursory view of the reign of Elizabeth of England in Hume's agreeable narrative, and in the valuable *Journal* of D'Ewes:[1] some economical speculations led me to this, but my attention was more forcibly attracted by the dawn of English freedom and of parliamentary privilege in the rude debates of the House of Commons; . . .⟩

1. Sir Simonds D'Ewes, *Journals of all the Parliaments during the Reign of Queen Elizabeth* (1682) (HL no. 203).

81. To the Duke of Somerset

BLPES i. 143–6   Edinburgh, 15 Sept. 1801

I was much obliged to your Grace for the particular account you sent me, of the loss of the Inclosure Bill: it showed me the individual actors, and their respective sentiments, in a much more distinct point of view, than I had been able to form from the ordinary communications to the public. I was rather mortified, though very little surprised, to find the dignitaries of the Law, ranging themselves with those of the Church, in opposition to salutary innovation. But it is indeed too hard a task to yield up inveterate habits, and at the end of a life exhausted in obedient reverence of established rules, to attempt the speculative examination of their reasonableness and justice. I have not learned whether the lay-impropriators would have proved as uncomplying as the Ecclesiastics: it was a fair opportunity to observe, whether our attachment to property, for the advantage of our heirs, is as strong as our attachment to the privileges of our order or corporation.

I fancy that very few people are now to be found, of liberal information and quite disinterested, by whom any doubts are entertained as to the expediency of commuting by this, and of rendering inclosures less troublesome and expensive. The mischiefs of the poor's-rate, indeed, are more unanimously and more feelingly acknowledged, because the class of the community, whose love of idleness is interested in the preservation of that system, cannot clamour learnedly enough to influence any part of the public. Even the ancient objection to inclosures, founded on the idea of depopulation, seems at length exhausted; perhaps it is overborne by the real weight of evidence. No prejudice was ever more obstinately retained by any nation, than that has been by the English; it is truly amusing, when we trace the steady progress of improvement and opulence, to meet with this complaint eternally reiterated, from the reign of Henry the 7th to the time of Dr Price. That learned, but querulous Economist yielded implicit faith to the notion, at the end of the 18th century; and Lord Bacon illustrated it with all his eloquence at the beginning of the 17th. It will no longer, however, be easy to disguise the evidence, or resist the conclusion, of two very plain facts: that in the same period of time, inclosure bills have rapidly multiplied, and the numbers of the people gradually increased. The argument against tithes, is much more obvious than that in favour of inclosures; but it has been very injudiciously managed, in some of the reasonings to which the attention of the public has been recently called. Instead of the distinct proposition, which Paley has copiously illustrated in two pages, and Smith has explained in a single sentence;[1] elaborate calculations have been formed of the import trade of corn, of the comparative produce of pastures and arable ground, and of the nutritive powers of various kinds of food: sometimes in order to prove that tithes have occasioned, within the last 50 years, a diminution of tillage, which is certainly not true; sometimes to prove that they have rendered the increase of tillage less than it would otherwise have been, which must be admitted without any such parade of difficult and ambiguous speculation. One instance of agricultural enterprise defeated by the exaction of tithes, or declined from the apprehension of them, is a complete demonstration; because every person will in his own mind generalize the example, who understands the nature of profit and loss. The late writers in defence of tithes, such as the Reverend Mr Morgan Cove,[2] are perfectly aware of this; and gain an apparent and easy advantage over the injudicious vanity of those, whose reasonings they endeavour to refute.

To carry these two salutary measures into effect, I cannot believe that much ingenuity or delicacy of adjustment is absolutely requisite. The most important care of the legislature is to recognize the principle of freedom, and not to embarrass the progress of emancipation by very minute regulations of procedure. These are best suggested in the course of practice, though it is a very natural error to think of defining them beforehand; this is one of the defects inherent in the character of a practical politician, more especially if he indulges a taste for project; it is perhaps the last incumbrance which enlightened legislators can shake off.

Will your Grace permit me still to trouble you with farther inquiries, on the subject of the late Bill? As the plan will be revived, I trust, in a similar shape, I wish fully to understand its merits. There is no branch of the Economics of this island, on which I find so little printed information, as that which the consideration of tithes and inclosures suggests. I have found no book yet, either of a legal or agricultural description, which gives a general view of the state of landed property in England, with respect to the several rights, claims, servitudes, etc. to which it is actually subject. I have been equally unsuccessful in the attempts I have made to learn a general idea of the manner in which inclosures have actually been conducted, and of the progress which proprietors have made in exonerating their lands from tithes. This confession of ignorance will excuse, I hope, with your Grace, the simplicity of my questions.

Why was the late Bill confined to wastes, and what circumstances render the inclosure of these an object of separate enactment from that of commons? It would seem, that the same principles, with very slight variation, must regulate the partition of all intermixed property, whatever be its peculiar tenure or state of cultivation.

I am not even aware of the reason why these measures constantly receive the name of *inclosure* bills, for that of *appropriation, allotment,* or (as it is termed in Scotland) *division,* would be more expressive, unless the acts impose regulations as to the construction of fences. That would be an impolitic constraint.

I do not distinctly perceive, why a provision for the absolute commutation of tithes was deemed indispensable in the general statute, unless it was meant, in the removal of one discouragement of husbandry, to make a partial attack upon an evil still more grievous. If the purpose of the bill had been limited to the facilitation of inclosures, by saving the expense and delays of a parliamentary application, I scarcely see that tithes should have proved a greater obstacle, than they are found to be in local acts; or that the chances were greater, in the one case than in the other, of the compensation not being accepted. If it is really less for the interest of the tithe-holder to yield to the commutation in the case of an inclosed waste, than in the usual circumstances of a partial inclosure, it would perhaps have been expedient to increase the rate of compensation accordingly. If it is more difficult to adjust the interest of the church and its lessees, when a waste is inclosed, than when the rights of a waste and common are allotted together; this might have been a farther reason for including both in the general bill.

After all, am I entitled to conjecture that the question of tithes was really started, with the view of favouring inclosures and cultivation by a still greater boon, than the remedy of delay and expense? If it was so, the event alone will decide how far it was prudent to hazard one measure upon the success of the other, which was sure to encounter a formidable resistance. Perhaps the clergy may effectually resist both. I cannot frame either a hope or fear, because I have no idea of their influence in affairs – perhaps their tithes may be rendered more odious to the nation at large, when they have been found to obstruct a necessary provision for the public good.

Your Grace thinks that the *general* abolition of tithes would endanger the Church, whose interests are interwoven with the rest of our constitution. As to the former part of this opinion, no doubt any plan of commutation, worth adopting, would eventually reduce the opulence which the establishment will otherwise accumulate, and depress accordingly the rank and influence of its members. In the present age, however, it is a very important question, whether such a consequence would be really a national detriment. The constitutional relation of Church and State, I have often heard asserted, never explained; for the divine right of Episcopacy, on which Mr Morgan Cove insists, does not thoroughly satisfy a Scotch presbyterian. There is unquestionably one point of view, in which every one will admit the intimate connection of church and State, who is influenced by the just principles of legislation; in so far as the actual existence of the establishment decisively excludes all idea of precipitate or violent suppression. But those who consider ecclesiastics of professional rank as a pernicious excrescence upon the political system, still more if they believe that parochial clergy (probably an useful order of men) may be more expediently upheld by private contribution than by public salaries, cannot regret that a measure, in every other respect wise, may provide a natural and easy death for the hierarchy; and, without any sudden change, prepare the gradual extinction of that useless and cumbersome institution.

. . .

1. The last paragraphs of chapter xi, 'Of Population and Provision', in Book VI of William Paley's *Principles of Moral and Political Philosophy*, and, presumably, *WN* III. ii. 13; but cf. *WN* V. ii. d. 2–3.
2. Morgan Cove (?1753–1830: *DNB*) was a leading defender of the establishment, whose major publications were *Essay on the Revenues of the Church of England, with an Inquiry into . . . the Abolition of Tithes* (1797) and *An Inquiry into the Necessity, Justice, and Policy of a Commutation of Tithes* (1800).

82. Notes of my progress in studying the system of the Economists[1]

Kinnordy MSS   October 1801

3. In forming a separate class of the *proprietors of land* were not the Economists misled by the prejudice of feudal habits? Does not the cultivator or farmer set apart a portion of the produce of his landlord, in exactly the same manner that he sets apart a portion of it for the monied capitalist who advanced to him the original stocking?

4. Is not the denomination of *classe stérile* improper on this account alone, that it is merely a negative?

5. In *Phys.* Quesnai betrays in various instances his habit of viewing too exclusively the system of political economy that prevailed in his own country; he might have enlarged his views to the more general aspect of affairs. His classing the *Décimateur* in the class of Proprietors is a remarkable instance of this. One of his

chief reasons for making a separate class of the proprietors, is, that they retain a certain superintendence of the cultivation, and therefore may be viewed to a certain degree as directly productive; this, which is also insisted on in *Philosophie Rurale*, is not understood in Scotland. In forming even a separate class of the *proprietors*, he has perhaps generalized a local and temporary arrangement, inconsistent with the perfect order most agreeable to nature; in which the real proprietors of the land would be the actual farmers.[2] 'L'ordre de la société, suppose [donc] *essentiellement* cette [troisième] classe de Citoyens', etc., p. 160.[3] Is it not enough, that, in the actual state of society, we describe the functions of the Proprietors in the distribution of wealth?

6. There is no room either to misunderstand or dispute that proposition of the Economists, in which they call manufacturing labour *barren* in opposition to the *productive* labour of the cultivators; because these terms have a reference to the sense, in which the same authors use the word *Production*, confining it to the produce of the earth. It is the propriety of this definition, that ought to be examined. – The epithets, *barren* and *productive* might be reciprocally changed, if a theorist were to restrict the term *productions* to those forms which manufacturing labour superinduces on the raw materials.

7. If the classification is well-founded, may we not consider the *Proprietors*, as really belonging to the productive class, but holding a more or less efficient part in that class in different countries, according to the degree of independence enjoyed by the *farmers*?

8. Though the fundamental position of the Economists may be quite correct, with respect to the source from which all national riches are distributed; it may perhaps be unnecessary to found upon that circumstance a classification of different orders of labourers.

9. Before entering into an examination of the reasoning by which the Economists have supported their leading principle, 'que la production est bornée aux seules richesses qui naissent de la terre' – it may be remarked that the language, in which they have expressed this proposition, is by no means precise.[4] I presume they do not mean to include all the productions of the earth, either of a vegetable or mineral nature; on the contrary, the phrase is limited, I fancy, to the esculent fruits and vegetables.[5] This being the case, it is from quality of nourishing human life that they are selected for this appellation. In all states of society, however, the human race generally derive their subsistence from other species of food beside the esculent vegetable; and in those forms of the social order, which precede the introduction of agriculture, they depend entirely upon fish, game, or cattle. If the principle of the Economists has a necessary reference to the idea of subsistence, it ought to be expressly mentioned; the proposition, as it stands at present, is in one point of view too general, and in another view too much restricted.

10. That wealth consists in exchangeable value, is a very false notion, and is indeed merely a different form of the old prejudice that the precious metals, which are the ordinary measure of exchangeable value, constitute wealth. The absurdity of the idea may be shown in the following light. If wealth consists of exchangeable value, it must consist in the exchangeable value of all commodities whatever, and it must increase directly with that value. Now the exchangeable value of a commodity

is said to be high, when a small quantity of that commodity will purchase a large quantity of any other. But as wealth consists in the exchangeable value of all commodities, great wealth must consist in the high value of all commodities; that is, in a small quantity of every single commodity being able to purchase a large quantity of any other commodity: which is a contradiction in terms. – Yet it seems to be an essential principle in the reasonings of the Economists, 'que c'est la valeur vénale qui donne aux productions la qualité de richesses.' p. 163.[6]

If by *productions* the Economists mean only the article of subsistence, and if by the preceding proposition they intend to assert, that these articles constitute national wealth only by the exchangeable value of the surplus, it would seem to follow, that in a season of dearth the sum of national wealth is at its *maximum*.

At present, I do not perceive that national wealth can be said to consist in anything else, than the supply of those commodities which satisfy human wants. As these wants differ much in point of urgency, the gratification of some being absolutely necessary to the preservation of life, there is a corresponding scale of subordination in the importance of the various articles by which they are supplied.

11. Quesnay admits, that manufacturing labour makes an *addition* of wealth to the raw materials on which it is employed, because it adds to their exchangeable value. He understands, therefore, that the raw material itself, which had likewise an exchangeable value, was likewise a part of wealth; and consequently that we are to enumerate, in the inventory of national wealth, all raw materials that have exchangeable value, though they may furnish nothing to human subsistence, and though they do not admit of reproduction. But why does any article acquire an exchangeable value, except because there is a demand for it, while the individuals who want it cannot directly supply themselves, and must therefore purchase it from others who have got it? Both these conditions must exist, before exchanges can take place; and the exchangeable value of a commodity is the result of its utility and its scarcity combined.[7]

The commodities, of which a man is in possession, are considered by him as riches or wealth, either because they minister directly to the gratification of his wants, or because they will procure for him by exchange such commodities as will directly gratify his wants. It is in the circumstance of gratifying his wants, either directly or after an exchange, that their character of wealth consists; they would not be wealth the less, because any bargain of exchange ceased to be necessary.

If this view of the subject be just, manufacturers may be said to make an addition of riches or wealth to the raw material on which they employ their labour, not because they augment its exchangeable value, but because they render it more serviceable and fit for the gratification of human wants. If this be true, the increase of exchangeable value forms no measure whatever of the real increase of wealth, occasioned by manufacturing industry: neither will it be correct to say, that the manufacturer neither diminishes nor augments the sum of national wealth, but exactly replaces what he consumes, or preserves the existence of wealth: for we shall then view him as consuming one kind of wealth, and producing another, which do not admit of any common measure or standard of value.

12. It does not appear to me, that there would be any inconsistency, in representing both agricultural and manufacturing labour as productive of national

wealth, and at the same time pointing out the former as the mainspring in the movements of national industry; though agricultural produce may not constitute in itself the whole of national wealth, it both forms the largest and an indispensable part of it, and it is the real stimulus to all that industry which contributes to the increase of national wealth in any other mode.

13. *Quesnai* observes, [Vol. ii], p. 165. that to call the increase of value which manufacturers give to the raw materials (on which their labour is employed) a production of wealth, and at the same time agree that the reduction of manufacturing expense is profitable by occasioning a diminution in the price of manufactured articles, is to assert two things which are contradictory. Nothing can be more just than this remark. The last of these two propositions is undeniably true; the fallacy must lie, therefore, in the first, viz., 'That the increase of value in manufactured articles is an increase of the whole sum of national wealth.' Taking this to pieces, there appear to be two opportunities of mistake; either in the general definition, that exchangeable value constitutes wealth; or in the particular application of it to manufactured goods. The general definition is assumed by Quesnai as a fundamental point of his doctrine; the fallacy of the foregoing contradiction, therefore, consisted, according to his opinion, in not attending to this peculiarity of manufactures, that every increase of exchangeable value which they occasion in particular substances, is indispensably preceded by the annihilation of an equal value of other substances.

In the preceding notes, however, I have mentioned some reasons for suspecting that Quesnai's definition of wealth is erroneous. If those suspicions are well-founded the fallacy, which is at present under investigation, will be found in a different part of the preceding proposition from that which Quesnai has pointed out. It will then be true, that the conversion of raw materials into manufactured goods, is a real addition to the sum of national wealth, not on account of the increase of exchangeable value, but on account of the multiplication of human comforts. And it will likewise be true, without any incompatibility, that there is a real profit in every saving of manufacturing expense, and in any consequent reduction of manufacturing price: to use other words, in the production of a maximum of manufactured riches by a minimum consumption of agricultural riches.

14. In that passage from Quesnai, which is criticized in the preceding note, that diminution of manufacture price is alone stated to be profitable, which is occasioned by a saving of manufacturing expenditure; in other words, by an improvement in the effective powers of manufacturing labour. ^^[8]

1. Continuing, in numerical sequence, the notes in Doc. 68.
2. *This, I now think, is a very doubtful proposition. In [Ch. ii, 'La source des Dépenses', of] the *Phil. Rur.*, I, p. 26, the author gives that the distinction of Proprietor and Farmer, as separate classes, is essential to a regular and complicated community and in the sequel of the same passage, he shows himself aware of the importance of making the farmer independent of all superintendence on the part of the Proprietor.
3. In Vol. ii of the 1768-9 edition of *Physiocratie*; the emphasis is Horner's.
4. Paraphrase of *Physiocratie*, ii. 156.
5. *The contrary, however, is stated by the author of the *Eloge of Quesnay*, which is printed in the *Nouvelles Ephémérides [économiques]* for 1775 [Paris], tom. V. 'Quesnay reconnut et fit voir, que l'agriculture, *la pêche et l'exploitation des mines et des carrières* étoient les seules sources des richesses.' p. 127.

6. *Physiocratie*, ii. 163.
7. This paragraph is dated in the margin 16 Oct. 1801.
8. Despite these insertion marks there appear to be no passages to be inserted. Paragraph 14 concludes Horner's notes of October 1801; paragraph 15 is dated 18 May 1802 (Doc. 86).

83. Journal

Kinnordy MSS ⟨Horner, i. 173–4⟩   23 Nov. 1801

My studies with Lord Webb, both of Bacon and of Adam Smith, still go on, though slowly, yet steadily. We have proceeded to the sixth chapter of *W. of Nations*, after having almost, though not completely, analysed the 5th; which abounds in violations of every rule of accurate reasoning and investigation. . . .

⟨. . . Though I become daily more attached to law as a study, I become daily more averse to the practice of the Scots Court. There are certain circumstances positively disagreeable both in the manner in which business is conducted, and in the manner in which success is attained; and these disadvantages are rendered the less tolerable, after comparison with the courts of the South. To speak out at once, therefore, whether it be foolish restlessness or ambition, I have for some time entertained serious thought of removing to another sphere of action, and of staking my chance in the great but hazardous game of the English Bar. It would take a great deal more patience than I have at present, to commit to paper the various views in which this plan has presented itself to my mind; as it occurs daily to my meditation, another opportunity will present itself for recording those sentiments of which I should be glad to preserve the history. At present, I shall only notice, that I came some time ago to the resolution of paying a visit to London in the Spring vacation, where, after a closer view of the scene, I shall form my final determination.⟩[1]

1. Sir James Mackintosh (1765–1832: *DNB*) visited Edinburgh in mid-September 1801 and renewed Horner's interest in London and the English Bar. On 22 Sept. Horner noted in his journal (*Horner*, i. 173), that he had 'lately spent two or three evenings in the company of James Mackintosh, author of the *Vindiciae Gallicae*, who was in Edinburgh for two or three days, and lived almost entirely with Sydney Smith. To one resident in the stagnation or poverty of Edinburgh conversation, the *beaux-esprits* of London are entertaining and instructive novelties.' On 16 Oct. 1801 Horner confided to Loch 'that a certain *bee* has been buzzing for some time in my head, which would carry me to the English Bar', and requested that Loch send him pertinent information (BLPES i. 147–8).

84. To the Duke of Somerset

BLPES i. 149-51 (copy)   Edinburgh, 19 Jan. 1802

At your brother's desire I will endeavour to make out a list of some books on Political Economy, which he told me you are desirous to have. The catalogue cannot fail to be very imperfectly executed both in point of number and criticism: because my reading on that subject, though miscellaneous enough, has been very cursory and inaccurate. I shall endeavour to recollect the titles of such publications as are either recommended by Mr Stewart in his lectures, or have fallen into my hands in the Advocate's Library.

Sir F. M. Eden, in his appendix to his ponderous but convenient compilation on the *State of the Poor*,[1] has printed a most extensive list of publications that have appeared in England on that department of Political Economy. Its very aspect furnishes a sort of proof that the evils resulting from our poor laws are equally great, lasting and difficult of remedy: I have noticed the omission of a few tracts in that list.

The Abbé Morellet, a liberal and perspicuous writer, published at Paris in 1769 a pretty large 8vo volume entitled *Prospectus d'un Nouveau Dictionnaire de Commerce*, at the end of which there is printed a scanty yet useful catalogue of works on Political Economy. The work itself is well worth reading, and gives me much room to regret that the project (as I understand) was never accomplished. Morellet both in this and many other works shows himself admirably qualified for the labours of distinct compilation.[2] He had the advantage too of possessing the copious MSS of Gournai, the famous merchant to whom the Economists ascribed the first systematic views concerning freedom of Trade.[3] In this *Prospectus* you will find a very elaborate treatise given by way of specimen on the Doctrine of Money and the principles of exchangeable value.

At the head of all works of Economical Philosophy I must place the few but invaluable essays of Turgot; because independent of the importance of the conclusions established in them, they present a model for the style of reasoning in this science. I allude especially to his *Lettres sur les grains*, and his *Formation et Distribution des Richesses*. There are also memoirs by him *Sur les principes de l'Administration politique, Sur la propriété des mines, Sur le prêt à l'Intérêt, Sur le commerce des fers* – etc. I have not found it easy to collect these different tracts, for there is no complete set of his writings; but with some pains they may be got. Lord Webb and I had engaged several of our friends here about 18 months ago, to translate all these Pieces and publish them together, but a London bookseller to whom I wrote did not relish the enterprise. I have heard Mr Stewart speak with much praise of the *preambles* to Turgot's *edicts*, promulgated during his Administration.

The study of the System of the Economists peculiarly so called forms a necessary part of the labour to be undertaken by every one who investigates this science. There is perhaps a pretty equal admixture of error and truth in their Theory: upon this I am not yet able to pronounce confidently. That their technical Nomenclature is awkward and unhandy, I should be very sorry to be forbid from saying, as some consolation for the pangs it has often cost me. But the great merit of the Economists, and the important benefit to be gained from their writings, consists in the strictness, precision, and simplicity which they introduced into the statement of Political reasonings, and the view of political phenomena. Adam Smith speaks of the little book of Mercier de la Rivière[4] as containing the best expositions of their doctrines, in which he appears to have greatly overrated it, if indeed he ever gave himself the serious trouble of studying their theory with attention. No doubt many of the arguments and illustrations of Mercier's book are stated with great neatness, but it is very unsatisfactory upon the whole. The *Philosophie Rurale* of the M. de Mirabeau is the most systematic and elaborate view of the Economist creed; but the large collection of Quesnai's writings published by Dupont under the title *Physiocratie* contains some excellent pieces, particularly three Dialogues in the second Volume, which appear to me written with remarkable force of argument. The writings in confutation of this System are innumerable, but very little known; I have scarcely looked into any of them. I recollect none of their names. I must make one exception however in favour of the ingenious Pinto, whose *Essai sur la circulation et le crédit*[5] abounds in valuable information and acute reasoning; it is not very easy to procure this book in the original but a very excellent translation by one Mr Baggs was published some years ago by Ridley in St James's Street.

I will endeavour in giving you the names that remain to refrain from such commentaries as I have absurdly enough given way to in describing those I have already mentioned. That I may preserve some kind of order, I shall run over my short notes from Stewart's lectures and copy the names of such authors as I find quoted under the different subjects.

POPULATION

Moheau's *Recherches sur la population de la France*: contains likewise a formal disquisition on the general principles.[6]

L'Ami des Hommes, par M de Mirabeau.[7]

Métrologie, par M Paucton.[8]

The Economical tracts collected in Price's book on annuities, and the various foreign works to which he refers, particularly the papers of Sussmilch, Wargentin, and Muret.[9]

Malthus's[10] *Essay on the principle of Population*.

The various tracts of Howlett, vicar of Great Dunmow, Essex, published by Richardson; these are sensible, candid and well informed, but seldom illuminated by any gleams of general principle.[11]

The Agricultural Reports,[12] especially Rutland, Middlesex, Kent.

Wallace on the numbers of mankind; an answer to Hume's excellent *Essay on the Populousness of ancient Nations*.[13]

A. Young's *Travels in France* and *Tour in Ireland*; the latter Mr Stewart considers as the best of his writings.[14]

The exquisite little essays of Franklin to be found partly in the edition of his *Essays* in 2 Vols 12mo and partly in a large 8vo volume of his *Miscellaneous Works*.[15]

Harte's *Essays on Husbandry*. Stewart quotes some extracts from this work with considerable respect, particularly a 'View of the Effects [of] Colbert's system of policy on the prosperity of France'. This author travelled with the son of Lord

Chesterfield, who speaks highly of the style of this work in one of his letters.[16]

Anderson's *Observations on National Industry*.[17]

Aiken's *View of the country round Manchester*.[18]

Rapport sur la Mendicité par le duc du Liancourt.[19]

The Statistical works of Sir W. Petty and Dr Davenant.[20]

Essai sur les Monnoies, par Dupré de St Maur.[21]

Recherches sur la population: divers ouvrages de l'Economie politique, par Lavoisier et de la Grange; a small but inestimable volume.[22]

Tracts on the Corn Trade republished in 1774, the author's name Smith.[23]

Dirom's tracts on the Corn Laws.[24]

Bibliothèque de l'homme public; published periodically to foment the political fervour at the beginning of the Revolution;[25] a slovenly compilation, but contains some information on the population of France, and the eloquent memoir of Condorcet *Sur l'Instruction publique*.[26]

Among the works that treat of the general Theory of the Science, I omitted Sir James Stewart's *Political Economy*,[27] a book valuable for curious and minute information, distinguished by great ingenuity, but of most troublesome perusal from the unfortunate manner in which it is composed. He has made a vocabulary of terms for himself, which is far from being happily executed. He is so overburdened with the propriety of being careful in the order and method of inquiry that he contrives most confusedly to interweave principles of Logic with his appropriate discussions; in the statement of an abstract subject, he rarely catches the point from which it may be seen most clearly and fully. In spite of the toil which these circumstances impose upon the reader, it is fully and amply repaid. There is an excellent little treatise published separately by the same Author: it was pointed out to me by Lord Lauderdale who thinks highly of it. 'The principles of money applied to the present state of the coin of Bengal [. . .] for the use of the East India Company, 1772.' It affords some very curious illustrations of the principles explained in Morellet's disquisition which I have already mentioned and which I have sometimes suspected to be written by Turgot.

MONEY

Rice Vaughan on Coins; a small volume which appears to have been written in the early part of Charles I's reign, and is curious on account of the precision with which at such a period several fundamental principles and reasonings are stated. It was published posthumously by a person ignorant of the subject who has left it very incorrect.

Harris on *Coins*; an excellent work.

Jeremy Bentham's *Defence of usury*.[28]

Locke's Tracts on Money.[29]

On this branch of Political Economy the publications are innumerable.

I recollect that your Grace got a list of Books on the Police of Grain when that interesting subject was under public discussion: there are a greater number of classical and standard Works on the Corn Trade than any other part of the Science. The recent scarcity added a number of Tracts, worthy of being preserved.

A great deal of important information with respect to the Political Economy of

England, is to be found in those pamphlets which are written for ephemeral purposes, and which in a few days become utterly forgotten except by those who cultivate the valuable talent of collecting, from the most trifling or corrupt sources, the authentic Materials of general speculation. It would be absurd to attempt any enumeration of these Tracts. It does not require much assiduity among the booksellers to accumulate the whole mass of them. They begin to be most useful about the time of the Revolution; but a few very curious and to us most instructive pamphlets are to be met with of the Reigns of Elizabeth and Charles I. I include in that class of Authorities the Reports of Parliamentary Committees. Some writers have exerted a very useful industry in compiling, upon a particular subject, the scattered information to be found in such books. This is the style of Eden's book on the poor, Anderson's *History of Commerce*,[30] and Smith's *Memoirs of Wool*:[31] all of them accurate and judicious as books of reference, and to me highly entertaining as so many tables of Inductive facts and experiments, which altogether thrown together in Chronological order, the most averse from Philosophical arrangement, yet in the perusal perpetually suggest either illustrations of principles already known, or excite attempts at further generalization.

From the hurried manner in which I have thrown these remarks together, as soon as Lord Webb proposed it, I am conscious you will have much reason to think the list very imperfect. The opinion I have hazarded on the merit of particular books may be very unfounded, because it is more frequently copied from vague impression than distinct remembrance. . . .

1. Sir Frederick Morton Eden (1776–1809: DNB), *The State of the Poor; or a History of the Labouring Classes in England from the Conquest to the present period* (3 vols, 1797), provided a detailed appraisal of British social legislation and the function of poor relief. The work contained information on wage levels, prices, and diet as well as a comparative appraisal of levels of poverty and want in a number of parishes.
2. The Dictionary outlined by André Morellet (1727–1819) in the *Prospectus d'un nouveau dictionnaire de Commerce* (Paris, 1769) was never published; although the *Dictionnaire universel de la géographie commerçante* (Paris, [1799–1800], by Jacques Peuchet (1758–1830), was based on the materials collected by the Abbé. Morellet's other major publications were *Réflexions sur les avantages de la libre fabrication et de l'usage des toiles peintes en France* (Paris, 1758) and *Mémoire sur la situation actuelle de la Compagnie des Indes* [Paris, 1769], which greatly influenced the suspension of the privileges of the Compagnie des Indes on 13 Aug. 1769.
3. Vincent de Gournay (1712–1759) opposed Colbert's system of close regulation of industry, protesting against the several monopolies, subsidies, and interest-free loans granted for the encouragement of new industries by the French state during the mid-eighteenth century, and arguing that the economy would expand and prosper if liberated from governmental interference. About 1755 Gournay used the term *laissez-faire* to describe the leading principle of his economic doctrine, and that term was subsequently embraced by the Physiocrats to express their plea for free enterprise and free trade.
4. [Pierre Paul François Joachim Henri le Mercier de la Rivière (1720–93/4)], *L'ordre naturel et essentiel des sociétés politiques* (2 vols, London and Paris, 1767), a three-part treatise considered by many to be the most comprehensive exposition of Physiocratic doctrine. It would appear that among the author's principal arguments none impressed Horner more than the assertions that the wealth of nations could be eroded either by a dearth or an overabundance of money (*ibid.*, ii. 368–9), and that a downward 'geometrical progression' of economic activity could result from excessive taxation on agriculture (*ibid.*, ii. 150–51).
5. Horner evidently means Pinto's *Traité de la circulation et du crédit*.
6. Moheau, an eighteenth-century statistician of whom little is known but who may have

been Baron Antoine Jean-Baptiste Robert Auget de Montyon (1733–1820) or the Baron's secretary, had published a two-volume work entitled *Recherches et considérations sur la Population de la France* in Paris in 1778.

7. The elder Mirabeau published the first three parts of *L'ami des hommes, ou Traité de la population* in Avignon in 1756. Horner seems to have used the first edition of these parts (though *HL* no. 163 gives Paris as the place of publication). For subsequent parts see Doc. 133.

8. Alexis Jean Pierre Paucton, *Métrologie* (Paris, 1780).

9. The writers cited by Price were: Johann Peter Süssmilch (1707–1767), an analyst of vital statistics and the first systematic student of political arithmetic, *Die göttliche Ordnung in den Veränderungen des menschlichen Geschlechts aus der Geburt, dem Tode und der Fortpflanzung desselben* (3rd ed., 3 vols, Berlin, 1765–66); Pehr Wilhelm Wargentin's *Mémoires abrégées de l'Académie Royale des Sciences de Stockholm*, in vol. xv of the *Collection Académique* (Paris, 1772), pp. 21ff (the original, 1766 article of this Swedish academician (1717–83) was translated into English and published as *Tables of Mortality* (Stockholm, 1930)); and Jean Louis Muret, *Mémoire sur l'état de la population dans le pays de Vaud* (Yverdon, 1766).

10. The copy, apparently in Horner's own hand, actually reads 'Melthurst'.

11. John Howlett (1731–1804: *DNB*) refuted in a number of tracts Richard Price's conclusion that the population of England and Wales had decreased by almost a quarter since the Restoration, arguing that inclosures improved agriculture and that an increase in population rendered them necessary. His major works were an *Examination of Dr Price's essay on the population of England and Wales* (Maidstone, 1778), *An enquiry into the influence which enclosures have had upon the population of this kingdom* (1786), *An Essay on the population of Ireland* (1786), *Enclosures, a cause of improved agriculture* (1787), and *The insufficiency of the causes to which the increase of our poor, and of the poor's rates have been commonly ascribed* (1788).

12. Perhaps Horner refers to *Annals of Agriculture*, which were initiated by Arthur Young in 1783 and eventually comprised 46 volumes.

13. Robert Wallace (1697–1771: *DNB*), *A dissertation on the numbers of mankind in ancient and modern times, in which the superior populousness of Antiquity is maintained* (Edinburgh, 1753). The work advanced arguments contrary to those put forward in Hume's *Political Discourses* and inspired Hume's later essay, *Of the Populousness of Ancient Nations*. Wallace also published *Characteristics of the present political state of Great Britain* (1758) and *Various prospects of mankind, nature, and Providence* (1761), both of which influenced Malthus.

14. Arthur Young, *A Tour in Ireland* (1780), and *Travels during the Years 1787, 1788 and 1799 . . . [in] France* (1792). Young also published, among much else, *The farmer's letters to the people of England* (1767), *A six weeks' tour through the southern counties of England and Wales* (1768), *The farmer's tour through the east of England* (4 vols, 1771), and *Political arithmetic* (2 parts, 1774–9).

15. Horner surely refers to Benjamin Franklin's *Observations Concerning the Increase of Mankind and the Peopling of Countries* (1755), a work contending, in opposition to Malthus despite several common ideas, that a large and swiftly growing population promoted the national interest. The other essays Horner had in mind may have been *A Modest Inquiry into the Nature and Necessity of a Paper Currency* (1729), which attacked bullionist doctrine, argued that an issue of paper currency would not depreciate the value of money so long as it was secured by land, and defined labour as the most viable standard for measuring value, and *Positions to be Examined concerning National Wealth* (1769). There were numerous two-volume editions of Franklin's works, including several in 12mo containing some of these essays. Horner does not specify which edition he used, and none of them was in his library when it was sold at auction. But, from the reference in Doc. 95 to Franklin's 'Remarks and facts relating to the American Paper-money', the 'large 8vo volume' would appear to be *Political, miscellaneous, and philosophical pieces*, published in London by J. Johnson in 1779.

   In a letter written nearly a decade later to a cousin visiting New York and Philadelphia, Horner commented (Horner to Harriet Baillie, 31 Jan. 1810, BLPES iv. 235–6):

   It is quite wonderful to me, that the Americans, who began with so good a writer as Franklin, should write at present such a clumsy, inflated, and low style, as appears in all their publications; both those of a literary nature, and the writings of their statesmen. Do not say a word of this, however, to any body; but wherever you go, preach to them the necessity of reading Franklin, and Addison, and Hume, till they can write something like a dialect of English: they enjoy the best government in the world, after ours; it is a pity that they do not add, to their freedom and prosperity, some portion of literary glory, without which their nation will never reach the fame which it already deserves.

16. The Reverend Walter Harte (1709–1774: *DNB*), who had once been tutor to Lord Chesterfield's son, published *Essays on Husbandry* in 1764. The work contained two essays. The first considered agriculture in general, the second the cultivation of lucerne; and the thesis of both essays, unsupported by data, was that agriculture was the principal support of all flourishing communities. There is no such heading as Horner describes, but he evidently refers to the passages on pp. 26–8, 66, and 178–9. Chesterfield wrote in his letter clviii of 3 Sept. 1764:

> I have received a book . . . from Harte. It is upon Agriculture, and will surprise you, as, I confess, it did me. The work is not only in English, but good and elegant English; he has even scattered graces upon his subject; and in prose has come very near Virgil's Georgics in verse.

17. A Scottish contemporary of Adam Smith and James Steuart, James Anderson (1739–1808: *DNB*) published *Observations on the Means of exciting a spirit of national industry [in] Scotland* in Edinburgh in 1777, his other major publications being *An enquiry into the nature of the corn-laws* (Edinburgh, 1777) and a *General view of the agriculture and rural economy of the county of Aberdeen* (Edinburgh, 1794). Anderson was generally favourable to free trade but advocated state protection in the early stages of development. Similarly, he championed the Corn Laws on developmental grounds and disagreed with Smith's assertion that corn regulated the price of all commodities. He was also the first to propound the theory of rent and indeed anticipated Ricardo's rent theory, though not so narrowly and abstractly.

18. John Aikin (1747–1822: *DNB*), *A Description of the country from thirty to forty miles round Manchester* (1795).

19. François Alexandre-Frédéric, Duc de Liancourt, afterwards Duc de la Rochefoucault, published a whole series of such reports in 1790–91.

20. Sir William Petty (1623–1687: *DNB*), an early proponent of the labour theory of value who embraced Bacon's inductive method and Hobbes's *logica sine computatio* in examining the distribution and flow of wealth within the 'political body', which he equated with the circulation of blood within the human body. Petty's leading works were *Political Arithmetick* (1690), *The Political Anatomy of Ireland* (1691), and *Quantulumcumque concerning money* (1695).

Charles Davenant (1656–1714: *DNB*), essayist on political economy and commissioner of excise from 1683 to 1689, espoused free trade principles early in life but later embraced the leading tenets of mercantilist doctrine. His major works included *An essay upon ways and means of supplying the war* (1695), *An Essay on the East-India-Trade* (1697), *Discourses upon the publick revenues and trade of England* (1698), *An Essay upon the probable means of making a people gainers in the ballance of Trade* (1699), *A discourse upon grants and resumptions* (1700), *Essays upon the ballance of power, etc.* (1701), *Reflections upon the constitution and management of the trade to Africa* (1709), and *Reports to . . . the commissioners for . . . taking the public accounts* (1712).

21. Nicolas François Dupré de Saint Maur, *Essai sur les Monnoies* (Paris, 1746).

22. From the later reference in Doc. 92 it would seem that Horner means *Collection de divers ouvrages d'arithmétique politiques, par Lavoisier, Delagrange, et autres* (Röderer, Paris, [1796]), which contains a number of essays focusing either directly or indirectly on the human and physical resources of the French Republic. In a letter to Richard Sharp dated 29 Mar. 1806 (Doc. 226), Horner mentions 'a fragment of a work undertaken by the famous Lavoisier at the desire of the National Assembly on *La Richesse Territoriale de la France*'. Lavoisier's 'Résultats extraits d'un ouvrage intitulé "De la richesse territoriale du royaume de France", . . . 1791' was among the essays included in the *Collection*.

23. A reprint of Charles Smith (1713–1777: *DNB*), *Three tracts on the corn trade* (1766), which appeared about 1774, contained the most important of his previously published tracts, *A short essay on the corn trade and the corn laws* (1758) and *Considerations on the laws relating to the Importation and Exportation of Grain* (1759), together with *A Collection of Papers relative to the Price, Exportation, and Importation of Corn* containing lists of corn prices between 1595 and 1765.

24. Alexander Dirom (d. 1830: *DNB*), *An Inquiry into the Corn Laws and Corn Trade of Great Britain* (Edinburgh, 1796).

25. Published in Paris monthly from January 1790 until March 1792.

26. *Rapport et projet de décret sur l'organisation générale de l'instruction publique* (Paris, 1792).

27. Sir James Steuart Denham (1712–1780: *DNB*), *An inquiry into the principles of political œconomy* (1767), a work that enjoyed a considerable reputation among continental, principally German, political economists throughout the nineteenth century but which was little read in Britain after the publication of Smith's *Wealth of Nations* in 1776.

28. This two-volume work, published in London in 1787, argued that the rate of interest on money should be outside the control of government.

29. *Some Considerations of the consequences of the lowering of interest, and raising the value of money* (1692), *Short observations on a printed paper, intituled 'For encouraging the coining silver money in England, and after for keeping it here'* (1695), and *Further considerations concerning raising the value of money* (1695) were all reprinted in *Several papers relating to money, interest and trade, etc.* (1696).

30. Adam Anderson, *An Historical and Chronological Deduction of the Origin of Commerce* (1764).

31. John Smith, *Chronicon Rusticum – Commerciale, or Memoirs of Wool, etc.* (2 vols, 1747).

Section II

The Edinburgh Reviewer
1802–1809

Introduction

HORNER made two crucial decisions in early 1802. The first, a resolution to go to the English Bar, was motivated by dreams of political honours.[1] The second, a hasty commitment to collaborate with his friends in founding the *Edinburgh Review*, allowed him to realise his political ambitions. For the unexpected success of the *Review* brought Horner literary fame, and his presence in the English capital enabled him to exploit it. Beginning in the winter of 1802, when the publication of his treatise on paper credit established his reputation as a political economist, and continuing until the winter of 1809, Horner pursued a calculated plan of manoeuvre that earned him a place at the dinner table of Holland House, a seat in the House of Commons, and considerable influence within the ranks of the Whig party.

Encouraged by Professor Stewart, Horner had practically decided to relocate in London by February 1802 and, despite his father's reservations, had made plans to visit the metropolis in late March.[2] Some two weeks before his scheduled departure from Edinburgh he found himself at Jeffrey's apartment in Buccleuch Place in the company of John Allen and Sydney Smith. The night was stormy, the conversation lively, and at some point discussion turned to the unsuccessful attempt of Adam Smith, Robertson the historian, and Hugh Blair the moderate preacher to establish a literary journal in 1755. The unemployed Smith proposed a second Edinburgh Review, a critical periodical altogether independent of booksellers and focusing on works of literature and science. Lawyer Jeffrey, who had no briefs, endorsed the idea enthusiastically. Allen, the impoverished physician, was also quite keen, and Horner too was taken with the prospect of exhibiting his intellectual ability.[3]

Subsequent consultations with the publisher Archibald Constable and a number of potential contributors made the venture seem feasible. Horner agreed to serve as the principal reviewer of economic literature, suggested the motto that was adopted for the journal, and began to meet with his colleagues in a dingy room off a printing office in Craig's Close owned by one Willison.[4] But in mid-March, while his fellow

---

1. See Horner's journal entry of 3 May 1802 (*Horner*, i. 197–9).
2. Horner's journal entries of 15 Feb. and 25 Mar. 1802, *ibid.*, i. 176 and 178.
3. *Brougham*, i. 251; *Jeffrey*, i. 127 and 136.
4. *Brougham*, i. 252 and 246; Clive, p. 26.

reviewers were still engaged in preliminary discussions, Horner left for London.

Fearing 'an imprudent sacrifice to ambition', Horner sought in London the society of English lawyers who might furnish 'matter for reflections of a personal nature'.[5] To this end he was assisted by Professor Stewart, who had given him a letter of introduction to the leading barrister at the Chancery Bar, Sir Samuel Romilly, and by James Abercromby, an admiring friend with whom he had been both at school and university.[6] Romilly received his visitor warmly, and Horner witnessed a performance of the great advocate in the Court of Chancery. Meanwhile Abercromby, seeking to connect his friend 'with persons who may be disposed to put him in situations where his acquirements may be displayed with advantage to the public', introduced Horner to John Whishaw and ensured that he also met Henry Hallam.[7] Both men were destined to become Horner's lifelong friends, but Whishaw was of immediate utility. On 10 April he introduced Horner to the society of the 'King of Clubs', an association of Whig lawyers who met periodically at the Crown and Anchor Tavern in the Strand.[8] There, in a party that included Romilly, Mackintosh, and Richard Sharp, Horner cultivated relationships that would bear heavily on his future. Afterwards he met privately with Romilly on several occasions, attended a dinner party at Romilly's home where he met George Wilson, the charming leader of the Norfolk circuit, and at last decided on a course of action.[9] He would return to Edinburgh for two years, and then remove to London in order to pursue a career at the Chancery Bar.[10]

On 2 May, as his coach neared Edinburgh, and again on 9 May, Horner outlined in his journal the strategy and tactics from which he would never depart. Successful legal practice was but a means to a greater end, he noted, a medium through which he might acquire enough financial independence and professional reputation to facilitate a political career. In the meantime he must curb personal ambition, steadily systematize 'all views and plans of life', continue his study of politics, and place himself in a position to exploit opportunities whenever an 'active scene' opened.[11]

Horner stressed the importance of examining 'other men's minds in conducting self-education' and recorded principles of conduct suggested by his recent visit to London. The political conversation of the Whig lawyers at the 'King of Clubs' in particular had left a deep impression. For there Horner had observed an absence of disputation, a spirit of compromise that resulted in uniformity of opinion on 'the

---

5. Horner's journal entry of 25 Mar. 1802, *Horner*, i. 178.
6. James Abercromby, afterwards 1st Baron Dunfermline (1776–1858: DNB); see also Doc. 296.
7. Abercromby to J.A. Murray, 29 Mar. 1802, *Horner*, i. 179–81. Henry Hallam (1777–1859: DNB), the future historian, was then a barrister on the Oxford circuit.
8. Horner's journal entry of 10 Apr. 1802, *Horner*, i. 183.
9. According to *Cockburn*, pp. 289–91, George Wilson (d. 1816) was, like Horner, a Scot by birth and education but an English lawyer by profession. He was a close friend of Bentham as well as Romilly; but in 1810 bad health forced his retirement to Edinburgh, where, however, he continued a very popular member of the Friday Club (for which see Doc. 125 n. 3).
10. Horner to J.A. Murray, 16 Apr., to John Horner, 17 April, and Horner's journal entry of 24 Apr. 1802, *Horner*, i. 188–96.
11. *Ibid.*, i. 197–99 and 360–61.

fundamental doctrines in religion and politics', an emphasis on retrospect to the virtual exclusion of 'present activity', and a curious reverence for the political doctrine of Edmund Burke. These were shrewd observations and they led Horner to important conclusions. At all times, he noted, one must regulate political and religious sentiments very carefully and demonstrate an 'acute sensibility to the proprieties of conversation, character, and company'.[12]

Already, it seems, Horner had identified a role model. Romilly, he had observed after dining at the 'King of Clubs' on 10 April, 'received from all an unaffected deference, and imposed a certain degree of restraint' on conversation. Romilly's extraordinary effect on other men, Horner had told Murray six days later, was owing, not only to his genius and learning, but also to his great independence, modesty, and polished conversational skills. Here was a self-educated man of relatively modest origins, who had risen by native talent alone and was now universally acknowledged 'to stand highest' at the Chancery Bar and, at a mature age, as a likely candidate for the highest offices of state. Romilly's advice had influenced Horner's decision to practise in Chancery; now, reflecting on the great barrister's example, Horner speculated that perhaps he might undertake political engagements at 'about fifty years of age'.[13]

Horner's plan also stressed the importance of cultivating advantageous political contacts. Before going to London his 'dreams of ambition' had been encouraged by the intimate relationships he had formed at Edinburgh University with Seymour and, more importantly, with Lord Henry Petty. Those aristocratic connections gave him a vital contact with high society and politics, and Horner was convinced that among the London lawyers also he had cultivated new friendships that 'must prove valuable to me throughout life'. Then, too, Abercromby, Mackintosh, Romilly, and Whishaw had encouraged his ambitions. Horner's English friends, his sister Frances afterwards recalled, were 'bent on his removing to the great field of London, and Parliament ultimately'.[14]

Horner took stock of his resources and contemplated the advantages of an accelerated timetable. All the pieces of the puzzle were in place, he concluded; nothing could be gained by remaining in Scotland for two more years. On 27 May he informed a friend that he expected to meet him in London in March 1803.[15]

Afterwards Horner was consumed by thoughts of politics. On 11 June he noted in his journal that 'Political *virtue*, political *sagacity*, political *science*, are three great branches of habit to be cultivated'.[16] His aspirations mounted shortly thereafter when John Allen accepted employment as personal physician to Lord and Lady Holland and almost immediately accompanied them to Paris in a party that included Fox himself. Such a connection, Horner realized, opened doors (Doc. 97); before long he was heaping lavish praise on the Whig leader in a letter to Allen

12. *Idem*, and Horner's journal entry of 10 Apr. 1802, *Horner*, i. 183–5.
13. *Ibid.*, i. 183; Horner to Murray, 16 Apr., and to John Horner, 17 Apr. 1802, *ibid.*, i. 189–90 and 193. *Ibid.*, i. 360–61. See also Horner's journal entry of 20 Apr., *ibid.*, i. 196.
14. Horner's journal, 3 May, and Horner to Murray, 16 Apr. 1802, *ibid.*, i. 199 and 189; Byrne Memoirs, p. 59.
15. Horner to Loch, 27 May, BLPES i. 162–3.
16. *Horner*, i. 362.

(Doc. 98) and attending the meetings of Edinburgh's Fox Club, a 'duty' he found 'stupid' but effective among 'a certain description of people' (Doc. 109).

During the spring and early summer of 1802 Horner continued to correspond with Seymour's brother (Doc. 90), surely realizing the potential importance of the Duke of Somerset in his plans, and during the rest of that year obtained political intelligence from his old friend Loch, who had migrated earlier to London. The letters Horner wrote to Loch between June 1802 and January 1803 addressed a wide range of political subjects – the rumoured reform of Scots judicature, British colonial and fiscal policy, the general election of July, the fragility of Britain's commercial wealth – but they are most notable for assessments of party alignments and an increasing focus on the party of Fox (Docs 91, 93, 94, 97, 103, and 105).

Meanwhile Horner began his career as an Edinburgh reviewer. According to Frances Horner, who witnessed the early deliberations of her brother and his collaborators in the parlour of the Horner household, the original goal of the reviewers was to resist 'the corruptive power' of Pitt and Melville and 'to elevate the tone of their countrymen'.[17] If so, Horner's view of the venture changed appreciably after he returned from London. For then he adopted a cautious attitude and fretted a great deal about the articles' 'tone and manner' (Docs 103, 104, 105, and 109). In this Horner agreed with Sydney Smith, who served as general editor for the first number, and a letter Horner wrote in November suggests that he agreed with Smith's insistence on the exclusion of the brilliant but reckless Brougham from the inner circle of reviewers (Doc. 103). At all events Brougham was kept at arm's length, Smith relying heavily on Horner's judgement and Horner apparently becoming quite active in evaluating and editing the several manuscripts that began to arrive in Craig's Close during the late spring and early summer of 1802.[18]

Initially Horner had considered writing a review of Canard's *Principes d'Economie Politique*, on which he hoped to hang a comparative analysis of Smithian and Physiocratic doctrine, and on 18 May he resumed his study of the 'Economists', making a number of notes on the nature of national wealth (Docs 85–6). Soon, however, he discerned 'some fundamental mistake' in Quesnay's reasonings, and being unable to 'solve the puzzle', concluded that the project should be delayed until he obtained the published works of other Physiocratic writers (Docs 87–8). He then projected a treatise on French commercial policy, but here too a dearth of information thwarted him. On 14 June he wrote to Allen in Paris, posing twenty-eight questions relating to contemporary French political economy and requesting assistance in procuring the works of Quesnay and his followers (Doc. 92).

While awaiting Allen's reply, Horner reflected on another recent publication, Henry Thornton's *Inquiry into the Nature and Effects of the Paper Credit of Great Britain*. The author was a successful banker, a member of Parliament since 1782, and a member of the Clapham sect. His 302-page work was awkwardly organized and abominably written; but it was the first judicious assessment of the causes and effects of the suspension of cash payments by the Bank of England, and it was written with attention to the money market, foreign exchanges, banking practice, and the present high price of bullion. Horner's earlier study of the theory of money had left

17. Byrne Memoirs, pp. 46–7. See Cockburn's similar account in *Jeffrey*, i. 82.
18. *Jeffrey*, i. 127.

him hopelessly confused, and by all appearances he was now reluctant to stake his reputation on a subject he yet regarded as 'obscure'. Within Thornton's practical treatise, however, Horner found a number of facts that tended to clarify his earlier researches.

He was helped along by the Duke of Somerset, who in late May had sent him a consignment of relevant parliamentary committee reports. The statistics within them provided 'a solid basis for accurate and important speculations' (Doc. 89); so Horner made arrangements to procure additional parliamentary papers and placed a standing order for economic literature with a London bookseller.[19] Towards the end of July – after an interval of more than a year – he returned to Adam Smith's chapter on money, considered the related works of Hume and Franklin, and took a number of notes (Doc. 95). But the subject continued to trouble him and in any case the French projects remained his first priority, his study of monetary theory being interrupted in August by a revival of his earlier plan to publish a selection of Turgot's writings (Doc. 98).

Evidently Horner made no firm decision about his contributions to the first number of the *Review* until early September, when Allen's reply to his letter of 14 June failed to provide the desired information on French political economy (Doc. 96). Now facing a short deadline, he resolved to postpone his articles on Canard and French commercial policy, make a review of Thornton his major contribution to the first number of the *Review*, and write cursory reviews of three other recent works (Doc. 100).

Horner seems to have written these reviews in about three weeks. His notes on Thornton, which drew heavily on earlier researches, are dated 5–16 September (Doc. 99). The writing of that review, he acknowledged, cost him 'considerable trouble', and he delivered it to the press in a form that required further editing (Doc. 100). He also noted on the 30th that he had finished all four reviews several days earlier. It would appear, then, that he completed the review of Thornton quite late in the month and then wrote the three shorter tracts very hurriedly, thereby meeting a deadline that allowed Constable to release the first *Edinburgh Review* on 10 October 1802.

The initial number contained twenty-nine reviews, of which, in addition to Horner's four, seven were by Smith, six by Jeffrey, and four generally credited to Brougham. Brougham's article on colonial slavery and Smith's on the French Revolution were lively, provocative pieces, but Horner had already decided that Jeffrey's reviews would be 'beyond any comparison the best' (Doc. 97). For his own part, Horner acknowledged that his short articles – on emigration, education, and country banks – were unexceptional. But the review of Thornton, he observed (Doc. 100), had 'served to break up the ground in one of the most necessary fields of political economy'.

Comprehending the importance of Thornton's bullionist doctrine, Horner had planned merely 'to mould the irregular materials of the original work into an useful arrangement' (Doc. 100). In that he had been successful, but the review, which in many cases contained passages lifted verbatim from Horner's earlier notes, also

19. Horner to Loch, 31 May, BLPES i. 164–5.

amplified Thornton's reasonings very expertly and advanced an altogether different view of the causes and effects of the suspension of cash payments by the Bank of England.

The article began with a refutation of the pervasive belief that negotiable paper did not form part of the circulating medium. Paper money, like precious metals, Horner argued, was nothing more than the representative of value; paper converted into value, and so long as public faith in its convertibility prevailed, negotiable paper was no less a part of the circulating medium than precious metals. Yet another fiction, he noted, was the idea, accepted even by Thornton, that a system of paper credit could not long command public faith unless paper could be converted into specie. Such a theory was disproved by the fact; a five-year suspension of specie payments had occasioned no discernible depreciation of paper attributable to a failure of confidence. Quite another matter, however, was whether an over-issue of paper such as had consequently been permitted to the Bank, had not undermined its value. Whatever the case, the suspension of cash payments by the Bank had carried the theory of money to a new juncture.

In 1802 these preliminary observations alone were quite bold, but Horner supported them with a very effective summary and analysis of Thornton's wandering comments on the relationship between metallic and paper currency, the price of commodities in the domestic market, foreign trade, and the price of bullion on the international exchanges. Thornton, somewhat like Hume before him, had contended that metallic and paper currency naturally held the same value in the domestic market so long as paper could be converted into specie. If the real or relative quantity of paper were augmented, however, the relationship of coin and paper would change. A real augmentation of quantity would come, of course, with an excessive issue of paper; but a relative augmentation, with precisely the same effect as a real one, would result from an unfavourable balance of trade.

Whether real or relative, an augmentation of the quantity of paper increased the price of consumer goods in the domestic market and set a ruinous cycle in motion. Inflation worsened the balance of trade. A trade imbalance placed a drain on the country's reserves of bullion, thereby increasing the price of gold in proportion to the circulating medium for which it was exchanged. And an upward spiral in the bullion price of consumer goods on the world market would continue until the return of a favourable balance of trade restored equilibrium between metallic and paper currency in the home economy.

Thornton had expanded on these reasonings with a detailed explanation of Britain's credit apparatus and then turned to the causes and effects of the suspension of cash payments in 1797. The suspension, he contended, had been necessitated by an unfavourable balance of trade that had diminished gold reserves and by bank failures in the north of England that had produced a run on specie. Afterwards the 'necessary influence of war' – accumulated taxes, scarcity, a resulting rise in the price of consumer goods – and an immense importation of foreign corn had compounded the commercial dilemma, turning the exchanges against Britain and so accelerating the drain on specie. The present high price of bullion, Thornton therefore reasoned, was owing, not to an excessive issue of paper, but instead to a continuing trade imbalance.

Horner disagreed. Initially, he pointed out, gold reserves had not been depleted by an unfavourable balance of trade. Rather, the war with France, like all wars, had occasioned a dearth of capital in the mercantile community, thereby creating an increased demand for credit. However, owing to the heavy loans to Government necessitated by Pitt's policy of subsidizing Britain's continental allies, the Bank of England, experiencing a progressive drain on specie, had progressively tightened its credit policy and reduced its issue of paper. That policy, of course, had forced London's banking houses and the country banks to follow suit. In the face of an already serious dearth of capital, therefore, the nation's credit apparatus had been disrupted, and the inevitable result had been mercantile failures, banking failures, and a run on specie. At last a chronic shortage of gold reserves had led to the suspension of all payments in specie, and to the issue of only paper credit by the Bank of England. However, a fearful Bank had not issued enough notes at first, and ruinous shortages in the circulating medium had ensued. Then, when the Bank realized it had not issued enough notes, it overreacted and issued too many. The resulting depreciation of paper had led to the melting and exportation of the remaining guineas.

Horner then turned to the bullion question and its relationship to British commerce. It was not, as Thornton suggested, the bullion price of goods that was raised by a real or relative increase in the quantity of paper credit, but instead the paper or currency price. The bullion price remained constant and, while inflation in the paper price of consumer goods mounted at home, the price of the same goods remained constant to a foreign merchant who paid in specie. Hence a real or relative increase of the quantity of paper, while having no appreciable effect on the balance of trade, had a considerable impact on the course of exchange:

> By that increase, our currency sinks in its bullion value, and a given sum of it will no longer purchase the same quantity of bullion; but the foreign currency … preserves its bullion value; and a given sum of that will still purchase the same quantity of bullion as before. The proportion, therefore, of the bullion value of our currency to the bullion value of foreign currency is altered … Our general exchanges might thus appear unprosperous, at the very time that the balance of trade was greatly in our favour; and if the issue of paper continued to increase, the exchange would appear to become more and more unfavourable, although the balance of exports and imports had remained unaltered. The difference, therefore, between the two cases, which Mr Thornton appears to have confounded, is very distinct. When the local rise of the price of goods consists in an actual increase of their bullion price, a real fall of the foreign exchange will generally take place, and will *occasion*, by the demand for bullion to be exported, a fluctuating excess of the market price above the mint price of gold. But when an excessive issue of paper money produces a nominal rise of prices, a nominal fall of the foreign exchange will always take place, and is a *consequence* of that steady excess of the market price of gold above its mint price, which originated immediately in the excessive issue of paper.

None of this, Horner insisted, could be explained away. Thornton had pointed to deficient harvests, heavy importations of foreign corn, and a resulting unfavourable balance of trade as the causes of a necessary suspension of cash payments. The suspension, however, had come well before the effects of deficient harvests were manifest. Nor were Thornton's explanations of subsequent inflation adequate. Accumulating taxes and a scarcity of provisions certainly increased the real or bullion price of goods, but those factors did not produce an excess or carry the market price of gold above its mint price. And Horner flatly contradicted Thornton's contention that there had been no increase in the amount of paper issued by the Bank of England. An unfavourable balance of trade, he asserted, could not have occurred 'without the depreciation of our currency, which originates in excessive quantity'.[20] Here was the general interpretation of the monetary crisis to which Horner would ever subscribe and the seed of the report of the Bullion Committee he would chair some eight years later. Essentially his doctrine repre-sented the nation's imbalance of trade as a monetary rather than a commercial phenomenon and laid the blame squarely on the failure of the Bank of England to pursue policies consistent with the wartime demands of a volatile commercial economy.

In advancing his arguments Horner displayed his long-standing concern about the internal consistency of Adam Smith's doctrine. He noted that what Thornton had observed about the velocity of circulation had escaped Smith's attention and that the *Wealth of Nations* had similarly failed to provide a suitable explanation of the determinants of price. Indeed Horner doubted Smith's assumption that every issue of paper currency must necessarily displace a like quantity of gold, and placed more confidence in Thornton's argument that psychological factors bore heavily on the state of public credit. Finally, Horner's conclusions suggested that changes in the institutional structure of the state necessitated a complete overhaul of Smith's entire theory of money.

No less significant was the political context of Horner's monetary doctrine. While Thornton had studiously avoided contentious political issues, Horner related the high price of bullion to Pitt's continental subsidies, thereby rendering his doctrine consistent with a major component of Fox's long-standing opposition to the conduct of the war against France. That point, emanating from a literary journal dressed in the buff and blue colours of the Foxite party, did not go unnoticed in Whig circles.[21]

As reports of the success of the *Edinburgh Review* arrived during the last three months of the year, Horner sought the opinions of Englishmen and discerned that the temperate views expressed in the first number had surprised and pleased the public (Docs 103 and 104).[22] More important, he began to sense the value of literary fame to his broader political objectives (Doc. 105). His object now was 'influence, in advancing the progress of the public mind and the public fortunes, as a political philosopher'. Such influence, he noted, might give him 'a chance for *acting* in public life', an opportunity to '*place myself* in a public situation, where the results of political philosophy may be applied to the exercise of the great duties of legislation'. The three 'great preparations' for this 'noble scheme' were 'a complete study of

20. *ER* i (no. i, Oct. 1802), 172–201.
21. See Fontana, pp. 56–9, and Chitnis, pp. 120–21.
22. See also Horner to Hewlett, 20 Oct., BLPES i. 186–7.

political science, and the acquisition of powers as a public speaker, and as a writer'.[23] He consequently resumed his political researches[24] and again attended Professor Stewart's lectures on political economy, hoping to enhance his 'visionary prospects' by acquainting himself more fully with the manner in which Stewart considered a subject. He also attended the 'Spec' regularly, following Brougham's example of preparing himself 'upon one or two of the best questions' (Doc. 104). The nexus of his scheme, however, was literary fame.

On 18 October Horner resumed his study of the Physiocrats, intent on completing his review of Canard for the second number of the *Review* (Doc. 101). But his researches were interrupted by lingering dreams of publishing a selection of Turgot's writings, and on 21 October he drafted a plan for yet another ambitious project, a 'Universal History' of the world with which he would dabble for the rest of his life (Doc. 102).

Horner did not resume work on Canard until 30 November, when he attempted to analyse Turgot's reasonings on the territorial tax,[25] and the surviving notes relating to the review suggest that he did not begin in earnest until about two weeks prior to Constable's deadline (Docs 106–108). Even then, however, the affairs of the metropolis, the character of Fox and, not incidentally, the opinions of Lord Grenville on the poor law, absorbed his thoughts (Doc. 105). Now there was not enough time to write a treatise comparing Smithian and Physiocratic doctrine, so Horner perused his earlier notes and applied many of the reasonings within them to a review of a manageable selection of Canard's chapters. Still, the resulting article, which appeared in January 1803, was a learned exposition of broad principles, and it contributed significantly to Horner's reputation as a political economist, if not to the popularity of his doctrine.[26]

Horner's article began with a brief tribute to Turgot, Mirabeau, and Quesnay, who were described as 'the friends of mankind', and then turned to a critical analysis of Canard's methodology and leading theoretical positions. Horner was especially critical of the author's exaggerated use of algebraic symbols:

> In its own province, the peculiar language of algebra will never fail to gratify those who can appreciate the admirable structure of the most perfect instrument that has yet been invented by man. But that injudicious and unskilful pedantry ought most severely to be censured, which diverts an instrument from its proper use, and attempts to remove those landmarks by which the sciences are bounded from each other. ... M. Canard has only translated, into a language less readily understood, truths, of which the ordinary enunciation is intelligible and familiar to all.

Here was an opinion that would always distinguish Horner among the political economists of even his own time, but the real importance of the review was his disagreement with a number of Canard's 'truths'. To Horner nothing was more dubious than the author's notion that the exchangeable value of a commodity was determined by the quantity of labour expended in its production. Such a definition

---

23. Horner's journal, 26 Nov., *Horner*, i. 362–3.
24. See, for example, his journal entry of 30 Nov., *ibid.*, i. 215–17.
25. *Ibid.*, i. 215–16.
26. *ER* i (no. ii, Jan. 1803), 431–50.

of value was 'certainly incorrect'. It had confounded even Adam Smith's analysis of price, and Horner thought it curious that Canard 'preferred the errors of our English writers to the accurate and precise notions ... which he might have found in various excellent works, published in his own language, particularly those of M. Turgot and of the Abbé Morellet'. As those writers had clearly established, exchangeable value was determined by nothing other than the fluctuating relationship of demand and supply in the market; the reciprocal value of any two commodities was merely a reflection of the 'proportion between the supply and the demand of each'.

Horner was no less adamant in refuting Canard's thesis that the wealth of commercial nations, checked by the waste and declining profits that accompanied the accumulation of a surplus of capital, was finite, and that the British economy, propped by an unsuccessful funding system, was in a state of decline. Such a view of national wealth, Horner snapped, was only a modern rendition of mercantilist doctrine, one that altogether ignored the invigorating effect of competition, and thus Canard's remarks on the demise of Britain were 'a *reductio ad absurdum*'.

Perhaps the most interesting part of the review was Horner's analysis of Canard's chapter on taxation, in which the author had asserted that taxes diffused themselves 'over all the different branches of revenue ... whether they are levied at the source of revenue or upon consumption'. Horner dismissed that point of view contemptuously and responded to it by incorporating a portion of the comparative analysis of Smithian and Physiocratic doctrine he had planned earlier. Adam Smith, he contended, had 'derived a much larger portion of his reasonings' from the Physiocrats than 'he himself perhaps recollected'. Indeed Smith's observations on the formation and distribution of national wealth 'approached more nearly to those of Quesnai, than he was himself aware', and his analysis of taxation, if carried 'a few steps farther', would have produced conclusions perfectly consistent with those of Quesnay. The reasonings of both writers, Horner argued, led inevitably to the conclusion that

> all taxes, however levied, are finally incident upon the neat produce, and are ultimately paid by the landlord either in a diminution of his rent, or in an increase of the wages and prices which, out of his actual rent, he distributes among the other classes of the community.

While Horner's doctrine was very favourable to the fundamental position taken by the Physiocrats, it rejected their proposal for a unified territorial tax and endorsed the Foxite argument that the centralized French system of taxation, like Pitt's much-abused wartime taxation policy, was 'despotic'. Thus in his review of Canard, as in his review of Thornton, Horner ended a scholarly treatise with a conclusion that coincided with the views of the political faction he courted.[27]

Although he complained of 'blunders' by Constable (Doc. 126), Horner was quite pleased with his single contribution to the second number of the *Review*. There was much merit, he rightly suspected, in his observations on Smith and Quesnay, and he was eager to develop his arguments in a subsequent review (Doc. 120). For the time being, however, his mind was on London and the extraordinary public reception of his article on paper credit.

27. See Fontana, pp. 53-4.

Horner apparently attempted to write a follow-up to his review of Thornton during his final months in Edinburgh. On 25 January 1803, the day the second number of the *Review* was released, he told Loch (Doc. 109) that he was reading a recent pamphlet on fiscal policy and requested assistance in locating publications 'in which the history of our funds is fully collected, and the principles explained upon which parliamentary loans are transacted'. Unfortunately neither Loch's reply nor any further correspondence relating to the project has been found, but as late as 4 March Horner recorded a number of conclusions relating to the theory of money among his notes on the *Wealth of Nations* (Doc. 110). In the end, however, the press of last-minute business in Edinburgh proved too demanding, and Horner's only contribution to the third number of the *Review* was two hurriedly-written pages on Sir John Sinclair's *Essays on Miscellaneous Subjects* that appeared with substantial additions by Jeffrey (Doc. 116).[28]

In late March 1803, following a farewell banquet at Fortune's Hotel, Horner left Edinburgh for London and, finding suitable chambers unavailable at the Inns of Court, took lodgings in Northumberland Street with James Brougham, Henry's brother.[29] He must very soon have been passed a brief; for on 2 April he made his initial appearance before a committee of the House of Commons, pleading none too happily in an appeal involving manure and turnpike roads (Doc. 111). Thereafter exploiting Mackintosh and his other English friends, he entered upon an active social life, meeting a number of influential public men,[30] and from the chambers he took in the Temple, began to execute the scheme for personal advancement he had formulated some ten months earlier.

Horner's affiliation with the *Edinburgh Review* served him well. Although Smith and Brougham were to follow him to London very shortly, Horner alone basked in the sunshine of the journal's early celebrity and was regarded as Jeffrey's principal agent in the English capital. Even *The Anti-Jacobin Review*, which began in the October 1803 issue a systematic if selective criticism of the first two numbers of the *Edinburgh Review*, praised Horner's contributions. The otherwise disapproving author, William Lisle Bowles, while generally ridiculing the reviewers as 'nameless boys', actually singled out for praise the article on Thornton as 'a very able review ... one of the best dissertations on the subjects, that have yet appeared in the English language'. Bowles continued his notice of the 'boys', moreover, with these comments:

> none appears to us more master of his subject than he to whom is allotted the articles on political economy. We have already mentioned one of those articles with approbation; and we feel ourselves called upon to express similar approbation of the review of Canard ... We were indeed disgusted with the critic's encomiums on the views of the French economists in general, and still more with his assertion that 'Turgot and Mirabeau, and Quesnai, were the

28. *ER* ii (no. iii, Apr. 1803), 205–211.
29. *Brougham*, i. 90, and Horner to John Hewlett, 16 Apr., BLPES ii. 10–11.
30. See Horner to Murray, 20 May 1803, *Horner*, i. 223–4, relating political gossip obtained from the Foxite politician Joseph Jekyll. See also *ibid.*, i. 226, for Horner's journal entry of 28 May revealing that he dined with Mackintosh and William Wilberforce at Sir William Grant's home in Russell Square, and *Wilberforce*, iii. 102, relating Wilberforce's account of the dinner and his opinion that Horner was 'a man of extraordinary talents'.

friends of mankind' ... Notwithstanding [all this] the article, on the whole, is ably written.[31]

Horner shrewdly exploited his association with the *Review* for social and political gain, but his correspondence also confirms that he provided considerable service to it during the first decade of the nineteenth century. He placed standing orders with London booksellers, perused new titles, posted his selections to Edinburgh, and suggested many of the reviews that appeared in the first few years' numbers (Docs 116, 120, 163, 164, 167, 184, 195, 210, 272, and 286). Sydney Smith, who later also migrated to London and lent a hand, reported in 1803:

> on the first day of every month Horner and I will meet together, and order books for Edinburgh – this we can do from the monthly lists. In addition we will scan the french booksellers' shops, and send you everything valuable, excepting a certain portion that we will reserve for ourselves.[32]

Often Horner's letters to Jeffrey and other reviewers included assessments of various published works and comment on literary figures. Especially interesting are his remarks on Bentham's works (Doc. 130), Campbell's poetry and the character of Malthus (Doc. 148), Mrs Barbauld's literary talents (Doc. 164), and on Coleridge, Wordsworth, and the Lake school of poetry (Docs 153 and 167). His correspondence also includes valuable comment on the authorship and public reception of the articles that appeared in the earliest numbers of the *Review* (Docs 114, 116, 125, 128, 139, 149, 184, 195, 203, and 268).

Always eager to broaden his influence with important personages, Horner of course heeded Jeffrey's plea to recruit 'journeymen for a third, and sometimes for a half, of each number'.[33] Among his earliest recruits were Whishaw, Hallam, Mackintosh, Elmsley, Pillans, and Thomas Moore. Later he led the poet William

---

31. William Lisle Bowles (1762–1850: *DNB*) began his review in the October 1803 issue and continued it in an appendix to *The Anti-Jacobin Review and Magazine, or Monthly Political and Literary Censor*, xvi. 213–23 and 515–23. After blaming 'the nameless boys' for a rash generalization in the first article (by Jeffrey on Mounier), he continued in a generally hostile vein. Stung by the review of his own work, designedly or not he was particularly hard on the contributions from that 'Scotch missionary or Jacobin' Smith, whom he variously described, somewhat inaccurately albeit understandably, as 'our rancorous pupil of Knox and Melville' and 'our presbyterian critic displaying his usual enmity for the Church of England'. Of Horner's piece on Irvine, on the other hand, he wrote:

> We pass over the 7th Article ... as comprising nothing worthy of detaining either ourselves or our readers. That, however, is not the fault of the Reviewer, but of the Author ... who with singular address, has contrived to divest of all interest a subject of no less importance than *the Causes and Effects of Emigration from ... Scotland.*

Others – on Parish Schools and on Country Banks – he passed over in utter silence. But having then singled out Horner's article on Thornton he concluded his remarks:

> Instead of a series of *reviews*, we have in fact a series of *dissertations* on subjects which have indeed been treated by the authors whose works are mentioned in the table of contents, and at the tops of the dissertations, but with very little reference to those works more than to others. ... The weakest of the corps is unquestionably the theological reviewer, whose articles are mere effusions of petulance, prejudice, and envy; and much the most valuable articles are those on political economy, and that which overturns (and it completely overturns) the Huttonian Theory of the Earth.

32. Smith to Jeffrey, [28 Oct. 1803], *Smith Letters*, i. 90.

33. Jeffrey to Horner, 8 Aug. 1803, *Jeffrey*, ii. 80.

Robert Spencer as well as Malthus into Jeffrey's stable, and in September 1805, when the death of Jeffrey's wife threatened to interrupt the scheduled publication of the *Review*, he encouraged and secured last-minute contributions from his friends (Docs 163, 183, 186, and 206).[34]

Horner also assisted Jeffrey in promoting, improving, and, on one occasion, saving the *Review*. Before moving to London he had solicited Allen's help in advertising the journal in France (Doc. 98). In October 1803 he met Longman, the London publisher, and suggested the list of recent publications that was subsequently to appear as a regular feature in the *Review* (Doc. 134). And in the spring of 1807, when Longman claimed a proprietary interest in the *Review*, scored a triumph in Chancery, and planned to continue with new reviewers, Horner seems to have led the counter-attack by proposing to establish a new literary journal and so helped forward the eventual resolution of the conflict (Docs 263, 268–70, and 272).

Horner was less enthusiastic about writing reviews himself. From the first he had regarded the *Review* as 'only a matter of temporary amusement, and subordinate occupation' (Doc. 105), and upon arriving in London he was anxious to get on with his professional and political plans. Indeed his first journal entry in London, that of 2 April 1803 (Doc. 111), expressed a desire to be rid of his commitment to write reviews, and his first letter to Jeffrey (Doc. 114) explained that he was simply too busy to contribute.

Horner, however, was reminded every day that his celebrity among Londoners was rooted in affiliation with the *Review*, and that his earlier reviews of Thornton and Canard had given him considerable stature in a vital branch of public policy. Within a week of his arrival in London, he asked his father to send down a paper he had formerly composed on Scottish poor rates, explaining that a politician who was to take part in the parliamentary debate on the poor laws had requested his assistance.[35]

Similar requests apparently led Horner to renew his economical researches. On 7 April he took notes on Scottish currency, the consumption of the metropolis, the prohibition of corn exports, and the theory of mercantilism (Doc. 113). By all appearances he conducted these researches, not with an eye to an article for the *Review*, but rather to enhance his conversational skills in political economics, and he abandoned them on the same day, evidently finding the political speculations surrounding the demise of the Peace of Amiens of more interest (Docs 112 and 117).[36]

In May, however, Horner began to reconsider his relationship with Jeffrey and to contemplate the wisdom of reclaiming his earlier station as principal reviewer of economic literature. His cautious scheme for the attainment of political honours had made him very sensitive about the content of the *Review* even before he had left Edinburgh, and the first two numbers, which he had helped edit, bore his conservative mark. But the third number was the first to be edited in his absence, and on 30 May, as it circulated in London amidst a degree of public criticism, he wrote Jeffrey a very revealing letter in which he protested 'undue severity, disproportioned criticism, and injudicious selection' (Doc. 120). Smith's flippant

---

34. See also Jeffrey to Horner, 2 Sept. 1803, *ibid.*, ii. 81.
35. Horner to John Horner, 5 Apr. 1803, BLPES ii. 8–9.
36. See also Horner to Murray, 20 May 1803, *Horner*, i. 223–24.

satire displeased him, to be sure, but Brougham was the real source of complaint.

Horner almost certainly had conspired with Smith to exclude his ambitious boyhood friend from the editorial board of the *Review* a year earlier, but now it seemed clear that Brougham was breaking free. On 11 May Horner had noted the savagery and 'poison' that characterized one of Brougham's reviews in the third number (Doc. 116). Two weeks later, a closer perusal, no doubt inspired by the critical remarks of those around him, embarrassed and incensed Horner, and he suspected that the problem might worsen. For Brougham had threatened to launch a rival literary journal unless he were admitted to the inner circle of Edinburgh reviewers, and an earlier letter from Jeffrey had given Horner ample reason to fear that flagging interest on the part of the original reviewers, himself included, might force the editor to honour the prolific Brougham's demands.[37]

Horner regarded that prospect with horror. For some time, he told Jeffrey, he had held a low opinion of Brougham, and now he was inclined to discontinue his correspondence with him. This was strong language, especially when one considers that Brougham's later correspondence with Horner, in which he attributed his exclusion from the editorial board of the *Review* entirely to Smith, suggests that he was altogether unaware of Horner's probable collusion or subsequent scorn (Doc. 124). Evidently Horner was not only concerned about literary indiscretions. Brougham, he knew, was brilliant, restless, and possessed of extraordinary energy; and soon he was to come up to London and pursue a career both at the Bar and in politics, perhaps as a competitor. Brougham also sought reputation as a political economist no less fervently than Horner: he was anxious to write articles on economic questions for the *Review*, and his first volume, *An Inquiry into the Colonial Policy of the European Powers*, was hot off the press.[38] Surely it was no coincidence that Horner chose this moment to renew his commitment to Jeffrey and to remark that generally he would restrict himself to works of political economy.

Jeffrey gladly accepted the offer and informed Brougham of Horner's renewed sovereignty over economic literature. Brougham, of course, was none too happy with the decision, and on the 27th he wrote to Horner, protesting against the absence of political economy in the *Review*, insisting that Horner either review or relinquish such publications, and hinting broadly that a review of his *Colonial Policy* should appear in an early number (Doc. 124). Horner, however, clung to his purview tenaciously, telling Jeffrey that a review of Brougham's book was an extremely delicate proposition (Doc. 134) and, notwithstanding Brougham's nudges (Docs 128, 135, and 144), refusing to touch it.

Brougham continued to protest about the dearth of political economy in the *Review*, and in early 1804 he insisted on reviewing Lord Lauderdale's *Inquiry into the nature and origin of Public Wealth*. Lauderdale's was a significant if ill-composed treatise on the nature of profit and, as such, well within Horner's editorial purview. The author was Fox's Scottish leader, however, and at the time Horner was collaborating with him in an unsuccessful attempt to secure for John Allen the chair of natural philosophy at Edinburgh (Doc. 147). Then, too, Horner had already

37. Jeffrey to Horner, 1 Apr. 1803, *Jeffrey*, ii. 67–8, and Doc. 120.
38. See New, pp. 13–14.

learned that Professor Stewart had a very high opinion of Lauderdale's treatise (Doc. 146), and that Brougham was likely to write an unfavourable review (Doc. 144).

So Horner graciously relinquished Lauderdale's treatise, thereby protecting himself at the same time as manoeuvring his eager rival into a political error that contributed significantly to his later difficulties with the Whig party. The correspondence relating to Brougham's scathing review, especially that depicting Horner's refusal to defend him against Lauderdale's bitter and easily assailable reply, reveals Horner's tactics very graphically (Docs 153, 165, 166, 169, 171, 173, and 178).

Horner's failure to produce reviews also forced him to relinquish publications on commercial policy to Brougham, but he did so reluctantly, continuing to nibble at that important branch of political economy and seeking simultaneously to undermine his rival. French commercial policy, of course, had interested Horner since the founding of the *Review*, and he was still promising Jeffrey a treatise on it in July 1803 (Doc. 126). Then, in September 1803, he listed 'Trade with the United States – Taxes on imports from' as a worthy subject.[39] However, with the possible exception of a short piece on Talleyrand's policy,[40] he wrote nothing, and Brougham slowly prized the general subject of commerce from his grasp (Doc. 163).

Horner had second thoughts in late 1805, when the publication of James Stephen's *Frauds of the Neutral Flags* inspired considerable public outrage concerning the illegal but lucrative American carrying trade with France. He never considered reviewing it himself. As London buzzed about it, rather, he wrote to Jeffrey, stressing its political significance and insisting that Jeffrey review it himself, and, fearing he might fail there, turned also to Reddie (Docs 210–12 and 223). Some two years later he apparently attempted to check Brougham's rising acclaim as an expert in commercial policy yet again, lecturing Jeffrey on the importance of West Indian affairs and the propriety of a judicious review of a recent publication on the subject; it was reviewed, however, by Brougham (Doc. 281).

All the while Horner berated Brougham in a number of letters to his friends. Normally he grounded the attack on the argument that Brougham's radical political views were destroying the credibility of the *Review* (Docs 181, 210, 369), and in 1808, when Brougham was wrongly thought to be the sole author of the infamous 'Don Cevallos' article, in which in fact Jeffrey collaborated, his reaction was vicious (Docs 313 and 314). He also protested that the *Review* was becoming a platform for his rival, represented Brougham as a political adventurer, and slandered his character (Docs 173, 177, 184, 228, and 231). On the other hand, employing a tactic that he would pursue with great success for the remainder of his life, Horner posed as a martyr, telling Jeffrey in December 1805 of Brougham's inexplicable coldness towards him and of a growing reserve in their relationship (Doc. 210).

Horner's campaign to neutralize Brougham surely accounts for the bad blood that later figured so prominently in their respective political careers, but it also largely explains the curious dearth of articles on political economy in the early numbers of a journal founded by students of Dugald Stewart. For, beginning in the summer of 1803, and continuing until 1807, Horner discouraged reviews by Brougham and

39. Kinnordy MSS.
40. *ER* vii (no. xiii, Oct. 1805), 151–5.

others by making idle promises, contributing relatively little himself, and clearly exploiting the *Review* to promote his own political agenda.

The first new economic work to interest Horner after his arrival in London was Lord King's recent publication on the restriction of cash payments by the Bank of England. King was a fawning young disciple of Fox who promised to be a politician of some weight among the Whigs, and his view of the Bank restriction accorded with that advanced in Horner's review of Thornton. As Horner told Jeffrey, such a review 'serves me a double purpose' (Doc. 120).

Horner's notes on the *Wealth of Nations* suggest that he had had his eye on King's tract since 6 May 1803, when he renewed his speculations on the relationship between rates of exchange and the balance of trade, and that he had resumed his studies later that month, when he considered the division of labour, the sources of national wealth, rents and the wages of labour, and the prices of precious metals (Docs 115 and 119). Then, with his economic purview reconfirmed, he began early in June to plan a comprehensive literary campaign on the subject of the Bank restriction. On the 11th he staked a claim to Wheatley's *Remarks on Currency and Commerce*, noting that its attack on Bank policy offered him an excellent opportunity to follow up his review of Lord King (Doc. 121).

As usual Horner attempted too much at once. A note among his papers at Kinnordy indicates that he was simultaneously engaged in an ambitious plan of research through which he hoped to identify 'Models for the art of communicating and popularizing truth', and two letters written to friends in Edinburgh confirm that Fox, Grenville, rumours of a change of ministry, and the foreign policy of the Northern Powers continued to absorb his thoughts (Docs 121 and 123). Moreover, he also wrote another article for the fourth number – a glowing tribute to a speech by Mackintosh, then his most valued contact within the Whig ranks, in defence of the accused libeller John Peltier.[41]

Horner apparently conducted no further research relating to his review of Lord King between 26 May and 26 June, when his notes resume for a single day (Doc. 122). That left him less than two weeks to compose a very demanding article. Not surprisingly, he complained to Murray of the difficulty of the project on 6 July, requesting at the same time copies of his earlier reviews, and the thirty-page manuscript he posted to Jeffrey the next day did little more than relate King's principal arguments to those advanced in the earlier review of Thornton (Docs 125 and 126). Yet the review was a significant contribution, one that again converted an untrained author's scattered thoughts and unhappy prose into a scholarly, coherent, and seemingly disinterested treatise. Brougham, while rightly describing the article on Mackintosh's speech as written even more 'con amore', found the review of King superior to Horner's former contributions, and Jeffrey thought it the best article in the fourth number.[42]

During the spring and summer of 1803 Horner planned two further treatises that, if completed, might well have altered the course of economic thought. The first was the comparative analysis of Smithian and Physiocratic doctrine that he had

41. *Ibid.* ii (no. iv, July 1803), 476–84. See also Horner to William Erskine, 4 Feb. 1804 (*Horner*, i. 257–8), acknowledging his debt to Mackintosh.
42. Doc. 128, and Jeffrey to Horner, 8 Aug. 1803, *Jeffrey*, ii. 78–80.

considered for the first number (Docs 120 and 126). He regarded that project, one must suspect, as the premier undertaking of his life. Professor Stewart's lectures had planted the seed; his own researches had led to significant conclusions; he had laid the foundation in his review of Canard; now he projected a grand vindication of Quesnay and his disciples.

Horner's notes on the 'Economists' resume on 24 May 1803 and reveal speculations on both the proper definition of wealth and the division of labour (Doc. 118). The difficulty of the subject confounded him, however, and he applied, apparently without success, to the Abbé Morellet for pertinent publications (Doc. 130). On 26 August he resumed his studies, this time citing the various definitions of wealth that had previously been advanced, and on 20 September he assessed the virtues of the Physiocrats, calculating their effect on Adam Smith's doctrine, and struggling with what he regarded as a troublesome semantical conflict in the reasonings of Quesnay and his followers (Docs 131 and 133). There, however, the notes end; Horner never completed the project.

The same fate befell his second major undertaking, a review of Malthus's *Essay on Population*. In all probability he had laid claim to it when the *Review* was conceived; surely nothing else can explain the omission of any notice whatever. On 7 July 1803 he sent Jeffrey a copy of the second edition, noting elusively that he might undertake the project, and a fortnight later he placed it at the head of his list of projected reviews (Doc. 126). Afterwards, however, he did nothing, although Malthus, learning that Horner was supposed to review his work, sent him a number of corrections projected for the next edition, requesting that they be noted in the review (Doc. 138).

In January 1804 Horner confirmed his intentions, telling Jeffrey that he was delaying a personal introduction to Malthus until the review was completed (Doc. 148). But it was not until the following July that he got around to sounding Jeffrey on the propriety of including Malthus's revisions in a review, and afterwards, while expressing reluctance to relinquish the project, he produced nothing but excuses and idle promises (Docs 163, 164, 171, 175, 227, and 244). Hence he never reviewed the most influential economic treatise of his age.

One can only speculate on the reasons for Horner's failure. Perhaps he felt unequal to the challenge posed by Malthus. On the other hand he might have been reluctant to criticize a man of Malthus's stature; a review would necessarily have included the critical remarks he had earlier recorded in his journal as well as his well-founded opinion that Malthus's writing lacked precision (Docs 30–32 and 310). Or perhaps he was simply too busy to complete the review and held on for fear that otherwise Brougham would claim it; his rival certainly pressed him about it (Doc. 144). After 1807, moreover, he was probably also deterred by his successful recruitment of Malthus as an Edinburgh reviewer, and by the personal relationship he gradually established with him (Docs 310 and 334).[43]

Horner's aborted analysis of Smithian and Physiocratic doctrine is perhaps more

---

43. Fontana, p. 56, suggests that Horner never felt secure enough to address the theoretical implications of Malthus's argument, and Mrs James (*Malthus*, p. 113), that he was nervous of openly revealing his fundamental disagreement with Malthus. (See also below, pp. 222–3.)

explicable; he absolutely ran aground on Quesnay, never comprehending the Physiocratic definition of wealth and being influenced perhaps by the fact that both Jeffrey and Brougham found his views suspect (Doc. 166). Probably more important was his perception that an attack on Smith, a necessary component of the projected treatise, might be politically imprudent. His review of Canard, in which he had criticized Smith's theory of value and hinted at plagiarism, apparently earned him a degree of criticism; at all events he came to appreciate Brougham's opinion that Adam Smith had 'become sufficiently famous to experience the fate of Bacon and Newton – to be quoted and sworn by, without being read' (Doc. 144).

In August 1803, when Horner was asked to contribute notes to a new edition of the *Wealth of Nations*, he refused because of a new-found reluctance 'to expose Smith's errors before his work has operated its full effect'. There was a 'superstitious worship of Smith's name', he told Thomas Thomson, and his 'plausible and loose hypothesis' on the nature and origin of wealth was 'as good for the vulgar as any other' (Doc. 130). He again voiced reverence for Smith in November, and in March 1804, when he briefly reconsidered a review of Wheatley, he observed that the author's career had to be cut short because of his Smithian 'heresies' (Docs 137 and 153). Shortly afterwards (Doc. 155) he told his brother of Smith's great influence on young politicians, and of a resulting appreciation of Smithian doctrine among senior statesmen, and that consideration in particular may account for his failure to complete the essay on the Physiocrats.[44]

Whatever the case, it is surely significant that Horner devoted a great deal of time during the summer of 1803 to an evaluation of his own qualifications as a writer and to the subjects on which he might best write. Concluding that he was suited only to 'the graver species of didactic writing', he decided to attempt nothing else.[45] The subjects he afterwards contemplated were therefore increasingly within the field of applied politics, and his principal concentration the political economy of 'practical' issues of state.

A document entitled 'Plans' and dated 19 July 1803 confirms his intention to review Malthus, the Physiocrats, French commercial policy, and the theory of national wealth, and to write a number of metaphysical essays as well. But it also lists other subjects recommended by their current political prominence – India, the poor laws, slavery, and the education of the lower orders. A second document, dated 2 September 1803, makes no mention of either Malthus or the French articles and instead enumerates the objects 'to which the attention of the practical Statesman is called, and for the right comprehension and government of which he can only be prepared, by the discipline of general principles and political philosophy'.[46]

Such a plan was perfectly consistent with that he had composed in May 1802, and already a review of the late parliamentary session had led him to important conclusions. Questions of foreign policy were notably absent from his list of priorities, although he did note public interest in Anglo-American trade, especially

44. Chitnis, p. 118, goes so far as to characterize Horner's apparently increasing reluctance to criticize Smith as 'hypocritical'.
45. Horner to Murray, 30 Aug., *Horner*, i. 243.
46. Horner's notes of 19 July and 2 Sept. 1803 are bound with a number of miscellaneous 'Memoranda' in the Kinnordy MSS. See also Doc. 127 n. 7.

Britain's tariff barriers. As for colonial policy, he found Britain's West Indian and North American possessions worthy causes, the former because of the African slave trade. His principal interest, however, was domestic policy.

Judicial reform was a promising Scottish question, and a 'general retrospect of conduct towards Ireland' was no less appealing. But questions of political economy had also cropped up frequently in the parliamentary debates – poor law, the tithe, parochial education, emigration, and the plight of the woollen industry in the west of England. For some time he had prepared for the debate on poor law; now he noted the necessity of examining 'particular administrations in different countries in respect of the attention paid to the comfort and improvement of the lower classes of the people'. Already he felt comfortable in the other economical questions that had concerned Parliament – 'Renewal of Bank Restriction – Income Tax – General retrospect of finance'.

Horner's next contribution to the *Edinburgh Review* appeared in the fifth number – a review of Helen Maria Williams's *The Political and Confidential Correspondence of Lewis the Sixteenth* (1803).[47] At first glance the article seems unexceptional; but the political commentary Horner added to an otherwise mundane review certainly reflected his earlier conclusions about the conservative cast and retrospective focus of British politics. Furthermore, his comments also meshed quite nicely with the Bourbon predilections of the Grenville faction with whom Fox then desired coalition; a letter to Thomas Thomson (Doc. 130) confirms that he was considering the views of Lord Grenville while he was at work on Miss Williams's volumes.

Given these facts, the review emerges as yet another tactic for political advancement. He found the 'plainness' of Louis's prose refreshing when compared with the 'finery and flippancy that prevail among French writers of the present school'.[48] He also recalled the 'first light and dawn of the Revolution ... which has since been overcast by so foul a storm'.[49] And Horner hailed the French King as a 'revolutionist' and a martyr:

> his name will be added by posterity to that memorable band of enthusiasts, who built their hope upon foundations unalterably solid, but attempted to realize the superstructure with incautious haste; who looking forward upon the prospects of the human race, saw, without illusion, what is disclosed by the light of philosophy, and is established in the laws of nature; but, with a benevolence too sanguine, grasped at possession prematurely, forgetting that the arrangements of nature are developed and perfected imperceptibly with the lapse of ages.[50]

This was curious language indeed for a man whose sister recalled his lifelong 'contempt of the Bourbon race'.[51]

Horner wrote nothing for the sixth, seventh, or eighth numbers of the *Review*. Rather, during the winter of 1803–1804 he reaffirmed the necessity of identifying and systematizing advantageous political views, and dreamed of a 'connection with

---

47. *ER* iii (no. v, Oct. 1803), 211–31.
48. *Ibid.*, p. 212.
49. *Ibid.*, p. 216.
50. *Ibid.*, p. 225.
51. Byrne Memoirs, p. 119.

the Whig aristocracy of England', again mentioning the utility of Burke's political doctrine.[52] But his ambitions remained unfulfilled, and his frustrations mounted after Brougham arrived in London, embraced Wilberforce, and launched an energetic campaign on behalf of the abolition of the African slave trade.[53] Horner tagged along at first but soon concluded that the 'Saints' were not a 'proper set of men', ridiculing Brougham's association with them and telling Murray that despite its celebrity in London, Brougham's pamphlet on slavery was an embarrassment (Docs 153 and 160).

At last Horner's political prospects improved. In late June 1804 he received an invitation, apparently at the instigation of Lauderdale, to dine with Earl Fitzwilliam. He consulted his friends but of course accepted and went along on 1 July. There he met Sheridan and Windham, and was asked to collaborate with Joseph Jekyll in writing squibs against the Government. Horner initially thought little of the proposal but quickly reconsidered, next day displaying enthusiasm for the Whig press campaign and labelling Jekyll 'the Jeffrey of the South' (Docs 163 and 172).

There followed yet another revival of interest in the *Edinburgh Review*. Horner contributed two articles to Jeffrey's ninth number. One was a review of John Quincy Adams's *Letters on Silesia* (1804), which had been written by the United States Senator when he had served as Minister Plenipotentiary to the Court of Berlin. Adams's unsophisticated observations on the Silesian linen industry, which he represented as an American alternative to that of Britain, were easy prey for Horner, and they allowed him to display his superior talents as a political economist, to flatter the 'great superiority of English workmanship', and to exploit what he rightly regarded as strong anti-American sentiment in Britain. 'The style of Mr Adams', Horner noted, 'is in general very tolerable English; which, for American compositions, is no moderate praise.'[54]

Horner's major contribution to the ninth number of the *Review*, however, broached a 'practical' issue of state – the bounty on grain bestowed by the Corn Bill of 1804 – and it may be significant that he resolved to review the new corn law shortly after his introduction to Fitzwilliam, Windham, and Sheridan. Whatever the case, he told Jeffrey in late July that he was composing the essay (Doc. 165), and got down to business about a month later.

Horner's notes (Doc. 168) reveal that he leaned heavily on a comparative analysis of Smithian and Physiocratic doctrine and considered the relationship between corn prices, the prices of other commodities, and the wages of labour. He drew on the theory of population as well; in mid-September, while working on the essay, he reported progress in reviewing Malthus (Doc. 171). But the subject was difficult for him: on 21 September, only days before his deadline, the article remained unfinished, and on the 24th he wrote to Loch, requesting historical data on the price of wheat on the Continent (Docs 173 and 174). On 1 October he posted the essay to Jeffrey, admitting that his ideas were not fully developed and speculating that his doctrine might offend one of Fox's old friends (Doc. 175). Later he confessed that inadequate prose had foiled his attempt to abuse Pitt in the review (Doc. 184).

52. Horner's journal entries of 8 Oct. and 29 Nov. 1803, and 9 Jan. 1804, *Horner*, i. 363–4.
53. Brougham to Horner, [28 June 1804], BLPES ii. 122–3.
54. *ER* v (no. ix, Oct. 1804), 180–89.

In the circumstances he did well enough. The essay advanced a coherent explanation of the effects of a bounty on grain, contended that Adam Smith's principles
were perceptible in the Corn Bill of 1773, and damned the more recent measure as
piecemeal wartime legislation arising from unfounded panic produced by an accidental coincidence of circumstances in the channels of trade. Once again, though,
he found it necessary to depart from Smithian doctrine, but this time he was more
prudent, dwelling less on the substance of Smith's errors than on their effect in
promoting misunderstanding. A bounty on corn would not lead to a direct and
immediate increase in price, as Smith had 'too readily assumed', but instead to an
indirect, gradual, and unnatural increase through the medium of foreign markets.
Such political contrivance was unnecessary and damaging, he concluded, and it
betrayed a profound ignorance of the nation's agricultural strength.[55]

Horner is generally credited with only four further articles in the *Review*. His
'Short Statement of Facts relative to the late Election of a Mathematical Professor in
the University of Edinburgh', which appeared in October 1805, marked the
culmination of several months of active involvement with Professor Stewart and
others in the controversy surrounding the eventual election of John Leslie to the
Chair of Natural Philosophy.[56] That review and Horner's extensive correspondence
shed much light on the continuing role of Hume's doctrine of cause and effect in an
unhappy relationship between Edinburgh University and the Kirk (Docs 190, 192,
197, 198, 201, 203, 208, 220, and 233). In the same number was Horner's review of
Lord Selkirk's treatise on emigration from the Scottish highlands.[57] It incorporated
a number of reasonings on population theory and betrayed a great deal of nostalgia;
but the then Whig affiliation of the author, Selkirk, is perhaps the most important
feature of the article. Then in January 1806 there appeared in the *Review* a single
page by Horner criticizing a new edition of the *Wealth of Nations*.[58] Thereafter,
excepting only his politically-inspired review of the French translation of Fox's
History in October 1809, a short piece on India, and two additional items considered
below, no more reviews are heard of from Horner.

Horner's retreat from the *Review* was occasioned by his increasing concentration
on contemporary British politics. Indeed, beginning in 1804, and continuing until
he entered Parliament in late 1806, his correspondence is a virtual chronicle of
political events. Letter after letter relates and speculates on the sequence of events
that brought Pitt and Fox together in opposition, that led to the fall of Addington,
the return of Pitt to power, and the collaboration of Fox and the 'New Opposition',
and that at last brought the 'Man of the People' to power in league with Grenville
and the rump of the old Rockingham faction.

Of special interest are Horner's accounts of the politics surrounding the
unsuccessful Foxite attack on the Lord Advocate (Docs 160–63, 172, and 178) and a
number of letters relating to Melville's trial (Docs 192, 195, 196, and 198). There is
also substantial comment on the fragility of Fox–Grenville collaboration, including
interesting assessments of the political liabilities of the Grenville faction (Doc. 159)

55. See Fontana, p. 118.
56. *ER* vii (no. xiii, Oct. 1805), 113–34.
57. *Ibid.*, pp. 185–202; see also Docs 195, 199, 207, and 208.
58. *ER* vii (no. xiv, Jan. 1806), 470–71.

and of the vital importance of Fitzwilliam in the attempt at coalition (Doc. 205).

Horner's journal entries and correspondence also depict the continuation of his consuming campaign for political acceptance. On numerous occasions he attended the gallery of the House of Commons, observing the styles of those who participated in celebrated debates, and arriving at remarkably accurate conclusions relating to the present and future structure of parties (Docs 151–2, 154–7, 159, and 162). His favourite subjects were Pitt and Fox (Docs 178, 185, 195, and 204), but he recorded his perceptions of other public men as well. Romilly remained a subject of careful scrutiny (Doc. 187), and Horner also commented interestingly on the characters and political views of Grenville (Doc. 159), Fitzwilliam (Doc. 205), Petty (Docs 150 and 196), Holland (Doc. 199), Melville (Doc. 196), and Canning (Docs 180 and 250).

The 'practical' issues Horner identified and pursued between 1804 and 1806 were also of future significance. The campaign to abolish the slave trade interested him, and certainly he regarded it as an important matter of state (Docs 192, 193, and 230), but he never displayed much personal interest in Abolition after Brougham embraced it in early 1804. Ireland was another matter. Early on Horner identified the Catholic claims and Irish policy in general as issues of monumental significance in British politics. In this he rightly perceived, as he later explained to Whishaw (Doc. 350), that the Catholic question was the only public issue that bound the Fox and Grenville factions together, and in the spring of 1805, as those groups collaborated ever more closely in opposition, he made a number of notes about the Irish policy of recent administrations (Docs 189, 191, and 194).

If the question of Ireland was fertile ground for the future, it was well beyond Horner's reach in 1804. In fact, questions of political economy constituted his only immediate prospect. There was, however, reason to be cautious. The Whig squirearchy had not been pleased with his essay opposing bounties, and one must suspect that even the gentle criticism of Adam Smith advanced in that article had raised some eyebrows. Perhaps that explains why Horner dropped the bounty question, saying little more about corn for almost a decade, and came to a final conclusion on Smith. Never again would he make direct attacks on his famous countryman; Adam Smith's reputation, notwithstanding the numerous errors, omissions, and inconsistencies that riddled the *Wealth of Nations*, was unassailable, and political prudence demanded an alliance. Thereafter Horner almost invariably appealed to the authority of the great man in propounding his economic doctrine.

Horner, however, perceived incredible ignorance of economic phenomena among leading public men and was convinced that fame awaited anyone who should accomplish a systematic study of political economy (Doc. 170). The challenge was to find an appropriate cause and exploit it. Among the 'practical' issues he had listed earlier, monetary policy and the state's arrangements for the poor remained plausible possibilities. The former was now exciting public interest because of the chronic derangement of Irish currency, and a parliamentary committee of inquiry had been appointed. The reform of poor law and other matters relating to the lower orders of society had commanded the attention of Parliament for some time, and currently there was much talk about the curious scheme of education advocated by Joseph Lancaster. Horner accordingly displayed great interest in those two 'practical' issues.

Horner had been confounded by Lord King's remarks on Irish circulation, and in the midst of writing his review he had twice asked his brother, who was about to depart for Ireland, to procure recent publications on the subject (Docs 154–5). Leonard Horner must have honoured the request because Francis told Murray in October 1804 that, notwithstanding continuing difficulty in understanding Irish circulation, he was reading Parnell's *Observations Upon the State of the Currency of Ireland* (1804) and working on a review of John Leslie Foster's recent *Essay on the Principles of Commercial Exchanges* (Doc. 176).

Horner probably wrote at least a portion of the review of Foster that appeared in 1806.[59] He said he was going to write it. He reported that he was working on it. The prose, or at least the bulk of it, is not unlike Horner's. The doctrine is Hornerian. Nobody else in Jeffrey's stable at the time knew a thing about monetary policy, and it is safe to assume that Horner would have opposed an invasion of his editorial purview over a lucid, enlightened treatise exposing the evils of the Bank restriction.

Furthermore, the absence of comment on the review of Foster in Horner's correspondence, or indeed in that of anyone else, is certainly curious, perhaps instructive. For Horner grew increasingly timid about the *Review* after his political fortunes began to improve in the summer of 1804, and he demanded anonymity as a reviewer some years later (Doc. 365). Given the political importance of Irish policy in 1805–1806, the fact that Foster's uncle was an important politician, and Horner's well-developed sense of caution, surely he would have made the same demand in 1806. Available evidence, therefore, suggests that he wrote the review of Foster, as usual sending an unpolished draft to Jeffrey insisting on anonymity, and that Jeffrey made stylistic changes, published the review, and kept Horner's secret.

The likelihood that Horner wrote at least a portion of the review of Foster is enhanced by correspondence confirming his continuing interest in the monetary crisis during 1805. In April he wrote to Mackintosh, then Recorder of Bombay, remarking on the utility of international data in theory-building and posing queries about the distribution of capital, the facilities of credit, the mediums of exchange, and the price of bullion in India (Doc. 193). A reply was not forthcoming, and in September Horner wrote again, complaining of a recent publication defaming Britain's country banks, renewing his request for economic data, and relating a plan to collect information on variations in the price of bullion in various parts of the world (Doc. 207). By 1805, it seems, Horner was convinced that the bullion question, the principal source of his fame as a political economist, would inevitably be forced on Parliament.

Similar reasoning apparently explains Horner's keen interest in Joseph Lancaster's scheme for the education of the lower orders. The first paper Horner presented to the Speculative Society had represented education as the only plausible check on the baleful effects of 'overgrown commerce'. Later he had expressed similar views, and his notes of both July and September 1803 had identified education and other arrangements for the poor as a proper subject for the 'practical Statesman'. Now, in the spring of 1805, he visited Lancaster's school, and having been impressed by the Quaker's philosophy of operant learning, immediately became a strong advocate (Docs 192 and 198).

Before he entered Parliament Horner planned, but never wrote, a grand treatise

59. See Docs 176 and 244.

on the Lancasterian system (Docs 203, 208, 212, 214, 227, and 244). He contributed to, and led a subscription for, Lancaster's school, and he promoted a related scheme of national education among his friends (Docs 193, 200, 205, and 221). Horner's correspondence of 1805 and early 1806, then, exhibits the views and the tactics of a young man who regarded national educational reform, like the Bank restriction, as a political cause of future importance.

Horner's shrewd exploitation of the *Edinburgh Review*, his fame as a political economist, his deportment, and his well-researched and closely-measured language all combined to make him very popular among Londoners. He was, in fact, by early 1805 regarded as a great ornament at the dinner table, 'a very happy man' whose 'worth and talents' were universally acknowledged.[60] He grew even happier in the summer, when Allen and the Hollands at last returned to England. Horner and Brougham appeared at Holland House on 5 July.[61] Lady Holland probably never really got on with Brougham, but she took to young Horner 'hugely'.[62] So did her husband, who shortly afterwards applied, surely at Horner's suggestion, to Lord Hawkesbury for an office in reversion for the poet Campbell.[63] Subsequently Horner corresponded with Lady Holland on the matter[64] and appeared in Kensington more frequently.

Horner's developing relationship with the Holland House circle ensured that he was privy to many of the discussions which attended the exciting developments of December 1805 and January 1806. His correspondence and journal entries include comment on the effects on British politics of the battles of Trafalgar and Austerlitz (Docs 209 and 214), on the political ramifications of Pitt's death (Docs 215–16), and on the events surrounding the formation of the 'Ministry of All the Talents' (Doc. 219).[65] Among his letters, too, is commentary on the canvasses of Petty, Althorp, and Palmerston for Pitt's vacated seat at Cambridge University, an account of the difficulties attending Cabinet appointments within the Whig Government, and remarks relating to the distribution of Scottish patronage (Docs 217, 221–2, and 224).

Horner's connection with Holland House of course occasioned the 'imprudent sacrifice to ambition' that he had promised to avoid before migrating to London. His plan had called for professional success first, then politics. With all the political cards falling into place well ahead of schedule, however, he fagged at law and daily assumed a greater political character. As early as 30 September 1805 Seymour reproached him for his 'continual fluctuation of motives, and of plans arising from them'.[66] Horner delayed a reply until 30 November, reporting that he was reading law and 'making very virtuous resolutions' concerning his profession, but also mentioning that later in the day he was to see Petty and Sharp at the 'King of Clubs'.[67] The

60. Smith to Jeffrey, ?16 Feb. 1805, *Smith Letters*, i. 102.
61. *Home of the Hollands*, p. 309.
62. *Holland House*, pp. 177–8; *Holland House Chronicles*, p. 83, citing a letter of 1 Oct. 1805 from Sydney Smith to Mackintosh.
63. Horner to Seymour, 11 Dec. 1805, BLPES ii. 241–2.
64. Horner to Lady Holland, [?Dec. 1805], BLPES ii. 251–2. See also Horner to Professor William Smyth, 12 Mar. 1806, BLPES iii. 30–31, reporting that Fox had agreed to give Campbell a pension.
65. See also Horner's journal entries of 26, 29, and 31 Jan., and 3 and 5 Feb. 1806 (*Horner*, i. 355–60), and his letter to Professor Stewart of 1 Feb. 1806 (BLPES iii. 11–12).
66. *Horner*, i. 342.
67. *Ibid.*, i. 343–4.

following week he was deprecating Pitt's foreign policy and hailing the sagacity of Fox's earlier prognostications on the folly of war with revolutionary France (Docs 209–210), and later in the month defending the Whigs in a letter to the critical Seymour.[68]

On 30 January 1806 Sydney Smith told Jeffrey that 'all the truly honest and able men' were rushing to the Whig banner.[69] Horner was among them. On 11 January, forgetting his earlier protests about partisan politics in the *Review*, he asked Jeffrey to publish a 'few lines' he had written about a speech on India by Fox's friend Sir Philip Francis; on 1 February he 'very anxiously' reviewed his 'original schemes' and considered 'future prospects'; and on the 11th he told Reddie, who evidently entertained doubts about Fox and Grenville, that, affiliation with party being a 'duty', he had made his choice 'long ago'.[70]

Speculations regarding Horner's future circulated widely in Edinburgh. 'Horner is as high as his merit deserves', Jeffrey told Reddie, 'and he is by far the most meritorious and most promising of any Scotchman that has lately emigrated South.' Others quite agreed. Horner's first emolument came in late February when Minto offered him a seat at the board of commissioners established by the East India Company to adjust the claims of the Nabob of Arcot. Horner accepted despite a number of professed 'scruples', assuring Murray that the position in no way impeded his professional plans or fettered 'the freedom of my opinions or future political conduct'. His closest friends, however, perceived correctly that the appointment threatened his legal career. Murray thought it would 'lead to some political situation'. Seymour predicted an early return to the Commons and felt the 'course of events' would carry Horner to 'high public station'. Jeffrey, who fully understood his friend's burning ambition for political honours, thought Horner might have done better. The commissionership, he noted, had not 'the splendour, nor the opportunity for display and great public service, which belongs to offices more purely political'.[71]

Jeffrey's opinion was not ill-founded, but it failed to contemplate Horner's rising stature at Holland House. There his cause was promoted by Allen, now emerging as Lord Holland's principal political adviser, by Petty, the young Cabinet Minister to whom Fox looked for future leadership in the Commons, by the much-courted Lauderdale, and by the flattered Lord King, who of course appreciated the Edin-

---

68. Horner to Seymour, 26 Dec. 1805, *ibid.*, i. 346. Horner's journal entry of 9 Jan. 1806 (*ibid.*, i. 348) notes Fox's favourable view of Napoleon's motives before the renewal of war and his remarks on Burke's opinions at the outbreak of the French Revolution. *Horner* omits a portion of the entry consisting of brief speculations on the authorship of articles in the *Morning Chronicle* in 1792 (Kinnordy MSS).

69. Clive, p. 83.

70. Doc. 214; *Horner*, i. 360; and Doc. 223.

71. Jeffrey to Reddie, 28 Feb., NLS MSS 3704, f. 26; Horner to Murray, 28 Feb. 1806, BLPES iii. 23–5 (an incomplete version is in *Horner*, i. 368–70); Murray to Horner and Seymour to Horner, 11 Mar., *Horner*, i. 371–6; and Jeffrey to Horner, 9 Mar. 1806, *Jeffrey*, ii. 105. See also Horner to Mrs D. Stewart, 11 Mar. 1806, BLPES iii. 28–9, betraying a good deal of defensiveness regarding the appointment. He resigned in the summer of 1809, telling Minto (6 June 1809, NLS MSS 11149, ff. 14–15) that he feared it would drag on interminably; but his resignation probably had at least as much to do with the attack on sinecures then being mounted by the radicals.

burgh reviewer's monetary doctrine. Horner's most ardent supporter, however, was Lady Holland. The motives behind her extraordinary regard remain speculative; but she certainly adored Horner from the first and actively sought to advance his interests. The warmth of their early relationship was revealed in late March, when the Whig Ministry briefly considered appointing Lord Holland Minister to Berlin. On the 25th Horner told Murray:

> Lord Holland is going as Minister to Berlin very soon; and his Lady, who is always very kind and attentive to me, has suggested that it would be a good opportunity for me to see a corner of the continent, and has offered me an apartment in their house at Berlin.[72]

Horner profited a great deal from the Government's decision to send someone else to the Prussian Court; for it allowed him to keep his finger on the pulse of politics, cultivate new relationships, and exploit the 'active scene' which he had contemplated in May 1802. Office, Horner complained, had a debilitating effect on the conversation of his Foxite friends, but he was more concerned about Brougham's courtship of Government men. Noting inconsistency in his rival's political opinions, Horner speculated unhappily that Brougham was writing a pro-Government pamphlet with Fox's approval (Doc. 228); and later, while reporting Brougham's unsuccessful attempt to secure a seat in Parliament, he sent Murray a remarkably perceptive account of Brougham's personal strengths, liabilities, and political prospects that concluded with what was by this time a customary diatribe (Doc. 231).

All the while Horner made himself useful to Ministerialists. Various references in his correspondence suggest that he was consulted on economic questions. In March 1806, for example, Richard Sharp requested and obtained from Horner a lengthy bibliographical essay on political economy. It is a remarkable document, containing considerable comment on Turgot, the Physiocrats, and the other writers who had influenced Horner's monetary doctrine, his view of grain policy, and his concept of the principles of population (Doc. 226).

There is also reason to suppose that Foxite leaders consulted Horner on Scottish affairs. Certainly he took a very favourable view of the Government's projected reform of Scottish judicature. He never encroached on the turf of Lauderdale, John Clerk, or other leading Foxites, to be sure, but his letters to friends in Edinburgh attempted to calm fears, and they contain analyses of the opinions of key men as well as reports of parliamentary activity (Docs 225, 228, 229, 234, 245, 252, 258, 260, and 261). Of course he also followed very closely the unsuccessful prosecution of Melville, and sent detailed accounts to Scotland (Docs 230, 234, and 235).

As late as 13 June 1806 Horner expressed reluctance to exploit the patronage of Petty, his sole personal contact within the Cabinet (Doc. 233), but a week later, as rumours of Fox's initiative for peace with France began to circulate in London (Doc. 234), Petty informed Horner of a proposal by Lord Kinnaird to bring him into the House of Commons next Parliament.[73] Kinnaird, however, was slow to make a

---

72. This passage in Horner's letter to Murray of 25 Mar. 1806 (BLPES iii. 34–7) is strangely omitted from *Horner*, i. 377–81.

73. Horner's journal entry – his last – of 23 June, and Horner to Seymour, 26 June 1806, *ibid.*, i. 387–91.

formal offer, the summer passed uneventfully, and Horner pondered the pros and cons of the opportunity.

Horner had little money; a closed borough was expensive, and somebody else would have to pick up the bill. Nor was Horner prepared to make political concessions; he was attached to Fox's principles but altogether unwilling to pledge himself on a public issue. Then, too, he apparently fretted about the sacrifice of his literary ambitions. Within days of his conversation with Petty, indeed, he began to collect materials for 'a history of the administration and affairs of Ireland' (Doc. 237), and on 18 September, shortly after Fox died, he was 'very far from averse' to a proposal to collaborate with Allen in editing a selection of Fox's speeches.[74]

The possible effect of Fox's death on the fortunes of the Whig party also gave Horner reason to pause and reflect. He had never had much faith in either Grenville or the longevity of the coalition Ministry. Now he noted the inexplicable failure of the Prince of Wales to attend Fox's funeral (Doc. 242), pondered the death of the old Whig faction, and in a flight of fantasy, actually entertained the thought that the Whigs might forge an alliance with the rising commercial classes, of which his own family was of course a part (Docs 239–41). His oldest friends, however, re-minded him of his yet unfulfilled professional plans, and of the wisdom of tending to first things first.[75]

But the allure of Parliament was strong, and Horner's Whig friends, notably Petty and Lord Holland, stoked the fire. The spectre of his old rival, the ambitious Brougham, probably influenced him as well; during the summer and autumn the two Edinburgh reviewers were 'continually dining' at Holland House. On 19 October, only days before the election, Kinnaird at last made his formal offer of St Ives, demanding neither money nor sacrifice of political principle. Horner consulted his father, who earlier had leased a house in Hampstead, and promptly came to a decision. On 23 October he accepted Kinnaird's 'unexpected generosity' and then proceeded to St Ives, where he survived a last-minute contest, and thereby achieved what he now admitted to be one of 'the earliest objects of my ambition'.[76]

The most striking feature of Horner's short career on the Government back bench was his low profile. He delivered his maiden speech in support of the Scottish Clergy Bill on 27 January 1807 but failed to rise again until 24 March, when he was ordered to assist Henry Bankes in bringing in an office in reversions bill, and he took the floor only once more during the session – on 24 April, when he briefly defended the bill he had helped bring in. He himself attributed his inactivity to fear, telling Murray that he had botched his initial oration, that he quaked at the thought of speaking again, and that his resulting silence was a source of great embarrassment.[77]

He was, however, quite active behind the scenes. Whig leaders, it was said, consulted him 'on nice points', to which he was 'ever ready with most pointed

74. Horner to Allen, 18 Sept. 1806, BLPES iii. 92–3.
75. Seymour to Horner, 7 July, and Horner to Seymour, 11 July 1806, *Horner*, i. 391–7.
76. *Home of the Hollands*, p. 201; Kinnaird to Horner, 19 Oct., Horner to Joanna Horner, 31 Oct., and to Kinnaird, 23 Oct. 1806, *Horner*, i. 403–407; Byrne Memoirs, p. 69. Accord-ing to the last (p. 94), John Horner made a very interesting remark immediately after his son departed: 'Now you will see an end of Brougham's friendship for Frank; he will never stand Frank's coming into Parliament before him.'
77. Horner to Murray, 20 Feb. 1807, *Horner*, i. 421–2.

answers'.[78] The first of them was Whitbread. Horner thought the brewer tasteless and somewhat vulgar and did not agree with all aspects of his scheme for a reform of poor law, but he certainly understood Whitbread's influence among Foxites in the Commons and collaborated with him very closely, notwithstanding protestations to the contrary.[79] As early as 5 December 1806 Horner queried Murray on the legality of Scots paupers being disfranchised for receiving parish relief; in early February Whitbread named Horner one of his committee on the poor law; and on 19 February the brewer revealed to the Commons that he had obtained most of his information on Scottish poor law from Horner (Docs 249 and 259).

Later in the year there appeared in the *Edinburgh Review* an article on the poor law.[80] Ostensibly it was a review of a pamphlet written by an unidentified justice of the peace; in fact it was a favourable review of Malthusian doctrine that applied Malthus's principle of population to the question of poor relief. It is said to have been written by Henry Reeve, a physician who had been at Edinburgh and in the Speculative with Brougham and Horner. But everything suggests that even if Reeve actually put it together, Horner supplied its substance.[81]

On 2 November 1806 Horner had promised Jeffrey that he would complete his review of Malthus before coming into Parliament; in the same letter he assessed the views of Whitbread and George Rose on the reform of poor law (Doc. 244). On 19 February 1807 he sent Seymour a detailed account of Whitbread's plan, and in it expressed objections that closely resembled those appearing in the review (Doc. 259).[82] And in July 1807 he disclosed to Seymour that he was evaluating Malthus's most recent speculations on the theory of population (Doc. 274).

The review in question includes Horner's opinion that the scheme of reform propounded by Pitt in 1796 was 'a most complex contrivance ... leading to every species of abuse'. The author, like Horner, also found much virtue in Malthus's recommendation that parish relief be discontinued for those paupers having children one year after the enactment of remedial legislation.[83] The review propounds Horner's grain doctrine as well, and relates it to population theory in much the same manner as Horner had done in his earlier notes, and as he would do again in a later document (Doc. 317).[84] A number of expressions in the review are also Hornerian. Two of them – the necessity of preserving 'the natural order of society' and the folly of 'artificial regulations and restraints' – are central arguments.[85]

Furthermore, all of the facts pertaining to the review of Foster's *Essay* are equally

78. Hunter to Constable, 7 Mar. 1807, *Constable*, i. 99 100.
79. Horner's letter to Murray of 29 Feb. 1807 (*Horner*, i. 421–2) denied active involvement with Whitbread.
80. *ER* xi (no. xxi, Oct. 1807), 100–115.
81. With the exception of the use of a technical medical term, and the vague assertions of his son, all the evidence cited by the *WI* for Henry Reeve (1780–1814: *DNB*) would apply no less well to Horner. Moreover, the two earlier contributions Reeve had made were both in the field of medicine and one of them, significantly, had been written in collaboration with Brougham.
82. Compare the negative remarks about Whitbread's plan in Horner's letter with those expressed in the review, *ER* xi (no. xxi, Oct. 1807), 112.
83. *Ibid.*, xi (no. xxi, Oct. 1807), 112–13.
84. Compare the remarks on p. 108 of the review.
85. *Idem*, p. 102.

applicable to the review of poor law. By all accounts Jeffrey then had access to no other reviewer capable of writing such an article, and surely Horner would in any case have protested against such an invasion of his purview. Finally, given Horner's involvement with the issue in Parliament, the absence of comment on the review in the Jeffrey–Horner correspondence is otherwise incredible. It therefore seems plausible that Horner exploited his notes on the *Essay on Population*, applied them to a 'practical' issue of state with which he was involved as a member of Parliament, and, perhaps, contrived with the aid of an old friend who had only recently returned from a prolonged residence abroad to take up practice as a country doctor, to place in the *Review* an article whose real origins were even more obscure than usual. After its appearance Jeffrey dunned Horner at least twice more for a review of Malthus (Doc. 313),[86] but Horner made no further promises and may well have considered his Malthusian debt discharged.

After February 1807, when Horner was named a member of the House of Commons Finance Committee, he actively involved himself in an investigation of the Bank of England and concurred in the committee's opinion that the rate of public allowance to the Bank be reduced (Doc. 266). In addition, he sought unsuccessfully to make the finance committee a vehicle for an attack on what he regarded as abuses within Sir William Scott's High Court of Admiralty (Doc. 262). His motive, it seems, was to temper Scott's hard line on neutral commerce, which adversely affected the Whig Ministry's attempted rapprochement with the United States. Following the lead of Lord Holland, Horner regarded improved Anglo-American relations as a vital component of British foreign policy after word of Napoleon's blockading decrees reached London. Among his papers is a note of January 1807 (Doc. 254) relating Spencer Perceval's critical opinion of the Government's American policy and a subsequent letter (Doc. 257) commenting on the implications of Napoleon's recent response to the merchants of Hamburg.

Horner also subscribed to Lord Holland's view that the Government should make an immediate concession to the Catholics (Doc. 251). On 4 January he resumed his notes on that subject, this time recording an account of the duplicity of Lord Rosslyn when Pitt attempted to bring on his Catholic Bill in 1801 (Doc. 253). He learned nothing from that note, however, for afterwards he emerged as a stout if silent supporter of the Government's suicidal attempt to commission Catholics as officers in His Majesty's armed forces.

One of the failings of the Whig Ministry was a reluctance to exploit the written word to mould public opinion. Horner had noted that omission as early as 19 May 1806 (Doc. 230), and during January 1807 he sought actively to make the *Edinburgh Review* a mouthpiece for the Government. On the 6th he encouraged Allen to write an article defending the Ministry's treaty with the United States (Doc. 255). There followed on the 14th a letter to Jeffrey requesting reviews supporting three leading Ministerial projects – the abolition of the slave trade, a softening of policy towards neutral nations, and concessions to His Majesty's Catholic subjects (Doc. 256).

Horner observed the progress of the Whig Ministry's modest Catholic bill with dismay, reporting the intrigues of Melville and Eldon to Murray and the events

---

86. See also Jeffrey to Horner, 2 Apr. 1809, *Horner*, i. 488.

surrounding the King's rout of Grey and Grenville (Docs 261 and 264). After the failure of the motion censuring the dismissal of the Whig Ministry, which Horner reported dutifully to Lady Holland (Doc. 265), Parliament dissolved. Horner then edited and expanded Henry Bennet's apology for the Whig Government, a threepenny pamphlet entitled *A short account of a late short administration* (1807) which predictably recalled Burke's account of the Rockingham Ministry.

A cry of 'No popery' undid the Whigs in the election of May 1807. Horner followed the campaign with undue optimism (Docs 267 and 271), encouraged Jeffrey to eschew foreign issues in favour of articles championing domestic liberties (Doc. 272), and was rewarded by word that he would not be returned to Parliament. Soon afterwards, however, the Grenvillite Lord Carrington, with whom Horner was only casually acquainted, brought him in for the closed borough of Wendover, apparently at the instigation of Petty and Holland.

From the re-assembly of Parliament in June 1807, through the session of 1809, Horner made nothing resembling a major speech. Rather, he contented himself with brief remarks that skirted central issues, and indeed failed to attend the Commons on a number of important occasions. The 'real cause', he told Murray in January 1809, was a continuation of the stage fright he had experienced earlier (Doc. 319). That explanation, however, does not ring quite true, and it did not satisfy a critical Jeffrey. 'Why do you not make speeches, if you will not write reviews?', he asked.[87] Horner, after all, had been among the finest debaters in the Speculative Society and was remembered as one who had engaged Brougham on almost equal terms.

The probability is that a number of very practical considerations combined to make Horner quite satisfied with relative obscurity in the House of Commons. The events of the spring and summer of 1807 left him with but little faith in an early return of the Whigs to power. That sagacious point of view led him instead to place renewed emphasis on professional success. He was called to the Bar in 1807 and, choosing the Western Circuit, thereafter plied his trade with great determination, if with but modest remuneration.

When Horner was not on circuit much of his time was occupied by the demands of the Carnatic Commission. Financially dependent on the commissionership,[88] he retained it unhappily until June 1809, resigning only after the City 'radicals' targeted him as a placeman. All the while he refused to compromise a very active social life, for he thrived on after-dinner conversation and treasured the company of intimate friends above all else. 'Our friend', Sydney Smith reported to Jeffrey in February 1808, '... has four distinct occupations, each of which may very fairly occupy the life of a man not deficient in activity: the Carnatic Commission, the Chancery Bar, Parliament, and a very numerous and select acquaintance.'[89]

Illness stole Horner's time as well. In January 1809 he was put to bed by a recurrence of the 'liver complaint' he had experienced as a child, and thereafter he was forced to endure a nagging cough and shortness of breath. These were symptoms

---

87. Jeffrey to Horner, 2 Apr. 1809, *ibid.*, i. 487.
88. Horner reported that his salary as commissioner was £1,500 per annum, half paid yearly and the remainder at the close of the Commission's trust (Horner to John Horner, 4 Oct. 1809, BLPES iv. 134–5).
89. Smith to Jeffrey, 16 Feb. 1808, *Smith Letters*, i. 133.

of the disease that would lead to his early death, and they produced in him despond-ency and frequent exhibitions of foul temper.

If illness and a busy schedule sometimes kept Horner away from the Commons, the speeches he delivered when he attended were closely calculated and well-rehearsed. For he regarded his early years in Parliament as an apprenticeship, as a necessary period of subserviency and deference to others, and that point of view made him conclude that infrequent, didactic orations were both prudent and capable of great effect. When queried about his failure to speak more often, he replied that 'he thought he had spoken too early and too much'. The result of his relative silence, his sister Frances recalled, was that he 'never rose to speak, without commanding the attention of the House'.[90]

Horner's behaviour during the 1808 session illustrates his concept of parliamentary manoeuvre. Ever deferring to those below him among the Opposition front bench, he took no direct part in the debates inspired by the Whigs' principal attack on Government. He did, however, deliver a number of short orations that elevated him well above his colleagues' prattle. In the debate on the offices in reversion bill of 25 January, for example, he seized on a remark by William Dundas and delivered a short, apparently set speech extolling the virtues of Edmund Burke, thereby acting on a principle of political conduct that he had formulated nearly six years earlier.

On other occasions he exploited his reputation as a political economist. In the course of the debate on a bill seeking 'to limit the excessive depreciation of Wages of persons employed in the weaving of Cotton', Horner endorsed the principle of laissez-faire advanced by those opposing the measure but remarked that such 'a numerous and deserving class of individuals merited every attention'.[91] His most impressive performance, however, came on 29 January 1808 when he pointedly dissociated himself from the war of words that raged over British commercial policy, moved for official accounts, and produced a degree of confusion among the Government bench.

Horner was evidently the first Whig MP to comprehend that the Portland Ministry's Orders in Council sought to control, rather than to prohibit, trade with the enemy. At all events Opposition spokesmen failed to heed either the pithy analysis of British commercial policy he provided Lord Holland on 14 November 1807 (Doc. 282), or the more focused assessment of commercial licences he subsequently sent Allen (Doc. 284). Instead the Whig bench attempted very unskilfully to draw a distinction between the unpopular and unsuccessful American policy of their own Government and the supposed negative reaction of Washington to the Orders in Council promulgated in late 1807.

Horner kept well clear of such folly. But on 29 January he called the attention of the House to the Privy Council's sale of licences allowing foreign merchants to import grain and other commodities to Britain and professed interest in knowing the extent to which the practice had been carried. For to Horner it seemed that the sale of such licences produced three lamentable results. First, the fees assessed for licences amounted to a tax on imports; it was 'a serious breach of the Constitution

---

90. Byrne Memoirs, p. 117.
91. Hansard, xi. 426; see also EW, p. 15.

that the Executive should thus take upon itself the levying of taxes'. Secondly, the sale of licences directly violated the provisions of the navigation laws, thereby playing havoc with ancient statutes 'dear to administrative England'. Worst of all, the licences were being sold to the enemy. That policy was both peculiar and hypocritical for a nation at war, and it created analogous situations in international law. These remarks, which questioned a policy promoting market considerations over higher interests of state, caught Perceval unprepared; the Minister actually admitted the illegality of some of the licences and their inconsistency with the navigation laws.[92]

One might speculate that Horner's remarks did not escape Brougham, who later earned fame by repeating them in the course of his successful attack on the Orders in Council, but in 1808 Horner was quite happy to wield a rapier and quickly sheathe it. Sydney Smith reported that Horner had 'spoken often and well, without however having as yet done anything decided'.[93]

Horner's failure to do anything 'decided' between 1807 and 1809 was also influenced by the fact that he found himself in a political vice. The Fox and Grenville factions agreed on very little indeed, but their views on the origins of the war with France, on the political objectives of hostilities, and of course on wartime policy were irreconcilable. Horner did not like the Grenvilles and anticipated an eventual breach in the Whig coalition, but after 1807 he could not escape from the unhappy truth that he alone among the Foxites owed his seat to a Grenvillite peer.

The plot was thickened by disagreement among leading Foxites. After Fox's death the peace negotiations with France had fallen apart, with Whitbread asserting that the Ministry had abandoned Fox's principles, and a nasty confrontation developing between him and Grey. Then an unsuccessful attempt, promoted by Grenville, to bring Canning into an already difficult coalition Government had threatened a complete separation with Whitbread. These events did not escape remark by Horner. A letter he wrote to Allen at the beginning of 1807 shows that he was no less appalled by Whitbread's attack on the abortive peace negotiations than by Grey's resulting warlike harangue in the Lords, and a note he made at the end of the year records his negative view of Grenville's flirtation with Canning (Docs 255 and 283).

Acrimony among the Opposition bench, which increased progressively after the fall of the coalition Government, led Horner to retreat still more. On the right was Windham, the self-styled disciple of Burke who loathed the Grenvilles but generally agreed with their politics. On the left was Whitbread, who went his own way with incessant appeals to a noble Foxite tradition and accordingly infuriated Windham and Grenville's surly brother, Tom. In the middle, representing little more than milk and toast, was George Ponsonby, or 'Snouch' as he was known, the ostensible leader whose status was owing to his very obscurity. Ponsonby was supported by Petty, still a youngster whose views blew with the wind, and by the former Addingtonian, Tierney, who posed rather ludicrously as a fiscal expert, coveting the leadership for himself, and competing for it with Whitbread. It was no wonder, then, that in January 1809 Horner should complain that he had witnessed 'but little else' than a 'petty war of political personalities' (Doc. 319).

92. *Hansard*, x. 183, and *Examiner*, 31 Jan. 1808; see also C.R. Fay, *The Corn Laws and Social England* (Cambridge, 1932), pp. 112–13.
93. Smith to Jeffrey, 16 Feb. 1808, *Smith Letters*, i. 133.

As always, Horner searched for common denominators and thought he found one in the person of Lord Holland. But the political views of Holland and his circle, like the 'principles' of the martyred Fox, were not always comprehensible.[94] Knowing full well that Holland was a stout supporter of the Catholic claims, Horner in the summer of 1807 ventured several critical remarks on Grattan's support of the Irish Insurrection Bill in a letter to Allen (Doc. 276). He failed to realize, however, that the coercive measure was a virtual carbon copy of one concocted by the late Whig Ministry, and he was yet to understand fully the hold of Fox's oldest friends on the Hollands. Allen's reply has not come to light, but clearly it chastised Horner in the strongest terms. Enlightened, Horner fired off a waffling retraction and followed it up with a letter hailing the integrity of Fox's adherents in Edinburgh (Docs 277–8).

Horner was also confronted with a good deal of inconsistency in Holland's opinions of time-serving Foxites. Grattan, Grey, and Lauderdale were thought sacred, and their frequent doctrinal lapses were excused; but Whitbread, whose lapses were few, was alternately loved and despised. Sheridan, who necessarily courted the Prince of Wales, was abused and ignored but regularly fed. Then there were the martyrs of the 1790s, Coke of Norfolk among them, who disapproved of Lady Holland; and the complexity of the thing was compounded still further by Lord Holland's regard for Fitzwilliam, who embodied the difficulties accruing from Fox's notion of coalition.

All in all the loyalties of Holland House were virtually incomprehensible, but the unhappy performance of Opposition during the 1808 session reinforced Horner's concept of men and measures. The Whigs agreed on almost nothing but the principle of Catholic Emancipation. Even there, however, a current of tension, checked only by the adhesive of the late Government's disastrous collision with George III, was discernible. Horner followed the debates very carefully, casting a silent vote in favour of the Catholic petition and reporting developments in the Commons to his friends (Docs 292 and 295). Thereafter, while never speaking on the Catholic question, he supported it zealously out-of-doors and came to the conclusion, expressed in September 1809, that the Whigs should regard Emancipation as a *sine qua non* in all negotiations for office (Doc. 350).

The 1808 session also revealed that the central point of dispute among the Whigs was foreign politics, and that an appeal to the legacy of Fox inspired considerable support among the bulk of the party's rank and file. Those truths were revealed vividly on 29 February when Whitbread, ignoring the protestations of the coalition's leaders and recalling the principles of Fox, moved resolutions for the re-opening of peace negotiations with France and secured the support of almost every Foxite MP. Sorely troubled by the warlike views of Carrington and his Grenvillite colleagues, Horner cast a silent vote for peace.

Subsequently Horner was loath to participate in contentious debates. Instead he gravitated increasingly towards Lord Holland and demonstrated greater loyalty to the elusive Foxite creed. He was admitted to Brooks's on 15 May 1808. In June he hailed Fox's fragment on the reign of James II, edited by Lord Holland, as a constitutional treatise of considerable importance (Doc. 296), but declined to review it,

94. For a useful analysis see *Holland House*.

encouraging Jeffrey to do it himself. Not approving of the first draft, he criticized and offended Jeffrey, but secured the inclusion of a remedial sentence.[95] In September, when the *Edinburgh Review* appeared, he remained displeased and told Murray that the review reflected the deteriorating quality of Jeffrey's prose (Doc. 305).

The Holland House dinner book lists Horner as an habitual guest during 1808. In October, after visiting Algernon Sydney's 'shrine' at Penshurst, Horner professed himself to be 'more Whiggish than ever' (Doc. 310). His emerging creed was expressed most notably by his keen support for the Spanish insurrection against Bonaparte. Horner's point of view is interesting. The good, he argued quite simply, had 'changed sides'. Formerly the French quest for liberty had commanded the respect of mankind. Now, however, it was clear that military despotism prevailed in France and that the Spanish 'patriots', a 'risen people' fighting to be free, deserved the same sympathy that French 'patriots' had deserved in 1789 (Docs 298–9).

Four weighty facts bear on this curious interpretation of events. First, it consulted Foxite ideology: like the English, the Americans, and the French before them, the Spaniards were good Whigs. Secondly, it coincided perfectly with the opinion of Lord Holland, a long-standing admirer of Spain who either influenced or was influenced by Horner. Thirdly, it represented a considerable shift in opinion: only months earlier Horner had supported Whitbread's resolutions for the opening of peace negotiations with the same Government he now deprecated for its military despotism. Finally, Horner's interpretation of events in Spain rescued him from the throes of pacifism, committing him to a more viable view of the war with France, and, logically at least, bringing him into line with the foreign politics of the Grenvilles.

Horner's correspondence in the final six months of 1808 is dominated by references to the Spanish civil war. He began reasonably well informed: Allen had kept him abreast of developments since April (Docs 289–90), and Horner outlined a scheme of Spanish policy in a letter to Loch as early as 13 June (Doc. 296). He became uncommonly enthusiastic in July, when word of the Spaniards' early military successes reached England (Doc. 297), and afterwards plotted military strategy with Holland and Allen. In September, when the Spanish deputies were entertained at Holland House, he recorded his impressions (Docs 302 and 303). Later he assessed the numerous manifestos emanating from Spain, the virtues and liabilities of various schemes of government, and the state of public opinion in Britain (Docs 304 and 306).

Horner's politics were not unreasonable, but his hopes began to evaporate in October. First Allen and the Hollands departed for Spain, thus depriving him of his fruitful evenings at Holland House. Then Grenville, having decided that Spanish peasants were no match for French infantry, called for the withdrawal of the British army, and was soon joined by Grey and Lauderdale (Doc. 310). Horner clung to his optimistic point of view, but by late October Whitbread was ironically the only Opposition leader other than the departed Holland who shared his views (Doc. 308).

In December 1808 Horner grew depressed when word of British reversals in the Peninsula arrived, and in the circumstances he professed to blame the Govern-

95. Horner to Jeffrey, 15 June, *Horner*, i. 453, and Jeffrey to Horner, 10 Sept. 1808, *Jeffrey*, ii. 124.

ment's mismanagement (Docs 314–15). Then in January 1809 he criticized Canning's hasty rejection of a French offer of negotiations and offered the theory that the Government was conspiring to blame everything on General Sir John Moore (Doc. 318). But Horner already knew better. Almost simultaneously he withdrew an earlier 'half-promise' to send Jeffrey an article on Spanish affairs; recent reports had cast uncertainty on the zeal of the 'patriots', he explained (Doc. 316).

Shortly afterwards Horner characteristically professed himself alienated from politics, bemoaning the folly of the Opposition bench, and making a personal note about the lamentable prejudices of the public and the unhappy state of political parties (Docs 318–20). The defeat of the British army at Corunna and the death of Moore in the retreat to the sea further depressed him (Doc. 322). He said nothing about the Peninsular War in Parliament during the 1809 session and virtually dropped the subject from his correspondence.

Politically isolated, Horner spent much time with Jeremy Bentham during late 1808 and the first months of the new year. He had met Bentham at Holland House in August 1805, and a mutual interest in the reform of Scots judicature had subsequently fostered a close, if not an intimate, relationship between them (Doc. 264). Now, in the autumn of 1808, they apparently met quite frequently to discuss the constitutional and legal issues confronting Spanish leaders. In late October Horner also accepted Bentham's invitation to meet the visiting Aaron Burr, and made an interesting note of the American's manner and conversation (Docs 309–311). Interestingly too, Horner came to appreciate Benthamite doctrine; 'the principle of utility', he told Murray in June 1809, was 'the sole foundation of moral reasoning'.[96]

Horner's letters of early 1809 contain vivid detail on the events attending the allegations of corrupt practices lodged against the Duke of York. There are assessments of the individuals involved, accounts of alignments in Parliament, analyses of the tactics of the adversaries, and opinions and speculations about the constitutional and political ramifications of the Duke's acquittal (Docs 321–7).

Finding the behaviour of the Whig leadership ridiculous (Doc. 327), Horner prudently took no direct part in the parliamentary discussions about the Duke of York affair, but uncharacteristically, and somewhat dangerously, allowed himself to be drawn into the resulting squabbles over economic and parliamentary reform. Among his correspondence on these matters may be found views about the degree of corruption in government and the crusade for reform (Docs 329 and 335), comments on the changing nature of parties in the Commons and the troubling events of the session (Docs 327–8 and 339), and, not least, indications of the thinking behind his own motions and speeches (Docs 330–31).

The most interesting commentary in Horner's correspondence in the spring of 1809, however, is that depicting his frustrations with the Whig hierarchy. He felt that concessions to the 'popular party' were necessary, and Windham's views reactionary, even boneheaded; but again he found himself in unhappy agreement with Whitbread and his band of followers in the Commons. None of this accorded with Horner's political plans. Collaboration with a group labelled 'The Mountain'

96. Horner to Murray, 2 June 1809, BLPES iv. 67.

was embarrassing; one simply could not find good men and good measures united in politics, he told a sympathetic J. W. Ward (Doc. 332).

Horner began to re-think matters in June, when it became clear that all the sound and fury of the City 'radicals' and of the 'popular party' in the Commons would come to nothing. On the 5th he wrote to Grey, soliciting an opinion of a harmless proposal for judicial reform.[97] On the 12th he encouraged Jeffrey, whom he knew to be writing an article on parliamentary reform, to reflect carefully on the wisdom of moderation (Doc. 334). The following month he experienced a change of heart on both economical and parliamentary reform, and taking a less favourable view of the reformers (Doc. 338), wrote twice more to Jeffrey to discourage an irresponsible article on reform (Docs 336–7).

Anticipating the Hollands' return to England, Horner also displayed a revival of interest in the Spanish 'patriots'. During July he co-operated with Holland to publish a pamphlet promulgating his patron's favourable view of Spanish affairs, and sent several related articles to the *Morning Chronicle* (Doc. 339). After the Hollands' return in mid-August, he resumed his place at their dinner table and became more politically active. Subsequently his letters record the political opinions of Holland and Allen, the folly of the British expedition to the Scheldt, and the unfolding difficulties of the Portland Ministry (Docs 342–6).

When Perceval opened negotiations with Grey and Grenville in September 1809, Horner exhibited a monumental shift in opinion. First, he told Allen that the infamy the Whig leaders had incurred by their apparent manoeuvrings was altogether undeserved (Doc. 349). Then, when rumour held that Grenville was yet again discussing coalition with Canning, he expressed his strongest disapproval and told Whishaw that he opposed coalition with any party (Doc. 350). As the intermittent Whig negotiations with Perceval continued into October, he became still more vociferous, his correspondence revealing a systematic campaign against coalition, against union with Canning and Wellesley, against compromise on the Catholic question, against anything, in fact, but the preservation of a political *status quo* he had found intolerable only months earlier (Docs 350–54 and 357). And when at last the Whigs came up empty-handed, he hailed the integrity of Grey and Grenville and remarked on the impossibility of a Whig Ministry surviving for any length of time in existing circumstances (Doc. 359).

The motivation behind Horner's remarkable shift in opinion is clear. Nobody was happy with Ponsonby or his colleagues on the Opposition front bench in the Commons, and there was much speculation afloat in mid-October about the health of the Marquess of Lansdowne raising the prospect of Petty's early elevation to the Lords. Opportunity, therefore, knocked. There were indications, however, that it would pass Horner by. Grenville's flirtation with Canning contemplated the void of leadership in the Commons, and Grey was eager to plug the gap by bringing Brougham into Parliament (Docs 350 n. 2 and 360 n. 1).

Surely it is this last that explains Horner's fierce opposition to union with Canning during the autumn, which included attacks on his character and past political conduct, and his gloating when Grenville's failure left Canning adrift (Docs 350 and 359). Combating Brougham was a more delicate matter. When

97. Grey MSS, Durham University.

Lansdowne died on 14 November, Horner immediately wrote to Murray about the sad state of the Opposition bench, speculating on the prospect of Brougham being brought into Parliament, and of course wishing him well (Doc. 360). An almost immediate deterioration in Brougham's relationship with Lady Holland ensued, however, and in January 1810, upon learning that the Duke of Bedford would bring Brougham in, Horner noted that his rival 'never could have found a more fortunate moment' and told Allen it would be 'very fortunate, for him personally, if he has some probationary years to pass on the Opposition side of the House' (Doc. 374).[98]

In the circumstances Horner's extraordinary efforts to please important men during the last months of 1809 are perhaps explicable. Shortly after hearing of Lansdowne's illness, he paid a rare visit to Lord Carrington at High Wycombe (Doc. 356). Simultaneously he apologized to an irate Jeffrey for a long break in correspondence and promised more active exertions as a reviewer.[99] Soon after this he posted a manuscript to Edinburgh, a review of the recent French edition of Fox's *History* that heaped fulsome praise on Fox and employed his 'immortal name' in a denunciation of Napoleonic France.[100]

During November and December 1809 Horner dined at Holland House even more often than usual, apparently feeling the pulse of Whig politics by associating with men of diverse political views.[101] He pleased the Hollands by securing preferential treatment at Edinburgh University for Lady Holland's son, Henry Webster, and communicated indirectly to the Duke of Bedford Professor Playfair's high opinion of young Lord John Russell, who only recently had begun attending classes at Edinburgh (Doc. 371).[102] Rosslyn, who was close to Grey, must have been astonished when he received a letter from Horner, with whom he had never corresponded, but he was probably pleased enough to learn that the studious back-bencher was devoted to the Whig leadership and deeply interested in Grenville's campaign to become Chancellor of Oxford (Doc. 358).

Creevey, too, was perplexed. On 8 November he noted that every Opposition MP except Horner spoke contemptuously of party leaders. That was odd, given Horner's active involvement with the 'Mountain' in the last session; now Horner damned the public as 'rank Tories', refused to commit himself on any political issue, and advocated 'nothing in the House of Commons this approaching session'.[103] The sudden shift in opinion was startling, and Horner knew it. On 24 November he told Murray that he was worried about appearing inconsistent in his political opinions (Doc. 362). In mid-December, amidst unprecedented feuding among Opposition front-benchers, he encouraged Holland to intervene, to 'keep us together'; for Whitbread had to be conciliated, and Tierney was 'not disposed to give Sam his full measure of consideration and deference' (Doc. 367).

Jeffrey was probably more surprised than anyone. There were even signs that the old Horner was back. His letter of 7 December (Doc. 365) promised a review of the

---

98. See also *Holland House*, pp. 177–8.
99. Horner to Jeffrey, 11 Oct. 1809, BLPES iv. 142–3.
100. *ER* xv (no. xxix, Oct. 1809), 190–97; Jeffrey to Horner, 10 Nov. 1809, *Horner*, i. 503–504.
101. HHDB.
102. See also Horner to Murray, 17 Nov. 1809, BLPES iv. 168.
103. *Creevey*, i. 111.

new French edition of Turgot's works and a much more active role as a reviewer. Here was a pledge to return to first principles, to the pursuit of literary reputation, to the subject of his earliest literary project, and to political economy. Horner, however, seemed overly cautious, requesting complete anonymity, and writing soon to Murray to seek his assistance in convincing Jeffrey that partisan politics had no place in the *Review*. He was especially concerned that Jeffrey might engage in a war of words with Canning's organ, the *Quarterly*, or allow 'indiscretions' by 'his most able and most entertaining colleagues' (Doc. 369).

Horner was at last plotting a political offensive. It envisaged what he regarded as unprecedented political opportunities created by a tottering executive, a weak Ministry, a leaderless Opposition bench in the Commons, and peculiar currents in public opinion (Docs 354 and 359). The plan had both defensive and offensive facets. Defensively, it called for the exclusion of Canning, for the neutralization of Brougham, and for the preservation of a balance of power among the existing Opposition bench. Offensively, it sought to please the principal Whig grandees and to exploit the successful tactics of earlier days.

Horner apparently regarded the review of Turgot as an opening salvo, a renewal of credentials. It was to be followed up by a parliamentary offensive, Horner's first, exploiting the 'practical' issue of state he had ever thought fruitful. A number of letters suggest that he had more or less pursued the research project he had mentioned to Mackintosh in September 1805 – a systematic study of the world bullion trade. In December 1806 he had sought official accounts of Chinese reserves and exports of quicksilver (Doc. 247) and had commented on the same subject in a letter to Allen (Doc. 248). In January 1808 he had asked Allen to obtain an account of Portuguese bullion imports (Doc. 284), and some six months later he had made further inquiries about the Chinese bullion trade (Doc. 299).

Other evidence indicates that Horner had kept a close eye on the British economy. In December 1808 he had sent Somerset an analysis of the unique wartime variables that had combined to bolster the nation's balance of trade (Doc. 315). In January 1809 he had written, apparently at the request of an aspiring Foxite author, a very full analysis of a paper addressing, among other political subjects, the effect of wartime taxes and mounting public debt on the wages of labour, the value of money, unemployment, criminality, and poor relief (Doc. 317). In late September of that year he told his father that the nation was perhaps nearing financial disaster. In the same letter he speculated on the Ministry's tax policy, and in a letter to Allen the following month he noted the mounting difficulties arising from Britain's commercial warfare with the United States (Docs 345 and 356).

By all indications Horner suspected that the expansion of Napoleon's 'continental system' in the wake of the Austrian military disaster at Wagram (Doc. 346), the accumulated effects of misguided British commercial policies, and a growing monetary crisis occasioned by the continuing suspension of cash payments were finally leading the country to ruin. At all events he had concluded before the end of 1809 that the time had come to voice on the floor of the British senate the bullionist doctrine he had propounded in his earlier reviews of Thornton and King.

85. Journal

Kinnordy MSS ⟨Horner, i. 204⟩   18 May 1802

⟨… Since dinner, I have worked hard for three hours on a few pages of Quesnai's *Analyse du Tableau Economique*, printed in the *Physiocratie:*[1] I am still repulsed by the difficulty of the subject, or the faults of his manner, or the weakness of my own intellectual powers; but I have commenced a regular siege, and mean to proceed methodically by lines of circumvallation. I keep in a separate set of notes a diary of my tactics. By persevering, with patient and painful thought, to examine the reasonings of Quesnai, and by a careful trial of his mode of procedure, by those views of philosophical logic which I have superficially learned in Lord Bacon's writings,[2] I trust I shall ultimately make out an opinion as to the truth, or error, or mixture of both, which prevails in these writings of Quesnai and his disciples.⟩

1. At this point Horner was using the one-volume, 1767, edition.
2. Horner and Seymour had continued to study the philosophical writings of Bacon throughout the winter of 1801–1802. In October 1801 Horner had written paragraphs numbered 62–72, all constituting responses to Bacon's concept of scientific method focusing on language and the ground rules for inducing generalizations from known facts. On 31 Jan. 1802 he added a short, unnumbered outline to these notes. The outline is headed 'Introduction, etc.', apparently referring to an intended treatise on the proper rules of philosophical inquiry, and contains sections entitled: 'Investigations of science consist in generalizing and classing the phenomena of nature – [mind and matter]'; 'General aspect of nature, and of the substance of phenomena which the mind has to arrange'; 'Must now advert to a most important fact in the history of human understanding, on which, as a leading principle, the whole of this system of Logic may be said to depend: instrumentality of language in general conceptions and reasonings – History of the mind in forming general terms'; 'Rules for the process of generalization, and for the promotion of general terms'; '*Rules of Experiment*'; 'Rules of evidence, in generalizing from definite observations and results of experiment'; and 'Habit of systematizing our acquired principles, in the due proportion of the evidence on which they rest, and of the degree in which the analogies of generalization have been legitimately traced'. Horner's final notes on Bacon, which are dated 14 Feb. 1802, contain paragraphs numbered 73–5, to which is appended a number of quotations from the *Novum Organum*. These final notes contain reasonings on inductive methodology including observation, analysis, arrangement, and conclusions.

86. Notes of my progress in studying the system of the Economists

Kinnordy MSS   18–21 May 1802

15. *Physiocratie*, p. 40.[1] Whether the Economists be well-founded in their speculation or not, it is evident that the language, which they use to explain it is too rhetorical. The Comte d'Albon remarks, though without any intention of suggesting either a censure or a suspicion, that if Quesnay had not been educated in

the country and early acquired a passion for rural occupations, we should never perhaps have seen his speculations in political economy.[2]

In examining the reasonings of this ingenious but perplexed system, we must cut off all that air of sentimental eloquence, in which the pursuits of agriculture are dignified and embellished. This page of Dupont's preface suggests a similar caution, which will not prove altogether useless, though the statement may appear almost ludicrously refined. In describing the productions of agricultural labour, the Economists constantly introduce the personified imagery of the Earth and Nature. This language may mislead our reasoning; in fact, where the deduction is so fine and is pursued through such a complicated subject, we cannot be too abstract, too algebraically correct, in the terms we adopt to guide our research. When the conclusions of philosophy are cautiously and securely developed, it may then be permitted to add those ornaments of expression, which are sometimes necessary to convey illustrations to a mind unaccustomed to abstract argument, or to insinuate persuasion into those minds of a still lower order which are unable to reason at all. Even then, the sacrifice should be as small as possible; and the illustrations, borrowed from eloquence, should be as nearly as possible adjusted to the truths of science, both in respect of minute accuracy and of comprehensiveness. It is but a narrow and cold personification of Nature, which sets her in distinction to man; man, and the labours of man, occupy as large a portion in that system of beings and that course of events, which the word Nature suggests to every mind habituated to the correct phraseology of science.[3]

16. *Physiocratie*, p. 45. If there were any of the *métayers* who advanced any part of the expenses of cultivation, would the Economists refuse to class them with the productive labourers, though the ground was cultivated by their hands, and though the rent passed through their hands to the landlord?

17. p. 46. It seems incorrect to say that the *neat produce* is paid, by the cultivator after reimbursing his several expenses, to the proprietor. This has no doubt been very much the case during the depression of agriculture. But in the prosperity of that art, the rent of the landlord is only a certain proportion of the neat produce, after all expenses are paid; and the lease is a contract adjusting the proportions in which the neat produce is to be divided between the cultivator and the landlord.

18. p. 47. 'Entière sûreté de la propriété des richesses d'exploitation de l'agriculture.' How fond Quesnai [was] of what Adam Smith has called the most abstract of the propositions! Thus on p. 45 also, 'qui fait les avances des dépenses des travaux de l'agriculture.' These instances indicate a mind powerful in the command of abstract attention, but clumsy in the use of the instrument by which abstract reasoning is performed.

19. *Physiocratie*, p. 52. The object of this chapter ['Analyse du Tableau'] is evidently to explain, synthetically, the order in which M. Quesnai conceives that the commodities or produce, which compose national wealth, are distributed among the different ranks of the people. This purpose coincides with what is announced in the title of Smith's first book.[4] Neither of them has been very distinct in the explanation of this subject, or rather in the description of this order; neither of them seems to have caught a simple point of view, till the fortunate discovery of which I am persuaded that this part of the science will remain in obscurity. As it is, these two

philosophers have adopted two methods distinct from each other. Quesnai has formed a classification of the people; Smith has made an analysis of price.

As I have a notion that this is the essential part of the doctrine of the Economists, and that the patient elaboration of it will lead me either to comprehend their discovery or to detect their mistakes, it is better for me to set down the ideas, however unconnected, that at present occur to my mind: viz.,

First, it is absolutely necessary to establish (by a scrutiny of the phrase already employed, and by an adoption of more correct terms if it is at all defective), what it is that is really attempted to be described, when we speak of 'the order according to which the produce of labour is distributed among the different ranks and conditions of the people'.[5]

Secondly, supposing the preceding object attained, it will be proper to consider (according to the rules of philosophical logic), what place such description is to hold in the science or general theory of political economy.[6]

Thirdly, the last point being ascertained, it will be in our power to conceive what inferences and conclusions may be derived from the description of such a fact.[7]

20. The Economists have made much use of arithmetic in their works; not always, I suspect, with a perfectly distinct conception of the kind of instrumentality which it furnishes to political reasoning.[8] Indeed there is reason to doubt whether this has ever been sufficiently explained by any writer. Smith says, II. 310,[9] without either explaining or qualifying the observation, that he has 'no great faith in political arithmetic'; on the other hand, Dupont, *Physiocratie*, p. 177, talks of it in the most unlimited style of panegyric. To explain the proper use of political arithmetic, forms a necessary article in the logic of political philosophy.[10]

So far as I understand the Economical Table at present, it seems to amount only to an illustration of the theory, without containing any other argument from which a theoretical conclusion is to be derived. It appears to me, that it does not even involve calculations; but is composed of a set of data, assumed for the purpose of making out a diagram or scheme, the numbers being all taken for granted, as well as the relations between different numbers.

If it is meant to be an illustration, it may at least be considered as very inadequate to the purpose of facilitating proper apprehension; and upon the whole I question very much the utility of illustrating in such a manner what ought to be more simply expressed in a series of abstract propositions. The mathematical doctrine of proportions, so accessible when completely generalized, is almost unmanageable by the imagination when illustrated, as Euclid has done, by lines.

My suspicion at present is, that the Economists, not aware of the just distinctions of philosophical logic, have introduced into political science a species of evidence, and a mode of reasoning, which belong to sciences of a different order. But I am very far from being clear on this point, and must carefully attend to it in the course of the investigation.

21. I will now set down all that I have as yet made out, with respect to this cardinal subject, the distribution of produce among the people.[11]

In a commercial country, where the sub-division of labour is systematically extended, every individual depends, for the supply of almost all his wants, on the labour of a great many other individuals. The produce of their labour he must procure, as he wants it, article by article, by means of equivalent considerations: and the commerce of a large and opulent society exhibits a picture of innumerable exchanges, constantly going on, ramifying from every point, and crossing each other in every direction. To describe the order in which the produce of labour is distinguished among all ranks of the people, is to give an analysis, or simplified description, of this vast system of exchanges.

The utility of such a description does not at present fall under consideration. We have nothing now in contemplation but the practicability of the description, and the different points of view from which the sketch may be delineated.

Now, from one point of view, we may no doubt give the following description. In the great system of sub-divided labour, every class of labourers furnishes commodities to every other individual labourer. The articles, produced or manufactured by any one class of labourers, are distributed among the rest of the people by a great variety of exchanges. Each class may be considered, therefore, as the source from which its productions or manufactures are distributed or circulated throughout the rest of the community. And as the same may be said, in exactly the same manner, of every class of labourers, we may view the complicated movements of national trade as composed of an infinite number of currents which radiate from every single class of labourers considered as a central point, to all the other inhabitants of the community considered as the extreme points of radiation. In this sense, it is unquestionably [true?] that the cultivators, or agricultural labourers, form one centre, the great and necessary source, from which their peculiar produce flows to the rest of the population; but then it is no less true that the woollen, or linen, or iron manufacturers, compose another centre, a great and a necessary source, from [which] their articles of manufacture are likewise distributed.

22. I will leave for the present that article in the *Physiocratie*, which I have dwelt on with so little success, the 'Analyse du Tableau Economique' – and proceed to the next.[12] My present impression is, that it is merely a synthetic statement of the theory without any proof being given of the fundamental principles, and with a very imperfect statement of the steps by which the remote conclusions are deduced. The political arithmetic, though apparently intended for something more, can only be considered as an illustration, and that an imperfect one; the deductions in that professed calculation are still more lame, being a series of near assumptions.

23. 'Maximes Générales', etc., *Physiocratie*, p. 99.[13] In the first of these maxims, two propositions are announced, both I presume as the results of inference stated elsewhere, which are, both of them, very contrary to the present bias of my opinions, and give a very unfavourable specimen of the political philosophy of the Economists. One is, that the utility of counteracting interests and counterbalancing forces is a consideration not to be admitted into the just theory of government. The other is, that, in an agricultural kingdom, every interest should be directed, by the frame of their political institutions to promote the prosperity of agriculture only.

1. A reference to Dupont's preface to the *Tableau Economique* in the one-volume edition. With the exception of those to pp. 99, 176, and 177, all subsequent references in this document are to the text of that 'table'.
2. Claude Camille François, Comte d'Albon, *Eloge Historique de François Quesnay* (Paris, 1775).

3. This section is dated in the margin 18 May 1802.

4 'Of the Causes of Improvement in the productive Powers of Labour, and of the Order according to which its Produce is naturally distributed among the different Ranks of the People'.

5. *I have some notion that the different descriptions of this order of circulation, which have been given by Quesnai and Smith, are not altogether irreconcilable. At least, the one seems to have been in some degree derived from the other; and perhaps, if stated with some modifications, might be given as approximate descriptions of the order of distribution. – In Quesnai's view, agricultural labour is represented as the centre of circulation, the source of the circulating matter, the heart of the system. In Smith's view, we have the branching of the system delineated without any common source or origin.

[The passage quoted from Smith ('Introduction and Plan', WN i. 5) should read: 'the order, according to which its produce is naturally distributed among the different ranks and conditions of men in the society'.]

6. *It is probable that an accurate description, of the order in which the produce of labour is distributed, would throw considerable light on the theory of money operating as the medium of circulation. [The location of this note is a guess, since the mark is lacking in the text.]

7. *I believe there is reason to suspect, that Quesnai's order of distribution was suggested by the desire of justifying a conclusion previously formed, with regard to the most expedient form of taxation. It will be proper to appreciate the justice of this suspicion by tracing the history of Economisme.

8. This is dated in the margin 19 May 1802.

9. WN IV. v. b. 30.

10. *In explaining this subject, something may perhaps be worked out of Dupont's very general and almost mystical remarks, Physiocratie, p. 176 [in the Preface to Pt ii, 'Discussions et Développemens'].

11. This is dated in the margin 20 May 1802.

12. This is dated in the margin 20 May 1802.

13. The beginning of 'Maximes générales du Gouvernement économique d'un royaume agricole'.

87. Journal

Kinnordy MSS ⟨Horner, i. 204–205⟩   19 May 1802

⟨Of this day I can give no better account, than that I worked as yesterday, and with little farther progress, on the same pages of Quesnai's Economical Table. I can make little or nothing of it. It is some consolation to recollect what Lauderdale once told me, that he had repeatedly left the study of the Tableau Economique, cursing himself for a blockhead. I scarcely entertain a doubt that the mode of reasoning, in which it is conducted, involves some fundamental mistake; probably in the misapplication of a species of logic and evidence, belonging to sciences of a different kind. I may be assisted, perhaps, in ascertaining this, by examining those writings which Quesnai produced on the general views of philosophy; such as his Preface to the Memoirs of the Society of Surgery.⟩[1]

1. The introductory discourse to the first volume of the memoirs of the Royal Academy of Surgery at Paris, concerning the vices of the humours, translated and abridged by a surgeon (1760).

88. Journal

Kinnordy MSS ⟨Horner, i. 205⟩   20 May 1802

⟨...

    ⟨Worked still at Quesnai. My notes grow voluminous, yet I cannot solve the puzzle.

    ⟨...⟩

89. To the Duke of Somerset

BLPES i. 160–61   Edinburgh, 21 May 1802

I have just had the pleasure of receiving your letter, together with the papers you enclosed for me, and I cannot lose a moment in returning you thanks for your great attention. When I asked you about the practicability of making an arrangement with some of the officers of the House of Lords, in order to procure the printed papers, I was sincerely very far from putting your Grace to any trouble; and yet from what you have been so kind as to do for me, I am afraid you may have had some reason to think me very troublesome and forward. The possession of these papers is to me invaluable; not only because they contain much information on the details of commerce and economy, but likewise furnish a groundwork and materials for political reasonings, which cannot otherwise be supplied. The genuine and legitimate use of Political Arithmetic has never been defined by any writer, whose observations I have met with. Some theorists have very carelessly neglected it altogether; while others, still more wrong, have considered it as all in all. Within a certain limit, I am satisfied that political calculation furnishes a solid basis for accurate and important speculations; and even beyond that limit, I believe it furnishes an instrument for the correction of reasonings that must originally rest on *data* of a different kind.[1]

    The sanguine confidence, which you describe Lord Hawke[2] to entertain with regard to the project of improving philosophical language, almost induces me to apprehend that he is unaware of the correct point of view, from which that speculation is to be considered. Indeed the letter you showed me from him gave me the same suspicion. Schemes of stenography, more or less commodious, might be invented without number; and a Real Character, in the strict meaning of that expression, appears almost impracticable, either with respect to invention, or introduction to general use. One or two branches of physical science, optics and astronomy, might perhaps admit of it; but the very perfection of our knowledge upon those subjects, which alone would render the design practicable, makes it less necessary. It is not so much as an abbreviated record of our knowledge already ascertained, that the improvement of philosophic language is so desirable, as because it would facilitate farther discovery and farther generalisation. It is in this point of view, that, as I formerly mentioned to you, the amelioration of established nomenclatures, and in some departments of science the introduction of terms entirely new, appears to me to present a most interesting object to an inventive and speculating mind. It is in fact the want alone of such an aid that we actually feel retarding us in many branches of electricity and philosophy; in Galvanism for example, as well as in the theory of national wealth and the natural history of mind. What was done by the French chemists affords a most flattering example;[3] yet I suspect it was conducted with a considerable portion of empirical good luck, rather than upon comprehensive views of philosophical logic. It is to this great speculation that I look for the improvement of science; I have little doubt that sooner or later the task will be overcome: the intellectual powers of the age, and the progress of philosophy, are already matured for such a discovery, as much as in the days of Fust for the invention of the press,[4] or in those of Lord Bacon for his improvement of Logic. Like those, the triumph is probably reserved for some individual of mighty genius.

I ought to beg pardon for turning prophet at the end of a letter which began in the character of a politician. But in predictions on the future achievements of philosophy, we are almost justified to any extent of confidence by its past triumph, and at any rate the prophet, however enthusiastic, may take shelter, from the mortification of personal disappointment, in the indefinite extent of time which he assigns.

1. Afterwards the Duke continued to procure the economic papers printed by order of the House of Lords and apparently sent them to Horner via Loch, who was in a position to obtain franks from the office of the Duke of York. Horner was 'in no hurry' to receive the papers and noted that his object was 'to have the materials of information in my own possession, to have recourse to in the regular course of systematic study, or upon occasional fits of curiosity'. Horner also had a standing order for all publications on economic subjects with Joseph De Boffe, the Soho bookseller who specialised in the import of foreign books. (Horner to Loch, 31 May and 25 June 1802, BLPES i. 164–5 and 176–7.)
2. Martin Bladen Hawke, 2nd Baron Hawke (1744–1805).
3. Probably a reference to A. Lavoisier, Claude Louis Berthollet, Antoine François Fourcroy, and Louis Bernard Guyton de Morveau, *Méthode de Nomenclature Chimique* (Paris, 1787).
4. Johann Fust was Gutenberg's associate.

90. To the Duke of Somerset

BLPES i. 170–71   Edinburgh, 7 June 1802

...

You appear to ask my opinion as to the study of chemistry, for the purpose of examining the principles upon which the modern nomenclature of that science has been contrived. There is not the smallest doubt, that a very adequate idea may be acquired of the chemical theory and terminology, without submitting to the inconvenience of performing a single experiment personally: which, as I know from a very slight experience, occasions not only an irreparable loss of time to the general scholar, but proves an ineffectual labour unless the mind and hands are wholly given up to it. It will be quite necessary, however, to *see* some other person exhibit a considerable number of experiments; for which purpose, I should think the most advisable plan for your Grace is, to form an acquaintance with some of the most active chemists in London, so that you can occasionally attend their laboratories. Your brother is particularly intimate with Hatchett, who has the reputation of being a very skilful analyst.[1] Davy, who lectures in the Institution in Albemarle Street, possesses a considerable share of genius as well as information, and appeared to me a very sensible man in conversation; it would be very easy for you, I make no doubt, to form an useful acquaintance with him for the purpose I have pointed out.[2] The Royal Institution itself is a very frivolous place; but if you have never seen the leading proofs of the modern theory, exhibited experimentally, it might be of some use to attend these now and then. As to the principles of the nomenclature, there are two or three books, independent of the large systems, in which they are explained in a very pleasing and satisfactory manner: Lavoisier's *Elements of Chemistry*, Fourcroy's *Philosophy of Chemistry*, the Preliminary Discourse of Guyton de Morveau to the second volume of the *Encyclopédie Méthodique*, and the article *Air* in that volume by the same author.[3]

If your Grace shall be tempted to examine, with reference to the introduction of similar improvements into other branches of philosophy, the principles upon which the chemists have invented their new language; I shall be anxious to learn what occurs to you upon that curious subject. It would be both a pleasing and most instructive exercise, by a critical application of the principles of philosophical Logic and Grammar, to distinguish, in that invention, what is judiciously contrived, from what is erroneous in consequence, if I may use the expression, of being *unprincipled*. You have heard, I suppose, one of the interesting anecdotes with regard to the history of this invention; that Lavoisier was led, to perceive the necessity of some such instrument in his favourite science, by the speculations of Condillac on the *metaphysique* of language.

---

1. Charles Hatchett (?1765–1847: *DNB*), chemist.
2. Horner had heard Humphry Davy lecture on animal substances at the Royal Institution in March 1802 and had met him in company on 2 April. For Horner's critical remarks on the Royal Institution but favourable opinion of Davy, see *Horner*, i. 182.
3. Fourcroy, the author of the *Philosophie chimique* (1795), and Guyton de Morveau, who wrote the introduction and contributed the entry on 'Air' in vol. ii of the *Encyclopédie Méthodique. Chimie, pharmacie et metallurgie* (6 vols, Paris, 1786–1815), were, with Monge and Berthollet, mainly responsible for helping to establish the system elaborated in Lavoisier's *Eléments de Chimie* (Paris, 1789). See also Doc. 89.

91. To James Loch

BLPES i. 166–9   Edinburgh, 7 June 1802

...

Your account of the intended changes is extremely interesting; you have not said, however, whether the scheme you explain has been definitively resolved on, and how far distant the time may be when it is to be carried into execution.[1] Your objection on account of the want of Juries is no doubt just.[2] I am only afraid that the plan, as it is, involves too vast a change, to be effectuated at once without perplexity. The transference of teind business to the Exchequer, is well thought of; as that court by its present constitution is already in part a ministerial board, the discharge of all functions of a discretionary and legislative nature (such as the commissioners for valuation of tithes and plantation of kirks are entrusted with), appears to be more wisely vested there than in the supreme court of common law and Equity. The permanence of a certain number of ordinaries in the Outer House will of itself, and if alone adopted, prove of great advantage, particularly by rendering dispatch more practicable; at present, the delay in that part of our procedure is insufferable. In fact, the Outer House may be described as a Court, which, upon an average, sits one hour in the week. But in the present constitution of our Judicature, there are many defects, the immediate remedy of which appears greatly desirable, and yet will not be provided by the mere establishment of two concurrent courts; because both of those courts must continue to proceed according to the forms already established by the common law of Scotland, unless they are authorised to amend that by an ordinance of the legislature. One of the evils I allude to, is our mode of investigating a cause complexly, without separating the discussion of the facts from that of the point of law; I am not aware how this is always secured by the forms of your Courts: but of this I am sure from our practice, that the rule of taking a proof before answer (as we term it) is productive of the most mischievous vagueness; and this I suspect from a theoretical view of the subject, that a mode of investigation, so contrary to the common rules of logic which we are forced to employ in all other inquiries, can rarely secure justice in the decision of a particular case, or lay a foundation for the establishment of general principles of law. I have repeatedly heard causes advised in the Court of Session, on which every one of the 15 delivered an opinion peculiar to himself: one took a certain view of the law, another a different view, though they agreed as to the facts; a second couple coincided in the law, but received different impressions from the evidence: and you are mathematician enough to know, that a question of law which admits of several arguments, and a narrative of facts which involves many circumstances, will furnish, by the rule of combination, a sufficient number of varieties to supply the illogical heads of a score of Scotch judges. Another great defect coincides, I believe, with what you call the want of special pleading; our summonses are drawn in the most careless manner, without any regard in general to the rules of pleading or the form of actions. You know we allow it to be amended at any stage of the proceeding; after the evidence is closed, after all the arguments of parties are concluded. Last winter session, in a great cause from Ayrshire about a lease of coal mines, the summons was actually amended after the opinion of the bench had been delivered seriatim upon the merits, and just before the Interlocutor was signed. Now these two irregularities must ever prove fatal, I apprehend, to the strict examination of a legal case. The greatest of all, however, is unquestionably the want of Juries; especially of special Juries in particular questions. Might not the benefits of this institution have been secured in some degree, by allowing certain cases to come into our Exchequer?

...

If this plan is adopted, the business of appeals to the House of Lords, will be lopt off; now this circumstance brings James Brougham's scheme to my mind, with some unpleasing ideas. He will be disappointed in the only plan of life, on which his expectations appear at present to rest; and I shall be sorely disappointed myself, if he is disinduced to settle in London. I have not yet spoke to him of this view of his case; on the contrary, when I saw him on Saturday last, before I received your last letter, he was quite sanguine, and we looked forward to the coincidence of his scheme and mine, in respect of residence, with much pleasure. I wish you would take this subject into consideration; and let me know what reflections occur to you.

I wish you would write to me a little more particularly, about your plans of drawing and special pleading. Mr Romilly assured me, when I spoke of the Chancery Bar as my own destination, that it would be a loss of time entirely, to go to a special pleader. And Whishaw, who is a well-informed and accurate lawyer himself, assured me strongly that even the knowledge requisite for a draughtsman may be acquired in a month or two, with moderate attention: yet you talk of three years, and then a year of special pleading.

Enfin, pour finir – I now recollect we met a Cheshire lady in Wimpole Street, but she appeared a very young girl. I heartily wish you joy of your first fee, and shall be happy to see your case; of which you may send me a copy by my father. The form of an appeal case is very favourable to a neat, close, argumentative statement. The first of October is fixed for the appearance of our first number;[3] as yet, I have done nothing.

...

1. In a letter to Loch of 31 May (BLPES i. 164–5), Horner had requested political intelligence concerning a rumour circulating in Parliament House and a subsequent division of opinion between the judges of the inner and outer houses relative to an alteration in the composition of the Court of Session.
2. One line has been obliterated here.
3. The *Edinburgh Review*.

92. To John Allen (Paris)

BLPES i. 172–5 (copy or draft)   Edinburgh, 14 June 1802

I am afraid the following queries are of too general a nature and too loosely conceived, to lead your attention to any subjects that would not of course have attracted your curiosity; but they may induce you to preserve for me such information, upon these topics, as falls in your way. For the sake of brevity, I shall now remark generally, that, in most of them, I have two objects in view; first, to have the particular fact, alluded to in the query, distinctly ascertained as at present subsisting; secondly, to ascertain how far that fact may have been affected by the Revolution.

QUERIES

1. What are the preferable modes of vesting free capital; in land, in trade, in the national funds, or at interest in private hands?

2. What is the average rate of profit, in those several modes of investment? And, supposing the rate to differ in any two of the four, what are the peculiar circumstances of greater or less security etc., which, added to the money rate of profit, establish the equilibrium of the actual profits?

The rate of interest?

The average rent of corn land?

The average price of land, according to the number of years' purchase?

3. During the Revolution, and at present, have any laws, limiting the rate of interest, been in force?

4. Arthur Young states somewhere in his *Travels*,[1] that the savings of the lower classes were almost constantly invested in the purchase of land. Is this the case still? Was it so, during that period of the Revolution, when so much land was brought into the market?

5. Are the *nouveaux riches*, who have amassed fortunes by contracts etc. during the war, understood to have vested much of those acquisitions in land?

6. Have many of the large estates been preserved, or entirely recovered, notwithstanding the Revolution? All information, with regard to the manner in which the ancient proprietors have returned, or the terms on which they have recovered their estates, will be highly interesting.

7. In a general description, may it be said, that the landed property of the country is much sub-divided?

8. In a general description, may it be said, that the agricultural prosperity of France has advanced or declined, since the fall of the monarchy? Has any change been particularly observed in particular districts?

9. Any information, concerning the condition and rank of the *actual cultivators*:

Does the class of *Métayers* still subsist, as before, in the southern and interior provinces; or has there been a sudden change, or is there a tendency towards a gradual change, in that respect?

In the flourishing districts, is the land generally leased, or cultivated by the proprietors?

If leases subsist, what are the usual terms, and what is the extent of the lessee's legal security?

10. By what description of persons were the lands in general purchased, under the Revolutionary confiscations?

Did the new proprietors usually take possession and proceed to cultivate under their own inspection?

11. Is agriculture at present esteemed an honourable and favourite occupation?

12. Have any of the military men returned, or betaken themselves anew, to this employment?

And is it said that these military farmers are introducing any improvements in the practice of cultivation; in consequence of having had opportunities of seeing foreign modes of husbandry, during their campaigns in Lombardy, Flanders, and Holland?

13. Under the new ecclesiastical establishment, are *tithes* preserved?

During the Revolutionary interval, were tithes collected by Government contractors? Was a servitude of tithes ever supposed to be conveyed in favour of a purchaser of church property? Or did the cultivators become all at once free from this tax, by the abolition of the old establishment?

14. Is it much the practice, among the lower ranks of cultivators (farmers or proprietors), to have household manufactures?

15. Are the manufactures of France prospering in any quarter? Are the manufactures, subservient to luxury or elegance, likely to be soon revived; or any manufactures, of a more permanent and substantial nature, likely to be established?

Has the taste for chemistry, and the study of the chemical arts, produced any degree of activity in this branch of national industry; or laid the foundations of any staple, such as that of iron, pottery, etc.?

16. Is the prejudice against commercial occupations done away, or strengthened by a new support derived from the honours and emoluments of the military profession?

17. I should like to receive information with regard to the state of the national coin, in respect of depreciation or scarcity.

18. And with regard to the facilities of credit, in the domestic commerce and transactions: whether the functions of that credit are performed by banks, or in the shape of bills, or by current accounts, or in any other form whatsoever.

19. During the years that have elapsed since the intercourse with this country was interrupted, has there been a general and progressive rise of prices? If so, what proportion does it appear to bear to the rise that has taken place here?

20. What arrangements are in force for the maintenance of the destitute poor; is this made the subject of general establishment, or left to local police?

Upon the destruction of the religious houses, was there any such increase of this unfortunate class, as to render some regulations immediately necessary?

21. What is the most prevailing, and what the most reasonable opinion, with respect to the influence of the Revolution on the population of the ancient territory?

22. Has any change taken place in the habits of the people, with regard to the connection of marriage?

Is a beneficial change in this respect perceptible, or acknowledged, in consequence of the abolition of convents?

Any change in the manners of the laity, with regard to the prevalence of celibacy?

Any perceptible indications that the catholic clergy may in time be induced to relax this rule of their order? And (as connected with this query) is the custom of confession as regularly kept up as ever by the women?

An author I lately met with, *Depradt*,[2] says, that the mode of recruiting the armies by requisition occasioned a violent multiplication of marriages, particularly among farm-servants and country-workmen, who thereby secured a certain degree of immunity; and that this unnatural increase in the number of marriages, beyond the encouragement held out by the natural supply of provisions, occasioned all over France a sudden and enormous increase in the number of exposed children: I am curious to have this fact particularly inquired into.

In the provinces, was as much advantage taken, as at Paris, of the law by which divorces were licensed?

23. Is the passion for military honours very prevalent?

Is it most so in the towns, or among the small proprietors and tenantry?

24. In what estimation is the profession of the law held at present? Is it supplied by men of activity and talents? What course of education is preparatory to it? Is it in alliance with the pursuit of political honours and official emoluments?

25. Has any change taken place with regard to the custom of Duelling; or generally with regard to the adjustment of those private quarrels, which are not objects of Law?

26. Among such of the literati as are addicted to metaphysical speculation, what are the leading doctrines: particularly with regard to the questions of natural theology, the foundation of moral obligation, and the freedom or necessity of will?

27. Is there any class of literati, who attach themselves to political economy? If there be, what are their leading doctrines, particularly with regard to the theory of national wealth, the freedom of industry, and legislative interference?

Is the peculiar system of the Economists forgotten, or does it still preserve some advocates?

In what estimation is the character of Turgot, etc. held?

28. Is there an extensive circulation of periodical works, either of political intelligence, or of literary composition?

Is this circulation to be traced throughout the country? in the provincial towns? among the small proprietors of land?

When I hear of your being in particular parts of the country, or of enjoying particular opportunities of inquiry, I may perhaps take the liberty of troubling you with specific questions upon the particular subjects that are, upon such occasions, under your command.

MEMORANDA

1. I wish you to collect for me any curious documents, that may fall in your way, on the leading branches of the political economy of France.

2. Purchase for me at Paris, *Collection de divers ouvrages d'Arithmétique Politique, par Lavoisier, Lagrange, etc.*; a very thin 8vo, published by Röderer.[3]

3. While you are at Paris, I wish you would inquire about the Abbé Morellet; whether he is alive? If so, whether he means to publish the *Dictionnaire du Commerce*, of which he long ago printed a prospectus; or if dead, what is become of the voluminous papers of Gournai, formerly in Morellet's possession?[4]

4. I wish you would likewise endeavour to meet with Dupont de Nemours: he had many of Turgot's MSS. On account of the republication proposed here, it is important we should know soon whether there is any intention of printing a collection of Turgot's writings; whether there are many pieces still in MS; and

whether any have already been printed, that are not generally known in this country?

Dupont himself was the great Evangelist of the Economists, and was formerly *Inspecteur général du Commerce*; has he any place under the present Government?

1. *Arthur Young's Travels in France During the Years 1787, 1788, 1789*, ed. M. Betham-Edwards (1889).
2. Perhaps *Les Trois Ages des Colonies* (3 vols, Paris, 1801–1802), or *De l'Etat de la culture en France et des améliorations dont elle est susceptible* (2 vols, Paris, [1802]), both by Dominique Georges Frédéric de Riom de Prolhiac de Fourt de Pradt.
3. See Doc. 84 n. 22.
4. See Doc. 84 n. 2.

93. To James Loch

BLPES i. 176–7   Edinburgh, 25 June 1802

… I have not seen the last Report of the India Company; I understand it was drawn up by Baring,[1] who has a mighty reputation for mercantile science, but in all his pamphlets that I have seen appears a very ordinary and middling man. Your account of the Report coincides with this character. I have heard that one able paper upon the private trade was composed by Charles Grant, a Director.[2] As to your dissertation on India politics, there is not a single argument in it which does not appear to me quite conclusive, upon the view of general principles. It nearly coincides with the aspect in which that immense subject has always appeared to myself, so far as my limited optics can comprehend such magnitude and distance. I have never been able to state to myself what the probable motives are, practically speaking, which give our Ministers and the Directors such an aversion to Indian colonisation. It is possible that the American Revolution alone has produced this impression, in opposition to the prejudice which was formerly so strong in this country in favour of Plantations? If so, it is a most singular fact in the history of public opinion. Or is there not some real or mistaken suspicion, in the breasts of the India Directors, that dangers of a more immediate nature, and likely to affect their individual interests, might result from the settlement of independent proprietors on the banks of the Ganges? You must have read in the *Morning Chronicle* a paper called 'Instructions from the Nabob of the Carnatic to his Agents in England'.[3] If authentic, it is a most important document; and whether genuine or not, it is a pleasing production. It is skilful throughout, and in some passages even eloquent; particularly in the description of English Ambition. I should suppose it to be written by an Englishman, for there are every where gleams of European thought; yet it has evidently been the design of the composer to give an air of Hindu character to his work, and he has preserved an almost dramatic effect.

Before lifting our eyes from off the East, I must fix yours on a very worthy object there; for I heard of Dis yesterday – his brother Adam told me had just received a letter from him. He had come down to Calcutta, in hopes of a short respite from excursions; but received orders to march against the Birmans. That I suppose is to be another scene of conquest and robbery; as it appears from the book of Major Symes, that the teak timber is too valuable to remain any longer the property of the natives of that country which produces it.[4]

...

PS Remember that I live by news from London.

1. Sir Francis Baring (1740–1810: *DNB*), the founder of the bank that bears his name and a director of the East India Co., was author of a number of *Observations*, on the establishment of the Bank of England and on its issuing of notes (both 1797), and on the writings of Walter Boyd (1801).
2. Charles Grant (1746–1823: *DNB*).
3. The *Morning Chronicle* of 18 June printed what its editorial said might be 'considered the official protest against that foul and dishonourable transaction', the deposition of the Nabob of Arcot.
4. 'Dis' was James Ferguson (1784–1859), the third son of Adam Ferguson (1723–1816: *DNB*), Dugald Stewart's predecessor as Professor of Moral Philosophy in Edinburgh. James Ferguson was an old schoolfellow of Horner's who had entered the service of the East India Co. in 1798. Like his eldest brother, afterwards Sir Adam Ferguson (1771–1855: *DNB*), he became a close friend of Sir Walter Scott and helped him compile his *Chronicle of the Canongate* (1827). Michael Symes was author of *An Account of an Embassy to the Kingdom of Ava sent by the Governor-General of India in 1795* (1800).

94. To James Loch

BLPES i. 178–9   Edinburgh, 26 July 1802

...

You can have no doubt that the turn, which the General Election has taken, has for the last fortnight afforded me daily pleasure. Whence all this? Moderation, or mismanagement on the part of Addington? If the latter, we shall see some awkward attempts made to excuse himself, or to counteract the consequences of his negligence. But I rather incline to the supposition of real moderation – in which case, the Minister will have no reason to repent. Whether it arises from imbecility or vigour of understanding, or (which seems more probable than either) from a fortunate temper, this moderation of Addington has been balm to our sores. It has already worked a charm upon the public mind, not by making it more enlightened, God knows, but by leaving it less exasperated – our fever is reduced – our nerves more quiet – our pulse more regular – our raw and irritated sores cooled and softened by the healing balm of Ministerial forbearance and moderation.

In all this interval, I am quite unsatisfied not to learn how Pitt is employed. That stupendous understanding must have now had sufficient relaxation in indolence. What active prospects and plans engage him in his retirement? Shall we again be scourged by mischievous and vulgar ambition for the possession of office, or having gained all the reputation or infamy that place can bestow, shall we find his passions turned towards nobler game?

As for Fox, I fear this continental expedition will retard the composition of his book; does Mrs Armsted accompany him, or is he to join Holland's party? For according to one account we have here, he is to spend the winter abroad.[1]

...

1. Although Fox had secretly married his mistress, 'Mrs Armistead', in September 1795, he did not acknowledge it until shortly before 29 July, when he left England with her following his re-election for Westminster. They joined the Hollands in Paris after touring the Netherlands, and returned to England in November.

95. Notes on Smith's *Wealth of Nations*

Kinnordy MSS   28–31 July 1802[1]

25. (p. 410) This chapter ought to be particularly examined.[2] Although it is cast in a very methodical form, and the language appears distinct enough, the principles are extremely obscure. Even the fundamental distinction of *circulating* and *fixed* capitals seems to be assumed without much necessity. But what will render the minute examination of this chapter most interesting, is, that this is the very ground upon which, if there really is any difference, Smith and the Economists are at variance. Some of the phraseology which he employs, and some of the principles which he insists on, are almost synonymous with their doctrines and language. The first eight pages of the next chapter[3] may be included, with propriety, in the same examination. I observe that Thornton[4] in his description of commercial capital, makes no use of the distinction between *fixed* and *circulating* capitals though he uses the phrase dead stock to express the former. He must have thought it unnecessary to distinguish the other by any peculiar appellation.

26. (p. 429 and p. 434) Mr Hume says I. 279,[5] 'Money ... is none of the wheels of trade: it is the oil which renders the motion of the wheels more smooth and easy.'[6] Smith calls money, 'the great wheel of circulation', and paper money 'a new and less expensive wheel'.[7] This opposition sufficiently exposes the absurdity of such metaphorical expressions.

27. (p. 434)[8] Smith seems to have nowhere explained the principles and history of that private commercial credit which is the foundation of paper money which would subsist though there were no paper, but which that kind of money contributes both to facilitate and to enlarge. There are some valuable hints and sketches to be found in Thornton's first chapter, which deserve to be prosecuted.[9]

28. (p. 441)[10] The saving occasioned by the substitution of paper does not consist merely in the different value of the materials of which the money is made. It is a saving too of time, of trouble, and of risk, which must always be considered in calculating the expenses of bringing commodities of every kind to market. By means of bills of exchange, both the expense and the risk of sending specie from one place to another, between which there is a reciprocal trade, are saved: the traders in both cases are thus enabled to give their commodities at a price proportionally less. Thornton, p. 25.

29. (p. 390)[11] This must be a mistake: a Decretal of Pope Alexander III in 1170, on the subject of tithes enumerates *preventus molendinorum* and another of Celestin

III in 1295 on the same subject, mentions *quæ de molendino adventum proveniunt.* See Fra Paolo [Pietro Sarpi], *Trattate delle materie beneficiarie,* f. 28. They had been introduced, therefore, into Italy at least, several centuries before the sixteenth.

30. (p. 466)[12] Thornton informs us, that the practice of drawing and redrawing is often carried on at much less expense than Smith imagines; because the transactions are often for the benefit alternately of each of the two parties. Each party, upon the whole, gains about as much as he pays in the shape of commission; so that the whole expense consists in the discount, which being the same as that on any other bill, money may be raised in this manner at an interest of only five per cent. – Thornton, p. 34.

31.[13] (p. 441)[14] The impossibility of such a determination does not arise merely from the difficulty of ascertaining the exact amount of circulating medium in a country, but from another circumstance to which Mr Smith appears not to have averted, that the same number of exchanges may be transacted by very unequal quantities of circulating medium, according to the different degrees of rapidity with which the circulation is performed. In proportion, too, as the commerce of a country is enlarged, various expedients are devised both for economizing the use of a circulating medium, and for abridged [?abridging] the time and trouble that must be spent in pecuniary transactions. Thus Mr Thornton remarks, and apparently with great truth, that the practice of transferring to London almost all the pecuniary transactions among the dealers of this country, must have lessened the number of guineas and banknotes that in the same extent of commerce, would have been necessary. [Thornton] p. 60.

32. (pp. 487, 488, 495)[15] Dr Franklin published a tract in defence of the paper currency of North America: *Misc. Works,* p. 206.[16] It is not remarkable for a very distinct statement of principles. Some of the facts vary from the assertions of Smith. In particular, Dr Franklin alleges, that it was the previous drain of gold and silver which rendered paper money absolutely necessary. He mentions that some bills were issued for so small a sum as 3d. The tract was published as an answer to the Report of the Board of Trade in 1764.

29 July 1802

33. (II, p. 142)[17] Smith has properly stated, that prior to that inspection, which the rulers of modern states have fancied it proper to assume over the balance of trade, they had recourse to several *ancient* schemes for accumulating the precious metals. He mentions, however, only one kind of scheme, the discouragement of exportation. There is some reason to suspect that they formerly endeavoured to further the same object by the still more preposterous means of encouraging the importation of bullion and foreign coin.

34. (II. p. 145)[18] By the qualifying article *perhaps,* he appears not to have been quite sure that he was entitled to call this part of the argument *sophistical.* Indeed a considerable degree of obscurity runs through his account of the effect of this state of exchange upon the balance of trade. He has evidently omitted an important remark of Hume,[19] I. 311[20] that an unfavourable exchange becomes an encouragement to exportation, by enabling the purchaser to purchase at a cheaper rate. Smith appears to be correct, on the other hand, in stating that the unfavourable rate of exchange will discourage importation. Both causes co-operate to restore the balance of trade.

35. (II. p. 235)[21] The golden rule of active benevolence, which preserves the communication of benefit in compatibility with personal interest, is practically illustrated by Ennius in two pleasing offices, the most valuable to the receiver, the least expensive to the donor:

> Homo qui erranti comiter monstrat viam,
> Quasi lumen de suo lumine accendat, facit,
> Nihilo minus ipsi lucet, cum illi accenderit.

The maxim is extended by Cicero to all the duties of private generosity, *De Off.* I. 16; we may enlarge on its sphere of action to the policy of nations.

36. (III. p. 147)[22] It seems to amount to something extremely like an exclusive privilege in favour of the two companies for insurance, that by the Act of Parliament which established them, no other joint stock company or private co-partnery can make a valid policy; and this privilege appears the more exclusive from the interpretation it receives in the courts of law.

1. The first date may possibly be 20 July.
2. 'Of the Division of Stock', *WN* II. i.
3. *WN* II. ii. 1–15, in 'Of Money considered as a particular Branch of the general Stock of the Society, or of the Expence of Maintaining the National Capital', deal with 'fixed' and 'circulating' capital.
4. Henry Thornton, *An Enquiry into the Nature and Effects of the Paper Credit of Great Britain* (1802).
5. Horner has subsequently pencilled in: 'used in my review of Canard'.
6. This is the opening of Essay III, 'Of Money', in Hume, i. 309.
7. *WN* II. ii. 14, and (paraphrase) II. ii. 26.
8. *WN* II. ii. 27ff.
9. Thornton, pp. 12–22: 'Of Commercial Credit; of Paper Credit, as arising out of it; of Commercial Capital'.
10. What follows is really a comment on *WN* II. ii. 39:
    When paper is substituted in the room of gold and silver money, the quantity of the materials, tools, and maintenance, which the whole circulating capital can supply, may be increased by the whole value of gold and silver which used to be employed in purchasing them.
11. *WN* I. xi. o. 12:
    Neither wind nor water mills of any kind were known in England so early as the beginning of the sixteenth century, nor, so far as I know, in any other part of Europe north of the Alps. They have been introduced into Italy some time before.
12. *WN* II. ii. 69:
    In a country where the ordinary profits of stock in the greater part of mercantile projects are supposed to run between six and ten per cent. it must have been a very fortunate speculation of which the returns could not only repay the enormous expence at which the money was thus borrowed for carrying it on; but afford, besides, a good surplus profit to the projector.
13. Dated in the margin 31 July 1802, though this is earlier than that for paragraphs 33–6.
14. *WN* II. ii. 40:
    What is the proportion which the circulating money of any country bears to the whole value of the annual produce circulated by means of it, it is, perhaps, impossible to determine.
15. *WN* II. ii. 89:
    In the currencies of North America, paper was commonly issued for so small a sum as a shilling, and filled almost the whole of that circulation.
    WN II. ii. 92:
    Those metals [gold and silver] are said to have become more abundant in America, since the suppression of some of their paper currencies. They are said, likewise, to

have been more abundant before the institution of those currencies.

WN II. ii. 102:

> Pennsylvania was always more moderate in its emissions of paper money than any other of our colonies. Its paper currency accordingly is said never to have sunk below the value of the gold and silver which was current in the colony before the first emission of its paper money.

16. See Doc. 84 n. 15.
17. WN IV. i. 5.
18. WN IV. i. 9:

> They were sophistical too, perhaps, in asserting that the high price of exchange necessarily increased, what they called, the unfavourable balance of trade, or occasioned the exportation of a greater quantity of gold and silver.

19. *Jacob Vanderlint [Money answers all things (1734)] observes, that an unfavourable exchange 'may be some small Encouragement to the Exportation of our Commodities, because they come so much cheaper to the Markets abroad.' p[p]. 29[-30].
20. In Essay V, 'Of the Balance of Trade' (Hume, i. 333n).
21. 'Of the Unreasonableness of those extraordinary Restraints upon other Principles', WN IV. iii. c. 2:

> Nothing ... can be more absurd than this whole doctrine of the balance of trade, upon which ... almost all ... regulations of commerce are founded. When two places trade with one another, this doctrine supposes that, if the balance be even, neither of them either loses or gains; but if it leans in any degree to one side, that one of them loses, and the other gains in proportion to its declension from the exact equilibrium. Both suppositions are false.

22. WN I. i. e. 34:

> The trade of insurance ... may be carried on successfully by a joint stock company, without any exclusive privilege. Neither the London Assurance, nor the Royal Exchange Assurance companies, have any such privilege.

96. From John Allen

BLPES i. 180–81   Paris, 18 Aug. 1802

...

Systems of political economy and systems of government are in pretty much the same sort of repute here. Few read them, and many look upon them with a mixture of dread and abhorrence. Many like you think the books of the Economists have produced all the horrors of the revolution, that they have had their day, and that the French People will not soon be persuaded to make trial of them again. That their day is really past in France can hardly be denied, when we find it among the prevailing and practised maxims of political economy at present, to stimulate the industry and ingenuity of the manufacturers at home by excluding the competition of foreigners, and to enrich the French People by making three fourths of them pay double price for every manufactured article which they consume, in order to encourage the remaining fourth to throw away the little capital they have left in a fruitless struggle against the superior machinery, skill, and credit of the English. Who may be the author or adviser of this system, I cannot tell you, but it has many zealous partisans here, some of whom boast that Chaptal is too enlightened a Minister and too sincere a friend to his country, ever to admit English manufactures into France.[1] Whether

Chaptal has interest with Bonaparte to introduce this or any other system of trade I have not been able to learn, but from the character of him which I have got from some of his personal friends and including too his proneur, it is very plain that Chaptal has been too long a superintendent of manufactures to be a good Minister of the Interior. So zealous a friend is he to the manufacturing interest of his Country, that on more than one occasion he has contrived to draw from its exhausted Treasury small sums of money, to enable a declining manufacture to struggle on amidst difficulties which neither he nor it could remove. But how far Chaptal or any other Minister or Counsellor here is responsible for the wisdom or folly of the measures of government, it is not easy to discover; for Bonaparte has the mania of doing many things himself, and consequently one half of the business of the interior government is ill done, and the other half not done at all. Instead of choosing men of talents and information, and leaving to them the details of administration, under the constraint of a popular assembly, he attempts to be that controlling power himself and to decide upon every question, from the Concordat to the best plan of building a bridge. France, in such hands, is likely to remain, which it is, in chaos; and that perhaps with the best intention on the part of Bonaparte to promote its internal welfare. His activity, temperance and perseverance merit the highest praise, but unquestionably their chief effect hitherto, at home at least, has been that of keeping such lazy, luxurious dogs as Talleyrand to their duty. He works them I am told to death. He has no idea that people should eat, drink or sleep, or need any other physical recreation but shooting. He takes no other himself. It is inconceivable, how he allows himself to be fretted with the animadversions on his conduct that are continually appearing in the English newspapers. The remarks which the *Moniteur* made some time ago upon the *Times* and *Courier de Londres* are understood to have been written by the particular command of Buonaparte; and this morning the Prefect of Police walked into the English coffee room in the *Palais Royale* and put under arrest the English papers which had just arrived. Our Government would do well to prosecute some blackguard like Peter Porcupine[2] for the first indictable paragraph in his newspaper and have him fined and imprisoned in terrorem for, considering the peevishness so manifest upon this side of the water, and the insolence which impunity will produce on the other, I should not be surprised to see disagreeable consequences to individuals and perhaps even serious effects to the public follow so contemptible and worthless an origin as the flippant and uncalled for animadversions of Messieurs the Editors of the *Times* and of the *Morning Post*. How does this jealousy of reputation affect your opinion of B[uonaparte]?
...[3]

1. Jean Antoine Chaptal, Comte de Chanteloup (1756–1832), a distinguished chemist, was French Minister of the Interior, 1799–1804.
2. William Cobbett, notorious for his anti-Gallicanism.
3. Horner subsequently copied an extract from a letter Allen wrote to Thomas Thomson from Paris on 28 Aug. which assessed the more remarkable of the men with whom Bonaparte surrounded himself (Kinnordy MSS).

97. To James Loch

BLPES i. 182–3   Edinburgh, 25 Aug. [1802]

...

The last letter from Allen mentions, that Lord Holland's party were waiting at Paris for the arrival of Fox and Fitzpatrick.[1] A most fortunate as well as agreeable circumstance for Allen; I hope these connections will lead to his establishment in London, which would afford me the highest pleasure. For after all, I begin to feel a considerable degree of regret at leaving behind me all the men, in whose society I have passed some pleasing and profitable years. Jeffrey and Murray are both rooted here, I am afraid for ever; but Brougham will certainly migrate Southward, and I wish Allen may be saved from ever returning to the North. At present, Lord Holland[2] proposes to winter in France; which is a great improvement on their original plan for either Spain or Italy would be, comparatively speaking, but an uninteresting residence. All the world is at Paris; so that we have a good chance to know it pretty well, as far as description will serve. I daily expect to hear from Whishaw, who is gone to the continent, and is admirably qualified to give a report of such a scene. The Dutch expedition has turned out wonderfully; you saw the parties in London before they set out. Their situation at present is, that Adam Ferguson is in London, Irving is in Edinburgh, and William Clerk was left upon the Rhine.[3] In the newspapers there was an account of three *Anglois* who went into a synagogue at Amsterdam; one of them broke into a fit of laughter, at some part of the ceremony, which was of course Adam Ferguson: they were about to be turned out, when another, certainly Clerk, knocked down a Jew. The catastrophe you may conceive.

The death of Lord Eglinton, which is reported, will occasion another election; I hope Lauderdale will be the man, and next to him Lord Elphinstone.[4] But the Court, I presume, will have a different person from both, equally ready to be proposed and chosen. Your anecdote of Addington is disgraceful: I shall maintain him to be moderate, no longer than his conduct proves it. I allow it not only to be possible, but even extremely probable, that a man, of an understanding unequal to his place, cannot preserve real moderation long, however inclined to it by temper. He may even be violent unconsciously; and he will sometimes do such things to conceal, sometimes to supply the deficiencies of his genius.

If you make any observations on the political economy of the counties you are about to traverse in your tour, I shall be glad to know them. Cornwall is a favourable spot for such inquiries; because it is placed in a singular combination of circumstances. You will have our review about the beginning of October; Jeffrey has written some excellent articles, which I am not [at] liberty to describe to you more particularly. But this I am both free and bound to tell you, that you will be at no loss to find out all of his, because they are beyond any comparison the best.[5]

...

1. Fox's friend, General Richard Fitzpatrick (1747–1812: *DNB*) arrived in Paris on 17 Aug.; Fox joined him two days later; and on 2 Sept. they were presented to the First Consul.
2. A few words have been obliterated here.

3. A sentence has been obliterated here. Like Ferguson, John Irving (1770–1850) and William Clerk (d. 1847), a younger son of John Clerk of Eldin (1728–1812: *DNB*), were close friends of Walter Scott's.

4. The rumour about Hugh Montgomerie, 12th Earl of Eglinton (1739–1819: *DNB*) and a representative peer of Scotland, proved false. But John, 12th Baron Elphinstone (1764–1813), was elected a representative peer in 1803 and again in 1806. Lauderdale had been elected a representative peer in 1790, but his anti-government views kept him out of the Lords from 1796 until he was made a British peer in 1806.

5. Jeffrey contributed at least six of the twenty-nine articles in the first number of *ER* i (no. i, Oct. 1802), on Mounier's *Influence des Philosophes*, pp. 1–18, Southey's *Thalaba*, pp. 68–83, Herrenschwand's *Addresse*, pp. 98–106, Bonnet's *Art de rendre les révolutions utiles*, pp. 122–7, Mackenzie's *Voyages*, pp. 141–8, Playfair's *Huttonian Theory*, pp. 201–216. A seventh, on Baldwin's *Egypt*, pp. 59–61, may have been written in part by him, although the Kinnordy set attributes it solely to Brougham; see also *WI*.

98. To John Allen

BLPES i. 184–5 ⟨*Horner*, i. 207–209⟩   Edinburgh, 1 Sept. 1802

⟨...

⟨You have managed the arrangement with regard to the publication of Turgot's writings in the best way; Constable has written, by my direction, to a bookseller in London about the business, and is willing to take for himself at the least 100 copies. I hope Dupont will be prevailed on to print some of the MSS he possesses; from the account he gives of them in his *Mémoire sur la Vie*, etc., they would be highly interesting.

⟨Our *Review* goes on tolerably well; in consequence of Constable's own arrangement, it is not to appear till the 1st of November, but more than half the first number is already printed. I wish you would advertise the publication in some of the Paris newspapers or journals, in the manner that you shall judge most likely, if there is any chance to excite a little curiosity about it. Jeffrey has written three or four excellent articles; and⟩ in consequence of Smith's residence in the country, ⟨Brougham is now an efficient and zealous member of the party.[1] We regret your loss to a degree that I shall not express to you, though we do not altogether despair of receiving a few short critiques on such foreign publications as you happen at any rate to read with care. I particularly wish we had from you a review of Ware's strange paper on the blind boy restored to sight.[2] Brougham has selected from the same volume of the *Philosophical Transactions* Herschell's discovery of the sympathy between the spots on the sun and the prices of wheat in Reading market.[3]

⟨...

⟨How much I envy you the opportunities you have had of being with Mr Fox: is your previous idea of that character varied at all (I do not mean lessened,) since you have surveyed it with your own eyes, or has it received no other change than that of being more definite? I have generally understood that his simplicity is what is most striking to those, who are introduced to him already full of admiration at his other great qualities.⟩

1. Brougham contributed at least four articles, on Horneman's *Travels*, pp. 130–41, Wood's *Optics*, pp. 158–63, Acerbi's *Travels*, pp. 163–72, and James Stephen's *Crisis of the Sugar Colonies*, pp. 216–37.

2. James Ware (1756–1815: *DNB*), a distinguished ophthalmologist, had published in 1801 his *Case of a young gentleman who recovered his sight when seven years of age*. It was not reviewed in *ER*.

3. Brougham's notice of William Herschel's famous contributions to the *Philosophical Transactions of the Royal Society* appeared in *ER* 1 (no. ii, Jan. 1803), 426–31, and dealt chiefly with his 'Observations on the two lately discovered celestial bodies'. It was a typically cavalier condemnation of Herschel's invention of the name 'asteroids' for Ceres and Pallas; but that was as nothing compared with the curt dismissal at the end (p. 431) of Herschel's suggestion of the connection between sun-spots and the weather: 'To the speculations of the Doctor on the nature of the sun ... we have many similar objections; but they are all eclipsed [sic] by the great absurdity which he has there committed, in his hasty and erroneous theory concerning the influence of solar spots on the price of grain.'

99. Notes on Smith's *Wealth of Nations*

Kinnordy MSS   5–16 Sept. 1802

37. (I. p. 67, and II. 335)[1] See in Thornton, p. 207, some strictures on this proposal of Smith's, which render the utility of it at least doubtful. I have not yet very carefully compared the arguments.[2]

38. (I. 437)[3] I suspect Smith had recourse to this metaphor of 'overflowing the channel', because he did not really see the principle that directs the operation which he is describing.[4] In the first place, he evidently offers no proof for the assertion, that the channel of circulation will remain no more than it before contained: upon this page, that appears a gratuitous assumption. In the second place, this assertion is contrary to the fact, that the discovery of the American mines caused a great additional quantity of money to flow into the channel of general circulation, and that in a much greater proportion than was wanted to distribute the additional increase of produce. – If Smith had attended to the influence of an increased money upon prices, he might have stated perspicuously and literally the manner in which paper-money causes gold to be sent abroad; which is the operation he means to describe. The addition of paper money, by flowing into circulation, and being received into that channel, produces a rise in the price of commodities; the gold, running in this channel, becomes exchangeable for a less quantity of goods than before, and than it is still able to procure in other countries. The gold will therefore be sent abroad, not because it would otherwise have been idle at home, but because it is more valuable abroad than at home. It will continue to be exported, until the equilibrium of prices is restored.[5]

In this note, I have only shown how Mr Smith's assertion with respect to the exportation of gold in consequence of the creation of paper money, might have been explained by his own principles. I have not quite made up my mind that the creation of paper money, while the gold remains at home, has the effect of raising prices; if it does not, the gold will not on that account go abroad.

39.[6] (I. 491) The instances, which Smith proceeds to state, are those of a *depreciation* of the paper currency; and by the phrase with which they are introduced, 'it would be otherwise, indeed', he seems to intimate that an increase of prices and a depreciation of paper money are one and the same thing.[7] In this, he has overlooked a distinction, which appears to be important. In the case of a depreciation of the paper, there is a difference between the paper-price and the coin-price of commodities; and it is in part this difference which is denominated depreciation. But Mr Hume has supposed, and in other circumstances than those which he has put it is a probable supposition, that multiplication of paper money may cause a general rise of prices, whether expressed in coin or paper, without occasioning any difference between the paper-price of a commodity and its coin price. The depreciation of paper proceeds from doubts entertained of its solvency, or of the character of those mercantile houses whose name it bears: the general rise of price proceeds from the increased quantity of the medium of circulation.

40. (I. 69)[8] See some strictures on this proposition in Thornton, p. 204.[9] Mr Smith's proposition might have been more comprehensively expressed, by using the word *currency* instead of *coin*; and he ought to have explained more distinctly the manner in which the difference of market and mint price is brought about, by stating that fall of the foreign exchanges which sometimes occasions the difference and always accompanies it. For Mr Thornton appears to me to be quite wrong, in asserting that that excess in all cases arises from a fall of the exchange, as I have endeavoured to show in my review of his work.

41. (I. 451)[10] Mr Thornton, p. 213, has criticized this passage minutely; but I am not satisfied of the justness of his strictures.

42. (I. 33)[11] In considering the place which the subject of money holds in that general inquiry, which is expressed in the title of Smith's book, and in examining the propriety of separating, as Smith has done, the subject of metallic from that of paper money; it may be useful to recollect the terms in which Mr Thornton [p. 260] has described money, as 'merely the instrument by which the purchasable stock of the country is distributed with convenience and advantage among the several members of the community'.

In prosecuting this point, it may likewise be proper to consider whether Smith has separated by a very distinct boundary the general subject of his *second* from that of his *first* Book.[12] In the general subject, that may be formed by the union of both, it is evident that a proper place ought to be found for explaining the principles of private or commercial *credit*.

43. (II. 215)[13] In my review of Thornton, I have made an application of the reasoning contained in these pages.[14] – An historical view of the different modes of computing exchange, which have [been] adopted in Europe, would illustrate this matter curiously.

1. On the first page cited (*WN* I. v. 39) Smith writes: 'A small seignorage or duty upon the coinage of both gold and silver would probably increase still more the superiority of those metals in coin above an equal quantity of either of them in bullion.' This is in substance repeated in the second passage cited (*WN* IV. vi. 19). Cf the note in Thornton's *Enquiry*, pp. 207ff.
2. Dated in the margin 5 Sept. 1802.
3. Horner is paraphrasing *WN* II. ii. 30.

4. Dated in the margin 10 Sept. 1802.

5. *It is important to correct this omission into which Smith has fallen, because the principle, in this erroneous form, is repeated in other parts of his work; as II. 158 [WN IV. i. 23]. I have lately seen a tract, in which the principle is correctly stated; Wheatley, *On Currency and Commerce*, Chapter I ['On the Utility of Money', pp. 1–36]. [This note is apparently of a later date since Wheatley's book was not published until 1803. See Doc. 113.]

6. Dated in the margin 13 Sept. 1802.

7. Having denied (WN II. ii. 96) that it was always true that 'the increase of paper money ... by augmenting the quantity, and consequently diminishing the value of the whole currency, necessarily augments the money price of commodities', Smith had gone on to state (97):

> It would be otherwise, indeed, with a paper money consisting in promissory notes, of which the immediate payment depended, in any respect, either upon the good will of those who issued them; or upon a condition which the holder of the notes might not always have it in his power to fulfil; or of which the payment was not exigible till after a certain number of years, and which in the mean time bore no interest.

8. WN I. v. 40:

> when ... the market price either of gold or silver bullion continues for several years together steadily and constantly, either more or less above, or more or less below the mint price; we may be assured that this steady and constant, either superiority or inferiority of price, is the effect of something in the state of the coin, which, at that time, renders a certain quantity of coin either of more value or of less value than the precise quantity of bullion which it ought to contain.

Thornton commented on this passage on pp. 203–205:

> Dr Smith appears to me to have treated the important subject of the tendency of an excessive paper circulation to send gold out of a country, and thus to embarrass its banking establishments, in a manner which is particularly unsatisfactory. ...
>
> It appears ... that he considers every permanent excess, whether of the market price above the mint price, or of the mint price above the market price of gold, as entirely referable to 'something in the state of coin.'

9. This passage is dated in the margin 15 Sept. 1802.

10. In WN II. ii. 53, Smith had asserted that 'Had every particular banking company always understood and attended to its own particular interest, the circulation never could have been over-stocked with paper money.' Thornton commented:

> even granting it to be just, it can be just only in a case which can scarcely ever occur among the country banks of this kingdom. I mean, that it can apply solely to the case of a single bank of which the paper circulates exclusively through a surrounding district: it obviously cannot hold in the case of many banks, the paper of all of which circulates in the same district.

Thornton then went on in the following pages to illustrate and elaborate his criticism.

11. WN I. iv, 'Of the Origin and Use of Money'.

12. Book I was entitled 'Of the Causes of Improvement in the productive Powers of Labour ...'; Book II, 'Of the Nature, Accumulation, and Employment of Stock'.

13. WN IV. iii. 7–8, deals with the effects of the different ways of computing exchange.

14. This passage is dated in the margin 16 Sept. 1802.

100. Journal

Kinnordy MSS ⟨Horner, i. 209⟩   30 Sept. 1802

⟨I finished, a few days ago, an account and criticism of Thornton's book on paper credit, for the *Edinburgh Review*; except three very short articles, Irvine on Emigration, Christison on Parish Schools, and an anonymous pamphlet on Country

Banks, it is the only contribution I have prepared for the first number of that publication.[1] The *Review* was concerted, about the end of last winter, between Jeffrey, Sydney Smith, and myself. The plan was immediately communicated to Murray, Allen, and Hamilton; Brown, Brougham, and the two Thomsons, have gradually been made parties. The analysis of Thornton cost me a considerable degree of trouble; but this labour has served to break up the ground in one of the most necessary fields of political economy. I have given the review to the press in a very rude form, although my aim was to mould the irregular materials of the original work into an useful arrangement; my style of writing is too formal and not sufficiently correct.⟩

1. Horner's reviews of Alexander Irvine, *An Inquiry into the Causes and Effects of Emigration from the Highlands and Western Islands of Scotland* (Edinburgh, 1802), Alexander Christison, *The general Diffusion of Knowledge one great Cause of the Prosperity of North Britain* (Edinburgh, 1802), *The Utility of Country Banks considered* (1802), and Thornton's *Paper Credit* appeared respectively on pp. 61–3, 92–4, 106–108 and 172–201 of the first, October 1802, issue of volume i of *ER*. All except that on Christison are reprinted in Horner's *EW*.

101. Notes of my progress in studying the system of the Economists

Kinnordy MSS   18 Oct. 1802

24. (After an unavoidable interval in this study, I resume it with a small book, which, according to the catalogue of our Advocates Library, is the composition of Forbonnais although it is not mentioned in the biographical notice of that author, which is given in the 7th volume of the *Memoirs of the National Institute*. The first volume of this treatise is entitled *Principes et observations Economiques*; the second volume, *Observations sur divers points du Sistème de l'auteur du tableau Economique*; and the third *Observations économique sur les articles Grains et Fermier de l'Encyclopédie*. The work is printed in 12mo, 1767.[1] – I shall begin regularly with the first volume, and examine it minutely.)[2]

25. 'Ad opera nil aliud potest homo, quam ut corpora naturalia admoveat et amoveat: reliqua, natura intus transigit.' Bacon, *Nov. Org.*, I. 4.[3]

1. The details Horner gives about the anonymous three-part work by François Véron Duverger de Forbonnais are substantially correct for the two–volume Amsterdam edition of 1767, save for some muddle between 'volumes' and 'parts'.
2. This section is dated in the margin 9 June 1802 but presumably was written much nearer to 18 Oct. (the following datemark) after the 'unavoidable interval' to which Horner refers above.
3. I.e. no. IV of the first set of aphorisms in the *Novum Organum*: 'Towards the effecting of works, all that man can do is to put together or put asunder natural bodies; the rest is done by nature working within.'

102. Notes for an Outline of Universal History

Kinnordy MSS   21 Oct. 1802

1. Both Bossuet and Voltaire appear to me to have mingled more of disputation and minute criticism, than is consistent with the plan of a general sketch. *vide* 4 [below].

2. The names of a few individuals should occur; of those only who have been leaders and revolutionists in empire, religion, science, or the arts; Alexander, Cæsar, Timour, Gengis, Buddha, Christ, Mahomet, Socrates, Aristotle, Bacon, Newton, Columbus, etc.

3. The picture must certainly commence with a view of the ancient civilization of Asia. This subject has not yet received that certainty, which the future labours of oriental scholars may give it; but we have undoubted materials for an outline of Asiatic history, anterior to the records of Europe.

The theory of Sir William Jones[1] has the great advantage in its simplicity. He supposes not only Arabia, but Hindostan, China, and the wastes of Tartary, to have been peopled from Iran. In an historical sketch, we cannot pretend to assume this; and it would be improper to mix critical dispositions. The civil historian, like the geologist, must content himself with tracing a series of great events backwards, though he never can approach the first origin of nations; cosmology is as foreign to the one as it is to the other. I believe the historical remains of India, China, and Persia, enable us to give a very authentic and distinct view of the state of Asia some four thousand years before the Christian era, as at times divided among several great and civilized Empires.

According to Sir William Jones, we may trace the history of Asia back a period, at which the Arabs, Indians, and Tartars, were quite distinct in language, aspect, and manners. He supposes them indeed to have all issued from one family, and to have lost their original languages entirely. We need not, in our sketch, go farther back than the period at which we find them distinct.

The religion of Buddha appears to have prevailed over almost the whole of Asia. At what time the Brahmeny rites were first systematized, I have not learned; it is certain, however, that about the period of the Christian era, the religion of *Buddha*, had the ascendancy throughout Hindostan. In consequence of the exertions of the Brahmans, it is now almost extirpated. (Hamn – *Edinburgh Review*, I. p. 36.)[2] According to Sir William Jones, Buddha came into India about 1014 before Christ; and probably came from Ethiopia, or some of the countries to the south-west. According to this view, it was a heresy, to which the Brahmeny faith yielded for a while. The religion of Buddha was introduced into China in the third century of our era; his name has been softened by that nation into Fo. The Lamas of Tibet are priests of Buddha; those that are to be found in Siberia, have gone from Tibet.

The proper history of Hindostan extends backwards from the Mahometan conquest, in the eleventh century, as far as authentic or probable records will carry us; that is, according to Sir William Jones, after the first settlement of the Hindus who emigrated from Iran. The history of Hindostan will be recorded in our outline, at different periods. A view of its original establishment and ancient civilization, will form a principal feature of that picture of Asiatic antiquities, with which the work must set out. The expedition of Alexander will give us from the banks of the Indus a distinct prospect of the country; but the conquest of the Caliphs will carry us into the interior of Hindostan; and a picture of their invasion must derive its chief forms of colouring from a retrospect of that wealth, and population, and felicity, which under the native government had accumulated (*Edinburgh Review*, i. 37). Our attention will be almost entirely occupied in the western world, until the British conquest in India gives us the occasion first of viewing the condition of the country under its Moslem rulers, and secondly of explaining the formation of that milder and more enlightened system to which it is now subjected.

The paramount uniformity of Chinese manners will render it unnecessary, to resume the history of that empire, after the first mention of it at the beginning of the work. The Tartar conquests, and the foreign wars of the late Tartar emperors, may be incidentally [?noted] when we explain the commerce of the caravans, or mention the discovery and settlement of Siberia.

The history of Persia forms an intermediate link between that of Asia and of Europe. Herodotus has constructed the unity of his work, by a reference to the destinies of that empire. We shall be insensibly withdrawn from Persia to the infant republics of Greece, not to be recalled until the march of Alexander leaves us to contemplate the subversion of the empire. In the same manner, we shall have nearly finished the view of Greece, before it is necessary to mention the growth of Rome.

4. *Voltaire* probably did not mean to confine himself to a general sketch. But I cannot help thinking that he has admitted too many minute anecdotes, and has sometimes descended to a style too familiar. His object no doubt was to paint the characteristic manners of the various ages and nations which he reviews, and the general turn of his composition is admirably fitted to that effect. But that popular sort of painting is inferior to the great object of general history, which is to present the great truths and principles of human manners, and to exhibit in a connected chain the revolutions of the world. There is certainly a juster philosophy in Voltaire than in Bossuet; yet the composition of the latter seems to me of a much higher order, and more appropriate to Philosophical History than that of the former. There is genius, unquestionably, in those characteristic sketches by Teniers in which local and individual peculiarities are imitated and fixed: but there is a higher merit and utility in the delineations, which Caracca has executed, of the general features of mankind.

5. The great uniformity of the feudal government of modern Europe is an important fact, which will deserve very careful explanation. The similarity of the circumstances, in which the different states were placed, will not alone account for it; nor even the original similarity of manners and origin, among the barbarous conquerors. I suspect a good deal must be ascribed to that uniformity of municipal constitutions etc. which the Roman Empire established throughout the provinces. The correct illustration of this part, and the precise limitation of its extent, will be very highly delicate but highly important. It supposes a minute study of the political facts which may be extracted, and combined from Theodosian, and feudal codes.[3]

1. Sir William Jones (1746–94: *DNB*), orientalist.
2. Alexander Hamilton, 'Asiatic Researches, vol. vi', *ER* i (no. i, Oct. 1802), 26–43.
3. In the margin Horner has dated this final paragraph 27 Jan. 1803.

103. To James Loch

BLPES i. 188–9 〈Horner, i. 210–11〉   Edinburgh, 7 Nov. 1802

〈... We are not a little amused by some of the guesses that are attempted by various shrewd readers; they blunder with the most ridiculous cross-purposes.[1] You will not be surprised that we have given a good deal of disappointment by the temperate air of our politics; nothing short of blood and atheism and democracy were predicted by some wise and fair ones, as the necessary production of our set. We shall go on to another number with considerable spirit, as a second edition of the first is in the press already: the first impression was 750, and as many more are to be printed. By all means, let me know whatever you hear said of it – good, bad, or indifferent; this is the main pleasure of such publications, and will indeed be our only recompense, as we give the MS for nothing.[2] Brougham has concluded a bargain about his book with Longman, who has been here making purchases of that kind; he talks of sending it to the press in about two months. The title, an *Enquiry into the Colonial Policy of the European Powers*. That it will do him great credit, I have no doubt; I hope it may be the means of introducing him into a respectable line of political connections. Old Liverpool wrote himself into notice by a seasonable, though puny, pamphlet on the rights of neutrals.[3] Should an active scene be opened to Brougham, I shall tremble with anxiety for some time, though it is what I very ardently wish; his information on political subjects, especially in some departments, is now immense; his talents are equal to the most effective use and display of that knowledge. But his ardour is so urgent, that I should be afraid of his being deficient in prudence. That he would ultimately become a leading and predominant mind, I cannot doubt; but he might attempt to fix himself in that place too soon, before he had gone through what, I presume, is a necessary routine of subordination.〉

1. Being anonymous, the articles in the ER excited much speculation about their authorship from the appearance of the first number in October.
2. According to a note by Leonard Horner (citing letters from Jeffrey of 11 May and Murray of 26 May 1803) on the copy in the MS 'Memoirs' at Kinnordy, the original agreement was that the first four numbers were to be provided free to the booksellers, but after the publication of the second number Constable and Longman proposed there should be a regular editor at £50 and payments of 10 guineas per sheet for the contributors. This is confirmed by *Jeffrey*, ii. 74.
3. Charles Jenkinson, 1st Earl of Liverpool (1727–1808: DNB), *Discourse on the conduct of Government respecting Neutral Nations* (1758).

104. Journal

Kinnordy MSS 〈Horner, i. 211–13〉   20 Nov. 1802

〈... I shall make a short memorandum with respect to the reception which the first number of our *Review* has met with in Edinburgh, for we have not yet got an account of its fate in London. Upon the whole, I do not think we have gained much character by it; it is considered as respectable enough in point of talents, but the severity, in some of the papers it may be called scurrility, has given general dissatisfaction. In the next number, we must soften our tone, and be more indulgent to folly and to bad taste. Jeffrey is the person who will derive most honour from this publication, and his articles in this number are generally known, and are incomparably the best. I have received the greater pleasure from this circumstance, because the genius of that little man has remained almost unknown to all but his most intimate acquaintances. His manner is not at first pleasing; what is worse, it is of that cast, which almost irresistibly impresses upon strangers the idea of levity and superficial talents. Yet there is not any man, whose real character is so much the reverse; he has indeed a very sportive and playful fancy, but it is accompanied with very extensive and varied information, with a readiness of apprehension almost intuitive, with judicious and calm discernment, with a profound and penetrating understanding. Indeed, both in point of candour and of vigour in the reasoning powers, I have never personally known a finer intellect than Jeffrey's, unless I were to except Allen's.

⟨...

⟨I wish to attend the Speculative Society very regularly, because I am satisfied that I have already derived great benefit from the exercises of that place, and still entertain hopes of receiving farther improvement. In general, I shall leave myself, as I have hitherto always done, to the extemporaneous efforts of the evening; but it would be very advantageous to prepare myself upon one or two of the best questions; this, I observe, is the plan which Brougham follows.

⟨I attend Mr Stewart's lectures on political economy, that I may complete my notes of his course, and that I may impress myself fully with the general manner in which he considers a subject, which, if my visionary prospects should ever be realized, will occupy in some degree the last part of my life; and which will continue to amuse and exercise my mind, though I should remain forever in obscure inactivity.

⟨...⟩

105. To James Loch

BLPES i. 190–91 ⟨Horner, i. 218–21⟩   Edinburgh, 12 Dec. 1802

⟨... The account you give of the projected improvements in London is very splendid;[1] too magnificent, I fear, to be carried into complete execution at once; but even a part of such a plan will be immense, worthy of such a metropolis: we may look upon these as the first fruits of that peace, which some[2] would labour already to deprive us of. These public works afford me a farther pleasure of a different kind; as I look upon our foreign commerce, in its present extent, to be only a temporary advantage, it is of importance that the wealth it at present produces should be fixed and embodied in our own country, either by multiplying the facilities of internal trade, or by enlarging the capital vested in agriculture. Whatever indeed is employed upon the first of these purposes, indirectly promotes the other.

⟨I am indebted to you for the pains you have taken to make inquiries about the reception of our review. Though to all of us it is only a matter of temporary amusement, and subordinate occupation, we cannot of course be indifferent about the fate of our attempt at reputation. We have certainly no reason to be dissatisfied with its degree of success; though, by the mismanagement of our publisher in London, it has scarcely got into circulation there. The opinions that have reached us as to its merits are pretty uniform; Jeffrey's papers being most admired, as they fully deserve to be; an exception being in general made to the tone and manner of certain articles, which most of us, before they were printed, considered as exceptionable on that very account.

⟨I am much interested by your notes of political intelligence, – never was there a period when one, who cares very little about men and parties, except as connected with the fate of leading objects, ought to feel a more lively curiosity: we are surely at a moment of crisis. The question of peace or war, except as determined by that of practicability, is surely far from being quite clear; if there is any foundation for what is called the doctrine of the Balance of Power, we have not, since the days of King William, seen an era when the application of that theory to existing circumstances was more important. Fox's second speech afforded me much pleasure; the older that man becomes, he seems to acquire a greater dignity of character, – the opportunities of retirement seem to have conspired with the growth of years, in cleansing his fine understanding of that intemperance by which it was often clouded, as well as in leading him to those comprehensive and philosophical views of political transactions, in which he appears to have been deficient in the early part of his life. For a long time I have not been so pleased with any circumstance, as the observation of this refinement of Fox's manner in parliament, coupled with the anecdote you give me of the lively interest he takes in the political events of the day. Has any thing more been reported lately about his *history*? Has the *second* speech been published? Send me a particular account of the debate on the Estimates, especially of Fox's leading positions and views of the subject; such, I mean, as the newspaper reporters never think of seizing.[3]

⟨...

⟨Have you good authority for your anecdote of⟩ Bogie[4] and ⟨the Poor Laws? I should like to believe it. If you have seen any thing published on that subject lately, let me know: I have got a paper to write during the holidays on a very general question, which has excited a good deal of interest among the tenantry and landed gentlemen, whether, under the existing Scottish Acts, relief was legally afforded, during the scarcity, to the industrious poor.

⟨...⟩

1. Perhaps a reference to the redevelopment of Bloomsbury, but from what follows more probably to the great reconstruction of London Docks.
2. A line has been obliterated here.
3. Fox had spoken in the debate on the King's Speech on 22 Nov. and again on 24 Nov. (*Parl. Hist.*, xxxvi. 951–9 and 1015–1027).
4. The nickname assigned by the Foxites to William Wyndham, Baron Grenville (1759–1834: *DNB*).

106. Notes on Smith's *Wealth of Nations*

Kinnordy MSS   12 Dec. 1802

44. (I. p. 102)[1] I think I have observed in most of the French writers a propensity to state the actual wages of common labour as at this lowest rate. The following expressions are used by Mercier de la Rivière, tom. II. p. 154: 'Examinez bien quel est l'état de tous ceux, etc.'[2] A late antagonist of the economists, M. Canard evidently makes the same assumption when he maintains the expediency of taxes on the necessaries of life.

45. (I. p. 154)[3] See Canard, *Pr. d'écon. pol.*, p. 10.

46. (III p. 256, p. 263)[4] This is evading the discussion of the system of the economists in a very summary manner.

47. (III. 265)[5] In all these proposed regulations, the author appears to have lost sight of the principle of perfect freedom, which, in other parts of his work, is the basis of so many important reasonings.

48. (III. 270) To speak of a tax as an unalterable regulation, and as a fundamental law of the commonwealth, does not perfectly accord with the language which we are accustomed to use in this country; which may not, however, on that account, be liable to well-founded objections.

49. (III. 276)[6] It would be an interesting article of historical inquiry, to trace in what manner the tythe has been abolished in some, and moderated in other, countries. Smith's phrase, 'upon that account' is surely too positive. Scotland is a Presbyterian country; yet the present state of our teinds does not appear to have followed *necessarily* from the establishment.

50. (III. 290)[7] It would seem more easy to reckon the hearths, than the windows, of a house, when the tax gatherer does not enter every room of the house.[8]

1. *WN* I. viii. 15:
   > Mr Cantillon seems ... to suppose that the lowest species of common labourers must every where earn at least double their own maintenance, in order that one with another they may be enabled to bring up two children.

2. The passage in Le Mercier de Rivière's *Ordre Naturel*, ii. 154–5, continues:
   > dont la profession est de servir aux différents travaux que la culture occasionne; en général, vous ne verrez en eux que des hommes réduits à des consommations qu'on peut regarder comme l'étoit nécessaire; il s'en faut bien qu'ils soient salariés en raison de l'utilité qui résulte de leurs travaux: leurs diverses professions sont communément d'une pratique si facile, qu'elles sont à la portée d'une multitude d'hommes, et d'hommes nés sans aucune sorte de richesses; par cette raison, la grande concurrence de ces ouvriers qui se forment promptement et sans frais, tient *nécessairement* leurs salaires au plus bas prix possible, je veux dire, à un prix au-dessous auquel on ne trouve que l'indigne et la misère, fleaux toujours destructifs des classes d'hommes dont ils forment l'état habituel.

3. *WN* I. x. b. 5 elaborates on the various particular costs of, for example, acquiring a craft or purchasing a machine: 'the wages of labour vary with the easiness and cheapness, or the difficulty and expence of learning the business.' The relevant passage in Canard runs:
   > Il faut distinguer dans l'homme deux espèces de travaux; savoir, le *travail naturel* et le *travail appris*. ... Toutes les fois qu'un art ou un talent est de nature à avoir un grand nombre de concurrences qui échouent, il arrive que la perte qu'ils font est au profit de celui qui réussit.

4. In *WN* V. ii. b. 3 Smith had written:
> Every tax, ... which falls finally upon one only of the three sorts of revenue [Rent, Profit, and Wages], is necessarily unequal, in so far as it does not affect the other two. In the following examples of different taxes, I shall seldom take much further notice of this sort of inequality ... .

In the latter of these passages about taxation (*WN* V. ii. c. 7) Smith had said that he would not enter into any 'disagreeable discussion of the metaphysical arguments' by which the 'very ingenious theory' of 'a tax upon the rent of land which varies with every variation of the rent, or which rises and falls according to the improvement or neglect of cultivation, is recommended by that sect of men of letters in France, who call themselves the economists, as the most equitable of all'.

5. *WN* V. ii. c. 12–13 criticised the practice of levying so-called 'fines' rather than raising the rent upon the renewal of a lease and of landlords prescribing particular crops, and advocated a special tax as a deterrent.

6. *WN* V. ii. d. 3:
> The cultivation of madder was for a long time confined by the tythe to the United Provinces, which, being presbyterian countries, and upon that account exempted from this destructive tax, enjoyed a sort of monopoly of that useful dying drug against the rest of Europe.

7. *WN* V. ii. e. 15ff, discusses and criticises the various methods of taxing houses.

8. Horner subsequently wrote in the margin: 'hearth-money abolished in Ireland, 1806 – See Debates 14 April that year.'

107. Notes of my progress in studying the system of the Economists

Kinnordy MSS   17–23 Dec. 1802

26. Any analogy between the sterility, which the Economists ascribe to certain kinds of labour, and that which Aristotle and the Schoolmen ascribed to money? This query suggested by a passage in Forbonnais, I. p. 107.[1]

MERCIER DE LA RIVIÈRE, *l'Ordre Naturel*, ETC.
(Chap. 36. Vol. 11. p. 249, to Chap. 44. p. 423.)[2]

27.[3] (p. 250)[4] In this proposition of the Economists' system the word measure appears to be used in a very strained and obscure sense: the reason assigned in demonstration of the proposition only proves that without the demand, created by consumption, there would be no reproduction; from which it may be inferred, or rather, in which it is implied, that the reproduction is proportioned to the consumption. But proportion is not expressed by the word measure; quantities cannot be said to be proportional, unless, by means of some third quantity, they may be reduced to a common measure.[5]

28. (Chaps 27. 28. and 29.) All this story of a *joint-property* in the disposable neat produce ['co-propriété des produits nets des terres'], seems extremely puerile; it cannot surely be any more than a very circuitous and very injudicious mode of stating, that, for the expediency of the state or rather for the existence of the social union, it is necessary that a certain portion of private property should be contributed to form a public revenue. With respect to this public revenue, derived solely out of

the disposable neat produce of land, the author is evidently quite conscious to himself of its impracticability, p. 64;[6] which surely might be deemed an objection sufficiently conclusive. He is not equally aware that it could never be carried into execution without injustice, and would never fail to be an arbitrary imposition. But there is a very strong objection to it, of a different kind from either of these: suppose it were quite practicable to fix and to levy the just proportion of the neat produce which ought to go to the Sovereign, it is evident that his annual revenue, or the amount of taxes annually levied, is determined without any reference whatever to the necessities of that year, or to the average [?] necessities of the state: provided the agriculture of the country is in a progressive state, the amount of annual taxes is likewise to increase, though the necessary expenses of the state may not have increased, but on the contrary may have suffered diminution. The contrary, however, appears to be a fundamental principle in the theory of finances.

29. (II. p. 116.) This page has slightly more than anything I have yet seen in favour of the fundamental principles of the Economists.[7]

30. Those parts of Mercier's treatises, and of the speculations of the Economists in general in which they express their confidence in the purity and illumination of their legal despot, evidently originates in an erroneous view of that great fact in human nature, the progressive tendency of improved minds towards just views of self-interest. The Economists have evidently considered this fact under an aspect of simplicity, which is quite fallacious; even as the ultimate though unattainable limit of that progressive tendency. The most general statement of the real fact involves necessarily a much greater degree of complication. The full elucidation of this truth would be very interesting; and the statement which it would enable me to give of the error of the Economists, would form an useful and splendid illustration for that discourse, which I have long meditated, on the necessity of making the science of human nature the basis of political philosophy.

31. {My late resumption of the subject of Economism, a third or fourth attack, has been occasioned by my having undertaken Canard's Essay for the *Edinburgh Review* which imposed the duty of examining the various arguments for and against the territorial tax.}[8]

32. Granting the fundamental proposition to be true, that all revenue flows from the territorial proprietors, and that therefore all taxes, however collected, are levied upon property that was originally in the hands of those proprietors; it does not therefore necessarily follow, that the tax should be directly levied at the original source, because there may be principles of political economy to prove, that, having a given tax to levy on a given mass of wealth, it is more expedient to levy it on that wealth as circulating and distributed, than at the original source.[9]

33. There appears to be a very puerile mistake in all those arguments against an indirect tax, which are drawn from the consideration of what is called *double emploi*. All those arguments resolve, I suspect, into this; that by the indirect imposte, a tax is raised from property, of which the public have already received the full portion to which they are entitled in name of tax. Nothing surely is more undeniable than that a farther tax ought not to be levied, if a full revenue has already been raised. But on the other hand, if the exigencies of the state require a further sum than has already been levied from the proprietors of land, a farther sum must be taken either from

them, or from those into whose hands produce is distributed. It can no more be called *double emploi* in the second case than in the first; if there is any meaning in the argument about *double emploi* it amounts to this nugatory proposition, that it would be inexpedient to raise a further sum of taxes than it is expedient to raise. I have very little doubt as to the manner in which Mercier de la Rivière has been led into such a fallacy; he sets out with a supposition that the sovereign has a joint property in the produce of land, and proceeding upon this *fiction* (I use this word as a lawyer) he soon forgets that it is only by the exigencies of the public expense that the share of the Sovereign can be determined.

34. In an agricultural country, it is the natural principle of negotiation, which is the main source of reproduction.

In a pastoral country, it is the natural principle of animal generation, which is the chief source of reproduction.[10] In a mining country, whether the minerals worked consist of the precious metals or the precious gems, or of the baser metals, or of fuel, or of other fossils used in agricultural and manufacturing processes, those operations of nature, by which the geological changes are affected (however indefinite their period of return, and however remote in the antiquity of the world the last change may have been), form the original source of production.

In a fishing country, it is the natural principle of animal generation, which is the source of production.

In a country, favoured by natural situation, and possessed of an established system of diversified industry and opulence, all these various sources of reproduction are open, from which an increase of consumable wealth is constantly flowing. –

In a *manufacturing* country, the mechanical powers of man, of animals, and of machinery, may perhaps be complexly considered as forming a natural principle which is a source of reproduction. Labour, or mechanical power, is as much a natural principle, as the law of generation or vegetable growth; and it may be no less considered as productive of wealth, since it renders natural productions useful and agreeable to our wants. It seems scarcely to be an answer to say, that nature creates those substances which she reproduces, while the labour of man only affects an alteration of form. In truth, nature herself only effects changes of form.

35. Granting that the annual reproduction is the source from which every increase of wealth is derived, and that taxes fall ultimately on the nett produce of the annual reproduction, it will not therefore be correct to say, that land is the only source of wealth, or that taxes are ultimately paid by the proprietor of land. In an agricultural and inland [?] country, this is probably an approximate statement of the truth; but is farther from it, the more we suppose a country to pay attention to its mines, fisheries, etc. The salmon-fisheries of the Severn and the Tay, the herring fishery of Loch Fyne, the coal mines of Newcastle, the salt mines of Cheshire, the lime quarries of Gilmerston, the marl pits of Berwickshire, the clay beds of Cornwall, the gravel pits of Kensington, and a thousand others, must unquestionably be considered as sources of production, from which a nett produce is yearly gained, over and above the reimbursement and profit of the capital employed in working them. Most of these are so situated, that this nett produce comes into the hands of a landlord; but in the herring fisheries in Scotland, and the whale and cod fisheries at sea, there has not yet been an appropriation of those parts of the earth's surface: in

these cases, the nett produce is confounded with the profits of stock, but does not on that account fail to be distinct from it in a theoretical point of view: any more than where land, as in America and the W. Indian colonies, is cultivated by the proprietors themselves.[11]

The Economists, natives of an agricultural empire, do not seem to have, in this respect, given their doctrine a form sufficiently comprehensive.

It might be curious, for the sake of illustration, to collect facts of the following class; viz.,

In the fisheries upon the coast of Holland, was any *rent* ever paid to individual proprietors, or to the public, by those who employed their capital in fishing?

Same query as to the oyster beds on the English coast.

Same query as to the pearl fishery at Panama, and at Ceylon.

In China, where the surface of the great rivers is a seat of permanent habitations, and esculent aquatic vegetables are raised, are the portions of that surface divided and appropriated, and is *rent* ever paid for them?

1. *[The passage from Forbonnais's *Principes* to which Horner refers is presumably: 'l'argent occasione qu'accidentellement et indirectement de nouvelles valeurs dans le commerce.' His own note reads:] (23 Dec.) I will hazard another query. Was Aristotle led to this position, which has been so much ridiculed, by any train of thought similar to that of the Economists? The interest of money is a profit upon the employment of so much capital; this is merely a transference of wealth from one hand to another, not an augmentation of national produce.†

   †Casting my eye over a few chapters of his work *De Republica*, Lib. I. c. 8–11, I have seen [?enough] to satisfy me, that this conjecture ought unquestionably to be prosecuted. In one or two points it appears to meet the Economists, and almost to use their language; it will be highly interesting to compare the two trains of thought. Mayow [John Mayow (1643–79: *DNB*), physiologist and chemist] anticipated Lavoisier; and the Economists, I make no doubt, were unaware of the authority of Aristotle.

2. Generally, the chapters on Commerce and Industry, together with the conclusion.

3. Horner actually entered 1, 2, 3, 4 from this point but evidently had meant to follow on from para 26 above, and so resumed at para 31 below.

4. '*La consommation est la mesure de la reproduction.*'

5. This section is dated in the margin 17 Dec. 1802.

6. Where Le Mercier de la Rivière refers to tax evasion.

7.   ... proscrivons pour un moment l'usage de l'argent, banissons-le du commerce, et n'y saisons plus entrer que des productions et des marchandises en nature. Dans cette hypothèse vous ne voyez plus que les premiers propriétaires des productions qui puissent communiquer des richesses aux autres hommes: c'est cette classe propriétaire qui fournit les matières premières des marchandises; c'est cette classe propriétaire qui donne des productions en échange des travaux de main-d'œuvre; une partie de ces productions peuvent passer de main en main jusqu'à ce qu'elles soient entièrement consommées; mais dans quelque main que vous le trouvez, vous ne voyez toujours en elles qu'une richesse qui provient de cette classe propriétaire.

8. The brackets are Horner's.

9. This section is dated in the margin 18 Dec. 1802.

10. *Aristotle's description of the pastoral state is singular and expressive: On account of the necessary change of pasture, he observes, shepherds must roam from place to place. ... *De Rep.*, I. c. 8. [John] *Gillies* translates it thus: 'Possessing *a sort of living farm spontaneously productive*, the shepherd, etc.'

11. This section is dated 23 Dec. 1802 in the margin.

108. Notes on Smith's *Wealth of Nations*

Kinnordy MSS   22 Dec. 1802 – 2 Jan. 1803

51. (III. 334)[1] This difference between the effect of taxes on the necessaries of the poor, and the effects of taxes on their luxuries, appears to be stated in too absolute a manner. The difference would be exactly so, if we could consider the luxuries and necessaries independently of each other. But so long as any luxuries remain within the reach of the poor, a tax upon necessaries will operate indirectly, in the same manner as a direct tax upon luxuries; so long as luxuries remain, these may be retrenched in order to meet the increased price of necessaries and in this manner, a tax upon necessaries may fail to produce any rise of wages.[2]

52. (III. 340)[3] What manufactures did Holland possess? What was the system of their manufacturing establishment? Can the progress of their decline be traced? – It would form an interesting picture, and a valuable repository of facts to the political economist.

53. (III. 354)[4] Some steps, towards the adoption of such a plan, were taken under the Administration of Mr Pitt, including some articles, formerly under the customs, in the administration of the excise. A still further approach to it is at present in contemplation, by the establishment of certain free ports. – While Holland possessed the carrying trade of Europe, what was their system of taxation of exports and imports?

54. (III. p. 292)[5] I cannot remember this principle as ever being explained or even stated in any former part of the work; though, if true (which I doubt), it ought to have been included among the results of that analysis, which is given in the first Book. – If it is a correct distinction, it should perhaps be otherwise expressed. Profit is a compensation for the risk and the trouble of employing stock; but this risk and this trouble, are sometimes not incurred by the same person, one person advancing the stock, and the other employing it. The profit must, therefore, be divided between these two persons; he, who has advanced the stock, receives that part of the profit which forms a compensation for the risk; he, who employs it, receives that part of the profit which forms a compensation for the trouble. To the former portion of the whole profit, a particular name, that of *interest* has been assigned.[6]

55. (III. p. 294) I can discover no reason for calling one of the portions, into which profit may be divided (see preceding note), a *neat produce* any more than the other portions; nor can I discover any reason for calling either of them so. Both of them taken together form a complete profit; each of them, singly, can be considered as nothing else than profit. The same principle of competition regulates the amount of each, according to the proportion of demand and supply. And with respect to the argument in this paragraph, which bears so much the form of a geometrical demonstration, it would be equally conclusive, according to my view of the subject, although the two portions into which the whole profit is divided were to change places. 'The whole rate of profit remains the same; but that portion of it, which goes to him who has advanced the stock, likewise remains the same; wherefore that other portion, which goes to him who has employed the stock, must necessarily remain the same.'[7]

It does indeed seem inexcusable that, at this period of his work, where he ought to be engaged in showing the synthetical application of his theory, we should all at once have a new principle brought forward, which, if true, would have formed a fundamental proposition.

56. (III. p. 255)[8] I have now read through this long review, and will state the general result. The object, which Smith seems to have had in view, was to present, under a convenient classification, a great deal of historical information as to the taxes which had been established in different countries, comparing (as he goes along) each kind of tax with the four preliminary maxims. He introduces only incidentally, and it would seem without any design to present it in a systematic form, that very curious part of the doctrine of taxation, which relates to their ultimate incidence on some one branch of revenue, or their diffusion over all the three branches. The opinion he entertained upon this point is nowhere absolutely stated; it may be collected however from a variety of passages, which would be found by the following references, viz., 255, 274, 282, 286, 292, 302, 323, 327, 333, 336, 372. The admissions, expressed in these passages, appear to me to lead, as an unavoidable consequence, to the conclusion of the economists, with respect to the ultimate incidence of all taxes upon the nett produce of land; perhaps, if they impart that conclusion, they do so by involving the fundamental principle of the economists with regard to the source of wealth. Various other passages in the *Wealth of Nations* appear to include that fundamental principle no less implicitly.[9]

He admits that no tax can fall upon the *wages* of labour; though advanced by the labourer, it must be replaced to him by those who employ him, and therefore is finally paid either out of the profits of stock, or out of the rent of land.

He admits further, that no tax can fall on the profits of stock: though advanced by the employer of capital, it must be replaced to him either by the consumers in an advanced price, or by the landlord in a diminished rent, or by the monied capitalist in a diminished rate of interest.

But if the remarks in the preceding notes are well-founded, it is a gratuitous and erroneous distinction which Smith has made between that part of profit which he here calls profit, and that which he here calls interest; both are precisely of the same nature; both are equally to be considered as the profit of stock. The taxes, that are laid on profits of stock, may therefore be considered as paid finally, either by the consumers in an advanced price, or by the landlords in a diminished rent.

Now the consumers form the whole population of the State; they can only pay taxes out of their respective revenue; and that must be derived from wages, from profit, or from rent. But it is admitted that no taxes can ultimately fall either on wages or on profit; those, which the consumers pay, are therefore all ultimately paid out of rent or nett produce.

Wherefore all taxes are finally paid out of the neat produce, either in a diminution in the rent of the landlord, or by increase in the wages and prices which out of his actual rent he distributes among the other classes of the community.

Though I am not at present aware of any fallacy in the preceding deduction, yet it is possible I may have overlooked some necessary step, and I may be deceived by the very strictness of form in which I have affected to state it. In order, therefore, to resume with advantage the investigation at some future time, I shall here note the three principles which are assumed in the preceding chain of reasoning:

First. In opposition to Smith, I assume that the interest of money is nowise different in its nature from the profits of stock.

Second. In coincidence with Smith, I assume that all the profits of stock are, by means of competition, kept as low as capitalists can possibly afford.

Third. I assume that an *indirect* tax upon wages or profit must be reimbursed to the labourer or the capitalist, no less than a *direct* one. Smith had not adverted to any distinction of this kind, so far as I observe. But, if there is any foundation for it, I may have stated his admission, with respect to taxes on wages and profit, more broadly than his own expressions would warrant.

57. (I. p. 139)[10] In reviewing Canard's 5th chapter, I was led into some reasonings upon the general point, in which this is involved. I shall only for the present observe, that the same conclusions are not applicable, without modification, to a state situated like Holland and to an agricultural territory.[11]

58. (I. p. 141)[12] I must collect facts with respect to the present condition of the American states, especially those which are furthest removed from their original colonial circumstances, in all these points.

1. *WN* V. ii. k. 6–7:
   > The rise in the price of the taxed commodities, will not necessarily occasion any rise in the wages of labour. … Upon the sober and industrious poor, taxes upon such [luxury] commodities act as sumptuary laws, and dispose them either to moderate, or to refrain altogether from the use of superfluities which they can no longer easily afford.

2. This section is dated in the margin 22 Dec. 1802.

3. In *WN* V. ii. k. 14, Smith had mentioned the view that the tax on milled flour in Holland had contributed significantly to her decline.

4. Horner inadvertently wrote '340' again but evidently meant *WN* V. ii. k. 36–40, where Smith proposed the reform of the customs on the lines of the excise, specifically by the introduction of a system of bonded warehouses.

5. *WN* V. ii. f. 1:
   > The revenue or profit arising from stock naturally divides itself into two parts; that which pays the interest, and which belongs to the owner of the stock; and that surplus part which is over and above what is necessary for paying the interest.

6. This section is dated in the margin 23 Dec. 1802.

7. This appears to be Horner's own alternative to Smith's conclusion to *WN* V. ii. f. 3: 'The residue, therefore, that portion which belongs to the owner of the stock, and which pays the interest of money, would necessarily remain the same too.'

8. 'Of Taxes' (*WN* V. ii. b); the specific references listed by Horner below are to: b. 1; d. 1–2; e. 4–5; e. 8–9; e. 20; g. 3–4; i. 2; j. 2; k. 9; and k. 58.

9. In the margin there is a note in pencil: 'I have made use of this note in my review of Canard.' (*Cf. ER* i (no. ii, Jan. 1803), 447–8 (*EW*, pp. 73–4).)

10. *WN* I. ix. 10, reflecting on the comparative richness of Holland. *Cf.* Canard's pp. 80–106, 'Des Causes de l'accroissement et du décroissement de la richesse', and Horner's comments on it in *ER*, pp. 440–43 (*EW*, pp. 66–9).

11. This section is dated in the margin 2 Jan. 1803.

12. *WN* I. ix. 11.

109. To James Loch

BLPES ii. 1–2 〈Horner, i. 221〉   Edinburgh, 24 Jan. 1803[1]

...

I go this afternoon, i.e. 16 hours hence to Fox's dinner, at Fortune's;[2] what sort of party we are to have in point of number, I have not heard. Sir W. Forbes is to be in the chair. I have always found it a very stupid meeting; but it is a kind of duty; and with a certain description of people, these things have some effect.

〈This day〉 too 〈we publish a second number of our review. I think you will find it free, at least nearly so, from some of the objections that were most strongly, and all of them justly, urged against the former. There are scarcely any insignificant books – no sermons – few personalities – the general train of criticism less abusive. We are not indeed quite purified of all our gross faults, but the opinion of our friends has made a considerable impression upon us. I think this number has no articles so good as some of the last; but there is a good deal of careful disquisition.〉

I got from London some days ago, gratis, but I do not know through what channel, a small pamphlet by G. Crauford of Rotterdam on our Finances; it is addressed as a letter to Addington.[3] Have you seen it? It contains an attack upon the sinking fund, not as ill-managed or as ill-planned, but as an injudicious system altogether for the redemption of debt. The arguments appear to me to have nothing in them; yet the author, I believe, has some name about London for his knowledge of money transactions. If the pamphlet has attracted any attention, I should like to know what is said of it. Pray, have you ever met with any work in which the history of our funds is fully collected, and the principles explained upon which parliamentary loans are transacted; I have only of late turned my thoughts at all to this branch of politics, and I am surprised not to find a good guide in it. The labour of putting together all the acts of parliament about the national debt, which seem to form the largest portion of good materials upon the subject, is more than I have at present time for. Adam Smith's chapter on public debts is a mere sham; and George Chalmers is after all a very meagre compiler.[4] Did you attend, at the time, to Addington's last transaction about the sinking funds and the loan of last year; I want to understand them: what end was gained by the consolidation of the two funds? and what particular advantages were proposed by the scheme of deferred annuities? I seem to be interrogating a stock-broker; but I know these things fall in your way, and you are never incurious about any of them.

...

1. Horner actually wrote 1802, which has been amended by his brother on the MS. At the end of the letter, following the signature, Horner himself added: '½ past one'.
2. An hotel in Edinburgh.
3. George Craufurd, A letter to the Right Honourable Henry Addington, on the finances of Great Britain (1802).
4. Probably a reference to An Estimate of the Comparative Strength of Great Britain (1782) and Opinions on interesting subjects of Public Laws and Commercial Policy arising from American Independence (1784) by George Chalmers (1742–1825: DNB), Chief Clerk at the Board of Trade. Horner evidently had a low opinion of this old-fashioned antiquarian and occasional pamphleteer on commercial questions. See Doc. 412.

110. Notes on Smith's *Wealth of Nations*

Kinnordy MSS   4 and 26 Mar. 1803

59. (I. 429, 483)[1] Beside the expense of collecting and supporting the metallic medium of circulation, we must likewise consider the annual loss of interest. The money in circulation must be considered as so much dead, unproductive stock. It is evidently quite unproductive to any one person, so long as it remains in his hands; and it remains unproductive, from the moment he receives it, till the moment he parts with it. But, however quickly it may change hands, it is always in the possession of one person or another. It is always, therefore, unproductive of annual interest to the nation.[2]

London,[3] 26 Mar. 1803

60. (III. p. 94)[4] This is doubtful; and a most important principle in legislation. I have some notes upon it, in the 2nd part of my Common Place Book. An important consideration on one side of the question is mentioned by Smith at p. 96, as well as a general historical remark to be found on p. 102.

60. [*sic*] (III. p. 96)[5] The first Turnpike Act for the County of Midlothian appears to have been constructed on a very different principle. It imposes a toll 'on every force with a load passing *each and every time*', and on 'every cart, wagon, or sledge passing, laden *or unladen, each and* every time, etc.' The only exemption in the Act is provided in the following clause: 'Provided always, that nothing in this Act contained, shall extend, or be construed to extend, to charge any person or persons, riding through the said county, or going in a coach, chariot, or chaise.'

1. *WN* II. ii. 13 and 86.
2. *But see Lord Lauderdale's *Inquiry*, p. 196 ['The labour of a manufacturing machine ... fixes itself in some vendible commodity, which makes the origin of its profit more apparent than that of circulating capital, whose services, like that of the menial servant, perish at the instant of their performance']. [Since Lauderdale's work was not published until 1804, this note must have been inserted in that year or later.]
3. So marked in the margin; see Doc. 111.
4. *WN* V. i. d. 2 (p. 94) had suggested that public works such as roads and bridges need not be subsidized out of public funds; *WN* V. i. d. 5–6 (p. 96) that by the application of appropriate tolls, the type of public works might be adjusted to the demands of either commerce or the luxury carriage trade; and *WN* V. i. d. 16 (p. 102) that 'in the progress of despotism the authority of the executive power gradually absorbs that of every other power in the state'.
5. *WN* V. i. d. 5: 'When the toll upon carriages of luxury ... is made somewhat higher in proportion to their weight, than upon carriages of necessary use, ... the indolence and vanity of the rich is made to contribute in a very easy manner to the relief of the poor'.

111. Journal

Kinnordy MSS ⟨*Horner*, i. 221–2⟩   London, 2 Apr. 1803

⟨I have now been about a fortnight in London, where I am at length fixed for life. But I have had no leisure to form any immediate plans of study, having been occupied for more than a week with some business before a Committee of the House of Commons. Yesterday I made my first speech in England; the subject was humble, manure, and a turnpike road. Such a committee is not a very formidable audience to address.

⟨I must now set myself to write a few articles for the *Edinburgh Review*, of which engagement I heartily wish I were rid.[1]

⟨…⟩

I am at present living in lodgings with James Brougham, who came with me from Scotland, upon a similar plan of settling in London.[2] His character is now intimately known to me, after long habits of intercourse. He has not the eccentric and powerful genius of Henry, but all his good-temper, much more steadiness, and upon the whole a more amiable and more domestic mind.

1. His only contribution to the next issue, no. iii of Apr. 1803, was apparently a small portion only of a review of Sir John Sinclair's *Essays on Miscellaneous Subjects* (1802), ER ii. 205–111. *Horner*, i. 222, claimed it all for him, but apparently it was mainly Jeffrey's (*Jeffrey*, ii. 73), two pages only being Horner's (Doc. 116).
2. At 27 Northumberland St, off the Strand, while waiting for rooms in the Temple or Lincoln's Inn.

112. To John Horner[1]

BLPES ii. 6–7   27 Northumberland St [London], Monday [4] Apr. 1803

…

In the way of politics, I have hardly any news. War, or peace, is still an undecided question; and nobody pretends to be in the secret, not even Maconochie.[2] Nobody believes that any other person is in the secret, or that there *is* any secret to know. Those who appear to talk most reasonably upon the subject, say there was no occasion for the late alarm, and that there have been no preparations in France which could be intended against this country.[3] The Doctor [Addington] had a mind to show us he was not altogether without spirit and vigour; like other feeble characters, when they are seized by these unlucky fits of resolution, he has bullied very unseasonably. This Doctor sinks every day deeper into disrepute; he is said to want even regularity and promptitude in the routine of ordinary business, and to practise a great deal of that chicane which is usually called in to the assistance of a weak head. Even people in office are not very scrupulous or decent in the way they speak of the Minister. Our Lord Advocate, for instance, declares that, though he must vote on that side as a crown officer, he is determined to give him no other assistance; this is quite agreeable to Hope's best manner of modesty and good sense. But he is enraged, at being left in the lurch, as he richly deserved, about Trotter's punishment.[4] Nothing could be more injudicious than the attempt to screen him.

…

1. Horner's father. His brother John had died the previous October.
2. Alexander Maconochie, afterwards Maconochie-Welwood, Lord Meadowbank (1777–1861: *DNB*).

3. War was, however, resumed on 18 May.
4. The Lord Advocate was Charles Hope, afterwards Lord Granton (1763–1851: *DNB*). James Trotter had been committed to Newgate for not attending a committee inquiring into the Dunfermline election despite Hope's plea on 28 Mar. for clemency.

113. Notes on Smith's *Wealth of Nations*

Kinnordy MSS   7 Apr. 1803

61. (I. p. 144)[1] According to the evidence of Mr Thornton before the Secret Committee of the House of Commons, p. 143., the average amount of the paper of Scotland was conjectured to be some one million two hundred thousand pounds, to one million five hundred thousand; the amount of gold about 60 thousand of which 50 [was] usually in circulation; the quantity of silver might perhaps amount to the same sum.

62. (I. 324)[2] I presume this is extremely vague. Wheatley, in his Essay on Currency and Commerce, p. 70,[3] estimates the consumption of London at three times this amount, and of the rest of the kingdom at only the same sum, making in all two hundred and fifty thousand pounds.

63. (II. p. 142 and p. 147)[4] I wish he had entered a little more specifically into the actual history of the mercantile system. In what country was it first proposed? Did it prevail gradually, or was it adopted at once? Was it long a tenet of speculative men, before it influenced legislative practice?

The prejudice that money constitutes national wealth is natural, and the policy of accumulating treasure, by prohibiting its exportation and by encouraging the importation of it, was obvious and coarse. On the other hand, the doctrine of the balance of trade, and of the circuitous means which that theory recommends for the accumulation of treasure, is somewhat refined and artificial, and involves a process of reasoning, which is by no means obvious. It is probable, on this account, that there was a struggle, before the theory of the Balance of Trade got the better of that more obvious policy, which adopts *direct* expedients for the accumulation of treasure. It might be curious enough to trace, in the different commercial countries of Europe, the circumstances of such a struggle; and to trace the conquest of an ingenious though false theory over a vulgar and strong prejudice, to the individual minds by whose efforts it was accomplished.

In some of the most commercial countries, the conquest, perhaps, is not yet completed. In the Statute Book of England, the prohibitions still remain against the exportation of our own coin. What is this, but a vestige of that old prejudice which subsisted before the mercantile system was promulgated?

In tracing the history of the mercantile system, according to the foregoing hint, it will not be difficult to introduce a notice of such individuals (they were very few), as looked beyond both the established prejudices of their times, and the more refined errors that were nearly coming into fashion. How much greater force of mind does it require to guard against the latter, than to overcome the former! Sir Dudley North[5] seems to have been one of those who, in this particular, avoided both errors. Mr Rice Vaughan, perhaps, is a good instance of those who saw the falsehood of the vulgar prejudice, but did not discriminate the fallacy of the new theory.

64. (II. 165)[6] The phrase *rude produce* is used here in too restricted a sense. It is quite true, I believe, that few countries produce much more *food* than what is sufficient for the subsistence of their own inhabitants. But unless many countries produced much more *rude produce* than what is sufficient for domestic consumption, there would be but little foreign trade.

1. *WN* I. ix. 14–15 compares the condition of various countries. Cf. the 'Third Report from the [Commons] Committee of Secrecy appointed to examine and state the Total Amount of Outstanding Demands on the Bank of England; and the Restriction on Payments in Cash', ordered to be printed 21 Apr. 1797.
2. *WN* I. xi. 30:
   > In the manufactures of Birmingham alone, the quantity of gold and silver annually employed in gilding and plating, and thereby disqualified from ever afterwards appearing in the shape of those metals, is said to amount to more than fifty thousand pounds sterling.
3. The *Remarks on currency and commerce* published in 1803 by John Wheatley (1772–1830), lawyer and political economist, were notable for their criticism of monetary expansion by the Bank of England, contending that exchange fluctuations were due exclusively to domestic price changes and that the Bank could therefore control prices and thus exchange rates through its credit policies.
4. *WN* IV. i. 5–7 and 10 outlined the mercantilist policies of England and France and the objections made to them by merchants and bankers.
5. Sir Dudley North (1641–91: *DNB*), an early advocate of Free Trade and author of a tract on *Currency*.
6. *WN* IV. i. 30: 'Few countries produce much more rude produce than what is sufficient for the subsistence of their own inhabitants.'

114. To Francis Jeffrey

BLPES ii. 12–13   [London],[1] 19 Apr. 1803

... The word *Review* never strikes my eye or ear, without heating and reddening my face; but it has proved indeed quite impossible for me to write while I have been in London.[2] I might have scrawled out a few paltry articles; and I read two or three books with that intention, but I had not courage to undertake work so unworthy of my associates. It is now, however, idle to apologize; all I can do is to promise some degree of reparation. I mean to write a *great deal* for No. 4th; and I have bought one or two books for the purpose. A tract on *Currency and Commerce*, by Wheatley (a young lawyer) is the only one I have yet [met] with which I think worth notice. Any others I hear of, I shall name to you; that I may not interfere with what is allotted to any other person. I have not yet heard much about our *Review*; though most of the literary people whom I meet appear to have read it. One person, a very good judge, mentioned to me, that we were generally thought to have fallen off in our second number. We had too little of Jeffrey in it. Longman, however, seems well pleased with the sale; which of course is all he cares or knows about it.

I have been thinking a great deal of that part of your letter, in which you allude to a more permanent connection.[3] There is a great deal of time yet, before it can be necessary to come to a resolution upon that point; and as I have not quite reflected as much upon the matter as I wish, I will defer saying any thing about it. I trust you will consider it very deeply. It is a point of most essential consequence to your future plans. I shall endeavour to examine it as candidly as I should for myself; and my dear Jeffrey, I will certainly communicate my opinion to you with the most faithful confidence. Murray and I have talked a little about it; it gives him much anxiety; I am sure there are not three men on earth who are more solicitous for the success of each other.

I hope you have taken some pains with your review of Gentz – the book has a very high character here. So has the author, who passed about two months in London last winter. He was formerly in the Prussian service, and [is] now in the Austrian – the civil service, I mean. Mackintosh told me, he appeared to be well read in the metaphysical writers of this island; he was originally a Kantian, but is now a sceptic. His first literary performance was a translation of Burke's *Reflections* into German.[4]

Who is to review Dumont? It should be done most undoubtedly. I hope Thomson will undertake it. I have met him, and am highly taken with his conversation; he is a very general scholar, extremely good-humoured, and has lived with a great many of those men who have within the last fifteen years made most noise in the world. With the vivacity of a Parisian, he has the plainness and apparent honesty which are more characteristic of England.[5]

I hope, my Dear Jeffrey, you will write me very frequently. It costs you no difficulty. I can now *read* perfectly well – and it will afford me much pleasure to send you all the literary or political news that I think may be interesting. You are one of the greatest losses I have suffered, in leaving Edinburgh, which even already I begin to look back to *cum desideris*. For the last six years, I lived with more happiness than I am entitled to expect again; and with as much profit, as my unconquerable indolence would permit me to take. You were one of my chief masters and improvers; I shall ever consider you as such, and love you on that account over and above every other. Remember me kindly to Mrs Jeffrey, and believe me ever most truly yours.

[PS] Mackintosh is made Recorder of Bombay – about £6,000 a year – he leaves England in July. He is to publish very soon his speech for Peltier; that is to say, he is to revise the short-hand writer's notes.[6]

1. Horner actually wrote 'Edinburgh'.
2. See Jeffrey to Horner, 1 Apr. (*Jeffrey*, ii. 67–8).
3. As editor of the *ER*.
4. Jeffrey's review of *Etat de l'Europe* (1802), by Friedrich von Gentz (1764–1832), appeared in *ER* ii (no. iii, Apr. 1803), 1–30. Aspinall, New, and the *WI* all err in referring to a later review by Brougham, in *ER* ix (no. xviii, Jan. 1807), 253–78, as though it were of the same work; Brougham's was in fact of Peltier's English translation of Gentz's *Fragments upon the Balance of Power in Europe* (1806). Gentz's translation of Burke had appeared at Berlin in 1793.
5. Horner was introduced to Pierre Etienne Louis Dumont (1759–1829), the Swiss editor of Bentham's writings, at John Whishaw's chambers on the morning of 3 Apr. (*Horner*, i. 222). After much dithering on the part of Thomas Thomson and Horner (Docs 120 and

126), Jeffrey reviewed Dumont's version of *Traités de Législation Civile et Pénale [et] Principes de Législation* (3 vols, Paris, 1802) in *ER* iv (no. vii, Apr. 1804), 1–26 (*WI*).
6. The review of Mackintosh's 'Trial of John Peltier, Esq., for a Libel Against Napoleon Bonaparte', *ER* ii (no. iv, July 1803), 476–84, was written by Horner (*WI*).

115. Notes on Smith's *Wealth of Nations*

Kinnordy MSS   6 May 1803

65. (II. 213)[1] J. Vanderlint says, p. 29, that the course of exchange 'is a *certain Rule* to know when the Ballance of Trade is for or against us with any Nation'.[2] – The history of opinions upon this point might be curious. Hume does not appear to have been aware of all the sources of error, which are here pointed out by Smith.

1. WN IV. iii. a. 4, argued that there was 'no certain criterion' by which to determine on which side the balance of trade lay and that both the most frequently cited criteria, custom-house books and the course of exchange, were 'very uncertain'.
2. The emphasis in this quotation – which appears in a footnote of Vanderlint's – is Horner's.

116. To Francis Jeffrey

BLPES ii. 14–15   London, 11 May 1803

...

I got your third number some days ago, but have had no time to read it, except in the most cursory manner. A great many people have been inquiring about it; when they have had time to express their opinions, I will endeavour to collect them for your amusement. In the mean time, I will mention what occurred to myself in my very hasty perusal. On the partition of Poland, you have done what I wished, to neutralize Brougham's poison; and your estimate of Cowper's merits and demerits is admirable.[1] I am upon the whole not quite so well pleased with your execution of the XXVIth art., though the train of opinions and criticisms is very consonant, as you know, to my own; there are some charming touches of expression, though sometimes 'disclosing a brave neglect'; but my chief objection is to the effect of the whole composition as a piece, which seems to me rather too elaborate, massive, and overloaded.[2] Brougham has been somewhat savage in his torturing of Ritson, and more than somewhat filthy;[3] so stupid and unnoticed a pamphlet, as *Guineas an Incumbrance*, hardly deserved 16 pages.[4] There is greater candour and good sense in the article upon the Egyptian Expedition; but I was a good deal surprised at the account of *Delphine*, which I have not read indeed, but have heard praised by some good judges.[5] It has been described to me, by people who have observed French manners, as containing some excellent sketches of Parisian society; and as abounding with specimens of that rapid and fervid eloquence, which distinguishes Mad. de Staël in conversation. All this may be unmerited panegyric, and our critic may by chance be in the right: for there was surely an unpardonable error in reviewing such a work through a translation. He [the translator] seems to have been quite unaware of the personal satire which runs through the novel; Talleyrand, one of the author's former lovers, is said to be happily caricatured in the figure of an old woman. I do not like – (now, my dear Jeffrey, do not think of my eyebrows as of old)[6] – but I do not like Brown's wit upon Dr Gall; and still less the unseasonable and inefficient levity of the gentleman (to me unknown) who has criticized Pinel; books of science should be censurèd, if they require it, in the tone of science, and not with such efforts of wit as might perhaps succeed in a party at a round game.[7] In your next letter, give me a list of the several authors; I am puzzled with Shepherd's *Poggio*, and I have no desire to be introduced to the *rédacteur* of *Charles et Marie*.[8] I was a little surprised to find two pages of my writing upon that great subject, Sir John Sinclair; I thought I had burned it, but must have left it by accident in the book: there is an absurd incongruity in the transition to your style from mine, from my formality to your ease and vivacity – like the change from a dead march to the jig-step; like – but you will furnish such similes as may be proper for the occasion.[9] I was glad to see the judicious praise of Prof. Dalzel;[10] we shall be rewarded, in the next edition, with a niche among his worthies. ...

You will call all these my remarks fastidious, and caustic, and *supercilious*; they are intended only for you, and I beg you will keep them to yourself. I dare say, many of them may be unjustly severe. But I was once an Edinburgh Reviewer.

Some few books have lately appeared, which ought to be noticed next time. I have desired Longman to send down Darwin's *Temple of Nature*, Dallas's *History of the Maroons*, De Lille's *Malheur et Pitié*, and Carnot's *Géometrie de Position*. I wish *you* would take both the poems; because each of them presents a good opportunity for a general criticism, such as none of us but yourself are qualified to give. Neither De Lille nor Darwin has yet received any public estimate of their poetical character; they are both good subjects for a picture, and their portraits will be suitable companions to those of Cowper and the school of Southey.[11] Carnot's new work appears to me of very great importance, and should be reviewed with no common care; it opens a new view of mathematical analysis, and will probably effect a beneficial change in the mode of stating the fundamental and elementary principles of that branch of logic. Carnot's book contains a general investigation of that subject, which Mr Ivory has touched very neatly, but superficially, in his review of Woodhouse's paper on negative quantities.[12] If Mr Playfair could be induced to undertake this article, a communication from him would be invaluable; I have reason to know that he has of late turned his attention very much to the same subject.

I meant to have written a great deal to you upon the subject, which at present more than almost any other interests me; the proposals made to you, of a permanent connection with the *Review*; but I have already proved so tedious, that I must again defer this till another time. Let me have your own thoughts about it; I can only give the impression that results from all my reflections, which is strongly, I had almost said *decidedly against* the proposal. I am sure that better and more conspicuous exertions are destined for you, if you will be true to yourself. But I will very soon take an opportunity of entering more at large into my various reasons and views.

...

1. The references are to Jeffrey's reviews of Gentz and of Hayley's *Life of Cowper* in *ER* ii (no. iii, Apr. 1803), 1–30 and 64–86.

2. This would seem to suggest that Jeffrey had at least amended, if not actually written, the review of Stewart's *Account of Dr Robertson* in *ER* ii (no. iii, Apr. 1803), 229–49, afterwards claimed by Brougham. The Kinnordy set attributes it unequivocally to Brougham. (Cf. *WI* and Doc. 120.)

3. So the MS appears to read; but possibly Horner wrote 'filschy', a Scottish word that would seem to imply that the article was padded out.

4. Brougham reviewed [Henry Boase's] *Guineas an Incumbrance on Commerce* and Joseph Ritson's *Essay on abstinence from animal food* (1802) in *ER* ii (no. iii, Apr. 1803), 101–116 and 128–36 (*WI*).

5. The reviews of the accounts of the Egyptian expedition and of Madame de Staël's *Delphine* in *ER* ii (no. iii, Apr. 1803), 53–64 and 172–7, were by Sydney Smith (*WI*).

6. Horner's full eyebrows had been a subject of jest among his set in Edinburgh; apparently his physiology was such that they betrayed his view of subjects of conversation, and Smith often referred to Horner as 'the Knight of the Shaggy Eyebrows'. (See Reid, *Sydney Smith*, p. 107.)

7. Thomas Brown had reviewed Charles F.R. de Villers, *Sur une Nouvelle Théorie du Cerveau* [Dr Gall's], and Henry Reeve Philippe Pinel, *Traité ... sur l'aliénation mentale* (Paris, [1801]) in *ER* ii (no. iii, April 1803), 147–60 and 160–72 (*WI*).

8. The reviews of William Shepherd's *Life of Poggio Bracciolini* (1802), and of Mme de Souza's *Charles et Marie*, in *ER* ii (no. iii, Apr. 1803), 42–53 and 184–91, were respectively by Brougham and Edward Percival and by Thomas Brown (*WI*).

9. See Doc. 111.

10. The review of Andrew Dalzel, *Collectanea Græca Majora*, in *ER* ii (no. iii, Apr. 1803), 211–15, was by William Stevenson and Thomas Wright (*WI*).

11. Robert Charles Dallas's *History of the Maroons* (1803) was reviewed by Brougham, and Erasmus Darwin's *The Temple of Nature, or the Origin of Society* (1803) by Thomas Thomson, in *ER* ii (no. iv, July 1803), 376–91 and 491–506. De Lille's *Malheur et Pitié* was reviewed by Jeffrey in iii (no. v, Oct. 1803), 26–42. (*WI*.)

12. Although he does not appear in Horner's 'Key', James (afterwards Sir James) Ivory (1765–1842: *DNB*), rather than Brougham, seems therefore to have been the author of the review of Robert Woodhouse, *The principles of Analytical Calculation* (Cambridge, 1803) in *ER* i (no. ii, Jan. 1803), 407–412. Lazare Carnot's *Géometrie de position* (Paris, [1803]) was not reviewed.

117. To Thomas Thomson

BLPES ii. 18–19 ⟨*Horner*, i. 224–6⟩   London, Monday evening [23 May 1803][1]

...

⟨I have inquired about Bentham's tracts, of which you wish to have a collection.⟩ But ⟨they are very scarce; I have only been able to get one. I shall not, however, despair of success; as I shall soon have a footing, if I go on, in every bookseller's shop and stall in and about London.⟩ I have met with one or two things in our way; Turgot's letters on Grain, a copy of Jacob Vanderlint, etc. Bentham has very lately circulated, but not published, two letters addressed to Lord Pelham, on the subject of

Botany Bay; from a review of Collins's book he draws a conclusion decidedly hostile to the continuation of that expensive system of punishment; and the best judges that I have met with here, consider his reasonings as invincible.[2] Bentham is a very singular character, but only to be known by description, he lives so reclusely; I have learned a great many particulars of him from George Wilson, who has lived with him very intimately for 30 years, and is the only person that now sees any thing of him. He told me an anecdote of Dumont's publication, which you will think singular; by far the greatest number of copies, no less than 300, were sold to *Spain*; scarcely any in this country.

I have not seen many new books of late; as to England, I begin to lose all hopes of seeing any thing new. There is nothing but bad poetry and politics. There is a work on commercial policy by M. Simond of Geneva, into which I have hardly had time to look; but it appears to be well done in some parts, at least as to the conclusions adopted and the tone of thinking; and considering the First Consul's creed in political economy, there is more praise than even a Frenchman can usually claim, in being liberal.[3] I am at present reading an historical sketch of the French revolution by Lacrételle, which I do not hesitate to recommend to you as extremely well done, particularly in what relates to the views and operations of the parties in the Legislative Assembly.[4] The style has very considerable merit; and some of the pictures are executed with great power.

‹I have seen a good deal of Mackintosh, since I came to London; he is at present quite full of his expedition to the East, and of his schemes of study there. He carries out such a library with him as never, I presume, was known in Asia; for his plans of metaphysical and political reading, it is admirably selected. He has fortunately no desire to make himself particularly acquainted with either the language or the antiquities of Hindostan; but he has got permission from the Board of Control and Directors to circulate, under their authority, statistical and political queries among all the servants of the Company in the different establishments. This may produce a little. In a few days the author of *Vindiciæ Gallicæ* is to receive the honour of knighthood!

‹You are indebted for this letter to a severe disappointment I met with this evening, in not getting into the House of Commons. A great display is expected, on account chiefly of the nicety and various embarrassments under which the question must present itself to more than one of the parties.[5] They are now in the very heat and pride of the debate; twelve o'clock. After waiting all the morning, I got no farther than the door of the gallery. Every body here seems to be of one mind as to the justice of the war, in respect of the case (as we lawyers may call it) that this country can make out against Bonaparte; but the *policy* of war at the present juncture is a different question, of which people take various views.

‹The old Opposition party held a meeting last night to discuss their plans; I learned a few particulars of it. Fox spoke with great moderation, expressed his anxiety for the preservation of peace, but acknowledged the difficulties of the conjuncture. He had to submit to the folly of some of his associates. Would you imagine that that great statesman Lord Suffolk[6] embraced this seasonable occasion of giving Fox a formal lecture upon some improprieties of his former conduct; beginning with the coalition, and ending with the evidence of Maidstone. This was meant merely as friendly advice. Sheridan was so drunk, that the first time he spoke he was unintelligible; he afterwards became more articulate, and dwelt a good deal upon the danger of throwing the Doctor, by too severe an attack, into the arms of Pitt. This idea I find very prevalent among many of the friends and partisans of the old Opposition. But Fox's observation was more manly; that they were bound to expose those errors and weaknesses of which they were convinced, and were not entitled to practise an over-cautious and temporizing forbearance upon a calculation of any contingencies. ...⟩

1. The date 24 May 1803 has been inserted and the letter is so franked. Possibly it was begun so late in the evening that it was re-dated and posted the following day.
2. Jeremy Bentham's *Letters to Lord Pelham on Penal Colonisation* were published that same year. The second volume of Lt Col. David Collins's *Account of the English Colony of New South Wales* (2 vols, 1798–1802), was reviewed by Sydney Smith in *ER* ii (no. iii, Apr. 1803), 30–42.
3. Jean Charles Léonard Simonde de Sismondi, *De la richesse commerciale; ou Principes d'économie politique, appliqués à la législation du commerce* (2 vols, Geneva, 1803).
4. J.C.D. de Lacrételle's *Précis historique de la révolution française* was completed in collaboration with J. P. Rabaut de Saint-Etienne (6 vols, Paris, 1801–1806). (See Doc. 120.)
5. Robert Banks Jenkinson, Lord Hawkesbury and afterwards 2nd Earl of Liverpool (1770–1828: *DNB*), had as Secretary for Foreign Affairs moved for an address to the King relative to the termination of discussions with France. On 20 May Horner had told Murray (*Horner*, i. 223) that he would attempt to attend in company with Mackintosh and Seymour and had added that he was 'studying this very critical and momentous question with as much anxiety, as I ever investigated any point of mere speculation; a trouble which I have hitherto very seldom taken with any of my political opinions'.
6. Gen. John Howard, 15th Earl of Suffolk (1739–1820).

118. Notes of my progress in studying the system of the Economists

Kinnordy MSS   24 May 1803

36. In *one* sense, we may say that *Land* is the only source of wealth; in *another* sense we may say that *labour* is the only source of wealth; but, since these two senses are different in kind, I do not think we may say, that the produce of 'land and labour' constitutes wealth.

37. It is quite true, as the Economists have asserted, that the number of manufacturers, etc. must be proportioned to the surplus food which remains over and above the subsistence of the actual cultivators and cannot increase beyond that surplus. But let that surplus be considered as a fixed quantity, and the number of manufacturers, etc. of course fixed likewise, the wealth of this actual population will vary with the effective industry of these manufacturers, etc., will increase as that industry becomes more effective, and will diminish when it becomes less effective. In this point of view, it would even appear, that no augmentation of the surplus subsistence can *permanently*[1] augment the relative wealth of the actual population, because that increase of surplus will encourage an addition of numbers and will be

absorbed by that addition. If such be the state of the case, it would seem to follow, that though subsistence is one part of national wealth (and in the order of necessity must be considered as the first part), yet in the relative wealth of a state it forms a fixed portion incapable of augmentation. An increase of surplus food adds no doubt to the absolute wealth; but it is relative wealth only, or the ratio of absolute wealth to population, which in the present discussion is to be considered.

Population itself is not wealth. An increase of population, under certain circumstances, indicates a previous addition to absolute wealth, and has[2] in truth the effect of levelling relative wealth to its former point. An increase of population, with the co-operation of other causes, may lead indirectly to the increase of relative wealth. In this manner, an increase of surplus subsistence may indirectly lead to an increase of relative wealth.

As an increase of surplus food leads directly to an increase of population, it is not improbable that this fact may have in some degree influenced the Economists in forming their conclusion, that the increase of wealth depends upon the increase of surplus food; because they were by no means free of the prejudice, which attaches so much importance to an increase in the numbers of the people.

38. With a view to investigate the classification which the Economists have made of the different kinds of labourers, we may consider, *first*, the proprietors of raw produce as distinguished from those who vary its form or prepare it for use; *secondly*, the producers of subsistence as distinguished from the producers and manufacturers of articles of less immediate necessity; *thirdly*, (if there is ground for such a distinction), those producers and manufacturers who add to the quantity of consumable produce as distinguished from the manufacturers who only alter the form of produce already existing.

The respective influence of each of these classes, by their industry, upon the absolute and upon the relative wealth of the nation, must be carefully considered.

1. *[Presumably Horner intended to make a note or insertion here but never did so.]
2. *[Presumably Horner intended to make a note or insertion here but never did so.]

119. Notes on Smith's *Wealth of Nations*

Kinnordy MSS   26 May 1803

66. (I. 75)[1] Wherever the land has been at all improved, that is, where a certain portion of moveable capital has been fixed on it, the *rent* received by the landlord may be considered as composed in part of the *profit* of that stock. This remark suggested to me by Simonde, *De la richesse commerciale*, I. p. 42.

67. (I. p. 326) 'Liv. VIII §42 des premières éditions; mais l'auteur a supprimé ce détail dans la seconde publication du même ouvrage, qu'il a fait en 1780.' Garnier.[2]

68. (I. p. 326) 'Liv. IX, 154 des premières éditions. Dans celle publiée en 1780, cette évaluation se trouve réduite de près de moitié. Voyez cette édition, Liv. IX 123.' Garnier.

69. (I. p. 106)[3] Bishop Berkeley mentions, *Misc.*, p. 102,[4] that 'in *Holland* a child five years old is maintained by its own labour.' I wish Smith had borrowed more illustrations, in this part of his work, from the State of Holland.

70. (II. p. 84)[5] If the question with respect to the expediency of primogeniture be considered in an enlarged political view, and especially in reference to our own country, the solution is not quite obvious.

In considering the effects of it, whether good or bad, we are not to limit our attention to the mere rule of law, which operates with respect to real property in the cast of intestacy. If this were the whole of the institution, its influence would be trifling; overruled (as it is) by the power of devise, and restricted in its operation to real property which bears so small a proportion to the mass of moveable wealth. But besides the rule of feudal law, we view as a part of the actual and subsisting institution, the prejudice and practice of the country in giving a preference to the elder male branch, even in exerting the prerogative of devise, and that with respect to personalty as well as land.

It may be a question of very nice determination, whether this prejudice has not in some measure contributed to maintain that body of landed proprietors, which form a large and efficient branch of the democracy in this country.

A number of pleasing views have often been given of the effect of gavelkind in Kent; I should like to ascertain what degree of truth there is in these. Personal observation and inquiries must furnish this light.

[6]A general review of the laws and prejudices of the rest of Europe, in this respect, would probably be a source of many new conclusions.

On this, as on the whole subject of landed property, the institutions of China would probably be a source of many new conclusions.

71. (II. 216)[7] In addition to these two illustrations of this important remark, may be stated the effect which resulted, to the price of bullion and rate of foreign exchange, from the extended issue of paper by the Bank of England during the restrictions. This is very cleverly made out by Lord King, in his excellent pamphlet upon this subject.[8]

1. WN I. vi. 9 dealt with the 'real value of all the different component parts of price', in particular labour and rent.

2. Earlier in the year Thomas Thomson had lent Horner Germain Garnier's recent edition (5 vols, Paris, 1802) of the *Wealth of Nations* (Horner to Thomson, 13 Mar., *Thomson*, p. 45). In the notes quoted in this and the next paragraph Garnier had pointed out that one of the authors cited by Smith (WN I. xi. g. 33) as a source of statistics about the import of gold and silver into Spain in the mid-eighteenth century, [Gillaume Thomas François Raynal], A *philosophical and political history of the settlements and trade of the Europeans in the East and West Indies* (Edinburgh, 1771), had substantially changed his estimates in the later French edition published in Geneva in 1780.

3. When writing of the comparative effect in England and America of the increase of population, Smith had stated (WN I. viii. 23: 'The labour of each child [in North American families], before it can leave their house, is computed to be worth a hundred pounds clear gain to them.'

4. George Berkeley, A *miscellany* (1752).

5. WN III. ii. 5–6 described entails as 'the natural consequences of the law of primogeniture' and condemned them as 'absurd'.

6. *What is the prevailing practice, in this respect, in those manufacturing parts of England, where a considerable sub-division of land has taken [?place] in consequence of the

overflowing of commercial capital; such as Lancashire, Norfolk, the West Riding of Yorkshire? – What is the prevailing practice in the devise of personalty, among the merchants of
London, Liverpool, Hull, Bristol, etc.? Information on this subject might be had from
conveyancers.

7. The 'important remark' is probably that on the preceding page, *WN* IV. iii. a. 9: 'the value
of the current coin of every country, compared with that of any other country, is in
proportion not to the quantity of pure silver which it ought to contain, but to that which it
actually does contain.'

8. *Another striking instance is given by Mr Foster in his tract upon Commercial Exchanges.
See his account of the adulteration of the Turkish piastre, p. 94. [This note must be of a
later date since John Leslie Foster's *Essay on the Principle of Commercial Exchanges* was not
published until 1804 and of a date after 3 Oct. of that year when Horner confessed he had
still not read it (Doc. 176). Lord King's *Thoughts on the restriction of payments in specie* was
first published in 1803; a second, enlarged edition with additional remarks on coinage was
published under a slightly different title in 1804.]

120. To Francis Jeffrey

BLPES ii. 20–21 ⟨New, p. 17⟩   London, 30 May 1803

... I consider myself bound by every consideration to furnish some articles for the
next No.; and I will endeavour to make out the 32 pages, which you demand as the
minimum of my contribution.[1] The books I mean to give an account of are these:
Garnier's translation of the *Wealth of Nations*, and Simonde's new publication *De la
Richesse Commerciale* – these will give me an opportunity of making some
observations on the fundamental principles of the Economists. The book, which I
brought up from Edinburgh, *Sur le Commerce de la France*, will furnish a good
occasion for making some strictures on the present policy of the Consul in that
respect, to which my attention has been more particularly directed by some speeches
published in the *Moniteur*, and by the Statistical Surveys drawn up by the Prefects of
the different departments.[2] Lord King has just published a sensible pamphlet on the
restriction of the Bank payments, the substance of the speeches he lately made in
Parliament; this I shall give some account of.[3] All these, you see, are in the line of
Political Economy; to which I wish very much to confine myself; the reviewing of
such tracts serves me a double purpose. I should like to add to these a criticism of a
short history of the French Revolution by Lacrételle, which I mentioned in a letter
to Thomson; it is not much in my way, as I am as yet very ignorant of the secret
history of that great event, but it would be a good exercise for me to make the
attempt.[4] I have thus, you see, made a large promise, to the performance of which I
mean to set myself immediately; and for your next number, I will at least accomplish
it to the extent of 30 pages. I have a very great desire to try Dumont, or rather to
examine his book with a view to ascertain whether I could venture to review it; it
would be a most useful exercise, and forms a great subject.[5] This, however, I shall at
all events postpone, till I have got through some work, in which I can more easily
rely upon myself. In deliberating about your acceptance of the editorship, we were
kept in a state of hesitation by very different views; I dwelt almost solely upon
professional considerations, which you appear to have slighted in comparison of

effects with regard to station and respectability, to which I can allow no weight at all. If the *Review* continues to maintain that character, with which it set out, for independence and candour, the respected editor of it must hold a highly respectable station in literature; such as was formerly filled by Le Clerc, and by Bayle a much greater name.[6] To preserve this tone and temper, it will no doubt be necessary for you, in the exercise of your monarchical discretion, to correct a great many irregularities which were unavoidable under our democratical constitution; such as undue severity, disproportioned criticism, and injudicious selection. I may be of some use to you in this particular, by conveying to you faithfully such remarks as are often made in my hearing by persons who know nothing of my connection with the work. For instance, I have heard many of the best judges, and favourers of us, reprobate most decidedly and warmly the side-blow in the review of Stewart against Currie's *Memoirs of Burns*.[7] But on this very important subject we must frequently interchange our thoughts; I am convinced that a Review (maintained in that spirit of candour and temperance, of which I heard Mackintosh call the critique of Mounier[8] a *chef d'œuvre*), would not only secure an immense circulation, but would gain a valuable reputation to its author, and have a most beneficial influence on the literature of the day. There is more good sense, liberality, and candour in the public mind, ignorant and prejudiced as it is, than such satirists as Brougham and Sydney Smith are willing to imagine. ⟨With regard to Brougham, I had suspected what you tell me, from a letter he wrote me some days ago in which he throws out indirect[9] hints and threats of a *rival* review and an *opposition*.⟩ He did not venture, or did not condescend, to communicate any notice to me unreservedly. You may easily believe that no proposals from that quarter upon such an undertaking would have received any countenance from me. Nothing ties me to your *Review*, but my engagement, and your editorship; for it interferes with my other plans of study. I shall certainly never have to do with any other. ⟨I do not want to know anything more particularly about Brougham's intrigues, for I have no interest in such pitiful anecdotes, and I do not wish to have any⟩ further ⟨reason to think more lowly of Brougham in some respects, than I have been forced to do for some time past, in spite of old habits of intimacy.⟩ I have bought his book, but have not yet read it, and shall not probably have leisure for such an undertaking for a considerable time. In your next number, if you can do with only half of his promised 50 pages, so much the better. As I am quite confidential with you, it is as well to mention, that when I write to Brougham (which I have never done yet and may not for some time) I shall not take any notice of that opposition for which he confederated. Unless I can be useful in composing differences, I do not want to hear any thing about the occasional quarrels that may take place among my old friends; at this distance from them, it is a comfort, of which I am not willing to deprive myself, if I can fancy them still as in former days unanimous and united. I am equally mortified and astonished at what all of you write me about Brown; I wish to heaven he were thrown out into the bustle of the world, where he might see the utility of common sense. What a pity, that such acute talents and amiable dispositions should become unprofitable by mismanagement! ...

1. In a letter of 11 May (*Jeffrey*, ii. 69–73) Jeffrey had good-naturedly assigned the 'blunders' of the second number of the *Review* to Horner's omissions and, renewing his plea for contributions, asked Horner to 'Inquire and look about among the literary men and

professed writers of the metropolis, and send us down a list of a few that you think worth ten guineas a sheet, and that will work conscientiously for the money.' The letter also contains Jeffrey's reasoning for being inclined to accept the permanent editorship of the *Review*.

2. The book Horner had brought from Edinburgh was perhaps Jean Blanc de Volx's *Etat commercial de la France au commencement du dix-neuvième siècle; ou, Du commerce français* (3 vols, Paris, 1803), a copy of which is listed as *HL* 128. For the statistical surveys see Doc. 193.

3. Horner's review of King's *Restriction of Payments in Specie* in ER ii (no. iv, July 1803), 402–421, was the only one to appear of those he mentions.

4. The second part of Lacrételle's *Précis*, two volumes on the National Convention (Paris, 1802), was reviewed by Thomas Campbell in ER v (no. x, Jan. 1805), 421–37.

5. In his letter of 11 May Jeffrey noted that Thomson hesitated about reviewing Dumont and beseeched Horner to 'Say positively whether you will do it or not' (*Jeffrey*, ii. 73). (See Doc. 114.)

6. Jean Le Clerc (1657–1736), theologian and man of letters, had been a severe critic of the famous *Historical and Critical Dictionary* of Pierre Bayle (1647–1706).

7. The review of Stewart's *Robertson* (see Doc. 116 n. 2) had contained (p. 233) a contemptuous aside against J. Currie's *Life of Burns*: 'Was it not Mr Stewart who sketched the only striking and living portrait that exists of Burns?'

8. By Jeffrey in the first number of *ER*.

9. Incorrectly transcribed as 'indiscreet' by New.

121. To J.A. Murray

BLPES ii. 24–25 ⟨*Horner*, i. 228–30⟩   London, 11 June 1803

⟨…⟩

Our friend Wm Adam has now commenced practice as a special pleader under the Bar.[1] From his father's connections, there can be no doubt of his success. He has drawn three declarations already. We celebrated this event by a dinner at the Crown and Anchor; four Adams, father and three sons, Loch and James Brougham. … You will be much pleased to learn that James Brougham has got some employment, which may introduce him into a very good line. In the new plan of taxation, there are to be separate bills for Scotland, which must of course be drawn by a solicitor; *Mundel* was proposed to the Treasury, but Mr Lowndes of the Tax Office, who had manufactured all the tax acts and budgets for several years, named Brougham and this experienced financier and legislator has been hard at work for more than a week. I am sure this will give you very sincere pleasure.[2]

⟨I decline Stewart's *Life of Reid*, for more reasons than one. I shall be much disappointed and really chagrined, if Jeffrey does not take it into his own hands.[3] Whateley's [*sic*] book on Currency I should like to reserve for myself; and I will review it, if I think it worth while after Lord King's pamphlet.

⟨I was so unlucky as not to hear the great debate. … By all the accounts I have collected, both Pitt and Fox made a very great display. Pitt's peroration was a complete half hour of his most powerful declamation, not lowered in its tone for a moment; not a particle of all this is preserved in the Report lately published, though said to be done by Canning. Fox's speech was quite of a different cast, and not at all in the tone which he usually adopts; no high notes, no impassioned bursts; but calm, subtle, argumentative pleasantry. He very seldom attempts to keep the house laughing; but in this speech, I understand, it was evidently his design throughout, and Mackintosh says he never heard so much wit. A good many of the points are repeated, none of which are in the newspapers, but I cannot pretend to give you them; I remember, however, the compliment he paid to Pitt's speech, that 'if Demosthenes had been present, he must have admired, and might have envied.'⟩[4]

I agree with you, it would be better that we should not receive payment for our contributions to the next number; and in this point I will be guided entirely by you. As the booksellers have already made a very handsome profit out of us, it would be idle to indulge any false delicacy, that would obstruct or retard Jeffrey's arrangement.[5]

⟨I do not believe there will be any change of ministers, unless some fatal blunder shall render it impossible for them to hold their seats longer. The King has two favourites – the war and the Doctor; but the Doctor has at present the preference, and even the war would be given up for him. Not that I believe there is any personal partiality for him, more than for his successors; but his manners must be delightful at Buckingham House. You would be surprised at Pitt's speech on Fox's motion about Russia;[6] the King had passed him in the park two days before without notice. About the same time Lady Fortescue,⟩ Bogie's ⟨sister, was so coldly and rudely received at court, that none of the ladies of that house attended the birth-day.[7] Such are the important trifles which, when correctly known, throw more light on the state of parties in this country, than all the harangues in Parliament⟩, or the dull discourses of Bob Adair in the *Morning Chronicle*.[8] Let me hear[9] how Brougham's book is liked in Edinburgh, and what his old enemies say of it; nobody here has read it yet. ...

1. William Adam's third son William George (1781–1839) had been a contemporary of James Brougham's at Edinburgh. Unfortunately, in these Documents, Horner refers to both as 'William Adam', and it is not always clear which of them he means.
2. Mundel has not been identified; but William Lowndes (afterwards Lowndes-Stone, 1752–1828), whose brother was married to Brougham's aunt, was a Commissioner of Taxes.
3. Jeffrey reviewed Dugald Stewart's *Account of the Life and Writings of Thomas Reid* (Edinburgh, 1802) in *ER* iii (no. vi, Jan. 1804), 269–87.
4. At this time Horner was studying the art of public speaking very closely. In his papers at Kinnordy is a document in his hand dated June 1803 and entitled 'Models for the art of communicating and popularizing truth'. It is organized into five sections: 'direct models of reasoning on political subjects', under which are the names of Adam Smith, Bentham, Locke, Turgot, Hume, Morellet, and Aristotle as well as a notation that Montesquieu 'rather teaches the art of conceiving political subjects, than of reasoning upon them?'; 'upon moral subjects that have a relation to Politics', under which are the names of Bacon, Stewart, Beccaria, Paley, Smith, and Hume; 'Models of argument the study of which indirectly beneficial', under which are a number of names headed by Milton, Hume, Smith, Buchanan, Erasmus, Grotius, and Bayle; 'Models of *Statement*', under which are the names of Hobbes, Swift, Berkeley, Franklin, and D'Alembert; and 'Indirect Models of reasoning', under which are a number of names headed by Copernicus and Galileo.
5. See Doc. 103.
6. For Pitt's speech of 27 May on Russia's offer of mediation, see *Parl. Hist.*, xxxvi. 1528–32.
7. Lord Grenville's sister Hester was married to Hugh, 1st Earl Fortescue (1753–1841).
8. Sir Robert Adair (1763–1855: *DNB*), diplomatist and friend of Fox.
9. 'Know' according to copy in MS 'Memoirs' at Kinnordy.

122. Notes on Smith's *Wealth of Nations*

Kinnordy MSS   26 June 1803

72. (I. 187)[1] Some curious light has lately been thrown on the history of this and some other similar statutes, in their application to one of our most important manufactures. A concise account of the information to be found, upon this point, in the Evidence before the House of Commons with regard to the woollen Trade of the west of England, must form a curious and valuable addition to this part of Smith's treatise. It would illustrate, also, the manner in which the necessities of commerce overcome and control the imperfections of law. It is probable that similar illustrations might be found in other branches of the manufactures of England.

> 1. WN I. x. c. 9 had examined the inconsistent application of the Statute of Apprentices, eventually abolished in 1813 and 1814. Cf. 'Report from the Committee on Woollen Clothiers Petition', BPP, 1802–1803, v. 243–67.

123. To James Reddie

NLS MSS 3704, ff. 7–8   London, 27 June 1803

I am very sorry to hear from Murray that you have been so much indisposed …

I fear this has retarded the progress of your work on Commercial contracts;[1] but you must really not keep it much longer from us. A general treatise on that subject is certainly much wanted by the profession in both parts of the island. Before you go to the press, I think you might find it of some use to see, for a short period of time, how the thing goes on practically here; and what the actual administration is of commercial law, by the system of London juries, etc.

You remember my prophecy about the other subject, which I have always considered as a much more important undertaking, as well as presenting a much wider field for reputation. The names of Lord Coke and Lord Stair are scarcely known beyond the limits of their respective countries;[2] that of Grotius commands all the lawyers and statesmen within the system of European relations. The question, which has already been debated (if one may use so improper an expression) by two Armed Neutralities, will again be brought forward. I can entertain no doubt that it has at present a very great influence on the diplomatic arrangements of the Northern Courts. It would be singular weakness, indeed, if Prussia and Russia were to overlook the fittest occasion that has ever offered itself, for the urging of their claim. The enlightened and systematic Bernstorff will not forget the bombardment of Copenhagen, or that he was one of the fathers of the measure in 1780.[3]

…

> 1. Reddie's known publications did not begin to appear until 1840 and do not include the work described here. (See Doc. 127.)

2. Sir Edward Coke (1552–1634: *DNB*), commonly known as 'Lord Coke', and James Dalrymple, 1st Viscount Stair (1619–75: *DNB*), were both distinguished jurists.

3. Christian Gunther von Bernstorff (1769–1835) was Danish Foreign Minister at this time; his father, Andreas Peter von Bernstorff, who had been Foreign Minister in 1780, had died in 1797.

124. From Henry Brougham

BLPES ii. 26–9 ⟨New, p. 18⟩   Edinburgh, 27 June 1803

I was sitting down to write to you when I received yours, so that I take credit for my punctuality of correspondence as much as if you had been two letters in my debt. The object of my intended letter was to quicken your reviewing powers by telling you that you are preventing a single article on political economy from being done. Some have come from Longman, but for fear that you may be about the same you must immediately perceive that nobody will venture his labour. From all which I draw two conclusions – first that the No. IV requires your speedy aid, otherwise it must want the whole of the above department, and next, that in future you ought as soon as conveniently you can, to make your election of articles in order that those you reject may be put in other hands. The truth of these positions must be quite obvious to you.

The more general subject of the *Review* requires a little commentary. Soon after my last to you (which if I remember was chiefly on the ill blood that then was clotting us) the matter came to open rupture, and I resigned. My reason was plain and I believe admitted by every one to be just, though it was needless to explain it. But Dupuis – for self and Allen – joined me, as did all our correspondents, so that the authors of 160 pp. of No. III were off.[1] I need not add, that from the beginning (in March 1802) I had perceived the existence of certain exceptions against myself, and had also discovered very plainly the Reverend quarter whence these came.[2] My friendship of Jeffrey (the most concerned) induced me to contribute and say nothing, though my backwardness at first must have been very apparent. But I soon observed that the same personal exceptions continued most indecorously to weigh, even after I had been the *immediate* supporter of the work for two numbers. I need not add that by supporter, I only mean, contributor of a certain no. of pp. necessary to the work within a given time. No one values the qualities of those contributions more lightly than I do myself, with the exception of the long article on Ségur.[3] I write them easily and care not a d—n about them. But still it appeared to me singular that one to whom the review was indebted for nothing but its worst parts, should have so much weight, and equally strange that the principle *Sic vos non vobis* should be recognized to the length of cyphers like T. Thomson counting more than those who had rounded the runs. I could not think of continuing in an unacknowledged capacity – only consulted when so many pp. were required within a certain no. of hours, and then *worked out* with very little ceremony. My ideas of the infinite unimportance of the concern being exactly like your own, I thought a quick cutting of the knot, the safest method and most likely to prevent coolness. But Jeffrey would not let me off thus, and the Bookseller made a splatter, so to the former I gave a full explanation, and he behaved as he always must – he cannot help it – with infinite honour and candour and every thing that is admirable and amiable. My requests were *explanation* and *concession*. The former he gave on the spot, and it confirmed every one guess that I had made regarding the internal structure of the junto. The latter he also gave in its full extent, for indeed he declared he should have nothing more to do with it if I did not recall my resignation. This concession was, that Allen should be assumed for editor of the scientific department and that Smith should be told in plain terms, that from the beginning to the end I had as much the management as if I had been formally considered one of the set. But, indeed, I did not wish to make the Parson say any thing, because I agreed with them *all* in considering my victory over him most complete. It is singular that he should himself be the person of the whole most remarkable for *indiscretions* of every sort – he has actually monopolized that commodity. I shall only add, that ⟨the most perfect good humour has all along subsisted between us two – a constant interchange of visits and walks and letters, while in our reviewing capacity we have been reviling each other, I dare to say, as cordially as if we had been poets, or players, or women⟩, or whatever is most given to bilious discharges. Jeffrey is too much on the conciliatory system. Murray and Smith and I are very angry at him for giving up Darwin to T. Thomson, who did *not* write [the review of Southey's] *Thalaba*.⁴ But, to make up for it, Jeffrey has reviewed the answer to Playfair,⁵ much to my discontent, for I detest, or rather despise ineffably, the *smattering* system. The objection made to the above work by all adepts is, that it is *written* with a useless knowledge of chemistry and a fatal ignorance of mineralogy. To this must now be added, that it is reviewed with a consummate ignorance of both the one and the other, although that deficiency will be wonderfully concealed and perhaps tolerably counter-balanced. I don't flatter you when I declare that more than *any* other the impending No. needs *your* aid. This much I was forced to say of the review, to rectify some mistakes which my last seems to have led you into. You never thought more lightly of the whole affair than I did, and still do (unless the money part of it, which my late calamity renders some little object to me).⁶ But when you say you don't see the use of being headman of a village, etc. you are *wrong*. Always be headman of your own village, unless you are thereby prevented from getting to the head of a larger town or city. But I admit your principle to apply in the case of the review, because being headman infers a salary and the married people ought to get all such things.

I thank you for your intentions of studying my book – pray communicate the result, and '*don't spare us, Good Lord.*' I am not surprised at people being *interested with the details of so very curious a subject,* nor at their thinking the composition hasty on the former point. I take the liberty of saying that there does not appear to me to be a single fact stated for its own sake, from beginning to end, and I particularly recommend to you in proof of this the III section of Book I and the two first parts of that section, because those appear prima facie to be the most seminal and yet I dare to say, they are altogether one exemplification of the two first sections. I thought it right to call your attention *thither*, because I rather used to consider your habits as somewhat too averse to details, and suspected you might pass over the above *portions of writ* without imagining they contained any points of *doctrine*. In the whole book, I have confined my *severity* to two classes of people – *sentimentalists* and *men of detail*, or as they are called, *'good plain matter of fact men.'* When they come in my way I cannot resist giving a solid[?] cut. So you see it is not in the *principle* that we differ here. With respect to the *haste*, I shall be very frank with you, as I was t'other day with Dugald [?Stewart], who was very inquisitive about this matter. Part of the beginning (on colonial character, etc.) was composed rather carelessly, after all the rest, but the subject was quite familiar, being in fact the result of *the whole*, as you may perceive. Part of Section III (Spanish and Portuguese policy) B[ook] I was *written* in greater haste, but all the materials were long concocted, as must appear from the nature of the subject. None of the first Book, except these parts, can plead *haste* in excuse of its composition. The fault (I admit its existence) belongs to the Speculative, the Parliament House, etc. If a compliment did not lurk in the word I should as a fact state that the rest of the first book was very elaborate, even in the mere writing. You will find some of it even *stiff*. I mean in the sense of mathematical readers, but that is the nature of the subject. I allude to Section II, especially Part II. As to the second vol., which is separate intirely [sic] from the first, the hasty part was the last section, on the slave system. It was too familiar to me and too easy to be carefully composed and was literally written as fast as I could talk in the Speculative, or dictate a paper. Some of B[ook] III was written rapidly too, and partly from the same reasons. The whole of B[ook] II elaborate (in the above acceptation), and the first section of B[ook] III with the discussion of Egypt, tolerably laboured, and Section I, B[ook] IV very much so indeed.

I know, that all this is cutting my own throat, if it is not so dull as to carry an antidote with it. But remember, the *haste* applies only to composition, for the substance throughout was, I declare (with the exception of the last section, which was easy to a degree and perfectly unquestionable I think) very maturely pondered[?] and severely chastened, altered, and modified according to facts. So now you are in possession of my whole secret. Only as an odd sort of thing I may add that the last sentence was written first, and the first last. When you read the introduction, which is *unintelligible per se* and I admit, altogether damning, look at the contents. Pray impute these *details* to their real cause – a wish not to seek shelter under the schoolboy excuse of 'Haste'. Now (excuse the shop) you might as soon expect to tear a Cuba blood hound from a Maroon's weasand [windpipe] as to sever an author from his book, when you have once let him take hold. Therefore I must turn from the *internal* to the *external* qualities.

Fox is reading me, as is also Windham.[7] I have had letters from both, though as you may believe, mere matters of politeness. But I am to receive farther communications. The former is an honest fellow. You can't think how roundly and hotly he writes (on the subjects that rouse him, as the slave trade, etc.) even to one whom he knows nothing of. The latter talks of enforcing some opinions by me, which would be a good advertisement but nothing more flattering – perhaps more ill than good. Billy Pitt (whom I conscientiously think the ablest of them all) has also got a copy, but I fancy he forgot to keep up his reading when in place and is too old to learn again. Besides, I sent it to him in a roundabout way, that he (who is proud) might not think it came from me. I shall therefore remain in ignorance of its fate in that house. To none of the *Idiotocracy*[8] have I sent any copy. They cannot read, and if they could, they would not get beyond the larger letters, which would convey to them no intelligible ideas. I must always except the Doctor himself, who I see is beginning to talk about '*things finding their level*' – which he applies, if I rightly remember, to 'The Speaker leaving the chair.' I gave no copies away here, except to Smith, for correcting the press of part of it which I left to his care when I went to Glasgow. But I hear now and then of it, though people are afraid to speak, least they should show their ignorance. From this I except Jeffrey, who is a convert to my general doctrines, and Dugald Stewart, who broached the subject, I thought very needlessly, t'other day, and must either be a very double man, or by no means so timid as I used to believe. You will be surprised when I tell you that he run out in praise of the composition, having read the greater part of vol I. But he had been prepared, I fancy, for something very execrable. What pleased me most was his very attentive perusal – and he bought another copy – but I find we differ [in some?] respect upon the economist theory, and the [quoted and underlined word illegible].

You prophesied wrong when you told me, 'the hour of anxiety would come'. Whether because I am tired of the thing or not, I can't say, but I am utterly indifferent, and never think of it unless it be by chance obtruded [?] on me, which is not above once a fortnight. I had always meant to interest[?] you in it, as I value your attention next to that of Dugald Stewart, and in some respects more. Your notice of the subject in your letter let out the torment, and it has proved Lethean, I doubt not.

Now to arms. In this crisis I am impelled to piss into the sea. So instead of dribbling as a volunteer I purpose to do as much as I can, and to overcome my theoretical repugnance towards the militia. In plain terms, I have resolved to take a company, if I can get one, only not in either the Scots, or Cumberland, or Westmorland. I have set matters in a train for the West York (i.e. one of the three) or the Lancashire, connected with which is leaving this place, and in my next I may probably trouble you to enter me in Lincoln's Inn. You will immediately glance over my whole plan. In case I find even the York and Lancaster disagreeable, I shall try southward, and shall thank you to inform me whether commissions (I mean companies) are going a begging in the southern counties as they are in the North. ...

1. According to the *Smith Letters*, i. 84, Sydney Smith called John Thomson 'Pus', distinguishing his other friend Thomas Thomson by the nickname 'Jus' (though this latter was also known as 'Timotheus; or 'Timothy'). But a note on Jeffrey to Horner, 1 Apr. 1803, in *Jeffrey*, ii. 67–8, states that the nickname was 'De Puis' and a note on the copy of that letter in the MS 'Memoirs' at Kinnordy explains that this was on account of Dr Thomson's frequent references to Charles François Dupuis, *Origine de tous les Cultes* (7 vols, Paris, [1795]).

     There were 268 pages of text in the third number of the ER. Brougham is believed to have contributed, in whole or in part, eight articles and Thomson one; but none has been claimed for Allen.

2. Sydney Smith.

3. Brougham had reviewed Count L. P. de Ségur's edition of *Politique de tous les Cabinets de l'Europe* (2nd ed., 3 vols, Paris [1801]) in *ER* i (no. ii, Jan. 1803), 345–81.

4. See Doc. 97 n. 5.

5. The anonymous *Comparative View of the Huttonian and Neptunian System of Geology* (Edinburgh, 1802), contained what Jeffrey's forthcoming notice in *ER* ii (no. iv, July 1803), 337–48, called 'a violent attack upon the doctrines of Dr Hutton'.

6. It is not known to what this refers, but possibly to the poor sale of his *Colonial Policy*.

7. William Windham (1750–1810: *DNB*).
8. Evidently Brougham refers to ministers.

125. To J.A. Murray

BLPES ii. 30–31 ⟨*Horner*, i. 230⟩   London, 6 July 1803

⟨To satisfy you at once about what I fancy is your principal object of impatience against me at present, I shall, by the mail coach tomorrow, send off a parcel for the *Review*. It will contain only one article, but a long one.[1] One or two more I shall send in time for publication. I hoped to have sent Lord King off this evening; but a knotty point has unexpectedly interrupted my progress, where I had taken for granted all was clear. You will easily discover this part of the article.⟩

Very soon after I got your last letter, I believe the second day, I took an excursion to Annereau's old stall in the Borough, to inquire for the pamphlets you wished to get. Instead of a volume, that number in the catalogue belonged to a parcel of loose tracts, and of these all the desirable ones were sold, except Sheridan's speech against Hastings, which I purchased for you with the sum of sixpence. I shall enclose it in the parcel tomorrow, so you may inquire for it next week at the shop of craft and suet. By the bye, I found t'other day that I had forgot to give you before you left London, a sheet of ms about Aikenhead's Trial,[2] which you lent me from your grandfather's papers; I have given it to William [Murray], that he may restore it when he goes to Scotland.

I am rejoiced to hear of your club; it is composed of excellent ingredients, and is placed upon a very judicious footing.[3] The *Aurora Borealis*, however, I shall not forget, the next time we take a raw herring and a bottle of port together. But for the love of God, conceal it from the profane; the Edinburgh reviewers have enemies enough, and sarcasms enough already against them. Do you imagine the club will have any effect in multiplying our valuable correspondents?

I meant to have given you a longer epistle; but I must fly to beef-stakes [*sic*] and then to foreign exchanges.

. . .

Has my cause about the poor rates ever been decided? Has Constable ever published the Aberdeen Trials?

I must impose a trifling commission on you. I wish to have a printed copy of my review of Lord King thrown off on a separate sheet, as I formerly had of Thornton; and if the second number comes again to the press, I should like to have the same of Canard. I find it convenient to sew them into my common-place book.[4] I shall be much obliged to you if you will negotiate this matter with the fat and Crafty, or with Brougham's friend the *Baillie*.[5]

1. Two articles by Horner appeared in *ER* ii (no. iv, July 1803), that on Lord King's pamphlet, pp. 402–421, and that on the Peltier trial, pp. 476–84. Since Horner defers the latter in Doc. 126, he presumably refers here to the other.
2. See Doc. 190.

3. The Friday Club was a literary society formed in Edinburgh at Walter Scott's suggestion in June 1803. It was to be limited to a select group of thirty and its sixteen founding members consisted mainly of Horner's friends, who met for supper every Friday and 'sat chatting until two in the morning'. (New, p. 19.)

4. A commonplace book of Horner's, covering 1799–1804 and bound in two parts, survives at Kinnordy but it does not contain any such offprints. (See also Doc. 183.)

5. A note by Leonard Horner in the Kinnordy 'Memoirs' explains with reference to the mention of 'craft and suet's' shop in the first paragraph omitted from this Document that: 'Archld Constable, the bookseller and publisher of the *ER*, was very fat, and used to be called "The Crafty".' Elsewhere he is also called 'Beefy' (Doc. 126). 'The Baillie', or 'Bailie', was the nickname given to his father by Constable's partner in 1803–1811, Alexander Gibson Hunter of Blackness (1771–1812). Hunter seems to have been called 'the Baillie' in humorous imitation of his father (*Constable*, i. 65n; see also Docs 144 and 263).

126. To Francis Jeffrey

BLPES ii. 32–3 London, Thursday [7 July 1803]

I have this day sent by the Mail coach 30 pages of MS which, with the few extracts, will print, I calculate, to about 17 or 18 of your cursedly comprehensive pages. This is too large for one review, I confess, but I had not time to make it shorter, and the subject is of considerable interest and importance. I must defer the other larger articles, which I mentioned to you, till another number; but I shall send you in a day or two, a short notice of Campbell's poems, [and] a similar one (with pretty large extracts) of Mackintosh's admirable speech for Peltier – these extracts will be what Beefy calls a *morceau*, a *bon bouche* [*sic*], to your readers, and by way of a supplement to composition, a considerable comfort to your humble and lazy reviewer. I shall likewise endeavour to give a summary flagellation of Mr Wheatley, for the petty offense of vulgar prejudice against country banks. And then I shall have done with you for this time.[1]

I wish to retain the French works I mentioned in my last; because I wish to give you a dissertation, sooner or later, on the French system of commercial policy, and on the relation between Smith's principles and those of the Economists. I will add to these works, the Reports of the Society for Bettering the Condition of the Poor; I have wished from the beginning of the *Review*, to give a fair estimate of the merits and demerits of this benevolent institution, but I was always deterred by want of practical information. This I have now a better opportunity of acquiring on the spot. There is no necessity, however, for hurrying on this article; as it may appear upon any number they publish of their Reports. I beg you will remember my right of retention upon these subjects.

I give up all thought of Dumont; chiefly on account of the probability that I may become intimate with him, as there are already several points of contact. But I must insist that you undertake it yourself, and entrust it to nobody else. I am pretty sure that the reputation of our Journal will be a good deal affected, at least among the most enlightened of our present praisers, by the manner in which that great subject is disposed of, the philosophy of legislation. I sent you down Malthus's great book;[2] I have not had leisure to look into it at all, so I know not whether I should like to review it or not. But you have perhaps by this time put it into somebody's hands. There is an elementary treatise on Mineralogy lately published in French, by Brochant, the first complete system of Wernerian nomenclature; it is liked very much here; perhaps Jameson might be got to examine it, but you must lay an injunction on him not to presume to *reason* about the stones.[3]

I wish Constable would give the *Review* a more clean, handsome garb; the last edition of the first volume is abominably ill printed upon more abominable paper. Ask him, if he is ambitious of surpassing Leipsick in dinginess; we shall not be fit even for the pastry cook, in the decline of our fame. There are some blunders in the impression of my *Canard*.

...

1. No notice of Campbell's poems appeared, and it was Brougham who eventually reviewed Wheatley's tract in *ER* iii (no. v, Oct. 1803), 231–52. But see Doc. 153.
2. The enlarged 1803 edition of Malthus's work, entitled *An Essay on the Principle of Population, or a view of its past and present effects on Human Happiness, with an Enquiry into our prospects respecting future removal or mitigation of the evils which it occasions*, while leaving the principles advanced in the earlier edition unaltered and attacking the operation of the poor laws, confessed that the 1798 work had taken too gloomy a view of human nature and accepted the hypothesis that by moral restraint squalid poverty might be greatly mitigated. It also analysed the relations of wealth to wages, of commerce to agriculture, and the effects of bounties on corn. The subject matter of the 1803 edition coincided with the mainstream of Horner's earlier researches in political economy, and his use of the word 'great' suggests that, despite his disclaimer, he may already have at least glanced at it and found its general doctrine invaluable. (See also Docs 138 and 226.)
3. Gregory Watt and not Robert Jameson (1774–1854: *DNB*), Professor of Natural History at Edinburgh, reviewed J. M. Brochant's *Traité de Minéralogie* (2 vols, Paris, [1801–1803]) in *ER* iii (no. vi, Jan. 1804), 493–7.

127. To James Reddie

NLS MSS 3704, ff. 9–10 ⟨Horner, i. 230–33⟩   London, 21 July 1803

⟨Your letter gave me the double satisfaction of hearing that your health was better, and that you had resumed your scheme of a work on international law, which I always regretted that you had for a moment suspended. I have been with several foreign booksellers about the contents of the list you have sent me, and have left an order both with De Boffe, and with Escher who is now (I understand) the most active in procuring books from Germany.[1] I am afraid, while the French Army retain possession of the Elbe, that there will be considerable difficulty in getting any works from the continent.⟩ Martens' Collection of Treaties[2] is now continued as far as *nine* volumes, and I have desired De Boffe accordingly to send you all after the 5th; which I understand to have been your meaning. There is in the press at Paris, a new edition of Valin's *Commentary*, published by order of Government;[3] there is a work also already published, which you may not have heard of, 'Decisions du Conseil des Prises';[4] let me know whether you wish these to be sent. In order to catch the titles of new books relating to your subject, you should look into the Jena review, the best (I am told) of the German journals, and executed by several men of reputation.[5] Of course, you get it at the Advocates' Library. Every new book, however, from that part of the continent, it would be profusion to purchase, as there is not a professor who does not print a text book.

⟨If you will allow me to offer an opinion, on a point which you must have considered much more deeply yourself, I should venture to question the propriety of the change you have made in your general plan. You remember the distinction which Bentham makes between the expository and critical treatises of law;[6] they ought unquestionably to be kept as distinct from each other, as the provinces of the judge and the legislator. Now in the present circumstances of Europe, I fancy that an expository treatise of international law is not only more wished for than one of a critical and speculative nature, but is more likely to be useful, and to extend the reputation of its author. So many incroachments have recently been made, perhaps by both parties, on the ancient course and maxims of the law of nations, that the primary object of importance is now to reinspire a deference to solemn precedents and established rules. I hardly know any thing more calculated to have this effect, than a learned and faithful exposition of the system. The execution of such a work will demand so much research, so much skill of arrangement, and such a firmness of temper, as may justly influence all your ambition. You must forget (for that object) that you are a citizen of a particular part of the European commonwealth, and consider yourself as a citizen of that commonwealth at large. In the present aspect of affairs, that is no ordinary effort; but it is absolutely necessary in your undertaking. In recommending you to adhere to your original plan of an expository treatise, I am supported by the authority of Mackintosh, to whom I mentioned your design generally, in order to obtain his opinion upon the point. I found him entirely coincide with my own ideas, both of the necessity of such a work at present, and of the vast field it presents for the acquisition of fame. Every lawyer, he told me, in the cockpit and Commons complains, that they have no book whatever which they can have on their table for constant reference.[7]

⟨With respect to Gentz's designs, you need not be in the least alarmed. I consulted Mackintosh about this too, because he knows him intimately, and was much with him when Gentz was in England. His work will be entirely *polemical,* and defensive of the rights of Britain against the prejudices and doctrines of the continent.[8] This being the case, there can be [no] clashing of your plans: but his work, if published earlier, may be of use to you in one part of your work. I shall without any delay make a collection for you of all the Tracts on the Armed Neutrality, that I can get hold of; if my books at Edinburgh were not packed up indiscriminately, I should have sent directions to give you my copies of them. I shall be glad to hear farther from you about this subject, to me, as you well know, most interesting, both for its own high importance, and from my sincere sympathy in your enjoyment and anticipation of reputation. I shall never forget an evening walk we had together, in the summer of 1801, when you sketched to me the outline of your intended arrangements. ...⟩

1. Henry Escher was a German bookseller and stationer established at this time in Clerkenwell Green.
2. Georg Friedrich von Martens's *Recueil des principaux traités ... depuis 1761* (7 vols, Göttingen, 1791–1801) was in process of being supplemented by his son Karl.
3. The editors have not traced any such edition. That sold from Horner's own collection (*HL* no. 159) was René Josué Valin, *Commentaire sur l'ordonnance de la marine du mois d'août 1681* (2 vols, La Rochelle, 1766). *Le Nouveau Valin, ou code commercal maritime*, by P. Sanfourche-Laporte (Paris, 1809), would seem to be too late, and Horner, perhaps, really meant the expanded version of [B. M. Emérigon], *Nouveau commentaire sur l'ordonnance de la marine du mois d'août 1681* (3 vols, Marseilles, 1803).
4. Perhaps the *Recueil de mémoires imprimés présentés au Conseil de Prises*.
5. The *Allgemeine Literatur-Zeitung*, published by Nicolai at Jena from 1785 until 1803.
6. 'To the province of the *Expositor* it belongs to explain to us what, as he supposes, the Law *is*; to that of the *Censor*, to observe to us what he thinks it *ought to be*.' (Jeremy Bentham, *A Comment on the Commentaries and A Fragment on Government*, ed. J. H. Burns and H. L. A. Hart (1977), p. 397.)
7. Horner subsequently wrote to Reddie (14 Nov. 1803: NLS MSS 3704, ff. 13–14) that he and Mackintosh agreed the success of the endeavour

> will turn upon the adaptation of the book to the use of practisers in the courts; ... I have already found, ..., even in ordinary literary conversation, the necessity of unlearning something of the manners which one imbibes in the metaphysical climate of Edinburgh: such as the inclination to theorize, and to present general principles or rules in a scholastic dress.

Reddie, however, responded (8 Dec., BLPES ii. 61–2) that he felt unqualified to write any such 'practical' book. His first known work, *Inquiries, Elementary and Historical, on the Science of Law*, did not appear until 1840, but was then followed in rapid succession by *An Historical View of the Law of Maritime Commerce* (1841), *Inquiries into International Law* (1842), and *Researches, Historical and Critical, in Maritime International Law* (Edinburgh, 1844). Fontana (p. 47) says that he became a contributor to the *ER*; but his name does not appear in *WI*, though Jeffrey did approach him on at least one occasion (Doc. 223).
8. The reference is perhaps to Gentz's *Vindication of Europe and Great Britain* (1803).

128. From Henry Brougham

BLPES ii. 34–5   Edinburgh, Monday [25 July 1803]

...¹ Authorship is not new to me. It is eight years *this* day since in consequence of correspondence with Blagden,² I began by writing what I knew would be published in the Royal Society transactions. Long before May 1796 (the date of publication) I was abundantly buttered by the men of the Society, who went upon the supposition that I was a person advanced in life. Consequently I was a little flattered, and the reviews repeated my dose. The papers sank into total neglect, even among Mathematicians. They were, I believe, never read, or at least speedily forgotten. *Therefore*, I have since that time had a great disregard of the fame consequent upon authorship, and conceive that any little applause which I may gain by my two tomes will be useless – soon over – incapable of buoying them up, and preventing them from the sepulture which tough works seem fated to undergo before they come to a joyful and durable resurrection. I am vain enough to suppose that all my buried brats will one day rise together, hand in hand, and partake of a blessed immortality. ...³ From the lounging habit of mind natural to me after being overfagged, ...⁴ I feel a degree of apathy which astonishes myself. I am, however, infinitely obliged to your friend Mackintosh for his liberal and handsome way of talking. If I knew him in the least I would, of course, desire you to thank him heartily for his kindness in sending the copies you mention and I need not add how pleasant it is to hear that he thinks my doctrine right, more especially that of vol I. I perfectly agree with whoever said that the 2nd vol. is inferior, but think that no small part of the difference is owing to the *un-neat* nature of the subject. The first is an entire and separate subject, complete in itself. The second – a jumble – unfinished – I believe unfinishable – I am sure, difficult and new. You'll also observe, that the novelty of the topics has a very extensive influence on the arrangement and management of the materials. The *logic* of foreign relations runs through the whole of it, and I don't believe that one syllable of that logic is to be found worth a farthing elsewhere – I mean, in a form at all scientific. I think Malouet will scarcely find translating me worth his while, but am equally obliged to Mackintosh.[5] My practice in writing French would enable me to give some useful directions if I saw a few sheets of any translation that might be (hereafter) found '*valoir la peine*'.

And now permit me to thank you, both as a reader and reviewer, for your article on Lord King. My taste is this – I think it, not only by far the best of No. IV – that is small praise – I even think it better than your own former articles, Thornton and Canard.[6] You are too indulgent, though. I would not have treated the theory in which Asiatic trade is brought *to serve* with half so much mildness because, instead of a *theory*, I think it is a *blunder*. There and in one or two other parts, you write *con amore* – I mean, of the author. In a future letter or interview, I shall talk to you farther upon this article, and the subject of it. As to Peltier, still more of the *con amore*, but, by God, the speech deserved much, and I don't see why a reviewer should be devoid of passions. You are very fond of the hysteron proteron at the end.[7] My prediction about Jeffrey's geological article is verified.[8] His ingenuity conceals and in part counterbalances his ignorance. Miss Baily (by the same hand) is a good article, but nothing striking.[9] And it is beyond all sufferance to see Tomy Thomson reviewing the Temple of Nature, and Jeffrey *battening* on Lady Molly Montague.[10] The Parson's Catteau (22 pp.) is heavy, inaccurate, and Smithish.[11] All my own articles are much below par. They are Defence of Order, Dallas and American Transactions. I ought to say Fuseli also.[12] Pray give me your opinion [of] Moore's *Anacreon* and who you think the author.[13] I rejoice to hear from Jeffrey that you work for the next no. I mean to be a better boy and shall instantly set about Black's lectures, [Abraham] Robertson's conic sections (sent by the author, Savilian Professor, with many compliments to the reviewer of the Edinburgh Transactions) and some political book.[14] I have not made up my mind about the review of my own book – but am extremely indebted both to you and the *confrères* here for the repeated suggestions they have made. If it is to be done, I am clearly of your opinion as to the *Quomodo*. Whether you or Jeffrey does it, must be to me and to the book a matter of indifference – which remark is a great compliment to you both. Poor Kinnaird! How lamentably he mistakes the thing! He will never be 'that terrible cornet of horse' – even to the Doctor. Making motions – and expressing opinions and returning thanks – will only do after a man has blazed in speeches, or in action.[15]

1. Brougham begins by acknowledging receipt of 'two very friendly letters' from Horner during the previous fortnight.
2. Sir Charles Blagden (1748–1820: *DNB*) was Secretary of the Royal Society.
3. Three and a half lines blotted out.
4. One line blotted out.
5. Baron Pierre Victoire Malouet (1740–1814), who was briefly Minister of Colonies under the Restoration, was the author of a number of works on colonies and on slavery; but there does not appear to have been a French edition of Brougham's book.
6. In a letter of 4 Aug. (*Thomson*, p. 47), Thomas Thomson told Horner: 'I am much pleased with your "Lord King", though a little surprised at the confidence with which you adopt his leading conclusion. I confess I don't feel the ground under me.' In a letter of 8 Aug. (*Jeffrey*, ii. 78), Jeffrey again encouraged Horner to recruit reviewers in London and remarked that 'your "Lord King" is the best article in the number'.
7. I.e., putting the cart before the horse.
8. See Doc. 124.
9. Jeffrey had reviewed Miss Baillie's *Plays on the Passions* in *ER* ii (no. iv, July 1803), 269–86.
10. Jeffrey had reviewed *The Works of ... Lady Mary Wortley Montagu* (5 vols, 1803), in *ER* ii (no. iv, July 1803), 507–521.
11. Sydney Smith had reviewed Jean Pierre Guillaume Catteau-Catteville, *Tableau des Etats Danois* (3 vols, Paris, 1802), in *ER* ii (no. iv, July 1803), 287–308.
12. The reviews of Josiah Walker, *The Defence of Order: A Poem* (3rd ed., 1803), R. C. Dallas's *History of the Maroons* (2 vols, 1803), and *Transactions of the American Philosophical Society*, appeared in *ER* ii (no. iv, July 1803), 421–8, 376–91, and 348–55. The reference to Fuseli's *Lectures on Painting* would seem to confirm that he shared the review in *ibid.*, 453–62, with Dr C. H. Parry. But it is strange that he makes no reference to John Davis, *Travels in America*, whose review in *ibid.*, 443–53, he later claimed (*Brougham*, i. 258). The Kinnordy set supports the attributions given in *WI*.
13. The review in *ER* ii (no. iv, July 1803), 462–76, was by John Eyre according to the *WI* and although it is attributed to Jeffrey in the Kinnordy set, the presence of Eyre's name in Horner's Key strongly supports the attribution to him since he is nowhere suggested as the contributor of any other article.
14. Brougham's reviews of Dr Black's *Lectures on Chemistry* and several other works appeared along with that on Wheatley in *ER* iii (no. v, Oct. 1803), 1–26 and 231–52; but the suppliant Robertson was not reviewed.
15. Kinnaird, who had been elected MP for Leominster just about a year earlier, had already been chided by Brougham and had snubbed Brougham in return. In July he was stirring himself again over the application of the property tax to Scotland. (*PH* iv. 339.)

129. To J.A. Murray

BLPES ii. 38–9 ⟨*Horner*, i. 234–6⟩   London, 6 Aug. 1803

⟨I like your *Beacon* well; it holds a strong, clear, and true light.[1] I hope it will guide your countrymen into the right harbour. The old Scotsman is well personated; the local circumstances are well hit. Pray have you engaged Walter Scott in these patriotic labours? His border spirit of chivalry must be inflamed at present, and might produce something. I wish he would try a song. I joined Mackintosh in exhorting Campbell to court the Tyrtæan muse; as yet he has produced nothing; not that I looked upon the success of his efforts with certainty, being not quite in his line; but a miracle produced *Hohenlinden*, and this is now the age of miracles of every kind.[2] You should reprint the different handbills that have had a great effect here; they are in general stupid and coarse, but it is the coarse souls which it is now most important to excite. The Declaration of the Merchants and Bankers was written by Mackintosh.[3] If you have any channel of influence over the Ballad Singers of your city, you should set them all a-singing 'Scots wha hae wi' Wallace bled'. I understand the spirit of the people in London is in general almost as good as can be wished, and better than could have been expected. The police magistrates can form a tolerably good guess, from their spies in the ale-houses.⟩ The only exception is among the Irish labourers, who (I am sorry to say) are said to amount to seven thousand. I was alarmed at the idea of the last Defence Act being executed in St Giles's and Marylebone; but the clause which gives the power to the crown of suspending the enrolment, where there is a satisfactory number of volunteers, has had a good effect, and has rendered it unnecessary (I believe) in either of those parishes to put arms into the hands of the unwilling. ⟨In the country, particularly along the coast, the spirit of the people is said to be very high. Indeed no other country of such extent ever exhibited so grand a spectacle as the unanimity in which all political differences are at present lost.⟩ I am not sorry that that senseless, misled fellow Burdett has been so absurd; he has served to prove that unanimity, in the most complete manner. Every one looks upon his political damnation as now quite complete: he made an attempt two nights ago to justify himself in the House, Fox being present, but he had not a single *hear-him*, and nobody deigned to answer him. I am not surprised at what you tell me of Lord Hobart; it is of a piece with the whole proceedings of government, which manifest throughout the most stupid indifference and imbecility. My only source of alarm is from the men who are to lead us in this eventful struggle; and my alarm on that score is indeed very great. Who could even have expected from them, such a dastardly jealousy as must have dictated the refusal of the Prince's services. There was a report yesterday that a council of war is after all to be formed; and you may judge of the confidence reposed in our commander in chief, when I tell you that this rumour seemed to cheer and encourage every body. You judge rather hardly of Byng; his sentiments seemed to me very manly and just, and his language as strong as the occasion and place required.[4] ⟨I am mightily amused with⟩ W. Erskine's[5] ⟨charge of plagiarism, which I scarcely indeed understand; he is a sensible neat man enough, and in his own way clever, but he has no measure for such understandings as Burke and Fox and Mackintosh; in the school of Burke, the last has certainly learned much of that practical sagacity and wisdom upon the politics of modern Europe, for which he is distinguished, and something too of the false taste in writing which may occasionally be objected to him; but to deny the defence of Peltier a merit and manner original and quite distinct from that either of Fox or Burke, seems to me to proceed from a deficiency in those feelings and that comprehension which are requisite for such large subjects. The speech of Peltier has mannerisms throughout, and one uniform cast of colouring; Mackintosh cannot then have stolen from both; for the manner of Burke differs so much from Fox's, as the style of Lucan or Milton from the style of Lucretius or Racine. You will perceive this charge of plagiarism has a little incensed me.⟩

... If we cannot ... found resolution on confidence, we must rouse it by despair; for if this country is to fall, there is no other now left in which one could endure to exist, with the remembrance of what we have enjoyed.

⟨Tell Jeffrey I have taken to myself, for the *Review*, Miss Williams's correspondence of Louis XVI. From what I see of it, I shall probably adore the unfortunate prince, and flagellate the conceited heartless woman.)[6]

...

1. From a letter *Horner* wrote to him on 29 July (*Horner*, i. 233–4), Murray evidently had a large part in the patriotic exhortations made irregularly during the August invasion scare by the *Scottish Beacon*. It seems to have lasted for only four issues; there are copies of three of them in the Edinburgh Public Library, the first (no. 1), dated 1 Aug., bearing the sub-title 'or Advice from an Old Scotsman to his countrymen', and the last (no. 4), dated 29 Aug., promising no. 5 'in a few days'. Offered at one penny each, 'or ninepence per dozen', they were printed by Willison, who also produced the *Edinburgh Review*, and no. 3 adds 'for Archibald Constable'. With them is a note by Cockburn that

> this periodical work was planned by Horner, Murray, Brougham, etc., and was meant to rouse the people to military virtue. It was written almost entirely by Murray, that is John Archibald Murray. They did not imagine it was to be succeeded by a Beacon of a different kind.

The name Horner has been crossed out by another hand and, indeed, it is clear that Horner himself later declined to contribute to Murray's propaganda campaign, though he expressed approval and himself joined the militia. (See Docs 136 and 137.)

2. Though depreciated by its author, Thomas Campbell's poem strongly appealed to Walter Scott's martial ardour.

3. The 'handbills' were probably more of Murray's patriotic productions; Mackintosh's 'Declaration' has not been traced.

4. The renewal of the war against France in May had been opposed by Fox, but the subsequent wave of patriotic volunteering had both alarmed the Government and divided the Opposition. Sir Francis Burdett (1770–1844: *DNB*), then MP for Middlesex, who on 29 July had publicly condemned the war at a dinner to celebrate the anniversary of his election, was very ill-received when he attempted to defend his views in the Commons on 2 Aug. and at a county meeting the same day. Reporters were excluded from the first, and the *Morning Chronicle* merely records that he 'concluded with complaining of the general misrepresentation of his sentiments'. At the county meeting, however, he was shouted down and excluded from the delegation to present a patriotic address to the King, the sheriffs being joined only by his parliamentary colleague George Byng (1764–1847), who was usually to be counted among the Foxites but had not joined them in voting against the war. (*MC*, 30 July and 2 Aug., *PH* iii. 304, and *AR* xlv (1803), 419–20.)

   Robert Hobart, Baron Hobart and afterwards 4th Earl of Buckinghamshire (1760–1816: *DNB*), Secretary of State for War and Colonies in Addington's Government, had given offence by circulating a letter deprecating any extensive volunteer movement.

   The Prince of Wales, who was nominally Colonel of the 10th Light Dragoons, had applied unsuccessfully for active service and on 2 Aug. the matter had been raised on his behalf in Parliament, but without any better success, in part perhaps because Burdett had used it as the peg on which to hang his own defence. (See *POW* iii. 348–9 and 386–96.)

5. Presumably William Erskine, afterwards Lord Kinneder (1769–1822: *DNB*), Sir Walter Scott's friend, rather than Horner's friend the orientalist, who was later introduced to Mackintosh and accompanied him to India the following year.

6. Horner's critical review of Helen Maria Williams's *The Political and Confidential Correspondence of Lewis the Sixteenth* (3 vols, 1803) appeared in *ER* iii (no. v, Oct. 1803), 211–31. His sympathetic view of the French monarch and of Turgot was reinforced by Mackintosh. (See Mackintosh to Horner, 26 Aug., *Horner*, i. 241–2.)

130. To Thomas Thomson

BLPES ii. 40–41 ⟨Horner, i. 236–8⟩   London, 15 Aug. 1803

...

⟨I hope I am not mistaken in inferring from your letter, that you have set yourself doggedly to an analysis and criticism of Dumont's publication. It will cost you some trouble; but it is a noble subject. Dumont himself has been very anxious, I understand, to see it noticed by us; and indeed it should have made its appearance earlier. The work does not seem to have been much read, or to have excited much attention, even in that small class of persons to whom such attempts are interesting. Bentham's name is repulsive. I never got through more than a half of the three volumes, and that not in a manner to have fixed much in my memory, or to qualify me for an opinion. The truth is I found that I did not assimilate much matter – I made very little chyle of it, and I lost appetite for the food. But I have always meant to attack it again; for though I am satisfied the system is quite devoid of enlarged views and comprehensive principles, there are possibly minute details both ingeniously contrived and admitting of practical applications. It is a curious fact, and to me almost unaccountable, that more copies of Dumont's book have been sold in Spain than either in England or France.⟩

I have not been able to get any more of Bentham's Tracts; they are so scarce, as only to be picked up by chance. He has lately printed, but not published, a tract on the Colonization of Botany Bay; founding his conclusions on the information furnished by Collins. I have not seen this piece, but those who have spoken of it to me agree in representing it as abominably ill written, and quite satisfactory.[1] ... ⟨There has been nothing new very lately in the line of political economy, though Brougham's work and Malthus's are a great deal for one year. An indirect application was made to me, to furnish a set of Notes for a new Edition of Smith's *Wealth of Nations*; this of course I declined, because I have other things to attend to: even if I had been prepared for such an undertaking, which I certainly am not yet, I should be reluctant to expose Smith's errors before his work has operated its full effect. We owe much at present to the superstitious worship of Smith's name; and we must not impair that feeling, till the victory is more complete. There are few practical errors in the *Wealth of Nations*, at least of any great consequence; and until we can give a correct and precise theory of the Nature and origin of wealth, his popular and plausible and loose hypothesis is as good for the vulgar as any other.⟩ I must tell you an anecdote of one of these vulgar: Lord Grenville is an implicit worshipper of Adam Smith; with him the *Wealth of Nations* is Gospel and ought to be law – and we were much indebted to this for the behaviour of the House of Lords during the last famine – yet this same Grenville admires to the very heavens a work on Currency by one Wheatley, a young lawyer connected with some bank Directors, which is a systematic attack upon country banks.

⟨I have some hopes of completing my set of the *Economiste* books, in consequence of an application by Mackintosh to Morellet at Paris. If I procure duplicates of any, I will take care of you. Morellet knows more of the matter than any other person living; as he has been a labourer in that line, and of the first class, for near fifty years.

I suppose you heard of the First Consul having nominated him to the *Conseil du Commerce*; but he complains sadly of the ignorance that is triumphant – all his representations and remonstrances are quite ineffectual. He has preserved his name unsullied through the Revolution, and a character for independence; the same can hardly be said of any other literary man at Paris, though they have upon the whole behaved less atrociously and servilely than the men of science. Morellet has likewise preserved his library, which is very rich and curious in our way; when it is dispersed, I hope we shall catch some fragments.

⟨The approaching invasion, and the circumstances of the country, have driven every other topic from conversation; questions are mooted, and possibilities supposed, that make one shudder for the fate of the world. But my habit is confidence. I have not been long enough away from Stewart, to have yet unlearned his optimism. But these intervals of ambiguity, and these suspensions of general laws, are dreadful while they last.⟩[2]

> 1. It is not clear what Horner intended, having, it would appear, omitted a word. Probably, he had meant to write 'but quite satisfactory', rather than 'and not quite satisfactory' in doctrine.
> 2. In a letter to Murray of 17 Aug. (*Horner*, i. 239), Horner observed recent patriotic demonstrations by Catholic peers and noted the probability that England was 'about to gain, for civilization and true democracy, a very splendid triumph over military despotism'.

131. Notes of my progress in studying the system of the Economists

Kinnordy MSS   26 Aug. 1803

39. '*Hands* being the Father, as *Lands* are the Mother and Womb of Wealth.' – Graunt's *Observ. on the Bills of Mortality*, p. 104.[1]

'The *Nutrition* of a Commonwealth consisteth, in the *Plenty* and *Distribution* of *Materials* conducing to Life.

'As for the plenty of matter, it is a thing limited by nature, to those commodities, which from (the two breasts of our common Mother) land, and sea, God usually either freely giveth, or for labour selleth to mankind.

'For the matter of this nutriment, consisting in animals, vegetals, and minerals, God hath freely laid them before us, in or near to the face of the earth; so as there needeth no more but the labour, and industry of receiving them. Insomuch as Plenty dependeth (next to God's favour) merely on the labour and industry of men.' Hobbes, *Leviathan*, chap. 24.[2]

This is a very distinct definition of the object of that particular branch of political science, which relates to the *wealth* of a nation. And the theory here sketched of the origin of wealth is probably the true one.

> 1. John Graunt, *Natural and Political Observations ... upon the Bills of Mortality* (3rd ed., 1665).

2. These are the three opening paragraphs of chapter xxiv, 'Of the Nutrition, and Procreation of a Commonwealth', *The English Works of Thomas Hobbes*, ed. Sir William Molesworth (11 vols, 1839–44), iii. 232.

132. To Anne Horner

Copy in Byrne Memoirs, pp. 72–5   London, 10 Sept. 1803

... I am glad you did not find the *Edinburgh Review*, so very dull as you expected; if you persevere, you will become as expert a critic as any of us, and I hope we shall have the honour of an article from your pen. What would you like to review? Suppose Miss Jackson[1] were to publish a novel. You could not resist the opportunity of *cutting her up*. You conjectured very rightly, that Smith wrote the articles on Irish Bulls.[2] ...

1. Not identified.
2. Sydney Smith had reviewed Maria Edgeworth's *Essay on Irish Bulls* (1803) in *ER* ii (no. iv, July 1803), 398–402.

133. Notes of my progress in studying the system of the Economists

Kinnordy MSS   20 Sept. 1803

40. The Economists can hardly be right, in asserting manufacturing labour to be unproductive of wealth. If we stop short of manufactures, the raw produce is not fit for consumption, and is not wealth. If we talk of any labour as productive of wealth, no distinction can be made between the labour which separates the raw material from the soil, and that which brings it into a consumable form. The successive labours applied to this material form a chain, of which the continuity cannot be broken: they all form a mass of labour, which is employed in the production of wealth.

I am not sure that the Economists have always presented an uniform and steady view of their theory; sometimes they include, as that produce of which agricultural labour is called productive, raw materials of every kind; on the other hand, when the manufacturing is called unproductive because *salarié* it seems to be understood that agricultural labour is made pre-eminent on account of the physical necessity of subsistence. These are surely two very distinct views of the relative subordination of the two kinds of labour: each view may be useful, and may be fruitful of conclusion; but they are distinct.

When the Economists consider subsistence as alone wealth, they seem to be misled by their incorrect notions upon the subject of Population.

But though they may have erred in describing manufacturing labour as unproductive, they seem to me to have made some essential discoveries in the theory of national wealth, with regard to the *first step* in the process of formation, with regard to the circulation and distribution of riches, and with regard to the influence of accumulated stock upon the increase of wealth. In the last particular, I suspect Smith borrowed more than he has acknowledged.

41. All the reasonings of the Economists, with regard to production and the productive class, must equally apply, and are in fact by them equally applied, to vineyards as to corn fields. Here then we have an *instantia* (so it would be called in the logic of Lord Bacon), in which we have the circumstance of first necessity. It is a proper and convenient use, therefore, to apply the reasoning of the Economists to, in order to appreciate the accuracy of their conclusions.

42. *Philosophie Rurale*, I. p. 46.[1] Some confusion is here occasioned by using the word 'superfluity' instead of the word 'surplus'. – The word 'transmutation', too, is used in this mystical definition of commerce for the appropriate word 'exchange'. The word 'source' likewise seems to be very improperly employed; the two *dépenses* spoken of are in truth reciprocally promoters of each other: there is a reciprocity and re-action between them.

PRINCIPLES AND REASONINGS OF THE ECONOMISTS.[2]

'C'est la valeur vénale qui donne aux productions la qualité de richesses.' p. 163 Quesnay.

'Puisque le travail des artisans augmente en effet la valeur de la matière première de leurs ouvrages, il s'ensuit, que ce travail fait une addition de richesses à cette matière première.' p. 161.

'La terre a été départie aux citoyens pour en tirer par leur travail, *les biens à leur usage; ce qui constitue la seule richesse.*' *Théorie de l'Impôt*, p. 6.

'Sans le Commerce, point de valeur vénale, et sans la valeur vénale, point de produit, que pour la subsistance bornée, journalière et informe.' *Théorie de l'Impôt*, 43

'... ce ne *sont point les hommes* quelconques qui sont sujets à l'Impôt ... Mais c'est de la masse des biens continuellement renaissans par le travail, qu'il faut extraire le montant des frais publics.' *Théorie de l'Impôt*, 56.

'Le Commerce et l'Industrie n'ajoutent rien aux produits, mais ils leur donnent la valeur; rien quant au fond, mais tout quant à la forme; rien à leur qualité de biens, mais ils peuvent seuls lui attribuer celle de richesse.' *Théorie de l'Impôt*, p. 74.

'En perdant de vue *l'existence naturelle des choses*, et leur place dans le grand cercle de prospérité, on s'égara dès le premier pas.' *Théorie de l'Impôt*, p. 92.

'La véritable utilité de l'Industrie est de faciliter la consommation: elle seule nécessite et *fait* valoir la reproduction.' Id. [pp. 92–3]

'Le produit provient de deux agens combinés. Ces deux agens sont le travail de l'homme, et le don de la nature. Cette bonne mère double, triple et décuple quelquefois ce que le travail de l'homme lui a confié. La totalité du raport [*sic*] s'appelle produit; mais dans le produit il n'y a que la crue et l'accroissement, la dépense prélevée, qui soit bénéfice.' *Théorie de l'Impôt*, 144[–5].

'All production originates from past/is procured by previous consumption, and is for the purpose of future consumption.

'Reproduction replaces the consumption, or expense, advanced,[3] together with a surplus.

'This surplus is called Revenue.'

1. Chapter 2 of vol. ii of the three-volume edition of the *Philosophie Rurale* was entitled 'La source des Dépenses'.

2. The following notes have been added on the left-hand facing page towards the end of paragraph 40. The first two notes, the second of which is a paraphrase rather than an actual quotation, refer again to vol. ii of the six-volume edition of *Physiocratie*. The remainder refer to the *Théorie de l'Impôt* by Victor de Riquetti, Marquis de Mirabeau. In a later reference (Doc. 226) Horner mentions two versions of that work. One of them, he says, was published as one of the additional parts of an edition of *L'Ami des Hommes*. That there was such a version seems borne out by the existence (Goldsmiths' Library no. 11,476) of a small volume entitled *Supplément à la Théorie de l'impôt* (La Haye, 1776) and including a half-title page that reads: 'L'ami des hommes. Huitième partie.' The editors have been unable to trace such a version of the *Théorie* itself, but it would appear that the version to which Horner refers in these notes was that published in viii + 422 pages in 1761, but bearing no printer, publisher, or place of publication, though the latter is believed to have been Paris; the Goldsmiths' Library has a copy (no. 9699). The emphases in the quotations in this Document are Horner's; the 'quotation' from pp. 92–3 is slightly adapted.

3. *(including the whole advances, both primitive and annual, together with 'les intérêts de ses avances pour les réparations casuelles qu'elles exigent.')

134. To Francis Jeffrey

BLPES ii. 45–6   The Temple, 15 Oct. 1803

I hoped to have dispatched Miss Williams to you by this mail, but I have suffered some intrusions, and cannot give her the *coup de grace* till the afternoon. This is provoking, as you will have to wait till Thursday, there being no conveyance tomorrow; at least, I believe not – about that, I shall make inquiries. I am very unreasonable, I confess it, and very unfair; and you are every thing that is merciful. I have trembled every day about post time; and the cold sweat broke upon my face, as I fancied I heard his foot upon my wooden stair. If you get one on Thursday, you will have time however to print; as near as I can guess, I shall fill about 15 pages. I hope never to be so very much behind hand again.[1]

Longman talked to me t'other day of a catalogue, and asked my opinion, which I gave him nearly in this way; that a list of the titles of all new books would be a valuable addition to our Journal, especially for those who live in remote parts of the country, and who in many cases get a Review rather to know what new publications there are, than to learn the opinion of an obscure critic. But to give, in addition to the list, a character of every book, appears to me a very hazardous plan: the expense will not permit all the trash to be sent to Scotland, and I hope you will never consent to employ as a pioneer and tester any of the hack workmen of London. For a passing criticism of that kind, nobody would think of reading the books carefully;

and your *Review* might be committed most fatally, by risking hasty and superficial judgements.[2] This blunder about Poggio should be a warning to us; we shall never hear the last of it.[3] As soon as we are convicted of a few such instances of want of information, which has a much greater effect than perhaps it ought, we are gone for ever. 'Ye have what I advise.'

Sidney [*sic*] is afraid his little boy has taken the whooping cough; which distresses him not a little. I have not heard of him this morning, but shall call in Doughty St before dinner; he gave me your last letter to him, which I read with shame for myself, and commiseration for you. Truly, we seem to be at the last gasp. I promise never to speak of your advertisement, which, from what you say of it, I reckon myself fortunate that I have not yet seen. The idea was not much to my taste, as you would surmise.

I have thrown myself so much out of time, by going down into the country, from which I found it difficult to return.[4] ... You have no title to find fault with me for my luxurious indulgence, and for preferring idleness and beds of roses to your *Review*, when you yourself did the same thing for such a cold, gluttonous, pedantic place as St Andrews. You shall have a great deal of Political Economy from me next number; if I had known any thing of the history of the Revolution, Miss Williams might have been a good occasion for showing it, but I have been forced to patch up a humbug thing, with some coarse abuse of her (not coarser than *she* deserves, though a little more than I like to inflict), and some formal ranting sentences in my most ancient and worst manner. What is Brougham afraid of, about his book; the delay, however, may not be a disadvantage. Mr Whishaw of [his] own accord, some days ago, offered to give [a review], and appeared disappointed when I told him you had undertaken it. He is full of its importance and value; and the idea occurred to him, he told me, at Bowood where he was living for some days, and where he found the object and utility of the work were not fully appreciated. You may think of this, and talk of it with Brougham; but let me know soon. For term begins soon, and Whishaw is a good deal in business. What is Thomson about with Dumont?

   ...

From what Smith has said to me, I suspect he has given the Treasury pamphlet most unmerited praise. I sicken at the idea of our contaminating ourselves with politics; still more, of showing mercy to such a stupid, blackguard production as that. But Sidney would make up his mind upon it, between his second and third cups of tea.[5]

   ...

1. In letters of 2 and 8–14 Sept. Jeffrey had beseeched Horner to contribute articles and to encourage others, the later letter in particular entreating him to review the 1803 edition of Malthus's *Population* in the next number of the ER (Jeffrey, ii. 80–85).
2. Beginning in Oct. 1803, a 'Quarterly List of New Publications' made its appearance in each number, divided into categories but otherwise without any comment or elaboration.
3. See William Shepherd, *Life of Poggio Bracciolini*, in ER ii (no. iii, Apr. 1803), 42–53.
4. He had been to Guildford for some ten days in late Sept. and early Oct. (Horner to Frances Horner, 6 Oct., Byrne Memoirs, pp. 75–7).
5. It is not apparent to what this refers. Quite possibly the notice was never published.

135. From Henry Brougham

BLPES ii. 47–8   Edinburgh, 24 Oct. 1803

I received yours of Sept. 23 (I am ashamed to say) and agreed with most of the remarks upon the subordinate nature of reviewing, and the dryness of scientific articles, to the bulk of readers. You seem however to have mistaken what I said about yours, when I told you not to be afraid of making them too slight. I meant that you was [sic] in no danger of carelessness; and when I called them elaborate, I intended to be very complimentary. You will see in No. V abundant proofs that lightness of hand is not always attained by careless execution. But, this needs not, indeed, any demonstration. The heavy, lax, prosing things to which I allude are Walter Scott's – above 40 pages on *Amadis de Gaul* and a man Sibbald's ballads.[1] I would rather be lame of both legs and write war songs to cavalry corps, and eat Dundas's toads, than have so digressive a head and such a vulgar taste as you will see exemplified in those effusions of criticism.

I am much delighted with your murder of that stupid woman Miss Williams, and also with your tenderness for Lewis, in which I think all readers will sympathize. One thing is sufficiently hyperbolical, viz., that the 10th of August, or even all that followed, was never equalled in the annals of any savage or civilized nation – St Bartholomew, Sicilian Vespers, St Domingo, are pretty well, and, not to mention the Russian assaults, Tartar and Turkish routs, and Indian famines, I don't think the every day fare of the Choctaws and Chickasaws so much amiss, in the way of atrocity. This mere trifle is the only hole I could pick in your whole article, and I must add that it satisfactorily refutes your assertion that your nature is abhorrent to light composition. If your logic on this score were to be adopted by every body, I am pretty sure that nobody except Jeffrey would write upon any subject unconnected with the plumb-line and scales.

...

My plans will, I should think, be finally arranged in less than a month. During that interval I wish to give Jeffrey my quota for [the] next No. – therefore, [I] wish you would look out for some good books at Cousin Longman's.[2] I have all along been shamefully negligent in not acknowledging your observations about the mode of reviewing my book. At first I thought it better to say nothing, taking it for granted that Jeffrey would see the propriety – I might say necessity – of either not reviewing it at all or of confining the review to an abstract. But learning that he meant to show the impartiality of the *Edinburgh Review* by a contemptuous thrashing, I told him (in one letter, he being out of town) that the consequences of such a piece of justice would be – all the cutting would count *a fortiori* with the public while any praise would go for nothing, which would rather place me in a ridiculous predicament – and, therefore, recommended him to give a short analysis. Since that I never resumed the subject and expected that he would make up his mind himself, as was proper. Three or four days ago he told me of your friend Mr Whishaw being [eager?] to do it, when of course it was too late for No. V. If the review is known not to be done by one of ourselves, I need not tell you that I don't care a button in what style it is conceived. Any disagreeable feelings were confined entirely to the former case.[3]

...

1. Scott had reviewed Southey and W. S. Rose's translations of *Amadis de Gaul*, and James Sibbald's *Chronicle of Scottish Poetry* (1802), in *ER* iii (no. v, Oct. 1803), 109–136 and 198–210.

2. *Brougham*, i. 248, mentions that the publisher Thomas Norton Longman (1771–1842: *DNB*) was related to Sydney Smith. Since it was addressed to Longman, this gives added flavour to Smith's famous refusal of an invitation to dinner (*Life of the Rev. R.H. Barham*, i. 283): 'I cannot accept your invitation, for my house is full of country cousins. I wish they were once removed.' Brougham had at least four articles in the January 1804 number.

3. In a letter of 19 Oct. (*Jeffrey*, ii. 85–7) Jeffrey informed Horner that Brougham had no objection to Whishaw reviewing his book and expressed relief 'to get rid of so delicate an engagement'. But see Doc. 144.

136. To John Horner

BLPES ii. 49–50   London, 26 Oct. 1803

...

We rather begin now to believe, that the Invasion will not be attempted on any part of England. Indeed such is the formidable aspect of defence that the country has assumed, it would appear to require more than even the madness of B[onaparte] to venture an attack. In the mean time, this defensive system, though very necessary, encroaches most lamentably on the industry of the country; we shall be a much poorer people, I suspect, at the end of the year than we were last spring – not merely from the additional expenses, which must have pressed severely on people of small capital, but from the consumption of time that would have otherwise been given to productive labour. I do not, for my own part, attend drills so well as I ought to do; but part of almost every day, and every now and then an entire day, is consumed in this way. This breaks in very much upon my schemes.[1]

...

1. Horner, who had previously served with the Edinburgh Volunteer Infantry, had joined the Bloomsbury Association along with James Brougham and begun drilling in July (Horner to Murray, 25 June 1798 and 29 July 1803, *Horner*, i. 60 and 233–4).

137. To Leonard Horner

BLPES ii. 52–3 ⟨*Horner*, i. 244–6⟩   London, 5 Nov. 1803

⟨...⟩

I hear a great deal of your soldiering, as you probably do about mine. It is no doubt a necessary evil, but it is a real and serious evil, encroaching very much upon one's time, and interrupting altogether the system of regular application. It gives bad habits too, and the red coat has a wonderful effect in turning the head. No doubt, you feel upon this subject just as I do, and at the same time that you discharge an irksome duty from a sense of its propriety and indeed necessity, are quite aware of the bad effects all this idleness and parade may have or rather to some degree *must* have upon one's habits both of thinking and of business.

⟨I am glad to find you have been reading Adam Smith; it is quite true, as you remark, that upon the subject of money he is not quite clear; the true reason of which is, that in some points he is not quite right, as you will be satisfied after you have studied a little farther. What I say now applies entirely to the fifth chapter, which I would not have you puzzle yourself with too much; it is sufficient for your present purpose, that you take from it the general idea of what distinguishes the *money-price* of commodities from their *real* price, or their price in other goods. This will fully enable you to understand all his subsequent reasonings with regard to prices, at least all such of them as are accurate and quite free from error; for you are not to take for granted all that is given you in this book, more than you ought to do in any other; and it should be your rule in reading, upon all occasions and all subjects, to examine the truth of every argument by the force of your own understanding. There is less chance, however, of being led into false opinions by the *Wealth of Nations* than by almost any book on that kind of philosophy.

⟨With respect to the time you are to divide between political economy and chemistry, you must, of course, judge for yourself. ... There are in London more than a dozen courses of lectures on chemistry, though none certainly so valuable as those at Edinburgh; but there are no lectures whatever on political science. ...⟩

...

138. From T.R. Malthus

Kinnordy MSS ⟨William Petersen, *Malthus*
(Harvard University Press, Cambridge, Mass., 1979), pp. 250–52⟩   [1][?1803]

⟨As it would always be my wish to acknowledge an error as soon as it was known to me, I should esteem it a particular favour, if in your widely-circulating review you could find room for the following remarks.

⟨In the 4th chapter of the 2nd book of the *Essay on the Principle of Population* I endeavoured to prove that the proportion of annual marriages to annual births instead of expressing the average prolifickness of marriages as it was usually supposed to do, expressed a different thing, namely, the proportion of the born which lives to be married. I was perhaps the more readily induced to adopt the train of reasoning which led to this conclusion, as it appeared to solve some difficulties in the registers of the births and marriages of some countries, which did not seem easily to admit of another solution. The suggestions of an able mathematical friend,[2] and my own further reflections on this subject, have convinced me that I was wrong, and that although the old theory is incorrect, that which I would have substituted is still more so.

⟨In a register, the births and marriages are of course contemporaneous; but the marriages in the register of any particular year cannot be contemporaneous with the births from which they resulted; nor are the births contemporaneous with the marriages from which they were produced: consequently the proportion of births to marriages in any register, supposing the population to be either increasing or decreasing, cannot represent either the number of births from which one marriage results, or the number of children to a marriage, but something between the two, though nearer to the latter than the former, on account of the distance of time being less between the marriages and the births which they produce in the course of their duration, than between the births and the marriages which result from them. In fact a note of Dr Price (*Observ.*, Vol. i, p. 270) respecting the inferences to be drawn from the different proportions of births and marriages, which I alluded to as erroneous, I am now convinced is correct; and if he has erred on this subject it is rather in his general and practical conclusions than in the reasoning on which they are founded.

⟨The proportion of annual marriages to annual births in registers is affected both by the proportion of the born which lives to be married, and by the prolifickness of marriages, and these two causes produce an opposite effect on the registers. The greater is the proportion of the born which lives to be married the greater will be the proportion of annual marriages to annual births; and the greater is the prolifickness of marriages, the less will be the proportion of annual marriages to annual births. Consequently, if, within certain limits, the proportion of the born which lives to be married, and the prolifickness of marriages, increase at the same time, the proportion of annual marriages to annual births may still remain unchanged; and this is the reason why the registers of different countries, in respect to marriages and births, are often found the same under very different rates of increase in population. At the same time it is impossible to reconcile so rapid an increase of population as is known to take place in some of the Russian provinces with registers which express a proportion of marriages to births as 1 to 3 and 1 to 3.6: for in this case it would appear, even after making every allowance for second and third marriages (a correction which should always be attended to), that all or nearly all of the born lived to be married which is impossible; and therefore it is necessary to suppose, that in the Russian registers and some others, the omissions in the births are considerably greater than in the marriages, a supposition which on other accounts does not seem improbable.⟩

1. This letter, which bears no date, has been slipped into Horner's copy of the second edition of Malthus's work preserved at Kinnordy; that quarto volume bears some pencil marks made by him as well as a very few minor comments in the margins, but hardly such as to warrant the description of them in *Malthus*, p. 112. The date of Malthus's letter is unknown; but it must have been before July 1804 when Horner evidently refers to it (Doc. 163), albeit not quite accurately as a letter to him. Malthus probably sent it to John Whishaw with instructions that it should be placed in the hands of the unknown party who was to review his work for the *ER*. The presumed reviewer was Horner. In a letter to Horner preserved along with that of Malthus and dated only 'Monday M[ornin]g' (not 'Monday Nov. 19' as *Malthus*, p. 113, states), Whishaw wrote:

   ... Malthus has lately sent me the Papers which I now enclose. They relate to an error in his Calculations which he has lately detected and which he wished to communicate (if there was no objection) through the medium of the *Edinburgh Review*. The letter which I send was intended for insertion.

   As you are engaged in reviewing the work, I send you the Papers in order that you may judge what use should be made of them. ...

Mrs James (*Malthus*, p. 114) suggests that Malthus was trying to encourage Horner to get on with his review, but points out that he entirely rewrote the chapter 'On the Fruitfulness of Marriages' for his third, 1806, edition. See William Petersen, *Malthus*, for further comment on this letter.

2. The mathematician is identified at the bottom of the page as the Reverend Edward Otter of Bolsover (1764–1837), the elder brother of Malthus's friend, William Otter (1768–1840: *DNB*).

139. To Francis Jeffrey

⟨*Some Letters of Lord Cockburn With Pages Omitted*
From The Memorials of His Time, ed. Harry A. Cockburn,
(Edinburgh, 1932), pp. 76–8⟩   London, 8 Nov. 1803

⟨The fifth No. is not yet published in Town but most of *our set* have either got their copies, or read the chief articles. We are all enamoured of your Millar;[1] the character is admirable, according to my recollections a perfect likeness, and finished with more felicity and pains than you bestowed on some of your last contributions.

⟨I must tell you at the same time that we all think you very heretical in some of the doctrines you have delivered under the head of De Lille.[2] You forgot Racine altogether when you spoke so contemptuously of French poetry, with respect to the description and language of passion; you ought to have admitted, too, when you spoke so generally that in the lighter classes of poetical composition, the French far excel all their competitors. Then it appears to us that De Lille, far from being more simple and chaste is more gaudy and meretricious than the great models of his own country; whose manner of composition is more severely classical than perhaps any that we can produce – such as Racine, La Fontaine, Moliere; and even Boileau may be added to these.

⟨In short, we think you have been too anti-Gallican. I am deemed so in another sense of that epithet by one or two of my stricter friends, who say I have been unwarrantably favourable to poor Lewis. I do not think so yet; it is possible enough, as I wrote that declamation very much under the influence of feeling that it blinded me to the cold historical partiality which might have been more becoming; but if it is so I am not yet recovered and the interval is not sufficient to have cured me of the delusion.

⟨We are most certainly attacked in the *Anti-Jacobin*; I suppose by the unfortunate Mr Bowles. We are, it seems, 'a parcel of nameless boys', who have sold ourselves to the Corsican Consul. Will it not be necessary that you, and Brougham, and I should draw lots to determine who shall wait upon Mr Bowles for an explanation. It is a pity Kinnaird cannot be of the party.[3]

⟨...⟩

1. Jeffrey had reviewed Millar's *Historical View of the English Government to 1688* in *ER* iii (no. v, Oct. 1803), 154–81.
2. Jeffrey had reviewed De Lille's *Malheur et Pitié* in *ER* iii (no. v, Oct. 1803), 26–42.
3. See pp. 205–206 for Bowles's criticisms in *The Anti-Jacobin Review and Magazine, or*

Monthly Political and Literary Censor, xvi (1803), 213–23 and 515–23. At this date Horner
would not yet have seen the second part of Bowles's notice, in which he was again singled
out for praise, and in his final remarks here was evidently drawing a parallel between
Bowles's otherwise hostile allegations and those lodged by Professor David Hume against
him, Brougham, Jeffrey, Kinnaird, and other students of Edinburgh University nearly six
years earlier. The remainder of the letter deals with an abortive scheme by Horner and
Mackintosh to secure Jeffrey a professorship at the planned College of Calcutta.

140. From Thomas Thomson

⟨*Thomson*, pp. 48–9⟩   Edinburgh, 17 Nov. 1803

⟨…

⟨We are much pleased with the whipping you have so lustily bestowed on Miss
Williams. I hear the emigrants in this place consider the letters as not genuine,
judging I suppose on the external evidence of the case. Monsieur must be able to say
something as to that part of the correspondence in which he is directly concerned.
Have you heard anything from that quarter?

⟨Have you heard of Lauderdale's intended publication?[1] He promises it in the
course of two months. I had no opportunity lately of seeing him, and have never
learned precisely what it is to embrace; but I take for granted it will give us all his
own leading notions in so far as they differ from Smith. It will fall on you to *review*
him, and the sooner after the publication the better. At second hand I have heard
some of his notions about the effects of the sinking fund in annihilating that vast
receptacle for capital, the stocks; but I have not been much impressed with any
opinion of their sagacity.

⟨…⟩

    1. An *Inquiry into the nature and origin of Public Wealth and into the means and causes of its
    Increase*, which was published in Edinburgh early in the following year. See Docs 147 and
    153.

141. To Thomas Thomson

⟨*Thomson*, pp. 50–51⟩   [London], 23 Nov. 1903

⟨I have now got a copy of Forbonnais, but not of Rice Vaughan; the latter I should
like to have.[1] It is very difficult to pick up Bentham's Tracts, and altogether impossible
to get those of Turgot which you and I want. I will think of Hobbes for you.

⟨… What do you think of a chair for lectures on political economy at Vilna in
Lithuania? Such a professor is wanted, and has been applied for. The person in
London, to whom the ambassador was directed to apply for advice, was requested to
have his eyes on Glasgow, and 'surtout sur Edinbourg'.

⟨…⟩

    1. Hitherto he had borrowed copies from the Advocates' Library.

142. To John Horner

BLPES ii. 54-5   The Temple, 23 Nov. 1803

...

I was in the House of Commons last night; but nothing occurred of any importance, except the sort of pledge which Fox gave, that he would in the course of the Session bring on a discussion with respect to the state and administration of Ireland.[1] He is particularly anxious, I understand, upon this subject; some time ago, he took an opportunity of stating his sentiments and views of it to the Prince, who dined with him at St Anne's Hill. And that there might be neither mistake nor forgetfulness, he next day stated the substance of his conversation in a letter; which, considering his habitual indolence particularly in writing, showed very unusual solicitude.[2] The present Chancellor of Ireland[3] is described, unfortunately, as a violent Orangeman; while that faction have the government uncontrolled in their hands, there will be no peace at all for Ireland, and no entire security for us. The question of Catholic Emancipation, and the late treatment of the Prince, are spoken of as the chief topics that the old Opposition means to urge. The former will be a good occasion for trying the political manhood of Mr Pitt; I think it not improbable that he will have a review of his volunteers fixed for the same day, which will render his absence indispensable. Last night, Fox spoke merely in the tone and manner of conversation across the table; he looks in excellent health, though enormously overgrown. The Grenville party were in strong force, but none of them spoke.

You will see by the papers that I am very soon to lose my friend Mackintosh.[4] ... I shall feel the loss very severely; because he has behaved with marked civility to me, ever since I came to England. His private conversation, which I have commanded almost at my own times, is full of talent and has been highly instructive to me on many branches of literature; and at his table, I have met many distinguished characters, and formed some permanent acquaintances, in whose way I might not have fallen otherwise. Had he been as stern and unshaken in his political connections, as he is enlightened and unprejudiced upon almost all political opinions, there could have been no limit to his success. Though he cannot be entirely defended, his error is far more venial than the malignant ill-nature of those who reconcile themselves to their own narrow capacity by aspersing the character of abler men, and conceive themselves quite consistent because they have not suffered their dogmatism to be shaken by the clearest result of experience. I shall ever think of Mackintosh with gratitude and admiration.[5]

...

1. In the debate on the King's Speech on 22 Nov. (*Hansard*, i. 21–3).
2. See *POW* iv. 402–406, for Fox's letter of 18 Aug.
3. John Freeman-Mitford, 1st Baron Redesdale (1748–1830: *DNB*).
4. Mackintosh was to go out to India that autumn as Recorder of Bombay.
5. Upon the departure of Mackintosh, Horner remarked that no man, not even Dugald Stewart, had so 'enlarged my prospects into the wide regions of moral speculation', and that had Mackintosh remained in England, 'I should have possessed ten years hence, powers and views which are now beyond my reach'. (See Horner to Erskine, 4 Feb. 1804, *Horner*, i. 258.)

143. To Leonard Horner

BLPES ii. 56–7 〈Horner, i. 249–52〉   The Temple, 26 Nov. 1803

〈... In recommending Political Economy to you at present, I was influenced by the single circumstance of your having but this opportunity of hearing Stewart. ...

〈I can easily pardon you for not being an enthusiast, as you call it, in Political Economy; at the first look it is somewhat crabbed and unentertaining. Then it seems probably to have too much ado with pounds, shillings, and pence, of which you have enough in your hours of business, and wish to forget them, when you come to amusement. At present I will refrain from attempting to undeceive you in this respect.

〈...〉

144. From Henry Brougham

BLPES ii. 59–60   Edinburgh, 8 Dec. 1803

...

I was much obliged to you for letting me know what Gentz wrote to your friend Mr Macintosh. It is very flattering and more, by a great deal, than my work deserved at *his* hands, who seems to be a proficient in political speculations and is certainly a man of more than German talents. Of the two reviews which I have seen, the one is written by a good man who knows nothing either of the subject or the book. The other in a literary journal is extremely dull and puzzlepated, but the author has done me the honour of perusing me with some care, an honour which he has not thought proper to bestow upon Doctor Adam Smith, although he is perpetually talking of him.[1] Smith, indeed, has now become sufficiently famous to experience the fate of Bacon and Newton – to be quoted and sworn by, without being read. He is used somewhat like the late Capt Grose,[2] the antiquary, whose prodigious maps you see inserted in the corner of almost every bad picture of a ruin, for the sake of increasing the likeness.

... Lord Lauderdale's book is in the Bailley's hands.[3] He has been showing it to all the world, who are utterly ignorant of these matters – as Dupuis, Sir H. Moncrieff, etc. – and talks of nothing else in the company of such men as H. Erskine, the Clerks, etc.[4] I should say this augurs ill, if one did not know the unaccountable absurdities of authors, who before delivery, are subject, apparently, to all the freaks of big-bellied women. Why are you not to do Malthus? Think twice before you do so much injury to the *Review* and consider that for this no. we have no political works, whereas for No. VII we shall have abundance. I rejoice to hear that Vansittart asked to be made acquainted with you, for I understand he is a reading man and conclude that his desires were excited by reading your articles.[5] Do work him up with a speedy and lurid display of the principle of population.

1. The second of the reviews to which Brougham refers was probably that in *The Literary Journal*, ii (Nov. 1803), 513-27, by James Mill who, of course, had also studied under Dugald Stewart. For a brief but useful critique of Brougham's book, and of his superficial understanding of Adam Smith, see Fontana, pp. 60-63. The book never was reviewed in *ER*, but see Doc. 175.

2. Francis Grose (?1731-91: *DNB*).

3. That is, with the publisher Hunter of Constable and Co. See Doc. 125.

4. That is: Dr John Thomson; James Moncreiff's younger brother Henry rather, perhaps, than their father, Sir Henry; Henry Erskine; and, probably, John Clerk, sen., and his son John, afterwards Lord Eldin (1757-1832: *DNB*).

5. Nicholas Vansittart, afterwards 1st Baron Bexley (1766-1851: *DNB*), was Secretary of the Treasury in Addington's Government.

145. To Mrs Dugald Stewart

BLPES ii. 64-5   [London], 19 Dec. 1803

... At Edinburgh, what an advantage you have over us; that you are now and then permitted to feel an interest in topics that are older than one day, and have life enough in them for more than another hour. However, I must tell you the last news I have heard; for, if true, it will make amends for many dull rumours, though I admit that the old proverb has something to allege against its probability. I have been assured, and I will tell you my authority, that Government has it in contemplation to suspend the Slave Trade for a certain number of years. Could you have guessed how this was to be brought about? The fertility of the late conquests in Dutch Guiana is so great, and so much capital is already pouring into them, that the owners of the old settlements in the West Indies foresee their ruin in the reduced prices of produce. To prevent the new acquisitions from being stocked with slaves, they are willing to make the experiment of keeping up their own stock without fresh importations. The way in which I first heard this, was that Fox mentioned to Lord King the information he had got upon the subject from Sir William Young, who is very anxious for the measure.[1] And on making farther inquiries of R. Sharp, he assured me that the same language is held in the City by the whole set, whose power, so few years ago, defeated the proposal.[2] I do not know that one ought to be so much pleased with this crooked dirty sort of sunk path to justice, as with the direct high road ...

I must give you a little scandal, and about the Doctor. A stupid huge fellow at the bar here has published a history of Ireland, as dull and as much out of dimensions as himself. Though a Catholic, he had been encouraged by Addington in the prosecution of his compilation; and yet the Doctor was so surprised to find that he favoured the Catholics and their cause, that he sent for Plowden to reproach him. 'Good God, Sir, did you not know that I live in this house by my opposition to that question?' This was one expression that fell from him. Among other papers in his appendix, Plowden has given the famous letter of Lord Castlereagh to Pitt, etc. which, by the bye, was given to the Catholic Bishop who first printed it, by Lord Castlereagh, in presence of Lord Cornwallis, at the Castle. 'Of all papers (said the Premier), that is the one which I regret most to see in your book.' I allow this is very incredible, but it is literally Plowden's account of the conversation to our friend Petty.[3]

...

1. Sir William Young, 2nd Bart (1749–1815: *DNB*), MP for St Mawes, was a West India proprietor.
2. Richard 'Conversation' Sharp (1759–1835: *DNB*), a West India merchant and friend of Mackintosh and the Hollands, was later, as a Whig MP, also a close friend and political associate of Horner. For Horner's high opinion of Sharp see his journal entry of 14 Jan., and for evidence of his reliance on Sharp's extensive command of information relating to the commerce of London that of 2 Feb. 1804 (*Horner*, i. 253–4 and 256–7).
3. This is a garbled reference to the attempts of Charles, 1st Marquess Cornwallis (1738–1805: *DNB*), as Viceroy of Ireland, and Castlereagh, as Chief Secretary, to placate the Irish Catholics following the refusal of the King to implement the Government's promise to follow union with Catholic Emancipation and Pitt's and Cornwallis's consequent resignations in February 1801. Castlereagh, who had come over to London in order to press the Government in person, composed various papers about the situation, including a letter written with Pitt's approval to Cornwallis on 9 Feb. (*Memoirs and Correspondence of Viscount Castlereagh, Second Marquess of Londonderry*, ed. Charles Vane, Marquess of Londonderry (4 vols, 1848–9), iv. 38–41). Although marked 'secret', extracts from this letter were then passed on by Cornwallis – not Castlereagh, who was still in England – to Lord Fingall and John Thomas Troy, the Catholic Archbishop of Dublin, in particular Pitt's assurance that he would 'do his utmost to establish their cause in the public favour'. It was this version that subsequently found its way into the newspapers and was reprinted, as 'Mr Pitt's paper', in a note (not an appendix) in Francis Peter Plowden, *An Historical Review of the State of Ireland* (2 vols, 1803). Plowden's book was reviewed in *ER* v (no. ix, Oct. 1804), 152–67, probably by Loch (*WI*).

146. From Thomas Thomson

⟨*Thomson*, pp. 52–3⟩   Edinburgh, 24 Dec. 1803

⟨... I hope you are to give us Malthus for next number, or what else. Lord Lauderdale is going rapidly through the press, – a *thumping* octavo. Stewart says it is better written than any of his former publications, and contains some good ideas, blended with a good many erroneous ones, – it is rich in valuable quotations. What a *bonne bouche* for your politico-economical maw. I long to see you munch it. ...⟩

147. To Dr John Thomson

BLPES ii. 72–3   The Temple, 10 Jan. 1804

I have great pleasure in telling you, that Sir James Mackintosh takes the most warm and active interest in our success.[1] He determined at once to write to Addington, but a more favourable opportunity presented itself, in consequence of the Minister having desired to see him in Downing St yesterday forenoon. At this interview, M[ackintosh] introduced the subject of Allen's canvass, which he found was already known; and placed it on the best footing. He does not feel himself entitled or inclined to ask any favour of them, because he never has had, and would not have, any political connection with the present people. He spoke of it therefore as a public measure of a literary nature, in which he was warmly interested; both by what he knew of Allen's high merits, and by his attachment to the university in which he had been educated – that that university had suffered much of late years by an absurd system of hereditary professorships, and by several unfit nominations of the Town Council – that the present was an occasion on which Government might introduce one of the ablest and most scientific men in the kingdom, and that it would be honourable to the King's Government to show that in their department at least the appointments were influenced by that consideration. Addington heard this with much attention, and observed that Tierney had already spoken of Mr Allen to him in the strongest terms of recommendation.[2] He must have heard of him, however, from *other* quarters; for he asked Mackintosh, whether Allen was sound in matters of religion and politics, and whether he had not in the late times shown some violence in these respects. Mackintosh said, those were times of prescription – that no man's character was to be taken from them – that subsequent events had moderated the opinions of most men.[3] This seemed to give tolerable satisfaction;[4] and, upon the whole, Addington appeared to have received an impression that Allen was the fittest man for the situation. He mentioned having been applied to, in favour of some other person, by Lord Buchan; the only danger from this quarter is, that Tom Erskine has lately been in the way of exerting some influence.[5] I hope Lord Lauderdale has done something to gain, or at least to neutralize him. In order to guard us farther against this danger, if it amounts to any thing, I have written to Mr Adam about it; unluckily, he is at present in Bedfordshire.

From what I can perceive, it is of much importance to us that the matter should be decided as soon as possible. If the cry of atheism and Jacobinism becomes very loud against us, it will frighten the Doctor. Besides this, it will be prudent to make it as little a question of political connections, as we can keep it; for it seems still the policy of the present Ministers, to do nothing that may personally and strikingly offend Lord Melville;[6] he [is a] great card for any of the players to wave and all of them have such assurance of his trimming nature, that no party despairs of gaining him.[7]

...

1. Horner refers to a canvass led by Lauderdale for the appointment of John Allen as Professor of Natural History at Edinburgh.
2. George Tierney (1761–1830: *DNB*) was Treasurer of the Navy in Addington's Administration.
3. Two words have been blotted out here.
4. Two lines have been blotted out here.
5. Thomas Erskine, afterwards 1st Baron Erskine (1750–1823: *DNB*), was the youngest brother of David Steuart Erskine, 11th Earl of Buchan (1742–1829: *DNB*).
6. Henry Dundas, 1st Viscount Melville (1742–1811: *DNB*).
7. The canvass for Allen was unsuccessful despite the support of Dugald Stewart and a number of other professors at Edinburgh University, of Lauderdale and the Scottish adherents of Fox, of Horner's closest friends in Edinburgh, and of a number of influential English Whigs. Further comment on the canvass is in Horner's letters to Loch of 5 Jan. and to Dr John Thomson of 7 and 16 Jan., and also in Brougham's letter to Horner of 10 Jan. (BLPES ii. 68–71, 74–5, and 80–81).

148. To Francis Jeffrey

BLPES ii. 82–3   [London], 26 Jan. 1804

In the present state of Thelwal's notoriety, I must agree with those who think that *nothing* should be done or written.[1] As I have not seen the pamphlet, I cannot be quite confident in my opinion; but judging from what it is possible from him to have said, and from what you describe to be the impression it has produced at Edinburgh, I am almost perfectly confident. It is not heard of in London, nor likely to be; for Philips told Rees that his name had been put into the advertisement without his privity, and that he was determined no copy of it should be bought at his shop.[2] I think this should set your mind entirely at ease – for the present at least. If any publisher can be found more blackguard than Philips, and any purchasers of any thing written by Thelwal, and any believers in what Thelwal should write against the Reviewer of Mounier and Gentz and Southey, then you shall hear of it; my ears will be anxiously alive to catch the faintest rumours, and we shall then deliberate on the measures to be taken.

You ask me what I have been doing? I have not of late been very busy, but have been going about a little. This is the time when society in London begins to be most attractive; and society is included in my plans of study. I find however that I hardly know my letters yet. From what you say of Tom Sheridan, I perceive he must be a good specimen of a class that is very numerous here; the *quizzers*, an amusing breed enough, and by no means unuseful in their generation. Quizzing, indeed, is almost the staple of London conversation. To a man just imported from Edinburgh college, it is so in a mortifying and terrific degree; for the most venerable reveries of his philosophy are set at nought, and treated with a levity which scandalizes his Presbyterian prejudices, like music on a Sunday. In this way, no doubt, a little mischief is done; as important topics and serious discussions are often exiled from the conversation of men the best qualified to treat them.[3] But upon the whole, we are much indebted to the quizzers; they are our only guards against a much more pernicious and offensive race, the quacks, who but for this vigilant police would over-run us. In every company you go into in this place, there are two or more canting empirics, ready to overwhelm all common sense with their music, or criticism, or charity, or pictures, etc., etc. I suppose this is a disease naturally incident to great cities – and on the other hand, quizzing seems to me the effort which nature makes, by virtue of her *vis medicatrix*, to keep down that disease. At the same time, I suspect she is a little assisted in the formation of such quizzers as we have, by the habits of common and combination rooms: whether quizzing might not become more refined, by becoming less collegiate, I leave to the examination of the curious.

...

I hope to see poet Campbell this afternoon, and will talk to him about the *Review*. I hope he will engage himself in it seriously, because it would bring him a little money, which he much needs; and though he would perhaps contribute little that would of itself make a reputation, the reputation he has already made and the *éclat* of his name would support his contributions. I think with you, that he would not review poetry well; yet I do not know what he would do better. And though he is unqualified for philosophical criticism, or to make a large estimate of unequal merits, he must have habits of minute observation, and has an instinctive fervour both in his verses and his conversation that would necessarily appear now and then in his prose. Besides, it would be of great service to himself to review poetical productions, by leading him to study his art; which I doubt if he has patience and formality enough to do, from remote and systematic views of ambition. All that Campbell wants is art; and it were a public calamity that for want of it the tenderness and fire of his genius should waste themselves in mistaken efforts.

In about a week hence I mean to set about Malthus for you, and mean to work at him very seriously; his book has made itself a great name among the thinking people here. That I may judge it with more freedom, I have declined one or two opportunities of cultivating the author's acquaintance; which I mean however to do, when I get loose from my task. He is a man, in conversation, of good sense, great candour, and liberality; the last is a rare qualification for an English clergyman, even after the splendid instance of our friend Smith. Apropos of the Sid; he is very well, and very merry, and by the roar of his animal spirits, and that happy combination of drollery and calm good sense, makes daily conquests in the society of London. ...

Where I dined yesterday, there was Wilkins the Sanscrit scholar;[4] who quite won me, by talking in the highest terms of Hamilton's knowledge and oriental attainments. He spoke of some institution for the promoting of that literature, which he wishes to be formed in London, and of which he wishes that Hamilton should be the head. ...

...

1. Jeffrey had criticized John Thelwall (1764–1834: DNB) in the first number of the ER and in 1803 Thelwall replied with a short pamphlet addressed to the editor which needlessly upset Jeffrey. See Clive, p. 144.
2. Richard (afterwards Sir Richard) Phillips (1767–1840: DNB), was a London bookseller and publisher, as was also Owen Rees (1770–1837: DNB).
3. The levity of London conversation had troubled Horner for some time. In a letter to Reddie of 14 Nov. 1803 (Horner, i. 247), he had observed: 'I have already found, I assure you, even in ordinary literary conversation, the necessity of unlearning something of the manners which one imbibes in the metaphysical climate of Edinburgh: such as the inclination to theorize, and to present general principles or rules in a scholastic dress.'
4. Charles (afterwards Sir Charles) Wilkins (?1749–1836: DNB), orientalist.

149. To Francis Jeffrey

BLPES ii. 84–5   The Temple, 11 Feb. 1804

Do not, I beseech you, publish a single line in answer to Thelwal. I implore you – do not; by every form and force of obtestation I implore you. This is the feeling of every body here; of all your friends, and of all who are their friends. Pray, be satisfied with the approbation of such, and do not attempt to satisfy those who can compose an audience for Mr Thelwal at Glasgow. I have not a low opinion of your powers of composition; yet I hold it quite beyond your powers, to tell the story so well for you, as Thelwal has already told it. I have consulted Whishaw on the subject, as well as divers others, scrupulous observers of decorum and all the proprieties of character. They are unanimously and strongly of this opinion. What would you have more? It is very natural for me, when personally attacked, to fancy that something ought to be done; but it is quite a delusive feeling; two months hence, you will see this subject exactly as Smith and I and all your other friends see it now. There is nothing on which a man can so ill judge for himself, as an occasion of this sort.

I have hardly considered your 6th Number. The only advantage I derive from having a copy before the general publication in town, is that I can gratify the curiosity of the impatient. I ought not to speak of your review of Stewart; because you plead guilty to haste, and seem to glory in being wrong on some points. If I were in the mood for it, you should have a bitter scold; I was very anxious about this article. You had a good opportunity, which you have despised. I should have easily forgiven your differing in metaphysics from me; but I cannot forgive, at least hardly, your being indifferent about your execution of so fine a subject. But, no more of this – only, in your next edition, alter that sentence in which you have, surely from inattention, coupled Condorcet's name with Stewart's. Alter it, at my request, and for my sake, if on no other account. It must have given a moment of pain to one, who is sensitive to an extreme, and whom I love and venerate so much that I would save him from a moment's pain at a considerably greater expense to my own blunt nerves.[1] The Public will certainly sympathize with the review of Godwin's *Chaucer* – which is amusing enough, after Scott's coarse manner;[2] the coarseness begins to border on something still worse, towards the end of the article, where there are some sentiments that might have been spared or at least softened.

...

1. Horner was of course aware how much suspicion Stewart had aroused by himself appearing to cite Condorcet with approval in his 1792 *Elements*. In a letter of 19 Feb. 1804 Jeffrey agreed to amend his errors, but told Horner that he was too sensitive, defending his own view of the limits of metaphysical discoveries and offering to 'take any wager you please, that when we are both eighty, you will be very much of my opinion'. The mention of Condorcet was not omitted from subsequent reprints. (Winch, pp. 32–3; *Jeffrey*, ii. 87–8.)
2. Walter Scott had reviewed William Godwin's *Life of Chaucer* (1803) in *ER* iii (no. vi, Oct. 1803), 437–52.

150. To J.A. Murray

BLPES ii. 86–7   The Temple, 17 Feb. 1804

I expected to have been in the Gallery all this forenoon, waiting for a great debate on the Volunteer Act.[1] But the King's illness has suspended that and other discussions. I have heard no farther accounts this morning, than what you will see in the Newspapers; but wait in hourly expectation of hearing the minute guns and the tolling from St Paul's, which is the ceremony (I understand) of announcing to

London the death of the Sovereign. Mr Addington said to the Prince on Wednesday, that he did not believe he could live beyond that day; this the P[rince] mentioned to the Duke of Bedford, and so you will conjecture how it came to me.[2] We have at present no other topic of conversation or curiosity. It is probable, indeed, that the event will be very important in its consequences; and the changes that at all events must ensue, will be very entertaining. Some of my good friends, the Whigs, are sanguine enough to look upon this as the very eve of a millennium and regeneration under {that Constitutional Redeemer, our Lord}[3] Charles Fox. But I begin to be very slow in taking up these hopes. It is more probable, that the said {our lord}[4] will be jockeyed by the P[rince] and Sheridan. We may even have a continuation of blessings under the house of Medici.[5] And at the very best, I cannot believe that Fox could be Minister to George the fourth for more than six months.

I was not in the House the other night when Petty made his first appearance – but the accounts I have got of it agree, that he spoke extremely well, and was listened to with most respectful attention. He has indeed established a high character for sense, propriety, and information. I think he was not a little timid in the conclusion he came to about the Irish Bank, and I have told him so. Old Foster had been talking him over. And Petty, it appears to me, is not yet sufficiently familiarized with these subjects, to see them in their real simplicity, or to hold them quite firmly enough. There was never so plain a case as this conduct of the Irish Bank.[6]

I have got Jeffrey's answer.[7] The parcel, if I am not mistaken, was directed in your handwriting. It is extremely well done; but, I still think, ought not to have been done at all. The temper of it is admirable. This answer will do Jeffrey no harm, but it can do him no good, because Thelwall has done him no harm.

...

1. For a short assessment of Pitt's controversial volunteer system, which Horner regarded as an apparent 'blunder', and of the respective positions of Pitt and Fox on that issue, see the journal entry of 18 Jan. in *Horner*, i. 254–6.
2. John Russell, 6th Duke of Bedford (1766–1839).
3. Scratched through, apparently by Leonard Horner.
4. Scratched through, apparently by Leonard Horner, and replaced by 'Charles'.
5. Addington's Ministry.
6. Lord Henry Petty delivered his maiden speech in the House of Commons, on the Irish Bank Restriction Act, on 13 Feb. (*Hansard*, i. 479–80). 'Old Foster' was perhaps John Leslie Foster (see Doc. 176), but more probably his uncle John Foster, afterwards 1st Baron Oriel (1740–1828: *DNB*), who had been the last Speaker of the Irish House of Commons and had just taken his seat at Westminster, where he harried the Government on the anomalous rate of exchange between England and Ireland and managed to get a committee with himself as chairman to look into it. He was also contesting the bill to extend the suspension of cash payments by the Bank of Ireland.
7. Contrary to Horner's advice (Doc. 149), Jeffrey had published *Observations on Mr Thelwall's Letter to the Editor of the Edinburgh Review* (Edinburgh, 1804).

151. To J.A. Murray

BLPES ii. 88–9   The Temple, 28 Feb. 1804

... To put myself in good humour with you again, I can think of nothing better than to give you some account of last night's debate.[1] I went there with Loch and Henry Brougham, who had never heard Fox speak; and he said that Pitt's voice would be balm to his soul. We went accordingly very early; and though we sat fifteen hours in that gallery, we agree that we purchased our entertainment very cheaply. The principal order of the day was the second reading of the Volunteer Bill; but the bulletin of Sunday from the King's physicians gave birth to a previous debate, which was extremely interesting on this account, that the game played by all the speakers was evidently to entangle the poor Doctor either in some undesigned confession or at least in a lie. In the latter, they perfectly succeeded; and Canning certainly was the person who had the merit of first casting the net over the unhappy animal, who looked very amazed and forlorn while Grey and Thomas Grenville were drawing the noose close.[2] Addington intended to say at first, I believe, no more than this, that any emergency indispensably demanding a personal exertion of the executive power was not immediately to be looked for; so that a little farther time might be allowed to Ministers, for the chance of a recovery. But he expressed himself in such a way, as half to suggest that there was nothing at present for the King to do, and half – that there was nothing at present which he might not be able to do. Upon the whole, from former instances of convicted prevarication, I presume that he probably had no objection to take advantage of either meaning. Canning, however, managed it so well as to fix the latter upon him explicitly; and you have now an assertion of the Doctor that the King is *compos mentis*. You will understand this account better, by referring to the reports of the debate; though, in the *Morning Chronicle* at least, there is not such a view of Canning's speech, as to give you the *progress* of this very amusing and skilful decoy. The Ministers were sorely badgered through the whole evening by Windham, Fox, and by Pitt who declared the most contemptuous and determined hostility. Fox's last speech is very ill reported; it delighted Brougham highly, which highly delighted me, as hitherto he never appeared to me to appreciate justly Fox's vast powers. As I am a great proselytizer, you know, to Whiggism – though I altogether despair of ever converting you – it gave me on Brougham's account a sort of vulgar Whig satisfaction that Pitt spoke rather dully and wordily. B[rougham] confessed he '*bothered damnably*'. Since he [Pitt] went a colonelling, he appears to have got all the boyish fondness for a new subject and for all the most theoretical parts of it. He dwelt very much on what he intends to propose in the committee upon the Bill; his former scheme of assistant field officers and adjutants, rules for enforcing attendance, as well as steadiness and *silence* during attendance, with a grand project of sending us all into quarters, with a marching guinea for our pains. All of which appears to me mighty childish – and quite unworthy of a great English statesman in the year 1804. I never heard Grenville till last night; he is very sensible, distinct, and acute in his matter; but after the first twenty minutes, his delivery becomes unpleasant. His indiscriminate emphasis comes to have no more effect in one respect, than no emphasis at all, at the same time that your attention is fretted and worried, by an eternal ringing of misplaced pauses and emphasis upon nothings. As to Charles Yorke and Lord Castlereagh, we agreed, after mature deliberation, that they do not deserve to be equalled to our third rate orators in the Speculative; at least then Masters Simpson and Kennedy had subjects worthy of their powers.[3] ...

1. The proceedings of 27 Feb. included the property tax, the King's illness, and the Volunteer Consolidation Act (*Hansard*, i. 507–567).
2. Lord Grenville's younger brother Thomas Grenville (1755–1846: *DNB*).
3. Charles Philip Yorke (1764–1834: *DNB*) was Home Secretary in the latter part of Addington's Ministry. The members of the Speculative with whom he and Castlereagh were unfavourably compared appear to have been James Simpson (1781–1853: *DNB*), advocate, friend of Walter Scott, and author of numerous works on education, and Robert Kennedy (1783–1805), who was also an advocate. The subjects of their various essays are recorded in *Speculative Society*, pp. 220 and 231.

152. To John Horner

BLPES ii. 90–91   The Temple, Thursday [8 Mar. 1804]

...

I was at the debate last night; though it was rather heavy, I remained till four o'clock this morning, chiefly from curiosity to know the division. For that on Tuesday almost gave one hopes that the house of Medici was tottering. The result last night was, I think, that Lord Hardwicke was *surprised* on the 23rd July, and had been culpably negligent. The government of Ireland, however, has been so mild compared to the former reign of terror, that I hardly wished success to the motion; though I should wish most heartily success to a motion that would remove from that government so unfit a person as Lord Redesdale. This man was so far from having any of this unseasonable and mischievous cant, before he married a Perceval (who are all canters) and got the Irish seals, that the lawyers of whom I have asked the question rather hint that he was suspected of not being righteous over-much. So much for the Orange piety, and for the poor misgoverned Irish.[1]

... You would observe that there is a committee on the subject of Irish circulation, Foster chairman; they are examining all the principal people connected with Irish remittances, Puget, Burrowes,[2] etc. A member told me that they have got some curious information; but have to extract it from unwilling witnesses, and on this account from very contradictory statements.

1. The long-expected motion for an inquiry into the causes of the Irish insurrection of 23 July 1803 had at last been brought forward on 7 Mar. and lost by a majority of 96 (*Hansard*, i. 738–806). Previously the Volunteer Consolidation Bill had been considered further on 6 Mar., when the Government had been forced to give ground on a number of amendments (*ibid.*, 719–34). Philip Yorke, 3rd Earl of Hardwicke (1757–1834: *DNB*), was Lord Lieutenant of Ireland in 1801–1806. Redesdale, the Irish Chancellor, was married to the sister of Spencer Perceval (1762–1812: *DNB*), the Attorney-General.
2. John Pujet was the London agent for the Bank of Ireland and Walter Borrowes also a London merchant. An extract from Pujet's evidence is conveniently reproduced (pp. 118–21) in Frank Whitson Fetter's edition of *The Irish Pound 1797–1826. A Reprint of the Report of the Committee of 1804 of the British House of Commons on the Condition of the Irish Currency* (1955).

153. To Francis Jeffrey

BLPES ii. 92–3   The Temple, 29 Mar. 1804

... I have spoke to Brougham about Lauderdale's book; he is quite resolute, and will not yield it. I don't wonder at this, for after reading it, I have felt as if I should like to have done it myself. There is novelty and error enough to give an excellent opportunity for a *critique raisonnée*. What he says about capital appears to me sound – though I have read it but once, and that superficially. The manner in which Smith is spoken of is the most reprehensible feature of the book, and I should have been willing to stand forward in reprehension of it. There may be some foundation for the censure of indistinctness in the theoretical exposition of his first principles; but there can be no apology for Lauderdale's petulance, conceit, and acrimony. Our gratitude never can exceed the benefits which we owe to Smith; and if the peer does not in time acquire more reverence for his memory, and a juster sense of his merits, he will remain, what he is at present with all his acuteness and readiness, a political speculator of the third or fourth class.[1] ... I hear Wheatley is about to publish another work in political economy, by which he is utterly to subvert, overthrow and demolish the speculations of one Adam Smith. This young man's career must be cut short, if he is to think of going on at this rate. Will you allow me to bespeak him for myself; Brougham treated him last time with too mild a regimen, though that is not *his* usual course of practice.[2] We are infinitely amused with Brougham's intimacy with the Saints here,[3] the salt of the earth; he has been dining with Wilberforce, and passing the night at Stephen's house where he had family worship to join in, morn and evening.[4] Would not you have given all your hopes of heaven (not a great price on your part), for a sight of Brougham upon his knees? ... Sydney [Smith] has now fixed his foot upon holy ground – as a morning preacher at an aristocratic chapel. I look upon this as securing his fortunes in that line; he so far excels all his competitors, that nothing but the opportunity of showing himself was wanting. He is quite determined, I believe, about the *Review*;[5] and after considering the matter as calmly as I could, I came to the opinion that he is bound to adhere to that resolution by every consideration of prudence. Concealment is out of the question; if it were practicable, he would not like it, and ought not to like it; and it would materially retard, if not permanently obstruct his success in the line he has chosen here, if he were known to write in a Review so independent and so odious as ours. When you have seen a little of London society, you will approve what he has done. Peter Elmsley and I do not often meet – scarcely indeed except at the monthly club;[6] we never took to each other very willingly on either side – and our reciprocal powers of attraction seem rather to weaken than gain strength. He has no doubt a liberal, acute, and full understanding; but the longer I live among men, the more I value and require those manners and dispositions which learning will not confer, nor atone for the want of. I should be sorry not to meet him once a month; but I am not solicitous to fall in his way more frequently. I saw Coleridge one morning lately – he has very extraordinary powers of conversation undoubtedly – as a man of letters – not in good taste as conversation – but with a certain fervour and exaggeration of expression, that is very imposing, and sometimes really eloquent. He is now gone on board the vessel which is to convey him to Malta – from which he proceeds to Syracuse, where it is his intention to remain a considerable time. He has professed, with a little of the fervour I speak of, his desire to be farther acquainted with Brougham and me; which, considering the *Edinburgh Review*, is curious. I don't admire these sudden affections. ...

1. For Horner's comments on Brougham's review of Lauderdale's *Public Wealth* and on some aspects of their respective views of Adam Smith, see especially Docs 165, 166, and 168 n. 4. See also Fontana, pp. 65–8.
2. This may perhaps be a reference to Wheatley's 1805 pamphlet, *Thoughts on the object of a foreign subsidy*, which was never reviewed. But it may well be a premature reference to Wheatley's *Essay on the theory of money and principles of commerce* (2 vols, 1807 and 1822), the first volume of which was reviewed in *ER* x (no. xx, July 1807), 284–99. That review has been tentatively attributed to Brougham or David Buchanan (*WI*), but whoever wrote it, it was so hostile as probably to have at least helped delay the appearance of the second volume for fifteen years.
3. Brougham's *Colonial Policy* had brought him some reputation as an opponent of the African slave trade. He followed Horner to London in Nov. 1803 and, apparently perceiving that opposition to the slave trade offered a road to political advancement, affiliated himself for a time with Wilberforce and the 'Saints', who were preparing to bring a motion for abolition before Parliament once again. In the spring of 1804 Brougham assumed a prominent role in the Abolition Committee and wrote an incisive pamphlet which was in the hands of every member of Parliament before Wilberforce made his motion on 30 May 1804 and which Pitt held in his hand when he spoke in favour of abolition on 7 June. (See New, pp. 21–6.)
4. Horner had met Wilberforce at Sir William Grant's house on the evening of 28 May 1803; afterwards Wilberforce noted in his diary (*Wilberforce*, iii. 102) that Horner was 'a man of extraordinary talents'.
5. To sever his connection with it.
6. London's Scottish Club.

154. To Leonard Horner

BLPES ii. 98–100   [London, late March 1804]

...

Your expedition to Ireland with Mr Baxter will be very agreeable to you;[1] and you may make it useful to me, if you will take the trouble to pick up in the Bookseller's shops at Belfast any pamphlets that you can find relating to the present state of the Irish currency, or the linen manufacture; particularly, any papers relative to the late attempts of the manufacturers to force the Notes of the Dublin Bank into circulation in the North. I do not know the titles of any such pamphlets, but you will easily get such as there may be by describing them in this general way. There was one published very lately at Dublin, which I should like to have; it is this: *Enquiry into the depreciation of Irish Bank Paper, its effects and causes, and a remedy proposed*, Dublin, printed for Mahon, 1804. Try also to get *two* copies for me of the Irish pirated edition of Adam Smith's posthumous Essays; it is in 8vo., and uniform in size with the editions I have of his other works. The title is, *Essays on Philosophical subjects, by Adam Smith, with his life* by Dug. Stewart, Dublin, printed for Messrs Wogan, Byrne, etc., 1795. ...

...

I must not let this letter go, without a little politics; as I know my Father loves to hear what is going on. We are made to expect three great debates very soon. Immediately after the holidays, Mr Fox is to make a motion about the Russian mediation. The Slave Trade is to be brought again under consideration, by a motion for a direct abolition; the abolitionists feel themselves stronger, in consequence of the recent changes in the West Indies, and are very sanguine of success: Brougham has seen a good deal of them lately at Wilberforce's house. The greatest debate of all will be on a motion for an inquiry into the State of the Nation; Pitt will not move it himself, but has thrown out repeated hints, and in such a manner that he was sure they would be repeated, that he thought such a motion was extremely proper, and was likely to unite more votes against ministers than any other question, etc. So that we expect to have rare amusement at the Doctor's expense. On the other hand he is endeavouring to muster all his forces – by writing to Scotland and Ireland for all his people to attend.

The new Chief Justice is not yet appointed; and the reports about it are still unsettled. One is, that old Mansfield is to have the place, but without a peerage. Another, that Lord Redesdale is to be brought there, Sir Wm Grant to go as Chancellor to Ireland, and Perceval to be made Master of the Rolls; which will keep him in the House of Commons, where the Doctors much need him. It must be settled somehow in a few days.[2]

...

1. Baxter had formerly been John Horner's clerk and, with Leonard Horner, was now his partner in London (Byrne Memoirs, p. 124; *Leonard Horner*, i. 3 and 10).
2. The Chief Justice of Common Pleas, Richard Pepper Arden, 1st Baron Alvanley (1745–1804: *DNB*), had died on 19 Mar. but was not succeeded by Sir John Masefield (1733–1821: *DNB*) until 8 May. Redesdale remained Lord Chancellor of Ireland until dismissed by the Fox Administration in February 1806. Consequently Sir William Grant (1752–1832: *DNB*) remained Master of the Rolls and Spencer Perceval survived to continue as Attorney-General under Pitt.

155. To Leonard Horner

BLPES ii. 101–102 ⟨*The Irish Pound 1797–1826.*
A Reprint of the Report of the Committee of 1804 of the British House of Commons on the Condition of the Irish Currency,
ed. Frank Whitson Fetter (1955) 118–21.⟩   The Temple, [?early April 1804]

...

⟨I have found in London the Dublin pamphlet I mentioned in my last, called an *Inquiry into the Depreciation, etc.*, so that you will be spared the trouble of getting it for me in Belfast.⟩ But you will oblige me very much by attending to my other commissions in that quarter. ⟨You would oblige me⟩ still more, ⟨if you would make yourself master of the subject of Irish exchange and currency, when you are on the spot, where particular inquiries can be made; not that I think your brethren the merchants are in general very skilful in the art of communicating their information. There are one or two points in this subject of Irish circulation, which puzzle me very much; and which I find puzzle some of my friends who are upon the Parliamentary Committee about it. The inquiries of this Committee will give us a good many curious facts. Thornton attends these constantly; and he understands these matters better than any body else in London. Lord Archibald Hamilton told me an anecdote very creditable to Foster, who is chairman.[1] When he came over at the beginning of spring, he knew only the facts and details of the business, and of course had very confident prejudices and errors – he has since studied it in the general view, and has come over entirely to the plain and liberal opinions which a general view gives and can alone give. It is a curious proof of the degree in which Adam Smith's speculations and others of the kind are studied by the young men in Parliament, beyond the attention that was paid to such topics by the politicians who were educated at an earlier period of the last century; that Mr Foster should have formed his opinion almost under the guidance of Hamilton and Petty, and Lord Grenville corrected his under Lord King.⟩

...

1. Lord Archibald Hamilton (1770–1827: *DNB*) was a prominent Opposition MP. He joined Foster's attacks on the Government's financial policy in Ireland and was a member of his committee.

156. To John Horner

BLPES ii. 94–5 ⟨*Horner*, i. 261–3⟩   [London, 24 Apr. 1804]

...

⟨... I was at the door of the House by half past eight; so that we had a pretty good seat of it, till three next morning.[1] But we were fully rewarded. I have not read the report in the *Morning Chronicle*; but if it is no better than they have been of late, you will receive but a feeble impression of the debate. Fox's opening speech was not eloquent; on the contrary, slovenly as to manner, and languid; probably from an express intention to restrain himself on personal topics, that he might not anticipate Pitt in this respect; he did not allude to ministers, but confined himself to the inadequacy of the present arrangements for national defence, and the means of improving them into a permanent system by a better plan of recruiting, and by regulations for military exercises among the peasantry. All the substance of his speech was excellent. Pitt gave us both substance and manner, as a debater of the highest powers; most explicit in his declaration against ministers, which he delivered, however, as if at last after much consideration and reluctance; but he enforced it with a good deal of grave vehement declamation in his way, and some touches of that bitter freezing sarcasm, which everybody agrees is his most original talent, and appears indeed most natural to him. His speech was very argumentative and full of details; throughout, the impression he left was, and he disguised very successfully his anxiety to make this impression, that every measure government had adopted for the national defence originated from his suggestion, which they had marred, however, by adopting them imperfectly, and carrying them still worse into execution. The speeches of ministers were confined, till the Attorney-General rose, to the defence of the different parts of their military measures that had been attacked; Perceval took a much more judicious view of the debate, and treated the motion as if it had been in terms for the dismissal of ministers. This was the true mode of treating it, if he could have executed his idea with skill; but his want of talent drove him to violence and extreme personality, so as to betray the fury and despair of his friends, or rather their convulsions in death. His personal abuse of Fox and Windham was vulgar and gross in the extreme. But we in the gallery were much indebted to him, for it produced a masterly speech from each in their very different styles. Windham repelled the personality, chiefly by the contrast of his own manner; with great fire, but perfect temper, a very polite contempt, and exquisite wit; he spoke not more than ten minutes, but he refreshed one's mind from all the bad feelings that Perceval had given us. Fox treated him after a different regimen; condemning, with much vehemence and indignation, the faction and ribaldry which he had introduced into the debate; and defending his own political connections and conduct with all the manliness and simplicity of his best manner. It is very likely that, so soon after the great entertainment I have had, I may be talking of it in a way that you will suppose exaggerated; but if it is so, you will know how to make allowances. One feature of the debate I must not forget; the fulsome adulation paid by Tierney, and the Attorney-General to Pitt; the latter of whom said, that no event could be more agreeable to the country than his return to power – a very strange expression to use in such circumstances.⟩ These two fellows will probably make a separate bargain, if they have an opportunity; what their opportunities will be, we shall know very soon – for ⟨after such a division as that of last night, nobody conceives the Doctor can any longer remain at the head.⟩[2]

1. On Thursday, 23 Apr., there had been a much-anticipated debate on a motion by Fox for a committee of the whole House to revise the several bills for the defence of the country and to consider further measures capable of making national defence more complete and permanent.

2. Fox's motion was defeated by 256 votes to 204, but with Pitt as well as Fox now in open opposition it was clear the Government was going to fall.

157. To John Horner

BLPES ii. 96–7   [London, 26 Apr. 1804]

...

The situation of political parties is at present very curious; the state of the King's health, and the still more ambiguous conduct of Pitt, keep them completely in suspense. The Doctor holds only by the misunderstanding of his enemies. Had there been a junction last night, he would have been left in a minority; and I suppose it is in consequence of that, that his usual voters have received this morning a circular note, requesting them to attend, though nothing particular is expected. The division last night appears a piece of great mismanagement on the part of Fox and Wyndham; for it does away, at least in some degree, the effect of that which took place on Thursday: an advantage that ought to have been pushed no doubt, but which it required great nicety to follow up well, while Pitt plays so entirely his own game.[1] He is playing it with great skill, no doubt, and with a great chance of having the sole nomination of his own cabinet; but even his immediate partisans, I am told, such as Canning and Sturges,[2] admit that a plainer and more decided line of conduct would be more becoming. He seems determined to unkennel the Doctor; but without the assistance, at least without any coalition of the other parties. All this while, there can be very little dependence on another personage, the Prince; last Saturday he sent for Fox to have an interview with him on public affairs, and nothing could be more favourable to Fox's views than what he expressed. Yet last night all the Prince's men, with Sheridan at their head, voted with Ministers. What is your Lord Advocate doing, that he skulks from Parliament? We have not been able to guess how he would have voted last Thursday.

You will think my head full of politics; I never in my life was more cool about them, because I have no hopes of any thing turning out as I should like to see it. But it is an amusing crisis of parties, at which to look on as a spectator; and the debates are a great school, where I am trying to learn something, that may hereafter be of use.[3]

1. A further debate on defence on 25 Apr., in which both Fox and Windham again spoke, again produced a majority for the Government, by 240 to 203, but it was their last in the Commons.

2. Presumably William Sturges-Bourne (1769–1845: *DNB*), afterwards Joint Secretary of the Treasury under Pitt.

3. As revealed by his journal entries, Horner's political ambitions mounted steadily after his arrival in London, and he studied the social and political manners of the English very closely during late 1803 and the early months of 1804. The entry of 8 Oct. 1803 noted the necessity of limiting and regulating ambition, of arranging remote views, and of maintaining 'a sedate, practical, calm prospect'. That of 29 Nov. 1803 noted: 'Systematic opinions, at least steady and systematic views of object of government, under form like ours; – regulated views of ambition; – strike just medium of approbation and feeling with regard to present state of affairs and opinions; – ambition of office under the Roman republic, compared with that under English monarchy; – ambition of legal office, in what respects similar to that of political office, and in what different; – rules, reduced into practical and ready habit, for judging of the political integrity of public characters; not even acquainted with the duties and proprieties of such a situation.' That of 9 Jan. 1804 noted: 'Form a connection with the Whig aristocracy of England. Upon what footing do I join? Upon what footing am I at present received or invited? As lawyer to be – as having already studied political philosophy; – preserve this independent character. Early part of Burke's life – Lord Somers's – Romilly's. Transfer of examples and maxims from Plutarch and Livy to England.' And that of 2 Feb. 1804 emphasized the importance of the 'art of listening'. (*Horner*, i. 256–7 and 363–4.)

158. To Leonard Horner

BLPES ii. 103–104   [London], 1 May [1804]

...

We had a party of reviewers at my sister's yesterday, where we were very happy and very noisy.[1] ...

I meant to-day to have given my Father a packet of political stories; but the proceeding in the house of Lords last night has put them all out of my head, till we hear it fully explained.[2] It was altogether unexpected: Pitt was on the steps of the throne, staring and biting his nails.

...

1. Jeffrey had visited London in late April and had stayed in Horner's chambers at the Temple (Horner to Frances Horner, 1 May, Byrne Memoirs, pp. 87–8). Horner's eldest sister Elizabeth was married to G. Leckie (d. 1812), a rich West Indian merchant. Apparently the Leckies had houses both in London and in Hampstead, John Horner senior and his family staying with them first in one and then the other for three months in the spring and summer of 1803. But from the summer of 1804 John Horner himself leased a large house in Frognal, until moving in 1807 to another in Russell Square. In the summer of 1813 they finally removed back again to Edinburgh. (Ibid., pp. 68, 69, 101, and 147.)
2. The Marquess of Stafford was to have moved a motion similar to that by which Fox had divided the Commons on 23 Apr., but on being appealed to by the Government, he agreed to postpone it. Apparently the Government recognized that it would have to resign but in view of the King's ill health, wished first to smooth the way for Pitt.

159. To John Horner

BLPES ii. 105–106   The Temple, 14 May 1804

...

So there is a fine end of all the struggles in the House of Commons – the old stern tyranny of Pitt, and the vulgar patronage system of old Lord Melville [?are restored].[1] It is not quite so bad as it would have been, if the Grenvilles had also gone into power; but they are a bad breed, and I have very feeble hopes of their being long out of it. They are well-placed in Opposition, to which they give the weight of large fortunes, extensive connections, and a fair proportion of talent; but their aristocratic character mixes but ill with Fox's principles, and still worse with his occasional language. Unlucky as the end has been, we are disposed to maintain here that Fox has only done his duty, in the assistance he gave to dislodge the Doctor; it is at least a partial triumph, to drive out the favourites of the court, though they may not be replaced by the favourites of the people. I have been a good deal surprised with the language I have heard from some people, who are the professed and zealous partisans of Pitt; they have no scruple in lamenting, that he yielded so easily to the King, and that he did not insist on forming a *broad* Administration. It is quite evident that his friends are ashamed of his late conduct; and that many of them really wished the experiment to be made, of having Fox along with him in power. Canning has certainly left town, and will have nothing to do with the new arrangements; though he was well entitled to a respectable station.[2] Even in the City, where Pitt has been worshipped as a sort of deity, a degree of dissatisfaction prevails; originating, I presume, in the feeling, that Pitt and war are inseparable, and that under the present circumstances of the continent, the union of the two greatest names in this country would have struck a great impression.

Lords Melville and Eldon, it is understood, managed the intrigue of last week.[3] You will not easily conceive how much Melville is hated by one description of Pitt's adherents; they look upon him as his evil genius, and it is certain he has a predominating influence over Pitt's mind. It was their dislike of Lord Melville, probably quite as much as their pledge to Fox, that prompted the Grenvilles in their late conduct. Lord Eldon is loudly abused by Addington's friends, as having betrayed him; when he saw them falling, he went to Buckingham House without concert, and has acted as the go-between in all the negotiation with Pitt. He attempted a visit at Carlton House, where he was not received quite as well; but on the contrary with a contempt that was perhaps too coarsely expressed.

...

1. On 12 May it had been announced that Addington had resigned office and that Pitt had been appointed to succeed him. Pitt proceeded to form his last Government without the inclusion of the Grenvilles, but with Melville taking the Admiralty.
2. On the contrary he became Treasurer of the Navy.
3. Eldon remained Lord Chancellor on the change of Government.

160. To J.A. Murray

BLPES ii. 113–14 ⟨Horner, i. 264–5⟩   The Temple, 8 June 1804

...

I quite agree with you about Brougham's pamphlet;[1] indeed all his most intimate friends, I observe, were disappointed, but every body else praises its distinctness and good sense. This is natural enough; B[rougham] could not on such a subject write without much information and much argument, and he ought (to please us) to have taken more pains with the manner. He is much flattered with the notice it has received, as well as with the attention the Saints show him. He is more with Wilberforce and the Thorntons at present, than in any other society; and has been a very active member of their Committee for conducting the Abolition-Bill. Both you (at least Jeffrey) and he attach more importance to this connection, than I can see in it; it is a very pleasant one, for they are well-informed and well-meaning men, and a very honourable connection, for the cause that unites them is truly interesting and great. But the Saints are not properly a political set of men; and their character is so entirely cast from their religious zeal, that there can be little community of sentiment between them and Brougham, when the object that at present brings them together is once gained. You must be anxious to hear of Brougham; I have not seen a great deal of him, but in the conversations we have had upon this and other subjects, nothing can be more perfectly sedate, orderly, and active. In plainness and sobriety, his understanding has been infinitely improved since I left Scotland; and from all I can hear, he has made a great impression in London. There are no symptoms yet of any intention to study Law. I have no doubt that if he gets a seat in the H. of Commons, he will very early establish a respectable name, for information, promptitude and power in debate; the choice of party and connections would perhaps give him some difficulty, and that difficulty he might not have views, sufficiently carried forward and systematized, to conquer completely.

Your Lord Advocate is a very pretty fellow; I thought I could not have under-rated his 'ardour of mind', and yet these proceedings, in senseless intemperance, go beyond my previous idea of his character. The feeling of the House of Commons is very strongly against him; so that you need not be surprised to see the minority, (if it is a minority), very large when Whitbread moves for his impeachment or removal.[2] We shall have Hope and the mad Irish Judge tied together.[3]

⟨Tell Jeffrey not to be so much alarmed; and that I wish to keep Stevens's new pamphlet, called *Opportunity* for a review.[4] Brougham and I have been discussing the subject a little; and I feel myself more inclined to agree with the author, than with Brougham, upon the subject. I wish besides to break a lance in this chivalrous cause, the Slave Trade, before it be quite forgotten; and to pronounce a panegyric on Wilberforce and Co., if they shall prove victorious, or to animate them to farther perseverance if they suffer another defeat. So that you may suspect me of a desire to be converted, if you please, and to labour, as Wilberforce said of Brougham when he introduced him to one of the brethren, 'in the same vineyard'.⟩

...

1. Brougham's anonymous *Concise statement of the question regarding the abolition of the slave trade* (1804) was reviewed by Jeffrey in *ER* iv (no. viii, July 1804), 476–86.
2. In a motion of 6 June Whitbread had attacked the Lord Advocate for his censure of a Banffshire farmer (Morrison) who had discharged a servant for attending the drill of a volunteer regiment. On 22 June a division on party lines rejected the motion by 77 votes, but in the course of the discussions several Ministers had commented adversely on the conduct of the Lord Advocate and he evidently felt he had been insufficiently supported by the Government.
3. About the same time as the vote on Hope's affair, complaint was also laid in the House against the conduct of an Irish judge, Luke Fox, in publicly censuring and humiliating a jury who had acquitted some prisoners of a charge of murder. Subsequently, in July, a whole series of further charges were laid against him in the Lords. But problems of procedure and constitutional nicety prevented any action by Parliament.
4. *The opportunity; or reasons for an immediate alliance with St Domingo. By [James Stephen] the author of 'The crisis of the sugar colonies'* (1804). See Doc. 163.

161. To J.A. Murray

BLPES ii. 117–18   The Temple, 23 June 1804

I take a large sheet of paper, because my text is last night's debate, and my discourse may therefore be long. The Advocate is not yet censured, and the minority, which thought he deserved it, was smaller than people expected. We had the felicity, however, to hear him well licked by able hands, and well exposed by himself. Pitt of course made it quite a party question; and for full assurance of this, let me tell you that the conscientious Wilberforce declared (you will guess to whom) that nothing indeed could be said in defence of Hope, but that 'in the circumstances of the case', that is, in the ticklish state of the new Ministry, he would vote with the Minister: so much for politics according to vital Christianity.

Neither Pitt, nor Will Dundas,[1] nor even the Attorney General, ventured to insult the House with an entire justification; they spoke in extenuation, from motives, from situation, from natural warmth of temper. There were 'indiscreet words', according to Dundas; in Pitt's phrase, there was something both to criticize and to regret, such as he wished had never happened, and trusted would never happen again.

The Advocate himself took a much higher tone; for he did not scruple to affirm, that on a similar occasion he would do the same thing again. He pleaded the high powers of his office, as an executive minister of government, subject to responsibility, and entrusted with a discretion on occasions of state necessity to supply or exceed the law. That it was not as *public prosecutor* he had any thing to say to Morrison, but as the executive minister of Scotland; that ever since the abolition of the Privy Council and state offices at the union, the whole of their powers had devolved upon the Lord Advocate, and that all the functions and power of the resident government at Edinburgh is concentrated in his person; all the superior departments of Government in London, and all the inferior throughout Scotland requiring constant information and assistance from him. He spoke of 'my administration of the government there'; he 'would not say the legality, but the necessity' of his conduct in Morrison's case. He 'was not to measure my official duty and personal responsibility by the cold and frigid forms of strict law'; and his office was not to be compared to 'the dry, dull, precise nature of that of the Attorney General of England.' I took down his words at the time.

The general tone of his speech was insolent and confident; there was a good deal of offensive egotism; and there was an entire absence of dignity or good taste. He was injudicious enough to try two or three feeble jokes, which had no effect but to make the silence more still; such as about that part of his letter, which mentions the return of his fee, which he commented on with a sort of hilarity and professional allusions that were very unsuitable to so grave an occasion. He was even so indelicate as to complain a little of the fees he lost by being brought away from the Session. As to the egotism, he spoke of himself, and his name, and his city; he dwelt repeatedly on his great popularity in his own country, and had the hardiness to assert that in his city had Whitbread coupled his name with violence and injustice, 'an hundred thousand tongues would have moved in my vindication, and perhaps as many arms.'

Windham had some reason to consider this last boast as partaking somewhat of a threat.

There was want of manliness, as well as dignity, in the manner he treated Morrison. He scorned, he said, to shelter himself under insinuations against the man's loyalty, such as he *might have* thrown out under the sanction of official information. But he repeated so frequently that he scorned to throw out such insinuations, and added so regularly that it would have been *easy* for him to have used them, that he did appear to me to be using them all the while in the least pardonable and least courageous manner. He went even farther than this; for though he made no direct charge of the slightest kind against Morrison, he spoke of seditious societies at Portsoy[2] in his neighbourhood, and of persons who might have influence with him having belonged to them some years ago.

Charles Hope has got, not an acquittal, but an *evasion* of the charge by the previous question. He has made an impression here, however, and in the House of Commons, even among those (I am convinced) who gave Pitt their votes, which will not easily be effaced. And the investigation has opened up a sort of bird's eye view upon the government and politics of Scotland, that in better times may lead to better things. In the meantime, my fears are for the worst. I can easily believe that Pitt may give him a private reprimand, because this has not been a very auspicious or very safe discussion at the commencement of so precarious an administration. But notwithstanding the 'curtain lectures' he may get from Pitt and Lord Melville, I mistake Hope's character from the beginning to the end of it if he does not return to Scotland triumphing in perfect self-approbation and victory, more confirmed than ever in his ideas of supremacy and his feelings for arbitrary government. And with the notions I entertain of Pitt's own maxims and feelings of government, I am not prepared to flatter you with hopes of a very effectual check from this quarter. Scotland is an admirable country for farmers, and metaphysicians, and friends; but I never think of your notions of constitutional policy, without feeling a very sensible consolation for all that I lost in leaving you.

Fox's speech was vigorous, and plain; Windham's delicious, quite calm, very contemptuous, and a tissue of close argument and fine wit woven together without a knot or a break. Kinnaird and Petty spoke both well enough to afford a fair contrast; Lord Henry with excellent composure, neatness, and much sense both of matter and manner – Charles with all the grievous faults of manner which we have often before talked of, petulance, undue impetuosity, unsuitable confidence, but with occasional felicities both of form and expression, such as a clever man is sure to display sometimes when he risks always, and such as Petty, a far *abler* man, will perhaps never reach because he will hazard very little.

...

1. William Dundas (1762–1845: *DNB*) was Secretary at War.
2. A seaport near Banff.

162. To J.A. Murray

BLPES ii. 120–21   [London], 27 June 1804

...

I am provoked to think that there was not so much diligence used by Opposition, in mustering their troops against the Advocate, as there might have been. I heard next day of three members who would have gone, if they had known it was to come on; and of course there were many more. Bob Adair is too lazy as well as too conceited and too ugly a fellow for his office of whipper-in.

...

We consider Pitt as pretty firmly seated now; at least, while the public interest about the King's health can be kept in the present state of indifference. I tremble for long war, severe government, and perhaps the revival of the old inquisition.

...

163. To Francis Jeffrey

BLPES ii. 126–7   The Temple, 2 July 1804

... For some time, I will say no more about Malthus; except to ask you whether there will be any impropriety, when the review does appear, in adding as a note a letter from the author to me correcting an error, of some importance, which he has himself detected.[1] There is a sort of precedent for this in a former number; I think in the review of Miss Seward's *Life of Darwin*.[2] It is not that I have had any direct intercourse with Mr Malthus, which I have avoided indeed, to keep myself independent in estimating his book; the application was made to me through Whishaw.

...

I hear of no new books, except Barrow's China, which seems to be much liked; you must take some pains with it therefore.[3] From what I have seen of the man in company and in former publications, he is not the person from whom I should expect any very successful speculations; he is the reverse of refined, and deduction does not appear very familiar to him. But he has a strong plain sense; and to be trusted, I should think, in telling what he has seen. He has taken the right view of the boasted civilization and wealth of China; and though people who consider such things have in conversation been long agreed about it, I do not know that the subject has ever been placed in that light by any author; unless De Pauw whose book I never read, has taken this line.[4] Stephen's new pamphlet will appear, I fancy, in your approaching Number; Brougham would not trust me with it, or I might have indulged myself in a wish which the perusal of it gave me.[5] I suppose he was anxious it should be done soon and positively, and in that case was very right not to run any risk by letting it fall into my hands, which are indeed so very slippery. Since that damned reproached [word obscured] again across me, I will insist against you, the distrust of myself has quite as much to do with it as indolence; I envy Brougham his security still more than his fluency.

I lately made an attempt to recruit for you at Oxford, which I hope may succeed; the two men I have in view are the Professor of Poetry with whom I have formed an acquaintance, a judicious and modest scholar, and the other is the gentleman who has published a critique of 'Horse' Kett's *General Knowledge*.[6] They are both of Oriel College. You must not mention this, for I believe they would both insist on concealment; indeed I am not yet sure of obtaining them for you. Classical literature of course would be their province. I shall call on Phillimore within an hour, and be your proxy at dunning.[7]

Tell Murray, that the epigram on Lord Amherst in Saturday's *Morning Chronicle* was written by Fitzpatrick, and the Three Bobbies by Jekyll; the same facetious little gentleman, the Jeffrey of the South, wrote the 'feast of the Statue' a few days ago.[8] Tell Murray also, that Lord Moira befriended the Advocate much on the late occasion; by his means most of the Prince's men were kept from the Division. ...[9]

1. In a letter of 6 May (*Jeffrey*, ii. 88–90), Jeffrey had encouraged Horner to forget politics and London society long enough to write his review of Malthus for the next number of the *Review*. Malthus's letter is Doc. 138.

2. Anna Seward's *Memoirs of the Life of Dr Darwin* (1804) had been reviewed by Thomas Thomson in *ER* iv (no. vii, Apr. 1804), 230–41.

3. John Barrow's *Travels in China* (1804) was reviewed by Jeffrey in *ER* v (no. x, Jan. 1805), 259–88.

4. Cornelius de Pauw, *Recherches philosophiques sur les Egyptiens et les Chinois* (2 vols, Berlin, 1773).

5. In what is evidently a mistranscribed letter to Brougham of 5 Aug. (*Brougham*, ii. 265–70), Jeffrey coupled the intention of himself saying 'a word or two' about Stephen's pamphlet, 'if the time be not past', with a similar intention of printing an abstract of Brougham's *Colonial Policy*, which, of course, also never appeared. The October number did, however, contain William Wilberforce's review of the pamphlet [?by R. Bisset] *A Defence of the Slave Trade* (*ER* v (no. ix, Oct. 1804), 209–241).

6. Henry Kett (1761–1825: *DNB*), nicknamed 'Horse' on account of his long face, was Fellow of Trinity College, Oxford and author of *Elements of General Knowledge* (2 vols, 1802). Some of the errors in the latter had been exposed in 1803 by John Davison (1777–1834: *DNB*), Fellow of Oriel. A later work of Kett's, *Logic made Easy* (1809), was so severely handled by another Fellow of Oriel as to make the author suppress it. This Fellow was Edward Coppleston (1776–1849: *DNB*), who in 1802 had secured the Professorship of Poetry that Kett had craved. Neither Davison nor Coppleston is given even a tentative attribution in the *WI*; and neither appears in Horner's 'Key' or in the Kinnordy set of the *ER*.

7. The first review by Joseph Phillimore (1775–1855: *DNB*), afterwards Regius Professor of Civil Law at Oxford, seems to have been of Dr Hill's *Latin Synonymes* in *ER* iv (no. viii, July 1804), 457–76.

8. The previous day Horner had gone to the London house of William Wentworth Fitzwilliam, 4th Earl Fitzwilliam (1748–1833: *DNB*), to attend a meeting of Foxites whose purpose, he noted in his journal, 'was that some association might be formed, for writing pamphlets, squibs, epigrams, etc., etc., against the Administration'. Lauderdale had evidently recommended Horner's inclusion in the 'club', and the invitation to attend was communicated by Lord Robert Spencer. At the meeting, where he met Sheridan, Windham, Fitzpatrick, and other leading Foxites, Horner committed himself to the party of Fox and thereafter had access to first-hand political information. William Pitt, 2nd Baron Amherst (1773–1857: *DNB*), an enthusiastic volunteer officer, who afterwards had a distinguished diplomatic career and was created Earl Amherst, had been reinstated as Lord

of the Bedchamber after being dismissed for voting against the Government in April. The 'Epigram on the late happy restoration of a L— of the K—'s Bedchamber' ran:

> When a K—g gives a Courtier a kick in the breech,
> And bids him get out for a son of a b—ch,
> A kiss from his hand, with an office to boot,
> Will atone for the injury done to his foot;
> Yet a kiss from the hand, unless honour's a farce,
> Is a very odd cure for a kick on the a—.

Joseph Jekyll (1754–1837: *DNB*), who was also present at Fitzwilliam's meeting, was MP for Calne and Solicitor-General to the Prince of Wales. A noted wit and an occasional contributor to Whig newspapers – he was dubbed by Bentham 'tale-bearer of the household at Bowood' (Lord Lansdowne's place) – he was recruited to write propaganda on behalf of the Opposition. His 'feast of the Statue' has not been found; but 'The Three Bobs', his skit on Pitt's partisans Sir Robert John Buxton (1753–1839), 1st Bart, Sir Robert Peel (1750–1830: *DNB*), 1st Bart, and Robert (Plumer) Ward (1765–1856: *DNB*), who was *not* knighted or made a baronet, ran:

> Three *Bobbies* rang their Major Bob
> In Billy Pitt's new peal;
> Sir *Bobby* Buxton, *Bobby* Ward,
> And Eke Sir *Bobby* Peele
>
> —
>
> Had each Sir *Bobby* staid at home,
> Nor grac'd a former lobby;
> Ten thousand pounds to one penny
> He had not been Sir Bobby
>
> —
>
> To make a third for honours fit
> Could both Sir *Bobs* accord;
> *Bob* Peel's hard cash, *Bob* Buxton's wit,
> Would knight Sir *Bobby* Ward.

(See the journal entries of 30 June and 1 July in *Horner*, i. 266–9; *MC*, 30 June; *George III*, iv. 201n and 273n; *PH* iv. 296–9; and Doc. 172.)

9. Gen. Francis Rawdon-Hastings, 2nd Earl of Moira and afterwards 1st Marquess of Hastings (1754–1826: *DNB*), an intimate of the Prince of Wales, was C.-in-C. in Scotland.

164. To Francis Jeffrey

BLPES ii. 128–9   The Temple, 12 July 1804

I do not wish to give up Malthus, because it would be childish to do so after such a pother about it, and because I really desire to perform the task. I am desirous too of giving it as soon as I can, that the subject may not become too stale, and that you may have another engagement over my head, which I shall most probably fulfil with the same fidelity and dispatch. I will not promise about Malthus again, having broken so many promises; but request you will let this book remain in my hands indefinitely, and for this one work allow me a privilege which I confess is not very suitable to the nature of yours. ...

You must give us an early account of Richardson's Letters. In the vols I have seen, there are more from a set of dull correspondents than from R[ichardson] himself, who after all seems but a dull writer of *real* letters. The life prefixed by Mrs Barbauld will afford you an opportunity, such as you wished for, of criticizing the Aiken style of writing. There is sense and talent, as in most things she has written, and even now and then a just refinement: enough of all this to merit a respectful treatment. But she is notwithstanding *une précieuse ridicule*, of the new school, and ought to be quizzed in a good natured way for the benefit of all those misses who in the fullness of time are to become maidens and gentlewomen. The solemnity and starch parade with which truisms and nothings are announced; the formal discussion to which she subjects some topics, that were all settled before we left the nursery; the prudery, mysticism, and cant of her virtue; her exaggerated, wire-drawn and yet clumsy sensibilities, will afford you a subject for a spirited and instructive sketch. I hope you will not forego the opportunity likewise of drawing a character of Richardson, and an estimate of his merits, such as you gave us in your review of Cowper, which I have read over and over again.[1] It is in these passages, that I find some consolation for your waste of talents upon such perishing productions as reviews; these passages will live, while the subjects live to which they belong; and at some future time, when you are engaged with other occupations, we must think how far it would be practicable to detach them from their present place, and bring them together in another form.

By the way, I must not forget to tell you, that young Drummond Home called here the other day, in return of a visit I paid him in Oxford.[2] He spoke very modestly (but as if he felt himself neglected) of having written to you without receiving an answer; he said, he supposed the paper he sent was not worthy of the *Review*. This I dare say was the case; and you must have a delicate as well as laborious task, in pacifying the mortified pride of these well meaning volunteers. ...

... Brougham is [as] active as ever, talks of going to the continent within a fortnight, and of writing in conjunction with Thornton, Stephen and Lord Teignmouth some large work on the Slave Trade, preparatory to the next Session. ...[3]

1. Jeffrey had reviewed William Hayley, *The Life and Posthumous Writings of William Cowper* (3 vols, 1803–1804), in *ER* ii (no. iii, Apr. 1803), 64–86, and iv (no. viii, July 1804), 273–84. He reviewed *The Correspondence of Samuel Richardson*, edited by Anna Letitia Barbauld (6 vols, 1804), in *ER* v (no. ix, Oct. 1804), 23–44.

2. Henry Home Drummond of Blair Drummond (1783–1867), afterwards MP for Perthshire, was one of Lord Kames's grandsons. But he does not figure in the *WI*, nor in the Kinnordy 'Key' or set of the *ER*.

3. Brougham went off to the Netherlands early in August 1804, partly in order to gather information about the slave trade (*Brougham*, i. 272). John Shore, 1st Baron Teignmouth (1751–1834: *DNB*), one of the 'Saints', was the first President of the British and Foreign Bible Society. Nothing seems to have come of the project for 'a large work' on the slave trade.

165. To Francis Jeffrey

BLPES ii. 130   [London, 30 July 1804][1]

... I have got the *Review* and find it an excellent number in all respects but one, that there is not enough of you; you must really give us one important article at least each time.[2] Lauderdale is masterly; erroneous, I think, in some of the anti-economical positions; but quite chastened enough in manner, and so far from severe, not sufficiently so, in my opinion, upon some parts. I object a little to Chatham's letters, which are extravagantly praised; what is there in all the religion of his Lordship, more elevating than when any old woman writes to her grand daughter? But Brougham wished, as they say, to blow [?in his] ear.

I am making out a little dissertation on the subject of a bounty on exportation of corn, suggested by the late new act.[3] I am trying to re-examine the grounds of my opinion.

...

1. The letter is so franked by William Wilberforce.
2. The viiith, July 1804, number of ER iv, contained, among others, reviews by Brougham of Lauderdale on *Public Wealth*, pp. 343–77, and of *Lord Chatham's letters to his Nephew*, pp. 377–86, as well as of Count Rumford on the nature of heat, pp. 399–415, and the phenomenon of glaciers, pp. 415–19, and M'Kinnen's *Tour in the West Indies*, pp. 419–27.
3. The act regulating the duties and bounties on imports and exports of corn received the royal assent that same day. (See Doc. 168.)

166. From Francis Jeffrey

⟨Horner, i. 269–70⟩   Edinburgh, 5 Aug. 1804

⟨I am glad there is anything in the *Review* to please your fastidious taste, and most glad to find that you are actually at work upon something to make the next number still better. Yours has been a deplorable desertion, my dear Horner; and has really weighed very heavily upon my spirits: for our sake, for my sake, for your own sake, and for God's sake, do set about Malthus immediately, and by the labour of one week save yourself from the penitence and reproaches of many months. I cannot vary my exhortations more; you have worn out my whole stock of obtestations.

⟨I do not dissent from Brougham's Anti-Economics, and I am almost perfectly certain that the doctrine of these theorists is absurd: and I am only confirmed in that impression, when *you* put on your most profound countenance, and tell me that neither of you nor I understand properly what it means. When you expound it, I engage to listen with the utmost patience, and to weigh it with the most respectful attention. But I do not quite agree with Brougham in what he has said of Lauderdale's view of the effect of capital. I am not sure that his Lordship has not blundered, and am persuaded, at any rate, that the thing may be simplified; but I do not think Brougham has done justice either to the author or the subject in that article, though I have not time now to tell you why. The article, however, is excellent, and takes a fine range. ...⟩

167. To Francis Jeffrey

BLPES ii. 133–4 ⟨Horner, i. 271–3⟩   The Temple, 13 Aug. 1804

⟨...

⟨How you still harp upon my fastidiousness! That, by the way, is a dogma of yours, on which a little of your spare doubts might by this time be spent to good purpose. I will venture to maintain, before the whole grand inquest of Edinburgh reviewers, that I have admired more that I might have slighted, and swallowed more that I ought to have choked on, than you will ever be able to do, if all the remainder of your existence, both in this world and the next, were to be occupied with a painful atonement of praise and acquiescence. I am comforted by what you promise in the next number for your omissions in the last; you have some excellent subjects, and do not, my dear Pyrrhonist, insist on disputing every position because it is not placed in the best light, or because your prolific brain bursts with nine farrow of objections. Barrow's view of Chinese policy and civilization, for example, always has appeared to me pretty nearly just, and a correction of the delusion which the missionaries have played upon us down to the days of Adam Smith; and yet a very plausible representation may be given of the other side of the question; and Barrow, though clear-sighted enough when he uses his eyes, is so unrefined a thinker, and so destitute of the materials⟩ for reasoning ⟨which general education gives, that the truth in his hands must appear both awkward and imperfect. I feel a little the force of your sneer against me on the subject of the Economists; but I put on my profound and oracular mask once more, and will wear it till I accomplish all my intentions in that way. I hope those fellows are well tormented in the shades for having done themselves so little justice in this upper region; and old Adam, for the contrary transgression of having done himself more than justice, ought to be set to teach such indocile scholars the art of writing. Southey's *Madoc* is in the press, I understand, and will make its appearance the beginning of winter. Wordsworth's Poems, for he has two great ones, that is, long ones, will not be published so soon. One of these is to be called the Recluse, and the other is to be a history of himself and his thoughts; this philosophy of egotism and shadowy refinements really spoils a great genius for poetry. We shall have a few exquisite gleams of natural feeling, sunk in a dull ugly ground of trash and affectation. I cannot forgive your expression, 'Wordsworth and Co.'; he merits criticism, but surely not contempt; to class him with his imitators is the greatest of all contempt. I thought our perusal of the *Lyrical Ballads* in the Temple would have prevented this; we found much to admire, but you will not admire. Sharp, however, is in the other extreme, I admit; but I insist it is the better of the two: he has been living at the Lakes, with these crazed poets; Wordsworth read him some thousand lines, and he repeated to me a few of these one day, which I could not worship as he wished me. ...⟩

168. Notes on Smith's *Wealth of Nations*

Kinnordy MSS   24–28 Aug. 1804

74. (II. p. 268)[1] In these three paragraphs, from 'It regulates' to 'price of corn', a very important and, if correct, a fundamental fact in political economy is for the first time (in this work) explained and proved incidentally. I have doubts, both of its being correctly expressed, and of the principle upon which it depends being correctly unfolded.

The word *regulate* seems to express too much; for the money price of corn is not the only cause that influences the money price of all other commodities, and *regulation* seems to impart an entire and undivided influence.[2] The money price of other commodities will vary, while that of corn remains the same, with the variations of the ratio between their supply and demand. On the other hand, it is true, that while the supply and demand of a commodity remain in the same ratio to each other, its money price will vary with the average money price of corn. This word *average*, or permanent, ought likewise to be introduced into the general proposition.

As to the principle upon which this great general fact depends, my doubt is, whether that consideration, which is stated in the second paragraph, ought to have been introduced at all. It was introduced, probably, from the plausible appearance of a sound formal demonstration, which is derived by its assistance in the third paragraph. But this, I suspect, is rather specious than solid. It does not strike me, that the money price of the other sorts of rude produce can be affected by the money price of corn in a different manner, from that in which the money price of corn affects that of other commodities. The whole principle is that, I apprehend, which is adverted to in the first of the three paragraphs; but which is not unfolded so distinctly as it seems to require.

It is evident, that, in the price of every commodity, one large ingredient is the direct price, or wages, of that labour which, immediately or indirectly, has been employed in its production or preparation. Beside this, there is only the profit of the capital, or the rent of the land, which has likewise been employed.

It is farther evident, that, in the price or wages of labour, one large ingredient is the price of that food or subsistence which is necessary to the labourer and his family. The quantity of food that is necessary to maintain him and his family, constitutes the minimum to which the real price of his labour can be reduced. Besides this portion or ingredient of his actual wages, there is that portion by receiving which he is enabled to purchase a few conveniencies [sic] or luxuries. He purchases these, by expending that surplus of his wages in the several prices of these conveniencies or luxuries. But in each of these several prices, one large ingredient, as before, is the price of the labour that has been employed in producing or preparing that article of convenience or luxury: and, in the price of that labour, one large ingredient is, as before, the price of the subsistence necessary to the workmen who employed that labour.

[3]The result of this analysis seems to be, that a *minimum is fixed, to the money wages of all labour, and therefore to the money price of all commodities*, by the money price of

that which affords subsistence to the labouring classes. Every rise or fall in the money price of that subsistence will occasion a proportional rise or fall in the money price of labour and commodities. The money price of commodities and labour is liable to be varied by other causes; but, the force of those causes remaining unchanged, that money price will *vary with the average money price of corn*.

The expressions, which Smith uses afterwards at p. 278, 'the real value[4] stamped upon corn by the nature of things', are very unphilosophical. They proceed from the mistake which runs through the 5th chapter of Book I; and give a metaphysical, or rather a mystical air, to what is very far from being either very abstract or very intricate. There is, as Smith remarks, a great and essential difference, in respect of price, between that subsistence which feeds the labouring classes of the world and all the other commodities which ease or gratify our secondary wants: and that difference is no doubt founded in the nature of things. This difference, and the principle upon which it proceeds, I have endeavoured to ascertain in the preceding part of the present note.

It might be worthwhile to ascertain the history of this proposition in political economy, from the vague opinions that loosely pointed toward it, to the almost accurate statement of it by Smith.

Before I leave this point, it may be useful to set down, for future investigation, a hint which now suggests itself to me. By means of the principle of population, as the economists long ago remarked, the supply and demand of food will be kept, with tolerable steadiness, *in equilibrio*, that is, at a permanent ratio to each other. If, therefore, the supply and demand of money should for any length of time remain likewise *in equilibrio*, in such circumstances the minimum, which is fixed for the money price of all commodities by the money price of corn, would continue unvaried; and there would be no other variations of prices, but such temporary changes in the price of single commodities as might be occasioned by the fluctuations of supply and demand, or such general changes as might resolve from a permanent change in the rent of land or in the profit of capital. – The effect of the money price of corn upon the money prices of commodities and labour, seems to open one view of the doctrine of the French Economists; it is an important view of the system of circulation; and it marks out one point, as of primary, or originating importance.

75. (II. p. 514)[5] There has never, that I know of, been any direct attempt to prohibit the exportation of British capital. There are establishments in Russia, Portugal, etc.

76. (II. 265)[6] This is true, as it [is] here very guardedly expressed: but the phrase which limits it is afterwards dropped, and the author proceeds to use the proposition in a more general sense, in which it is not true. 'In every particular year', no doubt, singly considered, the exportation of that year must cause the quantity in the home market to be less than it would have been, had the quantity exported been kept at home. But because this quantity would have lowered the price of that year, it does not follow, that the regular exportation has raised the average price from year to year; unless it be shown, that the quantity every year exported is subtracted from the quantity that would have been every year in the market, if there were no such regular exportation. Now the question at issue is, whether the bounty has a tendency

to produce a surplus above what is usually wanted on the home market. And the answer to this question, Smith takes for granted in his own way, when he says that the bounty raises the price in the home market.

77. (II. p. 267)[7] It may produce one effect or the other, but it cannot produce both effects at the same time. If the wages of the labouring poor rise proportionately to the advance in the price of their subsistence, they continue of course as able as before to bring up a family, and the population of the country will not be restrained. If the subsistence of the labouring poor is reduced by the advanced price, that is, if there is no proportionable rise in their wages, their employers continue of course as able as before to employ the same number of labourers; and the industry of the country will not be restrained. Smith, however, takes advantage of both, and describes the effect of this advance in the price of corn to be that of restraining the *population and industry* of the country. – This is another instance, it appears to me, of an erroneous conclusion and of an imperfect view of general principles, to which this excellent author has been led by affecting too curious a neatness, simplicity, and formality in the statement of his reasonings. The just principle of this subject involves a consideration, (which banishes this alternative form of the proposition), the reaction which the price of wages of labour and the supply of labourers have upon each other. A rise in the real wages of labour, proceeding from a temporary cause and not from the general diffusion of wealth, will soon be reduced by an increased supply of labourers; and a similar reduction in the real wages of labour will soon be corrected by a diminished rate of population. An advance, therefore, in the price of corn, as Smith himself afterwards states, cannot be permanent as a real advance, but, though it should appear to remain, will be in fact no more than a nominal rise of the money price.

78. (III. 103)[8] He might have gone on to mention the system which prevails over Germany, where the whole business of post-travelling is under the direction of government. There cannot be a better illustration of the consequences of such a violation of the natural order. In Silesia, for example, the farmers are obliged to furnish horses to the postmasters at the rate of three groschen a mile for each horse: for which the postmaster charges the traveller ten groschen. Farmers of course give their horses with great reluctance; and travellers have often to wait four or six hours at the post-house, till the horses, with which they are to proceed on their journey, are driven in from the adjoining fields. The regulations, which government has found it necessary to introduce for the relief of the peasant, serve to aggravate the inconveniences of travelling; the weight of baggage is limited by regulation, and the postilions are not bound to drive faster than at the rate of three English miles an hour. Adams, *Letters on Silesia*, p. 336.[9]

79. (III. 237)[10] The discussions that of late years have taken place in the British Parliament upon the debts of the Civil List, and provisions to the younger branches of the Royal Family, may furnish some general remarks and some useful illustrations upon a subject which Smith seems to have dismissed rather abruptly.

80. (III. 189)[11] The discussions that, within last year, took place upon the Volunteer System, and the probable use that might be made of that system if judiciously and moderately established, belong, as illustrations, to this part of Smith's treatise.

1. WN IV. v. a. 11–14 argued that the bounty on the export of corn 'regulated' the money price of labour and consequently of all other produce of the land and therefore of 'almost all manufactures'.

2. *See the objections which Malthus, Mackie in his letter to Dirom, and Anderson in his letter on National Industry, have made to this principle of Smith's; they have been evidently led by the word 'regulate', to misconceive altogether the principle. [A. Dirom, *An Inquiry into the Corn Laws and Corn Trade of Great Britain.* ... *To which is added a Supplement by Mr W[illiam] Mackie* (1796); the supplement was in the form of two letters, the second of which, pp. 216–62, began with 'an Examination of Dr Adam Smith's Theory on the Corn Trade'.]

3. *Until the rise (or the fall) of the price of corn is communicated to labour and to other commodities, the corn value either of labour or of one of those commodities is lower (or higher) than before, but the exchangeable value of labour and of any of those commodities, expressed in terms of each other, remains the same as before. The rise (or the fall) is communicated first to labour, and through labour to the commodities during the interval of the communication from labour to commodities, the exchangeable value of corn and labour with respect to each other will have regained its original rate, but both the corn price and the labour price of any one of those commodities will be lower (or higher), until the communication is complete. – See my analysis of the operation of Corn Bounties. [The date in the margin, against this note apparently, is 28 Sept. 1804. It seems that Horner appended the note after completing his 'Observations on the Bounty upon Exported Corn', published in *ER* v (no. ix, Oct. 1804), 190–208.]

4. *The word *value* cannot mean *exact value*; substitute what it really means, *usefulness*, and the proposition becomes intelligible, but appears to have no relation to the argument. See former remarks in these notes upon *value*; and my notes upon the discussion between Lauderdale and Brougham [not found by the editors]. If there were an index to all the words in the *Wealth of Nations*, I would go over all the cases in which *value* occurs. [WN IV. v. a. 23, criticizing bounties, actually reads: 'The nature of things has stamped upon corn a real value which cannot be altered by merely altering its money price.']

5. This paragraph seems to apply, not specifically to p. 514, but to Smith's general 'Conclusion of the Mercantile System', WN IV. viii. 45–7.

6. WN IV. v. a. 6:

> In years of plenty, ... the bounty, by occasioning an extraordinary exportation, necessarily keeps up the price of corn in the home market above what it would naturally fall to. ... In years of scarcity, though the bounty is frequently suspended, yet the great exportation which it occasions in years of plenty, must frequently hinder more or less the plenty of one year from relieving the scarcity of another. Both in years of plenty and in years of scarcity, therefore, the bounty necessarily tends to raise the money price of corn somewhat higher than it otherwise would be in the home market.

But he had then shortly gone on to say (WN IV. v. a. 8):

> whatever extension of the foreign market can be occasioned by the bounty, must, in every particular year, be altogether at the expense of the home market.

7. Having in the continuation of his attack on bounties on corn stated (WN IV. v. a. 8) that 'so very heavy a tax upon the first necessary of life, must either reduce the subsistence of the labouring poor, or it must occasion some augmentation in their pecuniary wages, proportionable to that in the pecuniary price of their subsistence', Smith had appeared to conclude in the same paragraph that both would occur 'in every particular year'.

8. WN V. i. d. 16 argued that when public works like roads and bridges were the responsibility of central government they were likely to suffer neglect on account of their unglamorous nature.

9. John Quincy Adams, *Letters on Silesia, written during a tour through that country in the years 1800, 1801, etc.* (1804), was reviewed by Horner in *ER* v (no. ix, Oct. 1804), 180–89.

10. WN V. i. i. 1–3 dealt very briefly and sympathetically with the 'expense of supporting the Dignity of the Sovereign'.

11. WN V. i. f. 59 emphasized the importance for defence purposes of sustaining 'the martial spirit of the great body of the people'.

169. From Francis Jeffrey

⟨*Jeffrey*, ii. 94–6⟩   Edinburgh, 4 Sept. 1804

⟨... here has been James Brougham, with his placid honest countenance, saying so many flattering and apologetic things of you ...

⟨The most acceptable thing that fell from his persuasive lips was, that you would have no objection to answer Lauderdale's pamphlet, provided it appeared unfit for reviewing.[1] Now, it is clearly quite unfit for reviewing. In the first place, it is rude and impertinent in many places; and in the second, the *Review* ought never to be made a vehicle of controversy, as it would soon be a vehicle for nothing else. We speak, of course, as judges, and of course must leave the bench when we are compelled to appear as parties. We could not consistently, or even with due regard to our reputation, affect to measure impartially the relative merits of Lord Lauderdale and of the *Edinburgh Review*, etc. With regard to answering the pamphlet, however, I urgently entreat you to do it, both for Brougham's sake, and also in some degree for your own sake, and the sake of the doctrines contained in that Review, for some of which I own I feel a sort of paternal anxiety. I have had time only to run over the said observations very slightly, but from what I have seen, I think them all very answerable. I am not quite clear about the pensionary and the sinking fund sections, but I have always shivered on the brink of those subjects, without venturing myself into their depths. However, if you will undertake to write an answer, I will engage to send you a few notes on the whole work, of which you shall be welcome to make as little use as you think proper. The pamphlet makes no great fame here, and seems scarcely to be read except by the political auxiliaries of his lordship. However, there is no presumption against it. For if my Lord Lauderdale were to write as prettily as Ezekiel, the Dundassites would affect to scoff at it.⟩

> 1. Lauderdale had answered Henry Brougham's critical review of his *Inquiry* with an angry but ineffective pamphlet, *Observations on the Review of his Inquiry* (Edinburgh, 1804). As Horner agreed in Doc. 173, it was thought best not to continue the controversy in the ER and so Brougham replied in turn the following year with his own pamphlet, *Thoughts suggested by Lord Lauderdale's Observations* (1805).

170. Note by Horner

Kinnordy MSS[1]   11 Sept. 1804

Subjects, suggested by the state and prospect of the age, to the investigations of philosophers, and of practical statesman, in Britain –
    The *whole* political economy and administration of *Ireland*
    The administration of law in *Scotland*
    Perhaps an increase in the provision of the Scotch clergy
    The whole subject of agricultural economy and police in *England*

Seminaries for the education of the lower classes in *England*

That immense subject, the administration of *India*

The general subject of *patronage* in Britain; considered with reference to public opinion, as well as to many other great considerations – purity – efficiency – Scotland; Ireland; India – the Army and Navy. This is a very important subject in political philosophy, to be treated generally; and in the constitutional politics of Britain, to be examined with a limitation of general conclusions by the peculiarities of our system. ...

To acquaint himself with the real circumstances of the times in which he lives, and calmly to anticipate the [word illegible: list?] of those which are to succeed.

A philosophical history of the politics of Europe from the Peace of Westphalia

To be master of the times, and breathe time's [?] full spirit

Changes that are likely to take place in the internal police of England, in the system of its wealth, in its commercial monopoly, in its constitution

Political Economy is science of practical application, not studied hitherto by any of our statesmen of the first genius. Not so well suited in truth – Fox, positive dislike. Even Pitt, not profoundly. Is it not probable that we shall see some such man come to business from a professed study of it as a science? Probable from the growing fashion among young men. Would effect a revolution in the science, by the practical modes he would introduce; and would immensely improve the financial and economical legislation of England, by the just principles he would bring into use – *Excoriatur!*

1. Bound with a number of miscellaneous scraps in a volume entitled 'Memoranda'.

171. To Francis Jeffrey

BLPES ii. 137–8   Frognal, Hampstead,[1] 12 Sept. 1804

... I was not aware of all your objections against prosecuting the argument with Lord Lauderdale any farther in the *Review*. Upon farther reflection, and considering what you have said, I am sensible that any retort of a *personal* nature would be unsuitable to your publication, and if it comes at all, ought to proceed from Brougham himself in a separate pamphlet, though I think he is entitled to treat Lauderdale with contempt and silence.

I am not yet convinced, however, that a review of the *Observations* might not appear in your next Number without impropriety; even though it assume *somewhat* of the air of an award between the disputants. Peculiar circumstances beget a propriety for themselves, and Brougham's absence upon the continent makes this a peculiar case.[2] I would set out with mentioning that circumstance, and without dropping the majesty of the first person plural, the corporate character might appear for the interests of a gild-brother, who happens for a while to be out of the liberties. All the personalities, except one, into which Lauderdale's senseless anger and mortified self-conceit have betrayed him, would be disposed of in a single sentence, expressing only wonder at such bad taste, and a total disinclination to follow so bad an example. And that one, the allusion to Brougham's political views, might furnish a sentence or two at most of general allusion to some testimonies, that might be given in defence of B[rougham] against a charge so unmanly in its form and so full of the lowest malignity of party, by persons who are not upon all occasions so much at variance with Lord Lauderdale's sentiments. The opportunity would not be unbecoming, I think, for such an act of strict justice; it would be understood sufficiently by those whom it would concern; and would not, it appears to me, be an inadmissible deviation from the *bienséances* of the *Review*. The multiplicity of our essence, and our hypostatic disunion, have been quite understood from the very first. The substance of the article would consist of dry economical discussion. I think I could show how completely L[auderdale] has misunderstood B[rougham]'s objection, to the blundering distinction between wealth and riches, and fortify the objection by a few additional remarks. Upon two or three points, I should give L[auderdale] some credit for useful acuteness; and to this candour, I think, there would be no objection founded on the existence of the former review, which would not be done away by the view in which I should endeavour to place myself at the outset. About parsimony and the sinking fund, I have not really brought my thoughts together; nor am I aware of the conclusion to which I shall ultimately be led; if in trying to make out the fair truth, I take an unexpected turn towards Lauderdale's side, I would honestly and explicitly declare it. For the conclusion of the article, if you permit me to write it, I meditate a very fine *adagio expressivo*, going off (as Puss[3] says) in the old way, to the tune of Adam Smith, to whose injured and disturbed manes I do not think Brougham has made an offering sufficiently solemn and splendid.

Lauderdale's *Observations* are not such as to justify a reply from me, in a separate form; his personalities against our friend Brougham are too much of course, and in the usual strain and language of all irritated scribblers, to require a very particular notice either from B[rougham] or his friends, and the discussions of a scientific nature are neither novel nor important enough to give me a respectable or even a reasonable occasion for thrusting myself forward. But the idea of such a review, as I have sketched, rather pleases me, I confess; and I shall go on with my notes upon the subject, until you give me orders to desist. It strikes me now, there is no medium between doing the thing in this manner, and abandoning the *Observations* to delight the Dunbar Committee at Edinburgh.[4] Thomson's heat amazes me; and as I have always had considerable respect both for his talents and his probity, I am sorry he should so impair my opinion of both, by a proceeding which is equally inconsistent with habits of scientific inquiry, and unbecoming one for whom upon a recent occasion all B[rougham]'s activity and zeal were exerted.[5]

I have written you a very short, trifling critique of Ambassador Adams's *Letters on Silesia* – rather abusive, I fear, and *précieuse*; and as dully ill-natured, as [the] work is good-naturedly dull. I have some copious notes, too, upon the corn bounty; a subject on which I found more difficulty in making up my mind than I looked for – I hope to shape it into a review for you, though I have no book to tack it to, but a short tract which was circulated and not published by Western the Member of Parliament.[6] Of course, I could only praise it. The Act of Parliament, to be sure, is a publication; but you would be afraid perhaps of a visit from the Sergeant at Arms. As to Malthus, you see, I am inexorable yet.[7] The truth is, I have only worked at these things for you by starts, stolen from other meditations and other musings. But I look forward to discharge my debt, before the *ish* of any of your short prescriptions. I shall not be surprised, and certainly not displeased, if I find some evenings in the winter for your work; but I shall then prefer lighter and more varied tasks than I have hitherto undertaken. I want to relax myself in some evening reading of voyages and travels, and shall perhaps ask you to give me some of the novelties in that line. But not, till I have done with Malthus.

... Let me hear soon, and give me as many of your notes upon L[auderdale] and B[rougham] as your clerk can copy. The [Sydney] Smiths are returned to town; and yet I have virtue to withstand the temptation; till they came, I thought of London with loathing, and am hardly there an hour in the fortnight. ... Lauderdale will probably be of the party; we must get to a side-table by ourselves. ... By the bye, will you let me review Playfair's *Life of Hutton*, and send it me when it is published; I have much to praise in it, and a little metaphysics to dispute.[8] This damned reviewing comes across all our fine discourses. ...

1. Presumably at his father's place.
2. A note about Brougham's absence (though of course without mentioning his name) appeared on p. 257 (the last) of the October 1804 issue in vol. ix.
3. According to *Smith Letters*, i. 84, n. 4, 'Pus' was Dr John Thomson.
4. So the MS appears to read; but Horner perhaps meant Dundas.
5. Albeit stressing the great merits of the work at both beginning and end, Adam Duncan's review in *ER* iv (no. vii, Apr. 1804), 120–51, of the second (1804) edition of Dr Thomas Thomson's *System of Chemistry*, in which theories about heat figured prominently, had (p. 121) expressed surprise and disapproval at an author who 'instead of returning thanks ... for the most unqualified approbation ... bestowed on his former edition, ... boldly sets the whole corporation [of critics] at defiance, and denies the competency of our tribunal. Indeed, it is not difficult to discern that it is the Doctor's honest opinion, that no person is qualified to judge of his performance but himself.' Between its few sentences of praise the body of the review then went on to criticize in some detail the organization, style, and substance of the work and consequently elicited some *Remarks on the 'Edinburgh Review' of Dr Thomson's System of Chemistry, by the Author of that Work* (Edinburgh, 1804). Perhaps Thomson and Horner both thought the review had been by Brougham.
6. Apparently, then, the author of the pamphlet, *Cursory Observations on the Act for ascertaining the Bounties, and regulating the Exportation and Importation of Corn*, 'by a Member of Parliament' (1804), which Horner noticed along with the Act of that year in *ER* v (no. ix, Oct. 1804), 190–208, was Charles Callis Western, the MP for Maldon and principal spokesman in the Commons for the agricultural interest.
7. The notice on the Corn Bounties contained a footnote apologizing for the delay in reviewing Malthus and offering 'reason ... to hope' that it would appear in the next, January 1805, number (*ibid.*, p. 191).
8. No notice appeared in the *ER* of John Playfair's biographical account of James Hutton, *Transactions of the Royal Society of Edinburgh*, vol. v, Pt 3, pp. 39–99.

172. To J.A. Murray

BLPES ii. 139–41 ⟨Horner, i. 275–81⟩   Frognal, Hampstead, 13 Sept. 1804

⟨...

⟨I remember having seen some inquiries about me in a letter to your brother, which I always intended to take a little notice of the first time I should write to you. Indeed, if I had thought the matter of much consequence to myself at the time, I should have satisfied you immediately; or rather have been beforehand with you, for in spite of your distance, you are the only one with whom I can communicate quite unreservedly upon all my private affairs. And I have always found that any thing interesting to me becomes of still more interest, in its relation to myself, after I have imparted it to you. This summer, I have allowed myself to be recognized more expressly as an adherent of the Opposition, than I ever had an opportunity of doing before. I did *not* dine at Carlton House; but at Lord Fitzwilliam's, with a set of partisans, 'black spirits and white.'[1] The advances were made to me, and, after taking the subject into serious deliberation, I resolved to take advantage of them. You have known, as long as myself, the cast of my political opinions, as well as my wish that politics should be joined to law in the occupations of my future life, if indeed my schemes of life shall ever be matured into real occupations. To hold an efficient character in politics, a man must choose a party, if the state presents one to whose leading declarations and views he can honestly subscribe. Now, though there are several parts of the former conduct of Opposition which I cannot approve of, and some men attached to it whom I never can esteem, yet the maxims and principles professed by Mr Fox are congenial upon all great questions to my feelings and conviction. I am not giving you this as an apology for myself, but as the deliberate mode in which I considered the subject before I came to a resolution. I accepted Lord Fitzwilliam's invitation, and permitted my name to be put down in the list of a new club to which Fox, Windham, Sheridan, etc. belong. It will be very comic to you, and therefore I cannot omit the circumstance, that this club meets at Budd's in Pall Mall, where Cobbett's works are published, under the sign of the Crown, Bible, and Mitre.

⟨I do not think that for a long time, my political activities will proceed any farther. For my view of the matter is this. Law must be my business and first object, because I have no fortune; I can permit nothing, therefore, to interfere with the necessary preparations for professional practice. Then again, I have no chance of getting into parliament these many years, whatever my chance may be at last. Now, to be an *active* politician out of parliament is, in my way of thinking, neither a very useful nor a very respectable character; and to be at the tail of a party is quite as much below my education and my schemes, as to be near the head of one is above my capacity, or indeed my inclinations. To be useful and eminent as a constitutional lawyer, and to turn to the public advantage those studies with regard to internal legislation which I still continue to prosecute, compose very nearly the ideal object which I long ago set before my ambition; I believe I have regulated my ambition, and sketched this 'beau ideal,' both calmly and with a desire to be right. As for the splendid hazardous pursuits of foreign policy and ministerial intrigue, into which our friend Brougham is plunging himself with a resolution to succeed that seems to insure success, and will at all events secure distinction, they are as unsuitable to the habits of my mind as to its powers; too bustling for the indolent predilection (which grows upon me hourly) for domestic and confined society, and not of magnitude, I will acknowledge, adequate to my idea of the highest sort of ambition. Lord Bacon and Dugald Stewart have made me a little of a visionary, as I believe you have sometimes thought; I am sure Brougham must have thought so always. But I have not yet reasoned myself out of those shades; the 'fantastic spell' is unbroken, so I must even go on still '*perque domos vacuas et inania regna*.' But I am forgetting the very humble subject, from which I have run off into a sort of declamation. It was under the impressions which I have been endeavouring to describe, and which you will not think new, that I took the step I lately did; deeming it advisable to form an *early* connection with the public men who maintain such principles and views as appear to me just, and that the opportunity offered was one which allowed me to form that connection in the most respectable manner, and without the imposition of any personal fetters. The first application was made to me by Petty, in name of Lord Robert Spencer, with whom I am not acquainted, at a time that a literary project in aid of politics was thought of, which is now dropped; and after I had signified my ready acquiescence, came the invitation from Lord Fitzwilliam, at the suggestion, I have some reason to conjecture, of Lord Lauderdale. Lauderdale, you know, is not a character altogether suitable to my taste, nor have I yet, in spite of his steadiness to an unsuccessful party, entire confidence in the purity of his politics; but I have traced him on more than one occasion speaking indulgently of me, with the intention of doing me a service; and I cannot be insensible to this unsolicited attention. I did not forget this consideration, in the subject which I have desired Jeffrey to consult you upon; but it appeared to me wholly eclipsed by the duty of acting with justice to Brougham, who in his absence has been so wantonly attacked.

⟨...⟩

1. See Doc. 163.

173. To Francis Jeffrey

BLPES ii. 142–3   Frognal, Hampstead, 21 Sept. 1804

...

The letters I have had from the Murrays and James Brougham, were so decided against any farther notice of Lauderdale in the *Review* that I had almost thought no more of my design. To this is added the distinct opinion of our most cautious man here, Whishaw, confirmed by Smith and even Playfair, that Brougham ought not to let so good an opportunity pass. I will add another circumstance to the effect of these, which was mentioned to me this morning by Adam; Miss Jenny Clerk, who is in London, asserts that her brother John has preserved a letter of Brougham's, upon the publication of Lauderdale's book, in which he praises it in unqualified terms. I suspect this is not the fact; but I must beg you to sift the report, if you can easily and without impropriety. If there has been any indiscretion or *mauvaise foi* of the kind, I will have nothing to do with the matter.[1]

For the present, I shall go on to write out my ideas upon the Corn Bounty; and if I finish it before I hear from you again, I shall try to compose such an article as I sketched out in my last. And it will be of no consequence what is ultimately resolved, as the general notes will [be] of use to me at any rate. My notice of Adams will not occupy above six or seven pages; and the bounty, about eight or ten. So you can reckon for me; and I will send them together.

In your review of Barrow, pray use your persuasive eloquence to forward the publication of those vols of Chinese Law which he speaks of. I hunger and thirst for them.

1. See Doc. 175 n. 2 and Doc. 177. Janet Clerk was probably one of the daughters of John Clerk, sen.; his wife was William Adam's aunt as well as a connection of Brougham's.

174. To James Loch

BLPES ii. 144–7   [London, 24 Sept. 1804]

...

I shall be curious to hear more news about the Jesuits; not that I am in the least alarmed at the prospect of their restoration. Superstition can do very little harm now in Europe, unless it comes in quite a new shape; and that is almost as unlikely, as the resurrection of the old errors in the countries where they have been suppressed. My conjectures about the Restoration are these; in the first place, that it may be conceived likely to bring back a system of education into France, which I fear has been absolutely without any such system for twelve entire years; secondly, that it is a price paid to the Pope for his journey to Paris, where he is no doubt to crown with oil thrice holy the new Charlemagne. Do you think it very unlikely that the Emperor of Austria may be *requested* to be present at the same ceremony, that is, threatened with being un-emperored and un-kinged too if he does not give his presence as a farther sanction?

... all I know of Brougham is, that he was for some days at the Hague, wrote to Jeffrey from Haarlem dated 5 September, said he had been feasted and flattered all through Holland, and was going to Frankfort on his way to Vienna.[1]

I tell you what you can likewise assist me in, if you have any such information in your head, or within reach of your hands. That is, the average price of wheat upon the continent, in the foreign markets; the average of the present times, particularly, and as far back towards the year 1764 as the means of intelligence will go. I have been considering the subject of Corn Bounties a little, and have got into a view of the subject which is somewhat different from the others that I have seen. But this point of information is almost essential.

...

1. About half a page has been obliterated here.

175. To Francis Jeffrey

BLPES ii. 150–51   [London], 1 Oct. 1804

I have just finished (strange to tell!) my dull prolix pamphlet upon Corn Bounties, and am upon my departure from Frognall to the Bull and Mouth to commit it to the mail. When I wrote to you last, I had only begun to bring my confused notions into order; and if I had foreseen the plague this was to give me, I should hardly have set about it.[1] I fear after all I have not succeeded in making myself quite right, or if I am so in making myself quite perspicuous; whether right or wrong, the article will probably spoil your sale in the county of Norfolk, and Jeffrey's health will not be toasted at Holkham sheep-shearing. I am unconscionably long, I know it; yet I cannot say what part I could willingly leave out, but I give you ample powers upon that point. The fundamental sin is, that it is not a review; the only apology for this is stated at the beginning, and if it is not enough you must send me the whole back again. I perform public penance, you see, for my Malthusian transgressions; but if you think this volunteering to the reporting stool, rather a piece of levity for one of my years, you may unstool me. Tell me what you think of my argument, and whether I have the right hand of Smith. You will observe a line about Lauderdale and Brougham – it came upon me so naturally, that I had some satisfaction in putting their names alongside of each other in this more honourable way, than they have been joined of late.[2] I am sadly formal as usual, and too much *in alto*; but I have had no time, to reduce it to natural language, *faire difficilement des périodes faciles*. I cannot shake off this pompous tawdry sort of garb that is somehow fastened upon me, nor can I contrive to change the undertaker's funeral step I have contracted into a common walk. Do give me your secret, my dear little Jeffrey, of tripping so lightly and so nimbly; I must have been cradled, I suspect, in Warwick Lane, and from my birth to be 'sad, slow, and profound'.

Adams looks so meagre now, I am ashamed to send it – you must not think the extract about education too long; I wish to have it all in.

As to Brougham and Lauderdale, that letter I mentioned to you in my last, ... quite brought me to a stand ...[3] From the thoughtless things which Brougham so often does with all his skill, it appeared to me far from improbable; and I should have appeared ridiculous if it were produced. ...

         ...

1. Horner made the following notation in his journal on 1 Oct. (*Horner*, i. 284):
    > Employed very closely for a week in investigating the policy of bounties upon exported corn; the results sent to Jeffrey. In this method of investigation, one cannot be without distrust, having no security that some necessary steps in the process may not be missed. The *method* must be improved, by the discovery of some principle, that shall at once abridge and make it more general.
2. Although Brougham's *Colonial Policy* was never reviewed in the *ER*, Horner had coupled it with Lauderdale's pamphlet in a complimentary comment in his piece on Corn in *ER* v. (no. ix, Oct. 1804), 205. Brougham, however, was far from pleased; see his letter to Murray of 2 Apr. (*Brougham*, i. 315).
3. The rest of the line has been obliterated.

176. To J.A. Murray

BLPES ii. 152–3 ⟨Horner, i. 284–6⟩   The Temple, 3 Oct. 1804

...

Foster's pamphlet on Exchange, I am ashamed to say, I have not read yet.[1] I ought to have done so, as he sent it to me. But one gets sick sometimes of a particular subject, and these details on foreign exchanges are so different from my usual thoughts, that it has always cost me an effort to fix my attention upon them, and excite an artificial interest. But I mean to go through the Reports of the Committee on Irish Currency, as soon as I clear my hands of other work; and if I can honestly approve Foster's book, I may frame a review upon the subject, which would form a suitable sequel to that of Lord King. But the truth is, I am over head and ears in business promised to others or to myself; literally buried alive; and I am pawing, and digging to get my nostrils once more above ground. I am not more guilty towards our acquaintance Foster, than to another Irishman who has been writing on currency and par – his friend Parnell, to whom I suppose he introduced you, and who sent his pamphlet to me.[2] He is a brother of Sir John's; not so sensible a man, I think, as Foster, who seems to me only Irish in the shape of his head, and very tolerably English in its inside and operations. If he goes on well, he has a fine course cut out for him; for his uncle has no son, I believe, and there is a hereditary character and influence to succeed to.[3] Character, I mean, in Ireland; for the *Spacker* [John Foster, the former Irish Speaker] is pretty well understood on this side of the water – a shrewd, able little man certainly – but quite unembarrassed by any political opinions. He has managed for himself, accordingly, with admirable sagacity; which never was displayed to more purpose, than in the advantage he took of Pitt's necessities upon the last arrangement, when he got the whole administration of Ireland, and reserved at the same time his engagements to the Prince of Wales.[4] I am persuaded, there is not a surer trade among all the crafts of London, than that of politics, if place and money are the object; I hardly recollect an instance of bad success.

⟨...

⟨... If you have resolution read my sermon upon Corn Bounties, and tell me what you make of my argument; I am not without my own suspicions of it. ...⟩

1. John Foster's nephew, John Leslie Foster (?1781–1842: *DNB*), an Irish lawyer who later became a judge and Tory MP, serving on the 1810 Bullion Committee, published his *Essay on the Principle of Commercial Exchanges, more particularly on the Relations between England and Ireland*, in 1804. In it he argued that the rate of exchange did not depend on the balance of debt but instead on the cost of transmitting specie. A review appeared in *ER* ix (no. xvii, Oct. 1806), 111–36, to which Horner probably contributed at least a part; see p. 217.

2. Henry Brooke Parnell, afterwards 1st Baron Congleton (1776–1842: *DNB*) and younger brother and heir of the dumb Sir John Augustus Parnell, 3rd Bart (1775–1812), published *Observations Upon the State of the Currency of Ireland* in Dublin in 1804. It was the first of four publications by Parnell dealing with the subjects of currency and exchange and the corn trade. In 1810 Parnell became a member of the Bullion Committee, and in 1813 he chaired the Committee on the Corn Trade.

3. Foster's uncle, however, had one surviving son who succeeded him as 2nd Baron Oriel and his mother as Viscount Ferrard.
4. In Pitt's second Administration Foster had secured the offices of both Chancellor of the Exchequer and First Lord of the Treasury in Ireland.

177. To J.A. Murray

BLPES ii. 154–5   The Temple, 25 Oct. 1804

I was quite comforted by your account of the alledged [sic] letter. B[rougham] has been unjustly slandered as upon very many occasions, and this is nothing but the old misfortune, that many women and many men cannot report a story as they heard it. It is one of the dispensations, so much admired, that B[rougham] should suffer by a vice, to which he is himself addicted. He contrives, one way and another, to make himself many enemies, in spite of his real and thoughtless good nature; his muse, to be sure, is very evil-tongued. In the sort of game he is playing, this is one of his capital and numerous oversights; for in that game, general and even vulgar popularity are not despised with impunity, any more than the minor proprieties of conduct. For one who makes conduct so much a matter of plan, he is wonderfully incautious and incomplete; and in spite of his vigorous talents, his extensive information, and his miraculous dispatch, I fear he precipitates in all things a great deal too much, and that severe disappointment awaits him. He seems not to have considered in the least the temper and manners of the country, where his ambition would lead him to figure, the staid and reserved correctness, the systematic principles, the slow approach to honours, which, in this lazy old order of things, are required of every political man who has not a hereditary name and fortune to give in earnest of all those requisites. I hardly think he is aware of the extent of public opinion, its immediate knowledge of all forward men, its scrupulous trial of their merits, or the weight of its sentence[?]. Under more absolute monarchies, than we may yet call ours, all these things are of less consequence to the political adventurer; the favour of the crown is all in all, public sentiment follows and does not dictate, and a man may be taken from a banker's desk at Geneva to the administration of the world. I trust this is not quite our case yet, though I have very little doubt we are approaching towards it; the fall of Addington is not entirely an unequivocal case, but the illustrations it yields rather preponderate on the favourable side. I hope we are not in our days to be governed by adventurers, whether they force themselves upon the crown by their talents, or wriggle into its favour by servility. New men are a most useful and necessary race, like projectors in trade; but we have no hold of them.

What do you make of this Spanish war? for we can call it nothing else, and indeed my main objection is that it does not get its right name.[1] If the Cabinet of Madrid has refused to satisfy us, upon inquiries that we were entitled to make, then we are entitled to commence hostilities; but if those inquiries were such as that Cabinet was entitled to refuse an answer to, then we had no right to attempt a detention of their ships. I cannot feel the difference between this detention and actual hostility;

for could the Spanish commanders submit to be detained, without being guilty of cowardice and a breach of duty? This Spanish war has very much the look of no better origin, than the love of dollars; Lord Melville felt for his brother tars, and thought it hard they should not be satisfied. Upon the principle of this war, we ought to have overlooked the ignoble and unwilling compliances of Spain to France, because they are out of hard necessity; and we ought, by all imaginable forbearance and tender care, to preserve, while we can, one more of the old limbs of the dismembered commonwealth. Nor ought we, even for retaliation, to violate a tittle of those salutary rules and forms of war, which we are fighting to restore. But the war was undertaken in madness, and is conducted with suitable want of skill; and we shall soon see the second empire of Charlemagne from the Atlantic to the frontiers of Russia. One cannot look a year forward, without terror and disgust.

I have been made very happy by Thomson's visit to London – whose liberal sense, unbroken good temper, and manliness, were always very high in my favour. We have lived together since his arrival, as much as his researches in black letter, and my very different pursuits will permit. ...[2]

...

1. Suspicious and resentful of Spain's subservience to France, the British had on 5 Oct. attacked and seized off Cadiz a small Spanish squadron of treasure ships. There followed on 12 Dec. a declaration of war by Spain.
2. Thomas Thomson visited London and, like Jeffrey before him, resided in chambers with Horner in the Temple.

178. To J.A. Murray

BLPES ii. 156–7[1]   The Temple, 3 Nov. 1804

... I believe you were quite accurate in all that you stated to [?William] Adam about Brougham and Lauderdale; there was once an attempt at intercourse which failed immediately, and produced a marked disl[ike] on both sides, and neither of them has any [for]bearance in the expression of that sort of feeling. I might say almost the same thing about B[rougham] and Adam, who never were made to come together; the one has no mind to appreciate the talents of the other, and this other is not very well prepared to value the coarse important virtues of the former. Adam with all his worth has as unfine a head as ever was attached to shoulders; and B[rougham], though surely a good-hearted fellow, so far as constitutional temper goes and the essential feelings of honour, wants that sort of understanding which the ancients supposed to reside in the heart; he is not *Cordeatas*.

As to Pitt's opinion of Hope, Lord Melville I believe can make P[itt] think any thing. But I recollect a circumstance Brougham repeated to me, on the authority of Wilberforce; to whom Pitt said, as the House broke up after the debate on Morrison's business, 'This Lord Advocate seems a man of talent – but his defence has been very injudicious – and his jokes abominable.' Your new story about Morrison I can hardly credit; if true, it would sink Hope for ever. If in the new appointments, Hope goes upon the speculation of the Chief Baronship, he may be bitterly disappointed; if the rumours that reach London about the King's state of mind have any foundation, the present Ministry are not perfectly well seated.

...

1. *Horner*, i. 286–8, prints other portions of this letter, reflecting gloomily on political conditions and prospects in Europe and England, but without indicating that any passages have been omitted.

179. To J.A. Murray

BLPES ii. 160–61[1]   The Temple, 15 Nov. 1804

...

... I have not yet met Mr Adam, but I am prepared to force him to a conversation about B[rougham], that I may possess him at least with all that I have to say. I wish we had done with this subject, but as it will probably be revived as soon as B[rougham] appears with a Reply, there is no other way of getting well rid of it, but by a vigilant sense of justice towards him. I rather regret now that I listened too easily to that story, which deterred me from writing something about it in the *Review*; though that would not have been the place to have expressed my sentiments except by a very general allusion. I could have done that with sufficient positiveness to have placed myself on the footing on which I wish to be with all the parties concerned, and to have satisfied L[auderdale] that B[rougham] had at least one compurgator among those who think very differently from him in politics. I may have another better opportunity.

...

1. *Horner*, i. 293–6, prints portions of this letter but without indicating that any passages have been omitted.

180. To Thomas Thomson

BLPES ii. 162–3 ⟨*Horner*, i. 298–300⟩   The Temple, 21 Nov. 1804

...

⟨... I hope the course of political economy is not given up for want of students; the number to be sure has always been small, but then it was composed only of such as take to the subject in earnest.[1] If peradventure there shall be twenty found there, for twenty's sake it ought to be saved. The effect which these lectures are already producing, by sending out every year a certain number who have imbibed a small portion of his [Dugald Stewart's] spirit, is so great that I cannot consent to any suspension of it.⟩ ...

... A brother Templar, I know not who, has published another attack upon Lauderdale's finance theory;[2] I have not seen it yet, and I do not expect much good from Galilee. Not knowing any thing of it, what are the odds that Lauderdale will reply?

‹What shall I tell you in the way of politics? Every morning, we have some new disgust or some new puzzle to swallow. This excommunicating bull of Talleyrand is the largest yet set before us;[3] is it to be bolted too? What an opportunity all these outrages, on *both* sides, would make for a Grotius, if we had one, to advocate the cause of sense and civilization! A slight change is now spoken of in the foreign department, on account of Lord Harrowby's bad health; Canning to have the green box, and Sturges to be Treasurer.›[4] This will leave all matters where they are; Canning is a very lively man, and I believe honest politician, but is an Eton wit a fit champion in such a contest?

...

1. In a letter of 14 Nov. 1804 Thomson had informed Horner that Professor Stewart, seeking more leisure time, had decided not to lecture on political economy during the winter of 1804–1805 (*Thomson*, p. 63).
2. Not identified.
3. Perhaps Talleyrand's second circular about the assassination plots against Napoleon, rejecting on 2 Sept. Hawkesbury's protestations of England's innocence of any complicity in them (*AR* 1804, pp. 657–9).
4. The Foreign Secretary, Dudley Ryder, 2nd Baron and afterwards 1st Earl of Harrowby (1762–1847: *DNB*), resigned on 20 Dec., and was replaced by Henry Phipps, 3rd Baron and afterwards 1st Earl of Mulgrave (1755–1831: *DNB*). Canning and Sturges-Bourne stayed where they were, the Earl of Buckinghamshire succeeding Mulgrave as Chancellor of the Duchy of Lancaster.

181. To Francis Jeffrey

BLPES ii. 164–5   The Temple, 29 Nov. 1804

I have very little book gossiping for you. The *Review* having made its fortune, one hears nothing of it in London any more; where there is no active relish for any thing that is not new. So that of this Number I have overheard nothing, except the abuse of some quotation Brougham has made from Cicero. I have lent my copy, so I have not yet looked at the passage; but I can believe a charge of that sort to be well-founded. For the same reason, that the work is quite established, one begins to catch the echo of its fame from country squires, rusticated peers, and provincial doctors. I was told of a bookseller at Salisbury, who swore indignantly there was nothing else asked for but the *Edinburgh*; and old Lord Pembroke remarked to Ward, as they proceeded together in a buggy, that it was the only Review he read.[1] What *do* you think of all this fame? And yet you have hypocrisy enough to cant against ambition, and all the other last infirmities of lost souls. Under this cloak of moderation, I suspect there lurks a most inordinate and aggrandizing spirit; and that when you have prostrated all your rivals here, even to the *Dublin Imperial*, you will aspire beyond the limits of this (*your*) little fame, and enter the lists of your giant competitors of Germany. I detected this from one of your emissaries, one Richard Heber,[2] who proposed in my hearing and Thomson's that our divine compositions should be translated into the gibberish of Saxony. Whenever that happens, I will pray that Tom Brown may be re-translated by Kant himself, and then we shall [have] a fair specimen of the dialect of the seraphim, the incomprehensible, the double distilled. By the way, there is a new French Review, to which great names are put, Suard, Morellet, etc. It is called *Archives de la Littérature*,[3] which is entertaining enough, the first time I heard of this was in a letter from Bombay; I have not yet seen it, but Romilly says it is poorly done.

Cousin Longman has played Philips with Philips, by bringing out before its time a set of Wilkes's letters – the birth seems abortive as well as premature.[4] The letters are well to have been written, but absolutely nothing; much good-nature and affection to his daughter, telling her how often he takes *beaume de vie*, and when he wishes to have a haunch of venison from Deputy Birch's. A very curious annalist of the present reign might glean two or three trivial notices, to which the name of Wilkes might lend a little interest. I own however that the very poverty of these letters gives me a little hope of entertainment from those which we are to have from Almon; because there is good sense in their manner, and letters to Miss Wilkes should show little else. Now and then too there breaks out an unbecoming hint of systematic Epicurism, which a profligate like you might enjoy if carelessly displayed in letters to some other person than a daughter. The Life prefixed is done in a very young manner, but seems to have the merit of honesty. The writer, as I was told in a sort of profound secret by Master Orme, is the husband of another daughter of Wilkes; he certainly does not affect to conceal the defects of his father[-in-law]'s morals.[5] ...

Our friend Smith has read two lectures, neither of which I have heard; not having time to share.[6] But I am very anxious, you may believe, to collect opinions about his appearances; the first pleased very much, the second has failed – failed, as I can perfectly understand, from his fear of being too dull, and therefore not being so dull as his hearers require him to be. I have not the smallest doubt he will get through the affair with *éclat*; though he knows next to nothing of metaphysics, he will do it with great cleverness and great sense. We have an established party almost every Sunday evening at his house.

... it is the faith and creed of all *Whig* believers ... that the Prince contrary to all expectation has behaved with firmness, and Moira with honesty; that the party is now very strong; and that the late farce of reconciliation is brought to its proper dramatic catastrophe, a serious dispute. It is a prerogative question; whether the King has a right to take into his own custody the young Princess Charlotte.[7] All the politicians are preparing themselves with law upon the subject. What a delightful fellow Lord Melville is. The Prince refused the offer of a military command by calling it almost in plain terms a ministerial intrigue; the wily Lord congratulated his friends on the P[rince] having given up all thoughts of so improper a thing as a command. ...

1. Major-General George Augustus Herbert, 11th Earl of Pembroke (1759–1827: *DNB*), and, probably, John William Ward, afterwards Earl of Dudley (1781–1833: *DNB*).

2. Richard Heber (1773-1833: *DNB*), book-collector and friend of Walter Scott.
3. *Mélanges de littérature*, ed. Jean Baptiste Antoine Suard (5 vols, Paris, 1803-1804).
4. *Letters from the year 1774 to the year 1796 of John Wilkes, Esq., addressed to his daughter, the late Miss Wilkes; with a collection of his miscellaneous poems. To which is prefixed a memoir of the life of Mr Wilkes*, published in four volumes in 1804 by Longman. Evidently Richard Phillips retaliated by bringing forward the publication of John Almon's five-volume edition of *The Correspondence of the late John Wilkes with his friends*, though the date on the title page remained 1805. They were both noticed by Jeffrey in *ER* v (no. x, Jan. 1805), 477-89 (*WI*).
5. Wilkes's legitimate daughter Mary, to whom the letters published by Longman were addressed, had died in 1802. He also had two natural children, a son and another daughter, Harriet, who was married to William (afterwards Sir William) Rough (1772-1838: *DNB*), the editor of the letters. Cosmo Orme (1780-1859) was Longman's partner.
6. Sydney Smith had begun his first course of ten lectures on Moral Philosophy at the Royal Institution on 10 Nov. (*Smith Letters*, i. 101, n. 1). For the better reception given to the second series, see *Homer*, i. 323.
7. A disagreement between the King and his son had blown up in the autumn of 1804 over the education of the Princess, who was then nine years old. Moira was understood by Pitt to have signified the Prince's consent to the King's taking charge of her and preparations were consequently made, not only for her care and education, but also for a general reconciliation of the father with his son. But the Prince apparently changed his mind at the last moment and Moira subsequently denied he had ever authorized any such statement.

182. To J.A. Murray

BLPES ii. 166-7 [London, 1 Dec. 1804]

...

    I have just been to hear Smith lecture; I liked the manner of it very well, as suited with great propriety upon the whole to his audience. One or two of his jokes failed; two or three took, and deserved to take; and three or four eloquent passages set off a piece of dull history to great advantage. There was a very affectionate and a very eloquent passage about Dugald Stewart, which produced a great effect.

    ...

183. To Francis Jeffrey

BLPES ii. 107-108 [London, 13 Dec. 1804][1]

I have been on the recruiting service for you. An old school-fellow of mine at Edinburgh, Mr Pillans, is come to London with a pupil at Westminster School; he is a man of application and of liberal opinions, but it is so long since we have seen any thing of each other, that I will not answer either for the extent or the nature of his acquisitions. But I think you may take him upon trial; put something into his hands that may be ill done without any serious consequences.[2] The other recruit I have enlisted is Mr Hallam, one of us here, a lawyer who has much leisure; he is an extremely well informed man in historical reading, and an eminent classic. He wrote a review for you of Plowden's *History*, which Elmsley says was elaborately well done; I have gone so far as to ask him to undertake Roscoe's new history, which I hope you will not disapprove of: he was entitled to some favour, after his disappointment about Plowden.[3] Tell me, however, what you think of my assumption of your prerogatives.

The new set of Wilkes's letters is out; quite as great a trifle as the other.[4] Your old friend Miss Baillie has published a new volume of plays, not in the course of her theoretic series, but miscellaneous; though she still declares her adherence to her own system.[5] I have read the first Tragedy in this volume, which appears to me bad. I suppose you have seen the new attack upon Brougham by Doctor Thomas Young; it is feeble to a contemptible degree, but Brougham should not have used all the expressions of contempt in which he has indulged himself.[6] At our Scotch Club some days ago, Davy asked me whether it would be a right thing to insert in the *Review* some account by way of *éloge* of our first deceased associate Gregory Watt, making his paper in the *Philosophical Transactions* an opportunity for introducing it.[7] The thing struck my fancy as well as his, if temperately executed; and I exhorted him to [do] it myself; if you see no more objections than I, you had better second the exhortation. Longman informs me you are to have a new edition of the first four numbers; tell me when you are to set about it, as I may be tempted perhaps to add a Note to my account of [Lord] King, in reply to the answer he has made in his second edition.[8] I should like also to have two or three copies of that and Canard taken for me, as I had of the last.[9]

...

Our season in London is now beginning; the old symposiac sets are re-assembling, and I have already seen one or two new faces. Of these, the most agreeable I recollect is Spencer, the author of some poems you may have read; whose spirit, variety, and elegance in conversation make him very nearly the first I have met with of that style, the fashionable (I mean) and dissipated style.[10] He has lived as much abroad as in his own country; is familiar with German and French literature, having been previously stored with longs and shorts at Harrow; and by the advantage of the blood in his veins, has had the run of the highest society all his life. When you add to these, much good nature, vivacity, and habits of pleasure, you have as full an idea as I can give you at present of this new acquaintance. I cling however to the old sets, of each of which you saw a little; the *faction* of good-sense over which Whishaw presides, *castigatque auditque*, Sharp's coterie of literature, and Smith's inexhaustible fun. At all of them, we often talk of you. ...

1. This letter is endorsed 16 May 1804, but the franks, while difficult to make out, seem to be 13 and 16 Dec. 1804. December is more compatible with the internal evidence, especially that the letter was written after Gregory Watt's death in October.

2. James Pillans (1778–1864: *DNB*), afterwards Rector of the High School and Professor of Humanity at the University of Edinburgh, had been second in class to Horner at the High School. In a letter of 11 January 1805 (BLPES ii. 174–5) Horner warned Jeffrey that he would 'have to unprovincialize any thing he may do'. According to the supplementary corrections in the *WI* Pillans did not write the notice of William Hayley's *Triumphs of Music*, *ER* vi (no. xi, Apr. 1805), 56–63. But since Horner unequivocally states that he did write such a review (see Doc. 188), Jeffrey must either have replaced it with his own or, as is perhaps at least as likely, considerably improved it. Whatever the truth, Pillans's contributions led Byron to revile him unfairly as the 'paltry Pillans'. Lord Holland's son said

of him in 1822 (*Fox*, p. 120): 'He is a sensible man, but sees everything with the eye of a schoolmaster.'

3. Hallam's first published contribution to the *ER* seems to have been the notice of Alexander Ranken's *History of France*, in vi (no. xi, April 1805), 209–228 (*WI*); and the review of William Roscoe's *Leo X* (4 vols, 1805), which did not appear in *ER* until vii (no. xiv, Jan. 1806), 336–58, is now attributed to Laing. Evidently, from the further mention in Doc. 206, Hallam was only considering a review of Roscoe at this time. See Doc. 145 for the review of Plowden by James Loch, whom Jeffrey is believed to have selected in preference to either Hallam or Brougham. See also Byrne Memoirs, p. 103.

4. See Doc. 181.

5. Joanna Baillie's *Miscellaneous Plays*, published in 1804 separately from her series of *Plays on the Passions*, contained two tragedies, *Rayner* and *Constantine Paleologus*, which were noticed by Jeffrey in *ER* v (no. x, Jan. 1805), 405–421.

6. Thomas Young (1773–1829: *DNB*) was perhaps one of the most distinguished scientists of his time. In the Bakerian Lecture on 'The Theory of Light and Colours' (1801), he had suggested an epoch-making doctrine of the interference of light. Brougham, whose scientific knowledge was superficial at best, had attacked the doctrine viciously and irresponsibly in the second, January 1803, number of *ER* (i. 450–56) and, following a subsequent experiment by Young, had renewed the attack in the ninth, October 1804, number (v. 97–103). Young then published a pamphlet – *A reply to the animadversions of the Edinburgh reviewers* (1804) – which refuted Brougham's censures but sold only one copy. Years later French scientists expanded on Young's work with important results. (See New, pp. 15–16.)

7. Gregory Watt, the youngest son of the engineer James Watt and an early contributor to the *ER*, had died in October 1804.

8. Lord King's second edition, which contained several introductory responses to Horner's review of the first, was published in 1804 under a new title: *Thoughts on the Restriction of Payments in Specie at the Banks of England and Ireland.*

9. In a letter to Constable endorsed April 1808, but evidently written rather about the same time as this Doc. (NLS MSS 7200, ff. 238–9), Horner made the same request direct, recalling that he had previously had such an offprint of his article on Thornton. That letter also reveals that Constable regularly sent Horner his *Farmer's Magazine*, which, Horner said:

> appears fully to maintain its character and merits, and I hope its circulation extends rapidly, both for your sake and that of the public; for I do not know any periodical publication that is calculated to be more useful. But I hope you will keep it always in the hands of real practical Farmers.

10. William Robert Spencer (1769–1834: *DNB*).

184. To Francis Jeffrey

BLPES ii. 170–71   The Temple, 29 Dec. 1804

...

I called at De Boffe's yesterday, and ordered two French works for you, the only novelties I met with. The one is the voyage of St Vincent to Madagascar and Mauritius, the other the Political Memoirs of the unfortunate Bailly.[1] I beg you will review the last yourself; if authentic, it ought to be a fine portrait of the modern fanaticism in its best state, the mistakes and enthusiasm of a man of virtue, knowledge, and eloquence. You may make a fine article of it; if you will wake again the little inspirer that dictated your Mounier, to which we always go back as the first and best of the *Review*. There wants something now to be said in favour of the first revolutionists; not much, alas! but something; both in palliation of their unavoidable errors, and in justification of their heroic hopes. The popular tide is at present set strongly the other way; why should not you, since you have coolness and clearness enough for it, anticipate [by] a few years the candid and indulgent sentence that will be definitive? There is the more reason for this, because Brougham has rung so many changes and so loud upon the song of the day, that the tune of the *Review* seems quite the same: yet the sentiments of most of us reach a little farther on. ...

I have been dipping a little, just to wet the tips of my fingers, into the last importation of books from Scotland. Lauderdale, I perceive, is to have a new pamphlet out very soon; Lord Archibald Hamilton has probably been grinding him to the subject of Irish currency.[2] Playfair has a passage most characteristic of himself, in his second edition of Euclid, where he has occasion to explain a principle of geometry which he and Legendre had both discovered about the same time:[3] the manly and modest candour of my ancient professor delights me like his scientific spirit. Why had you nothing of his in your last? For a long time I have not seen so fine a subject for a review of the first order, as the first volume of John Robison's *Elements*.[4] The science of course is very profound, and the range of his mathematical views is very grand; though as an elementary treatise its defects must be considerable. But the timid dotage of his philosophy whenever he quits geometrical ground, the want of taste in his digressions, the senseless mixture of politics with diagrams, the indistinctness of all his metaphysics and the fallacy of some of it, above all the illiberal manner in which he speaks of many eminent foreigners, and even the unsuitable idolatry with which he worships Newton, are faults that should not be overlooked at your tribunal. Yet I do not know where you are to find a person qualified for such a criticism; two or three you could name certainly, but I fear inaccessible, unless Playfair should be roused by Robison's sneer against Huttonian investigations. The book will come, I foresee, into Brougham's hands; who will do it very ably and very ill. I have not had courage to look into Forsyth's *Moral Sciences*, though stamped with the imprimatur of the Academy of *beaux-esprits* who used to hold their *séances* between the side-bar and the stove.[5] You must give some account of a metaphysical system, in an *Edinburgh Review*; though it be execrably bad, to disavow it. On this account, do not let an inferior hand do the work, dirty as it may be. A piece of dull 'pneumatology' will afford a new dull joke to those irrational prejudices, with which even the best informed Englishmen sometimes amuse their indolence and national vanity. If the book ought to be quizzed, quiz it by all means; you will do so much the more service to such as deserve better. I see advertised a new edition of Tucker's *Light of Nature*, so praised by our set of metaphysicians here; an additional chapter with Memoirs of the author by Sir Henry Mildmay may give you a sufficient pretext for an entire review. After what has been said of it by Paley, Mackintosh, and Parr, which I suspect to be exaggerated, it ought to be done with great care; the persuasion you know here is, that the Scotch school does not do justice to Hartley.[6]

I must not forget to tell you, that I have more than once heard regrets expressed that the *Review* is taking something too much of a cast towards party politics; and every one must agree that this is a departure from a purity and dignity of character, which it was the fair and proud boast of our Journal to preserve. I overheard this so settled, in a very strong manner, by two excellent judges who were discussing the subject; and I resolved you should receive the hint, to make the most of it. I recollect having myself felt a little remorse after I sent you my corn essay, on account of what I intended for a sarcasm against Pitt; the reputation of my taste has been saved, however, by the impotence of my rhetoric, for Cobbett has put his finger upon that very passage as a proof that the writer of the article is under the malignant influence and pay of Downing Street.[7] As I am solicitous that this, which is the truth, should be concealed, and never again surmised from my own awkward attempts to disguise it, remember I give you full authority to strike out every thing in any of my future communications that appears at all factious. I have no objection to party or its language in the proper place, and am quite prepared to use it where I think it may be useful; the *Edinburgh Review* has purposes of another sort to serve, which are impaired by such adulteration.

...

1. *Voyage dans les quatre principales îles des mers d'Afrique*, by J. B. G. M. Bory de St Vincent (3 vols, Paris, [1804]), was reviewed by Lockhart Muirhead in ER vi (no. xi, Apr. 1805), 121–37, and Jean Sylvain Bailly, *Mémoires d'un Témoin de la Révolution* (3 vols, Paris, 1804), by Jeffrey in the same number, pp. 137–61.

2. Perhaps *Thoughts on the alarming state of the circulation and on the means of redressing the pecuniary grievances of Ireland*, rather than *Hints to the Manufacturers of Great Britain on the Consequences of the Irish Union*, both of which appeared in 1805 though it was the latter Brougham reviewed in ER vi (no. xii, July 1805), 283–90.

3. Playfair's *Elements of Geometry*, first published in Edinburgh in 1795, was re-issued in an enlarged edition in 1804. Adrien Marie Legendre (1752–1833) was famous for his work on elliptic functions, the theory of numbers, and integral calculus, but best known at the time for his work on *Eléments de géometrie* which first appeared in Paris in 1794.

4. The first, and only, volume of John Robison's *Elements of mechanical philosophy* was published in Edinburgh in 1804; it was not reviewed in ER.

5. The first and only volume of Robert Forsyth's unsuccessful *Principles of Moral Science* (1805) was noticed by Jeffrey in ER vii (no. xiv, Jan. 1806), 413–36.

6. A second edition, with a life by his grandson, Sir Henry St John Mildmay, of Abraham Tucker's *The light of nature pursued* appeared in 7 vols in 1805. A sort of metaphysical humorist – Mackintosh called him a 'philosophical Montaigne' – Tucker was considerably influenced by David Hartley the elder (1705–1757: *DNB*) but, in turn, William Paley acknowledged his debt to Tucker in the preface to his *Moral and Political Philosophy*, and Mackintosh praised aspects of the work on several occasions. Although it was not noticed in ER, Dr Samuel Parr (1747–1825: *DNB*) reprinted some of Tucker's work in his *Metaphysical Tracts* (1837). See *Horner*, i. 285–6, for Horner's amusing sketch of Parr.

7. In a note to his 'Letter V to ... Pitt on the Causes of the Decline of Great Britain' of 8 Dec. (*PR* vi. 871), Cobbett had written: 'As to some points, and these not unimportant ones, I widely differ in opinion from the Edinburgh Reviewers, and for reasons that I may soon find an opportunity of stating, I am afraid that the long arm of Downing Street has reached them, and communicated to them its palsying effect.' That 'opportunity' he took in a long postscript in which he quoted at length from the last paragraph of the article in which Horner had written, with evident sarcasm, of 'the Master of the State'.

185. To J.A. Murray

BLPES ii. 177–8   The Temple, 24 Jan. 1805

. . .

We are all very impatient for the Spanish debate; the subject is an admirable one, particularly for Fox's sort of eloquence – that mixed case of policy and justice, in seizing the turns and combinations he appears to me peculiarly successful – resembling in *this* particular the manner of Demosthenes, and still more the cast of those speeches which Thucydides has composed for his *dramatis personæ*. From what I have heard and can guess from the old parliamentary registers, Fox was still more addicted to this style in early life than now; since the philosophical enlargement of his political views, and perhaps something of calmness from such a course of disappointments, have softened the vehemence of his manner. Perhaps, however, the fury of that vehemence drowned the effect of his better excellencies; while at present, the running tone of close, comprehensive reasoning, gives a bold relief to those occasional bursts of intellectual pathos, that give me a taste, I conceive, of what the ancients had in view as the highest excellence.[1]

1. On 21 Feb. 1805 Horner sent Murray a short account (*Horner*, i. 306–310) of the second day of the debate on the Spanish papers. The letter contains some interesting commentary on the speakers, notably on the peculiar style of Sir William Grant.

186. To Francis Jeffrey

BLPES ii. 179   [London], Friday [?15] Feb. 1805[1]

Brougham's pamphlet against L[auderdale] is probably in your hands by this time, where it is in every respect better placed than in mine. I should have had no objection to publish in the *Review* my own view of the controversy between these two champions, and to have given my own opinion in my own terms of the errors of his Lordship's reasonings, and the unjustifiable indecencies of his manner towards Brougham. But Brougham is warranted to use a language in reply to personal insults, if he thinks it worth while, which I should not be warranted to pass through my hands as editor. All this, however, is very fortunately out of the question; for Brougham has felt the sort of delicacy towards me which arises out of my very slight relations with Lord Lauderdale, and did not mean that I should be put to the dilemma of giving any opinion upon any part of his Reply. The MS was in London for a day or two, and was read by [Sydney] Smith, at whose house I happened to be when James [Brougham] called with it. Henry Brougham gave directions to his brother that Smith should read it.

I was vexed to hear that you had treated *The Sabbath* severely, before I learned from you the name of the author.[2] I read it some weeks ago, and though very unequal and in parts very bad there was enough to redeem it even to me, and I wrote indeed to Murray that you should bring to light the merits of what I conceived the obscure production of some obscure youth. Has Graham after all his philanthropy and Jacobinism taken to devotion? Not that I put this question on account of his subject, which is highly poetical, but because I was told by an acquaintance of mine here who corresponded with the unknown author, that he had sent two gilt copies for the Bishop of London and Wilberforce![3] I hear too you have accused him of plagiarism from Leyden's sonnet, which I do not feel to be a just accusation. Gray's 'sacred calm that breathes around' might have suggested the picture independently to both, even if it were not one which every body has seen and felt without the suggestion of any poet.

. . .

1. The letter, which has no surviving frank, is clearly dated 'Friday 5th Feb. 1805'. But 5 Feb. was not a Friday; so perhaps Horner meant to write '15th Feb.'
2. James Grahame (1765–1811: DNB) had published his poem anonymously in 1804. It had been noticed by Jeffrey in ER v (no. x, Jan. 1805), 437–42 (WI).
3. The Bishop of London, Beilby Porteus (1731–1808: DNB), was a supporter of the evangelicals.

187. To Francis Jeffrey

BLPES ii. 180–81   [London], Saturday [16 Feb. 1805]

. . . Romilly is at the head of the Chancery Bar, and the Solicitor-General (Gibbs) at the head of the *law* of the common law courts.[1] As to prejudices, etc., you may take it for granted that the Judges of the English Courts are full of collegiate prejudices, and have a great reverence for university charters and constitutions. . . .

. . .

1. Vicary (afterwards Sir Vicary) Gibbs (1751–1820: DNB) had just been made Solicitor-General. Samuel (afterwards Sir Samuel) Romilly (1757–1818: DNB) succeeded Gibbs on the formation of the All Talents Ministry.

188. To Francis Jeffrey

BLPES ii. 184   The Temple, 6 Mar. 1805

In case I forget it, I must begin with telling you, that I suggested to my friend Spencer to send you a review of the Abbé De Lille's translation of the *Eneid*; and he has promised to attempt it, indeed accepted the proposal with great readiness.[1] He should do this well, I think; for his taste appears to me very pure as well as susceptible, and he got his Latin at Harrow, and his French by many years' residence upon the continent. He is not profound, but very quick; so that you will have results and dogmas, probably, rather than *principes raisonnés*. Pillans has been asking me *when* it is necessary to send MS to you, so that I presume he has something for the next; and Drummond inquired *how* it is best, so that he ought by this time to have sent his dispatch.[2] I took something of a liking to the said Drummond, from hearing him speak of you as he ought. He has indeed been very civil to myself.

Pillans has since told me, that he has written a review of Hayley's *Triumph of Music*.[3] He is very modest about it, and I do not expect much; he has excellent powers, but execution requires practice as well as power. But in time, he may become a respectable associate; he has both knowledge and sense. Since I sent you the packet which was given me about Lord Strangford, I have met Moore *alias* Little several times in society; and feel somewhat sorry that he should be spoken of so severely in that critique.[4] He is perfectly unassuming, simple, and unaffected; no *Londony* vices in his manner: though I had expected much of all these defects, from the character of his poetry. He has no qualifications whatever for conversation, but he does not try to do what he cannot. All this good temper and modesty should secure a man from harsh contempt. I do not feel it right from particular circumstances to suggest to the author of the critique to make any alteration; but it may be within the province of your plenipotentiary discretion to alleviate a little. And you have this good ground, that Moore is not immediately the subject of criticism; an unjust side blow is the greatest offence, you recollect, that has yet been imputed to the *Review*, the savage sentence, I mean, against Currie's *Life of Burns*,

. . .

1. See Doc. 206 n. 4.
2. Presumably not Drummond-Home, but William Drummond (?1770–1828: *DNB*), who having early on made some reputation as a scholar and author, was now in between two brief appointments as a rather undistinguished diplomat. (The knighthood with which the *DNB* credits him was Turkish.) He is believed to have contributed some five pieces to the ER. But by the autumn of 1805 Sydney Smith was already calling him 'dull, wrongheaded, malignant and indiscreet', and warning Jeffrey not to use him too much, and before the end of the year Horner too was expressing his concern. Known to his acquaintances as 'Dry Drummond', he was, in fact, what his friend Ward later called a 'rampant' atheist. Even the sceptical Horner was offended by his profanity and blasphemy, which, he felt, merely played into the hands of their opponents. (*Sydney Smith*, i. 110 and 126; *Brougham*, i. 457; Horner to Murray, 23 Nov. 1811, BLPES v. 134–7; see also Docs 210 and 454.)
3. See Doc. 183.
4. Allen had sent Horner from Lisbon an anonymous review of the *Poems from the Portuguese of Camoens* published in 1803 by Percy Clinton Sydney Smyth, 6th Viscount Strangford (1780–1855: *DNB*), who was then Secretary of Legation at Lisbon. That notice, printed in ER vi (no. xi, Apr. 1805), 43–50, was by Bartholomew Frere (1778–1851: *DNB*), Strangford's predecessor at Lisbon and now Secretary of Legation at Madrid. Thomas Moore (1779–1852: *DNB*) had in 1801 published his amorous verse under the title of *Poems by the late Thomas Little*. Despite the sympathetic view expressed about it here, when a further volume of *Odes and Epistles* appeared in 1806 Jeffrey savagely attacked it in ER viii (no. xvi, July 1806), 456–65, and landed himself with a duel. (See Doc. 238.)

189. Political Anecdote by Horner

BLPES viii. 5   14 Mar. 1805

Lord Henry Petty mentioned to Seymour and me this morning, that he knew as a fact, upon undoubted authority, that very recently there was an offer from Bonaparte (through the Irish Directory at Paris) to the heads of the rebels in Dublin, of assistance by troops – that this offer was *deliberated* upon – and rejected, upon the expectation that Government would speedily grant the Catholic Emancipation.

Some days ago, Lord Henry Petty mentioned to me what he said he knew on the best authority, and said he had no doubt of when I ventured to express my suspicions: that when the Irish petition first came over and was talked of, the King said to his daughter, Sophia, that 'rather than yield the point, he would risk a civil war, and would be glad of it upon such a question – that he would leave the Duke of York here as regent – would go over himself with the Blues,[1] and take the Prince with him.'

1. *NB The King wears the uniform of the Blues at present. *Quidquid deliverant*, etc.

190. To J.A. Murray

BLPES ii. 185–6 ⟨*Horner*, i. 310–11⟩   The Temple, 16 Mar. 1805

⟨. . .

⟨Your account of Leslie's election interests me beyond any thing I have heard for a long while.[1] But you must tell me a thousand things more about it. In the first place, procure me, I beseech you earnestly, every document about it that you can lay your hands upon; especially the Protest, any paragraphs in the newspapers that may have been published by either party, Dr Hunter's letter if you can, or any other morsels of correspondence. I shall preserve them in the same bundle with my copies of Aikenhead's conviction, and Lord Anstruther's letter: and shall enjoin my heirs, in the whole line of substitution, to collect similar documents from century to century, by way of proving, some thousand years hence, that priests are ever the same⟩ and that Finlayson is an animal always to be found at Edinburgh. In the next place, I am equally delighted and amazed that these priests were not successful. What does this mean? Is Finlayson no longer the confessor of the House of Melville? Or the House of Melville no longer kings over Israel?[2] You must explain this to me; it is utterly mysterious. What influence moved the Town Council, that did not move to the same tune [as] Finlayson and his set? My curiosity is quite in earnest about all this, and I hope you will not refuse to satisfy it, though it should give you a little trouble. I shall write a few lines to Moncrieff, to get his father's edition of the part of the story in which he took a share.

. . .

Brougham is arrived – in excellent health, sobriety, and spirits. He has seen a vast deal, and written folio volumes: some hair breadth escapes he boasts of, and seems to have been in some foolish scrapes of no great importance.[3] I have no doubt that a faithful description of this *fier intriguant* was dispatched by every diplomat who got scent of him to every other. He talks in rapture of the blue sky of Italy, and with unmeasured contempt of all German heads. Dr Gall, however, has converted him to his theory of skulls. He describes the King of Prussia, as the very image in person, intellect and manners, of Cousin Longman.

. . .

1. Upon the death of Professor John Robison in January and the promotion of Playfair to succeed him in the chair of Natural Philosophy at Edinburgh, an unsuccessful attempt was made to exclude John Leslie (1766–1832: *DNB*) from the chair of Mathematics on the basis of a passage in his published researches on heat which represented Hume as 'the first who has treated of causation in a truly philosophic manner'. The attack was led by Professor Finlayson, and the resistance by Sir Henry Moncreiff-Wellwood (1750–1827: *DNB*), father of Horner's friend and a leading cleric in Edinburgh. The reference to Dr Hunter is explained by *Cockburn*, pp. 191–2. Thomas Aikenhead (?1678–97: *DNB*) was hanged for ridiculing the bible. The reference to him and to Lord Anstruther is explained in an appendix to *Horner*, i. 547–9. For the Leslie affair in general see Ian D. Clark, 'The Leslie Controversy, 1805', *Records of the Scottish Church History Society*, xiv (1962), 179–97.
2. A line has been obliterated here.
3. Brougham had returned from Italy about the end of January. *Brougham*, i. 271–308, gives a detailed account.

191. Political Anecdote by Horner

BLPES viii. 6   17 Mar. 1805

Lord Henry Petty has just told me, that he dined today where Windham and Lord Grenville were in company; they both mentioned, that Mr Pitt's letter to the Irish Catholics was never shown to either of them, nor did they know any thing of the promise or pledge he meant to hold out to that Body, until they saw it in print.[1] Yet they were at that moment resigning their places, along with him, upon this very ground.

1. See Doc. 145.

192. To Dugald Stewart

Lacaita/Shelburne MSS, William L. Clements Library,
University of Michigan ⟨Horner, i. 312–14⟩   [London], 6 Apr. 1805

. . .

⟨I take an opportunity of sending you two pamphlets on the education of the lower orders, written by a Quaker practically engaged in that occupation upon a very extensive scale; whose institution has excited a great interest among the people in London, that can be interested by such things.[1] You will form a pretty correct idea of his method, from his own account of it in these tracts; I have visited his school, and it exhibits a sufficient and very pleasing proof of its practicability. He seems to have introduced, or at least reduced more to system, one or two important principles, which are very little attended to in the ordinary course of elementary education. His scheme of rewards, and of punishment chiefly by withdrawing or delaying rewards, is both ingenious and very humane. And he has given greater activity to the emulation of children, than is commonly done.⟩ But the greatest novelty is the principle, upon which he has founded his new methods of teaching arithmetic and spelling; you will extract it from the explanation he has attempted. The advantage of these methods consists in keeping the little fellows all at work at once, and their attention engaged all the time they are confined in school. This is effected in a very simple manner; and besides the economy of time and expense, must contribute very much to the immediate happiness of the children. ⟨Nothing can be more pleasing than, on going into this school, that you discover nothing of the languor and sickly idleness which make a common parish school so melancholy to see.⟩ I saw here the other day more than six hundred boys, of the poorest people in the suburbs, taught for nothing, all in rags but cheerfully engaged; and writing, spelling, and cyphering as well as they need to do. The system goes on, by the classification of the boys and the selection of the best of them as Monitors, with scarcely any further trouble on the part of the head master, than that of general inspection. ⟨He has got a library too of almost 300 vols, in which there are books from Mrs Trimmer up to the *Lives of the Admirals* [by John Campbell] and Cook's *Voyages*; and the boys get these to take home with them from week to week. The man owned to me, that his boys always preferred the works of adventure or fun to scientific dialogues⟩, which Mrs Barbauld, etc. have been trying to substitute for them; but I did not get him to agree with me, that the boys know better what is good for them than Mrs B., etc.[2]

⟨I was at some pains to talk to Lancaster about himself. He was originally bred to be a Dissenting minister, but at the age of sixteen was converted by the Friends. He has no powers of understanding, but yet a practical way of turning his own subject in his thoughts; and he is keenly devoted to it by something which he honestly believes to be all philanthropy, but which is one or two tenth parts at least a very excellent ambition of notoriety. He is not so fanatical as the circumstance of his conversation might lead one to suspect; for he thinks with great liberality and justness, on the religious instruction of the lower orders. Yet I had an amusing specimen of his notions of inward light, on asking him rather too formal a question, about the steps by which his mind had been led to his views of improving education. He could trace no such steps, but talked of Providence, and quoted the Proverbs, and spoke of himself as an instrument in the hands of God for effecting a great improvement in the condition of the poor. He has groped out his system, he can't recollect how, and finds himself governing a thousand children very much to his own amazement.⟩

He is about to publish an enlarged edition of his book, and I found a subscription list for nearly two thousand copies; in which there were only eight names from Scotland, all sent by George Millar, a Quaker linen-draper at Edinburgh. This scandalized me not a little. And so with Lord Webb's approbation, and Petty's, when we were there together, I took the liberty of putting down your name for four copies.

⟨At Edinburgh, I suspect, you can form no conception of the impression which the Tenth Report[3] has produced here. There is but one feeling, and one language, among the adherents of all parties, beyond the immediate pedigree of Dundas himself. All the old topics against Placemen, and Scotsmen, are in full cry; and those who are most sincere in their attachment to Pitt, very rationally feel this indignation the highest.⟩ As to the event of Monday next, there is some reason to believe, that several of the Minister's friends will absent themselves, and that Addington's men will probably stay and do something more.[4] But the division, I confess, gives me very little anxiety; for ⟨an impression is already made upon the public mind which, with other matters daily accumulating, must work an effect. And at all events, the *historical* effect of the Tenth Report is decisively secured; a long shade is thrown back upon the former Ministry of Pitt⟩, and in a few years that period will show itself to every body with a hue and colouring, borrowed from Lord Melville's vulgar name. ⟨If Pitt had courage for it, one would think he ought to shake him off at once, and hold up his hands at such a disclosure of corruption which he could not have imagined: but that is out of the case; he must defend him, and he will try to do it in a very high tone.

⟨Since the persecution of John Home for writing a good tragedy,[5] or indeed since the murder of the medical student Aikenhead for his scepticism about the Trinity, there is nothing from the Presbytery of Edinburgh so worthy of them as their late intrigues against cause and effect.[6] We have had much mirth upon this story, in the King of Clubs; and long very much to hear it more circumstantially. Would it not be worth while that some body should put it into writing, with the relative documents, in order to preserve it in the chronicles that such things were done at Edinburgh in the year of our Lord 1805?⟩[7] The only inexplicable circumstance is, that Finlayson and his gang were not successful in the election.

We are to have another trial at the Slave Trade in a short time. Wilberforce has requested our friend Lord Henry to take it up, and the arrangements are almost made for a new motion. It was by mere negligence, the last was thrown out: that is, in the H. of Commons. There is very little chance of success in the other house. . . .[8]

1. Probably Joseph Lancaster's *Letter to John Foster, Chancellor of the Exchequer for Ireland, on the best means of educating and employing the poor in that country* (1805), and one of the earlier editions of his *Improvements in Education*, first published in 1803 and, as Horner mentions in a later paragraph, about to be re-issued in a much enlarged edition. (See Doc. 227.)
2. Sarah Trimmer (1741–1810: *DNB*) was a popular but pious author and critic of educational books for children and an active supporter of the SPCK and Sunday schools. Her attack on

Lancaster was but a part of her campaign of censorship, to which she dedicated her journal, the *Guardian of Education* between 1802 and 1806. Anna Letitia Barbauld (1743–1825: *DNB*), another popular author, was also devoted to the cause of children's education. (See Doc. 227.)

3. The report of the select committee inquiring into irregularities in the naval department dealing more specifically with the office of treasurer formerly held for a long period by Lord Melville, the present First Lord of the Admiralty.

4. Whitbread called the attention of the Commons to the select committee's report on Monday, 8 April, and at the conclusion of the ensuing debate the Speaker gave his casting vote against Melville, whose resignation was announced on the following Wednesday.

5. John Home (1722–1808: *DNB*), after the performance in Edinburgh and London of his play entitled *Douglas*, was forced to resign his ministry in 1757.

6. In the case of John Leslie.

7. Evidently this suggestion influenced Stewart's decision to write A *Short Statement of some important Facts, relative to the late Election of a Mathematical Professor in the University of Edinburgh; accompanied with Original Papers, and Critical Remarks* (Edinburgh, 1805). In a letter to Murray of 6 Apr. Horner discussed the propriety of sending documents to Government and Opposition newspapers and suggested that Jeffrey write a pamphlet disclosing the behaviour of Leslie's antagonists (*Horner*, i. 314–15). Omitted without acknowledgement from the published version of Horner's letter to Mackintosh of 8 Apr. (*Horner*, i. 316–22) is an account of events in Edinburgh relating to the case (BLPES ii. 191–2). In a letter to Murray of 16 May Horner laid out a philosophical defence of Hume's doctrine and of the context in which Leslie had referred to it (BLPES ii. 201–203).

8. Horner goes on to describe the extent of the famine that then existed in parts of British India, noting that the sources of his information were letters from Mackintosh and Bombay newspapers.

193. To Sir James Mackintosh[1]

BLPES ii. 189–92 ⟨*Horner*, i. 316–22⟩   The Temple, 8–9 Apr. 1805

⟨. . .

⟨I am glad to hear of your intention to survey statistically the island of Bombay; the *Archives Statistiques* shall be sent out to you certainly by these ships.[2] As to general queries, it would be idle to make out any such; and to frame such particular ones as would be pertinent, requires that some local information should be already possessed, which I can hardly say is my case, with respect to the political economy of Bombay. Yet I have a strong curiosity about it, and if I were taught a little, might make out questions to learn more. As the emporium of a very extensive and peculiar commerce, it must suggest many illustrations and many corrections of the theories which have been framed in this part of the world, from our own limited experience; with respect to the distribution of capital, the facilities of credit, and the contrivances for accelerating and economizing exchange. The theory of prices, and their variations, is the darkest part of our system; much light might be thrown on it, by considering the subject in various parts of the world, where the habits of consumption, and the medium of circulation, are different.

⟨You would confer a high favour on me, by communicating such views on these parts of the general theory as the peculiar facts to be observed in Bombay suggest: any books or papers, containing accurate details, I should look upon as invaluable.

⟨The trade of bullion connects all the parts of the world into one system; and there are some recent phenomena in the commerce of this quarter, which would probably be explained if we understood the state of the bullion market in Asia. Have you any means of ascertaining the variations of prices at Bombay, from one point of time to another? If there are, you may aid us much in solving this problem, how far the extraordinary rise of prices all over Europe within the last twenty years is to be ascribed to a change in the supply of the precious metals. Has there been a similar depreciation in India? Has it been felt in a general enhancement of commodities; in the collection, for example, of the revenue from the zemindars, with whom Lord Cornwallis compounded for a money rent? The *Ayeen Akbery* contains some very full and curious lists of prices;[3] a comparative set of modern tables would render both prolific of general results. . . .⟩

. . .

9 Apr.

⟨. . . We have hopes, some of us, that Lancaster's school may be the germ of establishments for a national education both in England and Ireland; he has got about 3000 copies subscribed for, of a new and enlarged edition of his book . . ., and Foster has proposed to take him over with him to Ireland this summer, in order to introduce his methods there. . . . I have already suggested to Lancaster, that he should procure a circulation of his book in America; he has likewise met with a person, who undertakes to translate it into German; and we shall give it the run of all our readers in the *Edinburgh Review*, from which it will get into the *Bibliothèque Britannique*.[4] There may not be novelty enough in the book to deserve all this; but there is importance enough in the subject to make a very little novelty a sanctified pretext for over-praising any book that relates to it. The interest already excited in London and some parts of the country, by this Quaker's school, is a sufficient indication, that some of the wounds inflicted on the English mind, by the terrors[5] of French principles, are already sloughing off.⟩

. . .

1. Stanhope (*Pitt*, iv. 310n) describes this as 'a remarkable letter'.
2. Probably a reference to the series of departmental reports emanating from France during the period 1792–1810 and described by A. de St Leger in 'Les mémoires statistiques des départements pendant la directoire, le consulat et l'empire', in *La Bibliothèque moderne* (1918–19) pp. 5–43; the HL includes in no. 166 a quarto volume of *Statistiques de la France* (Paris, 1804). Horner was probably responding to a request made in connection with the plans mentioned in Doc. 117.
3. *Ayeen Akbery; the institutes of Akbar*, translated by F. Gladwin (2 vols, 1800).
4. Founded by Marc Auguste and Charles Pictet in 1796, and afterwards retitled the *Bibliothèque Universelle*.
5. Horner actually wrote 'terror', which gives a somewhat different meaning.

194. Political Anecdote by Horner

BLPES viii. 6   26 Apr. 1805

At Drummond's, John Ponsonby mentioned to me (adding at the same time that perhaps he ought not to have mentioned it, but that he *knew* it to be the fact) that Foster offered at the first to be the agent to carry through the Union; and on Clare being preferred, he took the other side.[1]

1. Presumably John Brabazon Ponsonby (1771–1855: *DNB*), afterwards 1st Viscount Ponsonby and a distinguished diplomat, whose grandfather, like John Foster, had been Speaker of the Irish House of Commons. He had been a member of the Irish House of Commons from 1793 to 1800 and briefly, 1801–1802, MP for Galway in the United Kingdom Parliament. John Fitzgibbon, 1st Earl of Clare (1749–1802: *DNB*), had been Lord Chancellor of Ireland at the time of the union.

195. To Francis Jeffrey

BLPES ii. 197–8   [London], 3 May 1805

. . .

I have been reading the XIth number, and have read the introduction to the article [on] Bailly with a delight which I have not known, since the review of Mounier.[1] I hardly know a sentence in which I do not fully acquiesce with you; yet there is not one which has not extended my views of the subject, or corrected a little my former notions. There is no writing, in which you appear so worthy of yourself as in these general dissertations; and you must catch some other opportunities of the same kind, before you close your reviewing labours. These compositions will retain a value and an interest, after all the other articles are gone into oblivion after the books which they sent there. Your review of Scott, as I expected, errs in excess of praise; but you have given very plausible reasons for your praise, as you have been very skilful in counteracting by palliations the little censure you have hazarded.[2] I adhere to my original opinion that Edinburgh works had better be omitted in the *Edinburgh Review*. You must give *Madoc* in the next number; I have not read it, but I have heard Spencer and Rogers praise it more than I expected.[3] The former is a very candid and unenvious lover of excellence; when Rogers praises a living poet's composition, it must have merit undeniable. He spoke most in favour of the versification. Spencer has found the story interesting enough to read it twice. I tell you these little things, not to guide you, but that you may not overlook wholly what has most struck others. Our friend Sotheby, I hear, has a new poem in hand, didactic of the modern philosophy; in which there are said to be fine passages.[4] Little Moor [Moore?] too is at work upon a sort of Hudibrastic piece, to be called the 'Devil among the Scholars';[5] and Rogers himself will soon appear with his *Columbiad*.[6] I rather think Sharp will before long publish the little copy of verses, from which he quoted to us some lines in Kensington Gardens; they are elegant.[7] Drummond has published *Academic Questions*, which I think nobody should meddle with but yourself;[8] I have just got the book, and expect to find better writing than philosophy: in conversation at least, he is darkling.[9] I shall review Lancaster's book on education, as soon as it comes out, which I understand will be in the course of this month; and pray desire Constable to send me Lord Selkirk's pamphlet as soon as it comes out; that has long been a favourite subject of mine.[10] Did not you write to me long ago in favourable terms of Griffiths? His book is a meagre, contemptible performance.[11]

You see how we have been going on of late: the House of Commons vindicating its character as a great constitutional Assembly, and the Opposition as a party losing every advantage which fortune had showered upon them. Lord Melville is struggling a little yet, but the remains of political life in him will soon be extinguished – and he condemned to breathe out the rest of his natural existence in ignominious retirement. The Committee is not altogether composed of tools; nor if it were, would it be very practicable for them to give a new appearance to facts which the public has already considered, though they might suppress perhaps any farther evidence of criminality. But Lord Marsham, Lord Boyle, and Spencer Cowper, are not men who will lend their names to any thing dishonourable.[12] I do look upon this conviction and punishment of Dundas as a most important event; not only in affording an opportunity of breaking to pieces the provincial government of Scotland, but in its consequences upon the general administration of England. The mere correction of financial delinquency is of good example; but I see more permanent and extensive benefit in the disrepute, into which these inquiries will bring the name of Pitt and the history of his long Administration. I have no idea of his participation in any thing like Dundas's common pilfering; on the contrary, I feel a great respect for his proud and careless purity, as I do likewise for his vast powers of understanding. But his continuance in power and popularity is an obstruction to all liberal ameliorations of government, and daily renders even the public mind more vulgar and more unprincipled. There is a want of every thing like permanent deliberate maxims of policy, quite unworthy of this informed country, and quite unsuited to the situation of difficulties and perils in which it is at present placed. And there is, coupled with this want of system, such a morbid indifference in the man's mind to the great ends and purposes of a free government, that our whole system of civil economy as well as political constitution is falling into disorder. When his miraculous rhetoric ceases to ring in our ears, what reputation will be left to Pitt? . . .

1. See Docs 120 and 184.

2. Jeffrey reviewed Walter Scott's *Lay of the Last Minstrel* in *ER* vi (no. xi, April 1805), 1–20 (WI).

3. Jeffrey reviewed Southey's poem in *ER* vii (no. xiii, Oct. 1805), 1–29.

4. William Sotheby (1757–1833: *DNB*), was a prolific and personally popular, but on the whole, unsuccessful poet, who had, however, been much praised by Jeffrey for some of his translations in *ER* iv (no. viii, July 1804), 296–303.

5. There appears to be no such poem by Tom Moore; perhaps he contemplated but never fulfilled an intention of imitating Coleridge and Southey's *Devil's Thoughts*, as did Byron and Shelley.

6. Samuel Rogers's *Fragments of the Voyage of Columbus* was not published until 1812. An earlier version was privately printed at the beginning of 1810, when Rogers had already been at work on it 'for a dozen years'. (*Rogers*, i. 66; see also Doc. 483.)

7. None of Sharp's verse seems to have appeared in print until his 'Epistles in Verse' were privately distributed among his friends in 1828 and afterwards published along with a fragment of his correspondence in *Sharp*.

8. William Drummond's *Academical Questions* (4 vols, 1805) was reviewed by Jeffrey in *ER* vii (no. xiii, Oct. 1805), 163–85 (*WI*).

9. I.e., obscure.

10. Although Horner may have given up the attempt to review Lancaster (see Doc. 227), that in *ER* vii (no. xiii, Oct. 1805), 185–202 (*EW*, pp. 115–34), of Lord Selkirk's *Observations on the present state of the Highlands of Scotland, with a view of the causes and probable consequences of emigration* (Edinburgh, 1805) seems almost certainly to be his.

11. Macvey Napier is thought to have noticed J. Griffiths's *Travels in Egypt, Asia Minor, and Arabia* (1805) in *ER* viii (no. xv, Apr. 1806), 35–51.

12. This allusion is puzzling. For of those named – Charles, Viscount Marsham, afterwards 2nd Earl of Romney (1777–1845), Henry, Viscount Boyle, afterwards 3rd Earl of Shannon (1771–1842), and Edward Spencer Cowper (1779–1823) – only Boyle served on the select committee appointed on 29 Apr. to examine the report on the Melville case, and only Marsham on the committee appointed on 26 June to draw up the articles of impeachment (*House of Commons Journal*, lx. 222 and 424.) But there was much squabbling about the selection of members for the first and both Marsham and Boyle were proposed at one time or another.

196. To J.A. Murray

BLPES ii. 199–200　　　　　　　　　　　　　The Temple, 4 May 1805

I felt your reproach for having omitted to send you some account of the late very important, and very unexpected event, the parliamentary disgrace of Lord Melville. ... You must have derived great satisfaction from the praise which our friend Petty received, for his excellent speech in that debate; all accounts of it were the same, and his general reputation is much heightened and spread in consequence of these.[1] Fox said it was the best speech in the debate; and several persons who were present have assured me, that the compliment was deserved literally. I know that Fox has a very high esteem for Petty; Mr Ponsonby told me the other day, that he has repeatedly heard both Fox and Grey speak of him in terms of very high respect and attachment. Indeed I have seen Petty in Mr Fox's company, and he addresses him in a kind and distinguishing manner; as on the other hand, Petty's admiration and reverence for that extraordinary man rise every day. Nobody ever husbanded his powers so well as our friend Lord Henry: though by no means of the first order, they are in the first class of the second, and guided by his watchful systematic discretion will secure him always an eminent station among our political competitors. He will one day be Minister of the country, I look upon it as certain; unless some youth of genius shall start up, whom we have never yet heard of. All that I can learn about the nursery of our great families, gives no promise of such an appearance. If he remains steady to the principles and general views of his present party, he will soon possess that sort of character which is more efficient in England than the fame of original uncertain genius.

I shall now proceed to tell you such anecdotes, as have reached me from what appears good authority, about the event of the 8th ult. and its consequences. The result was not more unlooked for by those out of doors, than by the partisans on both sides of the House. The most sanguine hope of Opposition was, that the Court would gain the question only by 50. The infatuation of the other side continued so late, that when the Ayes went forth upon the previous question, Pitt harangued them about what he meant to do next, and the list was handed about of the Committee he meant to move for. The Duke of Bedford supped at Fordyce's that night, and went there from the House of Commons;[2] he told them what he thought the event might possibly be, from the appearance and tone of the House, for there never was known such a tumult of chearing [sic] to all the speeches against Lord Melville. Fordyce went over to the Admiralty, to inquire farther, but found M[elville] in the highest spirits, having just received a note from the House of Commons assuring him that his triumph was certain by a large majority. A great number of votes must have been determined by the speeches; which very rarely occurs in that deliberative assembly. Some of these were gained by Wilberforce, who made a great impression. Two or three, I have heard of by description and names, who had been convinced by the 10th Report, yet intended to vote with the Minister lest he should be endangered by the loss of the question, but brought themselves in the course of the evening to believe that his popularity would be still more injured by success in such a cause. Some persons look out always for the majority, and are always kept in the right by that habitual sagacity which appears to others like instinct. A few votes were added in still another way, by some members who were anxious to say Aye, if their colleagues had not said No; in this predicament were the Lascelles, I presume, who thought of the populous county of York:[3] and though I am not at liberty to mention the name, I know of a knight of an ancient shire, who was actually out in the lobby, but looking out for his brother knight and being told he was seated at the farthest corner of the House, made a push back and just got in. He had strength to push; another recreant was not so successful – the robust Secretary of the Treasury hustled him back to his first thoughts.[4] These are trifles in the scant history of the day; and had no preponderance, you may believe, in the contest. Such an effect, so unusual, so contrary to prejudices and interests, must have necessarily had a cause, as Drs Grieve and Finlayson will prove to you, proportionate and adequate.[5] That cause, was the irresistible evidence of the Xth Report, summed up and most strongly charged on in Lord Melville's own letter.[6] After deducting 140, the largest estimate to be made for the strength of Opposition as a party, there will remain a considerable number of members, most of whom, I really believe, gave their vote honestly and with pain to themselves. Such I consider the Saints to have been, who always make the most of their morality, when they have no religious motive to be immoral: to them you have to add several very independent men, zealous admirers of Mr Pitt, who have for several years looked upon Dundas as his evil spirit, that led him into all the mires through which he has been dragging himself and them: and then there are various Justices of Quarter Sessions, men of ten thousand a year, who are quite excellent judges upon a case of common honesty and keeping of accounts, though they happen very innocently to sanction whole systems of robbery and murder upon a grander scale.

You consider Lord Melville's fate in a temper of mind, which he little deserves, but which I expected in you. To me, it is only the ignominious end of a very vulgar man, about whom I cannot entertain either pity or resentment. The sentence of the Xth Report has only accelerated a little, and aggravated a little, the sentence which was already preparing for him in history without it. It is long since his character was settled in the House of Commons, and throughout England, as that of [a] common jobber.

. . .

1. Petty's speech of 8 Apr. (*Hansard*, iv. 289–93), which Horner had missed, made a great impression on the Commons. See also Horner's letter to Mackintosh of 19 Apr. in *Horner*, i. 324–5.
2. The Duke's second wife was the niece of John Fordyce of Ayton (1735–1809), Surveyor-General of Crown Lands.
3. Edward, afterwards Viscount Lascelles (1764–1814), was MP for Northallerton, and his younger brother, Henry Lascelles, afterwards 2nd Earl of Harewood (1767–1841: *DNB*), MP for Yorkshire.
4. Sturges-Bourne and William Huskisson were the Joint Secretaries.
5. Dr Henry Grieve was, with Finlayson, one of John Leslie's principal antagonists in the dispute over the succession to the chair of Mathematics.
6. Presumably that of 30 June 1804 to the Commissioners of Naval Inquiry, reprinted in *Pitt*, iv. 274–5.

197. To Francis Jeffrey

BLPES ii 206–207   The Temple, 21 May 1805

. . .

. . . Mr Knight has just sent round to his friends a work on the metaphysics of taste, which I have not yet seen; but in a party of the orthodox yesterday, I heard it charged with advancing some damnable heresies, such as that Thomson's versification is better than Milton's.[1] The Council of Edinburgh, not the Town Council though, will take good care of such a heretic, and deliver him over to the secular arm. The same Mr Knight is one day to prove that the *Odyssey* was not written by Homer. He is a good-natured, laborious, sensible, coarse man; of great erudition in virtue, famous for his collection of antique bronzes and for the best dinners (I hear) in London: he had the rare merit, as a man of fortune, of discovering at the age of 25 that his education was imperfect, and set himself down to elements with an extraordinary diligence in which he still perseveres. I have met him several times, and should never have given him credit for any delicacy of perception in the fine arts, or originality of judgement. Drummond's book I have not yet looked into; I heard Hallam express a wish the other day to review it, which you may indulge or not as you think proper.[2] . . . I have this morning had the satisfaction of reading Mr Stewart's pamphlet;[3] parts of which are quite admirable. . . .

1. The first (1805) edition of Richard Payne Knight's *Analytical inquiry into the principles of Taste* was reviewed by Hallam for ER vii (no. xiv, Jan. 1806), 295–328 (*WI*). The Scottish

poet James Thomson (1700–1748: *DNB*) still enjoyed enormous popularity at this time.
2. See Doc. 195.
3. On Leslie's case.

198. From Dugald Stewart

Kinnordy MSS   Newbattle Abbey, 8 June [1805]

I have remained very long in your debt for an excellent letter containing much information which interested me deeply. I was particularly delighted with your account of the Quaker's success in the Education of the lower orders, and with the details contained in his own pamphlet; and when I come to town I shall certainly pay him one of my first visits. . . .

The affair of Lord M[elville] has since the date of your letter assumed a much more serious aspect than it then wore, and I trust that it will terminate in a manner so decisive as to close for ever his political career; an event which I consider as synonymous with the emancipation and Salvation of Scotland. His friends . . . in the mean time, although disconcerted and mortified by the late proceedings in the House of Commons, are far from giving up his cause as desperate, and (for what reason I know not) their language has become bolder within the last week. You will probably have already heard that on the King's birthday, his health was given, among other public thanks, in the Parliament House, and I have this day learned that the same compliment was on the same occasion paid to him by the Magistrates of Glasgow. How the toast was received there, I don't know, but at Edinburgh I was told by a Gentleman who was present, that it was drunk with considerable enthusiasm.

. . .

After speaking of Lord M. whose fall is so interesting to the inquirer at large, and more particularly to any independent man in this part of the Island, I am ashamed to mention the miserable Kirk politics in which I have lately had the misfortune to be involved. And yet, circumstanced as we were it was absolutely necessary for the friends of liberality and of learning to submit to a combat with the Enemy however despicable; and I am not without hope that after the victory has been gained we shall be less *priest-ridden* in our Scotch universities, than we have been during the long period of Lord M.'s Administration. That all our College offices should in future be given to Clergymen (if Clergymen be found competent to fill them) was a system publicly avowed by some of his nearest relations and most confidential friends at the time when the Professorship of Rhetoric was last vacant. The general, I might almost say the universal sense of the public seems at present to be decidedly hostile to such an idea; and indeed the personal character of our ecclesiastical leaders has received a blow from this late defeat, which for some time to come cannot fail to lower both their literary and political consequence. The language they now affect to hold is, that after the decision of the G[eneral] Assembly the whole business should (for the sake of Mr Leslie's character and usefulness) be laid to rest; and I begin to suspect that they will have the effrontery to avail themselves of this pretence for declining any attempt to vindicate, by an appeal to the public, either their moral conduct or their metaphysical principles.

I am sensible at the same time that much is to be apprehended from their stabs in their [sic] dark; and I think it highly probable that something of this kind may be attempted through the medium of the English journals. Gleig of Stirling, Barclay the Anatomist and Thomson the Chemist are all of their confederacy, and I suspect that all of them are occasional contributors to the periodical publications in London.[1] Would it not be possible to guard against this by warning the conductors of the most respectable Reviews of the danger of being misled by false representations of facts? If a good report of the debate in the Assembly should appear, it would go far of itself, to accomplish every object I have in view, by laying open to the world the whole series of ecclesiastical intrigues, which have been carried on at Edinburgh since the moment of Robison's death; but even on that supposition I should wish that the friends of science and of free inquiry in England would make a common cause with their Scotch neighbours, by reprobating with that tone of Indignation which it deserves, so scandalous a persecution, originating in so odious a corporation spirit, and conducted with such matchless ignorance and stupidity. The journals most to be dreaded are the British Critic, and (if it still exists) the Anti-Jacobin Review.[2] There is a publication besides, conducted as I am told by a Scotchman of the name of Mill or Milne (I think it is called the Literary Journal) which is not unlikely to take the wrong side on this occasion.[3] Should any of these journals (even the most contemptible of the number) endeavour to palliate the misconduct of Leslie's accusers, or to sanction the outcry against the Atheism of Edinburgh (which I suspect is not unacceptable in some parts of England) it would not only do your friends here a very serious injury, but what would provoke me much more, would lighten in the opinion of many that load of infamy which can alone prevent this junta of unprincipled intriguers from again rearing their heads.

I shall send you in a day or two a few copies of the third edition of my pamphlet, to which I have annexed the correspondence between the University and the Presbytery about the Confession of Faith. I have also inserted a few additional notes of very little consequence. If you think it worthwhile to have the former article added to the copies destined for the London market, you will oblige me by calling on Mr Davies (Cadell's partner)[4] and requesting him to have it reprinted from your copy and stitched up with those which he has already received from Scotland. I confess it seems to me to throw a strong light on the spirit and temper which have dictated the various ecclesiastical proceedings with respect to Leslie, and when combined with the nonsense about Cause and Effect and necessary Connexion to place before every impartial judge, the conscientious scruples of the ministers of Edinburgh on both subjects, in that point of view in which they have been always regarded by those who know anything of the character of the parties.

. . .

1. George Gleig (1753–1840: DNB), afterwards Bishop of Brechin, was certainly a frequent contributor to the journals; John Barclay (1758–1826: DNB) was a cleric as well as an anatomist; and Thomas Thomson (1773–1852: DNB) was afterwards Regius Professor at Glasgow.
2. The British Critic was edited in 1793–1813 by Robert Nares (1753–1829: DNB); The Anti-Jacobin Review and Magazine until his death by John Gifford (1758–1818: DNB).

3. James Mill (1773–1836: *DNB*) was editor of *The Literary Journal* throughout its short existence from 1803 to 1806. Thomas Thomson, the chemist, was a friend of Mill's and a contributor to the journal. Evidently Stewart had no recollection of Mill as his pupil.
4. His publishers.

199. To Lord Webb Seymour

BLPES ii. 210–11 ⟨*Horner*, i. 325–7⟩   The Temple, 9 July 1805

⟨. . .

⟨I have been going on very much as you left me; meeting with new people every now and then, and drawing myself closer towards the old. I reckon that about one in ten is worth seeing a second time, and about one in fifty worth adding to the permanent list. I cling to Smith, and Whishaw, and Ward, and Mrs Spencer,[1] with a very short list of, etc.⟩ . . . Our friend Selkirk's book has made a great fortune; every body speaks of its good sense, valuable information, and pleasing style, with unqualified praise. Such is the language of our severest critics in this quarter of the world – Romilly, Whishaw, Hallam. Whishaw says, there is really nothing wrong in it. A very senseless and malignant allusion was thrown out in the House of Lords against Selkirk, a few nights ago, by the Duke of Montrose; which I am informed was repelled with effectual indignation by Lord Holland.[2] It is not worth telling you more particularly what such a thing as the Duke of M[ontrose] could say of any body, in the sourness and stupidity of his heart.

⟨I have had frequent opportunities of seeing Lord Holland, and am delighted with his spirited understanding, and the sweetness of his dispositions. In both respects, he resembles his sister very much; and both of them are of their uncle's make.[3] The strongest features of the Fox head are, precision, vigilance, and (if I may apply such a word to the understanding) honesty: nobody escapes from them in vague showy generals, or imposes by ostentatious paradox; you are sure of getting both fair play and your due, but you must give as much or you have neither chance of concealment nor mercy. Watchful, dextrous, even-handed, implacable sense is their law. I have shrunk from it often with shame; and this I have felt as often in conversation with Miss Fox as with any of them.

⟨. . .⟩

1. Presumably Susan, wife of William Robert Spencer and widow of Count Spreti, who was reputed to have committed suicide so that she could marry Spencer.
2. James Graham, 3rd Duke of Montrose (1755–1836: *DNB*), was President of the Board of Trade. The exchange with Holland on 4 July is recorded in *Hansard*, v. 735–6.
3. John Allen and the Hollands had returned from the continent in May, and Horner had immediately reestablished his relationship with Allen, now the Hollands' personal physician and librarian and an inmate of Holland House. In a letter to John Thomson of 20 May 1805 (BLPES ii. 204–205), Horner mentioned 'the great pleasure of seeing Allen very often'. Holland's sister was the Hon. Caroline Fox (d. unm. 1845).

200. To the Duke of Somerset

BLPES ii. 212–13   The Temple, 31 July 1805

. . .

Our friend Joseph Lancaster's book is published at last, and the subscription continued on so much beyond the number put to the press, 3500, that the booksellers have not one to sell. This is highly honourable to the public, and flatters one with the hopes, that his methods will speedily be diffused over all those parts of the country, where the population is crowded enough to render their adoption useful. Nothing has occurred for a long time in this country, which revives so forcibly our former visions of national improvement, as the pleasure with which Lancaster's success has been contemplated by all sorts of people. I have read this pleasure in the eyes of men, who six years ago would have argued against any education of the lower orders, and deplored the little they have as a source of public mischiefs. This is the best, though not the only symptom, of our returning, as Lord Clarendon says upon another occasion, to the old good-sense and the old good-nature of England.

. . .

201. To Henry Hallam

BLPES ii. 214–15 ⟨Horner, i. 327–9⟩   [London], 2 Aug. 1805

⟨I have this morning had the pleasure to read your article in the Critical Review; with which I am sure all those who heard of Leslie's affair, and are friendly to toleration, will be highly gratified.[1] . . .⟩

. . .

⟨. . . I have as yet met with very few who are aware of all that has been done for them by Adam Smith, whose work, however imperfect as a theory of moral sentiments, always seemed to me the most scientific and acute description we have yet received in any branch of what may be called the Natural History of the Mind. This analysis, I am persuaded, contains in it the means of explaining many of our difficulties both in criticism and morals. . . .⟩

1. Hallam, then, was evidently the author of the review of the second edition of Stewart's pamphlet on the Leslie affair in The Critical review; or, Annals of literature, 3rd series, v (no. ci, July 1805), 242–52. A letter from Hallam to Horner of 9 Aug. 1805 (Horner, i. 329–30) suggests that Horner, heeding Dugald Stewart's earlier plea, had encouraged Hallam to write it and provided him with pertinent source materials. In a letter of 25 Sept. 1805 to Mackintosh (ibid., i. 338), Horner also mentioned 'Brown's tract, which grew out of the same occasion', the initially anonymous Observations on the Nature and Tendency of Mr Hume concerning the Relation of Cause and Effects (Edinburgh, 1805). (See also Docs 220 and 233.)

202. To Thomas Thomson

BLPES ii. 216–17 ⟨Horner, i. 331–3⟩   Hampstead, 8 Aug. 1805

⟨. . .

⟨I don't know what to say to your account of Mr Stewart's plan of his book.[1] I should like to have *all* his metaphysics, and I should like to have all his literature, and I should like to see him pay both these debts that he might proceed forthwith to discharge his farther engagements in political economy. On all of these subjects, his views are original and profound; and their originality consists so much in the comprehensive form which they have assumed in his mode of conceiving them, that it can be preserved only in his expressions. His writing on literary and moral topics is the most popular in this part of the world, but Stewart ought not to write for this part of the world or for this age of the world; he is bound to feel more courage, possessing the art of writing as he does, which always makes such a conquest over time, to say nothing of that loftiness and sensibility which pervade his philosophy, and must insure its success for ever, if England has any pretensions to immortality. If I could have my own wishes gratified, I confess I should desire that he would make his view of mind, intellectually considered, as enlarged as he has ever considered it, including all his valuable suggestions for the improvement of logic in the various sciences, even though he should not have perseverance to mould these into a systematic shape; and that then he would proceed immediately to political philosophy, in which I am confident he would produce a work that would excite great attention, and impress a lasting influence. After all the mischief that has been done of late years, I am thoroughly convinced that the public mind, in England at least, is still sound and susceptible.

⟨. . .⟩

    1. Leonard Horner quotes a letter from Thomson to Horner dated 20 July 1805 (Horner, i. 331–2n), outlining the progress and evaluating the importance of Stewart's work on *Elements of the Philosophy of the Human Mind.*

203. To Francis Jeffrey

BLPES ii. 218–19   Hampstead, 10 Aug. 1805

. . .

    I intended to have sent you a short notice of Mr Stewart's tract for your last, and had nearly written it out. It is as well, however, to come after the English journals; whose opinions, so favourably and strongly expressed, form part of the case, and not to be omitted when we proceed to sum it up. I should like very much to see the Debate printed, before your next number; if faithfully reported, it must afford some choice flowers of rhetoric, and we shall be the finer for all that. The article I promised you on Indian politics is not written yet, not a word of it – I still have it in view, but there are points on which I have not made up my mind.[1] And by the way, you had enough for one No. on that subject in the spirited and intelligent review of Cockburn, which is very much spoken of among your readers.[2] The author of it has not given me leave to tell his secret, so I hope you will be very cautious. Brougham admires the article very much, which amuses me not a little, because he is in the habit of thinking with very undeserved contempt of the real author's talents; he is very confident that a certain very clever man, Cleghorn I think he calls him, must have sent you this contribution. Lancaster's book is just out, and I have been running it over with my pencil; in the mean time, I am actually employed for you upon Lord Selkirk – which you shall have very soon.

. . .

I have hardly looked into the 12th No., because I hear there is not one sentence by you; it is a sad substitute for your criticism and scepticism, to have such loads of rubbish as Herbert and Walter Scott can furnish to any demand.[3] Ostentatious learning is a very good seasoning; but one can't dine heartily without beef and solid pudding. I look forward to some of this next time, as I trust you will give us both Madoc and Drummond at least. I am rather sorry that Knight's book is not in your own hands; though Hallam will do it very respectably; but it would have been worthy of a more practised and versatile hand.[4] It is a book that has afforded me a more agreeable reading than any new one for a long time, though he has many heresies of opinion, and many vulgarities of manner. His philosophy is only skin deep, and not very clearly or skilfully cut; but there is a gallop in the style, and a charge of subjects upon you, besides great freedom of thought, learning, and ingenuity, that entice you more than once to many parts of the book.

I wish some fit person were to be had, to inflict a just chastisement upon Gifford, who has lately published an edition of Massinger, for the scurrility and malignity which he has uttered against many persons who have been much more useful to the public than himself. His affectation of puritanical morality is very suitable to the bitterness and rancour with which he violates much higher rules of good manners; for I look upon it, that Doctor Darwin's vegetable laundry,[5] though in bad taste enough, will do much less mischief than the utter neglect of literary justice and gratitude. In Gifford's preface, there is a passage about the late Lord Lansdowne, which is very disgraceful to appear just upon the death of a person, who, whatever his other demerits may have been, was in every respect liberal to men of letters, in none more than by the facility of access to his collection, to a degree that has always been uncommon in this country.[6]

. . .

1. See Doc. 214.
2. The notice of the Reverend William Cockburn's *Dissertation on the Best Means of Civilizing the Subjects of the British Empire of India* (Cambridge, 1805), which had appeared in *ER* vi (no. xii, July 1805), 462–77, was by Robert Grant (1779–1838: *DNB*) and contained a defence of Cornwallis's administration in India, with which his father Charles Grant had been closely involved.
3. The issue for July 1805 contained two reviews each by William Herbert (1778–1847: *DNB*) and Walter Scott.
4. Hallam solicited and Horner provided comment on the work. (See Horner to Hallam, 2 Aug., and Hallam to Horner, 9 Aug., in *Horner*, i. 328–30; see also Docs 206 and 210.)

5. Leonard Horner has substituted 'loves' in the MS; Erasmus Darwin was also author of *The Loves of the Plants* (1789).

6. The edition of Massinger's plays by William Gifford (1756–1826: *DNB*), formerly editor of the short-lived *Anti-Jacobin, or Weekly Examiner* (not to be confused with John Gifford and the *Anti-Jacobin Review*: see Doc. 198) and first editor of the forthcoming *Quarterly Review*, was, however, regarded as a valuable one, and for that reason perhaps not noticed in *ER* until William Herbert did so in xii (no. xxiii, Apr. 1808), 99–119. Even then, however, Gifford was accused (p. 100) of 'handling Lord Lansdown [*sic*] harshly' in having said in his preface that a small remnant of manuscripts surviving destruction in previous ownership 'are now in the library of the Marquis of Lansdown, where they will probably remain in safety, till moths, or damps, or fires, mingle their forgotten dust with that of their late companions'. The Lansdowne referred to was the unpopular Prime Minister who had had to concede the independence of the American colonies, William Petty, 2nd Earl of Shelburne and 1st Marquess of Lansdowne (1737–1805: *DNB*); he had died only a few weeks before Horner's letter, in May 1803. Gifford answered the review, which he thought 'dictated by personal animosity', at length in the 'Advertisement' to the second, 1813, edition of Massinger's *Plays*.

204. Journal

Kinnordy MSS ⟨*Horner*, i. 340–41⟩   August and September 1805

⟨Mr Windham, speaking of Pitt, described him as being without affectation in the least, much above vanity. He considers him as having suffered greatly by having been introduced too soon to office, and losing the opportunities of seeing men and manners, except as a minister, not the most favourable way (Mr Windham added) of seeing men: had he only seen them for a little while, as his father did, in the army. In preparing his measures, he thinks more of the House of Commons than of their operation; satisfied if they will look well in statement – like those improvers of ground, who will build you a house that shall look most picturesque to spectators on the outside, though within it be incommodious. Mr Windham instanced the Parish Recruit Bill, and said this was the most satisfactory solution he had been able to give of Pitt's failure in this and many other plans, when Mr Fox had observed to him, that surely these were occasions on which it was Pitt's interest to summon all his talents. Speaking of his going through military details – military cars, rockets, catamarans, etc., Windham observed, that Pitt's judgement on such matters was generally bad, though he had a great talent in stating them. On another occasion, with Ward and John Ponsonby, when there was a great deal of conversation about the exercises and sports of the common people, the impolicy of suppressing them, etc., and we ran over the names of the different public men in the state and the law, whose opinions upon such a point of policy might come to be of importance, I hazarded Pitt's name, – 'Oh!' exclaimed Windham, 'Pitt never was a boy; besides, such questions won't conduce to make a minister.'⟩

205. To James Loch

BLPES ii. 220–21   Hampstead, 5 Sept. 1805

. . .

One very unhappy piece of news was received in town yesterday; the dangerous illness of Lord FitzWilliam. Pitcairn is gone down to Milton. He [Fitzwilliam] was at Brighton lately with his militia, and became unwell after exercise on a warm day; he got somewhat better of this attack, and has now a worse relapse. If his death should happen at this particular time, it would be a severe blow to Opposition; for I look upon him as having brought the Grenvilles nearer to Mr Fox, than they can remain long if left to themselves. Notwithstanding his defection during the alarm, he is essentially a good politician; no lover of kings, a staunch hater of Pitt, perfectly disinterested, and very brave. It would be another sort of loss, to be sure, than what we suffered by the Duke of Bedford's death; but as we have no Duke of Bedford, we can the less spare Lord F.[1]

By all I can learn, politics were the least of all subjects thought of at Stowe; Mr Fox and Lord Grenville talked about Homer all morning, and played at chess in the evenings.[2] This is well enough, since no mischief was done; but really, the other games are not won by playing at chess – what were Talleyrand and Bonaparte employed upon, those six days? I dare say they spoke more of the Rhine than the Scamander. At the same time, it is more like great statesmen to be so amused, than to be busied as Pitt is with sky rockets and floating plat-forms. It makes one mad, to see such foolery; what has the Manager of the House of Commons to do with new projects of ordinance [sic]? What can he know of them? Pitt seems to think that some new and wonderful discovery, like gunpowder or Greek fire, is to be made out expressly for him at this particular moment that he may therewith annihilate Boulogne and Jacobinism in a moment. Murray and I were crossing the river the other day, and the machine passed us, out of which Castlereagh (as you read) got his wet skin; *there* was Sir Sydney Smith, in his Crescent Star, with a vast roll of plans and maps, on which he was making demonstrations to the Chancellor of the Exchequer, who sat with his fore finger between his front teeth looking as wise as Long, who sat by him, and the ex-member from Downshire, and Mr Congreve – this new light and fire-brand of the world, who after writing for a whole year a newspaper in praise of Addington, has betaken himself to the invention of ways and means for the deliverance of Europe.[3]

You say, some murmurs of coalition have reached you. There were some to that effect, but I hope they will come to nothing. One account is, which I heard only at third or fourth hand, and therefore have not much faith in it, that an offer came from Pitt to Lord Grenville, proposing a *broad-bottom*, to which the *contre-projet* required his resignation as an indispensable preliminary. One thing is certain, that our friends believe now, which I don't recollect they ever did before, that the King has prevailed upon himself, either from necessity or a growing indifference to public matters, to wave [sic] his personal exclusion of Mr Fox: and I rather imagine, that this has been signified in some roundabout way or other from Pitt. If it ever happens, as I hope not, that Pitt sits in the same Cabinet with Mr Fox, I shall tremble with anxiety.

. . .

The neighbourhood of Dunfermline seems to me well adopted for the introduction of some of Lancaster's methods of education. Can your influence be exerted in this way?

1. Francis Russell, 5th Duke of Bedford, a leading member of the Foxite group, had died in March 1802. However, Fitzwilliam, thanks perhaps to the ministrations at Milton of his physician David Pitcairn (1749–1809: DNB), survived to become President of the Council in the Grenville Government. For his 'defection' to Pitt in 1792–4 see L.G. Mitchell, *Charles James Fox and the Disintegration of the Whig Party, 1782–1794* (Oxford, 1971), pp. 194–202.
2. Stowe was the principal place of Lord Grenville's elder brother, George Nugent-Temple-Grenville, 1st Marquess of Buckingham (1753–1813: DNB).
3. Capt. (afterwards Adm. Sir) William Sidney Smith (1764–1840: DNB), who, as ever inclined to flamboyance, was wearing an order given by the Sultan of Turkey in acknowledgement of his services in the Eastern Mediterranean, Charles Long, afterwards 1st Baron Farnborough (1760–1838: DNB), who was a Lord of the Treasury, Castlereagh, the Secretary for War, who had been MP for County Down until he was defeated in July 1805, and the Prime Minister were all evidently attending a demonstration by William, afterwards Sir William, Congreve (1772–1828: DNB), of the Royal Laboratory at Woolwich.

206. To Henry Hallam

BLPES ii. 222–3   Hampstead, 7 Sept. 1805

I have this morning received a letter from Jeffrey; in which he wishes me to inquire if you can get the review of Knight ready for the Number now in preparation, and also if you have made up your mind about Roscoe.[1]

You have probably heard of the domestic loss with which Jeffrey has been recently afflicted.[2] This is the first letter I have had from him upon business. We are all very desirous that he should be relieved as much as possible of personal exertions for the next Number; and I hope you will forgive me for mentioning this to urge you as well as the rest of us, to contribute as much as possible.

I have not yet undertaken Herbert's long article, nor do I suppose myself qualified to read it with much advantage to myself.[3] I cannot refuse myself the pleasure of telling you, that I heard Mr Fox intimate his intention of reading it, in consequence of its having been highly praised by Lord Grenville; who considers, it seems, the doctrine of the article as wrong in some particulars, but treated with much ingenuity and learning.[4]

. . .

1. See Doc. 183.
2. The death of his wife in August.
3. Presumably his review of the second edition of William Mitford's *Inquiry into the principles of harmony in language, and of the mechanism of verse* (1804) in ER vi (no. xii, July 1805), 357–86.
4. In a subsequent letter of 10 Sept. Horner scolded Hallam for refusing to review Knight's

book and, evidently responding to Hallam's counter-offer to review works of French history, asked for titles so that he might procure them (BLPES ii. 224–5). Hallam's response of 13 Sept. listed a number of works, notably De Lille's translation of the *Aeneid* (Kinnordy MSS). Jeffrey seems to have managed to change Hallam's mind about Knight's book and to have himself reviewed De Lille in *ER* vii (no. xiii, Oct. 1805), 134–47. For the review of Lancaster see Doc. 227.

207. To Sir James Mackintosh

BLPES ii. 228–30 ⟨*Horner*, i. 335–40⟩   Hampstead, 25 Sept. 1805

⟨... Lord Selkirk's tract on the state of the Highlands, and emigrations, excited much attention; it is a valuable piece of descriptive history, as well as political economy, and though I had long known his accomplished understanding, it has raised my admiration of that as well as of his exalted and practical benevolence. We all lament that he did not make the account of his own colony longer. There was a much more perfect concurrence of opinion among our critics upon this book, than upon the last I mentioned [by Knight]. ... There is nothing else of value in political economy.⟩ Lord Liverpool has published an ostentatious volume on coinage, which he delivers as the work of his life; his opinions seem to have been picked up at the very beginning of it, for he inveighs against paper circulation and County banks like a Warwickshire Earl or Squire.[1] One Oddy has published a large 4to vol. on European Commerce, which I have scarcely looked into; his purpose is to describe the channels of commerce that may yet be opened in the North of Europe by English capitals, in room of those which the French arms have obstructed.[2]

⟨Roscoe's *great* history has made no name; it is universally considered a dull lifeless mass, in which the warm interests of the finest subject in modern story are obscured by tasteless accumulation, or diluted away in an insipid, colourless style.⟩ It is the very sample of provincial fine-writing. We must hear little more of Mr Roscoe. ...

⟨In a letter I wrote several months ago, either to you or to Erskine, I proposed some queries in order to obtain information about the change of prices in India.[3] I wish to arrive at a sort of inductive conclusion, from a comparison of remote facts, respecting the recent variation in the value of the precious metals, all over the world. If you can furnish me details enough, to give a sort of oriental tinge to my illustrations, I will humbly offer you a little essay for your infant society; where I observe, that statistics and political economy are to be encouraged. I hope you will infuse your own spirit into the mass which they are to collect for you about Bombay and Salsette;[4] and that you will direct them to include as much as possible the details of former times as well as the present. A statist does nothing for philosophical economy, unless he ascertains and describes *changes*, and such *relations* among his details as are matter of fact. Insulated particulars, however accurate, like those which the German statists are so fond of heaping together, lead to nothing; and perhaps the most faithful picture of the economy of a country, if it is taken only for a single point of time, may be considered rather as a curiosity for the library of a virtuoso, than the materials of reasoning. A series of such no doubt would give the relations and changes that I speak of; but I fear that in undertakings of this sort we cannot reckon upon successors precisely to our own work. . . .⟩

. . .

1. Charles Jenkinson, 1st Earl of Liverpool, A *treatise on the coins of the realm* (Oxford, 1805). Perhaps Horner's emerging political bias led him to underestimate the value of the book. It was originally written in 1778, with the co-operation of George Chalmers, as a draft report of a conference of the Privy Council appointed to inquire into the state of coinage. It provided a considerable amount of information respecting the coins of the kingdom as well as an exposition of the principles in which coinage should be conducted. The volume was ill-written and laborious but certainly no more so than Henry Thornton's *Inquiry*, and it was afterwards exploited by proponents of a gold standard. It was noticed by Brougham in ER vii (no. xiv, Jan. 1806), 265–95.

2. Joshua Jepson Oddy (d. 1814), *European Commerce* (1805), was noticed by Macvey Napier in ER viii (no. xv, Apr. 1806), 128–37.

3. Doc. 193.

4. An island to the north of Bombay.

208. To Francis Jeffrey

BLPES ii. 231–2   [Hampstead], Saturday 28 Sept. [1805]

As usually happens with me, these parsons have not only led me a much greater length than I foresaw, but have occupied more of my time than I like to confess to any body, but those who already know by an eternal repetition of the same promises and disappointment how tardily and toilfully I write.[1]

I fear I have not executed this article quite in the best key as to temper; my design was to be calm and contemptuous, yet I found such frequent occasions as I wrote on to interpose against myself for the purpose of suppressing more active indications of anger, that I am afraid I have not wholly succeeded in keeping them all down. But you know your powers in the commission of the peace, and I hope you will save me, I don't care as to libels, but from losing the aim of my blows by misdirection.

In the very first intelligence I received of this business, about the beginning of last March, I had a letter from one of you, which mentioned Finlayson's having preached a sermon against Leslie. On inquiry of Murray, I find he did not hear that sermon himself, nor ever received the story from any person who had actually heard it. Unless you have at least this second best evidence for the fact, I beg you will blot out the little sentence in which it is alluded to; it is at the foot of p. 8 of the MS. You can connect the next paragraph immediately, by writing for 'it' the words 'their intrigue'.[2]

You will find likewise upon p. 40 of the MS some phrases, which I threw down having Hermand and the President in my head; if you think them imprudent, I beg you will change them.[3] And I mention this, not as if you had not full power to change every thing that offends you, but because you might have incautiously overlooked these, they are so slight.

I always agreed from the first with what you mentioned in one of your letters, as to the falsehood of making a distinction between physics and morals in the application of this logic of invariable conjunctions. I have stated it therefore as the foundation of *all* inductive sciences, such as proceed by the methods of experiment or observation.

What I am most anxious about, is, that I may have kept myself in the safe and honest medium, upon these ticklish subjects. I should be sorry to have betrayed any of the scepticism, which is my real sentiment; and still more to have the appearance of assuming the language of the dogmatists. I wish you would pry narrowly into the last pages, which literally I have not revised; I was afraid that by keeping this till Monday, you might suffer farther inconvenience.

I shall proceed immediately to Selkirk, of which I shall give you little more than an abstract, for I have no difference of opinion to propose, and scarcely any illustrations to add. I hope to have done with it on Wednesday night; and then, for I am ashamed to say I cannot undertake Lancaster this time, I shall take a day or two of business in London . . .

. . .

1. As Horner had promised in early August (Doc. 203) he had delayed his review of the third edition of Dugald Stewart's *Short Statement* about the Leslie affair until the London journals had had their say and then summed up the case with a lengthy and very favourable review of his old professor's pamphlet in *ER* vii (no. xiii, Oct. 1805), 113–34, thereby complementing the earlier articles by Hallam and Brown and honouring Stewart's plea to combat the Presbytery's construction of facts in literary journals (Doc. 198).
2. This amendment was made (p. 115), and so too, presumably, was that suggested in the next paragraph.
3. George Fergusson, Lord Hermand (d. 1827: *DNB*), was a Scottish judge, and Ilay (afterwards Sir Ilay) Campbell (1734–1823: *DNB*), the Lord President of the Court of Session.

209. To J.A. Murray

BLPES ii. 237–8 The Temple, 2 Dec. 1805

. . .

We are all in gloom again, about politics. But for the sea fight, it would have been the panic of approaching destruction; and the best effect of that can be but temporary, if the same system is still persevered in.[1] Perhaps the time is already past, within which a change for the better was practicable. I say this, in settled despair; after reasoning against it with the assistance of as many English prejudices as I can summon. Not that I suffer myself to admit for a moment the imagination of this country being conquered; or that I look upon the landing of a French army as a certain event: but within a few years, it does seem a probable event, and the first consequences of it, I have great fears, would be calamitous and irreparable. Were it to be accomplished in the present state of affairs, I am terrified to think that a dissolution of the Government might be our only resource for safety, against such incapacity as our rulers have shown both in their political and military administration.

You see that I am at this moment in one of my low fits, which indeed come upon me now more frequently than before. Laying all considerations out of view but the most selfish, I feel that at eight and twenty one cannot look upon such prospects with the same consolations at heart, which one may find when a few years younger: the habits and technical learning of the Bar would become all useless, and the effeminate indolent constitution which conforms itself to an established order will be found a pitiable disability, for the fierce and coarse scenes into which we are perhaps to be cast. The acquisitions of a general education no doubt would prove an invaluable possession in some respects.

In the mean time, is nothing to be done by way of repairing if possible the past, or providing against future perils? Is Pitt still to be trusted, with Huskisson and the Duke of Montrose, after such a trial? I believe he will still be trusted; nothing seems more regular in the vicissitudes of politics, than the fatality which brings old governments to their end. 'De la chute des Rois funeste avancoureur.' I wish you would look back to the debates on foreign politics during this war; particularly the first debate in 1803, and the one last summer on the 5 millions subsidy.[2] Compare Fox's predictions with the projects and promises of Pitt; and then compare these last with the different steps in the history of this most wonderful campaign, which has been begun and achieved within the time we were together. We shall all be agreed about the political talents of Pitt ten years hence; but he must have a year or two more allowed him, to furnish us with a still larger body of evidence. The history of our part in this disastrous campaign will be no small part of it; when we have the full account of our 'rousing the continent', forcing Austria into a coalition by the influence of Russia against the opinion of the Archduke Charles and his brothers, forcing them forward into Bavaria that Pitt might open Parliament with a speech, delaying our own contribution of exertions till all was over, sending troops into the Mediterranean too late to get into Italy, others into the North which are not landed in Germany till after the peace is signed, and allowing ourselves to be again overreached by such a Cabinet as Berlin and to risk all Europe for such a changeling as Alexander. . . .

. . .

1. Horner refers to the battles of Trafalgar and Austerlitz and to Pitt's 'system' of subsidies to the continental powers.
2. Horner perhaps means the debates of 8–11 March 1803 (*Parl. Hist.*, xxxvi. 1162–9), in addition to that of 20 and 21 June 1805 (*Hansard*, v. 459–82, 490–532, and 535–47).

210. To Francis Jeffrey

BLPES ii. 239–40   The Temple, 6 Dec. 1805

. . .

. . . You cannot easily imagine at Edinburgh the effect which has been produced here by the Review of the Education of a Young Princess.¹ It is most unfavourable. All sorts of people speak of it; none are so strong in reproaches of it, as our best friends, for they consider it as a blunder which will impair irrevocably the utility and character of a work, whose best merit was unquestionably its advocation of moderate enlightened opinions. Nobody imagines you to be the author; but every body, I must tell you, gives you the blame of negligence at least.

I am glad to find that Brougham will review Mehée de la Touche;² I heard so from Allen. It appears to me very odd, and you may tell B[rougham] so if you please, that he should have forborne to ask me for the book at Edinburgh, when he knew I had it. What all this reserve is, I cannot know; I shall understand it perhaps some time or other. The review of M. de la Touche will be very creditable to the *Review*, especially if some extracts are given in the original French; since Government, that is the Under Secretaries of State, did all they could by means of the Custom house and Alien Bill to suppress it. I have not yet read Stephen's pamphlet, but most anxiously hope you retain your design of reviewing it yourself; the impression you had against its doctrine is the right one, from all I can hear.³ Part of this *all* is, that the said doctrine is adopted and praised by the Slaves and profligates at Lloyd's Coffee-House; and what is more, we had a stupid Lord of the Admiralty dining with us at the King of Clubs last Saturday, who could only pretend to speak the language of his masters, and who went so far in approbation of this tyranny against neutrals as to say we had better at present for our own interest be at war with America. I trust you are now too well aware of the influence your *Review* possesses, to leave an opportunity like this in unworthy hands. Lady Holland showed me the other day a remarkable plagiarism of Payne Knight's from Beattie's *Essay on Poetry and Music*; which I think you ought to notice, even though Hallam may have omitted it: it is in the famous description of the Homeric Achilles, which Murray will show you, if you do not know it.⁴ It is a passage which Mr Fox spoke in high praise of one day last summer. You will find Beattie's passage in his chapter on Poetical Characters. I am become quite nervous about this review of Knight; there is no book which has attracted so much notice among the higher race of men in London for a long time. It ought to [be] well scourged; but very judiciously so.

. . .

1. William Drummond was the author of the review of [Hannah More], *Hints towards forming the character of a Young Princess* (2 vols, 1805) in ER vii (no. xiii, Oct. 1805), 91–100 (WI).
2. According to AR 1804, p. 162, Jean Claude Hippolyte Mehée de la Touche (c.1760–1826), was a secret agent employed by the French to implicate British diplomats in plots against Napoleon; in fact he seems to have been a double agent. No review of his *Alliance des Jacobins de France avec le Ministère anglais* [Paris, 1804] appeared in ER.
3. James Stephen, *War in Disguise, or the Frauds of the Neutral Flags* (1805).
4. Hallam commented on the plagiarism in Knight's book of James Beattie's *Essays on Poetry*

and Music (Edinburgh, 1778) in a letter to Jeffrey of 13 Dec. (BLPES ii. 243) and a reference to it appears on p. 318 of his review.

211. To James Reddie

NLS MSS 3704, ff. 21–2   The Temple, 11 Dec. 1805

. . .

We have a pamphlet the subject of much conversation here, which will interest you much, *War in Disguise, or the Frauds of the Neutral Flags* – It is written by Stephen of the Prize Court, who wrote the *Crisis of the Sugar Colonies.*[1] There is much information in it, and much questionable doctrine. Azuni, who now holds an official place at Paris, has published *this* year a new edition of his book, quite new-modelled; I have not read it yet; it is called *Droit Maritime de l'Europe.*[2]

. . .

1. Stephen's earlier pamphlet had been reviewed by Brougham, *ER* i (no. i, Oct. 1802), 216–37; his new pamphlet was reviewed by Jeffrey in *ER* viii (no. xv, Apr. 1806), 1–35.
2. The expanded two-volume French edition of Domenico Alberto Azuni's *Sistema universala dei principii del diritto marittimo dell Europa*, published in Paris in 1805, was not reviewed in *ER*.

212. To Francis Jeffrey

BLPES ii. 243–41[1]   The Temple, 14 Dec. 1805

I have prevailed on Hallam to review Lancaster's book, instead of me; he has taken it with him into the country, where he went last night, and will send it to you in time for next No. I find it quite impossible for me to undertake any article which would cost so much pains as I should have wished to bestow on that; for I must get myself wholly immersed in law. I shall subjoin, however, a page or two to Hallam's review, by way of answer to a pamphlet of old Mrs Trimmer against Lancaster, in which he is accused of a design to corrupt the youth by making them both Quakers and rebels.[2] This would not be worth the least notice, if the old woman were not the voice of a large set, the Methodists of the Church of England, who are indefatigable, I find, in their insinuations against Lancaster. Their unreasonableness may be quietly and gravely exposed in a few sentences, which may therefore do good to Lancaster. I shall give you also a page or two, to destroy if possible utterly the sale of the new edition of the *Wealth of Nations* which Cadell and Davies have published with notes by W. Playfair; a very disgraceful instance of the cupidity of booksellers.[3] Let me renew my instances to you about keeping Stephen's tract in your own hands; Phillimore wants it I hear, but that would never do; he is a Doctor of the Commons and one knows how it must go there.[4] Since my last letter to you, I have read part of the tract, and he [Stephen] has shook me very much towards his opinion upon his main subject, the neutral carriage of *colonial* produce. There are very practicable distinctions to be made between that and the other branches of the neutral trade. But I have still difficulties, even upon the former; and the whole subject seems to me one that will require both your nicest discrimination, and your most sober judgement. Don't be in a hurry about it; the subject will last a while; but from the attention the pamphlet has attracted among thinking men of all classes, you are bound to consider it as an occasion not to be slighted.

. . .

1. The first page of this letter is taken up by one the previous day from Hallam. See Doc. 210 n. 4.
2. See Doc. 227.
3. *An investigation into the . . . wealth of nations. By Adam Smith. The 11th edition; with notes, supplementary chapters, and a life of Dr Smith* (3 vols, 1805), by William Playfair (1759–1823: *DNB*), the professor's younger brother, was attacked by Horner in *ER* vii (no. xiv, Jan. 1806), 470–71.
4. Phillimore was afterwards Regius Professor of Civil Law at Oxford.

213. To J.A. Murray

BLPES ii. 249–50   [London], 31 Dec. 1805

. . .

We have been in the strangest state about news for the last fortnight. The best part of the world might have been conquered by these French, without our hearing of the design till it was all over. A circumstance of our insular situation, not to be forgotten surely, when we lay down the doctrine of our continental interference.

I have never had a full day of hope, during this interval; had Prussia come into action, we might have flattered ourselves; but that seems never to have been intended on his side. Whatever his intentions may have been, it is all over now, and the whole of Europe is prostrated before this military despotism, which has overwhelmed the power and independence of nations, and by the necessary maxims and spirit of all military government will gradually barbarize and impoverish all that West of Europe, which boasted so fondly of the immortality of its sciences and literature.

What is to become of us?

One question is, whether the island is not to become a conquered province of France, even in our own time. Were it not for Ireland, I should believe not; but all the accounts we ever receive of that country, represent the disaffection of the lower orders as very formidable. The attention of the public has been withdrawn from Pitt's atrocious faults towards that unhappy country, by his grander blunders upon the continent. But it is too evident how they co-operate in one train of ruinous mismanagement. If Ireland were out of the question, I should feel a strong hope, that the actual subjugation of this country might be removed to such a distance, as to leave us in the mean time the chances of a contest among the successors of Bonaparte; or of insurrection in some of the continental provinces, or perhaps of a Tartar irruption. These are strange cases to put, and this is strange language; but is it not the true description of this new state of the world?

Supposing the worst extremity at too great a distance, to be contemplated by us; what is the best we can hope for with any reason? Nothing better, it seems to me, than the languid condition of a Kingdom, declining in its internal circumstances, impotent of all foreign operations, a helpless spectator of the slavery and barbarism of the continent, and conscious of a continual degradation at home in manners, wealth, constitution, and literature. This sounds very gloomy and sickly; but it is not in a fit of temporary sadness I write it: it is familiar to me in all states, in health and in gaiety.

. . .

214. To Francis Jeffrey

BLPES iii. 1–2   [London], 11 Jan. 1806

I hope you will have no objection to insert these few lines about Francis's speech.[1] It is not a review, but the *annonce* of a future one. I shall send you about as many on Playfair's Smith, if I can write them to night.[2] Mrs Trimmer I meant to have trimmed, but on examining the premises, it appears right that the rod should be pickled. You have got Hallam, which you will print if you have room for it, altering the allusion he makes to the article that is to follow. He has just been here; he says he wrote his in a great hurry, and seems to think he has not done it very well. I said to him, he had better in that case . . . have it again, and take more pains upon [it] for the April No. That he seemed to think would be a disagreeable trouble, but he desires me to refer the matter entirely to you and Lord Webb, whether it should be printed now or not.[3]

The accounts of Pitt's health are deplorable. There is said to be still a chance of Parliament being again prorogued, and public business still farther delayed on that account. Gout is not his only illness. He cannot sleep without opiates, and his voice has failed entirely; he is said to have shown more sensibility at the late bad news, than he used to do on similar occasions when in health. I tell you this from the information of those who are very Ministerial in their partialities. The story I have now for you came from the other quarter; that the old King is thrown into a quiet despair by this result of the war, the very next thing to indifference – he considers the conquest of his kingdoms as in the decrees of Providence. The Turks think it impious to take precautions against the plague. You shall have all my gossiping. Some body has written from the continent, that Bonaparte in his interview at the Mill spoke to Francis of his plans against England. Great (he said) as [were] his successes in the present campaign, they had interrupted him in the arrangement of those plans, which he had brought near to the moment of execution – that he had laid his measures so as to be almost certain of success – and that this interruption would only postpone them. Of all this, believe as much as you like. I cannot believe any thing that will make me more desponding, than I have been for some time, about the fate of our country, as we may yet continue to call it.

I have written out my oracle upon Playfair's *Wealth of Nations*. I only wish to stop its sale, and should have taken no notice of it but for this purpose – to inflict a merited punishment on the cupidity of the booksellers.

1. The short, two-page, notice in ER vii (no. xiv, Jan. 1806), 478–80, of Sir Philip Francis's *Speech on the War in India* (made in the Commons on 5 Apr. 1805: *Hansard*, iv. 225–40), which has been tentatively attributed to Robert Grant (*WI*), was, it seems, therefore really Horner's. From the following sentence, and from Doc. 227, it will be seen, however, that he by no means regarded it as fulfilling his promise to contribute an article on India. Indeed, the review itself (p. 479) stated: 'We mean to take another opportunity of laying before our readers the grounds of the opinion which we entertain upon this subject.'
2. See Doc. 212.
3. See Doc. 227.

215. To J.A. Murray

BLPES iii. 3–4 ⟨*Horner*, i. 349–51⟩   Gallery, House of Commons, 21 Jan. 1806

⟨We are all here in a corner together – your brother, Brougham, Loch, Frederick, and Dumont;[1] waiting with much patience for what the day may bring forth, but without a certain expectation of being repaid for our trouble. The amendment is to be moved here by Petty, and in the other House by Lord Cowper: the *Chronicle* is correct in this. It is possible that the speech may be of such an aspect as to render an amendment unnecessary or impolitic; though I hardly imagine that will be the case. For the speech must either omit all allusion to continental affairs, or speak of them in a style very different from what ought to satisfy those who have no confidence in the present Ministers: in both cases, an amendment is the proper course; and though the answer will probably be, that you ought to wait till the treaties and papers are laid before the House, yet there are sufficient grounds for an amendment in the objections that were formerly stated, against entering into *any* treaties of subsidy. There is another event, which may turn off the debate; the announced dissolution of the Ministry, which is not altogether out of the question, since the increased illness of Pitt. This is the point which at present occupies every one's feelings and attention; for no one, even with all his party antipathies, or with all his resentment for the mischiefs which have been brought upon the country, can be insensible to the death of so eminent a man. In the place where I am sitting now, I feel this more than seems quite reasonable to myself; I cannot forget how this space has been filled with his magnificent and glowing declamations, or reflect with composure that that fine instrument of sound is probably extinguished for ever. You observe I speak as if he were already dead.

⟨. . .

⟨If this event should take place, it must be followed by some very considerable effects on the state of our domestic politics. A numerous tribe of inefficient retainers, who have usurped important stations, will be swept off the field for ever; perhaps to be supplanted in time by another set of the same. But the very change is wholesome, and there is an interval always of something like qualification for offices, and deference to public opinion. There will be a new casting of parts among some of our state adventurers. And the removal of the old personalities, which have perhaps on both sides attached our speakers too pertinaciously to their respective systems, may render it more easy to enter upon that new system which seems necessary in this new position of our affairs.

⟨. . .⟩

1. Murray's elder brother William (1774–1854) was an English barrister; 'Frederick' was W.G. Adam's younger brother, afterwards Gen. Sir Frederick Adam (1784–1853: DNB).

216. Journal

Kinnordy MSS ⟨Horner, i. 351–3⟩   22 Jan. 1806

⟨I imagine that the illness of Pitt, and the belief that his life was despaired of, was not the only reason of postponing the Amendment last night, though it would have been a sufficient one. It had been understood for some time that the Addingtonians were to 'co-operate with the Opposition', according to their own phrase in what I believe was almost a communication from them. In the course of Monday, however, they sent notice that they could not support the Amendment; this must have been late on Monday, for at three o'clock that day Lord Cowper had no idea that the Amendment would not be moved. In consequence of this defection, it was probably deemed prudent not to push a division, especially as there was so good a reason for postponing the discussion for a few days. This sudden turn of the Addingtonians can only be explained, since the Amendment is so moderate, if not tame, by the report which we have had for some days, that the King wishes to make Sidmouth his Minister, since he is deprived of Pitt; and either from an understanding with the Court, already, or not to injure their chance by any thing offensive, they have agreed to relinquish the hostility they had resolved on. A few days will explain this; I shall not be surprised, in the least, if we have again the Doctor, Castlereagh, Hawkesbury, etc. I shall be surprised indeed, if, at such a crisis of peril, the country submits to it; but Whishaw says, 'the brute power of Government will do any thing.' Tierney is said to be very angry at this conduct of the Addingtonians, which of course means that the Prince is; certainly last Wednesday he was all for an Amendment.

⟨Since writing the above, I have inquired into the fact more particularly. Lord Cowper told me that the Addingtonians did give notice, that they would not vote for the Amendment; but that this had no effect in postponing it. A few hours before going down to Westminster there was a meeting at Mr Fox's house of a few of the principal persons of Opposition; Cowper was there; Fox stated to them that he thought it impossible they could enter into the discussion; he could not, while they had the idea that Pitt was in extremities; – 'mentem mortalia tangunt', he said. Cowper described him as appearing to feel very sensibly the calamity of his distinguished rival; and he described it by saying, that Fox appeared to feel more than Lord Grenville, who was present also.⟩

217. To Dugald Stewart

BLPES iii. 5–6 ⟨Horner, i. 353–5⟩   The Temple, 23 Jan. 1806

⟨Allen wrote to you yesterday, to inform you that Petty had begun a canvass for the University of Cambridge, in consequence of that very unexpected event, which, though not yet announced, is considered as certain.[1] Lord Spencer's son, Lord Althorp, is his opponent, and he set out last night for Cambridge; Petty thinks it more proper to wait till the death of Mr Pitt is declared, and it fortunately happens that the Cambridge address is to be presented to-day, and has brought the Vice-Chancellor and several of the Heads of Houses to town; Petty will go to St James's, and set out probably immediately after.

⟨Lord Althorp is a Johnian, and that college has always been formidable in elections, from the great number of graduates who belong to it, and who have always been more thoroughly disciplined to act together upon University contests, than those of Trinity.⟩ The Master of St John's, Craven, is supposed to have considerable influence over Pearce the present head of Jesus; but this Pearce is an intriguer at the same time who does not quite overlook opportunities of doing his own business. As far as I have yet been able to learn, this is the amount of Lord Althorp's strength; but if the Johnians make a point of it, you will understand how formidable they are, when I tell you that they brought Lord John Townshend within 9 of Lord Euston, supported by Pitt and the active interest of the Court. The Saints, headed by Dean Milner, are a strong phalanx; they will all vote together: we have considerable hopes of them, for Wilberforce has always been kindly in his advances to Petty. Our terror is, that they may think of starting the Attorney-General, who is one of the Lords of their congregation, and a member of Cambridge; but there has been no such report yet. It was said yesterday, that Lord Royston would try it, but I fancy it was said without foundation; this upon the whole would be an advantage, notwithstanding the great county interest and Cambridge reputation of the Yorkes; he must stand on St John's too, and of course divide it with Althorp who would ultimately throw the interest which could not seat himself into Petty's hands. ⟨We have great reason⟩, you see, ⟨to expect success; Lord Henry himself is very sanguine. It is on every account a most desirable object for him.[2]

⟨Since I wrote the above, I have been down to Westminster Hall. Pitt expired this morning at eight o'clock.

⟨. . .

⟨My anxiety about Petty's election is now much less than when I wrote the first part of this letter. He has had a letter from the Chief Justice,[3] flattering in the highest degree. Turncoats are volunteering to him; and a great many of the base worshippers of sunshine have, even since eight o'clock, turned their faces towards him. The very courtiers are showing such symptoms of kindness, as if they believed it possible to play over again the game of 1784, and set up a young one against the House of Commons and the public. They mistake their man; for if Petty has any good quality, on which I rely, it is a firm attachment to Fox and his maxims of government: any other conduct, to be sure, in the present circumstances, would be folly; but he has had praise enough to turn his head, if it were not a steady one.⟩ He is over-rated, I certainly think, in point of abilities; but ⟨he has information, diligence, and sense, that will make him an eminent statesman, if he preserves unimpaired his political consistency and probity. In this respect, I have the most sanguine expectations of him; notwithstanding the great disadvantages he may incur, if he is brought early into considerable power. I talk of him as if he were already a Minister; almost all the world talk of him as on the high road to it, and Mr Fox regards him as his successor in the only station *he* has ever held, or may perhaps ever hold. . . .

⟨. . .⟩

There has been a meeting of such Cambridge lawyers as mean to vote for Petty. Several unexpected ones appeared, and Whishaw says the Canvass seems as promising as possible.[4]

There is no account yet of the Attorney-General; I hope therefore we shall not hear of him at all.

I have no general politics worth telling you. Castlereagh is said to be Chancellor of the Exchequer, but merely for the necessary business. The King will indubitably try to give us the Doctor again; and just as people think him conceited still or taught by past experience, they expect or not that he will venture it.

⟨. . .⟩

1. Pitt's death forced a by-election for one of the Cambridge University seats, in which the eventual candidates were John Charles Spencer, Viscount Althorp and afterwards 3rd Earl Spencer, whose father George John, 2nd Earl Spencer, was to be Home Secretary in the new Administration, Petty, who was to be Chancellor of the Exchequer, and their Tory opponent, Henry John Temple, 3rd Viscount Palmerston. (*Palmerston Letters*, pp. 49–56.)
2. Horner was in error about Althorp, who like Petty and the Attorney-General, Spencer Perceval, had been at Trinity; it was Palmerston who had been at St John's, as had also Philip Yorke, Viscount Royston (1784–1808), the eldest son of the Earl of Hardwicke. The statement about Lord John Townshend (1757–1833), the sitting Whig member for the university, seems also to be incorrect; he had been defeated by 21 votes in the 1784 election. William Craven (c. 1730–1815), was Master of St John's, and William Pearce (1744–1820), Master of Jesus. Isaac Milner (1750–1820: *DNB*), an intimate of William Wilberforce, was President of Queens' College and Dean of Carlisle.
3. Edward Law, 1st Baron Ellenborough (1750–1818: *DNB*), was a Cambridge man.
4. As revealed in his letter to Murray of the same date (BLPES iii. 7–8), Horner actively encouraged his friends in Edinburgh to promote Petty among Cambridge men.

218. Journal

Kinnordy MSS[1]   23 Jan. 1806

. . . Brougham dined at Drummond's, who had sat for an hour with Lord Sidmouth, till four o'clock. Sidmouth expressed great surprise to D. that he (Sidmouth) had not yet been sent for by the King; and every knock at the door he seemed to think was the summons he expected.

1. Omitted without acknowledgement from the published journal entry of the same date in *Horner*, i. 353.

219. To Lord Webb Seymour

BLPES iii. 9–10   [London, ?3 Feb. 1806][1]

. . .

On Saturday evening about eight o'clock Lord Grenville was sent for by the King, who told him he had no objection to make to the list he had given in.[2] Grenville then proceeded to state, from a written paper, a few propositions with regard to such measures as must form the basis of their plan of government. One of these was to this effect, that in the present difficulties and danger of the country, it was necessary that the unreserved management of the Army should be committed to Ministers. The King seemed startled at this, as if taken by surprise; 'that's my own, (he said), and has been always so since the time of the Duke of Cumberland; does this mean that you are to turn out the Duke of York?' Lord G. replied, that he could only speak from the paper he held in his hand. Upon which the King said, that he must take the matter again into consideration.[3] There was very great civility in his manner to Lord G. This at least passed; and I believe nothing farther.

This morning Lord G. was with the King, and what is given out by *our* friends is that 'it is as good as settled.' G. is to see the K. again this evening.

The lists you have now seen in several of the papers, particularly the *Oracle* of this day, is nearly correct. Lord Moira has refused Ireland, and takes the Ordinance [*sic*]. Lord Auckland, I am sorry to say, is to have his place; a bounty, I think, for roguery to all coming adventurers. I know nothing about Buckinghamshire; but rather believe he will have nothing.[4] I cannot say any thing about Sheridan, except that he is not to be in the Cabinet.[5]

. . .

1. The letter is not franked and has been variously endorsed 1 and 3 Feb. The second seems to be in a more nearly contemporary hand and in any case more likely since 1 Feb. was a Saturday and on that day Horner would hardly have written as he did in the first line printed here.
2. The BLPES MSS contain political anecdotes by Horner dated 26, 29, and 31 Jan. 1806 (viii. 7–10) that provide information on Grenville's meeting with the King on 25 Jan. and

on the negotiations between Grenville, Fox, and Sidmouth that determined the composition of the 'Ministry of All the Talents'. Although represented as journal entries, all but a
few passages of these anecdotes were published in *Horner*, i. 355–8. The passages omitted
reveal that John Allen was the source of Horner's political intelligence and that William
Adam and his family were 'extremely dissatisfied, that he had not [had] the refusal of an
eminent station'.

3. Grenville backed away from this delicate question on 3 Feb. when the King produced a
paper asserting his prerogative in matters pertaining to the defence of the country and his
constitutional right to negative any governmental measure relating to the military establishment. See Horner's political anecdote dated 3 Feb. (misrepresented as a journal entry)
in *Horner*, i. 358–9.

4. Buckinghamshire became Postmaster-General jointly with John Joshua Proby, 1st Earl of
Carysfort (1751–1828: *DNB*).

5. Richard Brinsley Sheridan (1751–1816: *DNB*) became Treasurer of the Navy.

220. To J.A. Murray

BLPES iii. 13–14 ⟨*Horner*, i. 365–6⟩   The Temple, 3–4 Feb. 1806

I thank you for your copy of Mr Stewart's *Postscript*. Your two questions about it I
throw in to one, according to my view of the business; and I answer in the
affirmative that, for the sake of fastening a merited punishment upon Baird, it was
right to take notice of the Minister's pamphlet.[1] The head of a learned body, who so
disgraces himself and lends his aid to such mischief against the interests of learning,
ought to be punished, by the reason of all other penal proceedings, for the sake of
example to others in the same situation; and the appropriate mode of punishment is,
in such a case, to consign his literary and official character to disgrace in the annals
of the learned body to which he belongs, and in the local history of literature. This
Mr S. has done most effectually, and no doubt with the utmost severity; but I do not
think that there has been one lash too many. He flourishes his scourge, and lays
them on, most expertly. I have not seen any thing of his struck off with the same
spirit; it is better than any part of the *Short Statement*. I could almost wish he had a
little more controversy; he improves so fast. I hope you will send me Playfair's . . .

                                                                    4th Feb.
⟨I have not been from home this morning to gather news; and nothing has been
brought to me, except that Lord Eldon took leave of the Court of Chancery this
morning, Pigott, as the senior King's Counsel, returning an answer.[2] Petty is sent for
by express, to kiss hands tomorrow; he will thus avoid the trouble of a second
election.⟩[3] In the *Morning Chronicle* today, the list of the Cabinet is correct; in the
other, there are several mistakes. Creevey, for instance, is to be a Lord of the
Admiralty; the Duke of Bedford has not made up his mind; John King, from the
home department, is to be the other Secretary of the Treasury. Lord Wm Russell is
to be a Lord of the Treasury, and also Lord John Townshend; though there is a story
that Blandford is to be retained in his place, as well as Lord Chas Spencer. The
Marlborough family supports every ministry; but it is always bought. I believe Sir
Francis Vincent is rightly put down; he is a very amiable young man, who married

one of the Miss Bouveries, a delightful woman, whom he lost very lately; he has never been upon the continent, and will not be able, I should think, to give Mr Fox much assistance; but it is necessary he should have some person in that place, whom he can perfectly trust.[4]

⟨My chief objections to⟩ this new arrangement, ⟨though I have others,[5] are that the Sidmouth family has unaccountably got so much, that a Scotsman has the patronage of India, and that Lord Ellenborough has a seat in the Cabinet.[6] This last appears to me an objection of great moment, both upon constitutional grounds, and in point of party prudence. ...⟩ ...

1. George Husband Baird (1761–1840: DNB), the President of Edinburgh University, had sided with the Presbytery's interpretation of the philosophical issues surrounding the Leslie case, and John Inglis (1763–1834: DNB) had attacked Stewart's *Short Statement* anonymously in *An Examination of Mr Dugald Stewart's pamphlet relating to the election of a mathematical Professor*, by one of the Ministers of Edinburgh (Edinburgh, 1805). In late 1805 Stewart effectively criticized the behaviour of President Baird in a *Postscript* to his *Short Statement*. Early in the new year John Playfair contributed his *Letter to the author of 'An Examination of Stewart's Short Statement'* (Edinburgh, 1806), and shortly after Thomas Brown joined in the dispute by publishing *A Short Criticism of the Terms of the Charge against Mr Leslie in the protest of the Ministers of Edinburgh* and *An Examination of some Remarks in the Reply of Dr John Inglis to Professor Playfair*, as well as a second, enlarged edition of his *Observations*.
2. Sir Arthur Leary Pigott (1752–1819: DNB) became Attorney-General in the new Ministry.
3. See *Palmerston Letters*, p. 56, n. 1.
4. Thomas Creevey (1768–1838) became Secretary of the Indian Board of Control; the Duke of Bedford became Lord Lieutenant of Ireland; and John King indeed moved from the Home Office to the Treasury. Lord William Russell (1767–1840), the Duke of Bedford's uncle, became a Lord of the Admiralty; Lord John Townshend became Paymaster-General of the Forces jointly with Richard Temple Nugent Brydges Chandos Grenville, Earl Temple and afterwards 1st Duke of Buckingham (1776–1839: DNB); George Spencer, Marquess of Blandford and afterwards 5th Duke of Marlborough (1766–1840: DNB), gave up his place as a Lord of the Treasury, but his uncle Lord Charles Spencer (1740–1820: DNB) moved from the Post Office to the Mint. Sir Francis Vincent, 9th Bart (1780–1809), was appointed undersecretary to Fox at the Foreign Office. His wife Jane, a granddaughter of the 1st Viscount Folkestone, to whom he had been married for only a little more than three years, had died in April 1805.
5. Horner was also troubled by Grenville's insistence, stated to and accepted by Fox as a condition of their forming a government, that the accusation against Wellesley of maladministration in India should not be made a Cabinet measure nor any person be appointed President of the Board of Control who should bring it forward. (See Horner's political anecdote dated 5 Feb. (misrepresented as a journal entry) in *Horner*, i. 359–60.)
6. Sidmouth was notorious for getting places for his friends and relations. In addition to himself becoming Lord Privy Seal, his brother John Hiley Addington (1759–1818) joined the Board of Control, and his brother-in-law Charles Bragge-Bathurst (1754–1831) was led to expect a place on a suitable vacancy. Buckinghamshire, who was another of Sidmouth's cronies, also expected promotion at the earliest opportunity, but in order to give Sidmouth support where he might need it most, Ellenborough was brought into the Cabinet as Lord Chief Justice. The new President of the Board of Control, Gilbert Elliot, 1st Baron and afterwards 1st Earl of Minto (1751–1814: DNB), was not, however, one of Sidmouth's gang.

221. To J.A. Murray

BLPES iii. 15–16 ⟨Horner, i. 367–8⟩   The Temple, Thursday night and
Friday [6–7 Feb. 1806]

⟨. . . The election seems pretty sure, yet I cannot help feeling nervous about it⟩, and wishing that Raybey and your miserable Lloyd may have set out, though I hardly expect it of either of them.[1] Raybey's objections were too natural and indeed too reasonable to be overcome. ⟨Petty came to town yesterday to receive his seals; I did not see him; but I understand he was in high spirits about the election, counting three hundred and forty sure promised votes, if every one came.⟩ I fear Raybey's and Lloyd's were among them. But I have unbounded faith in the effect of his new dignity; you can easily suppose the instances that have occurred in the course of this canvass of the meanness and undisguised servility of various persons, but particularly the priests and college monks, who are 'of all Mankind that can read or write' the most selfish and shameless. But the letters that have been written, to Petty, and to his committee here, have exceeded all that my imagination at least had anticipated. I am just at present in an especial fit of indignation against these churchmen, who obstruct every thing that is desirable, in consequence of having three solid proofs of the mischief they do or try to do stated to me within an hour this morning: in the first place, their objection to Petty because he would emancipate the Catholics – Milner, I find, has on this account declared for Palmerston, though Brougham is sure he must have made the Viscount swallow the Abolition, which is supposed to be much against his stomach.[2] Secondly, there are objections stated against Romilly getting the honours and rights of his profession as if he were a dissenter, meaning by that a dissenter from their senseless piddling distinctions, and not in the comprehensive sense of the word which might have some justice in its application[3] – and thirdly, I have had that active, benevolent, intelligent creature Lancaster with me this morning, who finds obstacles in almost every parish, because the vicar declares that no poor man shall be taught to read, if the schoolmaster will not read with him the catechism and articles of the church. How perfectly true it is, what Clarendon says in his character of Laud, that 'Clergymen understand the least, and take the worst measure of human affairs, of all Mankind that can write and read.'

Friday 7th

I am panting for the *ana* [anecdotes] of Edinburgh on this trying occasion, and you will comply (I trust) with the earnest request I made on that subject in my last letter. There is one story I wish you would particularly sift; that the Justice Clerk and Sir Patrick Murray called on Moira, just before he left Edinburgh, and declared that they would consider themselves as attached to him if he should undertake the government and patronage of Scotland.[4] I am anxious to ascertain the truth or falsehood of this, because it is connected with the history of a sorry intrigue about Scotland, of which I shall give you the details some day hence. Try also to learn, how far Henry Erskine or any of the rest were brought to express themselves well inclined towards Moira.[5]

. . .

1. Probably Charles Raby (d. 1849) and Cynric Lloyd (d. 1822), both former pensioners of Trinity.
2. See *Palmerston Letters*, p. 55.
3. Romilly was, however, appointed Solicitor-General in the new Administration.
4. Charles Hope was still Lord Justice Clerk. Sir Patrick Murray, 6th Bart of Ochtertyre (1771–1837), who was also an advocate, was a relation by marriage of Hope's. Moira became Master-General of the Ordnance and a member of Grenville's Cabinet.
5. Henry Erskine (1745–1817: *DNB*), had just been re-appointed Lord Advocate.

222. To Dugald Stewart

BLPES iii. 17–19   The Temple, 8 Feb. 1806

Victory, and triumph beyond all hope; for Lord Henry, 331 – Althorpe, 144 – Palmerstone, 128.

Such of us here as feel an interest in the little politics of Scotland, are very much alarmed indeed at an attempt which is made to retain them under the old disgraceful and illiberal system of management. The Dundasses and Hopes have pitched on a most convenient person to effect their design; the Earl of Moira. Since his arrival here, he has put in a claim for the patronage of Scotland; in consequence of an understanding and agreement, before he left Edinburgh, with that set which is headed by the Justice Clerk, and with which Moira has been carrying on, while in Scotland, such a commerce of mutual adulation. The terms of this contract are said to be, that he is to preserve to the Hopes, etc. their present influence and share of patronage, and that they are to give him their support and consider him as their leader in the Government. This is perfectly intelligible to such as know Scotland, and the Hopes, and Moira.

In urging this claim, he is supported by the favour of Carlton House, and I fear by the intrigues of Sheridan. It can not be successful, however, if it meets with a proper resistance from Scotland. There should be but one voice from all those, who ever felt the mischiefs of the old system, or cares for the permanence of a new one. I feel very much alarmed on account of the facility and political indiscretion of Harry Erskine; and it is of the last importance, that he should be held firmly in the right by those who have a proper influence over him. And my anxiety is increased by this consideration, that, from faults on both sides, there is not a perfect unison between his sentiments and those of the persons who stand nearest to him in politics at Edinburgh, and who upon this occasion will take the just view. Cathcart is the lawyer who has most to say with him, and his excellent sense as well as resolution may be trusted perfectly; I have suggested to Allen the propriety of writing to him fully upon the subject.[1] You and Sir Henry Moncrieff have of course great weight with Erskine; you never could interpose with a more useful effect.

You must see at a glance what a crisis this is in the politics of Scotland; upon the settlement of this point it will wholly depend, whether it is possible so to embody the independent opinions of that part of the country, as to give us a barrier, when the Whigs are again out of place, against the illiterate jobbing cabal by which we have been so vulgarly misgoverned for the last twenty years.

The Whigs, believe me, will very soon be restored to their natural state of opposition to the Court. The surrender has been made with too good a grace, to be sincere even as a compliance with necessity, and the household will lie in wait for their opportunity. When that is presented, there can be no doubt what the Hopes would make of Lord Moira; we know well enough what they made of Addington, who had left them their seats and places.

Even if the circumstances of our external danger should give a longer duration to the new Government, would it not be an indelible disgrace upon its leaders, and a bounty against public virtue for ever, if all these slaves and jobbers of the old system should be retained? It is enough that we have Lord Auckland for England, without throwing the whole corruption of Scotland likewise into the scale.[2] It may suit very well the politics of the Court, whether the actual one or the future one, to make no distinction of parties or men, to confound the principle of uniting men of talents and influence together with the project of hiring all fellows who will serve, the principle of burying former differences of opinion when new questions and a new danger arise with the project of obliterating all rules of public opinion and conduct. One can easily understand how this should be relished at Buckingham House, or Carleton House, or Leciester [sic] House. But if the present opportunity of marking that distinction is lost, it is gone for ever.

. . .

Lord Moira has had a finger in Walter Scott's business.[3] We are assured that he promised to the Justice Clerk, that David Boyle should be Solicitor to the Prince of Wales.[4] Clephane, Member for Kinross, and Colonel of the 20th, received a letter from Sir Wm Keir, saying no more than this, that 'Lord Moira is the soldier's friend, and you cannot do better than stick to his Lordship.'[5]

If this is not enough, what would you have?

. . .

1. David Cathcart (d. 1829: *DNB*), afterwards Lord Alloway, was a Lord of Session.
2. William Eden, 1st Baron Auckland (1744–1814: *DNB*), who had been joint Postmaster-General under both Pitt and Addington, survived into the Grenville Ministry as President of the Board of Trade.
3. Scott had obtained one of the clerkships of the Court of Session.
4. David Boyle (1772–1853: *DNB*), afterwards Lord Boyle, succeeded Hope as Lord Justice Clerk in 1811.
5. As MP for Kinross-shire, Col. David Clephane (c.1760–c.1828) was a reliable, if silent, Pittite. Lt Col. Sir William Keir, afterwards Grant (1772–1852: *DNB*), was Moira's principal ADC.

223. To James Reddie

NLS MSS 3704, ff. 23–4   The Temple, 11 Feb. 1806

. . .

I regret very much that you have given up thoughts of writing upon the neutral question, for I should like to have seen your mode of putting it, and to have had your arguments to consider. We differ in opinion, I believe; at least so far as it is a question of political discretion at present. Stephen's pamphlet is an able work, certainly, in the distinct statement of a striking set of facts; but its practical tendency appears to me mischievous, and the reasoning is full of the zealous and unscrupulous fallacies of a mere advocate, who takes every advantage he can catch, instead of the sober reserve and diffidence of one who seeks only the truth in a complicated and difficult investigation. Even as a question of law, I am very far from being satisfied that Sir Wm Scott is right.[1]

... Nobody, that was not depraved by faction, could witness Pitt's fall from power without being afflicted; the very dramatic effect, of such a catastrophe, and the close of so eventful a career, must have touched every one who forgot, in the splendid delusion, the realities to which we are now to awake. But on the retrospect of his Administration, I can justify to myself what I felt throughout the whole period which I have observed, that his talents were mischievously employed in the devotion to an illiberal unenlightened Court, and after depressing all independence of mind at home, have revived the power and reputation of the state in its continental relations. How far I expect it to be possible that these should be repaired, is quite a different question from the confidence which I continue to repose in the majority of the persons who are to attempt it. But I trust at least that men of independent opinions will see that there is an opportunity for the attempt, and, whatever becomes of the Ministry, they ought to form in the country a strong embodied party, determined to resist the re-appearance of that system which prevailed for fifteen years. You wish me to tell you, whether I have committed myself by any overt act to a political party, and whether I have the wish to come forward in a public department. I am very willing to answer both questions explicitly. Nothing can tempt me to quit my profession, on which I must rest my independence, and I have added no new overt act, as you term it, to those which have for many years made it thoroughly intelligible to my friends, that I consider it a duty in every man who takes an interest in public affairs to lend his aid to those whose main purposes and principles coincide with his own, and that I had long ago made my choice.

. . .

1. Stephen's *War in Disguise* had appeared in the midst of a controversy sparked by a landmark decision handed down in 1805 by the Prize Appeal Court of the Privy Council. Prior to 1805 British commercial regulations had been aimed only at preventing direct intercourse between enemy colonies and their mother country, and indirect commerce carried by neutral bottoms was protected by the legal holdings of Sir William Scott, afterwards Baron Stowell (1745–1835: *DNB*), as Judge of the High Court of Admiralty (1798–1828). But even Scott's liberal exposition of the law, which created 'neutralization' through the 'broken voyage' doctrine, was evaded often enough to raise a furore in Britain, and these evasions led Scott, in the spring of 1805, to declare the American ship *Essex* and its cargo forfeited, despite the fact that the vessel had complied with established procedure. The precedent was quickly adopted by two others on the Admiralty Court, and the 'broken voyage' doctrine was thereby superseded. The US Government had protested vociferously, Canning and other young Pittite orators had attacked American pretensions in the House of Commons, and Stephen's pamphlet, a bitter and skilful denunciation of American claims, had fanned the fire of national indignation (Heckscher, pp. 105–108). Alarming tensions characterized Anglo-American relations in the early months of 1806, and the new Whig government, whose policy was to improve Britain's relations with the United States, was in February of that year actively promoting a revision of the Navigation Laws in the

face of a storm of protest (Taylor, pp. 61–4). Horner, who was loath to review Stephen's pamphlet himself, clearly sought to render the editorial opinion of the *Edinburgh Review* consistent with the Ministry's American policy. In Dec. 1805 he had encouraged Jeffrey to review Stephen himself (Docs 210–12), but Jeffrey demurred. Now, ignoring the obvious alternative of Brougham, Horner apparently encouraged Jeffrey to allow Reddie to do the review and tried to influence Reddie's view of the subject. On 28 Feb. Jeffrey asked Reddie to undertake the review, noting that he thought the author wrong and observing that the error of Stephen's doctrine could be underlined 'if we were learnedly and convincingly to disavow national usurpations and candidly espouse a cause that must be sooner or later successful'. He also stressed the importance of 'coming out soon in such a crisis as the present', and closed with an observation that Horner was 'by far the most meritorious and most promising of any Scotsman that has lately emigrated to the South'. (NLS MSS 3704, ff 25–6.) In the end Jeffrey himself wrote the review in *ER* viii (no. xv, Apr. 1806), 1–35, which generally supported the Whig point of view.

224. To Dugald Stewart

BLPES iii. 21–2   The Temple, 12 Feb. 1806

On the subject about which I wrote to you last Saturday[1] I have the pleasure to say, that there exists no longer any difference. The language to be held now to those who ask about it is, that Lord Moira makes no pretensions to the administration of Scotland, that whatever discussion there may have been for a moment upon the subject is at an end, and that that part of the arrangement is placed on the best footing. The fact of course is, that the pretensions have been *withdrawn*; but that is an ugly word, and not to be used, least it should do harm.

I need not congratulate you on the triumph at Cambridge; which, the more one hears of it, appears the more satisfactory in every respect. It was in truth a signal victory of the independent and therefore calumniated members of the University, supported by the young ones, over the formal authorities. Of the 16 heads of houses, only 3 were for Lord Henry. The good cry of Atheism was tried there, as every where else upon similar occasions; I believe they said of Petty, what old Lady Blair[2] said of John Allen, that he was 'not only a Deist but an Atheist.' The number of voters for Lord Althorpe was 144, as I named it to you, not 244 as it was given in some of the papers . . .

          . . .

1. See Doc. 222.
2. The widow of Sir James Hunter Blair, 1st Bart (1741–87: *DNB*). (See *Cockburn*, p. 59.)

225. To J.A. Murray

BLPES iii. 38–9   The Temple, 28 Mar. 1806

I seem to have frightened you more than I intended about the judicial reforms.[1] I have heard nothing more of them since I wrote to you, except that [William] Adam has the papers before him now, i.e. the different plans, with a letter from Lord Grenville to the Chancellor, urging the great importance of an immediate reply. Adam is a man of business and dispatch, that is, he knows the value (in pounds sterling) of getting through business speedily even if it should not be very nicely finished, and accordingly there will be no delay in his share of the deliberation. But to those who have seen Adam in legal business, it is thoroughly ridiculous, that he should have entrusted to him so nice a work as the repairing any of the machines for the administration of law. He has neither knowledge, nor speculation, nor ingenuity; and, though a man whom I respect very much for his worth and like for his good dispositions, I would not trust his understanding an inch out of the common road, first because he believes it to be fit for all things, and secondly because I believe it to be fit for nothing difficult or delicate.

I ought to have explained more particularly what it was I liked in Armadale's conversation upon the subject.[2] He had no specific scheme to point at; but he spoke as if the two great evils, in the present system, were, that the jurisdictions of law and fact are not separated, and that there is no competition of courts at the choice of suitors. I alluded to these as according very much with my notions of the sort of remedy that ought to be attempted.

. . .

If I am at all consulted upon the subject, which is not very likely, I shall do nothing but advise great deliberation, and the importance of bringing [as many] minds as possible to bear upon it. . . .

. . .

1. The reform of the Scottish Court of Session was afterwards undertaken by the Ministry of All the Talents and brought to fruition by the subsequent Tory Government only after long delay.
2. Sir William Honyman (1756–1825), 1st Bart and, as Lord Armadale, a Lord of Session.

226. To Richard Sharp

BLPES iii. 40–43   [London], 29 Mar. 1806

I conceive that the books in political economy, which you wish to have a list of, are such as would enable you to take a general view of the present state of such inquiries; that you may see not only what truths economists suppose themselves to have ascertained already, but what questions too are left half-solved, besides some that are no more than set down for future investigation.[1]

After all, *Smith*'s name must be at the head of the list; though I should not have thought of mentioning him to you, were it not that one must come back to his book after every other, or rather carry it always on in examining any other. The few tracts of *Turgot* that have been printed, are less valuable now for any conclusions or investigations to which we have to refer, than as specimens of methods; both in analysing such subjects logically, and in submitting to the respectful phlegmatic confutation of popular errors. Those I have are

Formation des Richesses
Lettres sur les Grains
Sur le Prêt à intérêt
Sur la propriété des mines et des carrières
Sur le commerce des fers

You know his articles 'Foire' and 'Fondation' in the old *Encyclopédie*; I expect we shall have very soon a complete edition of Turgot's writings, including some that have not yet been published, and are in the hands of M. Dupont de Nemours.

I will not condemn you to the works of Quesnai's sect, who write so abominably ill; you must look into some of them however, for they have done a vast deal for this science, though not exactly perhaps in the parts where they conceived their own merit to lie. For the shortest view of their system, the little book which Smith recommends is the best, Mercier de la Rivière, *L'ordre naturel et essentiel des sociétés politiques*, but take only the second volume; the first is occupied with their childish speculations about government, and a prolix mystical exposition of their views with regard to the order of nature – views which they had unquestionably the merit of first bringing to these speculations, and a high philosophical merit that is, but any one accustomed to generalize will catch the view as soon as it is stated. Besides, it is more properly a manner of considering the subjects of political econony, than capable of being stated itself in an abstract form.

There are two pieces by Quesnai himself, which are well worth reading; 'Sur le Commerce', and 'Sur les travaux des Artisans', published by Dupont in the first part of his *Physiocratie*. In these, there is a great power of subtle and dextrous reasoning. I am not sure that the faults of his style do not bear a resemblance to those of our favourite Bishop Butler.[2]

If these give you an inclination to look farther into the system of the Economists, the most useful books are the *Philosophie Rurale* and *Théorie de l'Impôt*, both by the elder Mirabeau; there are two editions of *Philosophie Rurale*, one in 3 vols 12mo, another in a single volume being an abridgement of the other; the *Théorie de l'Impôt* is printed separately, and also in one of the volumes of *L'Ami des Hommes*[3].

Hume's *Political Discourses*, Franklin's Miscellanies, Morellet's various tracts, and Bentham whenever he touches a subject of political economy, are full of instruction in the mode of treating the science; they may be read with great profit for another purpose, that of tracing the history of opinions while the science has been going on, which, in its present imperfect state, is the most satisfactory way of knowing what has really been done as well as what has been attempted.

I need not tell you of the new world which *Malthus* has discovered; but a great deal remains to be done, to describe it with more minute accuracy.

These are the original general writers whom I can recollect; as for systematic treatises, besides Sir James Steuart (whom I ought perhaps to have named in the first class, and who is full of ingenuity and errors), there are some excellent foreign books, particularly an anonymous *Traité des Richesses* published in 1781,[4] London and Lausanne upon the title page, and the recent publication by *Simonde* of Geneva, *Richesse Commerciale*. The little books of Count Verri in 1771, and *Condillac* in 1776,

Meditazioni sulla Economia Politica and *Le Commerce et le Gouvernement*, are worth having.[5]

A few subjects have been separately discussed with considerable success; at the head of these is the medium of circulation. Besides *John Law's* two well known books, there is a Memoir of his to the Regent Duke of Orléans, *Sur l'usage des Monnoies*, which is remarkable, among other things, for a distinct statement of the argument against the legal limitation of interest; it is printed in several collections; I have it in Forbonnais' book *Recherches sur les Finances de France*.[6] Then there is an ingenious treatise *de la circulation et du crédit* by Pinto a Dutch Jew, who seems for the time to have been remarkably well acquainted with the English finances. And I formerly told you of the article on Money in Morellet's *Prospectus of a Dictionary of Commerce*. These books are a good preparation for the discussions which have taken place, since the restriction of the Bank payments, and the disorders of the Irish currency. I might have mentioned too an old little book by Rice Vaughan on coinage, written during the usurpation, but not published till 1675, which gives a digest of the opinions of that day, besides a great deal of ingenious reasoning; this writer is the first, I believe, who stated that important principle in political economy, that the wages of common labour in money give us a measure or unit for tracing the theory of variable prices.

It is unnecessary to remind you, that there are a great many admirable tracts, both in English and in French, on the subject of the Corn Trade.

I shall only mention farther, two little books in what is called Political Arithmetic, which are both of great merit; the one is *Observations on the Bills of Mortality* by Graunt, one of the founders of the Royal Society, and I may add one of the fathers of the modern speculations in political economy; it is truly an original work: the other is a fragment of a work undertaken by the famous *Lavoisier* at the desire of the National Assembly, on *la Richesse Territoriale de la France*; it is the sketch of a great master.

I must leave this list imperfect –

1. This was not the first such exchange with Sharp. *Sharp*, pp. 132–40, prints two letters to Horner of 18 June and 1 July 1805 from which it appears that Horner had told him he had reflected 'again and again' on the subject of 'a singular conversation' they had had about the 'rules of probability'. Sharp suspected that there was no full-scale inquiry into the matter, not from 'a want of courage or of industry, but [from] a secret suspicion of the truth, that a complete, or even a very useful enumeration of such rules, is impracticable'.

2. The two 'Dialogues sur le Commerce et sur les Travaux des Artisans' comprise most of the substance of the second, not, as stated, the first, part or volume respectively of the two editions Horner variously used. The first collected edition of the works of Joseph Butler (1692–1752: *DNB*), Bishop of Durham, had been published in Edinburgh in 1804.

3. See Docs 84 and 133.

4. [Achille N. Isnard (d. 1803)], *Traité des Richesses* (2 vols, Londres, 1781).

5. Pietro, Count Verri (1728–97), *Meditazioni sulla economica politica* (Genoa, 1771).

6. John Law (1671–1729: *DNB*), like many other eighteenth-century economic writers, adopted a disequilibrium theory of money, viewing it as a stimulant to employment, output, and trade. Law's most celebrated work was *Money and Trade Considered: With a Proposal for Supplying the Nation With Money* (Edinburgh, 1709). The other 'well-known' work to which Horner refers was probably *The present state of the French revenue and trade* (1701). His *Mémoire* to the Duke of Orléans is printed in ii. 542–73 of [Véron de Forbonnais], *Recherches et considérations sur les finances de France depuis . . . 1595 jusqu'à . . . 1721* (2 vols, Basle, 1758).

227. To Francis Jeffrey

BLPES iii. 44–5   The Temple, 31 Mar. – 1 Apr. 1806

. . .

I am very sorry that I am unable to furnish any thing for you this No. though I will not let you shake me off altogether yet; I wish to hang on, by a slender tack indeed always, till I am called to the Bar next year, and I trust I shall in the interval furnish you with one or two articles that I am in arrear for by promise; India and Malthus at least. The third edition of this work is just published, and the author has sent me a copy.

I am very anxious, for public reasons, that an account of Lancaster's book should appear in this Number; you must even do it yourself at last, which is a great shame to me. But I am hardened in guilt. Poor Lancaster is likely to be a victim to the stupid prejudices of the high church; the Bishops have had a meeting to make speeches against him, and the effect of this is felt already, in the stop put to his plans, and to the public encouragement. He is almost broken-hearted. It is of no use swearing upon the subject; something more effectual must be done, but it is a delicate question to decide upon, in what way he may be served most effectually. We are talking of it here very much, and have not yet determined. If we decide to plunge into a controversy, and trust to the ultimate good sense of the public and the purity of the cause, you must give your powerful co-operation. In the meantime, it is of the last importance, that an account of the Plan, its vast advantages to the public, and a tribute of justice to the merit of the man, should appear without any farther delay in your Journal. After discussing the matter with Hallam, who, though the son of a churchman and acquainted (as Peter says) with nine bishops, is quite enlightened and indeed most zealous upon this point, we agree that it is better for the present at least to take no notice of Mrs Trimmer; and I trust very much to his judgement of the means of doing good 'in the tabernacles of the godly.' Sydney Smith, after being influenced at the club by some looks and words of Romilly, proposed to me to take Mrs T. in hand; but I told him at the time I thought he would perhaps not perform the business in the right tone, and I am quite confirmed in this by thinking more of it. He would catechize the old woman to her heart's content, but this would do no good to Lancaster, and only enrage the party we must try to convince or at least shame into silence. An abstract by you, with praise in your own manner, will be of infinite use and of all the use we can properly put ourselves to at present. You can patch up Hallam's sketch, with Seymour's assistance, who knows the subject much better than any of us, and will give you in a morning's conversation materials for an admirable article. . . .

1 Apr.

Your letter has played the devil with me.[1] I must try to do Lancaster myself, since you insist on it; though I run some risk of offending Hallam, and a much greater risk of executing the business imperfectly. I will set myself to it tomorrow, and think of little else till I have done with it.[2]

. . .

1. He had closed the previous paragraph as a letter from Jeffrey arrived.
2. Whether Horner ever did produce something about Lancaster and, if so, whether it was used remains unclear. Evidently Hallam had despaired of receiving Horner's contribution and had delivered his draft to Jeffrey late in December 1805 or early in January 1806 in the expectation that Horner would follow with a separate article, presumably aimed specifically at Mrs Trimmer. (Horner to Seymour, 26 Dec. 1805, *Horner*, i. 344–5, and Docs 212 and 214). Jeffrey acknowledged receiving Hallam's piece in January 1806 (*WI* no. 373), but was evidently as dissatisfied with it as was the author himself. Probably he had by the end of March still not received the revised version Horner had urged Hallam should supply (Doc. 214), and was too busy to take it on himself, as Horner suggested, and wrote in some desperation to Horner. If Horner did produce anything after this appeal, however, it must have been either too little or too late, for, despite the anxiety he expressed in the earlier part of this letter, there appeared in the *Review* only a few weeks later (viii (no. xvi, July 1806), 177–84) Sydney Smith's strong rebuttal of Mrs Sarah Trimmer's attack on Lancaster in her *Comparative View of the New Plan of Education promulgated by Mr Joseph Lancaster* (1805). It was then another eighteen months before the appearance of any direct notice of Lancaster's work in ER xi (no. xxi, Oct. 1807), 61–73, and then it was not of the later edition of his *Improvements*, but of his *Outlines of a plan for educating ten thousand poor children* (1806). That review, apparently, was also by Sydney Smith. But Hallam seems to have submitted a review, and though it was never printed it may perhaps have owed something to Horner. For in November 1806 Horner was still writing to Jeffrey about paying off his 'old debts' of Malthus and Lancaster, though it is clear from what he wrote then (Doc. 244) that he expected the appearance at any moment of the main article by another hand.

228. To J.A. Murray

BLPES iii. 46–7   The Temple, 10 Apr. 1806

I have seen very little of any political persons lately, having been very much at home; and indeed I find, or fancy I find, the intercourse of such people much less engaging while they are in office, than when they had the carelessness and keenness of opposition.[1] I cannot therefore tell you much about the projected reforms in Scotland, which probably do not occupy a great deal of the attention of Government at present. Thomson however breakfasted yesterday with the Justice Clerk, who told him that nothing more would be done this Session of Parliament than passing preliminary resolutions in the H. of Lords; to this effect, that the increase of population and trade in Scotland since the Union has rendered the system then settled for the administration of justice inadequate to the present business; that it has been found by experience to be inconvenient that so many Judges should sit in one court; and appointing the high officers of state in this country, with the eminent persons of the law in Scotland, to prepare a Bill for next Session. So far this seems all right enough, if the Justice Clerk really knows any thing of the intentions of Government. I walked with Armadale to the opera t'other night from a house where we met at dinner, and he talked a great deal upon the subject, and suffered me to talk a great deal; the only precise reform he seemed to have thought of, was, that parties should be entitled at their option to bring certain causes before a jury. This is vague enough; but it touches the material point, the separation of fact and law, and the alternative left to parties brings on the change by degrees.

The pamphlet I sent you the other day is professedly from the Foreign Office; little Orme told Thomson, he saw Mr Fox's corrections upon the proof sheets; the little bookseller was too vain of such a circumstance to remember his duty to keep the secret.[2] I am sure you will be convinced with me, from the internal evidence alone, that the main composition is by no other hand than Brougham's; though the conclusion from that, which would almost be strong enough of itself, is corroborated to me by a hundred little circumstances before and since the publication. There is great ability shown in parts of it, and the writing, though it has the peculiarities of Brougham's style, is upon the whole more corrected and even Anglicized than any thing he had done before. There are a few expressions too much for him, with respect to the errors of Pitt's Government *at home* and the *long* course of misfortune and mismanagement, which have accumulated difficulties upon his successors; which may all be said most justly, but not by all persons with perfect consistency; and indeed was not necessary for the argument against the Third Coalition, which stands apart as a folly by itself. I must keep you in mind, however, [that] Brougham denies the pamphlet.

. . .

1. Surely Horner's opinion was moulded by a perception that his stock at Holland House had decreased since the Whigs had come to power. Horner had first dined at Holland House on 26 May 1805 in the company of Lord and Lady Holland, Mr and Mrs Fox, Lord and Lady Bessborough, the lawyer John Lens (1756–1825: *DNB*), Grattan, Petty, Morpeth, Scarlett, Lord King, and Lord Archibald Hamilton. Thereafter, until the end of January 1806, the Holland House Dinner Books record Horner's presence on thirty-four occasions and reveal that he dined with virtually every Whig leader. Between 1 Feb. and 10 Apr. 1806, however, Horner appeared at Holland House only once, on 14 Feb. when he dined with a small party composed of Brougham and the Hollands (HHDB).

2. The anonymous pamphlet in question, *An Inquiry into the State of the Nation at the Commencement of the Present Administration* (1806), was, as Horner surmised, by Brougham, who also may have reviewed it in *ER* viii (no. xv, Apr. 1806), 190–206 (*WI*). Brougham had been introduced at Holland House in July 1805 (*Home of the Hollands*, p. 309, and HHDB), and having made an initially great impression there (*Holland House Chronicles*, p. 83) had dined at Lady Holland's table on three occasions during February and March 1806 (HHDB entries of 12 and 14 Feb. and 31 Mar.). Lord Holland had apparently suggested he write the pamphlet (New, p. 34). It was a sweeping indictment of Pitt's foreign policy and its execution, and it called for drastic changes in colonial policy, the amendment of the Navigation Laws, the abolition of the slave trade, juster rule in India, attention to the grievances of Irish Catholics, and a measure of parliamentary reform.

229. To J.A. Murray

BLPES iii. 50–51   The Temple, 7 May 1806[1]

. . .

Your Solicitor General told me the day before yesterday, that Lord Grenville had already agreed to their plan about the Scotch courts, and approved of every part of it. The resolutions will be moved in a day or two; and are to contain the outline of the plan. They have some reason, but I have never heard it stated, for beginning the subject in the House of Lords.[2] . . .

Clerk was very entertaining to me, in his conversation upon the subject. His own opinion is decided against any change; the original constitution of the Court of Session he thinks admirable, and quite adequate to all the purposes of legal administration, even according to the most approved order of procedure. In particular, he holds, and by his statement he made it very intelligible, that the jurisdictions of law and fact may be kept quite distinct by means of interlocutors of relevancy upon the different steps of the pleadings, and he asserts that formerly they were kept separate; so that the judgement of the court, after proof, was confined merely to the issue.

He considers Lord Grenville in this instance as the greatest of all innovators and Jacobins; and holds him very cheap for the promptitude with which he has approved of their plan. . . .

With this positive opinion, as to the inexpediency of setting about the change in this particular way, and his reluctance as he expressed it to break down an old splendid institution, he shows nevertheless an absurd affection for the thing he has helped to beget, though he was put to the act of generation against his will. Speaking of the Plan, 'it's a damned knowing thing' he said to me; and to Thomson 'By God there are great lines in it.' You must supply the accents and tune yourself; but for Heaven's sake, only sing them to yourself. You know how jealous he is, and how certainly a story gets round. Nothing can be more exquisite than his *naiveté*.

. . .

1. The letter continues with further sections dated 12 and 13 May, the first of which is that printed in *Horner*, i. 382–3.
2. Grenville made his resolutions about the reform of the Scottish Court of Session on 12 May (*Hansard*, vii. 93–4). The new Solicitor-General for Scotland was John Clerk, jun.

230. To Mrs Dugald Stewart

BLPES iii. 54–7 ⟨*Horner*, i. 383–4⟩   The Temple, 19 May 1806

. . . An express copartnery for the division of gains is *not* proved against Lord Melville; I never expected it would; nor did I ever quite believe that his guilt amounted to that, or had so much folly in it. But a corrupt participation in Trotter's gains, and the appropriation of public money, knowing it to be so, are fully proved: over and above the proof of having broken the Act of Parliament, and connived at Trotter's proceedings.[1]

The *whole* charge of corrupt appropriation is not established by *direct* evidence, but it is very far from being merely a case of circumstances. To a certain amount, and as far as [?concerns] certain specific acts of corruption, the evidence seems to me direct and positive; and then there proceeds such a tissue of circumstances, so infinitely multiplied and interwoven, as appears quite of one piece when viewed through that direct proof, but, in every other aspect, incongruous and confused.

You will be more curious, however, to learn what our hopes and fears are of the event. Melville's friends are of course very sanguine in their talk, and are probably as sincerely infatuated as they have been at every other crisis of his fate. Entertaining the very worst sentiments of the tribunal, by which he is tried, both as to public probity and intelligence, I am still most confidently of opinion, that an acquittal is wholly out of the question; that is, a complete acquittal. I do indeed feel some apprehensions, that the number of those who will of course vote for a complete acquittal, increased by those who will try a compromise between their honour and their inclinations, may be sufficient to reduce the conviction to a special verdict; declaring him guilty of the breach of the law, and the connivance of Trotter, and delivering him from the charge of corrupt participation. A conviction upon any one charge, enforced by the effect that will be produced upon the public mind as soon as the evidence is thrown into general circulation, will disable the man, I trust, for all future attempts in public life; and, whatever becomes of the verdict, the publication of the evidence will secure a correct judgement in history. But I am far from despairing even of a simple unmodified conviction.

It is very difficult to learn what the opinions are of individual members of the Court; many of course are still undetermined, and I trust very much to the exertions of those who will lead the debate on Wednesday se'nnight. In a case of complex proof, the honest indolent ones will trust their consciences to the Keeper of the King's; nobody can say for certain what Erskine's opinion is; it is understood however to be what we wish, though this is a point on which one is not at liberty to repeat what they have been given to understand on good authority.[2] It is a most fortunate circumstance, that he took no part in the proceedings in the House of Commons; and his deportment in the Hall has been so impartial, so patient, and so dignified, as to have drawn the admiration of all, and extorted a compliment from Lord Eldon in the House last Saturday. He feels it of course one of the great occasions of his life, in his own department, and crowning all the great judicial transactions in which he has performed so eminent a part. Lord Ellenborough leaves nobody in doubt of his clear unqualified opinion; Lord Redesdale has not thought it worth his while to come over from Dublin, till he has disposed of all his wines and houses; and Lord Eldon has not [the] boldness to act the part he would, if he durst. We have great strength, you see, among the law Lords. As for the laymen, Lord Sidmouth is reported by those who sit near him to have been almost indecent in his commentaries upon the witnesses; Lord Auckland very soon made up his mind, too, against the defendant; so also Lord Hutchinson, and Lord Carnarvon:[3] I mention these by name, not merely for the importance of their single votes, but because they may be considered as specimens of so many distinct classes in the House. It is even said, that Lord Chatham has evinced a disposition to convict Melville; though if this were so, it would be imputed to a spirit of personal animosity, that has rankled in his mind ever since he lost the Admiralty.[4] These little gossiping particulars will help you and Mr Stewart to conceive what our grounds of hope are; but I hope you will forgive me for requesting that the names may not be mentioned again.

Excepting Romilly's speech, this great occasion has been very little distinguished by any display of eloquence or ability. The nation owes a large debt of gratitude to

Whitbread, for his persevering ardour and industry; but beyond this, he has earned but little admiration. The conduct of the trial, as to the tactics of evidence, was not very remarkable for skill; and his reply in conclusion did not present, as it ought to have done, a perspicuous and impressive review of it. He is certainly a man of powerful good sense, and great force of reasoning, in all occasions of business in the House of Commons; but upon this opportunity he thought it incumbent on him to display all the varieties of eloquence, from grave to gay. He had pleasantries that made one's blood run cold; and flights of metaphor that made us hang our heads for shame and concern. I never suffered more discomfort in my life, than during the first day of his reply; there is not an epithet strong enough, to describe the badness of his taste. With all this, however, the earnestness of his manner secured him a considerable effect upon his audience, and so few opportunities have people of comparing different specimens of public speaking, particularly ladies and peers, that many of them, having a cultivated taste in other arts, thought him even that day very eloquent.

⟨Romilly's success was as great as his friends predicted. He spoke for three hours and a half, and his speech might be named as the model of the simple style. Had he hazarded more, he might have produced passages of more striking effect for a moment; had he been more declamatory, he would have collected more suffrages in the express praise of his eloquence. For I have heard it observed, that the speech had nothing but good sense, perfect clearness, and a strong cause. The fact is, he kept every one chained in attention, and made the whole case distinct to the dullest. Particular parts of the composition there certainly were, that might be enumerated, on account of their being more impressive, more indignant, more finely pointed, than the rest; but they were so in *keeping* with the whole, that the prevailing tone was only heightened, never interrupted. One might have said, his taste was too severe, too simple, if it had betrayed itself by a single false step; but it was so maintained throughout, and the execution all so uniform, and the general designing of the speech in so great a style, as to give it the rank of the highest order of compositions. It wanted only a finished conclusion; for he ended abruptly: he had one prepared, but something, he says, occurred in the course of his delivery, which prevented him from giving it, and he did not like to venture a composition of that formal sort upon the spot. I very much suspect, that the fastidiousness of his judgement, his great modesty and horror at any thing like display, rushed all back upon him about ten minutes too soon. His language is free from all ambition and curious adaptation, and therefore one never remarked felicities at the moment; and if he used any figurative expressions, they were so melted into the substance of his style, as to produce their effect without being noticed.⟩

. . . You asked me, in your last letter, about a good evening newspaper; there is none that I can recommend; indeed it is one of my complaints against the present Ministry, besides some that are of more moment, that they neglect the press a great deal too much. Even the *Morning Chronicle* is become intolerably fool[ish] since its friends got into power.

Do not let me end this endless letter, w[ithout] telling you that in the minority of 18 the other night against the Slave Trade Bill (a measure of partial abolition), there were *six* King's sons; being all the blessed family, except the Prince of Wales, who was absent.[5] The Duke of Gloucester voted on the other side, and made a very reputable speech. When Trotter was under cross-examination, and gave the lawyer a good plumping answer for Melville, the Duke of Cumberland called out 'hear, hear'. Yesterday the Bishop of London is said to have preached a decent Christian sermon against judging upon presumptions;[6] and it is farther said, that Lord Romney means to complain of it in the House of Lords.[7] What a gossip you must think me. . . .

1. Horner refers to the impeachment of Lord Melville on charges of misappropriation of public monies. Alexander Trotter, who had been his paymaster at the Navy Office, was one of those principally implicated in the affair. As the close friend of Romilly, the Solicitor-General, Horner was evidently privy to information of which the public was generally ignorant, and he attended the proceedings in Westminster Hall with some regularity. On 29 Apr. he had witnessed from the Chamberlain's gallery Whitbread's 'temperate, distinct, and weighty' three-hour opening speech which, he told Murray in a letter of the same day, was delivered with all of Whitbread's 'usual faults of bad taste, monotonous voice, and clumsy execution' (BLPES iii. 48–9). On 12 May he had told Murray that the trial had 'passed its critical stage' and had expressed anxiety about the first public appearance Romilly was about to make as Solicitor-General (BLPES iii. 51; Horner, i. 382–3).
2. Lord Erskine presided over the trial as the new Lord Chancellor.
3. John Hely-Hutchinson, 1st Baron Hutchinson and afterwards 2nd Earl of Donoughmore (1757–1832: DNB), was a soldier; Henry Herbert, 1st Earl of Carnarvon (1741–1811), was Master of the Horse.
4. William Pitt's elder brother, John Pitt, 2nd Earl of Chatham (1756–1835: DNB), had been First Lord of the Admiralty, 1788–94.
5. The Lords debate on the third reading of the Slave Importation Bill ended in its passing by 43 to 18 on 16 May (Hansard, vii. 227–36).
6. Beilby Porteus.
7. Charles Marsham, 1st Earl of Romney (1744–1811).

231. To J.A. Murray

BLPES iii. 58–61 ⟨New, p. 36⟩   The Temple, 26 May 1806

. . .

You will not be surprised to learn, that Brougham has declared his anxiety to get into Parliament; at least I have heard so from several quarters, for ⟨there is no degree of confidential communication between him and me, and we only see each other when we happen to dine on the same day at the table of a common acquaintance.⟩ I have been informed also, but not in a manner that entitles me to speak of it generally, that he has within these few days made an attempt, which has failed, to bargain with Lord Lowther about the vacancy made in Westmoreland by the death of Sir M. Le Fleming.[1] What the extent of his interest is, I do not know, but he must suppose it to be considerable, to warrant him in making an application which must have offered a sort of compromise: his idea, I presume, was not to offer himself for the county, but to give what interest he has there to Lord Lowther, on condition of a seat for one of the burghs. I could not conceal from you so important a piece of intelligence regarding a person in whose history you take so deep an interest, but I beg you will not repeat it to any body, unless you hear it from some other quarter. It cannot but very soon be universally known. The person who is to come in for Westmoreland is a Lord Munchester, a half saint – half debauchee – and whole raff, and a dear friend of Wilberforce.[2] Since Brougham has decided upon this, I wish him success most sincerely, and shall be very anxious till he attains his object; for the interval of that sort of expectation is neither very agreeable nor very advantageous in any respect. I think I see very distinctly Brougham's distinguished success as a parliamentary speaker, not by eloquence, but by his readiness and force, a prompt application of various knowledge which though never quite accurate is always given with that confident clearness which answers the same purpose in a popular assembly, and a powerful though never graceful fluency. I think I see too very distinctly that his success, as a political character, will be confined to the House of Commons; his dispatch in business is great, but it betrays him into inaccuracy and indiscretions; and he will never preserve the confidence of any party, or of any individuals who are not disposed to be entirely subservient. He will be a formidable debater; but he has neither comprehension nor refinement of mind to be the author of great measures of pacific policy, nor in a time of trouble (which God avert) would he be found, I think, to have courage for great enterprises. I guess he will always be inclined towards the party that is actually in power, or strong enough to seem on the point of getting it. I judge more harshly of him now, you will perceive, than I was formerly in the habit at least of expressing; but the late change of Administration was a sort of *experimentum crucis* to me, which I watched with attention. ⟨I cannot much respect the man, who could write both the review of Lord Chatham's letters, and the late *State of the Nation*, who reviewed Lord Lauderdale and gives that author an opportunity of expressing his surprise at the familiarity of old acquaintance with which his critic now accosts him.[3] There is a grievous want both of pride and principle in all this.⟩ I know, my dear Murray, you will not read this without some pain; but with you I have no secrets upon such subjects: and indeed I am anxious to be corrected by you, if you consider these sentiments about B. as in any measure unjust. ⟨I must confess there may be a shade of personal resentment mixed with my judgement of Brougham's public conduct;⟩ not on account of any interference between us, that either has or could possibly take place, for I have ever derived the most genuine satisfaction from the reputation he has so justly won, and my most favourite dream used to be, that we were to run on in the same direction with only that interval which his vast superiority would ever give him. But ⟨I have not been strong enough to throw off a little indignation at the neglect with which he has treated me and the indifference with which he has appeared to me to sacrifice the intimacy of a life-time. Perhaps this jealousy, which has still a good deal of affection in it, makes me[4] see things worse than they are;⟩ and makes me fancy a great deal of the adulation which I impute in some instances, and the malignant envy in others. I am on my guard against the danger of all this resentment of mine souring into animosity; ⟨and the subject has of late cost me some uncomfortable hours, both on account of the real loss I have suffered in Brougham's conversation which is so full of entertainment and instruction, and the disappointment of my plans of life which always included him,⟩ and because there cannot but be a certain loss of character to both parties in the alienation of two persons who were supposed to have travelled on together for so long a time. . . .

. . .

1. Sir Michael Le Fleming, 4th Bart (1748–1806), had been MP for Westmorland since 1774. Apparently William Lowther, 2nd Viscount Lowther and afterwards 1st Earl of Lonsdale (1757–1844: DNB), had been approached on Brougham's behalf by Wilberforce, but without Lord Grenville's authorization. Brougham's alternative schemes also badly backfired. (See PH ii. 406.)
2. John Pennington, 1st Baron Muncaster (1737–1813: DNB), was MP for Westmorland from 1806 until his death.
3. Lord Chatham's Letters to his Nephew Thomas Pitt Esq., afterwards Lord Camelford and Lauderdale's Inquiry into the Nature and Origin of Public Wealth had been noticed in ER iv (no. viii, July 1804), 377–86 and 343–76; Lauderdale's Hints to the manufacturers of Great Britain on the consequences of the Irish Union in vi (no. xii, July 1805), 283–90. Brougham's own pamphlet was reviewed, probably by Jeffrey, in viii (no. xv, Apr. 1806), 190–206.
4. New prints 'inclines me to'.

232. To J.A. Murray

BLPES iii. 62–3   The Temple, 2 and 3 June 1806

. . .

On Saturday morning I met Brougham at the west end of the town, and we walked together back to the King of Clubs. On our way, he asked me if I had heard any thing of his negotiation about Westmoreland, and proceeded to tell me his story. It is too long to give you more than the outline: his intention was to start for the county as the Government candidate, and to get Lord Lowther's acquiescence by a promise of support at Carlisle, where his Lordship's influence (it seems) is not quite secure. Through Fox, B. was to have the countenance of Lord Thanet, the D. of Norfolk, Lord Suffolk, and Lord Derby;[1] but Lord Lowther, having taken the alarm, got before him to Lord Grenville, and secured his support for his candidate, Lord Munchester. The end is, that Munchester, Lord Lowther's man, has the support of Government. Brougham holds himself very much obliged to Fox and Lord Holland for their zealous exertions in his favour; and what will not surprise you, as it has not in the least surprised me, he regards Wilberforce as having behaved to him, 'like a very saint and scoundrel', professing to be of service to him, and taking a decided part against him. So that this incongruous and (for that reason) most indiscreet connection is dissolved.

3 June

I have not heard yet what took place in the House of Lords last night, except that Lord Eldon is fighting for Melville through thick and thin, and sacrificing his own character for him. . . .

. . .

1. Sackville Tufton, 9th Earl of Thanet (1767–1825: DNB); Charles Howard, 11th Duke of Norfolk (1746–1815: DNB); John Howard, 15th Earl of Suffolk (1739–1820); Edward Stanley, 12th Earl of Derby (1752–1834).

233. To Francis Jeffrey

BLPES iii. 64–5   The Temple, 13 June 1806

. . .

. . . Except Petty, there is nobody in the Ministry or connected with it, of whom I would ask any thing. If I ever have any patronage myself, I think (like every body else who has none and the chance of none), that I shall do some good with it; but I will not, for the sake of good, go through the intriguing that seems indispensable in directing the patronage of others. . . . But we shall philosophize together upon all these matters after the dog days; I have not like you mounted so high, as to despise the globe and its existing race of inhabitants, or to view this goodly frame as a sterile promontory; but I am high enough to have great pleasure in looking at it, without caring to lose this indolent airy pleasure by descending again, and mingling with the other creatures upon the surface.

I have just looked into what you describe as John Forbes's answer to Selkirk; I should doubt that story of the authorship, for there is now and then a neatness of manner, which he must have acquired since I knew his hand, and there are insinuations about motives of which I am unwilling to believe him guilty. I have not determined yet whether it is worth making a separate article of; or may be thrown jointly with the other two into a general notice of the arguments that have been advanced against Selkirk's reasoning. The general subject is important enough to deserve this.[1] Have you seen a book on Mechanics by Olinthus Gregory, an under master at Woolwich; Rennie, the Engineer, told me there is some unhandsome treatment there of old Watt and John Robinson [sic]; if so, there are more reasons than one to punish that offence, against scientific good breeding, as well as public gratitude. I must mention it to Playfair.[2]

There is a pamphlet, I see, printed at Edinburgh upon civil trials by jury, and the reform of the court; take the trouble of telling Constable that I should like to see it.[3] Unless Leslie's affair has taken a new turn in the public opinion at Edinburgh, which I cannot suppose possible, I am against taking any farther notice of it. Here, we have utterly forgotten it, and will read no more about it. These brutal priests are kept alive by the controversy, and are very wise in their generation to have the last word, and as many last words as their antagonists will afford them. It is quite evident to me, that Inglis is conscious nothing but his being engaged in a controversy with great names will ever keep his own in the Gazetteer of the Cross. I will have nothing more to do with the subject. But after it is laid aside, I should like to see a scientific review of Brown's *Metaphysical Essay*; Playfair would execute such an article with admirable learning and logic.[4]

. . .

1. No such notice appeared in the *ER*, but its quarterly lists included three articles replying in 1806 to Selkirk's book, namely: R. Brown, *Strictures . . . on the Earl of Selkirk's 'Observations'*; *Eight Letters on the subject of the Earl of Selkirk's Pamphlet*; and *Remarks on the Earl of Selkirk's 'Observations'*. Whichever of the latter two Jeffrey may have meant, Horner seems to have been correct in thinking that John Hay Forbes was not its author, for apparently the third was also by Brown and the second by James Gordon.

2. John Rennie (1761–1821: *DNB*) had been an employee and John Robison a friend of James Watt. Olinthus Gilbert Gregory (1774–1841: *DNB*), mathematical master at Woolwich and subsequently Professor of Mathematics at the Royal Military Academy, had published a *Treatise of Mechanics* in which he supported the claims about a disputed patent made by another former employee of Watt's, Jabez Carter Hornblower (1744–1814: *DNB*). The second edition, published in 1807, contained an opinionated piece on steam engines by Hornblower and it was principally this that was noticed by Playfair in *ER* xiii (no. xxvi, Jan. 1809), 311–33.

3. Jeffrey's article in *ER* ix (no. xviii, Jan. 1807), 462–92, reviewed three anonymous pamphlets: *Reflections on the administration of civil justice in Scotland; and on the resolutions of the House of Lords relative to that subject* [by John Greenshields] (Edinburgh and London, 1806); *Thoughts on trial by jury in civil causes with a view to a reform of the administration of justice in Scotland* [by James Grahame] (Edinburgh, 1806); and *Remarks on the report of the Committee of the House of Peers, relative to the administration of civil justice in Scotland* (Glasgow, 1806). But none of them seems to have been published by Constable.

4. In his review of Stewart's *Short Statement* (see Doc. 208 n. 1) Horner had commented on the first, anonymous, edition of Brown's *Observations* that 'it would do honour to the most penetrating metaphysician of the age to have avowed this essay'; but no separate notice appeared in the *ER* of the acknowledged 1806 edition.

234. To J.A. Murray

BLPES iii. 66–73 〈Horner, i. 384–7〉   The Temple, 19 June 1806[1]

. . .

You will of course expect some account of Lord Grenville's speech and plan.[2] . . . It was not perhaps the best he can make, because the details of the subject, as well as its newness to him, stood in his way; but it was very clear, methodical, and grave, without a ray of great general principle (such as the occasion well deserved), and without a single originality or grace in his expression of the common places which he had recourse to. All this is his manner. . . .[3]

. . .

〈I am very far from agreeing with you in our feelings on the event of Lord Melville's trial. On the contrary, I consider his acquittal as a foul stain upon the records of parliamentary justice; bringing the mode of trial by impeachment into disgrace, and subjecting the House of Lords to the distrust and contempt of the public. Upon party occasions, I never pretend to speak otherwise than as a party man, because, for a time at least, I have given myself to that profession, with a view of being perhaps useful. I think I am sufficiently aware that the habits of that connection insensibly debauch our judgement, even for occasions that ought to be exempt from its influence: but I can perfectly and securely distinguish between the stronger bias, or the higher colouring, which party feelings communicate to my opinion and the substantial frame and fabric of that opinion reared out of the evidence laid before me by the natural use of my understanding. I am sure I am honest at least in stating it as the conviction of my understanding, whether accurate or not, that the acquittal of Lord Melville is a verdict contrary to plain strong accumulated evidence; and after that, I will farther say, that I consider that verdict to have been pronounced, by a great proportion of those who acquitted him, with a corrupt consciousness of its being contrary to evidence or a corrupt prostitution of the *honour* which they pledged without having considered the evidence. This is the opinion of many unbiased persons, who have no knowledge of parties, or interest in their passions; among the fifty-four peers, who thought him guilty of some charges as they were expressed in the articles, there were many of this description; and whatever Lord Melville's friends may say, or he *himself* may feel, such of his friends as are more sensitive to honour than he is (he has many such), cannot feel a very proud exultation, when they look at the sort of acquittal he has received, or look forward with much confidence to the future verdict of posterity and history. . . .

⟨. . .⟩ . . .

I suspect there is some foundation for the rumours of negotiation with France and Russia.[4] So far as I can learn, Lord Yarmouth is certainly gone back to Paris; though his relations and servants speak of him as being out of town. There are other circumstances which make me believe that there are communications between the Governments; and none more strong than the obvious interest of both, as well as of all the world, to come at length to terms.

. . .

1. Horner began the first part of this letter on 16 June.
2. Grenville had not followed up his earlier resolutions on the reform of the Scottish Court of Session, apparently because of illness, and so he had re-submitted them to the House of Lords on 18 June (*Hansard*, vii. 730–35).
3. There follows a lengthy summary of the speech roughly equivalent to that reported in *Hansard*.
4. In March 1806 Fox had initiated preliminary discussions with the French Government, and in June Talleyrand informed the British Government that France was willing to enter into peace negotiations with Britain and Russia on a basis of *uti possidetis*. The French offer was verbal and communicated to the Foreign Office through the medium of Francis Charles Seymour-Conway, Earl of Yarmouth and afterwards 3rd Marquess of Hertford (1777–1842: *DNB*), a close friend of the Prince of Wales and an old drinking and gaming colleague of Fox, who earlier had been detained in Paris with other British subjects by order of the French Government. The British Cabinet doubted Yarmouth's account of the French offer, but authorized him to return to Paris for the purpose of initiating informal discussions on the terms of peace. (See Taylor, pp. 67–73.)

235. To Mrs Dugald Stewart

BLPES iii. 78–9   The Temple, 30 June 1806

. . .

There is scarcely any circumstance in Lord Lauderdale's resignation of India, that gives me regret, except Matthew's disappointment;[1] and that, I hope, to his friends at least, carries its consolation along with it. His talents and activity will soon distinguish him for preferment, in a profession where the demand for those qualities is now so urgent. And Europe surely is in our present conjuncture the scene, where a man who gives himself to the public service would prefer being employed. It was for this reason, I never could understand how Lauderdale's ambition allowed him to wish for the government of India; and I am satisfied that his own reputation, the interest of his party, and the interest of liberty which is the proper business of his party, are all restored to better chances by his remaining at home. The chances for the last of these good things are much impaired, within these two weeks, by the state of Mr Fox's health; he is much better, however, since he received proper medical assistance; and the danger, with which we were threatened in consequence of the ignorance of a quack, is removed, I trust, to a great distance, and a more temperate application to business will restore our great man to health. But he cannot be permitted to engage again in the daily conflict of the House of Commons, and his place is not to be supplied.[2]

I had not heart to write to you again about Lord Melville's business; and you must hear far too much of it at Edinburgh, which must be at this time the most disgusting and melancholy scene of vulgar servility. If there is a meeting of the Faculty of Advocates to congratulate him, and about an hour ago I heard of such a thing, you will very probably see me for that day. Nothing could equal Lord Grenville's astonishment, I am told, at Melville's re-appearance in the H. of Lords. Lord Eldon had always been saying that his coming back again to public business or to public notice was quite out of the question, for hard as this venal lawyer fought for Melville he always spoke of him as guilty of that sort of criminal negligence, which the Commons might have impeached him for with success. The truth is, I believe, that till the report of Fox's illness, which was much exaggerated, Melville had made up his mind not to come down this Session: his absence from the critical and decisive division upon the Mutiny Bill is proof enough of this, but I know it [?is avowed] otherwise.[3]

1. Lauderdale had been nominated by the Government as Governor-General but the Directors refused to appoint him and a fierce quarrel ensued. However, when Fox became ill, Lauderdale withdrew from the contest and later headed the British delegation that conducted the abortive peace negotiation with France. Lord Minto was appointed Governor-General, and Mrs Stewart's stepson, Matthew, accompanied Minto as his ADC.
2. Horner's last journal entry, that of 23 June, noted that Lord Henry Petty had communicated a proposal from Lord Kinnaird to bring him into the Commons next Parliament, and that he had consented to consider it only on condition of being afforded complete independence of opinion (*Horner*, i. 287–9). See also Horner's letter to Seymour of 26 June, outlining his thoughts on the prospect of entering Parliament and noting that both his father and Whishaw had encouraged him to accept the offer, Seymour's reply of 7 July, discouraging acceptance but predicting that Horner's love of speculations in political economy would subvert his legal career, and Horner's reply of 11 July, expressing surprise at Seymour's assessment and advice (*ibid.*, i. 389–97). See also Doc. 246.
3. The Opposition fought a severe battle against Windham's military reforms and there were several crucial divisions in both Houses. But the reference here is probably to that of 13 June when the Lords followed the Commons in negativing an attempt to reject limited service as an invasion of the royal prerogative.

236. To Lord Webb Seymour

BLPES iii. 80–81 London, 5 July 1806

I have got into a little sort of scrape, from which it will be easy for you to relieve me. Among the names I gave to Count Pahlen,[1] as friends of mine at Edinburgh whom I wished him to call on, I added Walter Scott's; and I was just about to write to the minstrel, to request him to pay attention to my friend the Count, when these unhappy songs he has printed on a late occasion were brought to London, and became the subject of conversation.[2] In consequence of the very free discussion which one part of Scott's character has been subjected to, among my habitual associates here, I feel as if it would be very unpleasant to me to write to him for any thing like a favour. I must therefore request you to extricate me from this difficulty, by taking a very *early* opportunity of introducing Count Pahlen to Scott, which will set the whole matter right. You must not conceive that I am influenced on this occasion by a feeling of party resentment, which would be very unreasonable and very factious; it is really for the sake of sincerity. I cannot write to a man as a friend, whom I have just heard others call a sordid and profligate timeserver, without being able to defend him, or to refrain indeed from acquiescing expressly in the sentence of condemnation. In opposition to many of his acquaintances at Edinburgh, I had always considered Scott as a man who looked to his own pecuniary advancement almost solely in politics, and notwithstanding his poetical inspiration very much a son of the earth. But I never lowered my opinion of him so much, as to expect he would upon any occasion so prostitute his talents and his character, as he has lately done. I am happy to think that my intimacy with him never went so far as to render it necessary to assume a different degree of it in future; but if I had written now, as I did intend, it would have carried it one step farther.

. . .

1. Horner had met Count Pahlen, Secretary to the Russian Embassy in Paris, while dining at the London residence of the Duke of Somerset. He had offered to arrange introductions for him in Edinburgh, and had written to Murray for that purpose on 26 June (BLPES iii. 74–5).
2. Walter Scott's song in celebration of Melville's acquittal offended the Whigs very deeply, especially the line, 'Tally-ho to the Fox', which seemed to exult in their leader's approaching death (*Cockburn*, pp. 204–205).

237. Collections for a history of the administration and affairs of *Ireland* from . . . to . . .

BLPES viii. 12–13 17 July 1806

1. Lady Louisa Conolly told me, that it was always given out by Lord Clare, Foster, and their party, that the system of free-quarters [?compulsory and unpaid billeting]

was adopted by them with the sanction of Sir Ralph Abercromby's opinion, who gave it to them as his parting advice when he left the country that they ought to have recourse to that violent but necessary measure.[1] She said, this was always denied by those who knew Sir Ralph's character, as inconsistent with his principles and dispositions; but she was curious to know the real fact.

I inquired of James Abercromby today what he knew of this, and whether he believed there was any foundation for the falsehood. He said, as to 'parting advice', his father, when he quitted Ireland, was not on speaking terms with any one member of the Government, except Lord Clonmell;[2] and as to the free-quarters, he always considered it an unnecessary violence. He believed, he said, that there was a circumstance which might have been considered by these people as affording them a pretext for asserting his opinion to have been to the contrary. In a conversation with Foster or Clare, or both, they stated to him the necessity of having recourse to free-quarters, and grounded it upon an exaggerated statement of the condition of the country; his answer to them was distinctly this, and he had repeated it to his son; 'that if their description of the state of the country were true in point of fact, it might possibly become necessary to have recourse to such an extremity; but he did not believe the state of the country to be such; and even if it were, it was not in his opinion quite clear that it would even then be right or necessary to establish free-quarters.' This hypothetical acquiescence, upon a supposition of a state of things which he believed not to be then the fact, and, even with the supposition, so much qualified, is all the foundation for the assertion which they made so confidently.

Lady Louisa said, the *principle* upon which they justified the free-quarters, was to bring the rebellion to a crisis. Abercromby has told me too, that Lord Clare said to his father, he wished to see an hundred thousand rebels on the Curragh of Kildare, that he might try his strength with them.

The free-quarters, Lady Louisa thinks, besides the dreadful misery it occasioned, forced a great multitude to join the rebels, who were otherwise well-inclined to government.

Charles Napier, son of Lady Sarah (who was at his father's house in the country during the worst time of the rebellion, when they were all armed, the tenantry collected in the out-houses, and they were confined close to the house for months) said to me, that a great many of the tenantry were forced to join the rebels in appearance, and take pikes from them, in consequence of being abandoned by the gentry their landlords, who with great cowardice left their country seats.[3] The poor people were without arms to defend themselves; by the free-quartering system, their names were all written upon their doors, and when a party of rebels passed through, they called out the men from their houses, and forced them to take pikes.

Abercromby says, his father's great object was to restore the civil authority, and for that purpose to prevent officers from being justices of peace, and to have no military interference without the sanction of the civil power.

1. Louisa Augusta (d. 1821) was the daughter of the 2nd Duke of Richmond and widow of an Irish magnate, Thomas Conolly (1738–1803: DNB). Clare, the Lord Chancellor of Ireland, had been a staunch opponent of Catholic Emancipation. Gen. Sir Ralph Abercromby (1734–1801: DNB), the father of Horner's friend, had commanded the troops in Ireland at the time of the rebellion in 1798.

2. John Scott, Earl of Clonmell (1739–98: *DNB*), had been Chief Justice in Ireland.
3. Charles James (afterwards Lt Gen. Sir Charles) Napier (1782–1853: *DNB*), was the eldest son of Lady Louisa Conolly's sister Sarah (d. 1826).

238. To Thomas Thomson

⟨*Thomson*, pp. 112–14⟩   Ryde, Thursday evening [?28 Aug. 1806][1]

⟨. . . We are just arrived here from Portsmouth; we shall lounge in the island three days, and mean to reach Southampton on Monday evening. You had much better come down here, and assist Murray and me in our efforts to seduce Jeffrey from his resolutions of hastening back to London, that he may hasten away to Scotland.

. . . We had two days . . . of Rogers and Petty, who were more at their ease than in the midst of the business and fastidious terrors of London. We had no politics at all, and the scandal was not more than was very amusing, sixty miles off from all parties concerned, and tinctured with Sam's peculiar humour. . . .⟩[2]

1. *Thomson* dates it 29 Aug., but that was a Friday.
2. The 'scandal' to which Horner refers was the duel of 11 Aug. between Jeffrey and Thomas Moore in which Horner acted as Jeffrey's second and Dr Thomas Hume (?1769–1850: *DNB*) as Moore's. Apparently the quarrel concerned Jeffrey's interpretation of the motives behind Moore's poetry, and the confrontation occurred shortly after the arrival of Jeffrey and Murray in London, to which they had come with an eye to a tour of the south of England with Horner. In the Horner MSS at Kinnordy are various letters concerning the duel including the original holograph of Moore's challenge dated 9 Aug. There is also a letter from Jeffrey to Horner containing instructions to be followed in the event of Jeffrey's death and a memorandum by Horner and Hume dated 12 Aug. which seeks to explain how police officials at Bow Street Magistrates' Court came to find that only one of the pistols (Moore's) contained a ball. For further comment on the duel see *Moore*, i. 206–207, and Alexander Dyce, *Recollections of the Table-Talk of Samuel Rogers* (2nd ed., 1856), pp. 279–80.

239. To Francis Jeffrey

BLPES iii. 88–9 ⟨*Horner*, i. 397–400⟩   The Temple, 15 Sept. 1806

⟨It was the day you left us that Fox was again taken ill; and he is now no more.[1] . . . It is a cruel disappointment, if one thinks of the hopes so recently indulged;[2] and a cheerless prospect forward. The giant race is extinct; and we are left in the hands of little ones, whom we know to be diminutive, having measured them against the others. . . . I look upon what has been called Mr Fox's party, the remains of the old Whig faction, as extinguished entirely with him; his name alone kept the fragments together, after the party had been long ago broken to pieces. At the same time, I cannot resist the conviction, that, in spite of appearances, there is in the middling order of people in this country a broad foundation for a popular party, constituted by the opinions, interests, and habits of those numerous families who are characterized by moderate but increasing incomes, a careful education of their youth, and a strict observance of the great common virtues. No doubt, this is the genuine democracy, if they preserve their weight in that public voice, which government must obey. Many circumstances have occurred of late years to depress the just influence of that order of men; and it is melancholy to think, that they are the very circumstances which have brought other free governments to an end – an overgrown foreign trade, the dependencies proceeding from too bulky a system of finance, and an augmentation of the military force on account of foreign danger. These causes, I am persuaded, have already both undermined our institutions, and vitiated the sentiments and character of the nation. At the same time, it does strike me very forcibly, that the great number among whom wealth is diffused in considerable yet equal portions, the tolerably good education that accompanies it, the strength of physical and moral forces that are thus combined in a population to which both order and freedom are necessary, form a new case very different from any former example; and it is from this aspect of our condition, that I take my hopes of there being still a chance of defending successfully the liberties of England, chance enough to make it a reproach for ever against the present age if it does not make a trial at least. We are deprived, by this calamitous death, of our great leader in all popular principles of administration; no man of acknowledged and commanding talents is left to supply his place. But there are a few men whose integrity and steadiness have been tried; and a few others, younger men, who are confided in by those who know them best. Howick, Lauderdale, Holland, and Petty, are the persons in whom I am inclined to repose my confidence; though it seems to me, that they ought to yield the supremacy to Grenville, while he perseveres in the same honourable conduct to which he has adhered since his junction with Mr Fox. The new appointment will be a sort of test; not precisely the disposal of the seals, but the manner in which the vacant seat in the Cabinet is filled.[3] I look with very great solicitude to the course of parties during the next six months; it will be a period probably, though not at first, of severe and decisive probation. I have no fears of Lord Grenville himself; he is free from all levity or fickleness of conduct, certainly, and has given pledges which he has too much obstinacy as well as honesty to forfeit. A few years of opposition gave him some sentiments which will remain; and the circumstances of his family, their influence, fortune, and pretensions, make them now a knot of aristocrats, not ready to submit to the crown, but disposed to make terms.⟩ A little more of this is wanting; the corruption and separation of what there formerly subsisted, is one of the unfortunate changes that was effected during Pitt's reign. ⟨You perceive, therefore, that I consider an alliance with the⟩ unbending, grasping aristocracy of the ⟨Grenvilles as a measure of prudence for the Whigs; but my speculations will perhaps appear as fallacious, as you would think the subject of them unworthy of a *philosopher's* approbation, even if they were better founded in themselves. . . .

⟨I have this morning got Walter Scott's volume of Ballads; he has not mended that sad rhyme of Catchedicam, the absurdity and meanness of which spoils a very pleasing set of verses.[4] . . .⟩

1. Allen, who with the Hollands attended Fox during his final illness, wrote regular reports to

Horner between 1 and 13 Sept. that chronicle the last days of the Whig leader's life (BLPES viii. 14–28).

2. In a letter of 17 Sept. to Mrs William Robert Spencer, Horner identified these 'hopes' as peace and the abolition of the slave trade (*Horner*, i. 402).

3. The struggle which ensued revealed the internal weaknesses of the Whig coalition. Compromise between the Foxite and Grenvillite factions became possible when Fitzwilliam volunteered to bow out of the Cabinet to make room for Tom Grenville, who became First Lord of the Admiralty. Sidmouth climbed from the office of Privy Seal to that of President of the Council so that Holland could assume the former. Howick became Foreign Secretary and leader in the Commons with the understanding that the Foreign Office would go to Holland upon Howick's elevation to the Lords. Tierney succeeded Tom Grenville at the Board of Control, and Bragge Bathurst became Master of the Mint. These arrangements, which increased the relative strength of the minority Grenvillite faction, infuriated many influential Foxites (*Lady Holland's Journal*, ii. 185) and laid the foundation for future difficulties. The Duke of Bedford noted 'the vast chasm which the death of Fox has left in our political strength and consequence as a party' (Bedford to Howick, 29 Sept., Grey MSS, Durham University), and Sidmouth predicted with unusual sagacity that the loss of Fox would change the 'relation in which we stand to all foreign countries' (*Addington*, ii. 433). An account of the Cabinet negotiations is in the journal of John Allen, entries of 2 Aug. and 19 and 25 Sept., BL Add. MSS 52204A-1.

4. See *Horner*, i. 400n, and Doc. 241.

240. From Francis Jeffrey

⟨*Jeffrey*, ii. 110–13⟩   Edinburgh, 18 Sept. 1806

⟨. . . I agree with you entirely in thinking that there is in the opulence, intelligence, and morality of our middling people a sufficient quarry of materials to make or to repair a free constitution; but the difficulty is in raising them to the surface. The best of them meddle least with politics; and, except as jurymen or justices of peace, they exercise scarcely any influence upon the public proceedings of the society. The actual government of the country is carried on by something less, I take it, than 200 individuals, who are rather inclined to believe that they may do anything they please, so long as the more stirring part of the community can be seduced by patronage, and the more contemplative by their ease and their dread of violence and innovation. You must falsify the premises of this reasoning by a great moral reform before you can challenge the conclusion. You must make our adventurers and daring spirits more honest, and our honest and intelligent men more daring and ambitious; or, rather, you must find out some channel through which the talent and principle of the latter may be brought to bear upon the actual management of affairs, and may exert its force in controlling or directing the measures of government in some more efficient way than in discoursing in private companies, or lamenting in epistles. This is the problem. There is a great partition set up between the energy that is to save the country, and the energy that is to destroy it; the latter alone is in action, and the other cannot get through to stop it. I scarcely see anything but a revolution, or some other form of violence, that can beat down the ancient and ponderous barrier. . . . The antiquity of our government, to which we are indebted for so many advantages, brings this great compensating evil along with it; there is an oligarchy of great families – borough mongers and intriguing adventurers – that monopolizes all public activity, and excludes the mass of ordinary men nearly as much as the formal institutions of other countries. How can you hope to bring the virtues of the people to bear on the vices of the government, when the only way in which a patriot can approach to the scene of action is by purchasing a seat in Parliament? A correct view of our actual constitution, I have often thought, would be a curious thing, and a careful examination of it ought, at all events, to precede any attempt at reform. ...⟩

241. To Francis Jeffrey

BLPES iii. 94–5   Woolbeding,[1] 26 Sept. 1806

...

Allen, when I saw him last, desired me to let you know that George Lamb will send you for this number a review of Holcraft's tales in verse.[2] ...

I expected to have sent you something by this time; but I have you in mind. I have a great notion of trying a very short article on Walter Scott's volume of Ballads; and to better myself for it, I read his Lay over again on my way down here yesterday. I mean to try tonight what I can do. I have brought the Mysore Survey too.[3]

... I thank you very much for your political letter, though there is more revolutionary doctrine in it than I have relished for a long while; you and Cobbett are turned mere Jacobins. There is much truth, alas! in what both of you say of our actual condition, though the remedy needed is not so desperate; if others do not succeed, I have no doubt that [?the political establishment] will at length put itself upon trial. ...

...

1. Lord Robert Spencer's place near Midhurst: 'small, comfortable, and quite luxurious, from the perpetual attentions of its owners to the comfort and convenience of their guests and of themselves.' (Fox, pp. 185–6.)
2. This would seem to confirm the attribution made to George Lamb of the notice of Holcroft's Tales in ER ix (no. xvii, Oct. 1806), 101–111.
3. No notice of Scott's Ballads and Lyrical Pieces (1806) subsequently appeared in the ER. The 'Mysore Survey' is probably Mark Wilks's Report on the Interior Administration, Resources, and Expenditure of the Government of Mysoor (Fort William, 1805), a copy of which, bearing Mackintosh's signature, appears in HL no. 245. No notice of it appeared in the ER, and though a review of Wilks's later work on Mysore did appear in xviii (no. xxxvi, Aug. 1811), 343–70, its content makes it very unlikely to have been contributed by Horner.

242. To Mrs William Robert Spencer

BLPES iii. 95–7 (copy or draft)   [London], Saturday [11 Oct. 1806]

The ceremony of yesterday[1] is said to have been very well conducted; it seemed to me very solemn, and I found some parts of it very affecting – especially the sight of poor Holland and Lord Fitzwilliam, as they passed up the cathedral. The only complaint I have heard is against the Prince's absence, which is imputed to a notice on the part of the King that it would be contrary to rule to appear at a private funeral; but I have not heard on any good authority, that this was the true reason. If it be so, I cannot understand what rule there is upon the subject, or why the P. is seized all at once with a fit of obedience; and it would be truly contemptible to see them standing upon their miserable punctilios of monarchy nowadays, when it seems to depend so much on the men of talents in the country whether they are to keep their crowns or lose them. I look upon the funeral yesterday as a noble triumph; because it was given not to office, but to a life distinguished by opinions almost always unpopular: and to those who recollect the time when they were most so, it was no trifling satisfaction to see mixed together in the train those who were then in opposite extremes, Lord Grenville, etc. with Mess. Godwin, etc., and are now agreed in doing homage to the man who reprobated the violence of both, though he thought one more pernicious than the other. . . .

1. Fox's funeral.

243. To J.A. Murray

BLPES iii. 99–100 〈*Horner*, i. 404–405〉   The Temple, 27 Oct. 1806

〈. . .〉
The result of Lord Morpeth's dispatches yesterday, is, that between the 10th and 14th Prince Hohenlohe gained some advantage over Soult, but on the 14th the Prussians were defeated with great loss – Prince Louis killed, the Duke of Brunswick wounded, and (it was said) the King.[1] The Prussians, I take it for granted will very soon make whatever Peace Bonaparte will give them. Prince Louis is said to have been the only man of enterprising talents in the family; he was very popular in the army, and the war of which he has fallen the first victim, is said to have been chiefly instigated by himself. His popularity and abilities subjected him to the suspicions of the royal family; Prince Henri said of him to Lord Holland, 'C'est notre Duc d'Orléans'.
〈. . .〉
〈Brougham will receive orders for his return this week;[2] it is very much to be regretted that he was not at home at this time, for he left no instructions with any person about Parliament, and the sum necessary is too great for any of us to have become answerable for it. Had he been here, he would have judged for himself, and his activity would have carried his object through all obstacles. It cannot be long, however, before a good opportunity will occur; he is too well known now, for him to be suffered to lie unemployed: and that is the scene, I am sure, where he may be employed to the best advantage.
〈You will be glad to hear there is a report that Canning, Frere, etc. mean to back their parliamentary exertions with another newspaper of fun and wit;[3] some of our

friends will be scratched, no doubt, but the mischief will not be worse than that, and we shall have some merriment. . . .⟩

1. Shortly after illness had forced Fox to abandon the Foreign Office, and as peace negotiations between France, Britain, and Russia continued, the French Government, fearing the formation of a new continental coalition, resolved to crush Prussia before negotiation could settle King Frederick William's differences with Britain over Hanover. France demanded that Prussia disarm and ordered French troops in Germany to prepare for battle. Prussia appealed to Britain and Russia and the Tsar placed the resources of the Russian Empire at the disposal of his ally, but Britain hedged owing to disagreement between the peace and war factions in the Cabinet. At last, over the objection of Holland, Morpeth was sent as plenipotentiary to Berlin. He departed without the slightest idea of British intentions, and from Weimar he virtually begged Howick 'to speak more specifically' and for powers to negotiate an alliance. But in the meantime Napoleon engaged the Prussians on 10 October and by the 15th the Prussian army was in ruins on the field of Jena. (See Taylor, pp. 85–90.)

2. From Lisbon where he had acted as secretary to Lords Rosslyn and St Vincent.

3. Nothing seems to have come of this rumour, perhaps because John Hookham Frere (1769–1846: *DNB*), the friend of Canning and like his younger brother Bartholomew, a diplomat, was shortly recalled to service abroad. The first issue of the *Quarterly Review* did not appear until 1809, and that was hardly a 'newspaper of fun and wit'.

244. To Francis Jeffrey

BLPES iii. 103–104   St Ives, 2 Nov. 1806

. . .

I seemed to behave as shabbily as ever about the last review, but you had long ceased to put any trust to me, and I have no longer left to me the motive of a character to lose. I ought to explain however, the circumstance of your receiving half an article, and perhaps having had the trouble of ordering it to be printed. The day after I sent out those tables, which I thought might give the printer some difficulty, I received notice of the dissolution;[1] . . . I had besides no reason for reviewing George Rose's pamphlet, except that of taking an opportunity to argue against Whitbread's notice of a motion upon the poor laws, so far as he spoke of enforcing the statutes of Elizabeth with respect to employment.[2] It would not be becoming now to oppose him in *this* way. Of course, you will expect little or nothing from me, if I come into Parliament;[3] for every spare hour, that the law leaves me, I shall devote to the public business of the day – a poor exchange, I dare say it is, and I know you will say, for the idleness or easy work I have indulged myself with hitherto; but I have made my choice. One or two things I wish still to give you; my old debts of Malthus and Lancaster, but if you leave them to me, which perhaps you will not, you must likewise leave me my own time.[4] I hope you will not come to any sudden resolution of giving up the *Review*, without letting me know in time. Perhaps I shall find that Lancaster is already in this Number . . .

1. Horner made a similar reference to an incomplete article in a letter to Murray of 11 Nov. (BLPES iii. 107–108). There seems to be no trace of any 'tables' in the ER about this time; but the rest of the statement adds support to the notion that he may have been joint author

of the review of Foster's *Essay on Commercial Exchanges*: see p. 217 and Doc. 176.

2. George Rose (1744–1818: *DNB*), a close political associate of Pitt, had published in 1802 his *Observations on the Poor Laws, and on the management of the Poor, in Great Britain, arising from a consideration of the returns, now before Parliament*. In 1806, without collaboration with the Whig Ministry that had denied him Cabinet rank, Whitbread gave notice of a motion for the reform of the poor law (see Doc. 259), which found virtually no support but inspired Malthus's *Letter to Samuel Whitbread, Esq., MP, on his proposed Bill for the Amendment of the Poor Laws* (Mar. 1807). For an account of the poor law controversy of 1805–1806, which Horner prudently avoided, see Inglis, pp. 91–4.

3. At the time Horner wrote this letter he was engaged in the canvass at St Ives that first returned him to Parliament. For Horner's description of the successful canvass see his letters to his mother of 31 Oct. and to Murray of 4 Nov., *Horner*, i. 406–408.

4. See Doc. 227 n. 2.

245. To Thomas Thomson

⟨*Thomson*, pp. 114–16⟩ The Temple, 15 Nov. 1806

⟨We are in strict observance of our old ceremonious silence, but I am tired of it, and become very impatient to hear from you, and to hear ... of your judicial reformations, which I fear are most sadly and culpably neglected. It will be no justification of all this, when it comes to be judged of, that John Clerk's time was occupied with electioneering. It ought not to be left to John Clerk alone, not to any single person; least of all to one who knows the established practicks, but nothing of any other establishment, or of any theory. ... I cannot recollect an instance where the occasion was ever so open for important innovations. Lord Grenville is evidently desirous that his Administration should be distinguished by a measure of this high order, and, knowing nothing of the particular subject, he has no prejudices to embarrass him, nor any theory of his own to force upon you. He wishes to do what is best and comes best recommended, and is open to all plans and suggestions. I must say, then, that if the work is ill done, or half done, or not done at all (of which I have some fears), it will be for ever to the shame of the men who hold such means in their hands, and will not direct them. Everything else you can do in your own time is, for reputation, nothing, compared with the introduction of juries into your system, upon wise and practical principles. It is not to be done by saying the word, as Lord Grenville perhaps fancies, but the difficulties cannot be greater than to give honour to the achievement. I say all this in the way of exhortation, and hope we shall not have to repeat it in the way of reproach. A very short time will show.

⟨Jeremy Bentham is at work upon the subject, to what purpose I do not know yet, but I hope soon to hear. I have sent him, through Whishaw, all the pamphlets that have appeared, and the book called *Form of Process*.[1] He ought to be exhorted to print. Though his talent is much more to criticize than to build anew, he cannot fail to suggest many useful reflections. ...⟩

1. Doc. 285 indicates that this last was by Reddie. The other items presumably included those reviewed by Jeffrey (see Doc. 233). For Bentham's work see Doc. 264.

246. To J.A. Murray

BLPES iii. 110–15   The Temple, 15 Nov. 1806

I cannot help being uneasy at the account you give me of Jeffrey's health, and am made still more by some expressions about 'feverishness' which he uses himself. . . . That constant distress of mind, which he indulges (I must say) so wilfully, may have made inroads upon his constitution; and this fever, and loss of appetite, if unattended to, may gain upon him irrecoverably. His disease of mind, I own, is still a problem to me; with that understanding and temper so beautifully regulated, surrounded by friends who adore him more than he sees any one else adored, what is it that disgusts him so with the world? The loss of his wife is no explanation; and, whatever he may believe in his own mind, is but one feature of his melancholy. Fame he has got, as much as he has tried for it, and he is upon the road to professional success, if he would condescend to take it: he has only to give up that cursed *Review*, and try other things, to have as much professional employment or still higher reputation as the wishes of man can desire. I have often conjectured, and it gains upon me, that ambition, only disappointed because he would not step forward, lies at the heart of his mystery; and though he filled the void by the better pleasures of domestic confidence and indolence, the breaking up of his little household has left his mind lacerated by the double disappointment. But why is he not married again? I fear there is some secret in this, some vow or promise as we suspected at the first.[1] I would not pry into his sorrows; but yet I feel the greatest curiosity to understand what it is, that robs so much excellence of its natural reward, and leaves so unhappy the rarest union I have ever seen yet of the most penetrating talents and the most delicate virtue.

. . .

Paull's numbers have surprised me; for I have heard the number stated higher than 2,500, which any man who can make speeches may get in Westminster, provided he is very active; and this without expense.[2] What Paull has got more, he owes to the unpopularity of Sheridan among the tradesmen, on account of the swindling life he has always led. I do not believe Lord Wellesley's affair has affected the election one way or other. Paull has also derived some advantage, from the illiberal abuse he has met with, on the score of his origin and his father's trade – topics not very likely to be successful in a place where hundreds are rising in the same course, or have risen.

Different explanations are given of Lord Percy's conduct about Westminster; I do not hear what his friends make of it, or whether they have any thing to say. Among others, one story is that he was sickened and took fright at the noise of the hustings; another, that the Duke thought Sheridan, not being a man of family, an unfit colleague for his heir apparent; a third, that his Grace took offence at some neglect of Government in giving him notice of the Dissolution. They are all likely to be true; if indeed it is worth while to ascertain the conduct of a diseased capricious old peer, who has nothing in his head but gout, and whose conduct nobody ever relied on. The scene that followed at Cambridge, and the night-journey to Launceston, have completed the ruin of his son's character in public life.[3]

The Norfolk election will go right, we hope; and the Hampshire election will be as Government wishes it. The great triumph for us, the Foxites and Abolitionists, is Roscoe's success at Liverpool; that in Yorkshire is good too, though clouded a little by the warlike affected speech ascribed to Fawkes in the newspapers.[4]

I am amused with your credulity about Treasury money in the Scotch elections; as much as with the common-place credulity of [William] Adam in his reports from Scotland, as if it were any triumph to get numbers only in the Scotch representation, without looking to the men, and to make a new lease only with the old tenants. It is not necessary for Lord Melville to play the game for himself, when his antagonists play so stupidly into his hand. Of course you have heard of his circular letter to the peers, which is quite worthy of himself and of them.[5]

I have suffered considerable uneasiness from Kinnaird's refusal to be a candidate; don't mention this while there may be a chance of his being prevailed upon; but so the fact is at present. It would be infinitely more comfortable to me, to have him in London actively engaged in the same pursuit with my other friends.[6]

. . .

1. Jeffrey's wife Catherine, whom he had married in November 1801, had died in August 1805. Previously he had lost their only child and a favourite sister. He did not remarry until 1813; see Doc. 523.
2. James Paull (1720–1808: DNB), whose father had been a tailor, having as MP for Newtown, IOW, gained popularity by calling for papers relating to Lord Wellesley's dealings with the Nabob of Oude, had unsuccessfully contested Westminster in the General Election of November 1806. The successful candidates were Sheridan and Sir Samuel Hood (1762–1814: DNB), with 4,758 and 5,478 votes respectively, against Paull's 4,481.
3. Hugh, Lord Percy, afterwards 3rd Duke of Northumberland (1785–1847: DNB), had been elected unopposed as Fox's successor at Westminster in October 1806, but the electors were dissatisfied at the lack of a contest and the Duke thought it discreet to withdraw his son from the impending contest at the General Election against such powerful opponents as Sheridan and Paull. Percy had then considered standing for Cambridge and had made his pretensions public, but had abandoned the scheme abruptly in favour of a family seat at Launceston. Palmerston had been given fright by the prospect of Percy challenging his interest among the Johnians at Cambridge and on that account was no less prejudiced than Horner against Percy. (PH ii. 269–70; Palmerston Letters, pp. 68–70, n. 2.)
4. In Norfolk T.W. Coke and W. Windham were returned, keeping out the Tory candidate, the Hon. John Wodehouse, and though the election was afterwards declared void, Wodehouse refused to take advantage of it. At Liverpool the Foxite (and author of the despised Life of Leo) William Roscoe (1753–1831: DNB) dislodged Gen., afterwards Sir, Banastre Tarleton (1754–1833: DNB). William Wilberforce and Walter Ramsden Fawkes (1769–1825: DNB) were returned unopposed in Yorkshire. (PH ii. 228, 286, and 436.)
5. Lady Holland's Journal noted on 12 Dec. (ii. 191): 'The Scotch Peers elections have gone well; Ld Melville was cruelly disappointed, he expected to carry four, and only carried Ld Aberdeen.'
6. Kinnaird was elected a Scottish representative peer later in the year. For further evidence of Horner's uneasiness about accepting Kinnaird's closed borough see his letter to Murray of 19 Nov. in Horner, i. 408–409. See also Jeffrey's letter to Horner of 25 Nov., which scolds Horner for self-delusion and after a perceptive analysis of Horner's talents, ambitions, and tactics, encourages his commitment to a political career and predicts that he will become a minister of state. (Jeffrey, ii. 114–21; Horner, i. 411–12, gives an excerpt only.)

247. To James Loch

BLPES iii. 120–21   Cannon Row,[1] 1 Dec. [1806]

Are you able, from accounts already in your hands, to tell me how much quicksilver has at any time been exported from China in [the East India] Company's ships or others; if you have not such accounts, can you make an inquiry at the India House upon the subject?

What would come still nearer to the purpose I have in view, I wish you would learn from those who have such information, how much quicksilver *might* be procured in China, if it were made an object of our Indian trade.

   1. I.e. the Board of Control.

248. To John Allen

BL Add. MSS 52180, ff. 40–41   The Temple, Wednesday Morning [?Dec. 1806][1]

Is it true that a non-importation law was to take effect in America on the 15th of last month, and that the Government had no dispensing power? You see I am reduced to the newspapers for my intelligence.

I hope they are all wrong too in their stories about a prohibition, by the Privy Council, of transfers of stock (and I suppose private debts too) that stand in foreign names. It was done before, in the cases of Holland and Switzerland in 1798; but surely it is against all honesty, as well as policy. No principle seems so clear, as the obligation to keep faith and pay your debts; and if any motive were necessary to give it additional confirmation on the present occasion, it would be found in the wisdom of showing to all foreign capitalists, that there is one sure place for depositing their property in times of peril. These appear to be most powerful arguments against the measure; and what is there to be said for it? It can yield no indemnity to those who suffer by the violence of France; and as to the notion of keeping this property, that it may not go to increase the means and resources of Bonaparte, it is too puerile to be endured. And yet this last, I believe, was all that that profound statesman Lord Redesdale had to say for his bills in 1798, when he proposed them to the House of Commons, which appears to have allowed them to pass without discussion.[2]

I have not learned much yet respecting the China trade in quicksilver; but I understand, that whereas it used to be an article of export from that country, it has been quite otherwise since the year 1803, a large profit being gained by the captains of ships and private merchants who have carried out quicksilver from this country to Canton. It is not yet made an article of the Company's investments. The profit made by some of the adventurers in the last voyage, was as high, I am told, as 120 per cent; a monopoly price, of course, from the trade being a new one, and their getting the start of others. The Chinese merchants said to our traders, that they would continue to give as high a price; and explained the new demand for the article, by alledging [*sic*], that their own mines of quicksilver are worked out. As one may speculate upon every thing Chinese quite at one's ease, on account of our ignorance, it would not be very unreasonable perhaps, from the two facts put together – of a new demand for quicksilver – and a cessation of the demand for bullion, to conjecture, not that the mines of quicksilver are exhausted, but that those of the precious metals are become more productive.

Our private traders, and the captains of East India Ships, have likewise for a few years past carried out adventures of quicksilver to Bombay, which have always turned out profitable. Some persons have suspected, that from Bombay it may be carried to Manilla, and from thence to Spanish America. But the truth of this is not ascertained.

When I learn more you shall hear from me again.

1. The letter is endorsed '1807', but that was probably the year of receipt since the substance seems to refer to the Non-Importation Act of April 1806 which came into force on 15 Nov., though it was again suspended by the President on 3 Dec.
2. See AR xl (1798), 222, where the bill is said to have passed 'without opposition'.

249. To J.A. Murray

BLPES iii. 122–5   The Temple, 5 Dec. 1806

. . .

There is a very fine general question, at least I expect it will take the turn of a general one, in the law of parliament, which arises upon the petition against Cook Taylor's return for Barnstaple, who has asked me to be his nominee: viz. whether in burghs paupers are disqualified from voting, by receiving parish relief.[1] I wish you would turn it in your mind, and write to me the different views you take of it, and, what is always a material help, where your difficulties and doubts lie. The old cases are collected in Heywood; and the Colchester case in Peckwell is worth looking into.[2] . . .

1. The reference to 'Cook Taylor' is puzzling. William Taylor (b. 1782) of Ardmillan, Ayr, had been returned for Barnstaple in November 1806. There were individuals bearing the name 'Cook' or 'Cooke Taylor', but they had no known connection with the MP, who had been a member of the Academy of Physics and the Speculative with Horner's set. Taylor was thought to be a Whig sympathizer and the petition, if it was pursued, was unsuccessful. But he proved unreliable and more a supporter of Canning than anything else. (PH v. 344–5.)
2. See Samuel Heywood, *A Digest of so much of the Law respecting Borough Elections, as concerns Cities and Boroughs in general* (1797), and Appendix 'No. 1 The Borough of Colchester', in Sir Robert Henry Peckwell (afterwards Blosset), *Cases on Controverted Elections in the Second Parliament of the United Kingdom* (2 vols, 1805–1806), i. 503–511.

250. To J.A. Murray

BLPES iii. 126–7 ⟨Horner, i. 413–14⟩   The Temple, 25 Dec. 1806

. . .

⟨I have scarcely had time to write for some days past, but there has not been much to tell you of. Lord Howick's speech is reckoned the best he has ever made;[1] so Tierney says, and I overheard [Spencer] Perceval make the same remark. It seemed to me a speech of considerable ability, and parts of it were admirable in point of manner and sentiment; I particularly liked his account of Sir Home Popham,[2] and his asserting the honour and discipline of the service, in defiance of the low manufacturing popularity with which that⟩ freebooter[3] ⟨will be received. It is difficult to judge, from such a specimen as the moving an address, what powers Lamb will have for debate; he has evidently the most striking manner and voice of any person that is yet known in the House.[4] Your friend Canning made an able speech certainly, but a very injudicious one⟩, as is usual with him; and I suspect, if it was possible to lower his character for talents and discretion as a politician, that it is a good deal lower among those of his own side than it was before he moved that strange pamphleteering amendment.[5] ⟨It seemed a piece of personal ostentation; and perhaps a device to fix himself in the throne of Opposition, the settlement of which seems not yet regulated. I look upon it as a serious misfortune to the country, that it is for the present deprived of that important part of our political system; a party arrayed against the Ministers, for the purposes of popular vigilance and inquisition, upon fixed and assignable principles.⟩ The present set are the refuse underlings of the public offices; and have no other system, but to cavil vexatiously at every thing, till offers shall be made of taking them into place.

1. That of 19 Dec. on the Address (*Hansard*, viii. 61–76).
2. Rear Admiral Sir Home Riggs Popham (1762–1820: *DNB*) and General Sir David Baird (1757–1829: *DNB*) had been dispatched by Pitt in 1805 in command of an expedition against the Dutch colony at the Cape of Good Hope. In January 1806 the colony had surrendered, and Popham had proceeded without orders to Rio de la Plata. In June his force captured Buenos Aires, and afterwards Popham had announced the conquest in an extraordinary manifesto addressed to Britain's trading corporations that outlined the commercial advantages offered by the conquest of South America while simultaneously appealing to the British Government for reinforcements to attack Montevideo. After word of the French victory at Jena reached London, the British Government entertained a number of dubious schemes for the conquest of Spain's dominions in the New World but Howick paradoxically denounced Popham in the Commons. Enthusiasm for South American conquest was dampened on 2 Jan. 1807 when word arrived that Popham had evacuated Buenos Aires in the face of annihilation. (See Taylor, pp. 79–81 and 107–110.)
3. Leonard Horner substituted 'unscrupulous commander' in the printed version.
4. William Lamb, afterwards 2nd Viscount Melbourne (1779–1848: *DNB*), had moved the address of reply on 19 Dec. (*Hansard*, viii. 35–41).
5. *Ibid.*, viii. 44–61.

251. To Lord Webb Seymour

BLPES iii. 136–9 ⟨Horner, i. 414–18⟩　　　　　　　　　The Temple, 29 Dec. 1806

⟨. . .

⟨Our military arrangements remain still a very important subject of parliamentary discussion; though what is yet to be done rests more with the executive Government, Parliament having already furnished, in the way of plans and facilities, a great deal more than has been acted upon. The vigilant superintendence of the manner in which legislative measures are carried into execution, is no doubt an unceasing and imperious duty to the two Houses. I agree with you perfectly upon the subject of the Duke of York; and have always entertained an opinion, that the present Ministers are not aware of their own strength in shirking from a struggle upon that question, in which they would be supported very generally by the country, by all the best part of it, all but the most blind worshippers of the gracious sovereign.[1] At the same time, it is not doing justice to the men now in power, to forget that, upon the military arrangements, they have introduced a most important innovation, in opposition to the Duke of York, the King, the court, the old staff, and all the tribes of retainers that depend upon these; and that they put to hazard their power and their places, though one or two among themselves, whom the public, or at least history, will hear of at some future period, were cowardly and corrupt enough to think of abandoning the question. I am induced to mention this circumstance to *you*, that you may feel a little more confidence than I perceive you do, in the disposition of our present Administration towards useful innovation. In the present session, I expect, as we saw in the last, they are much more likely to be opposed for innovating what is called too much, than for a contrary line of conduct. With respect to military affairs, my apprehensions take very much that turn; and the language I sometimes hear used by those who call for new and great measures, fills me with disquiet.

⟨The sort of army, and the means of raising it, that some people want, would only be a less evil than conquest by a foreign invader; what I wish to see preserved from French subjugation, is not the physical England alone, with its two-footed inhabitants, but artificial England, the constitution, and that marvellous exception to all common experience – the freedom of the people. I have a great confidence in the efficacy of this system to furnish the means of its own defence; and those persons who think the same sort of exceptions and sacrifices necessary for us, as for the languid old monarchies of the continent, overlook, it seems to me, both the advantages of insular situation, and the resources that grow out of the established habits and feelings of political liberty. The present Ministers have difficulties which it will be the greatest of all glories to surmount; if they can steer their course with a firm hand, between the selfish prejudices of the court against improvements that touch its own immediate possessions and abuses, and, on the other hand, the clamours of the frightened public for innovation, disproportioned to a temporary danger. To recur to first principles, is to resolve our complex machine of immunities and privileges into its two simple elements of multitude and violence; and after deluding ourselves with the vision of a splendid military power, we should awake slaves in a camp. Depend upon it, the question is not so short as you have put it.⟩

I have not heard any thing till yesterday of the recruiting service, when I was informed, that it has gone on more actively since the new terms upon which it is now established, than it had done for years before.

I am as much in the dark as you about the *delicate measure* which the newspapers speak of; there is nothing, I dare say, to warrant the expression.[2]

⟨My anxieties are fixed upon quite another subject from that which occupies your letter – Ireland, where there is the fairest and surest opportunity of doing good, not only against the present danger, but through all the succeeding ages of this country, and where there are the materials of unceasing agitation, perhaps of some fatal explosion, if that opportunity be neglected. Since the present Administration came into power, they have adopted a new set of maxims for the government of that injured country, and have enforced them by including Catholics in their distribution of patronage, as well as by repressing, as much as possible, the hostile and malignant spirit of the Orangemen. While Mr Fox lived, whose power the Catholics regarded as a pledge that as much would be done for them as was practicable, the continuance of this impartial and mild spirit of Administration might have anticipated the effects of more decisive measures; but now, some of these are absolutely necessary, in order to renew a pledge which they lost by his death. It is something, that Ministers have been able to crush the late disturbances, without stepping out of the forms of the law; and to my mind, this is a contrast with the proceedings of former governments, that would alone attach me to the present. But I am persuaded the time is now come, when that which ought to have been bestowed long ago, as an act of justice to that country, must be conceded as a precaution for our own security. You know where the difficulty lies upon the subject; with our gracious sovereign again, and the bigots of the church establishment. Whether our Ministers have determined any thing upon the subject, I do not know; I speak only of my own wishes and fears. I shall regard it as a fatal oversight, if another session of Parliament shall pass away, without a most decisive measure being adopted with regard to the church revenues of Ireland, and the rights of Catholic subjects to rise in the army and the state.[3]

⟨. . .⟩

1. See Doc. 219.
2. Probably a reference to the Cabinet's recommendations to the King on the report of the 'Delicate Investigation' into the accusations made against the Princess of Wales by Major-General Sir John and Lady Douglas. (See *POW* vi. 104–110.)
3. Horner's interpretation of the Ministry's Irish policy is misleading. In opposition Fox had given the Catholics every reason to expect immediate relief in the event of a Whig ministry. Indeed, the Catholic question was the glue that held together his fragile union with Grenville and Fitzwilliam during 1804 and 1805 (Taylor, pp. 39–40), and upon coming to power he had told Windham that the Catholic cause was the only reason he had resumed an active role in politics in 1802 (Fox to Windham, [1806], BL Add. MSS 37843, ff. 241–2). As Foreign Secretary, however, he had regarded peace with France as a necessary prerequisite to any major domestic reform, and had therefore sought to delay the dangerous question of Catholic Emancipation until peace was concluded. He had successfully discouraged the Irish petition and promised piecemeal concessions with the remark that Catholic leaders must 'decide between a friendly ministry without immediate discussion of their claims, or an immediate discussion of their claims with a hostile ministry'

(*Holland Memoirs*, i. 213). Such tactics had, however, undermined his support in Ireland and led to the formation of a powerful and unfriendly Catholic association as early as March 1806, and afterwards the unfortunate Irish Administration of the Duke of Bedford had alienated Catholic leaders still further. In December 1806 the Whig Ministry was some three months away from its fatal decision to advance legislation enabling Catholics to be commissioned as officers in the armed forces, but the Catholic claims constituted a leading topic of discussion among the supporters of Government and Horner's view of affairs was consistent with that of Lord Holland and his circle. (See Roberts, pp. 7–13.)

252. To J.A. Murray

BLPES iii. 132–5 [London], 29 Dec. 1806[1]

I owe you many thanks for your very interesting account of the Dean's conversation upon the Court Reforms.[2] It is stamped with his own character, strong sense and strong prejudices. There is a great deal of what he said, which I have always felt since this question was first agitated; but he has debased it by a mixture of political resentments, which upon such a measure I can less easily pardon in a man of his high cast, than I pardon his very natural reluctance to see the profession very much changed in which he has spent his life and his talents. It is the topic of mere party animosity, to talk of the articles of Union, and a topic remembered from times when it was more effectual than it is likely to be in the present day. But I quite assent to his objection against altering the *general frame* of the Scotch institutions for the administration of justice, which, as already an established system, possess one of the most important requisites, in being adapted to the present course of transactions and the actual state of property. The Scotch law ought to be left unimpaired, because it is in many respects an admirable set of rules, simple, systematic, and comprehensive; and because in the rest, great facility has been experienced in introducing such ameliorations as were distinctly seen. On this view of the subject, I feel most decidedly as a Scotch advocate ought. And this enters most importantly into the consideration of the projected changes. It is much to be regretted, that a lawyer of such accomplishments as Mr Blair should not be ready to assist the improvements in the mode of procedure, which there is so valuable an opportunity of introducing. The silence which has been so mysteriously kept by Clerk, etc. gives me a bad presage of what is to originate with such mean and senseless jealousy. He would have fain consulted even his little fame, for executing the scheme, by courting interference. We must be prepared, however, when it makes its appearance to give it a candid and favourable consideration.

I am sorry that I cannot gratify your wish to hear about Brougham; for I have seen nothing of him since his return, nor do I know whom he lives with. I will not trust myself to speak of him yet; for though I try very resolutely to bring myself to think of him with the fairness of an indifferent acquaintance, I have not yet cast out all the resentful feelings of a neglected old friend. I shall soon come to what I wish, if we continue to live at the present distance from one another. But I never shall cease to regret this, as one of the disappointments of my life.

Petty's speech the Saturday before last was a very neat spirited reply. He was quite in order; the Speaker decided in his favour, and he did not lose the advantage this gave him against Canning.[3] You say you cannot endure the tone of Lord Grenville and Lord Howick; I did not hear Lord Grenville, and I have not read any of the newspapers – but if there was any peculiarity which delighted me in Lord Howick's speech, it was the temper, manner and spirit of it. It was modest, manly, and candid. I thought you had been too often in the Gallery, to take any unfavourable impression from the newspaper reports.

. . .

1. The letter was begun very late at night and, after adding a postscript not printed here, Horner redated it 30 Dec.
2. Robert Blair of Avonton (1741–1811: *DNB*), was Dean of the Faculty of Advocates, 1801–1808.
3. Petty had spoken on 20 Dec. in answer to criticisms of the King's Speech and Canning had interrupted him to object to a passing reference he had made by name to a petitioning candidate (*Hansard*, viii. 87–90).

253. Note by Horner

BLPES viii. 32   4 Jan. 1807

Lord Holland learned very lately – It was Rosslyn who confirmed the King in his prejudices on the subject of Catholic Emancipation; he saw him going that way, and he took advantage of it as a mode of keeping himself in favour. Pitt, however, made a stipulation with Addington, that he should turn him out.[1]

1. As Chancellor, Rosslyn – or Loughborough as he then was – had opposed Pitt on the issue of Catholic Emancipation in 1801, betrayed the confidence of the Prime Minister, and encouraged the King to resist, thereby becoming a crucial figure in Pitt's subsequent resignation. In early 1801, when Addington formed his Ministry, he went to great lengths to placate Pitt and indeed turned Loughborough out. Horner's contention that Loughborough's expulsion was attributable to an agreement between Pitt and Addington is plausible but by no means an established fact. (See Ziegler, pp. 91–2 and 98–9.)

254. Note by Horner

BLPES viii. 33–4   5 Jan. 1807

Perceval stated his strong suspicions that the American treaty would turn out to be one which sacrificed both the interest and the dignity of this country; the grounds of his suspicion are, the Intercourse Bill passed last Session, the very fact of treating at all 'with a pistol at your breast' (the Non-importation Act of Congress), and the circumstance of the Treaty being finally signed within three days after the news arrived in this country of that Non-importation Act being put in execution.[1]

He is of opinion that this country ought to watch most narrowly the conduct of Neutrals with respect to that Blockade which Bonaparte has lately declared. He is clearly of opinion that that measure of the enemy gives us a right, whatever the discretion may be, to retaliate; and to declare France in a state of blockade. We have a right to prevent neutrals from going to France, and from coming here if they have touched at any port of the enemy. He spoke of the *right*, not of the *discretion*.

See an Address of the Commons to the King, 1 July 1689, Journal, 10, 202, that 'in all his treaties with his allies for carrying on the war against France, there be an article inserted to prohibit all trade with that Kingdom.'

1. The American Intercourse Act, which transferred to the seat of government in London the long-standing discretionary powers of colonial governors in matters pertaining to the regulation of neutral commerce, sought to ease the tensions in Anglo-American relations that had arisen since Sir William Scott's decision in the case of the American ship *Essex*. That measure, which launched the Whig Ministry's policy of *rapprochement* with the United States, was complemented by an Order in Council of 16 May 1806 that, while declaring a blockade of the entire northern coast of Europe from Brest to the Elbe, in effect delivered an open invitation to American merchants to visit enemy ports if they did not carry contraband or goods owned by the enemy, and if they neither came from nor were bound for other enemy ports. Those concessions had led to promising Anglo-American negotiations during the last months of 1806 in which the Whig Ministry seriously considered the abandonment of Britain's contentious policy of searching American ships and impressing British seamen. Even after Napoleon issued his Berlin Decree in Nov. 1806 and word reached London that Congress had enacted legislation banning importations by belligerent powers, the British Government agreed to a treaty that, while reserving in blustering language Britain's right to retaliate in the event the US Government did not take effective action to resist the French blockade of British commerce, still left America's lucrative carrying trade intact. The treaty, which was never ratified, exposed the British Ministry to much criticism from Perceval and other Opposition spokesmen. (See Taylor, pp. 62-7 and 93-106; Heckscher, pp. 305-308; and Bradford Perkins, *Prologue to War: England and the United States, 1805-1812* (Berkeley and Los Angeles, 1961), pp. 83-4, 103-106, 126-8, and 132-6.)

255. To John Allen

BLPES iii. 140-43   [London], Tuesday [6 Jan. 1807]

Whitbread's speech[1] was in some parts very forcible, and of excellent sentiments; and it made a considerable impression upon many of the best men of the House. It was very far from being conclusively reasoned to my mind; for he completely overlooked the most important part of the case, the fidelity owing to Russia, and misunderstood the next in importance – the occupation of Dalmatia by French troops.

His speech however has derived a character of importance, which would not otherwise have been left to it, by the unpleasant, injudicious, and (to all my notions and recollections), inconsistent language of Lord Howick, with regard to the duration and principle of the war; which he stated with all the exaggerated declamation of the Pitt School.[2] I consider this as a most unfortunate error, in its consequences to the country, and to the character of those who act with Lord Howick; and it is the more to be regretted, since their case upon the papers was so strong, and not only admitted of being argued upon the true principles of Mr Fox's pacific policy, but could not receive full justice upon any other views.[3] I understand that Lord Grenville used no such language in the House of Lords; and I shall be anxious to ascertain the fact in this respect.[4]

[PS] Since I wrote in the morning, I have seen a new publication, which you might find it pleasant to review, in consequence of your studies in diplomacy last summer. *Actes et Mémoires concernant les Négocs qui ont eu lieu entre la France et les Etats-Unis de l'Amérique, depuis 1793, jusqu'à la conclusion de la convention du 30 Septr 1800.* It forms three very full duodecimo vols, and is published in London from the originals as published by the American Government. If you wish to have them sent down where you are, let me know. It would give a good opportunity of stating to the public what they ought soon to hear about the American treaty, as well as of entering upon the general principles of maritime neutrality.

1. On 5 Jan. Whitbread attacked Ministers for abandoning Fox's frankness and simplicity in favour of 'unimportant forms' in the recent abortive peace negotiations with France and maliciously moved resolutions for peace in the same words that Howick had used at the time of the rupture of the Peace of Amiens. Afterwards Whitbread published the *Substance of a Speech delivered in the House of Commons, on Monday, January 5, 1807* (1807). (See Taylor, p. 116, and Roberts, p. 107.)
2. Stung by Whitbread's resolutions and by the criticisms of Opposition, Howick angrily defended the Ministry's foreign policy and observed that 'until the Government of France changed its principles and character, there was no hope of peace for this country'. The Speaker was so struck by that remark that he recorded it in his diary. (*Colchester*, ii. 88–9; see also MC, 6 Jan.)
3. Horner's assessment of the effect of the exchange between Howick and Whitbread was sagacious. The debate signalled the detachment of the Foxite left in the House of Commons and would affect Howick's relationship with Whitbread and his supporters until the end of the war. The Duke of Bedford and Lady Holland agreed with Horner (Bedford to Holland, 18 Jan., BL Add. MSS 51661; *Lady Holland's Journal*, ii. 194–7). See the resulting editorials critical of Government in the *Independent Whig*, 11, 18, and 25 Jan. For analysis see Taylor, pp. 112–18.
4. Grenville's remarks in the Lords on 5 Jan. were more prudent.

256. To Francis Jeffrey

BLPES iii. 144–5 ⟨Horner, i. 418–19⟩   The Temple, 14 Jan. 1807

⟨...⟩ ...

⟨Before you read this, you will be delivered of your eighteenth birth; which I become curious to see, as I have heard nothing of its contents, except Don Juan's[1] abstract of the *Mercurio Peruviano*, and Murray's Essay on the Judicial Reforms, both of which promise me much pleasure.[2]

⟨Have you any good subjects in view for your nineteenth? There are two I wish you, *yourself*, would undertake, if you can pick up books that would admit of them; they are political perhaps strictly, but there is no objection to them on the ground of party politics, from which you must ever abstain. The subjects I mean, are, the policy to be pursued with respect to the commerce of neutral nations, and with respect to the grievances of Ireland. Many well-disposed people are in error upon these two great questions, who would be set right, or at least cured of the dogmatism and clamour of their errors, by a candid, plain, and forcible exposition of the conduct that is recommended equally by prudence and by kindness. I do not want an elaborate argument of *right* about the rule of 1756, nor an exhaustive disquisition upon all the points of the question of Catholic emancipation; but a perspicuous and pithy statement, drawn from the maxims of obvious policy and justice, which will satisfy honest thinkers, that the wild Irish ought not to pay a tithe on their potatoes, and that we ought not to aid and abet Napoleon in his plans for extirpating commerce and opulent industry. If you have given me the article I asked you for, upon the slave trade, it will come to London the week after next with most appropriate and beneficial effect.⟩[3]

. . .

1. 'Allen's' in *Horner*.
2. Allen reviewed the *Mercurio Peruano* in *ER* ix (no. xviii, Jan. 1807), 433–58, but that the article on the 'Proposed reform of the Court of Session' on pp. 462–92 was by Jeffrey himself (*WI*) seems confirmed by Horner's letter of 16 Feb. (Doc. 258), though the Kinnordy list also attributes it to Murray. See also *Jeffrey*, i. 176–7, and Horner's comment in Doc. 366 about a 'flippant' article.
3. On this occasion Horner stretched the truth to the point of breaking. For the abolition of the slave trade was most certainly a measure sponsored by the Ministry of All the Talents in opposition to a strong minority in Parliament, and concessions to the Irish Catholics and to the Americans were major policies of the Whig Ministry that drew opposition on party lines.

257. To Lord Webb Seymour

BLPES iii. 146–7 The Temple, 20 Jan. 1807

. . .

If you read in the newspapers an account of Napoleon's discourse with the deputies from Hamburgh, and from its extraordinary nature supposed it to be a fabrication, you will be surprised to hear that it is quite an authentic report. It was written by one of the deputies, M. Godefroi, an eminent merchant at Hamburgh, to his partner M. Mathieson, who made his escape to London, and whom I heard repeat the story. It is a most tremendous avowal of the designs of this new Gengis, who sees so distinctly the barbarism that must ensue from the permanence of the system he has established, that he makes that barbarism itself the object and purpose of his labours.[1]

. . .

1. The MC of 8 Jan. had printed a 'Private Letter' dated 27 Dec. reporting the unsuccessful mission of a delegation of Hamburg merchants to Posen, where they had tried to impress upon the Emperor how important it was to France to keep open her trade with their city, and relating how he had 'spoken violently against the English, declaring that the chief object of the measures he had adopted in regard to their city, was to distress the English and their trade'.

258. To Francis Jeffrey

NLS Acc. 6070   House of Commons, 11 o'clock, Monday night [16 Feb. 1807][1]

I have made my escape into the smoking room from one of Castlereagh's insufferable harrangues [sic], to take at last an opportunity of writing a few lines to you, which my daily engagement in the Shrewsbury Committee with my other business has prevented me from doing sooner . . .[2]

I have this evening heard Lord Grenville upon the plan of judicial reform in a sensible, superficial, candid speech. He scarcely went into any details; so that, not having seen the Bill yet, I know scarcely more of the scheme than I did last year from the resolutions. Full time is to be allowed for the discussion, and as I mean to devote some time to it as candidly as possible, I hope to have the benefit of your assistance. The general principle of the Bill I shall probably support, because it is a great occasion for remedying a great evil, but in the Committee there will be an opportunity of discussing in detail the regulations, and there the attempt must be made to improve the measure by the labours of those who were not made parties to its preparation.[3] I fancy there will hardly be much opposition in the House of Lords; for Lord Eldon expressed [himself] very much disposed to acquiesce in the leading provisions of the Bill, and entirely approved of the attempt to reform the Court of Session. Your article in the Review has made a great noise here, and is very much liked; the general views contained in it, and indeed on any of the particular schemes, are very much such as we have long ago agreed on.[4] I mean to write more particularly another day, than I can do at present.

I must end for the present; I will only tell you the piece of slipslop with which Castlereagh set me off. He spoke of the bad effect of peace in 'removing the presence of energy and the other qualities of fortitude that belong to war'. And this is a fair specimen of his usual style.

1. On 16 Feb. Grenville presented his Scots Judicature bill in the Lords and Castlereagh wandered on about the financial resolutions in the manner described in Horner's last paragraph. (Hansard, viii. 788–92, 794–7, and 821–4, especially 823.)
2. Henry Grey Bennet's election for Shrewsbury in November 1806 was petitioned against and declared void on 24 Apr. 1807 (PH ii. 338).
3. In a letter to Thomas Thomson of 15 Mar. 1807 (Thomson, p. 117) Horner professed himself especially anxious to see juries introduced in civil cases in Scotland but 'terrified at the mode in which this bill proposes to force them upon the country'. He also regarded the plan to have more courts than one sitting at the same time as indispensable; without that innovation, he observed, 'the whole scheme is nugatory, either in respect of increased dispatch or of the advantages to be derived from a competition of Courts'.
4. See Doc. 256.

259. To Lord Webb Seymour

BLPES iii. 148–51   [House of Commons], 19 Feb. 1807[1]

A plan has been opened this evening by Mr Whitbread, upon that most interesting and important of all subjects in the domestic economy of England, the Poor Laws. It is very comprehensive in the design; and though it contains a great mixture of what is perfectly good with what is objectionable, he has very sensibly and candidly avowed his intention not to abandon a single part of his plans, though the rest should fail. And it is fortunate, that the most important parts of it are easily separable, and may stand or fall singly. . . . Whitbread has done me the honour of naming me one of his committee to bring in the Bill; but as I knew nothing of its intended provisions till I heard his speech this night, so, that nomination does not in the least pledge me to the support of any part of it.[2]

As soon as the Bill is printed, I shall send you a copy of it; to satisfy your curiosity in the mean while, I propose to give you an outline of the heads of his statement tonight. And you need not consider this as a trouble which I unwillingly undertake, since it affords me a reasonable pretence for escaping from the dullness of Mr Bankes who is at present prosing to the knights, citizens, and burgesses all asleep.[3]

An abrogation of the poor laws, he [Whitbread] holds to be utterly impracticable; and none of the plans for a gradual abolition that have hitherto been proposed are advisable or likely to succeed.

The great purposes he places in view are the exaltation of the character of the labourer, a more equal distribution of the burden of poor's rate, and an improvement of the mode of administering relief. These three purposes formed the main divisions of his speech.

I. For the first of these purposes, he intends that there should be introduced a national system of education, so that the whole population of England may have the means of instruction. He spoke of Lancaster's inventions, and of the means by which he had simplified the process of education, with the highest praise; and I cannot help breaking off my story here to tell you, that Joseph and two of his pupils were in the gallery, and heard this just and gratifying tribute of public thanks to his unwearied and patriotic enterprise.

He proposes, also, to throw open in a certain degree the law of settlement, by enacting, that persons shall acquire a fixed settlement by having been householders in a parish for 5 years without receiving alms of any parish, and without suffering an infamous punishment in consequence of being convicted of a crime.

He proposes, farther, (what you and I will think otherwise of than of the preceding proposals), that the Quarter Sessions should give rewards to labourers in certain circumstances; once a year to those who have brought up six or more children without needing parochial relief.

The next object is to assist the poor in securing the savings of their own acquisitions. He acknowledged the important principle of not interfering by law in the affairs of the poor, and their own management of their property; but he added this qualification, until they come to the law for relief. And instead of trusting to the sure and rapid operation of the friendly societies, he projects a Poor's Fund, a national concern, established in the metropolis; to which every person shall be permitted to subscribe, who is certified by the minister of his parish as living by his own labour. He shall not remit less than 20/- at a time, nor more than £5; he shall not be allowed to accumulate more than £200, and he shall have the dividend of interest transmitted to him as soon as it amounts to 10/-. A system of insurance, without profit, is to be attached to this. The objections to this stare us in the face.

II. For a more equal distribution of the burden, he proposes that those parishes which are clearly unable to maintain their poor but by an enormous rate, as in Spitalfields where there [are] scarcely any but poor inhabitants, should be assisted by other parishes. This is to be effected by means of a general return, made every seven years, of the rate levied in every parish of each county; and those are to be assisted from other parishes in the same county, which, in spite of good management, have been forced to impose a rate more than double the average of the rest of the county. There is to be a new regulation of what is called the county rate. Personal property is to be made liable to the rate, instead of the land bearing it all; a principle which is to be found in the statute of Elizabeth, though it has not been generally acted upon.

There is a little scheme for building cottages to be let out to the poor; and there is to be a better constitution of vestry meetings, in respect of the right of voting.

III. With respect to the mode of administering relief, he professed himself a decided enemy to the system of work-houses and compulsory labour; and he proposes that the work-houses at present standing should gradually be converted into asylums for infirmity, or a temporary residence for those who are thrown out upon the world, until they can find a different habitation. Relief is, by the general system, to be administered at home; and the officers are to have the power of boarding paupers with their own relations. And the important principle is to be established, that a poor man may be relieved, though he has still some property.

I hope you will from this outline, which I have been obliged to put down in a great hurry, be able to form some idea of the schemes; enough to set your own thoughts immediately at work. Whitbread's chief assistant in the formation of this plan, is a Mr Wiltshire, formerly an eminent solicitor, and now a country gentleman in Hertfordshire.[4]

1. The letter is headed 'at night'; but in a postscript Horner apologizes for neglecting to post it until the 21st.
2. Rumours of Whitbread's scheme for a thorough revision of the Poor Laws had been circulating for some months, and Horner had provided Whitbread with 'a short note . . . stating the present law of Scotland on the subject, about which he had asked me some questions' (Horner to Murray, 20 Feb., *Horner*, i. 422). In his speech of 19 Feb. Whitbread said: 'Most of the information I have obtained on the subject of the Scottish law relating to the poor, I owe to an honourable member of this House (Mr Horner), who has been well known in the republic of letters, and at the Bar of Scotland; and who is sure to become an ornament of this assembly.' (*Hansard*, viii. 880, which prints Horner's note as a footnote to 878–9.)
3. Henry Bankes (1756–1834: *DNB*), an independent, was speaking on the new financial plan (*Hansard*, viii. 925–6).
4. William Wilshere of the Frythe (1754–1824) was a neighbour and business associate of Whitbread. (See *Whitbread*, pp. 94–5, and, for the poor laws, pp. 176ff.)

260. To James Reddie

NLS MSS 3704, ff. 178–9   Westminster, Monday morning [?March 1807][1]

I send you a copy of Lord Grenville's Bill, and shall be very much obliged to you if you will favour me with your observations, both upon the general plan, and upon the separate clauses. It is of the utmost importance that so great a measure should undergo an ample discussion, and that the sentiments of all those who are best qualified to judge of it should be freely suggested and made known. I shall consider it very kind of you, if you will communicate to me whatever occurs to you.

I have to acknowledge the receipt of a Memorial written by you, on the expediency of extending the new modes of trial to some of the Inferior Courts. ...

    1. Since Horner refers to a single bill, this would seem to concern Grenville's first attempt at
    the reform of the Court of Session, of which Horner himself still had no specific details in
    February. (See Doc. 258.)

261. To J.A. Murray

NLS MSS 1002, ff. 109–10   Shrewsbury Committee!! 17 Mar. 1807

There is very little for me to tell you of the debate last night. Lord Grenville's was a good speech, such as he always makes; I did not hear Lord Melville's, for I preferred hearing Windham and Sheridan on the Slave Trade.[1] Lord Eldon made some useful criticisms on the details of regulations, and pointed out some great difficulties in the introduction of jury trial in some sorts of cases. The prominent argument used against the Bill was, the breach of the articles of Union; in short, for such an occasion, the discussion was very slight and very far from giving any display either of knowledge, talent, or much interest in the subject. The fact is, I imagine, that there were other things in the heads of Eldon and Melville yesterday; of which you may hear bye and bye. We may have other matters to talk of very soon, than the greater or less merit of a proposed improvement. It will be something to have entertained pure intentions, and to fall in a great design of justice and liberty.[2]

...

    1. Windham's and Sheridan's speeches in the Commons' debate of 16 Mar. on the slave trade
    are in Hansard, ix. 136–8. On the same day, when discussion on the second reading of
    Grenville's Scots Judicature Bill was resumed in the Upper House, Montrose condemned it
    all as an infringement of the Act of Union and both Melville and Eldon indicated their
    opposition to that part of it proposing the introduction of juries. Grenville subsequently
    divided his proposals into two bills, so that if that concerning juries failed there would be a
    better chance of the other succeeding in making some administrative reform of the Court
    of Session. But these were overtaken by the change of Ministry and dissolution, followed by
    the substitution of the new Government's own bills. One, rather like Grenville's, proposed
    to divide the Court into chambers, but so far as juries were concerned the other only to set
    up a commission to examine when and how they might be introduced. (Hansard, ix.

109–114, 147–9, and x. 1345.) There is in BLPES (iii. 173–8) an unpleasant correspondence with Selkirk on this business, dating from the crucial period (July 1807) when the Government seized the initiative from Grenville. It is impossible to make out what had happened; but at the time Selkirk was a Scottish representative peer and probably it had something do with his not fulfilling a promise to help Grenville's bill in the Lords or to try and improve the Government's. For Selkirk had changed sides with the change of government and, as Gilbert Elliot wrote to his father on 14 Apr. (*George III*, iv. 531n), 'deserted us in the shabbiest manner . . . I always thought him a very wrong-headed man, but I really believed that he was always sincere in what he said. However, his speech last night was so directly in contradiction of the principles he has all his life professed that I am afraid it must be attributed to the *Scotch disorder*.' Leonard Horner merely added to the MS a pencilled note that 'Lord Selkirk had *ratted* in a very discreditable manner'.

2. A draft of the Whig Ministry's ill-conceived bill conceding to Catholics the right to be commissioned as officers in the army and navy, afterwards known as 'Lord Howick's bill', had been laid before the King on 10 Feb. On the 20th the scheme had been introduced in the shape of additional clauses to the Mutiny Bill, but on 4 Mar. Howick had brought a 'Catholic Militia Bill' forward as a separate measure. Prior to 11 Mar. the King had expressed neither approval nor disapproval of the measure, requesting instead clarification of its several clauses, but on the 11th he told Grenville that he opposed the measure and was prepared to make his opposition publicly known. Sidmouth promptly attempted to resign; and between 11 and 14 Mar., in the face of disunion in the Cabinet and unexpected opposition from Eldon, Melville, and the bulk of the former supporters of Pitt, Ministers had unsuccessfully sought compromise with the King and had at last abandoned the bill with the stipulation that they must express their opinions freely upon the introduction of the anticipated Catholic petition. The King was not content with this surrender, and on 17 Mar. he demanded 'a positive assurance' from Ministers 'which shall effectively relieve his mind from all future apprehension'. As Horner wrote, Ministers were hopelessly trapped and discussing a response to the King. Next day they would decline to give the required assurance but refuse to resign, and on 24 Mar., after learning that the King was attempting to form a new Government, they would deliver up the seals. (See Roberts, pp. 13–18.)

262. To Thomas Creevey

Creevey Papers, D.M.S. Watson Library,
University College, London   The Temple, 20 Mar. [1807]

I wish very much to bring Sir William Scott and his Court before the Finance Committee; to our general precept, he has made an evasive sort of answer. As I believe it to be a depot of inveterate abuses, it seems to deserve a thorough investigation. Will you have the goodness, if you collected any materials upon the subject when you proposed some motions some time ago, to put me in the right way for full inquiries; what accounts ought to be called for, and what the sources of abuse are that ought particularly to be looked to? Did you actually move for papers? and about what time, that I may look into the votes? Can you name any persons, from whom information may be procured?[1]

. . .

1. Horner had been named a member of the select committee set up on 10 Feb. 'to examine and consider . . . regulations and checks . . . to control . . . the public expenditure' (*AR* xlix (1807), pp. 104–105, and *Horner*, i. 412). Creevey's motions had concerned the work of the Commissioners of Naval Inquiry.

263. To Francis Jeffrey

BLPES iii. 152–5   London, 6 Apr. 1807

I have had two visits this morning on the subject of the *Review*. First, from the accomplished Constable; in great consternation at an opinion which Sir S. Romilly had given as to Longman's right in the concern. Next, from Sharon Turner, author and attorney for Longman & Co., who came to me as from Longman and as to a mutual friend, to see whether it was possible to accommodate matters; he produced Romilly's opinion, which is very clear and decided that Longman and Constable are joint proprietors. He had not the case to show me, upon which the opinion was given, and which I take for granted contained an erroneous statement of the facts, otherwise no such opinion could have been delivered.[1]

I told Turner, upon the point of accommodation, that I would undertake none nor recommend it, if his client Longman claimed any thing like a right of property in future numbers of the *Review*; and for this conclusive reason, that it would be a subversion of what I know to be the original constitution of the work, and what I thought still absolutely essential to its character and purpose, to recognize in any bookseller whatever a right of property in any but the numbers he had already published. I told him explicitly, that neither Longman nor Constable possessed, according to my knowledge and understanding of the facts, any claim against you for any future publication; that their property was from number to number, resting in the manuscript articles of each as they were delivered to them; that I held you to be at liberty to turn off either or both, to discontinue the work, or continue it with other publishers, at your pleasure; and that as the original ground of establishing the *Review* was to take that branch of literary work out of the hands of the booksellers, so we had clearly and systematically kept the property of the publication as a current one from being appropriated by any one of them. After this opinion, Turner said there was such a difference between my view of the subject and that which he entertained, that there could be no mode of discussing it but by a suit.

I advised Hunter to write this day to Edinburgh for a case to be fully and minutely prepared, in order to have the opinions of counsel; and I advised him to consult Alexander and Bell.[2] Of course you will take charge of the case; the important facts to state are those with respect to the first formation of the work and what took place when it first became a pecuniary concern on the side of the Reviewers.

There is no need of being under any doubt as to the publication of the next number at its appointed time. For the course matters will take is this, that Longman will file a Bill in Equity to make Constable account to him for a moiety of the proceeds and profits.

. . .

1. The long relationship between Constable & Co., the Edinburgh publisher of the *Review*, and Longman & Co., the London publisher, was a stormy one. It had something to do apparently with Alexander Gibson Hunter, Constable's partner. For Constable afterwards wrote on the file (*Constable*, i. 339):

    Mr Hunter was a high-minded and I must say honourable man, but of warm temper and out of that perhaps these quarrels originated, more than anything else.

Whatever the real cause of the difficulty, early in 1807, as the popularity of the *ER* continued to mount, the two publishing houses became embroiled in a dispute about their respective proprietary interests in it. Apparently it raged for some time before the reviewers themselves learned of it, but on 10 Mar. Hunter breakfasted with Horner and reported to his partner (*ibid.*, i. 104):

> We talked over everything about Longman and Co. fully, and about the *Review*. He did not seem to be properly informed about what had been passing, which I was much surprised at; but he referred me to Mr Brougham.

According to the account in *Murray*, i. 56–66 and 77–84, Constable had intended that Murray's firm, with which his own shared a family connection – Hunter's younger brother being an apprentice with Murray – and already co-operated to some extent, should take Longman's place with respect to the *Review*. But Longman had been given a legal interest in the *Review* and formally objected to the transfer of the London business, employing Sharon Turner (1768–1847: *DNB*), an attorney and historian much consulted on matters such as literary copyright, even though he was a close friend of Murray's. Turner succeeded in obtaining an injunction at the end of May (see Doc. 268), but when Jeffrey therefore finally threatened the oft-considered plan to begin a new journal in direct competition to the old one (see Doc. 272 and Jeffrey to Constable & Co., 1 June, *Murray*, i. 79), Longman's gave way and surrendered their rights for £1,000. The transfer was at once carried out and the London sales prospered. But before long differences of both a financial and a political and literary nature intruded and eventually in February 1809 Murray launched his rival *Quarterly Review*.

2. William Alexander (d. 1842), afterwards Chief Baron of the Exchequer, and John Bell were both equity draughtsman.

264. To J.A. Murray

⟨*Horner*, i. 424–7⟩   London, 7 Apr. 1807

⟨...

⟨I am much charmed with your decided expressions about the conduct of the late ministers. To be sure, no man of personal spirit, or who understands the constitution, can have a moment's doubt. The only part of the story I could have wished to be otherwise, is the withdrawing the Bill, and not resigning at once; but perhaps it was rendered unavoidable in consequence of that misconception originally about the extent of the measure. And yet, had the King closed with that compromise, they would have remained in power with tarnished honour: as it ended in a resignation at last, the appearance of moderation, in yielding to the King, may do them good with the country, which takes these transactions with a coarse judgement. Nothing but the impatience of the King's advisers to get into power, or his own impatience to get rid of the reformers and abolitionists, perhaps the Duke of York's to stop the reformation of barrack abuses, could have so blinded a practised artist in cabinet-making, like the King, as to make him overlook the advantage he would have gained, by keeping them, with their withdrawn bill, a little while longer in office, to be thrust out on the next opportunity.

⟨Do not think of undertaking a long journey for the sake of hot rooms and late nights. The debates ought not to tempt you, and would not reward you. We are no longer in the heroic ages; though Sheridan has awoke from his dotage, to show us again something of what they were. Had the great discussions gone on that were in view, upon measures of general and lasting benefit to the country, the interest of the subjects would have made up for the mediocrity of the speakers; but those seem all vanished. All the prejudices that have been skulking out of sight, will be advanced into broad day, avowed in Parliament, and acted upon in the Cabinet; it will be the language of the Treasury bench in the House of Commons, that the poor would be made worse subjects, and less comfortable to themselves, by letting them learn to read; the principles of toleration will be brought into question, and we shall have eternal chimes upon the wisdom of our ancestors and the danger of innovation. I will own a foolish secret to you: that I suffered more irritation from the sort of spirit and opinions that prevailed against Romilly's little bill,[1] than I have received in amusement from all my time in the House of Commons. There was something lost in the bill itself; but the symptoms that attended it were discouraging to every attempt of the sort in future.

⟨Like other good citizens, I do not quite despair; so long as the press is free, and men will devote themselves to the labour of instructing the public mind, there must be some impression made more and more in favour of just opinions; and, perhaps, upon the subjects that now embarrass us the most, some blame may be imputed to a neglect of this duty, especially upon the state of Ireland, and the real nature of the Catholic claims. I say, I do not quite despair; but I am very near it. That these opinions in these particular applications of them, will finally be acknowledged to have been just and salutary, I believe with the faith of a fanatic, and that those who in these days contend for them will be classed in one of the lower orders of martyrs to liberty and justice.[2]

⟨. . .

⟨I understand that Bentham's tract on the Scotch Judicature Bill will be published very soon, and you shall have several copies of it sent down immediately by the coach. Whishaw, who has seen it, speaks rather indifferently of its merits; but it cannot fail to present judicious hints, for the consideration of those who will condescend to be more soberly practical in their reasonings. It is some satisfaction to me, that you and Jeffrey are converts to my opinion of his book on French judicature; which, like all his other treatises, contains many important observations which may be taken in the very state in which he has left them, but is still more valuable for its irresistible effect in setting the mind of the reader to work by the boldness and restlessness of the writer's speculations. It is the most effectual exercise in the art of legislative reasonings.⟩[3]

---

1. To make the freehold estates of persons who die indebted assets for the payment of their simple contract debts (*Romilly*, ii. 179–80, 183, 186–7, and 190–93).
2. The MC of 8 Apr. contained a notice of Horner's election to the Whig Club. He told Murray that same day (*Horner*, i. 428) that it was 'of very little use' but that it served 'to keep together a number of very respectable Whigs, of the middle station of life, who reside in the counties near London' and 'to give the memory and the name of Fox still an influence over the opinions and conduct of many persons of that description'.
3. The two works to which Horner refers would appear to be Bentham's volume on *Scotch Reform* (1808) and the *Draught of a New Plan for the Organization of the Judicial Establishment in France* (1790). Horner (together with Brougham) seems to have met Bentham for the first time at a Holland House dinner party on 17 Aug. 1805 (*Bentham*, vii. 325) and by the date of this letter would no doubt have got to know him quite well through their mutual

friend Whishaw. He was, in any case, a recent convert to Utilitarian doctrine and an admirer of Bentham's jurisprudential works. On 10 Nov. Horner, in a reply to a letter from Bentham, assessed the demand in Scotland for Bentham's tract on Scots judicature and observed (*Bentham*, vii. 452) that 'though the people of that country are more addicted to reading than to buying, this subject has excited general interest and discussion'. Thereafter they seem to have co-operated closely on the Scots Jury Bill; see especially *ibid.*, vii. 463–4 and 483–7, and Doc. 285.

265. To Lady Holland

BLPES iii. 158–9 (copy or draft)
⟨*Horner*, i. 429⟩   House of Commons, 11 o'clock, 15 Apr. 1807

⟨None of the great ones have spoken yet on either side.[1] A great many new orators; the best on the Government benches, young Milnes of Yorkshire, who spoke very well.[2] Lyttleton, not with too much of youthful diffidence, but with more effect and better taste than I expected. The best speech by far is [J. W.] Ward's; you will set this down, of course, to partiality, but wait till tomorrow, and ask enemies, if there are any, as well as indifferent persons. I have always promised deep for him; but after what he has done tonight, I am ashamed of my imperfect sagacity in not promising a great deal more. Sir John Newport has been beating Castlereagh pretty hard; and Lord Holland will not be sorry to hear that the Union has been abused by Mr Tighe.[3] We are going to have a speech from Windham, if I can judge from appearances; he sits quite absorbed, and growls if any one disturbs him. I wish I could recollect more particulars, but I must go down to hear Tierney answer Bankes.⟩

1. Horner wrote while observing the debate on the motion of William Henry Lyttelton, afterwards 3rd Baron Lyttelton (1782–1837: *DNB*), 'That this House, considering a firm and efficient administration, as indispensably necessary, in the present important crisis of public affairs, has seen, with the deepest regret, the late change in His Majesty's councils.' The previous question was moved as an amendment and carried after considerable debate by 244 against 198, thereby leaving the new Portland Ministry with a majority of 46. (*Hansard*, ix. 432–75.)
2. Robert Pemberton Milnes (1784–1858: *DNB*) was later identified with the Canningite party.
3. Sir John Newport (1756–1843: *DNB*) was Chancellor of the Irish Exchequer; William Tighe (1766–1816) was MP for County Wicklow.

266. To John Whishaw

NLS MSS 11000, ff. 71–2   The Temple, Sunday morning
                                           [late April – mid July 1807][1]

As you have already got the amount of unclaimed dividends, and can require from the Bank all the other accounts necessary to direct the judgement of the Board upon the matter referred to them, none of the notes I have would be of much use to you.[2] We had the amount of unclaimed dividends stated in two points of view, as it stood upon the first day of every month for a year back, and as it stood at the period immediately preceding each quarterly dividend for a series of years; we ordered it from 1791 to the 1st January 1807, and received an account from 1794 to that date.

With respect to the establishment of the Bank, the number of offices and persons in its service in the year 1796 was 448, and this year is 846. They stated to us, that, from the best consideration given to the subject, it appeared that full one half of this number are employed on account of the management of the public debt.

The present rate of allowance to the Bank from the public was settled by Mr Pitt in 1786; we had the copy of a letter of his dated 11th March that year, to the Governor, in which he stated that 'considering the amount to which the debt has increased, and relying on the disposition of the Bank, to give every reasonable accommodation to the Public, he was inclined to hope that they would see no objection to establishing the rate of £450 for every million, instead of the sum then payable.'

In the course of last year, Lord Grenville and Petty formed some sort of agreement or transaction with the Bank, in consideration of its forbearing payment of what is owing to it by the public on advance. How far the terms or import of that transaction may prevent an immediate reduction of the rate of allowance, I am not aware: of course it must be kept in view. In the Committee, we were all of opinion, and nobody more decidedly than Thornton, that the rate ought to be very considerably reduced; at the same time that an advantage is still allowed, for the benefit of paying the dividends at a place more convenient for the public upon the whole, than any other that could be found.

You will have more than sufficient grounds for suggesting such a reduction to Government; that materials of the 14th Finance report are evidence and authority enough for such a recommendation.[3] I am very glad to find that the present Treasury does not withhold such references from your Board; they become responsible if your advice is not adopted.

PS Of course you will not forget the various balances of money lodged on the public account, among the accounts you call for from the Bank.

[PPS] Profits arising from the restriction of payments at the Bank may be incidentally mentioned.

1. Like Grenville's Scots Judicature Bill, the work of the select committee on public expenditure (Doc. 262) had been overtaken by the dissolution and as Horner was no longer an MP, he could not be included when it was reconstituted on 30 June (AR xlix (1807), p. 242). But it had had time to gather a good deal of material for its successor, whose second report (BPP, 1807, ii. 379–422) directly relates to the substance of the present discussion with Whishaw on the Bank of England. Since this second report seems clearly to have included the information Horner outlines, he would surely not have needed to provide it to Whishaw after the publication of the report on 10 Aug. 1807, and this places the letter between 10 Feb. and that date, probably, in view of the past tense references to the committee, after the dissolution of 27 Apr.

2. The 'Board' is evidently the Audit Board to which Whishaw had been appointed Commissioner in Oct. 1806.

3. This is a reference to the committee of 1797, of which that of 1807 was a deliberate imitation.

267. To Lady Holland

BLPES iii. 165–6 (?draft)   [?London, 26–28 May 1807][1]

I shall see Ward tomorrow, and settle some plan with him for coming down. We have already determined to come, and have only to fix when. It cannot be this week, for old Hobhouse is on permanent duty with his volunteers at Devizes, which keeps me in town all the *working* days; and on Saturday I am going with Petty to Lord King's.[2] Lord Henry has just been here, with rather uncomfortable news from Yorkshire, since Wilberforce is at the head of the poll; why are we giving him the second votes? I would not give him one till Lord Milton is secure. We have all too great a hankering for the Saint, who always has done, and always will do as much harm to us as he can without hurting himself. I am comforted by Lord Howick's return for Appleby, as I was afraid he might give up the game in disgust.[3] I hear the news from Ireland are very good; and that we shall have *forty*.

. . .

1. So the date would appear to be from the references to his journey the following week to join Lady Holland, to Howick's return for Appleby, and to the election campaign in Yorkshire. The poll in Yorkshire had opened on 20 May and lasted for fifteen days. Wilberforce was behind the other candidates, Henry Lascelles and Lord Milton, until the last week in May, but from then until the final result on 5 June remained on top. It was not until 1 or 2 June, however, that the contest for second place turned in Milton's favour. (*Wilberforce*, iii. 323–31; E.A. Smith, 'The Yorkshire Elections of 1806 and 1807; a study in electoral management', *Northern History*, ii (1967), pp. 62–90; *The Poll Book for the County of York, 1807* (York, 1807).)
2. Horner went down to stay with the Hollands at Southampton on 3 June (Horner to Jeffrey, 5 June, *Horner*, i. 430). Benjamin (afterwards Sir Benjamin) Hobhouse (1757–1831: *DNB*), MP for Hindon, was first Carnatic Commissioner and a captain in the Wiltshire Yeomanry. Lord King's place was Oakham Court in Surrey.
3. Howick had abandoned his supposedly safe county seat in Northumberland in the general election of 1807 when the Duke of Northumberland, hitherto his political ally, had decided without warning to put up his son, Lord Percy. Howick had then reluctantly agreed to transfer to Appleby, a pocket borough of Lord Thanet, where he was returned on 25 May. In July he resigned Appleby in favour of Tavistock, a family borough of the Duke of Bedford, which he held until his elevation to the House of Lords in November 1807. (See *Grey*, pp. 160–62, and *PH* iv. 110.)

268. To Francis Jeffrey

BLPES iii. 162–4   The Temple, 28 May 1807

I have seen Alexander this morning; he was not in court when the injunction was granted, but he conceives it to be rightly granted upon the principles which are established in the Court of Chancery with regard to property of this nature.[1] His own opinion, which of course you have seen, was formed upon the correspondence, which is held to establish a partnership in the adventure; and the profit and loss being shared, a property was acquired in the name and title page of the *Review*. The Court of Chancery recognizes such a species of property, and will therefore protect it. Murray's publication is held to be a piracy upon Longman's property.

I have had a long conversation also with Sir Arthur Pigott, who has paid most attention to the case. His view of the question is very nearly the same; but he lays particular stress upon the terms of Sydney Smith's letter of 12th April 1803, 'if *you* will give *your editors*, etc.' The result therefore is, however contrary to our most clear and positive intentions, that the *Edinburgh Review* is the property of the booksellers, Constable and Longman; which they may continue with what writers and editors they can find, or relinquish at their pleasure; and if either of those partners chooses to relinquish the adventure, the other may carry it on for his own advantage, or associate other partners with himself. On the other hand, it is perfectly certain, that there is no obligation upon you or any of us to write for this or any other Review belonging to these excellent gentlemen; since there is no engagement for time. The Chancellor made this express observation when he made his order.

The injunction is granted till an answer is put in to the Bill, when it would be argued in course; or it might be dissolved, upon affidavits stating sufficient matter to induce the Chancellor to make such an order before coming in of the answer. This is the shape of the suit. But Pigott is strongly and clearly of opinion, that we ought not to involve ourselves in any litigation; but come at once to the resolution of quitting this concern, and establishing another with a new name.

Longman & Co. believe that they will be able to deceive the public for a while, by having possession of the name, and they mean at present to practise that fraud. It is impossible, however, that it should avail them to any great extent; if proper measures be taken immediately to give due notice. An advertisement ought to appear immediately, announcing that the persons who founded and carried on the *Edinburgh Review* have withdrawn themselves wholly from all concern in that publication, and that the same persons mean to publish on a certain day, (make it a different day from that of the old work, say, the first of August next), the first number of a critical journal which shall be called so and so. This ought to be done immediately, and neither activity nor expense should be spared, in giving the most extensive circulation to the advertisement. It ought to be considered, very carefully, whether our names should be put to this advertisement; personally, I feel some small scruples of prudence as well as delicacy upon the point, and should rather dislike it; but I put myself into your holy keeping, and should wish you to do unto me as unto yourself. You will no doubt call in the sage counsels of Thomson, and the kind vigilance of Murray.

Since we are thus outwitted, and robbed by our own improvidence of the only principle that we did lay down at the establishment of the *Review*, it behoves us to be more careful of this new undertaking; and to guard our rights by express and unequivocal covenants. Since the common rule of property, at least in the Court of Chancery, for this species of adventure, is such as we have found it to be, we must shape the property for ourselves by an express stipulation, in such a manner, as to separate the right to the name from the adventure of profit and loss. It may be easily done, but it ought to be reduced into a written agreement. The operation of the contract ought to be no more than this, to vest the property of each number successively as a separate work in the publisher, but reserving to you the right of going with the very next number to any other publisher whose beard you like better.

The one pleasant circumstance in this broil is, that I hear the gentlemen of the Row have some hopes of our falling out among ourselves, and dividing our affections between Constable and Longman. I am apprehensive they will be deceived in this; and that Sharon Turner must take your post himself, and recruit his troop out of those who like himself have suffered.

In order to make our success in this business more complete, it will be necessary for the original parties to the *Review* to exert themselves particularly, and make the new first number a valuable one. I think none of them will refuse to exert themselves; but it is the stamp of your own hand that gives the work all its character. I must write upon this subject again, when I have seen Brougham, whom I have not been able to find today.

. . .

Your first article in this number is admirable and admired.[2] Petty says it is right all through; he agrees with you in every part of it, which is more than you do yourself by this time. There is a blunder he says in the article upon the new plan of finance, where your financier (who is he?) says it would have been all the same to have applied the supplementary loans at once to the liquidation of the war loans, without the circuitous machinery of the war taxes – forgetting that there would then have been no security to the lenders of the war loan.[3]

1. See Doc. 263.
2. Jeffrey had reviewed Stephen's *Dangers of the Country* in ER x (no. xix, Apr. 1807), 1–27.
3. The review of Petty's financial plan (pp. 72–85) was apparently by David Buchanan (1779–1848; *DNB*), the Edinburgh journalist who afterwards edited the *Wealth of Nations* (*WI*).

269. To John Allen

BLPES iii. 156–7   [London], Friday [?29 May 1807]

From the conversations I have had with Sir Arthur Pigott and Alexander, it seems to me that the most advisable course to take about the *Edinburgh Review*, is to leave Longman in possession of the name, and take another. He will attempt probably to continue the work with his own authors, and the public may for a while and to a certain extent be deceived. To resist this, there ought to be an immediate circulation of advertisements, announcing that those who founded the *ER* have no longer any connection with it, and intend to publish on a certain day the first number of another critical journal. To insure its success as speedily as may be, there ought to be an exertion made by all the original contributors.

. . .

If you have time to send him a contribution for the first number, you perceive of how much importance it will be. Though I am very much occupied, I will try to do something. You have repeatedly talked of giving some account of Jovellanos; your own work seems now postponed to so distant a day, that you might now say some thing about him in the *Review* without interfering with another immediate plan. Besides, a man of letters languishing in a dungeon ought not to be forgotten so long.[1] But you will easily find another subject also.

1. Gaspar Melchor de Jovellanos y Ramirez (1744–1811) had been in prison since 1801. See Doc. 300 for the review of his principal work.

270. To Henry Brougham

Brougham MSS, D.M.S. Watson Library,
University College, London, 24059   [London], Friday [29 May 1807]

My purpose in calling on you these two days was to concert measures about the *Review*, which must no longer be called The Edinburgh; and to tell you of a conversation I had with Pigott and Alexander upon the subject. We must be prepared, I fancy, to commence a new series under another title; and as the attempt will be made to continue the old work with the help of critics in the Row, and so to deceive the public as long as possible, we must endeavour to disappoint the fraud by circulating immediately, and as widely as can be, the notice of what we are to do.[1] I wrote to Jeffrey yesterday at full length; nothing, I suppose, ought to be done, till we hear from him. But I should like to talk with you on the subject, as soon as we can meet; if you are not to be at Lord Fincastle's this evening, I cannot say when that may be.[2] I am going out of town for two days.

1. Another London associate of Constable's, Cadell & Davies, suggested, as a possible solution to the dispute with Longman, a simple change of title from the *Edinburgh Review*, to the *Edinburgh Annual Register*, but Constable concluded that 'we need not think of getting either Horner or Brougham to engage in it'. (Hunter to Constable, 18 Mar., and Constable to Hunter, 22 Mar., *Constable*, i. 111 and 117; but see Doc. 263 n. 1.)
2. George Murray, Viscount Fincastle and afterwards 5th Earl of Dunmore (1762–1836).

271. To John Allen

BLPES iii. 171–2   Monday [?1 June 1807]

I hope you had an account of Lord Milton's victory this morning;[1] the mail was gone before my servant arrived at the place. I have not been in the way of hearing news today. Sir George Warrender writes, that Lord Elphinstone is almost sure of being returned; Lord Dalhousie has had special permission to vote for him. Lord Somerville was struck off the list for promising his vote the same way.[2] I am sorry to find that Loch was one of the five drunkards who broke into the town House at

Forfar and tore down Dundas's picture. They can give no better account of their exploit than this. The election dinner was in the Hall, and the squib of the 'extraordinary old woman' was fixed up under the picture; one of the baillies tore it down much to the indignation of the party, but so long as they remained tolerably sober they contented themselves with venting it by word of mouth. It was from the inn, after supper, about two o'clock in the morning, that they sallied and broke into the Town House. The five were, Maule, Ramsay, Loch, Rose and Proctor (two agents I believe). Besides the mortification of replacing the picture, they will probably be prosecuted for the breach of the peace.[3]

⟨. . .⟩

1. Milton's success in second place was not officially declared until 10 p.m. on 5 June and was known in London and the south the following day. But at that time Horner was with Allen and the Hollands in Southampton. Monday 8 June, on the other hand, would seem too late for such 'news'. Probably, therefore, in view of the exceptionally long-drawn-out canvass Horner may have been prematurely predicting victory rather than announcing it.

2. Sir George Warrender, 4th Bart (1782–1849), MP for Haddington Burghs, 1807–1812, and a strong pro-Catholic, generally sided with the Grenvilles, but deserted the Whigs after his marriage in 1810 to the daughter of a Ministerialist. On that account no doubt, but partly also because he had himself used the expression about others, some habitually called him 'Rat Warrender'. (PH v. 493–5; Creevey, ii. 74.) George Ramsay, 9th Earl of Dalhousie (1770–1838), and John Southey, 15th Baron Somerville (1765–1819: DNB), were Scottish representative peers like Elphinstone. Dalhousie survived until he was made a British peer in 1815; but neither Somerville nor Elphinstone was re-elected.

3. This incident, concerning the return as MP for Forfarshire of Loch's friend William Ramsay Maule, afterwards 1st Baron Panmure (1771–1852: DNB), is alluded to in an inaccurately dated letter in Brougham and Friends, ii. 308, and explained in PH ii. 541:

> Although Maule was returned unopposed, there was an unseemly incident at his election dinner when he and his cronies, the worse for drink, responded to the removal by a Mr Nicoll of a prominently displayed handbill lampooning Portland, by destroying a portrait of Melville which had been presented to Forfar council . . . Maule apologized and his opponents were evidently unable to make much useful capital out of the incident.

'Ramsay' was probably one of Maule's younger brothers.

272. To Francis Jeffrey

BLPES iii. 167–8 ⟨Horner, i. 429–31⟩   Southampton,[1] 5 June 1807

⟨. . .

⟨Though, at former times, I have often wished you to relinquish the Review, and betake yourself to your profession, I hold it to be a wise point of honour not to be driven off the field in this way; it is now become a most useful channel for the circulation of liberal opinions very extensively among the higher and middling classes of the people of England; they would regret the loss of it very much, and we seem bound not to throw it up, until we have established for other persons, who might be disposed to continue it, the right and practicability of preserving its absolute independence of the booksellers.⟩

I have talked with Allen about your two plans; and as your second scheme, of getting Longman to surrender for a valuable consideration the property he holds in the title, reserves the others to have recourse to at the worst, he thinks it ought to be tried. I see no objection to it, but it will probably end in nothing, so that a new work must be set a going. Longman, I should think, is confident of carrying on the *Review* with his own authors, of whose powers you cannot doubt he entertains a higher opinion than of yours; and as this negotiation will delay the appearance of the advertisement, you must be upon your guard that the sly tradesmen do not protract it for the sake of this advantage. Perhaps Smith might be of use in bringing his cousin to reason; but give him clear instructions. He is in Yorkshire at present, exercising his election franchise as well as the prerogatives of decimation. . . .

⟨. . .

⟨Elmsley has promised me to send you some short article for the next number, of whatever Review it is to be called; so has Hallam; and I have been exhorting Allen to be just and generous to poor Jovellanos, and to take charge of a late publication of American state-papers between France and the States: he scruples about the last, but promises fair for the other. I have given over promising, you know; but I own the only book I brought down with me is one about which I wish to write something. You must do the life of Kames, which is an excellent opportunity for you: grind yourself for it upon Thomson. There is a life of Hume too, with a⟩ blackguard[2] ⟨name on the title-page; but the occasion should not be missed. There are some historical works lately printed in America, which, if you please, I will send you; and a continuation of Lacrételle's little history of the Revolution, which gives the period of the Directory.[3]

⟨You talk with great contempt of our solicitude about elections, and our financial inquiries; and would have us think of nothing but Bonaparte. My system is quite the contrary: foreign dangers are always in this country sufficiently exaggerated; besides that this one is, I am persuaded, transitory: on the other hand, the decay of liberty at home goes on by imperceptible steps, requires a constant vigilance, and all the little successes that we gain by that vigilance are immediately productive of others. I quite believe, however, in your prediction of a great victory over the Russians. . . .⟩

1. The Hollands had taken a house by the water from the beginning of May to the middle of June and were visited there by several of their London friends (*Lady Holland's Journal*, ii. 228–9).
2. Leonard Horner substituted 'discreditable' in the published version.
3. Nothing is known of any contribution by Elmsley until that claimed for him on Blomfield's *Prometheus Vinctus* in ER xvii (no. xxxiii, Nov. 1810), 211–42. Nothing also is known to have been printed by Hallam in the July 1807 number, but he contributed the piece on Gillies's *History of the World* to the following number (xi (no. xxi, Oct. 1807), 40–61). The next known item by Horner himself was his review of the French translation of Fox's book mentioned in Doc. 361. Of the other items mentioned, including presumably Thomas Edward Ritchie's *Life and Writings of David Hume* (1807) and Lord Woodhouselee's *Memoirs of Lord Kames* (1807) as well as the continuation of Lacrételle's *History*, only Jovellanos was noticed in the ER (see Doc. 300 n. 1).

273. To the Duke of Somerset

BLPES iii. 169–70   The Temple, 26 June 1807

. . .

I can fully understand the indisposition which you express, to sacrifice to politics, in the present posture of our public affairs, any portion of the leisure which may be more agreeably passed in the tranquillity of literature and the country. The means of commanding even public opinion, at any rate of retaining the power of the state, are so abundant in the hands of the present Ministers, that the struggle against them is almost hopeless; and the doctrines to which they have sold themselves, are so vulgarly and childishly absurd, that one feels it like a sort of ignominy to have to contend seriously against them. At the same time, these are feelings which one ought to control, on account of the magnitude and mischief of the consequences which may ensue, if the enlightened and independent members of the Legislature shall throw up the contest in despair, or from contempt of those whom they have to oppose. The country is more deeply indebted to them for submitting to that trouble, when it is attended with disgusting circumstances; and how much soever the English public is always misled about the affairs actually going on, they are most fair and grateful judges of past services. I should be fearful of assuming too great a freedom with you, were I to state, as strongly as I see it, the importance of your name appearing among those of the persons of rank, property and character, who are making one effort, perhaps a final one, for the triumph of liberal policy and toleration over the worst prejudices and intrigues. It is by the exertions of the aristocracy that the spirit of the Constitution has, upon former occasions of this sort, prevailed; and in other countries, which have gradually lost their mixed forms of government, it has been owing almost invariably to the failure of exertion and vigilance in that part of the community.

There is an excellent tract just come over from Dublin, by Mr Parnell, called an *Historical Apology for the Catholics*; and a little quarto upon the trade with India has excited a good deal of attention and conversation, on account of the talent and information displayed by the writer, in his argument against the monopoly and sovereignty of the Company.[1] Shall I send them to you? I have not heard of any thing else very new, except the two additional volumes of Lacrételle's *Précis de la Révolution*. There is a novel indeed by Mad. de Staël, which is not much praised; I have not seen it. . . .[2]

We shall be extremely anxious till the decisions are known tomorrow morning. I have great fears indeed about the Commons, from the immense attendance; about 500 members had been sworn in yesterday. I should not be much surprised, if the Opposition is beat by 3 to 1; but their strength, independent of numbers, is very formidable to Government, and has excited much alarm, and occasioned (it is rumoured) some attempts to new-cast the Administration. The question is said to be, Canning and Lord Melville, or Perceval and the Doctor: The old Duke has been asked (it is said) to resign, but he does not think it necessary yet. What is supposed to give more solicitude to Ministers, than the force of Opposition, is the doubtful state of the King's health, which, according to this story, has of late shown appearances of constitutional decay; this is not idle rumour: I know it is confidently believed by some of the most cautious and patient of the politicians.

. . .

1. An *Historical Apology for the Irish Catholics* (1807), by Henry Brooke Parnell, 1st Baron Congleton (1776–1842), was reviewed by Sydney Smith in *ER* x (no. xx, July 1807), 299–306, and [George Grenville's] *Considerations on the Trade with India* by an unknown pen in *ibid.*, pp. 334–68.
2. Madame de Staël's *Corinne* was reviewed by Playfair in *ER* xi (no. xxi, Oct. 1807), 183–95.

274. To Lord Webb Seymour

BLPES iii. 179–80 ⟨*Horner*, i. 432–4⟩   The Temple, 6 July 1807

⟨. . .

⟨You have not yet given me the note of Alison's little scheme of Friendly Societies, which you said you would write down.[1] Give me the outline first, before you find him at leisure to fill it up. These discussions will be revived immediately by Whitbread, probably without leading to any result this session; but the attention of the public must be kept up, and I have no doubt we shall see some good done, if the King's conscience and Bonaparte do not settle the whole matter.

⟨Though the official details are not yet arrived of the last affair in Poland, no reasonable person seems to entertain any hope of its being short of decisive. What course will the conqueror take next? To the south-east of Europe, or to Ireland? At all events, he will probably give advantageous terms to the Northern powers whom he has subdued, and will march back an army to Boulogne. We shall have the autumnal alarm of invasion, with more of likelihood and a nearer approach to reality than we have yet known it.⟩ . . .

⟨Since you left us, Malthus has been a day or two in town; and gave me a little of his society, enough to enable me to judge of him; and I am happy to say, that a more philosophic candour, calm love of truth, and ingenious turn for speculation in his important branch, I have seldom met with.[2] It is quite delightful to find, how closely he has taught himself to examine the circumstances of the lower classes of society, and what a scientific turn he gives the subject. There is a new speculation of his, about the importance of the people being fed dear, which I wish you were here to discuss; it has the look of a paradox, and, like most of his views, is revolting to the common belief; but I have not yet detected the fallacy, if there is one. I will explain it to you in my next letter.⟩

1. It is not apparent what scheme this was, but a 'peculiar system' Alison had elsewhere devised for helping his parishioners to improve their lot is described by his son in Sir Archibald Alison, *Some Account of My Life and Writings. An Autobiography*, ed. Lady Alison (2 vols, Edinburgh, 1883), i. 12–13.
2. This meeting, in which Horner enlisted Malthus as a contributor to the *Review*, was apparently their first. Malthus's first review – 'Spence on Commerce' – appeared early the following year in *ER* xi (no. xxii, Jan. 1808), 429–48. There is in NLS MSS 580 (no. 323) what may well be Horner's first letter to Malthus, dated 5 Sept. 1807. If so, Horner was already helping him obtain parliamentary papers.

275. To Dr Alexander Adam

BLPES iii. 183–5   Exeter, 27 July 1807

I have just had the pleasure of receiving your kind letter of the 23rd inst. upon my arrival at this place for the Assizes. Before I left town, I put the management of the Schoolmasters' Bill into the hands of my old school fellow, and your pupil, James Abercromby; who very much to my comfort and pleasure is now a member of the House of Commons. He promised to take charge of the Bill, during the remaining stages in our House; from which I hope it is by this time sent up to the Lords. Brougham has had a good deal of trouble with Lord Walsingham, who is more strict than intelligent, and gives unnecessary vexation. He has made objections to more essential parts of the Bill than the clause for including other schoolmasters not Burgh or Parochial. These fundamental objections will be overcome I make no doubt, because they were quite unreasonable. But this particular clause, at least if it were to be made compulsory upon those other schoolmasters, is liable to objections which are not so easily answered, and which might come from higher authority than Lord Walsingham, and prove fatal to the Bill. I had a conversation with Brougham upon this point the day before I left London, and we settled it in this way; that as it was necessary to manage Lord W. it would be most advisable for Brougham to judge, according to circumstances, whether or not he would agree to strike out that clause, by way of a compromise against the other objections. If he should still make any difficulties, I advised B. to ask the favour of Mr Adam to speak to him upon this subject. I shall inform B. today of the substance of your letter.[1]

I receive your kind congratulations with great pleasure and sincere satisfaction.[2] The honour itself of a seat in Parliament is mixed with a large alloy, from the hopeless condition of the country; not merely from the tremendous chances of danger from abroad, against which one might find abundant securities in the valour and patriotism of our people, were it not that just at this crisis the Government is less provided than it ever was before either with talents or great principles. All the ills, of which our mixed monarchy is occasionally productive, seem to be collected together; from the old age of the sovereign, the predominance of court prejudices and of church craft, the treachery of public men to their party connections as well as to more important pledges, the possession of the most decisive stations in the public service by men allowed to be unfit, and in the nicest operations of government an insensibility to the greatest dangers and an infatuated contempt of all experience and authority. Rather than have recourse to such a measure as what is called Lord Howick's Bill, we will pass the Irish Insurrection Bill of which there is not a clause that does not freeze the veins of every man, who has a sense of common justice and humanity, not to speak of liberty and larger policy.[3] The history of the world does not furnish as yet the instance of such a miracle, as the preservation of a government that persisted in such a course of tyranny and folly. Even if we should not witness the last calamity, the ruin of our country by foreign conquest, it is melancholy to follow the gradual sinking of a free constitution into stupid despotism, such as our affairs exhibit at present: nor do I find, in my humble connection with public business, those feelings which I once anticipated while I yet believed in the progressive advancement of liberty and knowledge. I would not have given way to these gloomy reflections, if they did not haunt me the whole day through.

1. Abercromby had been returned MP for Midhurst at the general election. His patron, whom he now shared with Horner, was a relation of his wife, Robert Smith, 1st Baron Carrington (1752–1838: *DNB*). Thomas, 2nd Baron Walsingham (1748–1818), was Chairman of Committees in the Lords. Adam had evidently written at the beginning of the year to solicit Horner's assistance in promoting 'a Bill for the relief of the Widows and Children of the Schoolmasters of Scotland'. (See *Horner*, i. 420.)
2. On Horner's recent return to Parliament through the influence of Lord Carrington.
3. The Irish Insurrection Bill, which comprised a renewal of the Insurrection Act and a very stringent Arms Bill, had been formulated but not put forward by the late Whig Government. Designed to check the growth of the 'French party' in Ireland, the measure was adopted without alteration by Perceval and enacted to the embarrassment of the Whigs. (See Roberts, pp. 35–6.)

276. To John Allen

BLPES iii. 192–3 ⟨*Horner*, i. 434–5⟩ Ragland,[1] 19 Aug. 1807

⟨. . .

⟨I am very much satisfied in every respect with the circuit, and have found it a pleasant sort of party, though I should have gained more instruction from it if I had set out with a larger stock of legal knowledge, particularly in pleading. I never had seen so much of trials by jury before; and all I have now seen increases very much my admiration of the precision, sureness, and dispatch of that mode of trial. It is evident, however, that the establishment is too narrow for the business of the country. At Exeter, for instance, several causes were left, which the judge could not overtake; important causes of real property, and which must remain till the judges come round again. This is evidently a grievous defect in the system.⟩

Somewhat more than 30 barristers come from London to the Western circuit, and about ten more, provincials, join it at the different assize towns. Lens, whom you have seen, is at the head of the circuit, and deserves his eminence, from the great skill and discretion with which he conducts business. Jekyll is the other leader, having a silk gown; but his business is not what it would be, if he had any law to show, and I am sorry to hear it is growing less; his spirits are evidently affected by it: he is not the same man we see in town. The next to these are Dampier, brother of the bishop, a great Tory, but a very learned common lawyer; and Pell, a much younger man, whose politics seem to be very good. The Tories, I believe, have greatly the majority; though there are several among the younger ones, who hold very good opinions. Those I have remarked most, are two men whom I did not know till I joined the circuit, Taunton married to a sister of your Spanish traveller Townsend, and Larpent; they ought both to reach an eminence in the law, if that were to be reached by merit.[2] I am telling you these things, because you may like to have some account of the interior of a circuit, as well as to trace what men are getting on or likely to get on in the law – if indeed the law of England is destined to survive much longer, as any thing more than a customary in the Imperial Code.

⟨I have heard but little of the news lately, and very imperfectly; being reduced to the *Morning Chronicle*, and not receiving that very regularly. There have been some speeches in the House which I should have liked to have heard, and indeed some divisions at which I wish I had been present. Not even Grattan's authority, or that of the late Administration, would have prevailed upon me to vote for that Insurrection Bill, with the clauses it contains; which seem worthy of Charles the Second's Scotch Parliament. Can you explain to me Grattan's conduct, which appears so repugnant to the system of all his former principles? It is idle to talk of a necessity now, as different from what was urged formerly, and seemed then no justification of tyranny, or to talk of any necessity as justifying measures of that sort, which must perpetuate all the evils of discontent, if they do not bring them indeed to a crisis. Grattan's former conduct appears so uniformly excellent, and his view of the late Bill so inconsistent, that I am very anxious to understand his conduct.⟩[3]

1. Horner had arranged with Murray to make a pleasure trip to Wales after the conclusion of the circuit.
2. Jekyll was MP for Calne and Solicitor-General to the Prince of Wales. Henry Dampier (d. 1816), the younger brother of Thomas Dampier, Bishop of Rochester (1748–1812: DNB), and a distinguished ecclesiastical lawyer, became Judge of the King's Bench in 1813. Albert Pell (d. 1832) afterwards became a judge in the bankruptcy courts. Joseph Townsend (1739–1816: DNB) was the author of a *Journey through Spain* (1791); the AR xlviii (1806), p. 489, shows his daughter, not his sister, marrying on 11 Nov. William Leonard Thomas Pyle Taunton, barrister-at-law of the Middle Temple. Francis Seymour Larpent (1776–1845: DNB), according to his brother, made a lifelong friend of Horner: Sir George Larpent, ed., *The Private Journal of Judge-Advocate Larpent, attached to the head-quarters of Lord Wellington during the Peninsular War, from 1812 to its close* (3rd ed., 1854), p. viii.
3. The leaders of the Whig coalition had had little choice but to support the Irish Insurrection Bill, which after all they had conceived while in office, and under the lead of Henry Grattan (1746–1820: DNB) they had supported the measure to the chagrin of many among the Foxite rank and file. On 13 Aug. Sheridan had moved for inquiry into the state of Ireland, and contesting Grattan's point of view, ridiculed the Irish policy of the Ministry of All the Talents, and advanced the conciliatory policy towards Ireland that had ever characterized Fox and his supporters. (See *Hansard*, ix. 1185ff., and Roberts, p. 36.)

277. To John Allen

BLPES iii. 195–7 ⟨Horner, i. 438⟩   The Temple, 31 Aug. 1807

⟨I am very anxious to remove immediately all thoughts from your mind that I entertain, or ever for a moment entertained, any suspicions of Grattan's *integrity*.[1] On the contrary, all I have observed either of his public conduct or character since he came into England, has strengthened into most complete conviction an opinion I had formed of him from his transactions in Ireland, as one of the very few men of great talent in our day that have proved perfectly honest and pure in politics. I certainly regret very much and condemn the language he held, and the votes he gave upon the late Insurrection Bill; and nothing that I can imagine seems to me a sufficient explanation of such an inconsistency with the whole tenor of his former conduct.⟩

. . .

⟨Nothing yet of the Danish expedition: the delay is very much à la Duckworth.[2] Sir William Scott is said to have furnished Ministers with his opinion in favour of our right to search ships of war for deserters; such an opinion must be against all precedent, as well as all principle in the law of nations.⟩ But indeed the whole of that man's administration of that law has been an uniform sacrifice of the law and justice to the political interests and usurpations of one of the parties before him. He has never been sufficiently exposed.

1. Evidently Allen, subscribing to the compromised view of the Irish Insurrection Bill entertained by Holland House and the leadership of the Whig coalition, had responded in a very defensive manner to the very reasonable query about Grattan's conduct posed in Doc. 276, misrepresenting his friend's reference to apparent political inconsistency as an attack on the integrity of Fox's old Irish ally.

2. Upon receiving intelligence that a secret clause of the Treaty of Tilsit assured Franco-Danish naval co-operation, the Portland Ministry had almost immediately dispatched a large naval expedition under the command of Admiral James Gambier, afterwards 1st Baron Gambier (1756–1833: *DNB*) and Rear-Admiral Sir John Thomas Duckworth (1748–1817: *DNB*) to Copenhagen with orders to confiscate or destroy the Danish fleet. On 5 Sept. Horner condemned the expedition as immoral in a letter to Thomas Thomson (*Thomson*, pp. 118–20) and observed that Ministers 'take the chance of being condemned to shame, as well as the certainty of being abandoned by the mob, if they fail'.

278. To John Allen

BLPES iii. 197–8 The Temple, 22 Sept. 1807

. . . I shall be glad to hear from you what you find to be the political state of our friends at Edinburgh, as well as whether there is any prospect of the corps of liberal and honest men there getting a new reinforcement. It would have been well for us last year, if the honest men (there can be none more so than most of the Whigs at Edinburgh) had been equally enlarged in their views, and accommodating in their manners. There is a little band of the most enlightened and liberal men there, who are friends of liberty upon every question that has the least salt of generality in it, but who were repelled by the fanaticism, it may really be called so, as well as by the apparent selfishness of our own friends. . . .

279. To Leonard Horner

BLPES iii. 203–204 The Temple, 24 Sept. 1807

. . .

I know of no news worth sending; the story of Lord Malmesbury going to Paris I take to be an exaggeration, of some little truth at bottom: nothing I should think more likely than an overture to negotiate from Bonaparte.¹ I fear our Sovereign Lord the King has no thoughts of a sincere peace, and his present Ministers are all of the war faction, and not likely to be rendered more moderate by their success against Copenhagen.²

. . .

1. Beginning in April 1807 the effects of the commercial warfare between Britain and France and the encouragement of the *ER* and a number of Foxite newspapers including the *MC* gave rise to agitation for peace among the commercial classes of the North, and afterwards petitions to Parliament were prepared in Manchester, Bolton, and Oldham. In late September the French Government communicated a desire to negotiate to the British Government, and the Foxite wing of the Whig coalition became enthusiastic when the *MC* reported that the British Government would dispatch James Harris, 1st Earl of Malmesbury (1746–1820: *DNB*) to Paris. The flirtation between the two Governments, which would come to nothing, accentuated disagreement between the Foxite and Grenvillite factions within the Whig coalition. (See Taylor, pp. 157–9.)

2. The expedition was an unqualified success. The British fleet silenced the Danish shore batteries, bombarded Copenhagen, and made off with the entire Danish fleet in tow after Admiral Gambier had forced the Danish Government to sign a convention. See Taylor, pp. 149–54, for an account of the bickering in the Whig ranks occasioned by the success of the expedition.

280. To J.A. Murray

⟨Horner, i. 438–40⟩   Russell Square, 29 Sept. 1807

⟨. . .

⟨I have made up my mind upon this Copenhagen business; you will think it strange, perhaps, that I had it to make up. But I expressly put myself into double upon the subject, and endeavoured for a while to view it as one of the extreme cases of that necessity which has no law. I am returned from every deviation that I attempted into the intricacies of state expediency to the daylight of common justice and old rules. It was an unwise measure even for the purposes of the actual war; with any prospect of future character, or of future wars by sea, this impolicy becomes still more apparent; and then it is, beyond even all the proceedings of the Convention or the Directory or Bonaparte against neutral nations, a violation of the laws by which the society of the human race is preserved. Sir William Scott, however, told Sydney Smith that no *principle* is more *plainly* laid down than our right to take the navy of the Danes; and so he has been ready to say, and would be still ready, for any outrage or breach of the law of nations that the Government of this country has dared or is meditating to commit. What say your philosophers at Edinburgh on this occasion? . . .⟩

281. To Francis Jeffrey

BLPES iii. 205–206   London, 30 Sept. 1807

. . .

I cannot quite remember what coarseness or asperity I had perpetrated in my last letter, which drew from you so severe a reprehension; unless it was that I had spoken irreverently of your essay on household furniture, in which by the bye I am supported by all the good authorities.[1] Even your partial and mildest of all friends Charles Bell is so moved with indignation, that I verily believe he has composed a counter-piece, in which he adopts other principles of upholstery. Sincerely however, I ask your pardon, if I got beyond the limits of my accustomed licence; for I have always made a duty of saying what I thought of your articles, as well as of telling you what I found to be the general opinion of others. It would be a shame if little Tommy [?Thomson] were to make more words between us.

Tell me what you think of the Copenhagen business. If it is to your taste, I believe you will have more of the same sort; for Wellesley will very shortly be in the Cabinet, and his active restless mind will speedily take the ascendancy over the present set, in which all the men that have any talents have been bred for their whole lives to the habits of followers.[2] The pamphlet on the West Indies by one Lowe, is by the man whom you sent with a note of introduction to me, but who did not much captivate me; though his appearance of zeal for your *protégés* did him credit. He is the person, I understand, who answered Brougham's *State of the Nation*, as it is always called; and I think it is since I heard this, that I have not liked Mr Lowe so much. He is evidently an active person, and will make himself a name among the book-makers and newspaper editors. He was clerk in a West India merchant's counting house, when he wrote that answer, which succeeded so well that he has changed his trade. This West India subject ought to be carefully treated in the *Review*; for it is a momentous one. A speedy decision must be made by Government, and upon that decision much will depend. There is a good deal of information in the evidence taken before the Committee, and much that the Report would not lead you to expect to find there. The Report was manufactured by two or three persons who have West India property themselves, and are addicted to the creed of Perceval & co. on the rights of neutrals.[3]

1. Horner's previous letter to Jeffrey surviving in BLPES is that of 5 June 1807 (Doc. 272); it contained no critical remarks on the ER, but contested Jeffrey's criticism of the Whigs. The article to which Horner refers is Jeffrey's notice of Thomas Hope on *Household Furniture* (1807), ER x (no. xx, July 1807), 478–86.
2. Richard Colley, Marquess Wellesley (1760–1842: DNB), did not enter the Cabinet until he joined Perceval's Ministry in December 1809.
3. Joseph Lowe, the author of An *Inquiry into the state of the British West Indies* (1807), had retorted to Brougham's *Inquiry into the State of the Nation* (1806) with his own anonymously-published pamphlet entitled An *Answer to the Inquiry into the State of the Nation* (1806). This pamphlet and *The West India Commonplace Book*, by Sir William Young (1807), together with two other pamphlets on West India affairs by Charles Bosanquet (see Doc. 403), were severely mauled by Henry Brougham in ER xi (no. xxi, Oct. 1807), 145–67. The 'Report from the Select Committee . . . on the Commercial State of the West India

Colonies' may be found in *Hansard*, ix. cols lxxx–lxxxvi, and *BPP*, 1807, iii. 1–90, and is
commented on in Brougham's review of two further pamphlets on West Indian affairs in *ER*
xiii (no. xxvi, Jan. 1809), 382–413.

282. To Lord Holland

BLPES iii. 209–10   [?London], 14 Nov. 1807

. . .

The proclamation coming out tonight is not to declare Bonaparte's coasts
blockaded, but to instruct our cruisers to bring in every neutral going to them, that
they may be forced in the first instance to land their goods here and pay duties to us.
At least I hear it is so; and that this measure is preferred to that of direct retaliation,
as being more lenient. If this be the measure, it has probably been recommended at
least by more commercial motives, of getting the duties, and perhaps creating a
chance that the neutrals when they have landed their own cargoes may take off
British goods. It seems to be a much more foolish proceeding, than a general
blockade would be; and I have not yet found out the wisdom of that. Then there is
this difference between the two; that we have a right to do the one against neutrals,
and no right to do the other. Is this sound law of nations?[1]

. . .

1. The Orders in Council of 11 Nov. had asserted Britain's right to retaliate against Napoleon's Berlin Decree but struck at neutral trade by forcing all neutral vessels bound for Europe
   to stop first at a British port and pay duties. (See Taylor, pp. 181–6, for an account of Whig
   opinion on the issue in late 1807.)

283. Note by Horner

BLPES viii. 53   12–13 Dec. 1807

Canning's negotiation with Lord Grenville's Administration, a very short time
before their loss of office, which has been alluded to in several publications, had
gone so far as this. He gave them to understand, that he was very loosely connected
with his friends of that Opposition; that he approved of some of the measures of
Administration, and disapproved of the opposition that had been made to one or
two points, in particular to the vote of money for the Catholic College of
Maynooth:[1] he gave them to understand, in short, that he was a man afloat; but on
the other hand that he was not to be expected to give his support to Ministers,
unless he were received into their party as a considerable person, and that it would
depend upon the station to be assigned to him whether he would coalesce with
them. Among the other measures of Ministry which he stated himself to approve of

was Lord Howick's Bill for admitting Catholics to rank in the Army and Navy. While this sort of treaty was going on, Mr Canning, to use the vulgar phrase, smelt a rat: He found what was going on at Windsor upon the subject of that Bill, and saw very clearly that he had another game to play.

13 Dec.

Mr Canning never saw Lord Grenville in the course of this negotiation; the communication was made from the former through Lord Temple. What he stipulated for, was a seat in the Cabinet for himself, and considerable places for Huskisson and Sturges Bourne. He was given to understand, that the office of Secretary at War might possibly be soon vacant; but that it would be offered in the first instance to Whitbread: so there could be no promise made to him. Lord Grenville was inclined to take the proposition from Canning into consideration; Lord Howick and Lord H. Petty were averse to it. The vacancy that was likely to have been made in the Cabinet was by the retirement of Mr Grenville from the Admiralty in favour of Lord Holland.[2] Mr Canning, in the course of the above negotiation, gave the Ministers' friends some intelligence of the intrigue that was going on at Windsor against Lord Howick's Bill; and afterwards he complained that he was used by them rather harshly considering that he had given them the first intelligence: he has been considered by some of those, who were subsequently his colleagues for a time, as having betrayed them in giving that intelligence.[3]

1. The Whig Ministry had proposed, and Canning's colleagues in Opposition had resisted, a substantial increase in the Maynooth grant (*Hansard*, viii. 938–40 and 1079–88).
2. Thomas Grenville had remained First Lord of the Admiralty and Holland Lord Privy Seal until the fall of the Ministry.
3. For further comment on the Grenvillite flirtation with Canning see *Holland Memoirs*, ii. 196, *Dropmore MSS*, ix. 67, and *Buckingham*, iv. 125–8 and 140.

284. To John Allen

BLPES iii. 211–12   The Temple, 4 Jan. 1808

. . .

Are you in possession of any accounts of the imports into Portugal from the Brazils for the last two or three years, besides those of the bullion which I got from you? If you have such, I should like very much to look at them.

Robinson, the editor of Sir William Scott's decisions, has just published a collection of all the proclamations and orders of council, issued during the present war, relative to prize subjects and maritime war. There is another pamphlet just printed, which it may be useful for you to have, called 'An Exposition of the Orders in Council, digested into classes; by Mr Flowerdew', a city agent.[1] It is published by Black & Parry in Leadenhall Street; the former by Butterworth.

There is a subject, on which it has struck me that it would be proper to order some papers in the House of Commons, as connected, perhaps to an important degree, with the discussion of the late restrictions of neutral trade; I mean, the practice of Privy Council Licences for trading with the enemy. These are known to be a considerable source of fees to the clerks of the council; they afford opportunities also of favouritism and partiality. What has made me particularly think of making an inquiry into it, was hearing, that a considerable cargo of *indigo* went lately by licence from London to France. It is surely absurd to have orders of council, prohibiting the general trade of neutrals with the enemy and that for the purpose of depriving the enemy of supplies, if you permit exceptions in particular instances which yield him a supply of what he wants most.[2]

. . .

1. Evidently, then, Christopher Robinson, editor of *Reports of cases argued and determined in the High Court of Admiralty . . . with the judgments of the Right Hon. Sir William Scott* (6 vols, 1799–1808), was also the compiler of *Notifications, Orders and Instructions, relating to the Prize Subjects during the Present War*, published by Butterworth and White in 1807. D. C. Flowerdew's *An exposition of the Three Orders in Council of the 11th November, 1807* (1807) was indeed sold, if not actually published, by Black & Parry.
2. Dating from 1803, and continuing until 1813, licences issued by the Privy Council authorized trade with the enemy. Until 1809 general licences covering all but specifically restricted commodities were available; after 1809 special licences covering only grain were issued. Horner's attention was apparently focused on them by the provisions of the Order in Council of 11 Nov. 1807. (See pp. 225–6.)

285. To James Reddie

NLS MSS 3704, ff. 27–8   The Temple, 25 Jan. 1808

Will you oblige me so far as to give me another copy of that little book of process which you drew up for the Burgh Court of Glasgow?[1] I lent my copy to Mr Bentham, and he liked it so much and was so desirous that I should procure one for him, that I resolved to part with it and trust to your furnishing me with another. I ought not to omit telling you, that Mr Bentham said he was prompted by reading this little performance to ask me, whether you were not acquainted with some of his speculations on Judicial procedure as stated in M. Dumont's *rédaction*. That, I could not particularly answer for; but I recollected very well, and told him of it, that you were long ago a reader of his own compositions, and that it was you who first set me to study his *Principles of Morals and Legislation*. I directed a little project, for a court of Delegates to hear appeals, which he has explained upon a single sheet, to be sent to you last week.[2]

I do not know whether you remember a sort of promise you gave me last summer, to send me some details of information with respect to the progressive increase of poor's rates in Glasgow and the neighbouring district. That is so important a subject in many points of view in which I am repeatedly led to consider it, that if you could supply me with such information without giving yourself trouble, I should consider it a great favour done me.

. . .

1. See Doc. 245.
2. Horner had told Thomas Thomson on 1 Jan. that only two subjects – the improvement of the courts of justice and the reform of parliamentary representation – gave him any interest in Scottish politics and disclosed that he was attempting to unite Scotland's divided law reformers. (*Thomson*, p. 117. See also: Horner to Murray, 11 and 18 Jan., 12 Feb., 24 May, and 21 June, BLPES iii. 213–14, 218–20, 222–3, 252–5, and 269–70; Bentham to Horner, 24 May, and Horner to Bentham, 22 June 1808, *Bentham*, vii. 492–6 and 509–510.)

286. To Francis Jeffrey

BLPES iii. 224–7 ⟨*Horner*, i. 446–9⟩   The Temple, 17 Feb. 1808

⟨There is no chance (I fear) of my being able to write any thing for you next time, because the whole month of March I shall be riding the circuit, and till I set out I have my hands full. If I can meet with any person whom I can induce to assist you, and who is worthy of being admitted by you as an auxiliary, I will not forget your necessities. Since Malthus has begun to contribute, I hope it will not be for want of solicitation on your part, if he does not continue to supply you with articles. Of all subjects, political economy is at present the most productive of useful publications, and though his general views are sometimes imperfect, he is always candid and an advocate for what he believes to be most liberal and generous. You are good enough to ask me to recommend some subjects to you; I have long been a truant from literature, and find very little leisure to read any thing but black-letter and parliamentary accounts. But I will try to recollect some of your omissions, which ought to be supplied.

⟨There is Horne Tooke's work on language,[1] of which we talked long ago; a very fit subject for yourself, not because you have the learning that some would think indispensable, but because what is in truth required for improving that speculation is a more enlarged knowledge of metaphysics, and of the relations of the different sciences, than the acute inventor is himself possessed of. Dr Jamieson's new work on etymology[2] would give occasion for quite a different sort of dissertation; not on the philosophy of grammar, but on the actual history of the languages of Europe, with many curious illustrations of the philosophical history of manners and customs among the common people. The traditionary preservation of so many catholic, and even the most ancient pagan, rites of superstition, among the children and old women of your presbyterian country, is very whimsical, and must be very mortifying to the serious and feeble.

⟨The mention of the Presbyterians puts me in mind of a book, which I read last summer, and which has not been reviewed yet: the *Memoirs of Colonel Hutchinson*, one of Charles the First's[3] judges, by his widow.[4] It is a composition of much merit in various respects, and would give you an excellent opportunity for that characteristic criticism, which you ought to be very vain of; the personages who play what they thought a most important part in that day, are brought forward with strong effect; and the fanaticism of the times exhibited so far in a new light, that you see it in alliance with elegance of manners and accomplishments, mitigated by them, and corrupting them. If you could review Mrs Hutchinson without quizzing her, which I rather doubt, you might give a very gratifying and useful impression, of the practicability of accommodating even to the sternest times of civil war, the same domestic virtues, and the same love of letters and the arts, which thrive best, no doubt, in tranquillity. I do not mean that those times are coming to us; we shall live on in the tranquillity of a vulgar servitude and degeneracy. In the spring you will have many fine subjects;⟩ the three poets are all to bring forth. ⟨Campbell, I am told by his friends Richardson and Charles Bell, has written a charming poem of narrative and description,[5] and Scott, of course, will be very vehement with irregular success;⟩ and Rogers's polished little Columbus of five hundred lines, after the toil of twelve years, the gestation of a mammoth for the birth of a dormouse, will put it upon you, I fear, to destroy a very good friend. ⟨I hope you will review⟩ all of ⟨them with your own hand; nobody else has written a sentence of literature in the *Edinburgh Review* that can be endured.⟩

. . .

⟨I shall mention Buchanan's project to Mr Windham, who inquired of me the other day if I knew any thing about him. Encourage him by all means to try the experiment, at least, of a newspaper in Scotland; though I doubt very much whether your advice of mere impartiality will help him to a better sale, than his own propensities of Whiggism. The latter has but a poor chance in Scotland, and the former none anywhere. The man had better be left to his own opinions and inclinations; for he will give them more warmth and force, than if he writes impartially upon system: a heavy monotonous fairness is the last thing that people will read in their newspaper.[6] People read it to get their daily opinions and impressions; it is now a necessary of life, especially in the country towns, and a man feels himself as awkward if he walks out without his political creed for the day, as if he wanted his breakfast. Newspapers are a new means of influence to government in England; and no set of ministers ever understood this more practically, than the present; their indefatigable, systematic attention to the daily press is quite admirable: and the persevering activity with which the most palpable lies, the most atrocious calumnies and misrepresentations are circulated and repeated, after every refutation, is irresistible. Nothing ever equalled them, but the *littérateurs* of the French Revolution. It sometimes strikes me as quite ludicrous, to see the scrupulous, indolent leaders of our half-combined party, make a few feeble efforts to oppose this torrent, by good writing and virtuous indignation.

⟨I had some thoughts of saying something about politics before I ended this letter; but I have no time, and in truth little inclination. It is a subject in which all the interest I now feel, partakes of dejection and disgust. I have no fears, like you, about conquest; but I see the progress of a base servitude so rapid, and the degeneracy of the laws and constitution is now so sensible, that I despair of any good being done by any exertion.[7]

⟨. . .⟩

1. Part II of Horne Tooke's *Diversions of Purley* had been published in 1805. It was not separately reviewed in *ER*.
2. *The Etymological Dictionary of the Scottish Language* (1808) by Dr John Jamieson (1759–1838: *DNB*) was reviewed, perhaps by William Stevenson, in *ER* xiv (no. xxvii, Apr. 1809), 121–45.

3. The manuscript reads 'the King's'.

4. *The Life of Colonel Hutchinson* was reviewed by Jeffrey in ER xiii (no. xxv, Oct. 1808), 1–25.

5. John Richardson (1780–1864: *DNB*), a parliamentary solicitor in London, was a close friend of Jeffrey and Walter Scott as well as of Campbell. Charles, afterwards Sir Charles, Bell (1774–1842: *DNB*) was George Bell's younger brother and destined to become a famous surgeon. Campbell's *Gertrude of Wyoming* was reviewed by Jeffrey in ER xiv (no. xxvii, Apr. 1809), 1–19.

6. David Buchanan managed to start his liberal newspaper the *Weekly Register* in Edinburgh, but it lasted only about a year and in 1810 he became editor of the *Caledonian Mercury*.

7. Horner expressed these despondent views shortly after the parliamentary debates on the Orders in Council and on the Danish expedition had produced small Whig divisions (Taylor, pp. 196–203). He expressed them, moreover, in the midst of bitter disagreement on wartime policy within the Whig coalition. On 29 Feb. the last of Whitbread's three resolutions for peace negotiations with France had been opposed by the Whig hierarchy but supported by the most respected Foxites in the Commons, a troubled Horner among them. Horner departed for the circuit almost immediately after the division and prudently avoided political comment in his correspondence until April, when he returned to London. (For Whitbread's resolutions and the related debate see *Hansard*, x. 801–856. See also Taylor, pp. 203–207, and Roberts, p. 112.)

287. To John Allen

BLPES iii. 234–5   The Temple, Tuesday [12 Apr. 1808]

. . .

We were in the House till four this morning, dividing, I think very injudiciously, for an amendment of the Reversions Bill.[1] The conclusion of the debate took an unexpected turn. St Stephen,[2] whose animation as well as incoherence seem to border upon insanity, disposed of four or five matters of constitutional doctrine like the most servile Ministerial lawyer, and with great ignorance and vulgarity. He was answered by Burdett in a speech, which showed a talent for reply that I never conceived him capable of, and was in the most correct style throughout of parliamentary language and Whig sentiments. Windham however could not sit quiet under so much alarming democracy, and to save himself from the imputation of voting with Burdett upon common grounds, he delivered in a regular discourse the most extravagant defence of Government influence and corr[uption] turning chiefly upon the notable sophism, that in [cor]ruption there are necessarily two parties, and that the people must be bad before the government can corrupt. Sheridan in a forcible short speech protested against such doctrines. At the first I felt it uncomfortable that we should so expose our differences of opinion; but it is better perhaps even at that price to purchase the advantage of reviving occasionally in the H. of C. subjects which are fast becoming quite obsolete.

1. Prior to the third reading of the Offices in Reversion Bill on 11 Apr. Horner had conducted research on that question at the request of Lord Holland, and on 27 Feb. he had written Holland a letter which expressed generally hostile views to the granting of judicial and ministerial offices in reversion (BLPES iii. 228–9).

2. James Stephen.

288. To James Loch

BLPES iii. 236–40 (draft)   [?London], 22 Apr. 1808

. . .

. . . I am all for an establishment . . . both upon Hume's principle, and upon Bonaparte's (as expressed at the time of the Concordat) . . . though I derive them from a still larger view of human nature, and would assign a more permanent duration to those feelings and natural prejudices than is implied in the propositions of the philosophical and imperial scoffers. Being all for an establishment, I am all for residence too and for giving as much decency and independence as possible to the officiating parochial clergy.[1] . . .

. . .

1. Although some of Horner's closest political colleagues opposed the Stipendiary Curates Bill, which had been introduced by Perceval, he himself supported it despite his suspicions about Perceval's motives.

289. From John Allen

BLPES iii. 241–4   Holland House, 26 Apr. 1808

I have no news to send you either with respect to Spain or America, but I cannot refrain from expressing to you my very great satisfaction at the intelligence from Spain given in the *Morning Chronicle* of today.[1] I rejoice that a worthless minion is deprived of the power which he has so long abused, and that so excellent and enlightened a man as the Duke of Infantado is at the head of the government of the country. I have no doubt of this revolution having been effected, if not by the aid, at least with the consent of the French, but I do not see the possibility of any government maintaining itself in Spain in opposition to them, and therefore I am glad that these persons, whom I know to be warmly attached to the honour and liberties of their Country, have been skilful enough to procure the co-operation of France in measures, which if wisely pursued, must end in elevating Spain, at no very distant period, to her former place among nations.

It would be untrue to say of the Duke of Infantado that he has a predilection either for France or for England. He is devoted to his own country and has been long indignant at the mean, jealous and corrupt system pursued by the Court of Madrid. When we were in Spain he was distinguished as the only grandee of the first rank who had never had the meanness to pay his court to the Prince of the Peace by any other attentions than those which were due to him as head of the Army. He was educated at Paris, and for a man of his rank he is well versed in mathematics, chemistry and natural philosophy. He has established several manufactures on his estates, particularly a cotton manufacture at Santander but latterly he has applied himself more to agriculture and planting. He served in a very distinguished manner in the war against France, and I have heard him mentioned as one who gave proof on that occasion of uncommon military genius. He was a favourite officer under Union, who defended so long and so ably the Western Pyrenees against the French.[2] His age at present is about 40. He is unmarried and has an unencumbered estate (very rare among the Spanish grandees) of about £40,000 or £50,000 a year besides immense influence from his senorial [sic] rights, which (next to Medina Celi's) are the most extensive of any grandee in Spain.[3] He was never in England, but he reads English perfectly, and knows the works of some of our Poets and Historians. He is well acquainted with the ancient history and constitution of his own country, and should he be in a situation to attempt any reform of its present government I think that he will adapt his innovations as nearly as possible to its ancient, and though obsolete in practice, not yet forgotten institutions. I have heard him more than once express his admiration of the skill and prudence with which the English had proceeded in setting bounds to the Royal authority, and therefore I should expect that while he maintained the greatest exterior of respect for the new King, he would take the most effectual means to prevent the future abuses of his authority.[4]

I have no doubt that Jovellanos will be recalled from his prison in Majorca, and if his health permits, probably reinvested with the office of Secretary of the Home Department.[5] He is a very honest and most enlightened man, but too rigid about small matters, and one who sooner than yield a little to a friend would allow every thing to fall into the hands of an enemy. Saavedra, who was his colleague in office and Minister for Foreign Affairs, is a man of quick parts and extensive genius, but irresolute and unsteady.[6] Urquijo, another ex-minister, is a presumptuous coxcomb, and I hope will never more be heard of in a public situation.[7] Florida Blanca is still alive, but broken down with age and devotion.[8] Thank God, none of the others have a portion of bigotry – nor, except Urquijo, have they any portion of the intolerance which at one time disgraced the French and did so much harm to liberty and philosophy.

Every thing in the public news from America wears a hostile appearance, but I have not heard what private news Rose has brought with him.[9]

. . .

1. Following Bonaparte's invasion and popular demonstrations against the Prince of the Peace, Charles IV had in the middle of March dismissed his favourite and attempted himself to abdicate in favour of his son. One of Ferdinand's first acts was to appoint the wealthy but popular Pedro Mendoza de Toledo, Duke of Infantado (1773–1841) chief minister. But by this time the French were in possession of Madrid and able in May to force the abdication of both Ferdinand and Charles and then to seize the crown for Joseph Bonaparte.

2. Luis Fermin Carvajal y Vargas, Conde de la Union (1752–94), was killed in November 1794.

3. Don Luis Joaquín Fernández de Córdova, 14th Duque de Medinaceli (1780–1840), whose palace in his father's time is described in *Lady Holland's Spanish Journal*, pp. 136 and 197.

4. Here, well before the commencement of hostilities between Spain and France, Allen hints at the interpretation of Spanish affairs that would be embraced by the Holland House circle until 1815. Infantado, who later became a regular guest at Lady Holland's dinner table, was compared to George Washington and regarded as a good Whig involved in a Spanish constitutional struggle, while the Spanish 'patriots' who shortly resisted the French were supported in a vacuum, without reference to the broader context of European politics, on much the same ground as Fox had supported the Americans in their revolutionary war

against Britain. (See Taylor, pp. 224–9, for a summary of the evolution of the view of Spanish affairs embraced by Holland and his circle. See also Lean, p. 138.)

5. Jovellanos became Minister of the Interior in Joseph's first Ministry on 1 July, and when that attempt to reconcile the Spaniards to what had happened failed he became a member of the Central Junta.

6. Francisco de Saavedra (1746–1819) had been Jovellanos's colleague in 1797–8 and succeeded him as Chief Minister. In 1808 he became President of the Seville Junta, and Minister of Finance in the Central Junta.

7. Mariano Luis de Urquijo (1768–1817), who had several times been a Minister under Charles IV, was named Chief Minister by Joseph on 1 July, and unlike Jovellanos stayed with the French.

8. Don José Moniño, Conde de Floridablanca (1728–1808), another former Minister, in September became President of the Supreme Junta but caught a chill and died in December.

9. In November 1807 President Jefferson, making no distinction between the Order in Council promulgated by the late Whig Ministry and that of the succeeding Portland Ministry and referring angrily to the recent forcible impressment of seamen from the American ship *Chesapeake* by HMS *Leopard*, had obtained congressional authorization to expel British warships from American ports and followed up in December with the Embargo Act. Afterwards Congress had debated military preparations at length and Canning had dispatched George Henry Rose (1771–1855: *DNB*) to Washington as special emissary with orders to negotiate reparations for the *Chesapeake-Leopard* affair. Rumours of impending war with America had circulated in London dating from the autumn of 1807. The Whig attack on the Orders in Council of Nov. 1807 during the 1808 parliamentary session had included repeated warnings about war with America, and the British press continued to report alarming tensions in Anglo-American relations when Rose returned to England in the spring. (See Taylor, pp. 168 and 208–209.)

290. To John Allen

BLPES iii. 245 ⟨Horner, i. 449–50⟩   Wells, Thursday [28] Apr. 1808

⟨I thank you very much for your letter yesterday; not more for the information concerning the characters of the men brought into power by this revolution, than for the fit of hope which you have given me, that it may possibly lead to good. It is a doubtful and hazardous course, however, which the Duc d'Infantado has adopted for restoring liberty to his country, by the assistance of such invaders as the French troops are in the present age. And perhaps the hazard and uncertainty lie chiefly in this, that the further steps of such a course require harder and coarser virtues than usually belong to such a character as you describe the Duc d'Infantado's to be. As far as the individual is concerned, the success would be so glorious, as to be worth every chance and danger; and there have been so few moments lately, when one could find a pretext for indulging any hopes about the politics of the world, that I find it very agreeable to fall in with your sanguine expectations. It is so pleasant to dream again. . . .⟩

291. To James Loch

BLPES iii. 309–10 [London], Thursday [?5 May 1808]

. . .

The India Committee did not agree to the proposed loan of $2^1/_2$ million. I understood so at least; and that Perceval, who was present that day, objected to it – though it seems strange, that [Robert] Dundas and he should have taken such an opportunity of differing in any opinion. Creevey says it is quite evident that the wish and intention of Government is to get India to themselves, and though they will not incur the odium of appearing to overthrow the company, they will be very contented spectators of its fall. Mr Grant whispered to Creevey, 'mind how you lend yourself to the Government.' Sir John Anstruther, and Dundas, are vehement against too much exposure; and recommend a report in general terms. Mr Grant, like a bankrupt who knows it is come to the worst, is for making a clean breast. By the way, your usual sagacity failed in this instance; you rejoiced in Sir John's appointment, because he would be all for publicity. Grant has read, and read it twice, a long exposé of the state of the Company's affairs; Creevey has given notice that he will move to add this to the report; and Sir John has given notice that he will certainly oppose that motion.[1]

. . .

1. On 20 Apr. Charles Grant, the Deputy Chairman of the East India Company, had presented to the Commons its petition for pecuniary assistance to meet its deficit of £2,400,000 and the House had referred it to the Select Committee already examining the Company's affairs (Hansard, xi. 70–72). Creevey, Dundas, and Grant were all members of that committee, as was Sir John Anstruther (1753–1811: DNB). Creevey duly asked for the release of more information on 6 May and, after Anstruther had spoken against it, was duly refused (ibid., 128–31).

292. To J.A. Murray

BLPES iii. 246–7 [London], 12 May 1808

. . .

We had a strange scene in the House last night, as you will see by the newspapers; it is not very easy to guess what reason the Ministers had for saying nothing for themselves, or to justify such conduct even in point of prudence. The thing no doubt was quite indefensible; but that is hardly reason enough for not making a show of defending it. We made a larger division than we should have done, I believe, if there had been some speeches made, whatever they might have been; some of their voters went away, and one or two came out with us. Wilberforce and his friend Stephen went off; the former having expressed to several persons his entire disapprobation of the proposed appointment of Duigenan. It is curious that this man should have any name for political honesty left; it is almost a shadow indeed, now.[1]

The Duke of Cumberland, at his own solicitation, has been lately reconciled to the Prince; and the price he pays for being taken into favour, is to break off from the Princess, of whose wrongs he has been hitherto a busy and clamorous vindicator. The only inference that is made from this offer of reconciliation, is, that he must believe the King's health declining. But what base wretches they are, from first to last.

. . .

1. Dr Patrick Duigenan (1735–1816: *DNB*), the Protestant champion in the House of Commons and a critic of the Irish policy of the Ministry of All the Talents, had recently been made a Privy Counsellor. The promotion was greeted with considerable amazement and disgust; but, while utterly disdaining to explain itself, the Government nonetheless fended off its critics in the Commons by a vote of 179 to 107. (*Hansard*, xi. 145–57; see also Roberts, pp. 31 and 37.)

293. To J.A. Murray

BLPES iii. 248–9   [?London], 14 May 1808

. . .

I have seen part of the *Review*. Marmion appears to be very fairly judged of; but it is a criticism which will never be forgiven. I am very much struck with the extracts from Crabbe's poems; they show great power, though the subjects are not the most suited to poetry.[1]

. . .

1. Horner was correct about the review by Jeffrey of Scott's *Marmion* that appeared in *ER* xii (no. xxiii, Apr. 1808), 1–35 (Clive, p. 157). Jeffrey also reviewed Crabbe's *Poems* in the same number, pp. 131–51.

294. To J.A. Murray

BLPES iii. 250–51   [London], 17 May 1808

. . .

You will have seen from the newspapers that Romilly has given notice of some Bills he is going to bring forward, for the improvement of our criminal laws. The object is, to give a compensation, at the discretion of the judge who tries, to those persons who are acquitted and have been confined upon the charge. The other is, to diminish the number of capital felonies, by repealing some of the old Statutes respecting larcenies, which are in observance only as to the sentence of death and not the execution. Of course, he will be opposed by those who affect to dislike all innovation, and probably by the judges who are in general fond of severe laws. We shall probably have some returns moved for, from the Secretary of State's office, of the number of criminals committed as well as of convictions and executions, for some years back, which will give a striking picture of the state of criminal jurisprudence in England. I have seen such accounts for a few years, and they are curious.[1]

> 1. Romilly was to become the most active parliamentary reformer of penal law during the Napoleonic Wars, and in all cases Horner was to be among the handful of politicians who supported his campaign. On 18 May Romilly successfully moved for leave to bring in his two bills (*Romilly*, ii. 245–7).

295. To John Allen

BLPES iii. 256–7   [?London], Friday [27 May 1808]

. . .

   I was not surprised at the smallness of the division; but had indeed expected the minority to be still smaller, of a Parliament elected under the influence of the cry against Popery.[1] Grattan's speech was admirable, both in argument and eloquence; I am convinced no other person now in the House of Commons is capable of speaking in the same elevated manner. You will have heard how much reason the friends of Catholic emancipation have to rejoice, both at the composition of the minority in respect of Irish members, and at the improved temper and cast of argument with which the debate was conducted. I cannot help persuading myself that the Protestant bigotry has received its death-blow; and that the oftener the merits of the question are discussed, both in parliament, and by the press, the more speedily will the measure be finally carried.

> 1. On 25 May Grattan had moved to take the Catholic petition into consideration, and in debate George Ponsonby had avowed that John Milner (1752–1826: *DNB*), Bishop of Castabala, had authorized him to make the proposal. Although Petty and others would have preferred that the petition had not been brought forward, the Whigs generally supported their leaders. The motion was beaten 281–128, and among the minority were no less than forty Irish members. On 27 May Grenville made the same motion in the Lords and secured seventy-four votes including that of the Bishop of Norwich. (*Hansard*, xi. 643–94; MC, 28 May; Henry Grattan, *Memoirs of the Life and Times of the Rt Hon. Henry Grattan* (5 vols, 1839–46), v. 381; Roberts, pp. 42–3.)

296. To James Loch

BLPES iii. 262–4 ⟨*Horner*, i. 450–52⟩   The Temple, 13 June 1808

⟨In consequence of my being in the country, and my letters following me there and back again, I did not receive those you have written to me lately in their proper order. Two of them I have only now received, and the other yesterday.[1] I was down in Buckinghamshire with Abercromby, at Lord Carrington's;[2] and for four blessed days we were as idle in the open air, as it was possible for two men to be.⟩

Your criticism upon the length of Mr Fox's sentences is, I think, well founded; they are often too long, and sometimes involved too much.[3] Not that the effect of this is *obscurity* in the common meaning of the word; but the whole purport of the sentence, with the bearing of its several parts upon each other, does not perspicuously and easily present itself. This defect gives somewhat the air of a speech to many papers, which would have been more impressive and pleasing, if they had not that character. The same criticism in substance had occurred to myself, in another form: the periods are too rhetorical and of rather too artificial a shape, while the diction is often too familiar and even vulgar. Now for history, I should prefer a style, in which, while the expressions were a little elevated, the run of the sentences was natural and conversational. There are many passages of this very book, cast in that style; and these I think the best. But it would require a volume to tell you all I have to say about this admirable and delightful volume.

⟨I wish you would let me know *to whom* the King made that notable remark about Mr Fox's slovenliness in writing notes. Your conviction that this was said in order to give a tone to the court about the book, is a pleasant instance of the refinement you philosophers are fond of, in imputing profound motives to the most insignificant actions of great people. And yet you may be right. I rather think, that the tone of the courtiers is that of contempt for so flimsy and slovenly a performance; and, in the present circumstances, I am neither surprised nor sorry that they have taken this turn. The attachment to principles and examples of public liberty is so dead in this country, and even the recollection of the old sentiments and sounds of the English language in that cause is so slight, that it is very natural for better people than the courtiers to regard a piece, which breathes the very ardour of youth about freedom and justice, as belonging to some remote age or country, and having nothing to do with present interests or present purposes. This is my reason for not being surprised. And, very much from the same view of the present state of public opinion, I am rather glad, that the church and the Tories do not seem to think it worth while to raise a cry against the book; if it were to be stigmatized now as a mere party pamphlet, which would be a plausible criticism, an impression might be given which would last a long while; whereas, if it is suffered to get into every library, and considered, for the present, as curious from the fame of the author, rather than for its own merits, and as the fragment of a history of antiquated times, the day may once more return, when its immortal doctrines will be cherished even in England, and the style will be admired as a singular, but not perfectly successful effort, to recur to the purity of English writing, from the false taste and affectation of the age.

⟨I quite enter into your enthusiasm about Spain, and, in spite of Abercromby, whose calmer and colder judgement is an excellent bridle upon one's sanguine expectations, I have been dreaming wild in the same train of ideas.[4] To speak as coldly as I can upon the subject, I have not any strong hopes of success, even if the circumstances be made the most of, and assisted or guided in the most judicious manner. But, whatever the result may be, I cannot but rejoice that a people, who bear such a name as the Spaniards, should make a struggle, at least, for their independence; the example cannot be otherwise than beneficial, even if they should entirely fail, to their posterity at some future day, and to all the rest of mankind. It is the most detestable of all the enormities into which Bonaparte's love of dominion has plunged him; and more completely devoid, than any other, of all pretence of provocation or security. If I were a Spaniard, I should consider resistance, however desperate in its chances of success, and however bloody in its immediate operation, as an indispensable duty of discretion and expediency; to put the proposition in its most frigid form of expression.

⟨What the mode of our assistance from England should be, is quite another question. To judge of it in detail, would require more information than I have been able to gather concerning the real state of affairs in Spain. But my general principle would be, to make at once a cessation of all hostilities, and to declare to the Spanish nation, or to any provisional government which the insurgents may establish, that we renounce all projects against their colonies, as well as all views whatever of dismemberment or partition of any part of their dominion, that so long as they can maintain the struggle against France, they shall have the most cordial support, and supplies of all that is necessary. Indirect aid, I imagine, would be the best; that is, money, arms, provisions, etc.; for if the thing is to be accomplished, it is not by regular war, but by a protracted defence of the fastnesses of the country, and by the valour and perseverance of the Spaniards themselves. What a moment for a Spaniard of political and military genius!⟩ ...

1. Loch's letters to Horner have not been found.
2. Wycombe Abbey.
3. Loch was reading the recently-published fragment of Charles James Fox's *History of the Early Part of the Reign of James the Second.*
4. Following the outbreak in May of armed hostilities between French and Spanish troops, delegates from the Asturias had arrived in London early in June to ask for help. Allen, who remained Horner's principal source of information on Spanish affairs, had recently sent, in response to several queries by Horner, an optimistic account of events in Spain (Horner to Allen, [12 June], and Allen to Horner, 13 June, BLPES iii. 258–61). Horner had known Abercromby pretty well all his life but intimately only for about the last couple of years. Later he was to say (to Mrs W. R. Spencer, 4 Jan. 1811, BLPES v. 3–4) that Abercromby and his wife were 'two of the most sensible persons I know in the world'.

297. To Mrs Dugald Stewart

BLPES iii. 271–4   The Temple, 4 July 1808

As I sent you some particulars about the Spanish patriots in my last letter,[1] and as there is more good news today, I have sent you the *Morning Chronicle* which gives a translation of the most important paper, entitled *Precautions*, and the speech in the House of Lords which gives the word of our Government for the principles on which they are to act towards Spain.[2]

I read yesterday a mass of proclamations and hand-bills from Spain. The leaders of the people have had the good sense to employ the press immediately, in their cause; both at Oviedo and at Seville, as soon as a provisional government was organized, they established newspapers. And the addresses which they have circulated are not only full of the sentiments which are most natural on such an occasion, but composed with much judgement. . . . I like very much the language in which the Junta of Seville speak of the origin of their present authority; 'the people (they say) have transmitted to them all the rights, with which, in the present circumstances, the people consider themselves invested.'[3] One important means of success, they have already brought into operation, by dismissing both from military and civil commands, and appointing other persons; thus opening to every man of activity in Spain the prospect of serving his country in the most glorious of all causes. If they succeed, the Bourbons will return (if at all) to a people who have felt their own importance, and are all impatient for the revival of the Cortes.

I am (as you see) indeed very sanguine; though it is painful to think what chances there are against these excellent men, and what a protracted bloody struggle they will at the best have to maintain. But I own my political feelings are more roused by the prospect of their success, than they have ever been since Bonaparte destroyed the French constitution.

. . .

1. Not found.
2. The Supreme Junta's *Precautions which it will be proper to observe throughout the different provinces of Spain, in . . . resisting the unjust and violent possession . . . of the kingdom* [by the French], was also printed, along with various of the Junta's manifestos and the King's Speech of 4 July in the AR l (1808), 332–6. Horner and his friends at Holland House initially saw no alternative to the restoration of Ferdinand VII and thus were unconcerned about the context of the King's speech, which promised military aid to Spain on the principle of restoring 'legitimate' monarchs to their thrones. The assertion of the principle of legitimacy, however, cooled Foxite enthusiasm for the Spanish patriots almost immediately and troubled even Lady Holland (Taylor, pp. 233–7).
3. This appears to be a paraphrase, rather than an actual quotation, from the Junta's Manifesto of 29 May (AR l. 322–5).

298. To James Loch

BLPES iii. 275–6 ⟨*Horner*, i. 454–5⟩   Old Down,[1] Monday morning [?11 July 1808]

. . .

⟨Spain! Spain! I am in a fever till I hear more about Dupont and the passes of Sierra Morena.[2] It will be desperate, if they have failed in their first resistance, under favourable circumstances, in the very sort of war upon which all their hopes must rely.⟩ The accounts are very vague; but I much fear the truth will be, that Dupont has got possession of the road and defiles, and waits only for such an additional strength in troops as will insure him Seville, perhaps Cadiz. I own the news of his success in gaining that pass, threw me into a despondency which now makes me ashamed of my preceding confidence; and I have only recovered myself into a state of scepticism and anxiety. ⟨Till we hear how they will bear to be blooded, how they

can maintain themselves, after want of success, it is too hard to judge of the event. It is quite a new experiment, in which the powers are for the first time to be tried of a vast regular army, and an enthusiastic people. The circumstances are very favourable on both sides; this is indeed the very crisis of the fate of Europe, and the event (either way) will perhaps be the most decisive test of the genius and effects of the French Revolution. The one result would revive our original persuasion, in its first ardour, that the people are not to be subdued by foreign troops, unless the love of their country is lost in a contempt of their government. The other would sink me in final despair of ever living to see prosperity or liberty again in any part of Europe, or even of descrying, at any distance, the prospect of their return. For even the military empire might last ages, before its discipline degenerated; and ages more of darkness and idleness might protract the shame and misery of Europe. Suppose all this to take place, are you prophet enough to look beyond such an abyss? Will the Tartars once more over-run the West? Is there a circulation in the peopling and civilizing of the world, an alternation like those which prevail in its physical history; so that Europe is to oscillate from feudal institutions to military monarchy, and to catch only a short interval of laws and refinement, while it is passing from the one condition into the other? And shall we have future theories of the moral history of the earth, like Hutton's system of the changes upon the surface, tracing back many former transitions from civilization to barbarism, and presenting, in the future prospect, an endless, irksome succession of the same changes?⟩
... [3]

1. An inn at Old Down in Somerset was well-placed at a cross-roads en route to Wells and Glastonbury.
2. The movements of the French army under Dupont and those of the Spanish army under Castaños resulted in the first major battle of the Peninsular War and the astonishing surrender of Dupont near Baylen.
3. The letter continues with further passages written from 'The Court, Wednesday', and Bridgwater, July 14.

299. To James Loch

BLPES iii. 284–7   Wednesday night [?July][1] 1808

... I do not know whether I ever told you that Allen has a conjecture, that the forms of the English Parliament, and many of those forms especially which have ripened into constitutional principles, were directly borrowed from the Spanish Cortes by our Edward the First. ...

What Lord Holland seems now most anxious about, always supposing the patriots to be successful, is, lest the Junta of Seville by assuming the supremacy may disgust the Arragonese [sic] and divide Spain against itself. There is an hereditary jealousy ... The only wise plan is a general Cortes; such a one was summoned by Philip the 5th for the first time, and has since met by a sort of Committee of the Commons. A

general Cortes of all the Estates, and the hereditary right of Ferdinand the 7th, will
be the only chance for permanent regulated freedom to Spain. . . .

The friends of Ministers seem anxious to give assurances that the Duke of York
will not be sent with the troops to Spain. And Canning's friends would make you
believe that *he* has fought and won that point in the Cabinet. I shall not believe till
the last, that his Royal Highness will suffer himself to be disappointed, or that the
good old King will allow his favourite son to be thwarted in what he likes so well as
an expedition.

The Duke of Somerset met the Turkish Ambassador at Staines and had some
conversation with the Dragoman. They are sent to make up matters with us, and he
says they seemed very much disposed to do so upon any terms; if he might judge from
the strong expressions of admiration for this country, and detestation of the French,
which the Dragoman expressed both by words and gesticulations. He told the Duke
that the French force now contiguous to Turkey was about thirty thousand men.[2]

The proclamations, etc. at Seville, even the *Precautions*, are all written by a
monk; so I heard Lord Granville Leveson Gower say, who has all Canning's
information. He had forgot the name, however, of this excellent monk.[3] . . .

. . .

Pray let me know something more about the state of the Bullion market in
China; you must have pumped John [?Allen] dry by this time. . . .

I am determined in the course of the summer, after I return from the circuit, to
read all Davy's late papers, and make myself master of these new discoveries, which
seem to have quite changed the science of chemistry.[4] . . .

. . .

1. This letter has been endorsed in pencil '1 July 1808'; but that day was not a Wednesday and
   it seems more likely that this was one of the letters Horner wrote but did not send to Loch
   while on circuit in July and August. (See Doc. 301 n. 1.)
2. Fear of growing French influence in Turkey and therefore of her predominance in the
   Mediterranean had led Britain into hostilities with Turkey; but Canning had decided to
   make a new effort to construct an alignment against France with both Russia and Turkey. It
   was not until Jan. 1809, however, that peace with Turkey was formally restored, following
   renewed threats by England.
3. Lord Granville Leveson Gower, afterwards 1st Earl Granville (1773–1846: *DNB*). The
   monk is presumably the 'Padre Gil' mentioned in Doc. 304. Manuel Gil (1747–1815), a
   Franciscan monk, had taken a leading part against the French and become Secretary of the
   Seville Junta. (See *Lady Holland's Spanish Journal*, p. 269, and, as one of the signatories of
   the Manifesto of 3 Aug., the *AR* 1 (1808), 336–44.)
4. Employing a battery of 250 pairs of metal plates as an agent of electrolysis, Humphry Davy
   had succeeded in decomposing substances into their various elements, thereby establishing
   electrochemistry as a science of unlimited theoretical and practical possibilities. In 1806
   Napoleon had sent him a prize awarded by the Institut National, and in 1808, after Davy
   had discovered and isolated sodium, potassium, and a number of other elements, he went to
   Paris and received a second prize awarded by the Institut.

300. To Henry Hallam

BLPES iii. 288–90 ⟨Horner, i. 455–7⟩   Wells, 24 Aug. 1808

. . .

⟨The news from Spain for the last fortnight has been admirable indeed; much beyond my expectations, both in respect of the success itself, and of the prudence by which it has been secured. But it makes one quite nervous to reflect, how much more prudence will for a long course of time be required, how much wisdom, too, both military and civil, and (what is the most fearful condition of all) how great a stock of genuine active patriotism, in order to accomplish entirely, and permanently secure, the vast scheme which the Spaniards have before them.

⟨Like you, I have been reading a little in the language of the country which we have been all thinking of so much; but the summer circuit does not, without more self-denial than I have, allow much time for any regular study. I brought with me that memoir of Jovellanos, which, you may remember, was praised in one of Allen's articles in the *Edinburgh Review*, as worthy of Turgot's pen.[1] It contains many valuable details of the agricultural economy of Spain, and is perfectly of the liberal and enlightened school in all general doctrines, with the exception of one grand error upon the corn trade; for he is elaborately against exportation being permitted. The language is very perspicuous, and sometimes elegant; formed upon the model of what the French used to call their academic style. . . .

⟨Have you seen the pamphlet of which I have been reading extracts in the *Morning Chronicle*, called *A plain statement of the conduct of the Ministry and the Opposition towards his Royal Highness the Duke of York*, and supposed to be published under his orders?[2] If it have really that authority, I shall bind one forthwith with Burke's *Causes of the Discontents*; for if it has the Duke's sanction, it must have a still higher permission. And it would be indeed a very bold, but I do not for that conceive it a less likely step, that in the extreme weakness of his old age (but to be sure when all the men of genius who kept him at bay are no more), he should at length expressly avow, what has been so uniformly charged against him, and constantly denied; the existence of a 'domestic party – a kind of closet and family council, whom the monarch may occasionally interpose between even his Ministry and himself.' These are the words of the pamphlet. If it comes really from the court, this publication marks a new era in the history of our constitution.

⟨. . .⟩

1. The French edition of Jovellanos on agriculture and legislation – *L'identité de l'intérêt général avec l'identité individuel* . . . *Principe exposé dans le rapport sur un projet de loi agraire* (St Petersburg, 1806) – was reviewed, it is thought, by James Mill in *ER* xiv (no. xxvii, Apr. 1809), 20–39. But see Docs 269 and 272; it is also noteworthy that at the end of 1809 Horner and Allen seem to have been collaborating on an English translation of the original Spanish version, but none such appears to have been published. The comparison of Jovellanos with Turgot was made towards the end of Allen's review of Bourgoing's *Tableau de l'Espagne Moderne* in *ER* v (no. ix, Oct. 1804), 125–36.
2. Rumours of a plan to give the Duke of York the command in Spain had met with a storm of criticism in the press, including hints at the scandals that later formed the basis of the charges publicly brought against him (Doc. 321). (See *POW* vi. 304–307, and *Holland's Further Memoirs*, p. 16.)

301. To James Loch

BLPES iii. 291–4[1]   Wells, 28 Aug. 1808

. . .

From the manner in which you mention the renewal of the Indian charter, in the next session of Parliament, I conclude you have positive authority for it; and indeed the compromise you mention between the Company and Government is very likely to be true. In the Indian Committee I heard that Robert Dundas[2] and other persons connected with Government showed a manifest disposition, not to second the Company in all their views and pretensions; indeed nothing can be more natural than that Government should have a great desire to rob the Company of every thing but their monopoly, for an open trade would only benefit the subject, but to seize the patronage and particularly the military patronage is to enrich the coffers of the crown and fortify its influence. Now, it is just from contrary reasons, that the opinion I have dimly been wondering about for some time with respect to India, is that, if possible, it would be better for the whole patronage to be left in the hands of the Company and their trading monopoly to be taken from them. A strange unheard of monster this would be in politics, no doubt; not stranger, however, than the whole history of Leadenhall Street holds out; and perhaps not very different in any respect, except in what is good, from what the thing itself has lately become. I must own, that the single detached question of Charter or Not, is to me a perplexing one, under the circumstances that are to be left unchanged; and even when one speculates at liberty upon what circumstances might be changed, the various relations of the subject are so complicated as to leave one dissatisfied with every conclusion one attempts to form. As a mere question of trade, the charter would very soon be disposed of. After all, however, for any practical interposition in the discussion that you announce for next session, it is not absolutely necessary that one should come any thing near the perfectly correct and expedient view of the whole subject; it will be enough if one is ready to prevent a little more mischief being done, or to take an opportunity of inserting unseen a small portion of good. The relation of Ireland to the India trade is a new point to consider, and of material importance. So is the distinction which you point out between a monopoly limited to British India, and one extended as it is at present over all the coasts from the Cape of Good Hope to Cape Horn. . . .

. . .

I cannot understand your stories about Canning and the Duke of York; for when I left town, Canning's admirers were all in the firm belief, that he had opposed the Duke's appointment in the Cabinet; that he had risked every thing by that manly line of conduct; but that he had at length triumphed. This was their general language. I heard also Lord G. Leveson [Gower], who is supposed to be Canning's own Confessor, say in the most determined tone of voice and manner that the D. of Y. would certainly not be sent abroad, and a tone of voice that took a sort of credit to itself for the fact it was pronouncing. Now, by your story, the Duke considers C[anning] his best friend in the Cabinet. I wish you would inquire into the real truth of this, more particularly.[3]

1. The letter is unsigned probably because, as Horner explained in another letter of 5 Sept. (BLPES iii. 295–6), he had left unfinished a number written to Loch while on circuit, only one of which (perhaps this one) he then considered worth sending.
2. Robert Saunders Dundas (1771–1851: *DNB*), afterwards 2nd Viscount Melville, was President of the Board of Control.
3. The Government almost certainly from the beginning opposed the Duke's having the command in Spain; but it was afterwards alleged that Canning had been the prime instigator of the opposition to Moore (*POW* vi. 297; Wendy Hinde, *George Canning* (1973), p. 199).

302. Note by Horner

BLPES viii. 54–5   Holland House, 11 Sept. 1808[1]

Sangro the Deputy from Galicia dined there – only Lord H[olland] and Allen.[2] All the opinions which the Galiego expressed about the new state of affairs in his country were liberal and judicious: He regretted that at present the liberty of the press was not quite entire, that the Juntas assumed some direction of it, and allowed some things to be published, others not; He considered that when the French were completely expelled from Spain, peace with France would be most important, that all projects of invading France were to be blamed; upon Allen observing, that with a good government Spain would soon raise her population to 16 millions, Sangro said there was no means of increasing the population of Spain but *la tolérance*, and he dwelt much upon this as a necessary part of the new order of things if we were to expect good from it. Upon the whole, he seemed to me to despond too much on account of the difficulties which are to be surmounted, and to require too much at first to be done and to be done too fast. It seems clear, that the priests are not to be touched in the present crisis, and that the advantages of toleration must be the distant fruit of political liberty. But in Galicia, they are particularly overloaded by the church: *Sangro* stated, that $^2/_3$ of the lands of that province belong to the church, and that there are no fewer than seven bishops.

Sangro is a naval officer; and has some landed property in Galicia. He was at Paris for some time, two years ago; and it was probably from this circumstance of his being known, that he was named by Bonaparte as one of the Deputies to the Junta at Bayonne. But he preferred being loyal to his country.

1. Horner apparently wrote this note in the early morning of 11 Sept., after dining at Holland House the previous evening. The Holland House dinner book suggests that he arrived on the 9th and remained until the 14th or 15th. There is no entry in the dinner book for 10 Sept., but that for the 11th indicates that he dined there again that day with a very large party.
2. Five Spanish deputies had come over in July to ask for British help against the French. They were: José María Queipo de Llano Ruiz de Saravia, Vizconde de Matarrosa and afterwards Conde de Torreno (1786–1843), a member of one of the leading families of the Asturias and later the historian of the Spanish insurrection against France; Andrés Angel de la Vega; Francisco Sangro; Gen. Adrian Jacome; and Adm. Juan Ruiz de Apodaca (1754–1835). Apodaca afterwards remained as Spanish ambassador to the Court of St James and Don Rafael Lobo y Campo (d. 1816), who had accompanied the deputies as their secretary, also stayed on as secretary of the embassy.

303. Note by Horner

BLPES viii. 55   Holland House, 12 Sept. 1808

At dinner H[olland] H[ouse]. All the Spanish Deputies, Admiral *Apodaca* and General *Jachimo* from Seville, Viconde *Materosa* and Don Andres *de la Vega* from Oviedo, *Sangro* from Corunna; Don *Lobo* who came over with the Seville Deputies; the Dukes of Clarence and Kent.[1]

Of course in so large a company I had but little opportunity of seeing more than their looks. *Apodaca*, a fine looking man, with a manly countenance and mild expression, seems but 45, though he is in fact ten years older. General Jachimo is an older man in bad health; he has a good expression, and Lord H[olland] says he is sensible, and that both he and Apodaca speak of their country with the best principles and most judicious views. *Andres De la Vega* looks heavy, but reflecting and honest; he has not much the air of a man of the world. *Materosa* is boyish in appearance, but his conversation (the little I heard of it) was pleasing in manner and sufficiently full of matter. *Lobo* has the air of an adventurer.

The only one I had conversation with myself was *Sangro*; he spoke of the changes which it would be proper to introduce into the constitution of the Cortes, like one who both valued liberty and understood it, but his favourite point is the diminution of the political power of the clergy, and he is of opinion that circumstances have so diminished their influence in Spain as well as in other parts of Europe, that their prerogatives may with safety be abridged.

1. The dinner party of 11 Sept. included also Lord Henry Petty, Lord Henry Fitzgerald (1761–1829), elder brother of the tragic Lord Edward, and Matthew Gregory 'Monk' Lewis (1775–1818: *DNB*), the writer (HHDB).

304. To Lady Holland

BLPES iii. 303–304   [London], Thursday [15 Sept. 1808]

. . .

I have been reading the Padre Gil's Manifesto, which is in many respects very sensible.[1] But I fear these Andalusians will excite the jealousy of the other provinces; particularly of the *gentlemen* of the north. And by the bye, Padre Gil might have taken more notice of the Arragonese [sic]. I wish too that he had spoken in another manner of the practicability of a Cortes, and that their provisional government were more upon the cast of the ancient institutions. Their 28 Deputies will make a very bad sort of assembly, and the mode of their election a bad sort of government. But I am speaking very ignorantly perhaps, as much may depend upon what it is really possible for them under their present circumstances to accomplish.

. . .

I am going out to Ward's tomorrow till Monday. Perhaps he will enlist me in that grand new scheme of a popular party in the state, if he has heard of it yet.[2] Lord help us!

1. See Doc. 299 n. 3.
2. In June 1808 Whitbread had published *A Letter to Lord Holland*, which opposed the dispatch of a British army to the Iberian Peninsula and, raising the standard of Fox, represented events in Spain as a fortuitous moment for the opening of comprehensive peace negotiations with France. The reference to the restoration of 'legitimate' sovereigns in the King's speech of 4 July on Spanish affairs had led many Whigs to embrace Whitbread's point of view and to return to their original principles of peace abroad and reform at home. Brougham, reviewing Whitbread's pamphlet very favourably (*ER* xii (no. xxiv, July 1808), 435), had represented the 1806 peace negotiations of the Ministry of All the Talents as an occasion 'when the Whigs themselves manifestly deserted their ancient tenets, and, betrayed by false hopes of Continental victories, or debauched by the enjoyment of power, adopted the language and view of their ancient adversaries'. By the autumn of 1808 discontent with the Government's commitment to the Peninsular War and with the Whig leadership had spawned talk of the formation of a 'popular party'. (See Taylor, pp. 235–40, and Roberts, pp. 121–3.)

305. To J.A. Murray

BLPES iii. 297–8 ⟨Horner, i. 457–9⟩[1]   The Temple, 16 Sept. 1808

⟨. . .

⟨While I was at Exeter, I received from you the sheets of Jeffrey's review of Mr Fox's *History*; and before I had done with my travels, I wrote to him some remarks which had occurred to me.[2] Since I came to London, I find that the faults found with that article are chiefly on account of some inconsistencies; which are very intelligible to any one who knows in what manner Jeffrey writes his reviews, and with what carelessness in general he sets himself to do what all the world fancy he undertakes with an overwhelming sense of its importance.

⟨Though some of the strictures which I have heard upon the criticism of Mr Fox's history are, I think, well founded, the article pleased me very much, and still pleases me in its principal parts. I do not know, however, that it has occurred to you, but it has struck me of late, and strongly upon reading that piece, that though Jeffrey's powers of observation are strengthened, and his delineation of sentiments still more discriminating and refined, than when he first began these publications, his style of writing has suffered materially from the hurry in which he is usually left to compose. Some of his best-thought passages about Mr Fox are composed with a clumsiness that surprised me.

⟨. . .

⟨I wish very much to hear, whether any commission has yet passed the Great Seal, nominating the persons who are to prosecute the further inquiries relative to the improvements of the Scotch Judicature. I have heard nothing of it; but it is very likely that the first I am to hear of it will be from Scotland. The chancellor is slow, without being sure; and I have always suspected that there was a want of good faith in his undertaking to reform. It must go quite against his heart to make any change; though there is nobody so much addicted to the practice of criticising existing institutions in the law with severity: an inconsistency of character by no means rare. By the way, I should not be sorry to hear what remarks are current at your Bar upon the new Act;[3] it was something rash in me to take the part I did, though I was very anxious and scrupulous about all that I proposed, and contented myself with securing the alterations that appeared to me right, with less attempt at ostentation upon the general subject than I originally intended, and perhaps less than it would have been right for me to have attempted.⟩ . . .

1. Where it is misprinted 1806.
2. Horner to Jeffrey, 15 June (*Horner*, i. 453), and Jeffrey to Horner, 10 Sept. 1808 (*Jeffrey*, ii. 124–8). Jeffrey had reviewed Fox's *History* in *ER* xii (no. xxxiv, July 1808), 271–306.
3. Although Grenville's bill to reform the Scottish Court of Session had succumbed to the change of Ministry the previous year, another providing only for a cautious and limited resort to juries, was introduced by the new Lord Chancellor and passed into law on 25 June.

306. To John Allen

BLPES iii. 305–308   Wimbledon,[1] Sunday [18 Sept. 1808]

I did not fully understand the Seville Manifesto, until I read in yesterday's paper the address of the Junta of Valencia of the 16th of July, to which that of Seville refers for the description of the authority that is proposed to be vested in the Central Junta. By that it appears that . . . the provisional government to be formed, is to be a Republic. And indeed, though Padre Gil proclaims the principle of hereditary succession according to the fundamental laws of the monarchy, the Valencian Junta does not scruple to state the restoration of Ferdinand to be an uncertain event, which may never take place: so that there are not wanting persons in Spain who, in proposing this provisional government, think it not impossible that it may be rendered permanent.[2]

Now I do not like this republican project at all; for it will not succeed in the end, though during the first enthusiasm of the defensive war it may possibly be a vigorous administration. It does not strike me, even if a republic of the sort proposed would be well established, that it would prove a happy form of government for such a country as Spain; it would be an oligarchy, which is always tyrannical and prejudiced; and federative, which in so large a territory never can be kept free from distraction and delay in all important operations. But it is useless to consider, whether this would or would not be a prosperous government for Spain; it never will be established there. And the project of a republic, even a provisional one, if persisted in, will be sure to end in the utter disappointment of all the hopes we now cherish of a free constitution.

The Commanders who shall most distinguish themselves in the war and gain the attachment of the army, will soon acquire a fatal ascendancy in the Central Junta; to which they are to be eligible, as appears by the nomination of Palafox.[3] And then, according to the regular course of such events, and agreeably to all experience, some of those generals with this ascendancy will either establish a military reign in their own name, or make terms for themselves with the heir of the crown in which they will stipulate for their own aggrandizement and not for the rights of the people. The manner in which the Military Chiefs are already spoken of in these very Manifestos, shows that even now they have a weight in influencing the civil authorities, of which the utmost jealousy cannot too soon be entertained. In a protracted revolution, there seems to be no chance for liberty but by preserving the dependence of the military upon the civil authorities, and perhaps that can only be made sure by a distinct separation of the executive from the legislative powers.

I had indulged myself in the conviction that the men, who have influence in the present circumstances, looked to the formation of a controlling legislative assembly, formed upon the model of their ancient Cortes. For I cannot conceive that any other scheme will restore the liberties of their country, or rest them on good foundations. Why should not this Central Junta meet only to appoint a regency, in order to give a popular birth to the executive, which it is become necessary to revive? The regency ought to be invested by the Junta with all the legal prerogatives of the crown, and ought to be advised by the Junta (in effect commanded) to exercise forthwith its prerogative of convoking the Cortes. The Cortes, when assembled, will ratify the proceedings of the Junta, and make a settlement of the prerogative of the crown and the privileges of the several orders of the people. Notwithstanding what the Padre Gil says in his Manifesto, there cannot be more difficulty in bringing the provinces to agree to one Cortes for the whole kingdom, than to a central Junta for the whole; the sacrifice of mutual pretensions seems very much the same in both cases. By this order of proceeding, the ancient and beneficial distinction would.be preserved of an executive subject to advice and control, separate from the representative assembly whose business it is to inquire and to vote *pechos y servicios* accordingly. And then there is the trite, but most conclusive, argument in favour of this method of innovation, that, by working upon the ancient frames, you accommodate the new liberty easily to habits which will not be suddenly changed and to institutions which must be left standing for a while. An argument this, which ought to prevail, even if the old foundations were less excellent in their plan, than those of the Spanish constitution actually are.

. . .

There is some appearance of concert, in this place, between the men of Seville and those of Valencia. And yet, they speak very differently about the Council of Castille, both as to its recent conduct and with respect to the legal prerogatives of the Consejo. . . .

1. J. W. Ward had taken a place there.
2. The Seville Manifesto of 3 Aug. is printed in the MC of *Friday* 16 Sept.
3. José de Palafox y Melci, afterwards Duke of Saragossa (1776–1847), Captain-General of Aragon and the most distinguished of three brothers, of whom the eldest, Luis, Marquez de Lazán (1772–1843), was also a general. But it was the youngest, Francisco de Palafox (1774–?), who had been chosen to represent Aragon in the Central Junta.

307. To Andrew Gray[1]

BLPES iii. 299–300   London, 21 Sept. 1808

. . .

You cannot fail to be all of one mind in Scotland, as we are here, both about the cause of the Spaniards and the unfortunate issue of our glorious victory in Portugal.[2] The last business is quite unintelligible, and ought to be very closely inquired into; mere stupidity will not alone account for it, because you must suppose three men to have lost their heads all at the same moment. But the victory, in spite of this convention, is a most satisfactory event; it confirms that confidence in the British army, which Egypt and Maida had so justly taught us; and must establish upon the continent our character as a military power, which may be very salutary some time hence for the continent itself. But it is the conduct and success of the Spaniards that are most important; and I suspect that even among you Tories and Pittites, liberty will come a little into vogue, when it is found to do so much against Bonaparte. . . .

1. A daughter of Mrs John Horner's uncle George Baillie, whom Mrs Byrne calls a 'fanatical American loyalist', had married an Andrew Gray, who had a house called Southfield in East Lothian. But that Andrew Gray seems to have died in the summer of 1805 and Horner's 1808 correspondent to have been rather his son and namesake. A few years earlier Andrew Gray, junior, had wanted to move from the merchant or East Indian navy into the army, but as the military college was full to have gained through Horner's influence a cadetship instead; but if he ever took it up, it must have been for a short time only, since not long after his father's death, he sold Southfield and moved with his mother and sister to Dumfries. (*Horner*, i. 142n; Mrs Byrne's notes at Kinnordy; Horner to his father, 1 and 26 May 1804, and to Leonard Horner, 28 June 1805, BLPES ii. 103–104, 110, and 208–209; Horner to Andrew Gray, jun., 22 Sept. 1810, BLPES iv. 306–309.)
2. Sir Arthur Wellesley's victory at Vimiero had been followed by the Convention of Cintra, which allowed Junot's French army to withdraw from Portugal. The first news of the Convention came from indignant Portuguese sources and asserted misleadingly that Junot had been saved only by the folly of three general officers – Wellesley, Sir Harry Burrard (1755–1813: *DNB*), and Sir Hew Whitefoord Dalrymple (1750–1830: *DNB*). That view of the Convention was embraced by many Whigs who were perhaps too anxious to believe the worst. (See Roberts, pp. 120–21, and Taylor, pp. 238–40.)

308. To Samuel Whitbread

Whitbread MSS,
Bedfordshire County Record Office, 4203   The Temple, 21 Oct. 1808

. . .

In consequence of your letter, I have looked again at the *Review* and your printed letter to Lord Holland.[1] You have a good right, I think, to say that, in the passage referred to, the Reviewer has not done you the justice to make an accurate statement of your views. You have exactly proposed, and almost in the very terms, what the Reviewer would have you propose, and censures you for falling short of. The expression, 'Mr W. says merely', has the effect of leading his reader to understand that you were desirous only of 'conveying the terms to the Court at Bayonne', and that it was the critic himself who proposed the 'proclaiming them to the world.' I read the whole of this article in the *Edinburgh Review* with considerable pain; for I was one of those 'feeble fanatics' who were confident about Spain, from the very first appearances of a general unconcerted insurrection. Even if I had despaired of the event, I should have deemed it a sort of injury to the brave men who were still maintaining the struggle, to proclaim my despondency aloud.

Upon the subject which you mention towards the end of your letter, perhaps there may be a slight shade of difference between us, though I do not know that there is. Not that I have quitted, for an inch, the ground of your proposed resolution of the 26th February last;[2] for in my very short parliamentary life there is no vote on which I reflect with more satisfaction; indeed this sentiment is always joined with a real gratitude to you for the opportunity of giving that vote. But the events, which have since occurred in Spain, make the variance in my view of the question of peace; that to make sure the independence of Spain as a nation against the projects which France has attempted and will continue to cherish, I would make that independence an essential object of the negotiation, and for the attainment of it I should think it well worth while to prolong the war. The events in Spain, great as their consequences must be in improving the political prospects of the west of Europe, carry me no farther, than I have already stated, from the letter of your proposed resolution: for they cannot tend to make coalitions of Austria and Russia a whit more practicable. It will be time enough, when we see a free insurrection of the people of Italy or the North of Germany, for England to give them the succour they may deserve and desire: if they should ever attempt what the Spaniards have done, we shall of course feel for them in the same way; but I own there seems no probability of any such conjuncture.

. . .

1. Whitbread's letter to Horner has not been found. But the other reference is to Whitbread's pamphlet, and to Brougham's review of it.
2. Whitbread's unsuccessful resolution for peace negotiations with France that in effect declared the French Government legal and deserving of the treatment afforded sovereign states.

309. To Jeremy Bentham

BL Add. MSS 33544, f. 390
⟨*Bentham*, vii. 558–9⟩ [London], Tuesday [25 Oct. 1808]

⟨I am very much obliged to you for the opportunity you offer me of seeing Colonel Burr;[1] and as you allow me to name a day, I will mention the earliest – Thursday. But I am disengaged on Friday and all next week, so that if you have any preference I shall be happy to come to you any day.

⟨I know nothing more accurately of Lord Holland, than what appears in the ship news of this morning's paper; that the *Amazon* frigate, in which he goes, was to sail from Falmouth on Sunday last.[2]

⟨. . .

⟨I had not forgot your kind invitation into the country; but immediately after my circuit, I was obliged to come to London to attend my office, and though I have once or twice got a day or two of absence for idleness, I have never been able to carve out an interval large enough for a little country study. . . .

⟨. . .⟩

1. Aaron Burr (1756–1836), the former Vice-President of the United States who had come to England in the summer in an unsuccessful attempt to interest the British Government in his Mexican schemes, was at this time staying with Bentham.
2. Disheartened by the failure of most of his uncle's traditional followers and of his Grenvillite allies to support the Spanish patriots, Lord Holland, accompanied by his wife and Allen, had departed for Spain on 9 Oct. Holland's attitude was summed up in a letter of 20 May 1809 to his sister, Caroline Fox: 'If I cannot be a Whig in England I certainly shall be in Spain' (BL Add. MSS 51738). The Hollands were not to return until 12 Aug. 1809, and in their absence Horner stood virtually alone among Whigs as a supporter of Holland's view of the Peninsular War. (See Taylor, pp. 240–41, and, for the Hollands' interest in Spain in general, *Holland House*, pp. 217–39.)

310. To J.A. Murray

BLPES iii. 315–20 ⟨*Horner*, i. 460–64⟩   Carnatic Office, 27 Oct. 1808

⟨. . .

⟨I have been more Whiggish than ever, all this summer; for I have been full of sanguine expectations, and so far as I know myself, that is the state of mind in which I am most liable to think of politics. Some of my most confidential Whigs have treated me all along as too sanguine and somewhat Quixotic; and, to be sure, my castles were in Spain. Even still, my views of what the result is probably to be, are more confident than what I can find people ready to approve of.[1] Spain seems to me now to be quite secure from ultimate subjugation by France, even if large French armies should once more penetrate the country, and gain general battles; and indeed, from all I can observe of Bonaparte's conduct with respect to that country, or guess from comparing it with other measures of his policy, I am much inclined to believe that he has for the present relinquished the project. What a triumph for the principles of liberty is this revolution in Spain, and its extensive influence upon the present and future fortunes of the world! It may even make those principles be felt and regarded by men of property and education in this country, and deliver them from the suspicion and derision to which they are at present exposed.

⟨I passed a few days lately with Petty, in the beautiful country where he has taken an old house in the midst of old trees; and I cannot tell you how much I am pleased with Lady Louisa.[2] I believe you saw her; so I need say nothing of her beauty. The gentleness of her manner has a degree of shyness joined with it, but not the least reserve; so that you soon discover her good and well-informed understanding. She takes as much interest in his particular objects and pursuits as is natural and proper.

I could not fancy a wife better suited to him. They made no stranger of me, and allowed me to see how they lived daily; he went on, for instance, with the book which he was then reading through of an evening to her⟩ and her good humoured jovial sister Lady Charlotte.[3] ⟨Their scheme seemed to me very rational and tranquil, and likely, as far as depend upon themselves, to insure them an uniform happiness; I am only apprehensive of her health, which seems to require much attention.

⟨I went down on Saturday last with Whishaw to Hertford, on a visit to Malthus and little [Alexander] Hamilton. The Pundit is very happy, and gets very fat; in two years' time, I take it, he will have a figure in which it will be hard to say which is length, and which breadth, and which thickness. In a little comfortless lodging, I found him with Sanscrit proof sheets of a grammar, sitting in the most perfect content, and ready to discuss any proposition. He is very much liked, as he may well be, by every body, for his sense and his temper. I do not know that you have ever seen Malthus; remember, next time you come to England, that I make you acquainted with him; Whishaw, who has known him long very intimately, says he is one of the very best of men, and that you know is the judgement of Rhadamanthus; and there is no man with whom I like better to converse upon controverted subjects; not that he is remarkably original in such extempore exercises, or even satisfactory always in his manner of communicating his views, but then he has the mere love of truth, for which I would willingly exchange, when you come to serious matters, all the versatility, dexterity, and eloquence that can be displayed in the famous sport, which is so much practised at our learned university. I know this looks like a decision in favour of dulness; and so the ingenious gentleman would think it. You have seen in Malthus's review of Newenham's *Population in Ireland*,[4] some statement of those views of his with regard to the cheapness of the food of the common people, which we discussed together two years ago, and particularly, if I remember right, going from Ragland to Abergavenny. I think in this review you find the defect to which I have already alluded, and which affects all Malthus's writings; a want of precision in the statement of his principles, and distinct perspicuity in upholding the consequences which he traces from them.

⟨I am going to dine with Jeremy Bentham and Colonel Burr, and am very curious to see what sort of mixture will result from putting together pure philosophy and Yankee treason.[5]

⟨. . .⟩

1. Four lines have been obliterated here.
2. Petty had married in March Lady Louisa Emma Fox-Strangways (d. 1851), 5th daughter of the 2nd Earl of Ilchester, and taken as their country home Boundes Park, Lord Darnley's place near Southborough in Kent.
3. Lady Louisa Petty's elder sister Charlotte afterwards married Sir Charles Lemon, 2nd Bart (1784–1868), and died in 1826 very shortly after losing her second and only surviving son in a bathing accident at Harrow.
4. Thomas Newenham's (1762–1831) *A Statistical and Historical Inquiry into the Progress and Magnitude of Population in Ireland* (1805) was reviewed by Malthus in *ER* xii (no. xxiv, July 1808), 336–55. (See Doc. 286.)
5. Burr had allegedly been involved in a conspiracy to separate portions of the American southwest from the United States, for which he was tried and acquitted on a charge of treason.

311. Note by Horner

BLPES viii. 56-7   [London], 27 Oct. 1808

At Bentham's, Col. *Burr*, 6 hours

There are very few marriage settlements [in the United States] – the wife trusts to her legal provision. Yet, from the law of equal distribution, almost every bride brings a fortune more or less. B[urr] seemed to ascribe this to the spirit of commercial adventure.

Men of considerable property usually make a will. In general, a father leaves his children to take by the legal distribution. For one instance of a will, there are five of intestacy.

The Elections are determined, he says, by the force of numerical majorities; property exerts almost no influence. It is felt a little in the great towns; the great master shoemakers or warehousemen command their journeymen or carmen. In the country, property shows no influence. His inference was, that the strength of Government lies in pleasing the numerical mass; and he explained in this way the continuance of the Embargo, the pernicious operation of which have not yet reached the multitude, while the men of property who suffer by it have no voice. He said, that no men of property were in office, or were even members of congress; you may pass the whole winter at New York in what is called the best company, without ever seeing a member of congress; they do not belong to so high a class of society. There is no idle man of property; every one is engaged in trade, or agriculture. Quiet men, he said, could not bear the licence and tumult which must be undergone in the popular elections. He thinks at the same time, that, if the men of property were to combine and concert their measures well, they might command part of the returns in the elections; lately, he mentioned, there was a feeling among those of New York that some attempt of this sort ought to be made, arising from an apprehension that the Government [might?] fall into measures that seemed to endanger. Rufus King stood at New York for a seat in the House of Representatives; but lost his election, through mismanagement as B[urr] is of opinion.[1]

His appear[ance] [is] at first that of an underbred Frenchman, and upon nearer view of his countenance there is an expression of bad temper and even malignity. His manner when engaged in conversation is free from affectation, and also from vivacity; but it has that sort of quietness, which seems to show a constraint upon the natural temper. He was very ready to converse about America, and indeed did not appear to be ready for more general topics. His discourse very perspicuous and distinct, with something of the lawyer, which was originally his occupation before he became a banker and then a statesman. He seems to abound in practical political knowledge, such as, according to the American phrase, *will answer*; and his familiarity with subjects of a military nature, shows what his views have been and probably still continue. He has been here since the month of July, living all that time (I believe) with Bentham, and it is uncertain when he will return. Some things dropped from which I make no doubt that he has some intercourse with Government, if not with any of the Ministers themselves, with subministerial persons. They cannot surely be criminal enough to entertain his projects. Bentham is at present very curious about Mexico, asking for all kind of books, etc. about it; I should conjecture, that Burr's conversation has given him this direction.

1. Rufus King (1755-1827) had formerly been American Minister in London.

312. To J.A. Murray

BLPES iii. 323-6   Lincoln's Inn,[1] 3 Dec. 1808

... I am very much encouraged and confirmed in all my hopes of the Spaniards, by the accounts of these few days.[2] A thousand grave gentlemen have been saying all summer, wait and see how they will bear to be beat; we have seen it now, and whoever put his opinion upon that cast, must now be won over to the patriots, who are fighting as never men fought before. Such a people cannot be vanquished; they must in the end be triumphant. I was much alarmed by the long delay of intelligence, till it appeared that nothing came from Paris, from which we should have been sure to hear of any great advantage gained over Castanos or Palafox ...

... The transports at Corunna have certainly been detained, in case a re-imbarkation should be necessary. And Moore it is said has instructions most disgraceful to our Ministers, whatever Baird's may be, for he is desired to have always an eye to a retreat; the meaning of which I take to be, that if any disaster should befall his army, it should be easy for Government to throw the responsibility off themselves, upon an officer whom they dislike.[3] But I trust that neither Moore nor Baird will fear the responsibility of doing their utmost; I do not know what Baird's *political* courage may be; Moore's is said to be of the firmest. It was most unwise to send them upon such a march, perhaps to send men at all into the country; but being there, I hope they will not act upon the supposition that the error can be set right by flying before the enemy. I would rather hear of our army being cut to pieces upon the field, than of such a retreat.[4]

...

1. Horner had moved out of his rooms in Garden Court into Lincoln's Inn soon after 27 Oct. and on 11 Nov. was writing to Murray to say as yet that his new chambers were by contrast 'rather dismal' (*Horner*, i. 464, and BLPES iii. 321-2).
2. After his departure with the Hollands, Allen sent Horner a number of lengthy accounts of the Peninsular War and of Spanish politics. Two letters from Allen, written from Corunna on 11 Nov. and 3 Dec. 1808, are in the Kinnordy MSS.
3. General Sir John Moore (1761-1809: *DNB*), commander of the British expeditionary force which only recently had struck camp at Corunna and marched east to engage the French. General Sir David Baird (1757-1829: *DNB*) was his second-in-command.
4. Moore, who was then regarded as Britain's finest field commander, 'was in habits and opinions more connected with the Whigs than with their opponents' (*Holland's Further Memoirs*, p. 25). Moreover, while the British Government had in fact tried to advance Wellesley and jockey Moore by sending four successive commanders to Portugal during 1808, Moore for his part had made no secret of his contempt for Canning's policy, and by

the time he began his unfortunate advance into Portugal he had come in spite of himself to be seen as a 'Whig' general. His presence at the head of the British column also produced a predictable, if contradictory, point of view among the Whigs. On the one hand, his advance inspired a sudden renewal of support for the Peninsular War (Taylor, pp. 240–41). On the other, as Horner's letter reflects, many Whigs were suspicious of the British Government's motives towards a 'Whig' general and held from the first that Moore's advance was dangerous and threatened by mismanagement on the part of Ministers (Roberts, pp. 127–8).

313. From Francis Jeffrey

⟨Horner, i. 464–6⟩   Edinburgh, 6 Dec. 1808

⟨I see by the *Courier* that the combustion which the review of Cevallos has excited here has spread in some degree to London.[1] I am convinced, too, that it has damaged us a little; and am so much persuaded that it is necessary for us to make more than an ordinary exertion in this crisis, that I take courage to do that which is now very painful to me – to solicit your aid in my day of need. The Tories having got a handle are running us down with all their might; and the ghosts of all the miserables we have slain are rising to join the vengeance. Walter Scott and William Erskine, and about twenty-five persons of consideration, have forbidden the *Review* to enter their doors. The Earl of Buchan, I am informed, opened his street door, and actually *kicked* it out![2] Then, Cumberland is going to start an anonymous rival; and, what is worse, I have reason to believe that Scott, Ellis, Frere, Southey, and some others are plotting another.[3] You must see, therefore, that it is really necessary for us now to put on a manful countenance, and to call even the *emeriti* to our assistance. I entreat you to do an article for me during the holidays. We shall scarcely be out before the end of January, and I might even give you the whole of that month, if you need it. Now, I do not think that you would give me £100 if I was in great need of it; and this will cost you less work than you could do for £50 for any knave of a solicitor: and it is of infinitely more consequence and gratification to me than any £100 could be. Persuade yourself for once then, my dear Horner, that this is not a solicitation of custom, but that I make it with as much real anxiety and earnestness, and as much dread of a refusal, as if I were asking a pecuniary boon. You shall have your choice, of course, of a subject; but I wish you would put your notes and notions of Malthus together at last. It is a fine subject; and you are in a manner pledged to it. But if you can think of any thing more popular or striking, take it – only no party politics, and nothing but exemplary moderation and impartiality on all polities. I have allowed too much mischief to be done from my mere indifference and love of sport; but it would be inexcusable to spoil the powerful instrument we have got hold of, for the sake of teazing and playing tricks. Tell me, too, what you think I should do myself. I grow stupid from day to day; but I will cheerfully dedicate the holidays to this service, if you will condescend to guide me.[4]

⟨. . . Murray tells me that you have still hopes of Spain. I have despaired utterly, from the beginning; and do not expect that we are ever to see ten thousand of our men back again – probably not five thousand. The prospect is monstrous, and startles even my public apathy ...⟩

1. Jeffrey refers to the article, 'Don Pedro Cevallos on the French Usurpation in Spain' (*ER* xiii (no. xxv, Oct. 1808), 215–24), which supported the Spanish patriots but contained a blistering attack on the British and Spanish upper classes, a slur against the British monarch, and a demand for reform of the British Constitution that offended the Whigs no less than their political rivals. The article was apparently written jointly by Jeffrey and Brougham but it was universally credited to the latter at the time it appeared. Sydney Smith informed Lady Holland in a letter of December 1808 that Brougham had been 'bolting out of the course again' and that he 'should always remain between 2 tame elephants, Abercromby and Whishaw, who might beat him with their tusks, when he behaved in an unwhiglike manner'. (*Smith Letters*, i. 151; see also New, pp. 46–9.)

2. David Steuart Erskine, 11th Earl of Buchan (1742–1829: *DNB*).

3. The *London Review*, conducted by the dramatist Richard Cumberland (1732–1811: *DNB*), lasted for only two volumes (February-May and August-November 1809). But the outrage over Brougham's indiscreet article did of course lead to the establishment of the *Quarterly Review*, with Canning's friends George Ellis (1753–1815: *DNB*) and J. H. Frere as well as Scott and Southey taking a prominent part. (*Murray*, i. 98, 126, and 189; Clive, pp. 111–13.)

4. Horner's reply has not been found, but a subsequent letter (Doc. 316) confirms that he 'half promised' but later declined to write an article on Spain for the next number of the *Review*.

314. To J.A. Murray

BLPES iii. 327–30 ⟨New, p. 48⟩   Lincoln's Inn, 9 Dec. 1808

... The news of last night from Spain are quite heartbreaking;[1] I cannot bear to think of them, as far as the poor Spaniards and the general interests of the world are concerned. Nor can I control my indignation, that this country should be so disgraced in the eyes of Europe and to all future times, by such mismanagement of great means and such an incapacity for affairs as were never witnessed before in the most degenerate days of any other state.

⟨I have not time to say what I would on Brougham's review of Cevallos; I think it most reprehensible in its tone and spirit, and very unworthy of his knowledge and judgement, not only in what relates to the actual history of the Spanish insurrection, but also in the applications he makes to the constitution of our own country. Are all the fruits of a long continued study of politics, great opportunities of seeing both affairs and men very near at hand, and the best talents nature has to give, to be thrown away upon dashing declamations⟩ to suit a temporary purpose or give vent to the humour and fit of the day?

1. Probably the news of the imminent fall of Madrid. It occurred on the 17th.

315. To the Duke of Somerset

BLPES iii. 331–2   Lincoln's Inn, 9 Dec. 1808

... The productive state of the revenue at the end of this last summer, may be understood, it seems to me, without resorting to a miracle in the orders of council. Our commercial situation has been materially improved by the Portuguese and Spanish revolutions; not only in consequence of the vent for our commodities which the peninsula in the old world has afforded, but by the immense acquisition of a trade with all South America. Throughout the summer, there has been a good deal of commercial intercourse with Holland, vexed indeed and interrupted from time to time; and then I am informed that the rock of Heligoland has afforded facilities, which have been fully used, of smuggling goods of all sorts into the north of Germany.

With respect to the Orders of Council, it is not to be forgotten, that Ministers have hitherto kept from the eyes of the public, and from Parliament in spite of repeated orders of both Houses, an account of the trade and customs in the outports as well as London during the *first* quarter of the present year; the period when the Orders of Council were most fully in operation, and before that unexpected relief that was given by the expulsion of the French from the South of Spain.

But, independently altogether of Customs, the receipts of the Exchequer in the present year have been unusually augmented by the arrears of the property tax for several past years, as far back as 1805, which the improved methods of collecting and greater experience have enabled Government to draw together. I believe this will be found to be a very considerable sum.

The news of last night from Spain are very disastrous. Nor was there ever, it seems to me, such an instance of mismanagement with great means and resources, or such evidence of incapacity for affairs and particularly foreign operations, as is presented by the conduct of Ministers with regard to Spain. But the country is still asleep; and until it awakens to the sight of its disgraces and future danger, we shall live, as we have lived, under the feeble government of an absolute king worn out himself with age and served by ministers who are equally destitute of public talent and public integrity. It is frightful to compare, with the last days of other decayed states in history, our present insensibility and infatuation. The newspapers of today have made me quite sad and alarmed.

316. To Francis Jeffrey

BLPES iv. 7–11   Lincoln's Inn, 21 Jan. 1809

You will not be surprised to hear from me that I am not going to send the article on Spanish affairs, which I more than half promised you. I have been deterred from reducing my notions upon the subject to writing, in consequence of the uncertainty which has been thrown upon what I built on all along as my fundamental fact, the disposition and zeal of the people of Spain; an uncertainty which has been increasing by every account latterly received from that country, if the point is not already settled by sufficient evidence quite the other way.[1]

In addition to this, the case has now assumed that shape in which it becomes impossible to separate, in the discussion of it, the conduct of the English Ministers from the other causes which have co-operated in producing the disappointment of our hopes in Spain: and all examination of their conduct would be improper in the *Review*. The failure of the Spanish people in the defence of their country, might perhaps have been foreseen from the first if the country had been visited at that period by persons who are qualified to observe and report the real state of the popular mind: on the other hand, it may perhaps be ascribed, and that I am more willing still to believe, to a want of proper care and means being taken to nourish the first enthusiasm, and give it an organized direction. But without farther proofs than we are yet in possession of, I should be averse to any public condemnation of the individuals composing the new Government of Spain, how strong soever appearances are against them, or precipitately to express, in a shape that might by accident reach some of them, a distrust of men who have made great personal sacrifices to undertake such a trust, and may have been controlled by overruling circumstances in the discharge of it. When I proposed to you a statement of the grounds upon which I thought it had been reasonable to expect success to the cause of Spanish independence, I was still credulous about the active zeal of the Spanish people, and continued to rely upon an active administration at least by the Central Junta. With respect to the North, Old Castile and the province of Gallicia, it may be considered as established that their zeal has been in words only; but whether owing in some measure to the neglect of the Spanish Government, may be still a question. I have a great disposition to catch at every trifling probability, that it may be otherwise in the South: a very short time will determine this, for if there be any prolongation of the contest that would itself give just hopes and opportunities to the rest of the world, and the speedy termination of it would close the question and leave us nothing but acquiescence in the new state and order of things.

I am not well enough to attend Parliament, and shall not be able to go down till the weather becomes milder, so I know nothing of the debate but from report.[2] It is said to have been very flat in both houses; and I hear none of the speeches praised except Lord Grenville's, which is described to have been able though full of gloom and despondency about the future prospects of the country. Of course he will suffer some additional unpopularity, for his opinion that no troops ought to have [been] sent into Spain; an opinion in which he is supported by many competent judges, both political and military.[3] I am still, I own, with the mob and the Ministers upon this point; it being quite a separate question whether the troops have been sent in sufficient numbers, or to the proper places, or with due combinations and method.

A distinction of the same kind is necessary with regard to another subject, the reception of the overture from Erfurth: in substance, it seems to me, our answer is what it ought to have been; but nobody, except the little click [*sic*] round Mr

Secretary Canning, can approve of the intemperate manner in which his compositions are written; they have no resemblance to the customary style of state papers, and are more like the letters of a youth who begins to show a turn for fine writing but mistakes insolence for spirit. I do not know whether they will be admired; they are not plain enough perhaps for the public.[4]

... I have been amused by your alarm about a rival review; and you will not forgive me perhaps for rejoicing, as I do, in having another tolerable work of that nature to read, and to hear of its having a wide circulation in the country. I shall look upon its success as another of the good fruits of our little Edinburgh project, which has swelled to such unpremeditated importance, and has so outlived all calculation or intention. If this new one succeeds too, you have effected one great object of our scheme, the emancipation of the critical journals from those indulgent critics the publishers.

...

I am afraid from your utter silence, that I did not do what was quite agreeable to you in giving Col. Burr an introduction to you.

1. Horner wrote on the day that news of the death of General Sir John Moore reached London. Reports of Spanish apathy and cowardice had circulated for some time and were now being confirmed by wounded and emaciated British soldiers returning from the Peninsula. In addition, James Moore's publication of his late brother's *Narrative of the Campaign of the British Army in Spain* (1809) would shortly add further credibility to reports of unprincipled conduct by the Spaniards. (Roberts, pp. 133–4; Taylor, pp. 258–9.)

2. In either late December 1808 or early January 1809 Horner experienced the first serious effects of the malady that would take his life some eight years later and he consequently remained confined to his chambers in Lincoln's Inn until mid-February. Apparently his physician recommended a regimen of light reading, and Sydney Smith told Lady Holland on 10 Jan. (*Smith Letters*, i. 153) that upon searching his library Horner found that he 'had no amusing books, – the nearest to any work of that description being *The India Trader's Complete Guide*'.

   The debate to which Horner refers is that of 19 Jan., the opening day of the session. Although the bulk of the Whigs wanted to fight the French, there was great disagreement among them about tactics and so they moved no amendment to the Address. (See Taylor, pp. 245–58, for an account of Whig disagreement prior to the meeting of Parliament and a summary of Opposition speeches on 19 January. See Roberts, pp. 124–5, for an account of the contradictory and almost comical military advice advanced in the Lords by Opposition peers.)

3. Grenville, who was troubled no less by the implications of the mounting attack on the Duke of York for alleged corruption than by military reversals in the Peninsula, also announced a future reduction of parliamentary exertion on the part of Opposition (*Hansard*, xii, 1121 and 3854; see also Taylor, pp. 246–7.)

4. The speech from the throne of 19 Jan. announced that Britain had refused a Franco-Russian offer of peace negotiations because France refused to guarantee as a preliminary the restoration of Spain's 'legitimate' sovereign. A perusal of the related papers that had been laid before Parliament apparently formed Horner's opinion of Canning's diplomatic correspondence. (*Hansard*, xii. 1–4.)

317. To Lord —————— [1]

BLPES viii. 58–65 (unsigned draft)   Lincoln's Inn, 22 Jan. 1809

In the remarks which you have made upon the King's Declaration of the month of May 1803, and upon the contents of the papers which were laid before Parliament as its justification, I have found many strong and unanswerable reasons to confirm me in the opinion I have entertained from the first respecting the present war; that, upon the principles of the law of nations, it was at the time, and upon the grounds, which were chosen for breaking the Treaty of Amiens, an unjust war upon the side of England; and that, upon every view which could be taken either of the immediate or the lasting interests of England or the continent, it was a measure not merely of doubtful utility but manifestly full of the utmost hazard and danger.

Between the treaty of Amiens, and the period at which our incapable Ministry of that day thought fit to break it, France had given this country more than one occasion, it seems to me, of just remonstrance; and if redress had been asked and refused, of justifiable war, upon the principles of public law: but those occasions, the continued occupation of Holland and the new invasion of Switzerland, were passed by, and upon a review at this moment of the circumstances of the time it would appear inexpedient and unwise not to have waved the right of remonstrance and subsequent hostility.

The various grounds of complaint which France had given to this country, but which had been successively overlooked, could not properly enter into a statement of the ground, upon which we at length resolved to remonstrate, with a determination to follow it up by hostilities. You have very fully exposed this fallacy; I wish you had likewise shown that there was another fallacy, in the reasoning by which Mr Pitt defended the Declaration in this respect. He was obliged to admit, that those several grievances formed no distinct grounds of war, but he maintained that they were to be taken as auxiliary proofs of hostile intention; whereas it is certain, that no such indirect and remote evidence is admissible in judging of the question of right in war, otherwise there would be no chance of preserving peace between any two nations. That those acts of France were proofs of a spirit of aggrandizement, I do not deny, nor that there was evidence enough of that spirit to reduce it wholly to a question of expediency on our side, whether we were to take the first occasion of commencing war. But if we had satisfied ourselves of its expediency, we were bound to wait for the next just occasion; nor was it warrantable to take an unjust pretext, and to bolster up our imperfect case by recalling injuries which we might have resented at the time, but which we had not complained of.

From what I have said, you will perceive that I consider in a different light from you some of those preceding outrages of France, upon which I conceive that we might have been *justified*, in point of *right*, in renewing the war with her at an earlier period; though this difference of opinion does not affect our conclusion, with respect to the inexpediency of renewing the war at all. And even with respect to the question of expediency, I fancy that in general I should admit into the political maxims of England, a greater degree of continental interference than you would approve of; if indeed there existed any longer a system of European states. The conduct of France to Switzerland in 1802, and our right arising out of it, is put very erroneously in the Declaration; which states it as a *breach* of the treaty of Amiens, whereas it ought to have been stated as a *new* injury, and which would have been equally a ground of complaint though there had been no former quarrels and treaty.

There is one verbal criticism which I must submit to you, upon the composition of your work. Where you have occasion to show the falsehood of an allegation, or to impute motives to the actors in these transactions, your epithets are frequently too strong and direct. I well know how difficult it is, in the indignation one feels at the consequences of bad conduct in these great concerns, and at the sophistry by which it is usually defended, to restrain one's self from a precipitate imputation of the worst motives. Yet the worst motives rarely exist in these transactions; and the most pernicious proceedings against the tranquillity of mankind are much less frequently directed by deliberate malignity or even by cold calculating ambition, than they are the result of imperfect consideration, ignorance and ill temper. Besides, nothing is so difficult to be ascertained as the matter of fact, with respect to the motives of men. And for the sake of effect in writing, as well as for the sake of justice to the men whose conduct we examine in the deliberate review of any particular transaction, I am inclined to think it better to state the specific proofs and circumstances, so as that no reader can miss the proper inference, than to repeat the same epithets of condemnation; which, even if they are equally deserved in every step of the case, are not discriminating enough to leave so distinct an impression on the mind of the reader, as you can make by a perspicuous and skilful statement of circumstances.

p. 1. It is true, that Lord Hawkesbury had agreed to receive M. Coquebert Montbret, and to enter into negotiation with him respecting the commercial intercourse of the two countries; but you will observe, that the Commission given to Coquebert by his Government is not as an agent to negotiate, but in quite a different character. The delay on Lord Hawkesbury's part, to be sure, is unexplained; ought he not to have immediately noticed that the functions given to M. Coquebert were not in that character in which he had agreed to receive him? and to have urged M. Otto to explain why an agent to negotiate a commercial arrangement was not appointed?[2]

p. 6. It is not a proof of there being only two commercial agents sent over, that they were not ordered to quit HM's dominions; there were evidently more, as at Dublin. The story of the spies is childish; to be sure these agents had probably instructions to furnish their Government with all information that might [prove useful] at any future time, either in respect of commerce or war; because all such agents of all governments have such instructions: would a commercial treaty have rendered the persons resident, as commercial agents under its authority, less active as spies?

p. 9. At the conclusion of the Treaty of Amiens, France was under an obligation to Austria to leave Switzerland independent and free of French troops. The invasion in 1802 was a new aggression; which, upon the principles of the law of nations, gave

England a right (if she thought it expedient, which is another question) to complain against France; it was a *new* injury. In the Declaration, it is put differently, as if it were to be considered a *breach* of the Treaty of A. which is perhaps a refinement, but seems to me only nonsense; the Treaty had put to rest old quarrels; this was a ground for a new one, though there had never been any of those [quarrels] which rendered that treaty necessary to compose them. I would admit a greater degree of continental interference into the political maxims of England, than you seem inclined to allow of; if there were a system of European states, I would have England interfere to prevent an unjust aggression against any one (particularly a small and weak state) whenever she could interpose with success and effect for the preservation of the system.

p. 11. What is the date of the first demand made by the French Government to the English, to withdraw the troops from Malta? And what [is] the date of the election of a Grand Master at Petersburg? Without those dates, we have not proof of a false assertion; the first demand, for the withdrawing the troops, may have been before the Election.

p. 42. There are many propositions in this little paragraph, about which I must hesitate a good deal, before I admit them to be true.

1. Is it the fact, that by the war and taxation of late years 'the poor have been made to experience all the miseries of want'? By the necessary constitution of every society, where slavery is not instituted, the labouring classes are always, in peace as well as war, in a state of want from day to day; their wages may rise or fall, with the prosperous or unprosperous state of the community: war does in many respects tend to lower the real wages of labour, that is, the quantity of food and clothes which are paid for it; heavy taxation must in some respects do the same; but it is a very nice estimate to make in any particular case, if we wish to ascertain how far these causes have had the effect of depressing the labouring people, after giving due allowance to all the other circumstances which may counteract those causes. Such circumstances, are, a great increase of foreign trade by the peculiar turn of the war; and the progress of national opulence and industry, in spite of the war.

2. I doubt very much whether the increase of national debt has any influence in depreciating the value of money; I do not see how it brings immense sums into circulation.

3. The depreciation of money, it is to be observed, operates upon the amount of the debt and taxes, as well as upon the income of individuals. Annuitants are the persons who suffer by that depreciation; the annuitants in the funds like others; but what is lost by the person who receives a fixed money annuity, is gained by the party that has to pay it. A sum of debt in the present times is perhaps no more than equal to the half of it thirty years ago; and so it is of taxes; he who pays twenty shillings in taxes now, does not contribute more perhaps, is not burthened more, than he who paid ten, thirty years ago. After all this deduction, there remains an immense increase; but it is necessary to distinguish what is apparent only in the nominal increase from what is real. I have supposed the depreciation to be in the proportion of 2 to 1, for this argument's sake; it may not be exactly in that proportion.

p. 46. I believe it will be found that there has been a great *diminution* in the number of crimes: owing in a great measure to the drain of the army and navy, but in some degree (I am persuaded) to increasing industry among the people. The progress of this industry, and of the order which it introduces, are of course in spite of the war.[3]

p. 48. The great number of occasional poor, whom you very justly include in your estimate, is owing very much to a practice which has gained ground very fast of late years, and to the effect of that upon the wages of common labour. It is quite unconnected with the war or taxation, but arising out of an unlucky construction of the statutes for relief of the poor. They were intended to provide for the aid of 'impotent' poor, as they are called in the old statutes; that is, for those who are disabled by *infirmity*, permanent or occasional, from maintaining themselves and their families by labour. The scarcities that have repeatedly occurred produced a disability of a different kind; a disability in the strongest and most healthy labourer, by the utmost efforts of his labour, to procure bread enough for his family at so high a price as it rose to: to relieve this, though it was not a case of impotence or infirmity, the magistrates were led (naturally enough, but I doubt if legally) to give relief on account of the inadequacy of wages, and more, of course, in proportion to the number of children whom the labourer had to feed. This, though introduced (I believe) in time of scarcity, has not been confined to such periods of crying necessity; but has gradually been established into a rule, of giving relief whenever a labourer has above a certain number of children: it is chiefly since the last great dearth, and in the agricultural districts, that the practice and its effects have manifested themselves. Nothing can be more evident, than, that the unavoidable effect of such a custom is to prevent that rise of wages which would have taken place with the rise of all other prices; or rather to make the labourer receive that portion [of] what is in fact added to his real wages, from the parish under the name of relief, instead of the whole increased sum from his employer under the proper name of wages. If one adverts to the nominal rate of wages, in the agricultural districts, they have not risen in proportion to the rise of all other prices; but if one takes also into consideration the lists of occasional poor, it will be found, that what the labourer really receives in all, has been increased very much in the same proportion as the price of other things. This is a circuitous mode of paying the increase of wages, and therefore an expensive mode to the employer; and it is very pernicious to the moral character of the labourer, who does not know any thing of this reasoning, but only feels that the actual wages he gets from his employers will not feed his family, and that though he is in full possession of health for work he must be degraded to the pauper list. But the purpose for which I have made this long deduction at present, is, to infer that so far as this is to be stated as an increase in the number of the poor, it is to be ascribed, not to the war or to taxation, but to an injudicious administration of the poor laws, or rather a perversion of them from their proper purpose.

p. 47. I do not mean to enter into the discussion, which you avoid, about the original Compact: though I consider that doctrine to be an unlucky fiction, which is of no real convenience in any political reasonings, which leads to some wrong consequences, and which leads to no conclusions in favour of liberty or justice that may not be more clearly and simply deduced in another manner. But independently of this discussion, how can it be a natural inherent right to receive relief? Natural inherent right must be anterior to the supposed compact, for all the rights derived out of that must be those which have been agreed upon. Relief from indigence is a contribution to those who are unfortunate, from those who have had better luck or more foresight; but what natural inherent right has an unfortunate cripple to demand part of what belongs to a lucky able-bodied owner of wealth? I cannot figure any arrangement more strictly depending upon the arbitrary will of the state.

p. 48. In your note upon the Rights of Man, there *appears* to me to be a great deal of the most important truth, mixed with serious and hurtful error; and I do not know any subject, upon which it more concerns the interests of humanity, that those who may have an influence upon the opinions of others should have just notions, and see the real truth with all its necessary qualifications. That the only end of government is the good of the governed; that the theoretical form under which a government is to be classed, is rarely a test of its practical excellence; and that if the Administration practically secures property, and the free exercise of industry and talents, the people will remain attached to it: are all very great sacred truths, and the first of the three especially cannot be too constantly recalled and insisted upon. But it is not true, that God and Nature have not doomed the great mass of the population of the world to servile and painful labour; for that is their doom: it is the law of Nature, and as we are instructed it is, the sentence of God. It is inconsistent with both, that *mankind* should ever 'sit under the shade of their vines and figtrees'; for, in order that a few may enjoy that indolence and repose, the multitude must 'eat bread in the sweat of their face'. This is the unalterable constitution of mankind and society: and it would not be difficult to show, with the assistance of the great writers who have considered this subject, how many occasions of happiness, and how many opportunities of good, grow out of this which appears at first sight so deplorable an evil. But with reference to the fundamental principles of politics, it is most important to keep this truth in view; both that it may be the constant object of legislation and government to ameliorate and lighten the condition of the labouring orders, and that no visionary hopes or schemes may be held out to them which may disquiet them and embitter their condition. 'That those who think must govern those who toil', is the concise description of what will ever be the actual state of mankind; and the great principle of freedom in government, is so to model all the institutions of the state that it may be open and easy for individuals to rise, by superior industry and the better cultivation of natural talents, from the lowest station in the one class to as high as it is worth reaching in the other. Your quotation from the Bible brings to my mind a passage in the Apocrypha, which Mr Dugald Stewart first pointed out to me, and which describes very finely and philosophically the order of society upon the very principle which I have been stating.

p. 52. The concluding paragraph alludes, I presume, to Lord Grenville's Administration; but the memorandum on the cover, of the day when these Reflections were finished, would apply it to the Duke of Portland's.

1. The editors have been unable to identify the addressee or, if the document to which it relates was ever published, any such pamphlet.
2. The peace negotiations of the spring of 1801 were conducted through the medium of Louis Guillaume Otto, then in England as Commissioner for French prisoners. Coquebert Montbret was sent to London by the French in 1802 or 1803 as the Commissioner General of Commercial Relations, while a certain Mares went to Hull and Fauvelet to Dublin. (P. Coquelle, 'Les Responsabilités de la Rupture de la Paix d'Amiens en 1803', *Revue d'Histoire Diplomatique*, xvi (1902), 274–8, and *Addington*, ii. 264.) Gen. Andréossi arrived as ambassador in Nov. 1802.
3. This paragraph has been crossed out, apparently by Horner himself.

318. To Mrs Dugald Stewart

BLPES iv. 14–17 〈Horner, i. 470–71〉   Lincoln's Inn, 25 Jan. 1809

〈. . .

〈I am very much comforted by the account you give me of Mr Stewart's health. And, on every public as well as private account, I rejoice at the resolution he has formed to quit the college after this winter; for though I never think of the decline of that institution without a melancholy regret, yet its fall is now inevitable, and the continuation of its best remaining advantages would be no compensation to the public for a delay in the execution of Mr Stewart's other plans, or to those who love him and you, for your losing that freedom and power of retirement which you know so well how to enjoy. I shall regret only Mr Playfair's solitude,〉 among the ignorant and illiberal priests with whom he will be left alone; 〈but he is in the mean time establishing a new reputation, in addition to what he possessed before; and it is some triumph to expect, that the last glory of the college will be the exertions of those who protested against the system which has destroyed it.[1]

〈There is nothing new, I think, today; when any thing occurs, I will write you a little note. Though in truth I have not much heart for politics; and find myself more alienated than you would believe from the immediate questions and objects. It is not that I despair of what is to be the ultimate result; but there is such a prospect in this country of an interval, during which no exertions will avail, that it requires an iron fortitude to keep up one's interest in the details that are passing. I never felt any pleasure in the game itself, and care only for the object; and indeed if it were otherwise, there is so little capacity in any of the actors among us, and such a tone of illiberality in the successful ones, that my feelings as a spectator are often the very reverse of being pleasurable.〉

Genl Moore wrote a very hurried dispatch on the evening of the 13th, having first intended to make his report up to that time verbally, by Genl Stewart. This is the dispatch, asked for rather abruptly by Whitbread last night; the reason privately assigned by Ministers for their declining to produce the whole of it, is, that it contains a severe condemnation of the army for the want of discipline during the retreat. Their conduct was more than usually irregular. Genl Stewart asked Moore, before he came away, if he wished this part of the dispatch to be made public; to which he answered, that he never wrote any thing to the publication of which he had any objection, and that he should leave it wholly to Lord Castlereagh's discretion. The dispatch contains, I understand, one statement most important to Moore's reputation; that his second advance was contrary to his own military judgement. It will turn out probably that he was urged to it by the representations of that madman Frere, and the orders of our incapable Government at home. There is every appearance now, that they mean to save themselves if they can, by laying violent hands upon the memory of Sir John Moore, but from all I can collect, his conduct will bear any scrutiny, and will be found to be an unremitted course of skill, activity and firmness in the most trying circumstances. Confident as I am of this, it gives me the heartache when I think of the flippant sneers we shall have from Canning, and the cold malignity of Castlereagh; both of whom hated Moore, and intrigued against him in the basest manner. These are the things which often make attendance at the H. of C. painful to me, and have repeatedly sent me home disgusted and saddened.[2]

⟨. . .⟩

1. Professor Stewart retired later in the year.
2. As Minister to the Supreme Junta J.H. Frere had urged Moore to anticipate the French advance on Madrid or at least to retire through Galicia, and so was much blamed afterwards for the Corunna fiasco. Whitbread pressed for the publication of Moore's dispatches on 24 Jan. and again on 31 Jan. and received rather evasive replies from Castlereagh (*Hansard*, xii. 131 and 208–210). But a substantial extract from that of 13 Jan., Moore's last, brought home by Castlereagh's brother Gen. Stewart, was published (and reproduced in *AR* li (1809), 426–8).

319. To J.A. Murray

BLPES iv. 18–20 ⟨*Horner*, i. 472–3⟩   Lincoln's Inn, 26 Jan. 1809

⟨. . .

⟨Besides yourself, I can perceive that the more partial of my friends think me wrong in not making an attempt to speak in the House of Commons;[1] while the rest have given me up as incapable. Sometimes, I have been for a moment upon the point of agreeing with the latter in their opinion upon the subject, for every one has his moments of honesty and selfconfession. But, upon the whole, I am willing to believe that I might have done better, and that I have reason to reproach myself with a want of proper exertion. I have better resolutions for the present session; of which we shall see what may come. It would be an idle history of indolence, fastidiousness, dread of failure, etc., were I to give you my apologies for not making the trial on several occasions. There have been some discouragements of a different nature; the petty war of political personalities is exceedingly irksome to me, it disgusts rather than irritates me (being personally not implicated), and I have witnessed but little else since I sat in the House. I suspect too that I have not nerves for a hopeless unavailing struggle, where I have a contempt for my antagonists, and more than suspect the unfairness of their fighting. Then I have a great dislike for the audience in that place, in their present temper of stupid illiberality. I am made, or educated, for the sunshine of an improving community; and have not yet acquired the habits and resolutions that are more suitable to the present state of this country. I am learning them a little; and there is not one motive I have assigned for my silence in Parliament, that does not, I own, admit of a complete answer. I have one still to assign, which probably has but too just a foundation: my dread of finding it an effort above me, to discuss a large subject in public after many speakers, and with numerous details and arguments to manage. I have never made the experiment, and perhaps I should sink in the first attempt; though I am perfectly convinced that the power is to be acquired by practice, since men of very humble talents have acquired it. This, I take it, is the real cause, though confirmed and coloured by the others I have mentioned. Of course, you would not put me upon making a set speech, though fame for a day is to be had in that way; and rather than give such an express demonstration of my incapacity for business, I would sit contentedly under the doubts which my friends continue to entertain of me.⟩

I agree with you in all you say of Col. Burr. He is very strangely cherished by the underlings of our present Government; who must reserve him for some mischievous projects against America or New Spain.

. . .

1. Notably Jeffrey: see Jeffrey to Horner, 2 Apr. 1809, *Horner*, i. 486–8.

320. Note by Horner

BLPES viii. 66   [London], 31 Jan. 1809

TEMPER OF THE PUBLIC MIND

Devotion to the King – unpopularity of the Princes – Influence of newspapers, and state of the periodical press – No particular set of public men, nor individuals, looked up to or confided in – Hatred of the last Ministers, contempt of the present –

Distinction as to the different classes of the people – Readers of Cobbett; qu. has extinguished their ordinary cry for peace, but has (through odium of existing government) given them an indifference about French conquest?

INFLUENCE

Amount distributed annually in name of pensions, offices, etc. (independent of army and navy) – Number of places besides Colonial patronage, probability of deaths.

Hath not this influence made the manners of England less simple and pure?

Would not a steady course of measures, plainly effectual, and pursued with an intelligible system, do more than any other line of conduct, both to regain popular confidence, and to lessen the excesses of influence? Unpopularity from the dependants of office.

321. To J.A. Murray

BLPES iv. 24–6 Lincoln's Inn, 31 Jan. 1809

... Corunna, and Sir John Moore, and 'the universal Spanish nation', are now utterly obliterated from the retentive sensorium of this London; upon which there is no other impression but Mr Wardle, and Mrs Clarke and the Duke of York.[1] These giddy, headless people forget every thing for this. An important subject of inquiry, it unquestionably is, loudly called for, and which has been too long delayed. But it has been taken up in the most unlucky manner, for the [?integrity] of justice and serious investigation, which (I greatly fear) will be disappointed, not for want of truth enough in the charge, but of care and sense in the mode of stating and bringing it forward. An accurate examination of witnesses in a Committee of the whole house, in a case of such general curiosity, is quite impracticable; for a Select Committee, with all the chances of its being packed, would have been far preferable. It would have been more judicious not to have called the attention of the House to it, until the great subjects of discussion which have been proffered by the events of the last recess, had been in some measure disposed of; especially as it is understood that the new Report from the Commission of Military Inquiry, which is not yet printed, opens up some subjects of inquiry with regard to the Commander in Chief's conduct which would be a better ground on which to found a parliamentary inquisition, than information which has the appearance of being suggested vindictively by persons of infamous character. There is a story, that the information on which Mr Wardle acts was first laid before Sir F. Burdett and afterwards before Brand, both of whom declined having any thing to do with it.[2] I have every reason at present to believe that Mr Wardle is a man of respectability and is actuated by none but proper motives; and as the matter is brought before the House, it will be the duty of men who have any sense of duty to see justice done, and the inquiry made as full as possible.

1. Following the earlier rumours about the Duke of York (Doc. 300), the *Independent Whig* had on 30 Oct. 1808 published an article entitled 'Corruption and undue influence in the promotion of military officers the source of national disgrace', and a storm had broken out in Jan. 1809 when Colonel Gwyllym Lloyd Wardle (1761–1833: *DNB*) accused the Duke of conniving at the receipt of money by his mistress, Mrs Clarke, for her supposed influence in the procuring of commissions and the hastening of promotion, and moved for inquiry in the Commons. (See Roberts, p. 197, and Taylor, pp. 244–5.)
2. Thomas Brand (1774–1851), afterwards 20th Baron Dacre, was Whig MP for Hertford-shire. There seems to have been some truth in this story: see *PH* iii. 249.

322. To J.A. Murray

BLPES iv. 30–32   Lincoln's Inn, 2 Feb. 1809

Many thanks for the two letters of which you have sent me copies, which are interesting in the highest degree.[1] The account of Moore's death is related with a pathos and force of expression, which is seldom attained even by masters of writing. The general assertion in the other letter, that our army is fit only to fight and not to bear the hardships of war, was Moore's opinion too, and expressed in his last dispatch of which I have already told you what I have heard; it is a most important fact, and calls for the immediate attention of those who may take measures to improve the habits of our soldiery. Nothing but service in actual war will harden men sufficiently for its extreme privations; yet a good deal surely might be done, in the way of exercise and regimen.

The account I have received of the state of the Hospital at Portsmouth, corresponds with what one should expect from Col. Graham's general observation.[2] There are about 200 wounded men brought there, and above two thousand sick; some of the latter have bad fevers, but most of them are ill only of a dysentery . . . The wounds are all gun shot, none from the sabre or bayonet; and as most of them are in the upper part of the body, the number of wounded who have died before reaching the hospital is inferred to be considerable.

I have seen one or two Members of the H. of C. who heard all the evidence last night.[3] Several persons, not of the House, have been calling on me likewise this morning; and it is curious, though not very comfortable, to observe the discrepancy of their respective impressions. All the latter are satisfied from the newspapers that the Duke of York is guilty, and that the Opposition are in league with the rest of the House to screen the Duke.[4] On the other hand, one of the most considerate and disinterested of men, who is a zealous member of Opposition, who is accustomed to weigh and discuss evidence, and who sat out the whole proceedings last night, has stated to me his clear conviction that the case was not proved; that the money was proved to have been paid to the Duke's whore, but after the exchange had been already assented to, and that Mrs Clarke's assertion of her telling the Duke that she got the money was contradicted by the testimony of the other witnesses who stated that she was urgent with them about concealing the transaction. It will be an unfortunate and hurtful result, if the House of Commons should not have evidence on which a resolution condemning the Duke could in justice be founded, and the public should still believe the Duke guilty, and this is very likely to happen, because it is such a novelty to the people of this country, that a married prince of the blood should keep a strumpet, that their indignation at the adultery will be their verdict against him for malversation in office. I have not yet seen the Minutes of Evidence: if there be ground for convicting, the Opposition will show themselves the basest as well as most foolish of men, if they do not prosecute the matter with their whole force. Hitherto, they behave as they are bound to do in such a case, by maintaining a judicial reserve and holding out a presumption of innocence: though it has subjected them already, such is the violence of sensible and independent persons upon this topic, to the hasty (and as yet, I believe, unmerited) reproach of being disposed to shelter and protect a great delinquent.

. . .

1. These letters have not been identified.
2. Colonel Thomas Graham, afterwards Baron Lynedoch (1748–1843: *DNB*), who had been Moore's ADC at Corunna, had stayed a couple of days at Portsmouth after landing in England on 23 Jan. (Alex. M. Delavoye, *Life of Thomas Graham, Lord Lynedoch* (1880), p. 300).
3. On 1 Feb. the Commons began to hear evidence in the Duke of York's case (*Hansard*, xii. 264ff.), but Horner was absent due to continuing 'unexplained bad health' (Horner to Murray, Feb. 1809, BLPES iv. 279).
4. There was ample reason for such a view of Opposition. Grey and Grenville regarded the charges against the Duke as the entering wedge of an attack on all public men and feared that they could not control Foxites in the House of Commons, and on 2 Sept. 1808 the *Morning Chronicle* had attempted to refute the allegations against the Duke. At the time Horner wrote this letter, a fearful Grenville was actively encouraging his political colleagues to desist from attacks on Government. (Taylor, pp. 244–8.)

323. To J.A. Murray

BLPES iv. 36–7 〈*Horner*, i. 479–80〉 London, 11 Feb. 1809

〈. . .

〈I have not changed my view of the Duke of York's affair, since I wrote to you last; many more circumstances have come out in the evidence, which place his guilt beyond all question, without yet carrying the proof to the point of corrupt connivance, though making that the most probable inference upon the whole.

〈My sense of the critical importance of the proceedings that shall be had upon this case, is still farther increased by a rumour which I have heard, that the Ministers and the Duke of York together consider the matter as brought now to this alternative, resignation or impeachment, and that the Duke will not resign.

〈I shall consider the impeachment of the Duke of York by the House of Commons as the death-knell of the constitution. It will keep the whole country in a ferment for months; the House of Lords will acquit; both houses will be looked upon by the public as having concerted this acquittal: and then you have the alternative to expect, of an entire prostration of all public opinion and popular efforts before the Crown, or a democratical anarchy of which no man can see the end. I think these are distinct public grounds upon which the House of Commons should refuse to impeach the Duke; because the present case is one, not for punishment, but for future distrust and immediate removal, both from the nature of the evidence, and still more from the rank of the person. I do think, that the Ministers who advise an impeachment as the means of ultimately screening the Duke from the consequences of his conduct, will more criminally betray the public interests to serve an individual, than by any other act of which, in the present days, a minister can be guilty.

⟨The course for the House of Commons seems to me to be clear; to address, in the mildest and most general terms, conveying their wish to the King, that he would remove the Commander-in-Chief. I should like best to have it done by an address of the Commons, because even the formality and record of such a victory increase its value, by attaching it to the merits of the constitutional assembly; but even this advantage I would consent to relinquish, provided the substantial triumph of public opinion is secured by the voluntary resignation of the Duke, so much do I dread the consequences of a struggle between the Crown and the people.

⟨. . .⟩

324. To J. A. Murray

BLPES iv. 38–40 ⟨Horner, i. 481–4⟩   Lincoln's Inn, 16 Feb. 1809

⟨I can see by the change of opinion which you underwent in the course of writing your last letter to me, that the evidence in the Duke of York's business has wrought upon you gradually in the same manner as upon all the impartial persons whom I have had an opportunity of seeing. His character is now completely fixed, and for all political effects or measures the evidence against him is full. What the result is to be, forms a *crisis* in our constitutional history: if one could be calm enough to look on as a mere spectator, it would even in that state of mind be most interesting to mark what turn circumstances will take, in a conjuncture which one way or other must show the true condition of our government.

⟨But one cannot so forget our own interest and share in that government, as to wait coolly for consequences that must prove so important. It will now very shortly be decided, by an experiment not to be mistaken, whether the influence of the Crown is so powerful, and parliament such an instrument in its hands, as to defeat public opinion in a contest in which every possible advantage is on the side of the latter. And I assure you I feel such an uncertainty respecting this event, and am so little provided with the means necessary for a reasonable anticipation, that it gives me the greatest anxiety and uneasiness.

⟨There is not evidence yet, upon which I would say guilty, giving my verdict as a judge in a process which was to end in punishment. Because I would always carry even to an excess of caution, the presumption in favour of innocence, where it is a question of legal punishment: at the same time, I must observe that criminals are convicted every day upon evidence not stronger than has been produced of the Duke's corrupt connivance.

⟨There is a strong, consistent set of circumstances; and there is, besides these, the direct evidence of a witness, whose evidence, though to be weighed most scrupulously, cannot be rejected altogether. But, when the proceeding is such only as is proper to the House of Commons, there appears to me to be a great deal more proof than enough: there would be enough to ground an impeachment upon, if that were an advisable proceeding, which it is not in the present instance; there is much more than enough to justify a resolution that he is unworthy of trust in office, or (which is the mildest and therefore most prudent measure) an address to the King praying His Majesty to remove him from his employments.

⟨But will the House of Commons vote such an address or what would amount to the same thing, will it be averted by resignation? This is the doubt which makes me uncomfortable. If the House of Commons does what is right, by the accession of the Saints and Addingtonians and those who have the fears of a popular election in prospect, to the small party of honest and virtuous members, and the still smaller set who are against the Duke from party views or republican prejudices; if the thing is done, the country will be satisfied and will feel a returning confidence in the representative body. But if the King and the Ministers should blindly determine to try their strength in the House of Commons, I dread to think what a probability there is of their being strong enough⟩ there ⟨to carry even an exculpatory resolution; for I should, after such a vote, consider the permanence of our Constitution as very precarious, and expect it to be broken down into ruins upon our heads by democratical violence. The House of Commons alone protects the throne from the multitude; but that only by compromising and adjusting the claims of both.

⟨I see no means myself, in the present state of the world, of preserving our liberty but by the act of settlement and the House of Brunswick; but we are dependent even for that upon the family itself. And it is in their power, no doubt, by outraging every sentiment of public opinion and every decorum of English manners, to render it impossible to maintain them. It is a most serious evil, with a view to the public interest, that the House of Commons should be called upon to degrade a person who stands so high upon the steps of the Throne: but the matter cannot now be evaded, and to avert greater evils, that house must do its duty. I fear it will not.

⟨The stories which are mentioned of the King's behaviour, under these distressing and embarrassing circumstances, are very natural and likely to be true. The Duke of York went to Windsor after Wardle's original motion, and stated his case to the King; that is, stated the same lies to him which he has been repeating to the very last to his defenders in the House. The King said, the charges might be untrue, but the slur cast upon him would never be removed, and it was a greater injury to the family than they had ever suffered since they came to the throne. The poor old man, who is too blind to read, makes the newspapers be read to him by three different persons, that nothing may be concealed from him. The Duke was in waiting yesterday to receive His Majesty, but he would not speak to him. Such are the stories.⟩

I am afraid there is too much ground for believing that one of the Duke's brothers has evinced, by facts and deeds, too strong a disposition to encourage his accusers.[1]

1. The Duke of Kent was accused by Mrs Clarke of fomenting agitation in order to remove his brother from a position that he himself coveted. (See Mary Anne Clarke, *The Rival Princes, or a Faithful Narration of Facts* (1810), pp. 25 and 44.)

There follows in *Horner*, i. 484, a further paragraph which is part, not of the manuscript letter dated 16 Feb., but of Horner's otherwise unpublished letter to Murray of 18 and 20 Feb. (Doc. 325).

325. To J.A. Murray

BLPES iv. 41–3 ⟨Horner, i. 484⟩   Monday [Lincoln's Inn Monday, 20 Feb. 1809]

. . .[1]

One part of the proceedings in the Duke of York's case has been generally misunderstood, because the newspapers did not state it fully. The note in the possession of Capt. Sanden was not made the ground of an accusation of suppressing evidence, either against Wardle or any other person; nor was this matter brought forward by Perceval, with the view of making a new point in favour of the Duke. Quite the contrary. Col. Hamilton's information, which he meant well to the Duke (no doubt) but which has turned out most fatal to him, brought the matter to Adam's knowledge and Perceval's; very perplexing to them as advocates of His Royal Highness, because their duty as Members of the House compelled them not to withhold it. They have behaved most correctly upon this point, though the reason does not appear why Perceval did not make the communication to the House sooner. The state of the fact was however made known at the time to Whitbread, Petty and Fitzpatrick on the one side, as well as to Canning and Castlereagh on the other.[2] He is the more desirous to do justice to strict and honourable conduct, on account of the baseness and meanness which run through the greater part of the business.

⟨With the exception of one night, Perceval appears, from all I have heard, to have conducted himself with great temper and propriety in the Committee; and as upon several other occasions, has honourably distinguished himself from some of his colleagues, by greater manliness. He is an intolerant, bigoted, narrowminded little fellow;⟩ and his proper vocation would have been a Canon of Christ Church: ⟨But he has the best private virtues in an eminent degree, and in his public behaviour shows a courage, and upon the whole an honesty, that are respectable. The defence of this wretched Prince is a very embarrassing task to be thrown upon any minister; for in spite of the true theory of representative government, I fancy that, to speak practically, the minister (whoever he might be) would have had to take up the defence of the King's son against such charges. Perceval has done it expressly and explicitly; though the legal critics say he has managed his case very unskilfully.⟩

. . . I have received the *Review*; and have cast my eye slightly through the articles. Burns is one of great excellence; Warburton seemed to me upon the whole a failure, and upon the subject of the infidels injudicious: however, I must read it again, before I fix my opinion.[3] It is but fair to tell you, that [Sydney] Smith thinks the article of Warburton very good, and envies the writer of it. This would only make me peruse it once more; for he likes to see a bishop under flagellation, and his envy means that he would like to be whisking the lash himself. Jeffrey, I see, has given up all thoughts of writing to me, except upon the eternal subject of the Review; which I almost begin to wish out of the way for depriving me of the advantage of hearing from him upon subjects in which he might instruct me and would always delight me.

1. Several earlier paragraphs are headed 'Saturday night', i.e. 18 Feb.
2. Capt. Huxley Sanden or Sandon of the Royal Waggon Train appeared in a number of Wardle's charges as introducing to Mrs Clarke various supplicants for the Duke's favour. During the course of his examination he was caught out over a note which was suspected of implicating the Duke directly in Mrs Clarke's doings. At first he claimed to have lost or destroyed it but during the course of the hearing William Adam was approached by Sandon's commanding officer Col. Digby Hamilton and told about the note. Adam in turn went with Hamilton to Perceval and the matter was reported by them both to the Duke and to the Commons. Since Hamilton did not report the existence of the note to Wardle but to Adam, who was a confidant of the Duke and had by his own account warned him about Mrs Clarke and arranged their separation in 1806, and since they all reported to the Commons only after they had been led to believe by Sandon that he had at length destroyed the note, the suspicion remained that they had delayed until they were sure the Duke was safe. General Richard Fitzpatrick, MP (1747–1813: *DNB*), one of Fox's oldest and dearest friends and a regular at Holland House, was a steadfast supporter of Grey and the interests of the Whig coalition in the Commons. Perceval and Adam also informed the Attorney and Solicitor General.
3. Jeffrey had reviewed both the *Reliques of Burns* and Bishop Warburton's *Letters* in ER xiii (no. xxvi, Jan. 1809), 249–76 and 343–66.

326. To J.A. Murray

BLPES iv. 44–5   [London], Saturday [5 Mar. 1809]

. . . We are still in complete suspense, with respect to the probable result of the vote of next Wednesday.[1] The men who know the House best, make various guesses, so that I cannot give you any conjecture, on which I place much reliance. The nature of the question itself, unconnected as it is with the common party divisions, and presenting so unusual and disagreeable an alternative as between the unanimous public voice and the personal wishes of the royal family; this would have rendered it, at any period, an occasion of much anxiety and uncertainty in the House of Commons. But they are increased prodigiously in the present instance, by the total want of a leader on either side of the House, and by the insubordination which is the consequence of there being no eminent members, who have any ascendancy either from experience or superior sense. Every man follows what seemeth good in his own eyes; and the terrors of public opinion and popular elections, as well as the hopes and fears of ministerial changes, have their full sway. The usual force of opposition will be tolerably well united against the Duke, as far as one can judge in a case where there is no concert: Some of the Saints still boil with indignation which may subside perhaps before Wednesday, though Wilberforce seems kept up to effervescence by letters from Yorkshire: One half of the Addingtons have committed themselves against the Duke, the rest maintaining a proper reserve to see what can be made of it. The call will force county Members and those for populous places to vote. So that, upon the whole, it will not surprise me, if the vote should be carried; but it would be so great a good to the country, and so signal a triumph to the constitution, that I will not believe such a thing can be till it is past. Wardle's motion, it is said, will be what it ought; simply, an address to remove. There is still a notion, countenanced very much by the Duke's improper letter to the House, that the Ministers will move an amendment for an impeachment.[2] I have no doubt that is their best policy, for the purpose of saving the Duke, but it will be most criminal and wicked so to surrender the constitution, and will probably lead to very unpleasant consequences.

1. On the Duke of York's case.
2. On 23 Feb., the day after the witnesses had finished giving evidence, the Speaker read to the Commons a letter he had just received from the Duke avowing his innocence (*AR* li (1809), 131).

327. To J.A. Murray

BLPES iv. 46–8 ⟨*Horner*, i. 484–6⟩   Lincoln's Inn, 25 Mar. 1809

⟨. . .

⟨I am not surprised at the desponding tone in which you express yourself respecting the conduct of the majority of the House of Commons in the Duke of York's question.[1] At the same time, I do not feel the same degree of despondency, because the conduct of the House in general has been much more patriotic, and the vote of the minority has been much more effective, than I expected at the outset of this important inquiry, that either would be found to be. The practical measure has been obtained; and it can neither be denied, nor fail to be attended with a beneficial impression among all intelligent men, that this practical result has been accomplished by the united force of public opinion and of the respectable minority in the House. Had that minority been less, the Duke would not have resigned. That there should have been such a majority upon such a question, and in such a state of the public mind, is a disgrace to the constitution; and strengthens all former conclusions for diminishing the influence of the Crown, as well as the arguments in favour of a place bill. But the successful issue of the contest is a satisfactory demonstration of the vigour and virtue that still remain in the constitution, infirm as it is.

⟨In the midst of the satisfaction, which I feel upon the whole result of this affair, as it affects the popular interests of the constitution, I cannot disguise from you that the part which the Opposition leaders have taken fills me with concern; because there are no longer any men, not a single man in the House of Commons, in whom as a leader of the popular party I can repose confidence.[2] But this is a larger subject than I have time to explain myself upon at present; I will take another opportunity. This is entirely confidential; for I would not by a premature declaration of my apprehensions, run the risk of hastening the event which I dread. I am giving the most mature consideration to the present state of parties, and to the probable course of party relations, in order to be prepared for every turn it may take, and to be sure that my conduct will be right. I am so much a spectator only in the business, that I am not likely to have much trouble in attaining a correct view of what that conduct ought to be.⟩

1. Wardle had duly moved the removal of the Duke on 8 March, but Perceval proposed instead an affirmation of his innocence and a virtual vote of thanks for his services to the army! Before the debate was concluded the Duke resigned his command on 18 Mar. and the House voted by 235 to 112 on 20 Mar. to proceed no further. But the case unleashed the fury of economical and parliamentary reformers and forged Whitbread's 'Mountain' in the Commons.

2. The failure of the Whig leadership to take any 'distinct or manly tone whatever' during the parliamentary inquiry into the Duke of York's case was admitted even by Lord Holland. (*Holland's Further Memoirs*, p. 29; for further comment see Roberts, pp. 198–9.)

328. To J .A. Murray

BLPES iv. 48–9   Carnatic Office, 28 Apr. 1809

. . .

. . . there is nowhere that I can discover talent enough united with the necessary character of temperate and disinterested firmness, to lead us in the views we entertain, and, for the attainment of them, to gain an ascendancy over the rash and giddy enthusiasts of popularity on the one side, and the temporizing candidates for Ministerial place on the other.[1] A great deal of good, probably, will be accomplished in the end, though the immediate struggle is full of alarming and disgusting circumstances to spectators of our cast; what Englishmen are very fond of calling the good sense of England, will seem to prevail at last; that is, the reforming spirit of the commonality and the attachment of the professional orders as well as large proprietors to the ancient institutions, will be adjusted by mutual concessions. You will perhaps consider me as falling into my usual error of being too sanguine about the future, in expecting so happy a consummation.

. . .

1. Horner writes in the midst of the attack on corruption and sinecure places which followed the inquiry into the Duke of York's affairs and resulted in strong campaigns for economical and parliamentary reform both in and out of Parliament during the remainder of the year.

329. To Thomas Poole[1]

BLPES iv. 52 (copy)   Lincoln's Inn, 29 Apr. 1809

. . . I should find very little, upon which I could differ from your opinions, unless perhaps with respect to the extent in which, from the late disclosures, you suppose that corrupt practices have prevailed among the men who have held the offices of state during the last few years.[2] I am persuaded that if a rigid scrutiny could be made for the last twenty years, and for any other period of twenty years since the Revolution, the result would be greatly in favour of the former period; not from any other change, than the greater vigilance which has been exercised, both by the public, and by the House of Commons, with regard to the expenditure of public money, ever since the close of the American war. It is very natural, under a much greater pressure of taxation, that the same or even a less amount of peculation should be more resented; and after so long an interval, during which the mind and spirits of the people have been almost torpid, it is most fortunate that they should at length be roused, by so legitimate a subject of interest, to their ancient feelings for liberty and popular administration. The delusion, that any economical reforms can much reduce the national expenditure and the burthens of the people, does not, I should hope, prevail very widely, except among the uninformed multitude; and a conviction of their real utility and necessity, if well understood by the intelligent and disinterested classes of the community, cannot fail of being ultimately successful in establishing those constitutional amendments which will make our ancient laws and government more stable.

. . .

1. Thomas Poole of Nether Stowey (1765–1837: *DNB*), the friend of Coleridge.
2. In addition to the Melville and Duke of York affairs, attention had been drawn during the latter investigation to an avowed traffic in East India Company appointments and a select committee was appointed to inquire into that as well. The report of that committee in March had in turn drawn attention to a transaction of Castlereagh's regarding a parliamentary seat which as President of the Board of Control he had attempted to obtain for a friend in return for a writership. This last was brought to the attention of the House on 25 Apr. by Lord Archibald Hamilton, but in view of Castlereagh's frank behaviour not proceeded with by 216 to 167.

330. To J.A. Murray

BLPES iv. 55–6 ⟨*Horner*, i. 490–91⟩   Lincoln's Inn, 9 May 1809

⟨I gave notice in the House last night of a resolution which I mean to propose, in the committee of the whole House upon the third Report of the Finance Committee, for the purpose of grounding upon that resolution, if acceded to, a bill to render illegal the sale of all judicial offices by persons having the power of appointing to them.

⟨The grounds upon which I proceed, as far as England is concerned, are to be found stated and sanctioned by the greatest authorities, both in the state and the law, from Sir Matthew Hale downwards. You will find his opinion, in his tract upon the amendment of the laws. And the same sentiments are expressed in one of the Reports made by the Royal Commissioners, and presented to both Houses of Parliament in 1740. They are cited, with full concurrence, by the Finance Committee of 1797, in their 27th Report. I am desirous, of course, to make this a general law, equally applied to the three kingdoms. With regard to Scotland, it will be necessary for me to be put in possession of more detailed information than I can obtain here, or without your assistance, as to the number and description of offices of a judicial nature, which are in fact disposed of by the patrons, and as to the view in which such sales are regarded by the law of Scotland.⟩[1] . . .

1. Although Horner had spoken briefly on the subject on several former occasions, his motion to proscribe the sale of judicial offices constituted his first (albeit abortive: see Doc. 331) attempt to sponsor major legislation. Lord Holland's absence in Spain had relegated him to obscurity on the Opposition bench, and he almost certainly acted now without co-ordinating his measure with the leaders of the Whig coalition, though he evidently proceeded with the concurrence of Romilly and Bentham. For the motion was framed in the midst of Romilly's first systematic exertion for jurisprudential reform and at a time when Horner was communicating with Bentham about it and sending him pertinent parliamentary papers (Horner to Bentham, 2 and 31 May, *Bentham*, viii. 27 and 31-2), and in a letter of 2 June (BLPES iv. 67) he told Murray that the principle of 'utility to mankind' was 'the sole foundation of moral reasoning'. Furthermore, while the motion was well researched and moderate in nature, he hardly acted in a political vacuum. He gave notice of his motion on the heels of the unsuccessful one made on 17 Apr. by William Pleydell-Bouverie, Viscount Folkestone and afterwards 3rd Earl of Radnor (1779-1869: *DNB*), for a committee to inquire into the corrupt disposal of public offices (*Hansard*, xiv. 48ff.), thereby identifying himself with the political mavericks who at the time were carrying on a systematic assault on alleged corrupt practices in government, and perhaps nothing but the pervasive nature of that assault spared him the odium of a damning political label. On 11 May, two days after he had given notice of his motion, the radical MP William Alexander Madocks (1773-1828: *DNB*) moved for inquiry into the conduct of Perceval and Castlereagh in having bought a seat in Parliament for Quintin Dick (1777-1858) and then, as he wrongly alleged, forced him out of it. (*Hansard*, xiv. 493ff., and *PH* iii. 594.) Horner and Romilly voted with the minority in opposition to the wishes of the Whig hierarchy on that occasion, and Romilly felt that the division, 'coupled with some which have lately taken place, will do more towards disposing the nation in favour of a parliamentary reform than all the speeches that have been or will be made in any popular assemblies'. (*Romilly*, ii. 287.) Roberts, p. 235, lists Horner among twenty-seven Whigs who followed Whitbread's lead and voted for three or more motions for economical reform in opposition to the wishes of Grey and Grenville. See also *ibid.*, p. 316, for an analysis of Whig opinion on Madocks's motion of 11 May.

331. To J.A. Murray

BLPES iv. 61-2   Hampstead, 21 May 1809

. . . Perceval, I find, means to take the subject out of my hands, for among the Resolutions, which he is to propose in the Committee, as a substitute for Henry Martin's, there is one against the sale of appointments in Courts of Justice: I shall try to amend the terms of his resolution, so that it may more fully express the principle, and then I shall not dispute with him in whose name it shall go. I am satisfied, we should not have heard of it, if it had not been pressed upon him.

Those bargains, which you speak of, as made by resigning judges with their successors, form a separate subject, distinct from the sale of judicial offices. The former will fall under the operation of Perceval's Bill against the sale and Brokerage of offices, which makes punishable, by fine and imprisonment in Scotland, every person who shall agree to receive, or shall agree to pay, money, etc., directly or indirectly for the resignation of any office within the act. This, you observe, provides a punishment for the transaction; whether it was already an illegal one in Scotland, and whether the bargains formerly made can go on without subjecting the parties to this punishment, are questions which it may be very proper to consider.[1]

. . .

1. Henry Martin (1763–1839), a Grenvillite MP, had proposed such mild resolutions of reform regarding pensions and sinecures on 8 May as to have them readily accepted by Perceval; subsequently on 8 June he allowed Perceval to substitute the Government's own resolution on the abolition of law court sinecures. (Gray, *Perceval*, p. 150, and *PH* iv. 557.) The Sale of Offices Prevention Bill was a limited reform undertaken by Perceval in consequence of abuses recently brought to light by the inquiry into the affairs of the East India Company: it sought to make it a penal offence to solicit money for procuring offices, or to circulate any advertisement with that view. On 27 Apr., while saying he would not oppose that bill, Horner had made his point about the sale of court offices and Perceval had appeared to agree with him (*Hansard*, xiv. 268–70). But Perceval seems to have decided it was too difficult to extend the scope of the present bill and so over the protests of Horner and Folkestone it passed into law (49 Geo. III, c. 126) without any reference to the judiciary (Roberts, pp. 202–203). Afterwards Horner evidently considered an independent bill proscribing the sale of judicial offices but decided to desist after reading a letter from Grenville to Rosslyn expressing disapproval (undated but enclosed in Grenville to Horner, 10 June, BLPES iv. 77–80).

332. To J.W. Ward

BLPES iv. 54 (copy of extract) ⟨*Horner*, i. 492–3⟩   24 May 1809

⟨I am out of patience with the patriots, as they call themselves, and with the Opposition too; some reforms are become absolutely necessary, both with regard to expenditure, and in the representation of the Commons: but the patriots delude the people about the extent and nature of the evil that calls for remedy, and likewise as to the efficacy of the remedies which they propose; and the Opposition, by a timid, wavering, and ambiguous line of conduct, are losing all command of the popular party, both in the House of Commons and in the country. This has been a new sort of session in the House of Commons; the next, it is probable, will be still more remarkable, particularly if the Opposition leaders come to it, as they probably will, with the same want of explicit and determined opinions under which they labour at present. There is no evading any longer those discussions about sinecure places and the reform of Parliament; the questions must be met directly, and some considerable concessions must be made to the popular sentiments.[1]

⟨Windham is the only man who speaks out; with that contempt of popularity, of which the courage is quite admirable; but with that systematic repugnance to every proposition that savours of reformation, which turns all his wisdom into foolishness; and if it should guide the councils of Government, will speedily deprive us of the constitution, the living principle of which has always consisted in prudent and timely reforms. It is very irksome to me to have a middle sort of course to steer for myself; it feels so like trimming; and it is so completely ineffectual: but what else can I do, when I cannot find men and measures together? I like most of the parliamentary measures of the patriots, for I would make some exceptions; but the men I never can have any reliance upon; not so much that I suspect any of them, or rather I should say many of them, to entertain unconstitutional designs, but because they seem to me, one and all, wholly devoid of political ability. I like the men of the late Cabinet and old Opposition, but their proceedings in this session, their backwardness upon some questions, and their indistinctness about certain subjects that are fundamental and (what is more) will press upon every public man immediately for a declared opinion or conduct, have shaken my confidence, not in their views and intentions, but in their judgement and firmness. . . .⟩²

1. The Commons' virtual acquittal of the Duke of York had resurrected the cry for parliamentary reform among Cobbett and the old reformers of Westminster. In March 1809, at a meeting in Westminster held to vote thanks to those who had assisted Wardle, Whitbread spoke publicly, if vaguely, in support of a moderate reform of parliamentary representation. Afterwards Bentham, with whom Horner had by now become quite familiar, advocated radical reform in two pamphlets, *Elements of Packing* and *Parliamentary Reform Catechism*, both published in 1809, and a considerable movement for a substantial and immediate revision of representation, linked inseparably with the cry for economical reform, took hold in the City and gained a degree of popularity in the Commons, producing two unsuccessful motions late in the session. Windham and the Grenvilles were no less hostile to parliamentary reform than to economical reform, and the leaders of the Foxite wing of the Whig coalition opposed both economical and parliamentary reform in their private correspondence while voicing temporizing views in public. (See Roberts, pp. 235–65, for an excellent assessment of the issue of parliamentary reform within the divided Whig party during 1809.)

2. The following week Horner wrote to Grey seeking his support for a modest reform of the Northern Circuit, and received an encouraging response that ended by inviting him to visit Howick in the summer (Horner to Grey, 5 June, and Grey to Horner, 8 June, Grey MSS, Durham University).

333. To J.A. Murray

BLPES iv. 65–6   Thursday [1 June 1809]

. . .

The review of Sydney Smith's sermons in the 2nd Number of the *Quarterly* has given me much pain, and seems to me quite unjustifiable; no severity against his book could with reason have been complained of, for that might be a very warrantable retaliation, but this libel upon his professional character had no provocation. The article is surmised to be Gifford's . . . who is quite capable of malignant calumny, when he thinks it will serve the purpose of the party whose hireling he is; and the appeal to 'Philip of Foston' is in his manner.¹ Were I left however to my own conjecture, I should say, that nothing but theological rancour could engender so base a production. Will Walter Scott clear himself from all previous knowledge of the contents and temper of the article, or will he avow his responsibility for such flagitious calumnies upon Smith?

It was some compensation to find in this *Quarterly* so favourable a criticism of Campbell's poem. When two such rival oracles pronounce alike, they must be in the right.[2]

1. William Gifford, the editor, was joint author of the review of Sydney Smith's sermons in *QR* i (no. ii, May 1809), 387–98 (Shine).
2. The reviews of Campbell's *Gertrude of Wyoming* were by Jeffrey in *ER* (see Doc. 286 n. 5) and by Walter Scott in *QR* i (no. ii, May 1809), 241–58 (Shine).

334. To Francis Jeffrey

BLPES iv. 81–2 〈Horner, i. 493–6〉   London, 12 June 1809

. . .

〈Lord Webb and I have been down for two days at Hertford, and passed them very agreeably with the Pundit [Alexander Hamilton] and Malthus. . . .

〈I hope you will not commit yourself upon the subject of Parliamentary Reform, before you have fully made up your mind, after a careful view of the question. It is very fit that you should give your opinion upon it at large, before the next meeting of Parliament, but I should grieve very much if you were to take up in sport any side of the debate that first strikes you. I am a good deal of a reformer, and am prepared to go a considerable length; the question as to Scotland admits of no hesitation, and in England I would give Members to some important classes of the population who can scarcely be said to be represented. It is at the same time a perilous thing, either to change the qualification, or to take away franchises, or by compensation to recognize such a principle as the acquisition of that kind of property. I see a great deal of practical benefit result, even to the interests of liberty and popular rights, from the most rotten parts of the constituent body; and while I am satisfied that we should upon the whole be a more virtuous and patriotic House of Commons, if the deputies were more dependent upon the people, there are many occasions on which the clamorous and inconstant voice of the people would dictate a wrong course of conduct, and I cannot say upon a retrospect of parliamentary history even in the worst periods that the House of Commons has ever for a great length of time, or upon a system of measures, been at variance with the sentiments of the people. The close of the American war is the strongest case of that nature; and it was then accordingly that the remedy of a reform in the representation was most thought of. It is very fit to be considered also whether at any former period of our history, the formation of the House approached nearer than it does at present to the theory of our constitution, as drawn by general writers. With all this, I have a strong bias in favour of the proposition for rendering the representation more adequate and agreeable to that theory; and I only throw out these topics of doubt, that I may have the benefit of your mature consideration of them. It is a momentous question in its consequences, as likely to affect the permanent vigour of the constitution. It is no less so, on account of the circumstances of the time in which we may be forced to discuss it; not the most favourable certainly, for any measure of internal change. And I cannot therefore express to you how anxious I am, that you should take the utmost pains with the article you mean to write upon it; you ought to consider what it is, to send out eleven thousand prints of your doctrine on that subject, whatever that doctrine may be, with all the weight of your authority, and in the midst of such an agitation of the popular mind; and indeed the question has been recently connected so much with the irritating topics of the day, that you should not appear to enter into it, but with more remote views, and upon the largest contemplation of all parts of the discussion and of all the effects of the proposed measure.[1]

⟨Miss Edgeworth's *Tales of Fashionable Life*, *Alphonse* by Mad. Genlis, and Wordsworth's pamphlet on Spanish affairs, are the last new books I have heard of.[2]

⟨PS I hope no notice of the *Quarterly* will ever be suffered to appear in the *Edinburgh*. You must be above controversy, however provoked. You must be delighted with the accounts which have appeared lately in the newspapers relating to the state of opinions in Germany; they are quite your politics and mine; and they will ultimately restore the civilization and independence of Europe.⟩[3]

1. Horner presumably refers to Burdett's plan of parliamentary reform, which he produced in the Commons on 15 June. It advocated that those subject to direct taxation be required to elect MPs; that each county be subdivided according to its taxed male population and each subdivision required to elect one representative; that all votes be taken in each parish by the parish officers and reported to the Sheriff's Court; that all elections be conducted in one and the same day; and that Parliaments be brought back to a constitutional duration. Burdett's motion was beaten 74 votes to 15 in a thin House with Horner not voting. (*Hansard*, xiv. 1053ff.; see also Roberts, pp. 252–6.)
2. Jeffrey's review of Miss Edgeworth's *Tales* appeared in *ER* xiv (no. xxviii, July 1809), 375–88. But neither Mme Genlis's *Alphonse* nor William Wordsworth's *Concerning the Relations of Great Britain, Spain, and Portugal to each other, and to the Common Enemy* was noticed.
3. Reports of political dissatisfaction, patriotic fervour, and civil disobedience had emanated from the north of Germany for several weeks and were the entering wedge for the unsuccessful Austrian campaign against France during the summer of 1809.

335. To J.A. Murray

BLPES iv. 83–4   [London], 16 June 1809

. . .

After Curwen's Bill was so altered by Perceval, and evidently became an object which the Treasury pursued as something to be gained, I took a decided opinion against it, and voted accordingly.[1] In its present form, it will certainly do harm; and not a month of the next session should be lost, before an amending and extending Bill is proposed.

I should like to have your sentiments upon Lord Erskine's bill,[2] about which I wrote a hurried note to you . . . while I was still in doubt upon the question.³ I voted for throwing it out last night; and though the Bill, as amended by the Lords, was too unskilfully drawn in all its parts to be thrown into a proper form in the short period that remains of the session, which would have been a sufficient reason for not proceeding farther in it [at] present, I even went farther and voted against it upon the principle. I cannot see that this is a subject, on which laws can be made, with good effect.⁴

1. On 4 May John Christian Curwen (1756–1828), formerly a close friend of Burke and now the Whig Member for Carlisle, had introduced a bill which called for an oath against bribery and corruption by all elected persons, for the proscription of the sale of parliamentary seats and of the receipt by electors of any consideration for their votes at any time, and for the extension of the bribery laws to agents and others seeking to corrupt electors during elections. In introducing his bill, Curwen stressed the faltering confidence of the people in the House of Commons, the overgrown power of the House of Lords that had resulted from Pitt's large additions to the peerage, and the growth of the influence of the Crown, and remarked frankly that a general reform of parliamentary representation should precede the enactment of his bill (Hansard, xiv. 357–64). Only Windham opposed the bill on its first reading, but Perceval expressed dissatisfaction with several points on the second reading and in committee virtually every clause that promised to make the measure effectual, including the requirement of an oath by Members and the annexation of the penalties of perjury to the taking of such an oath falsely, were struck. On 12 June, when the amended bill was read a third time, the Government supported it, and though the Whigs opposed it to a man, it was carried by 98 to 83. Afterwards Folkestone introduced a motion for the substitution of the preamble, 'A Bill for the more effectually preventing the sale of seats in Parliament for money; and for promoting a monopoly thereof to the Treasury, by means of Patronage', and secured twenty-eight votes. Curwen's amended bill passed the Lords on 15 June by a vote of 32 to 9, the minority entering a formal protest (ibid., xiv. 1004ff.). (See Roberts, pp. 209–216, for a very thorough account of the progress of Curwen's bill and of Whig opinion. See also Romilly, ii. 292–3.)
2. The bill brought by Erskine into the House of Lords for preventing malicious and wanton cruelty to animals was introduced in the Commons on 13 June and defeated by a majority of ten on 15 June. (See Romilly, ii. 293–6, for a summary of the debate and an explanation of his reasons for supporting the measure. See Speeches in Parliament of the Right Honourable William Windham (3 vols, 1812), iii. 303–328, for the speech around which the opponents of the bill rallied.)
3. The note has not been found.
4. The letter ends abruptly here and is unsigned.

336. To Francis Jeffrey

BLPES iii. 311–12   Lincoln's Inn, Saturday [8 July 1809]¹

. . .

Parliamentary Reform is too big a subject for this occasion; I have very great anxiety to see what you will make of it, and indeed to know which side of the question you mean to espouse. But I have still a greater desire, that you would put into the form of a full exposition those opinions of yours with respect to the present state of the relations of people and aristocracy, upon which you gave me some of your views when we passed a morning together upon the road to Sydenham. There have been some accounts lately from the north of Germany, which would warrant you in extending your description beyond the limits of this country; and if it be destined that the French should at length be stopped in their career of conquest, perhaps the moment is at hand when those sentiments, of the existence of which in great force you seemed to have persuaded yourself, ought to show themselves in action and upon the continent infuse more of a popular composition into the new governments than was in any of the old.

. . .

1. This undated letter and the following one (Doc. 337) are misfiled with supposed dates of October 1808 in the BLPES. But 337 clearly refers to the Walcheren expedition of 1809, and seems almost as clearly to refer back to 336 as being written the previous day. An opening paragraph not printed in Doc. 337 and another letter to Murray of 7 July, moreover, show Horner to have been making a short trip to the sessions at Glastonbury on these dates. He then returned to London before going on the more extended Western Circuit in the middle of July.

337. To Francis Jeffrey

BLPES iii. 313–14 ⟨Horner, i. 459–60⟩[1]   Glastonbury, Sunday night [9 July 1809]

. . .

⟨I came here in the mail from London, before dinner; and have been enjoying a quiet evening in a scene perfectly rural, and equally singular and beautiful. . . .⟩

⟨Will you adopt the suggestion I made yesterday, of an article in some early number of the *Review*, upon the probable fate of the principles of liberty and good government upon the Continent? In our remoter views of the future, I fancy you and I come nearer to a coincidence than the terms in which we might compare our opinions would seem to show; while you, with a just caution and some mixture of despondency, suggest ultimate objects as what ought to be aimed at; and I, with more of sanguine credulity, and more too of indolence, would describe them as events which are steadily accomplishing themselves, and which will be realized as the result of a course which has never been suspended, but of which it is in truth the acceleration that has occasioned all this alarming violence.

'Kind nature the embryo blossoms will save.'

⟨All this, in my romancing, is equally probable, at a greater or less distance of time, whatever the immediate posture of affairs upon the Continent may assume. I do not allow myself to be very sanguine about that, for I find the best judges of such matters do not hope. Every thing, it is now manifest, depends upon the great operation upon the Danube; and the issue of that will either spread one conflagration over Europe, or plunge it once more, and until another crisis of similar uncertainty, in sullen submission.⟩

It is said that *our* expedition is to have purely a *British* object; the destruction of the ships and arsenal at Antwerp: an advantageous exploit at any time, except when there are French to be driven from Spain, or important discontents to encourage in the north of Germany. Sir Home Popham and Johnston the famous smuggler are both employed.[2]

. . .

1. Incorrectly dated October 1808 in *Horner*.
2. Horner evidently refers to Andrew James Cochrane Johnstone (1767–18??: *DNB*), the youngest son of the 8th Earl of Dundonald; but since he is not known to have served in the Walcheren expedition, he may be confusing him with Col. William Johnston (1773–1844: *DNB*), who commanded a regiment at the siege of Flushing.

338. To J.A. Murray

BLPES iv. 94–5   Lincoln's Inn, 15 July 1809

. . .

. . . The occupation of Cuxhaven seems to point out the object of the expedition, of which it is still said that the Duke of York is ultimately to have the command.[1] His victor, Mr Wardle, is to indict Mrs Clarke for perjury, which will probably be attended with as much success as any expedition under his Royal Highness. I believe the woman in this story, as I did in the former; not because she is worthy of credit, but because a very circumstantial detail has received direct confirmation.[2] The poor wretch is already hurled from his high estate, by the giddy unfeeling multitude, who never seem to have more exquisite enjoyment, even in their favourite pleasure of triumphing over ruined reputation, than when the victim is one of their own rearing. I cannot feel any regret that a popularity, so disproportioned to the real merit of the individual, founded originally on the very doubtful ground of activity in a criminating proceeding, and bolstered up by very unwarrantable practices upon the poor deluded public, should have undergone so speedy a dissolution; or that the party of reformers, as they would call themselves by distinction, should have received this check, for I never observed any set of men possessing more limited views or more ungenerous maxims of political conduct, at the same time that the extravagant purity which some of them would promise the public from certain measures, and the real usefulness of their vigilant inquisition against peculators, were conducive to give them a great ascendancy, and a power which they had not capacity to employ to any good purpose.[3]

. . .

1. Upon the outbreak of war between Austria and France in the early summer of 1809, the British Government resolved to assist Austria and to exploit long-rumoured reports of political dissatisfaction in the North of Germany by sending an expedition to the Scheldt to capture the island of Walcheren, the town of Flushing, and the fleet of Admiral

Missiessy, which was at the time lying shut up in the river. The large British expedition, which was destined to fail utterly, proceeded under the joint command of the Earl of Chatham and Rear Adm. Sir Richard Strachan (1760–1828: *DNB*). (See Roberts, pp. 132–3.)

2. Following his successful exposure of the Duke of York in January, Wardle had himself been the subject of action for debt in respect of furnishing Mrs Clarke's house. During the course of the case, which he lost, he was exposed as having offered the furniture as a reward for her testimony against the Duke. He subsequently prosecuted Mrs Clarke and two tradesmen of the name of Wright for a conspiracy to defraud him, but this trial, which was held in Westminster Hall before Lord Ellenborough and a special jury on 11 Dec. 1809, also resulted in a verdict of not guilty. For Horner's assessment of the results see Horner to Murray, 15 Dec. 1809, *Horner*, i. 508.

3. Horner's considerable shift of opinion on those who had carried the assault on the Duke of York and on the reformers who had exploited the Duke's acquittal by the House of Commons was generally consistent with a view of affairs that evolved among most Whigs after the prorogation of Parliament on 21 June 1809 (Roberts, p. 199). It would seem that the excesses and the failures of the 'popular party' during the 1809 session and the questionable characters of those who composed that party combined to recall him to a more conservative point of view.

339. To Lord Holland

BLPES iv. 96–7   Lincoln's Inn, 16 July 1809

I have received both your papers, the second two days ago. The first I printed verbatim as a little pamphlet, and sent copies of it to all the persons in the South of Spain whom you mentioned to me;[1] these I gave to Mr Gordon, a Spanish Merchant in the H. of C., who undertook to forward the several packets.[2] I am afraid they were to go by the *Donegal*, which was then expected to sail next day; but still waits for Lord Wellesley. I sent a little paragraph to the *Morning Chronicle* abusing Riquelme whom I take to be the very Plumer of the Junta, as I am inclined to make Jovellanos a Dugald Stewart of Spain.[3] It is very mortifying to find the lawyers so bad politicians in all countries. Your second paper I mean to cut into several paragraphs for the *Chronicle*.[4] Your account of the interior proceedings of the Junta is very interesting; though I have been much shaken in my confidence about Spain by their long uniform inactivity, I am still nearer to your hopes upon the subject than I can find any body else here to be. By this time, if you are still in Spain, you will have received the intelligence from the Danube of events, which may perhaps affect the deliverance of Spain even without any farther exertions of the Spaniards. If the country should once be freed from French troops, I see little reason from what has yet been done to infer that the enlightened patriots will be able to succeed in realizing their designs of a free constitution: But the violence of France has done, what the Revolution has accomplished for almost the rest of the continent; it has removed those institutions which excluded the people from all chance of ever influencing the measures of government; and though public opinion cannot be enlightened nor have its full operation without a free press, the great point is gained if it is once let in to act. The rest must follow, in time.

We have had strange doings at home, since you left us; not a little uncomfortable to a good Whig, on various accounts, but upon the whole satisfactory, because the effect has been not only to excite more of the popular interest in public affairs than had been since Mr Fox's death, but to abate very considerably that love of mere royalty which for some years past has been so disgusting as well as pernicious. The matter is not over yet, I am afraid, for all that is to follow can be but hurtful; Wardle, after being for a few weeks the god of the people, has been whirled from high, by the same Mrs Clarke too: he indicts her however for perjury, and the investigation, which that trial will render necessary, cannot fail to bring out more than has even yet appeared of the share which the Duke of Kent seems to have had in preparing and instigating the parliamentary attack upon his brother. We want you very much at home to do us good and keep us well together, and, what I must add, to keep some of the old Opposition more stoutly and consistently to popular courses. There is much to be considered and well settled, before the Opposition begins another session in the House of Commons.

. . .

1. There is in BLPES (iv. 85–91) a sequence of three letters Holland wrote to Horner in June and July; but they do not include the first mentioned here, which must have been written in May or earlier. That letter evidently enclosed the draft of a pamphlet Horner copied and prepared for the press, which he dated 'May 1809' and entitled *An Account of The Central or Supreme Junta of Spain, Its Chief Members, and Most Important Proceedings*. There is a complete draft in Horner's hand in the Kinnordy MSS and he may well have edited and even expanded what Holland had sent. But that it was essentially Holland's is borne out by the corrections and the anxiety he expresses in his surviving subsequent letters for his attack on Riquelme to be published anonymously, though he will send no more 'dissertations'. Although it was announced in the July 1809 number of the *ER*, no copy of the published version has been traced in the United Kingdom; but there is a copy in the University of Minnesota Library at Minneapolis.
2. The 'Spanish Merchant' was probably William Gordon, afterwards Duff-Gordon, 2nd Bart (1772–1823), who was a partner in his uncle's counting-house and handled its correspondence with Cadiz; he was also MP for Worcester (*PH* iv. 39–40).
3. Rodrigo Riquelme, a conservative member of the Central Junta from Aragon and a political adversary of Jovellanos who had been described to Holland as a lawyer with a 'bad heart and suspected of dishonest intentions', had been appointed one of five commissioners for the Cortes in May 1809. On 8 July the *MC* had printed a letter dated Seville, 3 June, and purporting to come from 'a native Spaniard'. After talking enthusiastically about military success and the convening of a general Cortes, it continued:
   > it would perhaps be ungrateful . . . to mix any doubts or suspicions with the sentiments of hope, gratitude and delight which the prospect of a free Government in this favoured country is calculated to inspire. But we understand here, that among the five persons named . . . to examine and prepare the plans for holding the Cortes, there is, indeed, one whom the public voice would designate for such an office, but that the wisdom of that choice, is counterbalanced (I trust it may not be counteracted and thwarted altogether) by the introduction into the same Commission of the man most notorious in the Junta for his opposition to every liberal measure, and to the Cortes in particular. You will easily suspect that the Member whom the Junta approve of is . . . Jovellanos . . . but I doubt whether the people of England have ever heard of one Riquelme . . . It is a fearful omen of the intentions or of the discernment of the Junta to have nominated such a man to prepare a system of liberty for the country, and though the friends of freedom in Spain are sensible of the disinterested spirit which has led to the adoption of the Decree of 25th of May, they cannot divest themselves of all uneasiness and distrust while

Riquelme is entrusted with such a commission, and while the laws against the liberty of the press, though not strictly enforced, remain unrepealed, to the terror of honest men, and the disgrace of a government which professes to be popular.
Whether or not their source was Holland via Horner, who was, presumably, comparing Riquelme to Sir Thomas Plumer (1753–1824: *DNB*), the Solicitor-General, similar letters from Spain continued to appear in the columns of the MC until about the time the Hollands left for home. (See *Lady Holland's Spanish Journal*, pp. 301, 322, 345, 347, and 408, and the MC, especially 8, 12, 19, 20, 25, and 31 July.)

4. Holland's second letter apparently enclosed printed papers that were presumably of Spanish origin and not of his own composition.

340. To Mrs Dugald Stewart

BLPES iv. 100–101   Wardour,[1] 25 July 1809

. . .

You will not expect news from me at this distance from town; the circuit produces nothing of that sort: though indeed the trial of Cobbett, which we had at Winchester, seems to make stir enough in London, to judge by the newspapers. Nothing could better manifest the importance which this man has earned in the estimation of the public; for in itself the case was any thing but important in any point of view. The charge was a very trivial one, though the circumstances proved him to be very harsh and tyrannical in his treatment of people under his power. The Attorney General has resolved, I hear, to file a criminal information against Cobbett for one of his late numbers, in which he commented upon the meeting of the Local Militia which was quelled by calling in the German Legion: the language of that paper was unguarded in the extreme, and spoke a very mischievous spirit, yet I question if such a prosecution can be regarded either as a discreet step or a necessary one.[2]

I understand that Lord Wellesley has at last left London, in proper person, and that he sets out in ill humour with his masters, in whose hands (he says) no cause can prosper. He is supposed to be tired in earnest of some of them, and of his own prolonged exclusion from power; indeed, the only credible solution that was given of his strange delay in going to Spain, was that he hovered over the Duke of Portland's sick-bed, who cannot live much longer. I shall be surprised, in that event, if any but Perceval succeeds to the helm; the reign of the Saints never was so near.

Have you seen James Moore's publication upon the subject of his brother's campaign?[3] All the documents are interesting, and so are some of the details which are given without that formal authenticity. It is a pity, that the style and temper of the connecting narrative is not equally worthy of Sir John Moore. . . .

1. Wardour Castle was the seat in Wiltshire of James Everard, 9th Baron Arundell (1763–1817).
2. The 'trivial charge' heard at Winchester Assizes on 20 July was one of assault and false imprisonment brought by relatives of one of Cobbett's employees who had run off. Dam-

ages of £10 were awarded against Cobbett and his co-defendants and Ministerial supporters naturally exploited the occasion, if indeed they had not actually contrived it, with pamphlets, newspaper articles, and posters about the 'Oppressions of Cobbett'. (George Spater, *William Cobbett: The Poor Man's Friend* (2 vols, Cambridge, 1982), i. 231–3.) But on 1 July Cobbett had provoked a much more serious attack by roundly denouncing in his *PR* the use of a guard of Hessian mercenaries during the flogging of an English soldier. Considering Cobbett's attacks on the Duke of York earlier in the year, his outrage at the Duke's acquittal, and the radical cast of his more recent editorials in favour of economical and parliamentary reform, a criminal proceeding based on an arguably patriotic editorial appeared shaky indeed and produced widespread charges that the Government sought really to silence a powerful critic. But the following year Cobbett was tried, convicted, and sentenced to both a heavy fine and two years' imprisonment for his allegedly libellous editorial.

3. *A Narrative of the Campaign of the British Army in Spain* (1809).

341. To James Loch

BLPES iv. 102–103[1]   Chudleigh, 5 Aug. 1809

. . .

. . . Nothing . . . can be more weak, or more blind to the demonstrations of uniform experience, than to expect any success against the consolidated power of France from any of the degenerate governments of the continent.[2]

There is a very striking article from Rome in the paper today, mentioning, from the *Journal of the Capitol*, decrees of the new Government abolishing not only the inquisition, but all the jurisdictions and temporal privileges of the clergy.[3] When one considers the French conquest in the light of such consequences, it is impossible to deny that the civilized world is reaping immense benefits from it; and that while its own mischiefs and miseries are probably of short duration and may pass quickly off, it has swept away, and perhaps was alone of force enough to sweep away, evils of inveterate obstinacy, which depressed and degraded mankind, and by the extinction of all free spirit left the nations an easy prey to this freebooter, who deserves however to be classed with those heroes of mythology who run over the face of the earth to rid it of monsters. In exchange for the complex tyranny of feudalities and the Church, the continent has for the present received the new grievances of universal monarchy and military law; but I persuade myself, that in their own nature these are but temporary, that the dissensions of the chiefs aided by the national antipathies will again break the empire into its former pieces, and that the several states under renewed dynasties will be wearied into an adjustment of distinct territories. In such a state of things, as we know from past history, the devastation of war will soon be repaired, and it may be felt, in the vigour with which mankind will resume their career of arts and liberty, that the violence, which shook the world for a while, cleared away many obstacles to improvement. The worst part of the prospect is that this happy termination is seen only through a long vista of desolating wars; and it is tolerably sad for ourselves to believe, that upon the most flattering prophecy that can be ventured, there is nothing to be known in our time but the extremes of violence and progressive degeneracy. I cannot say that these are not the dreams of a dreamer.

1. Unfinished and marked 'not sent'.
2. Horner writes in the immediate aftermath of the news of the Austrian defeat at Wagram.
3. See MC, 4 Aug.

342. To J.A. Murray

BLPES iv. 108–109   [London], 23 Aug. [1809]

. . .

    . . . Lord Chatham, it seems, keeps such hours in Walcheren as suit Boodle's and White's; never being visible to any body on *business*, till eleven or twelve o'clock. He is said to be the scorn of the whole army; and this account does not come from party prejudice, but as I understand from Lords Yarmouth and Lowther who have been over to see Flushing.[1]

1. Long before the unsuccessful result of the Walcheren expedition was known, the Whigs stopped at almost nothing in ridiculing every facet of it, most notably the supposed incapacity of the British commanders (Taylor, pp. 282–8). Evidently Horner heard this rumour shortly after his return to London from the circuit. He wrote to his father from Marlborough on 20 Aug., reporting failure on the circuit (*Horner*, i. 496–8), and to Murray from Speenhamland on the same day, discussing the reform of Scots judicature (BLPES iv. 106–107). He arrived at Lincoln's Inn on 22 Aug. William, Viscount Lowther, was afterwards 2nd Earl of Lonsdale (1787–1872: *DNB*).

343. To John Horner

BLPES iv. 111–14   Lincoln's Inn, 30 Aug. 1809

You will probably have some desire to hear from me what I have learned in conversation with Lord Holland and Allen, respecting the affairs of Spain.[1] The sentiments which they entertain respecting the past management of those affairs, both in what regards the Spaniards, and in what relates to the share which this country has taken, differ materially from the opinions which are held at present by most of their friends; though the view which they now take of what is likely to be the issue of the war, is far from being sanguine. They no longer doubt, that Bonaparte, if the state of Germany should afford him leisure, will be able to over-run the peninsula; and if he can spare so large a body of troops as will be required, and will incur the expense of fortifying the whole face of the country, that he may be able to retain it in subjugation. But almost the only advantage he can derive from the conquest, will consist in rewarding his generals with grants of territory; he can hardly within the period of his own life render it a productive dependency, as it was while he was content to receive tribute from the old Government; and the animosity of the Spanish people against the foreign soldiery is so irreconcilable, and so sanguinary, that the possession of the country, if not precarious, will always be a vexatious charge. Spain may be to France in this point of view, what Ireland in former times has been to England.

The antipathy of the French and Spaniards, always very great, is inflamed now to rage, and vents itself in a most inhuman warfare on both sides. An immense number of men has been lost to the French army, by assassination; every straggler is murdered; the women vie with the men, in taking advantage of every opportunity to slay a Frenchman. At Madrid, the women of the town dispatched so many, that there were general orders published to the army there, warning the men of their danger. The standing corns, particularly in La Mancha, afforded an ambush from which prodigious execution was done. In the course of every march, the peasants dispose of numbers, both those who loiter, and such as come off the road to the cottages for refreshment or plunder; and they are now very expert in burying the bodies quickly, where they think that precaution necessary. By this sort of treatment, the French, perpetually harassed, never secure by day or by night, are exasperated to fury, and practise horrors, which, though exemplified in their own Revolution and in their ancient civil wars, have never before been perpetrated by their army in any foreign country. The executions at Saragossa may be compared to those at Lyons in 1794; and with this aggravation, that the former have been perpetrated by the generals and marshals of a regular government, upon foreigners defending in arms their own country.[2] The men of letters, many of whom have very honourably distinguished themselves by adhering to the cause of their country and employing their pens in rousing their countrymen against the invaders, have been persecuted with the most savage hatred. ... Besides these sufferings of more eminent persons, the atrocities committed by the French soldiery in carrying on the war can only be compared to those of the wild Irish and American Indians. ...

. . .

With this mode of warfare against the conquerors, which (in a country half-civilized and every where intersected by mountains) may be interminable, it is important also to take into account the temper with which the Spaniards themselves look forward to the future. Allen's general observation is, speaking of the better sort and of those who are leading characters in the nation, that they are without foresight and without activity, but that their constancy and determination have never been shaken, nor their confidence of ultimate success ever damped, by any of the reverses or misfortunes of the war. They say their ancestors were six hundred years in driving out the Moors; which sounds as a very whimsical and ludicrous consolation, but considered more deeply may be taken as the expression of firmness rather than despair.

. . .

1. The Hollands and Allen had returned to Holland House on 12 Aug. Horner dined there on the evening of the 23rd, the day after his return from the circuit (HHDB).
2. The French reprisals against the defenders of long-besieged Saragossa following its surrender were among the most publicized of the war. See *Lady Holland's Spanish Journal*, pp. 300, 320–21, and 327, for the Holland House interpretation of the event.

344. To J.A. Murray

BLPES iv. 115–18 Lincoln's Inn, 11 Sept. 1809

. . .

. . . It is very possible that Lord Holland may not have been quite impartial about Moore, though I do not exactly know what he wrote about him last year; it was difficult at Seville to get exact information of what happened in the North, and he was surrounded there of course by persons who deplored and were therefore apt to condemn the retreat of the English. . . .[1] The only censure of Moore which I have heard from Lord H. is that he treated the Spaniards with excessive reserve and haughtiness, and thereby not only deprived himself of information and facilities which were within his reach, but continued to the last to misunderstand the real nature of the Spanish character and their peculiar spirit and mode of resistance in this struggle. An untameable antipathy to the French, the fierce instinct of an uncivilized people against foreign invaders, but actual ignorance of all the discipline of regular war, and the want of all those institutions, as well as habits of intercourse, which incorporate the different provinces of an improved country, formed a combination in which the general of an English army, or any other spectator accustomed only to the operation of public spirit in an enlightened and organized nation, might be at a loss to recognize what he had been led to expect by general descriptions of patriotic enthusiasm. It is a state of things, too, which would seem to recommend a different mode of assisting the Spaniards in the war, than by sending *small* regular armies into the heart of the peninsula. . . .[2]

. . .

1. The Hollands' Spanish sympathies had made them extremely critical of Sir John Moore after the retreat of the British army to Corunna, and Holland's point of view was altogether inconsistent with that of other Whig leaders who favoured making the Government's treatment of the General a principal facet of their attack during the coming session (Taylor, pp. 262–3).
2. Presumably Horner refers to the recent dispatch of Wellington and his small army to the Peninsula, a policy which Lord Holland's circle, including Horner, opposed despite the encouraging result of the Battle of Talavera and Wellington's subsequent victories; it also gave Holland House a point of agreement with the despondent Grenvilles and the pacific Whitbread.

345. To John Horner

BLPES iv. 118–19   Lincoln's Inn, 14 Sept. 1809

. . .

I suppose the paragraphs in the Ministerial papers, about changes in the Ministry, have set all heads agog in the country; they are strange paragraphs, but I hardly believe that they have any other foundation than the disputes among the members of the Cabinet, which naturally grow out of the failure of their absurd expedition, but which will as naturally subside from a common sense of interest if they feel there is any danger of losing their places. I do not see that any change is rendered necessary, by the state of public opinion upon the transaction; nor do I believe that there will be any material change. If Lord Wellesley should return in a hurry from Spain, Castlereagh would probably be turned out for him: though long before that, the public will have forgotten that there is such a place as Walcheren.[1] In truth, I feel very little curiosity or anxiety about any rumours of Ministerial changes; the state of the world in point of politics is almost hopeless and leaves little for the wisest and best rulers to do, and that little, though there are men in the country capable of securing it, is not to the taste of the English public in their present condition of selfish absurdity and levity. There is a wonderful healing power in the course of events, for which we must wait, however indignantly; and all I fear is, that the system of the present Government, which takes no care for futurity, may bring the finances into such disorder that we shall have no resources left to take advantage of a favourable turn of affairs. I do not hear that they mean to have any new taxes; and I should judge, that they have not courage to venture upon it: they will probably perpetuate another large portion of the war taxes, to liquidate the expenses of this summer, which have been very heavy, and to provide for the extravagancies of the next.

. . .

1. The Ministry was indeed nearing dissolution. It was now clear that the Walcheren expedition was a failure, perhaps a disaster; Portland was mortally ill and had recently been induced to resign; the feud between Canning and Castlereagh which had been brewing all summer had resulted in Castlereagh's resignation on 8 Sept.; and Canning, who remained in the Cabinet, looked to Wellesley for support in a contest with his rival Perceval, Chancellor of the Exchequer and Leader of the House, for the inheritance of Pitt. (Roberts, p. 347; see also Taylor, pp. 287–8, for an account of Whig opinion in the early stages of the Ministry's crisis.)

346. To John Horner

BLPES iv. 120–22   [London], 18 Sept. 1809

It is now quite certain, I understand, that there is to be a change of Ministry; but of what nature the change will be, I have not heard any probable conjecture, nor is it likely to be settled for some time.

The removal of the Prime Minister is rendered necessary, by the state of his health; for some time past, he has had no relief but by opium from the tortures of the stone, and is now incapable of the ordinary details of business.

But it is the expedition to Walcheren, which has broken up the Administration; the quarrels among themselves about its failure having gone so far that it would be difficult for them to keep together, even if they had not for the other reason a new chief to elect, and with the additional subject of difference it seems impossible that they should any longer go on.

The history of the expedition is likely to disclose a most ignominious scene of incapacity if there is any foundation for the stories which I have heard about it.[1] The officers of Lord Chatham's staff, at least some of them, pretend to justify him very positively; affirming, that the expedition was persisted in after he had declared his opinion that the object of it was impracticable, and in addition to this defence that nothing of what was necessary to be done by the Admiralty was effected. As an instance of this neglect, they assert, that for want of proper pilotage ten days were lost in sounding the passage up the Scheldt, and in towing the large vessels up by the small ones; that the information furnished to Lord Chatham by the Admiralty and War Secretary's office was grossly imperfect; and that Sir Home Popham, who has been the confidential adviser of this project of a *surprise*, actually printed a sort of sketch of what was to be done by the several divisions of the forces before they quitted the English shore.[2] The other point, however, is the most curious; for it is actually said, that Lord Chatham expressed his disapprobation of the expedition, or rather his opinion that it was no longer advisable, while there was still time to recall it; that the information which Government received of the Austrian armistice was withheld from him; and that after he did receive that intelligence, he expected, and to those near him expressed his expectation, to be recalled. I have not learned, whether, at this stage of the transaction, he remonstrated in writing against the farther prosecution of the object of the expedition. Another allegation is, that the publication made in the *Gazette* of extracts from Lord Chatham's letters and Sir R. Strachan's, is an unfaithful statement, and though it leaves no other impression (as we now read it) than that of blame imputable to the former and imputed to him by the latter, that the original dispatches would show that Sir R. Strachan agreed with Lord Chatham in opinion that the expedition was itself become impracticable.

This latter circumstance, whether a just accusation against Lord Mulgrave or only urged against him by Lord Chatham, would itself be sufficient to prevent them from continuing to sit in the Cabinet together.[3]

It has been nearly settled for some weeks that the D. of Portland should resign; that has been hastened by the late events. Lord Castlereagh is considered as already out, not attending the office, nor answering letters of business.

It would be idle to repeat to you all the idle stories and guesses, about who are to be brought in. Lord Wellesley is said to be sent for; Lords Bathurst and Harrowby have both been named for the Treasury;[4] Canning is supposed to wish to have it for himself; and the old joke against the poor Doctor is revived, that he sits in his dress coat and sword, expecting every minute to be sent for, and starting every time his door is knocked at. Nobody has any idea that any of the last Administration will be thought of; nor do I imagine that any of them think of it themselves. Lord Grenville is in Cornwall; Lord Grey in Northumberland; and Petty is gone to Ireland. I am sure none of them would listen to any proposal, without stipulating for the Catholic emancipation; and the King will surely try all experiments, even though so revolting to himself as submission to the ascendancy of Lord Wellesley or Canning, rather than come *informa pauperis* to any of L[or]d Grenville's Ministry. You will of course hear all sort of insinuations against them, among vulgar persons or those ignorant of the characters of those men. But you may be quite assured of their integrity.[5]

. . .

If Lord Chatham had not taken the command of the expedition, people who affect to know are confident that he would have succeeded the Duke of Portland. But I think the resignation of the latter could not have been looked forward to very long, otherwise Lord Wellesley would have contrived to prolong his stay at home. It is understood that our troops are to be sent for from Spain; and the resignation of Count Stadion is considered as evidence that there will be no more delay in the pacification between Austria and France.[6]

. . .

1. Horner apparently got most of his information from Holland House, which was much influenced by the critical reports Lowther and Yarmouth had brought back from the Scheldt in late August and more recently by Rosslyn, who had just returned from commanding a regiment there and, still full of indignation, had dined with the Hollands before proceeding to Howick. (Taylor, pp. 285–7.)
2. Rosslyn was especially critical of Popham, the commander of Chatham's flagship, and informed Grey on 28 Aug. (Grey MSS, Durham University) that Popham had 'put forward his plan, and then prepared and collected intelligence to support it; and I suspect that in like manner Ministers believed any thing that favoured their views'.
3. Mulgrave was First Lord of the Admiralty.
4. Henry, 3rd Earl Bathurst (1762–1834: *DNB*), became Foreign Secretary for a couple of months on 11 October, but Harrowby stayed President of the Board of Control until the middle of November.
5. On the day Horner wrote this letter, Perceval and his adherents met to review the political situation and concluded that they could not go on without an accession of strength in the Commons. After considering all alternatives they agreed to make a direct proposal to Grey and Grenville for the formation of a coalition government. (Roberts, p. 348.)
6. The resignation of Count Johann Phillipp von Stadion (1763–1824) as Minister of Foreign Affairs after the Austrian defeat at Wagram led to the appointment of Metternich on 8 Oct.

347. From John Allen

BLPES iv. 126   [London, 21 Sept. 1809]

. . .

Canning and Castlereagh have been fighting a duel and Canning is smote in the thigh, a bullet having passed through the fleshy part of his buttock, but I understand he is in no sort of danger. The cause of this most extraordinary event was a furious letter from Castlereagh concluding with a demand of satisfaction for the injuries he had received from Canning and couched in such terms that Canning thought he could not give him any explanation or offer him any satisfaction but the chance of shooting him. The parties met this morning at Wimbledon. Lord Yarmouth and Charles Ellis the seconds.[1] After an ineffectual attempt of Charles Ellis (unauthorized by Canning) to prevent matters coming to an extremity, both fired and both missed – but at the second fire the Minister of War was more successful in his own than he has ever been in his Country's cause, and the Minister of diplomacy was laid low.[2] This affair some people say is to be followed by others. Lord Chatham is to fight Lord Mulgrave, Lord Liverpool[3] any person who pretends to take his place from him, and to avoid being entangled by the precedent Rose and Huskisson have actually resigned their places, as the former says he wages war only with the dead, and the latter argues that if any [thing] were to happen to him, his friends could never show their face again in office as he does all their business for them.

This duel will make a great noise and must accelerate the breaking up of this scoundrelly Administration. . . .

1. Canning's friend Charles Rose Ellis, afterwards 1st Baron Seaford (1771–1845: *DNB*), was head of the West Indian interest.
2. For accounts of the duel and commentary see *PR*, xvi. 612, and *MC*, 28 Nov. and 1 Dec.
3. Robert Banks Jenkinson, who had succeeded only recently as 2nd Earl of Liverpool, was Home Secretary in the Portland Ministry.

348. From John Allen

BLPES iv. 126 [London, 22 Sept. 1809]

Nothing new concerning the duel. By what drops from Canning's friends it would seem that he means to assign as the cause of his resignation, the determination of the Cabinet to abandon the cause of Spain. And though the real difficulty as the *Courier* confesses is to settle who should succeed to the Duke of Portland, this pretence will pass with many as the true cause of his resignation. He, Perceval and Liverpool, were very lately at least, determined to stand or fall together, but perhaps this duel may alarm Perceval's morality and afford him an excuse if it should suit his interest to desert his associate. Chatham and Castlereagh are said to be together, and Chatham, as you know, is furious against Mulgrave. Westmorland is come to town to look after his place, and Lord Lonsdale to look after the Ministry.[1]

1. John Fane, 10th Earl Westmorland (1759–1841: *DNB*), was Lord Privy Seal. Lonsdale, who in 1807 had advocated the inclusion of Grenville in Portland's Ministry, would shortly demand that an effort be made to bring Grey and Grenville into a coalition government (Roberts, pp. 344 and 354).

349. To John Allen

BLPES iv. 127[1]   Birmingham,[2] 28 Sept. 1809

... I know nothing of the very important proceedings of last week, except the fact as stated in the *Courier* that Grenville and Grey are sent for . . .[3] I have no hope that this will lead immediately to their being in office; it is probably done for no other reason but to gain time, until Lord Wellesley can be brought home: Every thing seems to have prepared the way for him to [be] the head of the Cabinet. But it is surely a very fortunate occurrence for the other two, who will have this other opportunity of proving to the country their political consistency and integrity: they can make no coalition either with the remaining or the retired Ministers, without weakening as well as tarnishing themselves. You know that I have entire confidence in both of them; but I assure you, it is uphill work, whenever I have been in the country, to satisfy people that this is a well-founded confidence. The same persons, who never mention Mr Fox's name but with reverence, speak of Lord Grey as a man only desirous of office; and the Grenvilles are still more unpopular. This is monstrous injustice, and will be repaired in the end, [and] there can be no doubt, they have now an opportunity of showing their true political character.[4]

1. Unsigned and marked 'not sent'.
2. Horner, accompanied by Mr and Mrs Leonard Horner, had made a brief excursion into Warwickshire, 'half for political economy and half for geology' as his brother put it, and among other things spent a whole day with James Watt and his steam engines. (*Leonard Horner*, i. 14, and Horner to Lord Webb Seymour, 17 Oct., *Horner*, i. 502–503.)
3. The King had given Perceval permission to communicate with Grenville and Grey on 22 Sept., and the offer of a coalition Ministry had been made on the same day. Prepared to consider the offer, Grenville had returned from Cornwall with great haste. Grey considered a coalition with Perceval a practical impossibility, however, and without consultation with Grenville had promptly rejected the offer and refused to leave Northumberland. Upon learning of Grey's point of view, Grenville formally declined Perceval's offer on 29 Sept. (Roberts, pp. 349–50.)
4. In reply to a letter from Allen providing further information on the political situation in London, Horner repeated these views in a letter from Birmingham dated 30 Sept. (*Horner*, i. 498–501), and observed also that Grey and Grenville could not become Ministers without first obtaining the King's consent 'to the immediate relief of the Catholics' because they were 'committed upon it so strongly in the opinion of the public, that they must stand fast to that point, or forfeit all chance of ever regaining public confidence'.

350. To John Whishaw

BLPES iv. 130–31[1]   Birmingham, 30 Sept. 1809

. . .
    It is tantalizing not to be in London at this time, when the details of a strange turn of affairs, and one very critical for our friends if they do not conduct themselves

rightly, would be so interesting. I have no fears about their conduct; the part they have to perform is very plain; and nothing could induce them to deviate from the obvious line of their duty and their interest, but an appetite for place which they have never yet shown. Any negotiation with the remnant of the Ministry as such, is of course out of the question; and any coalition with any of that set ought to be equally so. My speculation is, that the accession of Canning to Lord Grenville's party is more likely to take effect, than any other junction; and, from the unaccountable manner in which he has saved his inconsistencies from being so notorious as those of some other persons, I do not think that there would be much sacrifice of character in a coalition with him: but I should not consider it as likely to answer in the end, or to prove even for a short time confidential or comfortable to either party. His personal ambition, it now appears, has no limit, though his qualifications are not such as to give him an easy ascendancy; his transaction with our friends towards the close of their Ministry, and still more his shabby conduct towards his late colleagues in all their scrapes, prove him deficient in good faith and fellowship: I hope therefore that Lord Grenville and Lord Grey will have nothing to do with him.[2] But it would be utter ruin to their character to make any arrangement with Perceval and Lord Eldon; though I have a better opinion of the honesty of Perceval than of any of the late Administration: but the principle of coalition has already been stretched as far as it ought, and any farther extension of it will completely extinguish all that remains of good party spirit in the country. Even if those men would consent to form part of an administration, which proceeded immediately to give relief to the Catholics, their prostitution could not fail to reflect disgrace upon their new allies; who have in truth no chance, either of regaining popularity, or of performing any permanent service to the country, but by standing firm together, rejecting all offers of coalition, and triumphing over the Court upon the question of Emancipation. This makes their chance of getting into office very slight; so I believe it to be; and I am satisfied they ought to cast out every other chance from their calculation. Not that there is not great room for amending the administration of public affairs in almost every department, and for saving the country from many mischiefs, independently of the Catholic question; because those who are most deeply pledged upon that claim, might be justified in waiting for a more favourable season, if they sincerely watched for such an opportunity, and Lord Grenville's Administration were in my opinion quite warranted in yielding to the King, when they found it vain to urge him. But their situation, as it seems to me, was wholly altered when the King refused to compromise the matter, broke with them upon that question, and made public what had passed upon it, in the *Protestant Letters*.[3] From that moment, the fate of that question and of their Ministerial life became identified; they are completely committed to the public, on that principle; if they do not hold it fast, the Catholics of Ireland will believe themselves again betrayed, and the people of England will think that there is indeed no attachment to principle among any public men: a party which has not the Court, must have popular confidence to support them; in reckoning their means of doing public good, that is essentially necessary, and some sacrifices must be made to effect a coalition with public opinion. I do not forget that there is still a great deal of popular prejudice against the Catholic claims; but not so much as ought to deter an honest ministry from granting them; and I am of opinion, that there is no chance at present of forming a set of public men to whom the public will look with confidence, but by a triumph over the Court and the multitude at once on this question. Though to those who will trust the good intentions of Lord Grenville and Lord Grey, the propriety, of taking the present opportunity to do as much good as may be and waiting for the first opportunity to do all the rest, may be accurately reasoned and set forth; and though their accepting office now without insisting upon the Catholic claims might be argued to be consistent with the line of conduct which they pursued in March 1807; yet the deduction is too long for the public, and what is more they do not feel the confidence upon which it proceeds. ... The public may be wrong in the argument; but they cannot be set right about it now; and the Whigs must have the public, or they will be nothing.

1. Unsigned and endorsed 'not sent'.
2. Since 1807, when Canning had conducted his brief, abortive negotiation with the Grenvillite wing of the Whig coalition, Lord Grenville had regarded Canning as a worthy successor to Tom Grenville as the family's representative in the Commons, and during 1809, as the Portland Ministry slowly went to pieces, a further flirtation between Grenville and Canning transpired. The anticipated elevation of Petty to the Lords generated a degree of support for Canning among Grenville's Foxite allies during August and September 1809, but the great majority of the Foxites, led by Lauderdale and Holland, rightly felt that the accession of Canning would set Whitbread adrift and lead to the detachment of the large Foxite left in the Commons. Hence passionate opposition to union with Canning developed and Grenville, faced with opposition even among his own supporters and a simple choice between the Canningites and the much larger Foxite party, abandoned his scheme (Taylor, pp. 296–8, and Roberts, pp. 342–3). Horner did his part to thwart the coalition with Canning. On 30 Sept. he wrote to Grey, telling him of a number of political liabilities arising from the past conduct of Canning's supposed ally Wellesley and suggesting that an attempt be made to bring it before the Commons. Grey's response of 10 Oct. stressed that any attempt to whitewash Wellesley should be 'vigorously resisted'. (BLPES iv. 140–41.)
3. [E. Cooke], Letters Addressed to Lord Grenville and Lord Howick, etc. (1807). Horner seems to refer to the vehicle employed by the King to disgrace the behaviour of the Ministry of All the Talents in putting forward Howick's Catholic bill.

351. To John Horner

BLPES iv. 132–5   Taunton, 2 Oct. 1809

...

The main point is settled, that Perceval is to be Prime Minister; Lord Harrowby is to be Secretary for Foreign Affairs, Robert Dundas (who came home from Ireland upon an invitation from Canning) is to be the Secretary for War and Colonies, and Lord William Bentinck will probably be Secretary at War. Long, the Paymaster, after vacillating for some time, at length agreed with himself to keep his place; so does old George Rose; but Huskisson follows the fortunes of Canning, and I do not know who is to succeed him.[1]

The substance of Perceval's letters to Lords Grey and Grenville, and of their answers, has been pretty correctly stated in the newspapers. The expression in Lord Grenville's answer, that he could not consent to form an *accession* to the existing Ministry, was taken up by Perceval in his reply, in which he observed that that was not what was desired, but that Lord Grenville would *assist* in forming a new Administration: to this second letter Lord Grenville made no answer whatever, judging, that this was only a repetition of the same proposal, and that any other communication except directly with the King, and especially a communication through the very person whom he might particularly object to, was not to be entered into.

It is said to have been Perceval's proposal, to write to those two members of the former Administration; that the King disliked the suggestion, and reluctantly consented to it; and that the Duke of Portland wrote to the King, to dissuade him from adopting it. Lord Liverpool and Perceval have acted together upon this part of the business.

The conduct of the Prince, in this affair, has been very satisfactory; and is of course very important. Lord Grey communicated to him his answer, and Lord Grenville also saw him after his arrival in town. The Prince wrote to the King, informing him that he had had those communications, but that they were only proof of personal respect, for that he did not mean (unless called upon by his Majesty to interfere more actively) to depart from the resolution which he had formerly expressed to his Majesty of abstaining from the immediate discussions of public affairs. The object of this letter, as I understand it, was to obviate too strong an inference from the intercourse which the Prince had held with Lord Grenville, and at the same time to leave an opening, if the King thought fit, for an interposition by the Prince: whose language is, that if Lord Grenville and Lord Grey were to unite with Perceval he would not oppose such an union, but that if they were to form an Administration without Perceval it should have his warmest support. Two strange overtures have been made at Carlton House, both without success. Canning sent Sheridan to explain to his Royal Highness all the circumstances of his quarrel with Castlereagh, in order that he might stand right in His Royal Highness's opinion upon that subject; the representative he selected has suggested a very reasonable inference, that he intended the communication to go farther, if there was an opportunity: but of course Lady Hertford[2] pleads Castlereagh's case with more effect, than Sheridan can state Canning's. Perceval too has had the meanness, after all his personal injuries to the Prince, to attempt to open the door of Carlton House, by means of Colonel Gordon;[3] but this advance has been rejected. The Prince sent the draft of his letter to the King, to Lord Grenville, before he dispatched it to Windsor; and Lord G. in the same manner communicated to the Prince the letter he wrote to Perceval.

The conduct of Lord Grenville and Lord Grey has been the best, indeed the only line, they could adopt; and I trust they have made up their minds to carry it one step farther, and not to accept of office without an immediate concession of the Catholic claims. They have already, by the manner in which they have rejected the late offer, raised themselves in the opinion of the public, though they have acted no better than those who had observed them nearly were quite certain they would act; and I am persuaded, that they cannot in any other way do so much service to their country, as by adhering firmly to the great principles involved in their quarrel with the Crown upon the Catholic question, and so placing themselves (as they in truth deserve to be placed) at the head of a true Whig party. The slight difference in their conduct, by one coming to town and the other refusing, arose from the blameable ambiguity of Perceval's letter, which did not directly state the King's commands, but used that expression in such a way as to leave the construction doubtful. I take it that Lord Grenville's course was the most agreeable to strict propriety; but I cannot help being glad, that Lord Grey refused to stir.

. . .

PS The Duke of York, who is supposed to be very desirous that Lord Grey should have a high rank in Administration, left town upon the breaking of the Ministry; the Prince was very anxious that he should be furnished with a full account of all that passed. . . .

1. Instead Bathurst became Foreign Secretary until Wellesley took over in December and Dundas succeeded Harrowby at the Board of Control, Liverpool becoming Colonial Secretary. Palmerston became Secretary at War, not Lord William Bentinck (1774–1839: DNB). Charles Long (1761–1838: DNB), afterwards 1st Baron Farnborough, remained Paymaster-General until 1826, and George Rose Treasurer of the Navy until his death in 1818. William Huskisson and Henry Wellesley were succeeded as Joint Secretaries of the Treasury by Richard Wharton (c. 1764–1828) and Charles Arbuthnot (1767–1850: DNB).

2. Isabella, Marchioness of Hertford (1760–1836), the mistress of the Prince of Wales, was distinctly Tory in her political opinions and evidently influenced the Prince on many occasions.

3. Colonel James Willoughby Gordon, afterwards 1st Bart (1773–1851: DNB), had been military secretary to the Duke of York as C.-in-C.

352. To John Horner

BLPES iv. 134–5   Taunton, 4 Oct. 1809

. . .

I think it next to impossible that Perceval should be able to carry on for any length of time the incapable system of administration, at the head of which he has had the presumption to place himself. The tameness with which the public seems ready to submit to it shows that there exists nothing like true public feeling. But the House of Commons, if he dares to meet it, will crush his ambition, which he has no talents to justify, or there is an end, at least for a period, of political freedom in this country.

. . .

353. To Lord Holland

BLPES iv. 136–7   Taunton, Thursday [5 Oct. 1809]

. . .

Even among the stupid Tory squires of this country, there is no hope that Perceval's Administration can possibly go on. Men who never before breathed against the Court, say it is too bad, and almost cry out shame. You may conceive how far this unfavourable impression is spread, from Lethbridge (the Member) saying to me this morning, that it could not last a month after Parliament meets.[1] This is a dismal omen for Perceval. There is nothing in the late business that I do not tolerably well understand, éxcept his sending to Lords Grey and Grenville at all; what could he look for but what has happened, and which has given Opposition so unexpected and important an advantage? Those two Lords stand now quite upon a different ground from what they did but the week before; one cannot call it popularity yet, but public confidence.

I am satisfied now, which I have not always been, that the Emancipation ought to be made a condition *sine qua non* of coming into power again. That is the true hold upon the only sort of popularity, the Whigs are likely to have in our day.

. . .

1. Sir Thomas Lethbridge (1778–1849) was MP for Somerset.

354. To John Allen

BL Add. MSS 52180   Lincoln's Inn, Monday evening [9 Oct. 1809]

. . .

It has been a Westminster Hall joke for a week past, that Canning has sent his Statement to Butler the Catholic conveyancer 'to peruse and settle', according to the phrase of that shop; and all the King's Bench men, who consider *libel* to be their peculiar province, wonder who could have sent Canning to such out of the way advice as Butler's. Whishaw has made it out, that Butler was consulted by Charles Ellis in the Howard peerage.[1]

. . .

1. Following their duel and resignations in September both Castlereagh and Canning published 'Statements' (*AR* li (1809), 562–7). Charles Butler (1750–1832: *DNB*) was a leading Roman Catholic lawyer. Charles Augustus Ellis (1799–1868: *DNB*), afterwards 2nd Baron Seaford, the eldest son of Charles Rose Ellis, had as an infant succeeded his maternal grandfather the Earl of Bristol as 6th Lord Howard de Walden.

355. To J.A. Murray

BLPES iv. 138–9   London, 10 Oct. 1809

. . .

. . . The great evil of our times is the distrust of the intentions of all public men; I think the late conduct of Grenville and Grey ought to soften that harsh and unjust opinion. Even if it were more founded in justice, it were greatly to be wished that such a distrust had never been felt; for its consequences to the public interest have already been injurious, and may be yet infinitely more so. In other times, it would be only an overflowing of the republican temper which is so important an ingredient in our public opinion, and might have no other operation than to enforce a greater purity of conduct and consistency in those who are candidates for the public confidence, which I conceive is one of its consequences at present. But with the crown so powerful by influence, and by the apprehensions of foreign danger, and with the representation of the Commons so manageable by the Treasury, the immediate and perhaps the only ultimate effect of this rejection of all the parliamentary leaders is to weaken and disappoint all their efforts to control the King. I am more clear however about its immediate effect, than about the ultimate consequences; for there is something so new in the present strange condition of the public mind in England, that I am very much at a loss in all my attempts to look far forward. What throws me out in trying to foretell the future operation of this public discontent, is, that it is not embodied upon any one political principle, except the vague and untrue persuasion, that great sums of the public money are corruptly misemployed; an opinion which scarcely admits of being set right, because it is fostered by the very vigilance and inquisition in Parliament which ought to satisfy it. The greater part of all this mischief we owe to the unjust acquittal of Lord Melville. Whether the condign punishment of the next conspicuous offender that is detected, and the reformation of several abuses which ought to be corrected without delay, would have the effect of restoring the attachment of the people to their Parliament, I cannot satisfy myself.

[PS] I wrote to Thomson about a subscription to Locke's monument: are the metaphysicians no longer Whigs, or the Whigs no longer metaphysical?

356. To John Allen

BLPES iv. 151–2   Wycombe,[1] Monday [16 Oct. 1809]

I was quite glad to hear from Whishaw this morning, that Brougham thinks quite with us, and very strongly so, upon all the late proceedings.

I read his review of Lord Sheffield, etc., on my way down here, for the first time; and think it most excellent.[2]

What strikes you on reading Champagny's letter to Armstrong?[3] The plain confession of the distress which France has suffered from the commercial privations, will be matter of triumph to the authors of the Orders in Council, though more properly to be ascribed to the non-intercourse act of America; which was the consequence indeed of those orders, but disowned by their authors. Can this country consider what is said about the Berlin and Milan decrees as any thing like an overture to us upon the subject, or is it only done to back the Americans in their proposition to us, that we should take the lead in repealing the restrictive orders? Nothing can be more false both in doctrine and fact, than the reasoning of Champagny's letter.

Lord Carrington has a story that Perceval has offered a seat in the Cabinet to the Duke of Northumberland, without effect.

1. Lord Carrington's place at High Wycombe, where Horner had gone with Abercromby for the weekend (Horner to Allen, [9 Oct.], BL Add. MSS 52180).
2. Brougham reviewed 'Lord Sheffield and others on foreign affairs' in ER xiv (no. xxviii, July 1809), 442–82.
3. See AR li (1809), 773–5, for the letter regarding maritime policies from the French Foreign Secretary to the US Minister in France.

357. To J.A. Murray

BLPES iv. 147–8 Lincoln's Inn, Tuesday [17 Oct. 1809]

I send you a copy of Allen's admirable *Suggestions*, which you must have already seen, and which you should have had from me before if I had been in town when they were first printed.[1] This little production will tell people who did not observe it before, what a superior understanding he possesses.

. . . It is now said that Lord Bathurst is to be the Secretary for Foreign Affairs, but whether for good or to hold only till Wellesley arrives, I cannot tell. Robert Dundas is to be put into Castlereagh's place, and after him any body may be made a Secretary of State. Lord G. Leveson [Gower] did not know last night who is to be his successor, and he mentioned a circumstance from which he inferred that it would not be Lord William Bentinck. Castlereagh says, I am told, there never was such *sporting time* in politics. Canning's friends talk as if he intended to start into flaming opposition the very first day of the Session; but upon what public ground I cannot devise: bad as his conduct was to Castlereagh, it was much worse towards the public. I shall be glad to hear your speculations, and your sentiments upon the conduct of Grey and Grenville; I am quite satisfied, and cannot help believing that the interests of our party and the cause of liberal principles of government have been much strengthened by the late turn of circumstances. The only thing that disquiets me, is, that the course of events may cast Canning upon us, which he is striving very much to effect; for though, upon my principles of party and coalitions, I would not reject him on any grounds taken from his past public conduct, yet I cannot help regarding him as a person with whom it is impossible to preserve either a comfortable or secure connexion in party.

. . .

> 1. Allen had recently distributed among his friends a printed but unpublished paper entitled *Suggestions on the Cortes*; there was also a Spanish edition entitled *Insinuaciones sobre las Cortes*. Both were dated 15 Sept.; but this 'little printed paper', as Horner called it (to his father, 4 Oct., BLPES iv. 134), was apparently composed at Jovellanos' request while Allen was at Cadiz and consisted of a short statement of political principles for the guidance of the Spaniards. Horner told Seymour in a letter of 17 Oct. that it was 'the best exposition I have ever seen, in so small a compass, of the principles of representative government' and a blueprint for a reform of parliamentary representation in Britain (*Horner*, i. 502).

358. To the Earl of Rosslyn

BLPES iv. 153–6 (copy)   Lincoln's Inn, 4 Nov. 1809

. . .

Lord Grenville's Oxford friends are very far from despairing even of success, and are quite certain now of making a good show. His friend the Pope has done him some injury in the canvass, but not near so much as was to have been expected.[1] The parsons seem to have too lively a sense of G.'s chances of being in office, to give wing to their fears of Popery. It is reckoned that 300 will be a majority; G. has already about 100 express promises. There is a great deal of languor and faintness about Lord Eldon even among the lawyers.

Wharton is to be Secretary of the Treasury. Lord Percy (I hear) is to be a Lord of the Treasury or Admiralty; though it is not three weeks since the Duke [of Northumberland] was writing letters to every body as if he were in decided opposition. George Johnston has refused a similar place, because they will not make him Right Honble.[2]

. . . Canning's second edition of his *Statement* was finished before the Duke of Portland's death, but as it was in the form of an address to His Grace, that event makes it necessary to write it anew; there never was any thing more elaborate apparently in the preparation.[3] He is said to be much out of spirits, having relied that many more of his friends would have followed him into opposition, than he can muster: I hear he will have *six* in the House of Commons, and *Lord Boringdon* in your House.[4] Sturges Bourne throws up his place, but is to vote with Government in order to keep his seat for Christ Church, which he holds from Rose.

. . .

> 1. Grenville's steadfastness in the cause of Catholic emancipation was put to the test in November 1809 when, in the midst of his successful canvass to succeed the Duke of Portland as Chancellor of Oxford University, the Irish Catholics again requested that he present their petition.

2. Percy was offered both offices in turn; but his father turned them down. A somewhat disreputable nabob, George Johnstone (1764–1813), MP for Hedon, was perhaps anxious for public honours. He was a member of the Bullion Committee and approved of its report. (*PH* iv. 312–16.)

3. Canning's September *Statement* explaining the circumstances that had led up to his duel with Castlereagh (see Doc. 354), had provoked a disclaimer of responsibility from the President of the Council, John Jeffries Pratt, 1st Marquess Camden (1759–1840: *DNB*), whose failure to communicate to Castlereagh what was going on Canning had blamed for giving the impression of a secret plot. Canning therefore felt obliged to issue a further 'Statement' in answer to Camden's, but delayed sending it until he had a chance to consult Portland about the Prime Minister's own role. After Portland's death Canning decided to send it in a revised form on 14 November. (*AR* li (1809), 574–88.)

4. John Parker, 2nd Baron Boringdon and afterwards 1st Earl of Morley (1772–1840: *DNB*).

359. To J.A. Murray

BLPES iv. 157–61 ⟨*Horner*, i. 504–506⟩   Lincoln's Inn, 11 Nov. 1809

. . .

Lord Wellesley is not yet arrived. That event, it is supposed, may occasion new arrangements of the Cabinet. My expectation is, that he will join Perceval at once, and that he will labour in process of time and one by one to make the Cabinet more suitable to his own partialities and purposes. Farther speculation is, that the King, who is said to have rather a prejudice against the Marquis at present on account of his profligacy in private life and probably also on account of his supposed talents for public administration, will in the end find Wellesley perfectly suited to his designs and wishes. He will find him entirely subservient on all questions of principle, and as bold as himself in carrying on government against both Parliament and people. Not that I have any very high opinion of Wellesley's political abilities; on the contrary, I suspect that none of that family will be found to have much capacity either for war or administration on this side of the Cape.

I hear that Canning is much dejected, with the issue of all his hopes and intrigues. He thought more persons in Parliament were attached to him; and he never imagined that his case, both against Castlereagh and towards the public, would be decided as it has been against him. He is still said to be at work upon a new edition of his statement.

We are likely to hear more of Ministerial dissenters. You saw it mentioned some time ago in the papers, that Lord Chatham had laid a memorial before the King, justifying himself for the failure of the Walcheren expedition: in this paper, he presses very hard upon the Admiralty for their inadequate assistance in the execution of the measure. This could not be left unanswered, and the first service Mr Croker has had to perform for the public in his new station, is the composition, with Sir Home Popham's aid, of a defence of the Lords of the Admiralty against the charges of Lord Chatham.[1] This is pretty well; but it is said not to end here. Lord Chatham has Perceval's promise, that his memorial shall be communicated by His

Majesty's command to Parliament; and Lord Mulgrave will of course insist upon the same justice being done to him. It is new in the history of our Cabinets, to find an administration begin with a paper-war among themselves.

⟨I have very little expectation that the unsettled state of the Government will end in a Whig Administration; and, upon the whole, I rather think that another attempt of that nature, in the present reign, is not much to be desired. In the precarious, unsure footing upon which they would have to act, with the Court hostile and deceiving them, and, on the other side an ill-disposed public, incapable of seeing their merit and public virtues, they could prosecute no systematic measures for the public good. They could not be efficient ministers, possessing neither the royal favour nor the public confidence; and until they shall have secured one or the other, it is better, both for themselves and for the country, that they should not attempt the administration of its affairs. Another experiment with this King, unless they are supported by the people, would speedily end as the last did, and with a farther loss of character; for their former experience in the closet ought to convince them, that honourable men cannot, with impunity, connect themselves, in public more than in private affairs, with a double-dealer; and in the present temper of the public mind, it would not be enough to govern better than others have done, nor would it be forgiven them if they only did as much good as they might find practicable. My own opinion is, therefore, that they ought not to accept office, except in the alternative, of either forcing the King's consent to the Catholic question, or of being loudly and distinctly called upon by the public to waive that question for the present in order to avert immediate danger.

⟨It is not very probable, under any circumstances, according to my view of these matters, that these men can retain for a length of time the favour of any king they are likely to serve. In a certain event, I expect that they will hold him just long enough to carry through one or two large measures, such as the Catholic emancipation, and an arrangement with regard to the Irish Tithes, which, like the abolition of the slave trade, and the limitation of military service, will mark them out hereafter to those who will appreciate their conduct more truly than their contemporaries in general are capable of doing. Not that I have not some faint hopes, in which you will probably think me both sanguine and partial, that a time may come in which they will acquire the confidence of the better part of the public; that is, a time when a taste and fashion may be revived in this country for the qualities and principles which entitle them to that confidence. My hopes of that sort are, however, but faint. The current of events, which has wrought such a change in the moral sentiments of Englishmen upon public affairs and characters, sets still in the same direction with unabated force. The old standards of public merit are broken; as the old feelings of constitutional control and order, as well as of national justice, are nearly extinguished.

⟨. . .⟩

1. John Wilson Croker (1780–1857: DNB), a friend of Canning and Secretary of the Admiralty in Perceval's Ministry, was regarded by the Whigs as the arch-propagandist against the Catholic claims.

360. To J.A. Murray

BLPES iv. 166–7   Lincoln's Inn, 15 Nov. 1809

Lord Lansdowne died last night. This is a great blow to the Opposition party in the House of Commons, and upon the whole it must be considered, happening just at present, as a misfortune to Petty. The vacancies in the House which this event will lead to, I hope and trust, will at length provide a seat for Brougham.[1]

Canning's statement is after all put into circulation, though not published. I have not seen it yet. It is a letter to Earl Camden.

Wellesley is not come yet. It is another pleasant incident in this comedy of errors, that he too finds Perceval's epistolary style ambiguous, and is upon the open sea at this moment with a firm persuasion that he has been invited to take the head of the Treasury. Frere is in the same ship, in whose favour the Central Junta have assumed the royal prerogative of granting a title; he is now *el Conde de Reunion*, which seems to mean *Count Coalition*.[2]

. . .

1. The several weeks that preceded and followed the death of John Henry Petty, 2nd Marquess of Lansdowne (1765–1809: *DNB*), produced much speculation and bickering among Whigs concerning the question of leadership in the Commons upon the elevation of Lord Henry Petty, Lansdowne's half-brother, to the Lords. George Ponsonby, the official floor leader since 1807, clung to his post tenaciously. Grenville continued to favour union with Canning and also considered coalition with Wellesley. Grey, regarding Brougham as 'the first man this country has seen since Burke's time', wanted to bring him into Parliament despite Brougham's recent break with Holland House. Holland, acting independently against the wishes of both Grey and Grenville, gravitated towards Whitbread. Tierney, hoping to secure the lead himself, opposed Canning and sought to undermine both Ponsonby and Whitbread. In the end, Ponsonby retained the lead and Brougham, at the request of Lord Holland and almost certainly with the active support of Grey, obtained Petty's vacated seat in the Commons, the Duke of Bedford's closed borough of Camelford. (Taylor, pp. 295–301; *Grey*, p. 190; New, pp. 49–51.)
2. According to Gabrielle Festing, *John Hookham Frere and His Friends* (1899), pp. 158–9, Britain's envoy to the Junta had left Seville in August with the title of Marquez de la Union.

361. To J.A. Murray

BLPES iv. 168–73   Lincoln's Inn, 17 Nov. 1809[1]

. . .

I have not read Lauderdale's book upon India;[2] but your account will induce me to take it up. He seems to have written every body out of taste for his compositions; yet he always knows a great deal about the subject he writes upon, and has always a way of his own in reasoning upon it.

The unprincipled proceedings of Lord Wellesley against the native princes of

India, and particularly in this instance which you mention of the deposed Nabob of the Carnatic, will be to all future times a foul stain upon the English name. One cannot read of them but with indignation; or remember, without the same feeling, the manner in which these questions were disposed of in Parliament, and the small minorities that appeared against Wellesley. The evidence, however, remains and will justify those who have the satisfaction of thinking that they were in those minorities. By far the best speech Romilly has made since he sat in Parliament was upon the Carnatic question when there [were] not above forty Members in the House.[3]

. . .

I have sent Jeffrey a very short and slight article, upon a translation of Mr Fox's history.[4] It is almost the only thing I have attempted to write for some years past; and I am quite sensible how much I am decayed in point of strength and fruitfulness, though my produce may have acquired more of an English race, by my growing so long in this soil. I have been most blamably indolent in not paying more attention to the cultivation of this habit. If *you* will point out to me any *short* subject, connected with more general politics or constitutional law, I will send Jeffrey another article for next Number.

. . .

1. Earlier portions of this letter were written the previous evening.
2. Lauderdale's *Enquiry into the Practical Merits of the System for the Government of India under the Superintendence of the Board of Controul* (Edinburgh, 1809) was reviewed in *ER* xv (no. xxx, Jan. 1810), 255–74, possibly by Robert Grant (*WI*).
3. This was the speech of 17 June 1808 on the last of Sir Thomas Turton's resolutions respecting the conduct of Lord Wellesley against the Nabob of the Carnatic. (See *Romilly*, ii. 256–7.)
4. *ER* xv (no. xxix, Oct. 1809), 190–97.

362. To J.A. Murray

BLPES iv. 174–7   Lincoln's Inn, 24 Nov. 1809

. . .

. . . Lord Wellesley, you will see, has decided to accept of Perceval's offer; which gives me very great satisfaction, for I regarded with horror the chance there was supposed to be, however slight, of his taking part with Opposition; because it might ultimately have led to a coalition, which would have been more ruinous to the character of public men, than even all that is past.[1] This must be felt as a new mortification by Canning; and it will be curious to see, what effect this incident, which I imagine *he* did not expect, and of which he has some reason to complain, will have upon his future course of conduct. I am not sufficiently acquainted with his character, to judge, whether the love of power, or resentment for personal slight, be the stronger principle in him. If he is well detached from Lord Wellesley and the

Wellesleys, one great objection to a junction with him is removed, so far as the expediency of that party measure is to be determined by a regard to public opinion and popularity; though the other very strong objections would still remain, which are founded upon the defects of his personal character as exposed by his former public conduct, and from which it must be inferred that a connection with him in politics will never be secure, but disquieted while it lasts by his restless and selfish vanity, and in danger of being sacrificed without any regard to faith if prospects open to him more convenient for his ambition.

After all this, I shall not say that the process of events may not bring us to a pass, when I should be of opinion that it would be right in the present leaders of Opposition to unite with this man: for coalition is always a measure of public prudence, and not to be governed in the determination by personal feelings or a regard to personal interests, except in so far as those form a part of the considerations upon which the public expediency of such a measure will turn.

It often occurs to me, when I hazard my speculations to you about politics and political men, that I run the risk of being found out to be often a changeling in such matters, if you should happen to remember from one time to another what my opinions have been. I have at any time but slight means of judging, and am not often very deliberate in forming a judgement; and indeed the interest I take, is of an intermitting nature, the fit coming upon me when leisure leaves me open to it, or occasion exposes me to impressions from those who are more systematically engaged. . . .

. . .

1. Wellesley returned from Spain and almost immediately became Foreign Secretary in Perceval's Ministry.

363. To J.A. Murray

BLPES iv. 178–9   [London], Tuesday [28 Nov. 1809]

. . .

In case any idle stories should reach Edinburgh, it may be as well to assure you that the rumour of a pregnancy or suppositious pregnancy is without foundation. The Chancellor has sent Lord Lansdowne his writ of summons. The woman has done him all the injury she could, and has tried more, having got a lease very recently executed, of the house in Berkeley Square to one of her daughters. . . . Under the leasing power of the settlement, it may be a question whether the lease is not good; but even in that event, which will be an unpleasant circumstance, Lord L. can suffer nothing by it in point of income.[1]

[PS] I hear that the evacuation of Walcheren, which would have been perfectly easy two months ago, is now likely to [be] attended with considerable difficulty, not only on account of the weather, but in consequence of preparations of the French. It will most probably however be effected.

There is to be a city meeting for an address on the subject of the Walcheren expedition; this I hear that citizen Waithman, who is lord of all there, has assented to, against the advice and remonstrances of his friend Cobbett.[2] Such remonstrances are a curious trait of the latter, and both prove his activity and the game he is playing.

> 1. The 2nd Marquess of Lansdowne, better known as Lord Wycombe, had married in 1805 – and not before time it was said – a middle-aged widow with three daughters by her first marriage. Lady Lansdowne, who was apparently even stranger than her very eccentric second husband, was described at the time as a large and 'vulgar Irish woman', whom Lansdowne himself habitually referred to as 'the old sow', explaining in due course that he had 'intended his strapping bride to be a barrier between him and the villainy of mankind'. As a younger son, Lord Henry Petty had been previously well provided for and was now assured of his succession to the entailed estates as well as to the family titles. But, although his half-brother had no children of his own, he was said to have left as much as he could to his widow and her daughters and to have attempted to make over also the remainder to them or others. These efforts apparently included a lease on Lansdowne House, as well as the furniture at Bowood. (See Lady Bessborough to Leveson Gower, 19 May 1805 and 24 Oct. 1811, Castalia Countess Granville, ed., *Lord Granville Leveson Gower (First Earl Granville). Private Correspondence 1781–1821* (2 vols, 1916), ii. 74 and 409–410; *Home of the Hollands*, pp. 131–2 and 236–8; *Lady Holland's Journal*, ii. 247.)
> 2. Robert Waithman (c.1764–1833: *DNB*) was a London linen-draper and common councilman who had distinguished himself in the City on the popular side earlier in the year and now held considerable influence among the Liverymen of London. The address was subsequently toned down by counter-resolutions.

364. To J.A. Murray

BLPES iv. 180–81   Lincoln's Inn, 4 Dec. 1809

. . .

It has been said, that Wellesley practised some degree of hesitation, real or affected, before he actually agreed to accept the seals of the Foreign Office. I am inclined to believe that this was not the case; for he went to Downing Street on Thursday, and has been regularly there ever since. But I take this rumour to have originated in consequence of a want of cordiality towards his colleagues, which he does not conceal even from strangers, upon all the subjects of their conduct prior to his joining them. It is very natural for him to wish to have as little to do with the Walcheren question as possible; but it is not very manly or fair to begin a co-operation with men who have that burden upon their shoulders, and to declare he will carry no portion of the weight. It might be a good reason for not joining them, till that discussion is disposed of; but he cannot be justified for taking a second part in the Ministry, and disclaiming the defence of the Premier, upon any question in which he will be called upon to defend himself.

. . .

365. To Francis Jeffrey

BLPES iv. 182–7 Lincoln's Inn, 7 Dec. 1809

. . .

There are new travels in Spanish America, by Azara, brother of the Minister, published since his death in France.[1] Perhaps Allen might be prompted to review these. I do not know that they would give the opportunity, but a good one is very much to be desired, to have his calm judgement and profound views upon the great question of South American emancipation, on which you have given us as yet only the enthusiasm of an advocate for Miranda.[2] It is one of the largest questions that have occurred in our day; infinite are the consequences which depend upon taking it rightly; the part of this country is yet to be taken; she will be called upon to decide very soon; and yet my conviction is, that very few even of our most active statesmen have considered it. You ought to urge all these things to Allen.

. . .

The state of literature in France at present is curious and equivocal. The exclusion of English books and of all foreign journals, even the scientific ones, the censorship which is exercised with the utmost strictness over the proof sheets of the Paris journals, even those of science, and the manner in which such books, as cannot be altogether suppressed, are mutilated, of which I have heard other instances mentioned besides that which I sent to your last number;[3] are all proofs of a tyranny, under which literature must languish and become enervated. The decay of classical learning, which was sure to be one consequence of the conscriptions, seems to have gone on more rapidly than even that system of destruction would account for. The editor of Bolingbroke's letters gives notice, in his preface, that he has translated all the Latin quotations that occur, because he was aware that the knowledge of that language was growing less and less every day.[4] And as another proof of the same fact, I observe that Dupont de Nemours in his edition of Turgot's works, makes an apology for publishing his academical exercises at the Sorbonne in a French translation, instead of the original Latin, because that idiom 'n'est pas familier aujourd'hui au plus grand nombre des lecteurs'; which of course means the majority of men of education, for none but such are likely to read Turgot's pieces even in his vernacular tongue.[5] On the other hand, the French press seems to be very fully employed; the most important works in mathematics pass quickly through numerous editions; some of the great compilations, which have been hitherto suspended by the Revolution, are now resumed, such as the great collections of historical memoirs, and the Benedictine collection of *Rerum Gallicarum Scriptores*. Of this last, two new volumes are already out; and it is amusing to see upon the title page, that they have been forced still to have recourse, for the execution of this task, to an *Ex-Benedictine Membre de l'Institut Impérial.*[6]

The new edition of Turgot's works in 9 vols, of which 7 are come over, suggests to me a subject on which I should like to make an attempt, if you will trust me with it, and give me a great deal of time. Indeed the labour of going through so many subjects minutely, would be such, that, in my unhappy state of multifarious occupations, I must ask for an unlimited period. But if you will not put it into better hands, I should feel an inclination to give you an account of these volumes, and a judgement upon Turgot; whose merits are but little known to common readers in this country, and even by the few who have heard of him a good deal misunderstood, from the exaggerated and fanatical portrait of him which was drawn by Condorcet. Let me have your pleasure upon this point.[7]

It is possible, however, that I shall send you another article before that, though I fear even this will not be for your next number. I have been looking into a sort of legal essay published by Luders, a retired barrister, upon that branch of the law of High Treason which relates to the levying of war; in which I find there are some just criticisms upon the constructive judgements which in this branch, appear to have encroached upon the statute of Edward the Third. Whether I shall be able to make any thing of it, I do not feel sure yet; of course, I mean not a legal, but a constitutional article; and the community of the law of Treason between the two kingdoms would remove any appearance of impropriety, even if it should have too much the appearance of a legal discourse.[8]

Both upon this, and my other project, I must request you to keep my secret from every body, and I make this request in good earnest; because, as you well know, there is much danger that I may never execute either of them.[9]

. . .

1. Horner has slightly muddled the two brothers. The major work of the naturalist Felix d'Azara (1746–1811), *Voyages dans l'Amérique Méridionale*, 1781–1801 (4 vols, Paris, 1809), had indeed been published for him in France, but it was his elder brother José Nicholas (1731–1804) who had died as Spanish Ambassador in Paris.

2. Francisco de Miranda (1750–1816), the Venezuelan revolutionary who solicited the support of successive British ministries, had assisted James Mill in reviews of several works on the 'Emancipation of Spanish America' and of Molina's *Chile* in ER xiii (no. xxvi, Jan. 1809), 277–311, and xiv (no. xxviii, July 1809), 333–53.

3. Horner's recent review of the French translation of Fox's *History* had focused on the omissions and misrepresentations of the anonymous translator in some detail and had attributed the 'corruption' of Fox's text to politically motivated censorship.

4. In an earlier passage omitted here Horner had encouraged Jeffrey to review an edition of Bolingbroke's letters recently published in Paris: Henry St John, Viscount Bolingbroke, *Lettres historiques, politiques, philosophiques, et particulières depuis 1700 jusqu'à 1736*, [ed. Count H.P. Grimouard] (3 vols, Paris, 1808).

5. Dupont published a 9-volume edition of Turgot's works in 1808–1811.

6. The surviving pre-Revolutionary editor of the *Recueil des histoires des Gaules et de la France*, Dom Michel J.J. Brial (1743–1828), had quit his monastery in 1790 but been engaged afterwards to continue the work by the Académie des Inscriptions. The first two such (vols xiv and xv) had appeared in 1806 and 1808.

7. In a letter of 21 Dec. Jeffrey authorized Horner to undertake the review. Horner was throughout his life fascinated by Turgot's economical works and it is likely that he at least began a review. But nothing ever appeared in print.

8. Alexander Luders, *On the Law of High Treason in the article of levying war* (1808), was never reviewed in the ER.

9. Clearly Horner's request for confidentiality also arose from his fear of being identified too closely with the *Review*. On 15 Nov., in the midst of his attempt to re-establish good relations with Jeffrey, Horner had told him frankly (BLPES iv. 162–5) that 'nobody should write in the *Edinburgh Review* or allow himself to be suspected of any intercourse with an

Edinburgh Reviewer, who has not made up his mind (for the sake of doing good) to be called an atheist and a Jacobin by ninety-nine in every hundred of the English parsons'.

366. To J.A. Murray

BLPES iv. 188–93 ⟨*Horner*, i. 506–10⟩   Lincoln's Inn, 15 Dec. 1809

⟨I have just heard of Lord Grenville's victory at Oxford, which I cannot but consider as a very important event in a public view; it is in truth a victory both over the Court, and over the worst prejudices of the Church.[1] The High Church is pulled down from its most ancient and formerly impregnable height: taken by storm in its strongest hold. The cry of No Popery is throttled. It will be found, I have little doubt, that it is the younger members of convocation, and those of the country together, who have defeated the resident monks of the University. And there is no prognostic so favourable and so sure, for the success of any improvement, whether in science or in opinion, as the distinct separation of the young ones in favour of the improvement, from the inveterate maintainers of the prejudice. What Black so liberally owned to Lavoisier,[2] is no less true in the history of political opinions among the people, ever since the press acquired its present power over those opinions; in our own times, we have seen instances, as in the case of the slave trade, and in some of the doctrines of political economy: the Catholic question has taken the same course, first among the Members of Parliament, and now throughout the people. The generation of those who are still sincerely afraid of the Pope, will quickly pass away; though it is by no means improbable, that the King and his *protectors*, as Perceval describes himself, will make one more desperate and convulsive struggle.⟩

Every body agrees with you, as to the dullness of Canning's narrative; Lord Ellenborough said, it was a log-book, to which Ward adds, there are many tacks in it. I cannot answer your question, as to the terms he holds with Wellesley. There are some stories about, that they are not cordial; and one very strange one, that among the papers of the late Duke of Portland has been found a letter from Canning, written at a turn of last summer's intrigues, when matters were going well for Mr Secretary, in which he says that he does not insist upon the Marquis being brought into office. But I have no good authority for this anecdote, which could not, if true, have got into circulation, without a very improper breach of confidence.[3]

I do not see why Canning should embarrass himself much with the defence of the Walcheren expedition. Wellesley ought, as I observed to you before, but will not. Nay he goes farther than this; for I know a man, to whom he said a few days ago, that he considered the late Ministers as having both misconducted, and wholly misconceived, the affairs of Spain, and that he would state that opinion in Parliament. This is pretty well for a new colleague. Castlereagh means to throw the failure of the expedition, not upon Lord Chatham, nor upon Lord Mulgrave, but upon Sir Richard Strachan; he will probably make little of that. There is a notion gaining ground, that we shall have an inquiry into this expedition. I cannot believe, that any thing so much like old times should happen in these, as a real parliamentary inquiry, not upon a mere production of papers from the public offices, but by witnesses in a Grand Committee. If the Ministers yield us that, they will not remain much longer Ministers.

⟨I am much vexed at the conduct of⟩ Sir John Anstruther ⟨in the commission, though not in the least surprised at any conduct in such a common-place jobber⟩ and Scotchman ⟨as I have long taken him to be. It is deplorable that such a person, equally ignorant of English law, Scotch law, and general principles, should have any thing in his power upon the most interesting discussion of a legislative nature that ever took place in any country.[4]

⟨The more I see of English law, and the practice of its various courts, and the longer I study the operations of politics, particularly as affected by the administration of justice, I gain new impressions in favour of trial by jury; of which I should find myself at a loss to say, whether the institution does most good, by preserving the poise of the constitution, or by accelerating the dispatch of private litigation, and by fixing the doctrines of law. ...[5]

⟨I never cease regretting, that the Edinburgh Review has wholly failed upon this momentous question; setting out with a clever, sceptical, flippant article against juries, and from that moment leaving the discussion to itself, that is, leaving it to the prejudices of the ignorant and the intrigues of the interested. It is not too late to repair in some measure this great neglect: why do you not write upon the subject?⟩[6]
...

The Duke of Sussex, who holds Opposition language at present, said yesterday, that it was not the City address which prevented the King from coming to town last Wednesday, but a new quarrel among the Ministers.[7]

1. Taking refuge in the veto, Grenville successfully combated the claim of his detractors that he was an enemy to the established church and was elected Chancellor of Oxford University despite a strong challenge from Eldon, who enjoyed the patronage and influence of both the Court and the Lord Chancellorship (Roberts, pp. 67–9).

2. Lavoisier's experiments had paved the way for Joseph Black's (1728–99) theory of 'latent heat'.

3. This is probably the letter referred to in Plumer Ward, i. 234–5.

4. Anstruther was a member of the commission on the reform of the Scottish Court of Session.

5. Horner goes on to discuss the principle of trial by jury and the feasibility of grafting that institution upon the law of Scotland.

6. The only previous article seems to have been that by Jeffrey in the January 1807 number; but Horner's characterization of it here is strange in view of what he had said about it shortly after publication (Docs 256 and 258). Murray shared Horner's criticisms with Jeffrey, who in a letter of 21 Dec. suggested to Horner that he write a tract on trial by jury (Horner, i. 511–12). But although Horner's letters to Murray continued to treat that matter at considerable length, no such article appeared.

7. London's Common Council, which on 5 Dec. had narrowly adopted resolutions calling for the recall of Parliament and an official inquiry into the failure of the British expedition to the Scheldt, had expected to present them to the King on 13 Dec. only to find the levee

cancelled. Like the Duke of Sussex, the MC of the following day suggested the postonement was owing to a serious rift in the Cabinet about the Walcheren fiasco; but it may well have been in the hope that a new meeting of the Common Council scheduled for the same day would lead to the withdrawal of the resolutions. As it happened, the resolutions were not withdrawn but at yet a third meeting on 15 Dec. they were toned down enough for the King to receive them on 20 Dec. Meanwhile a meeting of the Common Hall adopted resolutions of their own endorsing what their Council had originally decided; but when they sought early in January to present them to the King in person, they were told that he no longer held *public* levees on account of his failing eyesight. The City, however, refused to be fobbed off with a Secretary of State's letter-box and decided to complain to Parliament about the evasion of their privileges. Horner spoke about it when the matter was raised in the Commons on 7 May 1810. (Taylor, p. 299; MC, 6–21 Dec. 1809 and 10 Jan. 1810; and *Hansard*, xvi. 878–9).

367. To Lord Holland

BLPES iv. 233–4   [London], Friday [15 Dec. 1809][1]

From some things I noticed yesterday, I suspect that our more popular friends sneer at Tierney's activity about the circular letters, and that Sam [Whitbread] in particular thinks he ought to have been consulted both on that point, and about the amendment. The first is ridiculously unreasonable; but not the less to be attended to. On the other, I am sure you will agree with me, that it is very important, that Whitbread should not only have no reason to say that he has not been consulted, but that he should be very much listened to and yielded to if possible. It will do infinite mischief, if he brings out an amendment upon the amendment. No one has so much power as you to conciliate and keep us together; and I fear that Tierney is not disposed to give Sam his full measure of consideration and deference. The defeat of Wardle, and the victory of Lord Grenville, will perhaps put Whitbread in a more manageable train.[2]

. . .

1. The manuscript letter has been endorsed in pencil, probably by Leonard Horner, '25 January 1810' and, since that day was a Thursday, amended subsequently by BLPES to '26 Jan. 1810'. But in two final paragraphs it so closely follows what is said in Doc. 366 that it must surely have been written on the same day.

2. In the midst of the intrigues by Tierney and Whitbread to depose him as party leader in the Commons, Ponsonby had sent round anonymous circular letters to Whig MPs informing them of a meeting at his London house. This had infuriated Tierney and Whitbread (the latter of whom was also put out by Wardle's failure on 11 December to have reversed the verdict against him in his suit against Mrs Clarke: see Doc. 338 and T. Grenville to Lord Grenville, 12 Dec., *Dropmore MSS*, ix. 407), and relationships within Opposition had become even more strained when Grey and Grenville had agreed unilaterally to retain Ponsonby as leader in the Commons, to dodge the Catholic question, economical reform, and parliamentary reform during the next session, and to restrict the amendment to the Address on opening day to the failure of the Walcheren expedition and the management of the Peninsular War. Grenville later won Whitbread's support for the proposed amendment, but Whitbread failed to attend a meeting at Ponsonby's house on 22 Jan., the day before Parliament convened, and on 25 Jan. moved an amendment vaguely demanding economy, which was defeated by 95 to 54. (Taylor, pp. 306–310.)

368. From Francis Jeffrey

⟨*Horner*, i. 512–13⟩   Edinburgh, 21 Dec. 1809

⟨...

⟨Do, for Heaven's sake, let your Whigs do something popular and effective this session in Parliament. Cry aloud, and spare not, against Walcheren; push Ireland down the throats of the Court and the country; and do not let us be lost without something like a generous effort, in council as well as in the field. You must lay aside a great part of your aristocratical feelings, and side with the most respectable and sane of the democrats; by so doing, you will enlighten and restrain them; and add tenfold to the power of your reason, and the honour of your cause. Do you not see that the whole nation is now divided into *two*, and only two, parties – the timid, sordid, selfish worshippers of power and adherents of the Court, and the dangerous, discontented, half noble, half mischievous advocates for reform and innovation? *Between* these stand the Whigs; without popularity, power, or consequence of any sort; with great talents and virtues; but utterly inefficient, and incapable of ever becoming efficient, if they will still maintain themselves at an equal distance from both of the prevailing parties. It is your duty, then, to join with that to which you approximate most nearly; or, rather, with that by whose aid alone you can snatch the country from imminent destruction. Is this a time to stand upon scruples and dignities? Join the popular party; which is every day growing stronger and more formidable. Set yourselves openly against the base Court party; bring the greatest delinquents to serious and exemplary punishment; patronize a reform in Parliament; and gratify what may be a senseless clamour, by retrenching some unnecessary expenditure. I doubt whether all this can now save us; but I think it quite certain that we shall have rebellion, as it will be called, as well as invasion, unless something be done upon a great generous system. Cobbett and Sir F. Burdett will soon be able to take the field against the King and his favourites; and when it comes to that, it will be hard to say which we should wish to prevail. ...⟩[1]

1. The opinions advanced here by Jeffrey are very similar to those that appeared shortly afterwards in his article, 'State of Parties', *ER* xv (no. xxx, Jan. 1810), 504–521.

369. To J.A. Murray

BLPES iv. 194–5 ⟨*Horner*, i. 514–15⟩   Lincoln's Inn, 23 Dec. 1809

⟨...

⟨Somebody dropped a hint to me that there is to be a review of Canning's *Statement* in the *Edinburgh Review*. It seems to me, that such an article would be most improper; and I hope, if you agree with me, that you will use your influence with Jeffrey to prevent it.⟩[1] I would attempt to use mine, but that I think Jeffrey dislikes an interference of that sort from me. ⟨In my opinion, the *Review* has gone too much already into political reflections in their nature personal, and has too frequently overstepped the line by which it ought to bound itself in questions of politics, important on account of their general nature, but mixed also with those personal and merely party considerations, in which the *Review* never engages without a loss of its proper character and usefulness. In another point of view, I should object to it, as far as I am myself concerned; for I will not run any hazard of being supposed to be concerned in anonymous discussions of personal character, even in public transactions; and that is a point upon which I have made up my mind. The matter, however, ought to be decided by Jeffrey, upon grounds which do not include any personal feelings of mine, who have done so little for the work; and I beg you will urge the more general reasons only to him, if you think with me about it, and consider what I have said about myself as meant for you only.⟩ The turn which the *Quarterly Review* has taken as the mere organ of Canning's party, gives Jeffrey an opportunity of showing that his Journal is conducted upon higher views; ⟨I am never afraid of any thing that Jeffrey himself does; but I never open a new number without trembling for the possible indiscretions of his most able and most entertaining colleagues. ...⟩

1. No such notice appeared in the *ER*.

370. To J.A. Murray

BLPES iv. 198–201   Lincoln's Inn, 24–25 Dec. [1809]

. . .

[PS] Read the last article in the *Quarterly*, on the state of Parties; the irony not quite successful throughout, but the bitterness against Perceval, and the soreness about Wellesley, remarkable.[1] It gives some insight into the views and principles, if so they can be called, of Canning's party. It is utterly ridiculous to talk of Pittite principles for opposition. By the way, I do not know that I have mentioned to you, the authority which I lately saw for a very material anecdote of Pitt himself. In Lord Grenville's letter, upon the late occasion, to the Principal of Brazen nose, he states, that when Pitt came into office in 1804, he 'engaged', although retaining the same opinions which had governed his conduct and that of Lord Grenville, when they resigned in 1801, to 'forbear acting upon them': the letter states farther, that Lord Grenville himself at that time 'declined' entering into such an engagement.[2] Pitt's conduct, of course, implied such a pledge to the King; but till I saw this letter, I did not know that he gave an *express* one, in violation of all public duty, and of his very oath of office.

I have just heard that Staremberg was upon the road to Dover, and has been recalled by Wellesley. If this story be true, it would seem that the proposition of peace is not yet rejected; it is strange that offer has excited so little notice.[3]

1. 'Short Remarks on the State of Parties at the Close of the Year 1809', *QR* ii (no. iv, Nov. 1809), 454–60, was apparently by George Ellis and George Canning (Shine).
2. In the course of his successful canvass for the Chancellorship of Oxford University, Grenville wrote to Dr Frodsham Hodson, the Principal of Brasenose, disclaiming responsibility for the persistent agitation of the Catholic question and asserting, with references to his former political conduct, that he was committed to the security of the Establishment. The letter was intended for private circulation but later made public. (Roberts, p. 68.)
3. The Austrian Ambassador in London, Prince Starhemberg (1762–1833), had been recalled, following the Treaty of Schönbrunn. There may have been some short delay in his departure in the vain hope that Britain too would make peace. (A. Aspinall, ed., *The Later Correspondence of George III* (5 vols, Cambridge, 1962–70), v. 322, 468, 472, and 488.)

371. To John Allen

BLPES iv. 202–203 ⟨*Horner*, i. 516⟩   Lincoln's Inn, 28 Dec. 1809

Before I leave town, I cannot deny myself the pleasure of letting you hear what Mr Playfair says of Lord John Russell, in a letter I received from him this morning.[1] 'Lord J.R. is one of the finest young men I have met with, of very good capacity, great application and desire of knowledge, with perfectly good temper and entire command over himself. His society is so pleasant, that I had much rather have him for an inmate in my house, than not, even were all objects of interest quite out of the question.' I have sent the same extract to Adam, who is (I believe) at Woburn, in order that the Duke may have an opportunity of hearing so satisfactory an account of his son.

Playfair mentions Henry also, who (he says) is applying to study more than was to be expected. His private master in the mathematics is very well pleased with him; and Playfair thinks he will return to the South with some improvement from his winter in Edinburgh. He adds, that Henry must go into the army, but it ought to be into a regiment of infantry.[2]

⟨. . .

⟨I hope Lady Holland is now quite well. I liked Lord Holland's speech very much, as given in the *Morning Chronicle*; except that part of it about the *panacea*: no friend of Parliamentary Reform ever spoke of it as such; that exaggeration is only imputed to them by the other side; it is not necessary to disclaim it for the sake of the people, who are apt to misinterpret such guards and qualifications, as a proof of our being lukewarm.[3] No political measure, and especially no legislative one, ever could with truth be proposed as an immediate cure for many evils in the state; but perhaps none has ever been carried against prejudices, that was not prosecuted with as much ardour as if it were expected to prove a very *panacea*. The more I think about Parliamentary Reform, I am the more satisfied that good would result from making the representation more popular than it is: and if it is not done legitimately, the people of this country will one day have a fight for it. I shall get back to town about the 13th of January⟩; . . .

1. Lord John Russell, afterwards 1st Earl Russell (1792–1878: *DNB*), who had accompanied the Hollands and Allen to Spain and Portugal, had begun a three-year residence in Edinburgh in the autumn of 1809. He lived with Professor Playfair and attended Professor Stewart's last course of lectures in moral philosophy. (See Spencer Walpole, *The Life of Lord John Russell* (2 vols, 1889), i. 43–6.)

2. Henry Vassall Webster (1793–1847), Lady Holland's second son by her first marriage, who had a hankering to join the army, had been sent to Edinburgh for the winter in the hope, according to a letter Horner had written to Murray on 10 Oct. (BLPES iv. 138), that 'the society and air of Edinburgh may communicate to him some taste for information and reading'. He entered the army in 1810 and was ADC to the Prince of Orange at Waterloo. He was promoted Lt Colonel in 1831 and knighted in 1843. Like his father, he committed suicide. (*AR* lxxxix (1847), 51 and 223–4.)

3. The reference is to the speech Holland made at Nottingham on taking the oath as Recorder on 22 Dec. Nottingham's choice of Holland on the death of the Duke of Portland, 'however I may laugh at it', he said (*Holland House*, p. 56), 'I like very much because there never was a body of Men more firmly attached to the cause of freedom and in the very worst times more devoted to my Uncle than the corporation of that town'. Malcolm I. Thomis, *Politics and Society in Nottingham 1785–1835* (Oxford, 1969), p. 148, says it was 'a symbolic rejection of the local aristocrats and an assertion of the right to choose whom they pleased'. In his speech of thanks Holland said he took it as a tribute to the memory of Fox, and speaking of his devotion to civil and religious liberty declared: 'I am, and always have been, a Friend to a Reform in Parliament. I believe it would be a beneficial measure; but I by no means think it would prove a Panacea.' (MC, 27 Dec.)

The Front-Bench Politician
1810–1817

Introduction

T HE CONTINUING RESTRICTION of cash payments by the Bank of England was not an issue in British politics in early 1810. Indeed, nothing seemed more peripheral, more unlikely to inspire the interest of Parliament, than monetary policy. The war in the Iberian Peninsula increasingly commanded the attention of the nation, obscuring virtually all domestic issues; and besides, nobody of importance really seems to have comprehended economic philosophy or read the several contentious pamphlets inspired by the recent rise in the price of bullion on the international exchanges. Yet on 1 February Horner, emerging at last from the Opposition back bench, launched an attack on the Bank restriction that elevated him to a position of great influence in the House of Commons. For the remainder of his life, he was regarded as Britain's premier parliamentary economist and as a future minister of state. His correspondence therefore becomes of still more value to economic and political historians alike.

Horner's bullionist doctrine and the fame he achieved by propounding it in 1810 and 1811 are explicable only if analysed with reference to his objectives and to the broader political context of the controversy he precipitated. Two of his letters – of 3 and 22 January 1810 (Docs 372 and 376) – combine to throw much light on his strategic and tactical reasonings. Careful reflection had convinced him that the course of events was carrying British politics to a new juncture. The body politic, he perceived, had been dysfunctional for some time owing to a constitutional problem endemic to a period in which the evils of monarchy prevailed over its advantages. That problem was the manifest influence of the Crown in compromising the characters of statesmen, and thus the integrity of Parliament. At the time an unpopular, chronically weak Ministry held sway, the nation lacked faith in the steadiness of public men, and there was a ruinous breach between the aristocratic Opposition and 'the people'.

Horner, however, perceived among his countrymen 'a tendency to start forward, which cannot be repressed much longer'. This, he reckoned, was owing primarily to an 'agricultural revolution' born of the 'cupidity and luxurious necessaries of the gentry', and out of which the system of leases and the progressive rise of rents were daily strengthening the middle classes. Also promoting a coming age of reform was the progress of national education and the increasing influence of the press, which promised to make 'one democracy . . . of the whole population'.

Already there were signs of change. The strength of agitation for economical and parliamentary reform during 1809, especially out-of-doors, had impressed Horner very deeply. So, too, had the recent election for the chancellorship of Oxford University, which Grenville, a leading advocate of the Catholic claims, had won in a direct confrontation with the Court.

How might the forces of change be marshalled? What was needed, Horner felt, was the mobilization of a 'vast party' supported by the 'intelligence and activity of the middle orders'. That endeavour demanded parliamentary leaders who remained steadfast in all matters involving political principle, even if such a course of conduct were unpopular among the 'democracy'. Support for the Catholic claims, for instance, might well be a political liability at present, but a higher consideration dictated that any future Whig government must 'do something for the Irish Catholics without delay'.

Patience was a necessary political virtue. The present reign was nearing its end; at length a new monarch would be forced to grapple with the long-repressed political manifestations of economic and social change. Hence the arbiters of change must display a 'cool resolve'; what 'the people' liked, Horner sensed, was 'a great man who will not take office'. For the present, however, the process might be set in motion through 'a victory, by main force, over the Court, upon a great fundamental principle of liberty or toleration'.

Here the most fruitful causes were Catholic Emancipation and parliamentary reform, but Horner's correspondence of early January 1810 with Allen and Holland, who were engaged in political discussions at Woburn, confirmed what he already suspected – that the Whig party, as then constituted, was incapable of effectively exploiting either issue. Grenville was hedging on the Catholic claims in the wake of his victory at Oxford; Allen warned that even a modest proposal for parliamentary reform would divide the party; and the Opposition bench in the Commons was adrift (Docs 373 and 375).[1]

The situation left Horner with but three options. He could go back to square one – resign his seat, pursue his profession, and wait for the nation to 'start forward'. He could stand pat – retain his seat, remain obscure in the Commons, and until the course of events opened new vistas seek to avoid the bog of personal rivalries and compromised principles that at present so thwarted the Whigs. Or he could attempt to fill the void created by the elevation of Petty to the Lords. Certainly there was a rare opportunity for personal advancement; Allen reported from Woburn that there existed 'a most inviting field to any one who thinks he can distinguish himself in the ... Commons' (Doc. 373).

Well aware of that opportunity, Horner had for several months already been courting party leaders assiduously, all the while considering the political inertia arising from an unprincipled coalition among the Opposition and the embarrassment attending active collusion with the feuding Whig bench in the Commons. How might he break free? Again Romilly's example was instructive. For while he sat among the Opposition bench and was regarded very highly by Whig leaders, Romilly went his own way, refusing to be drawn into the quagmire of party politics, and his personal crusade for law reform, enhanced by his reputation at the

1. See also Horner to Holland, 15 Jan. 1810, BLPES iv. 217–18.

Bar, commanded the respect, if not the support, of the entire House. The answer, Horner therefore concluded, was an independent line in the Commons and a cause with a broad appeal that neither encroached on the territory of another nor offended any faction within Opposition.

But the political cupboard was almost bare. Disagreement among the Whigs excluded the major issues – foreign policy, Irish affairs, parliamentary and economical reform. Lauderdale had claimed the reform of Scottish judicature, Whitbread the reform of poor law. Indeed, among the several issues of state Horner had identified as worthy of the attention of the 'practical Statesman' nearly seven years earlier, only the Bank restriction remained unexploited.

That subject, however, troubled him for a number of reasons. First, the monetary crisis had not developed as he had anticipated. The commercial anomalies bred by the long war had created an altogether unprecedented situation in international exchange; even bullionists disagreed on the matter, and Horner was reluctant to enter such treacherous waters. Secondly, talk of depreciated paper, bullion, and the exchanges promised to excite nobody; the subject was likely to generate no more interest than Romilly's respected but desultory campaign for legal reform. Nor did the bullion question raise the prospect of a victory over the Court 'upon a great fundamental issue of liberty or toleration', and one could hardly hope to carry resolutions for a repeal of the Bank Restriction Act 'by main force' in the Commons.

However, in early January Horner was spurred forward by word that Brougham would be brought into Parliament by the Duke of Bedford. Worse still, his old rival was coming in as Grey's man, and almost everyone felt that Brougham's talents would soon deliver him the lead in the Commons. That was by no means a remote possibility, Horner realized, even if Brougham was certain at first at least to disappoint the extravagant expectations of others, and, as Horner also suspected, his unbounded ambition and woeful impetuosity were likely to cause 'irritation and uncertainty about him' (Doc. 374).

For the moment Horner retained the advantage, just as he had done earlier as a privileged founder of the *Edinburgh Review*, but he knew that he had to act promptly and decisively, that he must abandon his cautious ways and didactic speeches, and mount a parliamentary offensive. He reconsidered the feasibility of a campaign against the Bank restriction. Perhaps there was ground to argue that his earlier doctrine was being confirmed by the fact. For during the previous year there had been a re-emergence of inflationary pressures – a declining exchange rate for sterling and a marked rise in the price of specie in terms of Bank of England notes – and a number of commercial men had expressed concern.

Horner read Perry's *Morning Chronicle* regularly; no doubt he had noted in that Foxite organ the controversy inspired by Ricardo's letter of 29 August 1809 on 'The Price of Gold'. Then there had appeared Mushet's *Enquiry into the effects produced by the Bank restriction bill*, which included tables depicting Britain's faltering position in international exchange. And only recently Ricardo's *High Price of Bullion* had generated a considerable degree of interest among the money-men of the City and the commercial members of the House.

There was nothing authoritative or original in the extreme bullionist arguments advanced by Ricardo; he was as yet a relatively obscure stockbroker, and his doctrine, which in essence maintained that all problems were attributable to an excessive issue of domestic paper, hardly differed from that advanced by other writers earlier, notably by Wheatley in 1803. But Ricardo's attack and Mushet's evidence had elicited an interesting response from the Bank, denying that there had been an excessive issue of paper and attributing the exchange problem to the extraordinary foreign remittances necessitated by the war.

Horner thought that Ricardo's doctrine was essentially correct, and that the Bank's explanation was easily assailable; for of course there had been an excessive issue of paper. But he suspected that Ricardo's assessment was perhaps too narrow, that British commercial policy was a variable in the equation as well, and that at all events a broader avenue of attack was essential. He had practically dismissed commercial factors in his review of Thornton, and he remained convinced that the Bank restriction, an overabundance of paper, and the resulting depreciation of the monetary standard was at the core of the problem. But the commercial regulations advanced by the Privy Council certainly fettered trade and compounded the evils of a dubious monetary policy.

The real problem, Horner felt, had begun with Pitt's subsidies to Britain's continental allies, whose drain on precious metals had caused the Bank of England, and thus the country banks, to tighten credit. Diminished credit had in turn squeezed British merchants, leading to the closure of commercial houses and to banking failures, and forcing a disastrous contraction in the commercial community. The floating of sterling, and a corresponding increase in the issues of unredeemable paper, had served as a temporary lubricant; but the resulting depreciation of money had exposed British merchants to an ever-worsening crisis of exchange. Foreign merchants, fearing an unstable currency, had demanded payment in specie, thus accelerating the flight of precious metals and forcing British merchants to seek a continuing expansion of the channels of trade.

Napoleon had exploited the situation with his blockading decrees. The 'continental system' had not ended British trade with traditional European markets, but it most certainly had constrained commerce, and the Orders in Council promulgated by the Portland Ministry, which sought to control commerce with the enemy, had only compounded the problem. The Orders infuriated neutral nations, especially the United States, and their retaliation had squeezed British merchants still more. Spain's American colonies offered a commercial alternative, but that opening was closed by the demands of foreign policy. Hence the 'natural' lanes of trade had been constricted, the commercial base of the nation had narrowed, and the balance of payments had suffered. All the while the Privy Council had sold increasing numbers of licences to foreign merchants, even to those of enemy nations, who had exploited Britain's insulated, inflationary economy to undersell domestic producers.

The result was curious, to say the least. Within Britain prices, rents, and wages rose dramatically, creating an appearance of prosperity. Meanwhile, however, a ruinous cycle continued to evolve. Specie disappeared, the bullion reserves of the nation diminished, inflation and continuing issues of depreciated paper carried the national debt to outrageous levels, and the bullion ratio of sterling inevitably faltered on the exchanges.

The spiralling wartime economy also produced sad contradictions. Domestic producers of corn liked high prices while failing to comprehend that British commercial policy and the depreciation arising from an adulterated monetary standard collectively 'operated as a bounty upon importation' (Doc. 420).

Similarly, while landlords liked the 'name and show' of high rents, they did not understand that depreciated paper daily eroded the real value of their tenants' leases (Doc. 432). Indeed, a depreciated currency impaired all contracts, compromised the interests of all creditors, and was in fact an outright attack on property. Labour, also failing to think in real terms, liked rising wages, and many of the nation's capitalists, noting the happy effect of a depreciated standard on a profitable, if ever-narrowing, export trade, were content as well. Indeed, virtually nobody comprehended the inevitable long-term effects of the spiralling domestic economy. A continuation of the war would eventually inundate the nation with cheap foreign produce; prices, rents, and wages would fall, and unemployment would soar. The conclusion of a definitive peace would have precisely the same effect, only more rapidly. Moreover, convertibility would then of course be restored, and the nation would groan under the weight of a wartime debt that had accrued in an age of politically-contrived inflation. In the end, only bond-holders would profit.

All this made perfect sense to Horner. There was, he rightly suspected, a strong tendency for the commercial and monetary establishment's short-term interests, the landed classes' ignorance, and the national chauvinism born of a long war to combine to make his point of view politically unprofitable. But the debate of a decade earlier was heating up again, the Bank was on the defensive, and he was desperate for a cause. There was a viable issue of state here, he concluded, and it offered him an opportunity to follow up his earlier celebrated reviews of Thornton and King. Furthermore, while the prospect of an early political victory was slim, clearly cash payments must eventually be restored. Perhaps, therefore, he might hope to educate the House, and by following a course of 'cool resolve', later bask in the sunshine of vindication.

A more immediate consideration was the likely response of the Whig leaders. There were dangers, of course. Grenville's connection with Pitt's 1797 Government might lead him to resent an attack on a policy with which his name was associated. On the other hand, Grenville professed, if somewhat lamely, great admiration for 'established' principles of political economy, and his recent political opinions amounted mostly to grumbling about Ministerial policy.[2] Perhaps he could be brought round by the argument that the long continuation of the Bank's suspension of cash payments, rather than the suspension itself, was what was ill-advised. Such a construction, in fact, might blunt the opposition of all time-serving Pittites.

Grey might also react favourably. He knew nothing of monetary theory; but Lauderdale and King certainly did, Tierney thought he did, and all of them had applauded Horner's earlier bullionist doctrine. Holland, like his uncle, was ignorant of the principles of political economy, but he had listened attentively in the parlour as Horner had propounded his notions of 'true doctrine', and had a vague idea that the restriction was bad policy. The Whig peers, Horner therefore suspected, could be led. The essential thing was to ensure that his arguments were generally consistent

2. See Sack, p. 155; see also Doc. 130.

with the 'husbanding, defensive system' of wartime policy advocated by Grey and Gren-ville since 1806. That seemed easy enough; the Bank, after all, blamed the decline in the exchanges on the hefty foreign remittances necessitated by the Peninsular War, which both Grey and Grenville opposed as a waste of precious resources.

What, however, about the party rank and file? Their ignorance of economic phenomena was appalling, but perhaps the Pittite lineage of the Bank's policy might generate some little support among Foxite back-benchers, especially if, as earlier, Horner could link the monetary dilemma to the broader question of British war policy without offending Grenville and Windham. And surely the Whig squirearchy, indeed all landowners, might listen to arguments equating unredeemable Bank notes with the inflation that was compromising the integrity of leases and flooding the nation with foreign corn.

Active support among the Whig rank and file, however, was not essential. Of course Horner would welcome it, but above all else he must ensure that his campaign was not perceived as a party measure. For an attack on the Bank restriction otherwise promised to generate support among two important 'swing groups' in the Commons. Like Pitt before him, Canning professed admiration for the economic philosophy of the schoolmen, and his lieutenant, Huskisson, was known to favour a resumption of cash payments. Then there was Wilberforce's friend Thornton, whose views remained consistent with his 1802 treatise, and who promised to bring the 'Saints' in his train. Such support might weld together an impressive alliance and counter charges of partisanship.

No less significant was the fact that the Bank restriction was regarded by Britain's two most influential 'democratic' journalists as a legacy of Pitt's 'oppressive' policies of the 1790s. Hunt, the editor of the *Examiner*, propounded such a point of view, and Cobbett had been among the nation's most consistent advocates of 'hard' money. Indeed, Cobbett represented the Bank restriction as a conspiracy organized by Pitt to promote inflation, depress real wages, and encourage the purchase of Treasury bonds; and during the last months of 1809 his *Political Register* had begun a series of articles that ridiculed, among other commercial anomalies, the illegal exportation of bullion to France.[3] Horner realized the necessity of keeping well clear of Cobbett, and of dissociating himself from direct attacks on Pitt and the war. He was, however, influenced very profoundly by the bullionist doctrine of the *Political Register*. On 22 January 1810, less than a week before he launched his campaign in the Commons, he referred to Cobbett as 'that very sagacious judge of the popular sentiment' (Doc. 376).

Horner was encouraged to step forward by his rising reputation among Whig leaders. Grey and Grenville were desperate for leadership in the Commons, and Horner, perhaps at the instigation of Lady Holland, was included in the political discussions that were held in mid-January. On the 16th he was the only MP to dine at Holland House with Holland, Grey, and Grenville, and next day he dined there in a party that included the recently-elevated Lansdowne, the former Solicitor-General Pigott, and Fitzwilliam's lieutenants in the Commons, Windham and Elliot.[4] In all probability Horner broached the bullion question; for surely he would

3. *Cobbett*, pp. 170–71.
4. HHDB.

not have acted as he subsequently did without the sanction of at least the Foxite leaders. Two weeks later he went forward in the Commons.

Horner's remarks of 1 February 1810 were carefully measured. He began with an apparent falsehood, assuring the House that he had formed no 'clear or confident conclusion' on the causes of the high price of bullion, and it appears that he made no direct reference to the Bank restriction. Rather, he conjectured that the high price of gold 'might be produced partly by a larger circulation of the Bank of England paper than was necessary, and partly by the new circumstances in which the foreign trade of this country was placed'.

Within that broad construction, Horner recalled the Bank's own explanation – the continuing drain of bullion occasioned by the war – and noted that, contrary to the official explanations of Government, the problems of country banks were apparently mere symptoms of a disease at the central Bank. Both arguments were perfectly consistent with the doctrine he had advanced in his review of Thornton over seven years earlier, but his remarks on the possible effects of purely commercial factors were altogether new. In January 1808 he had produced confusion on the Government bench by questioning the wisdom and legality of selling commercial licences to foreign merchants, especially to those of enemy nations. He now reiterated that point, suggesting that such policy might well contribute to the monetary problem, and adding that Government had also failed to exploit the availability of precious metals from South America.

After giving notice of his intention of moving for a select committee, Horner successfully proposed that a number of papers be laid before the House. Among them were the very things he had sought, apparently with only partial success, since 1805: accounts of the imports and exports of bullion and foreign coins, the issues of Bank notes and dollars, the number of licences issued to country bankers, and the quantity of gold and silver exported by the East India Company to China and the East Indies.

Horner, it appears, very carefully co-ordinated the resulting debate. No Opposition front-bencher, not even Tierney, spoke, a fact which suggests that Horner had taken precautions to ensure that his proposals would not be perceived as a party measure. Indeed, only commercial members elaborated on the virtues of the several points he raised. Joseph Marryat expanded on Horner's suggestion that the monetary problem had been exacerbated by the policy of granting licences to trade with the enemy. Alexander Baring also dwelt on the negative effects of British commercial policy, reiterating Horner's emphasis on the availability of specie in the Brazils. And Davies Giddy, embracing an argument Horner had advanced in his review of Thornton, maintained that 'the great circulation of paper materially contributed to throw the specie into the market'.[5]

Hence Horner and every MP who supported him in the debate represented the

5. Joseph Marryat (1757–1824), father of the novelist, was MP for Horsham and, from 1811, Chairman of Lloyd's. Davies Giddy, afterwards Gilbert (1767–1839: *DNB*), the anonymous author of an 1804 pamphlet on the Corn Laws, was MP for Bodmin. Francis Baring's son Alexander, afterwards 1st Baron Ashburton (1774–1848: *DNB*), was MP for Taunton and a director of the Bank of England. Baring and Giddy both joined Horner on the Bullion Committee, Giddy publishing in 1811 *A plain statement on the bullion question.* (*Hansard*, xv. 269ff.; *AR* lii. 126–7; *Examiner*, 4 Feb. 1810.)

Bank restriction as only one of several factors leading to an increase in the price of bullion. That, to be sure, was Horner's intention, and the following day, after the Vice-President of the Board of Trade had attempted to refute his suggestions about the Government's commercial policy, Horner appealed to what he rightly regarded as the nexus of Whig opinion on foreign policy. The present difference between exports and imports, he observed, appeared resolvable into the increased foreign expenditure of Government; there must 'at last be a final equality'.[6]

Malthus, to whom Horner had apparently written just before he opened his attack in Parliament, and Ricardo, who was not yet personally acquainted with Horner, both responded to it with lengthy letters. Malthus, who had seen only an inadequate press report of Horner's speech, may possibly never have sent the only known version of his letter (Doc. 377); but in it he acknowledged that it seemed 'probable that our ideas on the subject may not materially differ' and then proceeded to elaborate his own developing position. Ricardo responded with two well-known letters on 5 and 6 February.[7] Displeased by the breadth of the bullionist doctrine advanced in the debate, he argued that the excess of the market above the mint price of gold bullion was solely attributable to an excess of paper circulation, and that the other arguments raised had merely confused the issue. Horner's reply, if he replied at all, has not come to light, but clearly he agreed with Ricardo's fundamental position. His plan, however, contemplated the political advantages of an eclectic monetary doctrine, and nothing was more immediately effective than his remarks on the relationship between the high price of bullion and British foreign policy.

Failing to grasp the political implications of Horner's remarks of 1 February, Perceval conceded on that occasion that the high price of bullion was probably attributable to 'the wars so long carried on', and the *Examiner* was quick to seize on that admission:

> The interruption of the supply of bullion, the Bank issues, and the *prophetic* demand of foreign merchants for our specie and nothing else but our specie, no doubt are very active *final* causes of the depreciation and ruin of paper-money; but the final cause is to be found in our wars, that is to say, in entering into enormous expenses, both for ourselves and *our allies, which we never retrieve* . . . We waste our money, we throw it over hill and dale into the pockets of princes waiting to be rifled, and then wonder where it can be gone. These are wounds in our credit which no paper-plaister can heal. The greater or less plenty of money in a state may be of no actual consequence, since the price of labour will keep place with it, and money after all is not a commodity but its representative medium . . . If it has really come to be an article of trade, Heaven help us . . . Paper-credit, which was first invented to conceal the wants of the State, has been kept up for the same purpose: paper does not truly represent riches; it conceals the defalcation and the bad application of them, and its credit has at last grown too thin not to be seen through . . .

The *Examiner* also endorsed Horner's view of the unexploited mines of Spanish America, lauded his capacity in fiscal policy, and called for inquiry under his leadership.[8] Shortly afterwards Cobbett's *Political Register* also voiced support for the

6. *Gentleman's Magazine*, lxxx (pt 1, Feb. 1810), 163.
7. *Ricardo*, vi. 1–10.
8. 4 Feb. 1810.

campaign, if not for Horner personally, defending country banks and representing the Bank restriction as a conspiracy by the arch-villain Pitt to feather the nests of bond-holders upon a resumption of cash payments. Clearly, Horner's opening remarks had tapped the strain of pacifism, exploited the discontent with lavish continental subsidies, and appealed to the hatred of Pitt that had characterized Britain's politically disaffected for some twenty years.

The short debate of 1 February aroused considerable interest. Speculation was rife in the City, and from Edinburgh Murray reported rumours that Horner would be named Secretary for Ireland in a new administration.[9] But Horner was aware that the breadth of his doctrine, and especially its strong appeal among the left wing of opinion, placed him on dangerous ground, so he moved quickly to solidify support on his vulnerable right flank, writing to Grenville on 11 February (Doc. 379). He was, he said, considering a motion for the appointment of a select committee to examine the causes of the high price of bullion; but he had yet to form any conclusions, needing advice on such a momentous issue and being reluctant to act without Grenville's sanction. Horner had read his man very well indeed. Grenville was not averse to an attack on the *continuing* restriction of cash payments by the Bank; that measure, he observed (Doc. 380), originally had been adopted 'to meet a sudden and very urgent pressure' but was 'ill calculated for any long continuance'.

Grenville's approval constituted the last piece of a very difficult political puzzle. At a stroke Horner had forged a very unlikely union of sentiment, if not a guarantee of active support, among an otherwise divided Whig party, while bringing himself into line with the leading voice of the 'democracy', Cobbett, and assuming a position that promised to attract the support of the Canningites, the 'Saints', a number of commercial members, and perhaps defectors among the squirearchy as well. Confronted by the Ministry, the Bank of England, the interested protectors of the commercial and monetary establishment, and the silent country gentlemen who supported every Government, the campaign had almost no chance of immediate success. That, however, was not Horner's goal. His primary objective was general political reputation; his secondary objective, which was certain to be enhanced by the attainment of the first, was advancement among the directionless Whigs; and, confident that cash payments must eventually be restored, he had every reason to think himself in a promising situation.

At the outset, however, Horner faced a number of daunting challenges. The first was how to convince Ministers that a select committee of inquiry should be appointed. How he did it remains unclear; perhaps the chronic weakness of the Government and the support of key men like Canning and Wilberforce influenced Ministers. Whatever the case, the Bullion Committee was nominated upon Horner's motion on 19 February 1810 and directed 'to inquire into the cause of the high price of gold bullion, and to take into consideration the state of the circulating medium, and of the exchanges between Great Britain and foreign parts'.

The second challenge was how to ensure the inclusion of friendly, or at least neutral, committee members. This, too, Horner somehow accomplished; indeed, given the Government's opposition to the restoration of cash payments, the compo-

9. Murray to Horner, 8 Feb. 1810, *Horner*, ii. 3–4.

sition of the Committee is almost incredible. For among its twenty-one members were Abercromby and Sharp, two of Horner's closest friends and political colleagues, as well as five other Whigs – Sheridan, Tierney, Earl Temple, Thomas Brand, and Pascoe Grenfell. Joining that core of supporters were Huskisson, Thornton, and Giddy, all of whom were known to be ardent bullionists, and Parnell, who leaned more towards Ricardo's particular view of the Bank restriction but agreed with Horner's conclusion. Hence Horner began with a stacked deck; a clear majority of the Committee was predisposed to his general point of view, and none of the remainder enjoyed any considerable reputation either as a statesman or as an economist.

Horner's third challenge was how to place himself in a position of predominant influence among the Committee. Given its composition, however, the fact that it was he who had moved for its appointment, the breadth and moderation of his doctrine, and the fame he had earned through his earlier economic treatises in the *Review*, that objective was realized with little or no difficulty; when the Committee met on 22 February it promptly chose him as chairman. Afterwards, until 25 May, it met on thirty days and examined twenty-nine witnesses. Horner was in the chair for twenty-one of those meetings, Huskisson generally taking it for some six weeks (19 March to early May) while Horner was away on circuit, and on 8 June the Committee submitted its report to the House of Commons.[10]

Horner's correspondence sheds much light on his influence in fashioning the final document. A recommendation for the resumption of cash payments was a foregone conclusion. The manner in which the Committee advanced that proposal, however, was still a matter of concern to him. His principal object, he told Murray (Doc. 406), was 'to impress the public with a notion that it is a state question, not one of trade, and to be decided by political considerations, not by the notions of the counting house'. And so he proceeded, from first to last deprecating the narrow, interested arguments of bankers and brokers, emphasizing the disastrous effects of an adulterated standard on private interests, and thus appealing to widely divergent factions.

Horner's entire frame of reference was retrospective. He wanted the report to declare, 'in very plain and pointed terms, both the true doctrine and the existence of a great evil growing out of the neglect of that doctrine'. His notion of 'true doctrine' was 'former experience and former doctrines'. He was unwilling to allow for either the exigencies of war or the related economic variables arising from an unprecedented state of commerce, and he sought to represent the anti-bullionist arguments of the Bank directors as mere theory. Furthermore, he was perfectly willing to sacrifice economic orthodoxy to political expediency so long as his essential objectives were realized. The Committee, he told Professor Stewart, based its case 'upon those grounds with which it was most difficult to mix any topics of declamation' (Docs 392, 397, and 402).

Notwithstanding the bullionist sympathies of a majority of the Committee, Horner experienced some degree of difficulty in imposing his point of view. Evidently Thornton clung to his earlier opinion that the original depression of the exchange had been owing to a trade imbalance. Horner had disputed this in his

10. *Ibid.*, ii. 2.

review of Thornton's *Inquiry*, pointing instead to a deficiency of credit, but Thornton had his supporters among the Committee, and Horner conceded a point he thought puerile but practically meaningless. There was also some disagreement on the relative issues of specie and paper that should follow a resumption of cash payments; several members of the Committee, it appears, opposed paper altogether. Here, though, Horner carried his argument that paper credit lubricated commercial transactions most beneficially, and that an 'actual interchange of a certain portion of specie circulating along with the paper' was necessary to secure the value of paper (Doc. 403).

Matters relating to the question of exchange were also contentious. A definitive line on that issue was not an essential item in Horner's agenda, however; so he argued successfully that the Committee should eschew comment altogether (Doc. 397). And while he was prepared to enhance the appeal of his bullionist doctrine out-of-doors by relating the monetary dilemma to British commercial policy, several members of the Committee were reluctant to tie the bullion question to the Orders in Council. Hence he was forced to consent to a much narrower point of view than he had originally espoused in the Commons, one that stressed monetary policy to the virtual exclusion of commercial policy. A letter he wrote to Grey (Doc. 388), however, suggests that he was initially undisturbed by the concession. For after all his talk about the unhappy effects of licences allowing trade with the enemy, he now confessed that perhaps he had overestimated their effect by relying 'less upon the facts' than on the 'probability' that Napoleon was shrewd enough to exploit Britain's 'senseless' American policy and 'avidity for imports and exports'.

The preparation of the Committee's report was also problematic. Horner, Huskisson, and Thornton each wrote parts of it, and the result, in Horner's opinion, was 'a motley composition' that was 'clumsily and prolixly drawn' and most unbecomingly 'tacked together'. But he attained his primary objective. The Bullion Report, he quite accurately observed (Doc. 392), stated 'nothing but very old doctrines' and assigned all the difficulties to a theoretical abstraction that flew in the face of tried and true principles. In essence, having pronounced depreciation to be a fact and attributed it to an excessive issue of paper, it drew attention to the ruinous effect of the resulting inflation on creditors and asserted that the only remedy was a prompt return to convertibility. Moreover, it dodged comment on the policy of the original Bank Restriction Act. As Horner pointedly told Grey (Doc. 389), he and his colleagues represented the suspension of cash payments as 'a measure which, however fit it may have been to meet a sudden and urgent purpose, was not calculated for any long continuance'.

Horner's behaviour between February and June 1810 suggests that he sought to screen the bullion question from the vicissitudes of partisan politics. In this he was probably influenced by a rumour, reported by the *Examiner* on 18 March, that the political articles appearing in the *Edinburgh Review* were being written at Holland House, but one must suspect that he also wanted to distance himself from his feuding colleagues in the Commons. Horner appeared at Lady Holland's dinner table on only four occasions between 1 February and 8 June,[11] and he exploited both his involvement with the Bullion Committee and his absence on circuit to emerge

11. HHDB.

unscathed from the Opposition's embarrassing failure to secure the passage of resolutions censuring the Walcheren fiasco.

That campaign, the central thrust of the Whig attack on Government during the 1810 session, was predictably undermined by personal rivalries among front-benchers, disagreement about virtually every other public issue, and unbecoming attacks on Wellington and his Peninsular campaign.[12] Opposition leaders were astonished by the failure, and J.W. Ward regarded it as the nadir of the Whigs as a political party;[13] but an analysis Horner wrote on 3 April (Doc. 382), when he was safe and secure on circuit, suggests that he was hardly surprised by the rout.

Three of Horner's letters – two written to Allen (Docs 383 and 384) and one to Professor Stewart (Doc. 385) – confirm that he played a double game calculated to enhance his position among the Whigs after returning to London in early May. To both men he bemoaned the absence of leadership in the Commons. Yet while the well-placed Allen was assured of Horner's abiding faith in Grey, Stewart was informed of the 'blameable reserve and hesitation' of Grey and Grenville 'upon those questions of economy and reform which so much agitate the people'. Indeed, Horner told him, the Whig leaders were lacking in 'popular feelings', resentful of the public, and inefficient.

Horner's political behaviour was also very circumspect. On 21 May he cast a silent vote for Brand's unsuccessful motion for a moderate reform of parliamentary representation, thereby aligning himself with the Whig centre in the Commons.[14] Two days later he navigated through 'a sea of difficulties' by siding with Grey and Grenville against Holland, 'the republicans', and the 'best lawyers' in the House – Romilly among them – on the question of parliamentary privilege raised by the Speaker's writ for Burdett's arrest and confinement.[15] Horner did this last very boldly, calling for the Committee's report to be referred back, with a view afterwards to moving resolutions in support of the utmost extent of privilege claimed. For he objected, he said, to arguments founded on the contention that the authority of common-law courts to proceed on summary attachment was analogous to that authority which sanctioned the privilege of Parliament, expressing concern that such a construction might throw doubt on the very existence of that privilege and observing that that doubt 'might have the most pernicious effect at a future period, if the time should ever arrive when the Crown might find it convenient to join a popular clamour against the House of Commons'.[16]

The opinions Horner expressed on the question of privilege reflected a tactic he would pursue for the remainder of his political career. Whenever possible, he would refuse to ground his political conduct on the wavering character of men. Rather, he would anchor his politics on an appeal to a noble Whig tradition of better days, thereby projecting himself as a man of fixed intellectual principle and extricating himself from the war of personalities and issues that confounded the troubled Fox–Grenville coalition. Hence his propounding the doctrine of both Fox and Burke that Parliament stood between the people and the Crown as protector of the constitu-

12. Roberts, pp. 144–6; Taylor, pp. 310–19.
13. *Letters to 'Ivy'*, p. 98.
14. Roberts, pp. 272–9.
15. See Doc. 386 and Horner to Holland, 9 May, *Horner*, ii. 13.
16. *Ibid.*, ii. 14–15; see also Horner's note of 6 May 1810, BLPES viii. 70.

tion, and that its independence must be supported in all circumstances.

Brougham opposed Horner in the debate on privilege, bringing on the first parliamentary confrontation between them, and Ward, who was 'very much diverted by seeing my friends the philosophers falling foul of each other in the House of Commons', thought Brougham got the best of the argument. Ward, however, failed to comprehend the broader political ramifications. Horner's uncompromising view of parliamentary privilege ran foul of 'popular' sentiment to be sure; but it placed him on impeccable Whig ground that pleased Grey and Grenville and also accorded with the views of the Government bench, thus enhancing his reputation for independence only two weeks before the report of the Bullion Committee was submitted to the House. Moreover, his arguments clearly 'un-whigged' Brougham. Indeed, Horner suspected that his friends found them 'more Whiggish than reasonable', and shortly after the debate Ward noted that Horner was more popular than Brougham among MPs.[17]

During late May and June Horner moved progressively closer to the Whig leaders in the Lords. On 24 May he sent Grey an account of British imports from the enemy (Doc. 388). On 10 June, two days after he had submitted the report of the Bullion Committee, he provided Grey with a summary of its contents and asked him to propound bullionist doctrine in the statement of political principles he was planning to deliver in the Lords on 13 June (Doc. 389). Thereafter he resumed a more regular attendance at Holland House,[18] 'lived a good deal' with Grey and Lansdowne, and embraced political opinions pleasing the Foxite peers. In late June, after Grey's public declaration of Whig principles had appalled almost everyone, Horner praised the speech excessively (Doc. 392). He also adjusted his view of the Peninsular War, endorsing the opinion of Grey and Grenville that the British army should be withdrawn. At the same time, however, he took care not to offend Holland, standing on his original assertion that the 'untameable spirit' of the Spaniards would prevail at last (Doc. 391).

Horner also waffled on parliamentary reform. While voting for Brand's motion and assuring Murray that he was 'keen' on a reform of Scottish representation (Doc. 390), he was very critical of the 'extremism' of English reformers. He delighted in Burdett's declining popularity with the 'liberty boys', remarking that he was most useful when he was least popular, and predicting that in time the 'radicals' would return to the Whig fold (Docs 391–2). All the while he posed as a Foxite martyr at Holland House, representing his campaign against the Bank restriction as a dangerous attack on the powerful war faction. Holland recalled that:

> He seemed to sacrifice the fairest objects of ambition, and to incur at the outset of his public life the private enmity of large bodies of men and great unpopularity with the public, by a patient, diligent, and determined inquiry into matters which, little attractive in their nature, led him, as he well knew, to conclusions unpalatable to powerful individuals as well as to the Bank and the Government. He foresaw that his opinions on this subject must lose him the seat in Parliament which he then held.

17. *Hansard*, xvii. 174–5; Doc. 427; *Letters to 'Ivy'*, pp. 108–9 and 111. See also Horner to Murray, [11 May 1810], BLPES iv. 251–2.
18. HHDB.

... All the supporters of the war, and some who, without approving its origin, profited by the spirit of speculation to which its continuance gave occasion, were for preserving a hazardous and dishonest system . . . [19]

Horner's tactics won friends in all the right places. On 1 July he was the only member of the Commons to dine at Holland House in a party that included the Prince of Wales, the Dukes of Sussex, Argyll, and Bedford, and the Hollands' Spanish friend, the Duque de Albuquerque.[20]

Horner began to prepare for the debate on the Bullion report during July 1810. Two letters he wrote to Jeffrey (Docs 393 and 395) confirm that he feared the *Review*'s 'mercenary troops', especially the 'deplorable heresies' of James Mill, that he wanted to keep the question in his own hands, and that he planned to write an article praising the bullionist arguments advanced by Ricardo, Mushet, and Blake before raising the issue in the Commons. They also suggest that he conspired with Huskisson to forge an unholy alliance between the *Edinburgh Review* and the *Quarterly Review* on the bullion question. He was eager to neutralize 'party politics' in the *Review*, especially Brougham's fetish for writing 'what he ought to speak in the House of Commons', and again he encouraged Jeffrey to eschew political disputation with the *Quarterly*. At the same time he failed to comment further on the review of Turgot he had planned in late 1809; the demands of 'practical' politics were apparently too great.

The celebrity of the Bullion Committee and the speculation that attended the lengthy delay in the publication of its report inspired in Horner both confidence and renewed interest in questions of political economy. In mid-September, while fretting about the possibility that Government might compound the monetary problem by interfering with the credit policies of the struggling country banks, he told Malthus that the evils of the Bank restriction would soon force a return to convertibility (Doc. 397). Later in the month, while visiting Ireland, he displayed great interest in its political economy (Doc. 398), and upon returning to England renewed his researches into the practical operation of poor law, writing that he planned 'to build a considerable measure' on them (Doc. 400).

The publication of the Bullion Report inevitably occasioned considerable debate among both bullionists and anti-bullionists. Allen provided Horner with intelligence regarding the activities and arguments of his adversaries (Doc. 399), and during October Horner apparently continued to work on his article for the *Review*. Later that month the publication of Huskisson's pamphlet summarizing and attempting to justify the doctrine of the report set the stage for exertions in Parliament. Horner's 'bullion fame' meanwhile reached a climax: Sydney Smith quipped that 'every ounce of him' was 'now worth at the Mint price £3. 17s. 4$\frac{1}{2}$d.'; Brougham unconvincingly expressed himself 'in raptures'.[21] Then, however, several unexpected events led Horner to re-evaluate his tactics.

First, Dugald Stewart offered an opinion of the Bullion Report that was lukewarm at best; then the Governor of the South Sea Company, Bosanquet, denounced it as 'wholly theoretical'. All this placed the bullionists on the defensive, and led Horner

---

19. *Holland's Further Memoirs*, pp. 103–104.
20. HHDB.
21. Smith to Lady Holland, 3 Nov. 1810, *Smith Letters*, i. 191.

very cautiously to solicit further comment from his old professor and to resume his own researches (Docs 401–403).[22] Then two political developments, one foreign, one domestic, stole the thunder of the report. Encouraging news from the Peninsula set London ablaze. Nobody was more excited than Holland and his circle, and in mid-November Horner wrote a memorandum for the Spanish 'patriots' on the English law of gaol delivery.[23] Thereafter he represented the Spanish war as 'the cause of European liberties', displaying renewed interest in the deliberations of the Cortes, and at length resurrecting the curious Whig interpretation of the Peninsular War he had advanced in 1808 (Docs 404, 405, and 412).

If victories in the Peninsula diminished the prominence of the bullion question, the report that George III was suffering another bout of mental derangement obscured it completely. Indeed Horner thought of little else during November and December 1810; his correspondence abounds with speculations about the King, the Prince of Wales, the prospect of a Whig Ministry, and Perceval's scheme for a restricted Regency (Docs 400, 402, 403, 407, 408, and 410). But the Regency crisis also offered him a splendid opportunity to score political points; so he decided to abandon the treatise he had promised Jeffrey in favour of bullionist articles from Ricardo and Malthus, and, postponing further debate on bullion in the Commons, to deliver instead a major speech displaying his devotion to constitutional whiggery.

On 3 December 1810 Horner told Jeffrey that, while Ricardo had declined his invitation to contribute to the *Review*, Malthus, who essentially agreed with his own position, had accepted (Doc. 404). Thus, placing the bullion question on the back-burner and entrusting the *Review*'s line to a friendly and famous party, Horner turned with Allen to research on the Regency question (Doc. 408)[24] and on 20 December delivered one of his most important orations in the House of Commons.

Horner's speech on the proposed Regency contended that the Government's bill threatened to usurp 'the whole of the sovereign power in all its branches' and drew a clear distinction between the principle of 'assuming the royal power' and that of 'conferring it'. Leaning heavily on the historical precedents afforded by the reigns of Henry III and Henry VI, he represented the issue to be a simple choice between the constitutional precedent of 1688 (an address to the Prince), 'which had been stamped with the sanction of an approving posterity', and that of 1788 (a Regency bill), 'which at the time and ever since had been condemned by high parliamentary authorities, and which was liable to the strongest objections both from express laws and from constitutional principles'.[25]

The older members of the House recalled a similar interpretation. For while Horner stopped short of advancing the rights of the Prince of Wales, he otherwise embraced the essential tenets of Fox's 1788 position. Furthermore, he prudently avoided direct reference to Pitt and Fox, restricting his remarks to matters of constitutional law and dwelling on the principles that had guided the patriots of 1688. The speech made quite an impression. Jeffrey reported much favourable

22. See also Chitnis, pp. 121–4.
23. BLPES viii. 71–3. See also Allen to Horner, [17 and 21 Nov.], and Horner to Allen, [21 Nov.], BLPES iv. 323–8.
24. See also *Lady Holland's Journal*, ii. 280, Horner to Allen, 10 and 15 Dec., BL Add. MSS 52180, and Horner to Grey, 24 Nov. 1810, Grey MSS, Durham University.
25. *Horner*, ii. 493–507.

comment in Edinburgh, and Brougham observed that it was 'full of instruction and sound argument, admirably delivered'. Cobbett, who at the time was confined in Newgate, believed that it 'was one of the most important of the whole' debate and applied to Horner for a draft.[26]

Thereafter, Horner postponed the parliamentary debate on the Bullion Report for yet another four months. His decision to delay was probably influenced by the persistence of an uncongenial political climate. For the Regency crisis continued to divert attention during early 1811, especially among the Whig leadership. Sydney Smith reported in late January:

> Never was such a ferment as Pall Mall and Holland House is in! John Allen, wild and staring, – Antonio [Lady Holland's page] and Thomas the porter, worked off their legs, – Lord Lauderdale sleeps with his clothes on, and a pen full of ink close to his bedside, with a string tied on the wrist of his secretary in the next room – Expresses arriving at Pall Mall every ten minutes from the House of Commons, and the Whig nobility and commonalty dropping in at all hours to dinner or supper![27]

The prospect of a Regency also inspired a good deal of anxious discussion about Cabinet arrangements among the hopeful Whigs. Especially disconcerting was Grey's refusal to come up to London, which alienated the Foxite rank and file no less than the Prince of Wales (Doc. 413), and Grenville's renewed interest in union with Canning, which excited outrage among Fox's oldest friends and threatened the very existence of the Whig coalition (Docs 414–15). Through it all Horner remained politically dormant. He flattered Grey most hypocritically in a letter to Sydney Smith, whom he knew to be intimate with Lady Grey;[28] but he failed to appear at Holland House for the first six weeks of 1811,[29] and in late January he hesitated only briefly before declining Grenville's premature offer of a secretaryship of the Treasury (Docs 415 n. 1 and 417).[30]

Horner's decision to delay the Bullion debate also reflected the desirability of first exploiting printed propaganda. Ricardo had published his *Reply to Bosanquet* in late 1810; Huskisson, probably with Horner's knowledge and perhaps with his assistance, was writing an article for the *Quarterly*; and Malthus was composing his for the *Edinburgh*. Horner sought to obscure the arguments of adversaries and to place himself on firm middle ground by co-ordinating attacks on the Bank restriction from both right and left, and by all appearances he hoped to promote a doctrinal dispute between Ricardo, who clung to his extreme bullionism, and Malthus, who felt that purely commercial considerations might well explain the monetary dilemma. Cer-

---

26. *Ibid.*, ii. 53n, quoting Jeffrey's report of Brougham's remarks to Horner, 14 [?4] Jan. 1811, and Cobbett to Horner, 30 Dec. 1810, *ibid.*, ii. 45–6.

27. Smith to Lady Grey, 24 Jan., *Smith Letters*, i. 202; see also Smith to Lady Holland, 24 Jan. 1811, *ibid.*, i. 203.

28. Smith to Lady Grey, 13 Jan. 1811, *ibid.*, i. 201, quoting a passage from a recent letter from Horner.

29. Among Lady Holland's dinner book entries of 1811, Horner's name first appears on 14 Feb. Thereafter, until after the Commons' debates in May, his name appears only once more, on 28 Feb. (HHDB).

30. Horner to Murray, 30 Jan. 1811, BLPES, v. 15–16, reveals that Abercromby was offered the secretaryship jointly with him and Brougham an undersecretaryship at the Foreign Office.

tainly he attempted with some success to influence the tone and content of Malthus's article, while simultaneously encouraging Jeffrey to write supporting reviews (Docs 411–12).[31]

Delay was also recommended by the fact that the exchanges were going Horner's way. Depreciation manifested itself very strikingly during the first months of 1811, especially after late February when he left for the circuit, and in mid-March, when the value of the dollar rose substantially on the exchanges, he concluded that personal interest might convert many Britons to the 'Bullion heresy' (Doc. 419).

All the while Horner gathered financial data with an eye to his forthcoming speech; and in early April, when he returned from the circuit, everything was in place. The political furore occasioned by the Regency debates had subsided. The exchanges remained unfavourable. Talk of depreciation was rampant. Huskisson had published his article in the *Quarterly*. And the debate between bullionists and anti-bullionists had been eclipsed by the doctrinal dispute among bullionists that Horner had apparently promoted.

Malthus's article in the *Edinburgh*, reviewing Ricardo's *High Price of Bullion* and *Reply to Bosanquet* along with the publications of Mushet, Blake, Huskisson, and Bosanquet, had appeared in February. Edited and influenced by Horner, it challenged Ricardo's extreme bullionist position and suggested that the exportation of gold and silver might be merely the effect of commercial causes. Now, in early April, Ricardo published the fourth edition of his *High Price of Bullion* and answered Malthus in an appendix, arguing that the flight of coin was the cause, not the effect, of the unfavourable balance.

Everything suggests that Horner sought to delay the debate until Ricardo's pamphlet appeared. He procured and read it immediately after it was published, and delighting in the public response to the dispute between Ricardo and Malthus promptly gave notice that he would bring on the debate in the Commons. While leaning towards Ricardo, he saw important political benefits in the position adopted by Malthus. For it blunted Ricardo's attack on the Bank, focused attention on the commercial policy of the British Government, and tended to please both bullionists and anti-bullionists. Malthus's doctrine, moreover, drove home a point of likely political advantage: it suggested that the combined effects of depreciation and British commercial policy were to the disadvantage of the domestic producers of corn. After reading the article Horner congratulated Malthus, sent him an historical account of British imports of corn, and observed that the depreciation of money had acted as a 'bounty upon importation'. A doctrinal dispute between men who essentially agreed with the recommendations of the Bullion Committee, he felt, was really trifling; the truth of the matter was somewhere between the two points of view (Doc. 420).[32]

On 5 April, when Horner at last gave notice in the Commons of an intention to bring on his motion, he observed that a postponement had been recommended by his opponents' claim that the monetary problem was of a temporary nature, that 'the interval which had . . . been suffered to elapse would be far from proving productive of any injurious consequences to the discussion', and that indeed the rise in the price of the dollar 'tended to confirm the doctrines of the Report'. Rose reproached him

31. See also *Malthus*, p. 198.
32. See also *ibid.*, pp. 202–207.

for his long delay in introducing the resolutions, and Perceval, unwittingly acknowledging the success of Horner's tactics, observed that the Bullion Report and the agitation produced by the delay in broaching the question in Parliament had occasioned a *'greater degree of public mischief and public calamity than any measure which he ever remembered'.*[33]

Three days later Horner informed the House of the substance of his resolutions and distributed a statement of pertinent facts.[34] Almost immediately afterwards he left London with Whishaw to spend a few days with Malthus at the East India College.[35] Unfortunately there is no record of their discussions, but the fact that they should have conferred together on the eve of Horner's bullionist offensive in the Commons is surely not coincidental.[36]

The influence of Malthus or, perhaps more accurately, Horner's exploitation of him, is an interesting sidelight on the bullion debates of 1811. Upon returning to London, Horner reread the first three chapters of the *Wealth of Nations* and made a number of notes that accord with Malthus's eclectic doctrine (Doc. 421). His opening speech in the Commons sought to strike a balance between the interpretations of Malthus and Ricardo. And he returned to Hertfordshire for further discussions immediately after the conclusion of the debates.[37]

In the weeks that preceded Horner's long-awaited motion, Vansittart distributed among the House the resolutions he would introduce in the event that Horner's were rejected. Wanting 'to have a concise counter statement of facts in the hands of members before the debate', Horner in turn printed and distributed proposed amendments to Vansittart's resolutions (Doc. 424). The circulation of the opposing points of view generated much discussion, both in and out of Parliament, and Cobbett, correctly perceiving that political contrivance was causing Horner to hedge on a number of essential points, observed: 'Here is fire against fire, you see. *Bang* for *bang*, except that Mr Vansittart returns one more shot than he receives.'[38]

On 6 May 1811 Horner moved sixteen resolutions. The first eight outlined the law and traditional monetary policy; the following seven assigned the monetary dilemma to departures from that law and policy; and the last called for the repeal of the Bank Restriction Act within two years, war or no war.[39]

33. PR xix. 873–4; *Horner*, ii. 62–3.
34. *Examiner*, 14 Apr. 1811; see also *Horner*, ii. 64–5.
35. Horner to Allen, [13 Apr. 1811], BLPES v. 30–31.
36. This view seems further strengthened by the discovery in the Malthus Archive at Kanto Gakuen University of the draft of an incomplete and unpublished essay on the doctrine of exchanges. Although intended to cover the Commons' debate as well as Ricardo's 'Observations' on Malthus's February 1811 article, the first part is lacking, which suggests that the rest was composed during the preceding holidays and at or about the time of Horner's visit. It was no doubt destined for the *ER* but overtaken partly by events and partly, perhaps, by a subsequent meeting with Ricardo. (See the forthcoming edition from the Malthus Archive of *Selected Papers of T.R. Malthus*.)
37. Malthus to Horner, 12 May 1811, *Horner*, ii. 69.
38. PR xix. 1061 (1 May 1811).
39. Horner's ninth resolution stated that Parliament had intended the 1797 suspension of cash payments to be temporary. The tenth declared that 'for a considerable period of time' the Bank's promissory notes appeared to hold an actual value 'considerably less than what is established by the laws of the realm to be the legal tender in payment of any money contract or stipulation'. The eleventh attributed the depreciation of the Bank's promissory notes and the paper of country banks to an over-issue arising 'from the want of

Horner's accompanying speech (Doc. 423), which was three hours in length, was moderate, informative, and persuasive. He carefully dissociated himself from the extremes of opinion on both sides of the question, especially from Ricardo, Parnell, and others who attacked the institutional status of the Bank, from the advocates of an exclusive paper standard, and from those who favoured a strict metallic standard. His complaint was with the policies of the present Bank directors, which flew in the face of the time-honoured views of the 'ablest and most practical statesmen' of former times, and with 'the merchants of the present day' who, unlike the 'old capitalists', failed to realize that their interests were dependent on the commercial credit of the nation.

Much of Horner's rhetoric related the depreciation arising from an unguarded standard to the rights of property. The policies of the Bank not only compromised 'that rank and station which property confers', but also attacked the sanctity of all contracts and injured all creditors, annuitants, and persons on fixed incomes. And while attributing the high price of bullion primarily to an over-issue of Bank paper, he exploited Malthus's theory of 'collateral causes' to broach British grain policy. In real terms, the 'great and paramount standard of value was corn', he argued, and the price of domestic grain had followed that of Bank paper, rising in an inflationary economy without benefit to landowners or tenants, and destroying the protections inherent in even the 1804 tariff on foreign grain.

Horner was answered by Rose, whose speech rivalled his own in length, and, after others had spoken, the debate was adjourned at half past one in the morning. It was resumed next day and continued on 8 and 9 May. At length Horner replied and his resolutions were put to the vote. The first division, which addressed the first fifteen resolutions, was lost by 75 votes to 151. The second, which was on the crucial final resolution, was discouraged by Ponsonby and Tierney, but Horner persisted in the face of their protests and lost the resolution for a resumption of cash payments within two years by a vote of 45 to 180. On 13 May Vansittart introduced counter-resolutions denying that the restriction of cash payments had anything to do with the unfavourable rate of exchange and proposing that the Bank Restriction Act be continued until six months after the conclusion of a definitive peace. The ensuing debate went on for two days. Horner spoke briefly on the 15th and, reversing a decision he had made five days earlier, proposed his amendments. After both these

that check and control on the issues of the Bank of England, which existed before the suspension of cash payments'. The twelfth stated the appearance of a long-standing and extraordinary unfavourable exchange between Britain and foreign countries. The thirteenth, while acknowledging that the unfavourable exchange had been influenced by adverse commercial circumstances and large military expenditures, laid primary responsibility on 'the depreciation which has taken place in the relative value of the currency of this country, as compared with the money of foreign countries'. The fourteenth declared the duty of the Directors of the Bank 'to advert to the state of the foreign exchanges, as well as to the price of bullion, with a view to regulate the amount of their issues'. The fifteenth declared convertibility upon demand to be 'the only certain and adequate security . . . against an excess of paper currency, and for maintaining the relative value of the circulating medium of the realm'. The sixteenth declared that 'it is expedient to amend the act, which suspends the cash payments of the Bank, by altering the time, till which the suspension shall continue, from six months after the ratification of a definitive treaty of peace, to that of two years from the present time'. (AR liii (1811), 295-7.)

and Tierney's had been rejected, Vansittart's resolutions were agreed (Doc. 424).[40]

British political history records few examples of an utterly unsuccessful campaign accruing so fully to the personal advantage of an MP. The Whig rank and file lent but modest support to Horner's resolutions, and indeed the division list is notable for the absence of Opposition members; yet afterwards no one in the Commons enjoyed a loftier reputation among the Whig leaders than Horner. To Russell Square, where his father had leased a house, came hordes of well-wishers. 'This man is destined to be the Minister of England', predicted George Wilson. Others quite agreed. Frances Horner recalled the large number of congratulatory letters received by her father, the many compliments paid her mother, and the 'high station' her brother held in the country. Francis, she wrote, was 'regarded as one of the first men of the age, and destined all believed, to be one day Minister of the country'.[41]

This extraordinary development is easily explained. Horner had planned and executed his campaign very shrewdly. While appealing to, or navigating around, discernible prejudices among Foxites, Grenvillites, Fitzwilliams, and 'radicals', he had succeeded in maintaining his independence in the perception of the nation. He had secured a sympathetic parliamentary committee and managed it magnificently. He had anchored his case on strong evidence. He had exploited the House's love of tradition, holding out a return to tried and true ways remedying a problem that damaged private interests. He had represented himself as a defender of the rights of property. He had appealed to the interests of creditors, the producers of domestic grain, and the commercial community. He had encouraged, co-ordinated, and exploited a well-timed paper propaganda by men of high repute. He had delayed bringing on the debate to great advantage. And finally, in league with eminent commercial members, the right-leaning Canning, the centrist Thornton, and a number of left-leaning Whigs, he had displayed, as Leonard Horner recalled, 'the extent of his knowledge, his eloquence and his inflexible integrity' in a speech that absolutely dazzled the House.[42]

The *Annual Register* found Horner's speech of 6 May 'elaborate, and very intelligent'. The *Gentleman's Magazine* described it as 'distinguished, as much by its eloquence as extensive knowledge of the subject'. The *Political Register* was less complimentary, labelling Horner 'a *lawyer* and a *placeman* at the same time', assigning his delay in bringing on the debate to political contrivance, and rightly observing that he had found the effect of the Bank restriction on the national debt 'too tender to touch'. But Cobbett was forced to voice begrudging approval. Horner, he remarked with some justification:

40. *Hansard*, xix. 833–1012, 1020–28, and 1151–69; xx. 1–128, 134–46, and 150–76.
41. Byrne Memoirs, pp. 105 and 132–4. Fontana, pp. 121–5, by contrast describes Horner's lack of support from the 'Whig grandees' as a 'desertion' attributable to his inopportune timing of the discussion, and emphasizes, rather, the success of Rose and Vansittart in representing him and his supporters as 'a clique of blundering philosophers' whose views had no 'practical relevance'. Apparently believing therefore that Horner's objective had been to 'rally the Whigs . . . around a set of proposals the political implication of which remained more than a little obscure', she concludes that the episode 'reveals the limitations in Horner's political performance', and that while by the time of his death he had 'undoubtedly acquired a solid reputation', that 'has to be accounted for in terms of his "Scottish" accomplishments rather than in terms of his political talents'.
42. Byrne Memoirs, p. 133.

made use of no one argument that was not used by me *nearly seven years ago*, in support of a proposition the same as that which he now brought forward, and for maintaining which I was abused like a pickpocket, and PAINE had before, for asserting the same, mixed with a little political fun, been burnt in effigy all over this *thinking* country.[43]

The broad appeal of Horner's speech was acknowledged by Abercromby and Malthus. Abercromby observed that, defeat or no defeat, 'all parties in the House', but especially those 'most acquainted with his talents', admired the oration. Malthus told him that his speeches of both 6 and 9 May 'far exceeded what possibly could have been expected from the subject' and wondered how he 'could contrive to treat a question, necessarily involving so many dry details, in a manner which seems to have so completely commanded the attention of your hearers'. Indeed, Malthus felt that he had convinced many who nevertheless voted against his resolutions.[44]

There was much truth in Malthus's assessment; Horner and his colleagues had undoubtedly shaken confidence in British monetary policy. But the Government bench had put forward a plausible defence and secured a large majority in the debates, which, as a writer for the *Annual Register* observed, had merely underlined that the theory of money was 'yet crude and undetermined'.[45] A vacuum therefore existed that demanded further enlightenment from Horner, while mounting commercial distress, especially in the north of England, gave the bullionists much reason for optimism.

Horner's friends encouraged him to keep up the fight, and initially he considered further literary exertions. Many important facets of monetary theory remained speculative, he told Murray; perhaps he would write a pamphlet. Yet he neglected to follow up. He had accomplished his personal objectives; no man among the Opposition bench now enjoyed greater stature in the House. He also thought the conclusions of the Bullion Committee had been 'established unanswerably', and that it was still only a matter of time before the continuing effects of depreciation would force Government to restore convertibility. There was, therefore, little to be gained, and perhaps much to be lost, by engaging in an extended battle of words with the likes of Rose (Docs 424, 425, and 427).

So Horner, relieved that he had 'at last got rid of bullion', published nothing, not even his recent celebrated speeches, and concluded that the best course was to await another opportunity to repeat his former arguments. Such a decision amounted to an abdication of leadership; and shortly after the bullion debates, when Lord King posted a letter to his tenants demanding rents either in specie or in its current paper equivalent, Horner began to lose control of his cause.

Horner's role in King's scheme is unclear. Perhaps he conceived it. King's letter to his tenants, after all, was nothing more than a practical application of the principal thrust of Horner's case against the Bank restriction; there was a 'general persuasion' in the House, Horner triumphantly told his father (Doc. 424), 'that something of importance to every man's own private concerns . . . was involved'.

---

43. *AR* liii (1811), 43; *Gentleman's Magazine*, lxxxi (pt 1, June), 570; *PR* xix. 1139 (8 May) and 1158 (11 May), and xx. 17 (6 July).
44. Byrne Memoirs, pp. 133–4; Malthus to Horner, 12 May 1811, *Horner*, ii. 69.
45. *AR* liii (1811), 43.

More likely, though, King had conceived the idea and sought Horner's advice. Whatever the case, King's letter attempted to promote and exploit the 'general persuasion' of the House, and Horner was aware of it from the first. Indeed, King almost certainly relied on him for legal advice, and Horner, apparently in league with Lauderdale, contributed to the tables depicting a progressive depreciation of Bank paper that King published in the summer (Doc. 431).

Horner probably involved Ricardo and Malthus in the bullionist ploy to some extent. He visited Malthus about the time King posted his letter; in June he and Ricardo took their seats on the board of the London Geological Society and moved, at least, towards social intercourse; and Malthus, inviting Ricardo to Hertfordshire on 16 June, suggested that 'perhaps Horner might be able to meet you'.[46] Although there is no reason to believe that such a meeting took place, Horner was certainly communicating with Ricardo and Malthus at the same time he was collaborating with King, and one may be sure that the subject entered into their discussions.

King's letter to his tenants seemed like a capital idea until Stanhope countered the conspirators by introducing a bill that sought to deny legal remedy to creditors. Horner happened to be in the House of Lords when Stanhope proposed his bill, and he immediately took fright, rightly perceiving that the very strength of King's claim, and the likely favourable result of litigation in chancery, might force Government to declare Bank notes legal tender. He encouraged King to desist, appealed to Grenville to contest the principle underlying Stanhope's bill, and probably inspired two separate protests entered in the Lords on 2 July 1811. One protest, deploring the compulsory circulation of a paper currency, was signed by Grey, Grenville, Lansdowne, King, Lauderdale, Cowper, Essex, and Jersey; the other, entered by Holland alone, went much further, representing the resumption of cash payments as 'the only measure which can cure the inconveniences already felt'.[47]

Stanhope's bill threw the bullionists on the defensive; the protests in the Lords, signed by nobody but leading members of Opposition, attached the stigma of political partisanship to their position; and Horner himself was soon immobilized by a recurrence of his 'old complaint'. Beset by a weak stomach, swollen ankles, coughing, and breathlessness, he took refuge at Torquay during August and September, at Tunbridge Wells and at Lord Robert Spencer's place in Woolbeding during October, and at Eden Farm in November, where Auckland found him 'uninformed ... respecting the true state and circumstances of the public world'.[48]

Auckland exaggerated. Horner was ill, to be sure, and his removal from London of course diminished his usual command of political intelligence. But his correspondence of the autumn of 1811 contains informed comment on Spanish affairs and on British policy towards Spain's revolted colonies (Docs 435, 438, and 443). He also wrote at some length on the growing controversy inspired by the competing

---

46. Malthus to Horner, 12 May, Horner, ii. 69, and to Ricardo, 16 June 1811, Ricardo, vi. 23.
47. Docs 430–32; and PR xx. 26–7 (6 July 1811), noting that Holland 'proceeds upon the notion of Mr HORNER and the Bullion Committee' and again criticizing the thesis of excessive paper on the ground that it failed to consider the dividends payable on the national debt.
48. Byrne Memoirs, p. 135; Auckland to Grenville, 12 Nov. 1811, Dropmore MSS, x. 179.

educational philosophies of the National Society and the Royal Lancasterian Institution, to which he had been admitted a member in May (Docs 448 and 453). But his principal interest, as always, was domestic politics, in particular Carlton House and the Catholic question (Docs 429, 433, 435, 438, 439, 442, and 445).

There was also a discernible attempt to keep his options open among the feuding Whigs. Whitbread's relations with Grey and Grenville had deteriorated badly during the previous year, but the brewer remained influential among the Foxite rank and file, and Horner corresponded with him on political strategy in both September and October (Docs 442 and 445). But he sought to please the aristocratic leaders of the party as well. In November a loving memoir of Fox written by his former private secretary initially earned Horner's praise, notwithstanding the author's assertion that the 'Ministry of All the Talents' had abandoned Fox's principles after his death. His opinion of the book changed dramatically, however, when he learned that it displeased a number of leading Foxites. After consulting with Lord John Townshend and Lady Holland, he posted Jeffrey a lengthy analysis of both the author and his book but failed to inspire the negative review he sought (Docs 446–7).

Although increasing numbers of British banks were failing and bankruptcies mounting throughout the country, Horner displayed only passing interest in monetary policy during the last months of 1811. In August he advised Seymour and his brother on the economic and legal viability of a sliding scale of rents reflecting the average market price of gold and corn (Doc. 434), and in November he wrote two interesting letters in response to Samuel Parr's queries respecting the relative value of money during the reign of Elizabeth (Docs 452–3). A letter he wrote to Reddie in October (Doc. 444), however, confirms that he was averse to a resumption of the campaign against the Bank restriction and quite content to await future developments.

Later developments were not encouraging. In November 1811 Grenville insisted that King proceed with litigation against one of his tenants, a Bank director who steadfastly refused to pay his rents in specie. Horner thought Grenville's point of view ridiculous. The only result of a legal victory for King would be a Government decision to resurrect Stanhope's bill, and legislation establishing Bank paper as legal tender might well be fatal to the public interest (Doc. 448). He was also concerned about the effect of King's lawsuit on the delicate political alliance he had forged against the Bank restriction. Aware of Grenville's unpopularity among the Foxite wing of Opposition, he stressed to Holland the prudence of keeping secret Grenville's role in the matter. Indeed, he thought it wise to promote the myth that King acted alone, and to hide the fact of disagreement within the bullionist ranks (Doc. 449).

The thrust of Horner's cause had thus changed from persuasion to prevarication when King decided to proceed in chancery, and that unhappy shift in tactics was followed in late December by an unanticipated rise in the rate of exchange with the Continent. Ricardo attempted to explain it away, but the improved status of sterling and the threat imposed by King's controversial legal claim hardly recommended a resumption of active exertions against the Bank restriction.[49]

49. MC, 2 Jan. 1812; Ricardo to Horner, 4 Jan. 1812, *Ricardo*, vi. 78–81.

Still hopeful that the Regent would bring in a Whig Government (Doc. 453), a yet sickly Horner attempted to resume his parliamentary activities in January 1812. Stripped of the bullion question and anxious about the uncertain result of Regency politics, he gravitated towards safe ground, aligning himself with Romilly. On the 9th he presented a petition on behalf of debtors gaoled in the Isle of Man, and on the 29th he spoke briefly on the inquisitorial powers of the Commons in criminal proceedings. Although he did not participate in the debate of 5 February on Catholic relief, he regarded the strong minority vote and the absence of 'Protestant rancour' as promising signs (Doc. 458). On 11 February he condemned Government for hamstringing the civil list revenue committee, and on 17 March he spoke 'at considerable length' on a bill extending the provisions of the Bank Restriction Act to Ireland.[50] Meanwhile he joined Romilly on a committee to inquire into the causes of delayed decisions in chancery.[51]

Horner was biding his time, cautiously hovering on the periphery of politics during a period of great uncertainty. Yet he remained quite ill, and in late February he retreated to his chambers. There he remained until mid-March, when he was thrown into a fit of despondency. A letter apparently written on the 16th (Doc. 460) suggests that his low spirits were influenced by the failure of Wellesley's recent negotiation with Grey and Grenville. But he was more upset with the state of the Opposition bench in the Commons. There was no leader, and he felt himself 'trimming'. Ponsonby and Tierney were inefficient; Whitbread went his own way; Ward and William Lamb were courting the 'Antijacobin dogmatism' of Canning; Brougham was 'giving himself over to Burdett and the Jacobins'. One could no longer pursue a middle course in politics, he complained.

Underlying these remonstrances was the fact that Horner thought his political plans were falling apart. He had cast his lot with Grey and Holland, but they were immobilized by disagreements within the Whig coalition, and Grenville's foolish criticism of Wellington and the conduct of the Peninsular War occasioned great embarrassment (Doc. 461). Canning was exploiting the resulting inertia and indeed making inroads among the Opposition bench. Brougham's growing political celebrity, however, was of more immediate concern.

As recently as 22 January Horner had commented without rancour on Brougham's talents and growing stature in the Commons (Doc. 456), but those remarks were made before he was fully aware of the magnitude of his old rival's planned parliamentary offensive against the Orders in Council. The fog lifted very shortly. The February 1812 number of the *Review* contained Brougham's opening salvo, an article entitled 'Disputes with America' that questioned the justice of British commercial policy and warned of 'the ruinous consequences of an American war'. Then, on 3 March, when Brougham moved for a committee to consider 'the present state of commerce and manufactures', he left no doubt that he planned an all-out assault. Indeed, on the 16th, when Horner was complaining about his leftward leanings, Brougham's name was on everyone's lips, and rumours were flying in London's clubs and galleries about the Ministry's fears of faltering support among commercial members.[52]

50. *Horner*, ii. 94. Unfortunately *Hansard* gives only a dozen lines to this speech.
51. *Romilly*, iii. 29–31.
52. New, pp. 60–61.

Horner had ample reason to be depressed. On 1 February 1810, when he first raised the bullion question in the Commons, he had conjectured that both an overabundance of Bank paper and the 'new circumstances' of Britain's foreign trade might account for the high price of gold. By 'new circumstances' he had meant the constraining influence of the Orders in Council, the licensing system in particular, and the commercial warfare with France and the United States. Followed in debate by Baring and Marryat, both of whom emphasized only commercial factors that might influence the price of bullion, he had sought initially to inspire a measure of support among the nation's capitalists. But as chairman of the Bullion Committee he had found it necessary to narrow his doctrine. Thornton and Huskisson, as supporters of the Orders in Council, presumably opposed arguments relating the price of bullion to the 'new circumstances' of trade. The same must have been true of those members of the Committee who subscribed to Ricardo's extreme bullionist position, notably Parnell. And the leading opponents of Horner's position out-of-doors were prominent capitalists who feared a diminution in the prosperous, if treacherous, export trade. Consequently the Bullion Report virtually ignored the commercial interpretation of the monetary dilemma to which Horner had initially assigned no less importance than a supposed over-supply of Bank notes.

Shortly after the Bullion Report was submitted to the Commons in June 1810, Britain had begun to suffer severe economic dislocation as a result of intensified commercial warfare with the United States and France, and the crisis had worsened after the promulgation of the American Non-Importation Act in March 1811. Observing growing unrest among the commercial classes, Horner had been troubled by his earlier sacrifice to political expediency, and had looked most favourably on Malthus's doctrine of 'collateral causes', which related the high price of bullion to the 'new circumstances' of foreign trade. Malthus's arguments, however, were advanced quite late in the game, and then only through the medium of the *Edinburgh Review*. Malthus, moreover, did not strike directly at British commercial policy, but instead merely suggested that commercial factors might account for the depreciation of money, and neither Horner nor any of his allies had sought actively to counter the opinion among Britain's capitalists that a depreciated standard had a beneficial effect on the export trade.

Hence commercial policy had emerged in the bullion debates as an ancillary consideration, as a mere component of the attack on monetary policy. Horner's speech of 6 May 1811 mentioned the superior wisdom of the 'old capitalists', and deplored the short-sighted opinions of the new ones, but his doctrine had found its greatest supporters among the landed interest.

Brougham's motion of 3 March 1812 made it quite clear that he was seeking to reverse the thrust of Horner's campaign against the Bank restriction. In effect he embraced Malthus's doctrine of 'collateral causes', pointing to commercial policy rather than to monetary policy as the source of the nation's ills. His motion for inquiry made particular reference to the effects of Britain's licence trade, thereby exploiting an issue raised by Horner in January 1808 and again in February 1810. He also repeated Horner's earlier remonstrance that Government had failed to open South American markets and represented the depreciation of money as an effect of ill-conceived commercial policy.

Brougham was joined by some of the same commercial members who had initially supported Horner's earlier attack on the Bank restriction; indeed, Alexander Baring was his principal collaborator. But perhaps the most depressing facet of Brougham's campaign was the revelation that he was making common cause with the merchant classes, anchoring his campaign on a flood of petitions to Parliament, and thus seeking to mobilize the 'intelligence and activity of the middle classes' of which Horner had written in January 1810.[53]

Ill and despondent, Horner went to Bath in March, but found no respite. For there he learned of the revival of Stanhope's bill, and of the apparent determination of Government to make Bank paper legal tender (Doc. 461). He grew still more despondent upon learning of the probable dissolution of Parliament in the summer. Carrington, it appears, had already told him that his seat at Wendover could not be guaranteed. So, speculating that he was to be turned out, he unhappily resolved (Doc. 462) to return to his original plan of life – to stay out of Parliament 'till I have done something for myself in the law'. Still quite unwell, he returned to London and on 20 April unsuccessfully opposed the Government's amended version of Stanhope's bill in a lengthy but ill-reported speech.

Stanhope's bill gave the Bank of England a virtual free hand, thereby constituting the political rout of Horner's bullionist position. Yet, as Horner's fortunes sank, those of Canning and Brougham rose. On 24 April Horner noted that Canning had given notice of a motion for Catholic relief without any previous communication with Opposition leaders, and observed that the Whigs no longer had any option but to follow his lead (Doc. 463). Four days later Brougham scored a major triumph when Government, besieged by petitions against the Orders in Council, consented to an inquiry. Next day Brougham, Baring, Perceval, and James Stephen began to examine witnesses.

The inquiry was to continue indefinitely 'from day to day', and with Brougham on centre stage, his triumph might well be long drawn out. Horner's political prospects, by contrast, were woeful. His *cause célèbre*, the bullion question, was no longer a viable issue of state. His long-standing attempt to follow a middle course in politics had left him mired hopelessly in the bog of 'trimming' measures championed by Ponsonby and Tierney. He was, in fact, likely to be turned out of Parliament, and meanwhile Brougham, employing his own arguments to great advantage, and Canning, stealing the only issue of state on which the Whigs agreed, seemed to be dividing the world between them. At this juncture, however, Horner apparently learned, perhaps from Allen at the meeting of the 'King of Clubs' on 27 April, that the Grenvilles might be willing to return him to Parliament in the event that Carrington denied him Wendover.[54]

On 7 May Creevey moved resolutions to reduce and fix at a definite sum the large incomes Buckingham and Camden received as Tellers of the Exchequer. After the

---

53. *Hansard*, xxi. 1092ff. See also New, pp. 61–2, and Taylor, pp. 341–3.
54. Horner's letter to his brother of 5 Apr. 1812 (Doc. 462) confirms that he had been already informed of the likely loss of his seat. Carrington had presumably communicated his intentions to his ally Grenville as well, and in that case Tom Grenville's rare appearances at Holland House on 1 and 8 Apr. (HHDB) might be significant. Horner returned from Bath around the 18th, Allen dined at the 'King of Clubs' on the 27th (*idem*), and it is very likely that Horner, who seldom missed a meeting, dined with him.

motion had been resisted by the Government bench and an amendment moved for a committee, Horner rose and delivered an extraordinary speech. 'No committee was necessary to prove what was an undoubted right', he observed. Indeed, nothing

> could be so clear, as that in all regulations for economical purposes, vested rights must be sacredly protected. . . . He was prepared to go as far in regulations which had economy for their object as any man; but in doing so, the rights of those having vested interests in such offices must be kept sacred. The property of the state was not to be protected at the expense of private property. . . . If this principle were once broken through by the House, temptation would grow upon them, and there would be no end to it. He reminded the House that such an interference had been one of the steps, taken by those frenzied politicians in a neighbouring country, to whom it was to be attributed, that that country had so long been the prey to anarchy, and every other description of horrors.[55]

Such remarks represented a considerable clarification, if not a reversal, of Horner's earlier view of sinecure places, and his reference to the excesses of revolutionary France was a tactic he ever abhorred in others.

Horner was breaking for daylight, towards the Grenvilles, and there were further remarkable shifts in his political behaviour in the days that followed. After 11 May, when Perceval was assassinated and Canning and Wellesley became major players in a series of complicated attempts to form a Government, Horner became extraordinarily active. He appeared at Holland House with uncommon frequency during May, dining with a variety of important politicians,[56] and he met elsewhere with Canning on at least one occasion (Doc. 465). Whether they discussed a political union cannot be ascertained, but on 22 May, when Wellesley made his offer to the Whigs, Horner emerged as a stout advocate of coalition.[57]

Horner justified his opinion by pointing to Canning's earlier support on the bullion question, to his recent 'manly' behaviour on the Catholic claims, and to a continuing void of leadership among the Opposition bench in the Commons (Doc. 467). But his new-found regard for Canning constituted a monumental change of heart. Hitherto he had been extremely critical, opposing coalition with him vociferously and warning that it would lead to the defection of Whitbread and a considerable portion of the Foxite party in the Commons (Docs 415, 458, and 460).

The explanation, it appears, lay in recent political developments. First, there was no longer a void of leadership among the Whig bench in the Commons. Brougham, Grey's man, was daily eclipsing his colleagues and, supported by Whitbread in his campaign against the Orders in Council, appeared to be forging an alliance between the Foxite left and the commercial classes. Secondly, as exhibited in his speech of 7 May, Horner was moving towards the Grenvilles, apparently looking to one of Buckingham's family boroughs, and at all events convinced that alignment with the Whig right was his only political card. Lastly, Grenville, hoping to check the more numerous Foxite faction in the Commons, had desired coalition with Canning since

55. *Horner*, ii. 94–5.
56. The HHDB notes Horner's presence on 14, 18, 20, 24, 26, 27, 29, and 31 May 1812. He had appeared only five times earlier in the year.
57. *Creevey*, i. 157, noting Horner's presence at Holland House on 24 May among a party that joked about Wellesley becoming 'our new patron'.

1806, and Horner, now regarding the relative parliamentary weakness of the
Grenvillites more sympathetically, had ample reason to reverse his former hostile
opinion of Canning.

Apparently he also attempted to ignore Brougham. The fact that he neglected
even to mention Brougham's celebrated campaign in his correspondence during the
first six months of 1812 is curious, perhaps instructive. So, too, is his failure to
support Brougham in debate; Horner, after all, had been among the earliest critics of
the Orders. But perhaps those omissions had nothing to do with Brougham; for
Canning, whom Horner was courting at the time, was a principal author and long-
standing advocate of the commercial regulations.

Yet Horner's hand was probably at work in the disinterest and rancour that the
Whigs exhibited towards Brougham and his cause. His earlier remark that Brougham
had gone over 'to Burdett and the Jacobins' is surely significant. There was nothing
Jacobinical about Brougham's political behaviour during the first months of 1812,
but most Whig leaders, and especially the Grenvilles, thought otherwise. Tom
Grenville, explaining his failure to support Brougham, expressed a reluctance to be
led by the left,[58] and Grenvillite MPs displayed little interest in the debates and key
divisions on the Orders in Council. The same was true of other leading Whigs. The
Speaker was struck by the vacant seats on the Opposition front bench during an
important division; and Brougham, while failing to mention Horner, reported that
Tierney and many other members of Opposition resented his exertions.[59]

Horner's correspondence of June and July 1812, the crucial months of
Brougham's parliamentary offensive, contains extensive comment on the various
negotiations that resulted at last in the formation of the Liverpool Ministry, the
exclusion of the Whigs, and the political isolation of Canning (Docs 468–72 and
474–5). Those developments, of course, required Horner to repair his bridges. He
accordingly hailed the 'honourable' behaviour of Grey and Grenville in rejecting
office, professed renewed confidence in the aristocratic leaders of the party, and
attempted to dissociate himself from both left and right. Whitbread's reputation, he
maintained, had suffered a great deal in the course of the negotiations for office, and
Canning's unprincipled, self-serving conduct had been deplorable.

Horner's attempt to return to the Whig centre is understandable, but he
displayed incredible hypocrisy when Ward, acting on Horner's own earlier
conclusion that one must choose between Whitbread and Canning, announced his
affiliation with the Canningites. On 3 August Horner wrote to Lansdowne:

> I am much vexed at Ward's conduct, not that I was greatly surprised at it, for he
> has long hankered after Canning, but this fresh instance of change sets upon
> him an indelible character for political inconstancy, which the very excellence
> and honesty of his intentions in politics will be sure to keep up by some further
> change hereafter; for though he has no well settled opinions, he is sure to be
> thrown off from Canning's course some day or other by the duplicity and trick
> which are so favourite a practice with that political leader.[60]

58. T. Grenville to Lady Grenville, 24 Apr. 1812, *Dropmore MSS*, x. 240–41.
59. *Colchester*, ii. 369; Brougham to Allen, 26 Oct. 1812, BL Add. MSS 52178. See also
    Taylor, p. 342.
60. *PH* iv. 280–81.

Horner's other correspondence about Canning's political liabilities and Ward's 'apostasy' (Docs 474–6) is also astonishing, but certainly no more so than his sudden display of affection towards Brougham. His old rival's great triumph came on 23 July 1812, when the Government, backed to the wall, revoked the Orders in Council.[61] It was an impressive victory, followed by an invitation from grateful merchants for Brougham to stand as a Whig candidate for Liverpool; and Horner, aware that Brougham was now a fact of political life, decided that a more reasonable attitude was in order.

Brougham must have been amused to receive Horner's letter of 25 July. It hailed his victory over the Orders in Council as 'unexampled in the modern history of Parliament' and expressed 'delight and pride' at the Liverpool offer. Horner, moreover, wanted to visit Brougham at his family home in the course of a trip to Edinburgh. Brougham responded with 'a most kind letter'; Horner professed deep gratification and revised his itinerary to include a stopover at Brougham Hall.[62]

The attempted *rapprochement* with Brougham, who was in a 'good tone of mind', went well, at least superficially. After several days of reminiscing, Horner travelled with him as far south as Preston, from which Brougham headed for Liverpool and a hot election, while Horner proceeded to London via Bowood, reading the latest number of the *Review* and finding in Brougham's articles on peace and parliamentary reform 'nothing but trash' (Doc. 478).

Horner took a keen interest in the General Election of 1812. Among his papers is a letter from Brougham (Doc. 479), written shortly after his arrival in Liverpool, which contains an optimistic account of the canvass and several remarks on the contest with Canning that he was destined to lose. Apparently Horner's reply has not survived, but among Brougham's published works is a note from Horner expressing surprise and regret at the result of the election.[63] In other correspondence Horner commented, not only on Brougham's failure, but also on the defeats suffered by Romilly, Tierney, Sharp, and other prominent members of Opposition (Docs 480, 482, 483, and 485),[64] and in one letter (Doc. 482) advanced an interesting interpretation of the election results. The Whigs, he reported, had gained in numbers, if not in quality, by their successes in Ireland, and the increased strength of Wellesley and Canning gave their combined parties the balance of power in the Commons.

Horner's correspondence chronicles the course of his own return to Parliament as well. He almost certainly had been told of Grenville's interest in providing for him some months earlier; but matters remained in the air on 11 October when he wrote despondently from Bowood that Carrington would turn him out in favour of a nephew, and that he had 'not money or popularity . . . to obtain a seat in the more regular and desirable way'.[65] Upon returning to London about the 17th, however, he found a letter from Lansdowne confirming that Grenville was attempting to find him a seat, and some two days later a second arrived, assuring him that Grenville

---

61. New, pp. 65–7; Aspinall, p. 25.
62. Horner to Brougham, 25 July, *Brougham*, ii. 23; Horner to Murray, 25 July 1812, BLPES v. 202.
63. Horner to Brougham, 21 Oct. 1812, *Brougham*, ii. 68–9.
64. See also Horner to Romilly, 15 Oct., Romilly to Horner, 18 Oct., and Horner to Holland, 19 Oct. 1812, *Horner*, ii. 116–19.
65. *Ibid.*, ii. 115–16.

was now confident he could deliver his brother's closed borough of St Mawes shortly after the meeting of Parliament.[66]

Although Horner was returned as a member for St Mawes on 17 April 1813, Grenville experienced more difficulty than he had anticipated. Buckingham had some qualms about it, and as late as 17 January remained reluctant to 'hamper himself by taking any engagement, or by entering into any explanation or negotiation with Horner'.[67] Later, when negotiations began, he rejected Horner's request that he be allowed *carte blanche* on matters of political principle. Indeed, on 16 March, when the offer of the seat was finally made, Fremantle, who wrote on Buckingham's behalf, required 'no stipulation or pledge of any kind' but nevertheless insisted that Horner must resign whenever his political views should differ from those of his patron.[68]

That proviso was constraining, even somewhat intimidating, but Horner apparently thought he could collaborate harmoniously with the Grenville party. The Catholic question was a strong adhesive, and the bond was hardly weakened by his new doctrine that equated sinecure places, and Buckingham's tellership more particularly, with the sacred rights of property. Grenville's high regard, however, was the most important consideration. Grenville admired Horner's command of economic philosophy and agreed with him on every major economic issue. He was a bullionist and a free trader who shared Horner's dark view of the corn laws, the property tax, poor law, and the commercial monopoly of the East India Company.[69] Indeed, as a political economist Horner probably had more in common with Grenville than with any other considerable figure within the Whig party, and surely Grenville's earlier offer of a secretaryship of the Treasury figured prominently in his deliberations.

Yet Horner was a Foxite, a man whose political base was at Holland House, and he was fully aware that the instability of the Whig coalition placed him in a position of some delicacy. The Fox–Grenville union was one of men, not measures, and some seven years of political collaboration had failed to cement the bond. Catholic 'Emancipation, a reflective Horner told Lansdowne in the autumn of 1812, was 'the only rallying principle that we have had for a long while' (Doc. 483).

Sources of discord were more numerous. Hitherto Grey and Grenville had navigated around their differences, and Holland, recalling his uncle's concept of political manoeuvre and Grenville's 'honourable conduct' after Fox's death, remained a stout supporter of the coalition. In the event of a schism, however, Horner's hands would be tied; he simply had to follow the lead of Holland House.

The most contentious issues among the Whigs were parliamentary reform and war policy. In the case of the first, Horner was committed to the moderate point of view propounded by Grey and Holland. Grenville disapproved, but Horner knew he could not hedge on reform, come what may. Disagreement on war policy was even more troubling. Grenville and his family wanted Napoleon's head, and for years Bourbon princes had been entertained lavishly at Stowe. The Foxites, however, had displayed on more than one occasion that they were susceptible to knee-

66. Horner to Holland, 19 Oct. 1812, *ibid.*, ii. 118–19.
67. T. Grenville to Grenville, 17 Jan. 1813, *Dropmore MSS*, x. 329.
68. Fremantle to Horner, 16 Mar., *Horner*, ii. 130–31.
69. For Grenville's economic views see *Grenville*, pp. 422, 427, 430, 439, 442, 445–7, 450–51, and 466.

jerk reactions whenever someone mentioned a peace negotiation with the French Emperor. Everything boiled down to fundamental disagreement on wartime goals.

Grey and Grenville attempted to neutralize their differences by advocating a 'husbanding, defensive system' of war policy that paradoxically rejected both an offensive war and a negotiated peace with France. Complemented by a great deal of grumbling about the British campaign in the Iberian Peninsula, their foreign politics did nothing to enhance the popularity of the Whigs. The coalition's leaders had succeeded in keeping the hawks and doves at bay for some time, however, and now the contending factions in the Commons were leaderless.

Earlier the war faction had been led by Windham and Tom Grenville, the peace faction by Whitbread. But Windham had died in 1810, Tom Grenville had stopped attending Parliament regularly, and Whitbread's influence had waned after the 1810 session. Indeed, the 'Mountain' – that curious meeting ground of disgruntled Foxites in the Commons – had lost its identity. Yet Horner saw trouble ahead. Mounting commercial distress at home, British victories in the Peninsula, and reports of French difficulties in Russia began to produce a considerable cleavage in the Whig ranks in late 1812. Whitbread and others on the Foxite left advocated a European settlement recognizing the sovereignty of Napoleon's Government as early as July. Two months later Holland joined Whitbread in calling for Franco-British negotiations based on the independence of Spain. In October the contest between Brougham and Canning at Liverpool revived the Fox–Pitt debate on the war policy of the 1790s, and by the spring of 1813 there was much speculation that the Whig coalition could not survive.[70]

Horner's woefully compromised view of war policy hardly equipped him to fight a successful two-front defensive action within the Whig party. After casting a silent vote for Whitbread's peace resolutions in early 1808, he had executed an abrupt about-face in the summer, arguing somewhat lamely that the 'good changed sides' when the 'risen people' of Spain, like those of France in 1789, sought to deliver themselves from military despotism.

Such a point of view, it appears, had been calculated to strike a balance between the party's doves and hawks, and in fairness to Horner one must concede that it was consistent with Foxite dogma. Virtually everyone except Holland had found the Horner thesis rather Quixotic, however, and the subsequently disappointing performance of the 'universal Spanish nation' had made Horner feel foolish. So in 1810, just before Wellington began to pay real dividends in the Peninsula, he had changed colours yet again, this time agreeing with Grey and Grenville that the British army should be withdrawn. Now, as he contemplated the prospect of becoming the only Foxite sitting for a Grenvillite borough, he was fully aware that, like the Whig leadership, he had no viable war policy.

Horner's response to these threats is interesting. Considering the delicacy of his political position, and perhaps of his health as well,[71] he resolved immediately upon

70. See Taylor, pp. 338–60, for an account of the mounting popularity of peace among the Foxites and the corresponding chagrin of the Grenvilles during late 1812 and early 1813.
71. On 16 Oct. 1812, shortly after he and Horner had parted at Preston, Brougham told Grey (*Brougham*, ii. 64) that Horner had 'no chance of living unless he is kept perfectly quiet'. By all appearances Brougham exaggerated; but after August 1811 Horner's health was never good, and his physicians warned of the dangers of over-exertion.

hearing of Grenville's offer to take 'a very slow, and a very quiet walk for a public life' (Doc. 480). That was to say that he planned to be cautious, to work discreetly to bolster his position within the weak Whig centre, and to dodge disputes whenever possible.

Horner's first priority was to stabilize his crucial connection with Holland House. The first letter he wrote after learning of his likely return for St Mawes was addressed to Holland. Its tone was defensive, and it dodged the question of war and peace altogether. But Horner found it necessary to add a postscript: 'let there be no doubt whatever left of my determination to vote for parliamentary reform, or of the full extent of my democratical tendencies and opinions'. So as to remove lingering doubts, he promptly descended on Kensington, appearing at Lady Holland's dinner table six times in November 1812 alone.[72]

Horner resolved to court Grenville via the medium of political economy. He had displayed little interest in economic issues for well over a year. Yet in November 1812 he was giving extensive advice on the preparation of charts, later published, that depicted the relationship between Bank notes in circulation, the rate of foreign exchanges, and the price of bullion, and in the months that followed, expressing renewed confidence in his monetary doctrine and keeping abreast of fluctuations on the exchanges (Docs 484, 491, and 510). In December 1812 he also expressed enthusiasm for an attack on the property tax, even going so far as to suggest the formation of corresponding committees of respectable Scottish farmers and, perhaps recalling Brougham's successful tactics against the Orders in Council, noting that nothing but a public demonstration could gain the attention of Parliament (Doc. 486).

Horner delivered his first two speeches as a member for St Mawes in mid-June 1813, shortly after visiting Malthus in Brighton.[73] Both of them broached economic issues, and both accorded with Grenville's point of view. On the 14th he challenged the pretensions of the East India Company, thus supporting, as a disapproving Lady Holland noted, 'Lord Grenville in all his E.I. doctrine'.[74] Next day he opposed a resolution, advanced on 11 May along with the report of Parnell's Select Committee on the Corn Trade and advocating a graduated scale of duties (Doc. 501).

The new Grenvillite MP displayed no timidity in propounding doctrine that was utterly opposed to the perceived interests of the Whig squirearchy and to the grain doctrine of Parnell and other bullionists. A graduated duty would render the price of corn dependent on the depreciated monetary value of the commodity, Horner argued, and the resulting 'artificial' price would make the poor a burden on the community. Earlier (Doc. 420) he had based much of his case against the Bank restriction on an argument that the resulting depreciation of money 'operated as a bounty upon importation' and opened 'the corn market of England to the free competition of foreign growers'. Now he opposed legislation that sought to address

72. Horner to Holland, 19 Oct., *Horner*, ii. 119; HHDB.
73. Horner to Murray, 9 June [1813], BLPES v. 309–10.
74. *Horner*, ii. 133; Lady Holland to Horner, [1–14? June 1813], BL Add. MSS 51644.

the problem he had himself described. Malthus found his arguments contradictory, and told him so (Doc. 502).

Horner went to considerable lengths to deflate tensions arising from disagreement on the course of the war. In that endeavour he exploited the Catholic question, the only major public issue upon which Foxites and Grenvillites had agreed since 1806. While awaiting Buckingham's offer, he had written several optimistic letters assessing the improved political prospects of the Catholics (Docs 487, 488, and 490), beseeching his friends to rally to the cause and on one occasion congratulating Somerset, of all people, on a good division (Doc. 491). After re-entering Parliament he refused to speak on behalf of the Catholics, instead deferring to Grattan and others, but he attended the key debates, joining his friends in the division lobby and continuing his behind-the-scenes encouragement. He pushed the principle of religious toleration to the very limits. Seizing on several vague remarks made by Grey and Holland in the Lords, he proposed in the spring that the party adopt the principle of universal religious toleration, and later suggested a Whig alliance with the English Dissenters (Docs 496–500).

Noting the growing momentum of the peace movement among Foxites, Horner concluded that his interests demanded an accession of strength on the Whig right. His zeal for Catholic Emancipation was influenced by hope that the issue might, as in 1806, weld together otherwise discordant factions and facilitate a coalition strengthening the weak Whig centre. The Catholic claims, he told Lansdowne as early as October 1812 (Doc. 483), constituted promising ground to 'draw closer our relations with Wellesley, whose force in the House of Commons is now so considerable'. Canning, despite his sins, also remained a worthy ally. Whatever his inclinations, Horner contended, 'he cannot help himself now, but upon the Catholic question he must be in Wellesley's train'.

Apparently Horner remained hopeful of coalition until July 1813. His correspondence of the first half of the year continued to exhibit an extraordinary interest in Canning and Wellesley, including, even, the 'discomfiture' he felt when Canning's negotiations with the Liverpool Ministry failed.[75] In July, when Canning announced that his party in the Commons was to be disbanded, Horner wrote to Grenville (Doc. 503) speculating that the event might signal Canning's desire to ally himself with Opposition.

Meanwhile Horner sought to check the Foxite left. The greatest threat from that quarter, he thought initially, was Brougham, notwithstanding his exclusion from Parliament. Brougham had collaborated very effectively with Whitbread and the more 'radical' Foxites in the Commons during the 1812 session. Later in the year he had published 'trash' in the *Review* that sought to revive the divisive issues of the 1790s. And then he had raised Fox's old banner of 'peace and reform' over the quays of Liverpool (Doc. 480).[76] Furthermore, he now enjoyed great reputation among the

75. An undated letter from Lady Holland to Horner, which was clearly written in June 1813 (BL Add. MSS 51644), contains the following curious remarks:

> I construed your silence exactly right. You would have no heart after such a discomfiture to write a line. How do the Canning squad bear up? To their chief it must be a blow, as nothing but success could justify the concessions he acquiesced in making. This will teach him that he does not hold the balance.

76. See also Taylor, pp. 343–7.

rising commercial classes, and he was therefore in the vanguard of what Horner himself regarded as the politics of the future. Holland summed up the position in the House of Commons about this time:

> The young speakers are numerous and full of talent, command of language, etc., etc., but there is not one who unites all those qualities which either constitute or promise to constitute a leader. Horner and Brougham come the nearest to it. The former is exceedingly popular in the House, and speaks with great weight and enjoys as he deserves the highest character for solidity of judgement, temperance and sobriety of disposition and inflexible integrity – but his health, his professional duties, his constitutional habits and perhaps even his scrupulous and fastidious notions of excellence prevent him from doing so much as his friends know he could and think he ought. Brougham's defects are of the opposite kind and consequently he is not so popular in the house or perhaps among those with whom he agrees most – but his activity, in which he equals Mr Burke or Whitbread, his readiness, his knowledge, and his perseverance have acquired him a great name in the country and rendered him a most formidable opponent.[77]

Brougham was likely to be brought back into Parliament as soon as Grey could find him a seat, and his re-appearance would be troublesome, at least, for someone constrained by the politics of the Grenvilles. But Brougham would be troublesome whether in or out of Parliament. Indeed, Horner reflected (Doc. 480), he might be more dangerous out than in. For last session he had displayed signs of 'becoming daily more a Whig'; but now his 'restless spirit' would lead him to embrace the 'fanatical faction', filling the *Review* with 'more of those intemperate declamations' and abetting their attempts at 'maiming the Whig party'.

Brougham began to make prodigious strides at the Bar during the last months of 1812. Horner attended several of his pleadings, and after sitting through his defence of the Hunts, acknowledged his rapid progress. But he was also extremely critical. Brougham's pleadings, he wrote, were 'not in the best style of legal reasoning' (Doc. 485).

Early in the new year, when the Regent's troubles with his consort began to command public attention, and as Brougham, legal counsel to the Princess, brought the issue to Parliament through the medium of Whitbread, Horner displayed almost predictable behaviour. The royal quarrel was difficult for him; the detested Prince was on one side, Brougham on the other. Initially he sided with the first. That ran foul of prevailing Whig prejudices, however, so he reversed his position, telling Lady Holland (Doc. 487) that he should be 'very shortly a downright partisan of Brougham's in this question'.

That, of course, was not to be. Finding the 'champions' of the Princess too numerous, Horner saw 'no chivalry' in defending her, professing that he had 'nearly gone over again to the other side', and apologizing for his 'trimming' opinions (Doc. 492). Shortly afterwards Whitbread lent a hand by attacking the commissioners of 1806 – Grenville, Romilly, and other prominent Whigs among them – and Horner stopped trimming. He criticized the brewer sharply in a letter to Holland (Doc. 493)

77. Holland to Minto, NLS MSS 11149, ff. 57–70, endorsed Sept. 1812.

and soon referred condescendingly to the 'Princess's party of the Mountain' in a letter to Allen (Doc. 498). Later, getting to the heart of the matter in a letter to Lady Holland, he reproached the 'childish vanity' displayed by Brougham (Doc. 533 n. 2).

Despite his efforts, Horner was incapable of suppressing Foxite passion for peace, and daily he was placed under more pressure to commit himself. A letter written in early December 1812 (Doc. 485) found him resurrecting his 'risen people' thesis – hailing the 'brute valour of Russians and Tartars' in a principled, popular rising against 'military science in perfection'. He learned very quickly, however, that Lord Holland was less enraptured with 'risen' Russians than with 'risen' Spaniards, and that a desire for peace negotiations was almost universal among the Foxites.

By all appearances Horner responded to this check by going into hiding. He appeared less frequently at Holland House during December 1812 and the first two months of the new year. He failed to show up at all between 22 February and 19 April 1813, and came only once between 8 May, when the presence of the warlike William Elliot probably unnerved him, and 15 November.[78]

In the meantime Horner either ignored the growing conflict within the party or vacillated about the war, though bending all the while in the direction of Holland House. On 20 May he deplored British policy in Sicily in a letter to Holland, and ten days later passed over the 'risen people' of Russia in a letter to Allen, reprobating instead the British Government's failure to open peace negotiations the previous winter. The following day he told an indignant Allen that French defeats had strengthened the Regent's resolve to oppose an armistice (Docs 497–9). By early June, when he learned that Whitbread would move resolutions for peace with Holland's full support, he was forced to come off the fence, and it was probably no coincidence that in the middle of the month he voiced Grenville's views on the East India Company's monopoly and on corn policy. For on 30 June, when Whitbread went forward in the Commons, Horner spoke briefly in favour of negotiations with France, voted with the Foxites, and no doubt fretted about the absence of Grenvillites among the minority.

The prorogation of Parliament roughly paralleled the signing of the armistice at Pleissburg, and thus Horner enjoyed a brief respite. He corresponded with Grenville, but neither mentioned the war, and Horner, perhaps fearing the inevitable, politely declined an invitation to visit Dropmore.[79] While on circuit he visited St Anne's Hill, walking about the grounds with Mrs Fox and leaving quite inspired.[80] From the circuit he proceeded once more to Edinburgh, where the society of his boyhood friends renewed his interest in the *Review*. He was fearful, however, of writing on any political subject, even anonymously, and could think of nothing but a review of travel literature (Doc. 504).

Early in September Horner expressed great anxiety about the renewal of hostilities, but was soon talking again about his warlike feelings having 'spread from Spain to Prussia'.[81] There followed an interesting exchange of letters with Allen,

78. HHDB.
79. Horner to Grenville, 22 July, and Grenville to Horner, 25 July 1813, *Horner*, ii. 135–6 and 138.
80. Horner to Joanna Horner, [?27 July 1813], BLPES v. 319–20.
81. Horner to Allen, 2 Sept. 1813, BL Add. MSS 52180; and Doc. 506.

who wrote criticizing the inconsistency of Grenville's foreign politics and warning he would advocate war when Parliament met in early November (Doc. 507). Horner's reply (Doc. 509) was astonishingly decisive, professing relief that Grenville would speak for war and contending it was time for the Whigs to admit their error in opposing the war in Spain and to take 'a right line of conduct' on German affairs.

Horner's almost scolding letter was totally out of character; evidently he was aware of several recent developments. Only days earlier Grenville had informed Grey that there could be no compromise on the question of war and peace, and his firmness had caused Grey, Lansdowne, and even Holland to re-think their 'principles'. More moderate views were beginning to prevail; and Grey, now opposed to a peace motion, was concerned about nothing but deterring Grenville from voicing his warlike opinions when Parliament rose.[82] Horner's new view of the war, therefore, gave the Foxite chiefs an avenue of escape that was rooted in their traditional dogma on foreign politics, and it recalled the very ground upon which Holland and Horner earlier had carried on their lonely campaign for the Peninsular War. In the end his point of view prevailed, open disagreement in Parliament was averted, and to Horner must go a measure of the credit or blame.

Horner's role in maintaining the public appearance of harmony within the ranks of Opposition considerably enhanced his political reputation. The visiting Madame de Staël, who never wasted her time on small fry, asked him to dine on 10 November (Doc. 512), and five days later he ended an absence of almost four months when he appeared at Holland House with Tom Grenville. The Hollands, who might reasonably have responded differently, welcomed him with open arms, and he returned three days later, this time dining with the pacific Creevey. Soon things were back to normal. Byron recorded that on 28 November he dined among a large party that included Lord John Russell and 'Horner – the Horner, an Edinburgh Reviewer, an excellent speaker in the "Honourable House", very pleasing too, and gentlemanly in company'; and on 8 December, apparently, Horner reappeared for what must have been an intriguing event – a dinner party featuring both Byron and Madame de Staël.[83]

Regularly now consulted by both Grey and Grenville, Horner displayed a rare outburst of activity during the short parliamentary session of late 1813. He delivered two speeches opposing a bill seeking to continue the penalty of death for the Luddite frame-breakers. He was less sympathetic with the plight of the nation's growing number of insolvent debtors; again rising in defence of the rights of property, he opposed a bill restricting the terms on which debtors might be imprisoned. Nor did he sympathize with the beleaguered local administrators of a failing system of poor relief, the House adopting upon his motion a standing order for the present session 'that no bill should be introduced containing any clause or clauses relating to the

82. Grenville to Grey, 21 Oct., Grey MSS, Durham University; Lansdowne to Lady Holland, 26 Oct., BL Add. MSS 51689; Grey to Holland, 24 and 27 Oct., BL Add. MSS 51552; Holland to Grey, 30 Oct. 1813, BL Add. MSS 51545.

83. HHDB; Thomas Moore, *The Life, Letters, and Journals of Lord Byron* (1860), pp. 208 and 213–14; and *Home of the Hollands*, p. 282. The dinner book does not list such a party on 8 Dec., but Byron describes it in his diary, and Ilchester, drawing on a source unknown to the editors, includes Horner among the guests.

settlement of the poor, or the corporal punishment of them, contrary to the law of the land'.[84]

A number of letters Horner wrote between early November 1813 and the fall of Paris in the spring of 1814 reflect the confusion and frustration that resulted from his compromised view of foreign politics. On 5 November he told Murray of the 'glorious victory' at Leipzig. He was quite satisfied with the warlike views Grenville had voiced in the Lords on the previous day and, curiously forgetting his own presence, expressed disappointment that nobody among the Opposition bench in the Commons had adopted the Allies' war (Doc. 511). Soon, however, he was expressing a very different point of view. The Whigs, he told his sister on 10 November, were 'highly pleased' with the 'pacific tone' and moderation of the Regent's speech. A Bourbon restoration was considered 'out of the question', and complete harmony prevailed in Parliament (Doc. 512).

Again Horner was trimming, agreeing with Grenville on tactics while clinging to Foxite strategy. He was convinced that the Regent, supported by 'the herd of the House of Commons', aimed at Napoleon's throne. Yet he believed, or at least said he believed, that a 'peace faction' within the Cabinet headed by Liverpool and Castlereagh contested the Regent, and that if matters came to an issue the 'bulk of Opposition' would give Ministers 'their whole strength' (Doc. 513). Holland shortly afterwards expressed an identical opinion.[85]

Horner also navigated very adroitly around the inevitable intra-party disputes that accompanied the French retreat towards the Rhine. In late November, upon hearing of the expulsion of the French from the Scheldt, he expressed great satisfaction with developments in Holland and very favourably assessed the characters of the Prince of Orange and his son (Doc. 514). That point of view coincided with Lord Holland's. Shortly afterwards, however, Grey sparked great controversy within the party by advocating a motion censuring Ministers for the restoration of the House of Orange,[86] and Horner had a change of heart (Doc. 517). Then, as the Allies continued their relentless drive across the Rhine, he defended Napoleon's reign and warned of the dangers of a Bourbon restoration (Doc. 523).

After the conclusion of the war, Horner's political behaviour was strikingly different from what it had been for some time. He was less manipulative, more direct, as if the weight of the world was off him, and he was determined to lead the Whigs rather than be led by them. His new attitude was manifested when Somerset met him in mid-April. 'Horner rather surprised me', the Duke told his brother on the 21st. For

> He was against the restoration of the Bourbons, which he seems to think a bad precedent on several accounts. It tends, he says, to confirm the prejudice in favour of the divine right of Kings. It holds up to reigning families the hope of being maintained on their thrones by one another, independently of the wishes of the people whom they are to govern. And it threatens France with the return of the abuses of the old Government, which he thinks by no means indifferent to the interests of the world at large.[87]

84. *Horner*, ii. 151–5.
85. Holland to Grey, 11 Dec. 1813, BL Add. MSS 51545.
86. Taylor, pp. 373–4.
87. *Two Brothers*, p. 133.

Such a point of view was hardly impromptu. It was, rather, well thought-out and absolutely impeccable on grounds of intellectual whiggery. Horner, it appears, had bided his time, employing a variety of tactics in his quest for political survival, yet always knowing that neither he nor the Whigs, any more than the nation at large, could prosper while the war continued. Now, for better or for worse, he was to anchor his foreign politics on the principle that had placed William and Mary on the English throne, cling to it in the face of attacks from right and left, and revive his long-frustrated political ambitions.

Lord Webb Seymour, who thought that the tendency of Horner's heart had been dampened by 'the remarks of some less liberal friends, such as must be found in every political party',[88] was the first to test him. Horner responded to Seymour's scolding letter very stoutly (Doc. 528), expounding his Lockeian opposition to British foreign policy and predicting that the restored Bourbons 'cannot fail to plunge France into new civil troubles, against which they will struggle to protect their throne by . . . foreign arms'.

The threat from the left was more troublesome, for the sympathies of Holland House were decidedly Bonapartist in the spring of 1814, as were also those of Grey, Bedford, and a considerable part of the Foxite faction in and out of Parliament.[89] Horner's stand on European politics of course gave him much in common with them, but he steadfastly refused to champion Napoleon. Indeed, surprised by the liberality of the French constitutional charter, he adopted a wait-and-see posture (Doc. 529), and a later letter to Lady Holland, in which he refers to her 'hero' Napoleon in a rather critical manner (Doc. 573), seems to confirm that he never pandered to her point of view.

In so far as Horner's own interests were concerned, a very significant recent development was his improved relationship with Grey. Formerly Grey had had good reason to regard him as a bright, if rather timid, sycophant who hovered dutifully behind Lady Holland's petticoats. But Horner had contested the foreign politics of Holland House and stood with Grey during the party crisis of late 1813, and now they regarded each other with mutual respect.

Grey remained hot on Anglo-Dutch relations, and was especially concerned about the reported displeasure of Princess Charlotte at her proposed marriage to the Prince of Orange. Horner had hitherto dissociated himself from the affairs of the Regent and his family. During April 1814, however, he gathered information on the young Princess and sent it to Grey in a confidential report (Doc. 527). Thereafter, for several months, his correspondence is sprinkled with interesting comment on the affairs of the Regent, Caroline, and the unfortunate Charlotte (Docs 531–4 and 549).

Upon the meeting of Parliament, Horner joined Grenville in resisting Parnell's revised resolutions, which still proposed a graduated scale of duties on foreign corn. On 13 May he observed that the 'real interests of the consumer and of the landlord were one and the same' and protested, as he had done in 1813 (Doc. 501), that the effect of the committee's recommendation would be 'to raise the price to the

88. Ibid., p. 135.
89. For an account of Foxite opinion in March and April 1814, see Taylor, pp. 375–82 and 386–9.

consumer'. When discussion was resumed on 16 May, he spoke in support of an amendment to postpone further consideration of the resolutions for three months (Doc. 530).[90]

In early June Horner was appalled to learn that the Allies had agreed to delay discussions on the abolition of the French slave trade for five years (Doc. 532). Abolition was Fox's old cause, the greatest single accomplishment of the late Whig Ministry, and Horner quickly moved to rally both factions of Opposition, and a united Whig bench soon took up the cause (Doc. 534 n. 7). In the Commons on 28 June, having expressed his doubt that Castlereagh had been firm enough on the slave trade question at the peace conference, Horner pressed for universal abolition and, concurrently with Grenville in the Lords, moved for information about the negotiations.[91] In July he was appointed to a committee of the African Institution formed to consider means of promoting the dissemination of abolitionist literature in France (Doc. 534). Later the same year he consulted Mackintosh on the possibility of exploiting existing provisions of French law to thwart the slavers (Doc. 540), and the following year he contributed to a special report by the African Institution.[92]

At the same time Horner did not overlook affairs at home. On 8 July 1814 he opposed on constitutional grounds Peel's motion to bring in a bill authorizing the appointment of superintending magistrates and additional constables in Ireland;[93] and five days later warned that the measure 'must tend rather to exasperate the people, and considerably exaggerate the mischief it proposed to remedy, than to produce any salutary consequences'.[94] The following evening, when the Under-secretary for the Home Department moved the second reading of a new Alien bill, Horner attacked it as an unnecessary and arbitrary encroachment on the constitution resembling the policies of continental despots.[95]

Horner's subsequent correspondence suggests that the continental tour he made in the autumn of 1814 influenced his plans for the forthcoming session of Parliament. On 28 October he wrote (Doc. 536) of his deep concern about the state of French politics, the threatening tone of public opinion in Paris, and the economic ills arising from an 'immense multiplication of landed proprietors' in France. His fears were probably fed by the negative assessments he received from Allen, who had accompanied the Hollands abroad.[96] At any rate Horner's opposition to British foreign policy was now more radical. He had no faith in 'this congress of sovereigns', those 'robbers at Vienna'; and while concerned about Grenville's point of view, he was convinced that the prospect of 'new wars and new revolutions' demanded active opposition in Parliament (Docs 538–9).

The miserable state of French agriculture, Horner wrote in November (Doc. 537), only strengthened his resolve to oppose duties on foreign corn. It made far

90. *Hansard*, xxvii. 524, 665–726, and 875–9; *Horner*, ii. 508–509.
91. *Ibid.*, ii. 512–18.
92. *Special report [of 12 April 1815] of the directors of the African Institution respecting allegations in the Letter to William Wilberforce by R. Thorpe.*
93. AR lvi. 162.
94. *Horner*, ii. 160–61.
95. *Ibid.*, ii. 161–2.
96. Allen to Horner, 2 Dec. 1814, BLPES vi. 139–40, and Doc. 544; see also Taylor, pp. 392–3.

more sense, he stressed, to terminate the ruinous American war, repeal the property tax, reform poor law, and return monetary policy to a proper footing. Foreign competition could only arise from 'something forced and unnatural' in the home market; never in political history had an 'unnatural state of prices' been cured 'by new artifices of taxation and restraint'. The British had best go to 'the root of the evil' and restore things 'to their natural course'.

Horner's plan for the session appealed to Foxite foreign politics and to Grenville's political economy. On 21 November he opposed the expenditure on the Russian alliance; next day he questioned the wisdom of the treaty with Naples and the cession of Saxony to Prussia; on the 25th, while withdrawing his opposition to Peel's Irish peace preservation bill, he accused Ministers of being unduly evasive on the principles underlying British foreign policy.[97]

Horner ventured these opinions without a clear understanding of Grenville's views or plans (Doc. 539). Soon, however, he was informed of a compromise between the Opposition leaders. It called for silence on European politics until Castlereagh returned with a definitive peace, and meanwhile for the harassment of Ministers on the American war.[98] In acknowledgement of Horner's standing, Grey and Grenville chose him to lead the assault in the Commons, and on 30 November and 1 December 1814, therefore, he attacked both the policy and the management of the American war.[99] In one respect he displayed great moderation, withholding his opinion that Britain had goaded the United States to war (Doc. 542). He was, however, unusually animated on 1 December, at one point, when he described Ministers as shufflers, inspiring 'loud cheers' from the Opposition bench.

After the prorogation Horner visited Edinburgh for the last two weeks of 1814, and then proceeded to Minto, where he remained several days. Afterwards he stopped by Dropmore for political discussions with Grenville, and returned to London in mid-January. A number of letters reveal that much of his time in Edinburgh was devoted to discussions with old friends about the propriety of introducing jury trial in Scots civil cases, and one from Grenville suggests that the reform of Scots judicature was among the several topics discussed at Dropmore.[100]

Horner was now approaching high tide, and his correspondence of early 1815 is that of a happy man of diverse interests. Even his financial affairs were in much better order, his law practice having prospered sufficiently by the summer of 1814 to make him, as he said, 'quite independent', and, from its surplus and with the aid of another loan from his father, to buy the lease of a house in Great Russell Street in the spring of 1815.[101] He still had an eye on Brougham, and in late January, after reading his rival's article on the slave trade in the *Review*, he vented his wrath on

97. *Horner*, ii. 203–209.
98. Taylor, pp. 389–91.
99. *Horner*, ii. 209–12.
100. Horner to Reddie, 29 Dec. 1814, NLS MSS 3704, ff. 68–9, encouraging active support for jury trials; Grenville to Horner, 12 Jan. 1815, BLPES vi. 151–2, giving a favourable opinion of jury trials and expressing 'the greatest pleasure in seeing you here at the time you mention'. See also Stewart to Horner, 1 Jan., Kinnordy MSS; and Horner to Mrs Stewart, 20 Jan. 1815, BLPES vii. 15–16.
101. Horner to John Horner, 10 June 1814, *Horner*, ii. 163, and 18 Feb., 26 Mar., and 10 Apr. 1815, BLPES vi. 174–5, 180–83, and 214–15.

Murray (Docs 546 and 548). Otherwise, however, he was quite satisfied with his political prospects. Originally the Whig chiefs had planned for him to renew the attack on the American war early in the new year, and Ponsonby, writing from Dropmore on 25 January, told him to go forward (Doc. 547). By then, however, promising news from Ghent recommended delay, so Horner, thrilled by word that Government would relinquish the property tax (Doc. 551), initiated the parliamentary campaign for which he apparently had gained approval at Dropmore.

The new campaign focused on three principal subjects: monetary policy, grain policy, and foreign policy. Horner opened it on 10 February with several brief remarks on the proposed renewal of the Bank restriction bill. On the 21st he made an 'animated' speech deprecating the transfer of Genoa to the King of Sardinia. On the 23rd he spoke twice, defending the integrity of the African Institution and opposing the corn bill in a 'luminous and logical speech'. After a week's rest he rose again, this time attacking Spain's newly-restored 'legitimate sovereign' so viciously as to inspire a later protest from the Spanish embassy.[102]

On 6 March Horner supported the Scots jury bill. On the 7th he renewed his opposition to the Bank bill, restating the recommendations of the Bullion Committee, dismissing the proceeds of the Bank as merely paper profits, and encouraging the Government to force convertibility on the directors. On the 9th he raised the issue again, successfully proposing an amendment calling for the resumption of cash payments when the market and mint prices of gold reached parity.[103]

For the historian of economic thought, Horner's most valuable speech is that of 23 February opposing duties on foreign corn (Doc. 553), together with the related correspondence published here. Horner's doctrine was remarkable. It was inconsistent with that of Adam Smith. Yet he invoked Smith's authority and, recalling the economic principles of Pitt and Burke, refuted his own earlier opinion that Smith had borrowed heavily from Quesnay and his followers. Indeed, Horner – surely hoping that nobody remembered his review of Canard – went so far as to represent Smith's opinions as 'the original growth of our own country' and stated that the Physiocrats had borrowed from Smith.

The speech is also a political curiosity. Horner's earlier monetary doctrine had won support among the landed classes. Now, tying the corn question to both the Bank restriction and the administration of poor relief, he argued for the manufacturer and for the labouring classes. He was at odds with Lauderdale and the entire Whig squirearchy, including the time-serving Foxites Western and Coke of Norfolk, whose wrath he had feared in 1804 when opposing corn bounties in the *Review*. And his views were almost diametrically opposed to those of his friend Malthus, who only recently had lent his powerful authority to the grain lobby in two celebrated pamphlets.

The principal thrust of the speech was more moral than political or economical – essentially it was a plea for public rather than private interest to be the guiding principle of the House. But it was also a defence of political economy. Here was a

---

102. *Horner*, ii. 519–22; Doc. 553; *The Gentleman's Magazine*, lxxxv (Pt 1, Mar. 1815), 263; and *PH* iv. 244.
103. *Horner*, ii. 534–43.

young man, educated in the finest tradition of the great Scottish Enlightenment, rising in defence of his heritage. Responding to the taunts and sneers of members who sought to discredit political economy, he asked 'upon what ground could gentlemen pretend to depreciate its character, unless they meant to deprecate the exercise of reasoning'. He defended Adam Smith, representing his work as 'sacred among the best writers this country had ever known'; he attempted to correct the mistaken view, asserted by an opponent in debate, that Mirabeau had supported protectionist doctrine. His speech was, in short, a notable example of the extension of Scottish metaphysics into British politics, and it was 'listened to with the most profound attention by his most zealous adversaries'.

Still more interesting is Horner's related correspondence. A letter of January 1815 (Doc. 548) shows that he thought his doctrine consistent with that of Smith, indeed with principles 'obvious to every one who understands the operation of demand and supply upon prices'. It also reflects his opinion of Malthus's opposing point of view. No man had 'a better or more informed judgement' than Malthus, and his was the 'single authority' that worried Horner; but within Malthus's philosophy was 'always a leaning in favour of the efficacy of laws', and Horner was certain that he could demonstrate, from Malthus's own principle of population, that his protectionist views were productive of misery among all labourers. Horner's greatest concern was the effect of 'a violent forced alteration' in the 'proportion . . . between agricultural and manufacturing population and capital'. The 'freedom of both', he concluded, had adjusted that proportion more effectively than the wisdom of 'all the squires of the island, with the political arithmeticians to boot'.

Horner's letter of 12 February 1815 (Doc. 550) was a detailed critique of Malthus's recent pamphlets on *Rent* and *Corn*. Malthus's reply (Doc. 552) contested Horner point by point, especially the charge that his protectionist doctrine gave a 'lift' to those who supported the Bank restriction. Still further light is shed on their conflict by a letter Horner wrote to his father after his speech (Doc. 554) and by another he received from Malthus (Doc. 558), picking up Horner's earlier analysis of the 'proportions' of population and capital distributed among Britain's various classes.[104]

Horner's spate of parliamentary activity, and his animated style in debate, astonished the House of Commons. Somerset told Seymour that Horner 'had made a shot in parliamentary eloquence beyond even our expectation', that his reputation was increasing rapidly, and that a member not acquainted with Horner had recently proclaimed him to be 'the best speaker in the House'.[105] Murray wrote that the 'best judges', Romilly and Mackintosh among them, voiced 'unqualified praise' for both speeches, and that Mackintosh had remarked that 'two such speeches had never been made in the House of Commons by the same person in one week; or, at least, not for a great many years'.[106] Whitbread, Tierney, and Morpeth all praised him, the last reporting that Horner 'bids fair at any rate more fairly than any of his contemporaries, to acquire great distinction'.[107] Furthermore, Horner's unsuccessful opposition to the corn bill won him friends in the City, with the Common Council

104. See also *Malthus*, pp. 262–8.
105. Somerset Papers, Exeter, 1815/9.
106. *Horner*, ii. 239.
107. Morpeth to Holland, 27 Mar., BL Add. MSS 51584.

voting thanks to him and Alexander Baring 'for their able and indefatigable exertions'.[108]

Perhaps the greatest irony of Horner's life lay in the fact that at this very moment – merely days after his oratory had set tongues wagging – word arrived that Napoleon had escaped from Elba. As the British Government moved towards war, Grey and Grenville reached an impasse, and the long-feared schism in the Whig ranks at last materialized. Initially Horner hesitated. He refused to attend a meeting at Ponsonby's place and absented himself from the House. By late April, however, he saw that he could not escape. Standing on his classic Whig interpretation of the political sovereignty of nations, he aligned himself with the 'old Fox party', voted for Whitbread's resolutions for peace on 28 April, and that evening offered to resign his seat (Docs 564–5).

Encouraged by Grenville, Buckingham deferred matters, and Horner resolved to carry on until a 'final separation' of the Fox and Grenville factions actually occurred and resumed his activity in the Commons. On 1 and 5 May he defended the London petition against the resumption of war with France; on the 2nd he moved for papers relating to British policy towards Naples (Doc. 565 n. 2);[109] on the 19th he again raised the Neapolitan question, boldly stating his preference for Murat over a Bourbon as ruler of Naples and accusing the Government of duplicity towards Napoleon's old captain. He was among a group of over seventy Whigs who met at Devonshire House on 22 May and adopted resolutions against the resumption of hostilities, and several days later he divided with a strong minority of ninety-two on Whitbread's motion.[110]

Horner's correspondence during the Hundred Days sheds some light on what is otherwise a lamentable gap in the historiography of the Whig party. The most important of it was with Grey (Docs 559–60 and 562) and Jeffrey (Docs 557 and 569–71), revealing the grounds of dispute and the intellectual basis of the Foxite point of view. Horner's stand on the Hundred Days, moreover, had a significant bearing on the short remainder of his life and on his place in history. On the one hand, its 'test' of his 'principles' was never forgotten by those who survived him; here, it appears, was a major source of his later reputation among the Whigs, a key factor in the inclusion of his name among the fallen 'martyrs' of the cause. On the other hand, his allegiance to the 'principles' of the 'old Fox party' brought him great discomfort and might well have contributed to his premature death. In March his friends had expressed anxiety about his fragile health;[111] by June the severe coughing and the shortness of breath had returned, this time permanently.

Further stress arose from the failure of some of Horner's closest friends to appreciate his political opinions. His stand on the corn duty had offended influential Foxite squires, especially Western, and now his foreign politics placed him on even shakier ground. On one side were Lord and Lady Holland, canting about the mistreatment of Napoleon and assigning to Wellington responsibility for the post-

108. *Horner*, ii. 533n.
109. *Ibid.*, ii. 258–9.
110. See Taylor, pp. 401–415, for an account of the Whig schism during the Hundred Days including comment on the role of Horner. On 6 June 1815 Horner spoke in support of Peel's bill to regulate the labour of apprentices in factories (*Horner*, ii. 266–7).
111. Morpeth, Whitbread, and Tierney to Holland, 27 Mar. 1815, BL Add. MSS 51584.

Waterloo policies of the Government. Horner firmly rejected such arguments, at the same time repelling attacks from friends who thought him unpatriotic (Docs 573 and 576).[112]

Whitbread's suicide shortly after Waterloo was also disheartening, and Horner wrote several letters that display the sense of loss he felt (Docs 575 and 577). His view of France, British foreign policy, and the Congress of Vienna darkened almost daily for the remainder of the year. In July 1815 he expected guerilla warfare and an extended Allied occupation of France, and wrote of the anxiety he felt because such men as Castlereagh and Metternich were to determine 'the fate of the world' (Doc. 577). In August he became obsessed with French politics and severely criticized both Wellington and the Regent (Docs 578-9). Shortly afterwards he sought to escape from it all, going north to Scotland and virtually ignoring politics. On the way he visited Grey, who reported that:

> He is one of the best as well as one of the most agreeable men I know, and I wish to God he was in a situation to take the lead in the House of Commons, which his character and talents would give him, if he could devote himself to that object. Yet why should I wish for him what would probably be much less conducive to his happiness than his present occupation.[113]

But after returning to London Romilly gave Horner a 'frightful impression' of France (Doc. 581), and then in November Horner spent several days among the politically disaffected at Woburn, after which he praised the 'hereditary' political virtue of the Russells but was thrown into a state of great agitation by the terrible accounts of European politics he had heard there and the 'atrocity and insolence' of the 'anti-revolutionary' treaty signed at Vienna (Docs 585, 588, and 587). Several days later he was writing of the 'breach of the amnesty' in France and of the employment of British troops 'in the most odious services for the Bourbons'.[114]

Meanwhile Horner's relations with the Grenvilles went from bad to worse. The events of the spring and early summer had left matters very unsettled, and thereafter he had had little or no communication with them. Now, in November, the 'radicals' of Westminster revived the old cry for economical reform, singling out again Buckingham's tellership, and apparently approaching Horner about it. The extent to which Horner involved himself is unclear, but he wrote a letter to Lady Holland which seems to have expressed a very negative view of Buckingham's obstinacy about the tellership, of Grenville for agreeing with him, and of someone within the Grenville family who had labelled their critics a 'Band of Cossacks'.[115]

Almost simultaneously Grenville took offence at several critical remarks about Oxford University that had appeared in Dugald Stewart's recent contribution to the

---

112. See also Horner to Hallam, 22 July, and Hallam to Horner, 26 July 1815, *Horner*, ii. 273-6 and 278-80.

113. Grey to Lady Holland, 22 Oct. 1815, Grey MSS, Durham University.

114. Horner to Bannatyne, 4 Dec. 1815, *Horner*, ii. 304-305.

115. Horner to Lady Holland, 2 Dec. 1815, *ibid.*, ii. 299-301. Leonard Horner deleted the names of the individuals of whom his brother wrote. They were almost certainly Buckingham and Grenville, however, and from the treatment of offending passages in other published letters, one must very strongly suspect that he also omitted other parts of this letter. Clearly Leonard Horner found it uncomfortable, and the disappearance of the original is surely not coincidental.

Encyclopædia Britannica. Unacquainted with the professor, Grenville insisted on communicating with him through Horner, and for several weeks an ill, unhappy Horner was forced to mediate a very lively dispute between his patron and his mentor (Doc. 590 n. 1).

As the meeting of Parliament approached, Horner was no doubt alarmed to learn of Brougham's return to the Commons. He worried also about Jeffrey's forthcoming article on the state of France and unhappily confessed to Murray that his own foreign politics were unpopular (Doc. 586). He proceeded to Dropmore in early January and remained for several days.[116] Grenville was cordial and quite eager to resume their earlier collaboration on economic policy. When discussion turned to foreign politics, however, Horner was dumbfounded.

Grenville had supported a war to restore the Bourbons in France. They themselves had been unable to command the allegiance of a single regiment, and the job had been done by foreigners. Obviously the foreign conquerors, Britain among them, thought an army of occupation necessary. Yet Grenville thought Opposition should focus on retrenchment in government, attack the cost and constitutionality of a peacetime military establishment necessitated by the success of a war he himself had supported, and, still more curiously, banish all reference to the war from parliamentary discussion.[117]

Horner appealed for guidance to Holland, who had now returned from the Continent, and received advice that only increased his apprehension. Holland thought it best to eschew discussion of the origin of the war and the right of interference in the internal affairs of France. Like Horner, however, he saw no way to avoid an attack on the principle of 'legitimacy' and on the restoration of the Bourbon dynasty by force of foreign arms (Doc. 592).[118]

After leaving Dropmore, Horner pondered his political dilemma and considered the points on which he and Grenville agreed. Letters of January and February 1816 (Docs 591, 593, and 598) disclose that he devoted much thought to the economic plight of the nation. Collectively they constitute no mean analysis of the problems he attributed to the 'artificial opulence' of the long war, and they largely explain the doctrine he recommended to Opposition leaders.

Essentially Horner regarded the British economic dilemma as the inevitable result of long-standing policies that had constrained the 'natural' growth of a healthy economy. His solution was simple: free trade, a substantial reduction in taxation, and a progressive restoration of cash payments by the Bank. Seeing no easy solution, he opposed raids on the Sinking Fund, saw little to be gained by attacks on sinecure places and, while opposing the Ministry's proposed 5 per cent income or property tax, looked very suspiciously on those who favoured tax relief in a vacuum.

Horner's comprehensive programme was entirely consistent with Grenville's point of view, and it was supported by Tierney and Abercromby among the Opposi-

---

116. Horner to Joanna Horner, 1 Jan. 1816, BLPES vii. 1–2.
117. See Taylor, pp. 426–7.
118. Horner's letter to Holland has not been found, but it was almost certainly written from Dropmore and seems to have included an assessment of the political opinions of Grenville, with whom Foxite leaders had had little or no contact since their confrontation in Parliament during the Hundred Days (Mitchell, pp. 87–8), and a plea for guidance.

tion. Yet free trade remained anathema to the party's dominant landed interest, few could understand how a resumption of cash payments might improve matters, and those seeking immediate relief found Horner's doctrine incomprehensible. H. G. Bennet, for instance, asked how the establishments were to be paid for if they were to get no money from either the property tax or the Sinking Fund. Fretting about the demise of agriculture, and infuriated by Horner's free trade doctrine, Western quite agreed: 'at such a moment, the sinking fund is not to be TOUCHED for the world, says Horner – no not a shilling of it: and yet – taxes to be taken off, rents to come down, cheap corn, cheap labour – how can a man talk of such IMPOSSIBILITIES?'[119]

Unable to agree on a comprehensive, dynamic economic policy, the party rank and file were inclined to react with a short-term solution – an attack on the proposed property tax and, by way of compensation, the transfer of considerable sums from the Sinking Fund. Brougham, who was determined to claim the lead in the Commons, exploited the opening. Refusing to be led 'by a coterie at Lady Holland's elbow',[120] he embraced doctrine that was diametrically opposed to that of Horner and Tierney. He supported the Corn Bill of 1815, and before Parliament met had resurrected an old alliance with Alexander Baring to solicit petitions for the complete repeal of the property tax. Furthermore, Brougham and Baring advocated a raid on the Sinking Fund, Baring assuring everyone that seven millions could be transferred without danger.[121] Fitzwilliam, whose politics at this juncture began and ended with opposition to the property tax, was keen on the plan, and soon Horner and Tierney found themselves on the outside looking in.

Meanwhile Horner's foreign politics continued to be attacked on the right and embarrassed on the left. Already his views of European affairs were tainted by the Bonapartist sympathies of Holland House. Now they were stained by the arrest in Paris of Grey's friend, Sir Robert Wilson, and by the French authorities' confiscation of imprudent letters Grey and Holland had written to him. Then Jeffrey's article on France, which circulated just prior to the meeting of Parliament, ridiculed Horner's concept of foreign politics, and essentially equated anti-Bourbon sympathies with an unpatriotic hankering for Napoleon (Doc. 595).

Horner's political prospects were grim, and his health was failing rapidly. Learning that the Foxites would move an amendment to the Regent's speech on the first day of the session, he informed Grenville that he must support it. Grenville's reply warned of the impropriety of such conduct, and emphasized that the proposed amendment was likely to breed renewed disagreement among the Whigs (Doc. 596). Horner's relations with the Grenvilles were increasingly tenuous. During January he had been none too discreet in deploring the persecution of eminent men by the restored monarchs of France and Spain (Doc. 594), the most celebrated of whom was Marshall Ney. According to Tom Grenville, Horner's sympathy for Ney incensed Buckingham. The impression he would give by turning out a man of such 'weight and consideration' as Horner and the likelihood that he would then join the more extreme faction of Opposition made Buckingham hesitate, and Horner himself

119. Bennet to Creevey, 2 Feb., Gore, Creevey, pp. 98–9, and Western to Creevey, 17 Feb. 1816, Creevey, i. 252.
120. Brougham to Creevey, 14 Jan. 1816, ibid., i. 249.
121. Bennet to Creevey, 2 Feb. 1816, Gore, Creevey, pp. 98–9; New, p. 162.

was unaware of his feelings.[122] But he had no illusions. On 29 January he outlined the causes of disagreement between the Foxites and the Grenvilles in a letter to the Duchess of Somerset (Doc. 597). The differences were 'irreconcilable', he concluded; a 'breach in the Opposition' could be anticipated.

Yet Horner again attempted to hold the middle ground on 1 February, when he joined the debate on the proposed amendment to the Regent's address. Brougham, who preceded him in debate, launched a fiery attack on the entire policy of Government and, seemingly oblivious to fissures within the Whig coalition, linked domestic and foreign policy in a speech of considerable length. Horner's brief speech was evidently calculated to embarrass Brougham and promote party harmony. Indeed, it practically refuted Brougham's entire agenda. A clear distinction must be made between issues domestic and foreign, he argued. The one demanded retrenchment in Government, and certainly the property tax was ill-advised; but he disagreed with his colleague's advocacy of sweeping fiscal reform, especially at the expense of the Sinking Fund. It was moreover premature for members to comment on the settlement of Europe before the treaties were laid before the House.[123]

Horner's remarks were hardly calculated to salve old wounds, and in the days that followed he attempted to match Brougham's extraordinary activity in the Commons, while maintaining great moderation. On 5 February he went to considerable lengths to appear patriotic in supporting the call for a monument to commemorate Trafalgar. On the 7th he sparred with Castlereagh on foreign affairs, hinting that the constitutional and financial ramifications of the treaty would be closely scrutinized, and two days later he again warned of the dangers of a costly military establishment.[124]

Horner was holding back, fully aware that party leaders were still trying to reach agreement on a plan for the session, but on 11 February there came two important developments. First, Brougham ended his long, self-imposed exile from Holland House, and actively sought to make his peace with Lord and Lady Holland.[125] Secondly, a shaky compromise between the two factions of Opposition was announced. It called for two attacks, one on the property tax, the other on the financial and constitutional implications of a British army of occupation in France. But it specifically excluded any reference to the policy of the war or to the principle of 'legitimacy' that framed the peace,[126] and so effectively gave Brougham the lead in fiscal policy and tied Horner's hands in foreign policy.

Next day Brougham forcibly asserted himself in the Commons, launching his attack on the property tax and giving notice of a motion on Spain – Lord Holland's pet subject – without prior communication with his colleagues on the Opposition bench.[127] On the same day Horner began to contemplate the treaties of peace,

---

122. *Buckingham*, ii. 114 and 117; *Dropmore MSS*, x. 409. Sack, p. 173, states that despite his strong feelings Buckingham never once in all his correspondence with his most intimate political confidant mentioned any intention to force Horner to give up his seat before the conclusion of Parliament.
123. *Horner*, ii. 320–23.
124. *Ibid.*, ii. 323–5.
125. HHDB; New, pp. 163–4.
126. Mitchell, p. 91.
127. New, p. 165.

which were now before the House. The subject was still a dangerous one, and the recent compromise of the Whig leaders imposed debilitating constraints, but his fears were no doubt assuaged on 13 February when the Grenvillite C.W.W. Wynn protested in the Commons against both the Government's fiscal policy and 'a war establishment under the name of peace'. Later in the debate Horner linked the 'appalling difficulties' of the domestic economy with a proposed peace establishment that was 'alien' to England and threatening to English liberties. A day later he played his Catholic card, bringing in the Irish grand juries bill which he had prepared the previous autumn.[128]

On the evening of 14 February Horner dined at Holland House among a party that included Holland, Bedford, Lauderdale, Jersey, Kinnaird, Mackintosh, and Ebrington.[129] Foreign politics were almost certainly the leading topic of conversation, and perhaps it was the doctrine of Bedford, whom Horner so greatly admired, that inspired him. Whatever the case, six days later he went forward in the Commons, boldly asserting himself in foreign affairs and, as he afterwards wrote, 'having . . . my breath out about the Bourbons and Castlereagh'.[130]

Horner's proposed address propounded the constitutional limits of treaties with foreign nations, and his accompanying speech (Doc. 599) was a shocking violation of the earlier party compromise. He broached the issue of the war and the principle of 'legitimacy' very directly. He anchored his remarks on Fox's 1793 address and resolutions (Doc. 599 n. 5). And, wrapping the traditional Foxite view of foreign politics in impeccable Whig dress, he applied the principles of the 1790s to the very event of which Fox had warned – British collusion in a treaty that expelled Locke from the English constitution.

Horner never spoke with greater effect in the Commons. The *Morning Chronicle* reported that 'he sat down amid the loud and repeated cheers of the House, having concluded a speech, whose power of eloquence, energy of reasoning, and profound and comprehensive views, it has been utterly impossible to convey'. Holland reported to Grey that he believed it was the 'best speech . . . that has been made this session or that he has ever made – firm judicious and eloquent'; Lady Holland, still more effusive, that

> The Town is ringing with Horner's praises, his speech is considered to have produced an astonishing effect. Lord Castlereagh was completely cowed, and since your absence from the House there has never been anybody equal to it on our side of the Question – old Piggott said it saved Opposition – and the little Speaker boasted of his own discernment in having predicted that Horner would be the greatest Speaker in the . . . Commons.

The Speaker also remarked that it was 'most powerful, argumentative, and profound, and altogether one of the most able speeches he had ever heard in that House', and James Macdonald, who found it a 'brilliant success', told Horner that it had confirmed the great impression he had made '*universally*' in the course of the session. Whishaw, whose close ties with Holland House gave him constant access to the opinions of Whig leaders, assured him that it '*establishes* your character and station,

128. *Horner*, ii. 325–9.
129. HHDB.
130. Horner to Joanna Horner, 21 Feb. 1816, *Horner*, ii. 340.

not only in Parliament, but with the public; and that it is universally considered as a most important event for the political party to which we are attached'. Several days later Whishaw informed a friend that Horner's speech

> both in the style, manner, and above all, in the excellent principles with which it abounded, was universally acknowledged to be one of the completest performances that has been witnessed in parliament for a great number of years. It derived great weight from the opinion universally and justly entertained of the sincerity and high honour of the speaker; and produced so considerable an impression as to mark him out for the future leader of the whigs, if that station had been consistent with his professional pursuits. Probably this speech did not influence a single vote; but it lowered the tone of the Treasury bench, and took away all the triumph of the reply. It was the universal topic of conversation for two or three days.[131]

While Horner's speech apparently failed to excite protest from the Grenvilles, it carried his conflict with Brougham to unprecedented heights. Brougham's quest for the lead in the Commons had led him to be very active even before Horner's speech; now he charged forward with compelling fury. He scored his great victory over the property tax on 18 March, and was honoured six days later at Holland House. Afterwards he sought an alliance with the reformers of Westminster, and was back on his feet in the Commons on the 27th, railing against extravagant and unnecessary public offices and calling for sweeping economical reform. He laid out his plan for the nation's recovery on 9 April, voicing support for duties on foreign corn, calling for a further reduction in taxation, and advocating an emergency invasion of the Sinking Fund. Meanwhile he appropriated one of Horner's cherished causes, obtaining a Select Committee to investigate 'the education of the lower orders in the Metropolis'. His energy was astonishing. By the end of the session he had spoken 147 times and delivered over fifty substantial speeches.[132]

Horner reacted predictably: he utterly ignored his rival. Certainly there was little or no social intercourse between them at this time. Between 1 January and 30 June 1816 Horner appeared at Holland House eight times and Brougham five, but never once were they there together.[133] Much the same was true of their political relations. Although one observer perceived a spirit of competition between them, and felt that Horner got the best of it,[134] after the first day of the session there was nothing in the Commons resembling a collision between them.

While Horner sat on Brougham's education committee, nothing suggests that he was active, or even interested, in its proceedings. He also lent only token support to Brougham's assault on the property tax, being absent on the day of the division and having nothing to say about a victory that, according to Ward, produced a 'prodigious' effect even in Paris (Doc. 605). Nor did he contest Brougham's contrary

---

131. MC, 21 Feb.; Holland to Grey, and Lady Holland to Grey, [?21 Feb. 1816], Grey MSS, Durham University; *Horner*, ii. 340–42; Whishaw to Thomas Smith, 28 Feb., *ibid.*, ii. 553–4.

132. New, pp. 164–9, 172, and 204; HHDB; Raymond G. Cowherd, *The Politics of English Dissent* (New York, 1956), p. 42.

133. HHDB.

134. *The Diaries of Sylvester Douglas (Lord Glenbervie)*, ed. Francis Bickley (2 vols, 1928), ii. 165.

economic views; apparently he was not even in the House on 9 April when Brougham laid out his programme.

Horner of course dissociated himself from Brougham's campaign, but merely by telling Lady Holland of his great distaste for debates on economical reform (Doc. 601). He also omitted to criticize Brougham's imprudent and universally condemned attack of 20 March on the Prince Regent,[135] and only once did he venture a critical comment on Brougham's increasingly ludicrous campaign to vindicate his 'injured innocent', the Princess of Wales (Doc. 611). Horner knew Brougham very well indeed, and he was probably confident that his rival would make indiscretions enough; at all events he refused to compete and went about his own business.

Horner was away on circuit for most of March, but he returned in early April eager to contest the renewal of the Bank Restriction Act. The difficulties attending the resumption of cash payments troubled him (Doc. 606), and he solicited advice from Grenville (Doc. 610), though not, it would seem, from Malthus.[136] Then, after criticizing the Alien bill on 25 April,[137] he delivered a major speech against the renewal of the Bank Restriction Act on 1 May, contending with some effect that every argument formerly advanced for continuing the suspension of cash payments had been overtaken by events following the conclusion of peace (Doc. 609). On 3 May he attempted unsuccessfully to insert a clause enjoining the resumption of cash payments after two years, and his subsequent motion requiring the Bank directors to prepare for resumption was also rejected. Pushed by Grenville, who thought his arguments unanswerable (Doc. 610), he repeated his motion on 8 May, but with no better success.

Horner was soon immobilized by a violent cough and an accompanying stomach disorder. Thereafter, for the remainder of the session, he attended the House less frequently, and remained in his chambers, at Holland House, or at the country houses of friends.[138] Notwithstanding Grenville's encouragement (Doc. 607), he never got around to a renewal of his attack on the East India Company. However, he reintroduced his bill for the reform of Irish grand juries and worked with Peel to overcome the opposition of the Irish bench (Doc. 613 n. 1).[139] On 27 May he spoke on behalf of the Spanish Liberals. On 13 June he made his final appeal to Jeffrey on behalf of his Whig friends, successfully discouraging a review of Lady Caroline Lamb's scandalous *Glenarvon*, which had thrown Lady Holland into a dither (Doc. 612).[140] And on 25 June he delivered his last speech in the Commons, encouraging 'a speedy settlement' to the 'grand question' of Catholic Emancipation.[141]

As the Whigs mourned the death of Sheridan, Horner proceeded north to Scotland in early July. Along the way he stopped at Woburn, and then at Stowe, where he was surprised to find Buckingham in good temper.[142] He was at Oxford on

135. New, p. 169.
136. Ricardo to Malthus, 24 Apr., *Letters of David Ricardo to Thomas Robert Malthus, 1810–1823*, ed. James Bonar (Oxford, 1887), p. 115.
137. *Horner*, ii. 555–62; *Romilly*, iii. 241.
138. For insight into Horner's activities and worsening health during May and early June 1816, see his letters to Thomson, 20 and 30 May (*Thomson*, pp. 154–7), Anne Horner, 20 May (*Horner*, ii. 355–6), and Somerset, 24 May, Frances Horner, 25 May, Mrs Stewart, [?late May], Stewart, [?late May], and Murray, 5 June (BLPES vii. 60–72 and 77–8).
139. *Romilly*, iii. 217–18.
140. See also *Moore*, ii. 104.
141. *Horner*, ii. 361–3.

the 14th, writing about the distress of farmers and manufacturers, the absurdity of Sidmouth's scheme of forced emigration, and the impossibility of maintaining the present military establishment (Doc. 614). From Wells he sent a despondent letter to Lady Holland on 18 August (Doc. 615). A poor wheat harvest was likely, the country gentlemen would respond with their 'usual blindness', and the content of periodical literary reviews had become shallow, he complained.

In early September Horner arrived at Dryden, a place his parents had taken near Edinburgh to help him rest and recuperate. A gossipy letter to Lady Holland of the 16th (Doc. 617) showed him under the doctors' care, living the life of an invalid and finding amusement in the visits of Jeffrey and other old friends. A letter to Allen of the 17th, however, displayed his continuing interest in politics, fretting about the cause of liberty in general and the fate of the Whigs in the coming election in particular; and he received in turn a steady diet of political intelligence from Holland House (Docs 618–20).

Lady Holland was anxious for Horner to spend the winter at Holland House, and offered to put three rooms at his disposal.[143] His doctors, however, diagnosing a 'pulmonary affection', advised that he spend the winter in a warmer climate, and after much procrastination he selected Pisa. On 6 October he left Dryden with his brother Leonard and proceeded to Holland House, from which he told Hallam of his travel itinerary and added a political diatribe (Doc. 621). In the face of an unprecedented economic dilemma, he complained, Britain was plagued with a feeble Government, dishonest Ministers, a 'diseased' public mind, an army of 'idle-headed reformers', an altogether 'unprincipled' body of country gentlemen, and the prescriptions of 'quack doctors' posing as political economists.

By late October Horner and his brother had arrived in Paris. Letters he wrote the 27th and the 29th (Docs 622–3) commented on Canning, who to Horner's chagrin was courting the Ultras, and on French politics; another written from Lyons on 6 November (Doc. 625) contained a melancholy assessment of the plight of French liberals but concluded with hopeful predictions.

Awaiting Horner upon his arrival at Pisa in late November was a large packet of letters from Holland House, and thereafter, excepting only a handful of his own, correspondence from friends in Britain constitutes the greater part of the Horner papers. His own letters often contained flashes of humour and hope; sometimes they were dour and despairing. He described his life at Pisa in a letter to Murray of 6 December 1816. He had 'entire liberty of study and reflection' at last, he said, and impatiently awaited the arrival of Adam Smith's *Moral Sentiments* and Addison's *Spectator*; but he continued to rant about the consequences of 'that sad job of the country gentlemen, the corn bill'. A week later he was reading Dante and Machiavelli's *Prince*, which, surprisingly, he had never previously read, and, interestingly, filled him 'with such disgust that I do not know I shall be able to open it again'.[144] On the 20th he doubted Lady Holland's report that Liverpool would resign or that Grenville would desert the Whigs (Doc. 629). His letter of the 21st to Lord

---

142. Horner to Lady Holland, [14 July 1816], BL Add. MSS 51644.
143. *Holland House Circle*, pp. 71–2.
144. Horner to Murray, 6 Dec. 1816, BLPES vii. 236–7 (extracts from which are printed in *Horner*, ii. 399–402 and as Doc. 628), and to Lady Holland, 13[–14] Dec. 1814 [*sic*], BLPES vii. 242–5.

Holland (Doc. 630), moreover, was a very comprehensive statement of his political principles; another to Murray of the same day (Doc. 631) commented at length on Scottish jurisprudence; and a further letter to Lady Holland of 4 January discussed the Whig amendment to the Address she had sent to him (Doc. 635).

Horner, his brother recalled, 'at no time appeared to despair of ultimate recovery'.[145] He did, however, anticipate a slow convalescence, and apparently spent much of his time drawing up a document that he eventually headed 'Designs, at Pisa, 2nd February, 1817, under the auspices of opium and returning spring'. Leonard Horner found much of it illegible, and included only selected passages in his memoir.[146] At first glance the published fragment resembles the many schemes of study Horner had composed as a boy, notably the one he had drawn up on the eve of his departure from Shacklewell in 1797. But on closer examination it becomes clear that he was laying out a plan for a very long and full life. The heart of the plan is a section entitled 'Political Preparations and Discipline', which, under the sub-heading of 'Questions', lists (and in some cases subsequently elaborates a little) 'Foreign Politics', 'Army', 'Catholics', 'Currency', 'Funds', 'Trade and Economy', 'Poor Laws', 'Parliamentary Reform', 'Church', 'West India Slaves', and 'Law Reform'. A further three sections are headed 'Classical Studies', 'Detached Subjects for Study', and 'Detached Subjects for Composition'. But his opening section shows that he had but two underlying 'Designs': to master the 'Theory of Jurisprudence', and to realize his earlier dream of becoming an eminent historian by following up his 'Hints for a History'.

As always, then, Horner entertained lofty designs, and on 4 February he told his father of his improved condition.[147] Two days later, however, his health worsened dramatically, and on 8 February 1817 he died.[148] He was thirty-eight years old.

145. *Horner*, ii. 433.
146. It is included as an appendix in *ibid.*, ii. 479–85.
147. Horner to John Horner, 4 February 1817, *ibid.*, ii. 429–33.
148. For Leonard Horner's account of his brother's last days, see *ibid.*, ii. 432–5.

372. To Lord Webb Seymour

BLPES iv. 206–209 ⟨Horner, i. 517–19⟩   Woolbeding, 3 Jan. 1810

⟨. . .

⟨The circumstances of the Oxford election,[1] and the line which Cobbett has recently adopted upon the question of Catholic Emancipation, concur in proving that the public of all classes, even as low as the multitude⟩ and the country clergy, ⟨have been most rapidly enlightened on that subject. There is not in my recollection a more remarkable instance of the beneficial power of the press; and I cannot conceive what greater encouragement we could have, to indulge hopes of the future prospects of England, than in so unequivocal a proof of the easy diffusion and reception of just opinions, when they are fully explained, and perseveringly and temperately urged. I consider it as utterly impracticable at present for the court to raise a cry about popery, though it is but so short a while since that wicked expedient met with the most complete success, and had nearly delivered up the Catholic inhabitants of England and their property to assassination and flames. The cry next attempted will be for pity to the King, and indulgence to his conscience, in his old age – a topic which is not calculated now to have popular currency, as appeared upon the occasion of the Jubilee, and which at any rate surrenders the subject of argument by asking for time and mercy. Before a great many more years are gone, we shall have the government of Ireland established upon just and generous principles, and that will give us a strength to defy the world, and an unlimited range for the development of all our internal resources. It is by a very perverse coincidence in point of time, that the greatest peril, we have ever been exposed to from foreign hostility, has fallen in just one of those periods, which are incident to our constitution by its nature, when the evils of the monarchical part prevail over its advantages: but if we overlive this crisis, there are numerous symptoms which begin to manifest themselves in each of the three kingdoms, but especially in England, of a tendency to start forward, which cannot be repressed much longer, but upon the next change of the individual whose character most affects the condition of the country, will enforce maxims of administration more adequate to the necessities of the time, and more corresponding to the sentiments of the educated part of the people. The immense influence of the press, in making one democracy (as it were) of the whole population, has been gained but within these few years; and possesses in itself a living principle of increase, the operation of which is farther accelerated by the progress of national instruction in England, which Joseph Lancaster's perseverance seems to have pushed now beyond all risk of being stopped: nor is it unpleasant to observe, how surely, and how unconsciously, the aid which the King has given to Joseph in his plans, and the diligence of the Methodists in spreading their absurd fanaticism, co-operate to the same end.⟩

Another symptom of improvement, which must have the most important effects, has shown itself still more recently, in the agricultural revolution that is now begun in England, and which the cupidity and luxurious necessities of the gentry will drive on, even if they shall be made aware, which they are not in the least at present, of the political consequences that must ensue. I will venture to prophesy, that the rise of rents and the system of leases will give more power to the commons of England, and contribute more permanent strength and stability in all their political privileges to the middling classes, than any revolution of economy that has taken place since the abolition of villeinage; more, than the establishment of foreign commerce and domestic manufactures.

⟨. . .⟩

1. The election of Lord Grenville as Chancellor of Oxford University.

373. From John Allen

BLPES iv. 210–11   Woburn, 4 Jan. 1810

. . .

I am anxious to know the result of the meeting of Lords Grey and Grenville. I was in great fear some time ago about their determination respecting the Catholic question, but I am now in great hopes that they will not flinch from it in the least but hold it up as it is the true bond of connection in the party.[1] *Here* there is great stoutness on the subject – the same at Panshanger, and Brocket Hall.[2] Wm Lamb shows a strong determination to come forward more actively than he has hitherto done. Lord Hy Petty's removal to the H. of Lords opens unquestionably a most inviting field to any one who thinks he can distinguish himself in the H. of Commons.

Have you heard of a letter from Perceval to Lord Melville which has given great offence to Melville and his friends? In this letter Perceval writes that he has HM's command to express to Melville how sensible HM is of the support which Melville has given to his Government, to express his hopes of a continuance of that support, to offer as a mark of his approbation to make him an Earl, and to give his son any situation he chooses to name in the Ministry, but that as to Melville himself he is sorry to add that no place can be offered to him 'on account of the slur attached to his character in public opinion.' Melville's friends in Scotland are said to be indignant at this gratuitous insult and to threaten no less than the pulling of Perceval's nose for his insolence. The fact of the letter I believe to be certain, as well as the offence it has given and the general strain of its content. What a fool this Perceval must be, and how ignorant of the ways of the world![3]

. . .

You are not the only person who is dissatisfied with the expression of *Panacea*. Major Cartwright in a letter to Lord Holland complains of it as implying an unfair imputation on Parliamentary reformers.[4] I think Lord Holland would have been more correct, had he complained of persons holding it up as a *sine qua non*, which is a most mischievous doctrine while it is impossible to carry it. When the country is decidedly for it, the object is so great that it might be worth while to break up the party to attain it, but to take it up prematurely would merely divide Opposition without advancing the cause of reform.

1. In the months immediately following his election as Chancellor of Oxford University, Grenville cooled on Catholic Emancipation, refusing to be led by Catholic leaders until they accepted a number of conditions designed to safeguard the Establishment. Consequently, while expressing willingness to present another petition, he refused to sponsor an accompanying motion and indeed opposed any agitation of the question during the 1810 session. Grenville's amended view of the Catholic question, which shortly was advanced publicly in his *Letter to Lord Fingal* (1810), threatened the very existence of the Whig coalition. Holland, the Russells, Whitbread, and other Foxite leaders felt themselves irrevocably committed to the Catholic claims, and Grey, always more sympathetic to Grenville's views, was caught squarely and unbecomingly between the extremes of opinion. (Taylor, p. 305; Roberts, pp. 69–72.)
2. The homes respectively of Earl Cowper and William Lamb.
3. Perceval's unfortunately worded letter of 5 Oct. 1809 was at first calmly received by Melville, but neither he nor his friends could long contain their bitterness, which ten days after Allen's letter broke out in the public press. (*Plumer Ward*, i. 255–63; Gray, *Perceval*, pp. 258–61 and 392.)
4. Major John Cartwright (1740–1824: *DNB*), the descendant of an old Northamptonshire family, had served in both the navy and the militia before emerging as an ardent reformer, a political pamphleteer, and an influential figure among the radicals of the City.

374. To John Allen

BLPES iv. 212–13 ⟨*Horner*, i. 520–21⟩   Bradley,[1] 6 Jan. [1810]

⟨I rejoice exceedingly at the news you give me of Brougham's coming into Parliament; and I am particularly glad that Lord Holland has had so great a share in effecting it.[2] Brougham never could have found a more fortunate moment for setting out upon his career, which, though it may appear less brilliant at first, on account of the expectations which are formed of him, will be very speedily distinguished: and, upon the whole, I would predict, that, though he may very often cause irritation and uncertainty about him to be felt by those with whom he is politically connected, his course will prove, in the main, serviceable to the true faith of liberty and liberal principles. For him, personally, it will be very fortunate, if he has some probationary years to pass on the Opposition side of the House.⟩

. . .

1. The Duke of Somerset's place near Bath.
2. Brougham obtained his seat in Parliament through the influence of Lord Holland, who apparently recommended him to the Duke of Bedford over the protest of Lady Holland. Interestingly, Holland's short description of the transaction is followed immediately by an account of Brougham's subsequent alienation from Holland House and of his 'unpardonable' conduct towards Horner (*Holland's Further Memoirs*, pp. 44–6). In their assessments of Brougham's difficulties with Holland House, neither Aspinall (pp. 17–20) nor New (pp. 49–51) take into account the heat in the Whig ranks on the question of leadership in the Commons or Lady Holland's close relationship with Horner.

375. From Lord Holland

BLPES iv. 214–16   Woburn Abbey, 9 Jan. [1810]

... I am afraid many of the embarrassments from which we thought ourselves extricated have been found to exist in full force. Pray tell me in what (Whitbread excepted) you think the difficulty of Ponsonby's continuing to hold meetings at his house and to act as leader consists.[1] As to measures I hear that if the Catholic question is moved we shall have many defaulters. Do you believe so? By the bye I heard Abercromby quoted as one of the persons who deprecated our sticking too pertinaciously by the question or at least for the whole of the question, and I ventured to express a strong disbelief of his ever having held so shabby and in my mind so very shortsighted an opinion. In doing so I relied more on his generally being in the right on such questions than on any recollection of his having said any thing upon it. Pray tell me if I estimated his strictness and inflexibility on such point too high.[2] Indeed I should like to hear the names of a few of our friends who think on this subject as you and I do, to be enabled to quote them as setts off to those of an opposite opinion.

As to Parliamentary Reform you were right in thinking I might have said some thing more in its favour, and I wish I had expressed my satisfaction at its again becoming popular, but I wished to mark that I did not think it a universal remedy or even a touchstone of a man's principles much less a *sine qua non* to any improvement of our present situation, and I wished to do so because I thought the tendency of Waithman's speech was to describe it as both a Panacea and a *sine qua non* to any thing good. Nothing can be so right in principle upon every topic as the master of this house – *dont je me rejouis grandement.*[3]

1. A meeting at George Ponsonby's house in London on 21 Dec. 1809 had revealed far-reaching dissension among Whig MPs about parliamentary tactics and their leadership in the Commons. Whitbread and Tierney flatly refused to follow Ponsonby's lead; Tierney refused to speak to Whitbread; and afterwards Whitbread demanded the acknowledged lead as the price of his support, threatening otherwise to take an independent line in the Commons. In early January 1810 discussions at Holland House had centred on the creation of an 'Opposition Cabinet', leaving Ponsonby 'the nominal leader without any substantial power' (Whishaw to Lady Holland, BL Add. MSS 51658), but Ponsonby 'suddenly sprung up in Arlington Street, with his sceptre in his hands . . . ready to lay [it] across the shoulders of any man who shall withhold all due allegiance' (T. Grenville to Buckingham, *Memoirs of the Court and Cabinets of George III*, ed. the Duke of Buckingham and Chandos (4 vols, 1855), iv. 418). Ponsonby's attitude caused Grey to favour the continuation of existing arrangements in the Commons, and Grenville, his long-desired alliance with Canning thwarted, concluded that Ponsonby was the lesser of evils. Hence the idea of an 'Opposition Cabinet' was dropped, and Holland set out to smooth the ruffled feathers of the feuding front-benchers. (See generally Taylor, pp. 302–308.)
2. See Doc. 376.
3. Holland was alluding to a speech of 5 Dec. in which Waithman had allegedly misrepresented Grey's views on parliamentary reform (*PH* v. 460–61). Horner's short reply to Holland of 15 Jan. (BLPES iv. 217–18) hedged on the explosive issues of parliamentary reform and leadership in the Commons and expressed 'great sadness and despair, at the temporizing and *balanced* views which some of my honestest friends in politics take on the Catholic subject'.

376. To J.A. Murray

BLPES iv. 223–30 ⟨Horner, i. 523–8⟩   Lincoln's Inn, 22 Jan. 1810

⟨I had some expectation of hearing today what is to be Pillans's fate.⟩ . . . ⟨It will be a very great satisfaction to both of us, to see so worthy and conscientious a man placed in a situation, in which he may be of the greatest use to thousands.[1] . . .

⟨I rather apprehend that you have not received a very clear account of the difference of sentiment which, to a certain degree, prevails among the chief members of Opposition, on the subject of the Catholic question.⟩ The subject ⟨has been discussed a good deal, and different opinions have been proposed and compared, but no decided breach of sentiment has taken place. It is only a precautionary discussion, with a view to an event which possibly (I should say probably) will never happen; another message from the present King to Lord Grenville, or Lord Grey. And the question is, whether, upon such an overture, Catholic emancipation should be stated to his Majesty as a *sine qua non* of their undertaking the administration of affairs? It never has been proposed by any one, or hinted at in my hearing, that the government, in the case supposed, should be accepted of in such a manner, that they might consider it open for them to oppose Catholic emancipation, as Members of Parliament, on the ground that the King is against it: that would be a degree of profligacy, and a surrender of the constitutional liberties, of which none of the persons I am speaking of can be supposed capable. But what has been thrown out for consideration, is, how far, under all the circumstances of the present time, it is consistent with their public duty to decline undertaking the management of affairs, unless the King makes a sacrifice of his individual prejudices upon that subject. Now, though the opinion which I entertain has appeared to some of my friends as too peremptory and absolute, yet I am far from thinking that there are no difficulties in coming to a clear determination upon the point⟩; I should be shook a little by the mere authority which stands against me, of judgements much better than my own, and no less guided by popular principles of government as well as by disinterested views; and I cannot deny that I feel the weight of many of the reasons which I have heard them urge. I cannot so well do justice to their mode of stating the argument, as by sending you two letters written to me by Abercromby, while I was last out of London; but which I will thank you to return to me, within a day or two.[2] ⟨However, after all the reflection I have bestowed⟩ both upon his reasonings, and ⟨upon whatever I have heard insisted upon by others, I return always to the same conclusion which I formed, when I first took the subject into consideration, at the end of last September, in consequence of Perceval's letter to the two lords. I would have them resolve, if they think of coming into office, to do something for the Irish Catholics without delay; and I would have them state such their intention fairly and explicitly to the King, when he sends for them. If they were to enter upon the government without that previous explanation, they would entangle their character in this dilemma; by abstaining from all mention of that irksome subject, their conduct would imply a pledge as dishonourable as an express one; or, upon the first mention of it, the King would again dismiss them with contumely, and with the most hurtful consequences to the country. What I look upon to be the great evils of our present political condition, are the bad opinion which the public entertain of the principles and steadiness of political men, and the loss of confidence between the aristocratical opposition and the democracy; even the waste of our finances and reputation, by the present incapable set of men, is in my mind a mischief of less momentous consequences, and more easily to be repaired by a change, than the crisis which may be dreaded from the farther growth of those former evils, especially the latter of the two. They would both of them receive a large increase, if the people were to take an impression, however incorrectly in point of strict conclusion, that the question of Catholic emancipation was abandoned for the sake of office; and I persuade myself, that a steadfast, calm adherence to that principle of administration would gradually restore the confidence of the honest and rational part of the people, in the honourable, enlightened, and sufficient men, who are at present the chiefs of the English aristocracy. What I regard as the greatest good that could happen to our constitution, in its present state, would be a victory, by main force, over the Court, upon a great fundamental principle of liberty or toleration; and though I agree that the chances of such an event are not very favourable, in the present strength of the Crown, and in the present bigoted state of the country in matters of religion, yet I do not even regard the chance of success as desperate; and it seems to me something very like acquiescing in despotism, for public men to govern their line of measures by an assumption, that particular measures, essential to the salvation of the country, cannot be carried against the individual opinion of the reigning sovereign. But next to that greatest good which could possibly happen, is the benefit to be derived from building up in the country a vast party, cordially united upon public principles, who, supported by the intelligence and activity of the middle orders, wait, with cool resolution, for the first opportunity, when they can demand, with decisive voice, the establishment of those laws and maxims of administration which are required by the necessities, as well as by the improvements, of the times.

⟨. . .

⟨What is most urged against this my position, of the loss of public character by temporizing about the Catholic question, is, that the people are not in favour of Catholic emancipation. But this is not satisfactory. In the first place, I am not sure that the people are so wrong, or at least obstinately so, upon that subject; for though there is still a good deal of bigotry, it seems to me so much weakened, and better opinions to have gained so much ground in the educated classes of the people, that it is now fit for those who are impressed with a sense of the urgent practical and immediate utility of the measure, to force it upon the people as well as the King. But in the second place, even if the Catholic claims be unpopular, I do not see that this will save the character of those who have hitherto maintained the necessity of the concession, and who would seem to relinquish it for the sake of power: it is possible, that that very relinquishment might make the claims more acceptable to the people, and I should conjecture from Cobbett's recent wheel upon the question, that that very sagacious judge of the popular sentiment felt that, in the expected abandonment of the Catholics, he would gain fresh materials for degrading the characters of public men among the multitude: besides, though the people like their Protestant prejudices, what they like much better now is a great man who will not take office. This may be carried, in some instances, an unreasonable length; but the sentiment has been gradually produced by circumstances, which make the imputation upon which it is founded not so unreasonable.⟩

. . .

1. At Horner's initiative and with his active support, his old friend James Pillans was chosen as successor to Dr Alexander Adam as Rector of the High School of Edinburgh in January 1810. (See Horner to Pillans, 23 Dec. [1809], and 19 Jan., and to Murray, 23 Jan. 1810, BLPES iv. 196, and *Horner*, i. 521–3 and 528–9. See also *Cockburn*, p. 249.)
2. Abercromby's letters to Horner have not been found, but Leonard Horner's exclusion of any reference to them here suggests that they contained strong opinions that, at mid-century, were thought to be damaging, though Abercromby himself, according to *PH* iii. 11, 'invariably supported Irish Catholic relief'.

377. From T.R. Malthus

Malthus Archive, Kanto Gakuen University[1]   Hertford, 5 Feb. 1810

Your letter was sent to the College at Haileybury, and as we have not yet removed from Hertford, I did not receive it till yesterday. I was very glad to hear from you on a subject which has excited my curiosity in a considerable degree without my having been able to satisfy it by any information that I could obtain; and I was quite pleased to see the notice of your motion in the papers, as I felt confident that in your hands the question would be put in the best train for solution. I have been looking at the *Morning Chronicle* of the 2nd, and congratulate you upon the deserved applause which you got for your motion, and the manner in which it was introduced.[2] I conclude that I see but a small part of your speech, but from what I can collect I think it probable that our ideas on the subject may not materially differ. I have no where seen the reasonings of Mr Ricardo and Mr Mushet to which you allude.[3] The view which on the whole I am most disposed to take of the subject is the following.

I think that the shock which Mercantile confidence has received from the present disturbed state of Europe, and the proceedings of Buonaparte, particularly during the last year and a half, or two years, has rendered the use of the precious metals in the transfer of commodities more necessary, and therefore more general than formerly. This increased demand arising from the increased use of the precious metals, has naturally increased their value on the continent; and if our circulation had been in its natural state, that is, if paper had continued exchangeable for gold at the Bank a considerable exportation of guineas and bullion would have taken place which would soon have raised the value of the currency of this country to a level with that of the continent; and then of course things would have gone on as usual. As our currency however, in its present state, consists so much of paper, and that paper not payable in specie, this equalizing process cannot easily take place. The small quantity of gold in circulation, even if it were all exported, would not be sufficient for the purpose; and if the increased issues of the Bank were merely to the extent of filling up the vacancy thus made in the circulation, the restoration of the level would be hopeless. Under these circumstances the value of the currency of this country must remain lower, [than] the currencies of the continent, the exchange be constantly and greatly against us, and a permanent premium continue for the exportation of the precious metals. This state of things you will observe might take place with little or no increased issue of Bank of England paper. It might arise indeed exclusively from the circumstance of a change having taken place in the value of bullion and currency on the continent, which the restriction of payments in Specie at the Bank had prevented from being communicated to our circulation in the ordinary way.

Should it appear by the papers you have called for that no increased issues of Bank paper have taken place, I shall be strongly disposed to attribute the present state of things to the cause I have mentioned. It is highly probable that the new channels of trade which British merchants have opened under the present difficulties have occasioned the necessity of prompter payments, and the consequent use of a greater quantity of the precious metals, than the old channels; but it should be remarked that such an increased use confined exclusively to British trade would not produce the effects observed. It would raise the market price of bullion in this country higher than on the Continent in general; and would tend to occasion a favourable exchange with those countries which were not particularly circumstanced with regard to the necessity of receiving payments in specie. One of the first inquiries which should be made therefore, is, whether the market price of bullion in this country is equal to the market price on the Continent; and if it be not, which I conceive must be the case, from its continued efflux, it is quite clear that the source of the difficulty could not originate exclusively in the peculiar wants of the British trade as at present carried on, but in some cause of a more general nature affecting the comparative values of British and Continental Currency. This cause may either be an increased issue of Bank paper, which would lower our currency compared with that of the Continent; or an increased use of the precious metals on the continent, which would raise the continental currency compared with ours. The effects on our foreign exchanges and on the market prices of the precious metals compared with their mint prices, would be the same in both cases, though they would imply very different degrees of culpability on the part of the Bank Directors.

It is important, however, to observe, that, though the Bank Directors would not be equally culpable in the two cases, they would not be entirely without blame in either; and whichever supposition turns out to be true, the remedy for the evil complained of, can be no other than a diminution of the issues of Bank paper. In the natural state of things previous to the Bank restriction a rise in the value of continental currency compared with British, from whatever cause arising, would be necessarily remedied by the influx of Bank notes, to be exchanged for gold, and the exportation of the gold so exchanged. And during the restriction, it should be the invariable rule of the Bank Directors so to regulate the issues of their notes as to make their value resemble as nearly as possible the value which they would have if they were exchangeable for specie. The great evil of the present circulation, is, that it does not naturally suit itself as formerly to the necessarily varying value of continental currency, but requires on the part of the Bank Directors great attention, great knowledge, and great disinterestedness, qualities which though they appear on the whole to have possessed in a greater degree than could have been expected, they have not possessed in a sufficient degree. It is not indeed very easy, under the present enormous payments, which the Bank has to make in discharging the half yearly dividends, and in the assistance which it is continually giving to Government, to restrict its issues sufficiently, without narrowing its discounts to private merchants in a degree which might occasion some embarrassment to the trade of the country, and very general complaints; yet still a diminution of notes in some quarter or other appears to me to be the only remedy; and in answer to the complaints to which it might give rise, it might be observed that in the natural state of the currency of any country, its merchants must always be liable to temporary embarrassments arising from the varying value of the precious metals, or the varying state of confidence, although they might not be quite so great as when an unnatural state of things had for some time been persevered in, and required to be remedied. At all events however the diminution should take place gradually.

The increased use of the precious metals in mercantile transactions, which I have supposed above to arise principally from the shock which commercial confidence has received, must undoubtedly have been very much aggravated, and may indeed have been in great part caused, by the number of armies in Europe requiring payments in Specie.

Any questions tending to elucidate the point of the increased use of the precious metals in Europe, from whatever cause arising, will materially facilitate the object of the inquiry.

You will also have an opportunity of ascertaining, whether bullion is frequently exported by the ordinary merchant in payment of the goods which he receives; or whether this export is conducted exclusively by the Bullion merchant according as he sees his advantage in the rate of exchange, selling under such circumstances a bill to the ordinary merchant, which he enables his correspondent to discharge by the transfer of bullion.

If the price of bullion in England has not yet reached the continental price, I conceive that very little has of late been imported, whatever Mr Rose may say to the contrary. Indeed his conclusions are perfectly absurd, and quite contradict the great acknowledged facts which have rendered the inquiry necessary. I don't exactly know how the imports are valued, but I suspect that the rate of exchange is not added to them, in which case with the exchange at 20 or 25 per cent against us, 55 millions of exports would be more than repaid by 45 millions of imports and a balance would remain to be discharged in specie by us, which accords with the actual state of things without rejecting the Custom House Accounts.

These accounts however are not much to be depended on, as they always involve (if not corrected in the way suggested, or some other) the absurdity which you have justly commented upon, of a constant balance in our favour.

All questions elucidating the manner in which our great exportations are paid for will be of considerable use. I don't know how we can receive bullion for any of them, in which case, as it seems to be acknowledged that we make considerable payments in specie, the drain upon our bullion must be considerable. In the present state of things if justly represented, the Bank may import Bullion on account of its double capacity but it can never answer to a private Bullion merchant to do so; he will be rather employed in buying up the plate of the silver smiths which he can get cheaper than foreign bullion.

I heard some time ago, but not from very good authority that an unusual rise had taken place on the continent in the value of gold compared with silver – is this so? it would prove that in the extended use of the precious metals, gold was found more convenient for distant remittances.

Excuse this long letter, and the desultory manner in which it is written. You shall hear from me again if I think of more questions. I hope politics go on tolerably. I should like to hear of your proceeding in the inquiry. Mrs M desires comp[liment]s.

1. This is thought to be the actual letter rather than a draft or copy, but since Malthus's other letters do not seem to have been returned after Horner's death, one that was never sent. The letter from Horner, to which it was evidently intended as the reply, has not been found.
2. Briefly reporting Horner's bullion speech of 1 Feb. See pp. 575–6.
3. Ricardo's *High Price of Bullion* had only just been published. Robert Mushet (1782–1828: *DNB*), an officer of the Mint from about 1804, had, by Horner's reckoning, published the first edition of *An enquiry into the effects produced on the national currency, and rates of exchange, by the Bank restriction bill*, late in 1809; the third edition was reviewed by Malthus in the *ER*, xvii (no. xxxiv, Feb. 1811), 339–72 (see Doc. 411).

378. To Sir Samuel Romilly

⟨*Horner*, ii. 4–5⟩   London, 10 Feb. 1810

⟨It appears to me to be very important that you should publish your speech of last night, if you can possibly find leisure for it while it is still fresh in your mind.[1] The irresistible argument for your particular bills, which is founded upon the returns, will not be seen in all its force, unless the numbers are all set down; and then I am quite persuaded, that, upon the subject of a reform of the criminal law, the public is quite ready for instruction, if delivered to them with the authority of your name, and with the attractions which your topics of reasoning and illustration cast over the argument. It is because you cannot know this so well as others, that I take the liberty of suggesting to you to make this exertion, always an irksome one, but which will be greatly and immediately useful. It will tend very much to make your future progress, in the same subject, more easy. Nothing seems to me so certain now, as that Parliament in all these matters of legislative improvement follows only the public opinion; and that to overcome in the House of Commons the resistance of which Plumer[2] is so worthy a leader, you must bring the weight of public opinion to bear upon the House, by enlightening it through the press. On the subject of the criminal law, the prejudices are all among the lawyers; the public in general seem to have none, and at the same time take a lively interest in such discussions.⟩

1. On the evening of 9 Feb. Romilly obtained leave to bring in three bills repealing provisions of the penal law. Romilly published later in the year the substance of the speech that

accompanied his motion along with some additional thoughts in a pamphlet entitled *Observations on the criminal law as it relates to capital punishment, and on the mode in which it is administered.* (*Romilly*, ii. 132–4, and Medd, p. 224.)

2. Romilly noted in his diary (*Romilly*, ii. 132–3) that Sir Thomas Plumer, the Solicitor-General, announced his intention of opposing the bills 'with his usual panegyrics on the wisdom of past ages, and declamations on the danger of interfering with what is already established'.

379. To Lord Grenville

BLPES iv. 237–8 ⟨*Horner*, ii. 5–6⟩   Lincoln's Inn, 11 Feb. 1810

⟨The unsatisfactory returns which are made to the orders which I moved for in the House of Commons upon the subject of Bullion and Currency, and the ready desire which was expressed on both sides of the House to see that subject fully examined, induce me to propose in a few days the appointment of a select committee. But before going so far in a matter of such public importance, I feel an anxious wish to have the sanction and benefit of your Lordship's advice as to the proper objects, as well as the best course, of investigation; in order that it may be conducted to an useful result. Hitherto, I have abstained from forming any conclusion, even in my own mind, respecting the causes of the present state of money prices; nor am I sure that I have yet gained a clear and exact notion of that change, whether depreciation or not, of which the cause remains to be ascertained. In this suspense of opinion, I have been desirous, before I enter into the inquiry, to collect the various solutions which the difficulty may seem to admit of at present while our information is incomplete, in order that the search for farther information may be so directed as to bring each of those explanations to the test. I fear that I ask too much of your Lordship, whose time is so filled up, in requesting that you would have the goodness to instruct me in the views, which your Lordship entertains upon this important question; but I am prompted to make that request, by my anxiety to get into the right track through so intricate a subject, and by my conviction that injury of no slight degree may be done to the public interest by taking a false step, and even by the publication of erroneous opinions.⟩

380. From Lord Grenville

BLPES iv. 239–41 ⟨*Horner*, ii. 6–7⟩   Camelford House, 12 Feb. 1810

⟨I saw with the most lively satisfaction that you had announced an intention of taking up a subject of so much difficulty and importance as that of the present state of the currency of the kingdom, and of the trade in bullion. It would give me great pleasure to have an opportunity of conversing with you on the subject at whatever time would best suit your own convenience. . . .

⟨The difficulty of arriving at any precise opinion as to the causes of the existing evil arises in great degree from the concurrent operation of so many circumstances wholly unprecedented. Nothing but a well conducted inquiry ascertaining as distinctly as may be the real effect (as it is now practically experienced) of each of these circumstances separately or combined with the others, can give one full satisfaction as to the application of those theories which one's general notions of the subject would lead one to form upon it. But on a general view, I am inclined to attribute the effect complained of, in a very great degree, to the stoppage of money payments at the Bank – a measure originally adopted to meet a sudden and very urgent pressure, but, I think, very ill calculated for any long continuance. While the necessity of money payments then continued, every increased demand for bullion which either the ordinary fluctuations of trade, or the extraordinary circumstances of these times occasioned, was immediately felt there, and was met (or ought to have been so) by adequate measures to diminish the circulation of paper, and by a corresponding issue and importation of bullion, by a body possessed at all times of a considerable store of that article and having both capital and commercial means for rapid purchases and importations.

⟨I am far from thinking that the question admits of so simple a solution as to be answered merely by a reference to this single principle – but I am inclined to believe that its operation will more or less be traced through all the complicated details in which the subject is involved; and I entertain sanguine hopes that under your conduct the inquiry will lead to an issue satisfactory both in the elucidation of this branch of political science, and in the practical measures to which it may lead.⟩

381. To Mrs Brougham[1]

⟨*Brougham*, i. 500–501⟩   House of Lords, 6 Mar. 1810

⟨You will naturally be very anxious to have some account of Henry's speech last night, which I had the pleasure of hearing. The manner in which he spoke was in every respect most parliamentary, and gave all his friends the most complete assurance of the success he will have in the House. His language and delivery were perfectly suited to the style which the House requires, and he showed himself to be in complete possession of it. It was well judged to begin with a speech which was *extempore*, and to give this proof of what he can do, before the great opportunity of which I trust he will avail himself upon the Walcheren inquiry.[2]

⟨. . .⟩

1. Henry's widowed mother Eleanora Brougham (1750–1839).
2. Horner's opinion of Brougham's maiden speech in the Commons is suspect. Some sixty years later Brougham also professed to recall that it had been favourably received and that it had been instrumental in the defeat of Ministers. But according to New it was 'purposely devoid of fire, sarcasm, and rhetoric', and was regarded as a failure by contemporaries as well as being a disappointment to Brougham himself. (PR xvi. 7; *Brougham*, i. 499–500; New, p. 51.)

382. Note by Horner

BLPES viii. 68–9 ⟨Horner, ii. 8–10⟩ 3 Apr. 1810

⟨In the late vote on the Walcheren question, there were many members, I doubt not, who voted with Ministers, though they condemned the whole of their conduct in that fatal expedition,⟩ yet ⟨from a sincere conviction of the superior fitness and excellence of the present set of Ministers for holding the Government, in the present circumstances, above any other set of public men.

⟨The vote of such men may have been given, in consequence of their perceiving, that if the House condemned that expedition by a vote of the majority, the King would be compelled to change his Ministers. I have no doubt that a sufficient number of men were influenced by this manner of considering the thing, to give the Ministers the majority they had, when added to their crowd of corrupt, devoted, or unthinking partisans. Perhaps this is far from being the only instance that might be mentioned, in which well-meaning and disinterested Members of Parliament have been deterred from voting in condemnation of a particular measure of Government, lest the effect of that vote should go farther than they wished, and lead to an entire change in the Administration.

⟨In this manner, it would appear, that the weight and importance which belongs to a vote of the House upon what is called a Ministerial question, is itself a cause of the House departing in particular instances from its professed and proper line of duty. And thus the power which the House has over the crown, does, in a certain respect, make it likely to fall into disrepute with the people. The regular division of political reasoners and public men into two distinct parties, in this country, has probably led to this state of things in the House of Commons.

⟨Whether such a state of things be more or less expedient, than that other, more agreeable at least to the theory of the constitution, in which the Parliament should exercise its controlling and inquisitorial functions, by adhering as nearly as human nature will permit to the exercise of a sort of judicial opinion upon the merits of each particular measure of Government, is a speculative question of some curiosity and difficulty. That it is not wholly a speculative question, however, may be seen from this, that a certain number of members in the House of Commons at present profess to act independently of party; and one or two of those who profess it, do in fact keep themselves independent. A considerable difference has taken place in the circumstances, by which the question of expediency is to be solved, since the increase of reading and of the daily press has brought almost every question of government and parliament to the bar of the people; who will of course pronounce upon each question separately, without looking to the distant operation of a more complex system of conduct, and may therefore come (as they have done) to look upon parties in Parliament as a juggle, and Parliament itself as uninfluenced in its decisions by any regard to the real merits of the questions which are discussed there, or to the interests of the public.⟩[1]

1. See the analyses and similar conclusions of Roberts, pp. 146–8, and Taylor, pp. 319–23.

383. To John Allen

BL Add. MSS 52180, ff. 51–2   Wells, Friday [4 May 1810]

. . .

I find that Romilly's excellent bills have been lost by our own people not attending, and particularly by our leaders (as they are called) going away.[1] This is but an unequal return for the exertions and sacrifices which are often made for them upon questions of theirs; when I recollect how often I have seen Romilly wait the whole night with all the business of next day awaiting him, it does appear quite inexcusable that he should have been so ill used upon this occasion. It was not felt, I suppose, that there [was] any thing in the question that would help them into office. Yet this perhaps was short-sighted; for the character and success of all the men who belong to the party, and especially of so eminent a person in the party as Romilly, is a part of their public character. That however is looking rather too far forward, for Tierney and Ponsonby. It is lamentable to see the interests of such a party, as the present Opposition in the House of Commons, in such incapable hands.

1. On 1 May Romilly's bills to mitigate the severity of the penal law (see Doc. 378) were defeated by two votes in a thin house, notwithstanding the warm support of the Master of the Rolls. 'Very few of the members of Opposition were present', Romilly recalled (*Romilly*, ii. 142–4). 'In general they wished well to the Bill, but not well enough to give themselves the trouble of attending upon it.'

384. To John Allen

BLPES iv. 245–6   [Lincoln's Inn], Tuesday [8 May 1810]

. . .

I heard Lord Grey's speech last night, with great pleasure for its eloquence, and, so far as a general statement could go, with satisfaction as to its substance.[1] The address will not deal, I trust, in vague and delusive generalities. An explicit and intelligible declaration of practical principles, and proposals too, may do us some good with the public, and give the public some chance of being saved: it is the only chance of any good. I hope you will attend to this proceeding, as by far the most important, in its immediate effect as well as future consequences, of any of the measures of the present Opposition.

1. On the evening of 7 May Grey gave notice that later in the session he would present an explicit declaration of the principles upon which Opposition acted. Horner thought Grey's remarks on that occasion the 'best specimen of his manner'. (*Hansard*, xvi. 846–9; Horner to Holland, 9 May, *Horner*, ii. 13.)

385. To Dugald Stewart

BLPES iv. 247–8 ⟨Horner, ii. 10–12⟩ Lincoln's Inn, 8 May 1810

⟨I have heard this morning with the highest satisfaction and pleasure, that you have accomplished your wish of having Brown nominated to be your successor.[1] On every public as well as private account, this event gives me the most sincere gratification. It does the Corporation of Edinburgh much credit, and almost inspires a hope that the University, and all the important interests which hang upon it, may be rescued from the ruin which so lately appeared certain. The appointment must be felt as a vital wound by that base church party, who under the conduct of the Dundas junto, have hitherto kept up so successful a contest against every person suspected of a free spirit, or of liberal opinions; and who must have looked upon the acquisition of the chair of Moral Philosophy as their final triumph.[2] I would write to you more frequently about our little politics, if I had any thing cheering to tell you. But I despond so disagreeably in my own views that I feel no disposition to communicate my impressions. The absurdity and the wickedness of the leaders of the democratic party in Middlesex have very recently brought matters to a worse pass than ever, in the result of which one cannot foresee any thing as very probable but a new accession of strength to the Crown, and the disappearance of all moderate notions of liberty, in a distracted but not doubtful struggle between popular frenzy and military force.[3] A faint effort you will observe in the proceedings of the House of Lords last night, is about to be made by the leaders of the Whig party, to regain the confidence of the public, by an explicit declaration of their views; but I fear they are hardly prepared to go as far as in the present circumstances they ought, and it is perhaps too late to recover, except by a very decisive tone, and by a very plain line of conduct, the effects of their blameable reserve and hesitation upon those questions of economy and reform which so much agitate the people. Never were men treated with so much injustice by the public as they have been, with respect to their Administration; but their resentment of this injustice, at variance always with the real liberality of their intentions and principles, has made them most indecisive and inefficient as leaders of the Opposition. The dangers of the time have at length awakened them to the necessity of taking a more marked and intelligible course; and this is rendered more easy indeed, by the plainness with which that small but noisy party of which Cobbett is the organ, have avowed their designs. But it is setting out with great disadvantages if, in collecting a popular party, you must exclude those who, in appearance only, carry popular feelings to excess; and I must confess to you, that we have a still greater disadvantage against us in this, that though our leaders in the House of Lords entertain very enlightened and even popular principles, they have very little of popular feelings. In the House of Commons too, where the main fight should be carried on, we have no leader at all. You will not wonder that, taking such a view of our situation, I should despair.⟩

. . .

1. Thomas Brown had been chosen in late April to succeed Stewart in the Chair of Moral Philosophy at Edinburgh and served for several months as his assistant before taking over towards the end of the year (Brown, pp. 186–8).

2. For similar views see Horner to Brown, London, 8 May, *ibid.*, pp. 188–9.
3. On 21 Feb. John Gale Jones (1769–1838: *DNB*), the conductor of a London debating society which recently had published materials critical of Charles Yorke for enforcing as teller in the Walcheren debate the standing order excluding strangers, was hauled before the bar of the House of Commons by order of the Speaker and committed to Newgate for contempt. On 24 Feb. Sir Francis Burdett, in a letter to the *PR*, attacked the action of the House and denied its power to imprison Britons who had elected it. On 5 Apr. the Speaker ordered Burdett to be committed to the Tower. Burdett refused to surrender to the Speaker's warrant and prepared to stand a siege in his house, but the Sergeant-at-Arms eventually broke through Burdett's defences and carried him off to the Tower. The reformers of the metropolis exploited the occasion to represent Burdett as a martyr who had defended the sovereignty of the people against the tyranny of a corrupt Parliament, and successfully stirred up the passions of the mob, most notably in Middlesex. The 'Burdett riots' were promptly quelled, but the issue of parliamentary privilege revived the cry for parliamentary and economical reform, inspiring numerous petitions to Parliament and largely dominating the proceedings of the Commons for the remainder of the session. (Roberts, pp. 265–70.)

386. To J.A. Murray

BLPES iv. 253–6 (incomplete copy or draft)
⟨*Horner*, ii. 15–19⟩[1]   London, 18 May 1810

⟨I am not sure that you will be of opinion that the House acted right in its vote of Friday last, respecting the question of privilege; resolving, that the Speaker should plead, with an understanding (not expressed in the resolution) that it should be a plea in bar.[2] I cannot say that I am so well satisfied, as not to have something like misgivings in my own mind, that we may have yielded up part of what I am convinced ought to be retained in full possession: but the most prudent persons think the course taken to be the right one, and I admit that I see no other course to which there are not more conclusive objections. Those who are against the House of Commons in its claim of privilege, among whom I am sorry to say are the best of our lawyers, quite concur in the vote; they think the privilege ought to be over-ruled by a court of law, and they are glad that this form of plea, by admitting the jurisdiction, will give the court an opportunity of deciding against the claim. These lawyers and the republicans are in unison about this. The Ministers, and we who concurred with them, think the Court will respect the privilege. The more rigid Whigs are alarmed by this very appearance of concert among such parties, who, how repugnant soever to one another in their ultimate views, are all of them more or less adverse to the constitutional power and authority of the House of Commons. It is of the essence of the republican spirit, to hate every semblance of discretionary power, and particularly the complex structure of a mixed government in which there is a conflict of such powers, and to insist that all authority should be reduced to the rules of a constant law administered in a course of judicial proceeding. The lawyers are brought to the same conclusion by the habits of their professional life, and resent, as a sort of reflection cast upon the perfection of their system, every departure from their modes. The present Ministers, who are almost all lawyers bred upon the lowest benches of the forum, are guided partly (I have no doubt) by their old habitudes, though much more by the convenience of taking that course which shall most easily bring to an end, or seem to bring to an end, their present difficulties. Both the republicans and the lawyers appear to me wholly mistaken, as to what it is possible for the law, judicially administered, to accomplish, as well as what the constitutional law of this country has provided for cases like that which has occurred. It is not in human nature possible to frame a government without leaving a certain power, not indeed arbitrary and wholly without rule, but discretionary, and to be exercised within certain rules according to circumstances. The peculiar character of the English constitution is, that that portion of discretionary power is shared among the several constituted authorities, instead of residing in one; and the chances of an improper exercise of it are lessened, by the checks which are thus established. The doctrine of the lawyers, and that of the republicans, tend to the establishment of a simpler frame, whether of democracy or of monarchy, in which they would speedily find that there would still be a discretionary power somewhere lodged, and that the universal dominion of the law would still be disputed, as the judicial law would still be inadequate. The only plan that has yet proved successful, in confining this discretionary power within proper limits, is the system of mutual controls, which results from the partition of this power among the several branches of a mixed government.

⟨My view of parliamentary privilege is this, that it is not a law to be applied (like the rules of criminal justice) to every case that occurs, and which is brought before the court, but a discretionary power to be exercised or not, and to the full extent of the rule or much short of it, according as it shall, upon a view of all existing circumstances and probable consequences, appear to be useful and necessary or otherwise that such an interposition of authority and punishment should take place. But then I have another doctrine, that this power is not unlimited and undefined, but of limits and a definition which may be certainly known, by consulting properly the records of parliamentary customs and usage. I think the House of Commons has an ancient and most necessary criminal jurisdiction, excluding all other courts, for the punishment of offences committed against itself and its members as such; and whoever will read the Rolls and the Journals, in the spirit with which all precedents ought to be studied (not to square the circumstances of particular cases, but to extract the principle which is implied in all of them, the principle which was aimed at in the precedents of good times, and which in those of bad times, was made the pretext of violence), will have no difficulty in collecting the evidence of this right of jurisdiction, as well as its fixed and due limits. I cannot at all approve of the doctrine, which Mr Ponsonby quoted the other night with approbation, from Blackstone, that it would be inexpedient and hazardous to the independence and authority of Parliament to have its privileges defined. They seem to me to be all very plainly defined already, as much as things of that nature can be; and if they were not, I should think it most wise to give them at length that definition. We have defined prerogative, which was, perhaps, a bold experiment in government; the success of it may satisfy us that there is no hazard in bringing privilege, if it be yet to bring, within the bounds of legal description. But by legal description, I do not intend a statutory enactment, and still less the more narrow conception of the law as administered in courts of justice, but in the manner practised in all ages by Parliament, by a resolution of the House itself.

⟨I have no manner of doubt, that the Judges in Westminster Hall will recognize this privilege in the present instance. They are bound, by the law, to recognize it; and unhappily the present instance of its exercise comes from that quarter, with whose feelings they are always found to sympathize.⟩ . . .

 1. This letter is wrongly dated 22 May in *Horner*; an excerpt from that to Murray of 22 May, none of which Leonard Horner printed, follows as Doc. 387.
 2. Imprisoned in the Tower, Burdett brought legal action alleging a breach of privilege on the part of the Speaker, the Sergeant-at-Arms, and the Constable of the Tower, and a deluge of petitions demanding his release descended upon the House. On 11 May the House, having received the report of a committee which had been appointed to search for precedents, reviewed Burdett's defence and concluded that the Speaker and the Sergeant-at-Arms should be at liberty to appear before the bar of the House and plead to the actions. For a note by Horner on this matter dated 6 May see *Horner*, ii. 10. See also *Romilly*, ii. 147–8.

387. To J.A. Murray

BLPES iv. 257–8   [London], Tuesday [22 May 1810]

I am sorry and somewhat ashamed to say that the Bill is gone from the House of Commons, without any animadversions having been made upon it. So little opportunity have we, in the present pressure of more general subjects, to discuss measures of a local nature. I watched the Bill several nights, till I was tired of such vigils, and your Lord Advocate on some favourable occasion stole it through. In consequence of your letter I have written to Lord Lauderdale, begging him to try either to send it back to us, or at least to stop its progress; and I have told him there is a chance of some resolutions against it coming from the Faculty.[1]

 . . .

 The debate on reform was a very poor one in every respect, and did not deserve so good a division.[2]

 1. Horner refers to a Government bill making some – but evidently unsatisfactory – changes in the inefficient and expensive practices of the Court of Session about which he and Grenville had previously complained. Afterwards Horner conducted, at the request of the Dean of the Faculty of Advocates, research on the exclusion of barristers from English juries and in matters pertaining to the reform of Scots judicature acted as an intermediary between Murray and Lauderdale, whom he described as 'the only peer who takes any charge of Scotch affairs'. (Horner to Murray, 29 May and 2 June, BLPES iv. 259–60 and 263–4.) On the third reading of the new bill in the Lords on 14 June Lauderdale reiterated his objections, but to no avail as usual (*Hansard*, xvii. 643–4).
 2. The debate of 21 May on Brand's motion for parliamentary reform: *ibid.*, xvii. 123–65.

388. To Earl Grey

Grey MSS, Durham University [?London], 24 May [1810]

The grounds on which I went, in what I stated the other day respecting the increase of foreign shipping in our trade,[1] were these –

That Marryat, the insurance broker, stated in the House some time ago, and was not contradicted, that *ten millions* were paid in freight last year to foreign ships for the import of commodities from the enemy's countries, under the system of Licences; he stated the number of vessels, on which such freight had been paid, at 4,000. On this occasion, Rose, not denying the statement to be true, said they were neutrals.[2]

In the Bullion Committee, a continental merchant, whom we examined, stated, that almost the whole of the enormous import from the Baltic last year was made in foreign ships, as well as the large imports from France of wines and brandies. This person explained the great amount of freight paid to these foreign ships, by stating, that the average rate of freight might amount to 50 per cent upon the original cost of the goods; instead of being between 10 and 20, which it would have been, if the importations had been made in British bottoms.[3]

And Rose himself, when he proposed his resolution for a duty on foreign timber, said, that 338,000 tons of foreign shipping were employed last year in importing this article, on which between two and three millions were paid for freight.

Perceval's answer to me was, from the annual accounts of trade and navigation, that the increase of foreign tonnage was not so great as that of British;[4] and those accounts certainly do not make the former so high as was to be expected from the other statements I have mentioned. To save you trouble, I will set the numbers down from the accounts.

	foreign ships	tons
1807	3,712	626,603
1808	1,829	269,970
1809	4,692	722,920

The number of seamen given, for the foreign ships of last year, is 36,420.

These accounts seem scarcely consistent with Marryat's story or Rose's. At the same time, the most important part of the question is not shown by figures; for it is the change from American ships and seamen, to such as lie more at the command of the French Government, which makes this increase of foreigners in our navigation a reasonable subject of jealousy.

There is reason to believe, that a certain proportion, I am told about a half, of this foreign tonnage is either actually British shipping or in the names of British subjects. So that I may possibly, in what I said the other day, have exaggerated the evil to be apprehended. Indeed I went less upon the facts to be learned from merchants and figures, than upon the probability that so able a statesman as the French Emperor would avail himself of an advantage, which seems most plainly to be offered to him, by our senseless policy respecting the American trade coupled with our avidity for imports and exports.

1. On 22 May: *Hansard*, xvii. 164–6.

2. The exchange had occurred in the course of the debate of 13 Feb. on Rose's bill to prohibit the use of corn in distilleries. But according to *Hansard*'s account (xv. 390–99) the amount stated by Marryat was a 'little short of a million sterling'.

3. Edwin Cannan, on p. xlii of the introduction to *The Paper Pound of 1797–1821*. *The Bullion Report* (2nd ed., 1925), conjectures that the 'continental merchant' was N.M. Rothschild.

4. On 22 May: *Hansard*, xvii. 166.

389. To Earl Grey

Grey MSS, Durham University   Lincoln's Inn, 10 June 1810

I have delayed too long to send you a note, as you desired me, of the result of our inquiries in the committee about the state of money. And I fear I am unable to furnish you exactly with what you wished to have; the general scope of our opinions and reasonings, you have seen in the resolutions; and any details in support of those conclusions would not admit of being compressed into so small a compass as to be of any use to you. If a description, in general terms, of the existing evil and the remedy proposed by us, would be enough, it might be put into something of the following form.

That there is too much reason to apprehend, that the current money of the kingdom is depreciated, in consequence of being too abundant, and from the want of the proper check to an over-issue of the paper, of which it now almost entirely consists. The unusually high price of the precious metals, for so considerable a period of time, and the extraordinary fall of the foreign exchanges, corresponding in point of time with the other circumstance, seem to demonstrate, that the value of our circulating medium is sunk below its legal standard. That the standard of money, which is the common measure and rule of all transactions of commerce, ought to be preserved as invariable as the nature of things will permit; but unless the issues of paper currency be kept within due bounds, its excess cannot fail to have the effect of lowering the value of our currency, and enhancing prices, and thereby deranging all money transactions in a manner the most unjust to creditors of every description. That no permanent and sure check to such excess can be found, but in the prompt convertibility of all paper currency into the coins of His Majesty's mint, according to the former law and usage of the realm; and by restoring our money system to that natural and sound state, in which it stood before the suspension of cash payments at the Bank of England, a measure which, however fit it may have been to meet a sudden and urgent purpose, was not calculated for any long continuance.

I have only suggested the substance of what I conceive might be stated, but must leave it to your Lordship to express it in the proper manner. As the remedy must be applied by Parliament itself, and not recommended to the King, I suppose the mention of the subject in the Address ought to be by way of promise or pledge to act in the next session. At all events, I am very anxious that this matter should be mentioned in your speech, that what we have been doing below may, during the prorogation, wear something like a sanction from those who have most authority and weight with the public. The evil is to be remedied most effectually and most easily, by the gradual force of public opinion.[1]

1. This letter, which was evidently written at Grey's request, preceded Grey's House of Lords address and resolutions of 13 June (*Hansard*, xvii. 535ff.). On that occasion Grey attacked the leading principles of Pitt's Government and, by Holland's description (*Holland's Further Memoirs*, p. 54), sought to

> recapitulate the dangers of the country; to expose the rashness of our policy . . . ; and to record the public principles of himself and his friends, by marking, on one hand, the difference between the system he recommended and that pursued by the Government, and on the other, a line of separation between himself and those reformers who were for circumscribing the powers of Parliament as well as altering fundamentally the basis of the representation.

390. To J.A. Murray

BLPES iv. 265–6 ‹*Horner*, ii. 19›   [London], Monday [11 June 1810]

I hear that the Scotch Bill will not pass without another fight against it on Thursday.[1] But of course the struggle is now ineffectual; none of the Lords, but Rosslyn and Lauderdale, care the least about it, though Lord Grenville would probably have taken some pains had he been able to attend; and the Chancellor will not stir, though he abuses the Bill as he sits on the woolsack, and damns it for being neither English nor Scotch. It will be very well worth considering, whether a bill to repeal it next session ought not to be talked of at Edinburgh immediately, and even perhaps mentioned in a Faculty meeting. This will keep the present opponents of it together – and, if it proves as burdensome as it seems likely to be found, will make them more watchful. . . .

. . .

‹Before the inhabitants of Edinburgh are scattered into the country, I wish very much you would take some opportunity of sounding them upon the question of Scotch Parliamentary Reform. The longer I live I become the more keen on that subject; both because I become daily more convinced that there is no part of the kingdom which would send more useful representatives than Scotland would, if there were a popular choice; and because it is manifest that none of the other great objects can be gained for Scotland, such as jury trial, until you have more active representatives. The measure will never be carried without a very decided opinion in favour of it, indeed a strong call for it from Scotland; such as there seems to have been, before the excesses of the French revolution stopped the progress of all our political improvements. I know there is no such anxiety upon the matter at present; but one should like to feel the pulse, and guess whether by administering proper materials the fever could once more be brought on.›[2]

1. See Doc. 387.
2. *Horner* wrongly indicates an omission here.

391. To James Loch

BLPES iv. 267–9   Lincoln's Inn, Monday [25 June 1810]

. . .

You had no business to think of politics; and I have a great mind not to tell you any. I must however mention, that Burdett appears to have impaired his popularity materially by his escape from the Tower; the liberty boys see he has not mettle for all they might want him upon occasion to do – the good humoured noisy mob, who enjoy the buzz and parade of election shows, as it is good for us they should, think he used them *ungenteel* – and the more rational and systematic democrats make unfavourable comments upon his apparent want of resolution. Upon the whole, there is a little tendency in the last description of Westminster people to fall back into their ranks as good old Whigs; but whether this disposition shall be improved by subsequent circumstances, or again be counteracted, will depend upon those circumstances, for we do not seem to have conduct enough to make them or to guide them. I own, Burdett's conduct has given me considerable satisfaction; both for the reason that it has injured his democratic popularity, which he was not likely to turn to any good purpose for the public, and because it shows that with his fondness for that intoxicating applause, and with all his headstrong vanity, he is neither the dangerous man in point of character and power nor in point of intentions which he has now and then seemed to be. Now that his glory is a little clipped, I can acknowledge that he is of some use to us in our mixed state of politics; that quick sense of indignation which he has against all manner of public injustice and oppression is one of the best elements of the true passion for liberty, though more knowledge than he possesses of the right means of preserving liberty is required in order to make that passion very useful to the public. I shall generally be for Burdett, when he is not too popular. He will never be very popular, if he shows such half measures as in his late transaction; for his own purposes, if he had such, he has gone too far to retreat; but, for the sake of the public, it is never too late to shrink from a purpose which has gone too far.

I fear there will be a dreadful battle in Portugal; though not quite so soon perhaps as most people expect. It seems unlikely, that Massena will risk a general action, until he can bring into the field an immense superiority of numbers; and in the cessation of all other operations upon the continent, there seems every probability that an immense effort will be made. I rather expect to hear that the Emperor has himself left Paris early some morning to be present at a decisive battle. Very few persons pretend to have any confidence in our Portuguese levies; they are improving very fast in discipline, but as they have not yet fleshed their swords it will be most hazardous to give them any important station on that day, or even to reckon their numbers as so many on our side. In our own troops, we have every reason to feel the most complete confidence; and I am convinced that they will not yield to any small superiority of numbers. But to risk that army for such objects as it is now practicable to gain in the peninsula, appears to be very unwise. The peninsula must be left to the untameable spirit of its population, which will never submit, though in a military sense it may be conquered by the occupation of the surface. The desolation of the interior is described by persons who have come from there recently, as being quite horrible; and at this moment, there are so many points of insurrection, that the French troops are called away from their regular lines of operation.

. . .

392. To J.A. Murray

BLPES iv. 270–75 〈Horner, ii. 20–24〉   Lincoln's Inn, Tuesday [26 June 1810]

〈The Report of the Bullion Committee is not yet out of the printer's hands; so that those who praised it to you were liberal enough to bestow that praise upon credit. I can let you into the secret, however, that the report is in truth very clumsily and prolixly drawn; stating nothing but very old doctrines on the subject it treats of, and stating them in a more imperfect form than they have frequently appeared in before. It is a motley composition by Huskisson, Thornton, and myself; each having written parts, which are tacked together without any care to give them an uniform style, or a very exact connection. One great merit the Report, however, possesses; that it declares, in very plain and pointed terms, both the true doctrine and the existence of a great evil growing out of the neglect of that doctrine. By keeping up the discussion, which I mean to do, and by forcing it again upon the attention of Parliament, we shall in time (I trust) effect the restoration of the old and only safe system.〉

. . .

You would have admired Lord Grey's speech very much, if you had heard him deliver it; the correctness, elegance and purity of his language, the perspicuity of his method, the practical yet elevated tone of his opinions, would have been all to your taste.[1] I heard little of the remainder of that debate; not Lord Lansdowne's speech: but there is no difference of opinion whatever between him and Lord Grey on any of the subjects that were discussed; at least none that I am aware of, and I have lived a good deal with both lately, particularly with Lansdowne. The Doctor's speech I did hear, and like all the late effusions of that blockhead, it was not very easy to see how his opinions and reasonings, if they can be so called, led him to his conclusion and vote: he voted against Lord Grey's motion. He is a temporizing, candid, empty, pompous jack-ass.

〈The story you heard of Lord Erskine and the Prince had some foundation, but was exaggerated, and the scene was mislaid. There was some argument between them about privilege, at a dinner at the Foundling Hospital, which was magnified by Erskine's enemies into a sharp and angry dispute. But I understand it was at a private dinner that the retort you allude to was made by the Prince, who, when Erskine said the principles he maintained were those which had seated HRH's family on the throne, said they were principles which would unseat any family from any throne.

〈I have no idea that there is any serious displeasure felt by the Prince against Erskine on this account; though Erskine has not left it to this day for him to prove, that rather than yield his public opinions he is ready to encounter that displeasure. His opinions upon this occasion are, I think, quite erroneous; his prejudices as a lawyer, perhaps an itch for popular favour, perhaps too a dislike of the House of Commons, all conspire to lead him wrong. The House of Commons was not his theatre of glory; he was perpetually losing there the fame he won in Westminster Hall.

‹I am more surprised at Romilly having erred, as I cannot but think he has done; and I regard it as a striking proof, how difficult it is for a man, whose mind is trained in the course of administering justice, especially if he be a lover of liberty, to allow the propriety or necessity of any thing like discretionary power being left anywhere. Both the habits of a lawyer's mind, and the sentiments which compose one's love of liberty, are in favour of the simpler system of constant and known rules and forms for every case that occurs; and the true theory of freedom is, unquestionably, to carry that principle as far as possible. For my part, this question came upon me by surprise; I hesitated a good deal, before I acquiesced in the doctrine of privilege to the extent to which I would now be prepared to state it; but I am satisfied now, after as accurate a view as I can take of what is the real necessity, that it is necessary for the efficient existence of the Commons' House, that they should be entrusted with the discretionary privilege of punishing by commitment those who either obstruct or libel them.[2]

‹I regret deeply that Romilly is on the other side of this great question; it weakens both the claim of privilege and his reputation that they are not found together. You need not, however, be under any apprehension, that he does not stand well with our party: no lawyer ever stood higher than he does in the House of Commons, or more thoroughly possessed the confidence of his party.

‹What a curious scene was exhibited last week in this city; and what would John Wilkes or Cardinal De Retz have said, to such a false step as Burdett has made, in failing to appear in the procession prepared for him. He has acted in that a more temperate and peaceable part, than I had previously given him credit for; but it is manifest, that his conduct is inconsistent with itself, that all he had done before required him to go on, and that he had advanced too far in the popular race to turn back. . . . His powers of doing mischief are diminished, therefore, if he ever had any mischievous designs, which I do not believe; and if the public were once satisfied that he is no longer popular with the multitude, and thereby formidable, I think he has qualities that would enable him, in his way, to do good occasionally, and to assist other public men in doing good in theirs. Vain he is, no doubt,› very ill-informed, ‹and always acting upon the suggestions of others, and those often inferior to himself; but he has a prompt indignation against injustice and oppression, one of the best elements of the passion for liberty; and by great and fortunate labour he has acquired a talent for speaking in public› infinitely above his understanding. ‹I believe he loves his country and the ancient institutions›, but he is neither enlightened nor very intelligent. ‹I think, too, he has considerable candour in judging of the talents as well as motives of other men; but there have been some symptoms of a very pitiful jealousy, towards those who have interfered with him in his own line of Westminster popularity. He has rendered himself a remarkable man, though I fear he is not likely to do any great or lasting service to the public: his late transactions have extended his popularity beyond the capital, to which it was confined before; but in the end they have lessened it in the capital.⟩

. . .

1. Horner's interpretation of Grey's speech of 13 June displays the extent to which he had cast his political lot with the Whig hierarchy. Though Grey's replies to Horner's letters of 24 May and 10 June (Docs 388–9) are in neither the Grey nor the Horner papers, Grey apparently commented on his prospective resolutions in a manner that alarmed Horner. In an undated letter to Allen (BLPES iv. 204–205), which was perhaps written on 11 June, he expressed fear 'that a capital and fatal error is likely to be committed by the aristocratic branch of the party; those whom I commonly think the most judicious, and know to be most honest, entertain views which appear to me founded in a total mistake of the present state of the public opinion, as well as to be in point of policy very short-sighted'. He then urgently requested a conference with Allen that may or may not have transpired, but at all events Grey's address and resolutions were most certainly a major, if not a fatal, error. Erskine condemned Grey on the floor of the House, Lord Douglas and the Duke of Gloucester both refused to vote, and Holland, who supported Grey, was described by Tom Grenville as 'not above half right upon the question'. A correspondent told Whitbread that Grey's speech ensured that he, Whitbread, now had 'the honestest part of the Foxites sincerely attached' to him; Creevey concluded that Grey was 'bona fide *Insane*'; and young Lord John Russell damned 'the aristocratical notions and vague arguments' that abounded in Grey's speech and observed that the political doctrine emerging from the Grey–Grenville coalition 'seems to be a Whiggy-Toryish mixture'. (Tom Grenville to Lord Grenville, [16 June], *Dropmore MSS*, x. 44; P. Payne to Whitbread, [?June], Whitbread MSS 2522; Creevey to W. Roscoe, 14 Sept., Roscoe MSS 1057; Russell to Holland, 7 Aug. 1810, BL Add. MSS 51677.)

2. Horner elaborated at some length on the principles at law that had led him to his view of parliamentary privilege in a letter to Murray of 17 July (*Horner*, ii. 27–30).

393. To Francis Jeffrey

BLPES iv. 276–80 ⟨*Horner*, ii. 24–7⟩   [London], 16 July 1810

⟨I am just returned to town, after an absence of about ten days. The Bullion Report, I am rather surprised to find, is not yet delivered from the printers; I revised the proof sheets before I left town. I would rather do something for you myself, if you will let me know the utmost time you can allow me; rather, I mean, than trust that subject [bullion] in the hands of any of your mercenary troops: one of whom was guilty of deplorable heresies in the account of a book by one Smith.[1] I will do a short article for you this time, to do justice to Mr Ricardo and Mr Mushet, who called the public attention to this very important subject at the end of last year.⟩[2] There is a tract by a Mr Blake also, of which I hear a favourable report.[3] Will you be contented with this? And in October, I should like to resume the subject, if the Report of the Committee produces any discussion. I should wish to keep the subject in my own hands, if I begin it again; for it would be only a continuation of the little I did before in the articles upon Thornton and Lord King. All the consequences which the Committee foresaw four months ago, are beginning to manifest themselves, both among the London speculators and the country bankers.

. . .

‹Will you allow me once again to protest against your suffering so much party politics in the *Edinburgh Review*? You knew my sentiments on that point long ago; nor would I now obtrude them, if I had not been led to feel with increased weight the justness of all my former objections, by the manner in which the last number has been received.[4] I am quite sure the character and efficient usefulness of the work is very considerably impaired; and it appears to me to be of great political importance, that that injury should be retrieved as speedily as possible. The power of the *Review* over the public mind, which was once so great, and is still very considerable, depended very much upon that general tone of politics, which, when it was the transcript of your sentiments, it almost uniformly preserved. But the turn it has taken of late, by descending to questions between Ministry and Opposition, and even to individual crimination, has lowered its name and given a prejudice against all its opinions and reasonings, even upon other occasions. Some time before I left town, I heard a long conversation about the *Review* between Lord Holland, Tierney, and Allen in which they all expressed the same opinion which I have now taken the liberty of representing to you. And I think you ought to give the more weight to a sentiment in which so many persons agreed, who would naturally feel very differently about the *Review*: you would hardly have expected that Tierney would refuse any party aid from the press; and in truth I believe his opinion upon the subject was taken up in this light, that a more powerful aid was given by the *Edinburgh Review* to the Whig party, composed as it is at present, and still more to the questions and principles to which that party is pledged, while the work preserved its independent judicial air of authority, than it can furnish by all its activity and skill as a partisan. I meant to have told you of this conversation before, which impressed me very strongly at the time, as conclusive evidence of the effect which the recent conduct of the *Review* had produced upon its own reputation. But I felt some reluctance in urging a topic which might be a disagreeable one to you, on account of the difficulty and delicacy you might feel in acting upon my view of the matter, even if you agreed with me. Brougham has been too useful and powerful an ally, to make it easy for you to point out any change you might wish for; but when I recollect the many admirable articles he formerly gave you upon more general subjects, I own that I regret very much that he should misplace his compositions so much, as to print in the *Review* what he ought to speak in the House of Commons.

‹I wish very much that Brougham and I were upon such a footing that I could state these things to himself; but that has been long otherwise: a consideration which more than any other has made me backward in stating them to you. But I have been latterly so much urged by other persons to use my influence with you, that I have been induced to make that effort upon this occasion.

‹I must not conclude without thanking you very gratefully for the pleasure I received in reading your extracts from Crabbe's *Borough*; some of which, particularly the 'Convict's Dream', leave far behind all that any other living poet has written.[5] Does not your critique, in some of its expressions and illustrations, break in a little upon the doctrines which you urged against Wordsworth? In the general principles, I am satisfied, you are consistent; and as far as I am capable of judging of such matters, I think you right; but a captious person might set you in some sentences against yourself. You must some day or other bring your thoughts on the philosophy of poetry and poetic expression into the form of a systematic essay; which I shall insist upon your polishing with much care. That, and a little treatise on the ethics of common life, and the ways and means of ordinary happiness, are the works which I bespeak from you for after-times.⟩[6]

1. James Mill had reviewed T. Smith, *Theory of Money and Exchange*, in ER xiii (no. xxv, Oct. 1808), 35–68.
2. Horner possibly refers to Ricardo's anonymous article, 'The Price of Gold', which was published in the *Morning Chronicle* of 29 Aug. 1809 and was followed by two letters answering critics (reprinted by the Johns Hopkins Press in 1903 as *Three letters on the price of gold, contributed to the Morning Chronicle (London) in August-November, 1809*), but more probably he refers to Ricardo's pamphlet, *The High Price of Bullion*, which had been published in January 1810. For Mushet see Doc. 377 n. 3.
3. William Blake (1774–1852), *Observations on the Principles Which Regulate the Course of Exchange; and on the Depreciated State of the Currency* (1810). Blake's *Observations*, which came to be regarded as the standard work on the subject of foreign exchanges despite an erroneous analysis of the actual rate of exchange, advanced a quantity theory of value very similar to that which Horner had deduced from his study of Hume and others at university. Blake reasoned that the actual or computed rate of exchange was determined by two different sets of causes: real exchange, or the demand and supply of foreign bills in the market, which was dependent on the foreign payments a country had to make, and nominal exchange, or those factors which affected the currency of a country such as the quantity and quality of metal in the coin and the amount of currency in relation to the amount of commodities that had to be circulated by it.
4. The April 1810 number of the ER contained three political articles advancing traditional Foxite doctrine. One by Jeffrey praised the French Revolution as the source of Napoleon's power, ridiculed the monarchies of the continent, and advocated British withdrawal from European wars, and two by Brougham championed parliamentary reform (ER xvi (no. xxxi), 1–30, 102–127, and 187–213). On 17 July Horner beseeched Murray (Horner, ii. 30) to use his influence with both Jeffrey and Brougham 'to keep out of the *Edinburgh Review* those party declamations, which are destroying its influence with the public'. 'Let them', he added, 'leave the last word to the *Quarterly Review*, and break off from this useless warfare at once.'
5. Jeffrey had reviewed George Crabbe's *Borough* in the ER xvi (no. xxxi, Apr. 1810), 30–55.
6. Jeffrey's reply of 20 July (Jeffrey, ii. 129–31) admitted that the *Review* was 'growing too factious' and expressed the hope that in future he could find reviewers 'of a milder and more disciplined character', adding with reference to Horner's projected article on bullion:
   I can give you till the 10th or 12th of August to transmit your first contribution. Make it as full, and long, and popular, as you can; and give us an outline of your whole doctrine, rather than a full exposition and vindication of its questionable and disputed points, which may come after.

394. From Lady Holland

BL Add. MSS 51644   Appleby Castle,[1] 30 July [1810]

... We made an excursion from hence to the Lakes ... at Keswick we saw Southey. He is as full of ardour and simplicity as ever. Do not cavil with the word *simplicity*. I only apply it to his feelings and character, certainly not to his writings as neither his style nor choice of subjects entitle him to that praise so applied. But he is of a frank open nature and does not conceal even his harmless vanities. He has in the press a poem consisting of five thousand lines in irregular rhyme. The subject is drawn from the Hindoo mythology very mild and obscure. It is called the curse of *Kihama* and proceeds upon the belief current amongst the Hindoos, that their Deities are compelled by an imperious necessity to comply with the prayers and entreaties of a supplicant, provided he undergoes all the penances of Prayer and self-mortification required by their *church discipline*, so that be it a blessing upon himself or a curse upon his neighbour a sufficient quantity of prayer and fasting must extract it from the fattened God.

Besides this poem he is [*sic*] has another nearly ready for publication. The Hero is the celebrated Don Pelayo whose adventures are to be sung in blank verse without any other machinery than the mere aid of Mortal Valour . . . We made no inquiry about Coleridge who is I suspect living with him, as there was a periodical work written by him lately published at Whitehaven. Wordsworth, is upon a visit to Sir George Beaumont.[2]

. . .

Lord Holland has a letter from the Marqués de la Romana dated Alverca British headquarters 4th July. He does not say what scheme has taken him there. He is full of complaints at the folly of his Countrymen whom [*sic*] he thinks might have got rid of the *french dogs*. He encloses a letter for Mr Canning! What could tempt him to choose Lord Holland for the medium of communication [illegible].[3] I hear that your friend Ward is very desirous of promoting a political junction with Mr C. and the Opposition. Will he when in the H. of Lords lead or follow Lord Boringdon, the life and soul and whole of the Canning party there?

. . .

1. The Hollands were on a seven weeks' excursion to the north, staying a few days at Lord Thanet's place in Westmorland (*Lady Holland's Journal*, i. 256–7).
2. Southey's *chef d'œuvre The Curse of Kehama* indeed appeared at last in 1810; but *Roderick, the last of the Goths*, in which Pelayo, the grandfather of Alfonso I, figured prominently, did not appear until 1814. The Coleridge reference is presumably to his abortive *Friend*, though it seems to have been produced at Penrith rather than Whitehaven and had ceased to appear in March. Sir George Howland Beaumont (1753–1827: *DNB*) was a distinguished patron of the arts and a friend of Coleridge and Wordsworth.
3. Pedro Caro y Sureda, Marqués de la Romana (1761–1811), the Spanish general whose military and political role in the Spanish civil war is mentioned frequently in *Lady Holland's Spanish Journal*, had gone to Wellington to appeal to him to do something to relieve the siege of Ciudad Rodrigo. Quite what Romana wrote to Canning – who, after all, had been a close friend of Holland at Oxford – is unknown, but Horner had written to Lady Holland on 25 July (BLPES iv. 289–90):

> Of course you have heard of Canning's intended voyage to Cadiz, on a visit to the Universal Spanish Nation. Perhaps Lord Wellesley may think it a fit occasion, if Canning left his letter to Lord Holland in the office, to copy that notable precedent.

395. To Francis Jeffrey

BLPES iv. 293–4   Salisbury, Tuesday, 7 Aug. [1810]

I am a good deal disappointed at not having yet received the report of the Bullion Committee, which is not distributed from the Vote Office. I have brought Mr Ricardo's pamphlet and Mr Mushet's with me, and shall send you some account of them – not so full as I intended; for I would rather do that after the Report is published; but enough to give them the credit which is their due of having called the attention of the public to this subject, and to make a short exposé of the chief reasonings upon it by extracts in their words.

My friend Sir John Cox Hippisley is anxious that the 2nd edition of his late speech, with the Appendix of very important and curious documents, should be well reported in the *Edinburgh Review*; particularly because it has been printed at the expense of the English Catholic Committee.[1] And he thinks it very material, that the import and conclusiveness of the documents, which he has added in the Appendix, particularly in the 2nd edition, should be pointed out. I have given him your address, that he may send the book to you.

. . .

Do not, My Dear Jeffrey, suffer any allusions to the *Quarterly Review*, or its doctrines or authors, to steal into yours. It is no longer a worthy adversary; and the true victory over such a rival, who shows so mean a spirit of malignity and such puny powers of attack, is by a scornful silence, and by persisting in your own better course. I expect that Walter Scott will be entirely reunited to you, by the malignant and feeble review of his last poem.[2] I hope you will review the Lady of the Lake yourself; it has not met with justice (I think) in London: that is, those who have hitherto overpraised Scott's poetry, begin to be tired of that and in the natural order of such things now praise it too faintly. There are passages in this, of the first merit; and though it is a great error in the management of his story, to have kept the reader out of the secret about Fitz James, I do not remember any other poem so long that one reads with so much interest and curiosity.

1. Sir John Coxe Hippisley (?1747–1825: *DNB*), MP for Sudbury and a Protestant well liked at the Papal Court, had conceived the compromise of a concession to the Crown of a veto on the appointment of Catholic bishops and had involved himself in a number of schemes designed to bring unity between the Whigs and the Catholics between 1806 and 1809. In 1806 he had published *The Substance of Additional Observations, intended to have been delivered in the House of Commons in the Debate on the Petition of the Roman Catholics of Ireland, on the 13th and 14th of May, 1805*. In 1810 he published *Substance of the Speech of Sir John Coxe Hippisley, on seconding the Motion of the Rt Hon. H. Grattan . . . Friday, 18th May, 1810*. Jeffrey's review of the enlarged second edition is in *ER* xvii (no. xxxiii, Nov. 1810), 1–39.
2. 'The Lady of the Lake' was reviewed by George Ellis (1753–1815: *DNB*) in *QR* iii (no. vi, May 1810), 492–517, and by Jeffrey in *ER* xvi (no. xxxii, Aug. 1810), 263–93.

396. To J.A. Murray

BLPES iv. 295–6[1]   Salisbury, 7 Aug. 1810

. . .

I quite agree with you about the review of the 'Lady of the Lake' in the last
Quarterly Review. Strange as it may well seem to you, it is certainly the production of
George Ellis. I shall think still worse of Scott than you know I have long done, if that
does not reconcile him to Jeffrey. You do not over-rate Scott's powers as a
descriptive poet; but I cannot permit you to speak of Homer – for Scott has no power
over the heart, and has no knowledge of the passions. He will be used with injustice
very soon in this country, the invariable issue of an excessive popularity. The fate of
young Roscius hangs over him. He is right to make his money fast: for his glory is
already in the wane. For myself, I shall always enjoy his splendid facility of diction
and measure, and those strong portraits of local manners which are the best fruits of
his limited but pleasing powers.

. . .

1. The following paragraph is one of several omitted without acknowledgement from *Horner*,
   ii. 30–31.

397. To T.R. Malthus

BLPES iv. 304–305 ⟨*Horner*, ii. 35–6⟩   Killarney,[1] 15 Sept. 1810

⟨I received last night your letter of the 7th instant in which you so very kindly invite
me to spend some time with you at Haileybury. . . .

⟨I am glad you are satisfied with the Bullion Report, so far as it goes. There are
still in the theory of the subject some points which give me difficulty, particularly in
what relates to exchange, and which I should like to try if they could be cleared up
by a little more thinking about them. In the Report, of course, we give the slip to all
such problems; as, for the useful and necessary purposes of the practical conclusion,
there is a plain road upon the principles that have been long well-settled. As it is,
the Report has more the air of a dissertation than was desirable; and any savour of
novel speculation, how just soever it might have been, would have tainted it to all
true born Englishmen. All the hopes I have of immediate success with the House of
Commons, and those are but very faint, are built upon what seems to be our strong
hold of former experience and former doctrines, in opposition to what we have
called the *Theory* of the Bank Directors. It will be very pleasant to prevail by raising
that cry. I have no doubt, that, at no distant time, the evils, proceeding from the
want of responsibility in the Bank, will get to such a pitch as to force upon
Parliament a recurrence to the old system; I am only afraid, that some mischief may
be done in the mean time by interfering unwisely with the country banks, and with

that diffused and subdivided credit afforded by their means to the enterprises of small capitalists in remote parts of the country. I have had no time to make political inquiries of any sort in this country; but the little I have learned, about the state of currency and credit at Dublin for the last few months, makes me expect to receive an ample commentary from that quarter upon all the doctrines of our Report.

⟨. . .⟩

1. Horner had met Murray at Birmingham in early September and proceeded to Ireland for a holiday. For details of their passage and first days in Ireland see Horner's letter to his mother of 13 Sept. in *Horner*, ii. 31–5.

398. To Andrew Gray

BLPES iv. 306–309   Waterford, 22 Sept. 1810

. . . I have been running over a great part of this country very rapidly with my friend Murray . . . The extent of cultivated land is astonishing, though the style of husbandry appears to be miserable, except in the article of potatoes. In consequence of the ground being let in minute parcels, and almost the whole population of the South of Ireland maintaining themselves upon the land, the rents they pay are higher than is known in England, or even in Scotland as far as I know. The general system seems to be, that the family live upon the potatoes they raise, and pay their rent out of their oats and pigs. All I had heard of the rags, filth, and hovels of the Irish, fell short of the reality as I have found it to be; but with all this, they seem a very happy, merry hearted, and clever people; and men, women, and children of them, universally healthy, robust, and handsome.

I have heard a good deal in letters from England of dreadful disturbances in various parts of Ireland, of which I have heard nothing in the country itself. There are no doubt some districts, where, for want of proper magistrates, the law is not so strong as it ought to be, and a lawless spirit is allowed sometimes to run riot, among the young men of a very crowded and idle population. But the stories we usually read of, are much exaggerated. The greatest defect, as far as I have been able to learn, in the administration of Ireland, is that the commission of the peace is not filled as it ought to be, with gentlemen of personal influence, as well as right character for that office in point of firmness and moderation. In some parts, this may be difficult, from the absence of many proprietors; but that difficulty is very much increased, by the unwise reluctance to put Catholic gentlemen into the Commission, even where they have property and are respected, but preferring protestants of neither character nor estate. As long as this foolish prejudice subsists, the law will never have its authority fully established.

I cannot find, that the repeal of the Union, which makes so great a figure in the newspapers, and about which the little shopkeepers of Dublin (who have no doubt suffered by the Union) make so big a talk, has any partisans throughout the country generally, or is even a topic of much consideration. The kingdom is unquestionably thriving very fast, and very much in consequence of the Union; and even those, who most regret the loss of their parliament and the absence of their men of talents and influence, admit that in point of wealth and prosperity Ireland is making a rapid progress. One consequence of the Union has been, that many of the smaller gentry, such as could afford to live in Dublin when it was a capital but not to come to London, now reside upon their estates; which is a most important benefit to the country. Nothing has more surprised me here, than the excellence of the roads in every direction, and the number of new ones that have been made of late years and are now making. This is at once a very satisfactory proof of increasing opulence, and will prove the cause of farther increase.

. . .

399. From John Allen

BLPES iv. 310–12   Portsmouth, Sunday, 21 Oct. [1810]

. . .

The merchants are very busy, I can perceive, in raising a cry against the report of the Bullion Committee, and the argument which makes the greatest impression is one used by Randall Jackson[1] – i.e., that the high price of bullion does not arise from a depreciation of bank paper, because 100 guineas will not buy a greater quantity of bullion than £105 in Notes, and therefore either Notes are not depreciated or guineas are equally so. The argument resolves itself into the general question of why is there not, if notes are depreciated, a metallic price for commodities different from the paper price – a point on which I should like to know what you have got to say, that is, whether you explain this circumstance from the smallness of the depreciation, the public confidence in the bank paper, or from what other cause. Besides thinking the argument to be nothing more than part of a more extensive one, though the part best calculated to make a popular impression, I should be inclined to doubt very much the truth of his statement, and to suspect that if you were to carry 100 guineas to a bullion merchant, accustomed to supply exporting merchants with that article, you would get from him *not* the weight of 100 guineas in bullion, but that weight *minus* what he judges to be a compensation for the risk and trouble of melting 100 guineas and sweating off their produce in bullion for exportation.

. . .

1. Randle Jackson (1757–1837: *DNB*), the parliamentary counsel for the East India Company, had published *The Speech of Randle Jackson, esq., delivered at the General Court of the Bank of England, held on the 20th of September, 1810, respecting the report of the Bullion Committee.*

400. To the Duke of Somerset

BLPES iv. 317–18 ⟨Horner, ii. 36–8⟩   Lincoln's Inn, 2 Nov. 1810

I am very much obliged to your Grace, for keeping so fully in mind the inquiries I wished to have made with respect to the poor of your parish at Berry.[1] Mr Edwards's answer, with respect to the relief given to those labourers who have more than 3 children resident with them under 8 years of age, is the important one; and his statement on this point corresponds with what I have heard to be the case in other agricultural districts. It is a fact, on which I propose some time or other to build a considerable measure; and your Grace will perhaps enable me, through the same channel, to learn a few more details. ...

⟨I was too short a time in Ireland to learn much more about the state of the lower orders in that country, than that it is very different from the condition of the people in either of the other two kingdoms, and that it is a subject of great curiosity, and which strongly invites speculation. Their immense numbers, their rags and dirt, exceed[2] in reality all the descriptions which I formerly believed to be exaggerated; and so does their gaiety of manner, their cheerfulness in the midst of all this show of indigence and misery, and their education. The only appearance of industry I saw was in the village schools, which seemed so many bee-hives in swarming time; I was only in the Catholic part of Ireland, and have not quite information enough to conclude what I rather presume to be true, that it is to the zeal inspired by religious persecution that this singular effect is to be ascribed. The instance would for the present appear to be one on their side of the argument, who deny the advantages of education: but the good fruits, I am convinced, will be reaped in due season. It was during the persecution of the Presbyterians in Scotland, that their system of parish education was founded and organized, and the lower orders of that country remained for many years after the union in a state of wretched beggary, idleness, and insubordination. Fletcher of Salton's description of them would pass for too high colouring in describing the present Irish.[3] They are generally speaking unemployed, and lawless; and the greatest political evil of Ireland is their excessive number. Nothing seems likely to remedy this but that change in the occupation of landed property, by the breaking down of vast territories held by absentees into smaller estates, and the reverse process of converting the present fractions of leasehold into large farms, which will take place in the natural progress of wealth. It is a revolution which will cause some violent struggles, on the part of the displaced tenantry. And there have been already some proofs of the change having commenced, and of the struggles which attend it. This progress of agriculture in Ireland will be accelerated, I expect, by two circumstances, which may be regarded as accidental. The peculiar circumstances of England in respect of population and wealth give Ireland a near and vast market for grain; and Sir John Newport's Act has rendered the trade quite free.[4] The other circumstance is that the rebellion of 1798 has led both government and the country gentlemen of Ireland to pay an extraordinary attention to the improvement of their roads, which are better in that country and more numerous, than in almost any other.

⟨The late unexpected turn of things here will probably bring your Grace sooner to town than you intended. I have not heard how the King is to-day, but I have good reason to believe that he was worse yesterday than was publicly given out. The pains taken at Windsor to conceal the real extent of his illness, only make one believe it to be much more severe and serious.⟩ There is a story, for which however I have not yet heard sufficient authority, that this derangement has been brought on by the drying up of a seton in his neck. If that be so, he may be expected to die very soon.

. . .

1. Berry Pomeroy was Somerset's seat in Devon. Mr Edwards was probably his steward there.
2. Changed to 'excel' in *Horner*.
3. Andrew Fletcher of Saltoun (1655–1716: *DNB*) published a number of pamphlets on the employment of vagrants.
4. Sir John Newport's Act had provided in the summer of 1806 for the free exchange of grain between Great Britain and Ireland.

401. From Dugald Stewart

Kinnordy MSS   Kinneil House,[1] 5 Nov. [1810]

Many thanks, my dear Sir, for your kind communication at the present very interesting and critical moment. I shall flatter myself with the hope of soon hearing from you again how the King really is, and what turn public affairs are likely to take if his illness should continue. I am scarcely less anxious to learn how the Cortes go on. If they continue as they have begun, and do not split into factions, I shall still indulge some hope for Spain, whatever may be the issue of the contest between Wellington and Massena.

I have received very great pleasure and instruction from the Bullion Report, although I have not yet had it in my power to read it with all the attention I mean to bestow on it. It is not yet in the Edinburgh shops, and the few copies which have reached this country are in such request that I was obliged to return the only one I have seen before I had half satisfied my curiosity. In one or two instances, when you have expressed yourself in more general terms than I would have wished, I can easily enter into the motives which prevent you from speaking out your mind more fully, or from following your argument through all its consequences. You have certainly said more than enough to suggest matter of most serious and alarming reflection. After I have had an opportunity of studying your Report more deliberately, if any thing should occur to me that I think at all worthy of your notice, I shall write to you at some length upon the subject.

. . .

1. Kinneil was a mansion in West Lothian loaned to Stewart by the Duke of Hamilton. According to *Fox*, p. 121, it was one of that family's oldest possessions and partly uninhabited: 'It is large and rambling, and is not an ugly building though irregular and odd.'

402. To Dugald Stewart

BLPES iv. 319–22 ⟨Horner, ii. 38–40⟩   Lincoln's Inn, 16 Nov. 1810

. . . You will see, from the proceedings of both Houses, that another adjournment for a fortnight has been agreed to, upon the faith of representations from the Ministers that the King is already in a state of amendment: Perceval's statement in the House of Commons seemed to me very faint and guarded, and the Chancellor's, by what I can hear of it, was neither confident nor explicit. They said nothing of a speedy recovery, nor of any time within which it is to be expected.

The general belief is, that the King will recover. My own impression, from all I have heard and compared together, is, that he will probably be restored to such a degree of recollection and reason, as to be used in the manner he has been for some time past in the forms of public business; but that his bodily constitution has within the last few months undergone a material change for the worse. All the suspicions which one founded upon the public reports made by the physicians, and all the surmises which have been afloat with regard to the immediate cause of this fit of insanity and the state of his health for some time before, have received considerable confirmation from the conduct of Ministers in not bringing forward the physicians to be examined in Parliament. They must have strong reasons for departing from Pitt's precedent of 1788 in that particular; and must have dreaded the questions that might be put respecting the general health of the King, as well as the state of his sight and hearing. If the physicians have nothing more unsatisfactory to state than what the Ministers yesterday reported as their opinion, they would have been produced to give it in their own words.

The conduct of the Prince, during the whole period of this illness, has been reserved, and quite consistent with an intention to act honourably towards the Whig party. He has very judiciously taken up his residence entirely at Windsor, and has had no communication with any person whatever. The Ministers are said to have made an overture, to explain to him their views and intentions; but his answer was, that they must have made up their minds with respect to their course of proceeding, and he saw no necessity of their consulting him.[1] Sheridan, on the other hand, is said to have made two attempts at Windsor to see him, but was not admitted. This quiet deportment, so unlike his usual bustle and fidgeting, has been considered by some persons as an indication that he thinks his object pretty sure and near him.

. . .

⟨I was much chagrined, upon my coming to London, to find that no copy of the Bullion Report had been sent to you from the Vote Office, though I wrote from the circuit expressly to desire it, and I had taken for granted that it had been sent. It is now out of print; but there is a copy which I have lent to a gentleman who is now in Yorkshire, and which, as soon as I can recover it, I will send to you; if I should not be fortunate enough to procure another sooner. I hope you have got Huskisson's tract, and pray let me know if you have Mr Blake's, which is very good.[2] The subject has produced much discussion in England, and, I have no doubt, will within a year or two, be practically settled agreeably to our views. Every day, I hear of converts. You could not do me a greater favour, than by communicating to me what particular points there are in the doctrine stated by the committee, on which you either entertain a different opinion, or feel difficulties; for myself I will own, that there are a few instances, in which I think the argument has not yet been placed accurately upon the right grounds, as there are some in which I contented myself (in drawing my part of the Report) with assuming what might have been deduced from principles, but not without an air of more theory and general speculation than I thought it prudent (on account of my own situation) that the Report should bear. I suppose it is with respect to the wages of labour, and the pay of the army and navy, that you wish we had spoken out more fully and followed out the consequences of our reasoning. I think the time will come, when all those consequences ought to be explained without reserve; but in first breaking the subject, against the prejudices of a large portion of the English public and against the arts of misrepresentation which Government and the Bank were sure to put in practice, it seemed more advisable to rest the argument upon those grounds with which it was most difficult to mix any topics of declamation; and the more so, as a single hint, with respect to those other momentous consequences of a depreciated currency, is more than sufficient for all who are already acquainted with the principles of such subjects.

⟨I was in the minority last night against the renewed adjournment.[3] The difference among us upon that motion, though it may be represented as party disunion, will have no bad consequences; I rather think the contrary. The constitutional principle is saved by so strong a protest; and the conduct of the rest of the Opposition secures the party from any charge of indelicacy towards the King, or undue eagerness to make the most of the present crisis.⟩

. . .

1. The Prince maintained this uncharacteristically prudent line until 18–19 Dec., when Perceval informed him of the restrictions the Government proposed to place upon him in their Regency plan (POW vii. 60–62).
2. In The Question concerning the Depreciation of our Currency (1810), Huskisson argued that the 'real bills doctrine' pursued by the directors of the Bank of England was not an adequate principle of limitation at times when currency was unconvertible. It ran to several editions and was praised by a wide range of economic thinkers including Ricardo and Horne Tooke. For Blake's 'tract' see Doc. 393.
3. The Government had proposed a fortnight's adjournment on account of the King's illness.

403. To J.A. Murray

BLPES iv. 329–33 ⟨Horner, ii. 40–43⟩   Lincoln's Inn, 29 Nov. 1810

. . .

You distress me very much by your account of Jeffrey's state of health. I should think that repose from labour is indispensable to him; labour of the head, I mean. I wish he would give up the Review. . . .

⟨Huskisson's pamphlet is excellent. There are still some points in the theory of this subject not quite cleared up; and I can put my finger now on one or two parts of the Bullion Report, from which I dissent. There is one especially, from which indeed I dissented at the time I drew up the Report, but adopted it as the sense of the majority of the committee, and particularly Huskisson, Thornton, and Baring; which is this, that the whole depression of the exchange was originally occasioned by the state of trade, and that the operation of the excessive and depreciated currency was to prevent its restoration. This way of stating it gives a confusion to the reasoning, and involves, I am satisfied, an error in principle; inconsistent, indeed, with the very foundation of the argument. Depreciation must produce, under all circumstances, its appropriate and proportionate effect upon the foreign exchanges; and produces that effect independently, though it may be combined in the result with the effect produced upon the balance of payments by political or commercial circumstances. It may in some instances require a good deal of address to separate, in a particular instance of the exchange with a foreign country, those other circumstances the effect of which is mixed with that of depreciation; and in some instances, from our imperfect knowledge of the state of the currency of the other country with which our exchange is stated, the case may stand for a while unresolved, and apparently as an objection, which it is not in reality, to the general conclusion.⟩

It does not do much credit to Lord Glenlee's understanding, that he pronounces upon such a question without informing himself. His prejudice against me has probably something to do with it. Lord Meadowbank's activity is characteristic.[1]

⟨I have not read the whole of Blake's pamphlet. It seemed to me very perspicuous and satisfactory. I shall read it in a day or two. I had dismissed the subject from my mind as soon as the Report was presented, but am now deep in it again. The discussion, which is in great activity in London, will do much good; and enable us to set a good many questions at rest. You cannot do me a greater favour than by stating to me any doubts or difficulties that you feel upon any part of the question.

⟨Bosanquet's⟩ very unfair but dextrous ⟨pamphlet has given me a good deal of exercise in this way: He leaves the main argument quite untouched, when his⟩ ignorant or unfaithful misrepresentations ⟨of the facts are explained.[2]

⟨The recommendation in p. 33 of the Report, that the Bank of England should be permitted to issue notes under £5 for some little time after the resumption of payments in specie, is founded upon this principle, that the former policy of the legislature ought to be resorted to, by prohibiting their issue of notes under £5. The reason upon which that rests, is, that it is important to have a certain proportion of specie in actual circulation, in order to prevent those sudden panics respecting the credit of paper among the common people, which are always attended with inconvenience. Smith's principle is, that the paper circulation should be confined as much as possible to the transactions among the dealers, and that there should be as much specie as possible for the transactions among the dealers and the consumers. If I recollect right, he grounds this principally upon the inconveniences which the consumers must suffer, when there is any sudden failure of credit, which diminishes the value, or impedes the circulation of the smaller paper. There is another thing to be⟩ considered, ⟨which I have not yet considered so fully as to have a clear view of it: I suspect, however, that convertibility alone of all paper into specie, without an actual interchange of a certain portion of specie circulating along with the paper, is not sufficient to secure the permanent value of the paper. The American states have nothing but paper in common circulation; it is all convertible by law into specie, but coin is seldom if ever seen: I suspect that they have an excess of this paper, and that its relative value is lower than it would have been if there had been always an interchange of specie. But, as I have already said, this is a part of the subject which I have not sufficiently examined. I am very anxious to get at the truth on every point of it; and I really think I have no prepossessions about it, nor have laid up any opinion which I am not ready to examine and to dismiss, if it will not stand the test. You know my declared hostility to all argument and controversy, but I delight to have materials presented to me for self-examination upon my opinions.⟩

. . .

⟨I am inclined to think that the King, if he does not die from bodily weakness, will recover from his present madness; but probably not for several weeks. The question for the Parliament seems to be, how long can the Government go on without the monarchy; in this respect, the royalists are playing rather a hazardous game. And as I am all for the monarchy, I wish the country and the Parliament were aware of this danger. In a mere party point of view, it is much wiser to let the Ministers have all the time they wish to gain; for nothing is more to be dreaded, in the present circumstances of the country, than a short interval of a new administration under a precarious regency.⟩

I remember, while I used to prowl in the Advocates' Library, finding two or three old volumes there, relating to a controversy about an alteration of the standard of the French money, in which the celebrated *Bodin* took a part, and on the other side a lawyer of the name of *Malestroit*. You will be able to find them, perhaps, without any trouble by the help of the Catalogue; and I will thank you to give me the titles of them, particularly those of *Malestroit*'s pieces . . . .[3]

. . .

1. Sir William Miller, Lord Glenlee (1755–1846: *DNB*), and Allan Maconochie, Lord Meadowbank (1748–1816: *DNB*).
2. Charles Bosanquet (1769–1850: *DNB*), governor of the South Sea Company and an eminent London merchant, published *Practical Observations on the Report of the Bullion Committee* (1810). It attacked Ricardo's *The High Price of Bullion* and the report of the Bullion Committee as 'wholly theoretical', and, denying the existence of a 'natural limit' in the variations of exchange, attributed high prices to the recent vicissitudes of the corn trade and to the increase in taxation, and advanced a wealth of details without reference to principles. To the second edition, which appeared later in the year, Bosanquet annexed a section entitled 'Supplementary Observations' which posed a number of riddles and challenged the members of the Bullion Committee to answer them if they could.
3. See Doc. 79.

404. To Francis Jeffrey

BLPES iv. 334–5 ⟨*Malthus*, p. 198⟩ [?London], 3 Dec. 1810

Ricardo has taken such fright at the notion of writing in the *Review*, that I have not succeeded in that point; he prefers publishing in a separate pamphlet.[1] ⟨Malthus has given me hopes that he will be able to scramble up an article this week; and I am very anxious to have the subject in his hands, and to engage him in the discussion, both because he agrees with me upon the fundamental principles of the doctrine, and because we have some differences, or rather difficulties which we try to solve differently, in some parts of the theory.⟩[2] All I beg of you, though I have no right to ask any thing, is not to let Milne lay his hands upon us.[3]

. . .

The news from Portugal this morning appears to be of very great importance; . . . A victory over Massena would be fatal to his whole army, and would be followed by the most momentous consequences to the cause of Spain; which, after all that the *Edinburgh Review* and many cold-blooded Whigs have said about it, is not yet desperate, and is the cause of European liberties.

. . .

1. The reference here is, not to *High price of bullion*, which had already appeared, but to Ricardo's *Reply to Mr Bosanquet's Practical Observations* . . . (1811).
2. Malthus's article on the 'Depreciation of Paper Currency', *ER* xvii (no. xxxiv, Feb. 1811), 339–72, evidently overtook the tentative proposals Horner had put to Jeffrey in Doc. 393. See also Docs 411 and 412.
3. Horner possibly means Joshua Milne (1776–1851: *DNB*), actuary to the Sun Life Assurance Society from 1810. But Milne is not known to have contributed any articles to the *ER*. More probably, therefore, he meant James Mill, whose name had been confused with Milne's on a previous occasion (Doc. 198) and about whose earlier review Horner had protested in Doc. 393.

405. To John Allen

BLPES iv. 338–9 Lincoln's Inn, 6 Dec. [1810]

Pray appeal from the Jokers [?] to the common public, who like the liberty of the press, and will not dislike the debates [in the Cortes] on account of the praises which are abundantly bestowed upon England. I think it a very great omission, that the debate has not been published in English; it would do a great deal to revive the languishing interest of the public for the Spanish cause.[1] All the good friends of liberty, who have attended to the proceedings of Cortes, have shown some symptoms of returning zeal. I am very anxious therefore that that particular debate should be published. If you will send the English report of it to me, I will see it through the press, if that trouble is the only objection.

. . .

1. After frequent delays the Spanish Cortes had at last met in Cadiz towards the end of September and, having proclaimed their loyalty to Ferdinand VII, proceeded to make various provisions for the better defence of Spanish rights and liberty. Following Horner's intervention, a lengthy report of the debate on the liberty of the press appeared in the MC of 11 Dec. There is also a brief report of the Cortes' proceedings in AR lii (1810), 215–18.

406. To J.A. Murray

BLPES iv. 340–41   Lincoln's Inn, 6 Dec. 1810

Do not be alarmed by my inquiries as to Malestroit and Bodin. I am not going to lose myself in antiquarian researches. But I wish to ascertain what views were entertained at that time in France, where the subject of currency was much considered, in consequence of the frequent frauds which were practised by the kings of that country, in altering their coin. It is material, in my view of this question, to impress the public with a notion that it is a state question, not one of trade, and to be decided by political considerations, not by the notions of the counting house. In our own English history, it has been always so considered; the little essay of Mariana which I showed you in the cathedral Library at York, and the controversy of Bodin and Malestroit, will furnish examples from the other two great states of modern history.[1]

The introduction of so many Scotch farmers into England, has set some of us, in this region of London, a-thinking upon the remedies which landlords ought to look to for enforcing the covenants of their leases. I may possibly trouble you, from time to time, to answer some questions upon points of your law, connected with that subject. For instance, I wish you would tell me, how far the Court of Session has gone in giving effect to an English judgement? Do you allow it to be conclusive, so that execution may pass upon it in Scotland without delay, or is it easy for a defender, by alleging objections to it in point of merits, to open the judgement, or at least obtain delay against execution? It might be important for a landlord, whose tenant had retired into his native country out of our jurisdiction, to know, whether he had best bring his action for damages in Scotland and carry his deeds and perhaps witnesses down there, or get (if he can) a judgement in England and send that to Scotland. The latter of course would only be practicable, where he could enforce an appearance to the action, which might perhaps be provided for by particular covenants in the lease.

Would it make much difference in the effect given to an English judgement, if, it was by default? I suspect it would . . .

. . .

1. Juan de Mariana's *De Monetæ Mutatiæ* (Cologne, 1609) severely criticized Philip III's adulteration of Spain's copper coinage. For this, Mariana was briefly imprisoned and the text expurgated, complete copies subsequently becoming extremely rare. According to John Laures, *The Political Economy of Juan de Mariana* (New York, 1928), p. viii, the tract was 'forgotten' for two hundred years until Pascal Duprat in 1870 pronounced it to be of great importance in the early development of political economy. To that extent Horner displayed a remarkable prescience in locating it and acknowledging its importance more than half a century earlier.

407. To Lady Holland

BLPES iv. 348–9   London, Friday evening [?14 Dec. 1810]

...

I hope Lord Grey will be in town for the debate on Thursday;[1] he owes it, I think, to the party, as well as to the Prince whose conduct has been so right, and I can perceive some symptoms of dissatisfaction rising among us on account of his absence. What people say now is, that others are married too and like their wives, which is a very uncourteous view of the subject: and then they add, that, in the circumstances of the Prince's situation after what has passed, the great Whigs ought to act as if there had been a direct communication, especially as the line then to be pursued is exactly the same conduct which on direct public grounds, without any regard to the party, ought to be observed. This is more the talk of others, which I am repeating to you, than my own idle speculation; though in that idle way I am disposed to think there is a good deal in it. I like Lord Grey so very much, and have such reliance upon him, that I am the more inclined to doubt whether things are right when he is not here.

1. On the King's illness, when Holland introduced a debate on the question of a Regency (*Hansard*, xviii. 229–41).

408. To John Allen

BL Add. MSS 52180   [London], Saturday 15 Dec. [1810]

I find that it was not till towards the latter end of the reign of Henry 6, that Acts of Parliament were drawn up in their present form of bills. Down so low as that reign, the petitions of the Commons did not contain the form of acts; but after the conclusion of the Session, the judges principally were employed, out of the petition and the King's answer to draw out a formal act, which was then entered upon a particular roll, called the Statute Roll. In the course of that reign, the Commons appear to have got into the practice of including in their petition the form of an act; and the entry of such, when brought to the Lords or delivered to the King, is made thus *quædam petitio liberata fuit etc., formam actiis in se continens viz.* Out of this, the present bills arose. My authority for this statement is Sir M. Hale in his tract on the 'Jurisdiction of the Lords House of Parliament', p. 62.[1]

I have been prevented hitherto from going through my books, on the subject of Guardians and Regents. But I shall see you tomorrow.[2]

I understand no communication has yet been made on the part of the Prince. Surely, the time to send for those whose advice he looks to, arrived, the moment that the Minister in the House of Commons declared that by next Wednesday it would be necessary to provide a *substitute* for the exercise of the royal authority: and upon the view which the Prince himself takes of his right, he ought consistently to regard every hour lost from that moment as a sacrifice of his rights and those of his family. If he is not intriguing with the others, he shows himself incapable of business. I do hope that a distinct line will be taken for the public on Wednesday, notwithstanding the silence of HRH, although there can be no doubt that the majority in Parliament will remain with the Ministers, and perhaps some of our own folks will begin to flinch, if the Prince does not by that time declare himself.

1. Sir Matthew Hale's tract had been published for the first time in 1796 under the title *The Jurisdiction of the Lords' House in Parliament considered according to Ancient Records*.
2. As Lord Holland's librarian and legal researcher, Allen was at this time immersed in research about the legality of a Regency. As was often the case, Horner assisted Allen, and on this occasion his researches were conducted with an eye to his own forthcoming speech on the Regency. On 10 Dec. he had posted to Allen a letter (BL Add. MSS 52180) containing a lengthy treatise on the history of the Great Seal, parts of which would appear in his speech of 20 Dec. opposing the Regency Bill (*Horner*, ii. 506–507), and he had concluded that letter with the following remark: 'I am decidedly against a Regency Bill, in the present circumstances, though I do not agree with you probably to the extent of all your reasons for being against it; as I cannot admit the *right* of the heir apparent, and am not much moved by the argument drawn from the statute of the 13th Car. II.'

409. To James Reddie

NLS MSS 3704, ff. 43–4   Lincoln's Inn, 18 Dec. 1810

. . .

In all the discussions relating to the economy of public offices, which for many years have occupied the legislature and which (I trust) will not be relaxed, one of the great principles which the reformers have aimed at, is the actual discharge of duty by the officer appointed, and (in furtherance of the same object) the actual enjoyment by himself of the emoluments which the public assigns him. It is difficult to carry the letter of a prohibitory law to the full extent of its principle; and in those which have been framed to prevent private arrangements respecting the salary or duty of offices, Parliament has not yet gone farther, in the application of forfeitures and penalties, than transactions in which some valuable consideration has passed. The principle, however, of those statutes, reaches beyond tangible considerations, and strikes at all arrangements, contrary to the public intent in the distribution of an office or the appointment of an officer, however honourable and disinterested the motives on both sides may be: and the public opinion, in its present wholesome state of vigilance and jealousy, and especially in this quarter, goes beyond the penal law and reaches to the full extent of this principle. I cannot but consider this a wise and salutary jealousy. Bargains of the most substantial nature will soon pass under the colour of a friendly arrangement, if that colour is allowed to be worn publicly; nor will any thing, but the disrepute cast upon it, secure us from its being used as a disguise for arrangements strictly illegal. Laws of this sort stand in need of support from opinion, and fashion, and as it were a point of honour among men of character. And it is the part of those, who would do their best to refine and elevate the public sentiment in this respect, or who at least wish to distinguish themselves from the herd by such purity, to take care how they engage in any arrangement, by which the general rule is departed from, and an exception made for unquestionable merit or from disinterested motives, lest they weaken the morality of the public on this head, by the sanction which their general character will give to their example in that particular instance, and lest it become a precedent under the shelter of which transactions a shade and a shade [?only] more incorrect may gradually go on.

All this argument is trite. One has often had occasion to apply it in censuring transactions, of which we know only the outside, without perceiving those private motives of generosity or partial judgement, by which they were made to seem venial to those who were concerned in them or contrived them. But the reasons appear to me of undeniable force and importance; and I could not justify myself for wishing to make an exception from them . . .[1]

. . .

1. Horner made these observations in response to a query concerning the legality and propriety of George Bell accepting a Scottish judicial appointment on behalf of Reddie, holding it while Reddie practised in the Court of Session for the required three years, and then vacating the office in favour of Reddie. He expressed similar cautious views some three months later when Murray declined the sheriffship of Peeblesshire (to Murray, 26 Mar. 1811, *Horner*, ii. 58–9):

> One of the lamentable consequences of the manner in which the patronage of Scotland has so long been dispensed, is, that it is hard for a man to act up to his own standard of public duty, who wishes to command the means of rendering service to the public by the weight of a character not only pure but never questioned. A part of Lord Melville's policy, in managing his burgh of Scotland, has been to make Sheriffships political gifts; and in this he has succeeded so well, and with respect to judicial offices indeed of a higher rank than the Sheriff's, that the vulgar here almost forget that they are judicial, and regard them much in the same light as he does who has so degraded them. The present rancour and illiberality of political differences make the vulgar a much more numerous and powerful body, than they have been in better times; and one of the evils of their ungenerous domination over public sentiment is, that the sphere within which a man may turn his talents, knowledge, and integrity to the public service is contracted, by the necessity of guarding against possible imputations; and his real usefulness diminished, by the prudence which is imposed upon him of foregoing small opportunities of being serviceable, in order to maintain that reputation which is to be the means of doing greater service.

410. To J.A. Murray

BLPES iv. 346–7 ⟨*Horner*, ii. 43–4⟩   [London], 20 Dec. 1810

. . .

⟨Perceval wrote to the Prince yesterday, announcing his plan of a limited regency, exactly like that of 1789; except that he is to be allowed to confer peerages for signal military or naval services, and that the duration of the regency so limited is fixed for a year and six weeks after the commencement of the next session of Parliament; like the restriction upon the distilleries. The Prince's answer was, in substance, this: that this communication was made to him, not like that of Mr Pitt after the two houses had passed certain resolutions upon which it was no longer fit for him to animadvert; but before such resolutions were proposed to Parliament, which he could not anticipate that Parliament would now agree to; if they should be passed, he would then refer to his letter of 1789 for the sentiments and principles which he still retains.[1]

⟨After he had sent this answer, he summoned in the evening all his brothers and the Duke of Gloucester; and stated to them what had passed. They drew up a letter to Perceval, which they *all* signed, protesting against a restricted regency. This is something like business.⟩

1. See *POW* vii. 108–13.

411. To T.R. Malthus

BLPES v. 1–2 ⟨*Malthus*, pp. 199 and 207⟩   [London], Friday 4 Jan. [1811]

⟨I send today the rest of your MS; in this part of it there is a great deal of very important discussion.[1] Your account of the operation of paper credit, in distributing capital among those who will employ it productively, coincides entirely with the view I have long taken of that question, so much agitated, whether paper credit gives a real or fictitious capital. And I am disposed to think that you have given a true solution of the difference between Hume and Smith, as to the rise of prices in Scotland.[2]

⟨Will it not be expedient to wrap up a little, in more general and less obvious expressions, the truth which you state in p. 33 as to the pay of the army and navy? I am afraid of telling it nakedly, for no other reason but because it is so true, and true to such an extent. Perhaps you will consider this timidity on my part somewhat prudish and unnecessary. But I own, that I should not like to have such allies in the argument, as we might obtain by such a proclamation;⟩ and though I would initiate without exception all who are capable of understanding the language of the mysteries, I am rather indisposed to an exoteric revelation of all the practical arguments, lest we should acquire some disciples who might be inclined to a mode of reasoning rather too practical.[3]

I am not convinced by the reasonings which begin at p. 21,[4] though they raise some doubts in my mind. You have correctly stated the fact, as to the difference between the circulation of Holland which was founded on the principle of a deposit bank, and that of this country: yet I cannot yet admit, that the circulation of the paper of the latter does not depend, as much as in the former, upon the faith which every holder of it reposes in the convertibility of the portion which he holds into gold on the instant of demand. Every holder, I think, believes this, and takes the paper because he believes it; it is the banker only who is in the secret, that only a certain number of the holders of paper need be expected to apply for gold at once, and that it is enough to keep gold for them. But as I have already said, I am not clear about this, for I cannot answer all the difficulties you throw upon it.

I have sent by the Guildford coach, which goes from the Golden Cross, Mushet's pamphlet and the Report, which you can give me back when you come to town. I have added to the parcel Ricardo's reply to Mr Bosanquet, in which you will find a great deal of excellent matter. It would be important to add to your article some notice of Bosanquet, and particularly because his new theory of a measure of value is a complete surrender of the whole question.[5]

I shall have the pleasure of meeting you on Thursday next.

1. Horner had begun a letter to Malthus on 3 Dec. (BLPES iv. 336), the same day he had written to Jeffrey (Doc. 404): 'I will send you the rest tomorrow.' It is utterly unclear, however, whether he meant he was returning an early, 'scrambled up' draft of Malthus's or sending some materials for it. But it is clear from the present letter and the next to Jeffrey (Doc. 412) that the draft version to which Horner now refers had been posted by Malthus to Jeffrey, who in turn passed it to Horner, and that afterwards Horner corresponded directly with Malthus on its tone and content. The published article included, as Horner had recommended, considerable comment on the recent pamphlets by Blake, Bosanquet, Huskisson, Mushet, and Ricardo, and embraced Horner's view, in opposition to that of Ricardo, that the exportation of gold and silver was perhaps the effect, and not the cause, of the current unfavourable balance of trade.

2. See p. 366 of the review, and *Malthus*, pp. 203–205.

3. In the event, Malthus seems altogether to have omitted the point about army and navy pay. Patricia James comments (*Malthus*, p. 199) that among all this 'patching and re-arranging', this was a 'regrettable excision' whose 'mystery will never be solved'.

4. See *c*. p. 351 of the review.

5. The third edition of Mushet's *Enquiry* had evidently appeared in Dec. 1810 or very early in the new year. In his *Practical Observations* Bosanquet reasoned that the standard value of a pound note was the interest of £33. 6s. 8d. three per cent stock.

412. To Francis Jeffrey

BLPES v. 5–8 ⟨Horner, ii, 47–54⟩[1]   Lincoln's Inn, 8 Jan. 1811

⟨I received Malthus's manuscript from you, and have since transmitted it to him, with such remarks as occurred to me in perusing it.⟩ I suggested to him at the same time the propriety of including Bosanquet in his review; and I am pretty sure he has been at work upon the subject for the last few days, for I sent some books at his own desire to him in Surrey where he is passing the holidays. I hope to meet him on Thursday, for he is to be in town for a day in his way back to Hertford.

I can nearly answer also for Allen's good intentions. He consulted me about the propriety of an article on the constitutional question of regency, in which he proposed to abstain from all considerations of present party or expediency, and to collect the learning which our history and the records of parliament furnish upon the general subject. I encouraged him much to do this for you; because he is full of the historical precedents, and if there is one thing more than another in which Allen displays the cleverness and strength of his sense, it is in the statement of the general rules of our constitution.[2]

⟨The *Quarterly Review* was sure to be right about Depreciation; being under the

command of Canning, who is under the command of Huskisson.³ I have heard it is
George Ellis, who has set Sir John Sinclair upon his black ram. By the way, I wish
you would take Sinclair's *two* pamphlets into your own hands, and make fun of him,
in a good natured way.⟩ He is too great a fool to be very harsh to. ⟨You would do me
a peculiar service, if you will deal with his currency, as you did with his longevity.
The inconsistency of his opinions at present, with those which he published in 1797
in a pamphlet against the Bank restriction, and which he repeated in the strongest
terms in 1803 in the second volume of his *History of the Revenue*, is rather a matter of
grave charge, for which he ought to be put upon the defensive. I am told that⟩ that
exquisite old zany ⟨George Chalmers has put forth a volume against us, more
extravagantly wrong than even Sinclair; perhaps you could contrive to put them
side by side into one frame, and exhibit the pair of portraits, like Noodle and Doodle
in their old tye and buckle and in the full complacency of conscious wisdom.⁴

⟨The subject you suggest of the present state of commerce, with all its
circumstances, and all the considerations both retrospective and in prospect that
naturally belong to it, is a noble one, but of very difficult execution. I do not know
what to say about peace: I should like of all things to have, for my own judgement,
the benefit of the views which you could suggest; but for the sake of the public, I
really think your opinion ought to be very deliberately weighed and confidently
formed, before you give the sanction of your authority to sentiments and
expectations, which, though remarkably dormant at present, may be raised any day
among the people to an unmanageable size.⁵

⟨Upon the question of peace, I parted company with some of my best advisers,
and you (I fear) among them, at the moment of the Spanish insurrection; thinking
that the circumstances of that event recommended an extension of hostilities, upon
the very same principle, which condemned the original hostilities on our part with
which this long war commenced. However persons may differ, as to the policy of
having acted upon this principle towards Spain, they must all, I apprehend, admit
that we have bound ourselves by our treaty with the insurgents, and that we cannot,
in good faith, abandon them, while they preserve any hopes. Besides this obligation
of good faith, in respect of which there can be no difference between us, I have not
yet myself relinquished such hopes, though you will probably regard me as somewhat
enthusiastic in retaining them so long; but miserable as our disappointments have
been, beyond all former estimates of the degradation to which a long course of
despotism could reduce a great people, I do not yet see that the affairs of the
insurgents in the peninsula are desperate. And I would have this country act upon
the same views, and if possible with the same magnanimity, as Elizabeth showed to
the rebels in the Netherlands, and persevered in at the lowest ebb of their fortunes.
This is an immediate consideration, which would prevent me from acquiescing in
any present proposal of peace, unaccompanied by a stipulation on the part of France
to evacuate Spain. But it grows out of a principle, which carries me a great deal
farther, and compels me almost to make up my mind to what you will call an
indefinite prospect of war; a prospect never to be avowed, however, even when it
appears most certain.

⟨In the situation to which the continent of Europe is reduced, and in the
situation which England commands, I cannot imagine a general peace of any

duration; and without it, we can have no peace with France. I rest very little argument now, upon the personal character of Bonaparte; the direct effect of his name and genius, so prodigious for a certain period of time, is at length almost sunk in that change of the state of the world which he has effected. I rest no argument at all upon his particular designs against this country, which is the grand reason with our vulgar for perpetual war; because, though to prevail over England must be the final scope and aim of his ambition, without which the absolute disposal of the whole continent leaves his love of glory unsatisfied, and would be insufficient to transmit his name to posterity as equal to those conquerors of former ages who overcame all that was great and civilized in their own time, and all that was opposed to them; yet his personal passion for making a conquest of us cannot be a better reason for war, than the national design pursued under all changes of government which France has ever entertained against us, and which we have ever entertained against France. It is the natural condition and infirmity of powerful neighbours; which never can become a reason to either of them for refusing to make peace with the other, as long as they preserve any thing near an equality of force for the maintenance of war. My view of our situation is taken from other circumstances. What is likely to be the state of the continent for many years to come? And in the probable condition of the continent, what must be the conduct of England; which (whatever her interest might be, if it could be managed for years together with perfect wisdom) cannot but be impelled by the voice of the people, and by the ancient habits of political as well as commercial connection? If the whole continent were to be tranquillized into one empire, and should slumber for years in repose under a vigilant and well-organized despotism, no fate could be intended for us but annexation to the mass; nor could we devise any safety for ourselves, but by adopting public institutions, and by fostering sentiments of individual ambition and conduct, of which defensive war and the most rigid prejudices of local patriotism were the constant objects. But it is seldom that human affairs fall into such a forced state. It seems infinitely more probable, that the new empire of France will be perpetually disturbed by efforts in one member or another to throw off the yoke; in the north of Germany, for instance, where military genius might win a fair kingdom, or in the hereditary states of Austria, where the natives cannot yet have despaired of recovering their ancient independence. Should such chances arise, even if the struggle of Spain were over, I conceive it would be the duty of this country, and I am sure it would be unavoidable at any rate, to contribute from our resources every aid and encouragement to the insurgents. It is idle to sigh for peace, if it cannot be had upon system, and for a period to be sure of; England forms a part of Europe, and must share its vicissitudes and agitations.

⟨The point to be considered is, by what mode and upon what principles the war may be conducted, so as to afford the best chance of contributing to the ultimate restoration of independence to some of those kingdoms, which never can be incorporated with France, from the diversity of race and languages. In my judgement, we have only to act upon the principles by which Elizabeth was guided, and afterwards King William; forbearing all little bye objects of gain and aggrandizement, and keeping steadily in view, through all fortunes and in the lowest depth of our despair, the ultimate partition of the continent into individual states and the revival of a public law in Europe. For such conduct, looking so far forward, much patience and constancy and public integrity will be required; but it is a part worthy of this nation, and no more, in proportion to its present means, than it has done before.

‹You will consider me very belligerent; I do not know that I ever before exposed to you, or indeed to anybody else, the full extent of my warlike disposition. It has been growing upon me, ever since the news of the memorable day at Aranjuez. I will not say that there is no inconsistency between my present views of the question, and those which induced me to give my vote in support of Whitbread's last motion for peace; but, besides having reflected more upon the whole subject, the main parts of it have undergone an essential alteration, both by the immense acquisitions of empire which Bonaparte has made since, and by the great example which the poor Spaniards have set to the rest of the world.

‹Before I quit the subject, I ought to say, that it would form an essential part of my plan of policy, to adopt Bonaparte's kings, without disputing their title; to teach them to look to England for support, if they have either a mind to show themselves ungrateful, or find him too exacting in the gratitude he requires. Bernadotte, therefore, and Joachim, I would make a point of gaining; as, if there had been any chance of assisting Louis with effect, I would have supported him in resistance to his brother. These, I will own at the same time, are operations of diplomacy, requiring more talent than I am afraid we possess in that department, and a more uniform course of foreign policy than we are likely to see pursued. . . .

‹I have not yet read your review of Stewart with sufficient attention to judge between you, which I mean to do with as much impartiality as my infirm nature will allow of, though I shall set about it with an old opinion on Stewart's side in the main question about which you differ.[6] I was much pleased with the just praise you have bestowed on him; and there is a kindness in the particular turn of those praises, which satisfies me that you now feel what sort of merit his is.

‹With regard to party politics, I have little to tell you; except that the Prince has sent for Lord Grenville, and that he and Lord Grey (who comes to London this evening) are the persons to whom he will apply for advice as soon as he is Regent. The Prince has conducted himself throughout the whole transaction, in very delicate circumstances, with eminent propriety, and with perfect honour towards the Whigs; who had in truth no right to consider him as owing any obligation to them. Whether the King will ultimately recover or not, and whether during the precarious interval of a regency administration, any good can be expected to be done, is more than I can tell you.

‹I am really obliged to you for reporting to me what Brougham has said of me; not only because I love praise dearly, but because it gives me more pleasure to hear of any thing like partiality in Brougham about me or any thing I have done, than even if I could be convinced that I had deserved his favourable testimony.[7] His alienation from me, for reasons which I never have been able even to guess, is the only considerable misfortune I have ever suffered in my life; and it would take quite a load off my mind, if he would give me a hint to catch at, for forgetting that I ever had suffered it. I have always cherished a hope, that we may in time approximate again.›
. . . [8]

1. The incomplete version in *Horner* is wrongly dated 18 Jan. 1810.
2. Allen's article on the regency question appeared in *ER* xviii (no. xxxv, May 1811), 46–80.
3. George Ellis had reviewed Huskisson's pamphlet in *QR* iv (no. viii, Nov. 1810), 414–53 (Shine).
4. Sir John Sinclair (1754–1835: *DNB*), who had a well-known interest in sheep-breeding, was the author of, among many other things, *Letters written to the governor and directors of the Bank of England, in September, 1796, on the pecuniary distresses of the country* (1797), and *The history of the public revenue of the British empire* (3 vols, 1803–1804). Horner, however, held a very low opinion of his economic writings: in 1803 he had contributed a couple of pages to Jeffrey's scathing review of Sinclair's *Miscellaneous Essays* (Docs 111 and 116). Most of those essays, the review had said, were 'extremely trite and puerile', and concluded that:

> Upon the whole there is not much to praise in this volume. . . . Sinclair would certainly be a useful man, if he knew how to set about it; though there will probably be always a considerable difference between his own estimate of his importance, and that which is adopted by the public.

Jeffrey had similarly so noticed Sinclair's *Essay on Health and Longevity* in *ER* xi (no. xxi, Oct. 1807), 195–214; this, he had begun, was 'the most diffuse, clumsy, and unsatisfactory compilation that has ever fallen under our notice'. Sinclair's immense conceit remained unabated. Late in 1814, when Horner heard that Sinclair had on his own behalf proposed a public subscription acknowledging his services to the nation, he wrote to his mother (BLPES vi. 130–31): 'It is a very great curiosity, not so much for the foolish independence of the proposal, which borders on lunacy, as for the grave and pleasant enunciation of his merits, from his writing the history of the revenue to his confutation of the Bullion Committee.' Similarly, when Sinclair, who was the first President of the Board of Agriculture, was elevated to the Privy Council in 1810 he had published a series of congratulatory letters and been ridiculed for it in two articles in *QR* (iv (no. viii, Nov. 1810), 518–36, and v (no. ix, Feb. 1811), 120–38). Although Ellis's name was associated with it, the first attack is thought to have been by Canning and Huskisson, with, perhaps, some contribution from Walter Scott; the second was by Ellis and Canning (Shine). The immediate subjects of the *QR*'s attacks upon him, however, were respectively the publication also in 1810 of his *Observations on the report of the bullion committee* and his further *Remarks*. No notice appeared in the *ER* of either Sinclair's new pamphlets or George Chalmers, *Considerations on commerce, bullion, and coin, circulation and exchanges* . . . (1811).
5. An article by Brougham on Rose's *Considerations on the .. War . . . and . . . Peace* appeared in *ER* xx (no. xxxix, July 1812), 213–34.
6. Stewart's *Philosophical Essays* were reviewed by Jeffrey in *ER* xvii (no. xxxiii, Nov. 1810), 167–211.
7. *Horner*, ii. 53n, quotes from Jeffrey to Horner, 14 [?4] Jan. 1811:

> I have really heard a great deal about your speech [of 20 Dec. 1810 on the Regency], and especially from Brougham, who says it was full of instruction and sound argument, admirably delivered. *This* testimony gave me a feeling of very unusual delight; and I think it will please you to hear of it.

8. Horner apparently wrote this letter after dining at Holland House with Lady Holland, Lansdowne, Lauderdale, Morpeth, Kinnaird, General Ferguson, Samuel Rogers, and Tom Grenville (HHDB).

413. To J.A. Murray

BLPES v. 9–10   Lincoln's Inn, Friday [11 Jan. 1811]

. . .

The general impression at present is, that the King will recover; at least that he is not to die this time, and that he has not fallen into a state of fatuity. I confess it will appear to me a very extraordinary event, if he is again restored to real sanity of mind.

Nobody denies, that he is still as mad as ever upon the subject of Lady Pembroke.[1]

At all events, I fear the Regency must now be formed. And a more difficult situation cannot be figured, than that in which the Prince is placed. Hitherto, he has conducted himself with a degree of sense and steadiness which I did not expect; and considering the grounds of complaint he might justly have urged both against Lord Grey and Lord Grenville, the one for his absence and the other for his unskilful obstinacy on the subject of restrictions, the Prince has (I think) shown much public spirit in sending for them as he has done.[2] They too are thrown into very delicate circumstances, as to the advice they ought to give him, on account of the uncertain state of the King.

. . .

1. The widowed Elizabeth, Countess of Pembroke (1737–1831), a member of the Queen's Household, was the lady to whom the King imagined he was married.
2. Apparently Horner had almost simultaneously expressed a contrary view to Sydney Smith. In a letter of 13 Jan. to Lady Grey (*Smith Letters*, i. 201), Smith quoted from Horner's recent letter:

> Lord Grey's absence (though scarcely excusable) has done no harm. He is decidedly at the head of the great aristocracy, including not only Whigs, but a great many Tories. I wish he were . . . he wants only *that*, to give him the power of doing more good, and commanding greater influence, than any man has done since the time of Fox. He deserves all the praises bestowed upon him. A more upright, elevated, gallant mind there cannot be; but . . . and will not condescend to humour them, and pardon them for their natural infirmities; nor is aware that both people and Prince must be treated like children.

Smith then continued:

> You may fill up the blanks as you like; but if you valued Mr Horner's understanding and integrity one-half as much as I do, you would, I am sure, value this praise.

414. From John Allen

BLPES v. 11–12   Pall Mall, 15 Jan. 1811

You will have seen by the newspapers that the great personage[1] who was expected here on Saturday came on Sunday and made a very long visit which ended in as satisfactory a manner as could be desired, Lord Holland being authorized to state to the two Lords[2] that 'the misapprehension had arisen from the different view which he and they had taken of this stage of the proceeding in which according to his notions they were not in a situation where his advisers were strictly and constitutionally responsible, but which they had considered as placing them in that situation.' So far so well. I wish I could add to this an account equally favourable of the consultations held for the purpose of arranging the new government. One great difficulty, but not the only one, arises from the earnestness with which some friends of the party urge the necessity of a coalition with Canning. Lord Temple and Fremantle have been urging this with great effect on Lord Grenville and among our own division of the army I find to my great surprise, not such men as Ward only, but Abercromby and Wm Lamb, who are pressing the same measure. Now a coalition with Canning is a separation from Whitbread and I leave you to judge whether any man who is a sound Whig can hesitate between them. In point of mere numbers I believe that you would lose more strength than you would gain by a connection with Canning. Coke of Norfolk goes in that case into decided opposition and he will be followed by Brand and others, besides disgusting and cooling the zeal of all the old members of the Opposition, so that to use a vulgar image on this occasion your coalition will be throwing away good money in the pursuit of bad. But while I state the very strong push which is making for Canning I ought to add that it is as firmly resisted by Lord Grey who I believe would sooner retire from public life than consent in the present circumstances of the party to such a connection. Lord Holland is also decidedly averse to it as well as Lord Lauderdale, Tierney, Whitbread, etc., etc.

But though this point were settled there are other difficulties to be overcome on which I cannot enter by letter, both on account of the length to which they would carry me, my imperfect acquaintance with them, and my doubts how far I am at liberty to communicate them to paper. You will be too late for the House of Commons but I hope we shall certainly see you before the end of the week. Something definitive will be settled before that time. . . .

Adam was the only person present at the interview on Sunday and Lord Holland was very much satisfied with his management of it. The Prince was in very good humour, and stated his case very ably and with much feeling. He too has been impressed with the idea of Canning being indispensable in the H. of Commons.

. . .

1. The Prince of Wales.
2. Grenville and Grey.

415. To John Allen

BLPES v. 13–14   Wells, Wednesday night, 16 Jan. [1811]

I am much obliged to you for your letter, and the information it contains. The difficulty, with respect to the answer, has been well removed; but the transaction proves a liability to influence, and a personal vanity to management, which will make the personage concerned more likely to be drawn aside by occasional private intrigues, than to pursue a steady course of confidence in the persons to whom the preference of his own judgement as well as the voice of the public directs him. It may be fortunate, that their connection with him begins with so express a protest; there will be many occasions for referring to it.

I lament very much the opinion in favour of Canning, which prevails to such an extent among many of our friends. It is a great error of judgement, though natural enough to those who sit much in the House of Commons; not that his powers are so transcendent, but because the want of a head is so much felt. But, with a great inclination towards Canning on account of his agreeable talents, as well as on account of the influence which he possesses being founded upon his talents alone, I am clearly of opinion that nothing, as a party and public measure, could be more imprudent than a *coalition* with him, if taking him into the party is worth so big a word. His faithless intriguing character, proved by his conduct to Castlereagh as well as by his negotiations in February 1807, and the general opinions which he holds – irreconcilable in every view with the Whig principles both of liberty and of foreign politics, are such as to make it next to impossible that he should maintain any permanent connection with that party. It will be a vast step, in his course of advancement, to be taken but for a while as our leader in the House of Commons; and his next step after that will be, as far as he can effect it, the depression and dismemberment of that party, by all the opportunities of which he can avail himself. I cannot understand, however, that there should be so much danger of his coming among us as you apprehend; if Lord Grey be averse to it, his negative must decide the question, or I wholly misapprehend his influence with the Opposition. Grenville, at least, can never consent to purchase Canning, at the expense of Lord Grey: for the loss of Lord Grey would I trust involve the loss, to Grenville, of every considerable person of the Whig party. The consequence of such a separation would no doubt be to leave us in a small minority, but one composed of the best materials. For my own part, I know, if I should happen to be in Parliament with Whitbread leading an Opposition, I could not help being very soon one of his followers; with all his fatal defects of manner, there is no politician whom I find so often in the right, at least in the present H. of Commons.[1]

. . .

1. In a letter of 22 Jan. (*Horner*, ii. 54–5) Grenville, anticipating the formation of a Whig ministry and his own return to the head of the Treasury, asked Horner 'to assist me as one of the Secretaries of the Treasury' and remarked that Horner's acceptance of the offer would create 'a universal impression, that I had in that way secured the assistance of the person in all England the most capable of rendering efficient service to the public in that situation, and of lightening the burthen which I am thus to undertake'. Horner's reply has not been found, but later correspondence (Doc. 417) confirms that he rejected the offer prior to 30 Jan.

416. From Francis Jeffrey

⟨*Jeffrey*, ii. 131–3⟩   Edinburgh, 25 Jan. 1811

⟨. . .

⟨Yes – *some* good will be done by turning out the present Ministry, if it were only for a day. But are they to go out? or is there *any* truth in the *Courier*'s stories of the dissensions of the opposite body? Our Whigs here are in great exultation, and had a fourth more at Fox's dinner yesterday than ever attended before. There was Sir H. Moncreiff sitting between two papists; – and Catholic emancipation drank with great applause; – and the lamb lying down with the wolf – and all millennial. [Dugald] Stewart came from the country on purpose to attend, and all was decorous and exemplary, etc. I think I shall come to town in April. If the Whigs be in power, it will be worth while for the rarity of the spectacle; like the aloe blossoming, a few days, once in a hundred years, etc.

⟨There is nothing new here. The meek, who inherit the earth, pass their time very quietly in the midst of all these perturbations, and I among them. I am a good deal with Playfair and Alison, – and teach them philanthropy and latitudinarian indulgence. Playfair is quite well this season, and not quite so great a flirt as he was last year. Stewart comes in sometimes, and has become quite robustious; – jogs on horseback two hours every day in all weather, and superintends transcribing as a serious business all the evening. He is an excellent person; without temper, or a sufficiently steady and undisturbable estimation of himself. And then he is an idle dog; – almost as great a *fainéant* as I or Cocky Manners.[1] You will call all this blasphemy; but it is very true, and I love him all the better for believing it. Murray is in great preservation – a little too bustling and anxious for my epicurean god state; – but in fine temper, and not at all low, nor so absent as usual. Thomson a thought bilious; and altogether discreet and amiable.

⟨I have written a long sermon about reform. It is something in the tone of my state of parties article, which you all abused, – and which I consequently think the best of all my articles, and the justest political speculation that has appeared in our immortal journal.[2] It is nothing but sheer envy that makes any of you think otherwise. However, this will not be so assailable.⟩

1. A bookseller in Edinburgh.
2. For Jeffrey's 'State of Parties' see Doc. 368; the article on parliamentary reform he seems to have written jointly with Brougham is in *ER* xvii (no. xxxiv, Feb. 1811), 253–90.

417. To J.A. Murray

BLPES v. 15–16 ⟨*Horner*, ii. 55–6⟩   London, 30 Jan. 1811

. . .

⟨Of course you, who know me so well, could not entertain any apprehensions, from what you may have read in the newspapers, that I was likely to be tempted to take a political situation. I wish, however, to let you know, but in confidence for the present, that I have been put to the trial, and have decided without any difficulty to adhere to the rule which I laid down for myself when I went into Parliament, not to take any political office until I was rich enough to live at ease out of office.

⟨There is a high probability that the Regent will form a new Administration, though the point is not yet settled; because the advice he has received upon the question is made to rest, upon what he shall find to be the real condition of the King, which hitherto has been concealed from his family and studiously involved in contradictory and false reports. My own conviction is, that he will be found so far from the appearance of a probable recovery, that the Regent will take his measures as for a permanency. With a view to the arrangement that would then be formed, I have been asked, in a manner very flattering to me, to undertake the office of

Financial Secretary of the Treasury: which I have declined. The opportunity there is at present in that department of rendering service to the country, both in meeting the difficulties which are coming on in its revenue as well as commercial concerns, and in conducting to a proper result the discussions which have been stirred respecting the state of the currency; the field which is opened by the present state of the House of Commons; the pleasure of having a man in whom I entirely confide for my colleague, and the gratification of accepting office with the rest of one's party at a moment when such a step is attended with such uncertainty and adventure: are considerations which would have strongly tempted me, if I had permitted myself to bring into doubt the propriety of my previous resolution. I decided therefore at once, and of course consider it a decision for life.⟩[1]

The person I have alluded to for my colleague is Abercromby, who will be Secretary of the Treasury, if an Administration is formed. I understand too, that Brougham has accepted the office of one of the Under Secretaries in the Foreign Office. . . .

1. Perhaps a more plausible explanation for Horner's refusal of Grenville's offer is the gloomy view he expressed of the formation of a Whig Ministry under a 'precarious regency' in Doc. 403.

418. To James Brougham

Brougham MSS, D.M.S. Watson Library,
University College, London, J.512   Lincoln's Inn, 23 Feb. 1811

Strickland was to write to you yesterday an account of Henry's great success in the Court of King's Bench.[1] But I cannot deny myself the satisfaction of telling you, that I believe he has by this exertion and the verdict he won by it established most firmly both his reputation and his fortune in the profession. I was prevented from going down to hear him, but I have received accounts of it from a great number of persons, who all concur in describing it as the best speech of the sort that has been made in the King's Bench since Lord Erskine left it. There has long been a vacancy in that department of the profession, which I trust Henry will at once step into; distinction in that line is both a great reputation of itself in this country, and will lead to every other. Besides the pleasure which Henry's friends derive from the event of yesterday as securing him a high professional station, it is with every body a subject of congratulation on public grounds, that at length some resistance is made to the indiscreet and oppressive prosecutions for state libels.[2]

. . .

1. Brougham's speech on 22 Feb. in defence of John and Leigh Hunt, who had been prosecuted for reprinting in the *Examiner* a criminal libel about flogging, secured their acquittal
in the Court of King's Bench. He made another shortly after at Lincoln in defence of the
original perpetrator, but failed to save him from a conviction. (New, pp. 54–6.) 'Strickland'
was probably either George Strickland, afterwards 4th Bart (1782–1874), or his younger

brother Eustachius (1787–1840), who were both barristers and former members of the Speculative.
2. A day earlier, before the verdict was known, Horner had lavished similar praise in a letter to Murray (BLPES v. 17–18, including a note to Murray from Charles F. Stewart).

419. To Henry Hallam

BLPES v. 21–2   Exeter, 21 Mar. 1811

Being no academic myself, I did not consider myself entitled to canvass; but I have made inquiry with respect to the Cambridge voters upon this circuit, and now send you the result. There are eleven Cambridge men, who have votes; and the greater number of them would vote both for the D. of Gloucester and for Smyth, if the management which has been used in fixing the days of election had not disfranchised almost all the lawyers.[1]

Lens, Harris, and Abrm Moore are all necessarily detained here by business; the last would probably be against us on both elections, the two first certainly with us.[2]

Larpent has written to Eyton, of the Oxford circuit, to propose to him to pair off for both; Standly, Lens's nephew, has paired off with Mr Rhodes a clergyman in this place.[3]

William Williams, Henry Bright, and Henry Tancred would all be for our friend Smyth, if they were to vote at all, though not zealous enough to make much exertion.[4] Lomax would vote for Smyth, Robert Grant and I believe Selwyn for Lord Palmerston.[5] Except as to the two pairs, all of this information is of very little use to you.

I am very much obliged to you for the paper you have sent me upon country Notes, which will be extremely useful to me.[6] How fast the depreciation is going on, and the consequences of it becoming manifest; this raising of the dollars will probably have more effect, than all the argument that has been used.[7]

. . .

1. The death of the 3rd Duke of Grafton on 14 March had created a vacancy both in the Chancellorship of the University and, by translating Euston to the Lords, in its parliamentary representation. In the event, the poll on 27 March secured the Chancellorship for the Duke of Gloucester against the Duke of Rutland, and that of 29 March the parliamentary seat for Viscount Palmerston over John Henry Smyth (1780–1822).
2. The lawyers Serjeant John Lens (1756–1825: *DNB*), John Greathed Harris (1774–1850), and Abraham Moore (1766–1822), who afterwards became an MP but had to flee the country as an embezzler, were all Cambridge men.
3. Thomas Eyton (1777–1855), Henry Peter Standly, formerly Poynter (1782–1844), and Rhodes (who was either Thomas or William (d. 1829)) were all Johnians like Lens. Standly's mother was Lens's sister.
4. William Williams (1774–1839), a Johnian regarded by some as a Jacobin republican (*PH* v. 586–7), Henry Bright (1784–1869), a Peterhouse man, and Henry William Tancred (d. 1860), of Jesus, all practised on the Western Circuit and were all afterwards MPs.
5. Edmund Lomax (1778–1847), Charles Grant's younger son Robert, and William Selwyn (1775–1855: *DNB*), a Johnian like Palmerston, were all lawyers in Lincoln's Inn.
6. Not found.

7. On 23 Mar. 1811 Horner expressed similar views to his father (BLPES v. 23–24): 'This rise
in the current value of the Dollar ought to have made some converts to the Bullion heresy,
and opened the eyes of people to their own interests. The Guinea must go in the same way
very soon.'

420. To T.R. Malthus

BLPES v. 27–8 ⟨*Malthus*, pp. 206–207⟩   [?London], 8 Apr. 1811

⟨. . .

⟨Your article is very popular in London.[1] Tierney spoke to me in particular
commendation of it, as giving what he thinks the most correct view of the subject;⟩
the admissions you have made upon some points of the argument, he considers as
both right and useful. ⟨The Governor of the Bank also mentioned the article to me,
and praised it for candour and fairness; upon which I took the liberty of telling him
by whom it was written.[2] So that you see you have the rare fortune, in this instance,
of pleasing both sides. I have a still better judgement to report in your favour;
Hallam, who has a great knowledge of the subject, and no bias whatever, said in a
letter I had from him lately that he thought your view of the question the most
sound as well as comprehensive he had yet read.[3]

⟨Ricardo's reply to your objections is not so well written, in point of clearness, as
his usual style.[4] I suspect that upon that dispute the truth lies between you, and that
a mode of expressing and stating what takes place might be hit upon, to which you
would both assent.⟩

I send you the account of importations of corn, in which you will see that the
import of last year was enormous, nearly as great as in the last period of dearth,
though there is no pretence for saying that last year was even one of scarcity. It is
probable that a considerable portion of this was for exportation again to Portugal. I
have a strong persuasion, however, that the depreciation of money has operated as a
bounty upon importation; though we are to be told, that the necessary importation
is a great cause of the rise in the price of gold. By the corn laws, 66/- is the price
above which wheat may be imported from all foreign countries, upon payment of a
nominal duty only of 6d. per quarter. Now, the average price has been considerably
above 66/- for several years; and, as Government has been forward to grant licences
for the importation of grain even from the enemy's countries, the importation has
been perfectly free. The depreciation of money, therefore, by raising the average
price above the limit fixed by law, has virtually repealed that law, and opened the
corn market of England to the free competition of foreign growers. It is probable,
that the real price of grain in France at present is so much below its price in this
country, that our growers cannot stand against those of France, if they meet in the
market. For the last few months, our farmers of the grain districts have been
complaining loudly of the low prices, and in some parts of the country are really
unable for want of a market to pay their rents. This is an unusual state of things to
find accompanying vast importations from abroad; nor can I explain it satisfactorily

otherwise than by the effect of the depreciation. I should like very much to know your opinion about it.

I shall move tonight for some accounts, to show how much was exported last year, and from what foreign countries the importations were made.

1. Jeffrey had evidently written otherwise about Malthus's February article on the depreciation of paper currency: see *Malthus*, p. 207.
2. John Pearse (?1760–1836) had given evidence to the Bullion Committee while still Deputy Governor in Nov. 1810 (*PH* iv. 739–40).
3. Hallam's letter has not been found.
4. Horner was responding to Malthus's letter of the previous day (*Ricardo*, iii. 12) referring to the appendix Ricardo had added early in April, as an answer to Malthus, to the fourth edition of *The High Price of Bullion*.

421. Notes on the *Wealth of Nations*

Kinnordy MSS   [London], 30 Apr. 1811

DESIDERATA;
SUGGESTED BY THE PERUSAL OF THE *WEALTH OF NATIONS*
BOOK I. CHAPT. I
['OF THE DIVISION OF LABOUR']

1. Beside the division of labour, are there not other general causes of improvement in the effective powers of human industry? (Accumulation of stock – [1]

2. Different manufactures, arts and professions, compared with regard to the degree in which they admit of the subdivision of labour, that is of being analysed and simplified in their operations: with a view to the development of general facts.

3. Different manufactures compared, with regard to their dependence upon the physical circumstances of climate and soil: with a view to the development of general facts.

4. Investigation of the degree in which agricultural labour is rendered more effective, in the course of what is understood to be the progressive improvement of husbandry; of the degree in which agriculture admits of, or excludes, a subdivision of labour; and historically, of the extent to which the subdivision of labour has actually been introduced into agriculture.

5. Are there not other circumstances beside these two, (we exclude the last mentioned by Smith), to which we may trace the effect of the division of labour in rendering labour more productive?

6. *Histoire Raisonnée* of the introduction and progressive improvement of machinery for abridging labour in the arts and manufactures with a view to the development of general facts.

7. If there is upon the principles of political expediency a maximum in the subdivision of labour, it would be a curious problem to determine the limits within which that maximum may, in general terms, be described to lie.

CHAP. 2

['OF THE PRINCIPLE WHICH GIVES OCCASION TO THE DIVISION OF LABOUR']

1. The subject of this chapter to be examined more profoundly and accurately; both in the metaphysical disposition, with regard to the principle in our moral constitution which gives occasion to the division of labour; and with regard to the *histoire raisonnée* of the progressive extension of that subdivision.

CHAPT. 3

['THAT THE DIVISION OF LABOUR IS LIMITED BY THE EXTENT OF THE MARKET']

1. To explain, from the situation, history and manners of those different nations, the policy which prevailed in Egypt, Hindostan and China, of excluding foreign commerce.

1. These last words appear to have been added at a later time, probably in the course of Horner's researches on grain policy in 1814 or 1815.

422. To J.A. Murray

BLPES v. 34–5   Lincoln's Inn, 4 May 1811

. . .

I have seen scarcely any thing of Jeffrey.[1] Before I got back to town, [Sydney] Smith had engaged him to all the dinners of foolish people that like to stare at eminent persons; and both of them seem to prefer that sort of high seasoned society, to quieter and more homely fare.[2] I had prevailed on Jeffrey to give me one day at my mother's, which I have unfortunately lost by the Bullion Debate being fixed for it . . . The oftener he comes to town, he makes a stronger impression upon all persons, whose esteem is an honour.

. . .

1. Jeffrey visited London during April and May 1811.
2. The HHDB confirms that Jeffrey and Smith dined there on 26 Apr. in the company of Adair, Grey, Lauderdale, and the American Senator William H. Crawford (1772–1834), afterwards Minister in Paris, 1813–15, and again on 12 May among a large party including Horner, whose last appearance at Holland House had been on 28 Feb.

423. Speech by Horner

⟨PR xix. 1148–52 and 1170–79⟩[1]   House of Commons, 6 May 1811

⟨Mr Horner rose, and moved, That the House do resolve into a Committee of the whole House, and that the Report of the Bullion Committee, with the different papers relating to the foreign exchanges, and the exchanges with Ireland, be referred to the said Committee.

⟨Mr Horner then proceeded to observe, that, in opening the subject before the

Committee, it was his intention to separate the consideration of the last resolution of those he should submit, from the consideration of those which preceded it. The latter consisted of a statement of the law, of the alleged evil, and of its cause, the former suggested what he conceived was the most proper remedy. Many Gentlemen, who might coincide in the opinions expressed in the first resolution, might not perhaps be disposed to concur with him in the propriety of his last proposition. It would therefore, he conceived, be advisable for him to keep the two questions as distinct as possible. And here he begged leave to observe, that although he designed to enter pretty fully into the view which he took of the general question, it would not be necessary for him to enter into all its details, or into many of those minute and various statements which were contained in the papers already on the table. Some of those which were essential to a clear elucidation of the subject, would probably be examined by the Honourable Members, who would follow him, and were much more competent to draw from them whatever was requisite for a clear exposition of the question. At the same time, the outline which he proposed to describe must comprehend all the most prominent and material points at issue; and he assured the committee, that it should be his endeavour to compress them into as narrow a compass as they would admit. – (Hear, hear!)

⟨Among all the various opinions entertained on the present and on former similar occasions, there had been some which proceeded to the most opposite extremes. Persons were not wanting hardy enough to assert, that a circulating medium, consisting entirely of paper, was perfectly adequate to the fulfilment of all the purposes of a metallic currency. According to their creed, the greatest of all modern discoveries in the improvements of commerce, was the exclusive substitution of a paper currency, founded, not upon the basis of the precious metals, but on the basis of confidence alone. On the other hand, there had been persons blind to all the experience of our commercial and economical history, blind too to all those important advantages practically derivable from the circulation of paper convertible into gold, who went so far as to assert, that the only remedy was to resort to the exclusive use of the precious metals, and to the anterior state of things. He wished, however, to revert only to the doctrines and opinions of the ablest and most practical statesmen of this country previous to the period of the Bank Restriction. The principle of those doctrines was, that the circulation of paper was in itself beneficial, and sufficiently guarded against excess by its constant liability of conversion into gold. There was another feeling also abroad in which he could not join, a feeling of jealousy of the Bank as an institution, and a disposition to condemn it as an unfair monopoly. He could not help thinking that all those who regarded the liberties of the country with a due attention, and who justly appreciated their value and their importance, could not contemplate the origin of the Bank without connecting it with an era memorable as the epoch when those liberties were secured, and placed on a solid foundation. (Hear! hear!) But beside this, all who had attended to the subsequent events of our political history must be convinced that at different periods, and on great critical emergencies, the Government of the country has derived from the Bank the most important assistance. If then the most extensive and essential resources had been drawn from that quarter for the greatest national objects, it was natural that with the present prospect of new difficulties to be encountered, and additional exertions to be made, we should look in future for a continuance of that aid, and of these resources, of which we had before availed ourselves.[2] Having thus disclaimed all these contrary opinions, he must now declare, that his great and ultimate object was to restore, with as much care and circumspection as might be fairly claimed by partial and particular interests, but at the same time with as much promptitude as still more urgent considerations might dictate, the circulating medium to its original state – a state attested by a long experience to be not less favourable to private than propitious to public prosperity – a state, every departure from which must be injurious, in proportion to its extent. He could not here forbear to notice a prejudice which had been excited against him, and those who coincided with him in opinion on this subject; a prejudice that represented them as mere theorists, and as setting up their theory against the conclusions of practice and experience.[3] If he was indeed a theorist, his theory was, however, that of those who founded the Bank of England (*Hear, hear!*). If he considered the convertibility of paper into specie as the fundamental principle of that institution, his opinion was in perfect unison with that of the most enlightened and practical statesmen who had conducted the financial relations of the country (*Hear, hear!*) and who concurred with the most eminent practical merchants of these times. They were consulted because it is the part of a statesman to acquire information from all descriptions of men, not to take it upon credit from any particular class. Such a question as that before the Committee was one peculiarly fit for Parliament to decide, because it was the province of Parliament to compare and distinguish different kinds of practical information, and to determine by their collective wisdom, the due application of general principles. If it was a charge against him to have entered upon the investigation with some preconceived opinions respecting it, it was a charge to which he must certainly plead guilty. But without considering if it was possible to commence any such inquiry free from any such preconceived opinions, he would venture to say, not only for himself but for the rest of the Committee, that no investigation ever was begun with a firmer determination to make the most ample, accurate, and impartial scrutiny, and to suspend judgement till that scrutiny was accomplished. (*Hear, hear!*) The names of the Members of the Committee were a sufficient security perhaps for this, and rendered it unnecessary for him to repel any accusations on that score. It would have been convenient for him to have been informed, before he began the discussion, which of his principles were denied, and which admitted by his right hon. friend (Mr Vansittart); but upon this point he was left entirely in the dark. If he looked at the last of his right hon. friend's Resolutions, he appeared to differ with himself only as to the remedy proposed; and when he turned his attention to those preceding it, he saw propositions directly controverting all the ancient and received doctrines of economical science. The primary object of the Committee had been to ascertain the causes of the high price of gold. The House of Commons, struck with the appearance of a gradual rise in the price of bullion, had appointed the Committee to examine and report its cause. If this was the object of the House at that period, how much more imperious had that duty become by the subsequent and progressive rise which had taken place? He meant to state broadly here, that although there had been collateral causes, the operation of which he was most ready to admit, yet that the high price originated in and was perpetuated by an excess of paper circulation. The Mint price was £3. 17s. 10¹/₂d., the market price has first risen to £4. 10s., and since the Report of the Committee had reached as high a point as £4. 14s. being somewhat more than 20 per cent of excess above the mint price. Now it was important to observe, that this excess was a departure to that amount from the standard value of our national currency, that standard consisting, according to law, of gold and silver of a certain fineness, weight and denomination. Bank notes were nothing more than stipulations to pay so much of this lawful money to the holder. The excess of the market price of gold proved, therefore, that bank notes purported to represent what they did not, viz. a certain sum of standard value. Measured by the market price, a pound note was worth 15 shillings and a fraction. To this degree the paper must be considered as depreciated. The maintenance of the legal standard had always formed a principal feature in the legislative policy of this kingdom. Parliament had hitherto, at all times, displayed the utmost vigilance upon the appearance of any derangement or undue alteration of the value of the circulating medium. Some of our ablest princes had on particular occasions attempted to debase the legal coin, or to raise its denomination, but Parliament had never failed to raise its voice and check the progress of the evil. The last operation of this kind took place in the reign of Queen Elizabeth, and since that period the standard has remained unaltered, both in fineness and in weight.

⟨His first Resolution contained a correct statement of the law, nor was there in the history of this nation, any reign that had been marked by a more watchful attention to the preservation of the standard value of the coin of the realm, than his present Majesty's. In evidence of this, it was only necessary to appeal to the new gold coinage, to the statute of the 14 Geo. III. enacting that silver should only be legal tender, for sums above £25 according to its weight, and not its denomination. There had been proclamations subsequently to the same effect, and the doctrine of Parliament fully coincided with this exercise of the Prerogative. The doctrine of the Legislative, the Royal Proclamations, the Rolls of Parliament, were all at direct variance with the new principles of recent theories. If we looked back to the 4th Session of Geo. I. we should find a Resolution of that House, importing that they would not consent to any alteration of the value of the current coin of the realm, and we should find them desiring a conference with the House of Lords, who came to a similar resolution. We were now told, however, that all this was error, and that the merchants of the present day had discovered its fallacy. This indeed was not asserted at first by those upon the Committee; they did not venture to commit themselves to such hazardous declarations, but contented themselves with strongly denying that any departure had taken place from the standard value from the currency. When this denial could no longer be supported, the advocates of the Bank denied the existence of a standard. One Gentleman, highly deserving of attention, had stated this principle in the first edition of his pamphlet; but had abandoned it in the second, in which he discovered that the standard was the interest of such sum in the public funds as would produce one pound, which pound being paid in paper, was thus of course the measure of itself. – (A *laugh!*) Deserting afterwards this original idea, he informed the public that the real standard was money of account, a proposition to which he (Mr Horner) could attach no intelligible interpretation whatever.[4] The next step in this curious series of reasonings was to assume the existence of an abstract currency, and in support of this doctrine, all the substitutes of the Aristotelian metaphysics had been collected and applied. There was something in this theory that furnished a striking resemblance to the attempts of the ancient school-men to substantiate essences, and embody the offspring of their imaginations. – (Mr Horner here read a passage from a late work, in which the nature of currency was illustrated by an allusion to a column of mercury in the tube of a barometer).[5] Another writer argued, that the only standard consisted in an ideal measure, and not in any tangible or material medium. From all these ingenious theories and amusing conjectures, he should make his appeal to the laws of his country. He was sure there was no lawyer in the House who would contradict him when he stated, that by all the statutes on the subject, no other standard was acknowledged but that of the precious metals. He must now advert to the admissions of the practical men, by which the fact of a departure from the legal standard was fully established. He could wish for no better evidence than this. The 3rd resolution of his Right Honourable Friend differed materially from his; and it was worthy of observation, that his Right Honourable Friend appeared to have been greatly embarrassed in drawing it up, as was evinced by his subsequent alterations. As that Resolution stood at first, bank-notes were declared 'to be held equivalent to the legal coin of the realm in all pecuniary transactions to which such coin is legally applicable.' In the new edition, however, they are stated 'to be held equivalent in public estimation and general acceptance.' (Hear! hear!) His Right Honourable Friend did not therefore meet his principle, but evaded it by a reference to a part of out criminal law, of very equivocal policy. (Hear! hear!) Now although his own principle was not denied, still must he positively deny the principle assumed on the other side. He affirmed that a difference did exist in the relative value of the gold and of the paper currencies, and that nothing prevented this difference from becoming manifestly notorious but the penalties of the law. (Hear! hear!) His Right Honourable Friend had also omitted one very important consideration, the undeniable fact that gold and paper do not associate; that the gold has actually disappeared, and is no longer in circulation. It seemed to be forgotten that the coinage was the King's assurance to his subjects – that the money was of standard value. The equivalence, therefore mentioned by his Right Honourable Friend, did not exist, and the only point in dispute was a question of fact, was the Bank of England note worth what it purported to be in the legal and current coin of the kingdom? He denied that it was, and no illustration could more powerfully demonstrate this than the reference, made by a Right Hon. Gent. (Mr Huskisson), which must be recollected by the House, of the preferable value of the light guinea over the guinea of sterling weight. – The point might be illustrated in a similar way in the instance of silver. Since 14th Geo. III silver by tale is not a legal tender for a sum not [sic] exceeding £25. If a debtor proposed to discharge a debt of £26 in silver, he must give, at the rate of 5s. 2d. per ounce, an hundred ounces of standard silver; £26 in bank notes would now purchase eighty-six ounces and a fraction only – he must therefore, in discharging his debt in standard silver, sustain a loss of fourteen ounces. To all these reasonings and examples he must say that he had never witnessed the shadow of an answer, and he was convinced that they were unanswerable. The bank note he stated to be worth no more at present than 15s.10d. He was not now discussing what was the cause, or where was the blame, but he hoped the plain assertion he had made, would be openly admitted or openly denied. Enough was certainly proved, to impose on the House the necessity of probing the question to the bottom. The determination of the measure of exchangeable value, was one of the most important institutions of civilized society. The precious metals, for various reasons, had been long selected as the best calculated for forming a fixed and permanent standard. In all modern commercial states they had in consequence formed the circulating medium. If then it appeared that within a very short time the standard had become deteriorated, it was impossible not to perceive the injury that must attend all contracts and fixed monied incomes, the loss to creditors, the irrecoverable impoverishment of annuitants and others, with the forfeiture of that rank and station which property confers, the mischief of the public interest arising from the decreasing value of the taxes, and a long train of concomitant evils. One very serious disadvantage too must arise from the public burdens appearing greater than their real magnitude, from the effect of a depreciation of their real amount. Here was an apparent increase of the national expenditure, without any real addition to the revenue. In turning their attention to the most expedient remedy for the existing evil, it was necessary for the Committee to ascertain its cause. All that had been urged by the adversaries of the Bullion Report in explanation of the present phenomena in our currency, appeared to be reducible to two points. It was said, that gold had experienced a rise in its real value from a positive scarcity – (Hear, hear!) and it was also stated, in the second place, that the unfavourable exchanges had caused a rise in its price at home. The first opinion implied, that the demand for gold had increased on the Continent – the other he held to be a complete fallacy. The money value of gold could not rise in this country. Its real price was unquestionably subject to all the variations arising from increased or diminished supplies; but its standard value as a measure of exchange, could not possibly fluctuate under any change of circumstances. In the East, in some places, salt was the common measure of value. It was obvious that salt was an article of which the real price must often vary; but used as a measure of value, it was as immutable as any other – and the apparent variations in it as a standard, were in fact variations in the prices of other commodities, estimated by that common measure. In those countries where silver was the standard, the money price of silver could never vary – and in Great Britain, where gold constitutes the standard, it was impossible that any change could be produced in its value as a measure in exchange. The only effect which could therefore take place, by any diminution of the amount of the circulating medium in any country, must be to make all commodities cheap, and he put it to the House whether any such effect had happened in this country. In 1795, there was a scarcity of gold arising from the large sums paid for foreign grain. In 1796, there was a great demand for internal purposes, and the practice of hoarding was carried to a great extent. During the whole of this period, not the smallest rise took place in the market price of gold. A very small quantity only was imported from Portugal, at £4. 8s. per oz. including the exchange and freight. From 1717 to 1790, there was no alteration in the market price of gold, as was shown by the very valuable document on the table from the Mint. With respect to the alleged rise on the Continent, he believed there had been some, but it was extremely small. In consequence of the excess of the importation of silver above gold, it had been found necessary to alter the relative Mint value of the two metals. Gold had accordingly risen somewhat as compared with silver in the states where silver was the measure of value. At Paris a new Mint had been established, and the alteration of the relative value of gold and silver was adopted there. It amounted to about 4 or 6 per cent. By an account which he had lately received of the current prices at Paris, dated 16th April, English pure gold was worth £3. 19s. 6d. per ounce. At Hamburgh the prices nearly corresponded. At Amsterdam the English guinea sold for 12 gueldres and a fraction – the bank note for little more than 7. But it was not only the gold which had undergone all this variation, silver had experienced the same. How was this to be explained? Our importations had been lately unusually large, we supplied the whole of Europe, and our export to India had been stopped. But the great and paramount standard of value was corn, and he would therefore beg leave to call the attention of the Committee to the rise within the four last years of its average prices. He proposed, for the sake of accuracy, to omit those years in which any extraordinary scarcity had been felt. It appeared, in p. 71 of the Report, that from 1771 to 1785, the average price was 46 shillings the quarter of wheat. From 1786 to 1797 the entire average was 52 shillings; but omitting 1795, and six years of peculiar dearth, the average would be 47 shillings and two-pence. Since 1797 a very different rate of increase would be found to have taken place. During an equal period of twelve years from 1798 to 1810, leaving out the two years of dearth, 1800 and 1801, the average price of the quarter of wheat was 71s. (Hear, hear!) and including the years of scarcity 79s. What could furnish more palpable or indisputable evidence of the fall in the value of the currency? – An unfavourable state of foreign trade had certainly a tendency to lower the foreign exchanges, but only to a certain degree. Admitting, which, however, he knew was not the case, that the whole of the depression of the exchanges was a real depression, he must yet deny that it could have the effect of raising the price of gold in this country. In the return from the Mint of the prices of gold for the last hundred years, no evidence could be discovered of the alterations of the exchange producing any corresponding rise in the prices of bullion. The present state of the exchange required itself explanation. It was a state, of which no example existed, except in those periods when the national currency had been debased. (Hear! hear!) With Holland the exchange had once fallen 25 per cent, and it was precisely under the circumstances which he had mentioned. He would not at present go into a detailed examination of the question relating to the balance of payments. He admitted that an unfavourable balance existed, and that in the last year a very enormous importation of grain had taken place, amounting to upwards of two millions of quarters. A most important consideration seemed to him to grow out of this fact, for if by any unforeseen interruption of supplies from the Continent, we should be left with an unsatisfied demand of corn to that amount, what must be the condition of the country? It was worthy of attention, while upon this subject, to observe that in 1793 an alteration was made in the corn laws, and a protecting price of 56s. was enacted for the home grower. In 1804, it was found necessary to raise this protecting price to 66s. and the same necessity clearly existed now for a further rise to 71s. These importations of grain must be paid for in some way; and although he was disposed to allow that the balance of payments was against us, when he considered the great excess of our exports above our imports, as shown by the papers before the Committee, he could not believe that the balance could be very considerable. The official value of the imports in the year ending 5th Jan., 1811, was £36,400,000 including Irish manufactures, and their real value might be £33,000,000. The exports amounted to more than £45,000,000 leaving an excess above the imports of £12,000,000. He was informed that the amount of cotton cloths exported in the last year, was £18,000,000 and with the addition of the yarn exported, made a sum of £19,400,000 thus furnishing a most triumphant proof of the impotence of the enemy's attempts to crush or destroy our commerce. Either it must be shown then that our military expenditure is so large, as more than to equal the excess arising upon our exports, or the statements of the quantity of bullion sent out of the country must be incorrect. He well recollected when a Right Honourable Gentleman, then at the Board of Trade, had given a most sanguine description of the flourishing and prosperous state of our commercial relations, he, at that time, had ventured to express some little distrust of that statement. He was told, however, that great as was the foreign expenditure of the country, the extension of our trade had more than counterbalanced it. What, however, he must continue to assert was, that whether our foreign trade had or had not declined, the present state of the exchanges could not possibly be produced by any such cause. That there was a necessary limit to the fall of exchange was a principle admitted by practical men themselves, and might be found in the evidence before the Lords' Committee and the Committee in Ireland. It was then stated that the expense of sending bullion to India was ten per cent. and that to no part of Europe it could exceed seven. The Bullion Committee were thus then compelled to resort for a solution of the difficulty to fixed and determined principles, since no circumstances of a partial or temporary nature could be found to explain it. The immediate inference was that it originated in the state of our domestic currency. The value of a domestic currency might be depreciated by debasement if it consisted of the metals, by excess if it consisted of paper. (*Hear! hear!*) During the whole of the seven years war the value of gold coin was depreciated by debasement in relation to bullion. Spain supplied at that time the rest of Europe with silver, and there the relative value of silver compared with gold was one per cent. lower than in any other country. A paper currency being liable to depreciation only from excess, was perfectly secure so long as its convertibility into the precious metals was free and unfettered. Any accidental tendency to excess was instantly corrected by its being exchangeable for gold. By this principle the Bank had been governed in their issues before the restriction. That restriction, by removing all control on their issues removed every limit to the depression of the foreign exchanges. The doctrine of the exchange was now as clear and indisputable as any question in mixed mathematics, and the only means of repelling its deductions was by the production of mutilated facts, and imperfect statements, with the quotations of parts of cases, the remainder being either unknown or studiously concealed. This practice had been pretty generally adopted out of doors; but at least it was incumbent on those who set up their new cases to account for those brought forward on the other side. The alteration in our currency had not communicated itself to the currencies of other nations. With Portugal the exchange last year was at par, and in Portugal there was then a paper currency depreciated 26 per cent. It was at an open discount to that amount. The Swedish exchanges had fallen 70 per cent., for she, too, had a paper currency depreciated to that extent. With America the exchange had been about 11, and was now 10 per cent. against us. The premium given for an English bill in the West Indies had been reduced from 15 to 5 per cent. [and] in the East Indies, it was about 22 per cent. against us. The exchange with Palermo and Lisbon when no obstruction existed to our intercourse, was equally low. He had likewise compared the exchanges on the Continent. Between Hamburgh, when there was no paper currency, and Vienna, when there was, the difference was striking. The par was at 144 guineas to 200 francs. The exchange had risen against Vienna to 950. Between Sweden and Hamburgh the par was 48 stivers for a dollar, the exchange was now 136. Between Copenhagen and Hamburgh the par was 125 rix dollars for 300 Banco, at Copenhagen they now paid 6 or 700. In all these places there was a depreciated currency. – Between Paris and Hamburgh, however, the exchange was 4 per cent. in favour of the former. In the period of issuing the assignats in France the exchange fell from 22 progressively to 17, 15, 9, 4, and nothing. Every body then ascribed this fall to the depreciation of the assignats. No such fall had ever been experienced in France since the famous Mississippi scheme in 1720. Even then, however, the price of gold never rose above £4. 1s. 6d. per oz. The depreciation of paper currency might proceed either from an issue of more than the circulation could absorb, or by not diminishing the issues according to any diminution in the amount of the metallic part of the currency. And here it was incumbent on him to state that although our trade and commerce had been represented as in so crippled and unfavourable a state, the Bank so far from restraining their issues had increased them by no less a sum than two millions since the publication of the Bullion Report. In 1809, the average amount of notes in circulation was 19 millions – in 1810, 21 millions two hundred thousand, and for the first 17 days of the present year, twenty-three millions and a half. He must term this a most wanton and unnecessary addition to the circulating medium of the country, since he was well assured money had never been more plentiful in the market. The recent doctrines and the practice of the Bank, unless checked, must inevitably soon bring down the most complete ruin in the financial relations of the country. The restriction in 1797 certainly placed the Bank in a novel situation; but the mischief was infinitely aggravated by its being afterwards made a permanent war measure. In his opinion it was much more dangerous in a time of war than in a time of peace. The task of ascertaining the precise quantity of circulating medium required by a nation, was one which no human wisdom could perform, and could only be properly regulated by the natural influx of the precious metals. Mr Horner then proceeded to read extracts from the evidence of Mr Whitmore and Mr Pearse, the late and present Governors of the Bank[6] in order to show that those Gentlemen acted on the erroneous opinion, that the issues of the Bank could not be excessive while confined to the discount of mercantile securities, and that they had contemplated as a possible event of no injurious tendency, the rendering the suspension of payments in cash a permanent measure. He did not believe, however, that all the practical men had fallen into this delusion, but that the old capitalists who had supported, in good and evil times, the commercial credit and prosperity of the country, looked with anxiety for a restoration of the ancient order of things. Among men of this description who had concurred in the conclusions of the Committee, was one (Sir F. Baring) not less eminent for wealth than for the characteristic enterprise of British merchants, but whose evidence on this important subject they were now unfortunately prevented from obtaining.[7] With respect to the remedy, he still adhered to his former opinion of the necessity of fixing some positive period at which the Bank should be compelled to resume their cash payments. Until that was done, we should continue to pay one fourth more of foreign expenditure than in a different state of the currency. But it was not only the disadvantages under which Government itself must labour in making those future exertions which might be necessary in the maintenance of our proper character abroad that ought to weigh with the Legislature. Let them also attend to the manifest shame of defrauding the public creditor, and of impoverishing the annuitant. Let them remember the obligations of public faith, the sanctions of parliamentary virtue, and all those principles on which the industry of the people, and the confidence between man and man so essentially depended. If the restriction had been necessary originally as a strong but salutary medicine to a diseased state of the circulation, it must infallibly prove a poison, if the application should be continued long after the disease had been removed. He was convinced, that if the House should content itself with a remonstrance on the negligence of the Bank Directors, in not sufficiently adverting to the appearances in the foreign exchanges in regulating their issues, it would not have the effect of checking the career which they were pursuing, and which threatened with the most formidable consequence, the most substantial interests of the empire. The Hon. Gentlemen, after a variety of further observations, concluded a very able speech, to which the lateness has prevented us from doing justice, by moving the first of his series of Resolutions.⟩

1. The report in *Hansard*, xix. 799–832, is fuller and includes quotations and other detail not reproduced in this version.
2. Horner thus drew a clear and no doubt tactical distinction between his own view of the Bank and the policy of its directors on the one hand, and the hostility expressed towards the Bank itself by Ricardo and Henry Parnell on the other. In his 'The Bullion Report Re-examined' (p. 657n.), Fetter notes that on 8 May Parnell expressed in the Commons his own hostility to the Bank but made it clear that Huskisson and Horner did not share his views.
3. Here Horner apparently refers to the charge levelled against the report of the Bullion Committee in Bosanquet's *Observations*.
4. Again Horner apparently refers to the first and second editions of Bosanquet's *Observations*.
5. Not identified.
6. Pearse had succeeded John Whitmore (1750–1826) the previous year (*PH* iv. 739–40 and 540–43).
7. Sir Francis Baring had died on 11 Sept. 1810; his son and successor Alexander was, however, both a member of Horner's committee and a director of the Bank.

424. To John Horner

BLPES v, 36–7 ⟨Horner, ii. 67–8⟩   [London], 10 May 1811

⟨I have been prevented from writing to you these few days, by being very busy. I have at last got through my share of the bullion question, which we have had for four late nights. I shall take very little charge of what remains to be done or proposed. Vansittart is to move his resolutions in the committee on Monday, on one of which Tierney will move an amendment; amounting to a declaration very much like one of my rejected resolutions, that the Bank ought (during the restriction) to keep the same principles in view which limited their notes before, and implying farther the principle (somewhat beyond mine) that the Bank ought to consider itself bound to be ready to resume cash payments at the earliest notice. I hardly think that I shall urge any of the amendments upon Vansittart's resolutions, which I printed some time ago; my chief purpose in circulating them was to have a concise counter statement of facts in the hands of members before the debate. I have nothing further to do, so far as I am at present concerned with the question, but to move my resolutions again in the House, for form's sake, that they may be put upon the Journals.

⟨The divisions were better than I expected, particularly upon the last; that division I took at a venture, contrary to the wishes of some who left me, but I am satisfied that good has been done by getting the forty-five names which I shall have to show for that.

⟨One is very apt to fancy the best of the argument on one's own side; and I am indulging myself at present in that belief. It seems to me that a very important impression has been made upon the House by the discussion, such as will not soon be worn out, and will be a ground work for a future attempt of the same sort to cure this great disorder. It is very creditable to the House, that so tedious a debate upon so uninviting a subject was heard with much attention and without any impatience; nothing perhaps could prove more strongly, that, however the votes have gone, from timidity, as well as from the usual motives that make majorities, there is a general persuasion that something of importance to every man's own private concerns, as well as the public interests, was involved in the question.

⟨The best speech was Canning's, which astonished every body, by the knowledge which he showed of the subject, which must be a very unpalatable one to him, and by the businesslike manner in which he treated it; he had all his fancy and wit about him too, and played with the most knotty subtleties of the question as easily as if it had been familiar to him.⟩[1]

. . .

1. On 8 May: *Hansard*, xix. 1076–1128.

425. To John Horner

BLPES v. 38–9 ⟨*Horner*, ii. 69–71⟩   Lincoln's Inn, 16 May 1811

⟨...

⟨I have at last got rid of bullion; the country, I fear, will not get rid of the necessity of resuming the question very soon. So far as the mere votes of the House of Commons go, mischief has been done by the parliamentary discussion; for we have concluded by two resolutions, one of which misrepresents, in a very dangerous manner, the prerogative of the King over the standard of money, and the other is a ridiculous evasion of the fact of depreciation. They will probably give birth to a new host of pamphlets. But in another point of view, [by] the impression made upon the public mind as to the importance of the question, I believe much good has been done; in the House, it was manifest, that we established unanswerably our conclusions, though the apprehensions naturally excited by such a statement, and magnified by the obscurity in which most persons find themselves upon such a subject, make them dread the effect of confusing its truth. I hear, also, that there has been a considerable change in the sentiments of the City. You must be sick, however, of this business.

⟨The King has been materially worse in point of bodily health lately, and the delusions of his mind are said to recur still very frequently. The Ministers speak rather diffidently now of his ultimate recovery, though the physicians are as ready as ever to swear to it. The session of Parliament will probably be drawn out till after the first week of July, when there will be another quarterly Report from the Queen's Council. He complains very much of being under petticoat government, and is much puzzled to make out why he should be subjected to this thraldom at present, when he says he is not worse than he has been for years. Such are the stories. There was a very affecting proof of his melancholy state, given last week at the concert of ancient music; it was the Duke of Cambridge's night, who announced to the directors that the King himself had made the selection. This consisted of all the finest passages to be found in Handel, descriptive of madness and blindness; particularly those in the opera of Samson; there was one also upon madness from love, and the lamentation of Jephthah upon the loss of his daughter; and it closed with 'God Save the King' to make sure the application of all that went before. It was a very melancholy as well as singular instance of sensibility; that in the intervals of reason he should dwell upon the worst circumstances of his situation, and have a sort of indulgence in soliciting the public sympathy.

⟨... I am going down with Whishaw for two days to visit Malthus in Hertfordshire, and hear his nightingales; we shall go on Saturday. ...⟩

...

426. To J.A. Murray

BLPES v. 40–41 ⟨Horner, ii. 71–3⟩   Lincoln's Inn, 24 May 1811

⟨I heard of the President's sudden death yesterday;[1] by some means, the intelligence reached London before it could have been brought by the post. It is impossible to figure any loss by which Scotland could have suffered so deeply, as by this afflicting event; whether what we have actually been deprived of be considered, or what we have to place in Mr Blair's room. I had no personal acquaintance with him, and have had no opportunity of seeing him in his judicial situation, but I have long felt the greatest admiration for his manly venerable character, and have indulged the most agreeable expectations of the beneficial influence which his administration of the law would have upon the jurisprudence and upon the public mind of his country.

⟨Short as his Presidency has been, I cannot but cherish a belief, that he has left a permanent impression. His example will remain a pattern for those who have been most sensible of his merits, and may hereafter have a similar opportunity of labouring in the public service; and his name and memory may even in the meanwhile be some check on those unworthy ones, who are likely to be his immediate successors. . . .⟩[2]

. . . I look upon . . . Colquhoun to be one of the meanest and lowest of human creatures; and his appointment, which cannot fail (I suspect) to take place, will be the last proof of the utter inefficacy of public opinion in Scotland, and will be the most galling indignity that has ever been inflicted on the Scottish Bar as well as upon the justice and property of the country.

. . .

There is a great disposition, I am told, at Carlton House to make an effort for Mr Erskine; and it is said that remonstrances have been made to the Chancellor, from the same quarter, against Colquhoun personally, as a man wholly unfit for such a station.

I look upon all such proceedings to be improper in the highest degree; the appointment of the Judges throughout the Kingdom is a trust for which the ministers are deeply responsible, and any interference on the part of the sovereign, that would fetter the free exercise of that responsibility, is most unconstitutional. In Perceval's present disposition to conciliate the Prince, and to project coalitions, he may practise possibly an improper compliance; though I think it more probable, if he finds this sort of interposition seconded by representations, from his own friends, of Colquhoun's incapacity and unfitness, that he may devise some compromise by a new arrangement of the bench, and by making only a common judge. But I speak without any knowledge whatever.[3]

1. Robert Blair, Lord President of the Scottish Court of Session, had died suddenly on 20 May.
2. The remainder of the published portion of the letter praises Blair further and lauds the conduct of the Scots Bar on the occasion of his death. It pledges a contribution in the event that a statue is erected by private subscription and suggests that the statue be executed by Westmacott. It then goes on to discuss Jeffrey's habit of doing justice 'to those whom party separates from him'.
3. Neither Henry Erskine nor Archibald Campbell Colquhoun (d. 1820), the Lord Advocate, but Charles Hope succeeded Blair as Lord President.

427. To J.A. Murray

BLPES v. 46–7 ⟨Horner, ii. 73–4⟩   Lincoln's Inn, 29 May 1811

⟨In my last letter, I omitted to⟩ . . . ⟨give you an answer, as to my intentions with respect to the publication of the speeches I made on the bullion question. All the reluctance which I felt about exposing myself in that shape to the public, has been so powerfully seconded by my indolence, that if I had any longer resolution enough to attempt it, it would not be in my power. I must be content therefore with such treatment as the newspaper reporters have bestowed upon me, and as I did not read these at the time, I shall know nothing of them till Cobbett's debates are published. The principal grounds upon which I rested the resolutions that I proposed to the House, are contained in the Report, and are indeed old and well established not only in the political writers of this country, but in the policy itself of our laws: there is nothing new therefore to record. Some points in the theory of money, and in the scientific explanation of some of its principles, are still indeed but ill settled; though not so as to affect materially the practical conclusions, belonging to our present question. I have sometimes had thoughts of writing a short essay upon these speculative parts of the subject, and mentioned it to my father, who seems to have misunderstood my intentions.[1] As for the practical question now depending, I shall confine myself to the parliamentary discussion of it. With respect to Rose's misrepresentations, it would be endless and discreditable to engage in a controversy of facts with him; he did not mention a single error of the least consequence in the statements of the Report, though I could have helped him to some, and it is ludicrous to scrutinize a paper of that sort as if it were a laboured composition.[2]

⟨. . .⟩ I suspect, that both you and Bell have thought me more Whiggish than reasonable upon the subject of interference by the Regent; yet the principle which I stated appears to be undeniable, if we have any constitution left, which (I own) may be a question. You remember I do not exclude either the right or the propriety of remonstrances, the more public in their mode and form the better, against the appointment of a particular individual, who is judged, by those most interested in the appointment, to be an unfit and improper person.

1. There is no reason to believe that Horner wrote such an essay.
2. George Rose had published the *Substance of a Speech on the report of the Bullion Committee.*

428. To John Horner

BLPES v. 48–9   Lincoln's Inn, 31 May 1811

What I told you (I believe) of the real state of the King is now become well known, and . . . his recovery and restoration to the crown may be considered as quite out of the question. Yet, I believe, from the quarter in which I was told so, that it was very recently the design of Ministers and their party in the Queen's Council, to make an

experiment of declaring him well, just before the prorogation of parliament, hoping
that they could keep him well enough, or conceal his real condition enough, to get
through the forms of royalty during the autumn. The Queen and some of the family
are said to have opposed this; the females having already suffered a great deal by
being exposed to his madness, in the intercourse with him which has been forced
upon them lately, for the purposes of the Ministers. It is a very curious fact, and
shows what sort of men have been trusted with so important a charge, that about
three or four weeks ago there was a division in the Queen's Council, upon a question
of immediately declaring the King well; the eight Counsellors were equally divided;
there being on the one side, for declaring him well, the Duke of Montrose – Lord
Aylesford – Lord Winchelsea – and the Archbishop of Canterbury, and against it
the Archbishop of York and all three lawyers – Ellenborough, the Master of the
Rolls, and the Chancellor. The Chancellor had, no doubt, the terrors of Lord Grey's
speech in his recollection.[1]

. . .

1. The Duke of Montrose, Master of the Horse, Heneage Finch, 4th Earl of Aylesford (1751–
   1812), Lord Steward of the Household, George Finch-Hatton, 9th Earl of Winchelsea
   (1752–1826), Groom of the Stole, Charles Manners Sutton, Archbishop of Canterbury
   (1755–1828: DNB), Edward Venables Vernon-Harcourt, Archbishop of York (1757–1847:
   DNB), Sir William Grant (1752–1832: DNB), Master of the Rolls, Ellenborough, the Lord
   Chief Justice, and Eldon, the Chancellor, were the eight members of the Queen's Regency
   Council. Whitbread moved for a copy of their report on 8 Apr. and the Government
   readily acquiesced (Hansard, xix. 738–9); on 25 Jan., towards the end of the debates on the
   Regency Bill, Grey had launched a violent attack on Eldon for his supposed conduct at the
   time of the King's illness in 1804 (ibid., xviii. 1008–1016).

429. To J.A. Murray

BLPES v. 54–7 ⟨Horner, ii. 76–8⟩   Lincoln's Inn, 24 June 1811

. . .

⟨I wish we could meet and have a gossip upon the present state of things; which
is very curious, and an excellent subject for speculation and gossip. Nothing of
importance has occurred for a long while, in the domestic politics; but the little
circumstances which pass daily and accumulate, give one by degrees a sort of history
which would be very untruly given without reporting all; and indeed of themselves
by their accumulation and gradual effect work a change in the position and
arrangement of political persons. Nothing can be more whimsical than the present
posture of what are still called parties; and the anxious, uncertain state of many of
the politicians of all descriptions. I expect that the prorogation of parliament will be
the signal for a more active course of intrigues at Carlton House; which, in a certain
way, have been going on a long while.

⟨I believe the Regent to be completely in the hands of Earl Yarmouth and the
Duke of Cumberland; two of the worst men, in point of principle, public and private,
that are to be found in this or any other country. The Lord Chancellor is intriguing

under the wings of the Duke of Cumberland; working out his separate salvation, and betraying Perceval (so far) just as he betrayed the Doctor in 1804. The Regent courts Lord Grey on the one hand, and Sir Francis Burdett on the other; and has adopted all the unjust and mean prejudices of the higher aristocrats and Windsor against Lord Grenville, to whom if the Whigs do not repay (as I trust and believe they will) the same fidelity which he has observed since their coalition, there will be an end of all honour in politics. Cobbett's silence about the Duke of York, which finally settles his character in point of honesty, is said to turn upon some expectations which have been held out to him of a remission of his sentence; he is said to have been talked to by Denis O'Brien, who is the friend of Bate Dudley, who is the friend of Sheridan, who is the friend of the Prince Regent.[1] Cobbett said he would not pledge himself, but has been silent on the subject. Do not be surprised, therefore, if Cobbett lies on in gaol; and in the end betrays the whole communication, and reviles the Duke of York and the House of Commons. I think it would have been a fair measure for popularity, to have given an amnesty to all the state libellers, with whom the King's Bench has crowded the prisons; but such negotiations with individuals, and making terms on the part of the sovereign with those whom the law has convicted, are not merely a great impropriety, but must give those unprincipled and ferocious persons such a hold over a nervous mob-led mind like the Regent's, as will prove embarrassing to him in the extreme.

⟨One may judge of a favourite's character by very slight circumstances. From what I saw of Earl Yarmouth and heard fall from him at the fete the other night, my conclusion was that he has no command or possession of himself, but must speedily render himself odious. I find this impression very general. The arrogance and assuming vanity, and rudeness of his manners, were very offensive. We shall have sport with him one of these days unless the Prince takes fright himself, before we have an explosion.⟩

. . .

1. Dennis O'Bryen (1755–1832: *DNB*), the dramatist, had been an intimate of Fox; Henry, afterwards Sir Henry, Bate Dudley (1745–1824: *DNB*) was founding editor of the *Morning Herald*. For the character of Bate Dudley's support of the Prince Regent see A. Aspinall, *Politics and the Press c. 1780–1850* (1949), pp. 169–71.

430. To Lord Grenville

⟨*Horner*, ii. 78–80⟩   Lincoln's Inn, 28 June 1811

⟨I happened to be waiting at the bar of the House of Lords yesterday, when Lord Stanhope presented a Bill, for maintaining and enforcing the value of Bank of England paper;[1] and I cannot resist the wish I feel to call your Lordship's attention to the great importance of what passed upon that occasion. The manner in which the extraordinary proposal of Lord Stanhope was received by Lord Liverpool and the Chancellor, and the opinions which the former intimated upon the subject of legal tender, convince me, that the Ministers have had the question of making Bank notes a legal tender under their consideration, and that they are prepared to take the first opportunity of effecting that momentous change in the system of our commercial and financial economy. I have been confirmed in the same conviction, by an expression which the deputy governor of the Bank used to me, just before the debate took place, in talking of Lord King's notice to his tenants, that he hoped Government would not be compelled to make their notes a legal tender.[2] The directors affect to deprecate such an alteration of the law; but they look to it as their ultimate protection, against the necessity, to which the general adoption of Lord King's notice by landlords, and of such actions against country bankers as have been brought lately in the West of England, would compel the Bank of limiting its issues in order to remove the depreciation of its notes. It appeared to me yesterday, that the discussion brought on by Lord Stanhope gave the Ministers an opportunity, not merely of feeling the pulse of the House upon this question, but of making an impression favourable to such an expedient, when they shall hereafter bring it forward; and I cannot but think it will be a great misfortune to the public, if the session of parliament closes with such an impression as will be left both in the House of Lords and upon the public mind, by such opinions, stated and not exposed, nor protested against, by those who have most weight and authority. The several successive steps, which have been observed in every country that allowed its currency to fall into a state of depreciation, are coming upon us faster than was to have been expected in this country; and as there will be no recovery after Bank notes are made a legal tender, the discussions which precede such a measure are evidently of the last importance.

⟨I take it for granted, that Lord King will attend on Monday: the turn which was given to the debate yesterday renders that indispensable. If your Lordship can make it convenient to yourself, to take a part in the discussion, I am persuaded that the expression of your sentiments will be of most essential benefit to the public interests in this great question, and, I would even flatter myself, might deter the Ministers from following so fast that course of measures, into which their own infatuation and the ignorance of their commercial advisers seem driving them.⟩

1. The Gold Coins and Bank Note Bill, introduced by Charles, 3rd Earl Stanhope (1753–1816: DNB) and commonly known as 'Lord Stanhope's Bill', sought, by denying any legal remedy to creditors who were offered depreciated Bank paper by debtors, to counter the legal principle underlying Lord King's recent letter to his tenantry demanding rents in specie or the paper equivalent of specie (AR liii (1811), 297–8). (See King, pp. 231–59, for King's letter to his tenants and his justification of it, together with two tables depicting the gradual fall in the value of Bank notes and the intrinsic value of money-contracts during each year of the Bank restriction. See also Holland's Further Memoirs, pp. 104–105.)

2. William Manning (1763–1835), the deputy Governor in 1810–12, was MP for Evesham. He had been a dissentient member of the Bullion Committee and on 8 May had openly criticized its recommendations (PH).

431. From Lord King

Lacaita-Shelburne MSS, William L. Clements Library,
University of Michigan   Minehead, 26 July 1811

I have just received your note and stop to write at the post office that there may be no delay.

The calculation of the number of guineas for 1810 – the price of gold being £4. 11s. is as follows

as 91 market price is to 78 mint price so is 100 guineas to $85^{65}/_{91}$ guineas

For 1811 the price being £4. 13s.

as 93 is to 78 so is 100 to $83^{81}/_{93}$

Therefore the weight of 85 guineas and two thirds is the real value of £105 contracted in 1810 and the weight of 83 guineas and $^8/_9$ is the intrinsic value of £105 contracted in 1811. I did not insert them because I had no occasion to make use of them or indeed for 1809 as I had not refused notes for any contract later than 1808 though the difference is very considerable since that date.[1]

I believe Lauderdale has moved for an account of the average of notes in circulation for 1810 and for those of 1811 but I may be mistaken and your average will answer the purpose as well. The page you propose to give to the Tables is as good as can be and I think they will be useful.[2] Pray add any explanation you please and alter and correct what I wrote for that purpose.

I hope to see you between the assizes but you will be much pressed for time.

I find many people here and in Devonshire are of our opinion on this subject.

1. King evidently refers to the tables depicting a progressive depreciation of Bank notes which he, Horner, and perhaps Lauderdale prepared during the summer of 1811, and which were included as a postscript to the published version of the *Speech of the Right Hon. Lord King, in the House of Lords, on Tuesday, July 2, 1811, upon the second reading of Earl Stanhope's bill, respecting guineas and bank notes* (1811) and reprinted in *King*, pp. 251–3.

2. Horner's proposed addition to King's tables cannot be identified with certainty. Considering his emphasis on precedents in monetary history, however, one might speculate that he proposed the inclusion of a short table summarizing the incidence in British history of political contrivance against the market value of the pound sterling drawn from the 1st Earl Liverpool's *Treatise on the Coins of the Realm* (1805). At all events, the tables which complemented King's reasonings on the Bank restriction and the resulting depreciation of Bank paper included a summary of Liverpool's account of the 'treasons against the pound sterling' by which Edward I, Edward III, Henry IV, Edward IV, Henry VIII, and Elizabeth I 'had degraded the coin for the purpose of defrauding their subjects'. King's tables were published in Aug. 1811. (*King*, p. 257; Doc. 434.)

432. To Lord King

BLPES v. 63–4 (draft or copy)   [Bulstrode,[1] ?31 July 1811]

. . . I would have given you my opinion before now, if I had not wavered several times about it. My first impression was, that you ought to go on with the action – but after talking with Lord Holland and reflecting upon the points he urged, I am now inclined to think you had better desist.[2]

It does not appear to me that you are individually engaged and committed, by what you have already done, in such a manner, as to make it incumbent upon you to proceed, against any reasons of a political or public nature to the contrary. Now, I think there really are such. In the first place, it is not a very favourable shape for the discussion of the main question, because it brings upon us the additional prejudices and alarms of the whole body of farmers, and nearly the whole body of squires who like the name and show of their high rents. In the second place, you will certainly drive Parliament to the adoption of the paper system, to the full extent of making it a legal tender. I do not deny, that I ought to have foreseen all this and to have urged it to you, last June when you first thought of the notice; for whatever weight such arguments have now, they had then: I fully admit it; but I could not then bring myself to believe that either Government or Parliament were so utterly ignorant of what is right in these matters, and in fact the turn that the discussion of Stanhope's bill took much surprised me. This, I am of opinion, leaves you at liberty to reconsider the thing; before you go farther, and drive them farther.

If you proceed with the action, the course will probably be this: if the judges think the law with you, as I persuade myself they must, they will make every delay that can be contrived to postpone a judgement upon this point, until there is an opportunity of having the law altered by a new Act; perhaps you will be treated with a bye battle in the Court of Chancery, upon an experimental bill of injunction against your action, grounded upon the equity that may be fancied to arise out of the circumstances of the times. There may be more or less delay; but I look upon it as certain, that, if the Judges cannot defeat you in Westminster Hall, Parliament will readily and eagerly pass a new Act. I own it strikes me, that the question, on which you have been consulting us, hinges chiefly upon this, whether, under such new Act – that is – under a system of forced paper made a tender by law, things would be worse for the public than they are at present, supposing Government to continue of the same mind, and more difficult to remedy, supposing the Government or its mind to be changed.

Viewing it in this light, I have no hesitation in thinking, that matters will be made much worse and rendered greatly more difficult to cure, if Parliament goes the length of a legal tender; and that the best that can be done meanwhile for the interests of private property, as well as for the finances, is by any sort of management to keep things at least from going on, if we cannot force them a little back. The Act, that is to be expected from Parliament if you force them to it, would release the bank from all apprehension, and would give them uncontrolled power; and as their certain abuse of such power would bring on more rapidly that crisis, which is likely enough to be the upshot even of the present state of things, it would be so distressful a catastrophe by the sudden vicissitudes and transfers of wealth that would first be felt and by the annihilation of almost all monied property which would be the ultimate result, that it seems to be recommended to us by every public reason to retard it as much as possible, and to give no handle to others in their ignorance to hurry it on. That they and Stanhope together may proceed to such extremities, even though you do not move, is very possible; but they will want the pretext at least of that necessity, which they urged with so much effect at the end of last session. We shall meet them, on more advantageous terms, if they make the first advance of their own accord; and, for the same reason, our parliamentary discussions of the Bullion question, which are certainly unavoidable, will stand upon better ground, if we have only to resist the continuance of Stanhope's Act, or bring it forward ourselves in a general form for the purpose of taking prospective measures.

If these reasons against your proceeding with the action are well founded, they furnish a distinct public ground which you have to assign for your change of conduct. You will forbear to follow up your legal rights, you will acquiesce in a certain loss of property, because you will not furnish Ministers and Parliament with a pretext for making the law more impolitic and ruinous to the public interests than it is already.

1. Then in the possession of the Duke of Somerset.
2. Horner refers to the litigation arising from King's demand for rent in specie or its equivalent.

433. From John Allen

BL Add. MSS 52180   [Holland House, ?Aug. 1811]

. . .

Moira has left town and what surprises me they say he has gone home tolerably well satisfied with the Prince's good intentions. After the desertion of Lord Leitrim and support given to Pole's proclamation this excess of confidence if faithfully reported astonishes me. Moira though sent for by the Prince was some days in town before he was admitted to an interview though favoured in the mean time with sundry civil messages to keep him in good humour.[1]

Lord Hutchinson has left town in disgust at not being able to obtain an interview with the Prince. Nothing augurs worse in my opinion of the intentions of Carlton House with respect to the Catholics than this exclusion of Lord Hutchinson. It seems as if the Prince had determined to take a line he knew to be wrong and inconsistent with his former professions and therefore declined an interview with Lord Hutchinson lest he should be reproached in plain terms with his treachery and insincerity.

Sheridan has also I suspect been kept carefully out of his presence ever since the late measures were resolved upon with regard to Ireland. Sheridan holds very high language on that subject and declares that much as he loves and long as he has been attached to the Prince he will break with him for ever if he abandons the Catholics.

Yarmouth in the mean time seems to be rising higher in favour every day at Carlton house and as the following story will show looks forward to a complete rupture between the Prince and the Whig party. In the first fervour of his grief and surprise at the death of the late Duke of Devonshire the Prince wrote a very warm and affectionate letter to Hartington, who was of course very much affected with receiving such a letter at that moment and answered it in the same strain professing the strongest and most inviolable attachment to His Royal Highness – On which Lord Yarmouth had the imprudence to say – 'Well if we should quarrel with the Whigs we shall at least have deprived them of one of their most powerful supporters. We are sure of the D. of Devonshire.' This conversation of Lord Yarmouth reaching the ears of Lord George was by him immediately repeated to Hartington who was of course extremely incensed at such a construction being put on his letter.[2]

Perceval and Arbuthnot you have probably heard have got permission to wear the Prince's uniform, which those who know the importance annexed at Carlton House to such a trifle consider as a strong proof that Perceval is gaining ground in that quarter.

1. Nathaniel Clements, 2nd Earl of Leitrim (1768–1854), the Prince's candidate to fill a vacancy for an Irish representative peer, was canvassed for energetically by the Hely-Hutchinson brothers, Lord Hutchinson and his elder brother Richard Hely-Hutchinson, 1st Earl of Donoughmore (1756–1825: DNB), who was himself a representative peer, against Perceval's candidate, Archibald Acheson, 2nd Earl of Gosford (1776–1849: DNB). In the end the Prince transferred his support to Gosford, Leitrim was beaten, and the Hutchinson brothers were infuriated. An effort by the Irish Catholics in 1810, moreover, to improve their organization had been contested by the Chief Secretary, William Wellesley-Pole, afterwards 1st Baron Maryborough and 3rd Earl of Mornington (1762–1845: DNB), so strongly that on one occasion the Perceval Ministry had been forced to disavow him. After Daniel O'Connell had outlined a new scheme for the election of delegates and offered to provide a test case in his own person at a meeting on 9 July 1811, Pole had responded with a hostile proclamation, ordering the arrest of those who had attended the meeting, and afterwards prosecuted them for violation of the Convention Act. In mid-August 1811, almost simultaneously with his desertion of Lord Leitrim and much to the chagrin of the Whigs, the Prince of Wales sanctioned Pole's proclamation and legal action against the Catholic leaders. (Roberts, pp. 81–90.)

2. William Spencer Cavendish, Marquess of Hartington (1790–1858: DNB), had succeeded his father as 6th Duke of Devonshire on 29 July 1811. Lord George Cavendish, afterwards 1st Earl of Burlington (1754–1834: DNB), was the new Duke's uncle.

434. To Lord Webb Seymour

BLPES v. 69–71   Torquay, 28 Aug. 1811

. . . You will be at no loss for documents to refer to, for the prices of corn. Under the present corn laws, weekly returns are made for all the districts to the Inspector, who publishes an abstract of those returns periodically, I rather think weekly, in the *London Gazette*. The inland and maritime districts are distinguished from each other, and Scotland is distinguished from England and Wales. I think, in calculating the price under your proposed contract, that Scotland and Wales ought to be thrown out; and the fairest average, for an English agreement of this sort, would probably be taken from all the maritime and inland districts of England put together.[1]

It is a nicer question, what number of years ought to be assumed for the average? And on this, I apprehend, Mr Morgan would be best qualified to advise you.[2] I have understood, that an average price of corn can hardly be considered, as including the proper compensation for all variations of season, if taken from fewer than nineteen years. But so large a cycle, though it may furnish an exact security against the fluctuations of the harvest, is obviously inapplicable to the case of a progressive depreciation of money; for it would always give a price greatly below the fair price of the year, for which the result of the calculation was wanted. For example, upon an average of the nineteen years preceding 1810, including even the four remarkable years of dearth, the price for 1809 would be only 59/2d.; whereas the real average price of 1809, not a year of scarcity, was 95/7d. It is evident, that a much shorter term of years must be fixed upon for your purpose. The shorter the term, however, the less is the resulting average to be depended upon as a security to both the contracting parties against the variations of the harvest in different seasons.

There is a peculiarity, however, in the present situation of this country as to its corn trade, the effects of which ought probably to be taken into account, in adjusting the number of years for your average; and which strikes me as operating, so as to affect it, in different ways. Our demand is considered as permanently exceeding the supply from our own fields; in the best years, it is said, we still stand in need of some addition by importation from abroad. In consequence of this, it would seem, that we cannot be said to have any years of excess and cheapness, because the demand is always enough to maintain the price. From which I would infer, in the first place, that as the irregularities of the season now to be guarded against in fixing a corn rent are fewer, a cycle of a smaller number of years may be sufficient to furnish a just average; and in the second place, as those irregularities are all on one side, on the side of scarcity and high price, it is the borrower only who need be careful to protect himself against them. These are very hasty remarks, which I have had but little time to consider; I rather throw them out to assist your own reflections.

The next query you put is, as to the number of bushels to be fixed on for the rate of interest? It does not occur to me, that the percentage should be different in this mode of arranging the payment of the interest, from the common one. You have only to ascertain what money is lent for upon mortgage, at the time you enter into your agreement. I wish you would say, why you think the interest ought to be lower at a corn value, than if the conversion were made into the market price of one of the precious metals. Some reasons must have weighed with you, which I have not been able to strike out.

Are you decidedly of opinion, that a conversion of the interest by the price of corn, is preferable to a conversion according to the market price of gold? The reasons, in favour of corn, are these, I apprehend; first, that besides the great depreciation going on so fast from the abuses of our paper money, there is a real depreciation proceeding all over the world from the increasing plenty and cheapness of gold, against which (it is very certain) that there is no security for maintaining the value of property so good as corn rents; and secondly, that there is no official return of the market price of gold, which could be appealed to in case of dispute, or in case the contract should fall into the hands of representatives. In favour of a conversion into gold bullion, I would urge the following reasons: the market price of exportable standard gold in bars varies exactly with the depreciation[3] of our paper, and its excess above the mint price of gold measures accurately the rate of depreciation, so that a conversion of interest according to that market price (if it can be affected) gives exactly a compensation for the fall in the value of money, neither more nor less; between two men who perfectly trust and understand each other, there can be no difficulty in ascertaining the market price of this commodity, because there are transactions enough among the bullion merchants in the course of a year to afford an average yearly price, if that be necessary, which can be learned upon 'Change; as between the representatives of the original contracting parties, it would be easy (I think) to introduce a clause into the deed, pointing out how the price of gold should be ascertained for each year, by the mercantile prices current, and in case of dispute by an arbitration of merchants; there is no occasion, as in a corn rent, to have an average calculation, because, if the principles from which I have reasoned are correct, the last quotation of the market price of gold ought to be taken at once, and you are freed therefore from the complex and indeed embarrassing considerations that must be balanced against each other in fixing a corn rent; lastly, the depreciation arising from the fall in the real value of gold itself, against which a conversion into gold will certainly not protect you, is so gradual as hardly to be worth taking into account except in contracts that are to operate for a very long period of time, and at any rate is so small in comparison of that arising from the other cause, that you can have no hesitation in choosing, if it is reduced to an alternative, from which of the two you will be protected. I do not pretend, that these arguments would be conclusive with me, in making a choice between a corn and a gold conversion; but I wish you to consider the whole matter, and have probably argued the latter most, because you had already decided for the former.

Lord King has just published some tables, as a supplement to his late speech, which you will find useful in this business.

. . .

1. Seymour and his brother Somerset had devised a scheme of leases requiring the payment of rents on a sliding scale reflecting the market price of either corn or gold and affording tenants protection from years of extraordinary dearth through the establishment of an average market price. The scheme, which was consistent with the view of depreciation advanced by Horner in the Commons on 6 May 1811, apparently pertained only to new leases, thereby avoiding the difficulties that had arisen from King's *ex post facto* claim against his tenants.
2. Presumably the actuary William Morgan (1750–1833: *DNB*).
3. *I.e. when there is either no gold coin of the King's in circulation, or when that gold coin is circulating in a perfect state undiminished by wear. If there be a worn gold coin in circulation, the market price of the above-named commodity will vary with this depreciation of the gold coin; which is in furtherance of the principle.

435. To Lady Holland

BLPES v. 95–6   Torquay, 5 Sept. [1811]

. . .

. . . I am almost reduced to despair now about Spain. If there is any thing more extraordinary than the patient perseverance of the people through these three terrible years, it is that no soldier or statesman among them has yet shown himself to lead them and keep the ascendancy. I am afraid it is made but too manifest now, that a Cortes will not expel the French . . .

. . .

There is nothing worth thinking of in politics now, but the cause of the Catholics, to whom I remember your great partiality. I fear they will not make much of it, however, with all their talking. I wish these were days in which we might see them make the Regent keep his word at the point of the bayonet. . . .[1]

. . .

1. In a letter to Allen of 7 Sept., Horner commented on the 'remarkable moderation' with which the Irish Catholics had conducted their county meetings. Allen's reply of 11 Sept. contains further information on the proceedings of the Irish Catholics and on the Irish policy of the British Government. (BLPES v. 97–103.)

436. From Lady Holland

BL Add. MSS 51644   [Holland House, 11 Sept. 1811]

. . .

We are busily employed in seeking a house for the Duke of Infantado, but nothing is more difficult. Lord Malmesbury is a Jew, and does not conduct himself like a grand seigneur, especially as he has been in Spain and ought to know better how to treat rich Spaniards.[1] He is pertinacious in being paid in *advance* and extravagant in his terms. The few who have seen the Duke are very much pleased with his manners, which are very easy and unaffected, and yet denote high breeding and polish. He is gratified with the attentions he meets with here, but he is quite dejected at the aspect of affairs in his own Country.[2]

The only *home* news, is that the Prince has cut off his tremendous painted whiskers, that his journey to Ragley was by bribery, kept out of all the newspapers, and that the operations at Carlton House under the guidance of Lord Yarmouth will cost half a million, and require half a year to complete.[3]

. . .

The Duke of Devonshire has added £2,000 to the Jointure, and made a present of £5,000 besides. Upon Mr Clifford he has settled £2,000 annually. He has given Mrs Lamb £5,000. The Jewels are under arbitration, to be decided by Sir Samuel Romilly to whom they are to belong, as the wording of the will is considered to be ambiguous.[4]

Mr Abercromby came here for one night only[5] to carry his boy to School. He returned yesterday to Tunbridge Wells, where there is still a good society of wit. Mr [J.W.] Ward has become greatly enamoured of a Mrs Tighe, a lady of the family of the Poetess of that name.[6] Lord Grey has had as he apprehends an attack of his old complaint.[7] It perhaps may only be an indigestion, but from what I hear I am afraid he is low spirited upon the occasion.

Sydney arrived here last night, and had the dreaded meeting with his brother. What past [sic] in that interview does not appear, but it was not of an agreeable nature, judging by the oppression and dejection of Sydney's mind afterwards. ...[8]

. . .

1. Malmesbury, whose intrigues had contributed to the overthrow of the Whig Ministry in 1807 (Roberts, pp. 23–7), had once been chargé d'affaires in Madrid.
2. A large party of Spaniards, including Infantado, dined at Holland House on the evening of 8 Sept. and returned frequently during the remainder of the month (HHDB).
3. See Doc. 439.
4. Augustus William James, afterwards Sir Augustus, Clifford (1788–1877: DNB) and Caroline (1785–1862), wife of William Lamb's brother George (1784–1834: DNB), were the children the 5th Duke of Devonshire had had by his second wife, but before the death of his first. During his lifetime the 5th Duke had already provided for the Lambs with a marriage portion of £20,000 and an annuity of £500; his half-brother also provided a handsome settlement for Clifford on his marriage in 1813. (PH iv. 354 and iii. 451.)
5. The evening of 9 Sept. (HHDB).
6. The poet Mrs (Mary) Tighe had died in 1810; that the reference is to her sister-in-law Marianne (d. 1853), wife of William Tighe, seems confirmed by Letters to 'Ivy', pp. 143 and 353, and Doc. 437.
7. Grey's 'old complaint' was a stomach disorder, perhaps an ulcer. Throughout his life its periodic recurrence seems often to have coincided with those instances in which Grey was depressed, loath to involve himself in politics, somewhat intolerant of the views of allies and rivals alike, and susceptible to charges of political inconsistency.
8. Robert Percy 'Bobus' Smith (1770–1845: DNB), Sydney's elder brother, had just returned to England after seven years in India. It is not apparent why his brother should have 'dreaded' their meeting. It would seem unlikely that it was merely a question of money; Bobus returned to England a rich man and, if anything, increased his financial support to Sydney. But see Doc. 437.

437. To Lady Holland

BL Add. MSS 51644   Torquay, 14 Sept. 1811

. . .

The Mrs Tighe you speak of must be the wife of a yellow little man in the House of Commons, who is very nice in the conduct of a black cane, and publishes much sentimental poetry about the vegetable world. She will contrive but ill for her future ease of mind, if she engages her affections very seriously with the person you mention;[1] however, it may answer very well for a little Tunbridge passion. ... What you say of Sydney's meeting with his brother vexes me, for it looks as if he had relied upon him in some way or other, and been disappointed: I did not know, however, that he entertained any expectations, in which he could be disappointed, with relation to his own affairs. Yet it would not account for the dejection you observed, that Bobus talks of literature and retirement, whereas Sydney has been building castles of politics and parliamentary success; because Sydney cannot put much faith in all that talking about retirement. It will be very mortifying to him and to all of us, if he must consign himself for life to Yorkshire; but all circumstances considered, I fear that the true prudence for him is to act as if he had no better chance. I am rather curious to see what his brother is to do, with all his activity and talents and acquirements, after having closed his professional pursuits so early in life. It is but an indifferent scheme, I take it, to lose any number of years in a profession, that is not to last through one's whole life; literature will not do for mere retirement, and a man has but a bad chance of distinguishing himself in it as a profession, who has employed otherwise his time from thirty to forty. Is Bobus connecting himself with Lord Wellesley since his return? If he takes to politics, will he renew his little warfare of jealousy with Canning? Against all of Sydney's sanguine predictions, I venture to think he would find Canning too much for him.[2]

. . .

1. Ward was a notorious womanizer.
2. Bobus Smith had been a close friend at Eton of both Canning and Holland and it seems to have been uncertain which he would support on his return. Ward wrote towards the end of 1812 (*Letters to 'Ivy'*, p. 185) that 'for some time he seemed to hang suspended betwixt Holland House and Gloucester Lodge [Canning's place], but Gloucester Lodge has proved the magnet of the strongest attraction'. This Doc. seems strongly to imply that Sydney Smith feared his brother might have political ambitions that would somehow blight his own. Bobus entered Parliament in 1812 but was a relative failure.

438. To John Allen

BLPES v. 104–7 ⟨*Horner*, ii. 90–91⟩   Torquay, 14 Sept. 1811

. . .

It is a curious attack in the *Times* of Thursday upon the Regent for the office given to McMahon.[1] I am not sorry for the attack; but the principle and reasoning of the article have all the baseness of that paper, which, in its system of adopting every sentiment good or bad of the prevailing public opinion, is driven into every sort of inconsistency. . . .

⟨It is very hard to believe that the transactions of Government in Ireland are not in the same character of a crooked intriguing policy, for the purpose of managing the Prince. Have you any hesitation in thinking that Opposition ought to take up this matter in Parliament in the most decided manner, without any more of that forbearance and reserve which they practised last session?

⟨If the Irish judges support their Government, in the construction of the Convention Act, we ought to move for the repeal of so abominable a statute, and in discussing it have no mercy for the judges. If by any unlooked-for turn of patriotism, or fear in the judges, they should construe the act as it seems to me it ought to be, then we shall have a much freer game to play, by an attack upon the Administration alone; but, in either event, I feel very anxious that Opposition should go resolutely to the attack, without any compromise towards the Regent. It is not unlikely that Parliament will meet before the legal question can be decided at Dublin; in that case, ought we not to act without any delay, assuming our own construction of the act to be clear and indubitable? I have not the least faith in any stories of secret intelligence possessed by Government, as to designs on the part of the Catholics; if Government is sincere, they may have been frightened by the appearance of a little more eagerness among the Catholics, when they believed the day of emancipation was at last coming on; and the show of a little more determination and system, when they found that day bring them a fresh disappointment. I am much more inclined to believe that Perceval and the Archbishop of Canterbury have worked upon Lord Manners,[2] who is a timid man and very bigoted. The conduct of the Wellesleys in all this business is very pitiful, for they have no bigotry on the subject.⟩

Is it certain, that our Government has entered into such a treaty with the Regency of Spain respecting South America, as is implied in a late decree of the Cortes, published by Blake stipulating our assistance for the subjugation of the revolted colonies, after 15 months, in consideration of our being permitted to trade with these same colonies during these same 15 months?[3] Nothing surely could be more imprudent than the former part of the stipulation, or more paltry and ridiculous than the latter. What resources shall we have left for carrying on a war in South America, fifteen months hence? What resources could we ever apply to such a wild project? On the other hand, what are 15 months of trading with such distant countries? Not more than enough to excite false hopes among our manufacturers, and to force a large exportation for which there will be no return. Besides, the publication of the other conditions of our treaty will most likely prompt the South Americans to disappoint us in that which regards trading with them. Such a treaty cannot have been made, unless the whole management of so momentous a question has been cast into the hands of a few grasping traders, who even in looking to nothing but their own interests have thought of nothing but their first cargoes. I cannot apprehend that it is very difficult for us, in the present circumstances of Spain and South America, to keep on trading terms with all the nominal dominions of Ferdinand the 7th, whom the revolted colonies, as well as those which adhere to the Regency at Cadiz, equally acknowledge for their sovereign. Our alliance with the Regency is, by a fiction which makes our line of conduct in this respect plain enough, an alliance with Ferdinand; and our guarantee of the integrity of his dominions leaves us a right of observing strict neutrality, between the different parts of those dominions which quarrel among themselves, while they recognize equally their allegiance to the King. After all this, there remains the still more important objection to such a treaty, that we are to take part against those who are in the right; as the colonies, who in the supposed renovation of the constitution demand equal rights, unquestionably are. The prejudices of the best men in Old Spain upon this subject are among the many lamentable proofs of their unfitness to save their country.[4]

⟨It would appear now, I think, that there is some relaxation in the violence of the King's disorder, and that the height to which it rose two months ago was probably owing to the heat of the season. As I understand he is better in health, I begin to think it likely that we shall have the question of restrictions to dispose of in Parliament; that will not fail to be a pleasant scene.

⟨I suppose the coronation of his wife is a matter that may be left to the new king's fancy. If he means any farther indignities or to impose any hardships upon her, it will be disgraceful to the nation to suffer them; with all her folly and low vices, she is a stranger; and though she has not conducted herself in her disgrace so as to deserve any respect, she has already been used very ill. . . .⟩

1. The Prince Regent had upset opinion by making official the appointment as his private secretary of Colonel, afterwards Sir, John McMahon (d. 1817). Since it carried a salary of £2,000 a year it was attacked by economical reformers out of Parliament for the remainder of the year; and since it was unprecedented it was challenged as unconstitutional in the Commons early in the 1812 session. The attack was broken off after an unsuccessful division in the Commons in Feb. 1812, with Horner voting in the minority.

2. Thomas Manners-Sutton, 1st Baron Manners (1756–1842: DNB), Irish Chancellor under Perceval's Ministry.

3. By a decree of 19 June the Cortes had accepted British mediation with the insurgent colonies, but on condition that if the mediation failed the British Government would not only suspend all intercourse with the rebels but actually aid in their subjection. Negotiators eventually went out to Spain but there was never any prospect of a treaty being concluded on such terms, or indeed of any significant improvement in Anglo-Spanish relations while the anti-British General Joaquín Blake was a member of the Regency. (AR liii. 162, and John Kenneth Severn, A Wellesley Affair: Richard Marquess Wellesley and the Conduct of Anglo-Spanish Diplomacy, 1809–1812 (Tallahassee, 1981), pp. 184ff.)

4. Horner's subsequent letter to Allen dated 19 Sept. (BL Add. MSS 52180) contains the following passage:

> I see from Henry Wellesley's note to the Regency, that we have offered our mediation with the revolted colonies. This project holds out an interminable course of fruitless and costly war, if it were possible for us to adhere to the principle of such an alliance, with the same honour which we have observed towards Spain for the last three years; but it will be next to impossible for our Government, or for this trading country, to resist the temptation we shall have to break off for the sake of a little trade.

439. To J.A. Murray

BLPES v. 108–109 ⟨Horner, ii. 88–90⟩   Torquay, 14 Sept. 1811

⟨I am very happy to have got some intelligence, though indirectly, of your projected journey. Jeffrey I hear is coming to London, and you are to be his travelling companion. This is a most agreeable arrangement for you.⟩

. . .

⟨You will get to London before the next quarterly Report about the King, which has always been a period of much political gossip, intrigue, and speculation; and a favourable time for using one's eyes and ears. The character of the Regent appears to be now thoroughly developed; he has evidently none of the ambition, good or bad, that his station inspires into all manly minds; but is as devoid of activity in public concerns as I always believed him to be of public principle. The life he leads is one of stupid, superannuated profligacy, which is disturbed by fearful anxieties, lest the public should discover his habits and haunts: he has been on a visit to Lord Hertford's at Ragley, and the newspapers were all carefully cautioned and paid to make no mention of it. Instead of the business and ardour which would have been natural to a man in the vigour of life becoming sovereign of such a people as this at such a moment of their history, nothing is known of him but such languid luxury and effeminate profusion as we read of at Paris in the last years of Louis XV.

⟨At present he is completely under the management of the Duke of Cumberland and Lord Yarmouth; of the former it is not a year since he used to express openly the worst opinion; the latter is by the general opinion of every body considered to be one of the very worst men living, wholly unprincipled in every particular, but with considerable talents from nature⟩, haughty, arrogant, cruel though fearless, educated at first in the kitchen and the stables in consequence of his mother having an aversion to him when a boy, and afterwards among all the sharpers of London and Paris, and who never exerted his abilities upon any other subject but making money in which he laboured like a tradesman at every species of gaming from the stock exchange to the halls in St James's until he ⟨ingratiated himself with the Prince not long before the Regency was formed and assumed the management of his household expenses and bedchamber politics. He will perhaps not have temper or manners to maintain his ascendancy very long; he disgusted many of the nobility at the fete in Carlton House by a vulgar insolence which he could not conceal; and the Prince is very likely to discard him on an instant for some unguarded freedom. In the meanwhile he has the direction of repairs at Carlton House, which are to cost half a million; though the Prince means, as soon as he is King, to remove to Buckingham House, which will also need repairs.

⟨. . .⟩

440. To Matthew Marsh[1]

BLPES v. 110–13 (copy or draft)   Torquay, 18 Sept. 1811

I owe you many apologies for having so long omitted to perform my promise of answering as well as I might be able your questions upon the laws relating to poor houses. As to the impolicy of such establishments in general, at least upon their present footing, how they poison the relief that is intended for the infirm poor, and what harm they do in many ways to the morals and happiness of all the rest of our labouring people, I perceive you and myself should quite agree: that however is not a matter of law, but a question for law-makers to consider, and entitled to a much more serious attention from them than they have hitherto thought fit to bestow on it. For upon the matters of law, on which you have referred to me, I fear it must be acknowledged, that a great deal of what would seem to be abuse and hardship, is not only permitted, but directed to be done, by authority of the acts of parliament which are at present in force on this subject. At the same time, the vigilance of well-disposed magistrates may do much good, not only in checking abuses which are contrary to law, but in mitigating and lightening what the legislature may have too much sanctioned.

. . .²

1. The Reverend Matthew Marsh (d. 1840), another friend of the Hollands who often accompanied them on their trips and was afterwards tutor for a while to their son Henry Fox, was at this time Chancellor of the Diocese of Salisbury (*Home of the Hollands*, pp. 176 and 337). Sydney Smith later remarked (to Lady Holland, [Oct. 1825], *Smith Letters*, i. 416) that for an intimate of Holland House he held remarkably illiberal opinions.

2. The remainder of this letter answers Marsh's queries about the legality of the poor house at Clarendon by reviewing the state of the law relating to poor houses.

441. From John Allen

BLPES v. 116–17   Holland House, Monday, 23 Sept. [1811]

. . . Jeffrey instead of coming to London is gone to the Highlands to refresh himself with the mountain air after the fatigues of the last number in which he has given us three very good articles and two of them without the least admixture of politics.¹

How much Brougham has contributed to the number I have not heard, but one article which is evidently his, viz. the Campaign of 1809, is very far from being in his best manner.²

There is so much egotism in many of his late articles and such carelessness and redundancy of style that one begins to regret less the little time or leisure he has now left for such compositions.

. . . The remaining part of Humboldt's *New Spain* has at last arrived.³ It contains a deal of very curious and interesting information concerning the mines, from which it appears that the annual produce of gold and silver from America is near 9½ millions sterling annually, while the whole amount of these metals brought into the commerce and circulation of Europe from all the other parts of the world does not much exceed £900,000 – making a total of near £10,400,000 exclusive of the mines of Japan, China, Tunysia and the interior of Africa and Asia.

. . .

1. In *ER* xviii (no. xxxvi, Aug. 1811), Jeffrey had contributed pieces on Ford's *Dramatic Works*, pp. 275–304, Scott's *Vision of Don Roderick*, pp. 379–92, and Mrs Grant's *Highland Letters*, pp. 480–510.

2. The only reasonably certain contribution by Brougham to *ER* xviii (no. xxxvi, Aug. 1811) seems to be that on the Report of the African Institution, pp. 305–325. In addition it is thought he may have contributed those on the 'Campaigns of 1809', pp. 392–425, and on Davy, pp. 470–80, and had some share with William Drummond in that on Hamilton's *Ægyptiaca*, pp. 435–47.

3. The first three parts of Alexander von Humboldt, *Essai politique sur le royaume de la Nouvelle Espagne* (2 vols, 1809–1811), had been reviewed by Allen in *ER* xvi (no. xxxi, Apr. 1810), 62–102; the next three parts in xix (no. xxxvii, Nov. 1811), 164–98.

442. To Samuel Whitbread

Whitbread MSS,
Bedfordshire County Record Office, 4607   Torquay, 29 Sept. 1811

. . .

I am not one of those who stood much in need of being undeceived, by the disclosures of character which the Prince Regent has made in the course of the last nine months. Whatever he may do now or hereafter in the choice of ministers, and though it may be the duty of all eminent public men to lose no opportunity which even his caprice may produce of doing as much good for the public as circumstances will admit of, however little that may be; it is manifest, that a novel course of affairs has commenced with his reign, through which the peculiarities of the sovereign's character and principles, totally dissimilar from those of his father, will require no less to be watched and on occasions resisted by the friends of liberty and just government.

. . .

443. To J.A. Murray

BLPES v. 118–19   Torquay, 5 Oct. 1811

. . .

This declaration of independence by the Carraccas [sic] is a remarkable event;[1] after such a measure, it is childishness to suppose that our proffered mediation can have any effect. Those colonies at least are lost, to the provisional regency of Old Spain; whether they will establish for themselves a tolerable government is another question. Many factious struggles, and much bloodshed, may be their first fruits of liberty; they have but little civilization and humanity as yet; and though their declaration is less stuffed with declamation and generalities, than other papers of the same sort which we have seen from other parts of the world, yet there is a project all through it of making every thing anew, that shows but little wisdom, and will probably come to a bad end. It would seem that the Spanish colonies are to separate at once into several independent states; Mexico, the greatest and best of them, adhering longest to the mother country. Nothing seems more certain, I think, than it is our duty and interest to observe a firm neutrality among them all, trading with every one of them; only taking care that the French take no part in these American revolutions, which we can easily prevent while we have the whole sea.

. . .

1. Venezuela had declared its independence of Spain in July.

444. To James Reddie

NLS MSS 3704, ff. 48–9   Tunbridge Wells, 18 Oct. 1811

. . .

I like very much your project of a course of lectures on commercial legislation and maritime law. Glasgow is a very proper situation for it; and the long attention you have paid to these subjects, would make it easy for you to convey in that forum most valuable information, and to make a solid improvement upon the system of legal education. What I would wish most would be to see you in Millar's chair; and in case a vacancy should happen, your having previously established a course of lectures would confirm and facilitate your claims.

I am not much acquainted with Prize appeal cases, or able to judge how far the printed statements with the mere judgement enable you to seize the principles, upon which the adjudication of the Court has proceeded. The few judgements that have been printed at length upon particular occasions, and the great fullness with which the decisions of the principal Court of Admiralty have of late years been published, furnish collateral lights undoubtedly that must assist you, if not in extracting the particular rationale of the other decisions, at least in judging how far such extracts as you can make may be depended upon. If the abridgement you have made of cases in the two last wars really presents a series of principles and rules, the publication of it must prove beneficial to those who are engaged in that department of law, however deficient it must necessarily be in the exposition of the reasonings upon which those rules were formed. It would be advisable, perhaps, to avail yourself of the advice of some experienced practiser in the Prize Court, that you may not fall into any of those minor inaccuracies, against which, in matters of law, nothing but daily practice gives a sufficient security. It is possible, too, that by inquiries at Doctor's Commons, some printed judgements of the Appeal Court, within your period, might be recovered; for I have now and then seen such; and it would be important for you to save them. Brougham is very well qualified, and I am sure would have a great pleasure, to assist you with respect to this publication.

I have derived great satisfaction from hearing of Erskine's good health, and, as I hear from all quarters, of Brown's distinguished success in his lectures. There would have been no impropriety whatever in publishing the speeches on the Bullion debate, which several of the speakers have done; but on the right side of that question there is so little new to tell, for there is nothing to do in the matter but to apply reasonings long ago completely settled to circumstances which have very little novelty in them, that when the argument failed in its immediate effect, there is but one course to follow, to wait for another opportunity to repeat it. I cannot say, that the Bar has occupied much of my attention or time; though waiting for the chance of being one day or other so occupied, is of course my whole occupation.

. . .

445. To Samuel Whitbread

Whitbread MSS,
Bedfordshire County Record Office, 4610   Tunbridge Wells, 20 Oct. 1811

. . .

I hear, that it is at present Perceval's intention to have the meeting of Parliament about the second week of January, so that there will be a fortnight more of restrictions for the Regent than by the Act is necessary. I hope the previous month of the Session will be employed to good purpose, for much will depend upon it; do not you think that we ought to proceed to the Catholic question at once, not waiting for any petition from the Catholics, but grounding our proceedings upon the measures of Government since the prorogation, and upon the notoriety of the King's state? . . .

446. To Lady Holland

BLPES v. 147–8   [!Woolbeding] Friday [25 Oct. 1811]

. . .

Coming down here, I read Trotter's book.[1] With all its bad taste, and malignity, it has much interest from the details to be collected from it about Mr Fox, as well as by the sincere admiration which is every where expressed. The letters at the end are delightful. I cannot help thinking the work calculated to increase, among the middle class of people throughout England, their affection and love for Mr Fox's memory.

1. John Bernard Trotter (1775–1818: *DNB*), the private secretary of Charles James Fox, published in 1811 *Memoirs of the Latter Years of the Right Honourable Charles James Fox*; it included an appendix of nineteen letters that tended to support the author's interpretation of Fox's principles. Trotter praised Fox profusely and argued that the Whig leader had enjoyed a relatively stable relationship with the King during 1806, that he had been a friend of agriculture who contested Pitt and Britain's capricious commercial classes, that his foreign policy towards France had been consistent with the principles he had advanced since the outbreak of the French Revolution, that his policy had inspired a genuine desire for peace in France, and that he had planned logically to bring on Catholic Emancipation as soon as a treaty of peace could be concluded. But Trotter was extremely critical of the foreign and domestic policy of the Whig Ministry after Fox's death, identifying the Grenvilles as the source of the problem and censuring Holland and the other Foxites in the Cabinet for abandoning their leader's principles. Such views were consistent with those of Whitbread and other Foxites but excited a hostile reaction among the Whig hierarchy.

447. To Francis Jeffrey[1]

BLPES v. 122–5   Woolbeding, 4 Nov. 1811

I have thought a little more about Trotter's book, and am still of the same mind as to the way in which it is desirable to see it reviewed.[2] I am much confirmed in this, by talking that matter over with Lord Robert Spencer, one of Fox's most attached friends, and one of those on whose judgement he relied habitually. He and all the rest of those friends, that I have either talked with myself or heard of their opinions, agree in regarding this book as a very malignant one as well as absurd, and quite contrary to the truth in many important particulars.[3] It is right you should know where it is wrong, but it will be better for the review to be confined to such observations as arise upon the contents of the volume itself. The author, to give himself more consequence, would represent Fox as abandoned in his last illness by all his old friends, not consulted by them on any public affairs, nay neglected as if they no longer retained the affection for [him] they had professed. All this is untrue; the persons he loved most were always near him, Lord Holland, Lord Fitzwilliam, Lord Grey and others; the rest of the Ministers were most anxious to have his opinion to the last on every important thing they had to do, and particularly in the foreign department he was informed of every particular to the latest moment, that he could attend to any thing, and expressed his approbation of what was doing.

The truth is, Mr Trotter, at no period of his connection with Mr Fox, was privy to any conversations on public business. Fox thought him a promising scholar, and that he had a natural taste for poetry, and he delighted in having a person near him with whom he could converse in his lounging way about his favourite books and favourite passages. When he went to St Ann's he dismissed politics from his mind, to enjoy his plants and poets and the open air. When he sent for Trotter to be his private secretary, he told Lord Holland he wanted to have some body to talk to about Greek, when he had done with the business of the day.

Lord Robert pointed out a trifling instance of Trotter's inaccuracy about facts, even where he could not fail to have once known them exactly. Fox was invited to dine with Bonaparte after the first levee which he went to, not the second, as Trotter has it; though it is true, that other persons were only asked at the levee subsequent to that at which they had first been presented. The ladies who are here mention another instance. He makes a fine anecdote, about Fox going to court without powder, and what he Mr Trotter said upon that subject. Now, they tell me he was all over powder when he went to court; I never was there, but I recollect very well seeing him once in the evening at the Duchess of Leinster's after a drawing room, and it [powder] made so great a change in his appearance that it is the circumstance by which I remember having seen him on that particular day. It is more important, however, to tell you that Lord Robert says, Trotter has described very exactly the sort of shyness with which Fox declined any attempt made to compliment or praise him.

Upon the whole (as we Reviewers always conclude), I take Trotter to be a little of a madman, morbid with self-importance, and with a notion of there being something better in this life than common sense and common feelings, which is to be attained by deliberate exaggeration and wilful melancholy. He seems to have caught nothing from Mr Fox, for his taste in writing and about manners and character are, in the most aggravated degree, the very opposite of all that Fox was himself or liked in others. Sincerely attached to that most extraordinary person, the book itself shows; and he appears to have sincerely felt and admired that 'negligent grandeur', as Grattan expressed it, which made Fox so difficult to be approached, and such an object of love to those who were near him.

1. This letter is unfinished, unsigned, and marked 'Not Sent' by Leonard Horner.
2. The *ER* took no notice of the book.
3. See Horner's note on Trotter's book and his related letter to Lady Holland (BLPES viii. 30 and v. 120–21).

448. To J. A. Murray

BLPES v. 132–3   [London], 18 Nov. 1811

. . .

Lord King has commenced his action against one of his tenants, who by good luck is a Bank director. The Bank of England have satisfied Perceval that the country silver tokens ought to be put down, which is to be done by Bill; upon exactly the principle, which the Bank disputes in their own case, that an inferior money will always banish the better sort. I have some reason to believe, too, that Perceval has made up his mind to legal tender; the renewal of Stanhope's bill will probably be used as the occasion of this alarming innovation, and very likely Lord King's prosecution of his action will be taken for a fresh pretext.

The church are in a most remarkable state of activity, upon the subject of education; compelled to it, much against their prejudices as well as their usual indolence, by the indefatigable exertions and daily progress of the Methodists. The Bishops have formed a national Board for the superintendence of the education of the poor according to the principles of the Church; and the Archbishop waited on the Regent, in the name of all the bench, to request that he would become patron of the institution. Circular letters have been addressed by each bishop to the parochial clergy of his diocese. The University of Cambridge, which has but a very poor chest of its own, has subscribed £500 to this object. I look upon all this to be the very triumph of Joseph Lancaster, whose single perseverance and zeal have spread the flame throughout the country. The church mean of course to suppress him if they can, but they can only do so (I hope) by being as active and persevering as he, in which case they would in truth be only the instruments of his success; it is more probable, that their fit will pass away, after a certain sum has been spent, and the more busy and forward promoters of the measure advanced to higher dignities; and that the bishops and prebendaries will relapse into their habitual slumber.

. . .

449. To Lord [?Holland]

BLPES v. 126–7   Lincoln's Inn, 19 Nov. [1811]

I believe Whishaw informed you yesterday, that Lord Grenville has decided, that Lord King ought to proceed with his action against the Bank director; an imprudent determination, I fear, and which we shall all repent of in the end, but King had left it to him, and he disposed of it in the most summary manner, and without a moment's hesitation. He gives no better reason in his letter, than that a contrary conduct would show a distrust in the propriety of what King did before; and that the farther steps which Ministers may take, upon the pretext of this action, they would take at any rate.

However we must lament that the thing has taken this turn, as it cannot be helped it seems to me important, both for Lord Grenville's sake and for the party, that it should not be known, that he has given this advice contrary to that of other persons. There is disposition enough already in all quarters to make a run at G[renville], and to collect pretexts to use against him. I should think it much better, therefore, that the determination should be talked of only as King's own, and that it should not be intimated that any of his friends have a notion he ought to have done otherwise.

. . .

450. To James Reddie

NLS MSS 3704, ff. 51–3   Lincoln's Inn, 26 Nov. 1811

. . .

You will participate in the joy which has been excited, almost universally, here, by the acquittal of the first of the Delegates tried at Dublin. It makes a new era not in the Catholic question only, but in the practical constitution of Ireland.[1]

1. On 21 Nov. a number of the Irish Catholic leaders who had been arrested in July and prosecuted by the Irish Government for violations of the Convention Act (Docs 433, 435, and 438) were acquitted (Roberts, p. 85).

451. To [?J.A. Murray]

BLPES v. 65–6 (copy or draft)   [Friday and] Saturday [late November
                                                      – early December 1811]

The poor King's delusions have lately taken a singular turn. He believes himself to have died, and to be in heaven; where he meets with several persons whom he knew or had heard of in his former life, and with whom he makes himself very comfortable, talking to them all at a prodigious rate. He holds conversations with Handel upon the subject of ancient music; but his chief companion is Lord Weymouth, his old Secretary of State, to whom he says many things about his present set of ministers, for he is all the while regarding our world below.[1]

. . .

Saturday

. . .

You have probably heard that the Duke of Cumberland has fallen into disgrace with the Regent. He had made his company rather too oppressive all the summer, and his bed-room at Carlton House was painted on purpose to drive him out. He still stuck fast, however, but it was reported to the Regent that the Duke had gone about saying, *he* made the Regent do this and that. To complete his folly, he went over to Windsor and said among his sisters that he thought the Prince was becoming as mad as their father. It is very likely that Lord Yarmouth has made the most of this for the ruin of his rival; his Lordship has sat by the bed-side at Oatlands constantly; in the absence of the mother, the royal tenderness overflows upon the son.[2] Lord Yarmouth will go soon, probably, after the Duke of Cumberland.

There is a story, but I know not on what authority it circulates, that the night before last the Regent decided at last in favour of Perceval for his Minister; and that this is after an intrigue of Wellesley's, enforced by letters from Lord Wellington, to bring Canning into office and displace Perceval. I do not know how much of this to believe; but I disbelieve as much of it as imports any thing like decision on the part of the Regent.

1. Thomas Thynne, 3rd Viscount Weymouth and afterwards 1st Marquess of Bath, had been Secretary of State in 1768 and 1775 and had died in 1796.
2. On or just before 16 Nov., the Prince Regent had snapped a tendon in his foot while attempting the Highland Fling and for nearly a month was laid up at Oatlands, the Duchess of York's place at Weybridge. In the absence of Lady Hertford her son attended the Prince's bedside. (*POW* viii. 225, 232, 251, and 252.)

452. To Dr Samuel Parr

⟨*Parr*, vii. 294–5⟩   Lincoln's Inn, 13 Dec. 1811

⟨I regret that I was unable to answer your letter yesterday by return of post, in consequence of being kept late at Guildhall. Your question is, 'What sum of money, as it is now valued and denominated, is equal to five pounds in the reign of Queen Elizabeth?'

⟨The *denomination* of our silver money has not undergone any alteration since the 43rd year of Elizabeth's reign; the sum of five pounds sterling consists now, as it has done from that year downwards, of 100 shillings, each of which is $^1/_{62}$ part of a pound Troy of standard silver. In that 43rd year of Elizabeth the silver money was debased a little from the denomination at which it had been fixed soon after her accession, by Burleigh's reform of the coin; for by his regulations, which subsisted from the second year to the 43rd of the reign, a shilling sterling was as much as $^1/_{60}$ part of a pound Troy of standard silver. This fractional difference must be added to any sum in our present denomination, to make it equal, in weight of standard silver, to the same nominal sum between the second and 43rd of Queen Elizabeth.

⟨The *value* of money, by which I understand the exchangeable value of silver for any thing else, has changed prodigiously since the reign of Elizabeth. To find in what ratio the value of silver has fallen *generally*, that is, as exchanged for all sorts of commodities and wares, is a problem of which many writers have often affected to give a determinate solution, but which does not appear to me to admit of a solution, even by approximation, near enough to be of much practical utility. The alteration of the value of silver in exchange for any particular article, corn for example, is of course a matter easily ascertained.

. . .

⟨You must feel much indignation at the course of political intrigues in our new court; they are more devoid of public principle than any that has been known in this country for a long period. . . .⟩

453. To Dr Samuel Parr

⟨*Parr*, vii. 295–8⟩   Lincoln's Inn, 20 Dec. 1811

⟨. . .

⟨Changes in the value of money may be estimated, with sufficient accuracy for all practical purposes, by comparing the money prices of a given measure of wheat. Your question, in this way, is reduced to a comparison of the price of the quarter of wheat in Elizabeth's days with its price in our own. But it so happens that, to make this comparison justly, an important distinction must be taken with respect to each of these two periods.

⟨With respect to Elizabeth's reign, it is to be observed, that during the course of it, the whole of that sudden and remarkable change in the value of money took place, which is ascribed to the discovery of the New World. This change was so great, that during the first part of the reign, prior to the year 1570, the average price of a quarter of wheat appears to have been no more than 10s. of our present money; and, for the rest of the reign, the average price was as high as about 32s. The answer to your question, therefore, will so far depend upon the particular date . . .

⟨With respect to our own times, a recent and extraordinary change has taken place in the value of our English money, which I should date from about the year 1800, though its progress has been most rapid in the course of the last three years. The cause to which this is to be ascribed is still a matter of controversy; but every body agrees that it is a depreciation local and temporary in its nature. It may be doubted, therefore, whether your candidate ought to take into account this recent and temporary change in the value of money.

⟨The average price of wheat in the first twelve years of Elizabeth, was 10s. During the rest of her reign 32s. The average price of wheat for thirteen years preceding 1799 (a fair average) appears to have been 62s. The price of wheat during the present progressive depreciation is progressively rising, so that an average from a number of years would mislead; but I conceive that, at the present rate of the value of money, the price of wheat, in an average crop, would be found to exceed 80s., perhaps considerably, if to the depreciation from excess of paper currency be added the effect of the increasing abundance of the precious metals in the general market.

⟨Upon these data, it appears that £5 in the first twelve years of Elizabeth was equal to £31 of our money previous to the year 1799; and to more, perhaps considerably more, than £40 of our present depreciated currency; and that £5 in the subsequent period of that reign (after 1570) was equal to £9. 13s. of our money previous to 1799; and to more, perhaps considerably more, than £12. 10s. of our present depreciated currency.

⟨. . .

⟨What judgement is to be formed of these late proceedings at Cambridge, and of these controversies about education and the distribution of bibles, which appear to be spreading the flames of religious discord over the whole kingdom? formed, I mean, by those who would maintain and strengthen the Church, but who are attached to it not upon the principles of the reformation and of toleration. In these present disputes, the Methodists seem to have the whole reason and argument on their side; yet they menace such a war against the establishment as may endanger its existence. The Saints are far from toleration in their real principles; yet there are symptoms of a disposition on their part to seek an alliance with that principle, and with those who would give fuller effect to it. I would go all that length with them; but I would not part with the Church, which is our bulwark against vulgar fanaticism. Excuse my stating to you, in the views of a Layman, the difficulties and doubts which I feel in consequence of these recent proceedings; which, though they have not yet attracted much notice, seem to me pregnant with weighty consequences to the peace of the State.[1]

⟨With respect to our Regent, my persuasion is, that there will be no material change of Ministers; not that he has made up his mind in favour of the present set of men, but because he has *not* made up his mind to dismiss them. It may be prudent, however, for the leaders of Opposition to act with forbearance a little while longer. It is a question of management and conduct which ought to be confided to their discretion. The most important thing for the country is to keep the Whig party strongly together in number and determination.⟩

---

1. A proposal to establish a branch of the Bible Society had been launched at Cambridge earlier that month.

In 1808, in a vain attempt to rescue Joseph Lancaster from his financial embarrassments, a group of sympathizers, more especially Joseph Fox, a philanthropic surgeon and dentist, and the Quaker William Allen (1770–1843: *DNB*) had constituted themselves as a board of trustees for both his private and his school affairs, and out of this had emerged the Royal Lancasterian Institution (from 21 Mar. 1814 the British and Foreign School Society), consisting mostly of dissenters and utilitarians and backed by the *ER*, and, in reaction to it, the National Society, which had been founded in Nov. 1811 to educate the poor in the 'principles of the established church' and was supported by the Tories and the *QR*. On 11 May 1811 Horner had become a charter member of the Lancasterian, but Brougham was the guiding force during its formative years, and all the charter members were either Foxite Whigs or men affiliated with the 'Saints'. The Foxite faction included Allen, Brougham, Horner, Lansdowne, Romilly, and William Smith; representing the 'Saints' were Clarkson, Thornton, and Wilberforce. Apparently Horner's remarks reflect his perception of the views expressed in the early proceedings of the Institution. (*Life of William Allen, with Selections from his Correspondence* (3 vols, 1846), i. 96ff., and 191; New, p. 204.)

454. To J.A. Murray

BLPES v. 155–6   Lincoln's Inn, 20 Jan. 1812

. . .

I dare say you found Drummond amusing; though I feel so much contempt for him, that I do not think he could amuse me again.[1] I do not know a human carcase, more completely destitute of all manly principle. As to his preaching infidelity, and proselytizing among the women, I have no patience for such unthinking vanity; the sure effect of which in the end is to give new activity to superstition. How incapable a man must be of judging with respect to such subjects, who has lived through the last twenty years, and does not see most surely, that philosophy can do nothing for mankind in their religious propensities, but make a compromise of peace and forbearance, and mitigate the fierceness and grossness of superstition . . .[2] It is to the indiscretion and impertinence of such sophists as Drummond, and to the abuse they made of their liberty while they were in vogue, that we owe that tide of fanaticism and hypocrisy which deluges England at present, and has converted the . . .[3] good sense which prevailed among men of education, and the unitarian dogmatism which was affected among the manufacturing classes of people, into a whining suspicious Calvinism, hostile to all the pursuits and habits either of literary refinement, or of a generous policy in public affairs.

. . . Had I any thing agreeable to say to you about politics, I would enter into that subject; but the great part that is occupied in it by the personal character of our Regent, and the despicable nature of that character, render the whole matter very disagreeable and one upon which I can hardly turn my attention without an irksome effort. . . .

1. William Drummond about this time was a frequent visitor to the Princess of Wales. He was a severe critic of the Christian view of the Bible and attempted to indoctrinate the young Princess Charlotte while a visitor in her mother's house. (New, pp. 86–7.)
2. Here a passage, evidently containing a derogatory remark about religious fanaticism, has been marked through by a pen other than that used by Horner to write the original letter.
3. Here a passage is similarly marked through.

455. From George Wilson

BL Add. MSS 52452   Forth Street, [Edinburgh], 21 Jan. 1812

. . .

   . . . I have never yet heard whether you carried into effect your intention of coming into the King's Bench. If you should continue resolved to abstain from office, at least you may command a silk gown and all the honour of the Profession which you can desire, and I have no doubt that you should take the first opportunity of getting forward. Your letter gave me great comfort. To know from good authority that the P[rince of Wales] has the present inclination to make a change, although his resolution may fail in effecting it, is a step of some moment. Many letters received here go still further but they are generally too sanguine. The new Ministry will have enough to do, the Catholics clear I hope of the Veto, the Bank, the India Company, South America, and I hope in time a reform at least in the Scotch representation. The present Ministry have no popularity here; on the contrary I think the few impartial people are tired of them, very much owing to the late law arrangements – but I know very little of this, living very retired.

   . . . The improvement of Scotland is no longer a topic. The late disturbances here shake one's faith as to the effect or at least the certainty of education among the lower classes. These are young men, apprentices, sons of respectable people, all reading and writing, yet enrolled in a book with an oath of association to the number of at least 300, binding themselves to all sorts of iniquity, going on for 6 months, with officers and signals, and watch words taken from the late murders in London.[1]

   . . .

---

  1. Preoccupied perhaps with the more serious disturbances at Nottingham, where the lacemakers had rioted in November 1811 and in the opening weeks of 1812, the AR makes only passing mention of the conviction of three conspirators for robbery and murder in Edinburgh on New Year's Eve, 1811. But it does comment at length on a series of unusually horrible murders in London in Dec. 1811. (AR liii (1811), 129–30, 138–9, and 141–3, and liv (1812), 11–12, 17–21, and 38.)

456. To J.A. Murray

BLPES v. 157–8 ⟨Horner, ii. 96–7⟩   Lincoln's Inn, 22 Jan. 1812

⟨I was unluckily prevented from hearing the whole of Brougham's speech last night; what I did hear was most excellent, and the rest, I am told by the best judges, was still better.[1] He has made an impression upon both sides of the House much more near the proportion of his talents and powers, than he has made by any former exertion of them in that place. He has done this, too, upon a subject of the first importance, and which has been waiting some years to be treated by so able a hand. The time for an adjustment of that matter with the Crown is not indeed till an actual demise; but it was desirable to have the ground broken up, and topics thrown out for discussion among the public, that when that time arrives the public may support its own interests, and second those who maintain them. It was objected by some of our critics, that he over-charged his statements; and it is true that his style in general has the fault, with another which is akin to it, of charging the different parts of his subject and argument with an equal weight of earnestness and emphasis.

⟨But the practical purpose to be effected last night, was not to gain the question, which would have been a premature success, but to make an impression as to the nature and importance of it. Besides this, there were names and possible cases held out *in terrorem*, which may stop in the mean while some abuses of this fund that were perhaps meditated. I was told by some of the members who sat near Lord Yarmouth, that the words mistress and minion were rung, till he looked black upon them. Since I came into Parliament, I have heard the Droits of Admiralty spoken of as the private patrimony of the king, not to be controlled, nor even inquired into; but by successive questions and discussions this doctrine has been utterly exploded, and the right of the House of Commons to order accounts of the distribution of it, established in full exercise. Such is the practical utility of Opposition.⟩

1. On the Droits of Admiralty (*Hansard*, xxi. 241).

457. To J.A. Murray

BLPES v. 159–60   Lincoln's Inn, 27 Jan. 1812

I send you a copy of a bill, the draft of which has been communicated to me by the gentleman who means to propose it in the House; and which, as it is to extend to Scotland and will introduce a new crime into the penal code, deserves to be well weighed by the lawyers north of the Tweed as well as on this side. In several instances, which in the last ten years have occurred, of failures in London banking houses, it has been found, that, in their distress, they embezzled securities deposited in their hands only for custody; such as exchequer bills, bills of exchange indorsed that they might receive payment of them when due, and every sort of negotiable security. The object of the proposed Bill is to punish this as a misdemeanour. I am far from being satisfied, that it is expedient to introduce any such law; which, if it ought to pass, will demand great care in expression of it, so as to render it efficacious. I wish you to contribute your assistance both upon the first question, and in describing and wording the offence properly. The Bill owes its origin to the London Bankers, who are willing to wipe off the imputation and distrust which those instances of fraud have occasioned.[1]

. . .

1. Horner expressed his doubts quite strongly when the bill – 'for more efficiently preventing the embezzlement of securities for money and other effects, left or deposited for safe custody, or other special purpose, in the hands of bankers, merchants, brokers, attorneys, or

other agents' – was introduced in the Commons on 25 Feb. by Henry Drummond (1786–1860: *DNB*). It was, he said, so sweeping as to be impossible to enforce; and most of its objects, he agreed with others, would be better met by even the most elementary precautions on the part of depositors. (*Hansard*, xxi. 943–7.) Nonetheless it passed into law that session.

458. To J.A. Murray

BLPES v. 162–5   Lincoln's Inn, 5 and 6 Feb. 1812

We finished our debate on the Irish question this morning, and the result in both Houses has been such, I think, as must give satisfaction to all those who feel a public interest in the conduct of the present Opposition, as well as the most sanguine hopes of an early settlement of the Catholic claims.[1] Our division in the Commons was good beyond our expectations, and on both sides of it; the numbers of the minority being higher, and those of the majority being considerably less, than were reckoned upon by either party. When you add to those who voted for the Catholics this morning, all those of the several flying squadrons whose leaders respectively spoke for emancipation though they voted against it, together with the tribe of followers without a name who are always in a majority, there is little doubt that even already there is a majority who wish to see the people of Ireland in possession of their rights. The tone and cast of the debate, and the composition of the minority, are still surer symptoms of a winning cause. In the last respect, it is very remarkable what a large proportion of young ones join us, as they come in. One vote of that sort we had this time, which gave me great pleasure, [was that of] young Charles Grant; who is a man of very fine parts and of very amiable qualities; though . . .[2] being tinctured with the contagion of the Methodists . . .[3] he might have been looked upon as hostile to the Catholic petition.[4] With regard to the debate, all those I have heard on this question in successive years have been more and more temperate each time, but on this occasion there was not the least trace of Protestant rancour, or of an outcry for the Church, from the moment that Doctor Nicholl, who tried his feeble voice in that strain, was stifled by Canning.[5] I cannot help suspecting, indeed, from the circumstance of Nicholl rising first and with an elaborate discourse, that Perceval's original intention in the debate was to address himself through the House to the country, upon the danger to the Church, and the abandonment of the veto; his own speech, however, turned out to be very moderate and calm upon those topics, a tone which either by reflection or from failure of spirits was imposed upon him by the whole course of the preceding discussion. I reckon it one of the signs of the time, that my friend Sutton, the Archbishop of Canterbury's son, declined in express terms committing himself to an opinion, one way or the other, whether there might be a time when the Catholic petition could safely be granted.[6] The strong sentiments which I have heard him formerly avow, contrasted with this forbearance, render it in his situation no equivocal token of the present indifference of the heads of the Church; the Regent has only to manifest a sentiment either way, and the breath of his mouth will be to the bishops the word of God. It is very amusing, that

Sir John Nicholl should have maintained on this occasion the character of the faculty to which he belongs; for all through the parliamentary history it appears, that exploded prejudices and abuses of every sort find their last advocates among the civilians of Doctors Commons. They come from their monastery in St Paul's Church Yard with opinions which all the rest of the world have rejected or begin to be ashamed of, and while our laws are in a constant flux, adapting themselves slowly indeed but surely to the changing circumstances of mankind, we have the Doctors always telling us that the Acts of Parliament which exist form the whole constitution; and in the last triumph of every innovation, some dignitary of the consistory court is still found clinging to the wisdom of former times. Nothing was ever more successful, than the malice and scorn with which Canning exposed the sophisticated imbecility of his Right Honble friend.

I hardly remember any debate, in which the principles and character of the several leaders in Parliament have been more brought to light. The manly and public-spirited line which the Whigs have adopted, upon this trial of their virtue, must make them respectable in the eyes of all those who can judge of such merits; and, while Perceval expressed with no less manliness his adherence to all his former opinions, bigoted and unfortunate as they are, it was impossible not to perceive, that he and his opponents entertained in this point of view a reciprocal respect for each other; and that they have in common infinite contempt for the temporizing conduct of Castlereagh and Canning, who have no ambition for any thing higher than office, and who render it manifest that no public interest, however they may be convinced of its reality and moment, can outweigh in their estimation any personal chance of being reinstated in power. Canning, I am of opinion, has missed a great opportunity of performing a higher part in Parliament, and has shown himself incapable of aspiring to it.

What effect these strong divisions will have at Carlton House, is a matter of some consequence; possibly they may have the weight, which plain and firm conduct sometimes has with the irresolute and timid. Whatever comes of it, I am satisfied that the leaders of Opposition have acted most virtuously, and wisely both for their own reputation and for the public interest. Some shabby people, who itch for little places, remonstrated against it; and some honest ones, of that sort of judgement which confides only in political management and balancing of measures, thought this direct course a hazardous one. Our division has silenced them all.

It ought not to be overlooked, that Burdett absented himself from these proceedings; a circumstance which has rejoiced me much, as every thing does that serves to show his political character in its true light, and may undeceive those excellent men in the House of Commons who have a hankering after him.

[PS] The speaking was all good: both Ponsonby and Whitbread better than I have ever heard either, and Canning with all the brilliancy which is familiar to him, and that depth and accuracy of reasoning which no man can excel – when it suits the little purposes of his tricking ambition to let his fine understanding have its freedom. Grattan did not speak till he and all his hearers were exhausted; but he struck out some sparkles of fire, that flamed with all the genius of his best days. He is the only speaker of the present time that gives a pathos and profound earnestness to his political declamation.

6th

... I find there is a very general satisfaction among the friends of the Opposition, at the course and result of the recent proceedings. ...

Canning is very anxious to have it understood by Opposition that he has had no communication with Lord Wellesley, and is somewhat vexed at the repulsive manner of Whitbread and Ponsonby towards him.

1. The debate in the Commons had concluded with a minority of 135 voting for Morpeth's motion for Emancipation (*Hansard*, xxi. 669).
2. Two words have been obliterated.
3. One line has been obliterated here.
4. Charles Grant, afterwards Baron Glenelg (1778–1866: *DNB*), the eldest son of the East India Company chairman, had been a member of the Speculative.
5. Sir John Nicholl (1759–1838: *DNB*), a judge and DCL as well as an MP, was a stern opponent of both parliamentary reform and Catholic Emancipation.
6. Charles Manners-Sutton (1780–1845: *DNB*), afterwards Speaker of the House of Commons and 1st Viscount Canterbury, was, however, subsequently to oppose the Catholic claims.

459. To T.R. Malthus

BLPES v. 166–7 ⟨Horner, ii. 97–8⟩   [London], Saturday [8 Feb. 1812]

⟨I am very glad it occurred to you, to offer Lancaster's committee the sanction of your name as a steward at our meeting; and I have written to Joseph Fox, telling him, that I have reason to believe you would not refuse to serve in that capacity, if it were proposed to you.[1]

⟨I entirely concur in your sentiments upon the subject, that both societies ought to be encouraged; nay I go a little farther, for if I could be convinced that the church would sincerely and zealously set themselves to accomplish the work of national education, the church should have the best of my wishes by preference; inasmuch as I regard the establishment as our best preservative against fanaticism, though I am persuaded it can only operate effectually to that end, or indeed subsist long as an establishment, by acting upon the true principles of the Reformation, of which educating the common people is the most important. It is impossible not to feel strong suspicions against the sincerity of all recent converts, especially from a prejudice which seemed but very lately so inveterate, as that of churchmen against the education of the lower classes. And even allowing them to be for the present sincere, it is hard to expect real and continued activity from that description of persons who have undertaken this charge. It is right, however, that they should have a fair trial; the result will speedily appear, for we can only know them by their fruits: and the public will be ready to hold them to a strict account, if they cannot, a year or two hence, give a satisfactory account of the efficient employment of the large funds which have been put at their disposal. In the mean time, they cannot crush the system of Lancaster, whose zeal is as unconquerable as that of John Knox; the only thing to be regretted is, that that zeal should have so large an admixture of polemic irritability, which begins, I fear, to disgust some of those persons whose taste is fastidious, and who cannot, for the sake even of the good that is effected, overlook the rudeness of the means by which such good has almost in every instance of the sort been accomplished.⟩

. . .

1. See Doc. 453. Although, as Mrs James has pointed out (*Malthus*, pp. 224–5), it seems to be the only source for Malthus's views on the matter, this letter has been used as evidence of his even-mindedness for a Church of England cleric towards the Lancasterian Institution and the National Society; but he may well have been more positively inclined to the former.

460. To J.A. Murray

BLPES v. 170–71   [London], Monday [?16 Mar. 1812]

. . .

I hope you have not thought me unkind, in omitting to write to you during the late political fracas.[1] The publication of the two letters made every thing public, which was worth sending to a distance; and the little personal details, that are connected with the main catastrophe, will be better to talk of than to commit to writing. We are fast approaching to a state of things, in which much more activity and much more public virtue will be required, to avert public dangers, than any that we have witnessed in our days. A new chapter of our history is in my opinion opened, for which not new maxims are necessary to be adopted, but a new determination to act upon the old ones. The state of the House of Commons is the least satisfactory part of our present condition; were there a powerful leader of the constitutional Whig party, I should hope for the best, because then instead of feeling ourselves trimming as it were not very pleasantly between opposite extremes in our own party, moderate and practicable counsels would take the ascendancy. But with Ward and Lamb on the one side courting Canning who brings all his Antijacobin dogmatism among us, and on the other Brougham giving himself over to Burdett and the Jacobins with all their hypocritical and impracticable pretensions, I see no success for the middle course where in my judgement both wisdom and honesty point to that we should all go. Honesty in all circumstances even of public calamity will be its own poor reward; but it is idle to be wise about public affairs, which are hurried on by circumstances with the most absolute fatalism. If one could cease to feel, as well as speculate, the latter would indeed be idleness.

1. On 13 Feb., only five days before the restrictions which the Regency Act had imposed upon him were to expire, the Prince had sent a letter to the Duke of York expressing his desire to establish a strong Ministry and authorizing the Duke to communicate its contents to Grey. Perceval had written the original draft of the letter, and the wording of that draft, which was amended by the Duke of York, suggests that the Prince had instructed the Prime Minister to produce reasons for not making an offer to the Whigs rather than reasons for a coalition Ministry. The final draft, which the Prince toned down considerably so as to

appear loyal to former views, was still calculated to offend the Whig leaders and in fact amounted to a simple if indirect statement of the Prince's decision to retain his present Ministry. For the letter commended Perceval's war policy, contained only vague reference to the Catholic question, and was delivered by a messenger who was distinguished by his strong Protestant leanings. Grey and Grenville had responded on 15 Feb. with a dignified refusal to unite with Perceval's Government, and Wellesley, seeing his hopes of heading a coalition Ministry of moderate men dashed, had responded by carrying into effect his long-rumoured resignation. The net effect of the 'fracas', as Horner described it, was to dispose of the troublesome Wellesley, to make the Whigs shut themselves out, to retain a Ministry committed to aggressive war in the Peninsula, and to postpone but not reject the Catholic claims. (Roberts, pp. 376–82.)

461. From John Allen

BLPES v. 172–3   Pall Mall, Thursday [19 Mar. 1812]

. . .

It is reported strongly that Lord Morton means to move the standing order for the exclusion of strangers in the debate of tonight and that Ministers are trying to prevent him, and as Perceval must be anxious to hear Wellesley's statement I should suppose they would be in concert in their application to him and of course in that they will succeed. Lady Buckingham's death will prevent Lord Grenville from being present which I think very fortunate as he could hardly have avoided alluding to the war in Spain and expressing opinions on that subject in which neither the Country nor a majority of his friends can possibly sympathize. His staying away on the Portuguese subsidy was a measure which he adopted with reluctance and considers as a sacrifice to the wishes of his friends. What a pity it was when he had been prevailed upon to do so that Fremantle should go down to the House of Commons and take the very line there which he [Grenville] had with difficulty been persuaded to abstain from in the Lords.[1]

Tierney thinks Perceval excessively out of spirits and suspects that he finds difficulties in his situation which begin to disgust him with it. Both he and the Bank directors showed great marks of despondence in the short debate on the revival of Lord Stanhope's bill. The latter were forced to confess that they were at present less prepared to pay in specie than they had been in 1797 – a confession which Tierney says appeared to make a great impression on the House.[2]

. . .

1. The Marchioness of Buckingham had died on 16 Mar., but quite unexpectedly and from Horner's account it would appear that it was on other grounds that her brother-in-law had absented himself from the debate that same day on the Portuguese subsidy. However, William Henry, afterwards Sir William, Fremantle (1766–1850: DNB), who was one of Grenville's most loyal assistants in the Commons, voiced for him his unpopular views on the war and, much to the general disgust, concluded by proposing the army be withdrawn from the Peninsula. (Hansard, xxi. 1298–1310; Plumer Ward, i. 465.)

The debate on the evening of 19 Mar., brought on by the motion of Canning's friend Boringdon for an appeal to the Prince Regent to form an efficient administration, proceeded without any obstruction from George Douglas, 16th Earl of Morton (1761–1827), and was designed, as Boringdon openly avowed, to give Wellesley an opportunity to explain his recent resignation. But Wellesley, though present, remained 'seated, and seated all the evening, for, to the surprise and disappointment of all who attended only to hear him, he was utterly silent from beginning to end, and never once braced himself to an endeavour to explain himself'. He did, however, subsequently issue a written statement. (*Hansard*, xxii. 35–89; *Plumer Ward*, ii. 469–71.)

2. On 17 Mar. Perceval had brought forward a bill for the purpose of continuing with certain amendments, and of extending to Ireland, the statute enacted during the previous session which made Bank notes legal tender. On 20 Apr., when the report stage came on, Horner is said to have spoken 'at considerable length', but *Hansard* gives his speech only twelve lines, probably because the debates in general merely rehearsed previous discussions. The bill then passed its third reading in the Commons and, after Lauderdale and Rosslyn had registered their strong protests against the third reading in the Lords, Bank of England notes became to all intent and purpose legal tender. (*Horner*, ii. 94; *Hansard*, xxii. 4–12 and 499.)

462. To Leonard Horner

⟨*Leonard Horner*, i. 19–20⟩   Bath, 5 Apr. 1812

⟨. . .

⟨I begin to be impatient to get back to town, both to see you all, and to be again in the midst of things, for this is likely to be an eventful summer. The activity of the French armies and fleets, portends some great measure that has been long in contemplation, and this is to be met on our part, by the wisdom of Perceval and the Doctor, and Lord Castlereagh. It is whimsical enough, that we are brought back by the Prince to the same Administration that in 1803 and 1804 was the ridicule of the whole world, with the difference only of Perceval changing his place from the law to the finance, and of our having young Dundas instead of St Vincent to superintend the distribution of the naval forces. At home we are to have this summer an attempt to raise another Protestant cry, and probably a dissolution of Parliament. In that event, I shall most probably take my leave of it for some time, and though this is of course for your confidence only, I have made up my mind, if I am left out at all, to the determination of staying out till I have done something for myself in the law. I would rather indeed go upon my present system, of uniting both pursuits, but in case of a break in one, I am resolved to give myself up for a considerable interval entirely to the other.⟩

463. To Henry Hallam

BLPES v. 174–5   [London, 24] April 1812[1]

... We made very little progress in the debate last night; except in clearing off
Duigenan and our friend Hippisley. Grattan's speech had some passages in a fine
strain of figurative and impassioned declamation; there were of course many arguments and statements repeated, that are familiar to every one on so exhausted a
subject; yet he gave it in some parts a degree of novelty by his peculiar and inventive
manner of representing them, and there is always in his speaking that earnestness
and public concern which are sure to interest.

Vernon spoke, and with very considerable success; he ventured on some of the
most delicate points of the question, particularly the Regent's breach of faith, and
the state of the King's mental health during the greater part of the time in which his
prejudices were held to be a sufficient answer to the Catholics; and he executed his
purpose in these hazardous topics, with much effect upon the House. His style was
too neat and academic for daily use in debate; but he showed some power of sarcasm,
which in the House of Commons will recommend any style.[2]

...

1. The letter is dated 'Thursday', but since it refers to the debate on the Catholic claims being
   'last night', which was 23 Apr., and, in the final paragraph not reproduced here, to the
   division expected 'tonight', the date must rather be early the following day.
2. George Granville Venables Vernon, afterwards Harcourt (1785–1861), was MP for
   Lichfield.

464. To Henry Hallam

BLPES v. 176–8   Lincoln's Inn, 8 May 1812

The only important event that has taken place since you left town, is the notice
given by Canning of a fresh motion on the Catholic question; which is to be in the
form of an address proposed to the Regent, that he will take into consideration the
claims of that part of his subjects, and the securities which it may be proper to
provide as an accompaniment of the concession. You probably heard that it had
been deliberated upon by Opposition, whether it would be proper to renew the
question after our great show of numbers; but upon consulting the delegates from
Ireland, as well as feeling the pulse of the most considerable of our new
parliamentary converts, it was decided by Mr Grattan that the question should not
be raised again this Session. Notwithstanding this, however, every exertion is to be
made to support the motion which Canning has brought forward; because his notice
leaves us no longer an option of meeting the discussion or postponing it. For my own
part, I rejoice that we are to have it again from that quarter; what might have been
indiscreet on the part of the Catholics and of Opposition, may be useful to their

cause when the movement is taken by their new advocate whose circumstances are peculiar to himself. The form also of his intended motion is such as may possibly please some members, who have been hitherto deterred by the prospect of the House instantly resolving itself into a Committee; while it is evident, that this mode of urging the claims could not have been proposed with the same propriety by those, who have hitherto called upon parliament to proceed at once to the subject.[1]

The notice was given by Canning, without any previous communication with any of the leaders of Opposition; which, under the circumstances of their previous decision for their own conduct, was perfectly right. He has had a motion of this sort in view a long while, though I cannot help suspecting (but it is entirely my own conjecture), that he was finally determined in bringing it forward by information, which Lord Wellesley some how or other obtained very lately, that Perceval is in communication with some portion of the Catholic body. If this be true, the motion must prove very embarrassing to the Minister; not only by reviving the argument at a moment when it will be impossible for him to resume his old tone of alarm and bigotry; but by putting him in the dilemma of refusing in Parliament to give advice to the crown which he is actually preparing to give himself, or of yielding to a measure which gives a direct victory to the Catholic cause. What degree of truth there is in the story, I cannot say; I understand that Lord Wellesley is positive as to the fact of a communication, but the mode in which he expressed himself (as it was repeated to me) leaves me in doubt, whether there was any thing more in it than a proposition made *to* Perceval *from* some Catholics.[2] Who these are, is another question, on which I cannot satisfy you, farther than that it is not any of the Delegates; the guess that seems to me most probable, is, that some of the Irish Catholic Bishops have thought it a wise course to make terms if they can with the Regent and Perceval. Grattan has been saying these three years, that Perceval would in the end emancipate the Catholics.

There is a rumour of a different sort with respect to this Notice, that it is done upon the speculation of its being agreeable at Carlton House; some pretend to say, even upon an understanding with the Regent: and that it is a measure of his with Wellesley and Canning. I do not give credit to this. I am inclined however to believe, that the Regent is by no means so well satisfied now, as he was before the Divisions, that the Catholics may be kept at arms' length, he saying all the while that his opinions are unaltered. Perceval undertook that the call of the House would yield such a decision as would be an answer to the Catholics, without prejudice to those opinions. The Regent cannot be unaware, that he has been deceived in this.

. . .

---

1. Canning had given notice on 6 May of a motion for an address to the Regent for the introduction of a measure of Catholic relief next session. Apparently it was not a Carlton House device; but his own idea. It was laid down for 28 May but being overtaken by Perceval's assassination was postponed until 22 June when it was carried easily.
2. There appears to be no evidence that Perceval had changed tack upon the Catholic question.

465. To J.A. Murray

BLPES v. 179–80   [London], Tuesday [19 May 1812]

. . .

. . . The last thing I heard last night was, that Canning and Wellesley had sent their answer to the Regent, from whom a communication had been made to them by Lord Liverpool: but it was still a secret, whether the answer was an acceptance or a refusal of the offer made to them. I was assured it was a positive and conclusive answer; though if I had not been told so, I should have conceived it much more likely that it would have stipulated either about men or measures in such a way as to lead to farther negotiation.[1]

Apropos of Canning, one day since you left town I met in his company your friend George Ellis, with whom I was quite as much pleased and entertained as you have always told me I should be.

. . .

1. Following the assassination of Perceval, the rump of his Government had resolved on 13 May to attempt to bring Wellesley, Canning, and their followers into the Ministry, and on the 17th Liverpool, on behalf of the Government, opened negotiations. Wellesley and Canning did not immediately reject the offer and rumour circulated that the coalition had been successfully concluded, but on the 20th the negotiation was broken off. (Roberts, p. 383.)

466. To J.A. Murray

BLPES v. 181–2   [House of Commons], Wednesday [20 May 1812]

. . .

Vansittart's writ has just been moved for; and upon that, Wortley has given notice of a motion to-morrow, to address the Regent for a strong and efficient administration.[1] There is a general feeling of the necessity of a strong government; particularly among the country gentlemen connected with the disturbed counties.[2]

. . .

1. On 20 May, following the unsuccessful termination of the Government's negotiation with Wellesley and Canning, a writ was moved making Vansittart Chancellor of the Exchequer. The moving of the writ gave notice of the Government's intention to attempt to carry on, and James Archibald Stuart-Wortley (1776–1845: DNB) at once gave notice of a motion for an address to the Regent, praying him to take immediate steps to secure an efficient Administration. On 21 May Wortley's motion was carried by a majority of four and on the following day Liverpool's Administration resigned. The Regent then asked Wellesley to attempt to form a Ministry. (Roberts, p. 384.)
2. Following the 'Luddite riots' at Nottingham the previous autumn, there were persistent disturbances among the cotton and clothing operatives of the north and midlands during 1812 that caused considerable alarm on account of their apparent organization as well as their violence.

467. To J.A. Murray

BLPES v. 183–4[1]   [London], 24 May 1812

I have for some time past been of the opinion which you say Mr [?George] Wilson has entertained, in favour of a coalition with Canning. I came into this more slowly than some of my friends; for the proposition of making advances to him was very seriously considered more than a year ago. I was then extremely averse to it, although I could not deny our ill condition in the House of Commons; because it seemed to threaten an irreparable breach with Whitbread, and still more because it seemed to me that Canning had not done enough in the way of opposition, to render an alliance with him either justifiable in the eyes of the public, or likely to prove useful and secure.[2] The share he took in the discussions upon the bullion question, was calculated to soften my opinions about him;[3] and from that time forward, it appeared to me that nothing was wanting on his part, but that he should take our test upon the Catholic question, and commit himself against the Court and to the country upon that primary subject. He did so manfully, at the commencement of the present Session; since which, I have been urging, as far as I have any little weight, the propriety of his being met half way by our leaders. It is one of their errors, that they sometimes do not move quite fast enough for the pace at which the course of circumstances has latterly been going on. They lost the time, in which their coalition with Canning might have been brought about in a way for them to make a merit of it; the events of the last ten days have given him a much higher rank in the state, than he seemed before to hold; and we must now submit to a necessity, which we might have anticipated by making it our choice. That necessity, however, to make the best of it and to repair the fault of our own procrastination, ought to be yielded to cordially and graciously; and I earnestly wish, and indeed I expect, that the discussions now pending with the Regent and among the several parties, will end in a real coalition with Canning and Lord Wellesley upon public grounds, either in office or in opposition.

A junction with Lord Wellesley is not rendered necessary to us, by any circumstances similar to those which make Canning so important in the House of Commons. The Marquis has little or no parliamentary weight of any sort in either house; one may say none, beyond his own power of making very rarely most effective speeches. In the country, even with the advantages of Lord Wellington's name, he brings but little strength to a party; the impression of his oriental proceedings is still so deep in the public mind, and for some reason or other there is so much distrust in his principles as a politician. I expect, therefore, if the coalition takes effect, that there will be a great outcry against the Whigs on that score. For myself I own, that I look upon an active and effective aid to the Catholic cause as a saving grace, to cover a multitude of sins; and that that vast measure of justice and wise policy, of which the Whigs must for ever have the merit and glory in future history, and by which they have done more for liberty and for the welfare of their country than by every thing else put together since the Revolution, is worth the price of a coalition with all the temporary unpopularity that it may bring down upon their heads.

1. The letter is unsigned and may therefore be a draft or copy.
2. See Doc. 415.
3. See Doc. 424.

468. To Henry Hallam

BLPES v. 185   [?House of Commons], Monday 5 o'clock, [1 June 1812]

Canning has just announced to the House, that Lord Wellesley at an audience with
the Regent this morning received his command to form a new administration.[1] Such
is the triumphant conclusion for Parliament of a protracted struggle against our vote
of the 21st. I shall have some curious particulars to tell you of this.

1. The conciliatory response of Grey and Grenville to Wellesley's offer of coalition surprised
   and distressed the Regent, and for a week he refused to make a decision. His closest advisers
   displeased him by recommending Grey and Grenville, but he secured a pledge of assistance
   from Moira on 26 May and some reassurance about Grey during the next three days. On 1
   June therefore he renewed Wellesley's commission, this time giving him full powers to form
   a Government. (Roberts, pp. 387–8.)

469. To Lord Holland

BLPES v. 188–9   Brooks's, Tuesday night, [2 June 1812]

I was told by William Adam this afternoon, who had just heard it from his father,
that the Regent, upon learning that the proposition made yesterday was not to be
accepted by Opposition, considered this as putting an end to the authority given
yesterday to Wellesley, and a proof that Wellesley could not form an administration.
He therefore sent for Lord Moira, to give him commands for this purpose; and Lord
M. went accordingly to Carlton House, meaning (as Adam understood from
himself) to decline it.[1]

As I find that Fremantle, who was at Camelford House an hour ago, knows
nothing of these circumstances, for which Adam's authority seems to be
unquestionable, it occurred to me that it might be useful to put you in possession of
the story as I received it. Do not mention Adam's name.

1. On 1 June Wellesley offered Grey and Grenville four Cabinet places if the Cabinet were to
   consist of twelve members and five places if it were to consist of thirteen, and stipulated
   that Moira, Canning, and Erskine were to be given places in a Cabinet which he would
   head as Prime Minister. Grey and Grenville declined the offer after short deliberation, a
   decision that alienated many moderates within their own ranks. But Adam was wrong
   about Moira who, rather, sought actively to bring the Whigs into a coalition Ministry after
   Wellesley had failed. On two occasions he attempted to renew discussions but was thwarted
   because he could not produce the Regent's express authority to treat. On 6 June Moira
   obtained that authority, but Grey and Grenville terminated the discussion when Moira
   expressed the opinion that it would be inexpedient to require the Household to resign upon
   the formation of a new administration. (Roberts, pp. 388–405.)

470. To John Allen

BL Add. MSS 52180   Lincoln's Inn, 4 June 1812

. . .

I am glad to find you speak of the thing having gone off well in both Houses last night. For the account in the *Morning Chronicle* of what passed in the H. of Lords, which was my first intelligence of it, had put me into a fright; it looked so like a blow up. Nor do I yet understand very well what Lord Wellesley meant by personal animosities, unless his purpose was to threaten the Regent with a disclosure of the animosities which HRH cherishes.[1]

I wish much to have for my private use copies of such of the papers, as may be had without impropriety. If you can assist me in procuring any of them, I will thank you. In the history of Whig politics this will form a memorable era, and it is very important for us to know all the circumstances of the transaction thoroughly.[2]

1. Although he had avoided entering into details when reporting his failure to form a Government to the Lords on 3 June, Wellesley had spoken of 'the most dreadful personal animosities' having thwarted his efforts. Grey and Grenville also declined to enter into details but strongly denied the imputation.

2. The ministerial negotiations of May and June ended with the failure of first Wellesley and then Moira to lure the Whigs into a coalition Government and the formation of Liverpool's Ministry on 8 June, thus retaining the rump of Perceval's Ministry despite Wortley's successful motion of 21 May. (See Roberts, pp. 404–405.)

471. To J.A. Murray

BLPES v. 190–91 ⟨Horner, ii. 98–100⟩   Lincoln's Inn, 18 June 1812

. . .

⟨I would have written to you more frequently during the late remarkable transactions in politics, if the nature of what passed, or the way in which I obtained from time to time some knowledge of it, had admitted of any intelligible communications in an abridged shape. The apparent changes of conduct succeeded each other so rapidly, that the story of one day looked like nothing but a contradiction of that before it, though all have in the end proved to be true. Nor was it possible, while the thing was going on, to adopt with confidence any conjecture that seemed to solve such contrarieties; until the most recent disclosures explained them by proving a depth of intrigue, which upon mere guess was hard to be believed. The result has probably been an unfortunate one for the country, because an administration with Grenville, Grey, and some others included in it, might perhaps have brought about successfully some of those changes in our policy, both foreign and internal, which they think so desirable: at the same time, the public voice would second them so reluctantly in those measures, and would be so much upon the catch to disappoint them if there was any difficulty to be overcome, that I trembled for my friends and for their cause when I thought them upon the brink of an administration, in which they were preparing to undertake the government under such difficulties as the present, without either court favour or a popular cry. From all this they are saved, not by any want of courage on their side, but by the triumph of the inveterate duplicity and the low arts of a palace over an inflexible and proud integrity. I believe the general opinion to be at present against the Whigs; and, with the usual sagacity of the public, they see nothing but a struggle for a few places in the determination not to accept office without power: at the same time, it is likely enough, that a very sincere disappointment is at the bottom of this rage, and the anger against the Whigs for not accepting the Ministry carries with it a strong dislike of those who have, and may produce a reaction.

⟨Being interrupted, I have only time to tell you, that Canning's motion is put off, in consequence of there not being members enough before four o'clock to make a House.⟩

472. To Henry Hallam

BLPES v. 196–7 ⟨Horner, ii. 100–103⟩   Exeter, 24 July 1812

. . .

⟨I regret very much, that you are not satisfied with the conduct of Lord Grey and Lord Grenville in their rupture of the negotiation. It is perhaps a nice question of conduct, and one of those in which there is hardly any other test but success to be resorted to. Upon the whole circumstances, particularly with what has been added to our knowledge of them by Lord Moira's subsequent conduct and by Lord Spencer's statement in the House of Lords, I think their mode of closing the negotiation was the most honourable and upright for themselves, though with a little more reserve they might have left it to be terminated with more disgrace to the Prince.[1] I was prepared, I own at the same time, to pardon them if they had been less sturdy about the Household, and thought, if there was a possibility of their getting power, with the views they had of using it, that they might be defended against the abuse that was in preparation for them if they should have yielded to the Court its pretensions respecting the Household. I am now satisfied, looking back to the whole intrigue, that they never had any chance of coming into office; and am somewhat inclined to apprehend, that the high tone of personal honour and the strict stoical maxims of political conduct, which the present leaders of the Whig Opposition are guided by in their negotiations about office, and without the observance of which power can have but little to gratify such men, are not calculated to obtain place for them except in a favourable conjuncture of accidents, or to win immediate favour for them with the public, whether they gain the places or are disappointed. I will not say that nothing of the peculiarities of temper was to be detected in their prompt and peremptory manner of negotiating; but on the other hand, they negotiated with all the odds against them, arising from their integrity and rigid honour being known to those who intrigued against them with fewer scruples. Never was there a time, in my remembrance of politics, which brought out in so strong a light the characters of all the persons engaged in the transaction; and I am sorry to say, that some of whom I was anxious to form or to keep a high opinion, such as Canning and Whitbread, sunk a great way in my estimation, before it was all over.

⟨I tremble, when I think of Spain. Surely, something more might have been done by us, particularly on the side of Catalonia, by sending into the Peninsula every company or troop that could possibly be spared, at the time that the forces of France are drawn to such a distance. But Bonaparte and all his army had crossed the Vistula, before we would suffer ourselves to believe that the price of corn would admit of his marching at all. I am very sorry to see such wretched talk in the House of Commons about the overture of April last; whatever it might have been reasonable to say about it then, while Bonaparte was still in Paris, and in our delusion that he did not think of leaving it, there can be but one language to hold now, respecting such a proposal. Sheridan's is nearest the right language; if he had not accompanied it with such baseness towards Whitbread, who has been slaving for a year and more in his private affairs to get him bread, and committed this ingratitude for the sake of patching up his ruined reputation by an address to popular sentiments. Col. Hutchinson's unjustifiable expressions about Bonaparte will be imputed, of course, to all the Opposition, and very likely to all the Catholics. It is incomprehensible to me, how any friend of liberty, as Hutchinson is very honestly, can help detesting the very name of this restless barbarian.⟩[2]

1. The publication of the *Correspondence and Documents relative to the late Negociation for forming a New Administration* had led on 19 June to a debate in the Lords during which Moira had testified to their authenticity and Spencer had explained his role in communicating Moira's views about the Household to Grey and Grenville. (*Hansard*, xxii. 593–9.)
2. The French had made a peace overture in April which had come to nothing when they neglected to respond to the observation that they seemed to expect the British to accept Joseph as King of Spain (*AR* liv. 420–23). Nothing was said about the exchanges at the time but they were subsequently revealed in the foreign press and taken up in the Lords by Holland on 17 July and in the Commons by Sheridan in what proved to be his last speech in Parliament on 21 July. Not knowing the full facts, Holland was cautious in his request for details; but Sheridan, who spoke in favour of rejecting the French overture, began by sneering at Whitbread for rushing up to town to denounce the Government's response before Whitbread had actually spoken in the debate, while Lt Col. Christopher Hely-Hutchinson (1767–1826: *DNB*), younger brother of the Earl of Donoughmore and MP for Cork, defended the sincerity of Napoleon's approach. (*Hansard*, xxiii. 1069 and 1123–62.)

473. To Leonard Horner

⟨*Horner*, ii. 103–105⟩[1]   Powderham,[2] 25 July 1812

⟨In consequence of your recommendation, I went with Adam to see Mr Poole's village school at Enmore, having first procured his book and read it.[3] The work gave me a great prepossession in favour both of himself and the method of his school: for though I never shall concede to any one the originality of Joseph Lancaster's inventions, and think that it is an act of injustice towards him to call Dr Bell the original inventor, (as Mr Poole does in his preface,) yet that preface is written in such a tone of good sense and genuine benevolence, that I do not recollect to have met with any composition, for a long while, that has afforded me a more real gratification.

⟨Independently of the improvements which he has added to the general method, his idea of the advantages to be derived from the mixture of farmers' sons with the peasant boys in the same school, is one of those thoughts that show a masterly sense for the business of life, apparently too simple to have much in it, but, in practice, fruitful of most useful consequences. The expectations we had formed from reading the book, were exceeded by what we saw at the school; which was indeed a most pleasing and satisfactory spectacle. We passed near an hour there, and were lucky enough to find Mr Poole himself. The achievements of the children in working sums by the head were quite astonishing, but what was of more importance, was the order, intelligence, and cheerfulness with which the ordinary business of the school was dispatched.⟩ . . . ⟨I was thoroughly convinced upon the spot of the good effects, resulting from the mixture of the farmers' boys with those of their ploughmen; the former, who bring a little more education from home, and stay at the school till somewhat a more advanced age, gain, in the usual competition of their learning, a superiority which appears to be owing to nothing else than their fate in this fair rivalry, while it puts upon the most pleasing footing that difference which is to last through life; at the same time, that the competition, and the level upon which they are all placed, gives both that just sense of equality which both ought to be taught, and the teaching of which in common to boys of the middling and higher ranks is one of the main advantages of the public schools of England. I like very much too the putting girls and boys in the same classes, at so early an age; it gives the boys a new spur to emulation, the girls are usually so much quicker. Of course Mr Poole's method will not have the same complete success as at Enmore, except where a person like himself will take as much pains. But I am convinced, that the dissemination of his work cannot fail to do infinite good, both in improving the schools where Bell's method or Lancaster's has already been adopted, and in setting a noble example to country clergymen of the Establishment, which is very likely to be followed in many instances.[4]

⟨. . .⟩

1. There is a copy only of this letter in BLPES v. 198–201, and that copy omits the whole of the text printed from the beginning of the second sentence of the first paragraph to the end of the second sentence of the second paragraph, ending 'satisfactory spectacle'. It is unclear whether the MS copy is defective or the additional passages were taken from another letter.
2. The place near Exeter of Viscount Courtenay, whom Horner's colleague on the Western Circuit William Courtenay (1777–1859) afterwards succeeded as 10th Earl of Devon.
3. The Rev. John Poole (c.1771–1857), the cousin of Thomas Poole (Doc. 329) and Rector of Enmore, near Bridgwater, had recently published The Village School Improved (1812).
4. In an undated letter to Mrs Dugald Stewart, evidently written from Powderham on 25 July (BLPES v. 213–14), Horner observed: 'Between Lancaster and the Church, whom he has goaded into an active though reluctant exertion, there appear to me very strong symptoms in the West of England, that a general system of parochial education will be established in the course of a very few years.'

474. From John Allen

BLPES v. 205–207   Holland House, 31 July 1812

. . .

Canning's little squad dispersed immediately after the last discomfiture of their leader so that we have not yet heard from any good authority what were precisely the points on which the second negotiation broke off; but if report is to be believed, it was his desire to humiliate and degrade the Doctor, that occasioned the failure of the projected accession to the Administration. Nothing is said to have passed on this occasion in writing, so that each party may tell his own story without danger of confutation. The Prince was anxious to have Canning and spoke most vilely of the Dr, who he said had been thrust upon him contrary to his wishes, and this language probably encouraged Canning to insist on turning out of the Cabinet all the Dr's followers and reducing the Dr himself to his old place of President of the Council. But what were the precise points on which the negotiation finally broke off, as I said before, we have not yet learned.[1]

You will have probably heard from Abercromby of the conduct of the Honble J. W. Ward. If you have not, prepare to blush that you ever thought well of him or admitted him to your confidence. The point to which I allude is one, that if you do not know it already, I cannot explain to you by letter, so that your curiosity, if you have any, cannot be satisfied till you come to town.[2]

. . .

1. The negotiations in July came near to success but broke down over the relative positions Castlereagh and Canning were to assume. So far as Sidmouth was concerned, something of a reconciliation with Canning transpired, partly through the efforts Wellesley had made at Cowes. (*PH* iii. 396–7.)
2. Allen refers to Ward's defection to Canning.

475. From John Allen

BLPES v. 208–209   Holland House, 1 Aug. [1812]

Canning's negotiation would not have failed if he had had more confidence in Ministers or they had had more reliance in him. Such is the account given of the failure of the late Treaty and as far as it goes it is not at all inconsistent with what one knows or suspects of the respective parties engaged in it. Ireland it is said was offered to Wellesley in the course of the second treaty, for during the first no communication was made to him. He refused it unless he had *carte blanche* on the Catholic question which Ministers would not give him, and his refusal formed with differences on *minor* arrangements which arose between Canning and Castlereagh after the great point of the H. of Commons had been settled, is said by Canning's friends to have broken off the treaty, which has ended in making Canning and

Castlereagh more bitter enemies than ever. There are others again who tell you that the treaty was insincere on the part of Ministers from the beginning, that it originated in the ruthlessness of the Regent and intriguing spirit of Canning, that Ministers, to gratify the Regent, were compelled to enter on the negotiation, but [that] they had previously determined to break it off on the first plausible pretext they could find.

Ward I am glad to find is laughed at by all parties for his conduct. The particular transaction to which I alluded in my last he has thought better of, and is now prepared to act in an honourable manner. . . .

. . .

476. To George Eden[1]

BLPES v. 212–13   Wells, 3 Aug. 1812

. . .

I know scarcely any thing of what has been doing in politics since I left London; having barely understood that there have been two negotiations for thrusting Canning upon the Ministers, in both of which the Ministers have intrigued too skilfully both for Canning and the Regent. Previous to all this, there was a sort of declaration made on Canning's part by those who speak with authority for him, that he would form no connection with Opposition as a party; his recent conduct has given publicity enough to the views he has of party connections: after all this, I trust we shall hear no more among the Whigs of the expediency of a union with him, whatever our circumstances may be, although no one was more prepared than myself to have rejoiced in such a union if it could have been effected, with any tolerable prospect of permanency or real confidence, at the time that Canning's tardy adoption of the Catholic cause made a sort of new era in his political adventures, and seemed to give a chance of his taking a new line. You must have heard of Ward's defection; I am not surprised that he has yielded to his love of wit, and fine sentences, and Eton reputation, for he has long hankered after them: but this inconstancy will injure him fatally in the House of Commons: It is ridiculous, as well as very blameable. It will not be his last change; for the leaning of his opinions and feelings about public affairs is too strongly toward what is honest and explicit, for a uniform approbation and following of Canning in all his doublings and intriguing contrivances.

1. George Eden, afterwards 2nd Baron and 1st Earl of Auckland (1784–1849: *DNB*), was MP for Woodstock.

477. To Frances Horner

Kinnordy MSS ⟨*Horner*, ii. 109–113⟩   Edinburgh, 9 Sept. 1812

⟨. . .

⟨I made a very agreeable journey with Serjeant Lens, the greater part of the way through country which was new; indeed, the only portion of it I had seen before was in Cumberland, from Kendal to Penrith, which it was very gratifying to see again. We had as fine a day as could be, and had views of Windermere, Grassmere, and Keswick Lake, in all their glory. At Keswick we found Rogers the poet, staying at the inn; he was good enough to take an evening walk with us, and led us to a favourite station of his, which gives the most striking prospect of the lake. As Murray could not meet me on the borders, I postponed my visit at Brougham till my return, when he will accompany me thither; I only regret that I lost our intended tour through Ayrshire; which I must delay till another year.

⟨Since I came to Edinburgh, I have been continually enjoying the society of my old friends, who have received me with all the affection that is most gratifying. It gave me a particular pleasure to find Mrs Murray so little the worse for seven more years of old age; she is a little thinner, but only a little; in every respect she is entirely in possession of her faculties and excellent understanding. Next to Murray I have lived most with Thomson, who since I was last here has fitted up a very pretty house, and put in order his valuable library. We all spent a very pleasant day at his brother's parsonage at Duddingstone;[1] and in the course of the morning, I went to the top of Arthur's Seat, with the two Thomsons and Pillans; the last of whom is, I take it, the most completely happy person in the Regent's dominions; having found exactly the corner that fits him in the world, where he can be most useful, and as universally respected. He has already done wonders with his school, and will yet do a great deal more: he thinks of nothing else. I have been for a couple of days also to Hatton, where Jeffrey lives in a great house, and writes his reviews in a little gilded closet; the Morehead family and his brother make up a household for him, in which he is perfectly comfortable, being strongly attached to them all.[2] When I was there, I rode to pay a visit to Mr Henry Erskine, who has retired from the Bar, and is living among the plantations he has been making for the last twenty years, in the midst of all the bustle of business; he has the banks of the river Almond for about four miles; he told me he had thrown away the law like a dirty clout, and had forgotten it altogether. It is delightful to see the same high spirits which made him such a favourite in the world, while he was in the career of ambition and prosperity, still attending him after all the disappointments that would have chagrined another man to death: such a temper is worth all that the most successful ambition could ever bestow.

⟨My greatest enjoyment in Scotland has been in the society of Mr Stewart and Mr Playfair, who have been growing younger all the while that their pupils had been turning grey, and are in such good health and such ardour of study, that the world will probably have the benefit of many years of their labour. It is a gratification which I enjoy more than I can describe, to be admitted to the confidence and unrestrained conversation of two such sages, who first imparted to me a true relish for literature. They have both many projects; Mr Stewart has already a great deal of manuscript quite ready for the press; we shall have two volumes of his *Philosophy of the Mind,* in the course of next year.[3] He is printing at present a memoir, which he read to the Royal Society of Edinburgh, upon the case of the blind and dumb boy, upon whose eye an operation was performed by Wardrop; it cannot fail to be a most interesting dissertation, in the way in which he has treated the subject.[4] My vanity will not let me conceal from you, that he has contrived, from the accident of my having sent him an old book, to pay me a very partial compliment, in a note to his memoir; it is not a little flattering, though I owe it to nothing but his good nature, to have his friendship for me recorded in writings which will live as long as those of Cicero and Plato, and will go down to distant times with their works.[5] We went to Kinneil, four of us in a landau (the same I suspect the bailies go in to the races), Murray, Thomson, Mr Playfair, and myself. The day being very bright and beautiful, we drove through Lord Rosebery's grounds, which are equal to any that I know any where for prospects and scenery.[6] The Romillys came to Kinneil the same day;[7] next morning all went away but Mr Playfair, with whom and Mr Stewart I passed an entire day. We went a mile beyond Falkirk, to see Mrs Dalzel.[8]

⟨You do not know Mr Wilson, but it has been no small addition to the pleasure which my visit to Edinburgh has afforded me, to see him upon the whole so well, and so comfortably settled with his nieces, who are in the best style of Scotch girls.[9] Lord Webb, too, arrived yesterday, and I have written this rambling scribbled letter in his room, waiting till the rain clears off.[10]

⟨. . .⟩

1. Thomas Thomson's younger brother John (1778–1840: *DNB*), the landscape painter, had been minister of Duddingston since 1805.

2. Jeffrey had become tenant of Hatton, a mansion near Edinburgh, in 1812 and for the next two years there lived with him his cousin and close friend Robert Morehead (d. 1842) and his wife (Margaret: d. 1849) and children, two of whom afterwards achieved distinction in India (William Ambrose Morehead, 1805–1863, and Charles Morehead, 1807–1882, both in *DNB*). Morehead had taken orders in the Church of England and as yet probably had barely enough to keep a family. Jeffrey's younger brother John (d. 1848), a merchant, was a widower like him. (*Jeffrey,* i. 59, 179, 213, 381, 403, and 404.)

3. The second volume of Stewart's *Elements of the Philosophy of the Human Mind* appeared in 1815; the third was not published until 1826.

4. Dugald Stewart, *Some Account of a Boy born Blind and Deaf* (Edinburgh, 1812), was reviewed by Mackintosh in *ER* xx (no. xl, Nov. 1812), 462–71. James Wardrop (1782–1869: *DNB*), a distinguished ophthalmic surgeon, had operated on the boy.

5. The 'old book' Horner sent to Stewart was George Delgarno's *Didascalocophus, or, The Deaf and Dumb Man's Tutor* (Oxford, 1680). Stewart's *Memoir* did not mention Horner by name but instead related that 'a friend' had purchased the book for him at a London stall. (*Horner,* ii. 112n.)

6. Lord Rosebery's place was Dalmeny Park on the Firth.

7. See *Romilly,* iii. 50–53, for Romilly's account of his visit to Edinburgh and brief observations on his meeting with Stewart.

8. Presumably the widow of Professor Dalzel.

9. Romilly, who also had a very hig' opinion of George Wilson, visited him in Edinburgh at about the same time as Horner. Recalling that Wilson had once prevailed upon his unlikely friend, Lord Ellenborough, to try and read the *Wealth of Nations* only to have it returned as 'impossible to read', Romilly doubted 'very much whether any other of the Judges, with the exception of Mr J. Heath, and, perhaps, Mr J. Leblanc, have ever made a greater progress in the study of political economy than the Lord Chief Justice'. (*Romilly,* iii. 52.)

10. While in Edinburgh, Horner and Seymour engaged in further discussions about the terms

on which Seymour and Somerset should lease their landed property with an eye to protecting themselves from rents paid in depreciated Bank paper. Seymour had first posed this question to Horner in Aug. 1811, and Horner had responded with a treatise evaluating the relative merits of rents calculated with reference to the market value of gold and corn (Doc. 434). Now, during Sept. 1812, Seymour and his brother exchanged several letters in which they discussed the contract recommended by Horner. Three of these letters are in the Bulstrode Papers at Aylesbury – two from Somerset dated 14 and 15 Sept. and one from Seymour dated 26 Sept.; the extracts from two of them printed in *Two Brothers* (pp. 98–101) do not include the relevant passages. Somerset's letter of 15 Sept. approved of the principle of the contract suggested by Horner and acquiesced 'in Horner's preference of gold to corn'. Seymour's letter of the 26th contains the following passage:

> All the letters you wrote, and those you were so good as to forward, have reached me. The last you sent in approbation of the principle of a loan of gold, came the very morning of Horner's last day in Edinburgh; he breakfasted with me, and so we had an opportunity of talking the matter over. For the average price of standard gold, he proposes that we should refer to *Wettenhall's Tables*, which are published regularly at short intervals, and that it should be stipulated that, in case the parties cannot agree about the price, they should refer the matter to two respectable London merchants, each choosing one, and these two, if they cannot agree, to obtain a final decision from a third, chosen by both. Horner says that two merchants could determine the price in half an hour. Horner says he cannot undertake to bring the contract into regular shape till he gets to London, which will be about the middle of next month. . . .

478. To J.A. Murray

BLPES v. 235 ⟨*Horner*, ii. 114–15⟩   Clifton, 4 Oct. 1812

⟨I had a very agreeable journey with Brougham as far as Preston; nothing could be more entertaining, or in better humour.[1] Indeed, since our old days of careless fellowship, I have never known him in so good a tone of mind, as through the whole of our late visit. After parting with him, I slept at Chorley, a dirty hole – Lancashire and manufactures; I strove to make it more endurable, by a vivid recollection of Dinwoodie Green. I was repaid for this the following night at Wolseley Bridge, a country inn of the right English sort; next morning brought me to Birmingham. All this journey I performed in a chaise by myself, but an indifferent sulky species of travelling, unless one has an interesting book, in which respect I had managed ill⟩ – trusting to the *Review* for Brougham's articles on Peace and Parliamentary Reform, which I had not read before, and which upon trial seemed to me nothing but trash – and trusting also to Jack Leslie's *Elements of Geometry*, but which I found almost as illegible, he has contrived so to adulterate the purest of all abstractions with his peculiar arrogance and inaccuracy, and to give all his own clumsiness to what one has never seen before but in the most elegant symmetry.[2] I was but badly off, therefore, for books. ⟨I tried in vain at Manchester to get the new volume of *Burke's Works*, for which I am thirsting, and again at Birmingham;[3] and then becoming desperate, I cast myself into the mail coach, and after a whole night of stargazing (for I never saw so fine a sky, or Sirius in such splendour) I came here this morning.⟩ . . .

⟨I was anxious, of course, to learn upon the spot what is likely to be the result of

Romilly's election, which begins on Tuesday; upon the accounts which I collected from several people in the morning, I had formed an impression, doubtful upon the whole, though inclining to the favourable side. This evening I have seen himself; he entertains scarcely a doubt of success, and thinks it not unlikely he will stand at the head of the poll: this is after a very minute scrutiny of all the information in possession of his committee, who have conducted their canvass and survey of the votes by parochial subdivisions; Romilly, however, is in all such things apt to be very sanguine. He does not complain of any fatigue or irksomeness in the canvass, though he has had four days of it from door to door; and they tell me he does it well.[4]

⟨You will be glad to hear that Abercromby is to be returned for Calne.⟩

. . .

1. Horner proceeded from Edinburgh to Minto, where he remained for several days, and from there to Brougham Hall, where he renewed his old friendship with Brougham and left with him in early October. Horner's letter to Seymour of 27 Sept. (BLPES v. 231–2), which was written from Brougham Hall, describes his visit to Minto and expresses the opinion that Gilbert Elliot, afterwards 2nd Earl of Minto (1782–1859: DNB), should be in Parliament again. His letter to Leonard Horner of 30 Sept. (BLPES v. 233–4), also written from Brougham Hall, relates that he himself had 'no reason to expect that I shall be returned to the new Parliament'.

2. Brougham's two articles on Parliamentary Reform and on the prospects of peace appeared in ER xx (no. xxxix, July 1812), 127–43 and 213–34, along with a third on the Sixth Report of the African Institution, pp. 58–79, and Playfair's review of Leslie's Elements of Geometry (Edinburgh, 1811), pp. 79–100.

3. Vols ix and x of the quarto edition of Burke's Works, edited by F. Laurence and W. King (16 vols, 1792–1827), were published in 1812. See also Doc. 483.

4. Romilly's scruples after the change of law making technically illegal the purchase of parliamentary seats (Curwen's bill: see Doc. 335) debarred him from seeking an extension of his tenure of Wareham. He had several flattering offers; but he dreaded the prospect of a popular contest and gave up Bristol after seven days' polling. (See Romilly, iii. 54–69, for his own account of the campaign at Bristol, Horner to Romilly, 15 Oct., and Romilly to Horner, 18 Oct. (Horner, ii. 116–18), for post-election comment.)

479. From Henry Brougham

BLPES v. 240–41   Liverpool, Tuesday [?6 Oct. 1812][1]

The entry yesterday took place in the most compleat style and finest weather – which you know for us mob-mongers is something important. I never saw as fine a show, nor so infinite a multitude. They say it doubled the last entry at Roscoe's.[2] The enemy made demonstrations by hand bills exciting riots since disavowed, of course, and reminding the people of their having beaten us by riot in 1807. They then made two attacks, but they were met by perfect preparation and so thoroughly beaten that we have since seen nothing but perfect quiet.

We were heard as if in a church by all this multitude, and the whole result has been so favourable that if Creevey were here I should have little fear for my own seat and think him in a very fair way, but 'tis rather hard to be weighed down by an absent man. He don't come till the 3rd day![3]

To show you what sort of work it is I only say that after speechifying yesterday to them all assembled, I set out on my nightly rounds (lasting till all is over) and visited during 7 hours of the night near 30 clubs, making literally long *speeches* in each! But so it is, and it is all a matter of course and not useful comparatively with the others, but done equally by all. The advantages it gives are only incidental. The whole day is spent in going round canvassing individuals. We are very popular especially *since yesterday*, and have all the women strong with us.

[PS] Canning is announced for the third or 4th time tomorrow, and tries a public entry too! It is quite good to see this appeal to the people and I look forward to his appearance among my sooty faced Club-men for no small diversion. At all events it quells him of his sneers at us poor reformers and mobbers, whether he wins or loses – I think he may win if he has courage – but still it is a most false move, so false that till I see him here I won't believe it.[4] There are 10 to one against Curwen being returned at Carlisle! I expect to see him give in, though we have done all we can for him both there and here.[5] . . .

1. A letter from Brougham to Grey dated Tuesday, and assigned the date of 6 Oct. by Professor New (p. 75), contains passages that seem to suggest that this undated letter was written on the same day.
2. After his success at Liverpool in Oct. 1806, Roscoe had made a sort of triumphal entry into the city at the dissolution in the following May. But it was an unfortunate example for Brougham to follow. For not only had it been opposed by physical violence; Roscoe's views on the slave trade and Catholic Emancipation had cost him his re-election.
3. This relatively favourable view of the value of Creevey as a running mate conflicts strikingly with that which Brougham professed in his correspondence with Grey at about the same time. Brougham and Creevey were not definitely nominated until 25 Sept.; and whereas Brougham came early to Liverpool and campaigned actively, Creevey, assured of a parliamentary seat elsewhere, was comparatively lukewarm about the contest, tardy in taking to the hustings, and inclined to think the worst of Brougham from first to last. (New, pp. 71–2.)
4. Canning entered the canvass and, after failing to conclude a pact with Brougham designed to assure the election of both parties, led the poll. General Isaac Gascoyne (1770–1841: *DNB*), an incumbent and a dependable Tory strongly attached to the corporation of Liverpool, was placed second and therefore returned along with Canning. Brougham and Creevey ran third and fourth, respectively, and General Tarleton, the other incumbent and a Whig too independent for the party leaders, ran last. (New, pp. 70–78.)
5. A general decline of popularity – among whose causes was included the seduction of a bishop's daughter – had led to Curwen's withdrawal from Carlisle, which he had represented almost continuously since 1796 and was to regain in 1816.

480. To J.A. Murray

BLPES v. 246–9 〈*Horner*, ii. 120–22〉   Lincoln's Inn, 21 Oct. 1812

〈I received both your letters from Liverpool, and am much pleased that you made the exertion of going there to assist Brougham, particularly as he tells me you did him an important service in an affair of some delicacy. His disappointment came upon me quite unexpectedly, for I looked upon *his* return at least as certain; and nothing, except Romilly's similar disappointment, has given me greater or more sincere distress. It is a great public loss, not to have Brougham in Parliament; it is rendered greater, by his failing in an attempt, to which he had been encouraged by the popularity of his eminent services last summer; and what aggravates it as a public misfortune, is, that Canning, the author of those same Orders in Council, should be elected, with such triumph, upon the very spot where their ruinous consequences were most severely experienced.[1] It seems clearly enough ascertained, that the real cause of Brougham's failure is the indiscretion of having joined Creevey with him, and attempted to carry both members upon the popular interest.[2] It is a mistake which has been committed over and over again, with the same fatal result;⟩ but Roscoe and Shepherd are just of that description of persons, whom neither the experience of other people nor their own will ever render practicable or reasonable.[3] ⟨It is among the very sincere and zealous friends of liberty, that you will find the most perfect specimens of wrong-headedness: men of a dissenting, provincial cast of virtue, who (according to one of Sharp's favourite phrases) will drive a wedge the broad end foremost, utter strangers to all prudence and moderation in political business, who are sensible enough when they find themselves in defeat that it is worse than partial success, but who, while the thing is in contest, imagine it would be a sort of treachery to their cause to accept in the first instance a whole half of the object they are contending for.

⟨If Brougham is to be out of Parliament, which I hope and trust will not be the case, I am very far from being able to accede to your opinion, that this public loss will be counterbalanced by advantages to him in a private point of view, such as ought to take away all regret from his friends and from himself. I cannot conceive any single private advantage he will gain by it, of the least moment. Money, to be sure, he may make in abundance by parliamentary business;[4] for that loose, rambling sort of practice is richly paid; but no professional fame or science is to be gained in that department; and what are a few hundred acres more in Westmoreland worth to Brougham? Depend upon it, he will not quit politics, even for the time he is out of Parliament; but will exert his boundless activity,⟩ and restless spirit, ⟨in another sphere and in other directions, where his exertions will be probably less advantageous to his own reputation, and to the welfare of the public.⟩ You will have more of those intemperate declamations in the *Edinburgh Review*, written to blow the flames for the day, which have ruined the literary character of that work, and have lent the semblance of its sanction to the doctrines of that incapable fanatical faction, which never can have any other success (and seems to care for no other) except that of maiming the Whig party, and frustrating their best exertions. In Parliament, Brougham was becoming daily more a Whig, in his sentiments and in his connections; as an active politician of his sense and public spirit is sure to become. Out of Parliament, I dread all this will be undone; he is very likely to have the lead offered to him, of that party which thinks it for the benefit of liberty to vilify and undermine the House of Commons; his temper, and his love of the lead, may throw him into that perilous post: and we shall have his powerful abilities and increasing labour cast as a contribution into that fund of faction and mischief, to which none of the other worthies bring any thing for their share, but indefinite views – ignorant exaggerations – malignant calumnies – fanatical and slovenly reveries about liberty and purity, more inimical in the mass to the real cause of popular freedom in this country, than all the designs of the Court and all the corruption of its retainers. We shall see Brougham's masterly sense the ally of Burdett and Lord Cochrane and Mr Fawkes;[5] and that is an alliance, in which the man of most sense is sure to be the slave. In the present state of politics, with Brougham's temper and defects, and the circumstances in which he is placed, such appear to me to be the too certain consequences of his exclusion from Parliament.

⟨I was made quite happy by your account of the manner in which he took leave of the contest when it became hopeless;[6] and I lost no time in communicating your account of it to such of our friends in London as were sure to take a proper interest in what concerns him.[7]

⟨I have some news to give you about myself: as I have now reason to believe, that very soon after the meeting of Parliament, when the double returns are disposed of, I shall have a seat in my power, which comes to me in a manner so perfectly satisfactory and agreeable to me, that I shall have no hesitation in accepting of it. I shall give you the particulars, as soon as I am at liberty; in the mean while, I wish not to say that I have any such prospect except to my nearest friends.[8] I suppose you will regret all this, according to your former opinions; which I am far from thinking as erroneous as that in Brougham's case appears to me; but which do seem to be mistaken upon the whole, though for quite other reasons. I am in much greater danger of losing all interest in party politics, than of carrying those feelings to excess; and have not the least doubt, that I could return, with undiminished enjoyment, to all the pleasures and luxurious tranquillity of speculative literature. But my choice, if a wrong one, was made long ago; and I do not permit myself now to canvass the propriety of it, but should regard it as a misfortune to be thrown out of the course in which that choice, aided by circumstances and connections, had directed me.

⟨If thrown out, I shall not find it hard to make up my mind to the change; but I would rather go on. A very slow, and a very quiet walk for a public life, is the only one for which I feel myself to be fit; though in such a one, with steadiness, I hope I may in process of time find some opportunities of rendering service to the country. One thing I feel more every day; that nothing but the alliance of politics, in the manner in which I take a share in them, would be sufficient to attach me to the pursuits of the legal profession, in which I have little prospect of eminence, and very moderate desires of wealth; but in which, by possessing the opportunities of legislative experiment, I do not despair one day of doing some good. The occasion has drawn from me too much egotism, which you must forgive.⟩

1. Horner ignores the broader context of the election, which because of Brougham's questionable tactics provoked an open confrontation between what the respective candidates represented as Foxite and Pittite ideology. In the wake of the American declaration of war on Britain and the British victory at Salamanca, Brougham and Creevey advocated not only a pacific policy towards the pugnacious Americans but also the conclusion of a general European peace. They also broached the highly controversial question of parliamentary reform, arguing as Fox before them that that would inevitably follow the conclusion of peace, and even the reformer John Cartwright (1740–1824: *DNB*) came to Liverpool and campaigned for them. These views and Cartwright's support appealed to the Liverpool Whigs; but the campaign of Brougham and Creevey was well to the left of the Whig centre and it was ill-calculated to appeal to moderates in Liverpool. It therefore attracted but little support from the Whig party at large and indeed infuriated such time-serving Foxites as James Perry and John Allen. Canning, on the other hand, profited from Gascoyne's close

association with the corporation of Liverpool and exploited his own impeccable Pittite credentials. Furthermore he capitalized on the jingoism spawned by Wellington's victories, appealed to the political establishment in Liverpool by opposing parliamentary reform, and dodged association with the Orders in Council by emphasizing his already well-known difficulties with Perceval and Castlereagh. Hence the election did not turn on the Orders in Council or the American war; rather, it was a contest between two powerful orators, both out of power, the one courting the local political establishment and supporting war to the knife with France, the other in effect advocating the overthrow of the local political establishment and urging peace. (See Brougham's speech of 8 Oct., the first day of the voting, in *Speeches of Henry Lord Brougham* (4 vols, Edinburgh, 1838), i. 481–7. See also Taylor, pp. 342–7.)

2. Horner expressed the same opinion to Brougham in a letter written on the same day (*Brougham*, ii. 68–9). See New, p. 72, for a concurring opinion.
3. William Shepherd (1768–1847: *DNB*), who was a close friend of Roscoe and, from this time perhaps, of Brougham too, was a unitarian minister of radical views.
4. 'Practice' in the manuscript.
5. Admiral Thomas Cochrane, later 10th Earl of Dundonald (1775–1860: *DNB*), was a persistent advocate of economical and parliamentary reform, and Fawkes was a metropolitan reformer who on 11 May 1812 had chaired the first dinner of the Hampden Club, the analogue of the Society of the Friends of the People.
6. Brougham closed his campaign with a tribute to Fox, to the great Whig families, and to the principles of peace and reform (*Liverpool Mercury*, 16 Oct.). Creevey reported (*Creevey*, i. 172) that the speech 'shook the very square and all the houses in it from the applause it met with', and a letter from Brougham to Grey dated Nov. 1812 (Brougham MSS, UCL) contended that after defeat was known 'an immediate and cordial reunion took place . . . between the high and low Whigs'.
7. See, for example, Horner to Allen, 19 Oct., BL Add. MSS 52180.
8. Interestingly, Horner's letter to Brougham of 21 Oct. (*Brougham*, ii. 68–9), which bemoaned the failure at Liverpool and expressed the hope that Brougham would obtain a seat elsewhere, did not mention the tentative offer of St Mawes that he himself had received through Lansdowne.

481. From Henry Hallam

Kinnordy MSS   Ryde, 21 Oct. [1812]

. . .

. . . I . . . do not know whether I am still to address you as MP. The elections do not seem on the whole to have added much to the strength of Ministers. Romilly's failure at Bristol was a great disappointment to me; it was the effect of a coalition, by which the Tory party have violently gained what they have long been aiming at, the return of two members. I regret also though [only][1] to a degree the fate of Brougham – and by no means that of Waithman.[2] This election has shown the impotence of that faction.

. . .

1. The MS is here torn away.
2. Waithman, an opponent of the war with France, was one of the unsuccessful candidates for London.

482. To Mrs Dugald Stewart

BLPES v. 250–51   Lincoln's Inn, 21 Oct. 1812

Now that there is enough of the new Parliament returned, to judge a little of its composition, you will be anxious to hear what our wise ones think of the result. There is nothing to compensate to Opposition the defeats at Bristol and Liverpool, which are both of them a very painful disappointment: besides Romilly and Brougham, many active and honest Whigs, and some of our most regular voters, have lost their seats and are not likely to find others, at least for some time; of these, I think our most serious loss is in Sharp.[1] In point of quality of votes, we are thus great losers; in number, hardly, if at all; unless Tierney has erred in his calculations. For he tells me, that upon the English returns Opposition does not appear to fall short of its strength in the last Parliament by more than three or four, and in the Irish and Scotch elections we are likely to make this up and even gain a few. If this turn out so, the Ministers must be the party that suffers by the Dissolution; for Lord Wellesley's forces in the House of Commons are very much strengthened indeed. His *following*, as it used to be called at Dublin, is spoken of by the followers themselves as amounting to twenty-two members; and Canning is said to have twelve. United, these will give a troop large enough to give the advantage to Ministers or Opposition at their pleasure; and though the two chiefs have hitherto professed the true principle of adventurers, not to be embarrassed by engagements to each other, it is now reported that, having been thrown together in the Isle of Wight this summer, they came into a convention of alliance offensive and defensive, which future historians will call the Treaty of Cowes.[2]

Next to the general election, I found London most interested about Drury Lane, and the 99 rejected addresses, and the 99 enraged poets. I must let you into a story of that most excellent Whig, the Brewer, because it is a rare example of the love of universal glory. When the Committee found, that not one of the compositions sent to them was fit to be spoken, what could Sam do in their distress, but pen some seventy couplets himself, all about the phœnix from beginning to end; the clumsiest, flattest doggerel that ever was pinched into rhymes. After Lord Byron volunteered for their deliverance, Whitbread contented himself with printing his verses with his initials, and distributing them very sparingly, though a few copies were suffered to steal out of Bedford during the election. It was upon some occasion similar to this, that Sheridan once said to Whitbread, 'You have the most extraordinary ambition, Sam – you try at every thing – you take your horses from the dray to run at Newmarket.'[3]

. . .

1. Sharp had been MP for the pocket borough of Castle Rising since 1806; but he now had to surrender it, his patron Lord Cholmondeley having gone over to Government with the Prince Regent. He did not return to Parliament until March 1816.
2. Following the failure of the negotiations for Canning's entry into the Government in July and August, Wellesley tried to rebuild their alliance but at their meeting on the Isle of Wight in September Canning refused to go so far.
3. The Drury Lane Theatre, burnt down in 1809, had re-opened on 10 Oct. To mark the

occasion the sponsoring committee had offered a £20 prize for a suitable 'address', only to reject all the entries – no less than sixty-nine of which had invoked the Phoenix – and, through Lord Holland, commission Byron instead; Byron's piece is printed in *AR* xliv (1812), 546–7. The story that Whitbread was himself among the disappointed competitors – offering according to Sheridan's well-known quip 'a poulterer's description of a phoenix' – is strongly refuted by Fulford (*Whitbread*, p. 284), since Whitbread could hardly have entered a competition in which he was one of the judges. He also thinks that it is possible but improbable that Whitbread took the relatively harmless course Horner describes of composing something after the failure of the competition. In any event the editors have not been able to trace any such printed verses. Some among the entrants were, as Horner says, 'enraged' at their rejection, one of them, Thomas Busby (1755–1838: *DNB*), a third-rate composer, publishing his protest and being cruelly satirized by Byron. (*Rogers*, i. 114–15.) Another with more sense, however, was given the bright idea of making a parody of the whole affair and on 10 Oct. too there appeared Horace and James Smith's *Rejected Addresses*. It was an immediate and long-lasting success, enthusiastically reviewed by Jeffrey in *ER* xx (no. xl, Nov. 1812), 434–51.

483. To Lord Lansdowne

BLPES v. 256–7   Lincoln's Inn, 27 Oct. 1812

In a letter I had from Brougham yesterday he tells me, that he was glad to find, by a letter from Romilly, that he had a seat in his power if he pleased. If he mentioned the thing in that sort of way to Brougham, I cannot doubt he was upon the point of accepting it. This, I think, may possibly be an offer from Lord Clinton; who had been thinking of making such a proposal to Romilly, before the Bristol election, in case it should end as it unfortunately did; at least so his friend Drake gave me to understand. At the time, I did not imagine any thing would come of it; and therefore did not, I think, mention it to you. I had more hopes from the Jockey, and could not help imagining that the double return he has made was for Romilly; in answer to applications that have been made to him about one of those seats, he has always hinted at a sort of engagement.[1]

It is now affirmed, that the Regent intends to open his Parliament in person: whether he will be able to execute his intention, may depend on the state of his nerves and the assize of bread.[2] I hear more every day of a determination to disappoint the Catholics, and not to redeem the pledge given by the last Parliament; perhaps, in the present untoward circumstances, nothing could happen so favourable to the Whig party as such conduct on the part of the Court. It would leave us still the only rallying principle that we have had for a long while; it must draw closer our relations with Wellesley, whose force in the House of Commons is now so considerable; and Canning, whatever his inclinations may be, cannot help himself now, but upon the Catholic question must be in Wellesley's train. The Regent said at dinner to the Duke of Gloster, that he was not pledged to the Catholics.

Of course you have heard that Mad. de Staël is coming to England, and is already at Stockholm on her way.[3] I look forward to this acquisition to London Society with much pleasure; I hope too she will be encouraged to write some books. Have you looked into the new volume of Burke's works; there is a letter there, addressed to Fox in 1777, the application of which to the present predicament of the Whig party, in many respects, though certainly not in all, struck me very forcibly.[4]

Rogers's 'Columbiad' crept into open day yesterday; not announced in a title page, but lurking at the end of a new edition of his other poems.[5]

1. Neither Romilly, in his diary, nor Patrick Medd, in his biography, mention an offer or the rumour of an offer (of Callington, in Cornwall) from Robert Cotton St John Trefusis, 18th Baron Clinton (1787–1832). But the young Lord Clinton was having problems about his inheritance and these may well have frustrated his good intentions, or those of his close friend and adviser Francis Drake. However, although there had been a contest at Arundel, the Duke of Norfolk's nominees had obtained both seats, and one of them was duly vacated for Romilly, the 'Jockey' requiring nothing but a dinner engagement once a year. So Romilly was elected without opposition. (*Romilly*, iii. 72 and 74–5; Medd, pp. 278–9; *PH* ii. 47–9.)

2. The new Parliament met on 24 Nov., and on the 30th the Regent went to the House of Lords and opened the session. Romilly recalled (*Romilly*, iii. 73–4):

> In his way to the House and back again, he was received with a dead and most humiliating silence; no marks of disapprobation, but no applause. The Princess Charlotte, who was present as a spectator of the ceremony, was recognized by the people on her return, and was greeted with loud and repeated huzzas.

3. Following the suppression of the first, French, edition of *De l'Allemagne* the Baroness de Staël-Holstein had at length fled Napoleon's harassment to her deceased husband's native Sweden before proceeding to England, where she stayed to be lionized until the restoration of 1814.

4. The relevant passages in Burke's letter to Fox of 8 Oct. 1777 (reprinted in *Burke*, iii. 380–88) ends:

> As to the Whigs, I think them far from extinct. They are, what they always were, (except by the able use of opportunities) by far the weakest party in this country. They have not yet learned the application of their principles to the present state of things; and as to the Dissenters, the main effective part of the Whig strength, they are . . . 'not all in force'. They will do very little.

5. Samuel Rogers's *Poems*, with 'The Voyage of Columbus' appearing as the last item in the table of contents, were published for the first time in 1812 and favourably reviewed by James Mackintosh in *ER* xxii (no. xliii, Oct. 1813), 32–50. A hostile review by Ward in the *Quarterly* for March 1813 provoked the famous retort from Rogers:

> Ward has no heart they say, but I deny it;
> He has a heart, and gets his speeches by it.

484. To Leonard Horner

BLPES v. 262 (copy)   Lincoln's Inn, 30 Nov. 1812

I think Mr Galton's idea of a Table is very well conceived for placing before the eye, at once, and in a striking manner, the main proof of depreciation; and the surprising coincidence of all the subsidiary proofs that have been referred to in the argument.[1] It will be very useful to publish this table, and I think it quite necessary that he should accompany it with an explanation, much as he has drawn up which is very perspicuous and neat.

Too great a size is, no doubt, an important objection; yet I question but that to avoid this he has lost something of the necessary distinctness of his table, by crowding into the centre part of it three things which are indeed different in their nature from one another. It would be much more clear, and would catch the eye better to have the exchange and the Amount of Notes in two separate divisions of the Table, parallel to each other and to all the rest. Besides, as I have already hinted, the way in which they stand at present (upon the same compartment with the price of Gold) is apt to suggest, what is not correctly true; that a given variation in the price of Gold is accompanied by a variation, arithmetically the same, in the amount of Notes and course of exchange. They do not hold a constant proportion. Indeed this objection might, in strictness, be carried a little farther. The whole table is at present ruled into equal spaces; every 5/- change in the price of Wheat being thus represented as exactly corresponding to a change of 1/- in the price of Gold, and 2d. in the price of Silver. Unless notice be given that the spaces, which for convenience were made equal, are not meant in the real theory of the table to be taken as such, the subject would be represented erroneously. The synchronism of the increments upon the whole, as it were, the near approach to parallelism in the lines which represent these flowing quantities is the thing that is intended to be illustrated; without pretending that they are all commensurable among one another.

I think Mr Galton has not adverted in the observations which accompany the Table, to the principle which makes Gold our present standard, instead of Silver as anciently. I conceive it to be this; that, if both the precious metals are coined into legal standard, but they happen not to be adjusted at the Mint in the same proportion to each other as the relative value which they bear in the market, men will only take that Metal to the Mint which is over rate and will also prefer paying their debts with the same. This was the case of Gold with us, for a long period prior to the late derangement of things.

. . .

1. S. Tertius Galton, A chart, exhibiting the relation between the amount of Bank of England notes in circulation, the rate of foreign exchanges, and the prices of gold and silver bullion and of wheat; accompanied with explanatory observations (1813).

485. To J.A. Murray

BLPES v. 263–6 ⟨Horner, ii. 123–5⟩   [London], Tuesday night and Wednesday,
                                                                         8 [and 9] Dec. 1812

⟨. . .

⟨There was not the slightest reason to believe that Tierney was going to Madras; that he either had thoughts of it, or had it in his power. Some of the Directors may have given out that they would be glad of such an appointment, as they would no doubt have reason to be. But Tierney, whatever faults he may have, is not the man to take an office of any sort from the present Ministers, or to avail himself of the untrue pretext that an Indian government can be accepted without being held under the actual Administration at home. His being out of Parliament is entirely owing to accident and bad management, which (I hope) will soon be remedied.〉[1]

. . .

〈Brougham's success at the Bar is prodigious, much more rapid and extensive than that of any barrister since Erskine's starting. I am going down to-morrow to hear him in defence of Hunt, which is a cause of great expectation.[2] I have been present at several arguments of his in Banc;[3] of which I should not, to say the truth, make a very high report; that is, in comparison of his powers and his reputation. Great reach and compass of mind he must ever display, and he shows much industry, too, in collecting information; but his arguments are not in the best style of legal reasoning. Precision and clearness in the details, symmetry in the putting of them together, an air of finish and unity in the whole, are the merits of that style; and there is not one of those qualities in which he is not very defective. But his desultory reasonings have much force in some parts, and much ingenuity in others; and he always proves himself to have powers for another sort of speaking, and a higher sort. What I say now, applies only to his appearances in Banc, having never yet heard him address a jury.〉

. . .

〈How deeply interesting is the Russian war now become![4] It seems hardly too sanguine to expect, that the world is to be set free from bondage, and that the justice of fortune is at length to be made manifest, in the signal punishment of the Conqueror, who has so long harassed the earth and subjected the fairest portion of it; *qui res humanas* (would we could say) *miscuit olim*. We cannot wish for a more signal vengeance to the cause of the liberties of mankind, than that he should fall, or at least lose his purple, in this unsuccessful aggression upon the independence of a great nation. It will be no small enhancement of this triumph, if we are really to enjoy it, because it will strengthen that sense of security, which is the best fruit of it, that the victory is due, not to the Government of Russia, which would have long ago submitted, but to the body of the Muscovite people, nobles and peasantry. Surely there is nothing in history so delightful to read or witness, nothing so useful in its example, as the successful resistance of foreign invaders; whether it be by the patriotism of a civilized and free state, or by the instinct of barbarians and slaves; whether it be Greek, or Dutch, republicans, whom we have to admire; whether it be the repulse of partitioning confederates by the enthusiastic Jacobinism of France, or the repulse of French genius, and military science in perfection, by the brute valour of Russians and Tartars. How vast will the events of our day appear, to those who shall be at a sufficient distance from them to see their real magnitude! Will not the march of the French host to Moscow be judged the very masterpiece of the military art, in point of execution: an achievement, that deserved no meaner disappointment, than by the barbaric magnanimity, which the people invaded have shown, in burning the ancient capital of their empire. One can hardly think of such things and not use big words.

Wednesday [9 Dec.]

〈The Hunts are convicted; but not without the jury retiring for about ten minutes. Brougham made a powerful speech, unequal, and wanting that unity which is so effective with a jury; some parts rather eloquent, particularly in the conclusion, where he had the address, without giving any advantage, to fasten the words *effeminacy* and *cowardice* where every body could apply them. One very difficult point of his case, the conduct of the Regent to the Princess, he managed with skill and great effect; and his transition from that subject to the next part of his case was a moment of real eloquence. Lord Ellenborough was more than usually impatient, and indecently violent: he said that Brougham was inoculated with all the poison of the libel, and told the jury, the issue they had to try was, whether we were to live for the future under the dominion of libellers.⟩

. . .

1. Tierney had obtained Bandon Bridge in County Cork in 1807 through an arrangement between the disputing patrons that they should alternate their interests and in 1812 it was not the turn of his patron (the Duke of Devonshire). The Whig leaders subsequently persuaded one of the sitting members for Appleby to stand down in his favour and so he was returned to Parliament on 29 Dec. (*PH* i. 637.) Abercromby's elder brother Lt Gen. John Abercromby (1772–1817: *DNB*) was appointed temporary Governor of Madras.
2. On 6 Dec. John and Leigh Hunt, publisher and editor of the *Examiner*, were placed on trial for a libel against the Regent. The prosecution's case was a strong one, and the Hunts this time were convicted and sentenced to two years' imprisonment. But Brougham – already principal adviser to the Princess of Wales in her conflict with the Regent – achieved great fame as their defence counsel. (New, pp. 90–92.)
3. I.e. in the full Superior Court of Common Law, rather than on circuit.
4. Previously Horner had had little confidence in the ability of the Russians to check Napoleon's advance and had viewed Wellington's victories in a vacuum, without reference to the broader European struggle, all the while lamenting what he considered to be incompetence in the British Government's management of the Peninsular War. (Horner to Murray, 2 Aug., and to C.R. Fox, 26 Oct. 1812, BLPES v. 210–11 and 258–9.)

486. To J.A. Murray

BLPES v. 267–8 ⟨*Horner*, ii. 126–7⟩   Lincoln's Inn, 16 Dec. 1812

. . .

⟨I entirely agree with you in opinion, that the property-tax as collected from the farmers in Scotland must have a hurtful effect upon agriculture, and is assessed by an unequal and arbitrary rule. The principle of the tax in other cases is, that of an assessment upon actual profits, and rackrent is no criterion of the farmer's actual profits. I cannot see that there is any greater difficulty in raising this tax from that class of men, by a requisition from them of their gains every year, than in the instance of mercantile and professional persons; on the contrary, a farmer's income from his proper business is far more ostensible to his neighbours than those of the other sort, and his actual rent affords such a check upon false returns, as would protect the revenue against them much more effectually, than it protects itself against them from merchants and men of professions. What you suggest, a corresponding committee including all the counties, is the most likely method of obtaining redress, if the matter is taken up by people of respectability and with resolution. And I should be glad to see this. Without a previous *demonstration* of that nature, it is of no use to call the attention of the House of Commons to it; it is very difficult to get their attention to any thing Scotch. The business was taken up with much spirit formerly by several of the counties, particularly (I think) Roxburghe; why did they let it drop? You may rely upon me, if you wish me to take any part about it; only give me timely information.⟩

⟨There is but one sentiment of condemnation, respecting Lord Ellenborough's intemperate and indecent conduct at Hunt's trial. This is not only universal among the Bar, who⟩, though Brougham is not popular with them, ⟨feel this as a professional concern; but among laymen, of all political denominations. I have reason to believe, also, that the other judges regret his conduct very much. The session of Parliament can hardly pass over, without some pointed notice of it.

⟨I am delighted to see, at last, another good number of the *Review*, worthy of its former name. There seems to be but one article of *monthly* politics, which is too short a life for a quarterly book. Allen is delighted with the orthodoxy of the review of Leckie's pamphlet, and says it is the best constitutional article Jeffrey has ever written. The *Musæ Edinenses* excite a very irreverent mirth among your colleagues, who instead of being disposed to give a liberal encouragement to our attempts, seem to regard it as improper ambition, and something out of the course of nature for Scotsmen even to try such excellence; I saw Bobus [Smith] and the Mufti [Whishaw] snickering together at the very mention of this title. This scorn of theirs makes me anxious that we should give them one more Buchanan.[1]

[PS] ⟨I shall not be returned to Parliament till after the adjournment; I expect it in the course of February.⟩

. . .

1. The *ER* for Nov. 1812 (no. xl, vol. xx) contained among other articles Brougham on the *Rights and Duties of the People* (pp. 405–425), and Jeffrey on Leckie's *British Government* (pp. 315–46) and, in lighter mood, on the *Musæ Edinenses*, a review of a volume of verse by Scottish schoolboys (pp. 387–405). The last reference is obscure but presumably means David Buchanan, the journalist and former contributor to the *Review*.

487. To Lady Holland

BLPES v. 278–9   Winchester, Friday 5 Mar. [1813]

. . .

Plunkett's success, and the triumphant vote for the Catholics, gave me the greatest pleasure. One's anxiety is now turned towards the Committee. It will be sad work, if agreement enough cannot be had, to outwit Bankes and brother Bragge, after getting the House to go so far. Is the vote very much disliked at Carlton House, or will there be any disposition there to let the thing take its course?[1]

The Princess's letter to the Speaker seems not a bad move, if she must go on; it compels a farther proceeding.[2] Though the wisest course for her and the most comfortable for the public would still be to hush up the whole story and be quiet, I own if it is to come to blows at last, I feel myself fast going over to the side of the lady. She is used with much harshness and insolence, in being denied her daughter's society upon such pretences; and it is more than one can bear, that such penalties for conduct should be imposed on her by [the] advice of Lord Yarmouth and his mother. So that if you do not look sharp after me, I shall be very shortly a downright partisan of Brougham's in this question.

. . .

1. Grattan's motion for a committee of the whole House 'to take into its most serious consideration the state of the laws affecting his Majesty's Roman Catholic subjects in Great Britain and Ireland, with a view to such a final and conciliatory adjustment, as may be conducive to the power and strength of the United Kingdom, to the stability of the Protestant Establishment, and to the general satisfaction and concord of all classes of his Majesty's subjects' had been passed in the Commons on 2 Mar. by a vote of 264–224 following a great speech on 25 Feb. by William Conyngham Plunket, Attorney-General in the Ministry of All the Talents and afterwards 1st Baron Plunket (1764–1854: DNB), who had been returned for Dublin University in the elections of 1812 after a lengthy absence from Parliament, and despite the speeches on the other side by Bankes and Bragge Bathurst. (Hansard, xxiv. 781–820 and 1072–3.)

2. Following the restrictions the Prince Regent had placed upon her visits to their daughter in Oct. 1812 and the Privy Council's rejection of her protest against them in January, the Princess of Wales had appealed to the Speaker.

488. To John Horner

BLPES v. 284–5   Salisbury, Sunday [7 Mar. 1813]

. . .

Every attempt will be made by the Chancellor and his assistants, to obstruct the proceedings in the Commons upon the Catholic cause; and very probably, they will be successful. But they cannot now deprive us of the unexpected advantage that was gained by the vote of the House for going into the Committee; which, under all the circumstances in which the vote was passed, is the greatest step that the Catholics have ever made towards the final recovery of their political liberty. And a proud thing it is for England, to be making such advances in the improvement of her laws and freedom, at a time when all the rest of the world is abject and retrograde.

The Princess of Wales appears to have come off with flying colours. The Prince must be mortified to the last degree, and has certainly not had all the advantages given him in the turn of the debate, that I apprehend he would have been entitled to upon the real merits of the Princess's case.[1] But I shall rejoice that the thing has taken this colour, provided it is suffered now to rest; nothing can be more injurious to the country, than these popular exposures of the royal family; at the same time the Princess has been used so harshly and insultingly, by those who have themselves no right to censure her conduct, that is very satisfactory to see them disgraced and humiliated.

. . .

1. When the debate on the Princess of Wales's appeal to the Speaker had come on in the Commons on 5 Mar., Whitbread, recalling the Delicate Investigation of 1806 and a Cabinet minute of late 1807 in which the Tory Ministers had practically cleared the Princess of the charges of the year before, had accused Eldon and his colleagues of the effrontery of basing a continuation of restrictions on aspersions they themselves had rejected in 1807. Whitbread's speech was among the most effective of his career; his arguments wrong-footed the Ministers, and Castlereagh had lamely to surrender. (*Hansard*, xxiv. 1148ff. See also New, pp. 96–7.)

489. To Lady Holland

BLPES v. 282–3 Salisbury, Sunday [7 Mar. 1813]

Though one cannot help thinking that the Regent has been used ill by his Ministers, in the turn which the business has taken, I rejoice exceedingly at the mortification and defeat he has suffered; the proper punishment for the want of manliness and generosity which he has shown in the whole conduct of it. First, in using the Princess so ill from the first; and next, in being bullied by her upon the original story. If the matter rests here, I shall be much surprised; the Regent's uneasiness under such an impression, and her restlessness with such a triumph, are both against that which is so desirable.

Wortley's strong speech ought to be a sign of the times to the Royal family; when the Tories begin to express such things, they are not far from one of those coalitions which work miracles in our government.[1] Wortley, however, is bolder and hotter than most of his set, and would probably have declared for the Prince of Orange before his landing. Will the Regent be thrown upon the Whigs at last, for personal protection?

. . .

I hope it is for Sheridan that the vacancy is made at Wootton Bassett. He has been mortified long enough, and most ungratefully used by the Regent.[2]

Our gaols upon the circuit are crowded with prisoners, and I hardly recollect on any former occasion so great a proportion of the worst description of crimes. I cannot believe that other countries are so bad as England in this respect; our metropolis is probably kept in better order than most of those on the continent, but the great atrocities are usually perpetrated by our peasants. In every calendar in the West of England there are half a dozen crimes, any one of which would make all Scotland ring for a year. . . .

. . .

1. Stuart Wortley had strongly criticized the Regent's treatment of his wife in a speech on 5 Mar.
2. Sheridan had tried and failed to regain his old seat at Stafford in Oct. 1812. A confusion of financial problems and personal considerations prevented his buying one of the vacancies created afterwards at Wootton Bassett, a notoriously rotten borough, and despite the further efforts of his friends he never returned to the Commons. (*PH* ii. 363–4 and 430; v. 164–6.)

490. To Henry Hallam

BLPES v. 280–81 ⟨Horner, ii. 128–130⟩   Salisbury, Sunday evening, 7 Mar. 1813

⟨. . .

⟨When we recollect the diffident language that we held about the Catholic cause before the debate came on, the advantages secured by the late vote seem immense. We thought for certain that some ground had been lost since the resolution of the last Parliament, whereas it is now manifest that we were gaining ground all along, and that the progress of temperate conviction had been steady and unremitted. What an illustration of the benefits of continued discussion, through Parliament and the press, where the great interests of justice and liberty are the subject of controversy; and what a pride it is for England, to have such a controversy leading slowly but surely to the truth, and to one of the most signal ameliorations of government in favour of civil freedom, during the terror and darkness in which the rest of the world is involved. I look with great anxiety to the Committee; not only on account of the arts which will be employed to embarrass it, but for fear of the unfavourable impression with which the late vote may be received throughout the country, even by liberal men, if it has the appearance of being followed by difficulties which the ablest men in Parliament cannot remove. I believe none such exist in the nature of the measure, though there may be in the habitual alienation and mutual repugnance which several of those members feel for one another. Yet I would fain hope, the public spirit which they all possess will on this great concern bring them together in earnest, and make them feel how much the reputation of all of them as statesmen is staked upon their skilful and successful use of the advantage which an honest vote of the House has put into their hands, and the final adjustment of this embarrassing claim will clear the great field of public affairs for other exertions of their ambition and patriotism, whether they are to be still adverse to one another or shall make an experiment of acting together. I cannot think that Grattan and Lord Grey and Canning would find it very difficult to agree upon a plan of emancipation and securities; and if they come to the Committee with a plan agreed on, that Bankes and Bragge Bathurst would find it easy to disunite them. Though the House, in its present temper, might perhaps be induced to pass a partial measure, I own it seems to me imprudent in any of the great leaders of the Catholic cause to think of originating any compromise of that sort; they may be forced to accept at present only part of their claim for the Catholics; but to preserve the strength of their cause, they ought to keep it entire, and there is no part of the argument which it is more important to impress upon the public mind, than that to do good you must give all.⟩

       . . .

491. To the Duke of [Somerset][1]

BLPES v. 286–7   Western Circuit, 9 Mar. 1813

... You are of course aware that there have been very considerable fluctuations recently, in the course of the foreign exchanges and in the price of gold; which, as far as I have had it in my power to inquire concerning them, illustrate and confirm, instead of shaking as will no doubt be asserted, the reasonings and principles which have been deduced from all former experience.

I congratulate you on the vote of the Commons in the Catholic question; it is the greatest step that has yet been made towards final success, in that great cause of religious liberty and political justice, and is a most signal encouragement in all such questions to perseverance in urging the claim temperately, and in informing the public patiently. It may still require a few years more; but success is now certain, if we will only go on repeating incessantly the same arguments. With people in general, who are not disciplined to reason for themselves, arguments make their way only by force of habit.

...

1. On 29 Mar. Lord Webb Seymour wrote to the Duke (*Two Brothers*, p. 108):
   I return Horner's letter, and expect to hear from you soon upon that subject. Horner can no where have so much leisure as upon the circuit.

492. To Lady Holland

BLPES v. 289–90   [Exeter], Thursday night, [18 Mar. 1813]

...

What is to be the end of all your violence in London? The Princess has now such a host of champions, that I see no chivalry in defending her, and I am nearly gone over again to the other side. I have made nobody but you the confidant of my trimming.[1]

1. On 10 Mar. the Prince Regent had published in the *Morning Post* and the *Morning Herald* the most damaging of the 1806 depositions against his wife, and Brougham had countered by publishing Perceval's 1806 defence of the Princess (New, pp. 97–8).

493. To Lord Holland

BLPES v. 395–6   Exeter, Sunday night, [?21 Mar. 1813]

In the last proceedings upon this unhappy affair of the Princess, there are some circumstances which I do not understand and which give me some uneasiness. I hear that Whitbread's motion for prosecuting the printers was settled at a conference at Camelford House; and one part of his speech, which is making much impression, consists of a laboured attack upon Lord Grenville, and his colleagues in the Commission, for their mode of examination, in the instance of Mrs Lisle;[1] that attack being founded upon the authority of a paper not official which had been put into his hands that same morning. Did he communicate that paper to Lord Grenville, and signify his intention of animadverting upon it? If he did not, his conduct appears such a breach of propriety as makes me quite uncomfortable. And if he had no other authority, than he assigns in his speech for considering that paper genuine, his making any use of it on such an occasion, without a previous reference to the persons concerned in the transaction, appears the most unlike a man of sense in business of any thing I ever knew.[2]

His speeches seem to have been very effective, and have made a great impression, among all the people whom I see at present, in destroying the character of Eldon, especially. He has done no justice to the Government of 1806, whose conduct in so disagreeable an affair appears to me to have [been] very nearly quite right. What I am most grieved at, is to see them given [?give] up, apparently by consent, as to that very important part of their conduct, the examination of the Informants upon oath. It quite amazed me, to see it stated, that the Douglasses cannot be prosecuted for their perjury. There was a sufficient reason for not doing so at the time, because it was of great moment to keep the whole concealed from the public for ever if possible. But can it be doubted, that Privy Counsellors and above all the Secretary of State have a lawful authority to take examinations upon oath with reference to informations of treasonable practices, and that those who swear falsely before them are liable to prosecution? I cannot think of any doctrine of the common law that I would mention as more indisputable. Yet by the recent discussions in the House of Commons, the law is held out as containing no such authority and imposing no such penalty; and Erskine, Ellenborough, and the two other Lords are represented as having acted in ignorance, or rather in violation, of the law.[3]

In the midst of all this odious work, it is a delightful consolation to hear that the concerns of the Catholics go on so prosperously.

[PS] Will you send the inclosed note to the two-penny post; it is to thank the Fox Club for electing me a member.

1. Mrs (Hester) Clapcott-Lisle (d. 1828), sister of the future 1st Marquess of Cholmondeley, was the lady-in-waiting whose evidence had justified the 1806 Commission's rebuke to the Princess for 'frivolous conduct'.
2. In the House of Commons on 15 Mar., after Ponsonby had remarked critically on the involvement of Whitbread and Brougham in the affairs of the Princess of Wales, Whitbread had delivered a singularly indiscreet speech in which he pointed out that the Princess had disclaimed all knowledge of any intention to publish her letter to the Regent of 14 Jan., produced an obscure document which he contended cast serious doubts on the propriety of the manner in which witnesses had been examined by the commissioners of 1806, and then launched a bitter and dubious attack on the commissioners of 1806, which of course included Grenville, Erskine, Romilly, and other prominent Whigs (Hansard, xxv. 142–80). Apparently Whitbread had had no previous communication with Grenville on the matter, and Horner's reaction to Whitbread's remarks reflected the consensus opinion of Whig leaders. Brougham rightly regarded Whitbread's speech as a serious tactical error, and thereafter, despite amicable discussions between Grenville and Whitbread, Horner

and other moderate Whigs were loath to follow Whitbread's lead in the Princess Caroline affair. (For brief comment on Whitbread's speech and its political ramifications, see New, pp. 98–9.)

3. See Doc. 251 n. 2.

494. To T.R. Malthus

BLPES v. 291–2 ⟨*Malthus*, p. 222⟩   Lincoln's Inn, Tuesday [20 Apr. 1813]

. . .

⟨I am anxious to see your defence of the College, which cannot but prove of great service not only at the present moment but to the future character of the institution. Nothing is so much to be regretted, as the view which Lord Grenville has taken of it; I think unjustly, after the best consideration I am able to give the subject. The general question of the education of those whom we send to govern India is one of the last[1] importance, and what you are going to publish cannot fail to obtain a more deliberate attention for it, than has yet been bestowed upon it by any body else.⟩[2]

. . .

1. Not 'first' as in *Malthus*.
2. The East India College at Hertford had experienced persistent disciplinary problems, which though by no means unusual in schools of the period were complicated in its case by internal conflicts of authority and of policy that in turn affected the debate on the renewal of the Company's charter. On 9 Apr. 1813 Lord Grenville, who was one of the Company's leading antagonists and wanted to suppress the College 'as a baneful influence' that separated the Company's civil servants from other, public-school educated Englishmen, had made a ferocious attack in the Lords, suggesting the College be closed and the Company recruit its civil servants from the public schools. This Malthus – who was of course a Professor at the College – answered about a fortnight later with *A Letter to the Right Honourable Lord Grenville occasioned by some Observations of His Lordship on the East India Company's Establishment for the Education of their Civil Servants*, in which he retorted that the College was a necessity, unless, as Grenville in fact wished, the Company itself were to be abolished. In the event the Charter was renewed for twenty years and the College given statutory recognition. (*Malthus*, pp. 214–21; but see Doc. 583.)

495. To Lady Holland

BLPES v. 299–300   House of Commons, Wednesday [12 May 1813]

I did not hear the first part of the debate, but I heard all Canning's speech; which was full of rough jokes about Hippisley, that kept the House in a roar of laughter against that mountebank for a full hour. It was an effective speech for the Division; with which we all seem to be very well satisfied, and still more with the explicitness of Lord Castlereagh's language. He has still some reserve about the particular securities which he would prefer; but he has expressed himself as strongly as the best friend of the cause could do, as to the importance of carrying into effect the principle which he considered the House as having settled, and likewise of allowing no delay that is not absolutely necessary. Six of our voters were shut out accidentally. There were one or two persons in the Division, Scotchmen, whom Abercromby regards as a sign that the Court is giving way; particularly old Ferguson, and General Wemyss, who changed last night from their former votes.[1]

. . .

1. On 11 May Hippisley had made a badly conceived and clumsily executed attempt to persuade the House to commission a far-reaching inquiry into laws affecting Roman Catholics, and Canning had pointed out that it was not only unnecessary but would also hold up the progress of reform, in particular the Irish Roman Catholic Officers Relief Bill, to which he then proceeded to propose a series of amendments. Castlereagh expressed a similar view and Canning's proposals were adopted in preference to Hippisley's. Major-General Sir Ronald Craufurd Ferguson (1773–1841: *DNB*) was MP for Kirkaldy burghs, and Lt Gen. William Wemyss (1760–1822) MP for Fifeshire. (*Hansard*, xxvi. 1–100.)

496. To Lady Holland

BLPES v. 295–6   [London], Sunday [16 May 1813]

. . .

There was a meeting with Castlereagh yesterday about the Bill.[1] Plunkett is the only one I have seen, of those who were present; and he told me last night he is not only convinced of Castlereagh's sincerity in wishing the measure to be carried, but he also thinks him very reasonable and tractable as to those points of regulation upon which there is some difference of opinion. I believe there is to be another meeting to-morrow. Plunkett, it is to be remembered, however, is more for securities than any well-judging man is found to be, who does not retain some nursery prejudices against the Papists.

I met the Attorney-General at dinner yesterday;[2] he said to Plunkett, that he supposed we should all fall out in the Committee, but that he should leave us to ourselves, as he understood too little of the matter to take any part in it. I cannot help thinking this an indication, that there is at present no very eager and determined opinion at Carlton House against the Bill, for Garrow is the mere creature of the Regent.

. . .

1. The MC reported on 17 May:
> A meeting took place at Mr Ponsonby's on Saturday of the Friends of the Roman Catholic Bill, at which Lord Castlereagh was present, and we rejoice to hear that they came to a perfect understanding on all the material clauses, so that there is little doubt of the Bill passing the Committee without much debate.
2. Sir William Garrow (1760–1840: *DNB*).

497. To Lord Holland

BLPES v. 302–304 〈*Horner*, ii. 131–2〉　　　　　　　[London], Thursday [20 May 1813]

... 〈Your argument, from the manifesto of the Regency, does not admit of an answer; yet the foolish people, who manage the No-Popery cause at present, were all delighted with the appearance of those documents.[1]

〈You and Allen must be right, I think, about the advantage to be derived from keeping the Dissenters and Catholics on the same footing, so as to give to each the services of the other in their common cause: though I was not prepared to go so far as he did some time ago, that the Catholics should not be relieved, if we could not give the Dissenters at the same time all they ought to have. It will be a great consolation to Lord Grey, to find what your sentiments are upon the omission of the words respecting the Sacrament in the Catholic Bill: for his chief apprehension on that point seemed to be, that you would think the Dissenters ill used by that omission. For myself, I would rather, I own, have given the Catholics that farther step, though one ahead of the Dissenters; for it seems that we can hardly expect to obtain our object of complete toleration by regular approaches, or by skilful management of parties, but that we must scramble for it, and make the most of lucky moments, and take as much for any description of sectaries as the accidents or humour of the day will let us have. And indeed, I think, if we had got an express release from the Sacrament Test to the Catholics, the argument for granting the same ease to Protestant Dissenters would next year have been found irresistible. However, it will be some comfort for the loss of this, if it shall have the effect of inducing the Dissenters and Catholics to pull together.

〈Have you heard enough of our doings in Sicily in March last, to have formed an opinion upon them? They have very much the cast of our Indian proceedings with nabobs and rajahs. There are stories of some arbitrary imprisonments which I do not like, and both King and Queen seem to have been treated with more violence than was warrantable without doing more; but I am imperfectly informed about this. Lamb, I suppose, has come home to give Government a full account of all that has passed.〉[2]

Creevey was brought up for judgement today; I was not present, but I hear he put in an affidavit, averring that in the publication he had no malice against the prosecutor, and denying that the Court had any power to take cognizance of him. Lord Ellenborough said, there was no doubt of their power; and then old Grouse proceeded to pass sentence, observing that the libel appeared to be more against the late spotless character [of] Mr Perceval, and therefore was bottomed in disaffection to the Government, for which reason Government itself ought to have proceeded against it as an affair of state instead of leaving it to the private prosecutor; the judgement was, that Creevey should be fined £100.[3]

Whitbread is to present a petition for him, stating that he has been fined and put to great expense by the proceeding of the Court against him, in a matter over which they had no jurisdiction. The petition will raise the question, though not upon such strong grounds as if the sentence of the Court had interrupted his attendance in Parliament. The question, however, is sufficiently raised for the principle. The consequences of such prosecutions seem to me likely to be very important and dangerous; the strong argument against us, is that according to former notions I fear it was a breach of privilege in a member to publish his own speech.

House of Commons, 5 o'clock

Creevey has just given notice to the House of his having been fined for the publication of words spoken in his place; and that he means tomorrow to present a petition and remonstrance against the Judges.

. . .

1. Hippisley had around this time (to most people's annoyance) both produced and demanded a mountain of information about the position of Roman Catholics at home and abroad. Among the latter, produced by Castlereagh on 21 May in response to Hippisley's particular demand for material illustrating how foreign governments fended off papal interference, was a translation of 'The manifesto of the Spanish Regency relative to the conduct of the Archbishop of Nicaea, the Pope's Nuncio in Spain, dated Cadiz, 23 April 1813'. (*House of Commons Journal*, lxviii. 509.)

2. Despite his earlier embarrassing failure as President of Madras, Lord William Cavendish Bentinck (1774–1839: *DNB*), had been sent by Wellesley to Sicily in 1811 as Commander-in-Chief of the Mediterranean as well as Minister to the Sicilian Court. An egoist who sought to rival Wellington as the saviour of Europe, Bentinck pursued a policy altogether inconsistent with that of the Foreign Office. While failing to exploit the military advantage created by the absence of Murat's Neapolitan army in Russia, he developed wild military schemes and employed a heavy hand in forcing a new constitution on Sicily, thereby deeply offending the Sicilian Court. (See Webster, pp. 74–86.) Frederick James Lamb, afterwards Baron Beauvale and last Viscount Melbourne (1782–1853: *DNB*), was Secretary of Legation at Palermo.

3. During his campaign in Liverpool, Creevey had repeated in public an attack he had made in the House of Commons on a Liverpool tax inspector as a 'common informer' of the Prime Minister and later published his remarks. A prosecution for libel resulted and Brougham was retained for the defence. Creevey was convicted at Lancaster on 29 Mar. despite a plausible argument that parliamentary privilege shielded him from prosecution and his appeal in the High Court on 20 May also failed. He was fined £100 just when his financial position was collapsing but his appeals to the House evoked very little sympathy. Whitbread does not seem to have presented any petition on his behalf and though Creevey gave the notice to which Horner subsequently refers, it was not until 25 June that he himself brought the matter before the Commons. The House's attitude then was patently unsympathetic and he was forced to declare himself content with having his version placed on record. (*Hansard*, xxvi, 252–3 and 898–921; *House of Commons Journal*, lxviii (1812–13), p. 604; *PH* iii. 527–8; see also Gore, *Creevey*, pp. 68–71.)

498. To John Allen

BL Add. MSS 52180   [London], Sunday [30 May 1813]

I sent the packet to the *Morning Chronicle* office this morning, and am very glad Lord Holland did not omit the opportunity of keeping Perry right, who is so liable to err on such occasions.[1] People do not seem to have made up their minds, upon the perusal of the bulletin, whether the victory of the French is to be regarded as a decisive one.[2] It is enough so, I think, to expose our want of prudence in not making an experiment of negotiation during the winter, and to suggest the propriety of still making an attempt of that sort. But our foreign affairs are now in the hands of Count Munster.[3]

The Princess's party of the Mountain are cast down by their factions in the City; they will hardly rally again, unless some fresh indiscretion be committed on the other side. . . .

1. The MC of 31 May carried the announcement of a dinner to be given on 10 June to the delegates presenting Irish Catholic petitions to Parliament by 'The Friends of Religious Liberty', and on 4 June it printed a list of stewards that included Holland.
2. *Colchester*, ii. 449, says that news of the battle of Bautzen, which had taken place on 20–21 May, reached London on 29th. There was heavy loss of life on both sides, but the result was indecisive.
3. Count Munster (1766–1839), the Prince Regent's principal Hanoverian Minister, was then a key figure in the formulation of British foreign policy. Later in the year he accompanied the Duke of Cambridge to Hanover and afterwards represented the Regent at Allied headquarters.

499. To John Allen

BL Add. MSS 52180   [London], Monday evening, [31 May 1813]

There is no account yet of the battle, more than we had on Saturday; but a firing on the French coast has been heard for two days.

You have probably been told already that when the news of the battle was told to the Regent, he expressed the greatest satisfaction, because it put an end to all chance (he said) of a congress or armistice.[1]

The General Assembly was moved to petition against the Catholics; Maconochie and Hill, with our friends, did not content themselves with throwing this out, but are to send us up a petition from the Kirk, with the Lord Jesus at its head, in favour of the Papists.[2] . . .

1. Through Austrian mediation a two-month armistice was, however, arranged at Pleisswitz on 4 June and was later extended until 10 Aug. so that a congress might meet at Prague to arrange a peace. But the French excluded England from the congress and it collapsed on 10 Aug.; two days later the Austrians declared war on France.
2. The General Assembly had on 27 May thrown out an anti-Catholic petition and instead unanimously adopted that proposed by Maconochie, who was now Solicitor-General for Scotland. George Hill (1750–1819: *DNB*), Principal of St Mary's College, St Andrews, was a distinguished moderate in the Assembly. The petition was presented by Castlereagh on 1 June (*Hansard*, xxvi. 485–6).

500. To Lord Holland

BLPES v. 293–4   [London], Friday morning, [11 June 1813]

I liked your speech yesterday much, and am quite glad you went the full length of the principle of religious liberty. It cannot fail to do as great service with the Dissenters, who both for the Catholic cause and for general politics deserve to be cultivated again by our party, as they used to be. Lord Grey's explicitness on the same point will probably do both the party and himself personally much good. I went away very soon after you spoke, but while I stayed every thing seemed to go off as well as could be wished. I see no reason to regret that Lord Grey reverted to the topic of 'violated promises'; it is both just and useful that that recollection should be associated with all our discussions of the Catholic cause, in the present state of the Court.

PS I wish the Duke of S[ussex] had not been so low in talking of his pension.[1]

    1. Grey, Holland, and the Duke of Sussex – among others – had all spoken at a meeting of the
    'Friends of Civil and Religious Liberty' the previous day. According to the MC of 11 June,
    Grey had said:

        He concurred most strongly with those who recommended moderation and temper-
        ance to the Catholic body, notwithstanding a recent event, at the same time that
        he had the utmost consideration for their feelings under all the circumstances of
        their case – under the irritation of defeated hopes, of repeated disappointments, but
        still more of violated promises. . . . he would continue to support the Catholic
        cause, as he had always supported it, because he deemed it the cause of religious
        freedom. He looked to it, however, as only a part of the great object to which the
        friends of religious liberty should direct all their efforts, and those efforts should not
        be relaxed, until all civil rights should be placed within the reach of every class of
        people unclogged by any religious qualifications whatever – until all Protestant
        Dissenters . . . should be relieved from every civil disability.

    Following him, Holland acknowledged that although he would not insist on total
    emancipation from the first, that was nonetheless his ultimate objective, for 'he looked,
    and would ever struggle for the attainment of that object, in the removal of every civil
    disability that was founded on religious distinctions'.

501. Speech by Horner[1]

⟨Horner, ii. 134–5⟩   House of Commons, 15 June 1813

⟨. . . It so happened, that though we had corn laws in our statute book, we had, in fact, no corn laws, and that there was the most perfect freedom in the trade of grain. Now, what was the state of the country with respect to agricultural improvement? The fact was, that tillage had never increased so much, and that prices had never been before so regular. For this, if reference was necessary, he would refer to the Report itself. With respect to the supply of grain from foreign countries, the evil was admitted to be, not in the supply itself, but in the danger to which it was exposed of being cut off. Now, it so happened, that at a time it was the policy of an enemy to prevent our supply, and when political circumstances were the most favourable for such a measure, the amount of foreign grain imported into this country had been greater then ever. The Report proved, that in spite of all the regulations of the enemy, whenever this country was in want of foreign grain, it could get it. There were several principles in the Report, with which he agreed; he had no hesitation in agreeing to exportation, and the abolition of a bounty. But the discussion of that night convinced him, that these principles were merely thrown out by way of conciliation, and the main object of the measure was to prevent importation from foreign countries, except when prices should rise to the enormous sums stated in the Report. At present, he contended, the price of corn was high beyond example, and was such as to afford a fair profit both to landlord and tenant. Supposing the measure of his honourable friend, the worthy baronet (Sir Henry Parnell), to be adopted, then would the increase in the price of grain go on, depending not on the value but on the depreciation of the commodity. The poor lists of the different parishes in the country, he contended, were loaded with persons perfectly able to exist by their labour, were it not for the high artificial price of commodities. It was only by those artificial prices that the poor were prevented from living, without being burdensome on the community.⟩

1. On 11 May the Select Committee on the Corn Trade of the United Kingdom had presented its report along with a series of resolutions, the most important of which provided for the free exportation of corn from the United Kingdom without duty or bounty and the importation of corn for home consumption under a graduated scale of duties. On 15 June Sir Henry Parnell, who had been chairman of the Select Committee, called the attention of the House to the report and moved for a committee of the whole House to consider the report. Lord Archibald Hamilton moved an amendment 'That the Report be taken into consideration this day three months'. The Chancellor of the Exchequer opposed the amendment and spoke in favour of the resolutions. Then Horner rose to express astonishment that the Chancellor of the Exchequer would lend his authority to the principle of a graduated tariff on imported grain, and expounded briefly. The amendment was nonetheless lost by a vote of 136 to 32, but after further discussions in the House the following month the intention to proceed with a bill was for the time being abandoned in the face of vociferous public protests. (*Hansard*, xxvi. 643–70, 812–15, and 986–7.) Parnell, however, produced revised proposals in May 1814 (Doc. 530).

502. From T.R. Malthus

Kinnordy MSS ⟨*Economica*,
New Series, xxi (1954), 331–3⟩[1]   Brightelmston, 16 June 1813

⟨I did not expect that the discussion on the corn trade would have come on so soon. I have just looked over the report[2] which you were so good as to send me, and should be inclined to agree with you in thinking that the present state of things does not seem particularly to require the interference of Parliament. I cannot however agree with you in the opinion you seem to hold, that restrictions upon importation have no tendency to encourage the growth of an independent supply of corn. There is certainly reason to doubt their policy on other grounds, that is on the ground of the wealth which you sacrifice to attain this particular object; but I cannot, without violating what appear to me to be some of the most fundamental principles of Political Economy, believe, that an increase in the relative demand for home corn will not produce an increase in the relative supply. In 1803 the price of the quarter of wheat fell to 56 shillings; and I by no means feel persuaded that the smaller importations of foreign corn which took place subsequently to 1804, were not occasioned by the laws of that year. There was no great change in the value of money from 1804 to 1809. With regard to the small importations of 1812, notwithstanding the enormous price of 124 shillings (a rise of above 30 percent) compared with the year before, it must, I think, chiefly be attributed to the difficulty of obtaining corn on the continent rather than to a growth at home equal to our wants.

⟨If there were no corn laws whatever I am decidedly of opinion that our general wealth would increase more rapidly, but I think that we should not so nearly grow our own consumption as at present. If Europe were like one large nation with regard to importation and exportation, its cultivation would proceed like the cultivation of a large nation; and it could never answer to bring *indifferent* land under tillage in one district, until the *good* lands in other districts, from which there was an easy communication, were first cultivated.

⟨England in reference to Europe may be considered as a large manufacturing district, with the natural tendency of such a district to import a considerable part of its corn, though with a power of growing it, if forced. In using this force there is reason to believe that we shall check our manufactures more than we shall increase our agriculture, and this it appears to me forms the true argument against the system; an argument surely of great weight although we allow that an independent supply is practicable by such means.

⟨With regard to moderate and steady prices I do not see how they are to be accomplished in this way. Until the independent supply is obtained the price will be at or above the price at which importation is allowed, and afterwards a little excess of supply not being relievable by exportations, on account of the general high prices of corn at home I doubt if prices would be steady. The great argument for the Report is an independent supply – not lowness or steadiness of prices.

⟨I don't quite agree with you about the interest of the landlords. High nominal prices of corn appear to me to be advantageous as it gives them a greater command of all their commodities the materials of which are foreign. But one never ought to hear the interests of landlords and farmers. The report and evidence is faulty in this respect, and conveys an improper impression. . . .⟩

1. Where it is printed as an appendix to G. S. L. Tucker's 'The Origin of Ricardo's Theory of Profits', pp. 321–31. The source is given simply as 'Horner Papers', which in the circumstances would have been thought to be the collection in the BLPES; but it is not there. The present editors have not seen the MS, having had made available to them at Kinnordy a typescript only; but that typescript differs only slightly from the printed version.
2. Not identified.

503. To Lord Grenville

BLPES v. 313–14 〈Horner, ii. 135–6;
〈Buckingham, ii. 36–7〉   Lincoln's Inn, 22 July 1813

. . .

〈A singular political event, and one not very intelligible, was announced last night; that Canning has formally, and with some solemnity, disbanded his party; telling the gentlemen who have been his supporters during the session, that they may for the future, consider themselves as unengaged; and that he is to no longer be regarded as their head.[1] Ward says they are all turned adrift upon the wide world, but as he has stayed a year in his place, he thinks himself entitled to a good character from his master. He had his discharge from the mouth of Canning himself, the day before yesterday; and the same notification was made to Mr Robert Smith yesterday. The only other circumstance I have yet heard, connected with this strange incident, is, that Wellesley Pole has been complaining very much that Canning did not bring matters to bear with the Ministry, and that he is now considered both by the Marquis his brother, and by Canning, as perfectly free to do what he can in that way for himself. Whether this is a deep measure, or the sudden effect of some ill humour; and whether Canning, in reducing his establishment thus abruptly, points towards Government or Opposition; I have heard nothing yet that enables me to guess. But very erroneous ideas these men must have of party connection, or indeed of political morality, who consider their parliamentary associations as held together and as dissoluble without any reference to opinions.[2]

〈. . .〉

1. Although he had enjoyed something of a triumph in his contribution to the recent Catholic debates, Canning himself had reason by this time to despair of ever regaining office and when approached by one peripheral member of his group – Wellesley's brother, William Wellesley-Pole – abruptly decided to relieve them all from their allegiance. (Wendy Hinde, George Canning (1973), pp. 265–6.)
2. Grenville's reply of 25 July, in which he lamented the negative effect of Canning's behaviour on all party connection and observed that Canning would be 'a desirable acquisition indeed to a government so unusually weak as this is in the House of Commons' debate', is published both in Horner, ii. 138, and in Buckingham, ii. 38–9.

504. To J.A. Murray

BLPES v. 332–3 〈Horner, ii. 140–42〉   Cheltenham, 31 Aug. 1813

. . .

〈Will you have the goodness . . . to give me some information with respect to the state of the Review, you being one (I am told) of the Commissioners for executing the office of Editor, during the absence of King Jamfray beyond seas.[1] If possible, I wish to make some contribution to the next number, because he particularly expressed a wish that I should, and that is my reason for passing next month, as I propose, in London, instead of coming to Edinburgh, which upon my father's journey thither being determined upon, I felt much inclination for. When is it necessary that articles should be ready for the next number? and can you suggest any thing for me to do? There are a great many subjects which I should be very averse from being known to write about anonymously, and almost all remaining subjects are beyond my means of information. If you could devise two or three short easy articles for me, that is what I should like best. Is there any new work, a mere analysis of which would be thought passable, such as Eustace's *Travels in Italy*? or must the evil fashion of the *Review* be still adhered to, of writing dissertations beside the work?[2]

⟨. . .⟩

1. Jeffrey, whom Horner had nicknamed 'King Jamfray' some years earlier, was visiting the USA.
2. A lengthy and generally favourable notice by Brougham and Edward Daniel Clarke of John Chetwode Eustace's *Tour through Italy* had appeared in *ER* xxi (no. xlii, July 1813), 378–424.

505. To Anne Horner

Byrne Memoirs, pp. 153–4 (copy)   London, 20 Sept. 1813

I picked up some scraps of poetical news from Rogers: Mr Moore, whose conduct lately has done him so much honour, is not wasting all his time upon the excellent squibs which appear in the *Morning Chronicle*, but is at work upon a large poem, by which he may bid for more permanent fame; it is to be a story, a Persian one – he has been reading hard for it.[1]

Lord Byron goes on adding a hundred lines to the 'Giaour' from day to day: it is now swelled to more than 1,200.[2] His habits of writing are peculiar, and show a rare facility. Rogers says, he often keeps his carriage at his bookseller's door all the morning while he stops to pour out some new verses. There may be some thing done in this way, but with all this show or reality of ease, Lord Byron lives a great deal alone, and works hard. There is no other way to such eminence as his. He describes himself, I am told, as pouring out his verses by the ear and tune, and then he sets himself to give them meaning. This of course is an exaggeration . . .

1. Moore made several unsuccessful attempts to supply a fashionable 'Eastern' poem, for which Longman's had undertaken to pay the highest price ever of £3,000, and *Lalla Rookh* was not finished until 1816.
2. By the date of the 5th edition in the autumn the *Giaour* had reached 1,400 lines.

506. To J.A. Murray

⟨*Horner*, ii. 145–6⟩   London, 29 Sept. 1813

⟨. . .

⟨I am impatient to have a talk with you about continental politics; about which, my warlike feelings have now spread from Spain to Prussia. It seems certain, that the immense loss of veterans and officers in the Russian campaign has, for a long time to come, impaired the vigour of the French soldiery; and also, that there is at last a strong national spirit roused into action in the north of Germany. The independence of those nations may yet be restored; and the Continent saved from that military despotism which two years ago seemed irresistible. But there are a thousand things to discuss, before you will allow me to acquiesce in this conclusion, I know; I am the more anxious to be kept right, because I suspect many of our Whig friends do not move so fast as I have been going for the last six weeks.[1] What a singular fate is Moreau's![2] The loss of his advice to the allies, an incalculable injury. His military fame will probably be heightened with posterity, by the last passage of his life, not only for the confidence which Europe felt in his name, but for the greatness of that design with which he opened the campaign. His moral reputation is, according to my sentiments of such conduct, stained with guilt, by taking arms against his country; though there are casuists, and I know some rigid ones, who deny there is any indefeasible allegiance, and hold him to have been absolved by banishment; I cannot, however, see it in that light; and his joining the allies, like a Swiss, or a Condottiere, whether excited by hatred of Bonaparte or by love of arms, strikes me as one of the many instances which the French Revolution affords, though on occasions mostly of a different sort, of that deficiency of moral principle without which no historical greatness is to be attained.⟩

1. Serious differences of opinion had appeared among Whig leaders several days earlier when word reached London that the armistice between the combatants in Germany had been broken by the Allies' rejection of a French proposal for peace. (See Taylor, pp. 360–62.)
2. Gen. Jean-Victor Moreau (1763–1813), who had assisted Napoleon in his *coup d'état* of 1799 but later become his rival and migrated to America after unsuccessfully plotting his assassination, had returned to Europe during the 1813 armistice and offered his services to the Allies as one who knew the secrets of Napoleon's strategy. He became a particular favourite of the Tsar, but was mortally wounded while observing the Battle of Dresden on 26 Aug. 1813.

507. From John Allen

BLPES v. 354–6   Holland House, 20 Oct. 1813

What progress is made in printing the *Review*? I have begun an article on the history of the Poor Laws, in which I hope to make out that they were not occasioned by the suppression of Convents but by the depreciation of money in the 16th Century. As far as I can make out, the ordinary wages of labour in the end of the 15th Century produced to the Labourer more than twice as much of the necessities of life as in the latter part of the 16th Century when the system of Compulsory Poor's rates was finally settled.[1] . . .

I fear there will be a small attendance of Opposition at the opening of Parliament. Lord Grenville however will be at his post and I suspect he will make a long speech. He is against any overtures for peace and yet seems not sanguine about the success of the War. He rejoices over the advantages that have been lately gained over France and yet laments over the sacrifices made in support of Spain. The Continent he thinks is now properly roused against France. This was the state of things which he always foresaw must sooner or later happen and for which he should have wished our resources to have been husbanded, instead of having lavished them as we have done in the Spanish war. He forgets that it was the resistance of Spain that encouraged Russia to resist, and that it was the misfortunes of the Russian Campaign that encouraged the Germans to take up arms.

. . .

Whishaw and Dumont left us on Monday. Whishaw is in town but Dumont is gone to Bowood.[2] He and Madame de Staël have come to an explanation about the *Principes*. She is no longer to attack the doctrine of Utility whenever she happens to meet with him in society. She and her daughter follow him to Bowood.[3] Now that Mackintosh is gone . . . her society in London, as far as I can learn, is composed of Ward, Perry, Curran and Godwin. Ward, as you probably know, is universally suspected of having written the review against Mr Fox in the *Quarterly*, and from the tone in which Perry of the *Morning Chronicle* speaks of him I am sure he has been doing something wrong, as nothing but fear could have made him behave with so much civility to Perry as from Perry's expressions with regard to him he seems latterly to have done.[4]

1. Allen's review of Juan Sempere y Guarinos' account of the poor laws in his *Biblioteca Española Económica-política* appeared in *ER* xxii (no. xliii, Oct. 1813), 184–98.
2. According to *Fox*, p. 79, Dumont was 'a constant visitor and universal favourite with the inmates of Bowood and Lansdowne House'.
3. For accounts of Madame de Staël's visit to Bowood by J.W. Ward and Dugald Stewart's daughter, Maria, see *Letters to 'Ivy'*, pp. 218–21.
4. The notice in *QR* ix (no. xviii, July 1813), 313–28, of the posthumous *Correspondence of Gilbert Wakefield with C. J. Fox, 1796–1801, chiefly on classical literature* (1813), had indeed been written by Ward (Shine).

508. From John Whishaw

Kinnordy MSS   Lincoln's Inn, 21 Oct. 1813

. . .

You have, of course, seen a very artful and malignant article against Mr Fox in the last number of the *Quarterly Review*. It is not exactly known who was the author of it, but it is universally attributed to Ward. Unfortunately it is very much the best article in the Number which upon the whole, is a very indifferent one.

It is now confidently stated that Abbot will be advanced to the Peerage; and Charles Sutton will of course succeed to the Speakership.[1] The principal business of Parliament before Christmas is expected to be financial – the sanctioning a new scheme for raising the amount of the necessary subsidies by Debentures payable 6 months after the next general peace and guaranteed by the three powers of Russia, Austria and Great Britain. This plan, originally devised by D'Ivernois, has been talked of for some time and was alluded to in the *Moniteur*, but it seemed so wild and extravagant that I gave no serious credit to it till I was positively assured by Sharp that it has been under the serious consideration of Vansittart, whose sole object it is to avoid immediate taxation.[2] The scheme is entirely disapproved of by A. Baring and all the intelligent men of the City, as being likely to cause great depreciation of the public securities, and ultimately to provoke the greatest financial disorders. You will, of course, understand that the payment of the interest as well as principal is to be postponed till after the Peace.

Sharp takes the matter very much to heart, and has talked to Romilly who says he will speak up it, though quite unaccustomed to financial discussions. I hope you will take some part in the debates on this most important question; which besides the interest naturally belonging to it is immediately connected with your Bullion question. . . .

1. Charles Manners-Sutton indeed succeeded Abbot as Speaker, but not until June 1817 when he easily defeated the Whig candidate. On 22 July 1813, when he had conveyed to him a strong hint from the Prince Regent that it might be time he retired, Abbot had replied that he 'had no such thoughts, and looked forward to a continuance of [his] present labours'. Later that same day, however, he made some unprecedented remarks in reference to the Catholic question when responding formally to the Prince's Address to Parliament and by them provoked the anger of the Opposition and a major procedural row. But he was a great and popular Speaker and in April 1814 a censure motion against his conduct in the matter was decisively defeated. (*Colchester*, ii. 452–64 and 483–96.)
2. Sir Francis D'Ivernois (1757–1842) was a Swiss exile in British service. The reference is perhaps to his *Effets du blocus continental sur le commerce, des finances, le crédit et la propriété des isles britanniques* (1809).

509. To John Allen

BLPES v. 357–8 ‹*Horner*, ii. 146–7›   Edinburgh, 25 Oct. 1813

I got your letter last night, upon my return from Kinneil. About one third of the *Review* is printed, and I am authorized to tell you that your article will still be in time, if it arrives in the course of ten days; as the number will not be published before the middle of next month.[1] The article upon the ancient constitution of Spain is printed, and I have read it with great satisfaction; it is very perspicuous, and the information it contains both important and new, particularly upon the origin of corporations. I would have you, for your own use hereafter, if not for the sake of all whom such curious information concerns, to make references, upon a copy of this dissertation, to the chronicles and other authorities from which the facts are drawn; for this purpose, I will desire Murray to return your MS. . . .

. . .

⟨Your account of the view which Lord Grenville is expected to take of Continental affairs, in a speech upon the first day of the session, has relieved me from an anxiety which I felt on that subject; for I have had fears, that we were to make the same false step respecting this German war, that has been so fatal to the party, and deservedly so, with respect to the Spanish cause. That the financial difficulties of the country will be increased by our embarking so deeply with the allies, as I think we ought to do, is true and ought not to be disguised; that the sanguine expectations, professed by the friends of Government, of a speedy settlement of the affairs of Europe, have apparently no just foundation in the present aspect of them, ought likewise in my opinion to be stated: but I cannot hesitate now in believing, that the determination of the French military force, and the insurrection of national spirit in the North of Germany, form a new conjuncture, in which the Whigs ought to adopt the war system upon the very same principle which prompted them to stigmatize it as unjust in 1793 and as premature in 1803. The crisis of Spanish politics in May 1808, seemed to me the first turn of things in a contrary direction; and I have never ceased to lament that our party took a course, so inconsistent with the true Whig principles of continental policy, so revolting to the popular feelings of the country, and to every true feeling for the liberties and independence of mankind. To own that error now, is a greater effort of magnanimity than can be asked for; but the practical effects of it will gradually be repaired, if a right line of conduct is taken with respect to German affairs.⟩

I wish you would be at some pains to ascertain what truth there is in the story, that Ward is the writer in the *Quarterly Review* of that rascally article upon Wakefield's correspondence; I cannot believe it – but am anxious to know, as I shall try to give a few pages upon the same subject.[2]

⟨. . .⟩

1. Allen's piece on the Poor Laws (see Doc. 507) appeared along with that on Dr Francisco Martinez Marina's *Essay on the Ancient Legislation of . . . Leon and Castile* in ER xxii (no. xliii, Oct. 1813), 50–67 and 184–98.
2. See Doc. 507. *Wakefield's correspondence with Fox* was not noticed in the ER.

510. To Lord Webb Seymour

BLPES v. 359–61 ⟨*Horner*, ii. 147–9⟩   Edinburgh, 26 Oct. 1813

⟨I received your letter of the 14th instant and took it very kind that you gave me some account of the proceedings of our Berkeley Street party, after I left it; in the fate of which, and all its doings, I felt so lively an interest.[1] Those few days, and the week we passed at Cheltenham, continue to afford me much gratification in the recollection of all we enjoyed, and in the confidence that I have added to the number of my friends Lady Carnegie and one or two of her daughters.² It was a very pleasing sequel to the period we had spent together, to have a couple of days at Minto, to communicate my impressions to Lady Anna Maria, and compare them with her judgements of her friends, which are so discriminating, and yet so affectionate.³

⟨Your guess was correct by halves, as to my occupations at Minto; the state of Europe I discussed with William Elliot, and found we entirely coincided in our view of the new conjuncture which marks the present year, as well as of the conduct which ought to be pursued in Parliament with regard to it.⁴ My notions I had imperfectly communicated to you before; it was delightful to me to have them cleared, and raised, and confirmed by Elliot's sagacious and comprehensive ideas.

⟨I spent the best part of two days at Kinneil last week; my two sisters, Playfair, Murray, and Thomson, formed the party. You will understand that I was highly gratified; with nothing more, however, than to see them both so well, particularly Mr Stewart, whose robust and tranquillised health makes me hope to see him live to the age of Plato, and continue writing to the last. I had 472 printed pages of his new volume⁵ in my hands, ran through a considerable portion of it cursorily, and read one or two chapters with ease; particularly one in which he has placed the doctrine of the Nominalists with regard to general ideas in so striking and clear a light, that no Conceptualist, I think, will any longer surmise that there is any shadow of a general idea; he has been remarkably fortunate in illustrating the use of signs in reasoning, by tracing the history of a student's mind, as he learns the first book of elementary geometry. We shall hear, however, what Dr Thomas Brown has yet to say for the conceptualists; Playfair, I was surprised to find, leans to the same heresy. It seems probable that Stewart's remarks upon the writings of Aristotle, and upon the use which has been made of them in modern times, will excite a little commotion and do a little good at Oxford. They will still make some fight for Dr Aldrich;⁶ but he is fast on his way to the catacombs. If the Stagirite himself could be *provoked* to hear such things, he would, I make little doubt, be far more proud of Stewart's estimate of his merits, and of the ground on which *he* rests his fame, than of all the⟩ ignorant ⟨devotion of all the doctors in convocation.⟩

There is a remarkable improvement in the export trade, and by consequence in the demand for manufactures. I heard something of this as I passed through Lancashire; old [James] Watt, who came from Glasgow the other day, says they talk of it there as a more sudden revolution than they remember in any former period; and I have seen a letter from Loch, who states, that the same change for the better has taken place in the Staffordshire potteries.

. . .

1. Seymour's letter of 14 Oct. has not been found.
2. The widowed Lady Carnegie had ten daughters, all of whom were then unmarried.
3. Apart from Lady Holland and, briefly in the winter of 1800–1801, a distant but beautiful relation called Charlotte Grahame, Lord Minto's eldest daughter, Anna Maria Elliot, afterwards Donkin (d. 1855), was the nearest Horner ever seems to have had to a female friend outside his own family. He had known her for some years, but by his own account had taken 'the first step in real intimacy' only during his Scottish trip in the autumn of 1812 when he stayed some days at Minto. He wrote to his sister Frances in a letter probably written in late 1813 or early 1814:

She has great merits of every sort, and I only rate her understanding inferior to her goodness of heart. She has seen a great deal of the world with quick eyes and a candid judgement. Her lively way of describing minutely all that is ridiculous, of which nothing escapes her, makes her a very agreeable companion, when one knows her real worth and benevolence, and how surely she is to be relied on.

Lady Anna Maria had something of a reputation as a bluestocking and nearly a decade earlier Horner had written, with reference to Sydney Smith's lecture audience at the Royal Institution: 'Your chemists and metaphysicians in petticoats are altogether out of nature, that is when they make a trade or distinction of such pursuits; but almost all women are well-made, and when they take a little general learning as an accomplishment, they keep it in very tolerable order.' His surviving letters to the learned but delightful Lady Anna Maria commence on 27 Oct. 1813 and terminate only a few days before his death. (Byrne Memoirs, p. 41; Horner to Seymour, 27 Sept. 1812, BLPES v. 231–2; to Frances Horner, 'Wednesday' [late 1813 or early 1814], Kinnordy MSS; to Murray, 15 Nov. 1804, BLPES ii. 161 ⟨Horner, i. 296⟩; and to Lady Anna Maria Elliot, 1813–1817, NLS MSS 11103.)

4. William Elliot of Wells (1766–1818), a distant relative but a near neighbour of the Earl of Minto and MP for Peterborough, had been an intimate friend of Burke and Windham and Chief Secretary for Ireland in the Ministry of All the Talents.

5. The second volume of *Elements of the Philosophy of the Human Mind* (1814).

6. Henry Aldrich (1647–1710: *DNB*) was the author of a small *Artis Logicæ Compendium*, which was first published in 1691 and despite Horner's predictions continued sufficiently in use as a text-book to be last reprinted in 1862.

511. To J.A. Murray

BLPES v. 362–5   Lincoln's Inn, Friday [5 Nov. 1813]

. . .

We heard of this glorious news, which changes the whole fate of the world, before we reached London.[1] Lord Grenville's speech last night quite satisfied me. It is lamentable that we had nobody in the House of Commons, to state the same views, and use the same language. Whitbread's speech was very well for him, and more discreet and reserved than was expected: but reserve is any thing but what I wished to hear; the Opposition ought to have adopted the war of the allies, and to have marked on the first day the sentiments which belong to the new conjuncture in which affairs are placed. I heard none of the young speaking except Charles Grant, if he can properly be styled a young one, for any reason but the youthfulness of his mode of speaking. It is not in the least to my taste. Considerable command of language, undoubtedly, he shows; but there is a very thin substance of thoughts in his declamation; and what is a more capital defect, his declamation last night seemed to me, with all his rhetorical talk of sentiment, really defective in point of feeling, public feeling (I mean) for the great interests he was set up to declaim upon.[2]

I think I have sufficient grounds to tell you for certain, that Ward is *not* the author of the article in the *Quarterly Review* upon Wakefield's correspondence. The remarks in the *Morning Chronicle* in reply to that article, were written by Adair; I have not yet seen them; Whishaw says they are very indifferent. Tell Thomson what I have said respecting Ward; the story was very current in London, and was considered as a very serious charge against him; I am really happy to find that I was right, in giving it no credit.[3]

The East India Directors, to my great delight, decided yesterday, by a majority of 15 to 9, to negative the appointment of Wallace as Governor of Madras. The Ministers had made a great effort to save him from this disappointment and disgrace: originally it was proposed to the Directors as a nomination by the Board of Control, and they rejected him by 23 to 1. Then the Ministers made it a Cabinet measure, and in that pure and upright body they contrived to gain over *eight* votes, but that was not enough. The Holy Ghost and his followers are frightened at the explanation of their own courage, and do not know what is to follow; Government threatens them with an act to take away their veto upon such appointments.[4]

House of Commons, 5 o'clock

There is no more news this afternoon, no account yet of Bonaparte's escape. It is understood that he pushed on with his body of cavalry, ten thousand strong, leaving the two columns of infantry to find their way. He must have got to Paris; there have been no papers from France for four or five days, which proves that the course of authority in the capital has not been disturbed.

1. The Battle of Leipzig (16–19 Oct. 1813).
2. Intent on preserving harmony among themselves, the Whigs moved no amendment at the opening of the session, and Whitbread expressed very moderate views in the Commons. Provoked by Wellesley's pacific remarks, however, Grenville violated his agreement with the Foxite leaders by adopting a belligerent stance and by representing the present difficulties of the French as a vindication of both Pitt's system and his own efforts as Pitt's Foreign Secretary. (For what is evidently a poor report of Grenville's speech, see *Hansard*, xxvii. 11–22, and for those of Wellesley, Grant, and Whitbread, *ibid.*, 8–10, 29–38, and 38–41. See also *Holland's Further Memoirs*, pp. 183–4, and Taylor, pp. 366–9.)
3. See Doc. 507. The MC of 25 Oct. had printed three columns of 'Remarks on the calumnies against Mr Fox in the *Quarterly Review*' by 'A Whig of the Old School'.
4. The opposition to the appointment of Thomas Wallace, afterwards Baron Wallace (1768–1844: *DNB*), an anti-Catholic and a member of the India Board, was led by Charles Grant, sen., the devout previous chairman of the East India Co. The minority vote in favour was presumably that of the current chairman Robert Thornton, who had canvassed Wallace's appointment, and whose own election Grant had also tried to prevent.

512. To Anne Horner

⟨*Leonard Horner*, i. 26–7⟩ London, 10 Nov. 1813

⟨. . .

⟨We of the Opposition are all very much satisfied, indeed highly pleased, with the pacific tone and moderation of the speech from the Throne, and *per contra*; there is much praise bestowed by the other side on Lord Grenville's, which I heard, and thought very able as well as right in all its doctrines. So that there never was such harmony and concord since I knew Parliament. How long it is to last is another story. From some things I have heard, I am inclined to believe that the real system of the Cabinet at present is an inclination to peace, and a determination to use all their influence with the allies in keeping them reasonable; and I have further heard, from a quarter entitled to some credit with respect to foreign politics, that up to this moment, there is a good understanding among all of them, and an agreement as to the propriety of offering fair terms to France. Pray tell Mrs Stewart all this, if you see her in Edinburgh, for I made her unhappy by my prophecy of continued war.

⟨My ground of incredulity still would be, that peace can hardly be agreeable to Carlton House; however, they may be satisfied for the present with Hanover, which the Duke of Cambridge is going over immediately to take possession of.[1]

⟨The Bourbons are considered on all hands, as out of the question, though it is not many months since our Regent, in the fullness of his heart, promised to restore them. Monsieur went over upon the strength of this assurance (it is said) to Bernadotte, but met with such a reception in that quarter that he came back without delay, and they have been crest-fallen from that day. It is a great object of curiosity now to see what course Bonaparte takes; there never was a drama, even in fiction, so highly wrought, as what is passing in our own times. I expect he will be stout, and not hear of peace, though if the terms offered be free of insult to the French people, that may prove a hazardous part. But the tones of his last Bulletins, in which he seems to me to express everything but despair, like a man who cannot feel it, makes me look for that part to be assumed by him. Nor should I be surprised, considering the peculiarities of temper he has shown on former occasions, if with this unconquerable spirit he should by degrees break out in all the violence and phrensy of a bloody tyrant, and in the end exhaust the submission of the French, as by his abuse of power, he wore out the patience of the Germans.

⟨Madame de Staël has asked me to dine with her today. I do not know who are to be there, except the Hollands.⟩[2]

1. The Duke of Cambridge, accompanied by Count Munster, shortly departed for Hanover and afterwards administered that state's government, if not liberally, with a degree of skill and tact (Webster, p. 33).

2. There is no further mention in Horner's surviving papers of a dinner engagement with the Hollands and Madame de Staël; but the Earl of Ilchester maintains (*Home of the Hollands*, p. 282) that he dined at Holland House on 8 Dec. in a party that included 'the great lady'. If so, he was surely privy to a warm debate on foreign politics. For Madame de Staël irritated the Hollands with her praise of Pittite foreign policy and her diatribes against Napoleon. Lady Holland despised her from the first, and as early as 17 Oct. Lauderdale had told Grey that Holland had forbidden his wife to associate with Madame de Staël because Lady Holland grew violent in her presence (Grey MSS, Durham University). Interestingly, after 8 Dec. Horner shared Lady Holland's low opinion of Madame de Staël. According to Lady Romilly, as early as August Horner had found Madame de Staël's son 'intolerable' (*Romilly–Edgeworth Letters*, p. 56). Now, in an undated letter to his sister Frances which was apparently written in late 1813 or in the first days of 1814 (Kinnordy MSS), Horner wrote:

   I do not know what authority Thomson has, for saying that I am become a great admirer of Mad. de Staël, after being otherwise. My opinion such as it is has not changed, but in truth I have not seen enough of her to form any fair opinion of her, or to have any thing more than an impression of her manner in large society, as it affects my taste. And certainly it is not of the sort that usually interests me, or leaves much desire to see more of it. Her display of understanding, and rhetorical accomplishments, is enough to make one wonder; but that is too great a strain to please long, and one cannot go day after day to gaze at a conjuror or a rope dancer. She wants gaiety altogether, and in this respect seems not in the least French, though she has wit. She is not feminine, and therefore never interests; and her intellectual exhibition never enlivens: in short, and I might have said it all in that one word, she is *tiresome*. Far better judges, however I must own, think very differently.

Later Horner was very critical of Madame de Staël's published works and displeased with Mackintosh's favourable review of *De l'Allemagne* in the *ER* (Doc. 515).

513. To Mrs Dugald Stewart

BLPES v. 404–405   London, [?18–20 Nov. 1813]

. . .

From what has passed in Parliament, as well as from what I have happened to hear by private conversation, my belief is that the present system of the Ministers, or at least of the predominant majority of the Cabinet, is reasonable and moderate, with respect to the use to be made by the Allies of their conquests in obtaining a continental peace. Their empowering the Russian Court to accept for them the mediation of Austria, if France had agreed to it, and that immediately after our successes in Spain, is a strong act in proof of that disposition; and the temperate, conciliatory language of the speech from the throne, notwithstanding the victory at Leipsic, is another confirmation of the same thing. To what this change of system is to be ascribed – how long it is likely to last – and how far the principles of the Cabinet are those of the Court, are other questions, on which I fear I can give you very little information.

It has been surmised, that the Regent and the favourites think the Ministry too pacific. Canning, you observe, has been bidding for office by declamation addressed to the alleged feelings of the Court, which, I am sorry to say, seem to me pretty prevalent too in the herd of the House of Commons. I should hope, however, that the bulk of Opposition would be prepared, if things came to an issue between Ministry and the Regent upon a question of peace, to give even this Administration their whole strength against him. Nobody as yet talks of the Bourbons; on the contrary, the language at present affected, even by some who most devoutly wish their restoration, is that such a turn of things is out of the question. There is much talk however of reducing France to her ancient limits, and of wresting from her both Holland, the Low Countries, and the Sardinian states.

514. To John Horner

BLPES v. 373–6[1]   [London], Monday [22 Nov. 1813][2]

. . .

The news brought yesterday morning from Holland is one of the most interesting events to this country that could take place, in the progress of undoing the conquests of France.[3] Some communication between this country and people of consideration in Holland must have been going on for a time; for they appear to have been prepared to act, as soon as the retreat of the French, which it was easy to foresee, began to take place. The frequent interviews which the Prince of Orange has had of late with the Minister no doubt were employed in arrangements with a view to this event; and indeed, when the Duke of Bedford took leave of him about ten days ago, the Prince said, he trusted that next time he saw him it would not be in *this* country. The gentlemen who came over yesterday in the character of deputies, are a Baron Perponcher and one of the brothers of M. Fagel the Greffier. They were sent to the Prince of Orange, as Stadtholder: five of the Provinces have declared for him. He is to leave London this morning, and it is expected that 4,000 troops will be embarked as early as Wednesday, to be followed by more.⁴ The French army were suffered to retire without molestation, though some of the Douaniers are said to have been massacred by the populace. As soon as the French troops quitted the several towns, bands of National Guards were instantly formed. The chief frontier towns are taken possession of . . . Even if these occurrences should not end in the restoration of Holland as an independent republic, upon its ancient constitution, they put the Allies for the present in possession of an invaluable military position. But I trust that the spirit of the Dutch people will render any future invasion of their country quite impracticable; the French can never have again that advantage, which laid all Europe open to them, the favour of the common people. The Prince of Orange has no reputation for abilities, but is esteemed for the propriety with which he has borne adversity; I dined once in company with him, with only three other men, and had some opportunity of judging of him; he made no shining figure in conversation, though he talked a good deal, but he seemed informed, and said nothing foolish or pretending; the only thing I remember of his conversation pleased me much; he was speaking of his son and how he had distinguished himself in Spain, and he said if he had had a dozen sons they should all have been called *William*. His son I have not seen since he was a mere boy; he seems to be popular among our young officers in Spain, which is a good sign; they call him *Dutch Sam*, for his spirit in fighting, and have sundry jokes about a pair of pantaloons given him by our Regent and which proved too tight for him. His campaigning in Spain, and the horses he has had killed under him, will be all in his favour if he has his father's dominions to protect; and a fine part he may have to perform.⁵

. . .

You will not be surprised that our heads are half turned with all this prosperity, and the rapid succession of such great events. People are already talking of Italy and that no peace ought to be made leaving B[onaparte] in possession of the title of that kingdom. His speech, by the mouth of his Senate, on the subject of peace, seems quite a riddle.⁶

. . .

1. A short, misleadingly paraphrased fragment of this letter is published in *Leonard Horner*, i. 30.
2. The earlier part of this letter, not printed here, was begun the previous day.
3. Inspired by news of the French military disaster at Leipzig and with the assistance of Prussian troops, the Dutch had overthrown French rule, opened the Scheldt to an English army, and paved the way for the eventual restoration of the House of Orange.

4. Gen. Baron Hendrik George Perponcher-Sedlnitzky (1771–1856) and Baron Jacob Fagel (1766–1835) had come over to invite the Prince to return. Fagel's elder brother, Baron Henry Fagel (1765–1838), was still known by the title of Greffier in virtue of his former office of Secretary of the States General. The Prince of Orange left England for the Netherlands on 25 Nov.
5. William, Prince of Orange (1792–1849), who became engaged in December to Princess Charlotte only to be twice rejected afterwards, succeeded to the throne of Holland in 1840 after the abdication of his father, William I.
6. The speech was the response to an informal, unsigned offer of peace dispatched by the Allies from Frankfurt on 9 Nov. 1813 which offered France her 'natural frontiers' – the Rhine, the Alps, and the Pyrenees. On 2 Dec. Napoleon accepted the offer through Caulaincourt, his Minister for Foreign Affairs, but by then the successful revolution in Holland had led the Allies to withdraw it.

515. To Thomas Thomson

⟨*Horner*, ii. 149–50⟩   London, [?27–30] Nov. 1813

⟨Allen is very angry, and I own with some reason, at a typographical blunder in the first page of his review of Marina's work on the ancient legislation of Spain.[1] His character of *Mariana* the historian is rendered useless and unintelligible, by the name being erroneously printed four times as if it were the same with that of the author of the work reviewed. You must set this right by putting it in as marked a manner as can be, into a table of *Errata* at the end of this number.

⟨I have read only Mackintosh's two articles, which contain many brilliant passages, and some original speculations.[2] The critique on *L'Allemagne* is an article of much interest, not as a judgement of that work, but as a specimen of Mackintosh himself; not a favourable one, I must own, in some respects; particularly in the bad faith, which scarcely hides itself, in what is said upon the subject of religion. It is very much to be regretted that the *Edinburgh Review*, 'that scourge of impostors, the terror of quacks', has upon this occasion laid by its thunders; when a work was before that tribunal which is calculated to make way for whatever it contains by the reputation of the author, as well as by the genius with which some parts of it are written, and which contains much that is repugnant to good sense and rational morality, as well as vicious in point of feeling. Jeffrey, however, himself set the example, in his account of the same author's work upon literature.[3] Much and lasting injury will be done, wherever the *Edinburgh Review* is read, by the unqualified approbation which it will be understood to have bestowed upon a great deal of nonsense, that looks like fine writing, and a great deal of paradox, artifice, and exaggeration that pretends to the character of good feeling.⟩[4]

1. See Doc. 509.
2. Mackintosh had reviewed Rogers's *Poems* and Mme de Staël's *De l'Allemagne* in *ER* xxii (no. xliii, Oct. 1813), 32–50 and 198–238.
3. Jeffrey had reviewed Mme de Staël's *Sur la Littérature* in *ER* xxi (no. xli, Feb. 1813), 1–50.
4. Horner offered further commentary on Madame de Staël's literary merits in a number of letters. In an undated letter to Mrs William Robert Spencer which was apparently written around this time (BLPES vi. 345–6), he observed that 'One of the most striking defects of

her writing ... is in my opinion the want of what we in this country call *feeling*'. In an undated letter to his sister Anne (BLPES v. 401–402), he noted 'a great deal of exaggeration, and false sentiment, and sometimes stark nonsense' in *De l'Allemagne*. 'There is', he added, 'a great air of presumption, too, in pronouncing upon subjects she has been at no pains to understand. Her ignorance of all English literature is surprising; yet she disposes of all parts of it as fluently, as she does with respect to German.'

516. To Mrs Dugald Stewart

BLPES v. 377   [London], Monday [29 Nov. 1813]

. . .

There seems a little uncertainty at the present moment in the Dutch business, which perhaps will cost some little fighting after all; the Admiral at the Helder having declared for France.[1] Nobody knows where to land. It is said, that the Duke of Cumberland has been intriguing at Hanover, to get himself elected Governor, which gives offence and even uneasiness at home.[2] Lord Yarmouth asked the Duke of Cambridge to let him accompany him, which HRH declined; his Lordship is gone by himself, to land where he can, nobody knows for what purpose, unless to be first in the Dutch market for some money speculations. There is a great reason to suspect, that the Chancellor and one or two others are disposed to support the Regent in extravagant projects of war, against the majority of the Cabinet who are disposed to be reasonable and even pacific.[3] Ministers are all of them, however, very suspicious of the designs of the Crown Prince; before there was any ground for this, if there be any now, the language of Carlton House was full of base ingratitude to the *parvenu*, to whom they are indebted for every thing.

. . .

1. Adm. Count Carel Hendrik ver Huell de Savenaer (1764–1845), the commander of the Texel fleet, remained faithful to Napoleon and held out in the Helder fort until ordered to withdraw upon the abdication.
2. The Duke of Cumberland, who was despised in England by Court, Cabinet, and public alike, had departed for the Continent in early 1813 when Princess Caroline threatened exposure of a number of his past letters abusing the Regent. Once on the Continent, Cumberland petitioned unsuccessfully for a military command, imposed himself on heads of state, and did his best at Allied headquarters to inflame the jealousies of the Austrians and Prussians of the Tsar's primacy in the military councils of the coalition. He entered Hanover as soon as the French had departed, intrigued to obtain the governorship, and was mortified when superseded by the Duke of Cambridge. (Webster, pp. 32–3.)
3. There were undoubtedly differences of opinion within the Cabinet about the peace negotiations, and more particularly over the question of a Bourbon restoration versus an agreement with Napoleon. The following March Liverpool was still complaining that 'it requires every effort of which I am possessed to keep anything like steadiness in our councils'. The Prince Regent was particularly difficult, allowing his support of the Bourbons to be publicly avowed, and to that end exploiting the national hatred of Napoleon. It was therefore by no means unreasonable for Horner to talk of a split in the Cabinet between a peace faction and a war faction; afterwards he and indeed the entire Whig party tended to interpret British foreign policy with an eye to that split. Certainly Liverpool and Castlereagh were less addicted to a fixed idea concerning the result of the war and more

willing to be guided by events than the Regent; and, like the Regent, some Cabinet Ministers no doubt sought from first to last to dethrone Bonaparte and restore the Bourbons. But the Whigs were wrong to think that there was in consequence a clear division within the British Government. All of them, probably, would have preferred a Bourbon restoration; but many were not yet convinced the French people would accept it. The main thing, as Liverpool later wrote to Castlereagh, was to keep the alliance together and for that they must be prepared to negotiate a peace with Napoleon; if the negotiations failed, however, the Bourbon plan remained as an alternative. The Cabinet, then, acknowledged that the course of military events and the need to keep the Allies together must dictate policy as well as tactics, and at length, on 26 Dec., they confided a wide discretion to Castlereagh. Hence also Eldon's role in making the Regent toe the line and the general relief when Napoleon abdicated in April 1814. (Webster, pp. 193–8, 238, and 529; Taylor, pp. 372–5.)

517. To John Horner

BLPES v. 378–80 ⟨*Leonard Horner*, i. 31–2⟩   Lincoln's Inn, 14 Dec. 1813

⟨. . .

⟨The late news from Holland of the usurpation of sovereign authority by the Prince of Orange, and the abolition of the ancient constitution of that state, throw a gloom over the prospect that we lately thought so promising.[1] Resistance to the French no doubt, and emancipation from a foreign yoke, is the first object and duty of the Dutch, and of all the other oppressed states, but nothing can be more unjust than to take advantage of this opportunity to subvert the constitutional freedom of an ancient government, and by an act of usurpation, under the stale pretence of an expression of the popular wishes to change a republic into a monarchy of undefined powers and prerogatives. It may in the end be found impolitic too; it is at all events unprincipled, and a bad omen of the disposition with which this country begins to exercise its influence in the pretended work of restoring Europe to its former institutions.

⟨We see few here but partisans of the House of Orange, who all approve of this measure; Baring, I am sorry to say, among the rest.⟩[2]

1. Upon expelling the French, the Dutch bestowed on the Prince of Orange, not the Stadtholderate, but instead the title of king, which his family had never held. The British Government disclaimed any direct collusion in the measure, but *Holland's Further Memoirs*, pp. 185–6, recalled that some of the Ministers and their supporters at Court 'could not suppress their triumph at the suppression of the very name of Republic, which the fashionable and servile seemed to regard like an indecent word, unfit to be mentioned in company'.
2. Interestingly, Horner eschewed comment in Parliament on European politics until the last day of the session, when he in the Commons and Holland in the Lords posed several questions respecting the terms offered France by the Allied powers in the Declaration of Frankfurt of 1 Dec. (AR lv. 211).

518. To John Horner

BLPES v. 383–5   [London], Thursday [23 Dec. 1813]

. . .

I am inclined to give credit to a story which is circulating today, that Castlereagh intends in person to go to Frankfurt to conduct the negotiation. Under the circumstances, I think he could not do better.[1]

An extract from Bonaparte's speech to the Legislative Body is handed about, in which he is made to say, not only that he has accepted the preliminaries of peace, but, strangely enough, that he does so 'on account of the people and Princes of France.' What this means, I do not pretend to understand; nor would I give any belief to there being an authentic extract from his speech, when we have not the whole, were it not that the gamblers of the City have unusual means of information at present – and upon the faith of this and the other story, the stocks have been rising greatly today . . .[2]

. . .

1. The Frankfurt Declaration included proposals so moderate that it was expected Napoleon would soon accept them; and on 21 and 22 Dec. Castlereagh sent dispatches to his ambassadors announcing his pending departure for the Continent. He left London on 28 Dec., proceeded to the Hague where he discussed the pending marriage of the Prince of Orange and the Princess Charlotte, arrived at the Allied headquarters at Basle on 18 Jan. 1814, and thereafter took personal charge of the negotiations. (Webster, pp. 188–9 and 198–200.)

2. Following the desertion by his allies and his retreat within French borders, Napoleon had informed the Senate on 19 Dec. that he had entered into negotiations for peace (AR lv (1813), 166–7). Evidently Horner learned of this and of Castlereagh's intention to go to Frankfurt at Brooks's; for in an undated letter to George Eden marked 'Brooks's, 4 o'clock' and almost surely written on the same day, he relates identical information as well as an account of Wellington's successful manoeuvres against Soult in the south of France (BL Add. MSS 34459, ff. 70–71).

519. To Sir James Mackintosh

BL Add. MSS 52452   Bowood, 29 Dec. 1813

I hear that Mad. de Staël has very lately, in speaking of our Ministers, been describing them as *all for war*, and that she has been giving some very curious, and, if correct, most important statements, respecting the terms of peace to which Bonaparte *adhered*. Her means of information are so good, and one feels so anxious an interest in this negotiation, that I trust you will pardon me for requesting you, if you can spare a few minutes, to let us know in this part of the world what you hear on these important points, of the real disposition of our Cabinet on the question of peace, and the conditions upon which Bonaparte has manifested a determination to treat.

I am sure that the allusion made to you in the *Examiner* of last Sunday, must have been read by you with the same contempt which all your friends feel about it, and with much more indifference than they can feel about any thing which relates to you.[1] It is evidently the production of some blackguard, who writes from personal animosity, and, provided he gratifies his own malignity for the moment, cares not how much he exposes his ignorance and injustice.

1. Mackintosh's maiden speech in the Commons on 12 Dec. had warned against Allied interference in Switzerland and the Netherlands.

520. From John Allen

BLPES v. 145–6   St James's Square,[1] Wednesday [?5 Jan. 1814]

. . .

I have not yet thought of any subject for a review. Those you mention would not suit me. They would give me more trouble than an apparently more elaborate work and I should do them very ill. I have some thoughts of writing some remarks on the new Spanish Constitution. Now that Spain is pretty sure to recover her independence the work of the Cortes becomes a matter of greater interest . . .[2] By the way have you seen Southey's 'Glory to God and deliverance to Mankind'? It is a very poor thing, garnished with quotations from Brougham's Edinburgh reviews and with sneers at the expense of the Sages of the North.[3] You must have heard of Brougham, Lord Byron and Mme de Staël having been brought together at Ward's. Brougham and Mme de Staël had much conversation. What impression the Lady made on the Gentleman I have not heard, but I suppose it was not a favourable one, for the Lady is not satisfied with the Gentleman, and as to Lord Byron I hear he declares that Brougham has the most odious expression of countenance he ever saw and expresses his satisfaction at not having been introduced to him – a ceremony which you probably know he thinks essential to forming an acquaintance with any one. Lord Byron by the way is again, as Lord Lauderdale calls it, in the press. He is printing a new poem called the *Corsair*, composed in the nature of Dryden.[4]

1. The Hollands rented a house in St James's Square at the opening of every Parliament, and it was there that the Foxites mapped out strategy.
2. Allen's piece on the Cortes of Spain in *ER* xxiii (no. xlvi, Sept. 1814), 347–84, was really a continuation of his review of Marina in the Oct. 1813 number (see Doc. 509).
3. Southey's *Carmen Triumphale*, celebrating the Allied victories of mid and late October 1813 and greeting the commencement of 1814, was reviewed by an unidentified writer in *ER* xxii (no. xliv, Jan. 1814), 447–54.
4. *The Corsair* and *The Bride of Abydos* were reviewed together by Jeffrey in *ER* xxiii (no. xlv, Apr. 1814), 198–229.

521. To T.R. Malthus

BLPES vi. 3–4   Cheltenham, 7 Jan. 1814

I have received both your letters, and have written to my brother . . . begging him to get all the information he can collect for us, respecting the prices of the metals at Hamburgh and Amsterdam, and the exchanges between the two places, first for the three last years, as what we wish most particularly to ascertain; then for the year 1796; for the periods 1761–69, 1775–77, 1781–83, if he can find the materials; and lastly what he can meet with respecting the prices of corn and other domestic commodities for the last four or five years.[1]

. . .

I have not yet read Lord Lauderdale's tract;[2] his general conclusion, in favour of an alteration of the standard, is one in which I do not yet find myself compelled to acquiesce.

I suppose you include me among those who are not disposed, upon those subjects, to take the mean course. My bias is against it, upon most of these subjects, as far [as] the speculative investigation is concerned; for the middle path, almost always the safe one for practice, is rarely the line of truth in general reasonings. At the same time, I own that some of my original opinions about the theory of Exchanges have received some qualifications.[3]

. . .

1. Leonard Horner, who was engaged in an abortive attempt to establish a trading house at Leith, was planning a trip to Holland. Neither of the Malthus letters referred to, nor any correspondence indicating whether Leonard Horner sent the statistics requested, has been found in the Horner MSS.
2. *Further Considerations on the State of the Currency* (Edinburgh, 1813).
3. See Doc. 609.

522. To John Horner

BLPES vi. 24–7   Lincoln's Inn, Wednesday [26 Jan. 1814]

. . .

You will see by the papers today what a progress the Allies are making into the interior of France. Unless however some vast success in a pitched battle, which is not very probable, should open new prospects to their ambition, we may expect to hear very soon of a peace being signed with Bonaparte. Since their armies crossed the Rhine, the allied powers have been undeceived in the idea which before had been impressed upon them, that they would find a disposition in the people of France to demand the restoration of the Bourbons; no symptom of this has manifested itself, or of any desire to exchange Bonaparte's Government for another, though there is a strong spirit of discontent against his wars.[1] It is said, that a dispatch from Lord Aberdeen, acknowledging these facts and stating the effect which this discovery had made upon the councils of Austria, has lowered for a time the insolence and folly of our drunken Regent, who had actually held that conversation with Monsieur about attending the coronation at Paris, which you saw mentioned in one of the newspapers.[2]

. . .

The belief of Government is, I have some reason to think, that Bonaparte has in fact a very considerable force in tolerably good order, particularly as to artillery. His cavalry is said to have fought well, in the affair with the Bavarians near Lunéville. All his marshals, too, appear to be in movement; had his state been quite desperate, we should have probably seen some defections among them.

The most important object to be gained now, either by the terms of the negotiation, or by arms before the treaty, is the possession of Antwerp out of the hands of France. In her hands Holland can have no real independence; and our naval means can hardly be reduced, with a French fleet in the Scheldt. This will probably be the subject of a keen contest.

Ministers disclaim expressly all countenance of the proceedings of the French princes. At a dinner some days ago at Fish Crauford's,[3] who has no delicacy in the measures he takes to satisfy his curiosity, Lord Liverpool and Lord Bathurst being present, he asked one of them directly about their knowledge of Monsieur's journey; and they seemed glad of the occasion to deny in the most pointed terms that it was done with their authority or knowledge. There can be no doubt, however, that the Regent has been giving those princes the most direct and unlimited encouragement. Monsieur is to go to Basle, the Duc de Berry to Guernsey, and the Duc d'Angoulàme to Lord Wellington's army.

The chance of peace depends very much, it is conceived, upon Castlereagh; and his disposition and wish are said to be in favour of it.

. . .

1. Horner's assessment was not entirely accurate; for after the Allies crossed the Rhine and entered France on 21 Dec. 1813, there were several manifestations of French discontent with Napoleon's Government. Perhaps the most notable example came on 29 Dec., when Laine, the member from royalist Bordeaux, read to the French Legislature a report criticizing the mistakes and excesses of Napoleon's Government, praising 'the happy sway of the Bourbons', and congratulating the Allies on 'wishing to keep us within the limits of our own territory, and to repress an ambitious activity which for the last twenty years has been so fatal to all the peoples of Europe'. The Legislature voted overwhelmingly to have Laine's report printed, and Napoleon immediately ordered the session closed. (See Will and Ariel Durant, *The Age of Napoleon* (New York, 1975), p. 720.)

2. Throughout the negotiations of late 1813 and early 1814, the British Government assumed that peace would be made with Napoleon; and despite several indiscretions by the Regent and a great deal of speculation in English newspapers, Liverpool and Castlereagh, convinced that the time was not ripe to open so delicate a question, ensured that no official document mentioned the possibility of dethroning Napoleon (Webster, p. 197). George Hamilton Gordon, 4th Earl of Aberdeen (1784–1860: DNB), formerly the ward of Pitt and Dundas, had been sent to Vienna as special ambassador in Aug. 1813.

3. John Craufurd (d. 1814), familiarly known as 'Fish', had been a friend and associate of Fox and MP for Renfrew in 1774–1786.

523. To Francis Jeffrey

BLPES vi. 37–8   Lincoln's Inn, 12 Feb. 1814

. . .

In coming back from the new world, you do not return to the old one which you left.[1] Was there ever so mighty a change in so short an interval? But the events which we have already witnessed, seem but a prelude to others still greater. Though my expectation at the present moment is that we shall have a peace signed, the future prospect beyond that seems altogether uncomfortable, and full of wars that must recommence after a short breathing. France is not a country that can submit long to a sense of being humbled and disgraced in its military character; and the partition of all the territories that have been so rapidly regained, with the adjustment of new forms of government and contested claims of property in the States that are to be erected again, will afford her Government, whatever it may be, ample opportunities for disturbing the continent and fomenting quarrels.

I never knew the public opinion of England in such a fever as it is at present. Though a peace with Bonaparte is the most rational measure that we could adopt, under the favourable circumstances which have arisen for making it, yet I am convinced that the bare majority of the Ministers who adhere to Lord Liverpool, and a small portion only of the Opposition, are all the numbers that, at this time, could be mustered in favour of it. Peace, I scarcely entertain a doubt, will be signed; but it will be received with execration in England, unless the allies should meet with some adverse fortune, which seems now quite improbable. It is not so much a wish to see the Bourbons restored, that actuates people at present, except the Court and its partisans, as a thirst for Bonaparte's blood. For myself, hating his character as much as they do, I should rejoice to see him fall by the just vengeance of the French people, if they had virtue enough to protect their own independence and establish a national government for themselves. But the restoration of the Bourbons by foreign arms would, in every point of view that I can take of the future fortunes of Europe, be the greatest of all calamities that *now* can happen to public liberty; and only second to that evil, from which we are now delivered, the military despotism of France.

. . .

1. Jeffrey had recently returned from the US with his new, American bride, Charlotte, a daughter of John Wilkes's American nephew Adm. Charles Wilkes and a close relation of Jeffrey's uncle. She was also not to everyone's taste, Henry Fox writing in May 1822 (*Fox*, p. 118): 'Mrs Jeffrey is a poor creature and not worth crossing the Atlantic for; she seems good-natured and inoffensive, but has St Vitus' Dance and is very silly.' Evidently Horner heard some such denigration and wrote to his mother on 6 Jan. (BLPES vi. 1–2):

    May I ask it of you, as a particular kindness, to show some attentions to his American bride; the gossips of Edinburgh are so unaccommodating, that unless she is to their taste at once, she will be made to feel herself in a new society without friends.

524. To John Horner

BLPES vi. 39–42   Lincoln's Inn, 18 Feb. 1814

... the difference of opinion which was known to exist before Lord Castlereagh's journey, has probably given the Regent a handle for intriguing with such of them [the Ministers] as are of his mind, and may have led some of those, in their language to him, to forget their honour to their absent colleague. The progress of events, too, has furnished the war party in the Cabinet with plausible grounds for rising in their language. The disputes and dissensions have much more probably taken place between the Regent and his Prime Minister; the former of whom has sworn upon his sword in a dress coat that he will restore the Monarchy of the Bourbons, and gave Monsieur a promise that he would not be among the last to attend the Coronation, provided they would have that ceremony at Paris instead of Rheims; the latter, on the other hand, knowing the necessities of the Treasury at home, and the views of the Cabinet of Austria, has a clear conviction that the only rational conduct for this country is to be included in the peace which Austria will make.[1] I am afraid, however, that Lord Liverpool has not nerves for a resignation, or even for a threat of that sort, especially in the present madness of the public opinion; and I therefore give a good deal of credit to what I find is the impression of some persons, that there has recently (that is, since Sylvester[2] the first messenger arrived from Chatillon), been a sort of compromise, by which the peace Ministers have yielded to the Regent a little delay in point of time, to see what the Allies can do for the Bourbon cause by occupying Paris. ... This compromise, if it has been made, is in truth a surrender of the whole question; and the delay may very probably deprive us of the opportunity there has been of bringing France to sign a peace in her state of humiliation, and may open to Bonaparte a new career of military successes. The result of the news brought last night seems to be, that he has turned the flank of the Allies, and cut off Blucher from the main army.[3] Some of our military critics speculate upon his having a plan of leaving Paris to its fate.

Orders have been ostentatiously published in Paris, directing the National Guard of the capital, in case of the last extremity, to consider their post of honour to be at the Tuileries, in defence of the Empress and her child.[4] And it is curious, that in all the little theatres Government have directed the old popular historical pieces to be acted night after night, the subjects of which are taken from the reigns of the favourite kings of the House of Bourbon; a proof, how little they apprehend any danger of the national feelings, that such representations must excite, taking any direction in favour of the present descendants of the family. There does not seem to be a corner of France, where there is the least sentiment in their favour, and hardly a knowledge of their existence. The Duc d'Angoulême, who is at Lord Wellington's headquarters, is there under another name.

I cannot make out, from any inquiries I have had an opportunity of making, that any body in this country, is in possession of information, respecting the comparative strength of the Allied and the French armies. There is a growing belief that the latter is in greater force than was at first apprehended.

1. Accurate reports were then circulating in London that while Prussia and the Tsar opposed further negotiations and advocated the conquest of Paris, Austria, fearing the territorial designs of her continental allies, alone stood by the Declaration of Frankfurt, refusing to march unless negotiations were first opened with Napoleon's Government, and indeed threatening to make a separate peace with France. On 17 Feb. Liverpool had written to Castlereagh:

> It was reported and believed yesterday that there were divisions in the Cabinet and that I had resigned. There was as little foundation for the first of these reports as for the last. Be assured everyone is disposed to support you in what you do. (Webster, pp. 202–203 and 523.)

2. Charles Sylvester, King's Messenger, 1795–1824.
3. Presumably Horner refers to Napoleon's victory at Brienne on 29 Jan., when the French surprised Blucher's army, defeating it and almost capturing Blucher himself in a sharp engagement, but failed to pursue the retreating Prussians and failed to cut them off from the other Allied armies.
4. On 23 Jan. Napoleon had assembled the officers of the National Guard in the Tuileries and entrusted to their care the Empress and the three-year-old 'King of Rome'. Next day, amidst defensive preparations in the capital, the Emperor had bid farewell to his wife and child, whom he would never see again, and left Paris to assume personal command of the army he had reconstituted for the defence of France.

525. To J.A. Murray

BLPES vi. 43–4 ⟨Horner, ii. 158–9⟩   Lincoln's Inn, 25 Feb. 1814

. . .

⟨I have read Mr Stewart's new volume with great satisfaction and instruction; it is full of matter, little to the taste of readers of the present day, but highly valuable for every person who in any intellectual pursuit or profession is called upon to correct and strengthen his understanding. Besides, I like these subjects. What seems to me the most complete, as well as original portion of the volume, is all that which treats of mathematical evidence and reasoning. The part I cared for least, is the dissertation upon Aristotle's logic, though it can hardly fail to have some salutary influence upon education in England, provided it provokes anger at Oxford. I wish he had examined more fully, and perhaps with rather more perspicuity, that curious but difficult subject, Analogy, on which he has made some observations that make one regret they are not farther pursued. In his remarks upon the use of final causes in philosophy, he is clear as well as just; but these he might have illustrated more at length; and it would have been a great service, as a practical guide to those who would profit by these remarks, had he brought us nearer to an express rule for distinguishing the use of that auxiliary in scientific inquiry, from the abuses of which it is susceptible in all the sciences. In the present low state of literature, while any thing is the mode but studies of a high aim, this volume may possibly draw less admiration than his former writings, where he had more occasions to illuminate his metaphysical reasonings for popular effect, by applications of moral and critical reflections; but it cannot fail to give greater solidity to his philosophical reputation.⟩

. . .

⟨I cannot pretend to give you any news; for I see nobody that knows more than the newspapers give us. The state of public opinion is an amusing subject of observation at the present moment; I never knew it more violent or more nearly unanimous, though I find myself, by the compulsion of all the reflections that I have been able to make upon this great crisis, in the small minority of those who dread the consequences of the restoration of the Bourbons, or the conquest of France. Some of the wisest men, I know, are praying for and even expecting the restitution of the church lands. The anxiety of this suspense is quite painful; it cannot last much longer.⟩

. . .

526. To J.A. Murray

BLPES vi. 45–6   Salisbury, 13 Mar. 1814

. . .

I perfectly agree with you in giving much credit to *some* of the Ministers, for their entertaining wishes and views for peace, at a time when the whole country has lost its senses upon that subject. Lord Liverpool and Lord Castlereagh, from what I have heard, are the individuals to whom this merit belongs. Unfortunately, a rational view of what is the real interest of England and of Europe in this great question of peace with France, was not enough to insure it, without a corresponding determination and firmness. Liverpool has no ascendancy, and lost every thing by granting to his colleagues and the Regent a little delay, though the whole was a question of time. When the facts of this negotiation come to be known, I suspect it will be seen, that the opportunity of making a peace with France, reduced to the old territories of the monarchy, has been thrown away, chiefly from the delays sought by this country, in opposition to the modest and honest intentions of Austria. That Cabinet, however, has shown much of its habitual feebleness of system, and has yielded in the confederacy of the allies to worse councils, just as Lord Liverpool has done at home in our Cabinet. She ought never to have consented to invade France, but upon a fair consent fully to try the experiment of the Bourbons; if she thought their cause desperate, which I still believe it to be in spite of Mr Descar's fictions from Vesoul and the fibs of Mr Croker in the *Courier*, or if she was disinclined to dethrone the husband of Marie Louise, she ought to have adhered to the [Frankfurt] Declaration of the 1st December, and have insisted upon a congress for peace upon the Rhine.[1] From whichever motive, perhaps from a mixture of both, this, I believe, was her view of what ought to be done; but, without being brought to act boldly upon the other scheme which the Russians and Blucher were for trying, she allowed herself to be induced to act with them upon their plan of invasion retaining still her own wishes as to the event, and accordingly has hitherto had just the sort of success that must pursue half-formed and inconsistent plans of action.[2] What the event is to be, seems now wholly uncertain; the increasing numbers of the allied forces may overwhelm France, and perhaps force upon her by foreign arms for a little while a Bourbon sovereign; I trust, but for a little while; for were such a measure to have permanent success, it would be a calamity, not to France only, but to all Europe, in its consequences to political liberty in every state. I am still sanguine enough to hope, that France may continue to maintain such a resistance against the invaders, as shall secure her independence and lead to a peace, not destructive of her as an integral power on the one hand, and on the other establishing the independence of Italy, Holland, and all the states upon the Rhine.[3]

How different from these views is the language which I am condemned to hear all day long, even from men of excellent understanding!

1. Croker was then contributing a series of pro-Bourbon articles to the *Courier*. Comte François Nicolas René d'Escars (1759–1822) was with the Comte d'Artois on the eastern frontier of France. Liverpool wrote to Castlereagh on 11 Mar. (Webster, p. 524):

    I send you a very curious correspondence in consequence of a letter from Comte François D'Escars on the subject of the reception of Monsieur in France.

    The whole statement I have no doubt is greatly exaggerated and there are some facts in it (such as the offer of the towns to capitulate to Louis, etc.) which must be false. It will show you, however, the temper of mind both of the emigrants and their friends in this country. Our master has got tolerably quiet and reasonable on this subject, but no effort has been spared to influence him upon it.

2. Horner's assessment was reasonably accurate. On 28 Jan. Castlereagh had sided with Prussia and Russia in opposition to Metternich's proposal for a cessation of hostilities while negotiations continued and had convinced Metternich that the changed military situation demanded that the Declaration of Frankfurt be abandoned as the basis of negotiations (Webster, pp. 204–205). That shift in British policy, which brought a degree of harmony among the Allied powers, in effect ended the possibility of a negotiated peace with Napoleon.

3. Horner's view of events on the Continent was largely consistent with that of Lord Holland, who in early 1814 accused the Allies of bad faith towards France, afterwards disparaged the Allies and depreciated the significance of French military defeats, and on 5 Mar. told Grey whimsically that his fondest wish was a coalition between Napoleon and the old constitutionalists and republicans (Taylor, pp. 375–6). On 1 Apr., after Allied forces had entered their capital the previous day, the French Senate convened to compose a constitution and appoint a provisional Government headed by Talleyrand, and a day later declared Napoleon deposed.

527. To Earl Grey

Grey MSS, Durham University   Lincoln's Inn, 16 Apr. 1814

Since you talked to me on Sunday about the Dutch marriage, I have received from another quarter a very strong confirmation of what I then stated, respecting the dislike of the P[rincess] to the residence abroad which is intended to be enforced.[1] A person, in whose accuracy as well as prudence I can perfectly rely, and who has the confidence of Miss Knight,[2] was assured by her some days ago, which assurances were repeated today, that nothing can be stronger than the repugnance of the P[rincess] to the thoughts of being sent into Holland, and the anxiety she at present suffers on the subject. They understand it to be a settled plan, that immediately after the marriage she is to be sent over, and put for two years, or some such period, under the tutelage of the Dowager Princess of Orange. Miss Knight made this communication to my friend, for the purpose of its reaching farther, because she is desirous that the P's sentiments should be known; but of course it is better for Miss K. herself that her name should not be repeated.

The P[rincess] is kept wholly in ignorance of all that is passing, and considers herself as treated with much neglect.

I am going out of town tomorrow morning; but I shall do what I can to arrive [back] in time to give my vote against the Speaker.[3]

1. The proposed marriage of the Princess Charlotte to the Prince of Orange had assumed more than ordinary political significance in view of the extraordinary context of European politics. The engagement had taken place on 12 Dec. 1813, but two days later, when the Princess learned that her future husband expected her to reside in Holland, she had protested violently. In March 1814 she had turned to her legal adviser, Brougham, who desired that the Princess be kept in England, and on 12 Apr., after an exchange of correspondence with the Prince of Orange had confirmed her greatest fears, the Princess had resolved to break off the marriage if it required her leaving England. Formerly Brougham had kept Grey apprised of the developing crisis, and now the Princess turned to the Whig leader for advice. Perhaps distrusting Brougham's account of the situation, and at all events wanting confirmation of the Princess's feelings, Grey, as this letter suggests, turned to the reliable and resourceful Horner. Before receiving this letter from Horner, however, Grey advised the Princess to express her feelings in a letter to her father; and the recommended letter, dated 15 Apr. and almost certainly composed by Brougham, insisted that she must receive an assurance that she would never be required to leave England without her consent. On 9 May the Princess sent an ultimatum to that effect to the Prince of Orange, asking that he seek to influence the British Government, and on 10 June the concession she desired was formally added to the marriage contract. (See New, pp. 101–102.)
2. Ellis Cornelia Knight (1757–1837: *DNB*), lady-companion to the Princess Charlotte.
3. In his prorogation address to the Prince Regent in July 1813, the Speaker, by adverting to a defeated bill, namely, the Catholic Bill, and, as some professed to think showing his approval, Abbot had broken with constitutional precedent. Consequently Morpeth had laid down a motion of censure for 22 Apr., which though defeated was afterwards deemed to have been correct in its view of the constitution.

528. To Lord Webb Seymour

Bulstrode Papers, Bedfordshire County Record Office   Lincoln's Inn, 5 May 1814

. . .

I wish I had leisure to enter into that subject on which you give me a friendly but undeserved rebuke, for suffering the murmurs of party to interfere with the exultation I ought to feel at the late revolution in the affairs of the world. I cannot quite let the opportunity pass, without showing you how nearly we feel alike, upon this great occasion, and hinting at the justification I have in my own mind for the mixture of doubt and apprehension that clouds my joy. It is true, that I have not given way to that unhesitating triumph which has been the almost universal, and I think the most natural feeling of the day; but so far is it from being true, that my coldness and scepticism have a factious origin, that of all the world the men who have exulted most fervently upon this crisis, and to whom I think also it was most natural to exult, are those friends of liberty to whose views of politics I lean habitually and by system. My hesitation and my fears are all of my own making; and are founded partly upon the caution which former disappointments have taught me, and partly upon an anxiety which carries me in all my reflections on politics into that futurity which is necessarily uncertain. Those fears are still strong upon me, though I do own that the moderation with which the allies have hitherto used their conquest has agreeably surprised me, and has convinced me that in the expectations I had formed upon that part of the subject I did them injustice. But though no man can feel more gladly the deliverance of Europe from the military despotism of France, and of France itself from a grinding Domestic tyranny, yet the restoration of the Bourbon family is an event which at the same time I cannot but regret, in the view which I take of its consequences to France and to mankind in general. Their perfidy and incapacity cannot fail to plunge France into new civil troubles, against which they will struggle to protect their throne by the presence of foreign arms. The restoration itself sanctions and confirms all those impressions, which kings and people both had too deep already for the happiness of the world, that men and nations are the mere property of their masters, by rightful inheritance, and that the national choice of governors is a Jacobin chimæra. The return of Bourbons and Emigrants to undisturbed power seemed, at the first, in my mind to threaten us with all the insolence and illiberality of an anti-Jacobin dynasty, under the thraldom of which all the opinions of the 18th century would be consigned to oblivion or to scorn. Some very recent symptoms, I admit, have rather comforted me upon this subject; for there are appearances, that some of the doctrines and truths, the propagation of which too ardently had contributed in some measure to the success of the Revolution, have settled themselves deeply and indelibly in the conviction of mankind, and have a practical influence upon the new arrangements that are forming in different countries. The most important symptom of this is the unquestioned establishment of religious toleration throughout France and the new state of the Netherlands.

I have said enough, I hope, to give you some idea of the state and temper of my mind in contemplating the present conjuncture, and its future probable consequences. If I am not as sanguine as you, you know enough of me to be sure that my inclination, if I would indulge myself, would make me more so; and that it is with a reluctant and impatient submission to what seems to me probable, in that portion of futurity which lies nearest our own days, that I postpone to a greater distance the realization of those improvements in government and in laws which I am confident are ultimately destined for the people of Europe. . . .

529. To Anne Horner

Kinnordy MSS   Lincoln's Inn, Thursday [?12 May 1814]

. . .

. . . I was very sulky about the restoration of the Bourbons, and my joy at the destruction of Bonaparte's power was clouded by its accompaniments, the conquest of France, the dictating a government by Foreign arms, and the injury done to the cause of political freedom by the recurrence to the rights (as they are called) of legitimate sovereigns. What has passed latterly, however, especially the constitution brought over yesterday, has in some measure reconciled me to the event: not that a paper constitution, given to France by a Russian Emperor, if it were guaranteed only by the sincerity of the Bourbon and by the fidelity of Talleyrand, would be calculated now-a-days to take me in. But, so far as it goes, there are some excellent provisions on many material points, and there appears to be a tolerable security for the permanence of these, in the interest to maintain them which is given to the new nobles and revolutionary generals and in the contrivance of the same legislature for two years. What pleases me most, is that there is no recognition of any right in Louis; the throne is offered to him upon conditions, and instead of his being restored to the same monarchy which his ancestors had, he is elected to one regulated quite in another manner. If this can be carried into execution, and substantially maintained, the benefits which France will have gained after all by the Revolution are vast; worth the sufferings she has endured, worth all but the crimes she has perpetrated. But I am far from being credulous about the future; we shall see strange scenes of incapacity and folly, for nothing can exceed the discontent and selfishness of the Emigrants, who cannot fail to have much influence in the new Court and are certain to use it ill; so that the stability of the new order of things depends upon circumstances which nobody can foresee. Talleyrand is for the present the lord of the ascendant.[1]

. . .

1. The constitution to which Horner refers was formulated by the French Senate and announced on 14 Apr. It called for amnesty to the surviving revolutionists, the prohibition of ecclesiastical titles and feudal dues, the confirmation of the redistribution of properties confiscated from the *émigrés* and the Church, the maintenance of a Chamber of Deputies and a House of Peers, the protection of civil liberty, and the sovereignty of the people. On 2 May Louis rejected Horner's favourite provision, the principle of the sovereignty of the people, on the ground that it was inconsistent with his hereditary rights as king by the grace of God and proposed, rather, to 'grant' a 'charter' instead of a 'constitution'. He also proposed a Chamber of Peers chosen by the King and a Chamber of Deputies elected by voters paying three hundred or more francs annually in direct taxes, the two Chambers controlling the revenues and expenditures of Government. The two Chambers accepted Louis' proposed amendments, and the new Government was launched officially on 4 June.

530. Speech by Horner[1]

⟨Horner, ii. 509–11⟩   House of Commons, 16 May 1814

⟨He was anxious to show his reasons for the vote he should give that night, begging this only to be kept in view, that if the principle of preventing the importation of grain was to be adopted, the most effectual mode in which it could be adopted was the best. The right honourable gentleman on the other side had failed in convincing him, that there was any occasion for departing from that system, in regard to the corn laws, which had hitherto prevailed. He was far from thinking that freedom in any trade was bad in itself, or that such a system was impracticable in regard to corn; but he thought it best that the system now in practice as to the corn trade should be kept in view, unless reasons were made out for the departure from it. He was aware that commerce should always give way to higher reasons of state; but it appeared to him that there was here no such reason; and, in addition, it also appeared to him that the present was the very worst season for proposing any change in this system. He could not help particularly remarking the great difference of opinion that prevailed on this second resolution, as to which no two members who approved of it concurred in the reasons on which that concurrence was founded. He was unwilling, therefore, to go into a detail of his reasons why he wished this resolution to be postponed. He did so, taking into consideration the state of the manufactures of this country, and the persons in foreign markets whom we were to meet with. He thought that this resolution ought to be postponed, not because there was not time enough to consider it; but because of the change of circumstances which might be expected to take place with regard to our foreign relations; and because there was not now time for us to see in what posture the trade of this country as to our foreign relations was likely to stand. If the House were to postpone this part of the subject, he should have the satisfaction of thinking, from reflecting on the Bill that had been brought in this day, and to which there was likely to be little or no opposition in any quarter, that the House had done enough in the present session on this important subject, in the recognition of the principle of a free trade in so essential a point. If that Bill was to be maintained and carried through, as he trusted it would, it would eventually, he hoped, improve one principal part of the trade of this country, particularly of the part of the kingdom in which he was satisfied every member of that House felt a deep interest – Ireland. That there was no danger that supplies of corn could at any time be withheld from us when we required them: he argued from this consideration, that at the very period when our enemy had vowed our destruction – when our crops had failed, and when the continental system was in full vigour, we were, in spite of that system, in full supply of corn. If so, what reason had we to be afraid of our agricultural interests on account of the cheapness at home? It was impossible that importation could ever be carried to such a pitch, as to drive out our home-grown corn. The expense of the carriage of so bulky an article alone must always render that next to impossible, added to which, there was the expense of double shipping from the one country to the other. As to the agriculturist, he would gain just nothing at all from the proposition of the right honourable gentleman; and as to poor-rates, there would, at no great distance of time, be occasion for a revision of them, for at present they could be regarded in no other light than as an inefficacious and circuitous way of paying the wages of labour. The extension of home demand and home market was the true stimulus of all agricultural improvement. He should conclude with stating, that this was not a merely agricultural country, but that we depended principally on our commerce and manufactures for that distinguished rank and preeminence which we held in the scale of nations; and he therefore thought it impolitic to adopt any measure, the tendency of which might be ultimately to throw discouragements on the commercial prosperity and resources of the country, from an exclusive and unwise preference of our agricultural interests.⟩[2]

1. On 5 May Parnell revived consideration of the Corn Laws by introducing what he had described as 'essentially different' resolutions, which were then discussed on several occasions during May. The first led to a separate bill, to permit the exportation of corn from any part of the United Kingdom without payment of duty or receipt of bounty, being introduced on 16 May and shortly passing into law. The second and third resolutions met with greater opposition. The second proposed a graduated scale of duties on imported corn of between 24 shillings per quarter when the price of wheat was at or under 63 shillings per quarter, and one shilling when the price should rise to 86 shillings and above; the third proposed that foreign corn should at all times be imported, warehoused, and re-exported free of all duty but made subject to the graduated scale of duties whenever introduced for home consumption. Horner had already spoken against the second resolution on 13 May, when, adverting to the proposed scale of duties, he observed that the 'real interests of the consumer and of the landlord were one and the same' and protested, as he had done in 1813 (Doc. 501), that the effect of the committee's recommendation would be 'to raise the price to the consumer'. Then when discussion on it was resumed on 16 May Horner spoke as follows in support of an amendment to postpone further consideration of the resolutions to that day three months. (Hansard, xxvii. 524, 665–726, and 875–9; Horner, ii. 508–509.)

2. The account of Horner's speech in the Gentleman's Magazine (lxxxiv. 608–609) suggests that he was far more direct in his remarks on the agricultural bias underlying, and the inflationary effects of, Vansittart's support for graduated duties on imported grain:

> Mr Horner begged the House to consider that the adoption of the resolutions would inevitably raise the price of Corn, and that would enhance the price of labour, so that when the cultivator came to cast up his accounts at the year's end, he would find that he had gained nothing for himself, though he had done so much injury to others. Our system was a mixed one, of agriculture and commerce; and it would be necessary to attend to every part of it, and not to endeavour to raise and keep up the one at the expense and the injury of the other.

The amendment was lost by a division of 144 against 27, and next day the second resolution, containing the graduated scale, was agreed to. But once again protests from around the country accumulated and on 6 June the necessary legislation was again deferred. (Hansard, xxvii. 935–55, 962–5, 1021–4, and 1084–1102.)

531. To Frances Horner

BLPES vi. 55–9 (copy of extract)   London, 1 June 1814

. . .

Every day brings some new person from Paris; I have just had a gossip with Francis Adam, one of the last arrivals.[1] My poor friend Eden came yesterday.[2] . . .

. . .

London is wholly occupied at present with two subjects, which rather cross each other: the new indignities cast upon the Princess of Wales, and the preparations for all the shows that are to be made for the Emperor.[3] The impression made by the Princess's letter is strong, and upon the increase; it is well written for effect, by Creevey, if I am not mistaken in the hand; and, to be sure, whatever her own indiscretions, and want of taste and propriety in her conduct have been, it is impossible to feel any thing but indignation at the unmanly behaviour of that poorest of all blackguards the Prince Regent. This is an ill-timed insult; for foreigners must laugh him to scorn for his taking such matters in that way and he will probably find it prudent not to expose himself much to the expression of any opinions on the part of the London multitudes, while the impression of her letter is warm; but must leave all the huzzas to the other Sovereigns. There is to be no limit to expense in all these gaieties. The fire works alone, it is said, are to cost a hundred thousand pounds; forty men have for some time past been employed upon nothing else at Woolwich; when they were first put to this harmless manufacture, they were so little expert, that they had to send for instructors from the play houses.

1. Francis James Adam (1791–1820), brother of W. G. Adam.
2. George Eden had had to return prematurely from France on account of the death of his father, whom he now succeeded as 2nd Baron Auckland.
3. The planned visit to London of the Emperor Alexander and other Allied princes inspired the Queen to plan two drawing-rooms for June. Upon hearing of the drawing-rooms, the Prince Regent informed his mother that, since he would have to attend them, his wife could not. That snub, which confirmed that the Princess of Wales would be barred from all social functions associated with the visit of the Allied sovereigns, served to reconcile differences between Princess Caroline and her daughter and produced letters of protest, written by Brougham and Whitbread on behalf of Princess Caroline, to the Queen, the Regent, and the Speaker of the House of Commons, all of which Brougham sent to the newspapers. The result was a great deal of popular sympathy for Caroline and further embarrassment for the Regent, who was greeted by hisses and groans everywhere he went. (New, pp. 102–103.)

532. To Lady Holland

BLPES vi. 60–61   [London], Friday evening, [3 June 1814]

. . .

The business in the House of Commons this evening took a very good turn, owing to a judicious speech of Ponsonby's, and a very clever one from Tierney in his best manner.[1] The motion for an address was withdrawn, upon the ground that a more parliamentary form (as we call it) may be given to the motion hereafter, if in the mean time the sentiments of the House and of the public, which are supposed to be nearly unanimous as to the folly of this last proceeding against the Princess, are not so made known to the Regent as to induce some change of conduct, at least a suspension of hostilities, and to render it unnecessary for Parliament to extend its protection to the Princess. I dare say it would have been more satisfactory at Carlton House tonight, to have had it over, with a large majority.

I hear sad things of the Treaty. They are to abolish the Slave Trade after five years; that is, they are not to abolish it, but to crowd into five years the horrors of many more for the sake of new peopling St Domingo and Guinea. Guadaloupe, by our treaty, is to be left with Sweden; but by a secret understanding, is to be ceded by Sweden to France.[2]

. . .

1. A discussion had taken place on an appeal the Princess of Wales had made to the Speaker about her treatment at her husband's hands (*Hansard*, xxvii. 1048–65). Tierney had protested against 'the unbecoming indignity, insult, and cruelty' she had been offered by

the Prince. But both he and Ponsonby had suggested that there were better ways of tackling the problem than, as had been proposed, by making a formal inquiry of the Prince, and the proposal had therefore been withdrawn.

2. See Webster, pp. 269–72, for an account of the negotiations which gave rise to the rumours reported here.

533. To Henry Hallam

BLPES vi. 72–4   Salisbury, Sunday [24 July 1814]

I have heard nothing from London, except what one can gather from the papers, of this movement of the Duke of Sussex. By the manner in which Lord Rosslyn put off the notice on account of the Duke's state of health, I am convinced that Brougham is actively at work in the affair, as indeed is ostentatiously proclaimed by himself in the *Morning Chronicle*.[1] This, if it does not throw the Princess Charlotte into the hands of that little busy faction, which it may do ultimately, unfortunately gives at the outset an unfavourable impression, I believe an untrue one, of all that has passed: How difficult it will be to satisfy people, that the same advocates have not been the advisers all along, and that the Princess has not been in the hands of those whom the Chancellor called her enemies.[2] In the Chancellor, who must know all the circumstances, that was as imprudent and malignant a falsehood as I can remember even in his own former conduct.

If the Duke of Sussex reads some of the letters, and tells part of the story, it seems to me no longer a question, that the whole ought to be made public in some other form and from some other quarter. All the reasons of propriety or feeling, or [those] founded upon a view of future consequences, which ceased to have any weight with me, as you know, from the moment when the story was imparted to the whole world by that unfortunate incident of the flight to Connaught House, must have ceased now to have weight with any body. At the same time, I admit, that the wishes and feelings of the Princess herself are chiefly to be consulted, and that a real objection on her part to the publication of her story ought to be conclusive against such a step: and indeed I am decidedly of opinion, that no consideration for other persons at the present moment, but the single consideration alone of what is best for the Princess Charlotte with a view to her permanent character and reputation in the country, and to the strengthening and maintaining the affection of the people for her person, ought to govern both in the measure of publication and the manner of it if it is adopted. The details of the transaction, when fully told, are calculated, I think, to throw all England into a flame; but what you suggested early in the business is most just, that it is far from desirable to draw upon the Princess early in her life a popularity of this particular sort, which would be hurtful to her own mind in the possession of it, and has nothing in it to last for better purposes; in addition to which, I own I feel, notwithstanding my extreme contempt for the Regent's character, that infinite harm is done, to the interests of good government and liberty, by the public degradation and persecution of that individual. It is to save his daughter from the misfortune of being early ruined in the public estimation, and because that would in the end prove a greater misfortune to the public itself than to her, that I think it proper and indispensable to weigh at the present moment for her the expediency of making known at once to the whole world all the circumstances of her case. I shall look with anxiety to the turn which the business takes on Tuesday in the Lords; the Commons are not to sit after that day, otherwise I should expect it to be brought forward also by Whitbread. Why he abstains, or rather why Brougham directs him to abstain, I do not understand. For stage effect, it is no doubt better that the uncle should seem to set the whole agoing; but by waiting till Tuesday, the opportunity is gone of doing any thing in the H. of Commons.

. . .

1. On 12 July the Prince Regent, reacting to Princess Charlotte's recent decision to terminate her engagement to the Prince of Orange and to reports that his daughter was engaged in a clandestine relationship with the King of Prussia's nephew, Prince Frederick (1794–1863), informed the Princess that she would no longer reside at Warwick House, but was to live with him at Carlton House for five days and afterwards at Cranbourne Lodge, where she was to have no visitors except Queen Charlotte once a week. Later the same day the Princess resolved to live with her mother, and fled from Warwick House to her mother's house in Connaught Place. Upon Brougham's advice, and under threat of force, the Princess submitted to her father's wishes but first signed a minute drawn up by Brougham stating that she would never willingly marry the Prince of Orange. Brougham published the minute under his own name in the *Morning Chronicle* and, in league with the Princess's favourite uncle, the Duke of Sussex, planned a parliamentary offensive. At Brougham's urging Grey undertook the long trip south from Howick, and on 19 July Sussex carried the popularity of the Princess and the unpopularity of the Regent to new heights by asking five embarrassing questions in the Lords pertaining to the terms of the Princess's forced residence at Cranbourne Lodge. Grey followed with a strong speech but, finding virtually no support among the Whig rank and file, agreed with Brougham that parliamentary discussions should be suspended. Rosslyn, citing illness by the Duke of Sussex, therefore abandoned his intended notice of a motion and Brougham departed for the Northern Circuit on 21 July, reducing Horner as well as others to speculation. (See *Letters of the Princess Charlotte 1811–1817*, ed. A. Aspinall (1949), pp. xvii–xviii, and New, pp. 103–104 and 108–110, where Prince Frederick is confused with his rakish cousin Augustus. Both princes were among a large contingent of the Prussian royal family in London at this time and both were mentioned as possible husbands; but Augustus's affections were engaged elsewhere.)

2. Horner's assessment of the situation was evidently consistent with that of most of his political colleagues who, notwithstanding the encouragement of Grey, were now loath to involve themselves in the affairs of the two princesses. Whitbread's attack of 15 Mar. 1814 on the Whig commissioners of 1806 had discredited the 'Mountain' and raised doubts about Brougham; and although Whitbread took no part in the parliamentary discussions of late July, Brougham's high visibility in the affairs of Princess Charlotte and a lingering distrust of his allies in the Commons discouraged public involvement by even those who supported the Princess. The day before he wrote this letter to Hallam, Horner confided to Lady Holland (BLPES vi. 75–6):

It is very hard upon the Princess Charlotte, that Brougham should so ostentatiously write his own name upon all his paragraphs about this unfortunate business. It is a sacrifice of her to a very childish vanity, and gives a false colour to the whole transaction. She has been most harshly used; but for her future success with the country, nothing can be more injurious to her than the impression which is thus attempted to be given, untruly as yet, of a connection with a faction personally hostile to her father.

534. To Mrs Dugald Stewart

BLPES vi. 77–80 ⟨*Horner*, ii. 166–71⟩[1]   Salisbury, 24 July 1814

⟨. . .

⟨I happen to know more of the Princess Charlotte's story than I usually care to do of the concerns or transactions of that uninteresting family; and though one never ought to be sure in any thing connected with them, that one knows the truth, my conviction is very strong, that she has been ill used in the extreme, and considering her education and the blood she has, she has conducted herself well, both in point of sense and of good feeling. The unlucky incident of the hackney coach and her flight to Connaught House appears to have been unpremeditated, in the despair and agitation very natural to so young a person, so ill brought up, in the confusion she was thrown into by a harsh and sudden notice to her, that she was to be separated at once from every one she cared for, and put under the custody of those whom she dreads. It is not worth while giving you the details; they are very circumstantial, and it is only from the whole that a fair impression can be taken; this motion announced by the Duke of Sussex will probably lead to a very general publication of them. The conduct of the Regent throughout has exhibited an entire absence of all natural affection for her as his daughter, a neglect even of the care and attentions which he owed to her as a young woman committed to his guardianship, and all the harshness, tyranny and want of nerves that belong to his character. The whole story of her education, projected marriage, and present imprisonment, is unlike English manners, and savours strongly of that taste and principle in domestic life which, by the Princess Wilhelmine's account,[2] were habitual in the German courts. I am quite persuaded that he had no other reason for wishing the marriage but to remove his next successor from his sight, and the galling popularity of a more youthful court than his own: to carry his point, it was a necessary part of the scheme to insure her residence abroad, though his real intentions on this head were concealed from her at first, and were, as I understand, detected, after her consent to the match had been obtained, by finding from the Prince of Orange that a different language was held to him on the subject, than had been used to her, in the single conversation which ended in that consent. From the moment of this discovery, she assumed a language which she maintained throughout; and she appears to have received from those who were about her at this time, very judicious and honest advice: she insisted upon a parliamentary security for her residence in England, and upon an establishment and house in England as the assurance of its being a practical security. To this she adhered to the last; and the match was finally broken off, upon her ascertaining that no house was to be provided for her, and that the Prince of Orange confessed he was under the necessity of residing in his own country. One of the most reprehensible circumstances in the Regent's conduct to his daughter, was, that after he found himself disappointed by her firmness of his purpose to send her abroad, he contrived to throw upon her the task and the seeming dishonour of breaking off the engagement; by getting the sovereign of the Netherlands to write such a letter to his son, as made his future residence there a public duty: the proof of this is very curious, and depends upon a comparison of dates, and upon the terms in which some letters that passed were expressed. Whether the scene that was acted at Warwick House in the beginning of last week, was merely dictated by the Regent's resentment for his disappointment, or is part of a scheme laid for still forcing upon her the marriage and foreign residence, I do not know. It had been threatened for some days, and yet was attended with much precipitation in the manner of its execution, as well as violence.[3]

‹From the day that her consent to the marriage was procured, I believe I might say very unfairly, she never, except at a public assembly at Carlton House, had a sight of her father for about three months: She was prohibited from having any intercourse with her mother. After his return from his freaks at Belvoir, she wrote to him inquiring after his health; he had not leisure to answer her note, but sent MacMahon with a verbal reply, and this mode of communication was all she was honoured with for some weeks.

‹She has some disorder in her knee; probably the family taint. Last summer, sea-bathing was recommended for her; she asked him to let her go; he said he could not make the necessary arrangements, and she did not go.

‹On the Saturday before the hackney coach scene, a certificate, prescribing sea-bathing for her, was written by Baillie, Cline and Keake; she communicated their advice to her father in a respectful letter, which I have seen, and which would melt your heart to read. There was no other answer given to this application, but his arrival on the Tuesday following, at the head of the three old ladies and the Bishop of Salisbury, to take possession of the house (that was his own phrase to Miss Knight), and to tell his daughter that Miss Knight was to be dismissed instantly; she must sleep that night at Carlton House, and then go with the same old ladies to Crauford [sic] Lodge, a lone house in Windsor Park. When the Duke of York carried her in the middle of the night from her mother's to Carlton House, he refused at first sternly, and was only prevailed on by the most urgent entreaties, to allow her maid to accompany her, a Mrs Lewes; His R. Highness said, It was not in his orders. Could a Prussian corporal have behaved worse? The Princess Charlotte is not yet gone to the sea. But after all this had passed, the Regent talked of his affection for her to Lady Ilchester for an hour together, and shed a flood of tears; another most characteristic trait.[4]

‹All this in answer to your single question, is she really ill used? You will suspect me to be getting deep into the secrets of the royal family, and will at the least suppose me to be much interested for this captive Princess. In truth, neither is the case. But enough of this subject for the present.›[5]

. . .

‹Will you ask Mr Stewart to turn in his mind what can be done by persons in this country to prompt any French men of letters to write against the slave trade. In the state of opinions upon the subject in that country, there is as much to be done, and as much glory to be won by those who will do it, as before Granville Sharp and Clarkson had started it in England.[6] Yet there is so little of colonial interest as yet organized against it, and there is so much in the arguments of the cause that would be captivating to Frenchmen if addressed to them in the modes and fashion of their own literature, that there wants, I should think, but a skilful hand to sow the seed in proper places. Except at Geneva, one knows not where to look for men of letters; but the press of Geneva may once more be rendered a powerful engine for the instruction of France. I am told that Chateaubriand is an abolitionist, and his way of writing is in vogue. I have been inquiring about the Huguenot clergy; but they are said to be very low in learning, and to be too much afraid of losing their toleration under the Bourbons, to be likely to do any thing that might be displeasing to the Government. The African Institution named a committee, of which I am one, to consider of the means of promoting the circulation of abolition tracts in the French language; nothing, I am satisfied, can be done to any purpose, but by giving an impulse to the French press itself. If Mr Stewart will have the goodness to suggest what occurs to him, I will use his communication in any manner and with any degree of reserve that he may desire. No one could be so useful to us . . .[7]

. . .

[PS] ⟨Have you heard that the King of Sardinia has signalized his restoration, by prohibiting vaccination as a dangerous novelty? This would be a match for the revival of the slave trade, and the re-establishment of the inquisition.⟩

1. Leonard Horner unaccountably extracted a considerable portion of this letter and represented it as a separate letter written to Mrs Stewart on the same day.
2. *Memoirs of Frederica Sophia Wilhelmina . . . Margravine of Bareith* (2 vols, 1812).
3. Horner seems to have been unaware that the Princess's demands about foreign residence had been substantially conceded and that the sudden breaking off of her engagement was her own doing. It should also be noted that Horner's interpretation of events, like that of the general public, contemplated neither the intrigues of Brougham, who for purposes of his own did all he could to prevent a foreign residence by either Princess Charlotte or her mother, nor the very understandable concern of the Regent about his daughter.
4. Horner's claim that he had seen Princess Charlotte's letter about the 'certificate' from her medical advisers – Matthew Baillie (1761–1823: *DNB*), Henry Cline (1750–1825: *DNB*), and Robert Keate (1777–1857: *DNB*) – suggests that his support had been solicited either directly by Brougham or one of his allies in the Commons, or indirectly through Holland, who like Grey was inclined to support parliamentary exertions on behalf of the Princess after she was forced to reside at Cranbourne Lodge. The 'old ladies' were presumably Lady Hertford, Elizabeth, Countess Conyngham (d. 1861), and Frances, Countess of Jersey (1753–1821). John Fisher (1748–1825: *DNB*), Bishop of Salisbury, had been the Princess's tutor. Maria, Dowager Countess of Ilchester (d. 1842) – not 'Rochester' as in *Horner* – was one of those appointed to replace the Princess's dismissed ladies. Mrs Louis, not 'Lewes' – or indeed 'Lewis' – was the Princess's French maid. Otherwise this account largely corresponds with that given in the *Autobiography of Miss Cornelia Knight* (2 vols, 1861), ii. 1–20.
5. This paragraph concludes the portion extracted and represented as a separate letter in *Horner*, ii. 168–71. The remainder, excluding an uninteresting first paragraph, is published in *ibid.*, ii. 166–8.
6. Granville Sharp (1735–1813: *DNB*) and Thomas Clarkson (1760–1846: *DNB*), the abolitionists.
7. Talleyrand and Louis XVIII experienced great difficulty in meeting Castlereagh's demand for the abolition of the slave trade in France's colonial possessions; for the French commercial classes argued that its purpose was to prevent the restoration of their colonial trade. Castlereagh therefore favoured a compromise whereby abolition would occur within five years, but this placed him and his reluctant colleagues in London squarely between the realities of public opinion in France and Britain. On 3 May 1814 the House of Commons had passed a resolution against the return of any colonies to France without abolition; and now, when word reached London that the treaty signed at Paris on 30 May stipulated a five-year extension of the slave trade, Wilberforce and his colleagues protested bitterly in Parliament and the African Institution initiated a campaign to propagandize France. The Whig Opposition, noting that 'the English Ministry was exclusively composed of men who, during the long controversy on that subject, had uniformly signalized themselves as the

enemies of the abolition', afterwards focused on Castlereagh's failure in their attack on the peace treaty. On 17 June the Duke of Norfolk presided and Grey, Holland, Lansdowne, and Whitbread spoke alongside Wilberforce at a great public meeting at Freemasons' Hall, and the Whigs continued an attempt to bind Castlereagh to abolition until the end of the session in July. (Webster, pp. 270–72; *Holland's Further Memoirs*, p. 196; *Hansard*, xxvii. 570, 637–42, 656–62, and 1078–84; xxviii. 55, 267–97, 299–351, 365–71, 384–413, 437–66, 466–70, 655–8, 803, and 846–7. See also *Wilberforce*, iv. 186–213; *Romilly*, iii. 136–42; and Taylor, pp. 384–5.)

535. To Anne Horner

⟨*Horner*, ii. 172–4⟩   Bodmin, 8 Aug. 1814

⟨. . .

⟨The only excursions I have made this circuit for sights have been in Devonshire . . . I have always heard of Ford Abbey since I first knew Devonshire, as an antiquity worth going to see; and who should have become the occupier of it but Mr Jeremy Bentham, who has taken a lease of the place for seven years?[1] He asked me to come and see him, and to bring Adam with me: we spent two days with him . . .

⟨There are some handsome rooms, furnished in the taste of King William's time; one of these very spacious and hung with tapestry, Mr Bentham has converted into what he calls his 'scribbling shop': two or three tables are set out, covered with white napkins, on which are placed two or three music desks with manuscripts; his technical memory (I believe), and all the other apparatus of the exhaustive method. I was present at the mysteries, for he went on as if we had not been with him. A long walk, after our breakfast and before his, began the day. He came into the house about one o'clock, the tea things being by that time set by his writing table, and he proceeded very deliberately to sip his tea, while a young man, a sort of pupil and amanuensis, read the newspapers to him, paragraph by paragraph. This and the tea together seemed gradually to prepare his mind for working, in which he engaged by degrees, and became at last quite absorbed in what was before him, till about five o'clock, when he met us at dinner. He permitted me to sit in the same room, for the purpose of looking over some old volumes which he had found in the house; but I was much more attentive to his own proceedings: this is his daily course throughout the year. Adam, who had never seen him before, was delighted with the suavity and cheerfulness of his manner. Besides the young man I have mentioned, Mr Cohen,[2] he has living with him Mr [James] Mill (a gentleman who writes a good deal in the *Edinburgh Review*) and his whole family.

⟨. . .⟩

   1. Bentham had moved for his health only that year to Ford Abbey near Chard, where he wrote his *Chrestomathia* on the educational principles of Bell and Lancaster, *The Church of England and its catechism*, and, perhaps with Francis Place, *Not Paul, but Christ*.
   2. Presumably an error of transcription for John Herbert Koe (1783–1860), Bentham's secretary and protégé (*Bentham*, vi. 365n).

536. To Dugald Stewart

BLPES vi. 124–9 ⟨Horner, ii. 196–201⟩ Bowood, 28 Oct. 1814

⟨I ought long ago to have thanked you for including me in the letters, by which you introduced Murray to some of your friends at Paris; particularly as I am indebted to all of them for the most obliging and marked attention.[1] M. Le Chevalier seemed to give us his whole time with a good humour and cordiality that made all of us feel most grateful to him. He is now librarian to the Lycée d'Henri Quatre, the modern transformation of the convent of St Geneviève. M. Gallois did us the favour of taking us to the Chamber of Deputies, on a day of public discussion; it would be well for France, if sentiments as liberal and enlightened as his were to prevail generally in that assembly, which I fear has not sufficient strength of materials yet, either in point of talents or connection with the people, to form the foundations of a popular constitution. I regret exceedingly that my short stay in Paris prevented me from cultivating the acquaintance of M. De Gerando; the first time you write to him, I wish you would assure him how much I feel myself obliged by his kind civilities and attention; he took the trouble of writing many letters, to render our travels in the south of France more agreeable; by one of which I had the satisfaction of seeing that excellent and agreeable man Camille Jourdan, at Lyons, one of the very few survivors who have gone through the Revolution, and the still more difficult trials of the late despotism, with an unsullied name, and an unimpaired attachment to the principles of moderate liberty.[2]

⟨You will be glad to hear that I saw both M. Suard and the Abbé Morellet in good health; I met them together at a party of Mad. Suard's, where Sir J. Mackintosh took me.[3] It was very interesting to see in person two men, who connect our day with names so memorable, and times so remote; for I think the Abbé Morellet was at the Sorbonne with Turgot in the year 1748. I had remarked his sturdy figure in the Chamber of Deputies.

⟨From what I could collect, though any judgement I could form in so short a stay is good for little, nothing can be more problematical than the future prospects of the new Government of France. That the Bourbon family will keep their place, unless they are exposed to the hazards of a new war, or commit some enormous indiscretion at home, seemed to be the growing opinion of the most intelligent persons.[4] But there appeared to be very little conjecture, and very little hope, with respect to the probable fate of what they call their constitution. In the King's Cabinet, it was said there were almost as many systems as there were ministers; some of them, and these the most trusted, urging the King to bring back by degrees all the old institutions of every description, at the head of whom is the Chancellor; others, such as Talleyrand, making a struggle, out of some regard to appearances of personal consistency, for as much of the improvements gained by the Revolution as can be retained; the Abbé Montesquieu is described as a mere creature of the Court, but liking to make his speeches at the bar of the Assembly.[5] The friends of the Court say, that Talleyrand attempted at first to surround the King with his own dependants, and to make His Majesty a cypher in the Administration; on the other hand, Talleyrand's account to a friend of mine was, that the King had the vanity to suppose himself capable of doing a great deal of business, in consequence of which it was in fact done by unfit persons. These stories are not inconsistent.

‹In the lower Assembly, there is nothing like party separation or connection. A remarkable symptom of this nature, however, showed itself in the senate, during the discussion of the law by which a censure of the press has been established; all the imperial marshals acting together, against the measures of Government. I was informed also that the young Duc de Broglie is an eager constitutionalist, and that he has always shown a predilection for popular principles, as much as that disposition could be made known during the reign of Napoleon.[6]

‹The discussion of that law excited a very lively interest in Paris, among all men of education and reflection; I was there at that time, and it appeared to me that its vast importance was duly appreciated and felt. I am afraid, however, that there is not in the country, or in the provincial cities, any degree of steady political feeling, connecting the middling classes of the people with their inferiors in a sentiment of common interest. The lower people in general, though more strongly in some districts than others, regret Bonaparte, and the loss of military glory, and that rapid military promotion which provided for their sons and held out to all of them prospects of ambition. The middling classes, who felt the conscription as a tyranny of the cruellest description, rejoice at the removal of their late ruler, but have no feeling of attachment either to royalty in itself, or to the Bourbons, who were literally forgotten. The priests are said to be very zealous in labouring to recall or create feelings of that sort, but hitherto without success. The populace of Paris are understood to be more disinclined to the present royal family, than those of any other part of France; they gave rather an unexpected proof of other attachments, upon the Duke of Orléans taking possession of the Palais Royal, for he was hailed with acclamations, and several voices in the crowd spoke to him of his father, and said he was always the friend of the people. Among the people of rank at Paris, the sentiment that is uppermost at present is that they are relieved from a tyranny which, though not sanguinary, pursued them through every interest and almost every incident of domestic life with incessant interference and vexation.

‹The only sure and permanent prognostic of civil liberty, that I could hear of in France, is the prodigious subdivision of land, and the unprecedented multitude of persons directly possessed of that property. An estimate, which seemed to come from authority, made it as high as three millions of persons. So great a proportion of this must be held upon revolutionary titles, or upon titles founded in the new law of succession, that one should hope that so much at least of the benefits earned by the Revolution, as consists in this equitable law, and in the salutary transfer of vast domains to the people, must be secured for ever, and fortified against the designs of the Court by an insuperable bulwark of such interests and such numbers. The Court have had the folly, however, to issue secret commissions to the bishops, for a return of the lands held by the church in 1791, and of the present proprietors by whom any of them are possessed: such a measure never can lead to any consequences, but against the Court itself. The fact is not much known in France, but there is no doubt of it.

‹This immense multiplication of landed proprietors has led to a great extension of cultivation, in point of surface, and probably in many parts has made the cultivation much inferior in skill and efficacy to what it was before.

⟨There are complaints, I observe, in all the statistical reports, of the unnecessary increase of vineyards, and of the diminution of the woods. I was assured, however, by a very intelligent and well-informed man, M. De Candolle, Professor of Botany at Montpelier, whom I was introduced to at Geneva, that of late years there has been a very great progress in the increase and management of artificial meadows.[7] He told me, at the same time, that such was the subdivision of lands in the south of France, that the footman you hire is commonly the owner of an estate. . . .⟩

1. Horner, together with Murray and Murray's brother William, had recently concluded a tour of the Continent. Upon finishing his business on the circuit in mid-August 1814, Horner had proceeded from Wells to London, where he met his travelling companions. They sailed from Brighton on 20 Aug., and after travelling through France, Switzerland, and the north of Italy, Horner returned alone to Brighton on 14 Oct. Copies of Horner's correspondence from the Continent, which amounts to several lengthy but uninteresting letters to family and friends, is in BLPES vi. 87–108, and portions of it were published in *Horner*, ii. 175–96. Horner's letter to Auckland of 28 Oct. (BLPES vi. 119) outlines the route of his continental travels; William Murray's journal of the tour is in NLS MSS 19737.
2. Jean Baptiste Le Chevalier (1752–1836) was an archaeologist and diplomat; Jean Antoine Couvin Gallois (1761–1828), having voted as a deputy both for the Empire and for Bonaparte's abdication, went into private life in 1814; Marie Joseph De Gerando (1772–1841) was a distinguished philosopher; and Camille Jordan (1771–1821) was the well-known politician and writer.
3. Jean Baptiste Antoine Suard (1734–1817) was Secretary of the French Academy.
4. Lord and Lady Holland were in Geneva when Horner visited Paris, and their absence perhaps explains why he reported no social contact with Benjamin Constant, Lafayette, Madame de Staël, Madame de Coigny, Madame d'Aguesseau, Sébastiani, Maubourg, or any other principal figure associated with the French opposition party. From Geneva Lord Holland sent him a letter of introduction to Lafayette which described Horner as one 'attached to my uncle's politics', but it was never presented (*Horner*, ii. 187–9).
5. Etienne Denis, Baron (afterwards Duc) Pasquier (1767–1862), had become Chancellor and François Xavier Marc Antoine, Duc de Montesquiou-Fezenac and Abbé of Beaulieu (1756–1832), Minister of the Interior under the restoration.
6. Achille Léon Charles Victor de Broglie (1785–1870), who had lost his father to the guillotine, nonetheless remained faithful to the Revolution and gave a sole vote in the House of Peers for the acquittal of Marshal Ney.
7. Augustin Pyramus De Candolle (1778–1841).

537. To James Brougham

Brougham MSS, D.M.S. Watson Library,
University College, London, J 513   [London], Tuesday 15 [Nov. 1814]

. . .

. . . I am not a convert yet to your Corn Bill; which, I am still obstinate in thinking, would in the end be injurious to the real interests of agriculture, and in the mean while to all the other great interests of the country. You corn-growers seem to me to look for a remedy at the wrong end, when you propose to tax the necessaries of life. Make a reform in your parochial administration of the poor laws, and press the

Government for peace with America that they may take off the property tax, and above all things insist upon a reformation of the money of the country. But you will do none of these things, I know, and will still clamour for a corn-law, which I dare say you will get in the end. I know well enough that it is not till you have had it some time, that you will be inclined to listen to any arguments that go to prove its inefficacy or inexpediency.

What a strange thing it is, that the farmers of this country, whose skill is so great and their capital so large, should be afraid of competition in their own home market with the growers of a distant country, whose cultivation rests on no capital and is in point of skill and science wretched. Though the whole surface of France is under the plough, it is cultivated most miserably and almost without stock. Such a competition can only arise from something forced and unnatural in the state of prices in that home market; and such an unnatural state of prices never, in the experience of governments, was cured by new artifices of taxation and restraint, but can be remedied by going to the root of the evil, and restoring other things to their natural course. All this you will say is theory; I think it the practical result of long and uniform experience. And so we are at issue; till there shall be a new addition made to that experience by the effect of this Bill, which may convince you after the event, but will not enable us, for all that, to meet any future device of the same kind with more success than we do at present. Experience goes for nothing in the conduct of nations. And so ends my discourse.

538. To Anne Horner

BLPES vi. 136–7 (?copy)   London, 25 Nov. 1814

. . .

If you have read the *Morning Chronicle*, I beg you not to believe that I used the word *disclaimer* in the H. of Commons. Because I am a lawyer, their reporter puts barbarisms of Westminster Hall into my mouth; they continue to give accurately enough, the heads of the substance of what one says in the House, but never the expressions in which we say it.[1]

. . .

Parliament is to adjourn until the 14th of February, by which time it is supposed the robbers at Vienna will have settled their division of the booty. I shall not be surprised, nor very sorry, if they fall out, to give the oppressed Germans and Poles another chance of getting their own.

---

1. On 21 Nov., following a motion for the House to go into committee on the army estimates, Whitbread had put some questions to Ministers relating to the proceedings at Vienna, especially with regard to the treaty between Austria and the King of Naples. Vansittart and Stephen had then urged the impropriety of public discussion, but Horner had emphasized that it was the duty of the Commons to seek information, especially on money bills, and remarked that 'he saw no difference, in the principle, between the annexations that were now making, and the tyrannical acts of that Government against which we had been so

long contending'. Next day, when Whitbread had again brought the subject before the House, Horner – in a speech in which he used the word 'denial', not 'disclaimer' – had pointed to apparent inconsistency in British foreign policy and suggested that Ministers were ignorant of developments on the Continent; and when the subject was resumed on 25 Nov., he argued that the House 'had a right to demand information, as it regarded the honour and faith of the Crown in its foreign relations, which should ever be dear to the House, whether we were not acting contrary to our treaty with the King of Naples'. That same evening (25 Nov.), upon the third reading of Peel's Irish Peace-Preservation Bill, Horner withdrew the opposition he had so strongly expressed upon its second reading in July the previous session when he had insisted it was both untimely and unconstitutional. This was a remarkable reversal of opinion, even if such legislation no longer froze his blood as in 1807 (Doc. 275). He claimed at the time that he had been won over by Newport, who had said in the course of the debate that he too considered it unconstitutional but that he had subsequently concluded from events that it had in practice 'produced salutary and beneficial effects'. In July Newport, being absent from the Commons, had in fact written to Peel to offer what Peel described as 'a qualified declaration of his approval', in contrast, he said, to 'Mr Horner and Sir Samuel Romilly and a host of enlightened and philosophic Scotch lawyers [who] think it very shocking to suspend, if necessary, trial by jury'. (*Horner*, ii. 160–61 and 203–209; *Hansard*, xxix. 522–3; *Peel*, i. 150–51.)

539. To Lord Auckland

BLPES vi. 138   [London], Monday [28 Nov. 1814]

. . .

Lord Grenville means to be in town on Thursday upon Lord Donoughmore's motion; but I do not [know] whether he means to go at large into the foreign relations, or merely to announce his intention of a motion after the recess upon the proceedings at Ghent.[1] I wish he would reprobate, before it is too late, the proceedings at Vienna; the animadversions that are made in Parliament cannot fail to impose some little restraint upon Castlereagh at least, if not upon others. I never expected any thing from this congress of sovereigns, but the plunder of Europe; they have far exceeded all my expectations in the shameless effrontery of their proceedings. The partition they are making cannot, one would fain hope, be maintained; new wars and new revolutions will be tried probably, to assert the independence of some of the nations who are disposed of at this auction. Dantzic has been surrendered, with Castlereagh's express assent, to Prussia; and Hamburgh is to be given in the same manner to the King of Denmark. I am assured it has been seriously entertained as a project, that a king should be set over the Swiss. There was a strong persuasion in the City on Saturday, that the negotiation at Ghent is to terminate very soon in peace; I found Baring decidedly of this opinion.

There have been some rumours of a new settlement of administration; which connect such a consequence with Lord Wellesley's arrival in town. He refused to go to Paris, it is said, not long ago; and assigned to his friends as his reason, that he would not attach himself to falling Ministers.

1. Donoughmore had intended on 1 Dec. to move for the production of the instructions to the British representatives at Vienna, more especially those relating to countries whose

liberties or independence were in jeopardy, such as Norway, Switzerland, Saxony, and Poland, but when the moment arrived he withdrew his motion on the grounds that though he had chosen the occasion with care and fully publicized its importance, the attendance in the Lords did not justify his pressing it. Holland, however, spoke warmly of his sympathy for Donoughmore's motion, and in the Commons Horner, as had been agreed, pressed home the attack he had already begun on 30 Nov. on the policy and management of the American war and successfully moved for papers. (See *Hansard*, xxix. 620–23, and, for Horner's speeches of 1 Dec., *Horner*, ii. 209–12.)

540. To Sir James Mackintosh

BLPES vi. 141 ⟨*Horner*, ii. 212–13⟩   Lincoln's Inn, 6 Dec. 1814

⟨You may remember, the morning I saw you at Coppet, that Madame de Staël expressed a desire to see at full length a letter of Burke's, which was mentioned.[1] I have copied it out of Hardy's book; and will thank you to give it to Madame de Staël with my best respects. It was with much regret that I found myself compelled to pass through Paris, without having time to wait upon her at Clichy.⟩

I wish much to have your opinion, upon a point of French constitutional law; if there may be such a combination of words. It has been reported, that, in consequence of the representations of the Duke of Wellington on the subject of the Slave Trade, the French Government have made an edict directing their subjects not to trade in slaves on any part of the African coast to the North of Cape Formoso. If such edict has ever been passed, it is made a sort of secret; for it was unknown to the ship-owners of Nantes less than a month ago. If it really exists and can be said to be in force, though a vast trade on the coast would still be left, this would be an important concession. What I am anxious to ascertain is, whether, under the new constitutional charter, the King could so issue a decree, restricting or regulating in this manner the foreign trade of his subjects, that the decree would have the force of law and be recognized as such by the Courts of Justice in France. If the edict makes it unlawful, by the French law, for the subjects of that crown to trade in violation of it, our cruisers (supposing an exchange of powers between the two crowns for that purpose) would be supported by our Courts of Admiralty in seizing for condemnation slaves so unlawfully shipped; but not otherwise. The Lords of Prizes, as you are aware, have laid down that rule.[2]

⟨Our short session of Parliament has not been inactive on the part of Opposition: Tierney, in particular, made considerable exertions, and gave us three or four speeches of great ability and effect. While we were protesting against the monstrous proceedings of the robbers at Vienna, I never ceased to wish you had been in your place to enforce our remonstrances. With what effect this expression of what I believe to be the public opinion of all England will be attended, rests with our Minister; upon whom parliamentary control is not wholly without effect, as is shown in the publication he has made at Vienna of a treatise on the slave trade – a treatise by Castlereagh in favour of the abolition, who to the very last opposed the Bill of 1807 in the House![3] . . .⟩

1. Horner, p. 212, identifies the letter as Burke to the Earl of Charlemont, 9 Aug. 1789, of which Francis Hardy, *Memoirs of the Political and Private Life of James Caulfield* [sic], *Earl of Charlemont* (1810), pp. 321–2, prints an incomplete copy; there is a full version in *Burke*, vi. 9–12.

2. Horner's queries were advanced with an eye to identifying a point of law on which British abolitionists could base their parliamentary campaign against the resumption of France's colonial slave trade. Evidently the queries arose from accurate reports of a circular letter, distributed in late September, from the French Minister of Marine to the Maritime prefects instructing them to grant no authorizations to vessels fitted out for the slave trade to the north of Cape Formoso, and from several other later communications of a similar nature addressed to the prefects and the *armateurs* of Nantes and Le Havre. After conferring with Wellington, Mackintosh replied with a letter of 12 Dec. (*Horner*, ii. 215–19), in which, after summarizing Anglo-French negotiations on the slave trade and outlining the several edicts of Louis XVIII partially restricting the operations of French slavers, he stated that:

> Lord Castlereagh and he [Wellington] had, it seems, suggested to Talleyrand the necessity of a law on this subject, and of course the concurrence of the two Chambers; but neither Talleyrand, nor any of the other Ministers, admit such a necessity. They represent commerce as being capable of being regulated by the King's prerogative. Your question is, I conceive, not put as a French Whig, but as an English abolitionist. If this *règlement* be held here to be a legal abolition, on the northern part of the African coast, it is sufficient for our purpose. To this information I venture to add, that, in my opinion, it would be wise to give the ambassador a reasonable time for obtaining this *règlement* on as good a footing as he can, before any thing be done or said on the subject in England.

3. The editors have been unable to identify any such 'treatise', although Horner refers to it again in Doc. 541. But Castlereagh is known to have circulated a translation of the voluminous evidence submitted to the Commons Committee on the Slave Trade in 1790–91, an *Abrégé* of which, by Jean de Carro, was published in Vienna in 1814. M. Gramagnac's translation of Thomas Clarkson, *Essai sur les désavantages politiques de la traite des nègres*, first published in Neuchâtel in 1789, was also reissued in Paris in 1814. (Webster, pp. 419–20.)

541. To Lord Auckland

BLPES vi. 143–4   [London], Wednesday [?7 Dec. 1814]

. . .

In Lord Oxford's case, it is clear the Government must have been in quest of particular letters. And if it turns out that the D. of Wellington has afforded him no vindication, one must conclude that the arrest was made with his previous assent.[1] I find this foolish Earl is understood to have arranged representations from King Joachim to the Regent; but in the present state of things, I do not see what particular suspicion the Court of France need entertain of an agent of Murat. Elba must be the sole and incessant object of their waking and sleeping fears. Did I mention to you, that Lord Holland tells Tierney in a letter from Florence, that the Emperor of that island has made a treaty with some of the Barbary States, and receives the pirate vessels into his harbour.

Castlereagh has written, and had it translated, a huge treatise in favour of the abolition of the Slave Trade; which he circulates at Vienna. This delights the Saints, and if it should have no effect upon the negotiating powers, it will mitigate the resentment of the voting powers in the House of Commons. Even tardy virtue has its merit; and there is some pleasure in seeing that the voice of Parliament and the country, in so good a cause, has force enough to make even Castlereagh work against the grain.

. . .

1. The French authorities in Paris had seized the papers of Edward Harley, 5th Earl of Oxford (1773–1848), on suspicion that they contained incriminating evidence of Muratist plots (*WSD*, ix. 547–8).

542. To J.A. Murray

BLPES vi. 147–8 ⟨*Horner*, ii. 213–14⟩   [London], Saturday [10 Dec. 1814]

⟨. . .

⟨As to the American war, the historical truth I take to be that we goaded that people into war, by our unjust extension to them, while neutrals, of all the unmitigated evils of maritime war, and still more by the insulting tone of our newspaper and Government language; and that when the English nation came to its senses about the Orders in Council, and the Minister was dead, who had insanely made it a point of honour to adhere to them, by that time the American Government believed that the continental system of Bonaparte had ruined the resources of this country, that he was to become lord of the ascendant, and that it was as well for them to be on the best terms with the winning side. What passed prior to the repeal of the Orders in Council may fairly be regarded now as matter of history only, and it is in that view of it that I consider the Americans as now aggressors in the war; the ground of complaint they had, we have relinquished; their pretensions against our maritime rights are matter of aggression.

⟨You ask me about the general feeling of London and England respecting the American war. I am convinced it is at present decidedly unpopular. The want of success, announced in so many repeated instances, had gradually weaned the public from their idle dreams of immediate subjugation; for that was the fancy, and, in this state of dissatisfaction, came that publication of the Ghent negotiations, which produced a great sensation. I have so little confidence in the steadiness or principle of the public sentiments, on matters of war, that if there were some signal successes won by our troops or our ships over the Americans, I should rather expect to hear again the old cry for chastisement, and all the old vulgar insolence. It is a sad misfortune to America, that they have not had for President of their republic, during this important epoch of their history, a man of a higher cast of talent and public sentiment than Madison; he has involved them without necessity in war, and has debased very much the tone, which a people destined obviously for such greatness, ought to maintain.⟩

543. To Macvey Napier

BL Add. MSS 34611, ff. 158-9   Minto, 5 Jan. 1815

I regretted very much that I had not an opportunity of returning your obliging visit, before I left Edinburgh, in consequence of some unavoidable engagements which occupied all my time.[1] If in the course of your laborious but most important undertaking, you think it possible that any applications or hints of mine might be of the least aid to you, I hope you will not scruple to communicate with me. I am only sorry that I have no leisure to offer you any contributions of my own; for I am convinced that the republication of our national Encyclopedia presents an opportunity, to which no other is equal, of forming and influencing the public opinion upon the most important subjects, and of diffusing among all the reading classes of the country the most improved knowledge of the age on all questions connected with individual or public happiness.[2]

1. Horner had visited Edinburgh during the last two weeks of 1814 and then proceeded to Minto, where he remained several days, and to Lord Grenville's at Dropmore, before returning to London in mid-January 1815. Evidently much of his time in Edinburgh was devoted to discussions with friends about the propriety of introducing jury trial in Scots civil cases and to the perusal of a manuscript that Samuel Parr had posted to Dugald Stewart for review and comment, and Stewart in turn had sent on to Horner, thinking 'his very characteristical criticisms might perhaps amuse you at some leisure moment before you return to London'. Parr's manuscript consisted of 'animadversions' he had made on some passages in Stewart's 'Essay on the Sublime' (*Philosophical Essays*, Edinburgh, 1810). Stewart was certainly not unimpressed. 'Some of them', he wrote to Horner, 'appear to me very acute, and stagger me not a little about my own too precipitate interpretations of the disputed passage in Longinus; but I must acknowledge that the conjectural emendation of Tonstal, sanctioned by Dr Parr strikes me as liable to still more obvious and insurmountable objections.' There were still greater objections, however. For *characteristically* Parr's 'animadversions' consisted, by one estimate of over one hundred pages, by another of two hundred and fifty of octavo print! Stewart was said by one of Parr's biographers (Johnstone) to have declined to incorporate so important a contribution in his own work; perhaps, rather, he resorted to delaying tactics, first referring Parr to Horner – the following year Parr appealed to Horner for help in recovering his manuscript from Kinneil – and then, in a footnote to a note in the second (1816) edition of his *Elements of the Philosophy of the Human Mind*, acknowledging (ii. 577) the 'instruction' he had received from Parr's publications and communications, and expressing the hope of 'being permitted to make a few extracts in a future edition' of his 'Essay on the Sublime'. Later that year 'a very imperfect abstract' appeared in the second edition of his *Philosophical Essays*. (Horner to James Reddie, 29 Dec. 1814, NLS MSS 3704, ff. 68-9, encouraging active support for jury trials in civil cases; Lord Grenville to Horner, 12 Jan. 1815, BLPES vi. 151-2, giving a favourable opinion of jury trials and expressing 'the greatest pleasure in seeing you here at the time you mention'; Stewart to Horner, 1 Jan. 1815, Kinnordy MSS, Horner to Mrs Stewart, 20 Jan. 1816, BLPES vii. 15-16, *Parr*, i. 713-20, and Stewart's *Works*, v. 455-65, for Parr's MS.)

2. Napier had undertaken the previous year to edit a Supplement to the sixth edition of the *Encyclopædia Britannica*, and had been provided for the purpose of enlisting contributors with a letter of introduction from Stewart to Horner (*Napier*, pp. 6-7). The project was completed in six volumes in 1824.

544. From John Allen

BLPES vi. 153–4   Rome, 17 Jan. 1815

. . . We have been now eight weeks at Rome . . . There have been a great number of English here this winter. The cold and damp of Florence drove them on and the fear of Murat has detained them here. Of late, however, they have taken courage and from the silence of the Congress presuming he is to be left at Naples, they are setting out in crowds to enjoy the niceness of his climate and witness the splendour and festivities of his Court, and nothing now detains the half of them who are still here but the reports of the expense of living and difficulty of finding houses at Naples. Byng set off yesterday with Mr and Mrs Blackburne and Rogers and Boddington are ready to follow as soon as they hear that lodgings have been secured for them.[1] . . .
. . .

We know nothing here of what is passing at Vienna and hear nothing worth repeating but from the isle of Elba – but you must have seen Vernon and have probably heard of Lord Ebrington's interview with Bonaparte.[2] He appears to be wonderfully good humoured and communicative, but the impression on my mind, I confess, from all I have heard of his conversation, is not at all in his favour. He seems to me more thoroughly a military despot, more indifferent about mankind and more insensible of the difference between right and wrong than even from the worst parts of his past conduct I had ever supposed him to be. He seems not as much to have been led astray from the paths of honour and duty by his passions and ambition as to be deficient in those fundamental notions of equity and justice which it is inconceivable any man of education, not born a Prince, can possibly want. He seems to have considered all those whom he had made his subjects to have been born for his use and to have regarded their happiness or existence as little as the pawns he might have parted with in a game of chess.[3]

All one can say of Italy is that the common people are in general satisfied and men of education discontented with the late changes. The former rejoice, as usual, at the downfall of their late masters, and will probably feel the same unfeigned joy when their next rulers are in their turn dispossessed. The latter find all their hopes disappointed whether of personal aggrandizement or of national glory. The reports from Naples are various and contradictory. The Lazzaroni are said to be unanimous in favour of Ferdinand and some English travellers who have lately returned from Naples assure me that many of the nobility are of the same opinion – but that I can hardly believe. There can be no doubt that it will [be] for the good of that country and of Italy and Europe in general that the Bourbons should not get a footing in it again.

1. From casual mentions in *Rogers*, i. 172, and *Ward*, p. 267, 'Byng' was evidently Frederick Byng (d. 1871), the Foreign Office clerk better known as 'Poodle' Byng. Samuel Boddington (1755–1843), Richard Sharp's wealthy friend and partner, was chairman of the King of Clubs from 1808 to 1819; in 1824 his only daughter Grace married Lady Holland's younger son, Henry Webster. The Blackburnes have not been identified; but were perhaps John Ireland Blackburne (1783–1874), MP for Newton, and his wife, rather than his parents John Blackburne (1754–1833), MP for Lancashire, and his wife.

2. George Vernon, the MP for Lichfield, was a distant connection of Caroline Fox's companion and Sydney Smith's sister-in-law Elizabeth Vernon (d. 1830). He and Hugh Fortescue, Lord Ebrington, MP for Buckinghamshire and afterwards 2nd Earl Fortescue (1783–1861), had recently visited Napoleon on Elba, as did shortly afterwards John Nicholas Fazakerly, then MP for Lincoln (see Doc. 640), Frederick Sylvester North Douglas (1791–1819: DNB), MP for Banbury, and Lord John Russell, MP for Tavistock. All were closely affiliated with the Hollands, who stopped at nothing in attempting to establish contact with Napoleon and his family during their extended residence in Italy. During the late summer and autumn of 1814 Lord Holland had expressed very favourable opinions of Napoleon and his reign. From Florence Lady Holland had sent Napoleon a consignment of newspapers and had received in turn specimens of iron ore; and in Rome, while living in Louis Bonaparte's mansion on the Corso, she had received poetry from Lucien Bonaparte. In late January 1815 the Hollands moved on to Naples, where they established close contact with Murat. (See Taylor, pp. 393–4, and Lean, pp. 144–8.)

3. Allen's opinion of Napoleon, which was evidently based solely on the impressions he formed after speaking to Vernon and Ebrington following their return from Elba, is in striking contrast to the impressions of others. In a letter to Lady Holland of 5 Jan., Elizabeth Vernon, presumably basing her opinion on her cousin's account, described the deposed emperor as 'a most wonderful person' (BL Add. MSS 51800). Lauderdale and Grey exchanged enthusiastic accounts of Ebrington's conference with Napoleon (Lauderdale to Grey, 24 Dec. 1814, Grey MSS, Durham University), and Whitbread, apparently drawing on the same reports from Italy, spoke warmly of Napoleon's character and genius while visiting Woburn (*Broughton*, i. 175–7). See also Taylor, pp. 396–9, for an account of the growing Bonapartist sympathies that arose among Foxites in Britain due to reports from Vienna and Italy.

545. To Anne Horner

BLPES vi. 155 (copy)   London, 19 Jan. 1815

. . .

I am much struck with the beauty of some passages, which are extracted in the *Review* from Wordsworth's new poem; they ought to have softened the barbarity of the critic. The plan of the poem is radically against all propriety and good taste, and his obscure inelegant Platonism must be wearisome; but the last few pages of the *Review* contain about half a dozen passages, that ought to shelter a multitude of faults. It is odd enough, however, that a much more favourable impression of this work is to be had, from the Edinburgh sentence of execution with all its savage texture, than from the *Quarterly*['s] studied panegyric of the Excursion.[1]

1. Jeffrey had begun his review of Wordsworth's *Excursion* in *ER* xxiv (no. xlvii, Nov. 1814), 1–30, with the famous phrase 'This will never do!'; Charles Lamb and William Gifford reviewed it in *QR* xii (no. xxiii, Oct. 1814), 100–111 (Shine).

546. To J.A. Murray

BLPES vi. 156–7   [London], Thursday [19 Jan. 1815]

. . .

Till I was in the Mail Coach, I had not read that article in the last *Review*, which treats of the Revival of the Slave Trade. Have you remarked two most extraordinary passages in it, about Party spirit and half-patriots; one at the end of the article, the other at p. 112. They are whimsical enough, considering, that party, which is here disclaimed, is the mortal disease of which the *Edinburgh Review* is dying. But I want to hear, whether any body with you annexes a meaning to them, or professes to explain them; for I find nobody here who can. Whatever be their real import, the publication of such passages at the present moment is not very creditable to the *Review*, and to the supposed writer of that article are very disgraceful; but he is a person of whom I have relinquished every good opinion I once entertained.[1]

> 1. Horner's comments give confirmation that the review in ER xxiv (no. xlvii, Nov. 1814), 106–133, entitled 'Revival of the Slave Trade', was by Brougham. It called on the people 'to speak out their sense of this last disgrace to their name, and no other minister will ever dare carry on a slave-trading negotiation'. The passage on p. 112 ran: '. . . what is commonly called Party, has of late years received . . . an extraordinary leaven from timeserving and wavering advisers, at least among the confidential underlings, and has shown itself . . . distracted by personal animosities and petty intrigues.'

547. From George Ponsonby

⟨Horner, ii. 219–20⟩   Dropmore, 25 Jan. 1815

⟨We who are here, Lord Grenville, his brother, Elliot, Newport, and myself, have been talking over the first operations fit to take place upon the meeting of the House; and we have agreed that the best motion to begin with (upon notice) is one relative to America; and that the best form will be to move for a committee to inquire into the conduct of the war. The papers which have been published, and the peace which has been concluded, since the adjournment, seem to render such a motion peculiarly expedient; for there can be no doubt that the feelings of the country must be strongly excited by the disclosure of the facts contained in those papers, and by the conclusion of a peace, justifiable only (in the opinion of those who concluded it) by necessity; a necessity arising solely from their own mismanagement of the war. We hope you will concur in our view of this subject; and that you will have the goodness to give, when the House meets, a notice of your intention of moving for the Committee upon Thursday the 16th of February.[1] I am myself persuaded of the utility of early and constant action in the House; and I am sure the public interest demands and the public expectation requires it. To our friends I have written some time ago, requesting their attendance; and I have every reason to be confident of their compliance.

⟨I shall be in town, to remain, on Friday, and will endeavour to find you at leisure, to converse a little upon these matters, very soon after.⟩

1. The decision to make the Treaty of Ghent a first priority in Parliament reflected Grenville's continuing opposition to attacks on British policy at Vienna and his desire to avoid public disagreement with his political allies. For several months Foxites throughout the country, and even several prominent members of Grenville's own party, had voiced mounting chagrin at developments on the Continent (Taylor, pp. 395–400). Now, with Holland still in Italy and Grey detained at Howick by the illness of one of his children, Grenville, while admitting privately that the recent conclusion of peace with the United States had disarmed Opposition, sought a plan of parliamentary tactics which dodged specific questions relating to Europe, centred on the 'mismanagement' that had resulted in the *status quo ante bellum* agreed to at Ghent, stressed the need for a low peacetime establishment, and included opposition to the retention of the property tax. (*Buckingham*, ii. 107; Grenville to T. Grenville, 3 Jan., BL Add. MSS 41853; T. Grenville to C. W. W. Wynn, 25 Jan., Wynn MSS, National Library of Wales, Aberystwyth.) Horner figured prominently in Grenville's scheme. He had visited Dropmore earlier in the month (Doc. 543 n. 1); now he was chosen to move for a committee of inquiry on the conduct of the American war. The plan adopted at Dropmore puzzled Mackintosh, who observed that it was foolish to sanction by silence the Vienna settlement while opposing the taxes that were necessary to enforce it, but Lauderdale comprehended that Grenville's views were adopted 'for the sake of mere display', and later a pessimistic Mackintosh came to appreciate that the plan was adopted with an eye to Whig unity (Mackintosh to Holland, 6 Feb., BL Add. MSS 51653; Lauderdale to Lady Holland, 6 Feb., BL Add. MSS 51698; Mackintosh to Lady Holland, [Feb. 1815], BL Add. MSS 51654). There is nothing in Horner's papers that suggests he ever attached importance to a parliamentary inquiry into the American war during 1815. See Taylor, pp. 399–401, for analysis of the factors that determined the Whigs' curious parliamentary behaviour in the early months of 1815.

548. To J.A. Murray

BLPES vi. 160–67 ⟨*Homer*, ii. 220–22⟩   Lincoln's Inn, 30 Jan. 1815

⟨I thank you for your kind attention to all my commissions, contained in my two last notes⟩, with the exception of the wish I meant to express, to have your opinion upon the strange passages in the last *Review*.[1] Though they stand unexplained, and probably have no real meaning except as an ebullition of personal momentary feelings, yet the publication of them in so important a work as Jeffrey's *Review* is not without its consequences. It appears to me the most signal instance of the injustice which the Whig leaders have met with, after all their sacrifices of personal ambition to principle, that such a stab should be aimed at them, by a hand that professes to be friendly; by which I mean Jeffrey's hand, and not that of the splenetic selfish individual who writes the particular article. If the public in general were in the habit of detaching particular articles from the general authority of the *Review*, or if they knew this individual as I do, the harm done could not be so great. However, one must suffer what cannot be prevented; a day will come, when this gross injustice will be compensated by posthumous reparation; and when intrigues will be thoroughly understood.[2] *Ohe! Jam satis.*[3]

⟨I never entertained any doubt that, upon the question of the unanimity of verdicts, a concession must be made to strong prejudice or misconception; as upon every other part of the Bill, or of any new measure that respects the administration of justice.⟩⁴ The only alternative is, between yielding to the popular error, or postponing your innovation altogether. What convinces me more than any thing of the propriety of giving way in the present instance, is, that, among those who voted for the English constitution of the jury, there were some who concurred in that vote with hesitation; because this shows that the prejudice reaches very high, among the best informed men of Scotland, and, what is of infinite consequence, among those who professionally must execute the new project. I shall regret it always; because I think it is admitting a defect into the system, which cannot at any future time be cured; and because I wonder that such a misconception should have taken hold of well-informed minds. ⟨The word *unanimity* has done the mischief, which is none of ours. The principle of the English jury is no more than this, that they should *agree* before they give in their verdict; which, practically, secures all those benefits of discussion, of a disposition in all to be reasonable and moderate, and of an opportunity still left to a single dissentient to have his arguments heard, that would be excluded by the rule of a majority. Substantially and practically, in nine cases out of ten, the verdict must go by the sentiments of the majority; but the operation is very different from what it would be, if it were *of course* by the voice of the majority. I cannot speak from much of what can be called experience; though, with something of that sort, and with a good deal more of reflection upon the principles that ought to regulate the constitution of courts of justice; but I own that my opinion is, without any hesitation, that the requiring of the jury to agree before they give their verdict, and the taking it from them as being said by them all, is a highly valuable part of our existing system.⟩ This I am sorry that Scotland is not to have; but even that is trifling, compared with many other advantages of the Jury system, which it is not proposed in any degree to communicate to Scotland.

⟨There is certainly no foundation for the rumour⁵ with which I am honoured, it seems, at Edinburgh, of being a convert to the Corn Bill.⟩ I dare say Rose is got over, for he never objected to it but because the particular mode of regulation was not to his mind, or rather because he was not consulted in settling it; regulation is his rage.⁶ ⟨The more I have read upon the subject, and the more I hear upon it, I get more firmly fixed in my original opinion, that nothing should be done. Of course it will be carried with a loud clamour, and with much abuse of all *lackland* theorists. It would be as absurd to expect men to be reasonable about corn, as to be reasonable in matters of religion.

⟨I do not imagine any new discovery is made about the relation of the price of labour to that of grain, or the effects of scarcity or plenty upon wages. The principles, upon which all such effects must depend, are obvious to every one who understands the operation of demand and supply upon prices; indeed, they are all an application of that single principle. A great many cases are necessary to be put, in order to distinguish the various effects of scarcity or plenty upon wages, according to the nature of the particular employment in which labour is to be paid for; but even when the effects are the most opposite, it is still the operation of the same principle. All this is stated well enough by Adam Smith towards the end of his chapter on the Wages of Labour [Book I, chapter viii].

⟨The most important convert the landholders have got, is Malthus, who has now declared himself in favour of their Bill; and to be sure there is not a better or more informed judgement, and it is the single authority which staggers me.[7] But those who have looked closely into his philosophy will admit, that there is always a leaning in favour of the efficacy of laws; and his early bias was for corn laws in particular. It was a great effort of candour, in truth, to suspend his decision upon this particular measure so long. I think I could demonstrate, from his own principles of population, that if this measure is effectual at all, it must be attended with great misery among the manufacturing classes, as well as among the labourers in husbandry; and with a violent forced alteration of that proportion, in this country, between agricultural and manufacturing population and capital, which the freedom of both has adjusted, and would continue to maintain, better and more lightly for all the people, than can be effected by all the wisdom of all the squires of the island, with the political arithmeticians to boot.⟩

. . .

1. Murray's reply to Doc. 546 has not been found.
2. It would appear from Doc. 557 that Horner later voiced similar protests to Jeffrey himself.
3. 'Oh! That is now more than enough' (Horace).
4. After seemingly endless stalling and delay, the Government had late the previous year at last introduced its own bill for trial by jury in civil cases in Scotland. (See Doc. 555.)
5. *Horner* prints 'distinction'.
6. Apparently there were rumours during the parliamentary recess that Rose, who like Horner had spoken against the proposed changes in the Corn Laws the previous May, had, as a result of interviews with Liverpool, changed his mind and, as Baring unkindly put it when they were discussed again in the Commons on 17 Feb., 'changed his title of "the Man of the People" for one of the new little crosses of the Order of the Bath'. Rose utterly refuted the accusation, adding later in the debate 'that neither on the present nor any former occasion when this subject was before the House, had he ever said one word against the principle of protecting duties'. (*Hansard*, xxix. 832–3 and 855.)
7. Malthus's *Observations on the Effects of the Corn Laws*, published in 1814, argued in the style of the Physiocrats that agriculture was more important than manufactures, stated the arguments for and against the protection of agriculture, and reasoned somewhat timidly that the political dependence arising from free trade was an evil. (See *Malthus*, pp. 253–7.)

549. To John Horner

BLPES vi. 168–9 Lincoln's Inn, 6 Feb. 1815

. . .

. . . The property tax is I believe given up, in consequence of the strong language of the country against it; though the Ministers had certainly formed their plans upon the continuance of this large revenue for another year. They will struggle hard against making any reductions in consequence of this defalcation of income, which they will endeavour to supply probably by a loan, of which they will charge the interest upon the sinking fund; a very improvident expedient. Notwithstanding the public poverty, the Regent is said to have in contemplation a very costly trip to the continent, to take possession of the new kingdom of Hanover, and to be present at

the coronation of the King of France; to enable him to go abroad, we are to have a
Bill giving him power to appoint Lord Justices. There have been rumours for the last
ten days of his health being deranged; one day it was a fit; another day, Willis had
been sent for;[1] and one edition of the story was that he had brought it on by a violent
paroxysm of anger against Wathier his cook for the soup being ill made. I do not
know that there was a foundation for any one of the particular stories; but the turn of
them all shows an expectation, among those who invent and receive them, that he
is not to be exempted from the family infirmity. Perhaps it would not be straining
very much to infer that the Queen herself is not without this expectation, from an
alteration of the most marked kind which has recently taken place in her behaviour
to the Princess Charlotte, which is all at once turned to great kindness and
indulgence. . . .

   . . .

   1. Probably Robert Darling Willis (1760–1821), the King's physician, rather than his elder
     brother John (1751–1835). Like their more famous father Francis (1718–1807: *DNB*), both
     had attended George III during his bouts of madness, and whenever rumours spread about
     the strange behaviour of one of the King's sons, 'Dr Willis' was said to have been sent for.

550. To T.R. Malthus

BLPES vi. 170–73 ⟨*Horner*, ii. 222–8⟩   [London], Sunday night, 12 Feb. 1815

⟨I have to thank you for sending me your two new publications upon the corn
question, which I have read, and am still reading.[1] You will think me very hardened,
but I must own that my old faith is not shaken by your reasonings; on the contrary,
I am even so perverse, as to think I have discovered, among your ingenious
deductions respecting rent, some fresh and cogent arguments in favour of a free corn
trade for this country; by which I always mean, as free a trade as we can secure by our
own good sense, however it may be impaired by the deficiency of our neighbours in
that qualification. If the consequence of 'high farming' and curious cultivation be a
progressive rise of the price of produce, an importation of partial supplies from
countries, which by a ruder agriculture can furnish it cheaper, seems the provision
laid by nature for checking too exclusive an employment of capital upon the land
least fit for culture. It would be a palpable sacrifice of the end to the means, if, for the
sake of extending our most finished husbandry to every sterile ridge that can be
forced to yield something, we impose upon the whole body of the people
extravagant prices for the necessaries of life. Nor do I see, upon your peculiar
principles, what other result there would be, if Dartmoor and Blackstone Edge were
laid out in terraces of garden ground, but a population always in some peril of being
starved, if their rulers will not let them eat the superfluity of their neighbours. I have
not leisure to write out in any systematic form what has occurred to me, but I wish
you would allow me to suggest some objections to you, and to request farther
explanations from you, on some points which I have marked in a very hasty perusal

of 'The grounds of your opinion.' I mean to put them down without any attention to order, and will stuff as many of them into this letter as I have time for; I have, in truth, very little time for these speculations.

⟨Why do you say, p. 28, that 'in all common years, France will furnish us with a large proportion of our supplies?' This affirmation is not founded upon the parliamentary evidence, which bears the contrary way. The witnesses were not examined till a considerable time after the signature of the Definitive Treaty; yet, in stating the various countries from which we are to look for imports of grain, during the subsistence of peace, none of them ever name France, or seem to think of it; although a great many foreign corn-factors are brought forward, and some whose experience goes back for years previous to the commencement of the long war. They say indeed expressly, that they know but one instance of an import from France, which took place after the harvest of 1809, and until the prohibition in July 1810. That exportation was allowed by the French Government, to relieve the pressure of an excessive plenty. But why did not the same motive operate more frequently, if you are right in what you state, p. 13, that 'prices have been often as low during the last ten years as they were after the last harvest?' And, by the way, in your statement of the French prices in the same passage, which is made, of course, for the sake of comparisons with our own, should you not have included the difference of exchange, when you converted their money into ours? You talk of the law, made by the two Chambers last summer, for the regulation of their export price, as if it had cast quite a new light upon the whole subject, and as if it for the first time had admonished you of having too precipitately made admissions of the favourable effects of a free trade. Had not the French always such a regulation, if not the very same?⟩

P. 5, you state, ⟨that, by the recent improvements of agriculture, 'we had become much less dependent upon foreign supplies for our support.' What proof is there of this? The excess of imports does not appear to have sensibly decreased of very late years; it never was so high as in 1810. The small quantity imported in 1812 (the accounts make it double what you state it to have been) is in the following page, not consistently, I think, used by you, not as a consequence of the increase of our home-growth, but as a proof of the difficulty of importation. A fact of this nature cannot tell both ways, it seems to me.⟩

P. 5. ⟨Speaking from recollection only, I should not say that it is a result to be gathered from the evidence before Parliament, that 'a continuation of low prices would, *in spite of a diminution of rents*, destroy farming capital and diminish produce.' The witnesses, who make this prediction, generally at least, if not uniformly, speak upon the supposition of the present rents being still to be paid. I may observe, too, that they generally take for granted, which is more fallacious, that with low prices, and continued low prices, all the expenses and outgoings of a farm are still to keep at their present rate; and so they prove, demonstrably to their own conviction, that a farmer will never be remunerated if he gets but 8s. a bushel for his wheat at market, while he is feeding all his ploughmen, and buying his seeds, and paying all the auxiliary labour of the farm, with wheat at 12s. a bushel.

⟨You have made a fair allowance for the partiality and interest of those who were *called upon to give* evidence.[2] You thought it would be indecent to give the same indulgence, or rather you could make no allowance for the bias of those who were appointed *to take* the evidence. There are some very gross instances of this: see, in our Commons' Committee, how they dispatch Charles Mant,[3] when he hints that the rate of the protecting price should be estimated, not according to the present expenses, but according to that very fall of grain and labour, which are anticipated; they huddle up that subject, and pass on in a hurry to other matters.

⟨I think some portion of the same fallacy, which I last mentioned, has slid into that part of your argument, p. 24, where you point out the advantages the labourer may derive from a high money price of corn, and consequently high wages to himself. Do not you assume that, though corn should fall and bring down wages, yet there will be no fall in the prices of any other articles of his consumption?

⟨In considering the influence of a low price of corn upon the condition and comforts of the labourer, you have wholly omitted this consideration, that such a fall will release thousands and tens of thousands from the parochial pauper list, and restore them to the pride of earning their bread by free labour. I could not read without indignation, in the evidence of Mr Benett of Pyt House, who seems the very model of a witness for Corn Committees, his cold-blooded[4] statement of the rule he makes, and unmakes, for the distribution of rations of provender and fodder among the prædial slaves of a whole district of Wiltshire.[5] It is this audacious and presumptuous spirit of regulating, by the wisdom of country squires, the whole economy and partition of national industry and wealth, that makes me more keenly averse to this Corn Bill of theirs than I should have been in earlier days of our time, when the principles of rational government were more widely understood, and were maintained by stronger hands at the head of affairs. The narrow conceit of managing the happiness of the labouring population, and of directing the application of industry, as well as the competition of the market, works in the present day upon a much larger scale than when it busied itself with the pedlar items of the foreign trade.⟩

P. 27, you have stated, ⟨rather like a skilful advocate than quite fully, the experience of the last hundred years respecting the fluctuations of the price of corn. You have shown but one side of that experience, which has two sides, very much alike. You take one period of fourteen years, and show a considerable fluctuation, by including remarkable years of dearth. This is during the time of imports being in excess. But take another period of fourteen years, while the excess was on the side of exports; for instance, the period from 1706 to 1720: the price of wheat in 1706 was 26s., in 1709 and 1710 was 78s., in 1719 was 35s. Take the first seven years of the last century, the average price was 30s.; in the seven subsequent years, the average price was as high as 57s. In 1740, the price I find was 50s., in 1743 only 24s., in 1757 again 60s. After this, it must be admitted, that the argument concerning *fluctuations* rests still in theory; and then my theory would be, that, upon the whole, nothing will contribute so much to make prices steady, as by our leaving our own corn factors unfettered by restrictions and regulations of our own making, and without embarrassment from that source, to make their own arrangements for bringing corn, when it is wanted, from the various large and independent markets, of which, in the present circumstances of the world, they have their choice. And though one may argue from experience, it can never be a sound inference, from the state of prices under the imports of the last seven or eight years, to conclude that there will be the same uncertainty in the new position of political circumstances.

⟨Though I have something more to object, I must release you for the present. Excuse the perfect freedom with which I have very hurriedly written these animadversions, and treat me still as one of whose conversion from heresy some hopes may be entertained. I should be sorry you should set me down for obstinate and beyond repentance; do not consign me to silence; I do not mind being consigned to the flames by Squire Western and the rabble of Irish economists.⟩

. . .

⟨PS By the way, I cannot part without saying how I grudge my adversaries on the bullion question the lift you have given them. Surely your corn zeal has lessened too much in your eyes for the moment the magnitude of that evil.⟩[6]

1. In early 1815 Malthus published two further pamphlets, *Nature and Progress of Rent* and *Grounds of an Opinion on the Policy of Restricting the Importation of Foreign Corn*. The first advanced the important principle that rents rose with the progressive cultivation of new land and the progressive improvement of old land, and fell with the abandonment of inferior land and the continued deterioration of superior land, and that the price of produce was therefore roughly equivalent to the cost of production on inferior land in use or to the cost of raising additional produce on old land. Reasoning from the thesis of diminished returns thus advanced, the second pamphlet advocated the temporary protection of British agriculturalists from foreign corn so as to keep prices high and thereby facilitate progressive cultivation. (See *Malthus*, pp. 259–63.)

2. *Horner* rather loses the sense by omitting part of the emphasis.

3. Charles Mant was a partner in the London firm of corn importers, Baker, Mant, and Page. His evidence is in *BPP*, 1813–14, iii. 284–6 and 311–12.

4. *Horner* prints 'cool'.

5. John Benett (1773–1852) of Pythouse was a large landowner in Wiltshire, which he afterwards represented in Parliament. Although a Whig supporter, he led the pro-Corn Law agitation in the county in 1814 and when he first contested the county seat in 1818 his opponents accused him of being a tyrannical landlord. His evidence is in *BPP*, 1813–14, iii. 253–65.

6. The Whig reviewers were plainly upset by Malthus's pamphlets which were quickly 'trounced' by Buchanan in *ER* xxiv (no. xlviii, Feb. 1815), 491–505. Henceforth, moreover, Malthus was given no access to or support by the *Review*, and had eventually to resort instead to the *QR*. Jeffrey himself had been sympathetic to his point of view and had even wanted to publish it in the form of an article. Professor Winch states that 'he allowed himself to be overruled by Horner's advice'. This may have been so, but the evidence cited does not appear by any means so clear. (*Malthus*, p. 264; Winch, p. 78.)

551. To Dr Samuel Parr

⟨*Parr*, viii. 298–9⟩   Lincoln's Inn, 14 Feb. 1815

⟨. . . It is a great satisfaction to me to see that the opinions I hold about the income tax, and the proposals of substitutes for it, are sanctioned by your authority. The victory which the people, by their constitutional vigour, have gained over the King's Ministers, a victory which the present House of Commons, if left to itself, never would have gained for them, will be left wholly incomplete, unless it leads to a systematic retrenchment, and to a considerable reduction of all the establishments, especially those of a military sort. On this view of the subject I suspect the public in general are by no means so much agreed as they have been against the continuance of the means of supplying the expenditure. Yet, in a financial light merely, much injury will have been done to the ultimate interests of the people, if, continuing the same heedless and pernicious profusion, we are to substitute for a very simple and efficient tax the spendthrift expedients of new loans in peace, and an encroachment upon the sinking fund. In all other respects, however, the repeal of the property-tax by the temperate and strong voice of the people, is one of those wholesome efforts of our constitutional liberty which must be attended with many and lasting good consequences. It is good to let the people feel that they can beat their rulers upon a wrong measure of government, particularly in the old line of supplies; it is no bad thing either to associate in the minds of the people themselves those two expectations, a renewal of the property-tax, and a renewal of Continental wars; but it is best of all, in the present circumstances of this country and its government, to put Ministers upon a short allowance of money, and force them, for want of ways and means, into a plan of frugal expenditure.

⟨I should have doubted the propriety of abandoning the idea of a meeting of your county. The Ministers still hold out a remote possibility of the property-tax as an alternative if their proposed substitute be rejected. The voice of the people cannot be too generally and repeatedly exerted; particularly if, besides the continuance of the tax, they will petition for economy and low establishments.⟩

552. From T.R. Malthus

Kinnordy MSS[1]   16 Feb. 1815

I am much obliged to you for the attention you have given my publication. I will not condemn you to silence for your heresies but I am at present so much behind hand with letters and business of all descriptions that I can only answer shortly. From what I saw in Town, I did not, I confess, expect to convert you with regard to the practical question; but I really did expect a little more favour for my essay on Rent. It is certainly a very curious and very important question, and I feel strongly that I am right in my theory on the subject, whatever inferences you may draw from it with regard to the policy or impolicy of importation.

I said what I did about France from the notoriety of the low prices of her grain which I had heard from all quarters. The corn factors could have no experience about France, as the state of France now with regard to corn is very different to what it was before the Revolution; and they have had nothing to do with her during the last 20 years, except in the peculiar trade by licence in 1810. I believe that at 'the' time corn was much lower than it is now; and I do not understand from our travellers that a people speak of this year as unusually cheap. It cannot, therefore, be doubted I think that we shall import largely from France in all commonly plentiful years. The corn factors intimate most justly that we could not rely upon France as a certain source of supply when we wanted it.

I confess that the present law of France has impressed me strongly, and brought home to me the reason why a free foreign trade in corn has never practically answered as well as one should have expected from theory. And such a law being passed by so near a neighbour (and in the actual state of France with regard to the growth of corn) cannot upon all general principles fail of producing great fluctuations.

If you will cast up the importations of the last seven or eight years ending with 1813 and compare them with the seven or eight preceding, you will find the diminution of importation one half, which is a great difference. I am so hurried at this moment that I cannot refer to papers, to be more accurate. I see no great inconsistency in using the year 1812 to prove both the improvements of our agriculture and the difficulty of importation. A small quantity imported (my tables say 115,811 quarters) compared with the high price show the latter; and our being able to get through a bad harvest without assistance, and yet without much starvation is a proof of the former.

I own my impression from the evidence with regard to rent is different from yours. Most of the lessors examined seemed to me to think the relief from a diminution of rent would be inconsiderable. The fact really is that a fall in price will affect produce much more than rent. The clay lands thrown out of cultivation might still yield the half or the third of what they did before but the produce might very likely be diminished to $^1/_{10}$th.

I agree with you that [our?]^2 farmers in their calculations did not take sufficiently into their consideration the fall of wages. Such a fall would undoubtedly take place but nothing I think can be more er[r]oneous than to conclude, that because a fall of corn would occasion a fall of wages, it will necessarily occasion a *proportionate* fall, not only in wages but in everything else. Here I think you are fundamentally and radically wrong in your general principles, and I feel myself quite safe in stating [that] in a rich country where the price of corn is high, a given quantity of it will almost invariably command a larger quantity of manufactured and foreign commodities than in poor countries where the price of corn is low.

I was certainly aware of the bias of the Examiners, and meant to include them in my general allowance.

I own I am not a little surprised at your arguments about thousands and ten thousands. You estimate that farming capital will not suffer, if wheat sells at 8/- a bushel, because labour having fallen in proportion, all the outgoings of the farm will be proportionately reduced, and the compensative [?]^3 gains the same. But if labour be reduced in proportion to the price of corn, how can the thousands and ten thousands be rendered independent? Is there any magic in the name of 6 or 8 shillings instead of 10 or 12 that can produce these wonderful effects[?] If labour did not fall in proportion, farming capital must suffer; and if it do fall, where is your relief and independence? You are on the horns of a dilemma.

You must be aware that no lessor can refutate [?*sic*] more than I do the rations of provenda [?*sic*] distributed by the country Justices; and I quite join with you in your virtuous indignation on the subject. But surely it is perfectly unfair and uncandid to mix the two questions together, they appear to me to have no kind of connection.

You really talk as if the Justices and Squires have now for the first time come forward with a proposal for corn laws, joined to the system of Parish allowances; instead of which, restrictive laws have (with a short period of exception) been the policy of the country for the last 130 years.

In stating the fluctuations of price which have actually occur[r]ed during the time we were most dependent on other countries, I really thought it quite fair not to go farther back than 100 years because we well know that the farther we go back the greater are the fluctuations, whatever system is adopted, and we can hardly percept to have established a steady system of agriculture till after the wars of Queen Anne. The variations you notice from 1743 to 1757 are certainly to the point, and to say the truth, they escaped my eye. Let us then go back to the theory of the subject; and I should say that according to the principles of supply and demand I should a priori expect greater fluctuations from a trade of corn like that which we are likely to have with France, the Baltic, and America, than under a system of restrictions; and certainly there is no experience to be adduced against the theory, if there be none for it.

If I have given our adversaries a lift on the bullion question, I really cannot help it. My object is the truth; and I should think myself a very bad theorist, and quite unworthy to be attended to if I did not keep myself always open to the lessons of experience. I consider what has happened since the Bank Restrictions as a very curious and instructive series of facts, lending to throw great light on the theory of paper money and the causes that effect the price of bullion.

If you do not now think that a much greater part of the difference between bullion and paper was occasioned by commercial causes and a peculiar demand for the precious metals, than was supposed by the Bullionists in general, it will, I confess, appear to me such an instance of adherence to an opinion once given in the face of the most palpable facts, as considerably to diminish the feelings of doubt and uneasiness which I have hitherto experienced whenever I have found myself compelled to differ from you in opinion.

Excuse the freedom and haste with which I have written.

1. The editors have seen only a typed transcript.
2. The typescript has 'for'.
3. The query is in the typescript.

553. Speech by Horner[1]

⟨Horner, ii. 523–33⟩   House of Commons, 23 Feb. 1815

⟨He should not pay much attention to the calculations on either side. From the manner in which the question was opened, he had no hesitation in saying, that the right honourable gentleman (Mr Robinson) had manifested a more statesman-like mind than any of those by whom his propositions were supported; for that right honourable gentleman had fully recognized the great principles which, according to the highest authorities, ought to regulate our commercial policy, admitting that a case of necessity should be made out for any deviation from those principles, and that the House had only to balance between difficulties – between the nature of the necessity and the deference that was due to the great radical principle of a free trade. That this principle was entitled to respect, was not, he maintained, the opinion of what were denominated mere modern speculatists, but of the soundest thinkers upon commercial policy, aided by the experience of practical men, who most naturally deemed the success of agriculture as the main basis of commercial prosperity. Those, then, who concurred with such thinkers, could not be regarded as theorists only, nor were they fairly liable to the attempts made to depreciate their judgement. He was indeed surprised at these attempts, as if the denomination of 'political economists' could detract from the authority of any gentleman who opposed the measure before the committee. But who were they who resorted to nicknames upon this occasion? Why, the very men who admitted that the knowledge of political economy required deep reading, and, that what appeared paradoxes to superficial observers were, upon further investigation, proved to be just and rational views. Those, indeed, who used the nickname alluded to, endeavoured themselves, by the legerdemain of figures, and a complication of details, to confer a rational character upon a proposition which had all the complexion of a paradox, which, in fact, appeared utterly irreconcilable with reason. But in reviewing these extravagances, he was glad to find that the report of the committee of that House was not disfigured by such observations as appeared in the report of the other House of Parliament; for, in the latter, he was really astonished to find these statements: first, that the price of provisions had truly nothing to do with the price of labour; and, secondly, that the amount of rents had no material influence upon the charges of agriculture. But there was another theory, still more extraordinary, from the advocates of the proposition before the committee, and which, he believed, had never been broached since the days of Cromwell; namely, that the land did not really belong to the proprietors, but to the community. – Nay, in addition to these strange doctrines, an honourable friend of his (Mr Preston),[2] who was among those by whom theorists had been decried, had that day sent him the tract of the Marquis de Mirabeau upon political economy, which he had alluded to in his speech, calculating, no doubt, that it would serve to produce an impression upon his mind: but his honourable friend was under a serious mistake as to the nature of that celebrated writer's opinion; for the Marquis de Mirabeau belonged to that class of economists, who maintained quite an opposite doctrine to that of the honourable gentleman; and also that all the taxes necessary to the support of the state should be drawn directly from the land.

⟨But as to political economy generally, upon what ground could gentlemen pretend to depreciate its character, unless they meant to deprecate the exercise of reasoning upon the subject under the consideration of the committee! However, in consistency with their system of depreciation as to political economy, they had thought proper to treat with levity the treatise of Dr Adam Smith, which was, in fact, but a collection or digest of maxims, which, instead of being any innovation, had long been held sacred among the best writers this country had ever known. But it was also well known, that the opinions contained in the work of Dr Adam Smith

were, after full examination, recommended by the sanction of our most
distinguished statesmen, – by Mr Pitt, for instance, and also by Mr Burke, who
traced the history of Dr Smith's opinions, demonstrating that those opinions,
instead of being, as some alleged, mere plagiarisms from those of the French
economists, were the original growth of our own country, from which they had been
borrowed by the economists of France. The justice, however, of Dr Smith's great
principles was recognized by the statesman-like view of the right honourable opener
of this question, who had not given the weight of his authority to the untenable
proposition, that because the manufacturers enjoyed some protecting duties, the
agriculturalists were entitled to the measure he proposed, which was a kind of
argumentum ad hominem. Still less did the right honourable gentleman manifest any
disposition to support the assertion, that the agriculturalists suffered by the
protecting duties granted to the manufacturers; and in what instance, he would ask,
could the British agriculturalists be conceived so to suffer? From what country could
they obtain any article of manufacture necessary for their consumption, at a cheaper
rate than they could purchase it at home, supposing trade perfectly free, and that
protecting duties, as to manufactures, were totally done away? Could coarse woollen
cloths, for instance, be purchased cheaper any where than in England? or could any
other article be had on better terms elsewhere? The only article, indeed, which
could be supposed cheaper elsewhere was linen, which was the manufacture of
Ireland. For himself, however, he had no difficulty in declaring, that all the
protecting duties (as they were called) at present in existence in this country, were
but so many clogs and impediments to our commercial prosperity; and that,
whatever might be the gain, which must be partial and comparatively insignificant,
derived probably to the most insignificant in trade, the effect of the whole system
must be, that the produce of our natural wealth was considerably diminished.

⟨But, reverting to the main question, and bearing in mind the grounds stated by
the right honourable opener, he maintained that no necessity was made out for any
departure from the main principles of trade, to the justice of which that right
honourable gentleman bore testimony. If the proposition before the committee were
merely a temporary measure, to relieve any temporary pressure upon the farmers, he
confessed that he should have felt much more difficulty in opposing it; but, as a
measure of permanent legislation, he could not hesitate to enter his protest against
it. Sympathy for the suffering of individuals would naturally dispose one to plead for
the former; but every consideration of sound national policy, which he was able to
appreciate, urged him to resist the latter. But the object of granting temporary relief
to individual distress had been disclaimed by the advocates for the proposition
before the committee, who thought proper to rest their pretensions upon
considerations of permanent policy; and here he was at issue with them. He was
aware of the distress of the agriculturists under existing circumstances, and he had
all due feeling for their situation; but, then, he recollected the cause of that
situation, which recollection was necessary to a due estimate of the policy of this
measure. The present distress of the agriculturists was owing to the great stimulus
which the circumstances of the war had given to agriculture; which stimulus was
now withdrawn. The operation of that stimulus, which offered a strong proof of the
prosperity and health of our commercial system, encouraged the farmers to offer

exorbitant rents for land, and also to lay out large sums upon that land; they must naturally suffer by the cessation of such a stimulus. They had, in fact, been too sanguine in their speculations, and hence the losses of which they now complained. But the farmers were not the only persons who suffered from too extensive speculations. Such sufferings, also, too frequently happened in every branch of trade, and did it therefore follow that an application should be made to Parliament to repair the loss? It would, indeed, be impossible for Parliament to make good such losses; and it would be unjust to make an attempt to withdraw from the profits of other classes of the community, to repair the losses sustained by any class of unsuccessful speculators.

‹But in considering the case of the agriculturists (as an exception was demanded in their favour), in looking at their present difficulties or losses, the House was called upon, in justice, to look also to the cause of that loss, which naturally brought into view their antecedent profits. The most interesting distress among the farmers – that which in his mind was most entitled to commiseration, was certainly the case of the agriculturists of Ireland; but that case also was the result of the artificial stimulus given to Irish agriculture by the peculiar circumstances of the war. No one, he believed, felt a more lively concern for the interest of Ireland than that of which he was sensible, and which should always regulate his conduct, as he thought it must the mind of every man who duly appreciated the general interests of the empire. He was therefore happy to witness the pregnant proof which the present situation of Ireland afforded of its advancing prosperity. For that situation served, in his view, to demonstrate that its commercial enterprise had of late years been considerably exerted, and that a great quantity of capital had been employed in that most useful branch of industry, its agricultural pursuits. Ireland had therefore experienced a check from the conclusion of peace (a smile on the other side of the House) – Gentlemen might smile, he said, but he would maintain that this check afforded a proof of the advanced prosperity of Ireland. For the present was notoriously the first instance on record, in the history of Ireland, in which that country had experienced any check in its domestic circumstances, from the conclusion of peace by the mother country; and this check he regarded as an evidence that it partook of our prosperity, the interruption of which naturally occasioned a participation of our losses. Then, as to the disadvantage resulting to the lands lately applied to tillage in this country, upon which a large sum must have been expended, he was fully aware that that disadvantage was entitled to consideration. This disadvantage must be universally regretted. But what relief could be expected by the sufferers from the proposed measure, especially if it were true, as the advocates of this measure alleged, that the effect of it must be to reduce the price of corn? According to the deposition of witnesses before the committee, 96s. per quarter was necessary to enable farmers to grow that article; nay, according to the allegation of some gentlemen, less than 135s. would be insufficient; and how then, in the name of common sense, could the sum be deemed an adequate remuneration for this species of culture? Or still more, how could the proposed regulation operate to reduce the price of corn? How, indeed, could gentlemen who supported these depositions and allegations, plead for a measure so self-destructive as the present? The light lands, or those lately devoted to agriculture, must still suffer all the distress that was deprecated, especially through the competition of the more fertile soil of Ireland, and the richer lands of this country; and the result must still be to throw those light lands out of cultivation.

‹With respect to our independence of foreign supply, he was ready to admit, that if a dependence upon foreign supply were likely to be the result of the existing system, that likelihood would form a legitimate ground for the proposed measure. (And here the honourable and learned gentleman took notice of the exception of Dr Smith with regard to our navigation law, which exception referred to a provision of our national safety, which was, in all cases, a predominant consideration. But returning to the apprehension of our dependence upon a foreign supply of corn, the honourable and learned member treated that apprehension as quite exaggerated and visionary.) Indeed it had been, he observed, most tenaciously maintained by the advocates for this apprehension, that it would be impossible for the whole navy of England to import any very large proportion, much less an adequate supply of corn, for our subsistence. This, however, these gentlemen seemed to feel an admission hostile to their own proposition, and therefore, in order to take off the weight of such admission, they asserted that even a small quantity of imported corn would have a material effect upon the market price. This, however, he could not admit. A comparatively small quantity of imported corn might affect the market price upon a particular day, or for a few days; but the price must ultimately and permanently depend upon the proportion of the supply to the demand, and the proportion of supply from abroad was in no degree likely to be considerable. But supposing the supply to be even considerable, the apprehensions expressed on this subject were still, in his mind, exceedingly exaggerated and fallacious; nor was it even probable that we should have to depend upon foreign supply to such an extent as to endanger the interests of our own agriculture. A great deal of this apprehension had been propagated, which was negatived by the papers on the table, especially with regard to the supply derived from what was called our natural enemy. He would readily admit, that if it could be rendered apparent, that in any event we should have to depend upon France for food, a protecting duty, as it was termed, should be immediately granted to avert such a calamity; and to this grant he would accede, not from any commercial jealousy, which he should always deprecate, but from political jealousy, to which it would, in such a case, be our duty to attend. But what was the fact? Was France a corn-exporting country? Did it not appear from the papers on the table that our great import of corn had been, not from France, but from Holland and from Belgium, the sovereign of which was our own creation? Thus we derived a supply of corn, not from a natural enemy, as France was denominated, but from our own probably permanent ally. But France could never be regarded as a great exporting country of corn. No; the poor country was always the exporter of that article to the rich, for which she received manufactures in return. France had, in fact, become for the last year an exporter of corn, in consequence of an exceedingly redundant harvest, and from the same cause she was an exporter in the year 1810. But France could never be expected to rival this country in agriculture; for from every information that had reached us, her system of agriculture was exceedingly inferior to our own, while her grain was also materially inferior in quality. How, then, could it be apprehended that we should have to depend upon that nation for supply in any event, especially when we had to look not only to Holland as a medium for furnishing the produce of the banks of the Rhine, but to Flanders, to the Baltic, to Poland, and to America also. With a peace, indeed, so consolidated, as the gentlemen on the other side promised, he thought all apprehension on this score quite visionary. But even calculating upon the renewal of war, or the reappearance of some extravagant tyrant, who, with a combination of all the powers of Europe, should speculate upon our total exclusion from continental commerce, he should still think such an apprehension groundless. For it was notorious from experience, that even when the experiment of this exclusion was made, namely from 1810 to 1812, a larger importation had taken place into this country, especially from France, than was ever known within the same compass at any former period. The apprehension, then, of depriving this country of foreign supply must, under any circumstances, be regarded as totally chimerical. As to a provision to guard against fluctuation of prices, which the advocates of the measure before the committee promised, it would be found that for the last seven years, when our importation of corn was greater than at any former period, the fluctuation was much less than during any period of the same duration since the Revolution; and this fact he had ascertained by examining the Eden tables.[3] Within the last seven years, too, it was notorious that our agriculture had been in the most flourishing state, much more flourishing, indeed, than when it was most the fashion to grant bounties upon the export, and to expose restrictions upon the import of corn. So much as to the pretence of a steady price, which was looked for by some gentlemen as the result of the proposed measure. In his opinion, however, the best security for a steady price – that is, for a fair price to the consumer, was not a measure the witnesses adduced to support which deposed that 80s. or even 96s. was necessary to enable the farmer to grow corn, while its advocates argued that its tendency would be to reduce the price of that article, but to leave the dealer in corn subject to this impression, that if he raised his price to an undue rate, corn would be imported. This impression, he conceived, and common sense would . . . be the best means of keeping corn at a fair price, and correcting all excesses. On these grounds he felt himself called upon by an imperious sense of duty to resist the proposition before the committee, more especially as no ground of necessity was shown to support it, and as all the arguments adduced in its favour appeared to him utterly fallacious. At the same time he begged it to be understood, that he was most anxious for the interest of agriculture, which he conceived essentially important to our domestic trade, compared to which indeed he regarded every other branch of trade as nugatory. But the proposition before the committee was in his view materially adverse to that interest.

⟨Having said thus much as to agriculture, he thought it proper, as connected with this subject, to advert shortly to the state of our manufactures, the condition of our labourers in husbandry, and the nature of our finances. As to the first of these, namely, our manufactures, he would ask, was it necessary at this moment to enhance the price of our manufactured articles? The necessary requisites to enable us to preserve our superiority in our manufactures were two, capital and skill. These were not necessarily domiciled in this country; but might, like any of the other goods of fortune, take to themselves wings and fly away; and it was no unfair or unreasonable thing to conjecture, that if to the difficulties to which our manufactures now laboured, were added the proposed regulations as to the price of corn, those would be

speedily followed by a departure from this country of the capital and skill which had
hitherto given life to our manufactures, seeing we were about in the same breath to
multiply the taxes on our manufactures, and to increase the price of corn. The
second point to which he had referred, was the condition of labourers engaged in the
affairs of husbandry. This, he agreed, did not depend on any defect in the system
itself, but on the poor laws, and the mal-administration of them, by which part of
the wages of the agricultural labourers was in some districts paid out of the poor-
rates. There could, he thought, be no difficulty in framing a law to reach this subject;
but certain gentlemen thought it more meritorious to pay such labourers out of the
poor-rates, than to suffer an advance of wages to take place; and the very same
persons who were outbidding each other in the purchase of leases of lands, seemed
the most misgiving as to the price of labour. It was the high price of corn which had
produced this, and would continue it. There was no other way of liberating our
peasantry from a state of villeinage than by restraining the price of corn. What could
be more degrading than that a man in the vigour of healthful labour should receive
the allowance of a pauper? It reduced our free labourers to a state of bondage; and
this enormous mischief the present measure had the strongest tendency to increase.
The third point to which he had alluded, was that of our financial arrangements.
The price of the necessaries of life must either enter into consideration in all the
arrangements of government, or of the greater part of them. It might be asked, How
would you pay the dividends on the national debt, unless you were to keep the rate
of provisions high? To this he would only say, that it was true the country had raised
large sums at a diminished rate, and that they would have to pay them at a higher
rate on account of the artificial state of their money; but was any man hardy enough
to say, that that artificial state ought to be kept up? If so, that man must be guilty of
a continual fraud on those great creditors of the country on whom this deceit had
originally been practised. Observe, then, what was our situation. With exhausted
manufactures, with a debt accumulating out of all proportion, and with our labourers
paid out of our poor-rates, were we still to lengthen out this artificial mode of
proceeding? The man who could look such a situation in the face, had stronger
nerves than he had. The best course, according to his idea, was to do nothing. Eighty
shillings per quarter was a *minimum* which, he was satisfied, even from the evidence
before the committee, it was not necessary to fix; but the *minimum* might have been
safely fixed at a much smaller sum.⟩

1. On 14 Feb. the Vice-President of the Board of Trade, Frederick John Robinson, afterwards
Viscount Goderich and 1st Earl of Ripon (1782–1859: *DNB*), moved that the House
should resolve itself into a committee to consider the state of the Corn Laws and announced his intention of then submitting a series of resolutions preparatory to the introduction of a bill. On Horner's motion a number of returns were ordered. Next day, when
Alexander Baring moved for another return, Horner encouraged the Chancellor of the
Exchequer to communicate full information to the House and to allow a thorough discussion of the issue before proceeding to a division. On the 17th Robinson brought forward his
resolutions. The most important of them called for foreign corn to be bonded and re-
exported without payment of duty; for the prohibition of the importation of foreign corn
for home consumption altogether until wheat rose to eighty shillings the quarter (and other
kinds of grain in the proportions that then existed); and for the same prohibition to apply
to the North American colonies until wheat rose to sixty-seven shillings. After a lengthy
debate discussion of the resolutions resumed on the 22nd, when Horner again encouraged a

full discussion, and the next day, after several supporters of prohibition had ridiculed the speculations of political economists, he delivered this speech.

2. Richard Preston (1768–1850: *DNB*), MP for Ashburton, was a belligerent supporter of the Corn Laws.

3. In the appendix to vol. iii of Frederick Morton Eden's *State of the Poor*.

554. To John Horner

BLPES vi. 180–83 ⟨*Horner*, ii. 237–9⟩   [Lincoln's Inn], Friday [3 Mar. 1815]

. . .

⟨The Corn Bill has been well discussed, though carried clamorously and precipitately.[1] It is in truth a most unwise measure, though I really believe that most of those who vote for it have brought themselves to believe that it may be serviceable to the agricultural interests of the country; at the same time, the most conscientious of them cannot but know, they will be no losers by it: for if it proves effectual at all, its operation will be merely to save rents a little in their unavoidable fall, and to gain this advantage to landlords by putting the people upon shorter allowance than they would otherwise have. Petitions are now coming from all quarters, and a good deal of heat is rising in the large towns; but the bill will probably be out of our House, before the petitions can be found in sufficient numbers to intimidate votes; and in the House of Lords the voice of the people is not likely to be heard. I hear we are in all probability to have wheat at a very high price, before the middle of summer; which may be attended with some inconvenience, if the popular impression should be, that that is owing to the new-made law.⟩

. . .

1. Robinson's resolutions were agreed to on 24 Feb., and after another lengthy debate on 27–28 Feb., a bill was brought in on 1 Mar. After long discussion in each of its several stages, it passed the Commons on 10 Mar.

555. From Lord Grenville

BLPES iv. 69–74   Saturday morning [4 Mar. 1815]

We received the report of the Scotch Jury bill yesterday and I think you will be of opinion that it has been much improved in the committee.[1]

I moved in the committee an amendment making the direction of juries imperative in the case of damages for personal wrongs. I withdrew it at the desire of the Lord Chancellor who undertook to consider the subject, and to move some such amendment on the report if he thought it possible to accomplish the object without material inconvenience.

He did not say much yesterday to satisfy me of the impossibility, but as he declined making the motion I did not think it worth while to press the subject further as I understand that this is the point on which the Scotch Judges and lawyers are in general most pertinacious.

I expressed a general approbation of the experiment, though not going so far as I thought it might.

From the strong impression which the Corn bill is making out of doors I feel very sanguine in obliging its supporters if not to relinquish it altogether at least to lose their support price. Every thing seems to depend on gaining time, and I wonder if that with that view the London people have not petitioned for liberty to be heard by Counsel, and to produce evidence on the many points in which the evidence is defective particularly

1. The real growing price under the reduced charges of agriculture

2. The manner of taking the averages, and their effect on the price of the loaf in London and elsewhere

and 3rdly On the actual proportion of the money price to the real price of the labour of those artificers and workmen who are not *constantly* supported (as our agricultural labourers are) by the Poor's rate, and of the comparison of that proportion with the rate existing from [?] the war.

On this point I have some very curious information and expect more. It tends to show that the *present* price of the loaf compared with the *present* wages places them exactly in the same situation as in the average of the last peace – and consequently that *any* fall in wages, or rise in bread must be injurious to them.

I thought that at the meeting in the city yesterday it would certainly have been resolved to apply to be heard by counsel and evidence. I am sorry now I did not suggest it earlier. Perhaps it is still not too late. I mention it to you as you may know, as I do not, when such a suggestion might be made with best effect.

Wakefield who is one of the witnesses they rely on, has been to me to state his decisive opinion *against* the bill – all his answers refer, he says, to the actual charges of cultivation – but he is satisfied they must fall, and that with them of course must fall the growing price.

It is curious that there is (comparatively speaking) scarce any information in the reports as to the growing price in Ireland, from whence the supply of England is meant to come.[2]

I return to you Sir I.C.'s opinion on the Jury trial.[3]

1. *Hansard*, xxix. 1206–1207, indicates that Grenville made a number of criticisms of the Government's bill, and that he tried in particular to limit the degree of discretion it gave judges to reject resort to a jury trial. For his part, Horner's sudden burst of parliamentary exertion continued on 6 Mar., when a committee of the Faculty of Advocates at Edinburgh, including Thomas Thomson, Murray, Jeffrey, and several others of his oldest friends, asked him to protest against the exclusion from the Government bill of a clause in the original draft stipulating that all judges be qualified to be senators of the College of Justice (NLS MSS 98, ff. 1–2); and that evening, while warmly supporting the introduction of jury trials in Scotland, he pointed out to the Commons the impropriety of allowing judges unacquainted with the peculiarities of the Scottish legal system to preside in the proposed courts (*Horner*, ii. 534–9). Although *Hansard* does not mention this speech it does those he made on 9 Mar. and 12 Apr., in the first of which, on the Bill's second reading, he again expressed great satisfaction, though like Grenville pressing for mandatory juries, and in the second for the eventual replacement of English by Scottish judges. (*Hansard*, xxx. 85

and 583–6. The *AR*, lvii. 318, prints a useful summary of the bill as finally passed.)

2. Edward Wakefield (1774–1854: *DNB*), the author of a statistical work on Ireland who was both farmer and land agent, had given evidence to both the 1813 and the 1814 Select Committees on Corn, whose reports and minutes of evidence are printed in *BPP*, 1812–13, iii. 479–529, and 1813–14, iii. 195–342. When the bill that had passed the Commons on 10 Mar. 1815 was introduced in the Lords on 13 Mar. both Grey and Grenville complained of its being insufficiently supported by facts, but equally to no avail (*Hansard*, xxx. 115–50).

3. Sir Ilay Campbell (1734–1823: *DNB*), the retired Lord President, had published under his initials *Hints upon the Question of Jury Trial as applicable to the Proceedings in the Court of Session* (Edinburgh, 1809).

556. To Dugald Stewart

BLPES vi. 184–5   [London], Friday 10 [Mar. 1815]

I little thought when I promised the other day to give the first news that occurred, that it would be to tell you of Bonaparte's escape from Elba. He landed, what day I have not learned, at Fréjus with 1,000 men; he was joined by about 800 who were on that spot, and took the direction of Grenoble. Our Minister at Paris has sent intelligence of the event to Government. Macdonald and St Cyr with the Duke of Orléans and Monsieur! are marched against him; and there is a proclamation setting a price on his head.[1]

It is idle to attempt to speculate about this extraordinary event, the issue of which must one way or other be very speedy. But while we are kept in suspense, it is lamentable to think that the unprincipled folly of the Allies at Vienna should have done every thing in their power to alienate the people of Italy and the north of Germany. It is on the disposition of the soldiery of France, however, that all will turn.

1. Alexandre Macdonald (1765–1840), who had risen to the highest echelons of French command in the campaign that immediately preceded the abdication of Napoleon and remained loyal to the Emperor until the end, had nonetheless accepted command under the restored Bourbon monarchy. Laurent, Marquis de Gouvion St Cyr (1764–1830), who had risen to be one of Napoleon's marshals before being taken prisoner in 1813, had been made a peer at the restoration and became Minister of War after the Hundred Days.

557. From Francis Jeffrey

⟨*Jeffrey*, ii. 150–54⟩   Edinburgh, 12 Mar. 1815

⟨. . .

⟨You need make no apology for your principles to me.[1] I have never for an instant considered them as other than just and noble. As an old friend and countryman, I am proud of their purity and elevation, and should have no higher ambition, if I were at all in public life, than to share and enforce them. I say this with reference to your attachment to party, your regard to character, and your candour and indulgence to those of whom you have to complain. Situated as I am, at a distance from all active politics, the two first strike me as less important, and I give way to my political and constitutional carelessness without any self reproach. If I were in your place it is probable I should feel differently, but these are none of the matters on which I should ever think of quarrelling with your principles of judgement.

⟨Neither will I deny that the *Review* might have been more firmly conducted, and greater circumspection used to avoid excesses of all sorts. Only the anxiety of such a duty would have been very oppressive to me, and I have ever been slow to believe the matter of so much importance as to impose it absolutely upon me. I have not, however, been altogether without some feelings of duty on the subject; and it is as to the limits and extent of these that I am inclined to differ with you. Perhaps it would have been better to have kept more to general views. But in such times as we have lived in, it was impossible not to mix them, as in fact they mix themselves, with questions which might be considered as of a narrower and more factious description. In substance it appeared to me that my only absolute duty as to political discussion, was, to forward the great ends of liberty, and to exclude nothing but what had a tendency to promote servile, sordid, and corrupt principles. As to the *means* of attaining these ends, I thought that considerable latitude should be indulged, and that unless the excesses were very great and revolting, every man of talent should be allowed to take his own way of recommending them. In this way it always appeared to me that a considerable diversity was quite compatible with all the consistency that should be required in a work of this description, and that doctrines might very well be maintained in the same number which were quite irreconcilable with each other, except in their common tendency to repress servility, and diffuse a general spirit of independence in the body of the people. This happens, I take it, in every considerable combination of persons for one general end; and in every debate on a large and momentous question, I fancy that views are taken and principles laid down by those who concur in the same vote, which bear in opposite directions, and are brought from the most adverse points of doctrine. Yet all these persons co-operate easily enough, and no one is ever held to be responsible for all the topics and premises which may be insisted on by his neighbours.   ·

⟨To come, for instance, to the topic of attacks on the person of the sovereign. Many people, and I profess myself to be one, may think such a proceeding at variance with the dictates of good taste, of dangerous example, and repugnant to good feelings; and therefore they will not themselves have recourse to it. Yet it would be difficult, I think, to deny that it is, or may be, a lawful weapon to be employed in the great and eternal contest between the court and the country. Can there be any doubt that the personal influence, and personal character, of the sovereign is an element, and a pretty important element, in the practical constitution of the Government, and always forms part of the strength or weakness of the Administration he employs? In the abstract, therefore, I cannot think that attempts to weaken that influence, to abate a dangerous popularity, or even to excite odium towards a corrupt and servile ministry, by making the prince, on whose favour they depend, generally contem-ptible or hateful, are absolutely to be interdicted or protested against. Excesses no doubt may be committed. But the system of attacking abuses of power, by attacking the person who instigates or carries them through by general popularity or personal influence, is lawful enough I think, and may form a large scheme of Whig opposition, – not the best or the noblest part certainly, but one not without its use, – and that may on some occasions be altogether indispensable. It does not appear to me, therefore, that the degree of sanction that may be given to such attacks, by merely writing in the same journal where they occasionally appear, is to be considered as a sin against conscience or the constitution, or would be so imputed.

⟨I say all this, however, only to justify my own laxity on these points, and certainly with no hope of persuading you to imitate it. With regard to the passages in last number, which you consider as a direct attack on the Whig party, I must say that it certainly did not strike me in that light when I first read it; nor can I yet persuade myself that this is its true and rational interpretation.[2] I took it, I confess, as an attack, – not upon any regular party or connection in the State, – but upon these individuals, either in party or out of it, to whose *personal* qualities it seemed directly to refer, – men such as have at all times existed, who, with honourable and patriotic sentiments, and firmness enough to resist direct corruption and intimidation, yet wanted vigour to withstand the softer pleas of civility or friendship, and allowed their public duties to be postponed, rather than give offence or pain to individuals with whom they were connected. This I really conceive is the natural and obvious application of the words that are employed, and I am persuaded they will appear to the general view of readers to have no deeper meaning. Certainly they suggested no other to me; and if they had, I would undoubtedly have prevented their publication; for I should look upon such an attack as that as a violation of that fidelity to the cause of liberty to which I think we are substantially pledged.

⟨. . .⟩

1. Evidently Horner had written, this time directly to Jeffrey, complaining of more evidence of an anti-Whig slant in the February number of the *Review* (vol. xxiv, no. xlviii).
2. This seems to refer to pp. 506–507 of an article by Mackintosh on France, *ER* xxiv (no. xlviii, Feb. 1815), 505–537.

558. From T.R. Malthus

⟨*Ricardo*, vi. 186–8⟩   East India College, 14 Mar. 1815

⟨Will you have the goodness to allow me to ask you a question in political economy, on which I should very much like to have your opinion.

⟨On the supposition which is generally allowed, that in a rich and progressive country, corn naturally rises compared with manufactured and foreign commodities, will it not follow that, as the real capital of the farmer which is advanced does not consist merely in raw produce, but in ploughs waggons threshing machines, etc.: and in the tea sugar clothes, etc., etc., used by his labourers, if with a less quantity of raw produce he can purchase the same quantity of these commodities, a greater quantity of raw produce will remain for the farmer and landlord, and afford a greater surplus from the land for the maintenance and encouragement of the manufacturing and mercantile classes.

⟨The Economists calculate that one third of the raw produce obtained by the farmer is advanced to the steril[e] classes. On this supposition let the produce of an acre be represented by 8 of which $1/4$ goes to the landlord, and $3/4$ are received by the farmer, that is, 2 go to the landlord, and 6 to the farmer, out of which latter sum the farmer expends one third or 2 in the commodities above mentioned. The farmer therefore retains 4 for his raw produce-expenditure, and profits; that is, he retains the value of the half of the gross produce.

⟨Let us now suppose the price of corn to double, while the price of manufactured and foreign commodities rises only one fourth. The whole produce will then be represented by 16 of which $1/4$, as before, or 4, go to the land and only $2^1/_2$ instead of 4 go to the expenditure in manufactured and foreign commodities; the consequence of which will be, that $9^1/_2$ out of 16 will remain to the farmer instead of 4 out of 8, that is about $3/_5$ instead of $1/_2$. Out of this increased produce the farmer will either receive proportionably in[creased] profits, or will divide them with the l[andlord] and thus a rise in the price of [corn] appears to increase the productiveness of all the capital previously employed on the land.

⟨This proposition appears to me to involve consequences so very important with regard to home demand, that I should like much to know whether you see any error in the premises or conclusion.

⟨The fault of Mr Ricardo's table[1] which is curious, is that the advances of the farmer instead of being calculated in corn, should be calculated either in the actual materials of which the capital consists, or in the money which is the best representative of a variety of commodities. The view I have taken of the subject would greatly alter his conclusions.

⟨I was much pleased with your speech the other night on the Bank Restriction. I can quite go with you. I remain firm in my opinion as to the Policy of some Restrictions, but though I would not yield to the mob, I should be disposed to yield to the prodigious weight of Petitions, and let the people have their way. What an enterprise of Bonaparte.⟩

    1. See the *Essay on Profits* in *Ricardo*, iv. 17.

559. To Earl Grey

Grey MSS, Durham University
(copy in BLPES vi. 194–5) ⟨*Horner*, ii. 243–4⟩   Launceston, 28 Mar. 1815

⟨I cannot say how much I feel obliged to you, for taking the trouble of writing to me so full and satisfactory an account of the sentiments of our different friends at the present moment.[1] They seem all of them upon the whole more pacific, than I was prepared to expect. The preservation of peace for any length of time is, I fear, a vain wish; considering the parties on all sides, with whom it rests. But the manner of our renewing the war is a point of principle, upon which I dreaded more serious differences of opinion. These may be saved probably by the immediate course of events, or rather by the conduct of the single man who guides or drives the events of our time. But if he should in the first instance think it for his advantage, to hold out terms of peace and moderation, a schism would seem unavoidable, at least for the interval of such a discussion, between those who are for an immediate invasion of France because Bonaparte is sure in the end to play his old part, and those who think that every thing is gained for the justice and popularity of the war throughout Europe, by forbearing to interfere in French affairs, till aggressions are again attempted. It affords me the greatest satisfaction to know, that the opinion I had formed, upon this turn of circumstances, coincides with that of your Lordship in all points.[2]

‹A war renewed now upon the footing of the Treaty of Paris will be in truth a war for the restoration of the Bourbon family; coupled with a still more indefensible principle, that of proscribing an individual to destruction. No successes would ever reconcile me to such a war; but by so recommencing[3] it, we should multiply all the chances against us. The entrance of foreign troops upon French territory will give the Emperor at once all the strength of French national enthusiasm, certainly not weakened by having been suppressed for a year, nor by the insults which it has recently submitted to. If the Austrians march across the Rhine, I suppose they will detain the empress and the young boy as hostages; and that cannot fail to give Bonaparte an advantage in the war, both among his own people and foreigners, of all the interest and sympathy which such a circumstance must naturally inspire. And all this is to be done, with the hope of forcing upon France a family, who in a year's possession of the throne could not secure a dozen bayonets to keep them in it, and who were so utterly insignificant that they were not molested in their flight.›

1. Grey's earlier letter to Horner has not been found, but Horner's remarks suggest that it had been written from London on either the evening of 25 Mar. or the following morning, when he was still cautiously optimistic that the Whig coalition might rally around a policy of non-interference in the internal affairs of France.

2. In league with Ponsonby and Tierney, Horner had successfully neutralized the threat posed by Whitbread's imprudent remarks in the Commons on 16 and 20 Mar. (*Hansard*, xxx. 114–15, 229–31, and 265–305). Grey had arrived in London on the 21st, and, following a conference at Camelford House, the two leaders of Opposition had displayed such unity in the Lords (*ibid.*, 305–306) that Horner's confidant Whishaw told Sydney Smith (*Whishaw*, pp. 96–7) that they were both 'entirely averse to any interference in the internal government of France, or even to a war for the possession of Belgium'. However, between 21 and 26 Mar., when official word reached London that Napoleon had entered Paris, Grenville grew increasingly warlike, and by all appearances Horner concluded early on that a breach between the Fox and Grenville factions was inevitable. As early as 16 Mar. he observed that Napoleon had re-established a firm grasp on France, and that discontent in Belgium and Italy would probably enable the Emperor to re-establish a considerable base of power in Europe. On the 24th he remarked that events in France constituted 'a wonderful and frightful revolution'. On either the 24th or 25th he met with Grey, and having committed himself to a policy of non-intervention in the affairs of France and requested Grey 'to apprise me of any indication that might appear in the party of sentiments more inclined to war', then departed London for the circuit, as was his wont in times of serious disagreement within the party. (Horner to John Horner, Thursday [16 Mar.], and to Leonard Horner, Friday [24 Mar.], BLPES vi. 187–8 and 189, and to John Horner, 18 Apr., *Horner*, ii. 251.)

3. The MS has 'commencing'.

560. From Earl Grey

BLPES vi. 196–7   Milman St, [London], 29 Mar. 1815

I have only a minute and can enter into no details, but I do not think it right to let a post go without telling you that the hopes I held out in my last (you would see that even then they were not unaccompanied with doubts) of an agreement between Lord Grenville and myself on the policy to be pursued by this Government, with a view to the preservation of peace, are completely at an end. A long letter from him this morning, in which he explains with the honourable frankness that I have always experienced from him the views that he entertains on this vital question, proves them to be so entirely different from mine, that this difference must appear on the very first discussion that takes place.[1]

I cannot give you a better idea of his opinion than by stating that considering Peace with Buonaparte to be *impossible*, and that the best chance of War depends upon its being immediately and vigorously undertaken, he thinks our object ought to be to renew the concert of last year *with a view to immediate action*.

I need not tell you how much this grieves me, or how entirely it destroys even the faint hopes which I might still entertain of any good arising in our political prospects.[2]

1. Grey's earlier optimism that he might reach accord with Grenville had been dashed at a meeting they had had on 26 Mar. (Grenville to Tom Grenville, 26 Mar., BL Add. MSS 41853). Here Grey refers to Grenville's letter to him of 28 Mar., which after remarking that long experience convinced him that peace with Napoleon was impossible, had advocated immediate Allied military collaboration for the express purpose of removing Bonaparte from his throne (Grey MSS, Durham University). Grenville informed Sir John Newport of his views in a letter of the same day, and a copy of that letter in Horner's hand is among Horner's papers (BLPES vi. 192–3).
2. Grey's response to Grenville of 30 Mar. (Grey MSS, Durham University), which essentially summarized the concept of foreign politics propounded by the Foxites since 1792, reprobated British involvement in the internal politics of a sovereign state and, borrowing from Horner's letter of 28 Mar. (Doc. 559), ridiculed a crusade to restore a Bourbon family 'which in the whole country could not muster a dozen muskets in its defence!'. A subsequent letter from Grenville to Grey dated 31 Mar., and a reply from Grey of 1 Apr. (Grey MSS, Durham University; copies in BL Add. MSS. 51551, ff. 1–25), portray the widening gulf between them. (See also Taylor, p. 405.)

561. To J.A. Murray

BLPES vi. 198–203
⟨Horner, ii. 244–8⟩[1]   Taunton, Saturday evening, [1 Apr. 1815]

⟨. . . God knows there is matter enough in public affairs for much anxious conversation. I begin to feel myself growing a mere fatalist about politics, we seem so much the victim and sport of uncontrollable events. I can bestow no thoughts at this moment upon the happiness of the French nation, as concerned in the last marvellous revolution of affairs; they are so sunk in my estimation, by their passive acquiescence under two such changes of government, that I feel no interest about their political or civil liberties. But the possible consequences to our own liberties, of the conduct that may be pursued by our Government in the present new conjuncture, do incessantly disturb and burthen my mind. So many persons, in whose judgement and public spirit I have the best confidence, are for hurrying into immediate war, that I am afraid almost to inquire about your sentiments on that point, lest I should find them differing from my own. But my impression from the first moment was, that we ought to give the Emperor of France an opportunity of maintaining the treaty of Paris if he would, and throw upon him the unpopularity of being the first to make aggressions and to break the tranquillity of Europe. These impressions were not shaken by the authority of all the names subscribed to the manifesto from Vienna, and they have derived of course some addition of strength from the formal declarations now made by Napoleon, of his relinquishing all former schemes of a mastery over foreign nations, and founding a great empire. Not that I place much faith in these professions, for in forming a practical decision as to what is best to be done, I would look upon them as entitled to none at all; although I think it not impossible that reflections in exile, and older years, may have given prudence some ascendancy in his plans, and not wholly out of his character that he should set his ambition as it were upon a new theory of greatness for its gratification. But in taking the practical determination, what I would be guided by is this, that if we are to open a new Iliad of war against the military power of France, it is of the last importance that we should so commence it, as to stamp upon it, in the opinion of the people of the continent, its true character of a war of defence merely against aggrandizement. By going to war now, we go to war for the Bourbons, to force that feeble worn-out race upon the French; we go to war too upon a still more hopeless, and in my sentiments unjustifiable principle, that of proscribing an individual, and through him the nation which has adopted him, as incapable of peace or truce. It is obvious that, proceeding in that manner, we do what we can to inspire into the French soldiery all the fire of enthusiasm, every feeling of pride for their national independence, and the utmost devotion for their great chief. The argument used on the other side is, that in prudence it must be assumed that he will act over again his old part as soon as he has collected sufficient means, and that the interval should not be let slip of overbearing him while he is unprepared with the whole combined numbers of the allies. In this reasoning there are more assumptions than one, of which I doubt the correctness. It is taken for granted, that he could not now make head against such force as the allies could push into his territory; in which I apprehend those who reckon the strength of armies by the tale of numbers might be proved, by the issue of such an experiment, to have forgotten in their estimate, that moral force which must be breathed into troops by the romance and marvellous [prestige?] that accompany this last enterprise of this extraordinary man. It is assumed, too, that the allies are all to be had as they were last year; now without considering the effect, which Bonaparte's declaration, that he will maintain the treaty of Paris, must have upon those powers which are in possession of what they have usurped in Italy and in Germany, it ought to be recollected, that these usurpations, and the indecent spectacle which the allies exhibited during the whole winter in their congress of plunder, have deprived them throughout Italy and

Germany of that moral force, which they boasted of last year, and with truth, as the foundation of their successes. But even if these things could be taken for granted, I question if it would not still be but a short-sighted prudence, to reject the opportunity which his professions of peace and moderation might afford of confirming in the public mind of Europe, an impression of the justice of our cause in that war, which, if it be renewed, will be one of no short duration, and must in the course of it involve in all the vicissitudes of fortune the best parts of the world. For England, I own, I cannot see, if we are to have another period of war, that ultimate success abroad, if to be hoped, would compensate our sure and irreparable losses at home; the inevitable insolvency of the Exchequer must, in one disguised shape or other, bring on a dreadful convulsion of property, with the ruin of all those families, whom the *Courier* (resuming the ancient Jacobinical phrase of its Editor when he was the hireling of violence of another sort) stigmatizes as the *drones* of society, the annuitants, those who live on the savings of former industry; and in addition to this calamity, we shall witness the acceleration of that change, which is already begun, of our old civil system of freedom and law, for a military government. Such are my present melancholy dreams; sleeping or waking, they are about my bed, and about my path, speaking most literally; for since this devil incarnate rose again from the dead I have known no comfortable day. Some differences of opinion among my political friends, are also come at last to add a little to the annoyance; but that is a trifle compared with the dismal prospects that one has before one's mind, for England and all that we are attached to. ...⟩

    1. Where it is misdated 3 Apr.

562. To Earl Grey

Grey MSS, Durham University (copy in BLPES vi. 204.)   Taunton, 2 Apr. 1815

On arriving at this place last night, I found your second letter;[1] which has filled me with the greatest concern, though I had in some degree anticipated this public misfortune. Nothing, I fear, can now occur to prevent the disclosure of this fundamental difference of opinion. For, even if Napoleon should have sufficient command of temper to adhere in spite of provocation to the policy which he seems to have resolved on,[2] that proof of his steadiness cannot be had till some lapse of time, and meanwhile these wretched Ministers and this hot-brained country will gain the sanction of Lord Grenville's authority, and the weight of his friends in Parliament, in support of the most fatal error, both in point of principle and prudence, that has ever been committed in the foreign politics of England. I shall feel very great anxiety till I know how a number of individuals are affected on this occasion; I try to flatter myself there can be no defection of any considerable name from the old Fox party, and if they keep together, they know what it is to maintain a high name with small minorities in Parliament. I cannot say how much I feel gratified and satisfied, to find myself on this occasion of an opinion entirely coinciding with that of which your Lordship will be the leader in Parliament and in the country.

I hope to reach town on Thursday next, and shall take the cordial opportunity of seeing your Lordship. How much I wish Lord Holland were at home.[3]

1. Doc. 560.
2. Trying desperately to contrast his behaviour with that of the European allies at Vienna, Napoleon had magnanimously freed the Duc d'Angoulàme, proclaimed a general amnesty, abolished the French slave trade, accepted the territorial settlement of the Treaty of Paris, and dispatched overtures for peace to Great Britain (*Napoleon's Memoirs*, ed. Somerset De Chair (1958), pp. 475-7).
3. See Horner to John Horner, 18 Apr., *Horner*, ii. 251-2, for an account of his correspondence with Grey.

563. To Mrs Dugald Stewart

NLS MSS 11103, ff. 26-7   [London], Thursday [6] Apr. 1815

You inquired about Lord Auckland. I am just come from Eden farm . . .

They tell me we are to have a message of war sent to the Houses today. Every thing I hear looks like immediate war; persons connected with Government speak impatiently of a commencement of hostilities, and very confidently of the result. Bonaparte, and France too, are to be put down. Poor France, and poor England, will both sink in the contest, I have little doubt, which ever way the victory goes among these military honours [?]; my only uncertainty in the whole business is, which result is to prove the worst for the world, the success of Bonaparte, or the success of the Allies.

We had at Eden Farm for a day Mr Crawford, the late American Minister at Paris. His account of the state of things there did not inspire any hopes; several individuals, of the old party of Constitutionalists, are doing their best and proving at this distance of time the steadiness and consistency of their character; but they have no real power. All the common people are for the Emperor and his military glory; the army in a state of enthusiasm; the people of property and education timid and acquiescing, not prepared to resist him nor to defend their country against foreigners. Mr Crawford was present at a conversation, in which Joseph Bonaparte laboured to impress La Fayette with a conviction, that his brother's system was now pacific and must necessarily be so from his age and the state of his health, etc. He confirmed the story I think I told you of Benjamin Constant's concealment in his house, and the message he received from Fouché; with some other particulars, which make me suspect that Constant's powers of mind will not carry him in politics farther than a clever pamphlet.[1]

1. Henri Benjamin Constant de Rebecque (1757-1830) had been extremely critical of Napoleon after the abdication, and as late as 19 Mar. had proclaimed in the *Journal des débats* that he was ready to die for the restored Bourbon monarch. Next day, when Napoleon entered Paris, Constant hid in the US Embassy. After Napoleon issued a general

amnesty, and Joseph Fouché, Duke of Otranto (1763–1820), who had resumed his old office of Minister of Police during the Hundred Days, had assured him that the Emperor was in a forgiving mood, Constant emerged from hiding. On 14 Apr. Napoleon would receive Constant, ask him to draft a liberal constitution, and, after considerable revisions, proclaim Constant's amended draft as the new charter of the French Government.

564. To John Horner

BLPES vi. 214–15 ⟨Horner, ii. 249–50⟩   Lincoln's Inn, 10 Apr. 1815

. . .

⟨. . . You would not be sorry, I am sure, to see my name in the small minority the other night, which voted that we ought not to begin the war by an attack on France.[1] The question is a very difficult one, and upon which different views may be taken even by those who are most agreed upon political principles and objects. My determination was not taken without a great deal of previous consideration, which my absence from London gave me an opportunity of pursuing at leisure, and I did not give that vote before my opinion was clear and satisfactory to my own mind. The consequences, in the event of immediate war, may be important to myself, with respect to my seat; but, of course, I saw all these consequences, and gave them no weight. There are some differences of opinion among our leaders, which may never come to a difference in Parliament; that depends upon events; but having had confidential communication with both the eminent persons to whom I allude, I have found in this instance only fresh occasion to respect the patriotism and public integrity of both. . . .⟩[2]

1. Upon arriving in London on 6 Apr., Horner had resolved to 'abstain from attendance in Parliament' and had prudently 'declined attending a meeting [of Opposition] held that night at Mr Ponsonby's'. At that meeting Grenville and his party expressed willingness to compromise and Horner, concluding that there was 'the most sincere anxiety on both sides to avoid, or at least to postpone as long as possible, any public declaration of the difference of opinion', resolved next day to attend Parliament for the Regent's address proposing military preparations. There the façade of Opposition unity was undone by 'a little forwardness on the part of Whitbread, but much more by the tone of Lord Castlereagh's speech'. The resulting amendment, which called for a purely defensive military posture by the British Government, forced Horner's hand. Many among the old Fox faction followed Ponsonby in opposing the amendment on the ground that a vote for military preparedness was not a vote for war, but Horner felt bound to support the amendment. (Horner to John Horner, 18 Apr., Horner, ii. 250–53; Grey to Wellesley, 6 Apr., BL Add. MSS 37297; and Romilly, iii. 161–2. See the Statesman, 8 Apr., for a division list and a report of the debate.)

2. Despite their differences, Grey and Grenville continued to communicate during April, actively seeking ground for compromise and encouraging moderation among their supporters. Every effort was made in Parliament to exhibit party unity, and on 19 Apr. Grenville, observing that a formal separation with Grey would become necessary only through the 'zeal and intemperance of others', noted that 'if we can avoid it I think we shall'. (Grey to Holland, 26 June, BL Add. MSS 51552; Grenville to Fitzwilliam, 30 Mar., Fitzwilliam MSS, Sheffield Record Office; Statesman, 13, 17, 20, and 28 Apr.; Grenville to William Wickham, 19 Apr., Wickham MSS, Hampshire Record Office; see also Taylor, pp. 409–10.)

565. To John Horner

BLPES vi 29–30 ⟨*Horner*, ii. 257–8⟩   [London, 3 May 1815]

⟨I have been prevented by a great deal of business of one kind or another from writing to you at the length I promised, and partly also by circumstances remaining still precisely as they stood when I wrote last. I cannot, however, delay showing you, for your own private perusal, the inclosed letters, which I will beg you to return to me after you have read them.[1] They will explain themselves; and I am sure you will agree with me in thinking, that nothing can be more liberal than Lord Buckingham's manner of seeing this business, or more strictly consonant to the honour that should be the foundation of such a relation as subsists between him and myself. I had a conversation to the same effect with Lord Grenville; and nothing can exceed the satisfaction which I derive from the footing on which this matter is placed. I shall continue acting in my own way, and upon my own opinions, until the event, which I do not now anticipate, of a final separation; and when that takes place, which I shall on every public account, as well as from private regard to those who have treated me with so much kindness, extremely lament, I shall then offer a second time my resignation.

⟨I fancy I made heavy work of it last night. My stings were drawn at the beginning, by hearing that the papers were to be granted.[2]

⟨. . .⟩

1. Horner enclosed copies of his letter to Buckingham of 28 Apr., in which he offered to resign his parliamentary seat due to disagreement on the question of immediate war with France, and of Buckingham's reply of the next day, declining the offer until such time as the course of events produced a 'radical and continued difference of opinion' between them. After voting for the amendment to the Regent's Address on 7 Apr., Horner had received a note from Grenville requesting an early conference. They had met the following morning and agreed that their difference of opinion was not yet so pronounced as to require a formal separation. Thereafter Horner had assumed a low profile in the Commons, but on 28 Apr. Whitbread forced his hand with a direct motion for peace. The resulting division produced the first public schism between the two factions of Opposition, and Horner wrote to Buckingham after dividing with the minority who supported Whitbread's motion. (*Horner*, ii. 253–7; *PR* xxvii. 564–74; Taylor, pp. 410–11.)

2. Horner had moved for papers relating to British involvement in negotiations between Austria and the King of Naples. His remarks on that occasion suggest that sources close to the court of King Joachim, probably the Hollands, had provided him with confidential information. Castlereagh acceded to the motion but observed that Horner's information 'appeared to have been drawn from the secret official sources of other countries, which were not the most creditable'. (*Gentleman's Magazine*, lxxxv (June 1815), 548–9 and 551; *Horner*, ii. 258–9.)

566. To Mrs Dugald Stewart

BLPES vi 231–4 ⟨Horner, ii. 259–62⟩   [London], 4 May [1815]

⟨I should not have been so long of writing to you, if there had been any one day on which I knew any thing for certain, or could form even a probable guess, respecting that frightful question which is suspended over us like a black threatening cloud. It is manifest, as far as our Government is concerned, that war, if the co-operation of others can be had, is decided on, and it is understood that our general, the Duke of Wellington, has been the instigator of those hurried and frantic denunciations which have been issued from Vienna. He thirsts no doubt for his old sport of war and military rule, as much as that appetite can be imputed to Bonaparte. His brother, the Marquis, who upon the question of peace as well as in the condemnation of the projects of the Congress is strongly in union with Lord Grey, says, that Arthur is a great captain of infantry, the greatest in the world, but will never be a statesman. Some persons still flatter themselves with a slender hope that one or other of the allies may shrink from the confederacy, and still avert the war; the diversion of the Austrian forces on the side of Italy, the growing jealousies between the court and Russia, and the absolute want of money of which both have reason to complain, being so many grounds for this speculation. Meanwhile, the state of Paris, and the position of Napoleon, are almost a mystery in this country. The most recent letters represent the friends of liberty, or those enemies of liberty the Jacobins, as acquiring daily a greater ascendancy: the new constitution is loudly condemned as savouring too strongly of monarchy, and the individuals who were employed in drawing it up are fallen into popular odium ... I must add a word about our own concerns at home. Though we are still in dread of a public declaration in Parliament of the difference of opinion which subsists between Lord Grenville and Lord Grey, I have much better hopes now than I felt originally, that this declaration, if made, will be so narrowed to the single point on which the difference has arisen, as to preclude the necessity of a permanent separation. This will depend altogether upon the turn of events abroad. In the mean time, nothing can be more consolatory, while there is a prospect of so great a public calamity as that separation would be, than the honourable frankness with which they have explained their opinions to one another, and the regret mutually felt on account of this unavoidable disagreement. ...⟩[1]

1. While Horner actively discouraged a public confrontation between the two factions of Opposition, he found himself ever more isolated. Lady Holland was informed (A. Raymond to Lady Holland, 9 May, BL Add. MSS 51585):

    At present there is an armistice and a constant interchange of Civilities between the two divisions of the Opposition Forces, but each party is busied in beating up for recruits against the day of attack. Reinforcements however come in but very slowly to the War Standard. In the Lords Gen[era]l Lord Grenville will not muster more than seven or ten at the utmost, and in the Commons Brigadiers Elliot and Plunkett will not command a detachment of above twenty-two or three.

567. To J.A. Murray

BLPES vi. 235–8   [London], Wednesday [24 May 1815]

. . . We shall make some fight . . . against these stamps, which are a most impolitic, indeed unjustifiable assessment, against all true principles of taxation, and indeed against the very first principles of government, of which the most inviolable ought to be the administration of justice. But by all the opposition we can make to it, we can hardly hope to do more than to show our individual disapprobation of the measure; for you have no representation of Scotland in parliament, except when some local job is to be done, as indeed you have very few other means or signs of public liberty.[1]

. . .

The division in the Lords last night was better than I expected, upon such a question. Besides Lord Grenville's family connections, there voted in the majority for war: Lord Erskine in his green ribbon, Lords Ossory, Stafford, Carrington, Cassilis, Bulkeley, and St Vincent. These were all I observed as defaulters from the Opposition. Lord Stafford I look upon as gone over to the Court for what he can get, and Erskine for what he has got: the rest are I believe honest opinions from fright. In the House of Commons, I expect we shall not fall much short of 90, though the debate unluckily comes on tomorrow, when several of our staunchest patriots *must* attend the Derby Stakes at Epsom: There were above 70 members of the H. of Commons, at the meeting at Devonshire house, a formidable number, in opposition to the commencement of a war, but doubly formidable by the property and influence which it includes.[2]

It seems to me that the public in general are much less aware at the present moment, than was even to be expected from their habitual improvidence, of the embarrassments of every sort which this war will bring upon the country. They may amount to a revolution in the property and government of the state. The readiness with which money can be borrowed and *made*, in the city, to any amount, as long as the interest of the loans can be paid, will lead us on till the difficulty of paying the interest becomes insurmountable; that is the only difficulty we have hitherto felt; it will soon be found to be insurmountable.

It is very difficult to form any thing like an opinion, of the real state of sentiments in France, amidst the contradictory reports that are given. Lord Liverpool said last night that 3/4ths of the whole population are against Bonaparte; he must have believed this too easily, for he cannot have rational grounds for such a conviction. Some of my friends are talking about La Vendée, as they must have done in 1795, and look to it as the hope of the world.

In the mean time, the allies do not talk of being upon the frontiers of France, in force for continued action, until the end of June. And it is certain, that upon the northern frontier the joint forces of Blucher and Lord Wellington are inferior to Bonaparte's, so that if he makes an advance the Duke must retreat behind the Scheldt, leaving all Belgium as free quarters to the French soldiery.

. . .

1. Before the end of the session large increases had been voted in the taxes on stamps in legal proceedings.

2. The long-delayed confrontation between Grey and Grenville had surfaced in the Lords on 23 May, with the announcement of the renewal of the coalition against France. Fearing a final separation with the Grenvilles, Grey went forward very reluctantly (Grey to Earl Spencer, 22 May, Spencer MSS, Althorp). His speech, which Caroline Fox found 'destitute of argument' (to Holland, 26 May, BL Add. MSS 51470), was most notable for its deference to Grenville, and his heavily compromised motion, urging a strictly defensive concert with the European powers and condemning a war to proscribe the ruler of France, secured only forty-four votes. Grenville, too, almost backed down (Grenville to T. Grenville, 18 May, BL Add. MSS 41853), and his short speech supported Ministerial policy without elaboration. For a report of the debate see the *Examiner*, 28 May 1815.

Erskine, whose silent vote for war constituted a remarkable change of heart that inspired charges of political apostasy among Foxites (*Romilly*, iii. 171–3), had recently accepted a green riband from the Regent, but Granville Leveson-Gower, 2nd Marquess of Stafford (1758–1833: *DNB*), who had been joint Postmaster-General, 1799–1810, was not made Duke of Sutherland until 1833, nor Archibald Kennedy, 12th Earl of Cassilis (1770–1846), made Marquess of Ailsa until 1831. John Jervis, Earl of St Vincent (1735–1822: *DNB*), had been First Lord of the Admiralty in the Addington Ministry and the leading figure in securing the inquiry into Melville's administration of the navy. The correspondence of Thomas James Warren-Bulkeley, 7th (and last) Viscount Bulkeley (1752–1822), with Auckland shows him to have been generally sympathetic to Grenville. John Fitzpatrick, 2nd Earl of Upper Ossory (1745–1818), was a regular at Lady Holland's dinner table and his vote was somewhat surprising. For the peace faction among the Opposition included Earl Spencer and his family connections, the Russells, the Cavendishes, and indeed every other peer identified with the old Fox faction except Erskine and Upper Ossory. The meeting at Devonshire House was held on 22 May. (*The Journal and Correspondence of William, Lord Auckland*, [ed. George Hogge] (4 vols, 1861–2), iv. *passim*; A. W. M. Stirling, *Coke of Norfolk and his Friends: The Life of Thomas William Coke, First Earl of Leicester* (2 vols, 1908), ii. 107; Taylor, p. 413.)

568. To Mrs Dugald Stewart

BLPES vi. 239–41 ⟨*Horner*, ii. 262–4⟩   [London], Tuesday 30 May [1815]

⟨I meant to have sent you a note after our division, and to have told you, while our gladness was still fresh, how well pleased we all were and continue to be, both with our strength in point of numbers, and with the excellent conduct of many individuals.[1] Persons long accustomed to parliament look upon the divisions, in both Houses, as large beyond example at the commencement of a war, and such as promise a speedy termination of it if success does not make us forget the principle of our opposition to it, or a change take place in the grounds upon which it is prosecuted. I place no great reliance on such speculations; the whole affair of war, and all the politics connected with it, being a mere chapter of accidents. But there is great comfort in the fidelity and steadiness of so many public men to their principles, after such repeated disappointments of every hope, and under such a change of circumstances as seemed to afford pretexts for being shabby. It is vain, in my opinion, to consider the present as any other than a renewal of the old coalition of 1793 against the objects of the French in their revolution;[2] it differs from that war only in this, that the coalition of the despots is more formidable, and that the

French are without the defensive enthusiasm arising from their possession or the near prospect, of liberty. The success of the allies will probably be fatal to the freedom of the world for an age to follow; and though I sometimes try to flatter myself there are chances against them, I cannot consider that as the result of any reasonable calculation one can form, and am filled therefore with the most gloomy apprehensions. There is an idle story in the streets today, of an expectation still entertained that somehow or other a settlement will be made without hostilities; it is the Bonapartists who circulate this speculation,⟩ General Ramsay for instance, supported by I do not know what authorities from Brussels and the coffee-houses of Paris:[3] ⟨but it is no more than their idle, confident interpretation of that pause and stillness, which must last some time longer, and which so dreadfully makes us sure of the calamities that are coming. The last account I have heard of Paris, is the detail of what passed in putting arms into the hands of the lower people, in the Fauxbourgs [sic] St Antoine and Marceau. It was a measure, it seems, of his [Napoleon's] own, without previous concert with any of his Ministers. He set out alone on horseback, in a brown coat, into that quarter of the town, was very soon recognized, and a cry set up that it was the Emperor, round whom a great crowd was speedily collected; he dismounted, entered into familiar conversation with the people, heard all their grievances; they told him they wanted bread; he promised to find them employment: they said they would have defended Paris for him last year, if he had trusted them with arms; he said they should have them now; a list of names was taken down, before he left the spot, on which five thousand men were enrolled. Next day a thousand of these were set to work on the fortifications of Montmartre. If this scene was so acted, of course there must have been preparation for it; it rests at present on the authority of Adams, the American Minister.[4]

⟨The effect of this movement, so like the Days of Terror, is said to have been very striking; all Paris became⟩ on a sudden ⟨silent and alarmed. A great many royalist families left it next day. There was a check immediately to the license of abuse against the Emperor, in speaking and writing, which, from pamphlets and handbills I have seen, was carried to an incredible excess.

⟨. . .⟩

1. The division in the Commons on 25 May had been on Lord George Cavendish's amendment proposing concert with the European allies only for defensive warfare and censuring a war seeking to proscribe a ruler of the French. In point of numbers the amendment was successful; ninety-two MPs supported it, and there were reportedly only nineteen defections from the ranks of Opposition (Bennet to Creevey, 31 May, Creevey, i. 215–16). But Horner's favourable opinion of the debate is very misleading. The only speakers rose from the Whig front bench, and the small war faction clearly had the best of it. Arguing that his old friend Fox would have opposed such an amendment, Grattan dominated the debate and so silenced the House that the Speaker almost called for a vote when he sat down (Farington Diary, viii. 3). Whitbread, curiously, and Horner, predictably, failed to respond, and Caroline Fox reported that the replies of Burdett, Ponsonby, and Tierney made no impression (to Holland, 16 June, BL Add. MSS 51470). Plunkett and C.W.W. Wynn declared their entire approbation of the war, and Lord Milton, who was identified with the 'radical' politics of Whitbread's circle, concluded the debate with a speech supporting Ministers (Examiner, 28 May). Romilly was offended by the 'extraordinary pains' taken by Grattan and Plunkett to display 'how much their former friends are . . . in the wrong', and he was puzzled the next day when only a handful of Opposition members attended to oppose the subsidies proposed for Britain's continental allies (Romilly, iii.

172–3). Mackintosh observed correctly that the substantive issue was sacrificed on the altar
of party unity (to Allen, 9 June, BL Add. MSS 52182), and Horner was obviously quite
happy with the sacrifice.

2. This point of view accorded with that of Lord Holland and his family connections.
   (Holland to Grey, 12 June, Grey MSS, Durham University, and to Caroline Fox, 14 June,
   BL Add. MSS 51739; see also Taylor, pp. 410–11.)

3. Perhaps Lt Gen. William Ramsay (d. 1827) or Major-Gen. George William Ramsay (d.
   1819).

4. Apparently Horner obtained this account either directly or indirectly through Auckland's
   friend and house guest, William Crawford, the former American Minister to France, who
   maintained contact with his successor, John Quincy Adams (1767–1848), later President
   of the United States.

569. To Francis Jeffrey

BLPES vi. 242–3 〈Horner, ii. 264–5〉   Lincoln's Inn, 2 June 1815

〈. . .

〈I wish much to know your sentiments about this new war in which we are
embarked. You were so fierce a warrior in 1803, that I almost dread to find you
differing in opinion from me on the present occasion; which seems, however, much
more nearly to resemble the conjuncture of 1793, though with many incidental
differences too, that may affect the success and result of the war.

〈But in principle, when you remove the specious pretexts which the allies affect
to throw over their proceedings, surely their object is substantially to prevent the
French from having any king but a Bourbon, and from consolidating the new
institutions and laws that have grown out of their revolution. An impracticable
undertaking, I believe, in the end; but they may have calamitous successes for a
while. My present terror is the conquest of France by the combined forces; which,
whatever turn they may give to it, must produce lasting mischief to the whole world.
Whether it be the fate of that country to undergo for some years a military
occupation by Cossacks and Pandours, or to be shorn for a similar period of the
frontier provinces necessary to its defence as an independent nation. This appears to
me at present the most probable danger that threatens the world. Don't suppose that
I see none the other way; the renovation of the French ascendancy in Europe, under
such a military government as is forming anew, would be a calamity worse than we
felt it before, for the soldiers who now lord it over the earth are becoming every year
more uncivilized and unprincipled. But this I feel for certain, that it is owing to our
forcing a war upon France in the present circumstances, that we are reduced to the
alternative of two such evils; when perhaps we might have contrived to shamble on
for a few years of peace until some of its old habits were formed again in all countries,
and the chances of mortality might have been improved to the advantage of mankind.

〈Let me hear what is doing, or meant to be done, about your Jury Court. That will
be a great field for you. The success of the new institution must in a very great
measure depend upon the exertions made by the Bar, and upon their skill in
gradually adapting the Scotch forms of pleading and the Scotch rules of evidence to

this new procedure. There is a great deal, too, to create; it must all be done by the Bar. And with so much genius and philosophy as adorns the Parliament House at present, it will be imputable to your indolence only, if you do not give the thing a right impulse at first, and lay those principles in the ground which will insure in proper time a fair and fruitful system.

⟨. . .⟩

570. From Francis Jeffrey

⟨*Jeffrey*, ii. 157–9⟩   Edinburgh, 9 June 1815

⟨Here I lie,
Shot by a sky-
Rocket in the eye.[1]

⟨This is literally true, except that I am not dead, nor quite blind. But I have been nearly so for the last week, or I could not have neglected your very kind letter so long. . . .

⟨I am mortally afraid of the war, and I think that is all I can say about it. I hate Bonaparte too, because he makes me more afraid than anybody else, and seems more immediately the cause of my paying income-tax, and having my friends killed with dysenteries and gun-shot wounds, and making my country unpopular, bragging, and servile, and everything that I do not wish it to be. I do think, too, that the risk was, and is, far more imminent and tremendous, of the subversion of all national independence, and all peaceful virtues, and mild and generous habits, by his insolent triumph, than by the success of the most absurd of those who are allied against him. Men will not be ripe for a reasonable or liberal government on this side of the millennium. But though old abuses are likely to be somewhat tempered by the mild measures of wealthy communities, and the diffusion of something like intelligence and education among the lower orders, I really cannot bring myself, therefore, to despise and abuse the Bourbons, and Alexander, and Francis, with the energy which you do. They are absurd, shallow, and hollow persons, I daresay. But they are not very atrocious, and never will have the power to do half so much mischief as their opponent. I prefer, upon the whole, a set of tyrants, if it must be so, that we can laugh at, and would rather mix contempt with my political dislike, than admiration or terror. You admire greatness much more than I do, and have a far more extensive taste for the *sublime* in character. So I could be in my heart for taking a hit at Bonaparte in public or in private, whenever I thought I had him at an advantage; and would even shuffle a little on the score of morality and national rights, if I could insure success in my enterprise. But I am dreadfully afraid, and do not differ from you in seeing little but disorder on either side of the picture. On the whole, however, my wishes must go to the opposite side from yours, I believe; and that chiefly from my caring more about the present, compared with the future. I really cannot console myself for the certainty of being vexed and anxious; and the chance of being very unhappy all my life, by the belief that some fifty or a hundred years after I am dead,

there will be somewhat less of folly or wretchedness among the bigots of Spain, or
the boors of Russia. One reads and thinks so much of past ages, and extends the scale
of our combinations so far beyond the rational measure of our actual interest in
events, that it is difficult not to give way now and then to that illusion. But I laugh
at myself ten times a day for yielding to it; and have no doubt that when my days
come to a close, I shall find it but a poor consolation for the sum of actual suffering
I have come through.

⟨. . .

⟨For God's sake get me a reviewer who can write a taking style. Suggest some
good topics and ideas to me . . .⟩

1. Jeffrey had been struck near his eye by a sky-rocket, while observing the celebrations in
    Edinburgh marking the King's birthday on 4 June.

571. To Francis Jeffrey

BLPES vi. 244–6 ⟨Horner, ii. 267–9⟩   [London], Tuesday, 13 June [1815]

⟨I had heard of your accident, but concluded it to be a trifling wound, from Murray
making no mention of it. Your epitaph on yourself is the purest specimen of the
lapidary style, since the death of Cock Robin. You must really leave off these very
youthful adventures; at least do not be doubly indiscreet by aping loyalty as well as
boyhood⟩; for you see by experience how awkwardly they sit on an old Jacobin. This
attempt of yours, to set off squibs in honour of King George, was a most audacious
mimicry of your Superiors, the David Boyles and Sandy Maconochies; . . .[1]

⟨I am not going to enter again into the argument of the war. It is a dismal subject
to talk of with those whom one agrees with about it; and an irksome one to differ
upon. We now understand one another's expectations and wishes; the upshot of a
thousand accidents will, a few years hence, decide which was more nearly in the
right. But there is one point on which I would rather not be mistaken by you. You
have an idea that I entertain more admiration and less of hate for Bonaparte than
you feel: you have given me a hint of this more than once, though I do not know
from what you can have collected it.[2] I am the more surprised that you should make
such a mistake about me in the particular instance, for my notions about him are
derived very much from my habitual sentiments respecting such personages and
characters. I have no admiration for any military heroes, conceiving it to be the least
rare of all the varieties of talent; and I have a constitutional aversion to the whole
race of conquerors. I never felt any interest in wars, either reading of them or
looking on in our own days, except on the side of the invaded; and whether they be
Greeks or Persians, Russians or French, my wishes have always been in favour of
each in their turn, for the success of their defence. You may apply this at the present
moment in its fullest force. Bonaparte never had any sympathy or applause from me;
besides his belonging to the odious herd of military disturbers of the world, his
genius is of so hard a cast, and his style so theatrical, and the magnanimity he shows

(which cannot be denied him) is so far from being simple and is so little softened with moral affections, that I never could find in him any of the elements of heroism according to my taste. Conceive me to hate Bonaparte as you do, but yet to wish (as I do fervently) for a successful resistance by France to the invasion of the allies, and you are pretty nearly in possession of all my present politics. Could I make the future to my mind, 'sponte mea *componere curas*', I would balance the success of the war upon the frontiers of old France very evenly, and would keep up the struggle for power at Paris between Napoleon and the constitutional party. For that there is something of a conflict and compromise, at the present moment, between the military chiefs and the partisans of civil liberty, seems undeniable; it may last only for the moment; but it is a glimpse of better days. I feel very happy at the distinction conferred on old Lanjuinais; particularly, if it be true, that Bonaparte wished the presidency to be given to that ruffian Merlin de Douay.[3] Though not occupying a place in the foremost rank, Lanjuinais is found at every crisis of the revolution from the beginning of the states general; ever moderate, rational, and intrepid. What an enviable old age! to have entered on the struggle for public liberty after fifty, to maintain all his consistency through all the horrors and all the disappointments of six and twenty years, and when at last there comes another snatch of sunshine to be honoured with the confidence of every one who thinks France still capable of freedom.⟩

1. Still respectively the Justice Clerk and Solicitor-General for Scotland.
2. Jeffrey's opinion was probably formed by accurate reports of Bonapartist sympathies among those who agreed with Horner. The context and the heat of the debate on the French Revolution had led many members of the old Fox faction, most notably the Hollands, Lauderdale, and Whitbread, to regard Napoleon as their champion, and as one possessed of almost supernatural powers. During the Hundred Days only Holland among the leading members of Opposition expressed direct support for the French Emperor (Holland to Caroline Fox, 5 Mar., BL Add. MSS 51740). But Grey was reported as feeling that Napoleon was 'formed for great purposes' and 'of a nature above the general standard of mankind, . . . in great degree above comparison' (*Farington Diary*, viii. 12), and Whitbread encouraged the Commons to 'Learn Justice, and do not despise the Gods.' These declarations, complemented by the Bonapartist sympathies expressed publicly by Burdett, Waithman, Cartwright, Capel Lofft, William Godwin, and other 'radicals', undermined Horner's reasonable but delicate concept of foreign politics and identified him as having subversive views. (Lean, pp. 65, 103; Taylor, pp. 403 and 407–408.)
3. Comte Jean-Denis Lanjuinais (1753–1827), a fervent enemy of Napoleon, had been elected president of the French Chamber of Representatives on 3 June. Comte Philippe Antoine Merlin (1754–1838) was commonly known as 'Merlin de Douai'.

572. To John Horner

BLPES vi. 247–8   [London], Friday [23 June 1815][1]

. . .

The loss is such as was never known in the British army; it is said that the number of officers killed and wounded [at Waterloo] will amount to eight hundred, and Lord Wellington, besides his description of the loss as 'immense' in the *Gazette*, speaks of it in strong terms both in conversation at Brussels and in his private letters; a loss, he says, in that most important arm, the British Infantry. So many families in London are involved in the calamity, that I never remember any splendid victory received here with such a mixture of depression with their political joy. The value of the victory, in giving splendour to the British arms and efficacy to the British name throughout Europe, is inestimable; its consequences in the war are matter of various speculation even to those who think alike respecting the war.[2]

The Duke of Wellington says, that he never felt so much anxiety in any action, and never was so near being beaten; his admiration of the conduct of his troops is unbounded; 'My God! The Guards', he exclaimed to a friend of mine who saw him at Brussels on Monday Evening. They defended a particular post assigned them in a Garden, in a manner that never was seen before. The Duke says of Bonaparte, that he did his duty; this expression he uses, I am told, in a letter to his brother Pole today, adding that nothing could have given him the victory but the physical courage of the British troops. Bonaparte, it seems, was on a scaffold commanding the field of battle the greater part of the day, till the fortune of the fight turned against him; he then mounted his horse, and led several charges in person; the last charge made by the French was by the Imperial Guards, cavalry, with the Emperor at their head; this was received and repulsed by our foot Guards.

. . .

1. Though endorsed '26 June 1815'.
2. The allied victory at Waterloo astonished many members of Opposition. Addressing the Commons only four days before the battle, Tierney had predicted a lengthy war, and several key politicians depreciated the significance of the battle even after official reports reached London (Taylor, p. 415).

573. To Lady Holland

BLPES vi. 339–40   [?London], Sunday [?2 July 1815]

. . .

I was anxious to hear Abercromby's way of justifying Napoleon for leaving the army; but it is only a very anxious argument, to make out that it was the best thing he could do, and does not turn upon any particular facts that we did not know before. He has not convinced me; so I must remain some while longer of opinion that in that part of his history your hero falls short of heroism.

. . .

Why does the Morning Chronicle, with its usual fatality, throw the blame of running with Louis from Ghent on the Duke of Wellington, instead of keeping it to Ministers?[1] In the first instance, at all events, they are responsible for the errors which have brought them into their present embarrassment; and it is not our business to insist, till it appears otherwise, that the Duke of W. is any thing but a soldier, with whom political measures do not originate.

I rejoice to see that Sir Nathaniel Wraxall advertises an answer to all the

Reviews.[2] He will of course give them fresh advantages, and it will be hard if they do not extinguish the credit of his memoirs. *La Belle Alliance!* when the *Edinburgh, Quarterly, British Critic* make common cause.

1. On 30 June the MC published Wellington's Proclamation of the 27th that the army was entering France as the ally of the King of that country and criticized the policy of the British Government. But the following day it made a direct attack on the Duke's Proclamation, as well as rejecting the notion that Louis was welcomed back.

2. Mackintosh had published a ferocious attack in *ER* xxv (no. xlix, June 1815), 168–220, on the first edition of the famous *Historical Memoirs* of Sir Nathaniel Wraxall, 1st Bart (1751–1831: *DNB*), and in August Wraxall replied to it and similar attacks with his *Answer to the Calumnious Misrepresentations of the Quarterly Review, British Critic, and Edinburgh Review.* Mackintosh responded in turn with another article in *ER* xxv (no. l, Oct. 1815), 527–41.

574. To Joanna Horner

BLPES vi. 257–60 ⟨*Horner*, ii. 270–71⟩   Winchester, Tuesday [4 July 1815]

⟨. . . I left town yesterday with Adam, who is remarkably well. From this place we must cross to Bridgewater for the sessions, which will fall this time in the second week of the circuit.

⟨ . . .

⟨We have lost Jekyll from our circuit; he is made a Master in Chancery by the Regent. The Chancellor delayed the appointment in a manner the most disagreeable to Jekyll's feelings, and then wrote him a very fulsome letter, full of the pleasure he felt in conferring the office upon him.⟩[1] There is another anecdote of this base man, very much talked of in London. Sir Thomas Picton had applied to him for a Welsh living for his brother, and after repeated applications which Picton at last grounded upon his public service, the Chancellor finally, a short while before Sir Thomas went to Flanders, by letter promised that his brother should have the living. Since his death at Waterloo, the Chancellor has given the church to another person.[2]

⟨The Duke of Cumberland's disappointment will give universal satisfaction.[3] Never was the value of general character so proved. The conduct of the House of Commons makes an excellent contrast with their liberality to the Duke of Wellington. The old Queen is said to have been as eager against her son Ernest, as any of us of the Opposition who had an old score against him to pay off; I know that several of her old cats from Windsor were very busy abusing him all Saturday and Sunday.

⟨. . .⟩

1. The Prince Regent was said to have exerted indecent pressure to ensure the appointment, and *Romilly*, iii. 186–7, observing that Jekyll was 'deficient in almost every qualification necessary to discharge properly the duties of a Master in Chancery', reports that the appointment was known as early as 13 Apr. but that the Chancellor, apparently displaying 'his sense of the impropriety of the appointment', waited until 23 June to write to the appointee.

2. Lt Gen. Sir Thomas Picton (1758–1815: *DNB*) was killed while leading his brigade at

Waterloo. His brother Edward (c.1761–1835) remained until his death in the modest living he had held since 1798.

3. In what was regarded as the only meaningful Opposition victory during the 1815 session, Western had moved an amendment postponing for six months the Ministry's bill to provide for the marriage of the Duke of Cumberland (Mitchell, p. 86).

575. From Henry Hallam

Kinnordy MSS   London, 11 July [1815]

You desired that I would write to you on the passing events of this extraordinary time, and the state of public opinion. I have had no opportunities of judging of the latter – you will pretty well guess how persons think and speak in London. But, among all the victories and revolutions, no event has made such an impression as the fatal death of Whitbread.[1] It created, as far as I saw, a kind of consternation which almost prevented the expression of regret; but the latter has now had time to prevail, and it is satisfactory to perceive that his memory is treated with a general respect which it well deserved. Such a tremendous visitation of intellectual disease must make us all serious – it is an awful proof of what you lately observed to me, the progress of insanity among men of ardent and reflecting minds. To me it was merely astonishing – I could not have less anticipated such a circumstance in any one individual, but those who knew him nearly and especially Tierney, had perceived the rise of this malady for some time. I do not know if you had made the observation. His loss will be keenly felt, notwithstanding his faults, which, considered as a public man, were numerous enough.

You will see the curious position of affairs in France; and probably will agree with me in thinking that Fouché has been intriguing with the King, probably betraying Bonaparte into his abdication. I believe I told you that this expectation prevailed two months ago among the royalists. It would be equally base and impolitic in Louis not to trust or employ him, and I am almost sorry the Duke of Wellington has asked him to dinner. Nothing can more strongly show the deprivation of moral feeling in France, than that a man should hope to find his interest in a course of marked infamy. Ney seemed to have the same idea.

With the views that you know I have taken of these matters, you must suppose I am not much interested in the state of these new legislators. It is to be sure a fine reflection for them that they have sacrificed the lives of fifty thousand men, and thrown away their national honour, in order to set up a constitution, which as far as I see, differs in nothing from that the King gave them, except the colour of a cockade. The liberty of France is certainly in jeopardy, and she must depend for it on the temper and moderation of Louis. However, I think he will hardly innovate on the constitution of 1814, which was quite good enough to allow France to flourish. Amnesty he neither can nor ought to grant; not even as to capital punishment, if he can get hold of a few persons most concerned against him. It is a very certain truth, though one of which I should not wish governments to be convinced, that nothing strengthens them like public executions . . .

1. On 6 July, the day after he heard of the fall of Paris, Samuel Whitbread committed suicide. Upon learning of the death of his colleague, Horner had been 'thrown into very low spirits'. (Horner to Mrs William Spencer, 7 July, *Horner*, ii. 271–2.)

576. To Lord Webb Seymour

BLPES vi. 269–72   Exeter, 18 July 1815

. . .

Have you again, as last year, another vision of the return of order and justice and liberty to the earth, in the train of the Bourbons? It would be some consolation to me, in my dejected views of the future, to know that any of those whose judgements I rely upon thought better than myself of the prospects of Europe. One thing seems manifest to demonstration; that the Bourbons cannot maintain themselves on the throne of that country, if left to themselves and to such an army as they can form out of the French people. Another thing seems certain, that France in the possession of a foreign soldiery for the purpose of upholding a particular government, is no longer France, a separate independent member of the European system; but a dependency of the worst kind on those whose soldiers are in possession of the territory. Now how long does any reasonable man expect that such a state of things can be maintained? The military habits of the French people seem lost for the present; owing probably to the very circumstance of their having been so long accustomed to great standing armies; for that institution seems to habituate the people to rely upon it entirely as all that can be set up for defence, and to acquiesce in the result of what has passed in the regular field of battle; whereas the true defence of every country against invaders is in the knives and pitchforks and fierce antipathy of the whole body of peasantry. This saved Spain: and there may be a reaction in France.

I look upon the attempt to restore Louis 18th, with his Charter, to be only a prolongation of the revolutionary miseries of France, and of the agitation which her internal revolutions must for ever communicate to all countries around. Prostrate and conquered and depraved as she is, France will have something for her revolution, and will not submit to the old *regime* of courtiers and priests. King Louis and Castlereagh and the Duke of Wellington, depend upon it, have no better views than to force that submission as far as it can be enforced; this is what your trading bond of the North means, by the effect of the victory of Waterloo upon the *liberty* of the world. Your ingenious candid adversaries of freedom say, and say very justly, that the true undoubted triumph of their great principle of *legitimacy* is the restoration of Ferdinand of Naples; who has nothing personally, or in the recollections of his former government, to recommend him to the choice or affections of his patrimonial subjects; on the contrary, against whom every thing may with . . . truth be alleged that would unfit an individual for being a king, except his being the legitimate heir. In the former age, this was called *divine* right; the world has some- how or other got into a state of thinking, that will not admit of that particular mode of expression; but the thing substantially, the principle, seems to be just the same.

. . .

577. To Henry Hallam

BLPES vi. 273–7 ⟨Horner, ii. 273–6⟩   Exeter, 22 July 1815

...

⟨The event that has most agitated me since I parted from you, is the death of
Whitbread, which you mentioned with sentiments that gave me a real pleasure; for
I shall ever respect his memory, and with something like affection too, for the large
portion of my life which in a certain sense I consider as having been passed with
him, and for the impression he had made upon me of his being one of the most just,
upright, and intrepid of public men. As a statesman, I never regarded him at all; he
had no knowledge of men or affairs, to fit him for administration; his education had
been very limited, and its defects were not supplied by any experience of real
political business: but he must always stand high in the list of that class of public
men, the peculiar growth of England and of the House of Commons, who perform
great services to their country and hold a considerable place in the sight of the
world, by fearlessly expressing in that assembly the censure that is felt by the public,
and by being as it were the organ of that public opinion which in some measure
keeps our statesmen to their duty. His force of character and ability, seconded by his
singular activity, had, in the present absence of all men of genius and ascendancy
from the House, given him a preeminence, which almost marks the last years of
Parliament with the stamp of his peculiar manner. His loss will lead to a change of
this: in all points of taste and ornament, and in the skill too and prudence of debate,
the change may probably be for the better; but it will be long, before the people and
the constitution are supplied in the House of Commons with a tribune of the same
vigilance, assiduity, perseverance and courage, as Samuel Whitbread. ...[1]

⟨Pray give me your speculations upon the present state of France, so
problematical, so pregnant with future consequences. ... It is evident the present
state of things cannot be lasting; the occupation of such a country as France by
foreign troops. They may be kept there long enough to devastate the surface of the
territory, and to keep the Bourbons a few years nominally upon the throne. But do
you believe it practicable for the Allies to accomplish the restoration of that family,
and then to leave them to carry on the government with French hands and French
guards? Or, on the other hand, do you consider it as practicable for the French to be
permanently subjugated by the foreign soldiery? It may be a long while before the
peasantry, and the townsmen, betake themselves to assassination in detail; but to
that horrible extremity I think it must come at last, if the Prussians and Russians
remain. The geography of France is not very advantageous for *guerillas*, but there are
other advantages in the habits of the people, from their discipline and docility.
Depraved as the French are, the reaction of French patriotism will be dreadful and
resistless. And I must own that my wishes are decidedly for the deliverance of that
country, by the exertions of its own people, from the conquest of their invaders. I am
conscious that I can honestly and purely cherish this wish, without abating a jot of
that wholesome distrust of France which we must always keep up, as our enemy in
Europe; but along with this distrust, I retain also so much of the notions of the old
school, as to feel persuaded that France, as a separate country, is an essential member

of the European system. But how idle it is to speculate, when the fate of the world is in the hands of Metternich and Castlereagh.

⟨. . .⟩

1. For further comment on Whitbread and the political ramifications of his death, see Horner to Somerset, 18 July, *Horner*, ii. 272–3.

578. To Mrs Dugald Stewart

BLPES vi. 286–7   [London], Wednesday [22 Aug. 1815][1]

In these times a piece of really good news so seldom occurs, that I must tell you without delay what I have just learnt for certain, that the French Government, after much reluctance and opposition, has at length agreed to an entire and immediate abolition of the Slave Trade. Lord Liverpool has communicated this important event to Wilberforce, and the person who told me of it has received the intelligence from the Duke of Wellington.[2]

All accounts coincide in representing France as in a state of great disorder, and except where there are foreign troops absolutely without a Government. Three hundred houses of Protestants have been burnt out at Nismes; they are considered as Bonapartists; and in fact they always considered themselves as sure of toleration under him, and have had reason to distrust the Bourbons on that point.

Le Désiré[3] is now called at Paris *L'Inévitable*, and somebody who would be more smart has given him the name *Le Biscuit*.

Talleyrand was very urgent with the King to be more explicit in his Declaration, respecting those who had been engaged in the last revolution, that individuals might be more precisely notified of the intentions of the Government towards them; Your Majesty, he said to him, does not know 'toutes les delicatesses d'une mauvaise conscience.'[4]

Upon that Declaration being published, Carnot wrote to Fouché a billet in genuine French, 'où me rendrai-je, Traitre?' The answer was, 'où tu voudras, imbécile.'[5]

Is there another people on earth, or was there ever one, that in the midst of national ruin and convulsion could show no spirit but for nicknames, and sayings, and stage trick?

There is an expedition going to Africa, in the footsteps of Park, but with a considerable military escort of negroes from the interior. The persons employed to conduct it are two Scotch officers, Pedie and Campbell, of whom I know nothing; they are to leave London by the beginning of next month. It is a pity they should not be supplied with hints and instructions from every body that is competent to furnish them. General Gordon of the Horse Guards is the promoter of this expedition; he is Colonel of the Black Corps at Sierra Leone, from which the escort is to be taken.[6]

1. Horner evidently wrote this letter after dining at Holland House in the company of Mackintosh and Sheridan on 22 Aug., his first appearance since the return of the Hollands from the continent on 6 Aug. (HHDB).

2. The French had undertaken at Vienna to abolish the trade, but only within the next five years, and after the Hundred Days they continued to prevaricate and to demand compensation for an earlier abolition. Eventually, towards the end of July, they agreed to complete an immediate abolition, thanks largely to pressure from the Tsar. On 31 July Castlereagh wrote to Liverpool from Paris (WSD xi. 83):

> I have the satisfaction to send you the Abolition complete. In reply to a succession of inquiries from Wilberforce, I have by this messenger referred him to you for information, apprising him that the point has been conceded.

3. Louis XVIII.

4. Talleyrand objected to the declaration the King had made on 25 June after re-entering France as likely to make him appear to his people as coming too much in the baggage of the Allied armies. Consequently he drafted a second declaration which the King signed on 28 June. His version of the story, with the text of the two declarations, is given in *Talleyrand*, iii. 129–57.

5. Fouché, having resumed his old office of Minister of Police during the Hundred Days, retained it also for a short time upon the second Bourbon restoration. The story told here was confirmed by one of Wellington's secret agents (WSD xi. 108).

6. The object of the expedition led by Major John Peddie and Capt. Thomas Campbell was to follow up Mungo Park's last explorations and locate the mouth and course of the Niger. The instructions addressed to him on 23 Aug. (C.W. Newbury, *British Policy towards West Africa: Select Documents 1786–1874* (Oxford, 1965), pp. 54–7) directed him to recruit volunteers from captured negroes in the British settlements or from the Royal African Corps, whose Colonel-Commandant was Willoughby Gordon, the Quartermaster-General at the Horse Guards and, afterwards, a founding fellow of the Royal Geographical Society. In a letter to his sister Frances of 22 Nov. 1815 (*Horner*, ii. 292–3) Horner mentioned that the expedition had sailed and commented that the Government had after all been 'stingy' only on one point, though that a vital one in his opinion – the reward to the black soldiers for returning safely with their officers. The expedition was an utter failure and neither Peddie nor Campbell returned alive.

579. To Mrs Dugald Stewart

Lacaita/Shelburne MSS, William L. Clements Library,
University of Michigan   London, 26 Aug. 1815

. . .

There is no decided opinion yet, among those who can determine such things, whether the extraordinary paper signed Fouché, which you saw in the *Morning Chronicle* some days ago, is really a genuine document. Of course it could only make its appearance in a suspicious manner through the English press, even if the King was a party to it; for no such publication would be suffered by the Allies. Whether strictly genuine or not, in the official sense of the word, it probably comes from Fouché, for the purpose of exciting the spirit of France, if it has any left.[1]

There is probably exaggeration in the accounts given of the Protestant massacres in the South. But the newspaper which mentioned them was immediately suppressed. Frederick Lamb who came very lately from Paris, where he had lived in the midst of the diplomatic and military personages, says they talked of as many as three thousand Protestants put to death.[2] The number of foreign troops and plunderers, let in upon the soil of France, was estimated by Sir Charles Stuart at about nine hundred thousand.[3] Of all these the Prussians behave the worst, and, what is very satisfactory, the English the best. Lamb and Abercromby, and others whom I have seen, agree that there is manifestly a feeling of suppressed indignation, which is gradually assuming more of a national cast and includes all the enemies of *La France*. There is a terrible phrase that passes from mouth to mouth, 'qu'ils attendent le bouc'. Nobody at Paris, or even in Carlton House it is said, pretends to believe that Louis *le désiré*, *l'inévitable*, *le zéro*, (for that has been the progress of his title) can be long maintained even in name upon the throne. Were the foreign troops to go, he could not muster two hundred men, or collect two hundred pounds. It will be to my mind an inestimable consolation for all that is happening, if the principle of legitimacy receives so signal an overthrow. There is much talk there, and here too, of the Duke of Orléans, who is prudently keeping out of the way at Richmond, and leaving events to take their own course which he cannot pretend to give any direction to, either by his talents or by the position in which he is placed. I do not understand there is the least individual preference for him, except as a Bourbon who cannot claim by right, and whose family name is connected in popular recollections with the earliest events of the Revolution; for low as France is, I believe from all I observed myself last year, as well as from what has happened since, that the people of all ranks cling to the substance of what has been gained by the Revolution, and will revert to that after all difficulties and sufferings.

By all accounts, the Russian takes a part at Paris which thwarts the other allies in their plans. One account is, that he was about to withdraw his troops, in consequence of some unpleasant movements at home, and the discontent of his Russian nobles on account of the new arrangement he has made about Poland. Another story is (and this I have fresh from Sir Robert Wilson, who arrived from Paris last night),[4] that he declares himself the Protector of the integrity of France, 'et qu'il a encore du monde,' with whom he threatens to take up a position in Poland that shall influence the politics of both Prussians and Austrians at Paris. The two stories are consistent enough; and have probably this foundation in common, that, in his remote situation, he has no direct interest in the dismemberment of France, but rather in the preservation of that as a great power.

Lamb says you never hear a Frenchman say 'les alliés', but invariably 'nos ennemis'.

We may look forward to a dreadful winter. It was one objection to this most unprincipled war, that success was improbable; our very success itself has proved the reasonableness of that expectation: the other objection was, that success to the allies would be found unmanageable. How they have confirmed this! They had one opportunity of avoiding the embarrassment they have brought upon themselves, by negotiating with the provisional Government, and keeping the old man at Ghent till they had gone through the farce of appearing to act upon their Declaration, and of seeming to take the advice of the French about their King. But the Duke of Wellington scorned this; he took it upon himself to put Louis at once in possession, for which he has now been reproached by the other Allies, and (now that this measure seems unlikely to succeed) by our own sagacious Regent – who is reported to have lately given pretty strong indications of favouring the Duke of Orléans. He is to be the restorer of the Bourbons; and whichever Bourbon events seem to favour,

His Royal Highness must make haste to favour too, for fear of being left behind by those same events; which in all our time, I think, have never been guided by any one politician among them, with the exception of Napoleon at one or two epochs of his history. – What have you brought upon yourself by telling me you are pleased with my gossip.

PS Lady Granville says she went to an evening party at Mad. de Coigny's, from which all the French company withdrew, when the English appeared.[5]

1. The MC of 24 Aug. 1815 had printed a 'Report to the King on the situation in France, and on the Relations with the Foreign Armies, by Fouché, Minister of the General Police', complaining of the general attitude of the Allies, and a protest from both Talleyrand and Fouché about the Allied order to disperse French troops throughout the country. The Ministerial papers subsequently questioned their authenticity, but Wellington had already been given secret intelligence of them and Talleyrand afterwards accused Fouché of deliberately leaking them. (WSD xi. 107–10; Talleyrand, iii. 174.)
2. Frederick Lamb was then between diplomatic appointments.
3. Brougham's old friend had been made ambassador at Paris earlier that year.
4. General Sir Robert Thomas Wilson (1777–1849: DNB), whose unduly negative assessments of military affairs in the Peninsula and elsewhere had deluded Grey and other leading members of Opposition since 1810, was violently and imprudently anti-Bourbon, and he now disseminated inflammatory information on French affairs among Foxite leaders. See the Wilson–Grey correspondence in BL Add. MSS 30118.
5. Harriet (d. 1862), wife of the politician and diplomat, Viscount Granville, was a close friend of Louise Marthe, Duchesse de Coigny (1759–1832), a handsome and witty member of society in Paris and in London.

580. To Mrs Leonard Horner

⟨Leonard Horner, i. 79–80⟩   Bowood, 29 Oct. 1815[1]

⟨I have spent a most agreeable week here, in spite of unsettled weather, and leave the place with much regret ... I hear from town today, that Admiral Fleming has received a letter from Sir George Cockburn, dated off Madeira, who reports Buonaparte as having been in good spirits during the voyage, but lethargic, which prevents him from much reading or writing.[2] He sleeps fourteen out of the twenty-four hours. But he has taken a great deal to card-playing, of which he was ignorant when he left Plymouth, but now he beats everybody. Sir George had lost a hundred and thirty napoleons to him the night before, and says, if he went on, he should lose all his pay. Buonaparte had ingratiated himself with everyone in the course of the voyage, and was universally popular.

⟨Sir Hudson Lowe is to take out for him to St Helena a considerable collection of books, many of his own particular choice, especially mathematical works, and a set of the best French translations of the classics.[3] ...⟩

1. Early in September Horner left London by mail coach and proceeded to Brougham, Howick, Minto, and Edinburgh. He remained in Edinburgh until mid-October and then went south to Bowood, where he spent the last week of the month. Available manuscripts and published sources contain nothing but chatty letters to friends and relatives written

during September and October. Such letters written to Lady Anna Maria Elliot during September are in the Minto MSS (NLS MSS 11103). See also *Horner*, ii. 285–90, for letters written from Howick to his mother on 11 Oct., from Taunton to Murray on the 20th, and from Bowood to his sister Frances on the 26th. See also Horner to Grey, 27 Oct., and Grey to Horner, 1 Nov., *Horner*, ii. 290–92.

2. Admiral Sir George Cockburn (1772–1853: *DNB*) daily invited Napoleon to dinner during the voyage of HMS *Northumberland* from Portsmouth to St Helena. Admiral Charles Elphinstone Fleeming (1774–1840) was the son of the 11th Lord Elphinstone and nephew of William Adam.

3. Sir Hudson Lowe (1769–1844: *DNB*), who succeeded Sir George Cockburn as Governor of St Helena in April 1816, first dined at Holland House on 22 Sept. 1815 (HHDB).

581. To Mrs Dugald Stewart

BLPES vi. 297   [London], Thursday [2 Nov. 1815]

. . .

The Romillys are returned quite well; with a frightful impression of all that is passing at Paris, and a conviction that it cannot possibly last.[1] Impressions from those who have been upon the spot outweigh every judgement found at a distance; otherwise I should have been inclined to dread, that by means of the foreign force this tyranny will be maintained. It is the greatest disgrace yet that England has ever inflicted upon herself, to be a party to such transactions, indeed the leader of them.

. . .

1. See *Romilly*, iii. 210–12.

582. To Anne Horner

BLPES vi. 298 (copy)   London, 7 Nov. 1815

. . .

Since I returned to London, I have seen a little of the celebrated Italian sculptor Canova, who is come here for a fortnight. His look is quite worthy of a man of genius, his forehead and eye being particularly fine; and what is a still surer physiognomy, his manners and temper of mind are remarkable for simplicity, calmness, and good nature in talking about artists. I am going to Holland House today with Whishaw, to meet him again in a party of our London artists; Lawrence, Westmacott, etc.[1]

. . .

1. Antonio Canova (1757–1822), who headed the commission appointed by the Pope to restore to their original owners the art works that had been sent to Paris by French generals, dined with Horner at Holland House on 4 Nov. The dinner party of 7 Nov. included the

sculptor Richard Westmacott (1775–1856: *DNB*) and the painter David Wilkie (1785–1841: *DNB*). Sir Thomas Lawrence (1769–1830: *DNB*), the current rage of English portraiture, declined the invitation. (*Home of the Hollands*, pp. 302–303; Horner to Frances Horner, 22 Nov., *Horner*, ii. 292–3; see also *Holland House Circle*, pp. 239–41.)

583. To T.R. Malthus

BLPES vi. 299–300 ⟨*Malthus*, pp. 231–2⟩   The Temple,[1] 16 Nov. 1815

⟨I am very much grieved to hear, that the peace of the College has been again disturbed by your young men.[2] From your letter to Whishaw, which he has shown me, it would seem that they have proceeded farther lengths this time than ever, and the attack upon the servants appears to have been attended with circumstances which require the interposition of some stronger authority than college discipline. It struck me, last time, that there was no certain remedy for outrages of this description, except in the ordinary process of the criminal law; and I apprehend there can no longer be any hesitation in resorting to that sure[3] expedient. If you cannot punish your pupils as boys, you must subject them to the punishments by which other men are kept in order; and as the particular plan of your Institution, together with the situation of most of the lads, make rustication and even expulsion nugatory as correctives, you have nothing else left but recourse to the law. The servants attacked ought to be directed to prefer indictments, and in my opinion there ought to be no false delicacy about the employment of the most effectual means, which Bow Street and the Old Bailey can furnish you with, for tracing out evidence. A conspiracy and riot of the most aggravated sort is one of the offences that have been committed; and the wounding of the servants with the sharp instrument which you describe is, by the law, a capital felony in all who were concerned.

. . .

1. Horner had had to change his chambers as well as his lodgings.
2. Despite the successful resistance to the attacks on the East India College in 1813 (Doc. 494) the disciplinary problems continued. There were further disturbances in May 1815 and then, on 9 Nov., what has been called 'the most serious riot in the College's History', when fourteen masked students physically attacked a couple of unpopular college servants. Horner's advice on this occasion was taken: the servants were induced to complain to the magistrates; the principal offenders were unmasked; and three of them spent a day or two in prison before being discharged (though unfortunately one of them died very shortly afterwards). All this gave further ammunition to the Company's enemies, who renewed their attacks the following year and provoked in turn a second pamphlet from Malthus, *Statements respecting the East India College, with an Appeal to Facts, in refutation of the Charges lately brought against it in the Court of Proprietors*. This was sympathetically noticed in ER xxvii (no. liv, Dec. 1816), 511–31. (*Malthus*, pp. 230–39.)
3. Not 'same' as in *Malthus*.

584. To T.R. Malthus

BLPES vi. 300–302   The Temple, 21 Nov. 1815

I am very clearly of opinion that you ought not to hesitate to make any improvements in the new edition of your work, which farther time and reflection have suggested to you, either in the form and arrangement of the treatise or in point of additional matter. Every reader, who has appreciated the book near its value, will only be thankful to you for farther assistance and instruction. At the same time, I think it will be expedient, if possible, to print on a few separate sheets the substance of the new additions, together with some explanation of the changes you make in the order of your work; to be purchased by those who have the former editions, just as you did before upon the first octavo edition.[1]

I hope you will be able to come to the Club. The first is always one of the best.[2] I mean to go out of town early on Sunday, into Bedfordshire.

. . .

1. Malthus was already at work on the fifth (1817) edition of his *Essay on the Principle of Population*, in which he seems to have followed Horner's advice: see *Malthus*, pp. 370–71.
2. Apparently Horner refers to the King of Clubs and to its first meeting of the new year on 3 Feb. 1816 (HHDB).

585. To Joanna Horner

BLPES vi. 303–304   Woburn Abbey, 28 Nov. 1815

. . .

I came down here on Sunday, and shall remain till Thursday. I had often been invited before, but never had it in my power to accept till this time, and I was very glad to be able to come down for a few days. The Duke I have known and liked a long while; and now that I have seen the Duchess in her own house, it is impossible not to be pleased with her lively good humour and cleverness, and the pains she takes to make every body pleased and at their ease. The house and park are very magnificent; but I am a bad describer of such things. The most agreeable of the visitors are the Hollands, John Allen, Rogers, and a Mr Binder, a young Italian of very amiable manners, one of the many foreigners drawn to England for refuge from the present disasters of the continent.[1] Besides these, there is Prince Esterhazy the Austrian Ambassador, a good-natured youth, very little like an ambassador; and with him, a Hungarian Magnat [sic], young also, whose opinions upon the present state of things are rather stronger than I should think his own country could bear.[2]

1. Giuseppe Binda, a friend of Ugo Foscolo and a former civil servant under the Roman and Neapolitan Governments, became acquainted with the Hollands in Italy and followed

them to London in 1815; he was about this time a regular inmate of Holland House. (*Home of the Hollands*, pp. 300–302.)

2. Prince Paul Anton Esterházy (1786–1866) had just arrived to take up his post as Austrian ambassador in London. It is not known who was the 'Hungarian magnate'.

586. To J.A. Murray

BLPES vi. 305–308 ⟨*Horner*, ii. 294–6⟩   Woburn Abbey, 28 Nov. [1815]

⟨. . .

⟨I am impatient to see the *Review* . . . to know what Jeffrey's speculations are about France; for he seems to have given different persons in London, with whom he talked about them, the most contradictory impressions of his opinions.⟩ Of course, we shall have his impressions at least in the *Review*, for they hardly remain long enough with him to acquire the stability of settled opinions; a sad consequence of his dialectical habits, and of his too easy and prolific ingenuity. But ⟨his ingenious powers of diversifying the views of a great subject are a copious source of instruction to those who submit to the duller task of patiently forming a judgement that is to remain on their minds; and the assistance which one derives from his inventions and reasonings is always accompanied with a delightful confidence, at least upon serious and great occasions, that his sentiments, however transient they may prove, are honest and conscientious at the time. For, though Jeffrey often trifles with a subject expressly, and often argues for exhibition, he never leaves me in doubt, when he means to do so, and when he is for the time in earnest. I am therefore very impatient to see what he has to say about France; for as the new state of affairs in that unhappy country, and our deep participation in them, must be a constant meditation in every reflecting and feeling mind, so I conclude from the opinions he held about the war in May last, that I am not likely to find him judging of these matters at present in the light in which I see them.

⟨It was a very painful circumstance in my last visit to Scotland, from the little politics I talked with any body, to find myself so far asunder from my best friends in our views of foreign affairs. To me, it is losing the chief relish of life not to feel alike with them upon things which make us all feel strongly. And I have laid nothing so much to heart for many years as the difference which I imagine exists among us, respecting the nature and character of the present crisis of European politics. All the opinions which I have ever cherished seem on this occasion concentrated, and all the principles which have been gaining strength and confirmation in my mind every year of my life, seem put in peril at once. It is a question, whether all the good fruits of the French Revolution, dearly and cruelly as they have been earned, are to be lost to France; and whether it is not to be settled in the instance of that country, that the greatest and most civilized people may, by the confederacy of courts and the alliance of armies, be subjected to the government of a family whom they despise and detest. It is a question whether the very first principle of slavery, that the people are the property of certain royal families, is not to be established as a fundamental maxim in the system of Europe; and whether the vital principle of our English liberty and our revolution is not to be antiquated as a Jacobinical heresy by the force of English arms. The degradation of our army in being the main instrument of this warfare against freedom and civilization, the stain upon the national name in making so ungenerous a use of our triumph over our rival in arms, our keeping the police of Paris to protect the Bourbons while they are murdering with judicial forms those who tried the fortune of war with us, and to whom we in words and they by fact and deed gave warrant of an amnesty;[1] these are incidental subjects of grief and shame, which embitter the pain with which one contemplates the course of events, and which will leave wounds upon our honour even if the future struggle should take a favourable turn; but the struggle to which I look, is that of the French people against the Bourbons and against the confederate sovereigns. And the most anxious and the most depressing reflection that perpetually recurs upon me, is the conviction, that for the success of this great contest the principles of liberty must rely for their principal support upon the enlightened men of England, while most of these are not yet awakened to a sense of what is doing, and of what the consequences will inevitably be.

⟨You will think me very serious; but I cannot write otherwise to you on these matters, if I write at all; for there is no day that is not saddened by every thing I read and hear.⟩[2]

1. Frenchmen who had borne arms for Napoleon during the Hundred Days were guaranteed impunity under Article 12 of the Capitulation, but the French Government held that the provision did not apply to political acts and proceeded via courts martial against a number of eminent personages. At this time Lord Holland and his circle were outraged by the execution on 9 Aug. of Charles Huchet, Comte de Labédoyère (1786–1815), a recipient of the Cross of St Louis under the Restoration who had been promoted general, ADC, and *Pair de France* by Napoleon during the Hundred Days. Other distinguished proscripts whose fate remained in doubt, and whose causes were soon to figure prominently in Whig politics, were Marshal Ney, Antoine Marie, Comte de Lavallette (1769–1830), and Auguste Charles Joseph, Comte Flahault de la Billardrie (1785–1870). Several days later Horner described the executions as 'murderous', as 'cold-blooded' as the Reign of Terror, and as a 'direct breach of faith' by the restored Bourbon King (Horner to the Duchess of Somerset, 2 Dec., *Horner*, ii. 303).

2. For similar views, including comment on the 'illusion of military success that seems to have blinded many, who used to be guided in their judgements of foreign politics by some regard to justice and to the cause of liberty', see Horner to Thomas Thomson, 29 Nov., *ibid.*, ii. 296–7.

587. To John Allen

BL Add. MSS 52180   The Temple, 1 Dec. [1815]

. . .

Has not the anti-revolutionary Treaty exceeded in atrocity and insolence all that you expected?[1] If this attempt is not put down, or [does not] fail by its own inherent weakness, there will be a speedy end of all political liberty and civilization throughout Europe. One understands now, how even Gentz found the thing too strong. The Emperor Alexander said to an Englishman at Paris, talking of the revolutionary sentiments of the Prussian army, that he might soon be called upon to perform the same service at Berlin, which he had already rendered to his brother Louis. Will this be borne? Can it be successful?

I heard Lord Lansdowne is of opinion that the convention of Paris can only be construed as an amnesty for Ney and his associates. This is better than I expected; for he justified to me the death of Labédoyère – a case to be sure not within the articles of that convention.

> 1. The treaty forming the Quadruple Alliance on the principle of legitimacy, as well as the Second Peace of Paris, had been signed on 20 Nov.

588. To Frances Horner

Kinnordy MSS   London, 2 Dec. 1815

. . . I made a very pleasant visit indeed at Woburn. I could not have believed that so much magnificence could be united with so much ease. Then what comforted and satisfied me more than all, in the midst of these the most gloomy and hopeless prospects of politics that I have ever known, the Russells with all their hereditary virtue: both see justly the real nature of the questions which our proceedings at Paris have raised, and are ready to meet the discussion with the resolution that becomes their name . . .[1]

> 1. For similar comment see Horner's letters of 2 Dec. to Thomas Thomson and the Duchess of Somerset in *Horner*, ii. 301–304.

589. To Mrs Dugald Stewart

BLPES vi. 315 (incomplete)   [London, 5 Dec. 1815]

. . . What we shall do in Parliament in point of numbers . . . I am not yet able to say; but I have heard nothing to give me any distrust about it: in the country, I am afraid, for want of Parliament and of an active press, there is but little sound opinion on foreign affairs and on the disgrace of our name at Paris.

The Dissenters have taken up, with a proper warmth, the sufferings of their Protestant brethren in the South of France. There has not been time yet to see, whether this will have a run among the whole body of the Methodists. It may rouse a detestation of the Bourbons throughout this country. I am not without some apprehensions, however, of its re-acting perniciously for the poor Catholics of Ireland. The leaders of the Calvinist sects, with whom the proceeding originates, are perfectly well disposed to guard as much as possible against that consequence; but the Wesleyan Methodists, the Arminians, hate the Papists as the High Church does. These religious passions are edge-tools to play with; but the people of England seem now to have no other public passion.[1]

The agricultural distress is universal, and attended with a great destruction of the capital possessed by the tenantry, and an evil influence upon their character. Insolvency is the general description of their present condition; and where they contrive to pay, it is generally at the expense of their stock and savings. I believe there will be no effectual remedy for the evil, which is one of long growth, but in a very substantial and perhaps violent reduction of taxes. Before it comes to that, we shall have many projects from the country gentlemen and the Ministers. I heard Western say, but he is apt to exaggerate on this occasion, that, at the present price of grain, the land of England pays no rent at all, but defrays only the expenses of cultivation.

. . .

1. Following the Hundred Days, during which they had been generally well-disposed towards the Emperor's return, the Protestants in the South of France, in particular in the vicinity of Nîmes where they were most numerous, had suffered a good deal at the hands of vengeful royalists and resorted to armed resistance. Towards the end of the year they had appealed to their co-religionists, more especially in England; but order was soon after pretty well restored. (*AR* lvii (1815), 87–9 and 92–3.)

590. To the Duke of Somerset

BLPES vi. 327–30 ⟨*Horner*, ii. 309–10⟩   The Temple, 16 Dec. 1815

. . .

⟨I hope you have by this time read Dugald Stewart's Preliminary Discourse to the new Supplement, published at Edinburgh, to the *Encyclopedia Britannica*; because it must have afforded you much pleasure, from the magnificent survey which he takes of the history of human knowledge in several of its most important branches, and from the splendid eloquence and choice details with which he has rendered attractive and interesting even the progress of metaphysical doctrines. It seems to me written in a freer spirit of criticism and more copiously ornamented than any of his former compositions; yet the ornaments are not excessive, but give the work a character of majesty and richness quite appropriate to the height of his subject. The work has still another charm for me, borrowed from the times in which it has made its appearance. It is the tendency of all Stewart's writings to impart to his reader a sanguine belief in the real progress which practical knowledge and human improvement are steadily, even when most imperceptibly, making, through all the political troubles and all the philosophical follies which at particular periods seem to throw every thing back into its original disorder and ignorance. In none of his former treatises, had he so direct an opportunity of proving and illustrating this pleasing opinion. And I have been seduced, perhaps by his eloquence, but by what I feel at present like unanswerable arguments, to apply even to the dismal prospects of our own days that confidence in the ultimate prevalence of truth and liberty, which he extracts from the struggles of the Protestant Reformation, and from the whole subsequent history both of opinions and of legislation in Europe. If this should prove an idle hope, at least it ministers some present relief; and if all these promises about the future are visionary, I for one would not forego the luxury of dreaming now and then, and escaping for a while from the realities of the age in which we live.[1]

⟨. . .⟩

1. See Horner to Macvey Napier, 4 Dec., BL Add. MSS 34611, acknowledging receipt of two copies of the dissertation sent to Horner at Stewart's request, one of which Horner posted to Lansdowne, and Horner to Anne Horner, 15 Dec. 1815, and 29 Jan. 1816, *Horner*, ii. 308 and 317–18, for further comment on Stewart's work. Horner procured a third copy for Lord Grenville, and thereafter mediated a modest dispute between Stewart and Grenville arising from Stewart's critical account of the expulsion of John Locke from Oxford University. See Grenville to Horner, 6 and 10 Dec., *ibid.*, ii. 306–307; Grenville to Horner, 14, 15 Dec., Horner to Stewart, 19 Dec., and Stewart to Horner (copy), 23 Dec., BLPES vi. 320–26 and 335–6; and Horner to Grenville, 31 Dec., *Horner*, ii. 310–13. See also *Buckingham*, ii. 132–4, for Grenville's letters to Horner of 6 and 10 Dec., as well as comment on Grenville's later tract, *Oxford and Locke* (1829), in which he sought to vindicate the University.

591. To J.A. Murray

BLPES vii. 3–4   Wells, 8 Jan. 1816

. . .

The distress in this part of England is peculiarly great. I cannot make out that any thing else is at the bottom of it all, but the taxes; which have been eating away so long the capital of the country, and have now brought the expenses of cultivation to such a pitch, that the plentiful produce, resulting from successful exertions in agriculture, is become the very cause of agricultural distress. At such a price as the taxes keep up, we cannot dispose of our surplus produce in any other part of the world; and a very small surplus, therefore, is sufficient to occasion a ruinous depression of the market. A bad year would give temporary relief; but no permanent relief can result but from a diminution of the pressure of taxation on the one hand, or from a permanent reduction of our annual growth on the other. I fear the latter is the most likely of the two to happen. For it would be difficult to effect at once a substantial diminution of taxes; and as those farmers and landowners suffer most at present, who have recently brought poor and high lands into corn, an immediate check will be given to that cultivation.

592. From Lord Holland

BLPES vii. 5–6   [?Holland House], 10 Jan. 1816

Nothing can be clearer, I wish I could add more satisfactory than your letter.[1] It would I think be easy to avoid all discussion on the origin of war and even to smooth matters on the subject of interference or at least on the abstract question of the right of interference – but the dreadful consequences of a general alliance of Princes to guarantee Governments against revolutionary principles, the evident intention of exerting the means of that combination in favour of what they are pleased to term, *legitimate* Governments, i.e a few families reigning (at least in their own opinion) on the exploded principle of divine right and the disgusting breach of all honour and faith in imposing Lewis 18th on France after such frequent and solemn pledges that we meant not to interfere with their choice, further [than] to put a Veto to Bonapartes, are topics impossible to compromise and not easy to suppress, indeed quite impossible for me even to be silent upon if any amendment is moved. One can on the score of policy postpone speaking on such matters but if we move any amendment expressive of our opinions on public affairs the most material part of our opinions cannot and must not be omitted. This is my view of the subject. At the same time I do not like to be the man to take such a step and Grey must come and our friends (you are one) must write to tell him so.

The latter part of Grenville's opinions on the constitution of the country, the effect of Military establishments and the designs of the Court are all sound and I do not much quarrel with the idea of a farther dismemberment of France if that had been practicable, but these questions especially the last are subordinate in importance. It is not our business to find inconsistencies in those opinions of our friends in which we agree but I cannot comprehend how they reconcile the notion of reducing establishments with that of governing Mankind by force.[2]

1. Horner's earlier letter to Holland was passed on to Grey and by him to Lauderdale (Holland to Grey, [Jan.], and Grey to Holland, 14 Jan., Grey MSS, Durham University) and has therefore not been seen, but it was almost certainly written from Woburn or, more probably, Dropmore, where he had been staying for a few days from 3 Jan., en route to the Sessions (to his mother, 1 Jan., BLPES vii. 1–2). It seems to have included an assessment of the political opinions of Grenville, with whom Foxite leaders had had little or no contact since their confrontation in Parliament during the Hundred Days (Mitchell, pp. 87–8).

2. Lansdowne and Bedford, with whom Horner had recently conferred, were also perplexed by Grenville's point of view, which supported the forced restoration of the Bourbon family but opposed the resulting British commitment to a standing army in France. (Lansdowne to Holland, 19 Dec. [1815], BL Add. MSS 51686A; Bedford to Grey, 2 Jan. 1816, Grey MSS, Durham University.)

593. To J.A. Murray

BLPES vii. 7–12 ⟨Horner, ii. 314–17⟩   Great Russell Street,
[London], 18 Jan. 1816

. . .

⟨. . . It requires but a superficial observation of what is passing to be convinced, that, independent of the check which all eager enterprise in the employment of capital must occasionally meet with from its own excess, there was for some time an artificial state of prices and credit in this country, which (even if it could be revived once more for a little while) cannot be much longer maintained, and that our unexampled wars have made an encroachment upon the substantial wealth of the whole body of the people, which could not fail at last to become visible to the dullest eye, and be felt everywhere. The distress, as a national one, will soon, I believe, pass off, except in what regards the finances of the Government; because the real wealth that is accumulated and remains is immense, and is shifted and applied with a promptitude and confidence never known among any other people. But the present crisis must be felt severely by individuals, and, as in the progress of our artificial opulence, there was much derangement of property, and many a sudden as well as unjust transfer, something of the same sort is to be expected while things are falling back towards a more natural state. I believe it to be very fortunate for us, that they have been forced back so soon, and in a manner which to me at least was wholly unlooked for. For, if I am not wrong in my way of seeing it, it is the very prosperity and improvement of the country in its first of all branches, the agricultural, which has wrought the sharp but sure remedy for all the errors of our policy. What I mean is this. The great exertions made in husbandry have at length given us so large an annual produce, that for three successive years (no one of which has been very remarkably fine) we have had some surplus of our own growth. That surplus, in the comparative state of our prices and those abroad, could not be sold to any foreign consumer. The smallest surplus, it is well known, if thrown back upon the market and kept there, may depress it almost indefinitely. The great fall of prices we have experienced brought a very sudden embarrassment upon the farmers and proprietors. This not only alarmed all the reasonable bankers in the provinces, but actually withdrew great part of the foundation upon which both the reasonable and the foolish bankers had so long maintained their large issues of country paper. By far the greatest banker in the west of England[1] told me the other day, that their circulation was not now much more than a fourth of what it had been. The reduction in the quantity of money has been followed by a fall in the nominal price of the precious metals, an improvement of all the exchanges, a fall in the wages of labour, and one after another of various commodities, some being reached much sooner than others. Here then we arrive at a point, at which matters begin to take a favourable turn; the low money price which the grower gets for his corn, being already a better price in reality than the same money price would have been, while money was more abundant. Unfortunately things cannot go quite round, at least not smoothly. The public debt that was contracted while the money was abundant and low priced, and the taxes that must continue to be raised to pay the interest of that debt, will still make our expenses of cultivation so high, that we cannot grow corn for the price of the foreign market; so that it would seem that, as long as the expenses of cultivation are kept up to that rate, we must, in order to secure our farmers a fair price, grow less than we actually can consume ourselves. Tell me, how many blunders there are in this deduction. Of course, I have stated it but roughly. I need not add, that the only practical measure to which I can look, as holding out any promise of easing the present suffering, would be such a reduction of establishments, as would render it practicable for the Government, without violating any of its engagements to the public creditor, to remove a large proportion of the taxes that press most directly and heavily upon the capital employed in cultivation.⟩

. . .

I agree with you about Jeffrey's note. It contained a statement grossly unjust, in the manner in which it has been read and understood by every body, who supposes him to write deliberately. I know he writes such things flippantly, and therefore did not accuse him of any intentional injury to any body. It is too late to have regrets about the *Edinburgh Review*. The note is not what I regretted most in that article.[2]

. . .

1. Not identified.
2. The October number of the *Review* had not appeared until December. In the course of an article on France (*ER* xxv (no. l, Oct. 1815), 501–526), Jeffrey had appended a note (p. 510) about 'the strange partiality [for Napoleon] among some of those who profess to be lovers of liberty in this country'.

594. To Frances Horner

BLPES vii. 13–14 (copy)   London, 19 Jan. 1816

. . .

I believe the Quintana who is sentenced to imprisonment by Ferdinand, is the author of the book you mention, and the Editor of the specimens of Spanish poetry which you have from me.[1] It is a horrible tyranny. But we shall have much more of it in other countries as well as Spain, if the Bourbons make good their possession. Arguelles is in the list of those arbitrarily condemned by Ferdinand, after being acquitted by two different tribunals; I have seen him repeatedly while he was in this Country, a man of great acquisitions in literature, of a lofty and refined spirit, full of patriotism and of ardour for the liberty and improvement of his country, and in the Cortes a very eloquent speaker; his sentence is, to serve as a common soldier in Africa for ten years.[2] I must give you a trait too of France. There is a gentleman just come over, whom we saw at Geneva, and were much pleased with: M. Decandolle, Professor of Botany at Montpelier, very much distinguished as a man of science; though hostile to Bonaparte in his opinions, he had gained some promotion in his College during the time of the last short reign of Napoleon; for which reason simply he has been displaced, and his Chair given to a Royalist who knows nothing.[3]

Decandolle went to Paris, and presented himself to the King; who told him he was the greatest botanist in Europe and was an honour to France, but they had found it necessary to lay down a rule that nobody should retain any office who held it under Napoleon. The stupidity and imprudence of such a rule are delightful. Such incapable drivellers cannot remain much longer where they have been thrust; at least I hope not; for in spite of disappointment, one goes on hoping.

1. Manuel José Quintana (1772–1857), the Spanish lyric poet from whom Lord Holland obtained information and advice in composing his *Life of Lope de Vega* (*Home of the Hollands*, p. 218), had helped stimulate the revolt against the French in 1808, but had nonetheless shared the common fate of liberals by being imprisoned on the restoration of Ferdinand in 1814.

2. Agustin Arguelles (1776–1844), the Spanish orator and constitutional reformer, had been leader of the liberal party in the Cortes in 1812–14.

3. Candolle had succeeded Cuvier at the Collège de France in 1802, afterwards moving to chairs at Montpellier. In 1816 he removed to a chair in his native Geneva, where he remained for the rest of his life. Since his name appears in the Holland House dinner book entry of 4 Feb. 1816, Horner's version was presumably taken at or near first hand. But conventional accounts do not quite confirm that given here. Rather, it is claimed, Candolle was not removed from his chairs but from the position of Rector of the Department, and that, not at the direction of the central government but by the act of the local authorities. Such was his pride and sensitivity, however, that he chose of his accord to leave Montpellier altogether, as he had out of personal pique moved from Paris earlier.

595. To Mrs Dugald Stewart

BLPES vii. 15–16   The Temple, 20 Jan. 1816

. . .

I was angry too at the note you mention, and should have been more disturbed if I did not know how thoughtlessly my friend Jeffrey hazards such things.[1] It is no new misfortune to the Whigs, to be used unjustly by their friends. The injury done by that imputation to some individuals in the judgement of the vulgar, seemed to me a far slighter offence in that review, than the manner in which the interests of European freedom are abandoned in the author's course of reasoning.

This arrest of the three Englishmen at Paris is the great subject of interest here at this moment.[2] It has brought out a good deal of the personal violence which has been gathering for some time. Strong hints are given of discoveries made in Sir Robert Wilson's correspondence, and the letters found in his possession from Lord Grey and Lord Holland; in which I dare say there will be found the expression of very free opinions and a generous indignation.[3] One cannot but condemn Wilson very much for the mode in which he has conducted himself in this enterprise, particularly for his want of discretion in allowing himself and his assistants to be taken; had they all got safe away, I should have envied them their feelings for successfully withdrawing one victim from a faithless tyranny, and after all it is not to be forgotten that while they neglected their own safety they delivered the object of their concern.

I am very grateful to you for confiding to me the report of Paris news, which is interesting, and has so much authority.[4] I wish it would console us for the evils that are present, to be told of conjectures that seem probable with respect to the future course of particular events and individual fortunes. If the Duke d'Orléans is not to be taken immediately, by the will of the French people and with conditions for a popular government imposed upon him, I feel it difficult to care about having the way opened for him in the end by the death of Lewis. The prolongation of Lewis' reign I regard as the chief evil; nor do I see but that the submission of a few years may bend the little that remains of resistance in that country, to an acquiescence in the succession of Monsieur and his sons, odious as they are at this moment.

In consequence of being at Dropmore lately, I have another letter to write to Mr Stewart, for which I hope to have leisure to-morrow (Sunday).[5]

1. See Doc. 593.
2. In Dec. 1815 Sir Robert Wilson, Captain John Hely-Hutchinson, afterwards 3rd Earl of Donoughmore (1787–1851), and the ne'er-do-well son of an English banker, Michael Bruce (1787–1861), successfully conspired to engineer the escape of Lavallette, Napoleon's former aide, who had been sentenced to death by the French Government. Wilson was closely identified with the Foxite leadership; and after personally escorting Lavallette to the frontier, returned to Paris and wrote a detailed account of the conspiracy to Grey, which he foolishly committed to the French postal system. On 13 Jan. Wilson, Hely-Hutchinson, and Bruce were arrested and charged with conspiracy. (Lean, pp. 178–82; see also Doc. 601.)
3. Letters to Wilson from Grey and Holland expressing anti-Bourbon sympathies were indeed among the papers confiscated by French authorities; and the political implications of the affair were compounded by the fact that Holland House had emerged as a sanctuary for disaffected Frenchmen, the most prominent of whom was another of Napoleon's former ADCs, Comte Flahault. Flahault's escape to England had been facilitated by the collaboration of Holland and Talleyrand, and he had appeared openly at dinner in Holland House with Whig leaders on 15 Dec. 1815. At the time of Wilson's arrest Flahault was a regular at Lady Holland's dinner table, and Lauderdale and Holland were attempting to protect him from the provisions of the Alien Act to the chagrin of the British Government. (Lean, pp. 172 and 176–7.) Flahault afterwards married a great Scottish heiress and their daughter married Lansdowne's younger son and successor.
4. Mrs Stewart's letter has not been found.
5. No copy of the letter promised to Stewart has been found.

596. From Lord Grenville

BLPES vii. 17–18   Dropmore, 25 Jan. 1816

Lord Holland's letter conveyed to me the first intimation of any intention of forcing a question upon the prorogation to a division in the House of Commons on the first day.[1] I cannot satisfy myself of the propriety of such a course. It is I believe generally held that divisions on amendment to the Address are seldom advantageous to those who press them, though they are sometimes unavoidable. And in this instance Ponsonby's absence,[2] and the known contrarieties of opinion respecting the War and its consequences seemed to me to afford strong additional objections to that mode of proceeding.

Then as to the question itself, consider how it stands. The House knows nothing on the first day but the fact that they have been more than once prorogued since the signature of the treaty of Peace. Were this all, it would be improper, no doubt, and a fit subject of animadversion. But what gives to this fact a constitutional importance almost unexampled, is that the Treaty stipulates for the maintenance of a standing Army in Peace, and in foreign pay, and that the Crown has openly assumed the Prerogative not of contracting only, but of executing this engagement without the sanction of Parliament.

It is not the Prorogation that is illegal or unconstitutional, but the unauthorized execution of the Treaty. On the first day neither the stipulations of the treaty nor, still less, the fact of their execution can be before the House. You might certainly advert to the thing as notorious, and in this shape you might have a desultory debate *about it*; but a decision *upon it* you could not have, not even if the House unanimously agreed with you in principle.

To whom then, in a case of such real and paramount importance, will this mode of incidental and mixed discussion be favourable? Surely to those who have the worst side of the cause to defend: Who wish to weaken its impression and divert attention from it. Their desire must be to blend it inseparably in the public mind, with the general and temporary politics of the day; with measures which have been singularly successful and are therefore almost universally popular.

In this endeavour I have no doubt that by such a form of discussion they must succeed. A debate on an amendment to the Address cannot by any possibility be confined to the simple and abstract point of law and constitution. It must extend to the policy or necessity of the stipulation itself, and from thence not improbably to the justice and expediency of the object for which the stipulation purports to provide. And in either case, I need not tell you what differences of opinion will be found, and what difficulties they may create as to any concurrence in a vote concluding such a debate.

1. The letter to which Grenville refers has not been found. It would seem, however, that Holland had informed Grenville that a group of Opposition MPs, meeting in London in mid-January, had agreed unanimously that the usual letter should be written to solicit a full attendance for an amendment to the Regent's Address on the first day of the session, its precise wording being left open (Mitchell, pp. 88–9).
2. Ponsonby had been detained in Ireland by family business (*ibid.*, p. 89).

597. To the Duchess of Somerset

BLPES vii. 19–20 〈Horner, ii. 319–20〉   [London], 29 Jan. 1816

〈From all I can hear, there is no chance of a division in the House of Lords on the first day.[1] The first important debate there will probably be upon the Treaties, after they have been laid by the Crown before Parliament; and it can hardly take much less than a fortnight to read and consider them. Lord Grenville will bring forward, I expect, a specific question upon the violation of the constitution, of which he thinks the Ministers have been guilty, in not asking the sanction of Parliament to their treaty of peace before they proceeded in execution of it, particularly with so new a stipulation contained in it, as the maintenance of an English army in France during peace. But he will of course give ample notice of this motion, which is no doubt one of high importance.

⟨I fear we are not likely to go on long very harmoniously in opposition; there are such wide and irreconcilable differences of opinion between those who, on the one hand, will hear of nothing but a return to all that was undone by the French revolution, and who in the present moment of success declare views of that sort which they never avowed to the same extent before, and those who, on the other hand, think that the French people have some right to make and mend their government for themselves, and who are not prepared to adopt, under a new and not a much better name, the old exploded doctrines of divine right, kingcraft, and passive obedience. If this was only a speculative interest felt by us in the affairs of France as spectators, we might differ in sentiment and go on together with respect to the concerns of our own country, with which those of France ought not to be so much mixed; but this treaty for putting down by force of arms whatever the kings combined may think, or choose to call, revolutionary movements, is such a conspiracy against the rights and liberties of mankind as it is impossible to refrain from condemning and resisting. You may expect very soon to see a breach in the Opposition; I think it cannot be averted much longer. It is this circumstance which makes Lord Grey's absence[2] at this moment so peculiarly unfortunate for those who, as I do, agree with him in the way of seeing all these things, and look up to him as their head. . . .⟩

1. This suggests that Holland, almost surely informed of the sentiments expressed in Grenville's letter to Horner of 25 Jan. (Doc. 596), was wavering as early as the 29th. Two days later he told Morpeth (Carlisle MSS) that he had decided to remain silent in the Lords 'partly for peace sake and partly for personal convenience'.
2. He was ill.

598. To John Horner

BLPES vii. 23-8   The Temple, 7 Feb. 1816[1]

. . .

You ask my opinion about the distress of the country, and what is likely to be done by Parliament. There is a very general distress among the whole body of the actual farmers, which extends of course, but not so universally, to their landlords: It consists, I believe, solely in this; that the prices of grain have been so much reduced, that in the last year the sale of the produce of corn lands has hardly been sufficient to do more than replace to the farmer the expenses of cultivation and the taxes, leaving him little or nothing out of the yearly produce for rent to the landlord. This has been almost literally and universally the situation of *arable* farms throughout England. Where the farmers were opulent, and had either large stocks or money saved, they have paid their rents out of that fund: and I know many great proprietors, who have received their rents without defalcation. Where the farmers were not provided with such resources, either from their poverty (as in the unimproved parts of Devonshire and the other old counties), or from their capital being all in advance for speculative improvements (as in those tracts of light poor soil where experimental farming has been pushed farthest), they have failed altogether, or nearly so, in their rents. The immediate distress of landlords, who are in this last predicament, is extreme; and it has been aggravated for the time by the difficulties which they find in borrowing money upon mortgage: the vast loans of Government in the last two years having absorbed so much of the loose capital of the country, that there was not enough left to satisfy all the demands for private loans upon mortgage or heritable security; this of course would have raised the market rate of interest, but then the usury laws stood in the way; accordingly, the country gentlemen have been driven last year to the ruinous expedient of borrowing in the way of annuities, and, from transactions of which I have seen something, they have not effected these loans even with the most respectable insurance corporations at a less cost than ten per cent. But though the temporary distress of those landlords, whose rents have fallen off, is the most severe, my opinion is that a much deeper and more lasting injury has been inflicted upon the wealth of the nation, by the payments which the other class of tenants have exerted themselves to make; there must have been a very wide destruction of farming capital, to effect these payments, and a permanent loss therefore of the means of future reproduction. Such, as far as I have hitherto been enabled to understand it, from very limited and imperfect inquiries, is the nature and description of the agricultural distress as it exists.

The *cause* of it, is another matter; and an inquiry attended, of course, with a good deal of uncertainty. I have formed a theory about it, but in which I do not feel very confident, till I have farther opportunities of information. If it should turn out to be well founded, it will carry with it this comfort, that the present suffering is only of a temporary nature. It is upon the first show of matters rather singular, that our distress appears to be connected with abundant harvests; and whereas the dearness of provisions and labour seemed to be the very evil, that upon the return of peace we had most to dread in our commercial competition with the rest of the world, one is apt to suspect there must be something factitious and temporary, in an obstruction to industry, and to the growth of capital, which results from plenty and cheapness. I explain it, or rather attempt to explain it, in this way. For a course of years, our prices of grain have been forced up very high, partly by the various taxes which make the minimum price at which our grower can bring it to market a much higher price than prevails in any of the foreign corn markets, and partly by that excess of paper currency which raised our money price of grain greatly above even that minimum rate which is fixed by the taxes and other necessary expenses of cultivation. Such was the state of prices, when we began at last to reap the fruits of the great exertions that have been made in the application of capital and skill to husbandry, in an augmented yearly produce; which became more manifest to us in consequence of the exportation of an artificial branch of the home demand for corn, which our wars in Spain and other distant parts of the world had forced. Here then was a state of things, new, and sure to be attended with inconvenience; the combination of a price rendered necessarily higher than those of any foreign markets, with a surplus produce. The surplus was not to be disposed of; finding no vent abroad, its certain effect upon the home market was to work a depression of money-prices, down to the very minimum fixed by the taxes and expenses of cultivation. Had that minimum been nearly upon a level with the prices abroad, we should have come to our relief, when the price was lowered to that. But, our misfortune is, that that minimum is above the foreign prices; so that, although the price is depressed as low as it can be brought, we have still the surplus of our produce hanging upon our own market, and, by a permanent excess of supply above the effective demand, depriving the sellers of such a price as will replace their advances. In such a state of things, there is no alternative, but a diminution of produce on the one hand by throwing lands out of cultivation, or a reduction of taxes on the other hand which would diminish the expenses of cultivation. The former is already begun; whether Parliament, or rather I ought to say the country, for it has in these matters the control of Parliament, will make any material sacrifices of establishments and of the ambitions and visions of foreign politics, for the purpose of lowering taxes, will very soon be made manifest.

What has lately happened, with regard to the paper circulation of the country, appears to me very curiously and importantly connected with the agricultural question. There has been an immense reduction in that very important branch of the present currency, the country bank paper; from inquiries I have made among some great bankers of the West of England, and also at the Stamp Office, I am inclined to think that the country paper is considerably less than a third of what it was, and it is daily lessening. The Bank of England circulation is probably much the same as last year, perhaps a little greater. The contraction of the country circulation I conceive to have been, both in the first instance, and also in the progress of the thing, caused by that fall in the price of agricultural produce, the cause of which I have already attempted to assign. The paper of the country banks was issued chiefly upon the confidence of rising prices, which had the effect of permanently maintaining, or rather of continually improving, the value of all that farming stock and produce to which they looked as a security for their loans to the farmers. A fall in the value of the produce, followed of course by a fall in the value of all farming stock, presented to every prudent banker just an opposite prospect. What he was prompted to do by prudence and foresight, was soon forced upon him by necessity; for the diminution of the farmer's means led to a demand of all those deposits, which the more thriving farmers had been enabled in better times to place in their banker's hands. The loss of the loans which they used to get from the country bankers is very much complained of, accordingly, by the suffering farmers, and has no doubt aggravated their embarrassment: and many farmers, and many gentlemen, are simple enough to have declared it to be their opinion, that Parliament or Government 'ought to encourage a liberal system of bank discounting': the very same persons who called it a sort of sedition some years ago, and who very likely will call it so again, if any body asserts that a liberal issue of bank notes had the effect of raising prices at all. In the mean while, so little are they aware of what is for their good, it is certain that the improvement which has already taken place in the real efficient value of money, in consequence of part of the excess of country paper being withdrawn, tends in some small degree, and will gradually tend more, to lighten the pressure of their misfortunes. The sixty shillings they get now is worth more than the sixty shillings they had two years ago; it will already purchase more labour and more meat; and their other necessaries and conveniences of life will more slowly, but surely, one after another, accommodate themselves to the price of the first necessity and to the value of money. You ask me about the Irish exchange. I take that to be a satisfactory proof of the improved value of our currency. Their Banks have never been so prudent and skilful as ours. They had got into excess before us, and first gave the proofs of it by the enormous fall of their exchange with this island. The first symptom of our excess was an apparent improvement of that exchange on the side of Ireland; and for the same reason, one of the first symptoms of an improvement in the value of our money is the re-appearance of the former exchange against Ireland.

. . .

I have taken the liberty to make use of your name and Leonard's, in a subscription which we are going to try for the poor Spanish patriots, who have been exiled or otherwise persecuted by their restored King. . . .

> 1. The letter is headed and endorsed 7 Feb. by Horner himself but postmarked 6 Feb. and therefore written before dining the following day at Holland House in the company of Lansdowne, Abercromby, Mackintosh, and the Grenvillite, Ebrington (HHDB).

599. Speech by Horner[1]

⟨Horner, 11. 540–53⟩   House of Commons, 20 Feb. 1816

⟨. . . It had, since the Battle of Waterloo, been admitted, even by the confession of an enemy, that the infantry of England had no equal. He did look on this as a great acquisition of glory, a great acquisition of strength; and his prayer was, that the military strength thus acquired might be properly made use of. The proper use of that strength was, first, to reserve it for the defence of our country; and, next, in foreign interposition, when that interposition should be clearly and absolutely necessary to our welfare; but we were to remember that it would be employed unnecessarily in continental quarrels, or in projects of unjustifiable ambition. It was obvious that they had mixed up the whole of their transactions with French politics; and though it was impossible for the House not to entertain some feelings on that subject, yet they ought to interfere with it as little as possible. By an unnecessary interposition, they would be unavoidably led to involve themselves in the factions and views of their neighbours, and be drawn out of the circle of their own affairs, which were quite enough for them without considering whether this or that form of government was most beneficial to the people.

⟨His main objections, however, to the treaties were, that they did not provide that security which the country had a right to expect; and it demanded the most serious consideration, that in prosecuting the war to an end, his Majesty's Ministers had at last disclosed that important project which they had so anxiously disavowed at first; namely, the determination of forcing the Bourbon family on the throne of

France, contrary to the faith of the Crown, contrary to the pledge which had been given to Parliament, and in direct violation of the solemn engagement and promise to the nation of France at large. On former occasions the noble lord [Castlereagh] had expressly avowed, that the professed object of the war was of a very different nature. The idea of forcing any particular person on the French had been repeatedly disclaimed, on the principle that it was carrying their measures further than the justice of the cause allowed: but now, forsooth, it was openly, and without a blush, acknowledged, that however the national honour had been violated, it had always been considered that such a result of the contest would be satisfactory. It was now too late, indeed, to say, that they had not resolved to interfere with the internal government of France; but they excused themselves by saying, that they might interpose on a necessary occasion.[2]

⟨It must, indeed, be within the recollection of the House, that when it was put to the noble lord, whether the restoration of the Bourbons was the object of the war, he distinctly and repeatedly disclaimed it. It was notorious, that upon this understanding, several gentlemen in that House voted for the war. Why, then, was not this object openly and manfully avowed at the outset? With what view was it disguised? Why, obviously for the purpose of obtaining votes in that House, and practising delusion upon England, upon France, and upon Europe.

⟨The effect of this delusion and duplicity upon France was, as he understood from the best authority,[3] to dispose the well-informed and the reflecting part of France, who belonged to no faction – who were as hostile to Bonaparte as they were indifferent to the Bourbons – to look to the allied armies as deliverers, as about to afford the French nation an opportunity of choosing a government agreeable to its own wishes and interests. The effect was indeed such as to neutralize a great and respectable portion of the French, who, instead of supporting Bonaparte, rather endeavoured to keep down the spirit of the people, and induce them to confide in the declarations of the allies. Many Frenchmen believed those declarations, confirmed as they so often were by the solemn pledges of the Ministers of England. But the believers were dupes. For himself as well as for several of his friends, he could state that he never was duped by these declarations, or by the pledges of the noble lord, because he always thought that to be the sole object of the war, which events had demonstrated. But he would ask some gentlemen in that House who thought differently, who grounded their votes upon an entire credit in the professions of the noble lord, how they now felt? He would appeal to the whole House, to Parliament, and the country, what ought to be the feeling of a proud and honest nation, tenacious of its character for good faith, upon comparing the pledges of its Government at the commencement of the war, with the conduct of that Government at its conclusion. Was there to be no faith, then, in these solemn promises? Could it be a satisfactory feeling to any honest Member, who possessed the generous spirit of an Englishman, to know that the engagements of Ministers with the French nation had not been kept? His Majesty's Government had declared manfully, boldly, and plainly, what their purposes were; but it was one of the most melancholy features of the times that the bonds of political faith were not so strong as they used to be.

⟨Whatever doubt might exist in some minds as to the import of the declaration on which the war was commenced, there could be no possible misunderstanding as to the object of the treaties. It was no longer to get rid of the dangerous ambition of Bonaparte; it was not to prevent the military power of France from encroaching on neighbouring states. No! it was to maintain the family of the Bourbons on the throne, whatever might be the feelings of the people towards them. If it were pretended, as he understood it had been somewhere said, that the conduct of the French army in invading the Netherlands released the Allies from their pledges not to force a government upon France, he would ask the noble lord and his colleagues, whether they, who always alleged that the French people were hostile to Bonaparte, and that he was supported only by the army, could consistently maintain that the conduct of that army could release the Allies from their solemn pledges to the people, not to force any particular government upon them? But yet this Government was imposed upon France, and it appeared that with a view to maintain it, certain precautionary measures, as the noble lord termed them, were adopted.

‹Among those measures a large pecuniary contribution was levied, and this contribution the noble lord called, rather singularly, a main feature of the tranquillizing policy to be acted upon towards France. This was really a most extraordinary view, perhaps peculiar to the mind of the noble lord; for it was the first time he had heard, that to subject any people to a large pecuniary contribution was a good mode of producing their tranquillity. Certainly the noble lord could not have learned that doctrine in England, where a large pecuniary contribution was not very apt to produce popular tranquillity. Indeed, he rather apprehended that a rather opposite feeling would rise in this country, if that contribution were enforced by a foreign army. Why, then, should the noble lord calculate upon a different result in France? But upon this point it seemed that according to the doctrine of some gentlemen, the contribution raised in France, instead of falling into the pockets of the people, and being placed under the control of Parliament, was to become the property of the privy purse, to be applied, perhaps, to enable the Pope to carry home some works of art from Paris, or to erect a statue to Henry IX (Cardinal York). He wished, however, that this novel doctrine might now be repelled, as inconsistent with the constitution and laws of this country.

‹But as a further precautionary measure to keep the Bourbons upon the throne, it appeared that 150,000 men, composed of different nations, were placed in France. So it was calculated that the presence of this foreign force, under the command of a general, who was a native of a country always the rival of France, was likely by degrees to reconcile the French people to the Government which that force had imposed upon them. But what could be the character of the minds which entertained such a calculation? Would not every rational being rather conclude that the presence of such a force must serve to form a perpetual fester in the breast of France, instead of contributing to the tranquillity of that country? But, according to the express opinion of some gentlemen, that which was most galling and offensive to the French formed an argument to justify the expectation of order and repose. Those only, however, who entertained such a singular notion could, he believed, concur in the views of the Allies in placing an armed force in France. And what estimate must those gentlemen have formed of the character of the French people – distinguished as that people always were for national pride and military spirit? How, he would ask, was that proceeding likely to operate upon them, which was calculated to rouse the most sluggish nation upon earth? How were the French people to feel towards a sovereign twice forced upon them by an army of foreign bayonets? For when that army was on the first instance withdrawn, that sovereign was soon compelled to quit the country; and he would put it to the candour of any man, if the French people were friendly to that sovereign, why should it be necessary to maintain him on the throne by the assistance of a foreign army? The dilemma was obvious; – either the French were friendly to the King, or they were not. If the former, the foreign army was unnecessary to the maintenance of the King; but if unfriendly, the presence of this army was calculated to augment their dislike. For what could be more galling to a Frenchman, than to suppose the King guilty of that which was the greatest treason any sovereign could commit, namely, that of inviting the assistance of a foreign force?

‹While the French were our active enemies in war, we must rejoice in their defeat; but now that they were completely fallen, must not every considerate man feel for a people so circumstanced? Was there, besides, no danger to be apprehended from the result of a national movement against the army by which the French were so grievously oppressed? The great power of the Allies would no doubt defeat such a movement; and could any man doubt that the effect of such defeat would be the dismemberment and partition of France? What, then, would be the consequences? It would, perhaps be said that no danger whatever was to be apprehended from the ambition of any of the Allies – that none of them were capable of meditating any wrong. But the noble lord had written much against the plans of aggrandizement entertained by Prussia. . . .[4] If [France] should be dismembered – if it should cease to be a substantial power in Europe, by the division of its territory among the despots of the North, what then would be the state of this country? In such an event what must be the amount of our establishments, both naval and military, in order to guard against the dangers naturally to be apprehended from the occupation of France by those formidable powers?

‹Now, as to another point. It was stated by the noble lord, that he was pressed by several reflecting persons in France to secure the guarantee of the Allies to the maintenance of the constitutional charter. But this the noble lord refused to accede, while an unreserved guarantee was granted to maintain the King upon the throne. No stipulation was made to support the constitution, which, by the bye, had since been repeatedly violated. While every arrangement was made that appeared to the Allies necessary to provide for the maintenance of the King, nothing was done to preserve the privileges of the people. The Allies, in their eagerness to support the former, overlooked the conciliation of the latter, although that conciliation would have been the best policy. But such policy was not within the consideration of despots.

‹Here he felt it necessary to make a few remarks upon the assertion of the noble lord, that the whigs of the present day forgot or departed from the doctrines of those whom the noble lord called their progenitors. But this assertion was grossly erroneous, as would appear upon a review of the address moved by Mr Fox in 1793. For in this address that great man did not propose to protest against our interference in the affairs of any foreign state as a general principle, but against such interference under existing circumstances.⁵ The effort, therefore, to fix any imputation upon those whom the noble lord denominated the modern whigs, was totally ineffectual. The noble lord's cry of victory was quite groundless – was indeed clumsy.

‹But it was strange that the noble lord should quote precedents from those whom he never before affected to admire. It happened, however, that in all the noble lord's reference to the conduct of the whigs, he betrayed a total want of historical accuracy. This want of accuracy was indeed particularly evident in the noble lord's reference to the quadruple and triple alliances, for neither furnished any precedent in favour of the noble lord's cause. On the contrary, it was notorious that, in the former, the whigs obtained a guarantee from the Allies, that they should not interfere with the right of this country to choose its own government, which choice was made decidedly against the doctrine of legitimacy and the divine right of kings; for this country on that occasion dismissed King James with his hereditary rights, and selected William, with a view to establish a government congenial to the constitution and assent of the people. Then, again, as to the triple alliance, the object of that confederacy formed by the whigs, was to withstand the principle of legitimacy by preventing the House of Bourbon from becoming possessed of the throne of Spain. How, then, could either of those alliances be said to furnish any precedent in favour of the conduct of the noble lord and the Allies, in forcing a government upon France according to the doctrine of legitimacy?

‹But there was a precedent on the occasion of the triple alliance, which the noble lord might have quoted in support of his views: for Louis XIV at that time sought to force a government upon Spain, according to the principle of legitimacy; and the noble lord, in overlooking this circumstance, showed that he was quite as ill versed in tory as he was in whig precedents. The noble lord should, therefore, before he ventured to quote again, study history with more attention.

But, with respect to the principle of legitimacy, he fully concurred in what the House had heard so eloquently urged by an honourable Member (Mr Law) upon that subject, namely, that hereditary right was not essential to the maintenance of monarchy. It was, in fact, but subsidiary to that object, as our own history demonstrated. For the maintenance of this principle was subordinate to the preservation of the constitution and laws of any country, and meant not that the direct lineal descendant should be preferred, but that some such member of the family of the monarch should be selected, as might be best disposed and best calculated to maintain the laws and liberties of the country. This was the true sound doctrine sanctioned by the wise example of England. But the sole object of the late war and of the treaties which followed it manifestly was, to place a monarch upon the throne of France, without any regard to the laws, the liberties, or the wishes of the people. . . .

‹The noble lord, no doubt, also wished to put down all the principles of the revolution, which he might conceive a very desirable end, and it was consistent with his views that every thing that could be accomplished should be done for sovereigns, and nothing for the people. That such was the intention was pretty evident from what had taken place within the last two years. A great statesman had often observed, that of all revolutions a restoration was the greatest, and that of all innovators an arbitrary monarch was the most dangerous. This, indeed, was fully evinced in what had taken place in Wurtemberg, in Prussia, and in certain states upon the Rhine, where nothing whatever of right was restored to the people, while the authority of sovereigns, whether crowned since or before the Revolution, was established and confirmed. The total disregard, indeed, of popular rights was manifested in various parts of the recent arrangements; but it was sufficient to refer to the instances of Venice and Genoa.

‹But the most odious part of the late arrangements, which appeared from a treaty on the table, was the league of arbitrary sovereigns to meet annually for the purpose of considering their interests; for what rational man could doubt what such sovereigns would, in the long run, consider their interests, how they would decide upon every indication of popular feeling, or upon any movement in favour of popular principles? The noble lord even, who was the advocate of every act of those sovereigns – who was ready to take up the gauntlet in that House for every one of them, could not be much at a loss to decide upon their probable views, if he would only take the trouble of looking with but common attention to history.

‹Let him look, for instance, to the conduct of Austria towards Hungary and the Low Countries; let him look at the conduct of three of those sovereigns with respect to Poland. Hence it might be concluded how these sovereigns were likely to decide for their own interests, and against the privileges of the people. But it appeared, from the noble lord's own statement, how these sovereigns felt with regard to popular privileges, from the jealousy which they expressed respecting the freedom of debate in that house. He should like to know whether these sovereigns expressed that jealousy in the noble lord's presence, and whether they obtained his acquiescence. It would, indeed, be surprising if the noble lord, who had himself acquired so much distinction as a parliamentary orator, especially in favour of popular privileges, and who was said to have made such long speeches to these sovereigns themselves, no doubt in the same strain, could silently listen to such an expression of jealousy with regard to the freedom of the British Parliament. Yet the noble lord had observed, that these arbitrary monarchs were truly indisposed to follow up some arrangements which they had in contemplation for the establishment of popular privileges, in consequence of some speeches in that House.

‹What a compliment did the noble lord thus record in favour of the virtue and firmness of these sovereigns. So, they were dissuaded from doing that which they themselves thought proper, in consequence of parliamentary speeches in England! They declined to do right, because some of them might have been censured for doing wrong – because, for instance, such an able senator as the late Mr Whitbread – because that great man, who had, perhaps, more of the good man in his composition than any great man who ever existed, felt it his duty to expose and reprobate some act of oppression or injustice. He trusted, however, that such a feeling of duty would ever be found to prevail in that House.

‹But, seriously, could it be believed that the sovereigns alluded to could have been prevented from making arrangements in favour of popular liberty, by any thing that happened to fall from an obscure minority in that House, seconded as their dispositions must have been by the noble lord himself at the head of his immense majorities? The opinions of these military despots, on this, as well as upon other subjects, he entirely disregarded. No prospect could be entertained that any thing would be done by them for the rights of mankind. His hopes of improvement were derived from a different quarter. They were not directed to innovation, but to a beneficial change effected through the medium of constitutional organs, and the wholesome operation of public opinion.

‹Even though there was reason to believe that the sovereigns appointed their meetings with no pre-concerted designs against the liberties of the world – even although they formed no deliberate conspiracy against the rights of their subjects, still he could not but view the close association, that would appear to be established between such great military powers, without great jealousy. The great object of our late struggle was avowed to be the destruction of the military principle in Europe, which was incompatible with the liberties, the happiness, and the social tranquillity of mankind. By unparalleled efforts, by persevering and heroic sacrifices, we had extinguished the great military despotism, which agitated and conquered and oppressed the nations of the Continent; but was the situation of Europe much improved, if the present system was to be carried into complete effect, and the late arrangements were henceforward to be universally adhered to? We had, indeed, annihilated the most extensive, the universally felt despotism, but there were now three or four to spring up and to occupy its place. Their union, for purposes connected with their own support and extension, might be nearly as dangerous as the one from which we congratulated ourselves on being delivered.

‹These military sovereigns were to meet and consult for their common security or mutual interests. . . .[6] He wished to meet the question of security fairly and impartially; but he could not help inquiring at first, what were the evils against which security and guarantee were required? What were we to guard against?

‹We were at the end of five and twenty years of convulsion, revolution, and war. In that period the institutions of society, the political arrangements, and the relative condition of the different orders in the civil state, had undergone great changes. A new spirit was created, and had operated powerfully in bringing about the present circumstances. There might be different views entertained, and there were certainly very different opinions delivered on our present situation. Some thought that the revolutionary spirit, which produced such atrocities in its first display and subsequent operations, still existed in France in all its malignity, and that its existence, in any degree, was inconsistent with national tranquillity or civil order. This opinion had been declared by many Members in the House, and was entertained by a great party out of it; but he thought that it was entertained upon false and narrow views. There were other persons who took views entirely opposite, but equally distant from reason and sound policy. They would not be satisfied, if France did not at once carry into practice all those ideas of political freedom that they entertained: they would not be contented with less than seeing France in possession of all those institutions, and that free constitution, that this country enjoyed, without taking into consideration the difference that existed between the state and the ideas of the two nations.

‹It was needless to say that he disapproved of both these extremes. Whether the Revolution in France was good or bad, whether it had contributed to promote the liberties and rights of the nation or not, it could not be denied that there had arisen out of it a state of things which could not be altered, a spirit which could not be entirely extinguished. If the restoration of the Bourbons proceeded upon the supposition that every thing was to be restored to its former condition, and that every new interest was to be destroyed, the project could not be realized; and those who entertained it were not aware of the obstacles they would have to encounter in attempting its execution.

⟨Every thing was changed in the Revolution – property had been transferred to new hands – the people had acquired new ideas – the privileged orders had been abolished, or their claims reduced – political institutions were altered, and a new distribution of political power had established a spirit of inquiry, and a disposition to discuss the conduct of rulers was every where diffused. It was difficult to calculate the power of these changes. We might guard against the effects of them, but we could not bring things back to their former situation. Happily this was not necessary for our security, as it certainly was not practicable in its execution.

⟨The real security which was required from France, after the destruction of that military monarchy which oppressed the greater part of the continent of Europe, combined the integrity of that kingdom with the establishment of a government agreeably to the wishes, and deserving of the confidence of the people. ...⟩[7]

⟨The French Revolution had exhibited many scenes of cruelty, atrocity, and horror, and its principles had been often dishonoured by the profligacy of those who held them, or professed to carry them into execution; but it arose at first from a love of liberty, and had been attended by consequences of the most important kind. Any man who had examined the state of France before the Revolution, and after it, would perceive the good effects that it had produced. The great body of the people, whose interests were the most important, were raised by it in education, in character, in property, and in independence. No revolution since the Protestant Reformation appeared so important as that of France. The people of France might, therefore, expect that some attention would be paid to their wishes, and that all the advantages for which they had suffered would not be extorted from them. They might expect that they should be allowed a free constitution, and would it be honourable in us to obstruct them in that object? The first men in this country had anticipated great good from the Revolution. ...⟩

1. Delivered in the course of the debate on Lord Milton's resolutions of 19 Feb. countering those, proposed on the same day by Castlereagh, expressing satisfaction with the treaties of peace.
2. Here Horner surprisingly broached an issue on which Grenville remained extremely sensitive (Grenville to Grey, 10 Feb., Grey MSS, Durham University), but one that, *faute de mieux*, was pivotal in any reasoned attack on British foreign policy.
3. Perhaps from Benjamin Constant, who was in London and had dined at Holland House on 11 Feb. (HHDB).
4. Here Horner briefly digressed, citing examples of Castlereagh's earlier efforts to counter the territorial designs of the Allies and recalling his 'rage' whenever Opposition had remarked negatively about them.
5. It is not insignificant that Horner referred to Fox's address and five resolutions of 18 Feb. 1793. For those resolutions, which had been a frame of reference among Fox's followers for twenty-three years, essentially constituted the blueprint for Horner's speech. Traditionally a strong 'northern man' in foreign politics, Fox had indeed grounded his opposition to the British declaration of war against France on the peculiarities of existing circumstances. His

resolutions (*Charles James Fox: Speeches During the French Revolutionary War Period*, ed. Irene Cooper Willis, n.d., p. 92.) had opposed as unjust a war seeking to suppress or punish principles and opinions or to establish a particular type of government in France; declared that the complaints lodged against the French Government were no just cause for war; reprobated the failure of Pitt's Ministry to state 'distinctly to the French Government any terms or conditions, the accession to which, on the part of France, would induce his Majesty to persevere in a system of neutrality'; criticized the Ministry for lodging no complaint and for making common cause with continental allies who recently had engaged in illegal and unjustifiable acts of aggrandizement against Poland; and declared it to be the duty of Ministers in the present crisis

> to advise his Majesty against entering into engagements which may prevent Great Britain from making a separate peace whenever the interests of his Majesty and his people may render such a measure advisable, or which may countenance an opinion in Europe that his Majesty is acting in concert with other powers for the unjustifiable purpose of compelling the people of France to submit to a form of government not approved by that nation.

6. Horner then examined the specific securities established in the treaties.
7. Horner then summarized his principal arguments against forcing the Bourbons on France and maintaining them by foreign arms, contested Elliot's contention that the Chamber of Deputies was a dangerous republican institution, and briefly disparaged Fouché and his influence in the selection of deputies.

600. To J.A. Murray

BLPES vii. 31–4 ⟨*Horner*, ii. 342–3⟩   The Temple, 27 Feb. [1816]

⟨My circuit begins on the 5th of March, but my engagements in the House of Lords will not permit me to join it early, perhaps not before the 18th. I shall be back from it by Friday the 5th of April, and from that time I shall remain in London.⟩ . . .

. . .

⟨It is no common degree of gratification to hear from you, that you coincide with me in the opinions which I have been lately expressing in Parliament, if you include in that approbation my sentiments upon the Treaty of Peace. For I was afraid that there perhaps you might think me too unfavourable to the principles and views upon which the precautionary measures of the allies are founded. My disapprobation of what has been done, and my apprehensions concerning its future consequences, are no doubt derived out of opinions which I have long held fast; yet I cannot accuse myself of having failed, upon the present occasion, to review and reconsider them with some coolness and anxiety. There are changes in the whole frame of European politics, and in our domestic scheme of liberties, which are going on much faster than politics ever before seemed to me to move. It is a movement, perhaps, which has resulted from causes that were put in action long ago, though their force has been compressed for an interval by counteracting circumstances, which have been suddenly removed. In the most formidable periods of the French military power, my dread never was of its prevailing against us in this island by conquest, but of the inroads that our system of defence was making upon the constitutional forms of our parliamentary government, and upon the constitutional habits of the English commons.

⟨We are nearly declared to be a military power. If this design is not checked, of which I have slender hopes, or does not break down by favour of accidents, we shall have a transient glory for some little while; the bravery of our men, the virtues which the long enjoyment of liberty will leave long after it is gone, and the financial exertions of which we are still capable, will insure us that distinction; but it is a glory in which our freedom will be lost, and which cannot maintain itself when the vigour, born of that freedom, is spent. Do not tell any body of these gloomy visions of mine; they will appear absurd and insincere; above all, do not tell them to Jeffrey, or I shall see myself niched in some sentence against moping Whigs who love Bonaparte. I have in my heart infinitely more apprehension, about the future fate of English liberty, than I ever permit myself to express in public; one chance of preserving it, is to keep up the tone of the public sentiment, particularly in Parliament, to the consciousness and confidence of still being free. ...⟩

601. To Lady Holland

BLPES vii. 37–8   [Dorchester], Friday night, [15 Mar. 1816]

... It is very teasing to be taken away from the midst of things, without any better reason for it than the chance of what may be gained about the close of life by adhering to the routine of the profession. But upon the whole I believe I am right in doing it. My absence however will not injure the vote on Monday; for I believe young Bankes would have been induced to go up for that propose, but I have settled with him a pair for the rest of the circuit.[1]

...

I suppose all this activity in the House about economy will prove of use. We have no actual savings by it yet, nothing tangible; and I dread every day, from the time it has taken, we are to see a re-action for the Court. I confess to you, it is a part of politics for which I have a great distaste; these discussions, I mean, of individual jobs and salaries, which are never managed in such a way as to effect any real retrenchment for the public, and always lower the character of Parliament with the people. I am not sure that the thing could be done in another manner, and it is very right that it should be done, but for my own gratification and comfort I would rather be away while it is doing. This is only for yourself.

I begin to wonder that no hint is given in Parliament of the state of the Regent's health; for it can hardly be doubted any longer, that he is in a very dangerous way; and this precarious state with his absence from London must be excessively inconvenient to the Government.

From nothing being said in either House about Sir Robert Wilson's case, I have been flattering myself that Ministers have consented to interpose in his behalf to some extent; notwithstanding the denial of this in the *Courier*. Yet I am sorry to say, I have not observed any correct feeling upon this subject since I left town. Wilson's folly prevents people from seeing the generosity of the exploit, or the horrible violence of the French Government in their fever of change.[2]

1. He wrote in a similar vein to his mother two days later (BLPES vii. 39–40), about having 'to drudge on at the circuit' and also about having missed a vote a couple of weeks earlier on account of a cold. This latter was a division on the army estimates on 6 Mar., after having been present earlier in the day (*Hansard*, xxxiii. 1209). Rather more important was his absence for the vote on the property tax on Monday, 18 Mar., when Brougham scored a triumph against the Government. He had, as he says, secured a pair with George Bankes (1787–1856: *DNB*), Henry Bankes's son and a fellow barrister on the Western Circuit, who had been unexpectedly returned for Corfe Castle only the previous month. But evidently Horner was in any case really rather relieved to be away from it all.

2. According to Ian Bruce, *Lavallette Bruce: His Adventures and Intrigues before and after Waterloo* (1953), pp. 210–12, Grenville and Grey went together to see Liverpool on 8 Mar. and secured his undertaking to intervene officially. But while the British Government made it clear to the French that they wanted no executions, they were quite prepared for imprisonment and in any case were anxious not to encourage by public support any embarrassing antics in court by Wilson in particular. The three defendants were convicted on 24 Apr. and received the lightest possible sentences, three months' imprisonment, while Kinnaird, whose earlier unsuccessful plot with Wilson to rescue Ney had been hushed up but was wrongly thought to have been involved in the Lavallette affair, was this time ordered to leave France. (*Ibid.*, p. 234, and Lean, pp. 178–82.)

602. To Henry Hallam

BLPES vii. 41–5 ⟨Horner, ii. 344–5⟩   Sidmouth, 17 Mar. 1816

⟨. . .⟩

From nothing having been said upon the Message the other day, I conclude that all is going on harmoniously for the present. But I confess I shall be anxious to see that a parliamentary enactment is made, with regard to the P[rincess]'s *right* of residence in England.[1] If this is not proposed, there must be an intention of removing her Court abroad, as soon as a plausible opportunity occurs; and if she is induced by her present happiness and confidence to overlook the necessary securities for this essential point, she will not be able to make resistance when the time comes, without a risk of appearing in the wrong. In kindness and fairness to her, it ought to be done, without putting upon her the necessity of seeming to insist upon it. And I would rather hear of its being done, if Lord Liverpool would agree to that, by a proposal on the part of the Ministers themselves, than that there should be any appearance of a parliamentary party for the P[rincess] distinct from her father's Government. That is an evil which we shall probably have soon enough; it will be hard to keep clear of it, if she continues to reside at home as she ought to do: but I never was more sure of any thing than of these two, that she ought to be in England, and that she ought to abstain from political connections during her father's regency or reign. For her own peace and honour there is no other safe course, and to the country nothing ever has resulted but harm from political dissensions between the sovereign and his heir expectant.[2]

⟨I fancy you will not⟩ so much ⟨agree with me, in being sorry to see, that nothing has been said by any body, upon the bills relating to the prisoner at St Helena, expressive of a regret that it was cast upon this country to execute so odious a part of the arrangements to which the victory of Waterloo has led.[3] You know all my sentiments about the man, how little I share any of that admiration which his extraordinary fortunes and character have imposed upon some persons, and how much I execrated all along his tyranny and military ambition and enmity to all civil liberty. At the height of his power, I expressed myself more strongly against him than I should permit myself to do publicly now. In the treatment he has met with, I feel no inclination to deny, that the sparing of his life is an act of humanity, such as is not recorded of any of those former ages in which such characters and events are to be found. Yet I cannot but feel at the same time, that, when a few years more are gone by, and we can all look back upon these transactions from some distance, it will be our regret and mortification that the Government of this day could see no safety for Europe against a single man, but in transporting him to a rock in the ocean, and that in leaving him his life we have taken all that can make life any thing but a torment. I do not mean to make a stronger imputation, than that we have been wanting in magnanimity, where the opportunity was obvious and commanding. But this country has reached too high a station, to be at liberty to miss such opportunities. Our virtues must rise with our fortune, or we shall be thought to have been unworthy of it: a large and secure generosity, is one of the conditions by which we are to hold our greatness. Instead of this, we have treated our captive with the timid severity of a little republic; and have lowered ourselves to the notions of our despot allies, who know nothing of safety but in force and bonds. Perhaps, some years hence, at the point of view which I anticipate, I shall soberly discover all this to be a romance. I can say without any affectation, that I shall have nothing but pleasure in seeing the glory of the country quite clear of the stain which I think I see upon it at present.[4]

⟨Do you hear any thing of Canning's coming into office? I wish he were back in the House of Commons; it would refresh one's mind, to hear something like eloquence again, and to see a man at work, who, with all his faults, owes his means of greatness to his powers in that House. His faults, it must be owned, and especially his late errors, are miserable.⟩[5]

. . .

1. Princess Charlotte's engagement to Prince Leopold of Coburg had again raised the question of a residence abroad, and Whig leaders feared that the Regent's divorce and remarriage, followed by the birth of a child, might compromise the Princess's right of succession unless her right to residence in England was established by a declaratory statute.
2. Horner wrote this letter the day before Brougham, who was legal counsel to the Princess Caroline and the likely parliamentary advocate of her daughter's claims, scored his great victory over the extension of the property tax proposed by Government.
3. Horner refers, of course, to the parliamentary bills regulating the conditions under which Napoleon was confined on St Helena.
4. Hallam replied on 19 Mar., reporting the surprising Commons vote the day before of 238 to 201 against the property tax and disputing Horner's attitude towards the Government's treatment of Napoleon. Seymour also wrote, contesting Horner's view of foreign politics and attributing it to party prejudice. Horner eventually responded to Seymour on 15 June, maintaining the integrity of his opinions but declining to enter into a disputation. (Hallam to Horner, 19 Mar., Seymour to Horner, 27 Mar., and Horner to Seymour, 15 June, *Horner*, ii. 345–7, 347–53, and 359–61.)

5. Although Canning had resigned the Lisbon embassy the previous summer, after only a little more than six months there, the appointment continued to be attacked as a Government 'job' and in May 1817 was eventually to be the subject of an attempted censure in the Commons. In the meantime he returned to England to become President of the Board of Control in June 1816.

603. To Leonard Horner

⟨*Leonard Horner*, i. 91–2⟩   Taunton, 30 Mar. 1816

⟨The enclosed letter to you from Mr Poole has been in my hands for some days after having made a journey to town.[1] I detained it, by his permission, to read it, for which purpose he left it open. The distinction he has pointed out between the Saving Banks and Friendly Societies, is just, and important to be kept in view. His reasoning about the poor laws is not so sound or distinct, though the practical conclusion, in favour of retaining those laws in England, is the opinion which I have long held, but upon principles somewhat different; in one respect, indeed, widely so, for whereas he seems to approve of the modern conversion of the poor rate into what he calls a labourers' rate, I look upon that recent change in the system to have been one of the most pernicious corruptions it has ever undergone, and to be upon all principles, both moral and economical, quite indefensible.[2]

⟨. . .⟩

1. Poole's letter has not been found. But see Mrs Henry Sandford, *Thomas Poole and his Friends* (2 vols, 1888), ii. 106–116, for his interest in the poor laws.
2. The Opposition's current parliamentary campaign against the fiscal policy of Government included an attack on the system of poor relief. Burke's old friend Curwen was protesting against the fact that the nation was spending some one-sixth of its tax revenues on the relief of the poor, and shortly a parliamentary committee would begin to collect evidence. (See Inglis, pp. 111ff.)

604. To Lady Holland

BLPES vii. 46–7   Taunton, Saturday night, [?30 Mar. 1816]

. . .

I should like much to be up for Tierney's question on Wednesday, because it is his; but I fear that is impossible.[1] . . .

You probably think me ill-natured and unamiable on the subject I wrote about in my last letter. And indeed the apprehension, not so much of being thought so, as of being in some degree really so, is what has given me much uneasiness in thinking of this business. For I feel ashamed to think how many little low feelings are always trying to get the better of me, when he comes across me. On these occasions, I often long to transfer to myself some portion of Lord Holland's temper and magnanimity.[2]

. . .

We all dislike the new judge we have had with us, Park.[3] He has no knowledge, and no good manners; chattering, canting, and confused. What we shall not forgive, is a piece of rudeness to Lens.

I have been looking every day for a speech from Lord Grey. Every body asks why he has not appeared this session.

1. Tierney had kept up the harassment of the Government during Horner's absence, moving from his unsuccessful attacks on the army estimates to the more promising field of salaries and sinecures. Horner's reference is probably to Tierney's motion of 3 Apr. for the abolition of the Secretaryship of State for Colonies. Horner returned to London the following day. (*Tierney*, p. 176; Horner to Mrs Leonard Horner, 3 Apr., BLPES vii. 48–9.)

2. In the opening paragraph Horner mentions letters he had written from Exeter and Cornwall, which, unfortunately, have not been found. But the reference may very well be to Brougham (see Doc. 601) and, specifically, to the speeches he had made in the Commons on 18 and 20 Mar. The first was widely credited with gaining the great victory over the income tax; the other with throwing away the gain by an ill-timed attack on the Regent.

3. Sir James Alan Park (1763–1838: *DNB*) had been made justice of common pleas in January. His bad temper was notorious, but contrary to what Horner says, he was generally regarded as sound and sensible.

605. From J.W. Ward

Kinnordy MSS   Paris, 30 Mar. 1816

It occurs to me that you might like to see de Pradt's book about Spain which has just appeared.[1] It is reported that the Police mean to prohibit the sale of it, and in that case it may be difficult hereafter to procure it – Cavendish Bradshaw set off this evening – sent for, it appears, by an express from Carlton House – and I take this opportunity of sending you a copy. . . .[2]

So you have played the very deuce with his Majesty's Ministers. The effect which the victory your friends have gained has produced here is prodigious[3] – people thought that the old English Constitution was dead and gone, and are quite astonished to find it all alive and kicking – and in that point of view no doubt the event is satisfactory, though I confess I should have voted with the minority.

1. Dominique Dufour de Pradt, *Mémoires historiques sur la Révolution d'Espagne* (Paris, 1816).

2. Augustus Cavendish Bradshaw (1768–1832), younger brother of the 2nd Baron Waterpark, was Groom of the Bedchamber to the Prince Regent.

3. Presumably the recent defeat of the property tax.

606. To John Horner

BLPES vii. 50–51   [London], Monday 15 Apr. [1816]

. . .

Vansittart must be very much embarrassed about his finances; even if every reduction were made, that is practicable, it will be difficult to defray the expenses of the peace establishment and interest of the debt, with any taxes that the present condition of the country can bear. We are now to suffer, and some time hence we shall all acknowledge, the consequences of that long continued system of finance, which has been so heedlessly persisted in. I confess I am quite at a loss to see how we can get through the difficulty.

607. From Lord Grenville

BLPES vii. 52–3   Dropmore, 25 Apr. 1816

I return you many thanks for the trouble you have been so good to take in sending me the paragraph from the East India Act. It seems to be beyond all question that the form now adopted in presenting the account to Parliament is a complete evasion of the Act, and I think it extremely important that it should be noticed, and that endeavours should be made to oblige the East India Co. to bring annually before Parliament and the Public the real state of their commercial transactions in the same form of profit and loss which any other merchant would adopt in stating his accounts.

If they make difficulties about this, I submit that the best course would be to move for the plan prepared by the Company in pursuance of the *express* directions of the Act and approved by the Board of Commissioners – and then to refer that plan to a Committee with instructions 'to examine and report how far the [case?] is, and how it may be made effectual for the purpose, intended by the said Act, of bringing annually before Parliament a distinct and separate view of the territorial and political receipts and disbursements of the East India Co., and of the profit and loss on the respective branches of their Commerce.'[1]

1. On 22 Mar. Grenville had reminded the Lords that when they had been considering the renewal of the Company's charter in 1813 they had discovered that its commercial accounts were so mixed up with its 'territorial revenue' as to make it impossible to calculate the amount of its commercial profit or loss, and queried whether the Company had ever put into practice the provisions they had included in the new Act in order to remedy the defect. (*Hansard*, xxxiii. 522.)

608. To Joanna Horner

BLPES vii. 54–5   [London], Tuesday night, 30 Apr. [1816]

. . .

We have been engaged tonight upon Lord Cochrane's impeachment of Lord Ellenborough, an unfounded and frivolous accusation, which has been very properly disposed of: Lord Cochrane and Sir F. Burdett his seconder had no ayes to tell for his motion, and then the House ordered the charges to be expunged from their Journals.[1] There was not so great an attendance on the part of Opposition in this business, as there ought to have been; but it was very satisfactory to me, that Mr Ponsonby took a lead in what was done. There is a personal dislike of Lord Ellenborough, which weighed with many on this occasion; a feeling very much warranted by some parts of his conduct, but which ought not to have weighed against doing him justice. There can be no reasonable expectation, that Judges will act independently of the Court, if even when they are attacked and accused without a shadow of cause, they can look for none to protect them but among the retainers of Administration.

. . .

> 1. Ellenborough had presided as Lord Chief Justice at Cochrane's notorious trial for fraud in 1814 and pronounced a savage sentence, including an hour in the pillory. Consequently on 5 Mar. and 1 Apr. 1816 Cochrane had presented in the Commons fourteen charges of 'partiality, misrepresentation, injustice, and oppression' against Ellenborough. His motion, seconded by Burdett and put on 30 Apr., was defeated by 89 to 0. But in the same session an Act was passed abolishing the pillory.

609. Speech by Horner[1]

⟨Horner, ii. 563–75⟩   House of Commons, 1 May 1816

⟨It was a matter of great convenience that he had been enabled to bring forward the proposition which he had then to submit to the House before the bill for continuing the restriction act came under discussion, because it was his opinion, as it had been that of many gentlemen in the House, that when it was proposed to renew the restriction on the bank payments for two years, their attention should be called in detail, and on a specific motion, to the reasons why this restriction should be continued under the present circumstances; and on what principles, or under what motives, it was adopted as a permanent part of our peace system of finance. The surprise which he had felt when he heard of the proposition to renew the restriction on cash payments in time of peace, had been generally felt throughout the House and the country; because if any thing could be collected from the former declarations of Ministers, and from the enactments themselves, it was this – that at the end of the war the system adopted in time of war should be abandoned, and that we should revert to that state of law and practice, on which alone any secure system of finance could be founded.

⟨The proposal to renew the Bank restriction, for so long a period as two years, had had this effect – that he doubted the sincerity of the professions which had been all along made by Ministers, of their desire to effect the renewal of the cash payments. . . . But, if he felt a doubt with respect to Ministers, no doubt whatever existed in his mind with respect to the Bank of England. Were they not told, year after year, until they could scarcely hear the declaration with gravity, by gentlemen connected with the Bank, that their not resuming their cash payments was all a matter of compulsion – that it was against their system – that nothing was so painful to their feelings, as their being prevented from paying their notes, of every denomination, in gold and silver? He always thought, if it were a measure of compulsion, that never was resistance so weak as that which was opposed to it by the Bank. And he was of opinion, that if they were really desirous to renew, as soon as Government would permit them, their payments in silver and gold, they had given, under the resistance which Ministers opposed to their wishes, an example of the passive grace of fortitude which never had been exceeded. Therefore, from this day forth he should think, whatever professions that body might please to make, that they would be very well contented to enjoy all those vast and almost incalculable profits which grew out of the adoption of this measure. For, from the trammels created by it, arose a subserviency in the Government to the Bank, which rendered Ministers incapable of fairly going into the money market. He would not go farther into this subject, because it had already been ably discussed by an hon. Member (Mr Grenfell), whose luminous statement, founded on the most authentic documents, was on record upon their journals, and showed such an example of rapacity on the part of a corporate body, and of acquiescence on the part of a government, as stood unrivalled in the financial history of any country in Europe.[2]

⟨He believed, that his right hon. friend, the Chancellor of the Exchequer, had no settled system of opinions at all on this subject. He had a sort of notion, that if cash payments could be resumed, without altering his plan of finance, it would be as well if things were restored to their old order. But sooner than attempt this reform, he thought it was better to rub over this year and the next year, and to make up, by the assistance of the Bank, any defalcations that might arise in the finances of the country, however exorbitantly he was to pay for the accommodation.

⟨He had no doubt, from the renewal of this measure, being for two years, that it was intimately connected with the financial arrangements of his right hon. friend. His right hon. friend said, that his plans and the renewal of the restriction were coincident in point of time, and had no other connection. But any man who recollected what took place at the meeting of the Bank proprietors, would form a different opinion. Early in the year, when the first bargain was about to be entered into, the proprietors were told that Ministers meant to renew the Bank Restriction Act. Why was this statement made, unless to induce the proprietors to agree, to the loan which was demanded of them? But what other effect had the information which was given on this subject? When it was afterwards stated that the bill was introduced, there was an immense and immediate rise in the price of Bank stock. It was said, that the Bank had no interest in the renewal of the restrictions. If that were so, it was strange that the most ignorant person in the market should at once perceive that his property would be benefited by it, and that, therefore, it was advisable for him to speculate. He believed on the occasion to which he alluded, that Bank stock rose about 18 per cent.

⟨The proposal to renew the Bank Restriction Act for two years was a most extraordinary measure, when compared with the extension of it at a former period. It was known with what trembling anxiety, in 1797, six weeks and six weeks had been added to the term of the act; and with what caution in 1802, the Government, suspecting the peace of that year to be precarious, had proposed short extensions of the restriction. Even after the principle (a mischievous and fatal principle he conceived it to be) of making the restriction a war measure had been adopted, it had always been determined that it should cease six months after the conclusion of a general peace. And last year, when surely the peace did not present such a prospect of duration as at present, it was only extended to a fixed day – the 5th of July – in the following session. But now it was to be extended two years, without any reason, unless it was to be understood as the price of the loan which the Bank was to advance.

⟨The question of the restriction had of late been put on a new ground, by connecting it with the agricultural distresses. But if the Bank restriction was to be grounded on the agricultural distresses, why was it to be continued for two years? Was not every one more and more convinced every day, that the distress would be a temporary evil? Why, then, was not the restriction of a short duration? – Only with a view to the bargain between the Bank and the treasury. He knew this would not be avowed; but he would put it to all who were anxious for the security of the country, or desirous of preserving their own property, whether, after they had considered the circumstances he had explained, they could imagine, that this measure had nothing to do with the bargain entered into between Government and the Bank? Would they vote for inquiry this evening, or give their assistance to a measure, the true object of which was not avowed, and the only reason for proposing which he conceived he had stated?

⟨On what ground did his right hon. friend mean to call on them to accede to these restrictions? And how did he mean to defend himself from the charge of not having taken any steps to compel the resumption of cash payments? These were points on which the House was ignorant, but on which it ought to be informed. And here he wished to correct an error which had been unjustly imputed to him and to those gentlemen who coincided with him in opinion. It was said, that they wished the cash payments to be immediately resumed. They never harboured such a sentiment. They always stated that it could not be done, without precautionary measures; but they conceived that no time should be lost in giving the country full assurance that payments would be renewed, and in taking speedy measures that this might be done with safety. The measures which had been successively proposed to Parliament, were to be put off, not only the cash payments, but the consideration of the means of again bringing them about.

⟨He would ask the House, did they not feel some anxiety on this head? Had they felt no evils from the long suspension of cash payments? Were they sensible of no evils after all that had passed in the course of the discussions of the agricultural distress, during which no one had been hardy enough to deny that a great evil had arisen from the sudden destruction of the artificial prices? Would any man say that there had not been a great change in the value of money? What this was owing to might be disputed; but, for his own part, he had not the least doubt. From inquiries which he had made, and from the accounts on the table, he was convinced that a greater and more sudden reduction of the circulating medium had never taken place in any country, with the exception of those reductions which had happened in France after the Mississippi scheme, and after the destruction of the assignats.

⟨He should not go into the question how this reduction had been effected, though it was a very curious one, and abounded in illustrations of the principles which had been so much disputed in that House. The reduction of the currency had originated in the previous fall of the prices of agricultural produce. This fall had produced a destruction of the country bank paper to an extent which would not have been thought possible without more ruin than had ensued. The Bank of England had also reduced its issues; as appeared by the accounts recently presented. The average amount of their currency was not, during the last year, more than between twenty-five and twenty-six millions; while two years ago it had been nearer twenty-nine millions, and at one time even amounted to thirty-one millions. But without looking to the diminution of the Bank of England paper, the reduction of country paper was enough to account for the fall which had taken place.

⟨Another evil which had resulted from the state of the currency, which he had foreseen and predicted, but which had been deemed visionary, was, that during the war we had borrowed money, which was then of small value; and we were now obliged to pay it at a high value. This was the most formidable evil which threatened our finances; and, though he had too high an opinion of the resources of the country, and of the wisdom of the Government to despair, he was appalled when he considered the immense amount of the interest of the debt contracted in that artificial currency, compared with the produce of the taxes.

⟨These were the two grand inconveniences which had resulted; and it was to be remembered, that the great difference during the former discussions on these subjects, was not so much in the theoretical as in the practical question. The late Minister, Mr Perceval, who had no general principle on the subject, thought, that to revert to cash payments in time of war would be so difficult that it was not worth the hazard. But he (Mr Horner), though he thought that the renewal of the cash payments was a matter which required caution and preparation, thought that the true policy was to meet the difficulty at once, and that it was a fallacy pregnant with evil to suppose that any lasting benefit could be derived from so factitious a state of the currency.

⟨The event had decided the question. But, turning from these results, and looking forward to the operation of this restriction in time of peace, it would be found to leave us without any known or certain standard of money to regulate the transactions, not only between the public and its creditors, but between individuals. The currency which was to prevail was not only uncertain, but cruel and unjust in its operation – at one time, upon those whose income was fixed in money, and to all creditors – at another time, when by some accident it was diminished in amount, to all debtors. Was not this an evil sufficient to attract the attention of a wise, a benevolent, and a prudent government?

⟨If they looked at the agricultural interest, was not a fluctuation of prices the greatest of evils to the farmer? For, supposing prices were fixed and steady, it was indifferent to him what was the standard. As long as we had no standard – no fixed value of money – but it was suffered to rise and fall like the quicksilver in the barometer, no man could conduct his property with any security, or depend upon any sure or certain profit. Persons who were aware of the importance of this subject must be surely anxious to know whether there were any imperative reasons for continuing the present system, to know whether it was intended to revert to the old system, and if not now, when that system would be reverted to, and what would be the best means for bringing about that measure. This was the object for which he proposed to appoint the committee, that the House might know something of the true state of the case before they plunged headlong into the system of the Chancellor of the Exchequer.

⟨He hoped they should hear the opinion of his right honourable friend, and learn from him on what grounds the bill was now proposed, and what were the circumstances under which they might revert to cash payments. If he looked at the professions of former times, he was at a loss to know how to apply them. The reasons for continuing the restriction had been said to be our great foreign expenditure, the necessity of importing corn, the high price of the precious metals, and the unfavourable state of the exchange. These subjects had created much controversy, which he should not now renew, but which he did not shrink from, and which he thought it probable he might have an opportunity again to discuss; for, if the present system were persisted in, the exchange and the price of gold would be very unsatisfactory to the Bank and the Chancellor of the Exchequer.

⟨The opinions which he had formerly given had received a strong and unexpected confirmation by late events; but he had already modified the opinion which he had formerly given as to the price of gold. When, by the depreciation of the currency, gold was permanently separated from paper, it was subject to all the variations in price of any other article of merchandise.[3] On this subject it was to be remarked, that in the last year, a year of peace, gold, though lower than it had previously been, was never below £4. 8s., which was equal to the whole of the alleged depreciation; but now that the country banks had called in their paper, it had fallen nearly to, and would soon be quite as low as, the Mint price. Let not the right hon. gentleman flatter himself that if the Bank of England were to issue their notes to that extent, which they were likely to do upon the enactment of his bill, the country banks would not return to their former practice, and the rate of prices be affected by that practice. The House should therefore be prepared for such consequences, and in due time consider how to provide against them. To afford an opportunity for that consideration was the object of his motion, and he hoped the House would see the propriety of acceding to it.

⟨The high price of bullion, the rate of exchange, the importation of foreign grain, and the amount of our foreign payments, which were on a former occasion pleaded as reasons for the restriction of cash payments by the Bank, could not now be urged, because those reasons no longer existed. Therefore his right hon. friend, who urged those reasons on the occasion alluded to, was called upon in consistency to support the present motion, in order to ascertain how it became necessary, after the cessation of those reasons, to continue the restriction. For himself, he could not conceive, after those reasons had ceased to exist, [how] the measure could be justified.

‹He had heard of publications, copies of which were pretty widely circulated, and the object of which was to show, that if bank notes were issued in the same abundance as they formerly were, prices would again rise, and the farmers be consequently benefited; that this therefore would be a good thing for the country, and that grain might probably again rise to 100s. a quarter. But he could not suppose the right hon. gentleman prepared to support his measure upon such grounds; or that he would be an advocate for the issue of bank notes, with a view to raise the price of grain. For if the right hon. gentleman would do so, he must become the advocate of one of the most monstrous projects that had ever been imagined. Projects somewhat similar had no doubt been brought forward and tried during the Regency in France, and about the same time in this country, but the result proved their fallacy. Both Governments were, however, in these cases, then dupes and projectors. But if his right hon. friend should press such a project as that to which he alluded, he would not be the dupe – but the fallacious projector himself. This course, however, he could not suppose the right hon. gentleman prepared to pursue.

‹In what he had said, he did not wish it to be understood that his object was to have cash payments resumed immediately, but that steps should be immediately taken with a view to that resumption – that the Bank should set about it – that the directors should prepare for the resumption – that indeed both Government and the Bank should set about measures to relieve the right hon. gentleman from the dilemma in which he was placed by the removal of those causes which he had formerly assigned to justify this restriction. He would not specify any time within which this restriction should be removed – he would not even mention two years – but he could not help thinking that it was the duty of Government and the Bank at once to set about the means of accomplishing that object which the public had a right to expect. Necessity was the only reason ever urged in justification of this restriction; and when the necessity ceased, the country naturally expected that the restriction should cease also.

‹He should now proceed to discuss the second branch of his motion; namely, the best means by which the Bank might be enabled to resume its payments in cash. He ... thought it should be enacted, that the Bank should gradually pay its several notes according to their value. Thus, as the Restriction Act was to expire in July, it might be provided that the Bank should pay all notes of £1 within six months; afterwards, its £2 notes within the next six months; its £5 notes within the succeeding six months; and all its notes above £5 after that period. By such an arrangement, the Bank would be guarded against the consequences of any sudden change, while the just claims and expectations of the public would be gratified. But before the committee which he proposed, this subject might be fully considered, after an examination of witnesses, including the directors of the Bank and others, competent to afford every necessary information.

‹Another subject, which would properly come under the consideration of such a committee, would be the state of our metallic currency. He had heard that it was in the contemplation of Government to have a new silver coinage, with a view to relieve the country from that sort of bad English, and still worse French silver, with which it was at present inundated. This silver was indeed so very base, that it would probably be better for the country to have no currency at all, than be subject to suffer by such a circulating medium. But, in considering this subject, it would be very material to ascertain whether the new silver coinage should be according to the old standard, or whether any new standard should be established. For if the system of paper currency were to be restored to the rate at which it sometime since prevailed, it might be inconvenient and unjust to re-establish the old Mint standard of silver; for by such re-establishment, Government, as well as individuals who sent silver to the Mint for coinage, would be very likely to suffer a considerable loss.

⟨It was idle to expect that good money and bad would circulate together. The Mint might be constantly at work, but not for the benefit of the public; its new coinage might be poured into circulation, but it would not continue in circulation. It would, if some regulation with respect to our standard did not take place, immediately vanish, and the expense would be incurred in vain.

⟨He had now come to an end of the two objects of his motion – the expediency of resuming cash payments, and the most proper method of doing this. He hoped that the House would make some inquiry on the subject: he did not ask them to adopt his opinions, but at least to make some inquiry, and not to pass on as a matter of course. If the House did grant what the Chancellor of the Exchequer proposed, they would in fact pass a bill to continue the restriction for ever. He must be an idle dreamer who could suppose, after what had passed, that the Chancellor of the Exchequer or the Bank directors ever meant to resume cash payments at all. If, then, this bill were sanctioned, as a matter of course, they made the system permanent. They set their seal to it, and must answer to the country for the consequences. . . .⟩[4]

1. On 24 Apr. Horner, giving notice that on 1 May he would move for the appointment of a . committee to inquire into the expediency and most propitious means of a resumption of cash payments by the Bank of England, had successfully moved (*Horner*, ii. 563):

   that there be laid before the House an account of the nett weekly amount of the Bank of England notes in circulation, from the 9th of February, 1815, to the latest period to which the same could be made out, distinguishing post bills from notes, and distinguishing those under the value of £5.

2. This is probably a reference to the speech made by Pascoe Grenfell (1761–1838: *DNB*) on 13 Feb. 1816 when he denounced the Bank for understating its profits and overcharging commission on the public business it handled. But he made further speeches on the related Bank Loan Bill on 14 and 29 Mar. (*Hansard*, xxxii. 458–93 and xxxiii. 265–9 and 721–2.)

3. On 24 Apr. Ricardo had told Malthus (*Letters of David Ricardo to Thomas Robert Malthus, 1810–1823*, ed. James Bonar, Oxford, 1887, p. 115) that Horner had come round to his own point of view on the price of precious metals and, noting that the value of silver had fallen below the mint price, had observed that 'There cannot be a better opportunity than the present for the Bank to recommence payments in specie.'

4. Horner then moved 'That a Select Committee be appointed to inquire into the expediency of restoring the Cash Payments of the Bank of England, and the safest and most advantageous means of effecting it'. After the Chancellor of the Exchequer, supported by Castlereagh, Huskisson, and others, had spoken against the motion, Horner made a 'luminous reply' that, while unfortunately reported very poorly, evidently exploited Castlereagh's muddled reasoning quite successfully. Horner's motion was then defeated by 146 to 73. (*Horner*, ii. 573–5.)

610. From Lord Grenville

BLPES vii. 56–7   Dropmore, 3 May 1816

I think there can be no doubt that when the Bank are [sic] left under their natural and legal liability to pay in Cash, as far as respects their small notes, they should be relieved from any obligation to discharge the larger notes in small ones. Without this provision one great advantage of the plan of gradual usurpation would be defeated. I mean the security it affords that no accidental run upon them in the first moment of Cash payment could at the very utmost go beyond the amount of small notes actually in circulation, an amount which they could with certainty command the means of meeting by the issue (*if necessary*) of larger notes to a greater extent than before.

The clause of option would as you truly state it be so ridiculous an abandonment of the whole pectoral of compulsory restriction that I do not think it can really be intended. Yet some such measure seems absolutely necessary to give any thing like sense or substance to some of the arguments which I see used against you.[1]

1. Horner's reply has not been found, and there is no further mention of the Bank restriction in his correspondence during the spring.

611. To John Horner

BLPES vii. 73–6 ⟨*Horner*, ii. 356–7⟩   Holland House, 5 June 1816

⟨. . . I have been here for three or four days, during our Whitsun holidays; Lady Holland taking almost as much care of me, when she fancies I need it, as if I were⟩ almost ⟨in my own dear mother's hands. I am still a little plagued with a cough, in which there is nothing at all material, except the circumstance of its continuing so long, which I think is owing to the cold weather. To be quite sure of this, I have (by Lady Holland's desire) seen Dr Warren, who thinks there is nothing in it; but considers the stomach, as of old, chiefly in fault, and has given me some directions to observe on that head.⟩[1]

. . .

⟨My sisters seem to have taken it for granted, that I have fixed upon my summer plans, to the exclusion of Scotland. But that is by no means the case. I rather think, if I travel at all, it will be to see you; but I am not without thoughts of staying quietly at home, in order to read a little law, for which I have but few opportunities at other times of the year. But I have made no resolution yet.⟩

The only piece of news I have to give you, is, that it is now rumoured that something is to be done, for the trial of the Princess of Wales, or her divorce. What is certain is, that Lord Exmouth has sent home strong evidence against her, having, it is said, secreted his spies behind the hangings while she was with one of her lovers.

This is not a very honourable service for him; it will get him another step in the peerage.[2] Whether this detection was made in Sicily, or elsewhere, I have not heard; but the lover is not the Italian servant, that has been so much talked of; for, when he got tired of his Princess, he took her diamonds from her, gave her a beating, and left her. The poor profligate wretch must have the madness of her family. What John Bull, or Henry Brougham, will have to say now for their injured innocent, I am at a loss to guess.

. . .

1. This was probably Pelham Warren (1778–1835: *DNB*).
2. Adm. Edward Pellew, 1st Baron Exmouth (1757–1833: *DNB*), had been C.-in-C. in the Mediterranean during the Princess's travels, and a number of naval officers were to give evidence at her so-called trial in 1820. Exmouth was promoted Viscount on 10 Dec., but for his operations against Algiers.

612. To Francis Jeffrey

BLPES vii. 83–6   The Temple, 13 June 1816

In a note which I received yesterday from Allen, he mentioned there was some chance of an article appearing in your *Review*, upon a scandalous novel, lately written by a woman of fashion in London; and he added that he regretted this so much, that he had written to request you would not insert any notice of it.[1] I so entirely agree with him, that I cannot help adding my dissuasions to his; because the impressions which we have who are upon the spot, may at least assist you in forming your determination.

I say nothing of the insignificance of the work itself in point of literary merit, nor of the currency that would be given, by your notice of it, to the personal slander and the indecencies in which it abounds; for these considerations would occur to yourself. But without knowing the character of the shameless little strumpet, who is the author, you can hardly conceive how much she would be encouraged to commit farther outrages of the same sort, by any degree of notoriety that is to be acquired, either by approbation, or by severe censure. To be the talk of the world, to be the object of interest and conversation, is the rage that has depraved her to what she now is; and there is no punishment for which she has any sensibility left, but neglect. Her publication has been read with much avidity, not only by those who having the key to the real characters can enjoy the secret history, but by the women in general, who are not so scrupulous as they used to be about their reading. But if your *Review* and the *Quarterly* pass it by, the mischief will be but for a day. There are a good many persons, you may believe, her own nearest relations, and other friends to whom the worthless woman owes the most real obligations, that are kept in a very irksome state of fidget, while the public attention is alive to the stories true and false which she has put in print about them. Among these, are her own husband, and her own mother; the former of whom she has outraged in a manner as unexampled, as his own good nature in not turning her away for it. I cannot see any good you can do, by any reprehension you can express of the work; you will do any thing but amend the author, who is past all amendment; you will give pain to many persons, by prolonging the life of her libels; and, however moral and indignant your censure might be, you know enough of the public appetites [?not] to doubt that you would only excite curiosity where it is not yet felt, and spread wide into the country the corrupt and corrupting secret histories of Whitehall. I feel very earnestly upon this point; for knowing as much as I do of most of the parties concerned, and living with many of them, I see very clearly that an article in the *Edinburgh Review* upon this unhappy book will cause a good deal of pain, and give both a triumph and farther encouragement to the wretch who has already caused much pain. Just before the publication of this novel, she had brought herself into what seemed a worse scrape; having wounded dangerously a poor page she has of ten years old, by laying open his skull with a fire-shovel; his life was for a week in a state of uncertainty, yet those who know her best say, she would not have disliked the éclat of a trial at the Old Bailey, if she could have been sure of acquittal.

. . .

1. Allen's 'note' has not been found, but the 'scandalous novel' was presumably Lady Caroline Lamb's *Glenarvon* (1816), which portrayed Lady Holland as the odious 'Princess of Madagascar'.

613. To John Horner

BLPES vii. 79–82 〈*Horner*, ii. 357–8〉   The Temple, Thursday [13 June 1816]

〈There is nothing I should like better than the plan you propose, for spending the autumn in a house at some little distance from Edinburgh. . . .

〈. . . I shall probably be released from the circuit on the 23rd August at Bristol; and I may arrange matters so as to set out at once for the North. I have concealed nothing from you about my health; . . .〉

I am carrying through the House of Commons, with ease, a very important bill of reform for Ireland; by which the Grand Juries and Judges in that country will be compelled to do their duty according to law, by finding their indictments upon evidence, which, by a very slovenly and immemorial practice, they have hitherto found without evidence in most cases. All the Irish Judges, with one exception, have been vehement against my measure, and even irritated about it; and I am sorry to say, that even Plunkett had allowed his mind to follow in their train. But against their prejudices, I have the prejudices of the English lawyers on my side; and with that assistance, and Castlereagh's knowledge of the Judges he made at the Union, I have had great odds in my favour. If it is not thrown out by the Law Lords in the other house, I shall effect a very important reformation in the course of Irish criminal law, which requires more to be purified and strengthened, than almost any other part in the bad system of that government. I have been obliged, unwillingly, to consent to a compromise in the manner of immediately effecting the change; but I think it better to take what I can get at present, than lose the whole; only I must keep an eye to the operation of my act, if it passes, and chase a good opportunity hereafter for making it more complete.[1]

⟨. . .⟩

1. Having had his attention drawn to the fact that in Ireland it was common practice for grand juries to consider only depositions and so deny themselves and counsel the opportunity of questioning witnesses, Horner had given notice the previous session that he intended to bring in a bill to declare it contrary to common law. So on 14 Feb., shortly after the opening of the new session, he had proposed his bill only to find it meet a good deal of opposition, on the grounds of the 'physical impossibility of its execution' because of the heavy and often conflicting demands of criminal and civil litigation in Ireland, and the possible legal implications of a statute exposing the failure of Irish judges to operate on an impeccable principle of the common law. As a result he was reluctantly persuaded by Peel to abandon his earlier insistence on a declaratory statute in favour of a remedial measure, and it passed into law that session. For a detailed account of the origins and progress of Horner's measure, see Horner to Murray of 9 July, with accompanying comment in *Horner*, ii. 329–36, the latter part of which also summarizes a communication from Spring-Rice of 1830 (not 1831 as stated), of which there is a fuller version in the Kinnordy MSS, including copies of correspondence between them of June 1815 (further copies of some of which are also in BLPES vi. 251–2). See also R.L. Edgeworth to Romilly, 21 Feb. 1816, *Romilly–Edgeworth Letters*, p. 129, and *Romilly*, iii. 217–18.

614. To Henry Hallam

BLPES vii. 116–18   Oxford, 14 July 1816

. . .

Wherever I go, I hear very deplorable descriptions of the distress of the country, both in the manufacturing and agricultural classes; and it is every where said to be upon the increase. It would be very important, with a view to the propriety of devising any practicable palliatives that are within the competence of Government, to ascertain, from the circumstances of all this suffering, whether it is a temporary suspension only of commercial relations, or a change of a lasting nature. That is a very difficult judgement to form: and yet essentially necessary. Lord Sidmouth, who is Minister for this purpose, has no very deep or sound view of it, I fear; as you shall judge from this anecdote. The Duke of Bedford waited upon him, on the part of the proprietors of the fens, where crowds of labourers are thrown out of employment, to ask pecuniary assistance from Government in executing an important line of drainage, which would give immediate work to these men. The Doctor said, 'the country was in a most alarming state; his Grace could form no conception of it; but the only thing the Government had thought of, for its relief, was to afford liberally every possible encouragement to emigration.'[1]

A forced emigration of our peasantry and artisans, coupled with a tax upon polite travellers to prohibit *their* escape, forms a sagacious and enlightened system of policy; the last result of all the political reasonings, and liberal ideas, of the eighteenth and nineteenth centuries.

Let me hear your political gossip. I am no believer in Ministerial changes, or dissolutions of Parliament: but I begin to feel very anxious about the internal state of the country, and the prospect of our finances. No ministry can save us, I fear, from some unprincipled attack upon property and all the consequent misery and confusion, that is not strong enough to compel the Court and the Duke of Wellington to consent to a reduction of the army. It will seem much easier to put down that confusion by using the army in that service.

> 1. Early in 1815 the Government had sanctioned a scheme of assisted emigration for demobi-
> lized soldiers and had avoided the subject in Parliament until Horner challenged them on
> 21 June that year with 'encouraging emigration'. The Government then denied that they
> had tried to do anything other than to induce those already committed to change their
> destination from the United States to British North America and early in 1816 they had
> suspended even some of that assistance. But the question was agitated again by the
> deepening agricultural recession and by the riots – and consequential hangings – in East
> Anglia in June. (*Hansard*, xxxi (1815), 917; Helen I. Cowan, *British Emigration to British
> North America: The First Hundred Years* (Toronto, 1961), pp. 41–9.)

615. To Lady Holland

BLPES vii. 127–8   Wells, 18 Aug. [1816]

. . . There is no appearance of any wheat ripening. The farmers I believe and country gentlemen, with their usual blindness, are comforting themselves with the thoughts of high prices; but if there is not more heat in the rest of autumn than can with any probability be expected, things will be so bad next winter, that *they* will have their share even of the immediate suffering.

I have been reading the *Review*. Allen's article is quite admirable, so full of good sense and sagacity, and of well selected learning, arranged and expressed with the greatest perspicuity. One only regrets to see it lost in a periodical work, where nobody looks for any thing like careful discussion, and which nobody thinks of beyond the passing quarter. I conclude the crucifixion of the Laureate to be Jeffrey's, and the exaltation of Mr Brougham to be his own. There is a useful account of the Stuart papers, which I suppose is Mackintosh's, for nobody else would have found good-nature enough to suppress all mention of the editor's comparison of King William's revolution to that which has lately *demoralized* Europe, especially with the temptation of making such a sentiment as dated from Carlton House.[1]

. . .

> 1. Allen had published an article on the 'Constitution of Parliament' in the *ER* xxvi (no. lii,
> June 1816), 338–83, and Jeffrey was indeed the author of the savage attack on Southey's
> *The Lay of the Laureate* (pp. 441–9), but that reviewing (along with another by Western) of
> Brougham's House of Commons speech of 9 Apr. and entitled the 'Distresses of the
> Country' (pp. 255–81), was by Lord John Russell. The author of the review (pp. 402–430)
> of the *Life of James II* (2 vols, 1816), edited by James Stanier Clarke (?1765–1834: *DNB*),
> domestic chaplain to the Prince Regent, is generally thought to be Mackintosh.

616. From John Allen

BLPES vii. 131–2   Holland House, 12 Sept. [1816]

. . .

You have probably seen a short but clever pamphlet on the divorce. From internal evidence I think it Brougham's, but I have no other ground for that or any other conclusion with respect to its author.[1] It is said that Liverpool, Eldon and Castlereagh are against trying the divorce, but that the Doctor is strenuously for it, and that he is anxious to have Wellesley in the Cabinet to support him in that measure. I have farther heard that one of the Duke of Wellington's objects in coming to England was to remove the political connection between Wellesley and Canning and bring his brother into office, and that he so far succeeded as to have [had] a meeting between Canning and Wellesley, in which the latter after many civil expressions to Canning and professions of regard to him personally ended by saying that nothing could induce him to act with men whom he had publicly stigmatized for their incapacity. But this I give you as mere common report having no means of ascertaining its truth.[2] A dissolution is still talked of, but does not seem generally to be credited. If Ministers have any such intentions the approaching contest for Lincolnshire will enable them to feel the pulse of the public. If Sir Robert Heron perseveres in the contest, he comes forward as a Whig and reformer, while nothing can be found less of either than his opponent Mr Cust.[3] Lord Ebrington is still in Devonshire canvassing the County and from what his friends say with a good chance of turning out Sir Thomas Ackland.[4] Lord John Russell is returned from Spa. He brings a sad account of the bad odour in which the English are held throughout the Netherlands. They have become so noted for wrangling at the inns about the amount of their bills, that at Aix la Chapelle, Cologne and other places the principal innkeepers have made a rule to admit no Englishman into their house. Montron says he used formerly to pass himself for an Englishman wherever he went, but now a days before he gets out of his carriage he takes care to let the people know he is a Frenchman.[5] This is not an unnatural consequence of a parcel of ignorant boobies travelling with a view to economy. Their ignorance of the places through which they have passed is I hear truly diverting. Their recollections of what they have seen are faint as well as circumscribed and their notions of locality far from distinct. They have no conversation among themselves except comparisons of what they have paid at different inns. In short, they are as much condemned as their Government is hated. Of the late great change in the internal administration of France it is impossible as yet to form a judgement.[6] It is said to have been required by Russia, who threatened to abandon the Bourbons to their fate if the power of the ultra royalists was not put down. Whatever may be the ultimate consequence I am glad to see dissolved the assembly of Brigands whom they had lately got together, but if moderate and steady measures are pursued I fear the legitimates may after all weather the storm. I have great hopes however in the duplicity of the King and incurable bigotry of his family.

. . .

1. Two such pamphlets appeared about this time: *The attempt to divorce the Princess of Wales impartially considered* and *A Letter to John, Lord Eldon, lord high chamcellor of Great Britain; on the rumour of an intended royal divorce.* New, p. 175, mentions, but does not identify, a pamphlet by Brougham.
2. Nothing seems to be known of any such meeting.
3. According to his published *Notes* (2nd ed., Grantham, 1851), Sir Robert Heron (1765–1854: *DNB*), 2nd Bart and MP for Grimsby, considered offering himself for the vacancy in Lincolnshire caused by the death of Charles Chaplin, sen. (1759–1816) but the election came on too soon for him to vacate Grimsby, leaving William Cust (1787–1845), the brother of the Lord Lieutenant, Earl Brownlow, to come in unopposed.
4. The sitting Members were Sir Thomas Dyke Acland (1787–1871: *DNB*) and Edmund Pollfexen Bastard (1784–1838), both nominally independents. Lord Grenville's nephew Ebrington had stood unsuccessfully against Bastard in the by-election in May. But in the following months Acland had lost much of his popularity among the constituents and in October Ebrington accepted a formal invitation to stand, dislodging Acland at the next general election in June 1818. (*PH* ii. 96–8.)
5. Casimir, Comte de Montrond (1768–1843), the confidant of Talleyrand, had taken refuge in England from the summer of 1812 until the Hundred Days.
6. Louis XVIII had dissolved the Chamber in September and so reduced the number of members as to ensure a majority of moderates in the ensuing elections.

617. To Lady Holland

BLPES 133–4 〈*Horner*, ii. 367〉   Dryden,[1] 16 Sept. 1816

. . .

〈I am living at a retired and very beautiful place seven miles from Edinburgh, where I have only been once in the morning since I came. The weather has been cold and disagreeable, till within these two days; after a very sudden change, it is now deliciously warm and genial. This has given me a release from coughing; but〉 I am still broken-winded. 〈I am taking the advice of Drs Thomson and Gordon, who do not alarm me much about the nature of my illness, but have imposed upon me a great many cautions against cold and fatigue.[2]

〈I must expect to spend the greater part of next winter in the character of an invalid. My friends here have been very kind to me, coming from Edinburgh very frequently.〉 Jeffrey is in great force, and his French politics are in a better state than they were last year. I delivered your message to Thomas Thomson, but have no copy of your letter to Lady Caroline Lamb, which I should like much to have shown him.[3] I have had a visit too from William Elliot, and from old Adam. John Murray is not yet returned from the Western Isles, and the gossip of Edinburgh is that he has found a Calypso in Lewis. He wrote me word from there, that there had not been two rainy days from the middle of June, which I rather took for a proof of the enchantment.

. . .

1. Dryden, a place near Edinburgh belonging to an East India merchant, George Mercer (1772–1853), had been taken by Horner's family from the end of August to help him rest and recuperate after the persistent illness from which he had suffered that year. He remained there until 6 October.

2. The first was probably John Thomson.

3. After the appearance of *Glenarvon* Lady Holland appears to have severed communications
with Caroline Lamb. So perhaps this was the letter of mild rebuke sent only a short while
before the appearance of that book. (See Sonia Keppel, *The Sovereign Lady: A Life of
Elizabeth Vassall, Third Lady Holland, with her Family* (1974), p. 199; see also Lady Holland
to Horner, [7 Nov. 1816], BL Add. MSS 51644.)

618. To John Allen

BL Add. MSS 52180   Dryden, 17 Sept. 1816

I rejoice to hear you are once more engaged in your historical studies. None of us will
consent again, to your putting off your results in the *Review*, where they are admired
for half a quarter, and then carried down by the weight of the stuff that is mixed with
them. In the last number, yours is the only article that is spoken of, or that deserves to
be. But nobody reads Reviews a second time. It is quite waste, to put any thing there
that is of permanent value, either for the research that has been used, or for original
reflections. I wish reviews were brought back to their proper business, that of giving us
an account of the contents of new books, and sometimes helping the public to form a
right judgement of their merits. It is much better, on every account, that the materials
of new and valuable works should appear by themselves in their own form.

. . .

Is there any hope of Sir Robert Heron's success in Lincolnshire? it would be a
considerable victory over the Tories. That veteran Whig Sir Thomas Miller is dead
I see; the Dissenters are strong enough, I believe, in the Corporation of Portsmouth,
to replace him properly: a gentleman by the name of Carter used to be spoken of as
his successor.[1] Who is that Mr Webb, that stands for Gloucester? Will the present
election there afford any indication as to the continuance of the Howard interest in
the borough?[2] What I understood in Devonshire was, that Ackland was more likely
to be the victim than Bastard, which I shall regret; for the former is the better
parliament man of the two, and, though both Toryish and what is worse Ministerial
in his propensities, has some liberality in his disposition, and has had the virtue and
sense to vote for the Catholics. But any regret for him is by the bye. The only thing
I really care for about Devonshire, is Ebrington's success. Ackland's friends give out
that he will not yield without an expensive struggle. He lost many of his supporters,
and even in his own family, by his want of firmness and distinctness about the
petitions on the property tax last Session. The struggle in this county is going on
briskly; Dalrymple has gained a few new votes this year; and the corporation of
Edinburgh have been contriving some out of their superiority for the Arniston
family who begin already to express their dissatisfaction with their own creature, Sir
George Clerk, in order (I conclude) to pave the way for the Chief Baron's son by the
time he is of age.[3] I fear that General Ferguson has lately lost hold of Kinghorn,
which is gone over to Admiral Durham; but this, if true, does not decide the next
election, for the two burghs, the General still has, have the two next turns as
returning burghs.[4]

The late change of French politics is curious. We have still to see, whether the Ultra royalists will prevail in the elections. It is a pleasant commencement at constitutional liberty for France, when the King is compelled by the threats of a foreign power, and that Russia, to alter by his proclamation the numbers of the representative assembly. It appears to me mere idleness and trifling, to consider any thing that happens in France at present, in its relation to political liberty. I should like to know for certain, if that story is true, of a criminal being broke upon the wheel at Turin.

The Jury Court seems [to be] making its way, as well as a new institution of the kind could be expected to do.[5] The Chief Commissioner expressed himself perfectly satisfied with his progress, and is struck with the talents he finds at this Bar; they are not very skilful yet, he thinks, in the examination of witnesses, and he has apparently some reason to complain of the extreme length of the speeches of counsel, faults which must wear off with the novelty of juries, and when business of this sort increases so much as to enforce dispatch. The barristers, on the other hand, though they do ample justice to Adam's excellent temper and strict sense of justice and impartiality on the bench, say that he really has not law enough even for this branch of its administration, and that the juries seldom receive any aid from him in the way of observations upon the weight of evidence or credit of the witnesses. These mutual criticisms are not urged on either side with any tone of complaint or acrimony. All agree now, that no difficulty has ever occurred, or seems likely to occur, from the unanimity required of the jury; a triumph to the practical men over the theoretical reasoners. What is natural too, the Court are now become of all people the most enamoured of the thing; they find it saves themselves so much trouble: The writers on the other hand are running it down, it shortens so much many promising law-suits and bills of costs. The country seem disposed to give it a fair trial; more talent and reputation on Adam's side would ensure it immediate popularity; but if the scheme, as first drawn out in their crude plan, be improved by degrees into a real system of trial by jury, its ultimate success and the advantages to be derived from it are certain. The loss is, that there is no direction of the great abilities that are to be found at this Bar, to the study and improvement of this institution as a novelty rather violently introduced into their jurisprudence, and which requires, to be adapted to it, some application of skill and contrivance and learning. The rules of evidence, for example, cannot remain the same, when the matter is to be decided upon the spot by men of plain unprofessional understandings, who have the advantage of seeing and confronting the witnesses; as when it was collected out of depositions, taken in absence of the judges, and which they have repeated opportunities of considering at leisure, and to the discussion of which they bring minds habituated to such examinations. The mode of trial by jury will also necessarily lead to a new method of stating and preparing, for the application of evidence to it, the question in dispute between the litigants; which is practised in the English system with much logical address and subtilty [sic], but in a form that belongs to the peculiar method of actions in that law, which is essentially different from the Scotch. It would be worth while, in some of the distinguished men that abound at this Bar, to seize the present occasion for examining these subjects deeply and upon principle, with a view to make the most of so remarkable an innovation as the legislature has been betrayed into; if turned to the best account, these juries are a foundation for something like popular liberty in Scotland. But all our friends are busied about other things, or do not see the importance of this.

1. Sir Thomas Miller (1731–1816), 5th Bart of Froyle, Whig MP for Portsmouth since 1806, had just died and on 9 Oct. was succeeded unopposed by John Carter, sen., afterwards Bonham-Carter (1788–1838), who also held the seat until his death.
2. Robert Morris, one of the MPs for Gloucester, where, until the Duke's death the previous December, the patronage had been shared with the Whig corporation by the 11th Duke of Norfolk, had also died in 1816 – the weather that year, winter and summer, was one of the worst on record – and was succeeded in an expensive by-election by Edward Webb (1779–1839), nominally independent but really a partisan Whig, who held the seat until 1832. (PH ii. 175–6 and v. 498.)
3. Robert Dundas of Arniston (1758–1819: DNB) was the fifth successive head of his family to have risen to the supreme bench of Scotland and to have represented Midlothian in Parliament. But he had married only in middle age and when he became Chief Baron in 1801 he had passed the seat to his cousin and brother-in-law, Robert Saunders Dundas, and, when Dundas succeeded as Viscount Melville in 1811 to Sir George Clerk, 6th Bart (1787–1867: DNB). This last may well therefore have been intended only as an interim arrangement until Dundas of Arniston's eldest son Robert (1797–1838) came of age. But in 1816 Robert Dundas junior was still only nineteen and even later on seemed far from anxious to resume the seat for his family. Clerk held Midlothian against Lauderdale's protégé, Sir John Dalrymple, afterwards 8th Earl of Stair (1771–1853: DNB), until the General Election of 1832, when his defeat, according to Cockburn (Journal of Henry Cockburn. Being a Continuation of the Memorials of his Time 1831–1854 (2 vols, 1874), i. 42), 'struck a blow at the very heart of Scottish Toryism'.
4. Despite the efforts made by Adm. Sir Philip Charles Durham, afterwards Henderson Calderwood Durham (1763–1845: DNB), Gen. Ronald Craufurd Ferguson of Raith (1773–1841: DNB) managed to hold on to Kirkcaldy Burghs from 1806 until 1830.
5. For extensive comment on the new Scottish jury court, see Horner's letters of 2 and 3 July to Murray (BLPES vii. 96–101).

619. From John Allen

BLPES vii. 135–6   Holland House, 20 Sept. 1816

. . .

. . . Abercromby is to arrive at Paris today. I am anxious for his return to know what is the opinion at Paris of the late measures of the Government and what is likely to be the complexion of the new Assembly. The want of money I hear was the real cause of the dissolution of the last, the moneyed men positively refusing to advance a shilling to the Government unless the Assembly was dissolved. The King seems already to be repenting of his own act and will probably pursue the same half measures that brought his brother to the scaffold. We have lately had accounts of Napoleon. He is busy with the history of his own life and has already brought down his narrative to the battle of Eylau, and I am told he is desirous of publishing it without delay. . . .

I have a letter from Brougham who is in Milan. He says the Princess of Wales is coming home, but she is detained somewhere in a long quarantine, so that he has no chance of seeing her, with which he seems not to be at all dissatisfied. . . .

620. From Lord Holland

BLPES vii. 141–6 ⟨Horner, ii. 369–70⟩   [Holland House], 28 Sept. 1816

⟨. . .

⟨. . . I conclude you have heard that they have had the meanness to abridge some of the few comforts which they had left within the reach of Bonaparte and even thrown new obstacles in the way of his acquiring intelligence of what is passing and securing to himself the satisfaction of communicating to the world and posterity his views and knowledge of what has passed.[1] We must at least take care that some of the base lies of 1815 shall not receive the same credit with posterity as they have done in our time.⟩ . . .[2]

⟨We hear no more of dissolution. The King was seriously ill some few days ago, which would force one. There is a report of bad news from North America.[3]

⟨I think sinecures will not be able to stand the clamour. Apropos to that subject, I and your friends ought to take shame to ourselves for not stating when first the subject was started the real state of the case with respect to your commissionership.[4] It was natural to hold such vulgar calumny cheap but I believe the people are in a temper where they listen to such lies with such pleasure and even draw inferences as to public measures of men upon them, more than they have done for years.⟩

I don't think Brougham or the pamphlet will make much of the Princess of Wales. I know not how you feel on these subjects but I am determined never to consider the squabbles of that race, as any criterion of party principle or opinion, and think that it [is] as foolish as it is base to use them as instruments.

1. A statute of April 1816 had made unauthorized contact with St Helena a capital offence, and Holland had entered a Protest on 8 Apr. declaring the policy of the British Government 'unworthy the magnanimity of a great country'. (Lean, p. 186.)
2. There follows in the manuscript letter a lengthy account of French politics as well as a tirade against the principle of legitimacy and the conduct of the Allies.
3. The 'bad news' from America was perhaps the protectionist tariff.
4. As Horner had apparently feared early in the 1816 session (Doc. 601), the Whigs had proved incapable of controlling the campaign for economical reform. By the autumn Henry Hunt and his 'radical' colleagues were attacking all public men, and Horner's earlier lucrative appointment as one of the commissioners for the payment of the debts of the Nabob of Arcot was among the sinecures he criticized. (S. Maccoby, *English Radicalism, 1786–1832* (1955), p. 314.)

621. To Henry Hallam

BLPES vii. 176–80 ⟨Horner, ii. 378–80⟩   Holland House, 14 Oct. 1816

⟨. . .

⟨I have made up my mind to a system of exclusive attention to my health, for some time.⟩ . . . ⟨From all I hear, Pisa, or some one of the small towns in that part of Tuscany, will be the best residence for me during the three or four months of winter;

if my health improves, I shall be tempted to go farther south about the end of March, for I do not mean to come back till the east winds have ceased to blow here. . . .⟩ . . . ⟨I shall be anxious and nervous about public matters at home, till this lowering winter is over, and most of all about the state of the public mind, which I look upon as very diseased at present, and much inclined to give ear to quack doctors and to try the experiment of violent prescriptions. As the people never dies, we shall get through the actual malady, and become prosperous again; but I dread what sacrifices we may be tempted to make of essential principles of policy, and especially of those which guard and consecrate property.

⟨Upon the subject of the public debts, I look upon the whole body of country gentlemen to be altogether unprincipled; as eager and sharp set for rapine, as the Jacobins ever were for their acres.[1] Then you have a very feeble Ministry, and,⟩ with the exception of Lord Liverpool himself and Lord Harrowby, not composed of men of honesty. ⟨Between their financial difficulties on the one hand, and the clamours of the idle-headed reformers on the other, I fear they will be base enough to make compromises that will produce no real ease to the state, but which will leave the lasting mischief of bad example and violated principle. Never were virtue and good sense on the part of the House of Commons more fervently to be prayed for. If under such a conjuncture as the present they shall compel the reduction of the army, and at the same time strengthen the Government with an efficient system of taxation, abstaining from all predatory inroads upon property of any description, they will make our liberties immortal; and if they do not do all this, these liberties have not much longer to survive.

⟨. . .⟩

1. As Horner later explained to Lord Holland (Doc. 630), his reference to the Jacobinical tendencies of the squirearchy arose from a growing opinion among them that Government should renounce the payment of interest on much of the public debt contracted during the war, a cause which Cobbett ironically embraced and included among the ten reasons for parliamentary reform he listed in Oct. 1816 in his famous *Letter to Sir Francis Burdett* (*Cobbett*, pp. 207–208).

622. To Lady Holland

BLPES vii. 192–3   Paris, Sunday evening, [27 Oct. 1816]

. . .

Canning is here. He is looked upon by the ultras as their best friend. I have never seen the discourse which he preached at Bordeaux on the principles of legitimacy, but as it was translated and circulated by order of the King, some of my friends in the House of Commons ought to look into it before the meeting.[1] . . .

. . .

1. Canning had visited Bordeaux earlier in the year in order to establish his family there before returning to England to take over the Board of Control, and again in October to bring them home. But, while some unfavourable mention of a speech he made on the first

visit afterwards appeared in the English press (MC, 27 May and 22 Nov. 1816), the editors
have found no copy or summary of it. On the way back from the second, he spent six weeks
in Paris – his first visit.

623. To Lady Holland

BLPES vii. 194–5 ⟨Horner, ii. 384–5⟩   Paris, 29 Oct. 1816

⟨. . .

⟨Ward lives within three doors of us, and has been here repeatedly, very pleasant
and entertaining; he sat by my bedside yesterday, that is my sofa, while Leonard
went to see Talma in Hamlet.[1] His master, he says, is to remain some time longer
here; a fortnight or more: and he seems to suspect, that Canning, besides
reconducting his lady home, has some political reason for being here at this time,
but he evidently makes no confidences of that sort with Ward. Canning is of
opinion, that the Ultras are about to commit a great fault, in declaring themselves
for a free press; and he tells them so: the spirit of a party question carries them for the
moment so far out of their own element, that an old emigrant magistrate, whom I
knew in London, a *President à mortier* of one of the Parliaments, and who in all his
opinions is for every thing of the old regime, maintains that nothing will save France
but the liberty of the press. This is not founded, that I can hear, upon any
speculation that the country might be roused by the press to any declaration in
favour of their views; but was suggested first by the proceedings against
Chateaubriand's pamphlet,[2] and is kept up by feeling that they have here a change
and a general question to debate in which they will have the general feeling of the
nation with them against the Ministers. But besides this, and accusations of undue
and unconstitutional influence in the elections, with which they are to open their
campaign, they talk of other popular questions, such as abolishing the qualification
of age for the chamber of deputies, enlarging the number of that assembly, and
giving it the initiative. I am afraid the ultras have more of the discipline as well as
zeal of a party, than any of their rivals.

⟨I told you of Madame de Souza's kindness to me, in preparing for my arrival, and
coming to see me immediately; she has paid me a visit every day, and while she had
the goodness to amuse me by conversing in my hearing, she enforced your
instructions in prohibiting me from taking a part. There is something very pleasing
in her affection for her son and her anxiety on his account. . . .⟩[3]

1. The celebrated actor François-Joseph Talma (1763–1828).
2. During the Hundred Days François René, Vicomte de Chateaubriand (1768–1848), had
   published a *Rapport sur l'état de la France* (Ghent, 1815), proposing among other things a
   more liberal policy towards the press. A falsified edition was subsequently published in Paris
   in which he was made to advocate almost precisely the opposite.
3. Flahault's mother (d. 1836) had married, as her second husband, Dom José Maria de Souza
   Botelho Mourão y Vasconcellos (1758–1825). No doubt Horner had repeated to Lady
   Holland what he had written to W. Adam from Dryden on 27 Sept. (BLPES vii. 137–8):

I certainly do not get worse, and have no symptoms yet that appear to be more than warnings to take care of myself. I have been consulting Drs Gregory and Hamilton, and am to see them again on Sunday, when they will pronounce judgement; I expect it to be a sentence of imprisonment without hard labour. Gregory said already, 'No vociferation, Sir, even if you are paid for it.' This is hard enough upon one of my craft.

624. From John Allen

BLPES vii, 200–201   Holland House, 4 Nov. 1816

. . .

. . . The riots and disturbances of the Country will I fear be a strong and prevailing argument against any farther reduction of the Army than the Ministers themselves choose to propose. Cobbett seems so thoroughly persuaded that parliamentary reform is at hand, that he is at pains to persuade the people to trouble themselves about nothing else, and he is fool enough to think that that [sic] by a few fine words he can console the Clergy into an approbation of his views.[1] Ministers or at least their newspapers are evidently enjoying the present bustling activity of the reformers as the best security against any change whatever. In the mean time the distress of the Country increases. Rents are worse paid than they were last year, and the crop is turning out so ill, that in many parts of the Country they have not a bushel of corn fit for seed.

. . .

1. For accounts of the riots in the industrial cities of the north and of Cobbett's campaign for a reform of Parliament in late 1816, see *Cobbett*, pp. 201–213.

625. To Mrs Dugald Stewart

BLPES vii. 206–207 ⟨*Horner*, ii. 386–7⟩   Lyons, 6 Nov. 1816

⟨. . .

⟨I saw Ward at Paris, where he talks of remaining during the winter; and I could not help envying him the opportunity of seeing so near at hand the proceedings of a most critical era in the history of French liberty. Not that we should probably take the same sort of interest in the same things. When I talk of the moment as critical for French freedom, it is not that I expect any sudden turn of affairs, or that I have heard of any thing like a party politically formed in favour of liberal institutions. Quite the reverse. The few friends of rational liberty that are to be heard of, seem broken-hearted, and they are systematically excluded from the public assemblies. But I cannot believe that a deliberate assembly, with a party in opposition to the existing Administration, can regularly meet and debate in the present circumstances of this country, without gaining some ground for the action of public opinion; however ill the assembly may be constituted, and however miserable the views and intrigues of the contending factions that compose it. The accidental jostling of their wretched interests has produced this whimsical and fortunate combination, that the Ultra-royalists are to attack the Ministers for breaches of the law in the late elections, and to press upon them the urgency of more freedom for the press, and of a better constitution for the chamber of deputies. Is it not reasonable to conclude that these things are considered as deeply seated in the wishes of the nation at large, when such a party as the Ultras force themselves into topics so revolting to their real sentiments, in order to play the game of popularity against their antagonists? The nation at large seems quite idle and calm upon all those political discussions; but there is a preponderating weight of settled opinions and habits; and, what is as good, of proprietary interests, all leaning one way. I am inclined to think that it is as much at this day, as it was in 1789, a question between the whole people on one side, and a handful of nobles and priests on the other; with this difference, that the contest is not with the nation wild and zealous and full of ardour for immediate action in politics, but with the nation in full possession of equal rights sanctioned by law, and conscious of a real enjoyment in the possession of that civil equality. No counter-revolution can destroy this; however the presence of foreign forces may retard the acquisition by the people of a direct share in the political administration of their affairs. It is impossible to see and hear of the present condition of the French people in detail, without a conviction that the solid benefits sought by the Revolution for them are permanently secured and already substantially enjoyed.

⟨. . .⟩

626. From John Allen

BLPES vii. 225–6   Brighton, 20 Nov. 1816

. . .

. . . The distress of the agricultural and manufacturing districts continues unabated, but trade, I am told, begins to revive a little, and there never was greater plenty of money in the City. Stocks rise very slowly in consequence of vague apprehensions of some measure being adopted at the meeting of Parliament that may prove injurious to the stockholder, but Exchequer bills bear a high premium, as they are conceived at present to be the safest mode of investing capital. Cobbett, Hunt and other fellows of that description are doing what mischief they can, but I have not heard as yet that they have excited any serious alarm. Burdett, I am told, affects to be offended at finding himself coupled with Hunt, but he must either submit to the co-partnership or break with his coadjutors. He is at Brighton at present with his son, who has met with an accident. They talk of a Wiltshire meeting for retrenchment and economy. . . . And I should fear that the Duke of Somerset, Paul and Gordon will hardly be equal to a contest with Hunt unless they have some other assistance.[1] Lord Lansdowne's absence is in this view most unfortunate at the present crisis. Indeed there never was a time when the Whigs might do more good to the country by calling and attending public meetings. But to do so with effect, they must have, what they have not at present, some definite and intelligible system of politics, foreign as well as domestic. In the latter subject parliamentary reform is the difficulty, on which it is impossible they can ever agree with the present agitation of the populace, but on which they must be prepared to give an opinion at any public meeting where they come forward. ...

. . .

1. The radical Henry Hunt lived in Wiltshire and was politically active there. Somerset was a Wiltshire magnate, as was also of course Lansdowne; while John Dean Paul, afterwards 1st Bart (1775–1852), was a banker with west country interests and Robert Gordon (1786–1864), MP for Wareham and a strong retrenchment man, had considerable property in Wiltshire as well as the West Indies and was toying with the idea of offering himself for the county. Gordon acted as Whig spokesman at the Wiltshire county meeting about this time. (PH iv. 37–8.)

627. From John Allen

BLPES vii. 234–5   Holland House, 5 Dec. 1816

. . .

This country is at present in a most deplorable state. The corn deficient in quantity and bad in quality – the potatoes spoiled by the frost – no work for the poor – no rents for the rich – a deficiency of 17 millions in our revenue and no reduction of our expenditure. Cobbett infusing his weekly poison into the ears of a starving population and Parliament prorogued to the 28th of January. Whether Ministers wish for disturbances in order to stifle the cry for reform, or seek merely to put off the evil day as long as possible or require time to make the Ministerial arrangements that will be necessary if Lord Liverpool should go abroad, as it is confidently reported, I cannot tell you, but the delay in assembling Parliament at a time when the country is in general ferment from distress is most inexcusable, as nothing but Parliament is capable of allaying discontent when it is groundless or of satisfying the people where they have reason to complain. In the mean time it is most essential for the Whig party to settle what course they mean to follow with respect to reform, and now that Tierney has returned from France the subject I hope will be taken into serious consideration.[1] They cannot too soon or too strongly draw a line of separation between themselves and Cobbett, Hunt and other partisans of annual parliaments and universal suffrage, but if they wish to retain any character or influence in the Country, they must also make up their minds as to what reforms, both economical and parliamentary, they are ready to support, and having done so, to leave the public no longer in doubt with respect to what they will do and what they will not do. If there are no disturbances or plots that excite alarm as in 1793 I have little doubt there will be great economical reforms in the next Session of Parliament. The distress of the country and the opinions of the public will enforce measures of this description, whoever may be the Ministers, unless people are scared out of their wits as at the beginning of the French war by fear of the mob. And with the same reservation of no alarm being excited by Cobbett and his associates I think there is a chance of measures being carried to reduce the influence of the Crown in the House of Commons, provided they are chosen with judgement and brought forward with moderation, not as part of a general plan, but as separate measures, distinct and independent of one another.

All these hopes may be destroyed in one moment. Cobbett is working up the people to a frenzy in support of visionary and impracticable reforms. The general misery is procuring him a favourable hearing in every part of England. No one answers him except the Ministerial scribblers in the *Times* and *Courier*, who appear purposely to seek occasion to exasperate the people by reviling and abusing them. And Parliament which could alone allay this spirit is prorogued for two months. I am sometimes inclined to think that Ministers ask for disturbances in order to excite alarm and consolidate their own power without the necessity of any reform at all. But if it is so, they are playing a desperate game. The dissatisfaction of a single regiment might involve them and the nation in destruction, and who can answer for the troops, surrounded as they are and will be by scenes of misery on every side?

Vansittart intends, it is said, to cover the deficiency of the current year by a loan and to pay the interest out of the sinking fund, and a general idea has gone abroad that the whole of the sinking fund must be sacrificed, either to a reduction of the taxes, or to defray the expenses of the Government. And many persons, who used formerly to be steady supporters of Government but are now partakers in the general distress and full of apprehension from the state of the Country, declare themselves openly in favour of such a scheme. To mention only two persons whom we have seen lately, Lord Sheffield and Lord Egremont are both in favour of this measure.[2] Lady Liverpool's health, which requires, it is said, a milder climate during the winter, is the reason assigned for Lord Liverpool's intended resignation. And Bathurst and Castlereagh are reported to be competitors for his place, but all this may be unfounded rumour as well as another report in circulation that Lord Grenville has declined an offer made to him of being taken into office.[3] I have heard another report which I repeat to you as it was told me without vouching for its truth. It is said he [Grenville] has written to Lord Liverpool to say he was ready to give up the salary of his auditorship provided it was accompanied by other retrenchments of the same sort.[4]

. . .

---

1. Tierney had been in France on private business since July and had only returned on 1 Dec.
2. George O'Brien Wyndham, 3rd Earl of Egremont (1751–1837: *DNB*), and John Baker Holroyd, 1st Earl of Sheffield (1735–1821: *DNB*), were both large landowners in England and Ireland.
3. There were indeed anxieties about Lady Liverpool's health that year and the Government was somewhat demoralized. The Prime Minister therefore was apparently anxious for some sort of junction with the Grenvilles, but while Buckingham was more than willing his uncle was not. (See Sack, pp. 170–78.)
4. On 7 Feb. 1817 Castlereagh announced that the Cabinet was prepared to surrender unnecessary offices and sinecures expenditure and, in emulation of a substantial voluntary reduction in the Prince Regent's personal income from the civil list, that the Ministers too

would forego 10% of their salaries and invited others to do the same. The general opinion of the House, however, was that this was not enough and Ponsonby responded at once by undertaking to match in his pension the larger proportionate reduction taken by the Prince; others, including subsequently the two Grenvilles, declared their willingness to take the 10% cut in their income from sinecures. The Government then headed off further motions for retrenchment by announcing on 19 February their intention on the death of the present incumbents to abolish a number of sinecures, including those of the Grenvilles and the four Tellers of the Exchequer. (See Mitchell, p. 104.)

According to the *DNB*, when an unsuccessful attempt was made in 1812 to limit the income of the Tellers, one of them, Marquess Camden, a Teller for over fifty years, from 1780 until their abolition in 1834, 'from that moment' relinquished all the income amounting (presumably over the whole of the period 1812–1834) to over a quarter of a million and received the formal thanks of Parliament for it. The facts, however, seem rather more complicated and a little less impressive. Following the 1812 attack, Camden and one of his fellow Tellers, the 1st Marquess of Buckingham (whose income from it he himself estimated to be £14,500 a year – an amount even his brother suggested had outstripped the value of his services to the state: see *Grenville*, p. 428), undertook for the duration of the war only to forego one-third of the income, and, in addition, in the event that that income in any year during wartime should exceed that of 1812, the whole of the excess. In 1819, when the amount thus donated by Camden was calculated at £45,000, he undertook to give up for life what was described as 'the surplus income of his office, amounting, in time of peace, to about £9,000 a year', for which voluntary action he received many congratulations but not, apparently, any formal vote of thanks. (*AR* liv (1812), 150–51, and lxi (1819), 70–71.)

Buckingham's office of Teller had passed on his death in 1813 to Perceval's eldest son, but the younger Grenville brothers Thomas and William still held respectively those of Chief Justice in Eyre, worth £2,000 a year, and Auditor of the Exchequer, worth £4,000 a year. When in paid office, the recipients were expected to forego some part of their combined emoluments, and this was often a sore point in Lord Grenville's various negotiations for office, since he considered his income otherwise inadequate. (*Grenville*, pp. 300 and 435–7; *Colchester*, ii. 603.) Tom Grenville's sinecure was abolished in 1817, but William's survived until his death in 1834.

628. To J.A. Murray

BLPES vii. 236–7 ⟨Horner, ii. 399–402⟩   Pisa, 6 Dec. 1816

. . .

⟨It gives me great pain to hear such distressing accounts as are sent from England and Scotland of the scarcity, and the want of employment for the people. Their sufferings are, I fear, most severe, and will not admit of relief for months to come. In addition to other evils, we shall experience on this occasion one of the worst consequences of that sad job of the country gentlemen, the corn bill; for England will by its operation get no foreign grain till the prices are at the highest, and after all other countries have supplied their wants; and that means nearly all Europe. At Leghorn there is great activity in the corn trade, bringing wheat from the Levant and the Black Sea, the most from Alexandria: Leghorn is no doubt a port of deposit, where our merchants may still find it, when the declaration of the average at the end of the right number of months (such formal nonsense⟩ and interested hypocrisy ⟨makes one angry at the words) shall apprise them that they may send out orders;

but from what I could learn, what was brought from the East was sent away again very quickly to the coasts within the straits, Italy itself, the south of France, and to Spain, in all of which countries the harvest is short.⟩
      . . .[1]

1. There follows a passage relating to Murray's collaboration with Holland in framing a bill to mitigate the severity of legal punishment in Scotland. For further comment see Doc. 631.

629. To Lady Holland

BLPES vii. 248–9   Pisa, 20 Dec. 1816

. . .

   I am not quick to believe the stories of Lord Liverpool's resignation; indeed, how could he with honour give up the government, at a moment of such difficulties and disaster? It would be a reproach for the rest of his life. I feel still more certain of another thing, that neither Court nor Courtiers will succeed in talking over Lord G[renville]; who has made up his mind, if any man ever did, to his own view of matters, which unfortunately does not coincide with ours on the grand subject of interference abroad, but tallies still less with that of the Court on others which they think more important.
      . . .[1]

1. The letter was completed on 21 Dec.

630. To Lord Holland

BLPES vii. 252–3 ⟨Horner, ii. 412–17⟩   Pisa, 21 Dec. 1816

⟨. . .

   ⟨I rejoice to hear you say, that the system of maintaining legitimates in foreign countries at the expense of English treasure and character has lost its popularity; I feared it was too early for that subject to be seen by the English in its true light, for though they always get at the true sense of things in the end, they rarely come to it in time, nor until they have paid deeply for it. It is the great theme for parliamentary discussion, coupled with that of the reduction of the army, which is closely connected with it, both upon the grounds of economy, and upon all the true and enlarged principles of political liberty. I hope when Parliament meets, these questions, so joined together, and taken upon their broadest ground, will be urged repeatedly; not merely in the protest of one solemn debate, which saves the consciences of the speakers, but does not work upon the public. What I dread is, that in the House of Commons there will be nothing but the old song of sinecures and reversions; which we learned from the unreasonable narrow-minded democrats, and in our turn have been teaching it so exclusively to the excellent Whig party among the gentry and middle orders of England, that more general and generous notions of constitutional liberty and foreign politics are no longer so familiar or acceptable to them as they were formerly. As to sinecures, the line we have hitherto taken on that subject seems to me still the most reasonable, and it ought to be adhered to with firmness; to concur in their abolition or regulation, but to protect all existing interests as property. As long as the subject would bear discussion, I think the argument was much in favour of sinecures, under our form of government; and that their existence, as a fund of distribution by statesmen among themselves (to put it in the plainest terms), was an additional security given to the democracy, for the efficacy of what we justly reckon one of the best marks of our freedom, that a man may rise from the humblest rank to the highest office: the democracy, however, have scouted all such arguments, and I take the discussion to be at an end; at least while the present stigma is upon such places, no man, who hopes by means of public confidence and reputation ever to do any public good, would be indiscreet enough to come near them.

⟨But though this view of the subject would carry me so far in the cry against sinecures, as to join in their future abolition, no outcry, nor any public pressure, should ever prevail upon me to touch them in the present hands of those who got them, and hold them by a legal title. I cannot see this in any light but robbery; which may be committed by Parliament, with as much injustice and violence as by a highwayman. It is a ticklish thing to begin to draw subtle distinctions about property; and the last philosopher I would trust with such a perilous experiment, is a popular assembly in an hour of national necessity and heat. Perhaps one grudges⟩ such a dolt ⟨as Lord Camden his vast drafts of public money; with the same feeling, one might still grudge the Pagets, for instance, their exorbitant grants from Henry VIII for no one service rendered to the people, and no one memorable action performed by the family in any age of our history. If the House of Commons take away Lord Camden's grant of the Tellership, which was given him perhaps fifty years ago, why should not they proceed to take back also to the crown Lord Somers's manor of Ryegate which was granted about fifty years earlier? The greater length of time is nothing in the argument; for prescription is the mere creature of law, which by the argument is to have no efficacy against reasons of state necessity; besides, the law has created no prescription in this case, judging it unnecessary, the grants being good in law from the first moment. Then it may be said, Lord Somers's ancestor did great things for the country, and earned great rewards: will it be for the democratic purists of the present day to say, that the first Lord Camden deserved none? I think this is a point of the very first importance, considering what sort of discussions may be broached in the ensuing session; and the principles, by which property is guarded from public rapine, ought to be inculcated with authority and a strong hand.[1]

⟨The question of parliamentary reform is with me a far more doubtful one, and attended with many difficulties which I have never yet solved to my own satisfaction; at least that part of it which respects the rotten burghs, which is the only thing the democrats are struggling for, and that out of their envy and hatred of the aristocracy, not from jealousy of the crown. I have sometimes thought their object a salutary one for our liberties upon the whole, but I am ashamed to say I have no clear nor fixed opinion yet upon that part of the subject. There are others, and important ones, in which the reformers are clearly right; though for other reasons, than they commonly assign. I do not know what I should think justifiable, if I were a radical reformer, and were bold enough to make the experiment of a new scheme of representation, but in my present views of that question there is nothing I would do more resolutely, than to disclaim, if I had any name to carry weight with it, the idea of forcing this subject upon Parliament, when such mighty difficulties of immediate pressure demand all its attention, and the folly (in some individuals, the palpable wickedness) of connecting the present sufferings of the people with any thing in the state of the representation. Pitt was the first demagogue who propagated this fallacy, which has been flung back upon his own course of measures with ample retribution. It is used at present so falsely, in my opinion, that, ever since I have sat in the House, I should say, that, in its worst votes upon all great state questions of peace and war, it has been in unison with the passions of the people: there is but one seeming exception, the vote on the Walcheren business, but which when looked at a little deeper than the surface, instead of proving the power of the Ministers of that day to carry a question in the House against the sense of the public, really proved the sense which the House had of its own power at that crisis to choose ministers, and its decided preference, in concurrence with the public one must say, of one set of men over the other.

⟨I am not at all surprised to hear that Lords Egremont and Sheffield, two names oddly coupled but very well for this service, are declared against the sinking fund; they are just for the expedient of the day that will help things on another year, at whatever sacrifices of the reasons, and pledges too, involved in their former votes. To the extent of a certain sum, there is a positive pledge of Parliament to the creditors that the fund shall not be touched. Taking what remains beyond that, is only shifting for half a year, and giving up for that the certainty of a great future relief for which we have been paying annually for thirty years large sums. If the sinking fund is let alone for a few years, there will be in our financial history a rare example of provident, persevering, and successful forbearance; if it is violated, and by Pitt's own creatures, it will be just as remarkable an instance of extravagance, facility, and deception. While there is a regiment or an office to reduce, I would not touch a hair of its head. The country gentlemen in the House of Commons are, upon this subject, some of them, the most arrant Jacobins; they consider the whole body of the stockholders as fair game; that is, they have gone on borrowing from monied men, campaign after campaign, without thinking of the consequences; and when the whole amount of interest to be paid for the money they have spent presses hard upon them, they say, these men who ask for their interest are a set of plunderers who have been making money by the war.

⟨On the reduction of the army, it seems to me we cannot wish for any thing better in debate, than that the Ministers should dare to use as an argument for their high establishment the existence or probability of riots. That would put the discussion upon great topics, such as the public ought once more to hear from their Whigs in Parliament. The civil force must of course look for its radical support to military hands; but to pretend, that England needs for that purpose any thing like⟩

even ⟨so many forces as we should consent for other reasons to vote, would be a sound so new in the English Parliament, that I hope you will make the whole land ring with it.

⟨ . . .⟩

1. As one of the principal advisers of Henry VIII, William, 1st Baron Paget (1506–1563: DNB), had obtained considerable grants of property from the King, but also as a member of council during the minority of Edward VI. Similarly, John, 1st Baron Somers (1651–1716: DNB), Lord Chancellor under William III, had been rewarded, among other things, with the manors of Ryegate and Horley.

631. To J.A. Murray

BLPES vii. 256–7 ⟨Horner, ii. 407–12⟩ Pisa, 21 Dec. 1816

. . .

John ⟨Clerk's opinion will not make me think that there was no injustice done in the Ayrshire case.[1] There was an absolute failure of justice, upon a point of form, after infinite delay. If he and others think nothing wrong in the existing laws, I am certain that was not the opinion of Lord Eldon in that cause; and I should have expected some of those you name to have been at least as quick as he to see and admit defects that touch the liberty of the subject.⟩ If your Act 1701 is perfect, or at least not to be touched without doing harm, the subsequent Acts of Parliament, which altered some parts of it, and raised the penalties on one side but not on the other, do not seem under the same protection of professional prejudice. I hope Lord Holland will at all events bring forward his bill; and that you have drawn him one for the objects he had in view, if it do not embrace those farther objects which I think it might; he cannot but consider himself as pledged to the measure by his notice, and if you dislike putting the thing into form because your friends have given you reasons against it, I shall regret very much indeed that my incapacity last summer for any exertion made me leave it undone. It was a relief to my mind, to think I had left it in so much better hands.

⟨Of all persons, those who give you the least aid, when any thing is to be done by legislation, are your ancient barristers; the two operations of mind, knowing what the laws are, and seeing what they had better be, seem almost incompatible.⟩ I have seen something of Clerk's disposition for mending the laws, in the progress of the jury business, from the first opportunity that offered itself in 1806; and as I felt then, that it was to his want of interest in that great question, coupled with a very inconsistent rashness, that the prejudices of the public were so harshly encountered, so I am sure on the recent occasion, if the command that his connection gave him had been used with any thing like knowledge of principles or a similar anxiety for improving the laws of Scotland, the measure would not have been so mutilated, and deformed with so little living principle in it, as it now appears.[2] ⟨But it is idle to regret the obstacles that exist to any amelioration of the constitutional laws of Scotland. Similar improvements in England have⟩ never[3] ⟨been the work of lawyers, but have been forced upon them, or carried through in spite of them, by the public voice upon some crying instance, like that Ayrshire case, or by the efforts of individuals unconnected with the legal profession. In Scotland you have no public voice; for you have neither a popular meeting nor a political press.

⟨You leave me in doubt, whether you adopt Clerk's opinion, when you state it, that the laws of Scotland and their administration are particularly lenient to all persons liable to imprisonment. Under the actual administration, ought to be included the state of your prisons; which, from what I have seen of some, and heard of many others, are a reproach to a civilized country. Another branch of actual administration is the practice, upon your circuits, of 'deserting the Diet', at the discretion of an Advocate-Depute; by which, I have been assured, in numberless instances, the imprisonment of persons accused has been prolonged from year to year, until it appeared that they had suffered confinement long enough even for guilt, and upon that principle they were discharged as persons, not tried indeed, but punished. You have the means of correcting me, if these are fictions. Another rigour in the administration of your laws, is the practice of committing indefinitely for further examination; under which I have been informed there have been recent abuses to a great extent. Let me add one more; the power your magistrates exercise, if legally or not I do not know, of condemning to long and even solitary imprisonment, upon their own conviction, without a jury, persons charged with police offences, or even offences of another description, such as that of the servant who assaulted and kissed his mistress. The things I have spoken of actually do happen; so much for lenient administration. I am not one of those theoretical innovators who are for squaring the letter of the laws to the ideal rules of a perfect justice; the correction and prevention of practical grievances is the best we need aim at. But there are some branches of the law, in which the possibility of wrong ought to be prevented, if by fresh guards the law can effect it; and the most important of these is the liberty of the subject. A single instance of abuse and oppression, like that from Ayrshire, on which I must insist still, ought to raise every voice for a law to make the repetition of such conduct impossible. To quit that instance, the capital defect of your law of imprisonment upon a criminal charge is, that it does not provide a certain infallible course of proceeding, to bring the accused person to trial, as early as the preparation of evidence will admit of. The law, which throws an innocent man into gaol, ought of itself to determine speedily whether he ought to be discharged or punished. Then you tell me of your act 1701, and that every man may run his letters; that is, with money he may, if he sets about it with good professional advice. But why should it be rendered necessary for him to take any steps? why do not his letters run by operation of law, without any movement or payment on his part? The law has made the first move, in taking him from his labour, his family, his liberty; ought it not to go on, and, with every degree of speed that is consistent with a due execution of justice, ascertain a point so important to this man, if he is innocent, the question of his innocence or guilt? Here then is a principle, the introduction of which would be a practical improvement of your law; keep the phraseology of the act 1701, but let the letters run by operation of the statute. Reverting here to the actual administration again, I speak with very imperfect information, but my impression is, that it is not a matter of course for every prisoner to take immediate steps for running his letters; that when he has recourse to it, there are difficulties and delays from his having already lost time, and from the formalities of the law; that there is a sufficient field for the chicane of such practitioners as minister to the wants of prisoners; and that the amount of fees is such as cannot fall light upon a man in the condition of living by his daily labour.

⟨I see nothing in Clerk's other arguments: he dreads discussion: you will not learn that of him. Is any good ever done in England but by discussion? This is a hint worthy of some of my present acquaintance in ecclesiastical habits on the Lung'-Arno. But jurisconsults, after a certain age, get wonderfully ecclesiastic in their ways of thinking. 'It will be a long time before the new law is understood and executed' – that is an argument I will not answer. He thinks it better to preserve the present severity of penalties against the magistrate who misconducts himself; that is the part of the new bill on which I am least anxious. One use of it was to conciliate the magistrates in favour of the rest. I question, however, the solidity of Clerk's reasoning; he ought to show that the penalties have, in any instance, been enforced, and that the court has never shrunk from doing justice upon a complaint on account of their severity. I believe they are an instance among a thousand, that there is no surer device for impunity, if that is the real drift, than to enact a punishment such as nobody could think of enforcing.

⟨I ought to ask your forgiveness for worrying you at such length upon this subject. I feel it to be mere Utopia, to talk of improvements in the law of Scotland; one has nobody to go to but the lawyers, and they never favoured in any country the improvement of the law. This would be too saucy, if I were not a bit of a lawyer myself; and if I had not, in more instances than one, caught myself sliding down into Westminster Hall superstitions.

⟨. . .⟩

1. John Andrew, an Ayrshire shoemaker who had been incarcerated for supposed seditious practices, had unsuccessfully brought an action for wrongful imprisonment under the provisions of the statute of 1701, against John Murdoch, sheriff-substitute of the county.
2. Clerk had been connected to the Lord Chief Justice since 1810 by the marriage of a cousin to Ellenborough's niece. For his role in the jury court business see *Cockburn*, p. 207.
3. Leonard Horner changed this to 'seldom'.

632. From Lady Holland

BL Add. MSS 51644   Holland House, 27 and 28 Dec. 1816

. . .

L[auderdale] writes me word that Lord G[rey] is full of ardour and ready to believe anything, stories of Castle pilfering, etc., etc. Ponsonby writes that Trade in Ireland is reviving but the Revenue growing worse, rather an Irish proposition to maintain. L[auderdale] says he will come up to consult with our friends before the meeting, but despairs of any good being done as neither parliament reform nor the abolition of sinecures, the grand remedies suggested by popular clamour, can cure or palliate the diseases of the Country; the only wise line he allows will be to confine their efforts *solely* to insist upon Parliamentary investigations of the real state of the Country and of its *Finance*.[1] From all I hear the distress of the country is quite insufferable, and it has produced a mass of discontent which is unfortunately ill-directed, as the people pretend to believe that a parliamentary reform will dissipate their distress, and seeing this object of relief only, are indifferent about the real pinching causes, such as large establishments, foreign policy, home expenses, etc., etc.

Friday

The sudden arrival of our great military man gives me hopes of some mischief brewing from whence he comes. The sudden arrival of the Duke of W[ellington] puzzles – he came unexpectedly in the night. The contributions avowedly are delayed for two months. . . .[2]

1. Owing to insurmountable disagreement within the ranks of Opposition on every public issue, domestic and foreign, Grey shortly embraced Lauderdale's call for a 'strict and solemn inquiry into . . . the state of the country'. (Grey to Lambton, 17 Jan. 1817, Mitchell, p. 102.)
2. By the Second Peace of Paris of 20 Nov., France was subjected, among other things, to a three-to-five-year occupation by 150,000 troops under Wellington and fed at French expense. This last seemed an impossible burden to some who thought it could most easily be lightened by reducing the size of the army itself. For a time Wellington wavered between immediate or deferred concession, but on 26 Dec. he had made a lightning visit to London in order to tell Castlereagh he had changed his mind about the necessity of maintaining the army in France, and now advocated a substantial reduction. (Longford, pp. 34 and 36.)

633. From John Allen

BLPES vii. 258–9   Holland House, 28 Dec. 1816

. . .

We go to . . . Woburn, where . . . we shall stay till Lord Grey's arrival . . . and there Tierney has agreed to meet him and concert measures for the ensuing campaign. It seems agreed there should be an amendment and a division in the Commons on the 1st day. Every one is agreed on the necessity of economy and retrenchment, but these are the only points on which one does not meet with a diversity of opinions. There is a very general cry against sinecures in which many of the friends of Ministers participate, and Lord L[iverpool], who has a pleasure in opposing any thing that is popular, is the only person I have yet heard who is inclined to defend them. The violent reformers will have few or no supporters in the House. Even Burdett is said to be disgusted with them. But there are many who will declare themselves friends of moderate reform, without however agreeing in any one plan or affixing the same ideas to that word. Some are for a place bill – others for biennial parliaments, and Lord Folkestone I hear is for annual parliaments, but objects to every other sort of reform. If Tierney is encouraged by the aspect of the

House, he will be disposed I think to bring forward again, with alterations, his old bill about non resident Electors. Abercromby wishes the reformers would try their hand on Scotland, and for this session at least confine their labours to that part of the United Kingdom. But reform is not the only point on which men are divided. There are not two who are agreed as to the sort of relief that all agree must be found for our financial difficulties. Vansittart it is said means to propose a loan for the present year and to trust to Providence for the year following. The Country gentlemen who have got no money in the funds are desirous to take the whole or the half at least of the sinking fund and apply part of it to the expenses of this year and part of it to relieve the Country from some of the more oppressive of the taxes. Some have taken up Lord Lauderdale's plan and recommend a change in the value of the Currency[1] and others directly propose a reduction of interest on the national debt. Before any of these violent measures are adopted one should wish to see what can be effected by retrenchment. Much might be saved in the Ordnance, the army and the Household, and Ministers are said to be busily employed at present in devising means to lessen the expense in their different departments. The Prince is living soberly and economically at Brighton. Lord Bathurst has signified to the West India Colonies that they must contribute largely to the Military force necessary for their own defence, as it will be *impracticable* for the Mother Country any longer to maintain and pay the troops necessary for their protection. Reductions have been taking place in the regiments stationed in Ireland, and Clerks innumerable have been dismissed from all the public offices. But what the whole of this saving will produce, has not yet been stated. France has in the mean time stated her inability to pay the contributions settled by the last treaty, and has requested, 1st that part of the Allied force should be withdrawn, and 2ndly that the period for paying what is called the indemnity should be extended from five years to eight. The Duke of Wellington came to London, but whether on this business or not, is unknown, and this day he was to return to France. He is very much averse, as it is said, to any reduction of the force under his command. But if Russia agrees to it, both he and his master must submit to it. This is a very judicious step of old Lewis and will gain him much popularity in France, where the prevailing passion now, I am told, is hatred of the Allies and more especially of the English.[2]

1. See Doc. 521.
2. The letter is completed with a paragraph of 29 Dec.

634. From Lady Holland

BL Add. MSS 51644   Woburn, 30 Dec. [1816]

. . .

The most probable conjecture as to the cause of the Duke of W[ellington]'s sudden appearance is that it was to consult personally with him upon strengthening the Ministry, as he was expected to arrive the night of the day on which he came in

the morning. So Lady Castlereagh told the Duke of Bedford. Besides the Duke of
Sussex the day he dined with us (22nd Dec.) mentioned as a piece of news that
Ministers had sent to Cambray for him, and the day of his coming tallies exactly:
this makes me afraid we are not likely to cease being the mercenaries of the
Bourbons against their Countrymen, I cannot call them subjects.

. . . The brave indiscreet Knight is very busy in promoting his scheme of coming
in for Maidstone, where he is to stand upon the popular sentiment and rely upon
'your Voices, your Views'. Mr Palmer (Lady Madeline's husband) is actively
employed upon the same grounds at Reading. Allen has been writing a *grave* squib
for him against Mr Weyland a dull pamphleteer.[1] Many of the staunchest
Government members have answered the circular Treasury summons in the
negative, upon the score of being obliged to watch their re-elections and that were
they to attend their votes would not be of use to Ministers as they should consider
the wishes of their Constituents; in Hampshire Mr Heathcote has written to the
Treasury to say he shall not in future require their influence; if Lord Carnarvon were
in England Algernon Herbert might be started with a certainty of success.[2] The
Regent is much altered in his habits, especially as to his diligence and love of
business. His temper is become quite abominable, [and] insufferable to his servants.
Most of his old ones are dismissed and his Household new modelled by the
interference of Lady Hertford: the severity of the sentence against young Stanhope
was entirely his doing, as the officers and others were inclined to a more lenient
decision, but he was peremptory, chiefly to please the Lady on account of her
grandson, and partly from hatred to Lord Harrington, whom he has never pardoned,
since he declined voting with Ministers upon the Catholic question, a question he
told him that none could support but those who wanted to dethrone his family.[3]

. . .

[PS] The Duke laments your absence most sincerely. Lord Grey, Tierney [and]
Morpeth are coming here on the 6th to have a *Council* and it is confidently believed
that the present Government may be expelled, but who is prepared to succeed and
your absence from the House of Commons renders it impractical for our friends to
think of it.[4]

. . .

1. Gen. Sir Robert Wilson had been adopted as prospective candidate for Maidstone earlier in
   the year, but, warned by Grey that it was a 'dangerous place', he eventually opted for
   Southwark, free of all expense (*PH* ii. 218). Charles Fyshe Palmer (c.1770–1843), an
   advanced Whig who had an estate nearby and was married to Madelina, daughter of the
   4th Duke of Gordon, was returned for Reading in 1818 and held the seat until 1834 and
   again from 1837 until 1841. His unsuccessful opponent in 1818 was Sidmouth's friend,
   John Weyland (1774–1854: *DNB*), a barrister and writer on the poor laws.
2. Algernon Herbert (1792–1855: *DNB*), a scholar, was the youngest brother of the 2nd Earl
   of Carnarvon. The Herberts had already spent a good deal of money on the constituency,
   but gained for another brother William (1778–1847) only a brief tenure in 1806–1807. In
   any case the suggestion was abortive, Thomas Freeman-Heathcote, afterwards 4th Bart
   (1769–1825), the sitting Member, appearing after all in the Ministerial interest in 1818.
   (*PH* ii. 180–81.)
3. At a court martial in Cambrai in November, Lt Augustus Stanhope (1794–1831), the
   youngest son of Charles Stanhope, 3rd Earl of Harrington (1753–1829), had been found
   guilty of inveigling the sixteen-year-old Lord Beauchamp into a game of cards, in which

some £15,000 was lost, and discharged the service. (Bernard Falk, '*Old Q.'s Daughter: The History of a Strange Family* (2nd ed., 1951), pp. 92–4.) Richard Seymour, Lord Beauchamp (1800–1870), was Lady Hertford's grandson, the future 4th Marquess. Although the Prince Regent indeed confirmed the verdict, Harrington, who was Constable of Windsor Castle, seems to have remained the Prince's friend, and was his standard bearer at the coronation.

4. In a letter to Grey of 10 Jan. 1817 Holland advanced a similar view of Whig prospects, and having mentioned Horner's health and that 'he by the bye is nearer to Lauderdale's opinions about sinecures and mine about foreign politics than any of our friends', asked whether they should not make it clear to the public that they could and would form a Ministry, being prepared both with a First Lord of the Treasury and a Leader in the Commons. Grey's reply of the 17th did not overtly refer to Horner, but he accused Lauderdale of being 'quite wrong-headed' about sinecures, which he himself wished to attack for economy's sake, and felt that it was 'a little premature' to be talking about personnel. 'A Leader of the House of Commons you [already] have at present', he pointed out, 'though not perhaps possessing all the qualifications that you would wish for in that situation. But can you displace him, and appoint any other? If not, that question . . . is answered.' (Grey MSS, Durham University; Mitchell, p. 100, is a little misleading about this correspondence.)

635. To Lady Holland

BLPES vii. 265–6   Pisa, 4 Jan. 1817

. . .

The reasons for an amendment to the Address this Session, I have been trying to make out, but with no success; every argument seems against such a measure. The year 1810 was a period of war and war proceedings, that upon principle we opposed in the whole system. All the circumstances of the present day seem to me to concur in pointing out quite a different course, for the opening of opposition at this meeting. Surely our leaders are not to be led at this time to bring forward Parliamentary Reform, because Cobbett and the Sunday newspapers and Mr Hunt harp upon it, while it has no real place in the attention or thoughts of the country at large. If any of the gentlemen in the House of Commons who must shoot their bow for that sort of popularity, force on the question, the discussion to a certain extent becomes unavoidable, improper as the time is for it, with the country nowise for it, and so many other immediate objects pressing upon Parliament.

636. From Lord Holland

BLPES vii. 271–2 ⟨*Horner*, ii. 422–4⟩   Holland House, 10 Jan. 1817

⟨. . .

⟨We had persuaded Grey to come up soon, and prepared plans for consultation on the course of proceeding for the session, as well as the measures to be taken, both about men and things, if beyond our expectation, but not beyond all probability, the

Ministers should be beat. But, alas! the only time that I ever saw a prospect of good sound previous deliberation, a fortnight before the meeting of Parliament, Lord Grey is most painfully detained at Milton, nursing Lady Grey, who is taken ill of the scarlet fever, and fretting about his children, whom he has separated from her and the infection.

⟨I agree with you in most of your points, but not quite in the same degree. Retrenchment and economy, which must include suppression of sinecures in future, and as far as the rights of property (established by legal decision) admit, the reform of those now existing, as well as the reduction of many useless places, miscalled the splendour of the crown, are absolutely necessary to give any party, who wishes to do good, authority and weight with the people. They must go. The community are punished, and severely punished, for their base acquiescence in liberticide wars, by their present distresses. I am not so sorry for that as I ought to be, but let Ministers and the Court be punished too, and a useful lesson will be inculcated, that rash and unprincipled wars cannot be entered into without (even in the case of success) the people risking their prosperity, ministers their power and influence, and kings and courts a part of their beloved splendour. It is through the unpopularity of the expenditure that we must get at the foreign system of politics, which, in my conscience, I think the cause of it. As to parliamentary reform, the industry of the violent party, and the talents, I must own, of one among them,[1] seem to have made a deep impression; but I do not despair of getting over that difficulty well. There are many of our best friends out of Parliament, and many, too, who were not our friends till now, who are anxious to support retrenchment, and to change foreign policy, and to dismiss ministers, and yet, though reformers, are no great sticklers for any very violent reform, and are both disgusted and alarmed at the language of Cobbett, Hunt, and Cochrane. They are, I hear, of their own accord, and without any concert with us, to have a great dinner in Westminster, at which their resolutions will be such as we must all approve; though perhaps, on the subject of sinecures, some of them will be a little more peremptory than we could wish; but the fact is, they are eyesores, neither beautiful to the sight nor useful to the body; while they remain, we can make no progress in courting the community, and they must be lopped off.⟩ In Parliament I hear of many falling off from Ministers and more staying away. Of positive accessions to Opposition I have only heard of Lord Huntingfield[2] . . .

1. Apparently Cobbett, to whose 'able mischief' reference is made in *Holland's Further Memoirs*, p. 249.
2. The immensely wealthy Joshua Vanneck, 2nd Baron Huntingfield (1778–1844), had succeeded to the family seat of Dunwich only a few months before and was probably as ambiguous a supporter of Government as his father before him. For apparently he left no trace of any parliamentary activity whatever in the short period up to his retirement in February 1819. (*PH* v. 434–5.)

637. To Earl Grey

Grey MSS, Durham University
(copy in BLPES vii. 277–8) ⟨Horner, ii. 424–6⟩   Pisa, 14 Jan. 1817

⟨. . .

⟨You will think it natural for me to look forward, with great anxiety, to the meeting of Parliament: the future safety of the country depends so much, not only upon the measures relative to finance and expenditure which shall be adopted in the ensuing session, but upon the views of their real situation, which the intelligent and effective part of the community may be taught, by those statesmen in Parliament to whose opinions they look. Our financial embarrassments, I fear, are now of a very serious nature. Those in trade and agriculture, I am persuaded, have already past the worst, and at all events cannot be otherwise than of a temporary nature; the other difficulties, if not met on the part of the country with great firmness, and on the part of the legislature with the right measures, may endanger the Government itself and the whole system of our liberties. I have vast confidence, however, in the resources which are found in the freedom of our government for a contest with political calamities, and in the soundness of public opinion in England, when it is honestly instructed and trusted. The delusions, which appear to have spread among the lower classes of the people, unemployed and suffering, respecting the efficacy of indefinite reforms, as a cure for their actual misery, may, by neglect, and in a long continuance of such distress, rise higher, and threaten us with convulsions.

⟨But this is an evil for which a sure preventive has always been found hitherto in Parliament. When the first day of the session is over, I shall feel great impatience to know what has passed; for the sentiments and views given by leading men that day have more weight with the public, than the result of many subsequent debates. What I trust is, besides giving a right direction to the public anxiety, that the opposition to large votes of supply and establishment will be pursued in detail, from day to day, in the House of Commons, and that time will not be given to the Ministers, by propositions of inquiry upon a large scale, which have always ended in nothing. It is very presumptuous, however, in me, at this distance from what is going on, to suggest even my wishes upon these subjects.

⟨I have heard today of the Duke of Wellington's sudden journey from Cambray to London, and then to Paris. This looks like a prelude to some immediate measure of importance. The suspension of the contributions is a more important event, for the restoration of common sense in England upon foreign politics and military establishments, than one durst have hoped for so early.⟩

638. From Lady Holland

BL Add. MSS 51644   Holland House, 17 Jan. [1817]

. . .

I would willingly give you the particulars of the scene at Paris, but my impressions are very indistinct upon the subject. Indeed I think Tierney himself was not as clear as usual in his statement: as far as I recollect a few groups were drinking coffee and some waiting for their carriages. T[ierney] in his little corner heard some loud tones issuing from a party of which Tally was one. Attracted by curiosity to see what could cause the phlegm of such a man, he went up and heard him charge P[asquier] with the indecent interference of the Police upon the elections. This was repelled with vehemence and a disrespectful *oubli* of their former relative situations. Pasquier's carriage came first and he went in a straight line to the Thuilleries [sic] and reported to the King what had passed, a proceeding worthy of the worst *délateur* who ever came to his own office. The King ordered his Gentilhomme de Service to write to the Grand Chambellan and forbid him the Court. The Courtier obeyed, but paused and remonstrated observing that as a loyal subject he felt such gratitude to T[alleyrand] for having assisted in bringing about the present felicity of the country, that he could not write such a mandate without the Royal Warrant or Contre-seing [sic] or some such authority to justify the measure. I sent you the paper containing T[alleyrand]'s letter to Lord Castlereagh.[1]

. . .

This is from A. Baring's letter to me upon other subjects. After saying he goes to Paris tomorrow he adds

> I am not occupied with all the mischief which the Finance World of Paris and London impute to me, but in these times of dullness and distress I can not quite refrain from the indulgence of occupation.[2] Thanks for your account of Horner. I shall write to him from Paris any thing I think likely to amuse him.[3] {The accounts from [Lord] Milton are highly satisfactory.}[4] I have had a conference out of the window with Milton. He says both Fitzwilliam and Elliot seem rather averse to amendment, on the supposition that Ministers will promise largely on the subject of retrenchment. To my suggestion that they probably would add to those promises opinions such as they have expressed in their answers to addresses, and that the distress is temporary and is owing to the change from war to peace, in which it would be impossible for us to acquiesce; Milton admits that in that case, we might have an amendment. He is himself quite right; but I can see that both Fitzwilliam and Elliot have a hankering after the Army in France.

A[bercromby] will have told you all Tierney's hopes and of the dinner today, etc.[5] Waithman has opened a correspondence with Lord Holland in a very temperate and serviceable mood, but the reforming branch I leave to Allen and the amateurs and believers in the greasy Plebs. Lord Holland at the suggestion of some people wrote a friendly easy letter to Dropmore urging the necessity of attendance on the first day in the Commons and requesting his influence to bring up the Troops in his Wing of the Army. The reply is stiff and repulsive, rather confiding in the intentions of Government. Upon the frightful military establishment he [Grenville] says

on this subject necessity has proved as I am told a powerful ally to our cause, and if I am not misinformed there is now a real intention of bringing the Army within limits more consonant to our true policy, etc. . . . [sic] While people are mooting in conversation and in the newspapers whether we shall touch the Sinking fund, we have already actually taken the whole of it. This state of things presents a new and most difficult consideration, and one by [which the] calmest reflection of the most dispassionate man might and must feel itself infinitely embarrassed, but it surely is not one of party hostility.[6]

His great anxiety about his own consistency to which as we have seen he will at any time sacrifice the most important measures, increased love of solitude, the effect of court cajoling upon his mate, the duplicity and ruse of Wickham,[7] dislike of Mr Citizen [Tierney] as you call him, soreness upon sinecures and fifty other minor considerations make a formidable combination. Grey says upon this letter

I am not very much surprised at his backwardness. The truth is that he must feel that he has had his share in producing our present distresses, and that they necessarily and unavoidably bring the original principle and policy of the war into discussion.[8]

Enough of these dry chapters, but which are I know to you valuable and interesting and that God knows would make me read and learn finance even to please you.

. . .

1. Talleyrand's outburst, supposedly inspired by personal jealousy, took place at an official dinner at the British Embassy and consequently attracted the attention of the press. The *Courier* gave a critical account on 27 Nov. and on 13 Jan. the MC printed Talleyrand's dissimulating letter of 6 Dec. 1816. (See also Mrs Edward Stuart Wortley, *Highcliffe and the Stuarts* (1927), p. 250.)
2. French finances were now so badly strained that Wellington had proposed a loan from Baring's Bank. The contract for the first such loan was signed in Paris on 10 Feb. (Longford, pp. 36 and 38.)
3. A subsequent letter from Baring is not among Horner's surviving papers.
4. This seems to be an interpolation or paraphrase by Lady Holland. Fitzwilliam's son Charles William Wentworth Fitzwilliam, Viscount Milton and afterwards 5th Earl Fitzwilliam (1786–1857: DNB), was MP for Yorkshire.
5. After being approached by a group of moderate reformers from the City, including Alderman Waithman and the Lord Mayor (Matthew Wood), Tierney came to regard moderate parliamentary reform as feasible and encouraged Foxite leaders so to pledge a future Whig Ministry. He attended Wood's reform banquet on the evening of 17 Jan., and it was this that no doubt alarmed some of his colleagues. (Mitchell, p. 101, and *PH* v. 394 and 646.)
6. Grenville to Holland, 14 Jan., BL Add. MSS 51531.
7. William Wickham (1761–1840: DNB) was Grenville's lifelong friend and nothing is known to have separated them for even a brief period. What Lady Holland probably meant therefore was that Wickham was thought to have worked on Grenville to withdraw from active politics as he himself had done. Grenville wrote to Buckingham on 16 May that he intended to withdraw from 'parliamentary attendance'. (*Grenville*, p. 7n.)
8. Grey to Holland, 16 Jan., Grey MSS, Durham University.

639. From Lady Holland

BL Add. MSS 51644   [Holland House, 23 and 24 Jan. 1817]

I enclose the amendment such at least as it was settled at Mr Ponsonby's the other night, present only Romilly, Elliot, Piggott, Abercromby and Tierney. The original draught was stronger but to comply with the squeamishness of E[lliot] it is toned down to the insipid thing you see; the word *embarrassments* was cavilled at, as it was liable to the interpretation of being caused by the war, that war for which *he* voted. Many of the eager ones have heard there is no mention of reform and are grumbling. E[lliot] declares if it is inserted he must withdraw from a Party which raises that as a standard. Lord Grey came up today and spent his evening here. He is in excellent health and ready for any thing. He describes Lord Fitzwilliam as full of the Burke mania as ever, saying of the Army in France that if the Government there wish it withdrawn and can fully prove their ability to maintain a civil government which will ensure the maintenance of the present quiet order of things, he would in that case agree to the removal of the troops, not otherwise, as he dreads another *Statocracy*. His son is more reasonable and admits the inutility of acting upon these old principles, but says he will be for any thing prospectively: as to Reform they will not hear of it, and there perhaps they are wiser than upon the other points.[1] The Address is to be moved by Lord Valletort and seconded by a Mr Dawson who was Peele's private secretary;[2] this Paddy was yesterday entrusted with the speech by Lord Castlereagh in order that he might frame his own discourse. Soon afterwards he met a friend and read him the speech. Said friend went to the Cocoa Tree and repeated verbatim the speech. In the corner of the room sat Huskisson, who was all dismay at the disclosure and began questioning how it was obtained. This imprudence will probably cause a change in the speech, which as it stood yesterday was an entire admission of all the difficulties of the Country, and assurances of their being met with retrenchment, reduction, etc. Tierney has a story of Vansittart having issued illegally two millions of Exchequer bills, for which he must have a bill of Indemnity but some think it impossible, more especially as Lord G[renville] must know it from his office which when called a sinecure he said was one of efficient control.

   ... Brougham is in England ... There is some anxiety to know how he will be upon the subject of Reform. Little O, Maxwell and other wrong heads look to him as a champion.[3] Lambton is a little awry.[4] It is comical enough to see Cobbett, Hunt, etc. squabbling and calling the Hampden Club a set of scavengers. I send you the account of the meeting.[5] You will have seen that Curran destroyed the effect of a dinner by a rhapsody in which he says that a superficial compliment is best answered by an *insolvent* bow ....[6] A letter from Lord Thanet today mentions Brougham being with him, he adds *il a l'air heureux*.[7] We shall see as he is to be in Town this evening ... The meeting previous to the House of Commons will take place at Devonshire House. ...

   Snouch is more dull than ever. He has not sent or written properly to persons for attendance.[8]

1. The meeting, which was held on 21 Jan., also included Morpeth; and while Elliot did indeed deliver an impassioned harangue against parliamentary reform, Grey had already decided to avoid that issue and to frame an amendment with an eye to party harmony, leaving such contentious issues to individual initiatives and declarations. The draft amendment Tierney brought to the meeting therefore said nothing about reform, making little more than vague references to Ministerial extravagance, and discussion centred on semantics, so that the amendment that emerged was, as Lord Grenville observed, both harmless and unnecessary. (Mitchell, pp. 102–103.) The amended draft, which Lady Holland enclosed on a separate sheet, is substantially on the lines of that moved in both Lords and Commons on 29 Jan., save that the latter included the call for a general inquiry into the state of the nation mentioned in Doc. 640.

2. William Richard Edgecumbe, by courtesy Viscount Valletort (1794–1818), was MP for the family borough of Lostwithiel. Peel's private secretary and brother-in-law, George Robert Dawson (1790–1856), MP for County Londonderry, was an Orangeman and notoriously indiscreet (PH iii. 578 and 666).

3. The diminutive Charles Augustus Bennet, Lord Ossulston, afterwards 5th Earl of Tankerville (1776–1859), MP for Knaresborough, and William Maxwell of Carriden (1768–1833), who had been MP for Linlithgow Burghs until 1812 and had some hopes of regaining his seat, were both advanced Whigs.

4. Pointing to a lack of party discipline, Grey's new son-in-law, John George Lambton, afterwards 1st Earl of Durham (1792–1840: DNB), opposed the compromise, advanced by Lauderdale and supported by Tierney, of following the Address with a motion for a committee on the state of the nation (Lambton to Grey, 17 Jan., Grey MSS, Durham University).

5. The large number of local Hampden Clubs founded by Cartwright to advance the cause of reform between 1813 and 1817 was criticized by Cobbett, who argued that such organizations invited measures of repression on the part of the Government (PR 15 Feb. and 27 Apr.; Cobbett, p. 214). Lady Holland's account has not been found, but the MC of 23 Jan. reported that the meeting held the day before of the delegates from the various bodies petitioning for parliamentary reform had been 'orderly, calm, and deliberative'. However, it also recounted how Cobbett and Hunt had disagreed about the details of reform, in particular the ballot, and how, when a vote of thanks for its suggestions was proposed to the Hampden Club, Cobbett had protested that, 'with some respectable exceptions, . . . it consisted of determined enemies of reform', and called them 'the dirtiest scavengers in England'.

6. The MC of 18 Jan. reported that at a dinner the previous day of the 'Friends of Economy, Reduction, and Parliamentary Reform', Curran had begun a long and extravagant response to the toast of his health: 'On ordinary occasions a superficial civility is sufficiently rewarded by an insolvent bow. But something more is necessary in return for the introduction of my name, at a moment when the liberty of England is in question.'

7. Lady Holland, whose spelling, even in English, was unreliable, seems to have written 'heurent', and her meaning therefore remains uncertain.

8. George Ponsonby ('Snouch') assured Grey on 8 Dec. 1816 (Grey MSS, Durham University) that he had already begun to write round, and while the Opposition leader in the Commons did not arrive in London until the second week of January, there is no reason to believe that he was remiss in summoning Members to the meeting of Parliament.

640. From Lady Holland

BL Add. MSS 51644   25, 27, and 28 Jan. 1817

I have had my room as usual thronged which you know is what I like in these devoted months. The morning began with a very early visit from the Duke of

D[evonshire], who is just come up eager in politics, and anxious to have the cry for reform checked. Then came Lord Essex full of Drury Lane, grumbling at Lord Grenville's not coming to Town or instructing his friends how he wished them to proceed.[1] ... I left them ... On my return, found Brougham and Allen in deep confab. Augured well of his temper and disposition by finding him *here*; my first question was whether he had been at Pisa. Shuffled a reply that he had waited at Florence for an answer to a proposal of going to you, no intercourse between those Cities, irregular Posts, assured at Florence you disliked visitors; soon after Lord Grey came. B[rougham] was civil to every body, even to Mackintosh. Went away appointing a meeting at night with G[rey] and T[ierney] to consider over the Amendment. ... The petitions came.[2] B[rougham] wanted instead of an Amendment to add to the Address an inquiry into the state of the Nation. Said there was a precedent in 1691, warmly objected to by the others.[3] He grew warm and made a long offensive oration against fox hunters, as it was observed the Members would not remain in Town unless questions were pressed early, especially if the weather continued open. He is violent and abrasive against Lambton for some offence he took last Session.[4] Reports in Town of change of Ministry. Boasts of Ministers that if their friends are slack, yet the divisions amongst Opposition will so weaken *them* that they shall be able to ride the storm. Such people as little O, Sir Ronald, Maxwell and Sir Robert do a world of mischief.[5] It seems agreed that Reform shall not be named in the Amendment. I prevailed upon Lord G[rey] to write to the little Marquess[6] ... to invite him to *Council*. He received the finest and most direct manly reply, and an offer of coming tomorrow. Hertford is vacated by Mr Spencer Cowper, and Lady Salisbury says that Lord Cranbourne will pay the people the *Compliment* of canvassing for one day. Richard Wellesley is to go out of Parliament immediately. ...[7] Lady Melbourne came here with Luttrell after the opera.[8] The Regent besides calling Lady Hannah dear Hannah, talks of the Opposition as his old friends though he has not seen them *much* lately.[9] Quarrel between Lord Liverpool and Duke of York. Rumours of the abolition of the office of Commander in Chief, and of great debts and distress in that quarter ... The story of the Exchequer bills is not exactly true as I was told but there is something ... This operation of Baring's has saved a crash in France, and had there been one at present, they [Ministers] could not have faced Parliament. If this is true how abominably unlucky to have one's throat cut by a friend, and an odious Government preferred, all 'for the indulgence of a little occupation in this time of dullness and distress'. B[rougham] offended Perry mortally here today, by begging he would sacrifice his advertisements on Wednesday for the debates. Perry fired and said he had enlarged his paper, yes, but you have diminished your letter press. The war will wage. Lord Folkestone is very anti-reform, indeed all except some wrong heads.[10] I am sorry Lord G[rey] is to see the deputation from Westminster tomorrow.[11] Sir Robert [Wilson] is very officious and will lead him a sad dance with one absurd scheme or other.

Monday night [27 Jan.]
Yesterday morning Lord Holland went to Lord Grenville. He found him in a high state of dissatisfaction against the Country and House of Commons on the subject of sinecures, quite sore, rather soothed by finding he met with so much lenity and reason from his companion both upon that subject and that of reform. On foreign

policy they were so widely different that they agreed not to touch. Lord Holland's impression is that he was very unwilling to oppose the Government. At one o'clock Lord Grey had his interview with the City Whigs Waithman, Lucas, etc.[12] Upon the subject of taking up Reform of Parliament as a principal measure, he referred them to his speech of 1810, said he could not make it a party measure or clog himself with such a pledge, and stated hypothetically that if he were offered the Government he was convinced he would more essentially serve the country by changing the system of expenditure and the present foreign policy, but were he to urge the other he should not carry it and sacrifice thereby real benefit. They said they came to him to make a barrier against Anarchy and Revolution. He observed these were formidable words, but that he must act as he thought his duty. They added that Reform in Parliament ought to be a *sine qua non* and so they parted. I made Lord G[rey] state the conference he had had to Fazakerley: who was in raptures with his manly frank mode of proceeding, but today *Achates* has given a very different version to the Town and frightened Calcraft out of his wits.[13] Lord G[rey] then went to the other King of Bradford [Grenville] who held much the same language as he [had] done to Lord Holland. Friendly personally, but not conciliatory or yielding, begging against an amendment as he would not he thought vote for it. Brougham dined here with Elliot, Duke of D[evonshire] and Morpeth, and Abercromby and Mackintosh. A gulp to all. However he rattled away and told such excellent stories that they laughed in spite of their spleen towards him. He is less enduring of contradiction or even of a difference in opinion than he ever was. He lays down his opinion and will not easily listen to that of another person.

Lady Castlereagh's mother is dead, so he is not to be in the House, and Canning will officiate as Minister. There was a meeting at D[evonshire] H[ouse]. The only novelty was the presence of William Smith and his son in law Mr Carter.[14] Elliot was not there. About 65. The Ministers have not all their troops ... Lord C[astlereagh] wrote to Lord Wellington to hand over all the officers in Parliament. Lord William Russell said as he was one he should come, and he is come ...[15]

Tuesday 28th [Jan.]

... There will not be a great assemblage in Parliament St ... Hunt has hired a room in Palace Yard, and much hissing and pelting is likely to ensue which will be very mischievous in its effects. Poor Lord John [Russell] is so oppressed by cold that he could not come up today, but will come up for Lord Althorpe's motion on Friday. There was not a single Cavendish at D[evonshire] H[ouse] nor will there be any in the discussion tonight.

[PS] Mde de Staël is called the *Pie conspiratoire*.[16] She says there must be a change in the dynasty, as the people must fancy their King is of their own choice, but she varies in her language and prophesies every day ...

1. George Capell, 5th Earl of Essex (1757–1839), known as the 'Prince of Gossips', was a long-standing associate of Grenville and at this time a member of the Drury Lane Theatre Committee.
2. The first of over 600 petitions for economical and parliamentary reform received by Parliament during the 1817 session.
3. There appears to have been a compromise by incorporating in the proposed amendment a concluding call for such a general inquiry.

4. It is not known how Lambton had offended Brougham; but they were both of course very difficult men and were to have more famous differences later.

5. Presumably, in addition to Ossulston and Maxwell, Col. Sir Ronald Craufurd Ferguson of Raith (1773–1841: *DNB*), who was MP for Dysart Burghs, and Sir Robert Wilson.

6. Wellesley.

7. Edward Spencer Cowper, who had been MP for Hertford since 1802, had just vacated his seat, probably on account of ill health. It then passed to James Brownlow William Cecil, Lord Cranborne and afterwards 2nd Marquess of Salisbury (1791–1868), a Government supporter and opponent of Catholic Emancipation, who was until then MP for Weymouth but had previously contested Hertford. Wellesley's eldest natural son, Richard Wellesley (1787–1831: *PH* v. 508–509), the following month vacated Yarmouth, Isle of Wight, on account of a growing rift with his patron.

8. The noted wit and satirist, Henry Luttrell (?1765–1851: *DNB*), the natural son of the 2nd Earl of Carhampton, was one of the Holland House set and an intimate of the formidable Elizabeth Lamb, Viscountess Melbourne (d. 1818).

9. Grey's younger sister, Hannah Althea (d. 1832) was married to Edward Ellice.

10. After years of open association with such as Cobbett and Burdett, Folkestone had in recent years behaved with much greater reticence, probably on account of differences with his father. However, although against parliamentary reform, he remained, he told Holland about this time, 'a stickler for annual parliaments'. (*PH* iv. 826–32.)

11. Tierney had earlier reported that 'a large body of Westminster tradesmen' who were disillusioned with Burdett and Cochrane wanted to place themselves under Grey and to mark it with a 'grand dinner' before the meeting of Parliament. But Grey was unwilling to have a dinner and evidently substituted a private meeting, perhaps jointly with the similar deputation from the City mentioned below. (E.A. Smith, *Lord Grey 1764–1845* (Oxford, 1990), p. 211.)

12. Matthias Lucas was, like Waithman, a London common councilman.

13. John Calcraft (1765–1831: *DNB*) was then MP for Rochester. Whomever Lady Holland meant by her sarcastic reference to Grey's supposedly faithful friend (Achates), it seems unlikely to have been John Nicholas Fazakerley (1787–1852), then MP for Lincoln, a moderate reformer, much liked and admired by his friends but often absent and inactive in Parliament. Horner told Lady Holland in Mar. 1816 (BLPES vii. 46) that he thought him one of the most intelligent people he knew and in Jan. 1817 (*PH* iii. 732) that he was 'one of the best as well as the cleverest creatures in the world'. See also Horner to his mother, 1 Jan. [1816] (*Horner*, ii. 313–14), where, however, he made the common error of assuming Fazakerley was descended from the Jacobite Nicholas Fazakerley (d. 1767: *DNB*), though he was related, his father having been his heir at law and taken his name. Fazakerley's eldest daughter married 'Bobus' Smith's grandson.

14. John Carter, afterwards Bonham-Carter, had married on Christmas Day the previous year Joanna Maria (d. 1884), daughter of the old Foxite William Smith (1756–1835: *DNB*), then MP for Norwich.

15. Lord John Russell's elder brother, Lord (George) William Russell (1790–1846: *DNB*), MP for Bedford, was ADC to the Duke of Wellington in Paris at this time.

16. I.e. the conspiratorial windbag.

641. From Earl Grey

BLPES vii. 291–2   Portman Square, [London], 3 Feb. 1817

. . .

The papers will inform you of the result of the debates on the Address, and of the circumstances which preceded it. These have been unfortunate to the highest degree to every body but the Ministers, who are endeavouring to turn them to the same account that Pitt did similar occurrences in 1795.[1] Neither the time, nor the circumstances of the Country, nor the Minister, nor the character of the Sovereign are the same, and I hope this attempt, by a new alarm, to divide and divert the attention of the public from the causes of its distress, and the misconduct of the Government will not have the same success; and indeed I think I see strong symptoms of its failure. The experience of that former period however forbids us to be sanguine on this subject, though the same experience will, I trust, guard us against some of the errors by which the Opposition then greatly assisted the views of the Government. I very much fear that one of the consequences, against which it will be hardly possible entirely to guard, may be some division amongst us, upon measures which must necessarily produce a recurrence to our former opinions. I need not tell you that it will be my endeavour, if I cannot entirely avert, to mitigate this difference as much as possible, and to prevent its interrupting our co-operation on those points on which we agree. Even on these, however, at least in the degree and manner in which they should be pressed, I am not without apprehension that it may have some influence.

What the measures of the Government will be can at present be only matter of conjecture. I suppose they will certainly extend the laws for the security of the King's Person to the P[rince] Regent; to which ... there can be no objection.[2] They probably will also revive the Bill to restrain seditious meetings; to which I must object; still more to the suspension of the H[abeas] Corpus Act, if they should propose it, as many expect, but which I do not yet believe. There seems to me no necessity for any new powers in the Government, and surely nothing can be more impolitic in a moment of such distress and complaint, than to show this eagerness to adopt coercive measures.[3] As to the distress itself, I wish I could see any good ground for your opinion that with respect to our Commerce, Manufactures and Agriculture it is in its nature temporary. I shall rejoice sincerely to find that the fears I have are without foundation; but I certainly see nothing to allay them in the conduct of the Government. As to the mode in which our Parliamentary operations should be conducted, your opinion seems to me to be as correct as it could have been if you had been on the spot. I shall urge our friends in the H[ouse] of Commons to pursue it with all my influence. . . .

1. Ponsonby moved the heavily compromised amendment to the Address in the Commons with a strong attack on Ministerial extravagance, while in the Lords Grey launched a far more comprehensive attack that boldly embraced foreign policy. Despite the support of all factions within Opposition, the amendment secured only 112 votes in the Commons because of the alarm occasioned by reports of widespread disturbances in the northern industrial areas. (*Hansard*, xxxv. 19 and 54; Mitchell, p. 103.)

2. On his way to open Parliament the Regent was hooted and attacked by an angry mob; and that development, Thanet told Grey on 7 Feb., 'made a very serious impression upon our friends as though it had made all opposition useless'. (Grey MSS, Durham University; Mitchell, p. 103.)

3. On 5 Feb. secret committees were appointed in both the Lords and the Commons to consider evidence of a conspiracy against the constitution.

Index

This index is primarily one of persons, literature (with published works listed by author, if known), key events, institutions, and words and terms of likely interest to historians of economic thought, and intellectual, literary and political historians. Words and terms appearing frequently in the text but denoting nothing of consequence have not been included, and references to places have been excluded unless the place mentioned in the text includes substantive comment of potential interest to scholars.

Whenever pertinent, entries include, first, the page number(s) on which the reference appears in the narrative introductions and, secondly, the document(s) in which the reference appears. References to the former are preceded by 'intro', those to the latter by 'doc' or 'docs'. An asterisk (*) following a document reference denotes a letter written by, or a note relating directly to, the person or subject of the entry.